Fusion 360

Mastery Bible

From Beginner to Pro

The Complete Step-by-Step Guide to CAD Modeling, Simulation, CAM, Assemblies, Drawings, 3D Printing, Electronics & Manufacturing

Gally Renders

Disclaimer and Terms of Use

This publication is an independent work and is **not affiliated with, authorized, sponsored, or endorsed by Autodesk, Inc.**, or any of its subsidiaries or affiliates. *Fusion 360* and *Autodesk* are registered trademarks of Autodesk, Inc., and are used here for identification and educational purposes only.

The author and publisher have used their best efforts in preparing this book but make **no representations or warranties** regarding the accuracy, completeness, or suitability of the information contained herein. The content is provided for educational and informational purposes only. The author and publisher shall not be liable for any loss or damages arising from the use of this material or the software discussed.

Printed in the United States of America

TABLE OF CONTENTS

INTRODUCTION

Every product begins as an idea.

A sketch on paper. A rough concept in the mind. A problem waiting for a practical solution. But in today's world of engineering, product development, and digital manufacturing, ideas alone are no longer enough. To compete, create, prototype, and produce effectively, you need the ability to transform concepts into precise digital models, test them intelligently, refine them efficiently, and prepare them for real-world manufacturing.

That is exactly where **Fusion 360** becomes a game changer.

Fusion 360 is far more than a standard CAD program. It is a powerful, integrated platform that brings together **3D modeling, sketching, assemblies, simulation, rendering, drawings, CAM, CNC preparation, additive manufacturing, electronics design, collaboration, and workflow customization** in one unified environment. For students, engineers, designers, makers, manufacturers, entrepreneurs, and innovators, it provides the tools needed to move from concept to production with remarkable speed and precision.

Yet for many new users, the first encounter with Fusion 360 can feel overwhelming.

The interface is rich with commands. The workspaces are extensive. The possibilities are enormous. Sketches, constraints, parameters, components, joints, simulations, toolpaths, renderings, electronics, APIs—without a structured roadmap, it is easy to feel lost before you ever begin. Many users do not struggle because they lack talent. They struggle because they lack a guide that explains the software clearly, logically, and in the right sequence.

This book was written to be that guide.

Fusion 360 Mastery Bible: From Beginner to Pro is designed to take you on a complete learning journey—from the essential foundations of the interface and sketching environment to advanced workflows in modeling, assemblies, simulation, CAM, rendering, additive manufacturing, electronics, and customization. Rather than giving you fragmented lessons or disconnected tutorials, this book provides a structured path that helps you build skill upon skill with confidence.

You will begin by learning the fundamentals: how Fusion 360 works, how to navigate its workspaces, how to create and constrain sketches, and how to build accurate 3D forms. From there, you will move into more advanced topics such as construction geometry, feature-based modeling, patterns, fillets, lofts, sweeps, parametric control, assemblies, animation, and technical drawings. As your confidence grows, you will explore manufacturing workflows, CAM and CNC strategies, simulation and FEA, rendering and visualization, sheet metal design, additive manufacturing, PCB and electronics integration, collaborative workflows, and even the use of scripts, add-ins, and APIs to extend the software.

In other words, this is not a surface-level handbook.

It is a serious, in-depth resource built to reflect the true scope of Fusion 360 and the real demands of modern design and manufacturing. Whether your goal is to design consumer products, prototype mechanical systems, prepare CNC toolpaths, create production drawings, develop printable models, integrate electronics, or simply become highly capable in one of the world's most versatile design platforms, this book is meant to equip you with the knowledge to do so.

Just as importantly, this book is practical.

Throughout these chapters, you will not only learn what tools exist, but also why they matter, when to use them, and how they connect within a professional workflow. You will see how sketches drive models, how parameters drive design intent, how assemblies drive motion, how simulations drive improvement, and how manufacturing tools drive production. By the time you reach the later chapters, you will not simply be using Fusion 360—you will be thinking like a designer, engineer, and maker who understands the full design-to-manufacturing pipeline.

This book is for:

- beginners who want a clear starting point
- students who need a strong technical foundation
- makers who want to prototype and build
- designers who want to model with precision
- engineers who want to simulate, document, and manufacture
- professionals who want a broader, more integrated command of Fusion 360

If you are willing to learn step by step, practice consistently, and stay curious, the reward is enormous. Fusion 360 can become more than just software in your toolkit. It can become the bridge between imagination and execution—the place where ideas take shape, problems find solutions, and innovation becomes tangible.

So whether you are opening Fusion 360 for the first time or returning to master it at a higher level, you are in the right place.

Open the software.
Study the process.
Build with precision.
Create with confidence.

Your journey from beginner to professional-level Fusion 360 mastery begins here.

PART 1

INTRODUCING FUSION 360 AND DRAWING SKETCHES

CHAPTER 1

INTRODUCING FUSION 360

Fusion 360, because of the one-of-a-kind capabilities it offers, is quickly becoming one of the most popular Computer Aided Design (CAD) products available on the market for casual users (hobbyists). It is a single, collaborative platform that is cloud-based and can be used for engineering, CAM, and design. Its capabilities are comparable to that of Inventor, SolidWorks, or Catia. The user can carry out the whole of the product design and development process on a single (cloud-based) software thanks to this functionality.

Autodesk, which is one of the largest businesses in the computer-assisted design sector, is responsible for the development of the CAD application known as Fusion 360. They are also responsible for the development of the well-recognized software programs AutoCAD, Inventor, and Revit, which are used by millions of working professionals worldwide. They are venturing into uncharted territory with the release of their most recent product, Fusion 360, which is a tool designed for hobbyists and other infrequent users.

What Is the Function of Fusion 360?

Cloud-Based

You should be aware that Fusion 360 is a cloud-based modeling program at this point. When a model that is now being worked on is saved, the file is not stored locally on the device that it is being worked on, but rather it is saved on a server. If the project has to be accessed offline, it may be exported onto a hard drive, which can also be used as a way for turning the model files into the OBJ and STL file formats. Since it is cloud-based, this also implies that one's models and projects can be seen online from any computer or device. This is a significant advantage. Users now have access to a more portable and remote method of assessing models while they are on the move, thanks to mobile applications that are accessible for both Android and iOS. This, in turn, fosters improved team cooperation. This eliminates a significant portion of the headache that is often associated with team collaboration on larger projects in which design choices, markups, and comments are continuously being exchanged. It does not make a difference what device you are using to view Fusion 360, what version of the application you have installed, or whatever file format you wish to work with. Fusion 360 stores all of this information inside itself, and a click of the "**Share Public Link**" button makes it simple to send files to other people. In 3D CAD software, the concept of exchanging data so easily is unheard of.

Manufacture

As a result of Fusion 360's inherent support for computer-aided manufacturing (CAM), your CAM design may be manufactured in real life on a machine that uses computer numerical control, or CNC for short. It provides tools to create cuts, either by utilizing the software's default tools or by allowing the user to manually input the qualities and specifications of a tool that the user has previously earned. In addition to this, it utilizes a method known as Adaptive Clearing, which enables significant chunks of the material to be removed.

After a toolpath has been constructed, you will be able to see a simulation of the process of the model being created and examine the slicing operation. Because of this, difficulties in the cut may be avoided, and any last-minute design adjustments can be changed before any real machining is carried out. Because it minimizes mistakes in design and decreases the amount of wear and tear on machines and equipment, efficiency may result in significant cost and time savings.

Part Modeling

Fusion 360 integrates some distinct working environments, each of which offers a unique set of customization possibilities and other capabilities. When you launch the software for the first time, a blank modeling plane is displayed to you since the Design environment is the choice that is set as the default. Within this environment, 3D modeling is then done, and one of the most impressive aspects of Fusion 360 is that it provides the ease of having direct, parametric, freeform, and surface modeling all in the same area. While modeling in one environment, switching from, for example, a freeform workspace to a parametric one requires nothing more than the click of a button. This is one of the features of Fusion 360 that will save you the most time.

Rendering

When a design is developed on any computer program, there is always a need to know what it would look like in the real world as an actual product. This is something that can be accomplished by using a rendering application. The chosen model can be seen in an extremely lifelike fashion thanks to the Rendering tool that is included in Fusion 360. This feature generates a real-world setting that is based on your precise preferences and then displays it. The user can customize the surface by adding material properties, such as wood, marble, metal, glass, and many more. It is possible to download additional plug-ins, such as Key Shot, that will provide an even more realistic final render.

Simulation

When digitally evaluating a design, simulation may be a vital tool for analyzing how the design responds depending on the forces and external pressures that are given to it. A model's performance in real-world scenarios, as well as whether or not it would break under certain loads or pressures, may be evaluated using simulation, which can also reveal whether or not the model is imbalanced.

Within Fusion 360, the following is a list of some of the variables that may have their values altered:

- Modal frequencies
- Static Tension
- Temperatures
- Buckling of the structure
- Stress nonlinear under static tension
- The effects of heat stress

This might be challenging for users without prior knowledge, but if it is used appropriately, it can be a helpful tool in the design process.

Installing Fusion 360

System requirements

System requirements for Autodesk Fusion 360	
Operating System	Apple® macOS • macOS 12 Monterey • macOS 11 Big Sur • macOS 10.15.7, or newer, Catalina **Note**: macOS 10.14 Mojave support was deprecated on March, 2022. (More details) Microsoft® Windows® • Windows 11 • Windows 10 (64-bit) • Windows 8.1 (64-bit) (until January 2023)**
CPU Type	x86-based 64-bit processor (for example, Intel Core i, AMD Ryzen series), 4 cores, 1.7 GHz or greater; 32-bit not supported Apple silicon processors require Rosetta 2 - see this post for more information.

Recommended specs for complex modeling and processing	
CPU Type	3 GHz or greater, 6 or more cores
Memory	8-GB RAM or greater
Graphics	Dedicated GPU with 4 GB or more VRAM, DirectX 11 (Direct3D 11 or greater)

Step 1: Sign up for a Fusion 360 License

The first thing you need to do is determine what kind of license you need for Fusion 360 and sign up for that.

- Fusion 360 Commercial Subscription
    - Before committing to a paid membership, users may take advantage of a fully functional trial period that lasts for thirty days.
- Fusion 360 for Educational Use (free for qualifying students and educators)
- Fusion 360 for personal use, hobby use (free, for non-commercial use)

- Fusion 360 for startup use (free for eligible venture-backed, angel-backed, or bootstrap startups that are less than 3 years old and have 10 or fewer employees.
    - **Take note**: You will be required to apply for a start-up license. It is not granted permanently, and the request may be turned down at any time.

Before a certain license may be activated, the specific sign-up procedure that corresponds to that license type must first be completed in its entirety. Visit your Autodesk Account after you have your Fusion 360 license to access all of the licenses that are currently available to you. If you do not already have an Autodesk Account, you will need to establish one first. Commercial subscribers who have acquired a license may also examine the subscription and invoicing information, as well as control the users of the license they have purchased.

Step 2: Download and Install Fusion 360

You are now able to download and install Fusion 360 once you have successfully secured your license for the software. Because it is a cloud product, Fusion 360 automatically downloads the most recent updates to operate on the most recent version.

To get started right now, just follow the steps that are outlined below:

1. Go to **manage.autodesk.com** and choose the option labeled **All Products and Services**
2. Select the product you want to download and then click the **Download Now** option. Since Fusion 360 is bundled with several different services, ensure that the **Download Now** button is selected.

3. When you click the **Download Now** button, you will be sent to a new website where the installer will be downloaded without any more action required on your part. Note that the website can determine what operating system you are running and will either supply a Windows install file or a Mac install file depending on which one it determines you need.

4. When the file has finished downloading, you may begin the procedure by running the installer.
5. When the installation of Fusion 360 is finished, the program will launch on its own for the first time, and you will be prompted to sign in to your Autodesk account using the email address and password that you have associated with that account.

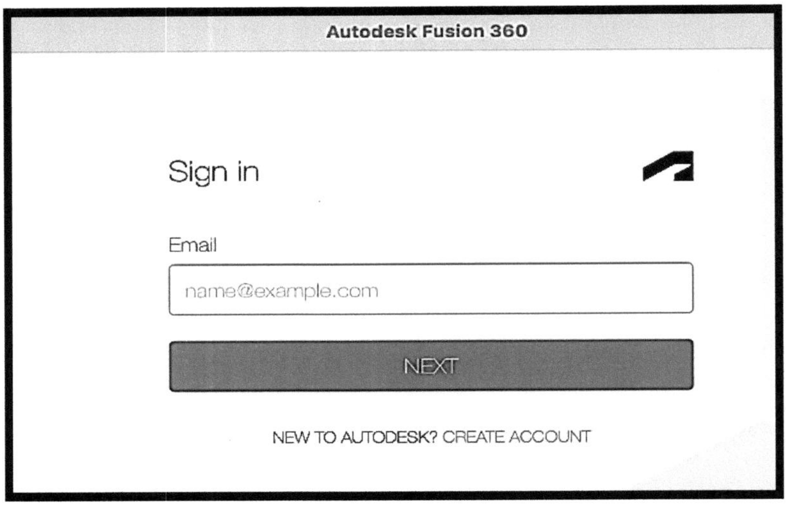

Getting Started with Fusion 360

Working with the User Interface of Fusion 360

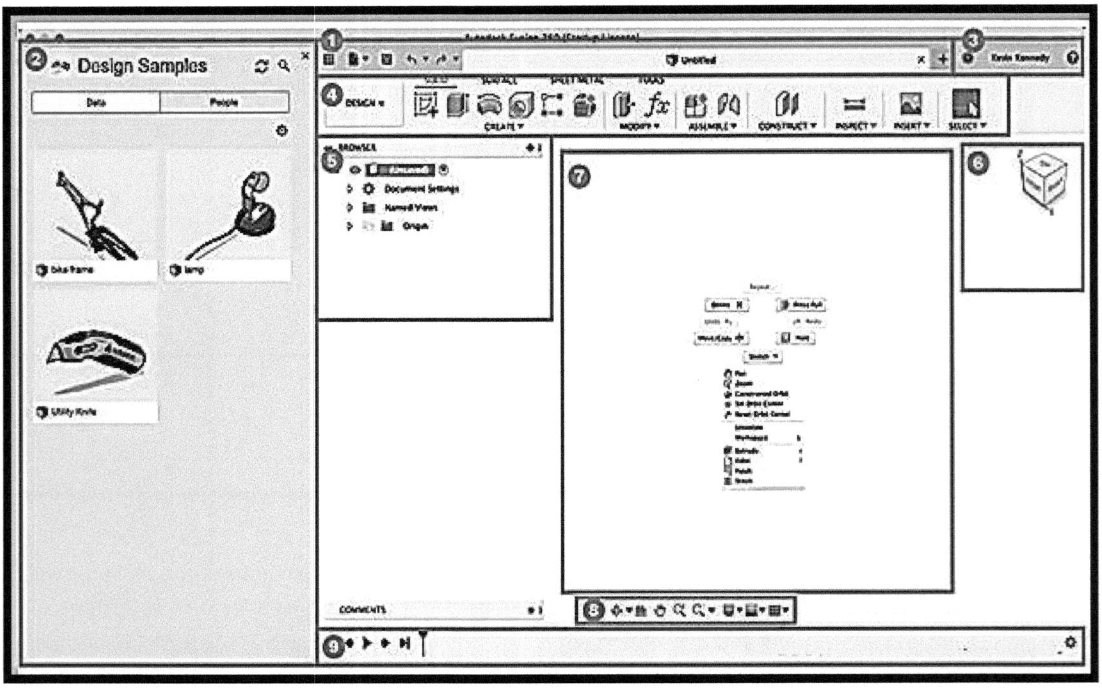

1. Application Bar

The location of the Application Bar can be seen in the top left corner of the screen.

There are four primary components included inside the application bar.

- **Data panel** - contains your design files.
- **File menu** - create, export, or share your creations.
- **Save**: This allows you to save your designs together with descriptions of their versions.
- **Undo and Redo Buttons**: These allow you to undo or redo your most recent activities.

You will see tabs that reflect each design file across the top of the window. On the tab, you will see both the name of the file and the number of the version. On the other hand, if you have a big number of files open, you won't be able to view the name of the file until you hover over it. This operates in a way that is similar to how the tabs in your web browser function.

2. Data Panel

Your whole collection of design files may be found under the Data Panel. You may further organize your files by creating new projects and folders inside the data panel, which is located on the left side of the screen. You are also able to manage other users who are working on your projects using the data panel. However, depending on the kind of license you are using, there may be limits applicable to this functionality. You may open a project at any time by double-clicking on the file or right-clicking it and selecting the "open" option from the context menu that appears.

3. Profile and Help

Notification Center - Notifications will occur (a few times a year) with critical alerts, such as scheduled maintenance.

These notifications will be shown in the Notification Center.

- **Job Status** - View job status, Fusion 360 update status, and online/offline status.
- **Profile**: Click on your name to:
    - Access your Autodesk account.
    - Adjust your Fusion 360 preferences
    - Alternate between the two teams.
    - See or make changes to your profile.
    - Sign Out

4. Toolbar

The toolbar gives you the ability to choose the kind of working environment that best suits your needs. It is essential to keep in mind that the tools available on the toolbar will vary from one workspace to the next. There are additional tabs inside each toolbar, which further arrange the tools into logical categories. Tabs may be found in each toolbar. You will be able to personalize and rearrange the components of your toolbar as you get more familiar with your routine operations.

5. Browser

The Browser panel provides a summary of the document's settings as well as its views, as well as the origin, axes, and planes. To access the units, click the Document Settings button; here is where you may make adjustments to them. To show the model from the top, front, or side perspective, click the Named Views button. By clicking the origin, you can examine the multiple planes, which is helpful when picking an orientation for a drawing. There is one component that is always present in a Fusion document; this component is referred to as the **root component**. The top field of the browser displays the name of the browser, which reads Unsaved until you save it. You may access its functionalities by right-clicking on it. Everything that is added to the model, including drawings, bodies, components, and assemblies, is listed on the Browser panel as the model develops. You can adjust the display of these things and change them directly via the browser. Items are shown with names such as **Component 1:1, Component 1:2,** or **Body** as their default. The number that comes before the colon denotes the version, and the number that comes after it denotes the copy number. You can rename every entry in the browser, which is a useful practice for differentiating between them as their number increases. A new name can be entered by clicking the text box to activate it, typing it in, and then pressing the Enter key to complete the process. You may undock any panel by moving the bar at the top of that panel. To redock, move the panel to the border of the workspace, hold down the mouse button until a green line appears vertically, and then let go of the button. You may keep the browser window open, or you can minimize it by clicking the minus symbol **(-).**

6. Viewcube

You can see your design from a variety of normal view locations as well as revolve around your design using the viewcube. You have the option of clicking and dragging the viewcube in any direction, or you may choose to choose certain faces, corners, or arrows. You may also see the model in the default home position by clicking the home icon, which is located next to the viewcube in the interface.

7. Canvas and Marking Menu

You'll be conducting all of your design work and sketching in the center portion of Fusion 360, which is where the app's name comes from. Because of this, we refer to this part of the picture as the canvas. The "**marking menu**," also known as the right-click menu, is accessible from inside the canvas and may be accessed by clicking the right mouse button. If you right-click, you'll be able to access commonly used commands, as well as the option to switch between different workspaces; this saves you from having to go to the top left corner of the screen. You'll need to commit the location of the various marking-menu elements to memory if you wish to make full use of the menu. Users have the option to right-click and drag (in the same direction) to fast reach the function that they wish to utilize. This is done via the marking menu. To activate the press, pull command, for instance, right-click the mouse and move it toward the two o'clock position.

8. Navigation Bar and Display Settings

You may zoom, pan, and orbit using the tools that are included inside the Navigation panel. In addition to that, it features display options that may alter the workspace as well as the way the model looks. You may, for example, alter the size of the grid, adjust the way the mouse snaps to the grid, see the model as a wireframe, and see many versions of it on the same screen. This section explains the various navigational tools. To see the available choices, choose the arrow with the downward pointing triangle next to each icon.

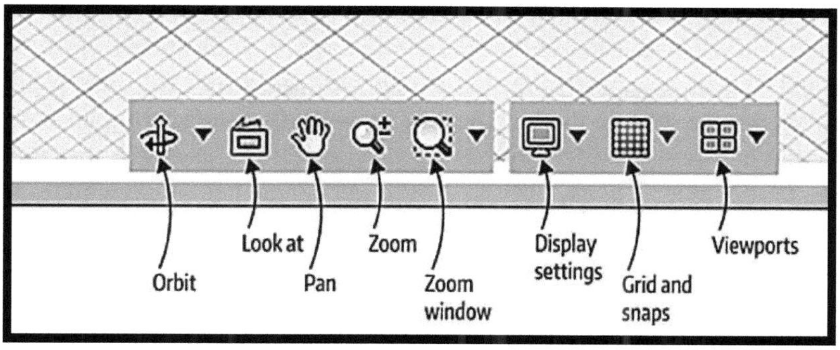

Orbit: This is a view that rotates the viewer around the model, allowing for a comprehensive examination of the object from a variety of perspectives. It is not the model itself that is moving, but rather your location about it. You have the option of orbiting freely or being bound. Orbits that are constrained around either the xy plane or the z-axis. Free to go in whatever direction the user chooses. To release orbit more quickly, you need first to depress and hold the Shift key, and then you should depress and hold the scroll wheel on your mouse.
Look At: First choose an area on the model to click, and then select this icon. The location of the model will adapt itself appropriately.
Pan: The model will move across the screen as you pan the camera. You can pan more effectively by depressing and rotating the scroll wheel of the mouse while holding down the mouse button.
Zoom: This provides you with either an enlarged view of the model (think of it as a telephoto lens) so that you can notice minute details or a reduced view of the model (think of it as a wide-angle lens) so that you can see the whole picture. To zoom in or out with more precision, just scroll the mouse wheel in the desired direction.
Zoom Window: This allows you to look at a certain spot in more detail by allowing you to drag a window around that location. When you choose the **Fit** option, the model will occupy the whole screen. If your model disappears after you click it, it's because there are still bits and parts of it that you sketched previously that are sticking around.

Find those files and delete them to make your model appear again. Using Clicking Fit, you may find "lost" components of your puzzle.

- **Display Settings**: This allows you to change the appearance of the working area.
- **Grid and Snaps**: You may choose whether the grid is shown or not, and you can also change its parameters and the snap increments.
- **Viewports**: Show the workspace either as one huge workspace or as many smaller workspaces at the same time using viewports.

9. Timeline

The timeline provides a listing of the operations in the sequence in which they were done on your design. The timeline is a row of icons that shows at the bottom of the screen if you are creating in a parametric manner. This row of icons is sometimes referred to as the history tree. There is a corresponding symbol for every activity that is carried out. The timeline expands along with the project; however, it may be made more comprehensible by grouping many icons (to do this, click the first icon in the timeline, then while holding down the Shift key, and click the final symbol). If you double-click on an icon, the feature that corresponds to that icon will be selected in the model. If you right-click on an icon, you will have access to a context menu, and if you drag an icon to the left or right, you can change the order in which operations are calculated. By moving the slider to the left, you may "**travel back in time**," which means you can review actions that occurred previously. If a feature has a yellow indicator, it indicates that there is a caution associated with it; for example, you may have destroyed something that Fusion requires to maintain the integrity of the design, but Fusion cached it, which allowed you to continue working. A red indicator indicates that there is a problem; one example of this is that an edge that a fillet utilized has been erased, which implies that the fillet can no longer be created. It is in everyone's best interest to address warnings and mistakes as soon as they appear.

You can disable the timeline by right-clicking the title field of the browser and selecting the **Do Not Capture Design History** option from the context menu. This puts you in direct modeling mode, which, compared to parametric modeling mode, you may find to be more straightforward. To bring up the timeline again, right-click the title field of the browser and choose the **Capture Design History** option from the context menu. When you enter Direct Mode, the timeline will begin from that moment, and you will permanently delete any timeline icons that were there before you entered **Direct Mode**.

Invoking a New Design File

When you launch Autodesk Fusion 360, the program prompts you to create a new design file and gives it the default name "**Untitled**." Earlier on, many components of the starting user interface of the new design file were covered. These included the **Application Bar, Toolbar, BROWSER, and Timeline.** In addition to the design file that is loaded by default, you can load a new design file by selecting the New Design tool from the drop-down menu in the application bar that is labeled File. When this is done, a new design file with the name "**Untitled**" as the default name is called, and it is automatically set to the active state. You can also start a new design file by clicking on the plus symbol that is located next to the name of the current design file that is open. The tools that are accessible in the Toolbar change depending on the workspace that is now active. The **DESIGN** workspace is the one that is active by default. As a consequence of this, the tools that are required for the creation of 3D models, surface models, and sheet metal models may be found inside the different tabs of the Toolbar.

Working with Workspaces

DESIGN Workspace

You can generate and modify the solid, surface, and T-Spline model geometry in the Design workspace, which is controlled by the geometry of 2D sketches. This workspace is the one that most closely resembles a conventional 3D CAD environment. In this setting, you may develop history-based features (such as extrude, revolve, loft, and sweep) that adapt to changes in the design.

Sketch contextual tab

The Sketch tab is a contextual tab that provides tools that allow you to generate and change 2D drawings that drive the 3D geometry of a design. These sketches may be found under the tab named "**Sketch.**" Within the Design workspace, the Sketch contextual tab may be accessed in a variety of different places. The most typical location to find it is under the Solid tab's Create panel under the Create Sketch menu item.

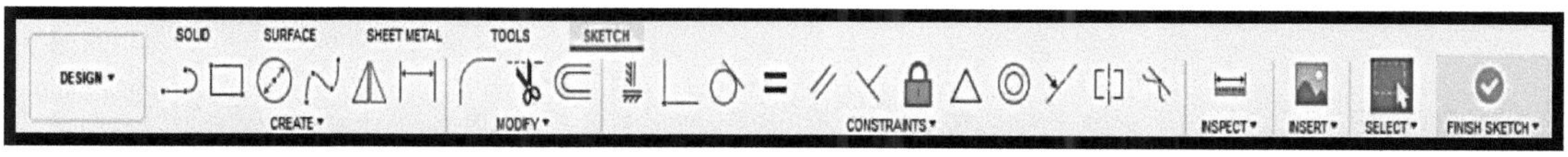

Since you can create a Sketch inside many tabs in addition to contextual tabs, Sketch is treated as a special case and shown with the other non-contextual tabs also visible. This is because you can build a Sketch within multiple tabs. When you choose Create Sketch, a new contextual tab titled Sketch appears. This tab has a dedicated toolbar that, by default, is stocked with the sketch tools that are used the most often. By default, the toolbar will additionally display the sketch limitations that are now active.

You will see that the tab itself as well as the button labeled Finish Sketch will be marked in blue to let you know that you are now operating in a temporary mode. In contrast to the other contextual tabs, the Sketch contextual tab does not prevent you from switching to other tabs while it is active. This is the primary distinction between the Sketch contextual tab and the other contextual tabs. This is because you can use modeling commands (like Extrude, for example) even while your sketch is currently active. Performing this action will cause you to be taken out of Sketch mode and into the command itself automatically.

Solid tab

Tools that enable the creation and modification of solid models may be found under the Solid tab.

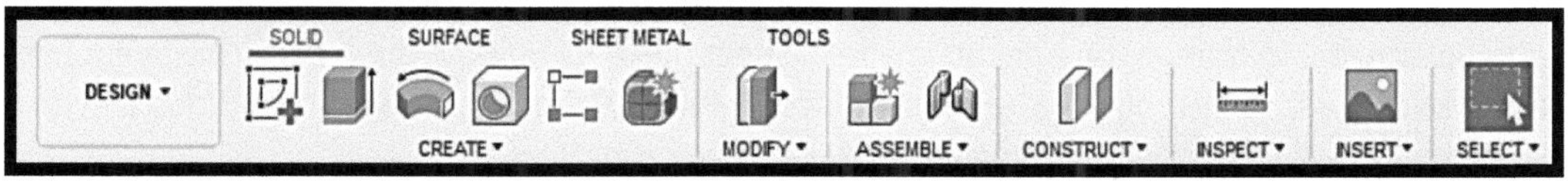

Form contextual environment

The form is a contextual environment that gives you the ability to push and pull T-Spline bodies' faces, edges, and vertices to form intricate organic features. The tools are analogous to those used for sculpting clay. The Form contextual environment can be accessed via the Create panel of the Solid tab in the Solid editor.

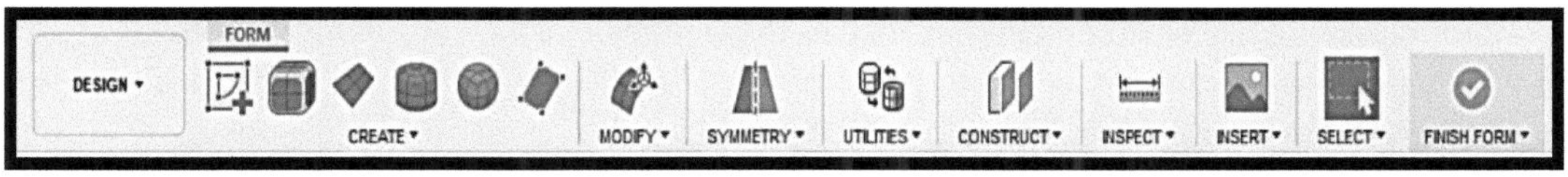

Surface tab

Tools that enable the creation and modification of complicated parametric surfaces may be found under the Surface tab. The exterior contour of a design is denoted by its surface, which is flat and devoid of depth. You may also use the tools on the Surface tab to patch or fix openings in a model. These tools are located on the Surface tab.

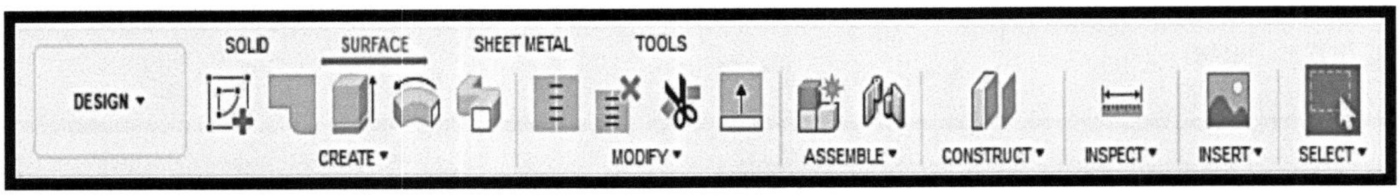

Mesh tab

Tools that enable the creation and modification of parametric mesh bodies may be found under the Mesh tab. A mesh body is a collection of polygon faces that are formed from vertices and edges of the polygons. A mesh does not have any thickness to it. In the process of additive manufacturing, meshes are often employed. You can insert new mesh bodies, repair existing ones, and change existing ones by making use of the Mesh commands to get them ready for manufacture.

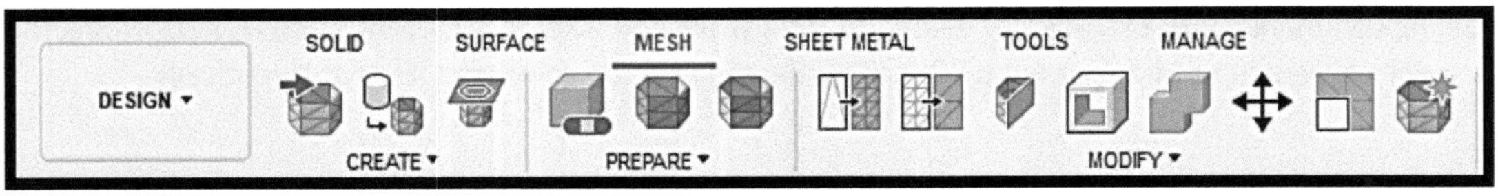

Sheet Metal tab

You may construct and change components made of sheet metal by utilizing the tools in the Sheet Metal tab, which are organized according to sheet metal rules. Utilizing 2D drawings and various cutting processes, flat designs may be documented and manufactured using these methods.

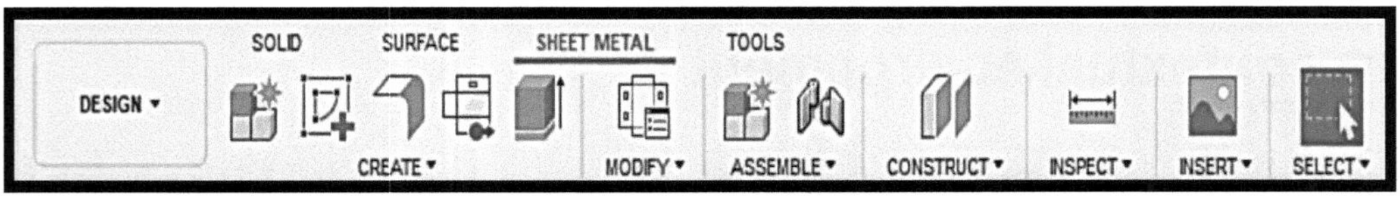

Flat Pattern contextual surroundings

Flat Pattern is a contextual environment that enables the creation of a flat pattern for sheet metal starting from a folded design. Through the Create panel of the Sheet Metal tab, you will have access to the contextual environment of the Flat Pattern.

- **Flat Pattern Solid tab**: To build and change Flat Patterns with solid geometry, use the tools on the Flat Pattern Solid tab, which are located in the tab's name.

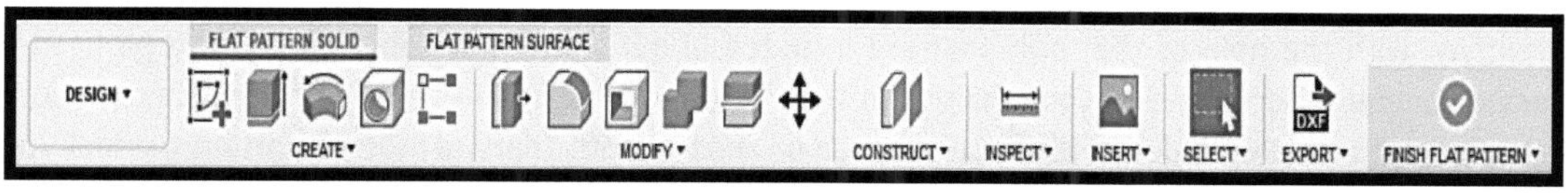

- **Flat Pattern Surface tab**: To build and change flat patterns with surface geometry, use the tools on the Flat Pattern Surface tab, which are located in the tab's name.

Base Feature contextual environment

Base Feature is a contextual environment that provides you with the ability to enter a direct modeling sandbox and inserts a feature in the Timeline that does not have any history associated with it. You get access to modeling tools as well as surfacing tools when you use the base feature. Through the Solid tab's create panel, you will have access to the contextual environment known as the Base Feature.

Base Feature Solid tab: To construct and change solid geometry, use the tools that are located on the Base Feature Solid tab.

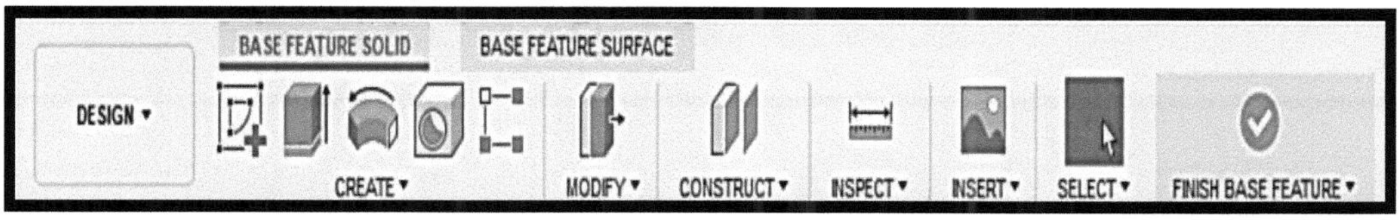

Base Feature Surface tab: To develop and alter surface geometry, you may use the tools that are located on the Base Feature Surface tab.

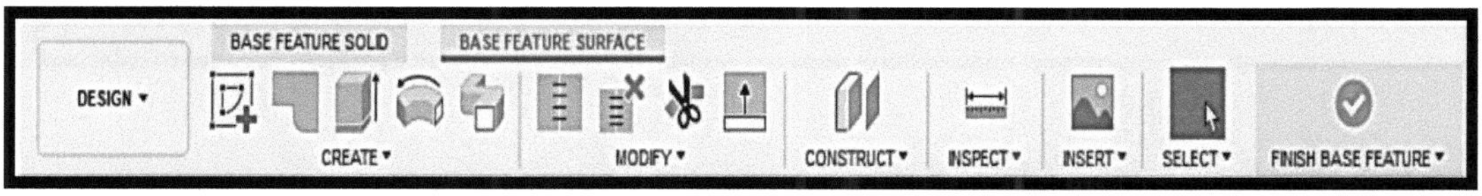

Generative Design Workspace

You can develop various CAD-ready design solutions all at once with the help of the workspace known as Generative Design, which is determined by the manufacturing and performance criteria.

Define tab

You may build up design studies with well-specified objectives, limitations, materials, and production alternatives with the help of the tools that are included under the Define tab. Tokens may be used to generate several different design possibilities in the cloud that are process and performance conscious. Investigate and assess each design alternative based on the tradeoffs that are most important to meet your requirements. After that, export your ideal design, and then import the geometry that is suitable for CAD into Fusion 360.

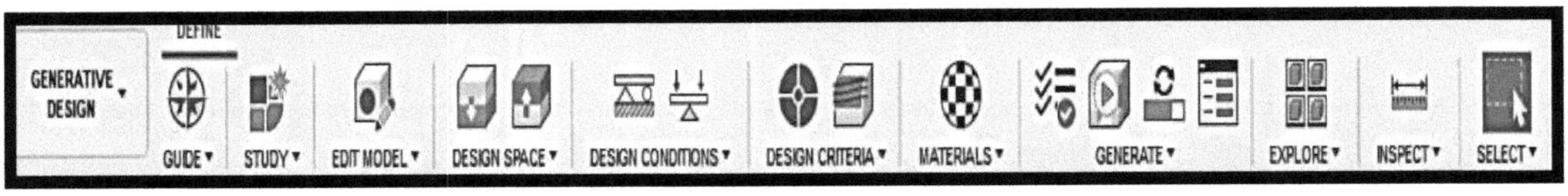

Edit Model contextual environment

Within the context of the Change Model environment, you can utilize the usual modeling tools that come with Fusion 360 to build and edit model geometry, as well as to construct obstacles and preserve geometry. Through the Define tab's Edit Model panel, you will have access to the contextual environment of the Edit Model panel.

Edit Model Solid tab: The Edit Model Solid tab includes a set of tools that, when used, enable users to edit the geometry of solid models without having to leave the Generative Design workspace.

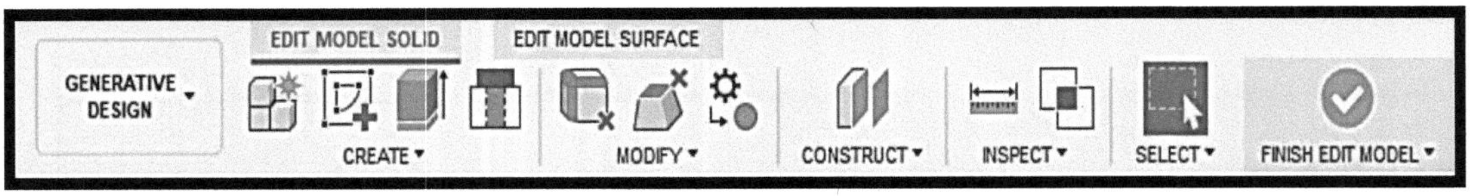

Edit Model Surface tab: This is where you'll find the tools that will allow you to edit the surface model geometry without having to leave the Generative Design workspace.

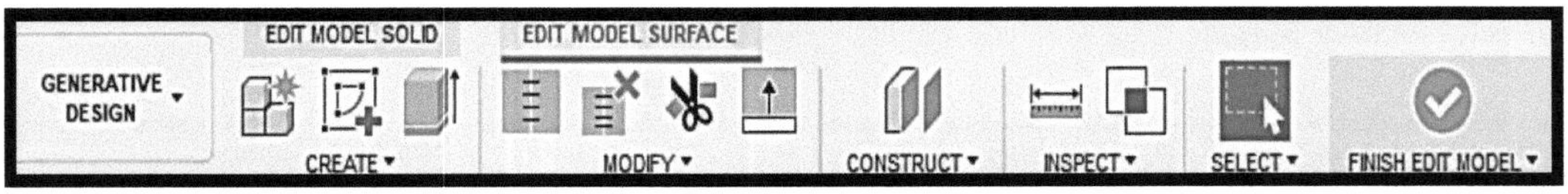

Explore contextual environment

You are given the ability to show the model, stress, export preview, and design space views of a result inside the Explore contextual environment. Additionally, you have the option to view the Comparison View. Through the Define tab's Explore panel, you will have access to the contextual environment known as **Explore**.

Outcome View contextual tab: Within the Explore contextual environment, the toolbar will switch to the Outcome View contextual tab when you select one or more outcomes to explore in the 3D View or Comparison View. This tab includes a variety of tools that allow you to display, compare, and export outcomes. When you select one or more outcomes to explore, the Explore contextual environment will begin.

Render Workspace

You can get a more accurate and thorough picture of what your final product will look like by using renders. These renderings have the potential to serve as an invaluable resource for product marketing as well as the idea and depiction of products. To go over to the render workspace, just right-click on the current work environment you are in and pick **Render** from the menu that appears.

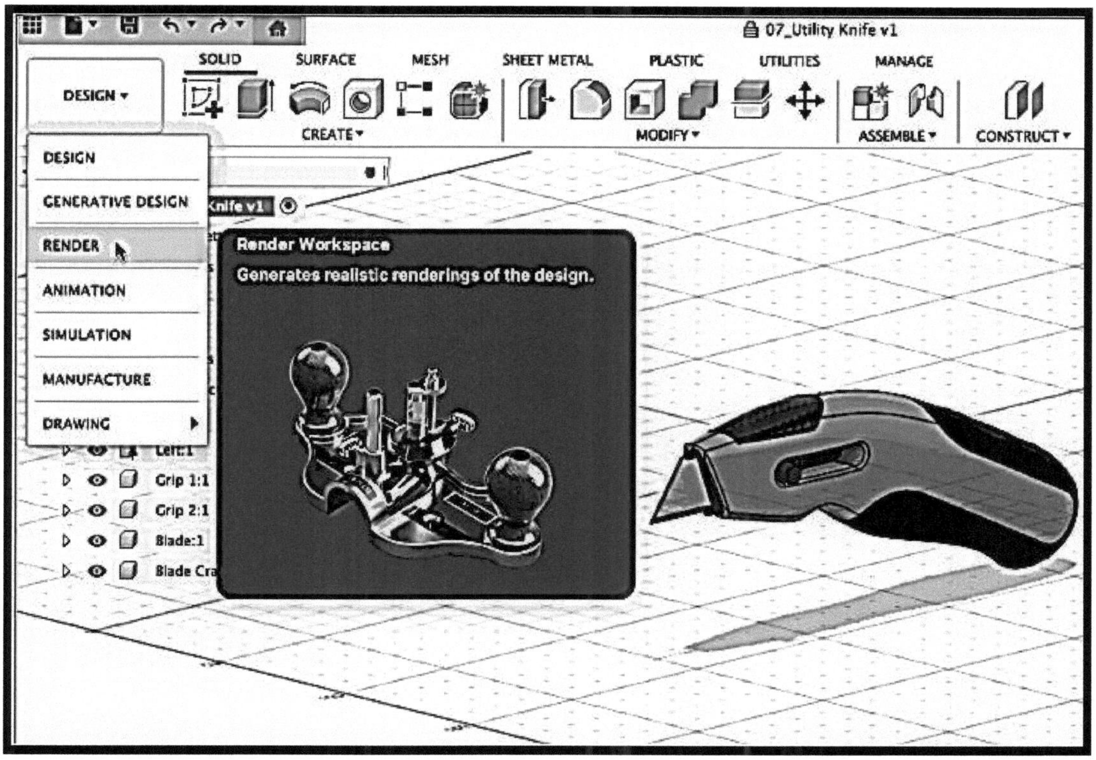

The appearance of your model will abruptly undergo a significant transformation if you apply this change. Let's look at the instructions to have a better understanding of how to make use of this area.

Appearance

You can change the kinds of materials that your model is made up of by using the Appearance command. Within this menu, in addition to the ability to choose a material from a list that includes leather, liquid, metal, plastic, wood, stone, and other alternatives, you can also modify the color, texture, and feel of your material.

You can edit the content by either right-clicking on it and selecting Edit from the context menu, or you can double-click on the part of the material that you want to change. When you click this button, you will be sent to a new dialogue where you will be able to modify the fundamental features of the look of your material. After you have finished the fundamentals, you may select the **Advanced** button to dive into more specifics about the texture, bump pattern, sheen, and feel of your material.

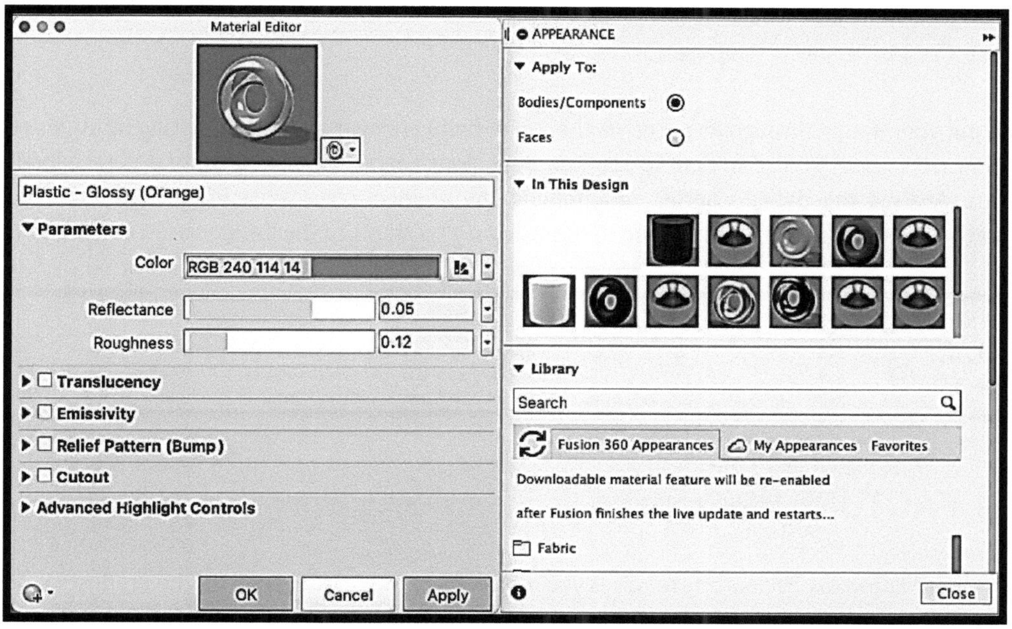

Understanding the Advanced settings dialog

- **Reflectance**: This is the amount of light that is reflected from a surface.
- **Roughness**: This refers to the degree to which the surface is abrasive, which in turn determines how glossy the surface looks.
- **Translucency**: This determines how much of the surrounding environment can be seen through the material.
- **Emissivity**: This is the property that transforms a substance into a source of light.
- **Relief Pattern (Bump):** This displays the bump map that has been applied.
- **Advanced Highlight Controls**:
  - **Color**: This allows you to alter the hue of the highlight. For the most part, you will want to keep this white for a more authentic appearance.
  - **Shaping**: Alternate between highlights that are smooth (Long Falloff) and highlights that are sharper (Short Falloff)

ANIMATION Workspace

Your ability to describe your design using 3D exploded views and animations that illustrate design assembly are both facilitated by the Animation workspace. You may assist your teammates and customers in better understanding and assessing your design by sharing videos with them.

SIMULATION Workspace

You can put your design through its paces via the use of finite element analysis by setting up studies in the Simulation workspace (FEA). Simulate to see how your design fares under a range of different loads and situations. Analyze the data to better comprehend the physical constraints imposed by your design. Investigate a variety of design options, and then settle on alterations to the design based on your findings.

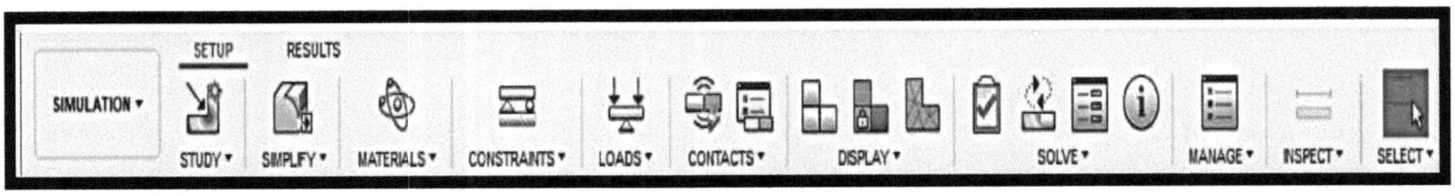

MANUFACTURE Workspace

The workspace known as "Manufacture" gives you the ability to design toolpaths for the production of your components using methods such as machining and turning (also known as "subtractive manufacturing") or 3D printing (additive manufacturing).

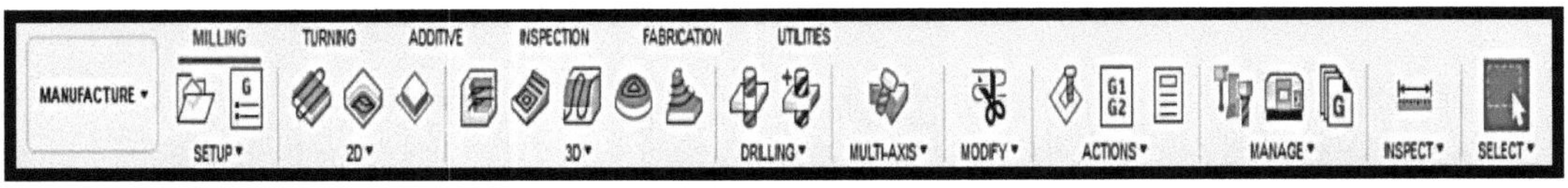

DRAWING Workspace

Documenting production requirements via the use of integrated, associative drawings and animations for both parts and assemblies is possible when you use the Drawing workspace.

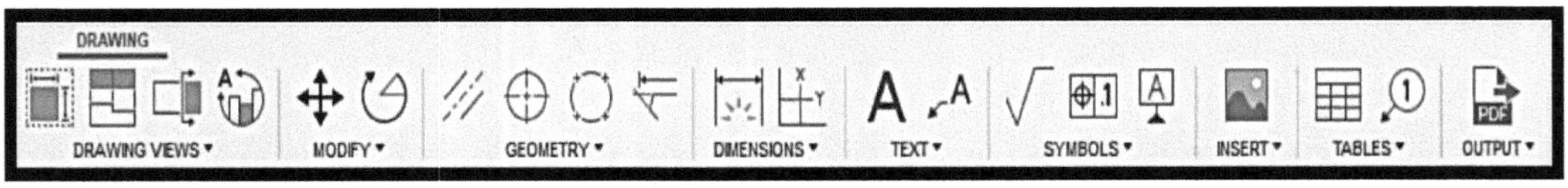

Managing Data by Using the Data Panel

- You can get access to your Fusion 360 projects and design data, as well as organize and share it, by using the Data Panel.

- The Data Panel provides access to your designs and allows you to manage projects.
- By default, the Data Panel will not be shown. To access it, you need to choose the Show Data Panel icon from the toolbar.

A helpful hint is that you can reveal or conceal the Data Panel by pressing **Ctrl+Alt+P** (on Windows) or **Option+Command+P** (on macOS).

You will be able to examine both your projects and designs using the Data Panel. Additionally, it provides you with sets of samples that you may use, such as CAM samples.

Make the projects you want to see more or less apparent by using the project filter:

- **All projects:** the full list of projects in the current Team
- **Joined by Me**: only the projects you have joined
- **Pinned**: only favorite projects
- **Owned by Me**: only projects you started
- **Shared with Me**: only projects to which you've been invited

Join a project

It's possible to start or end a project. An open project welcomes participation from any member of the team. In a closed project, team members may only join if they have been invited by a project administrator or have been authorized by a project administrator. Even while everyone on the team can see open and closed projects on the list, to view the contents of a project, you will need to join it first, even if the project is open. To participate in an open project, position your mouse so that it is in the top right corner of the project, and then click the Join button. To participate in a project that is currently full, move your mouse to the top right corner of the project, and then click the **Request Access** button. Your request will be looked at by the administrator of the team. The project will display Access Requested until the administrator decides whether or not to grant you access.

Grant access to a project (Administrators Only)

When someone requests access to a project, you, as the administrator of the team, are told about it.

- Position your cursor so that it is in the top right-hand corner of the project, and then choose the **View Access Requests** option.
- Take a look at the permission requests.
- Either click the **Approve** button to allow the requester access or the Reject button to refuse the request.

Open a project

If you want to access the data that is stored in a specific project or sample folder, you can do so by double-clicking on the name of the project or sample. Take note that the name of the team is shown at the very top of the data panel. Simply go to your team inside the online application by clicking on the team's name.

Creating a New Project Folder and Sub-Folders

1. Within Fusion 360, first expand the Data Panel and then click the **Home** icon to navigate to the top of the data structure.
2. Select **New Project** from the drop-down menu, and a fresh entry will be added to the project list.
3. Give the project a name and give it a number.

4. If you would want the project to be moved to the top of the list, you should "**pin**" it (optional)
5. To launch the project, just double-click on its icon.

When you use the Data Panel to establish a new project, the Project Type setting will automatically be set to **Closed**. This ensures that the project can only be accessed by members of the team that you have invited to participate. During the process of creating a project in Fusion Team, you will have the opportunity to pick the **Project Type** and select a **Project Avatar**.

You can submit any data linked with the design to the project, and you can also invite other members of the project to participate. To launch Fusion Team and access the project, you may alternatively choose the **Open Details on Web** button from the toolbar. After that, you'll be able to use a web browser to control the project's settings, members, and content.

How to Create a Folder Structure

The newly created project does not have any kind of folder structure, to begin with. You can save a fresh design and then instantly begin working on more manageable jobs. On the other hand, if you're working on a more involved project with several people, you should devise a plan right from the start that will help you keep both your team and the project organized.

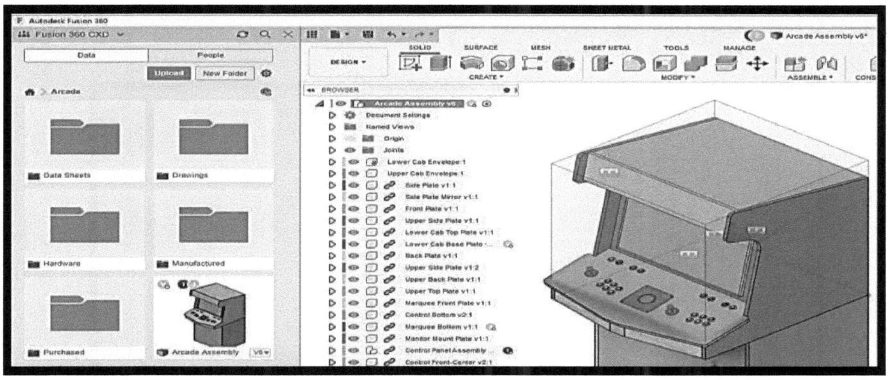

1. While the project is still open, go to the Data Panel and select the **New Folder** button. This will cause the creation of a new folder inside the project.
2. Give the folder a name and click the **Save** button.
3. Repeat the steps for every other folder and subfolder that you need.

For the sake of this illustration of an arcade, you may wish to design a:

- **The manufactured** folder will include the components that you will develop and build in-house.
- **Purchased** folder for components, such as controllers, that you will buy off the shelf, such as in this case.
- **Drawing** folder to be used to store any designs that will be sent to third-party manufacturers
- **Data Sheets** folder that will include any specifications or data sheets connected with components in the design.
- **Hardware** folders that you may need, such as hinges, fasteners, and threaded inserts

Uploading Existing Files in a Project

To upload a file to the Data Panel, do the following:

1. If the Data Panel is not already open, you may expand it by clicking the grid symbol in the top left corner of the screen.

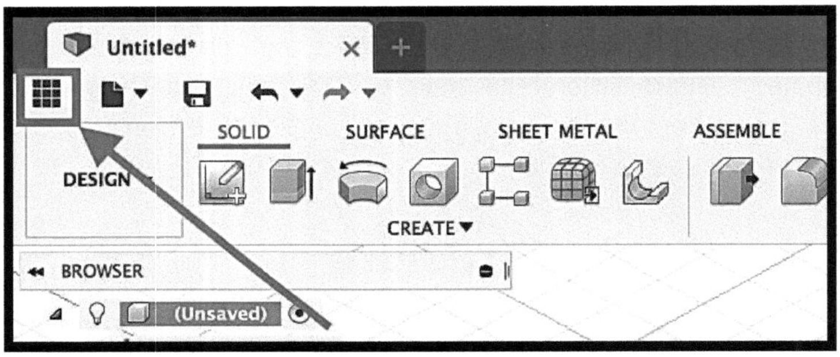

2. Launch the project where the design will be stored after the Data Panel has been enlarged and then click the **Save** button.

3. Select the file to upload by clicking the icon as shown below;

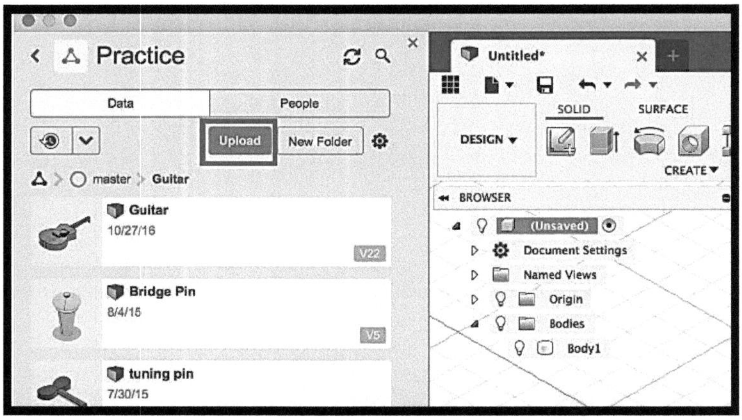

4. In the Upload dialog box, click the "**Select Files**" button, as shown in the figure below;

5. On the personal computer, pick the directory where files may be uploaded, then open the file you want to upload by clicking the "**Open**" button.
6. After clicking "**Open**" to upload the design to the cloud, the design ought to be listed on the following screen.
7. After the file has been successfully transferred to the cloud, the status should have transitioned from a progress bar to the word "**Complete.**"

Organize and find projects

All Open, Closed, and Secret projects that you are a part of are shown on the Projects tab in Fusion Team. The projects are organized alphabetically.

Projects can be pinned for organization. Projects can be located by:

- Browsing the projects list on the Projects page
- Sorting
- Filtering

Pin projects

You may easily identify projects that you are interested in or those you are working on by pinning them. You can pin both projects you are a part of and all Open projects.

Fusion 360

1. Launch the Data Panel first.
2. Hover your mouse over the project in the project list.
3. Select the **Project Pin Icon**.

A new filter called PINNED will become accessible on the Projects page when you pin a project.

In Fusion Team

- Choose the ALL filter on the Projects page.
- Hover your mouse over the project in the project list.
- Select the **Project Pin Icon**.

Unpin a Project

You may unpin a project if you no longer want it to appear in the PINNED filter.

- Choose the **PINNED** filter from the Projects page.
- Hover your mouse over the project in the project list.
- Select the **Project Unpin** icon.

Wherever the project is displayed, the Unpin option is accessible. You may do this, for instance, by hovering over the project on the page for all projects, in OWNED BY ME, or SHARED WITH ME.

Find content in the content

From the Project Home page in Fusion Team, you can access all the material in your project.

By default, a project's material is shown in the following order:

- Folders are displayed in alphabetical order
- Files displayed in alphabetical order

In your projects, you may modify how the material is displayed. To switch between the List view and Grid view choices, click the corresponding icons in the upper right corner of the Project content area.

Search for content

You may search for files by utilizing letters or phrases that are present in either the file names or the content of the files themselves. You may search for certain letters, characters, or phrases by clicking the search button that is located on the top right of the navigation bar and entering the information that you are looking for.

Filter projects

By default, the following filters are applied to the projects to organize them: **ALL, OWNED BY ME,** and **SHARED WITH ME.** Click the **OWNED BY ME** link to see and access all of the projects that you have established, and click the SHARED WITH ME link to see and access all of the projects to which you have been invited.

If you choose a filter, the default view will switch to the filter you choose the next time you sign in, regardless of whether you changed it or not. Using the Filter box that is located at the bottom of the Data Panel in the Fusion 360 app, you can filter the project list. The filter looks at the names of projects and the descriptions of those projects. As soon as you type a character into the Filter box, the filtering process will begin. Filtering may be done with anything from a single character up to multiple words. Either choose the Clear button that is located at the very end of the Filter field or erase the text that is included inside the filter. If the filter requirements are not met by any project or description, then all of the projects will be hidden.

Organize the contents and the projects.

You can arrange projects in descending order based on the project name (**Name**), the creator (**Owned by**), and the creation date (**Created On**). Simply click the column heading in the header row located directly above the list of projects to sort the projects in the list.

You can organize the project's files and folders according to the following criteria:

- File name (Name)
- Who was the uploader? (Owner)
- File type (Type)
- File size (size)
- The date of the most recent update (Last updated)

Take note that files and folders are organized in different ways. If you choose to sort by Owner, for instance, folders will be shown in alphabetical order according to the name of their respective owners (**ascending or descending**). Additionally, files will be arranged according to the owner's name in alphabetical order (**ascending or descending**). Folders will always come before files in the directory tree. These criteria are shown in the List view on the row that serves as the heading for the list of items. To sort the material, click on the header of any of the columns.

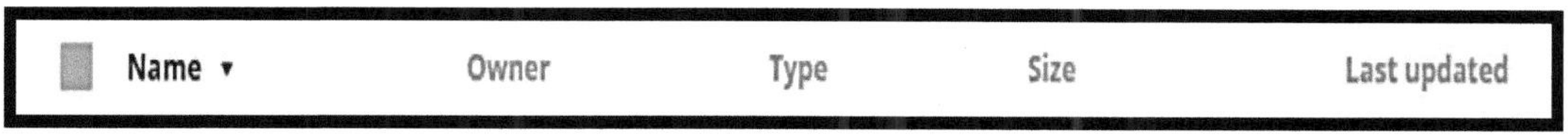

To sort the data, choose a criterion from the drop-down menu located in the Grid view.

Saving a Design File

Click the **save (disk)** icon that is located in the upper-left corner of the toolbar to save a design file. You may also use the keyboard shortcut **CMD + S (Mac OS) or CTRL + S** (Windows) (Mac).

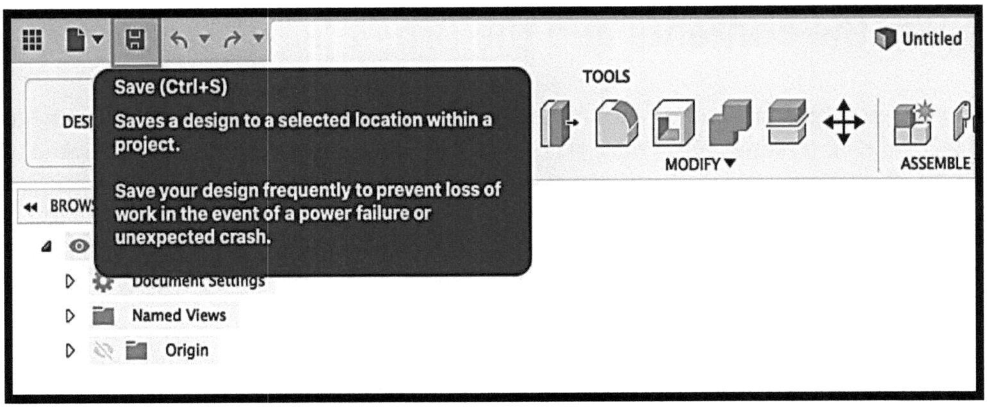

When you save a design file for the first time, you will be required to provide the file name as well as the location where the file is going to be saved. Later on, using the data panel, you will be able to alter either the location or the name.

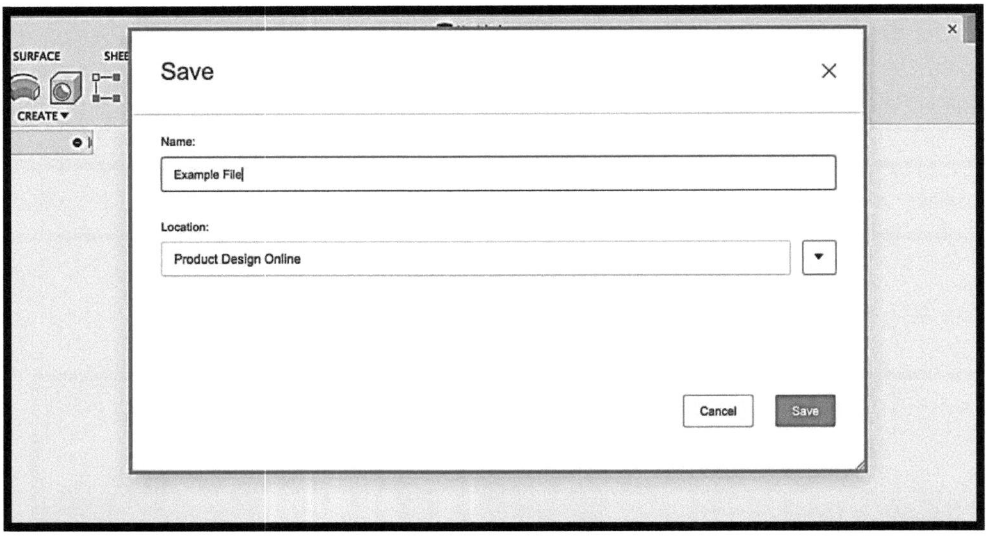

After you have successfully saved the file, the save icon will be disabled until the file is modified.

Exporting a Design to Other CAD Formats

Native vs. Neutral File Formats

If you have ever used Fusion 360 to open a generic CAD file, you have probably seen uneven results. On the other hand, one could not show up at all, while the other might be made up of hundreds of surface bodies. And why did some of the intricate details from the first model get lost in the translation? Translation problems can arise whenever a CAD file of any sort is imported or exported. The flexibility of design files to be exported and imported into a variety of tools raises the risk that quality may be compromised. Keeping this in mind, it is essential to choose the appropriate file format to ensure that the quality of your design is maintained even when it is passed from one engineer to another. The file formats used by CAD programs may be divided into two distinct categories: native and neutral. The file formats that are native to a tool are inherently compatible with that tool. This indicates that the creator of the program controls the technology behind the file format, and they can make any modifications to it that they see fit. The creation of neutral file formats often occurs inside a standards-setting group of some type. This group takes into account not only one tool but also how their file format will be utilized across the board in terms of CAD software. The intention is to make it simple for any CAD tool to switch between using any of these file formats.

Keeping all of this in mind, let's discuss some of the most common neutral file formats that you'll want to think about using when exporting your next design:

STEP

The **International Organization for Standardization** (ISO) governs one of the most used neutral file formats, which is known as the **Standard for Exchange of Product Data** (STEP). Probably, you are already familiar with the STEP file format if you have dealt with almost any kind of 3D CAD.

This format, in comparison to other neutral forms, provides a variety of benefits, including the following:

- **More data**. Tolerance information is included in STEP files, which offer valuable data for applications requiring accurate machining.
- **More versatility**. The STEP format, which is defined by ISO standards and has been updated throughout the years to serve a wide variety of specialized engineering specialties, may be found here.
- **More intelligence**. STEP files reference each unique component included inside a design rather than reproducing the same part an arbitrary number of times; as a result, this format is ideal for use with assemblies.

IGES

Before the release of STEP, the dominant CAD file format was known as the **Initial Graphics Exchange Specification** (IGES). STEP was developed to replace IGES. This particular file format provides geometry data for a model, but it does not include any information about the connection that pieces have with one another inside an assembly. Additionally, it does not provide built-in support for solid modeling. There is a possibility that IGES files are still in circulation; nevertheless, we do not advise that you use these files to translate your contemporary CAD drawings. As of the time of this writing, the IGES standard will not be undergoing any more revisions in the foreseeable future.

Parasolid

The **Parasolid** file format is owned by Siemens, and any other corporation that is willing to fork out the necessary cash may get a license to use it. This format has a CAD kernel, which assures that it is compatible with a wide range of different tools.

Among the many modeling approaches that may be used with Parasolid are the following:

- Solid modeling
- Modeling of freeform surfaces and sheets
- Support for the rendering of graphics, including tessellation

DXF

The **Drawing Exchange Format**, known as DXF, is AutoCAD's default file format for 2D drawings. We have decided to include it here because AutoCAD is one of the most popular CAD programs, and practically all CAD programs support DXF. This format is wonderful for bridging the gap between old and modern applications; but it does not support the most recent technology such as solid modeling.

STL

The **Standard Tessellation Language** (STL) file format is used extensively in 3D printing, scanning, and even certain CAM software programs. This model is represented in this file format as a pure triangular mesh; however, none of the object's extensive parametric data is included in the representation. Because of these constraints, STL works well for 3D printing, but it is not recommended for use with 3D CAD tools.

Importing a CAD File in Fusion 360

To get started, you'll need a CAD file to practice importing into so you can hone your abilities. The process of uploading a Fusion 360 design and importing standard CAD files are functionally identical. You will need to start by bringing up the Data panel, selecting a project from the drop-down menu, and then clicking the Upload button.

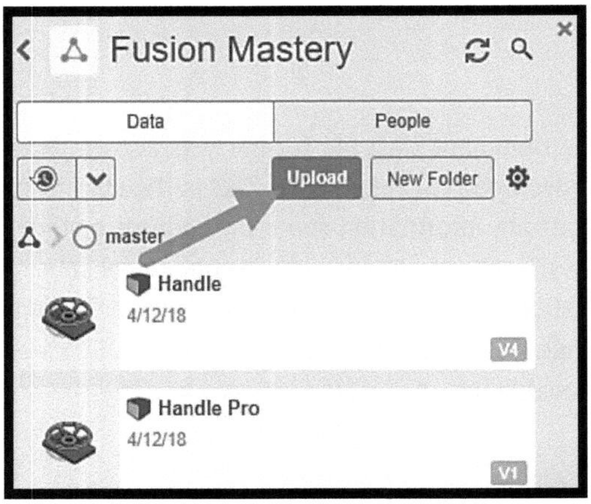

You may now choose the IGES file you just downloaded and then click the option labeled Upload from this screen. After the file has been completely uploaded, you may then go ahead and shut the Job Status window. **When you open the example IGES file in your canvas, you should see a model that has a fancy appearance similar to the one below:**

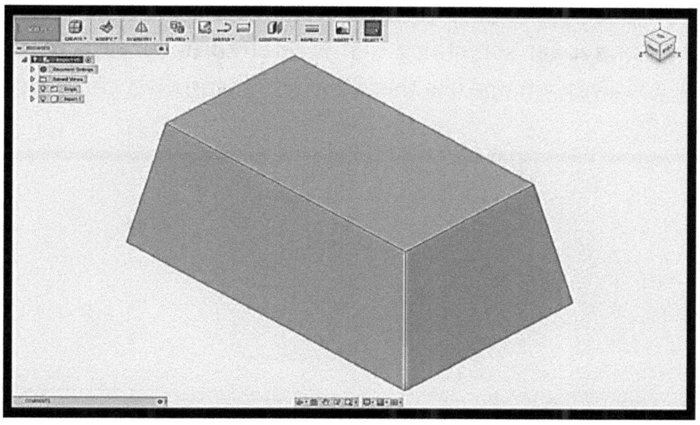

When it comes to importing generic CAD files like this one, there are a few important factors to keep in mind. To begin, the Sculpt workspace will be selected as the default when you have finished importing your file. **This may be altered in the settings of Fusion 360, as seen in the following example:**

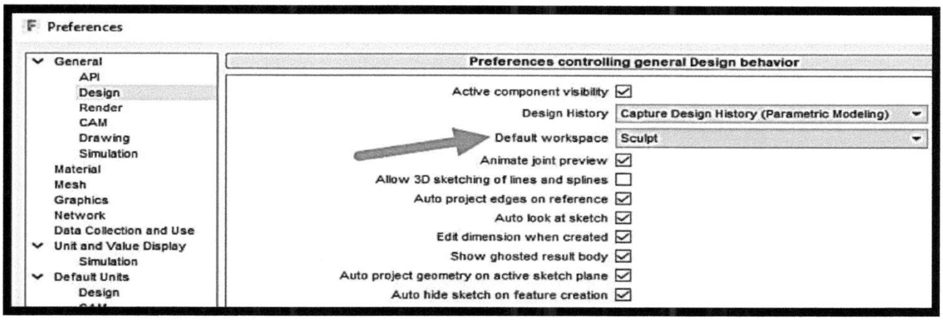

You'll also note that there isn't a design timeline at the bottom of the canvas in this particular file, which brings us to our second point. To activate this feature, right-click the file name while in the Browser, and then pick the **Capture Design History** option from the context menu.

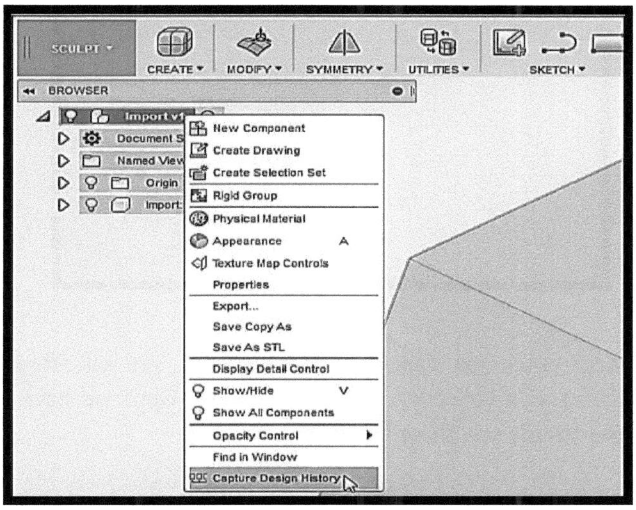

When you choose the plus sign on your newly added timeline, you will notice two entries: the first is for the original import, and the second is for something that is referred to as **Base Feature 1**. When a solid or surface body is imported, it is given a name like this, which is essentially a generic name.

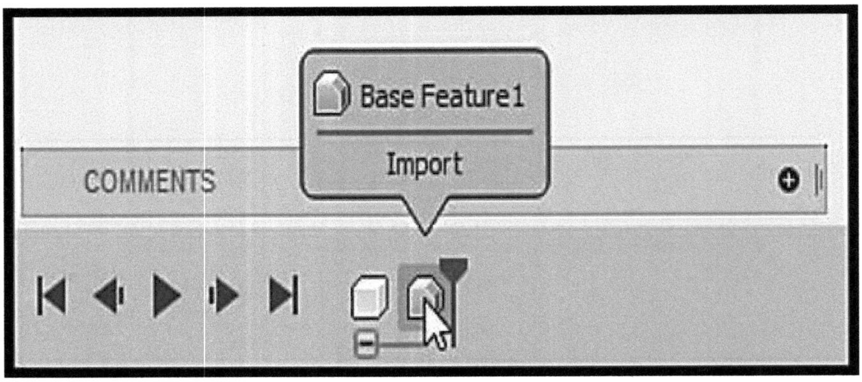

Last but not least, Fusion may recognize some imported objects as a collection of separate bodies rather than a single solid body. First, open the **Import: 1** folder on your browser, and then expand the Bodies folder. You will notice a folder labeled "**Unstitched**" that has six separate bodies within.

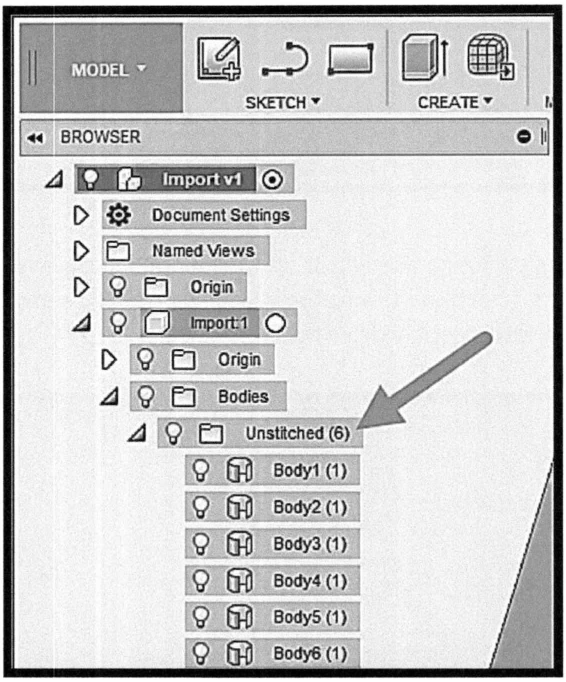

What led to this occurrence? When you want to save an IGES file, you will often be given the choice to either save it as a surface or as a collection of surface bodies. Once we have switched to the Patch workspace, we will be able to easily sew these bodies together.

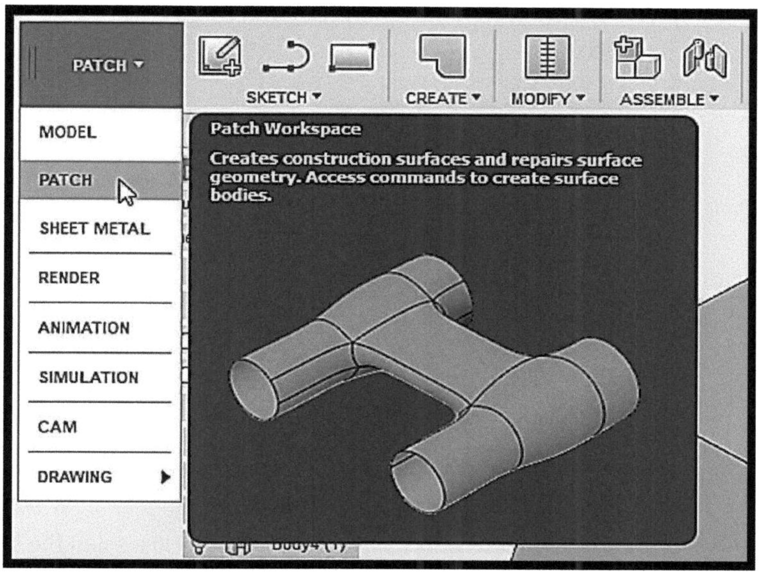

Using the shift key and the left mouse button, select all of the bodies that are found in the **unstitched folder** inside the Patch workspace. When you have all of them chosen, expand the Modify choices on the toolbar of the Patch workspace, and then pick the **Stitch** option. In the Stitch dialog, we are going to leave all of the settings as they are, and then click the **OK** button.

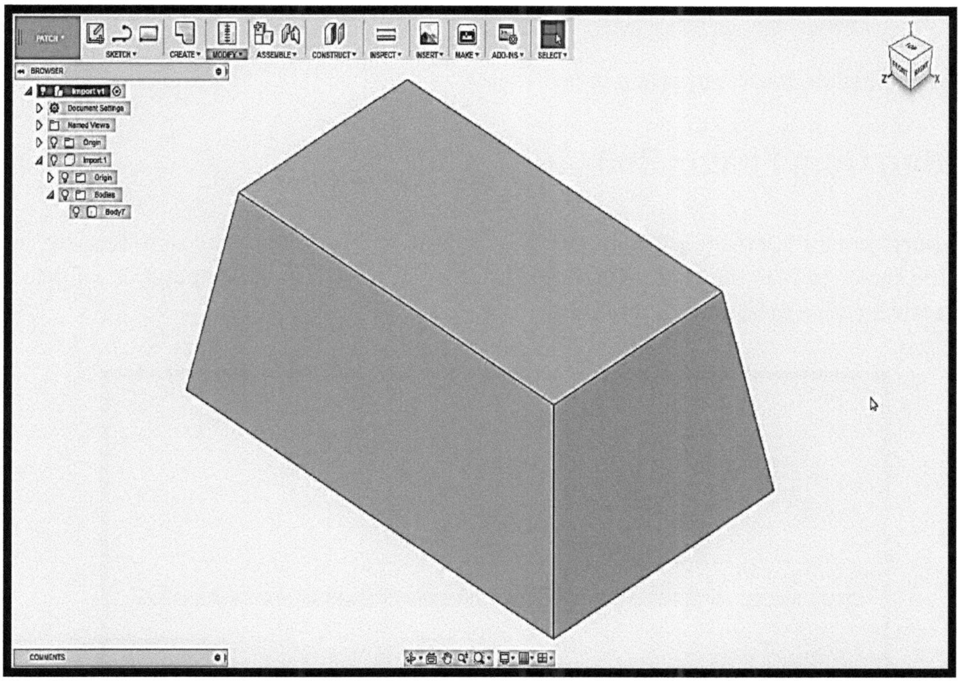

Once the stitch is finished, you should check out the results on your browser. These six unstitched bodies need to have been combined into a single Body 7 at this point.

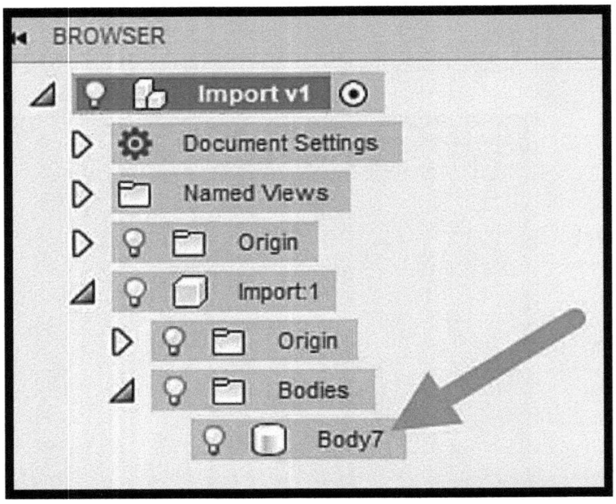

At this stage, our IGS model has been loaded into Fusion 360 without incident and the components have been successfully joined together. You are now working on V2; just be sure to save the file and give it a description that reflects the change.

Exporting a CAD File in Fusion 360

The process of importing a standard CAD file has just been covered; the next step is to learn how to export the same file to a different CAD user.

There are two possible courses of action to investigate:

Exporting from Fusion 360

Choose **Export** from the File menu while your IGES file is still open. The Export window will appear, providing you with the choice to save the file to either the Fusion cloud or your local computer. It will also provide you with a few file-type options to choose from.

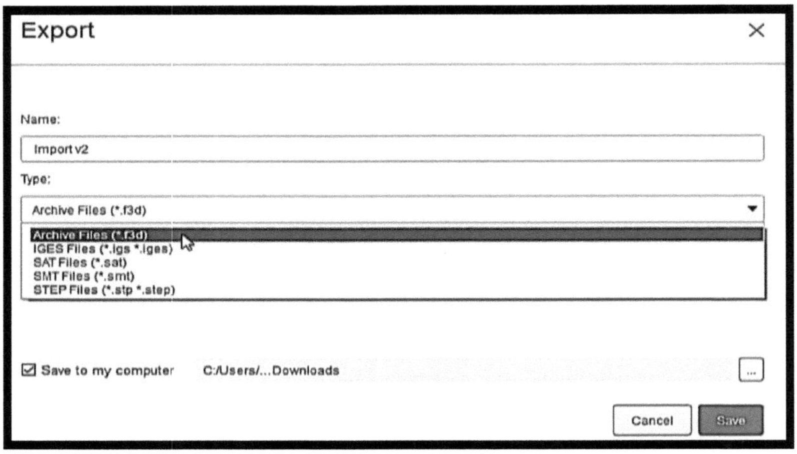

You may have seen that the list of supported file formats in the dropdown is quite limited. If the format you want to use isn't on the list, it's time to step into Fusion Team.

Opening an Existing Design File

The file may be an existing Fusion 360 design that has been saved in the past, or it can be a file that was saved locally on your computer by following the procedures below:

1. Click **File**.
2. Click **Open**.

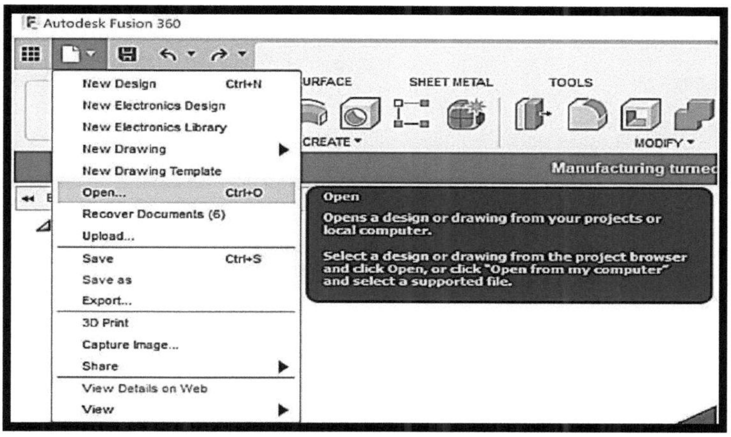

3. A dialog window labeled **Open** will then open, displaying your cloud data.
4. To access a file that is listed in your cloud data, go to the file's location, and then click the Open button.
5. Select "**Open from my computer**" to load a file that has been stored locally on your computer.

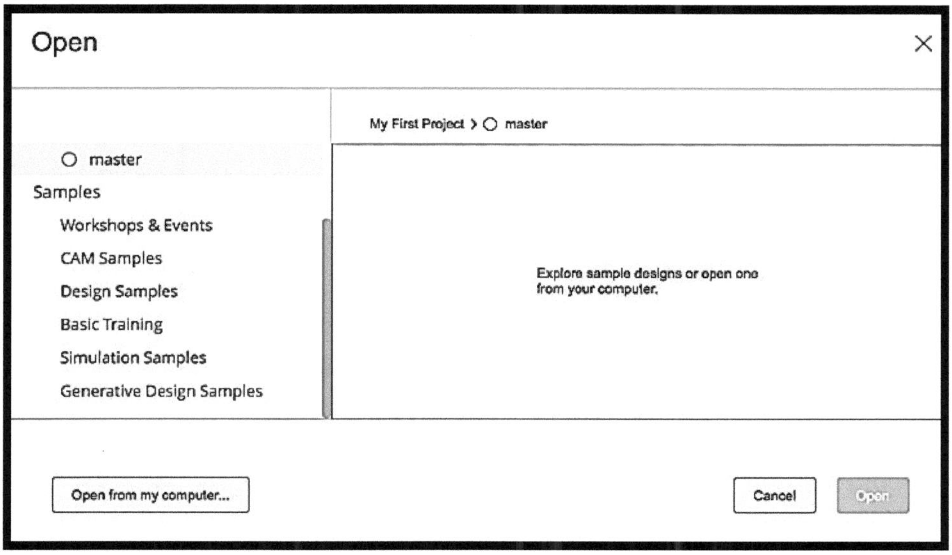

6. Once you have located the file, click the **Open** button. For a list of the many sorts of files that can be read by Fusion 360.
7. When the translation of the file in the Cloud is finished, you may open it in Fusion 360 by clicking the "**Open**" button in the Job Status box. This will bring up the file.

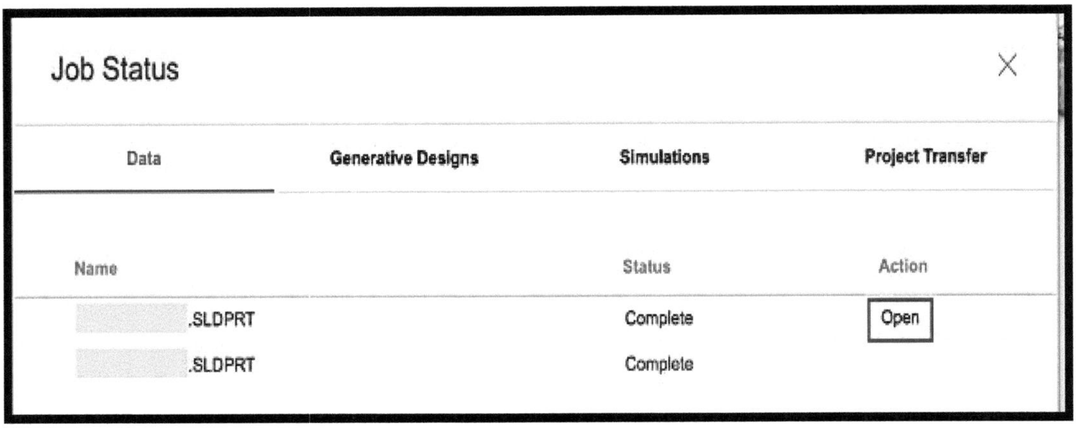

Opening an Existing File from the Data Panel

Simply select the Show Data Panel option on the Application Bar. This will allow you to access an existing design file of a project from inside the Data Panel. The Data Panel is brought into play. The next step is to go to the location of the file that needs to be opened, then double-click on the file itself. Fusion 360 will now open the specified file in its workspace. Another way is to right-click on the file that needs to be opened, then click on the **Open** option that appears in the shortcut menu that pops up.

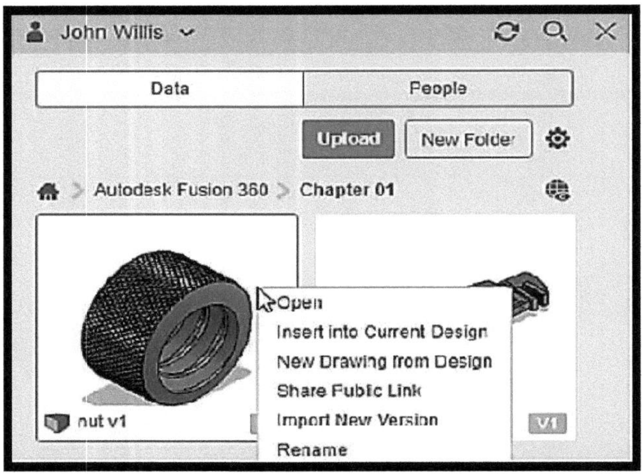

When you open a design file in Fusion 360, the program will automatically open the most recent version of that file. Nevertheless, you also have the option of opening the file in an earlier version. To achieve this, choose the design thumbnail in the Data Panel and then click on the Version icon that is located in the bottom right-hand corner of the thumbnail. The Data Panel contains representations of all the different versions of the respective design file. Move the mouse over the version of the file that you want to open and leave it there. In its immediate vicinity are the buttons labeled **Promote and Open.** When you click the **Promote** button, the older version of the file will be upgraded to the most recent version of the file. The Open button is what you need to click to open the earlier version of the file. To access the file, choose the **Open** option. Fusion 360 will launch with the version of the file that you choose already open. If the Data Panel does not display all versions of the files that have been chosen, you may make them show by selecting the option to Show all versions inside the Data Panel.

Opening an Existing File by using the Open tool

To use the Open tool to access an existing design file associated with a project, first, choose **File** from the menu located in the Application Bar, and then select **Open** from the menu that appears. The dialog window labeled Open will now appear. In this dialog box, you need to choose the project by clicking on its name, which is located on the left panel of the dialog box. The right panel of the dialog box displays all of the subfolders and files that are associated with the currently chosen project. Choose the necessary design file to open from the list located in the right panel of the dialog box. Note that if the design file that is going to be opened is saved in a subfolder of the project that is now chosen, then you will need to double-click on the subfolder to see the files that are stored inside of it. After choosing the file that contains the design, click the **Open** button that is located in the dialog box. The application will open the specified file.

Opening an Existing File from the Local Computer

You also have the option of opening a previously stored file on your local computer, such as a Fusion file **(*.f3d), IGES file (*.iges; *.igs), SAT file (*.sat), SMT file (*.smt), STEP file (*.step; *.stp),** etc. To do this, bring up the Open dialog box, and then choose the option to **Open from My Computer** from the menu that appears. There is a new instance of the Open dialog box appearing. Use the "**Browse**" button in this dialog box to go to the location of the file that needs to be opened. You will be able to open files created in Alias, AutoCAD DWG, Autodesk Fusion 360, Autodesk Inventor, Catia V5, NX, IGES, and STEP, amongst other file formats. Following the selection of the necessary file, the **Open** button will become active in the dialog box. When you click on the Job State window, you will see the current status of the file shown in the Status column. Click the **Open** option in the Action column of the dialog box when the status of the file displays as Complete in the Status column of the dialog box. This will allow you to access the file. Fusion 360 will now open the specified file in its workspace. When you access an already-created file, you will have the ability to update it by adding new features. It is advised that before you add the new features, you switch on the process of recording design history in the Timeline for the newly added features. This should be done before you add the new features. To do this, right-click on the name of the file (the top browser node) in the **BROWSER**, and once the shortcut menu opens, choose the tool titled "**Capture Design History**" from the list of available options. In the same manner, if you do not want to record the design history for a particular design, you may use the tool that allows you to do so by selecting it from the shortcut menu that displays.

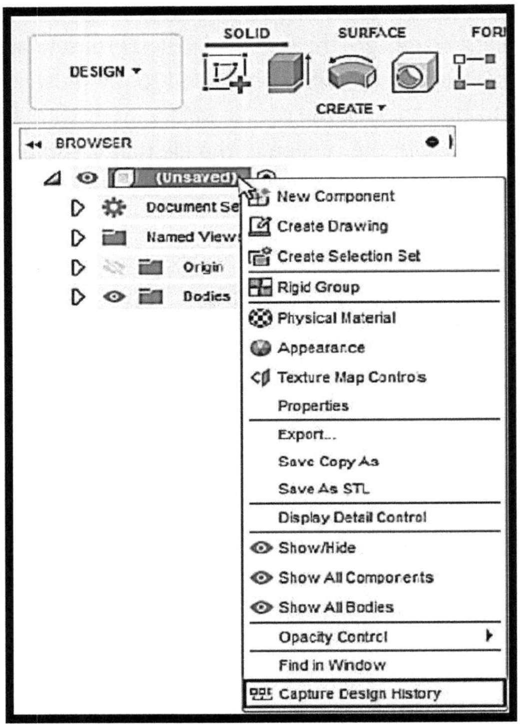

Working in the Offline Mode

When you are not connected to the Internet, when your Internet connection is lost, when an unexpected outage is detected, or when the service is being maintained, Fusion 360 will switch to the offline mode automatically. Nevertheless, Fusion 360 enables you to continue working on your ideas even when you are not connected to the online platform. In addition, you can manually toggle between the online and offline modes. To check the current status of your job, go to the top right corner of the screen and click on the button labeled "**Job Status.**" The flyout for the Job Status will show. To begin working online, choose the icon provided in this flyer. When this happens, the offline mode is enabled, and an icon denoting "**Working Offline**" shows in the flyout.

Recovering Unsaved Data

If you want to identify a file that can be recovered, you may try using one or more of the following solutions: To examine the designs that were recovered from the file, use the Recover Documents command.

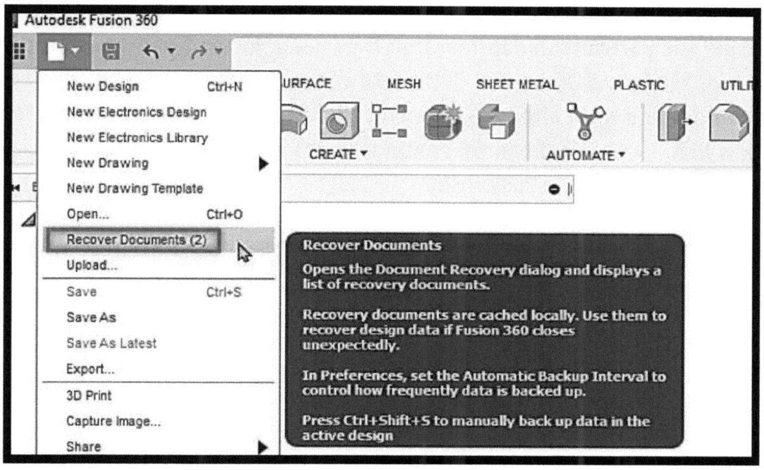

Use the arrow keys or the mouse to go to the next place. Make use of the upload command to successfully upload the necessary ***.f3d file**. Please take note that the files and folders in these directories are hidden. By default, backups will occur every 5 minutes (although this interval can be changed in the Fusion preferences). While you are working on the document, there is a chance that the save will be delayed until after the current operation has been finished. For instance, an automatic save will not begin if there is a dialog box for the Extrude command that is now active.

Sharing a Design

Sharing Design Using a Link

This public connection may be generated in one of two different places: either from inside Fusion 360 itself or from A360 within a web browser. Launch Fusion 360, open the Data Panel, and go to the location of the Design you want to share. Use the context menu to choose **Share Public Link** after right-clicking on the design.

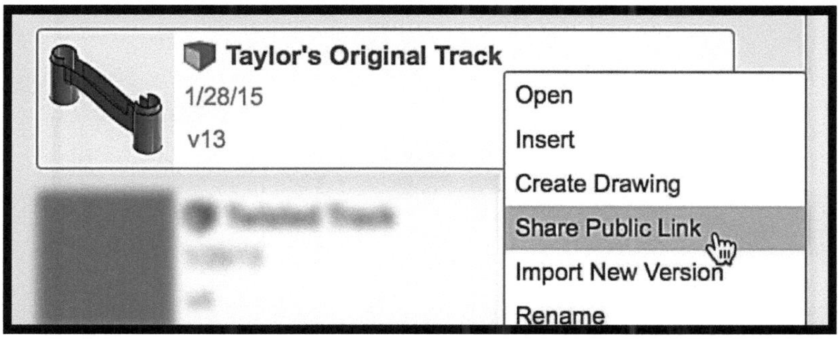

To make the public link active, you will need to tick the first box that appears in the following dialogue window. After that, you'll be able to choose whether or not the Design may be downloaded, as well as whether or not a password is needed to access it. When you make the Design accessible for download, you are not only posting the.f3d file so that it may be downloaded by others, but you are also making it possible for anybody else to get the particular file format that they need. Instead of manually submitting files with extensions such as.f3d, STL, and.STP, let the cloud take care of this translation for you instead! You may start sharing with anybody you want after you have copied the link that is located at the top of the dialogue box. The public link will, for your convenience, continue to lead to the most recent version of your Design even as you make new versions of it in Fusion 360.

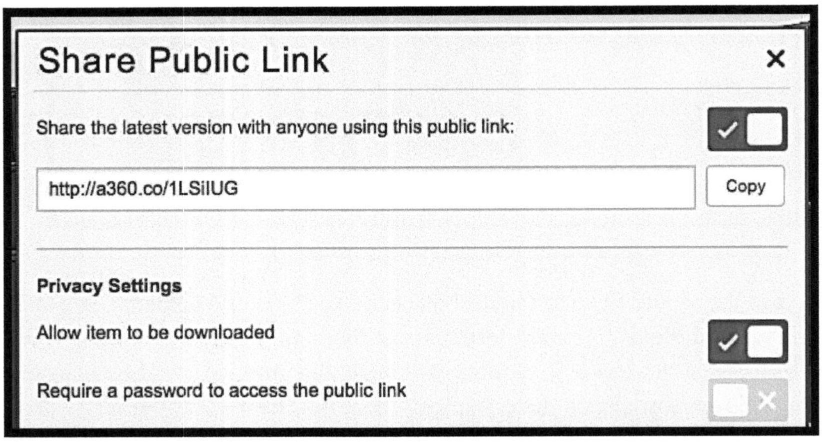

The use of A360 inside a web browser constitutes the second method for producing a public connection. Open the **A360 viewer** and browse the design inside A360 that you want to share once you have done so. There will be a **Share** button at the very top of the screen, and clicking it will bring up the identical dialogue that can be seen in the actual product. In conclusion, the A360 viewer enables users to produce HTML embed code, which can then be included in any website of their choosing to add a 3D viewer that does not need the use of a plugin. To do this, choose the share dialogue box and look for the Embed option. The only thing left to do is choose the size of the viewer you want, copy the HTML code, and then paste it into the HTML code of your website!

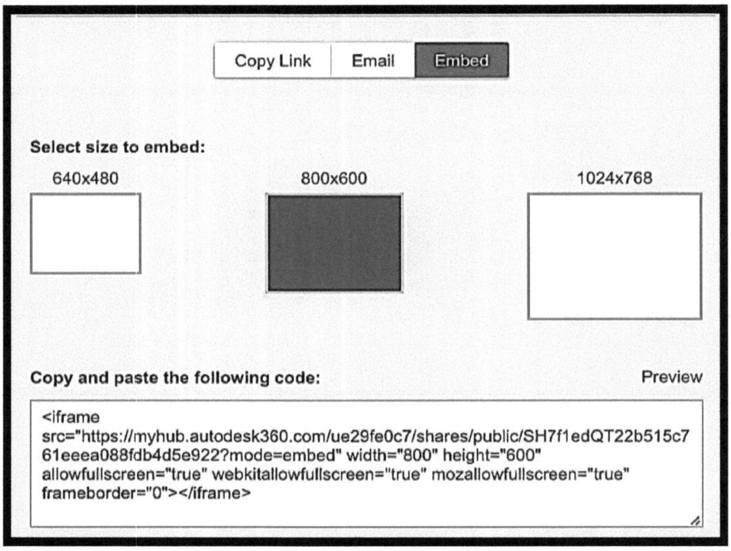

Sharing Design to GrabCAD

To publish or share your design on GrabCAD (www.grabcad.com), go to the **File** menu and choose **Share** before selecting **GrabCAD** from the drop-down menu. The dialog box labeled **PUBLISH TO GRABCAD** will now display. You may publish your design to all registered members of GrabCAD by logging in to your GrabCAD account via this window and then selecting the Publish button.

Sharing Design by Recording Screen

Using the Screencast Recorder, which is included in Fusion 360, you can record your screen and produce a movie of your design, which you can then send to anybody. To accomplish this, go to the application bar and click on the File menu, then choose Share, and then select Launch **Screencast Recorder**. The Screencast Recorder program is going to be downloaded; thus, the Autodesk website is going to be viewed. Get the Screencast Recorder program by downloading and installing it. After the Screencast Recorder application has been installed, you can open it by double-clicking the Screencast Recorder icon that is located on your desktop. The screencast window will now open.

After that, all you need to do to begin recording your screen is click the **Record** button located in this window. When you have finished recording all of the steps of your design workflow, you can end the recording by clicking the **Stop** button in the Screencast box. The preview window for the screencast recording is shown. To save and upload your changes, click the button located in this window. A dialogue window labeled Screencast Details is shown.

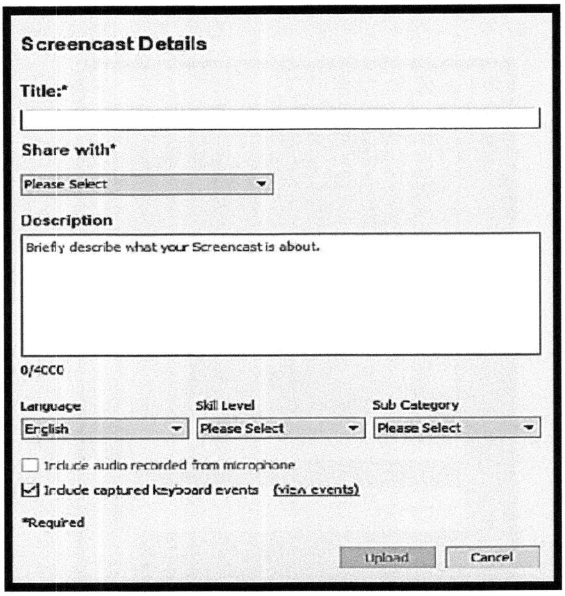

In this dialogue box, you will need to provide the necessary data, such as the title name, and description of the video. After that, in the Share with drop-down box, choose the option that corresponds to what you need, and then click the **Upload** button. The video will be uploaded and shared following the option that was chosen from the drop-down list located in the dialog box labeled Share with.

Invoking a Marking Menu

The Marking menu is a radial menu that gives you rapid access to commands that are used often.

- If you use your mouse's **right mouse button** anywhere in the canvas, the Marking menu will show around your cursor.
- To execute a command, you must first move the mouse in the direction of the command and then click anywhere inside the highlighted wedge.
- To close the Marking menu, either click anywhere outside of the menu, inside the center of the menu or hit the Esc key on your keyboard.

There are three distinct subsections inside the Marking menu:

- The radial menu on the first level
- The radial menu on the second level
- The context menu

First-level radial menu

The radial menu on the first level includes commands that are used often. There are eight predefined commands available in the radial menu of the first level in the Design workspace.

- Restate last command.
- PressPull
- Redo
- Hole
- Sketch
- Move/Copy
- Undo
- Delete

Workspaces, toolbar tabs, contextual environments, and active commands

The commands that are shown in the Marking menu are dynamic and alter depending on the workspace, the toolbar tab, the contextual environment, and the command that is now active.

Examples:

When you transition to the Surface tab in the Design workspace, the Hole command is replaced with the Patch command. This change takes effect immediately.

- The **Flange command** replaces the one that was there before when you switched to the Sheet Metal tab.
- The **Edit Form** and **Face commands** are shown when the Form contextual environment is selected.
- The **Generative Design workspace** shows instructions that guide you through the process of setting up generative research.
- The **Render workspace** presents instructions that are relevant to rendering, appearances, and textures, as well as scenarios.
- The **Animation workspace** provides access to commands that facilitate the creation of animations and their distribution.
- The **Simulation workspace** provides command prompts that guide you through the process of establishing simulation studies.
- The **repeat, undo, redo, and import functions** are not available in the **Manufacture workspace**; however, this workspace does provide a more detailed context menu for configuring and maintaining toolpaths.
- The **Drawing workspace** provides you with commands that assist you in documenting and annotating your design, in addition to tools for annotation that are accessible through the context menu.

Second-level radial menu

When you move the cursor over the bottom command in the radial menu of the first level, the radial menu of the second level appears around the pointer.

The second-level radial menu in Sketch has default access to eight different commands, which are as follows:

- Complete the Sketch
- 2-Point Rectangle
- Fit Point Spline
- Project
- Line
- Offset
- Sketch Dimension
- Center Diameter Circle

Your productivity may be substantially sped up and made more efficient if you access the Sketch commands via the second level of the radial menu. By moving the mouse above the up arrow, you may access the radial menu on the first level again.

Context menu

A context menu that includes the following items is displayed underneath the radial menu:

- Operation controls for navigation such as Pan, zoom, and Orbit
- Isolate/Unisolate
- A list of available workspaces will make switching between them much simpler.
- Saved shortcut keys

Choose the command you want to execute from the menu that appears when you right-click.

Gestures

You may start to use gestures to pick commands in the Marking menu after you have started to learn the placement of commonly used commands in the Marking menu. This allows you to select commands without having to bring up the whole Marking menu. Any command that is accessible through a radial menu may be executed using gestures. You may also use gestures to pick contextual instructions such as **OK** and **Cancel** while a command is active. This is particularly useful for the radial menu on the second level of the Sketch program. You can access the Sketch commands by right-clicking, holding down the mouse button, and dragging down, followed by dragging in the direction of where the command appears on the second-level radial menu of Sketch.

Examples:

- To create a 2-Point Rectangle, drag in the downward direction and then to the top right.
- To create a Fit Point Spline, drag in the form of an L.
- **Line**: Move in a downward direction.
- To adjust the offset, drag in the down and left directions.
- To complete the sketch, drag the cursor down, then halfway up.
- To do this action, within a command, right-click and hold, then swiftly drag to the right.

3D Printing

Form Feature

The form feature, which is represented by a purple cube, makes it possible to build intricate organic forms. It offers up a new workspace that comes equipped with a broad variety of tools for sculpting intricate designs. Using this function, one may easily create organic and creative models that can then be printed using 3D technology.

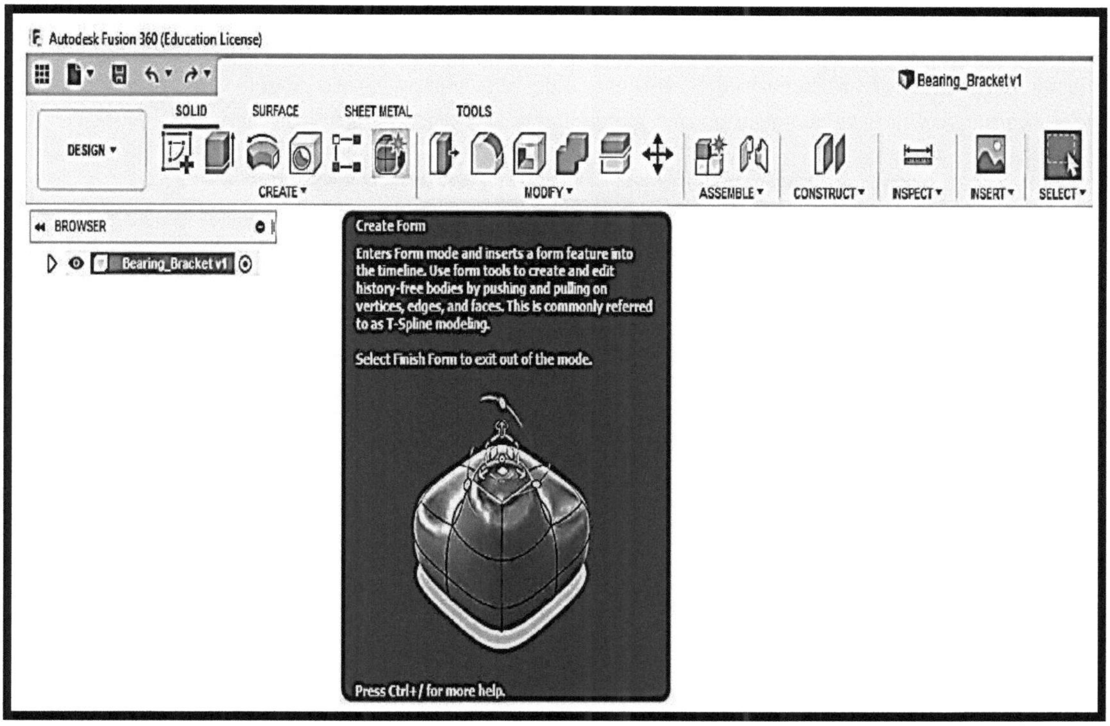

Surfaces

The user can fix models in preparation for 3D printing using surface tools. To reshape the component, the surfaces may be stitched closed, extruded, pulled, or pushed. A watertight model that does not have any holes in the shell may also be created with the assistance of the surfacing tools.

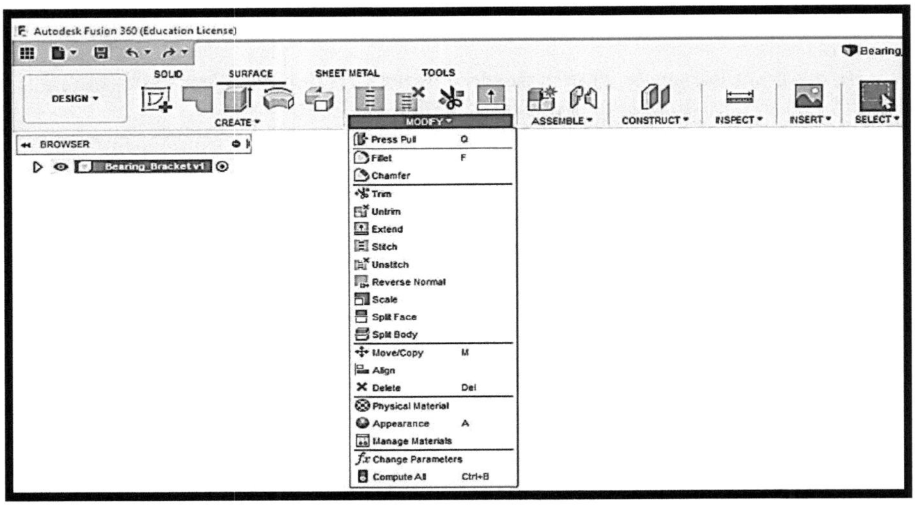

Event simulation

This tool helps model how your 3D print will react under time-dependent loads and velocities so that you may make any necessary adjustments before it is printed. For instance, snap-fit joints may be modeled to indicate what loads are encountered by the clip while it is being pressed closed. This provides a good understanding of where the weak areas are, allowing the design to be optimized more effectively.

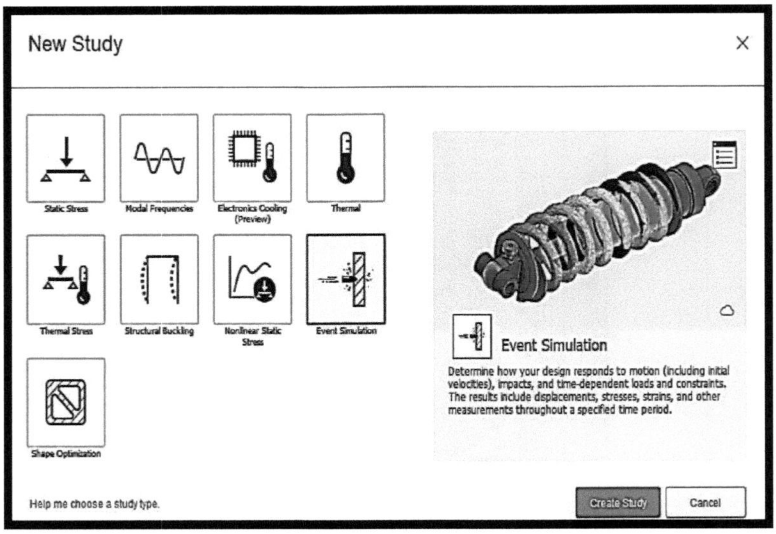

Non-Linear Stress

Certain 3D printing procedures, such as fused deposition modeling (FDM), result in the creation of components having non-linear material characteristics, which can only be modeled using a finite element analysis (FEA) tool that offers a non-linear study type. If the appropriate material data is input into Fusion

360, the extremely competent nonlinear study type that it offers can produce an accurate prediction of the stress that will be placed on a component.

3D Printing from Fusion 360

When the **Make** icon is clicked in the Design workspace, the 3D print menu appears. From this menu, you may make a variety of adjustments to the model to improve its readiness for printing, and then you can submit the model to a 3D print utility.

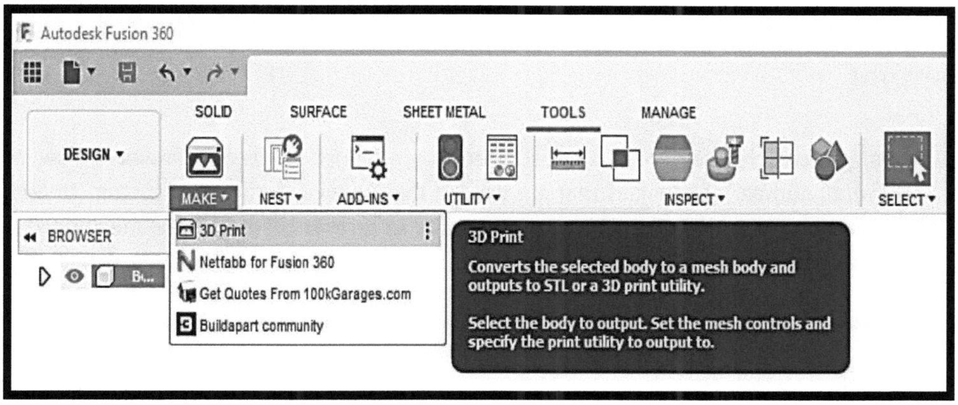

The following is a list of the many choices that may be selected from the menu:

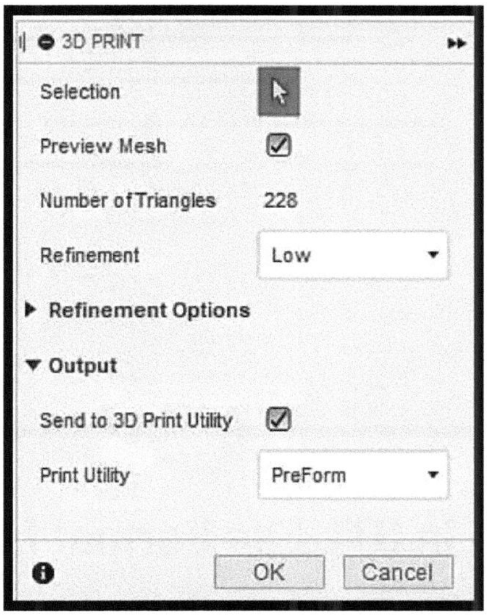

Selection

The user is given the ability to pick the model to be 3D printed via the usage of this option.

Preview Mesh.

This checkbox displays the model's mesh, which is helpful for the user if the user wishes to see what impact modifications to the parameters have on the model.

Number of triangles

This reveals the total number of unique triangles that are used to construct the model. This number will rise when the fineness level is raised.

Refinement

With this option, you can choose between three different predefined levels of refinement: low, medium, and high. The overall number of triangles that are used in the model is determined by this. **In addition to this, there is a custom option that gives the user the ability to further customize the mesh depending on the following parameters:**

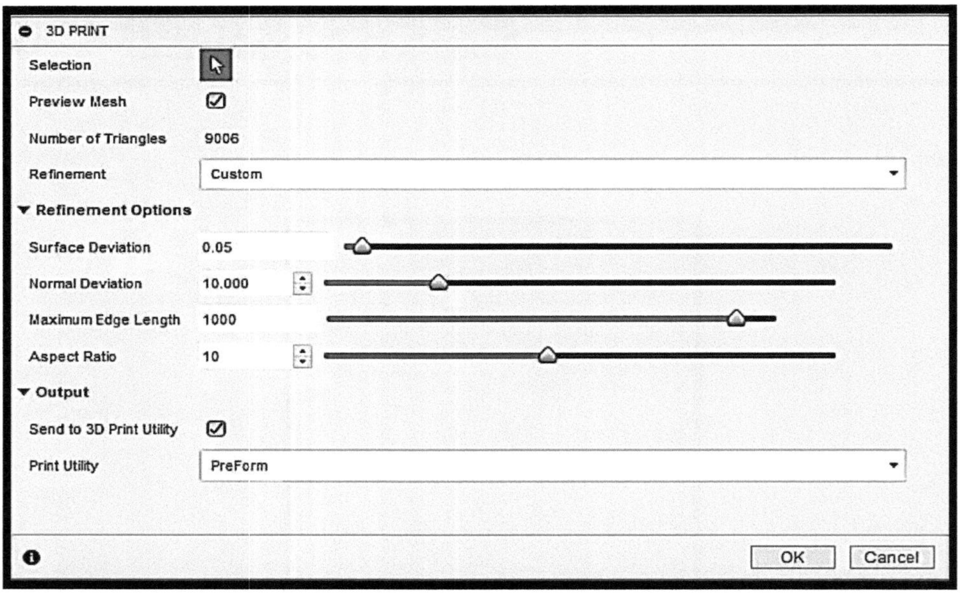

Exporting a Design in STL File Format for 3D Printing

Method #1: Exporting an Entire Design

Using the model Browser tree, which is located on the left-hand side of the screen, you can export a full project, which will include all of the bodies and components that make up the project. Simply right-click the top branch of the tree, which is where the project name is located, and then pick "**Save As Mesh**" from the drop-down option that appears.

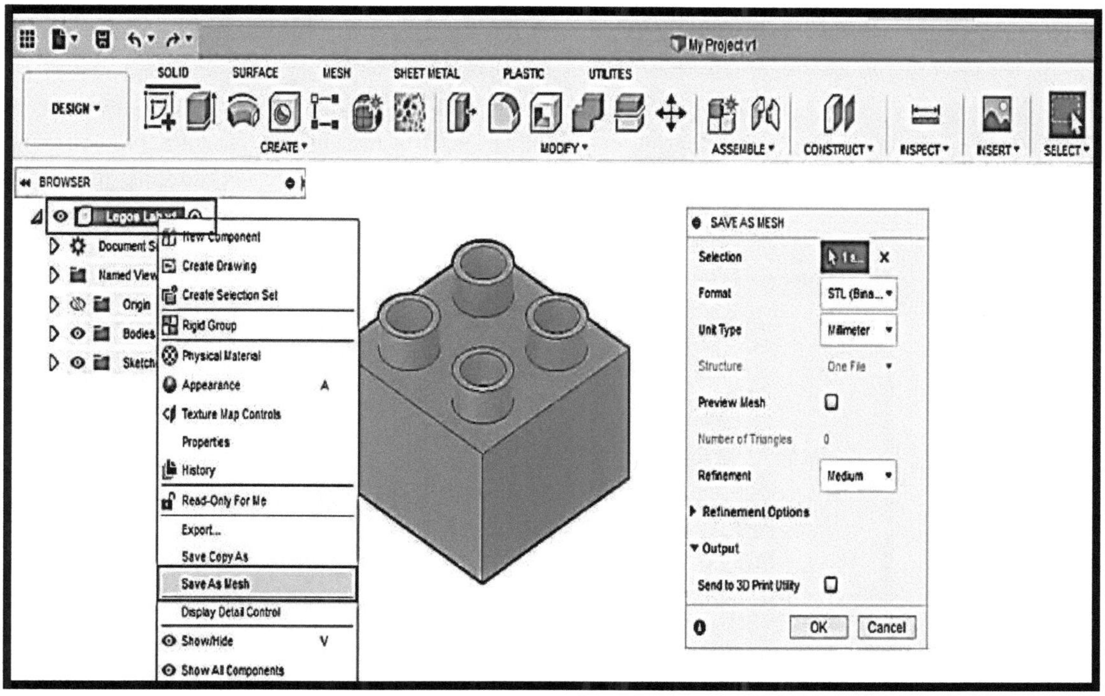

After you have chosen this option, a panel labeled "**SAVE AS MESH**" will appear on the right-hand side of the screen.

Within this panel, you will be able to customize the parameters for the mesh. Let's quickly go through the available choices:

- **Format**: This option allows you to choose the file format that will be exported. The STL, OBJ, and the more recent 3MF formats are available to choose from here.
- **Unit Type**: This allows you to choose the measurement units that will be used for the exported file. STL files are not affected in any way by this in particular since the STL format does not retain any information about unit measurements.
- **Structure**: This lets you choose whether the complete design will be exported as a single file or as a collection of individual files.
- **Preview mesh:** This enables the user to have a sneak peek at the final mesh file that will be produced by Fusion before it is saved.
- **Refinement**: This allows the user to choose the level of refinement that will be applied to the generated mesh. In the "**Refinement Options**" section, you have the option of selecting one of the presets (Low, Medium, or High) or manually adjusting the numbers for the deviation.
- **Output**: This contains the "**Transmit to 3D Print Utility**" option, which allows the user to send the file straight to third-party software such as Cura, Meshmixer, PreForm, and other applications as the user has configured them.

If you want to merely export the model in the STL format, make sure that the "Send to 3D Print Utility" box is ticked, and then click the "**OK**" button in the "**SAVE AS MESH**" window. This will complete the process. You will be given the option to choose the location where your export file will be saved.

Method #2: Exporting Individual Components or Bodies

Simply right-click the component or body you want to export in the Browser tree, and then pick "**Save As Mesh**" from the drop-down option that appears. This will export only the selected component or body. This will open the "**SAVE AS MESH**" tab, which allows you to define your mesh settings in the same manner as the earlier technique.

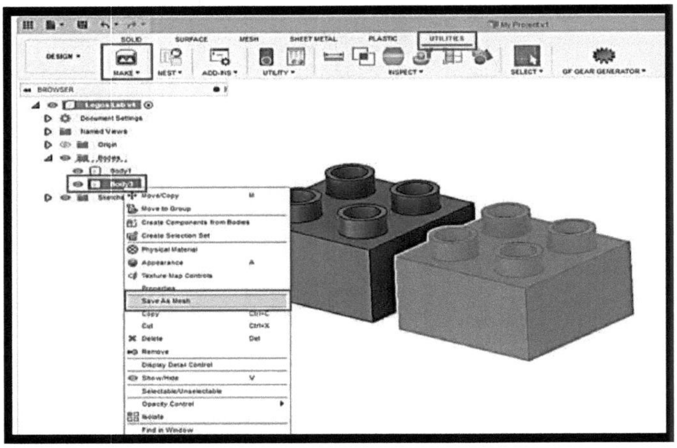

You also have the option of opening the panel by selecting "**3D Print**" from the "**Make**" tool, which is located in the "**Utilities**" tab of the toolbar that is located at the very top of the screen. You will be able to pick the component or body that you want to export from this location.

Method #3: Exporting Multiple Bodies as a Single STL File

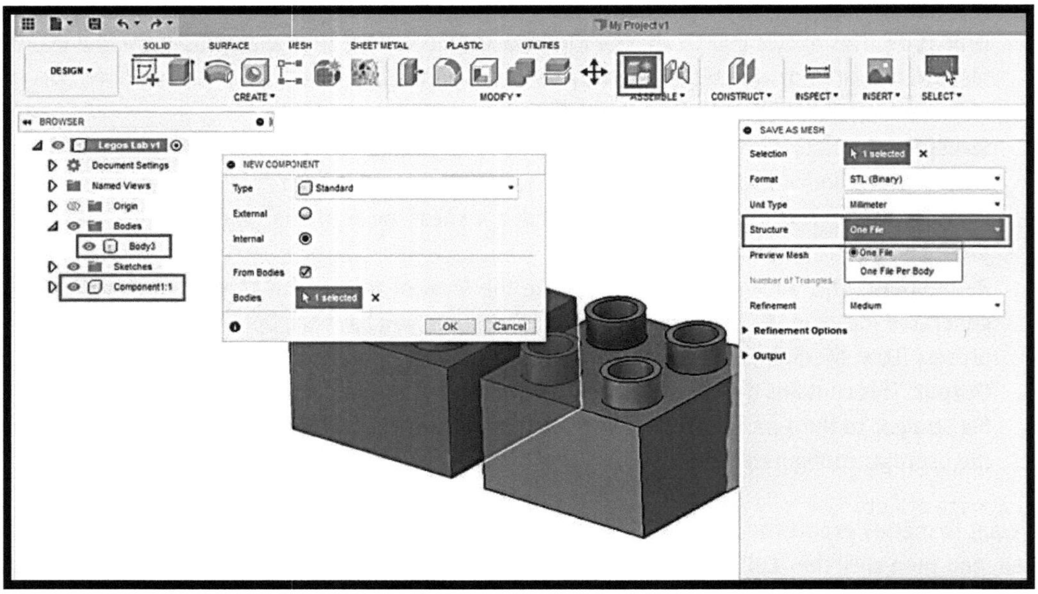

If you want to export several bodies as a single STL mesh file, you may do so by building a single component that includes all of the bodies that you want to include in the STL file. This will allow you to export numerous bodies as a single file. This may come in handy when setting up a print-in-place configuration or when situating pieces on the build platform in preparation for sending them to the slicer. Create a new component by either clicking the icon labeled "**New Component**" (located in the toolbar) or choosing it from the "**Create**" menu (also located in the toolbar). This opens a window on the right side of the screen that allows you to pick one or more corpses from the design. You may select as many bodies as you want.

Make sure the switch labeled "From Bodies" is turned on, and then choose only one body to work with. If you pick more than one body, an equal number of components will be generated, one for each body; however, this is not what we want to happen in this case. Just hit the "**OK**" button. When the new component has been successfully constructed, it will be added to the left-hand side of the Browser tree and shown at the very bottom. If you want to add more bodies to this component, all you have to do is locate the bodies in the tree, then drag and drop them onto the branch of the tree that represents the new component. After that, you will be able to export them all by right-clicking this component, then choosing "**Save As Mesh**" from the menu that appears. If you go into the Structure setting and make sure that the "One File" option is chosen, you should be able to go from there without any problems.

Extra: The Ability to Export an STL File from the Cloud

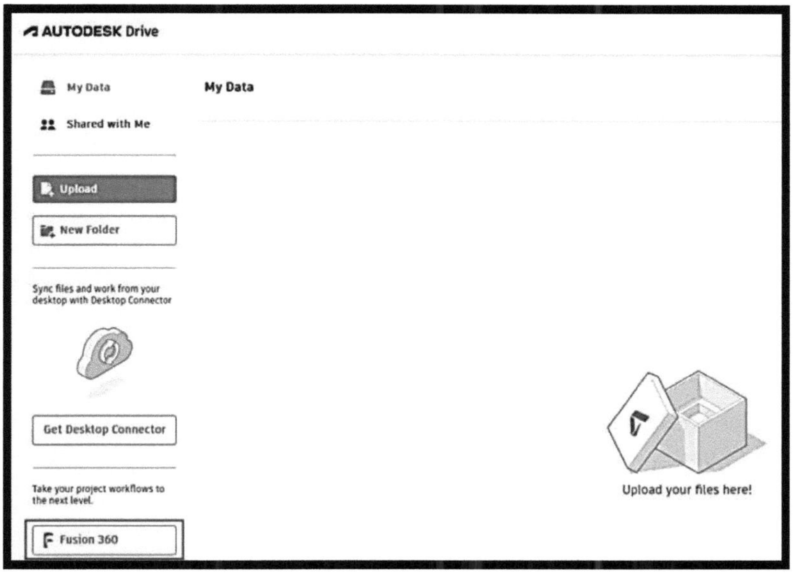

There is even another approach, which does not even need access to the program itself, to convert and export an STL from Fusion 360. In most cases, Fusion 360 design files are stored in the cloud hosted by Autodesk. As a result, these files are accessible from any internet browser. The Autodesk Drive platform gives customers the ability to generate STL files from existing drawings as well as download those files. Visit the homepage of Autodesk Drive and login into your A360 account to do this (the same used in Fusion 360). After logging in, go to the left panel of the interface and choose the **"Fusion 360"** button.

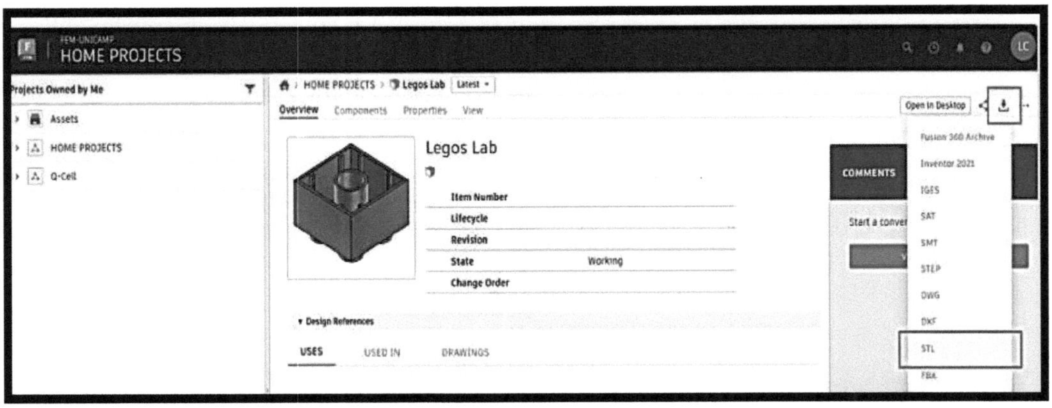

You will then be led to the core of your Fusion 360 account, where you can browse through all the projects and designs you have already created. You may discover the precise design you want to export as an STL by searching through the file system that is shown on the left. After you have located the 3D design you want to use, click on it to get to that model's specific page. Simply click the little download button that is found in the upper right corner of the screen to export the file to STL (or any other format). Then, from the option that drops down, choose the format of the file that you want to export the design as.

When you choose "**STL**," a link to your exported file will be sent to the address that is associated with this account, and your file will be produced. You will have access to the download URL for one week, during which time your STL file may be downloaded from any computer, regardless of location.

Questions

1. The workspace that consists of many sets of tools that are used for creating solid models is called?
2. The tool that is utilized to turn on the process of capturing design history in the timeline for an imported design?
3. Which workspace is used for creating exploded views of an assembly as well as an animation of design?
4. Which tool is used for making a design from an existing fusion (.f3d), IGES (.iges, .igs), SAT (.sat), SMT (.smt), or STEP (.step, .stp) file?
5. How do you store all your designs in the cloud in Fusion 360?
6. Does Fusion 360 allow you to work in offline mode?
7. What happens whenever you save a file using the save tool?

CHAPTER 2

DRAWING SKETCHES WITH FUSION 360

Sketches

In Fusion 360, a design begins with a geometric profile called a **Sketch**, which serves as the basis for the 3D geometry in the design. Creating the underlying sketch profiles that will drive the general forms of the parametric solid, surface, or T-spline bodies that make up your design is the first step that must be completed before you can go on to the next step of creating 3D objects in your design. The first step in any future parametric modeling process is the creation of sketches. If you make a detailed drawing profile, you may streamline your work process and reduce the likelihood that your design will have problems further down the line. You can draw sketches on a plane or an existing planar face on a body. Additionally, you can build geometry about the **XY, YZ, and ZX** planes, or at any arbitrary point in three-dimensional space. Lines, circles, arcs, points, and splines are all examples of two-dimensional geometry that may be found in sketches. You have the option of either drawing sketch geometry or projecting edges from previously drawn geometry onto the sketch plane. To completely specify sketch geometry, you may additionally make use of parameters, constraints, and dimensions. This means that you will have complete control over the shape of any 3D bodies that are derived from your designs.

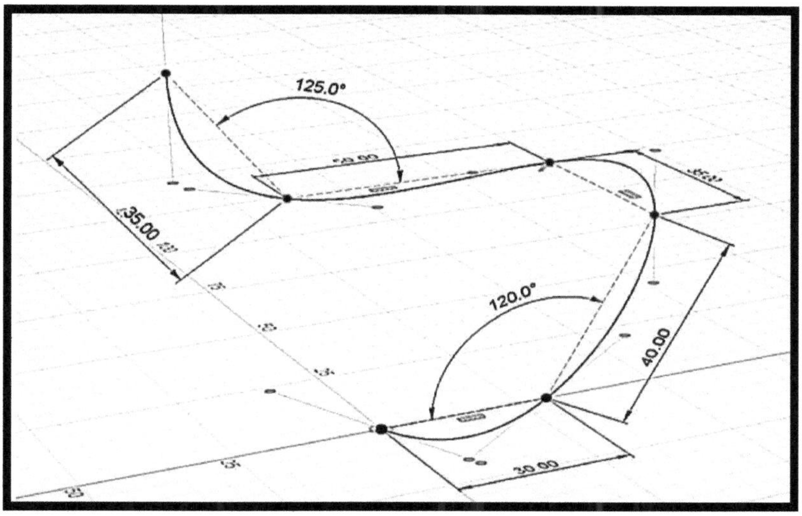

Sketch profiles

In Fusion 360, you may create two different kinds of sketch profiles.

- A sequence of linked two-dimensional geometry that does not create a closed border is referred to as an **open profile**.
  - Open profiles may be used to direct some modeling processes like Loft as well as to build surface bodies, extrude thin solid features, and create surface bodies.

- A set of linked two-dimensional geometry that creates a closed boundary is referred to as a **closed profile**.
  - When a sketch profile is closed, it becomes a shade of blue and may be used to extrude three-dimensional forms or conduct three-dimensional Boolean operations such as **join, cut, and intersect**.

Unconstrained and constrained sketches

You have the option to make drawings in the Sketch environment that are either completely unconstrained, moderately confined or constrained.

An unconstrained sketch has geometry in it that is nevertheless able to move about freely in space. The drawing does not have all of its limitations and dimensions set in place.

- The symbol that appears next to the drawing in the Browser will change to reflect whether or not it is limited.
- In the first stages of the design process, unrestricted drawings might be helpful. When you want to be able to explore and have freedom in the early geometric design decisions you make, unconstrained drawings are the way to go. As you develop your design, you may iteratively refine a drawing by giving it more limitations and dimensions. However, in complicated parametric assemblies, referencing unconstrained sketch geometry in downstream design features might lead to unanticipated consequences.

In a constrained sketch, the geometry is held in place by the limitations and dimensions of the sketch itself.

- The symbol that appears next to the drawing in the Browser when it has all of its constraints applied indicates that it is completely constrained.
- You are unable to move constrained sketch geometry in the canvas when you attempt to drag it there. When you are familiar with the particulars of a design and are aware of the goals you want to accomplish with it, constrained drawings may be helpful. Their behavior is more predictable even in sophisticated parametric designs. Be cautious, though, that limited drawings have the potential to lock elements in your design more strongly than you would want so early on in the design process. It is important to remember that the earlier in the design process you add limits and dimensions to a drawing, the less useful they will be.

Working with the Selection of Planes

The gridded surface on which you draw is referred to as the **work plane**. There is a horizontal plane, as well as two vertical planes. In addition to that, you may build a work plane at any angle that you see fit. Selecting the work plane that you want to sketch on is the first stage in the sketching process. When you choose a sketch or solid (a solid, which is a three-dimensional object, is often referred to as a body), the origin planes and axes will become visible. Cartesian coordinates are used on the work plane, with the center circle serving as the point of origin (point 0, 0, 0).

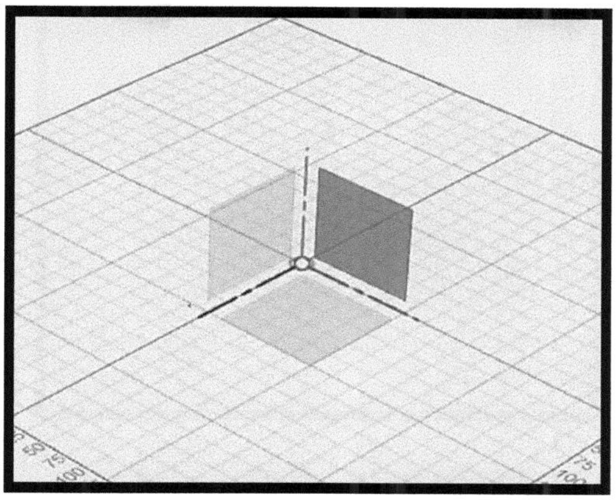

Specifying Units

The most popular unit for 3D printing is the millimeter, which is also the default unit that Fusion uses. However, there are a few different ways that the units may be altered. In the Preferences menu, you may do this by selecting the down arrow next to your name, and then selecting **Default Units > Design** from the option that appears. To begin working with those units, choose **File > New Design** from the menu bar. The modification will take place on the new design, not the active one. Click the Units field in the Browser (which can be found under Document Settings), and then click the image on the right. This is an alternative method. Pick the new units from the drop-down menu that appears in the dialog box. The open file will be updated instantaneously with the new unit designations.

Specifying Grids and Snaps Settings

The grid is adaptive by default, which means that the space between grid cells adjusts proportionally as you zoom in and out of the image. However, the parameters for the grid may be altered. To assign fixed numbers to the grid, for instance, choose the Navigation panel at the bottom of the screen and click the button labeled "**Grids and Snaps.**" To establish the primary grid space and the desired number of subdivisions, choose **Set Increments > Fixed** from the menu.

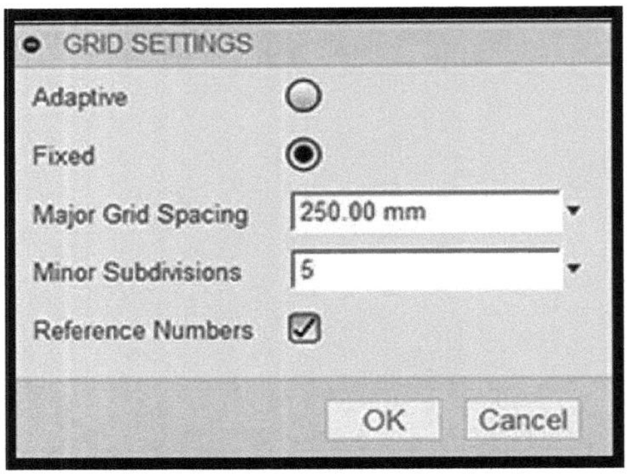

Movement is limited at predetermined intervals when snapping is used. You'll be able to model more precisely if you align your sketches and bodies with the grid lines. You can choose the increments that are used for linear and rotational motions. To glide over the workspace instead of moving in increments, you have the option to turn off the incremental move function entirely. When using a gadget that continues snapping beyond the point you desire, this comes in handy. When you are sketching a form, snapping is vital because if the shape does not snap to a grid or a line that you have drawn, it is possible that you have not sketched a closed shape.

THE SKETCH MENU

To see all of the available options in the **Sketch** menu, click the arrow that points down. When you move your mouse over a tool, pop-ups will emerge that provide a concise explanation of how to use that tool. Some of the tools include arrows that shoot out from the side that allow you to reach the submenus. This menu has a variety of tools, some of which are predefined forms like rectangles, circles, ellipses, and polygons. Some others, such as Spline and Arc, provide you with the ability to create your forms. **Fillet, Trim, and extend** are editing functions that can be applied to sketches; Offset copies and places a sketch at a specified distance from the original; Mirror flips the orientation of the sketch; **Circular Pattern and Rectangular Pattern** copy and arrange the sketch, and Project places a sketch onto another surface.

Creating Sketches

After selecting a Sketch tool, the majority of drawings may be created with only three clicks. The first step chooses the drawing plane, the second chooses the beginning point for the sketch, and the third chooses the terminus or the size of the sketch. Select the **Line** tool from the menu. There will be three image planes visible. Simply choose the plane you want to doodle on by clicking on it. I selected the horizontal one. It will reposition itself on the screen so that it is facing you. After selecting a starting point, you may begin to sketch a form. To quit the tool without leaving the drawing, either press **Escape or Enter**, or right-click the line and choose **Cancel** from the context menu. Without leaving the sketch means that all of the sketch curves will be created on the same drawing. To pick up where you left off sketching, click the **Line tool** once again.

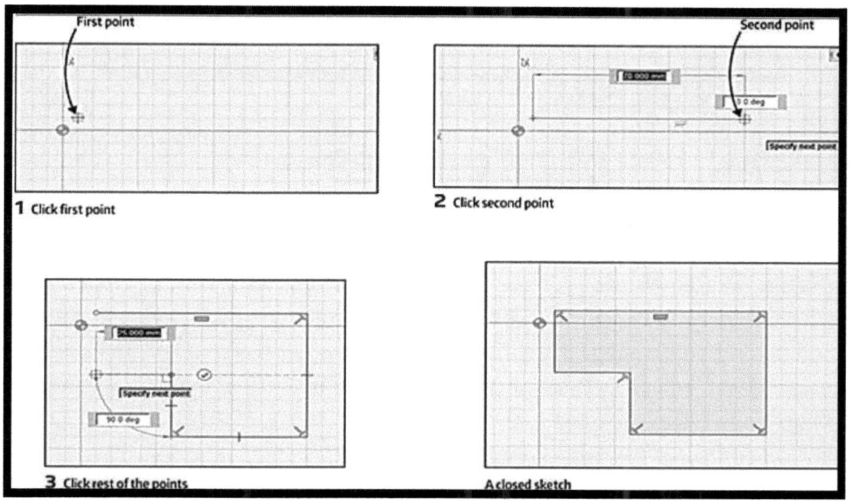

When all of the endpoints are joined, a face, or a darker surface, appears between the lines of the structure. This kind of drawing is referred to as a closed-loop sketch or a closed sketch. An open drawing does not have any connecting endpoints, and as a result, it does not have any faces. A closed drawing is required for the majority of procedures to be carried out. When you are through creating the drawing, either right-click the canvas and choose OK from the context menu or click the symbol that looks like a stop sign in the upper-right corner of the screen.

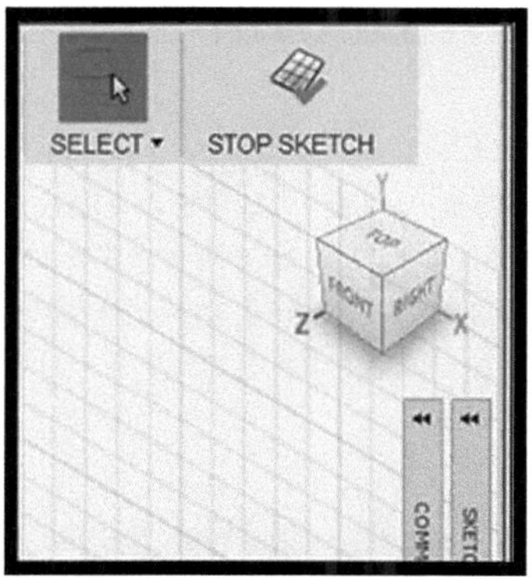

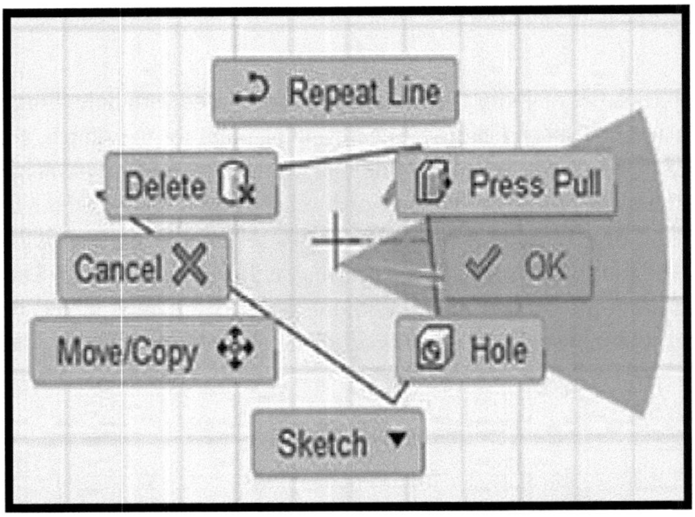

SKETCHES AND SKETCH CURVES

There is a lot of interchangeability between the phrases sketch and sketch curve. A "sketch" refers to an entire drawing, while "**sketch curves**" refer to individual portions of a sketch. Because it's only a line segment, a sketch curve may be straight, curved, or any other form you might imagine. Certain procedures may be performed on certain drawing curves but not on the overall sketch itself. The outline of a drawing is made up of curves. When you draw them all during the same operation, before you click the button that says "**Stop Drawing**," they are all included in the same sketch.

If you want to add additional sketch curves to an existing sketch, instead of clicking the grid, you should click the drawing itself. It is not immediately clear from a visual inspection whether the curves on two distinct drawings belong to the same or different sketches; nevertheless, this will become clear as you continue to interact with the sketches. To modify and act on the drawing as a whole, all of the sketch curves need to be on the same sketch. For instance, if you wish to trim overlapping sketch curves, those sketch curves need to be on the same sketch for you to be able to trim them. If they are not on the same sketch, you will not be able to trim them. It depends on what you want to accomplish as to whether or not you will want to sketch curves on the same drawing. Sometimes you will want them, and sometimes you won't.

INFERENCES AND CONSTRAINTS

During the process of sketching, inference lines and symbols will develop. These are small geometric shapes that indicate, for example, center points or perpendicularity, as well as dashed lines that indicate that a line, you're currently drawing matches the length of an existing line. Additionally, there are small geometric shapes that indicate that a line you're currently drawing matches the angle of an existing line. You can see inferences of perpendicularity, midpoint, and terminus, as well as dashed line inferences, in the drawing that we just produced.

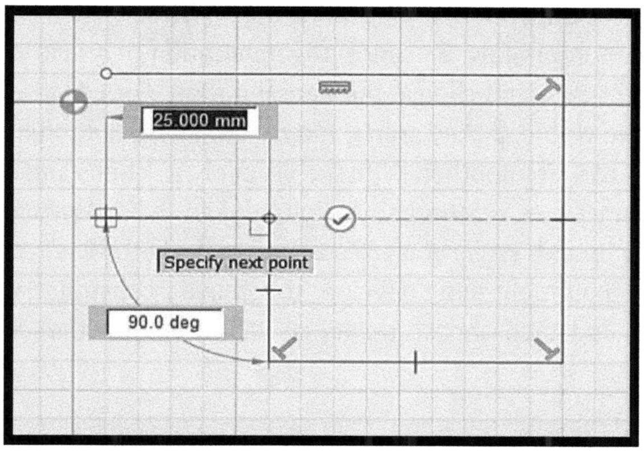

The drawing shown in the previous picture additionally includes notations referred to as **geometric limitations** in the four corners. These are the restrictions that you place on the form of the drawing. The relationships between the various components of the form are constrained geometrically. You may limit a drawing, for example, to ensure that two lines are always parallel or perpendicular to one other. As soon as you begin drawing, a palette including geometric limitations displays.

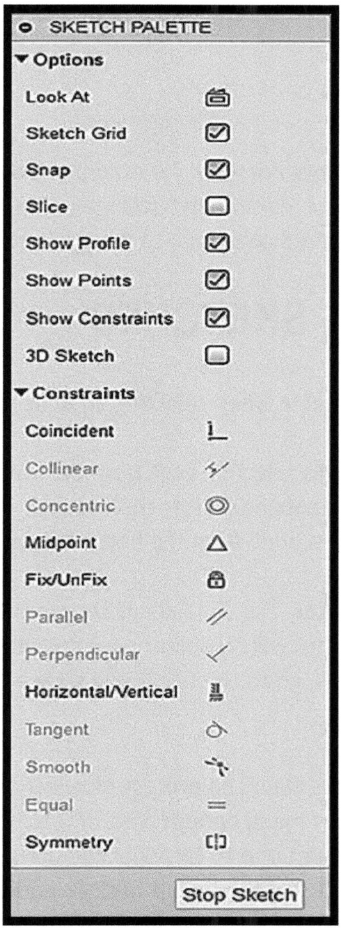

To apply a constraint, first, click the symbol representing the constraint, then click two sketch objects. The lines will adapt themselves appropriately. To cancel the application of a restriction, either hit the Escape key on your keyboard or right-click and choose the Cancel option. For constraints to operate effectively, sketch dimensions need to be visible; if they aren't, the constraints will do things that you probably don't want, like extend one sketch curve to another. With the proper restrictions and dimensions, a drawing may be constrained, which is sometimes referred to as fully define. It is also possible for it to be entirely unrestrained or just partially bound. While you are creating each sketch line, you should keep the **Ctrl** key down and held down so that limitations don't develop. To remove a constraint, you must first click the icon that looks like a constraint and then choose **delete**. It will be shown that it has been chosen by the appearance of a blue circle.

Tap the **Delete** key on your keyboard. That particular drawing line will be exempt from the limitation going forward. If a constrained sketch is included inside a body, you must first deactivate the body by using the Browser (click the light bulb in front of it to change its color from yellow to gray), and then you may erase the constraint. If your drawing is completely confined, it means that you may click anywhere on it to move it, and the sketch will continue to maintain its original form even as it is repositioned. There is no way for any of its lines to move on their own. When a drawing isn't restricted to its fullest extent, parts of the sketch are free to move and transform. When you conduct additional operations on a completely constrained drawing, such as mirroring its features, you will get predictable results, which is one of the benefits of using such a sketch. It will always keep its shape, which is the objective of the design.

TIP

If attempting to restrict two drawings does not work, for example, if one sketch does not move to the other in the appropriate sequence or if the size of the sketch changes, try applying the Fixed constraint to one of the sketches, and then applying the desired constraint to the other sketch.

SELECT AND DELETE SKETCHES

There are many different options available when selecting an item. You can:

- **Drag the selection window**. This selection goes from the top left to the bottom right and includes everything that is completely contained inside the window.
- **Drag a crossing window**. This is done from the bottom right to the top left, and it selects all that the window encompasses.
- **Choose its entry in your browser**. This will reliably choose the complete item every time.
- **Choose the Timeline option**. This will reliably choose the complete item every time.
- To access the available choices, go to the top of the screen and choose **Options** from the **Select** menu.

Items that have been selected look dark blue. The process of selection is not always an easy one. You will be presented with a varied set of context menu options according to how you pick an item. It's also possible that you didn't choose a sufficient amount of it to carry out the procedure; this is more of a problem with bodies. It's possible that you haven't picked the body's back or underside yet. To see all of the drawings included in the file, click the arrow that is located to the right of the term "**Sketches.**" If there is a gray bulb in front of the drawing name, it indicates that the sketch cannot be seen. Simply clicking on the lightbulb will cause it to change from white to yellow, revealing the drawing.

You can't choose a drawing by only clicking on its face; instead, you have to select all of its edges at the same time. You may also choose to choose the whole drawing using the Browser panel as an alternative to the selection window. There are occasions when this is the only way to remove some elements, such as a sketch point or a sketch curve. If selecting the item, right-clicking on it, and selecting Delete from the context menu do not work, then this method will. In most cases, you can delete a drawing by dragging a selection window around it and then pressing the **Delete** key on your keyboard. You may also right-click the drawing and choose the Delete option from the context menu. Pick the sketch you want to edit, then right-click on it and select Edit Drawing from the context menu. This should remove the sketch. Then you may delete it after making a selection of it by dragging a window around it.

CREATE A SELECTION SET

You may choose lines and then store that selection so that you can return to update it at a later time. Make numerous choices by pressing and holding the Shift key while selecting the lines, then right-clicking on one of the lines and selecting the **Create Selection Set** option from the context menu. This pick will appear in the Browser panel, where you will be able to give it a new name. When you move your mouse pointer over the entry for the selection in the Browser panel, two icons will appear: one will allow you to choose all of those lines again, and the other will enable you to update any modifications that have been made to the selection set.

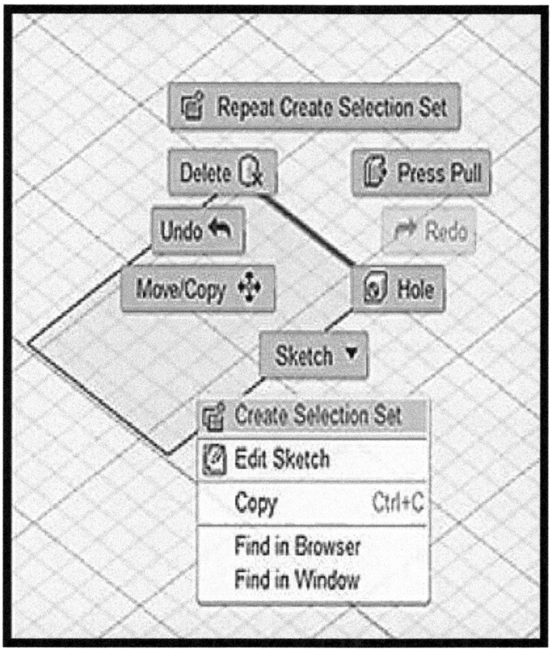

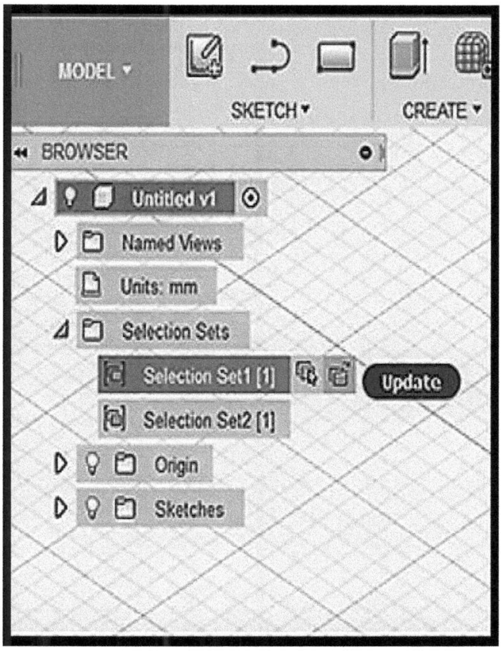

DIMENSIONS AND SKETCH EQUATIONS

If you are sketching and attempting to work out a design, you can count grid squares and click drawings into the grid lines, or you can simply eyeball the proportions of what you are drawing. This provides accuracy, but without the tedium of always having to type in the measurements. When drawing a sketch, it is simpler to count the grid squares if you begin at the origin. Changing your grid spacing to fit the grid lines for what you are trying to accomplish is beneficial; if you know that your snap points will be at a specified interval, you can specify that. Changing your grid spacing to accommodate the grid lines for what you are trying to do is useful. When it is necessary to be explicit, type the dimensions. These determine the size of things as well as their distance from one another. While you are sketching, text boxes will display, and you may change between them with the Tab key. When you put a dimension into the box, a note and a dimension line will automatically appear on the drawing. This will also add a constraint to the sketch. When you click the Stop Sketch button, the dimension lines and the notes will disappear from the drawing.

When you are in the Edit Drawing mode, the dimension lines and comments on the sketch become visible. You must have these elements visible to write equations into the sketch. These are formulae that rely on the size of another sketch curve to determine the size of the first sketch curve. To establish this link, first, activate a dimension text field by clicking on it, and then click on the dimension note of another sketch curve (do not click the sketch curve itself; rather, click on the dimension note of the sketch curve). After that, the dimension remark in question will show up in the text area that has been enabled. The picture below depicts a dimension text field that has been enabled. It allows you to input dimensions and also allows you to draw equations. The figure below illustrates a sketch equation. The length of that line will change to 27 millimeters when you hit the Enter key. To complete, type Stop Sketch in the box.

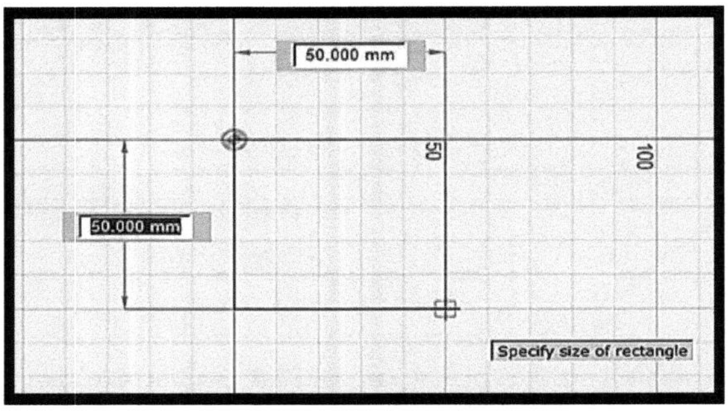

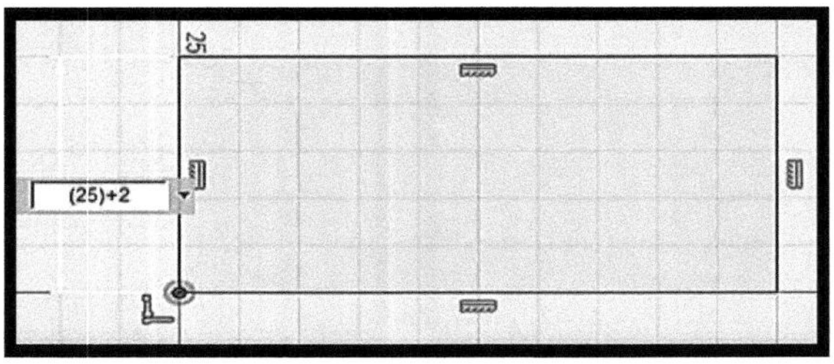

Entering **Edit Sketch mode** will allow you to make changes to the dimensions at a later time. After that, pick a sketch line by left-clicking on it, going to the context menu for that line, and selecting **Sketch Dimension** from there. It will show up as a dimension line; just drag it off the drawing. The current length of the line is shown in the text box. Type a new length, if you like. The length of the drawing will be adjusted to match that value, and if it has any horizontal or vertical limits, the overall form will not change. You may also add a new unit to the dimension by inserting the name of that unit after the number. For example, if the file is already in millimeters, you might add an entry for an inch to the file, and Fusion would automatically convert the new unit to the file's existing units.

Drawing a Line Entity

- To use the **line** tool, either choose it from the toolbar or use the **L** key on your keyboard.
- Proceed now to the drawing area, and while you're there, point out the origin, also known as the starting point, from which you will draw the line.
- Move the mouse away from the beginning point so that the appropriate amount of space is shown in the dimension box; this will indicate the distance between the cursor and the starting point.

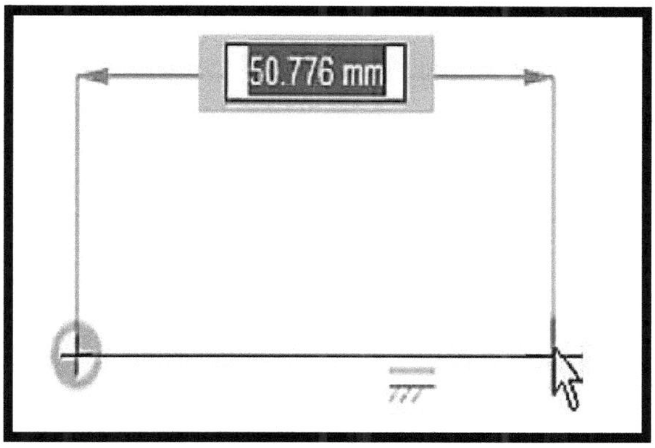

- Now, while dragging the cursor away from the starting position, hit the left mouse button at the place where you want the line to finish to establish the endpoint of the line. You can see that your line is being formed right now.
- To finish the sketch, tap the right check mark after you have created several lines and obtained the required design. This will bring up the next screen. Because the line tool is still selected, to deactivate it, you may either use the ESC button or right-click on the drawing area and then press the OK button. Both of these actions will result in the same result.

Drawing a Rectangle

You may build a variety of rectangles in an active drawing in Fusion 360 by using the rectangle tools included in the **Sketch > Create** panel. These rectangles can be used as sketch geometry or construction geometry.

When working with an active drawing, you may generate rectangles by entering the following commands:

- **2-Point Rectangle**
- **3-Point Rectangle**
- **Center Rectangle**

Note: Before you can generate sketch geometry, you will need to either right-click an existing sketch or choose **Edit Drawing** from the context menu to enter the **Sketch** contextual environment. Alternatively, you may use the Create Sketch command to create a new sketch.

2-Point Rectangle

Create a rectangle with two points of definition with the 2-Point Rectangle command. The two points are the corners of the rectangle that are opposite one another. After clicking once, you'll be able to position the first corner point, and then clicking again will position the second corner point. You also have the option of specifying the values for the width and height.

3-Point Rectangle

Using the 3-Point Rectangle command, a rectangle that is specified by three points may be created. The width, orientation, and height of the rectangle are all determined by these three points. To position the first corner point, you click, and then you click again to position the second point. You also have the option of clicking first to set the point, after which you may choose the initial distance number. After that, you click to either set the third point or give the second amount for the distance.

Center Rectangle

The Center Rectangle command generates a rectangle whose boundaries are determined by the center point and one of the points that define the rectangle's corners. After clicking to set the first point as the rectangle's center, you may click again to set a corner point or to input values for the rectangle's width and height.

Create a 2-Point Rectangle

You may make a rectangle by positioning two corner points that are opposite one another.

This will establish the location of the rectangle as well as its size.

1. Select **Create > Circle > 2-Point Rectangle** from the contextual menu of the Sketch tab.
2. Click anywhere on the canvas to set the beginning point of the corner.
3. **Indicate the dimensions of the rectangle as follows:**
    a. Use the mouse to position the corner point on the other side.
    b. Alternatively, you may choose either the length, the width, or both of the values, and then click to position the rectangle.
4. Steps 3 and 4 may be repeated indefinitely to generate more rectangles.
5. To finish the instruction, press the **Enter** button.

Displayed in the canvas are the rectangles, together with any construction geometry, restrictions, and dimensions that have been applied to them.

Create a 3-Point Rectangle

You may make a rectangle by setting three points at its corners. These points will specify the location of the rectangle as well as its size.

1. Select **Create > Circle > 3-Point Rectangle** from the contextual menu of the Sketch Tab.
2. Click anywhere on the canvas to set the beginning point of the corner.

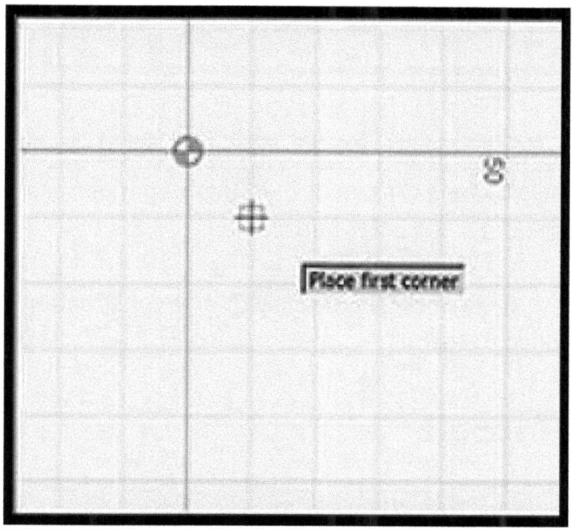

3. Indicate the length of the rectangle in the following format:

- Use the mouse to position the second point of the corner.

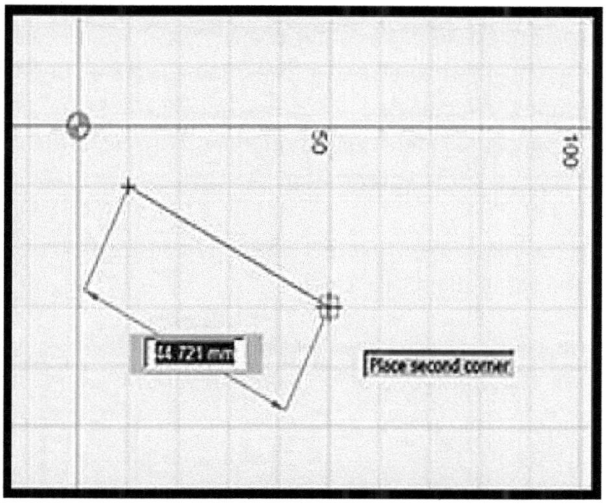

- Alternatively, you may click to insert the second point after first specifying the length value.

4. Indicate the width of the rectangle using the following:

- Use the mouse to position the third point of the corner.

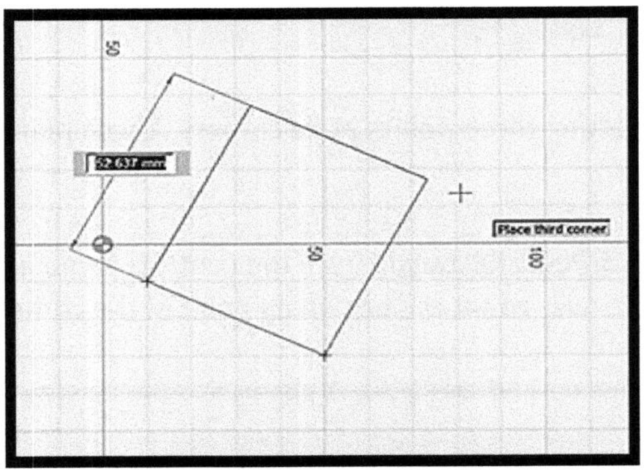

- Alternatively, you may click to insert the third point after first specifying the width value.

5. Create another rectangle by repeating steps 2–4 (this step is optional).
6. To finish the instruction, press the Enter button.

Displayed in the canvas are the rectangles, together with any construction geometry, restrictions, and dimensions that have been applied to them.

Create a Center Rectangle

Establish a rectangle by locating its center point and one of its corner points. This will allow you to determine the dimensions of the rectangle as well as its location.

1. Select **Create > Circle > Center Rectangle** from the contextual menu of the Sketch program.
2. Within the canvas, use the left mouse button to position the center point.
3. **Indicate the dimensions of the rectangle's length and width:**
    a. Use the mouse to position the corner point.
    b. Alternatively, you may choose either the length, the width, or both of the values, and then click to position the rectangle.
4. Steps 3 and 4 may be repeated indefinitely to generate more rectangles.
5. To finish the instruction, press the **Enter** button.

Displayed in the canvas are the rectangles, together with any construction geometry, restrictions, and dimensions that have been applied to them.

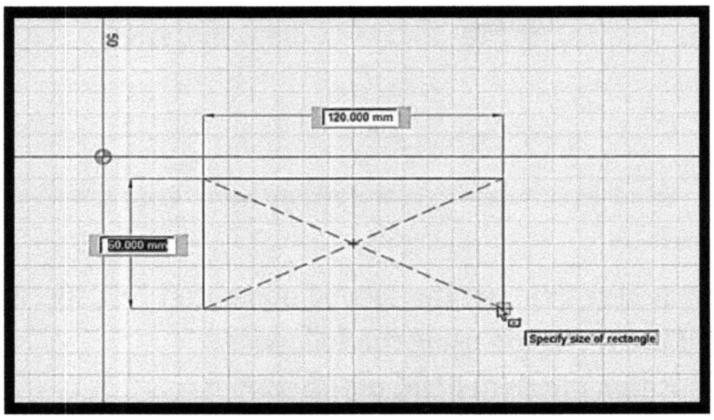

Tips

- While any rectangle command is active, you can switch between different kinds of rectangles by navigating to the Feature Options area of the Sketch Palette window.
- When you snap to the sketch grid or other geometry in the design, object snap symbols will show near the geometry as you move the mouse pointer. When you snap to a certain place in the drawing, the logical restrictions are applied to the sketch immediately thereafter.

Drawing a Circle

You may add several sorts of circles as sketch geometry or construction geometry to an active sketch in Fusion 360 by using the circle tools in the Sketch > Create panel.

The following commands may be used to draw circles in an active sketch:

- **Center Diameter Circle**
- **2-Point Circle**
- **3-Point Circle**
- **2-Tangent Circle**
- **3-Tangent Circle**

Note: To access the Sketch contextual environment, you must either use the Make Sketch command to create a new sketch or right-click an existing sketch and choose Edit Sketch.

Center Diameter Circle

To set the location and dimensions of a circle, place the center point and input the diameter.

1. Click **Create > Circle > Center Diameter Circle** in the Sketch contextual menu.
2. Click on the canvas to position the circle's center.
3. Enter the circle's diameter value, then click to position it.
4. You may optionally make another circle by repeating steps 2-3.
5. To finish the command, press **Enter**.

The circles appear on the canvas along with any building geometry, limitations, and measurements that are put on them.

2-Point Circle

To specify the location and size of the circle, place two points on each end of the diameter.

1. Pick **Create > Circle > 2-Point Circle** from the Sketch contextual menu.
2. Click on the canvas to position the diameter's initial point.
3. **Identify the circle's diameter:**

   - To position the circle, click a second point.
   - Alternatively, enter a diameter value and click to position the circle.
4. You may optionally make another circle by repeating steps 2-3.
5. To finish the command, press **Enter**.

The circles appear on the canvas along with any building geometry, limitations, and measurements that are put on them.

3-Point Circle

3 points that are located on the circumference may be used to define a circle's location and size.

1. Pick **Create > Circle > 3-Point Circle** from the Sketch contextual menu.
2. Click on the canvas to position the first point that is on the edge of the circle.
3. Click to place a second point on the perimeter.
4. Click to place the third point on the perimeter.
5. You may optionally make another circle by repeating steps 2-4.
6. To finish the command, press **Enter**.

The circles appear on the canvas along with any building geometry, limitations, and measurements that are put on them.

2-Tangent Circle

By choosing two lines and entering a radius, you may determine the location and dimensions of a circle while still maintaining tangency with the sketch geometry you've chosen.

1. Pick **Create > Circle > 2-Tangent Circle** on the Sketch contextual menu.
2. To make a circle that is tangent to two lines on the canvas, choose the lines.
3. **Identify the circle's radius:**
   a. For the circle to be placed, click a point.
   b. Alternatively, enter a radius number and click to put the circle.
4. You may optionally make another circle by repeating steps 2-3.
5. To finish the command, press Enter.

The circles appear on the canvas along with any building geometry, limitations, and measurements that are put on them.

3-Tangent Circle

To determine the location and size of a circle that preserves tangency with the chosen sketch geometry, choose three lines.

1. Pick **Create > Circle > 3-Tangent Circle** on the Sketch contextual menu.
2. Pick three lines on the canvas and draw a circle that is tangent to them.

3. If desired, repeat step 2 to make an additional circle.
4. To finish the command, press **Enter**.

The circles appear on the canvas along with any building geometry, limitations, and measurements that are put on them.

Note: To pick many lines at once, utilize the window selection feature or click on individual lines to do so.

Tips

- While any circle command is active, you may switch between Circle kinds in the Sketch Palette dialog's Feature Options area.
- When you snap to the sketch grid or other geometry in the design, object snap symbols appear close to the geometry as you move the mouse cursor over it. The logical limitations are immediately applied to the drawing if you snap to a certain location.
- When you are certain of the size and placement of the circle, use the Center Diameter Circle to draw it. The center of the circle may be placed using snap points and construction geometry.

Drawing an Arc

You may build several sorts of arcs as sketch geometry or construction geometry in an active drawing in Fusion 360 by using the arc tools in the Sketch > Create panel.

In an active drawing, the instructions listed below may be used to produce arcs:

- **3-Point Arc**
- **Center Point Arc**
- **Tangent Arc**

Note: To access the Sketch contextual environment, you must either use the Make Sketch command to create a new sketch or right-click an existing sketch and choose Edit Sketch.

3-Point Arc

To determine the location and size of the arc, place the end points and a third point that sits along the arc.

1. Pick **Create > Arc > 3-Point Arc** from the Sketch contextual menu in step 1.
2. Click on the canvas to position the arc's initial end point.

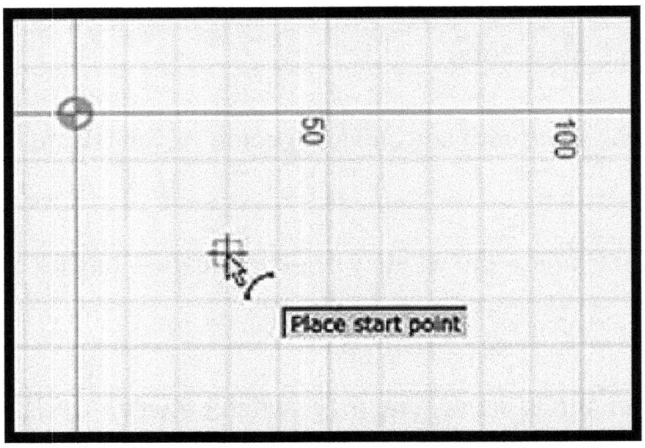

3. **Enter a distance, then click to position the arc's second end point.**

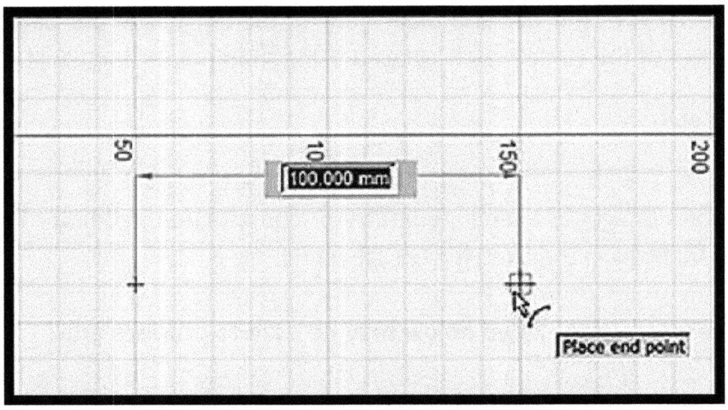

4. Click to place a third point that is situated along the arc.

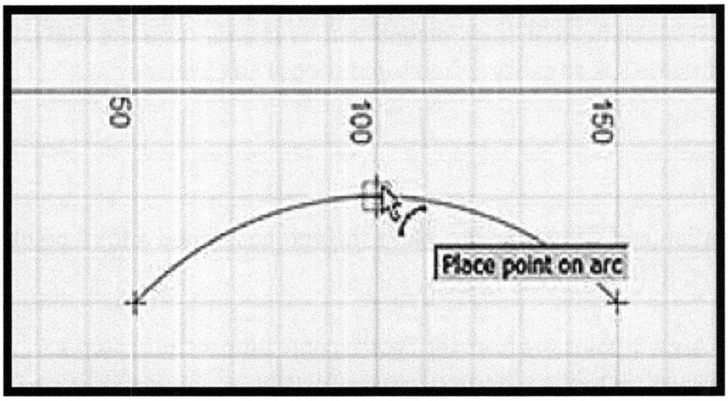

5. You may optionally make another arc by repeating steps 2-4.
6. To finish the command, press **Enter**.

The arcs appear on the canvas together with any construction geometry, restrictions, and measurements that are applied to them.

Center Point Arc

To determine the location and size of the arc, place the center point and end points.

1. Click **Create > Arc > Center Point Arc** on the Sketch contextual menu.
2. Click on the canvas to position the arc's center point.
3. Use your mouse to position the arc's initial end point.
4. Click to position the arc's second point or provide an angle value.
5. You may optionally make another arc by repeating steps 2-4.
6. To finish the command, press **Enter**.

The arcs appear on the canvas together with any construction geometry, restrictions, and measurements that are applied to them.

Tangent Arc

To create an arc that preserves tangency with other sketch geometry, place the end points to specify the location and size of the arc.

1. Choose Create > Arc > Tangent Arc from the Sketch contextual menu.
2. Click on the canvas to position the arc's initial end point so that it lines up with the sketch geometry that will be subject to the tangent restriction.

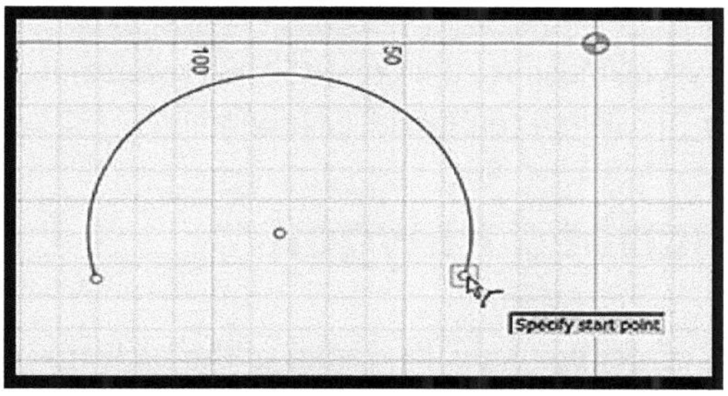

3. Click to position the arc's second point or provide a radius value.

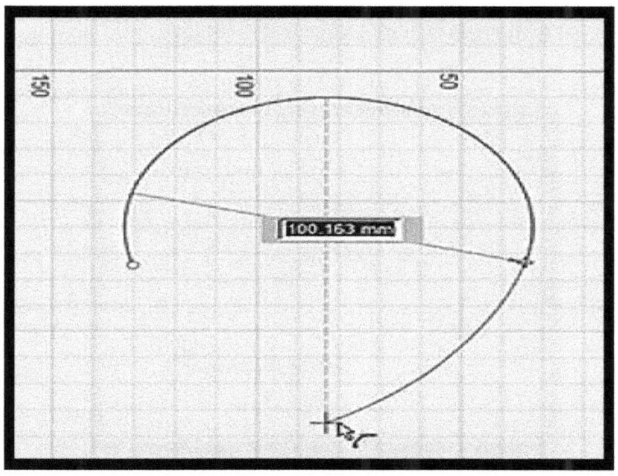

4. **Optional:** To make another arc, repeat steps 2-3.
5. To finish the command, press **Enter**.

The arcs appear on the canvas together with any construction geometry, restrictions, and measurements that are applied to them.

Tips

- While any arc command is running, you may switch between Arc types in the Sketch Palette dialog's Feature Options area.
- When you snap to the sketch grid or other geometry in the design, object snap symbols appear close to the geometry as you move the mouse cursor over it. The logical limitations are immediately applied to the drawing if you snap to a certain location.

Drawing a Polygon

In Fusion 360, the polygon tools in the Sketch > Generate panel allows you to create several polygon types as drawing geometry or construction geometry in an active sketch. **The following commands may be used to build polygons in an active sketch:**

- **Circumscribed Polygon**
- **Inscribed Polygon**
- **Edge Polygon**

Before creating sketch geometry, you must use the Create Sketch command or right-click an existing sketch and choose Edit Sketch to enter the Sketch contextual environment.

Create a Circumscribed Polygon

Create a polygon by defining its center point and the radius of the circle that will circumscribe it.

Each polygon's midpoint is located on the circle.

1. In the contextual tab of Sketch, pick **Create > Polygon > Circumscribed Polygon**.
2. In the canvas, click to insert the polygon's center point.

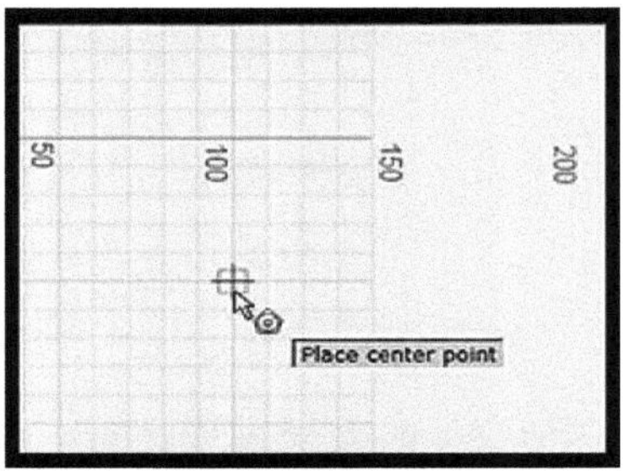

3. The radius of the circumscribed circle must be specified.
4. Press **Tab** to choose between the radius and number of sides.
5. Indicate the number of sides.
6. Drag the mouse cursor to adjust the polygon's orientation.
7. Click to position the polygon.

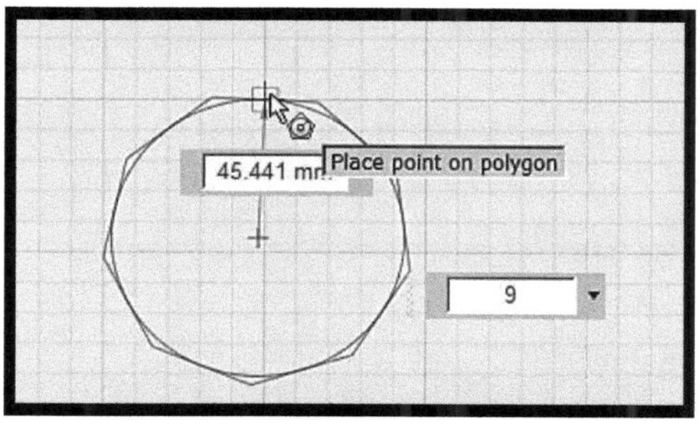

8. Repeat steps 2-6 to build another polygon if desired.
9. Press the **Enter** key to execute the instruction.

Canvas displays the polygons and any building geometry, restrictions, and dimensions attached to them.

Create an Inscribed Polygon

Create a polygon by defining its center point and the radius of the circle that will include it.

The intersection points of the polygon edges lie on the circle.

1. On the contextual tab of Sketch, choose **Create > Polygon > Inscribed Polygon**.
2. On the canvas, click to insert the polygon's center point.
3. Specify the radius of the circle inscribed.
4. Press **Tab** to choose between the radius and number of sides.
5. Indicate the number of sides.
6. Drag the mouse cursor to adjust the polygon's orientation.
7. Click to position the polygon.
8. Repeat steps 2-6 to build another polygon if desired.
9. Press the **Enter** key to execute the instruction.

Canvas displays the polygons and any building geometry, restrictions, and dimensions attached to them.

Create an Edge Polygon

Create a polygon by specifying its perimeter and orientation.

1. On the contextual tab of Sketch, choose **Create > Polygon > Edge Polygon**.
2. Click on the canvas to set the first point of an edge.

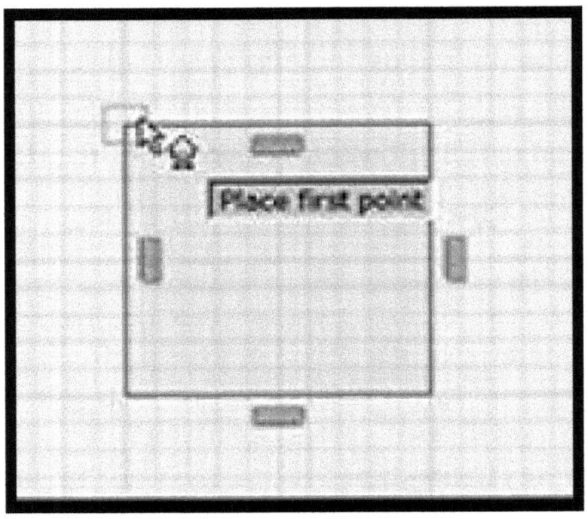

3. **Place the second edge point:**
    a. Indicate the length of the edge.
    b. Press Tab to swap between length and angle.
    c. Specify the edge's angle.
    d. Click or press Enter to set the second point.
4. Indicate the number of sides.
5. Dragging the mouse cursor to either side of the edge will rotate the polygon.
6. Click to position the polygon.

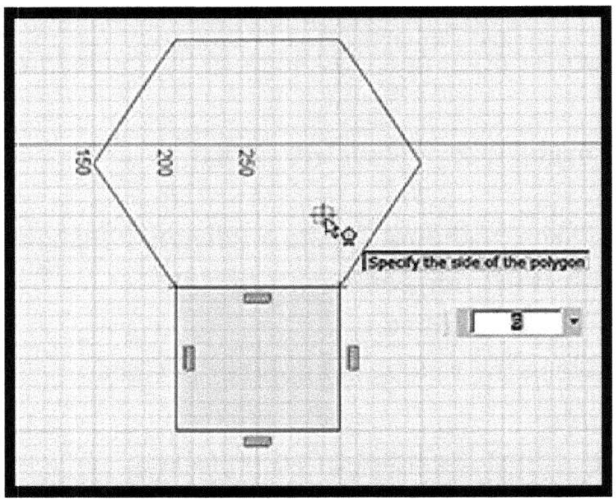

7. Optionally, repeat steps 2 through 6 to build a second polygon.
8. Press **Enter** to finish the command.

Canvas displays the polygons and any building geometry, restrictions, and dimensions attached to them.

Tips

- In the **Feature Options** area of the Sketch Palette dialog, you may toggle between Polygon types while any polygon command is running.
- When snapping to the sketch grid or other geometry in the design, item snap symbols appear as you move the mouse cursor near the geometry. Snapping to a given point immediately adds logical limitations to the drawing.

Drawing an Ellipse

The Ellipse tool in the Sketch > Create panel allows you to create ellipses in an active sketch as sketch geometry or construction geometry.

1. On the contextual tab of Sketch, pick **Create > Ellipse**.
2. Click the canvas to position the ellipse's center point.

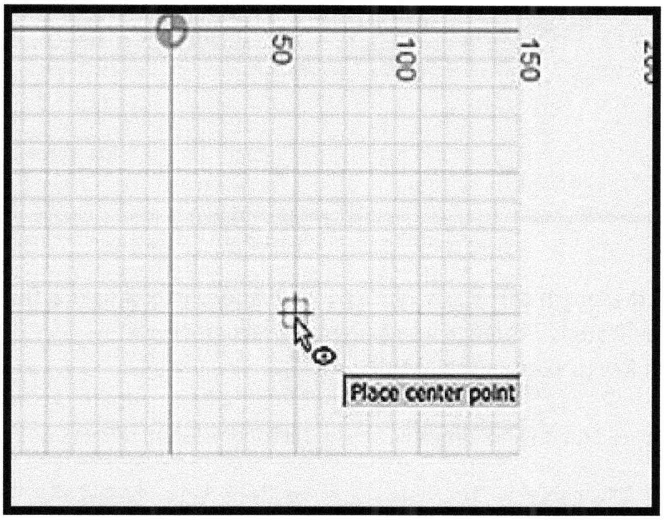

3. **Indicate the first axis point:**

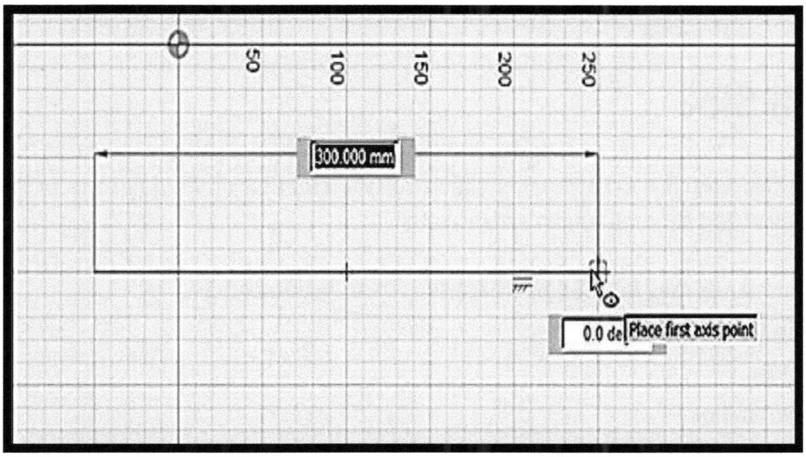

   a. Indicate the size of the axis.
   b. Press Tab to swap between length and angle.
   c. Indicate the axis's angle.
   d. To insert the first axis point, press Enter or click.

4. **Indicate a point on the ellipse:**

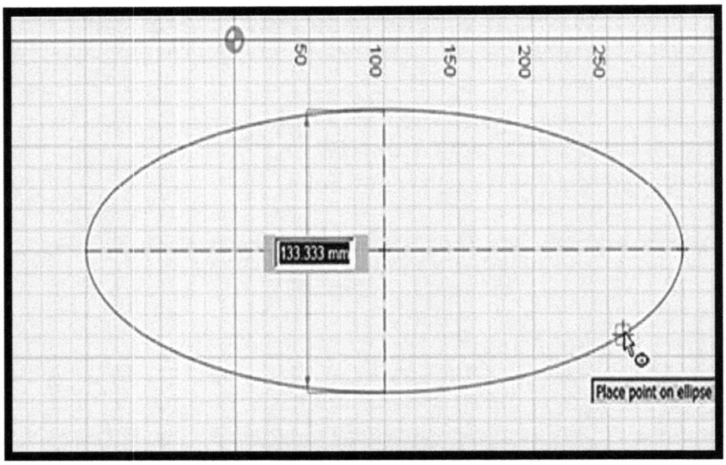

   a. Enter the length of the axis, or click to add a second point along the ellipse.
5. Optionally, repeat steps 2 through 4 to generate a second ellipse.
6. Press the **Enter** key to execute the command.

Canvas displays the ellipses and any building geometry, restrictions, and dimensions attached to them.

Tips

When snapping to the sketch grid or other geometry in the design, object snap symbols appear next to the geometry as you move the mouse pointer. Snapping to a given point immediately adds logical limitations to the drawing.

Drawing a Slot

The slot tools in the **Sketch > Create** panel allows for the creation of various sorts of slots as drawing geometry or construction geometry in an active sketch.

The following commands may be used to create slots in an active sketch:

- **Center to Center Slot**
- **Overall Slot**
- **Center Point Slot**
- **3-Point Arc Slot**
- **Center Point Arc Slot**

Before creating sketch geometry, you must use the **Create Sketch** command or right-click an existing sketch and choose **Edit Sketch** to enter the Sketch contextual environment.

Center-to-Center Slot

Create a linear slot by defining the center points at either end of the slot, the distance, and angle between the center points, and the slot's width.

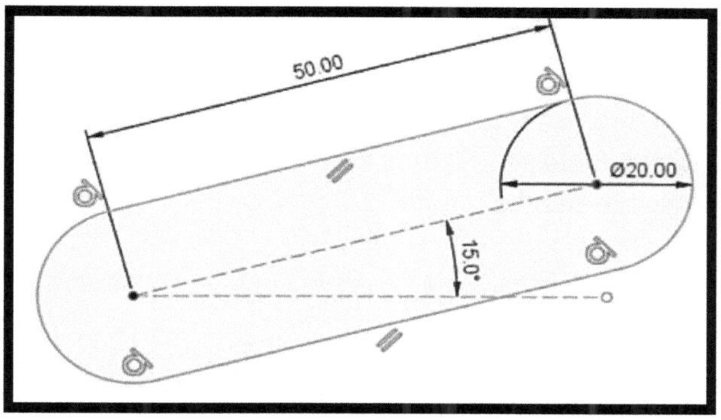

1. On the contextual menu for Sketch, choose **Create > Slot > Center to Center Slot**.
2. On the canvas, click to set the center point for one end of the slot.
3. **Place the second end of the slot's center point as follows:**
    a. Indicate the desired distance.
    b. To define the angle value, press Tab.
    c. Click to position the spot.
4. **Specify the slot's width:**
    a. Provide the distance value.
    b. Click to position a point that falls along the slot's linear edge.
5. Optionally, repeat steps 2-4 to get a second slot.
6. Press the **Enter key** to execute the command.

Canvas displays the slots and any building geometry, restrictions, and measurements attached to them.

Overall Slot

Create a linear slot by positioning two endpoints, describing the distance and angle between them, and defining the slot's width.

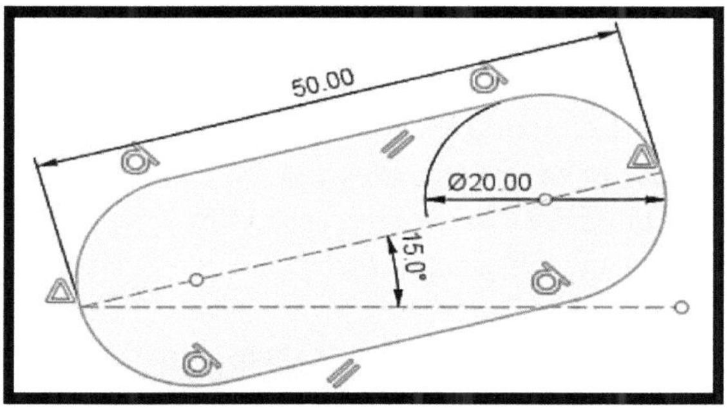

1. On the contextual tab for Sketch, pick **Create > Slot > Overall Slot**.
2. On the canvas, set the initial end point of the slot by clicking.
3. **Place the second endpoint of the slot as follows:**
    a. Indicate the desired distance.
    b. To define the angle value, press Tab.
    c. Click to position the spot.
4. **Specify the slot's width:**
    a. Provide the distance value.
    b. Click to position a point that falls along the slot's linear edge.
5. Optionally, repeat steps 2-4 to get a second slot.
6. Press the **Enter key** to execute the command.

Canvas displays the slots and any building geometry, restrictions, and measurements attached to them.

Center-to-Point Slot

Create a linear slot by defining the slot's center point, the distance and angle between the slot's center point and the center point of one of its ends, as well as the slot's width.

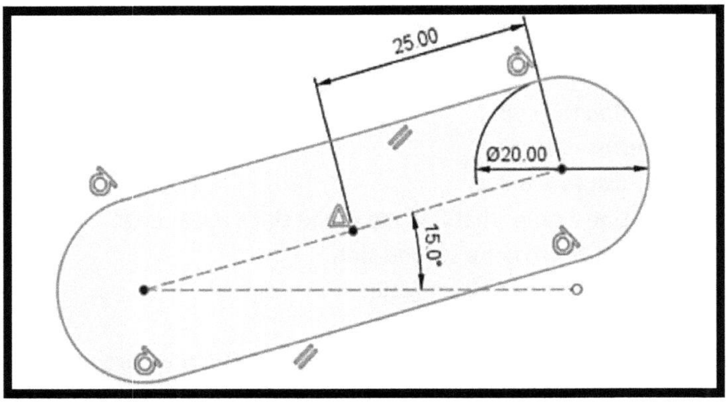

1. On the contextual tab for Sketch, pick **Create > Slot > Center Point Slot**.
2. On the canvas, click to position the slot's center point.
3. **Locate the center point of one of the slot's ends:**
    a. Indicate the desired distance.
    b. To define the angle value, press Tab.
    c. Click to position the spot.
4. **Specify the slot's width:**
    a. Indicate the desired distance.
    b. Click to position a point that falls along the slot's linear edge.
5. Optional: Repeat steps 2 through 4 to create a second slot.
6. Press the **Enter key** to execute the command.

Canvas displays the slots and any building geometry, restrictions, and measurements attached to them.

3-Point Arc Slot

Place the center points at each end of the arc slot, define the distance between the center points, place a point along the arc between the two center points, and select the slot's width.

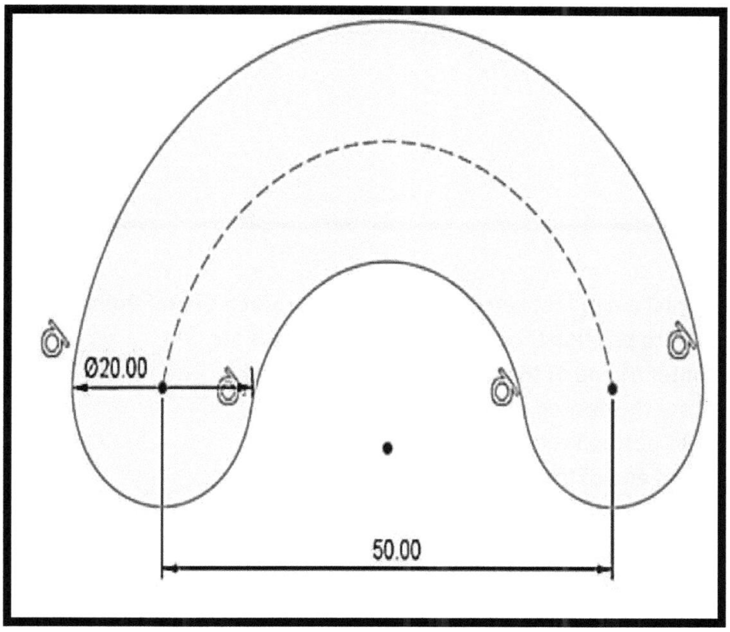

1. On the contextual menu for Sketch, choose **Create > Slot > Three Point Arc Slot**.
2. On the canvas, click to set the center point for one end of the slot.
3. **Place the second end of the slot's center point as follows:**
    a. Indicate the desired distance.
    b. Click to position the spot.
4. Click to position a point along the arc connecting the two center points.
5. **Specify the slot's width:**
    a. Indicate the desired distance.
    b. Click to position a point along the arc of the slot's edge.
6. Optionally, repeat steps 2-5 to generate a second slot.
7. Press the **Enter** key to finish the command.

Canvas displays the slots and any building geometry, restrictions, and measurements attached to them.

Center Point Arc Slot

Create an arc slot by defining the center point for the arc of the slot, the distance between the center point for the arc of the slot and the center for one end of the slot, the angle between the centers for the two end points, and the width of the slot.

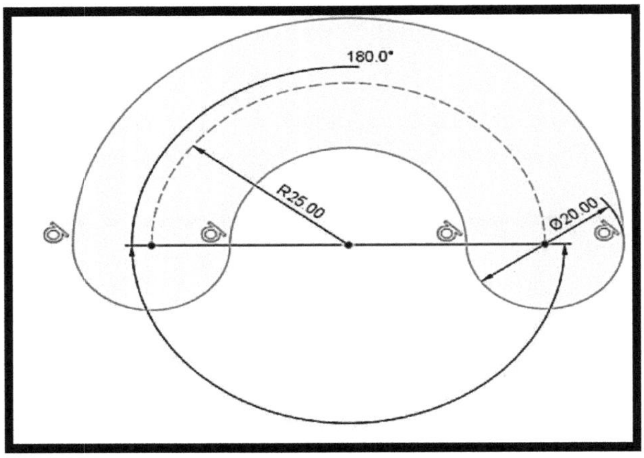

1. On the contextual menu for Sketch, choose **Create > Slot > Center Point Arc Slot**.
2. Click the canvas to position the center point of the slot's arc.
3. **Locate the center of one of the slot's ends:**
    a. Indicate the desired distance.
    b. Click to position the spot.
4. **Place the second end of the slot's center point:**
    a. Specify the angle between the two ends of the slot's center points.
    b. Click to position the spot.
5. **Specify the slot's width:**
    a. Indicate the desired distance.
    b. Click to position a point along the arc of the slot's edge.
6. Optionally, repeat steps 2-5 to generate a second slot.
7. Press the **Enter** key to finish the command.

Canvas displays the slots and any building geometry, restrictions, and measurements attached to them.

Tips

In the **Feature Options** area of the Sketch Palette dialog, you may toggle between Slot types while any slot command is active. When snapping to the sketch grid or other geometry in the design, item snap symbols appear as you move the mouse cursor near the geometry. Snapping to a given point immediately adds logical limitations to the drawing.

Drawing Conic Curves

In Fusion 360, the **Conic Curve** tool in the **Sketch > Create panel** enables the creation of conic curves as drawing geometry or construction geometry in an active sketch. The Conic Curve command generates a curve whose endpoints and Rho value are specified. The ends specify the curve's location. The shape is defined by the Rho value. The curve might be elliptical, parabolic, or hyperbolic, depending on the amount of Rho.

You click to put the starting point, ending point, and vertex. Utilize the instructions to establish a tangency restriction, and then define the Rho value to construct the appropriate form.

1. On the contextual tab of Sketch, pick **Create > Conic Curve**.
2. Click in the canvas to insert the first endpoint.

3. Click the second end point into position.

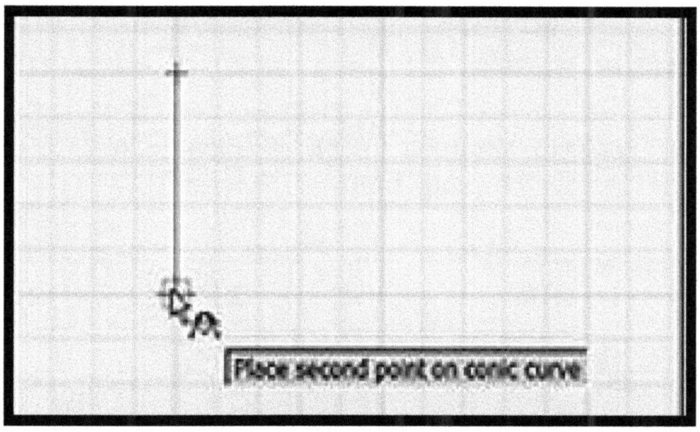

4. Click to position the vertex.

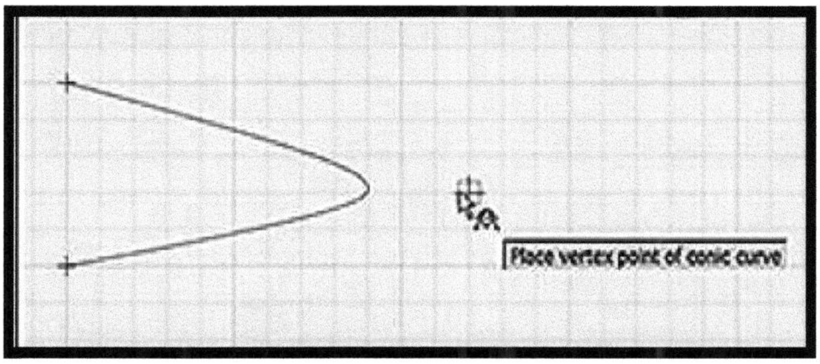

5. Move the Rho manipulator handle or enter a specific Rho value.
6. Press the **Enter** key to execute the command.

Canvas displays the conic curve, its endpoints, and its vertex point.

Tips

When snapping to the sketch grid or other geometry in the design, item snap symbols appear as you move the mouse cursor near the geometry. Snapping to a given point immediately adds logical limitations to the drawing.

Drawing a Spline

The spline tools in the Sketch > Generate panel allows you to create various spline types as drawing geometry or construction geometry in an active sketch in Fusion 360.

A spline is a smooth, freeform curve that travels through or near a collection of points that impact the curve's shape. There are two types of splines available in Fusion 360. You can create either open or closed splines.

The following commands may be used to construct splines in an active sketch:

- **Fit Point Spline**
- **Control Point Spline**

Before creating sketch geometry, you must use the Create Sketch command or right-click an existing sketch and choose Edit Sketch to enter the Sketch contextual environment.

Fit Point Spline

The Fit Point Spline command generates a smooth curve that connects many points.

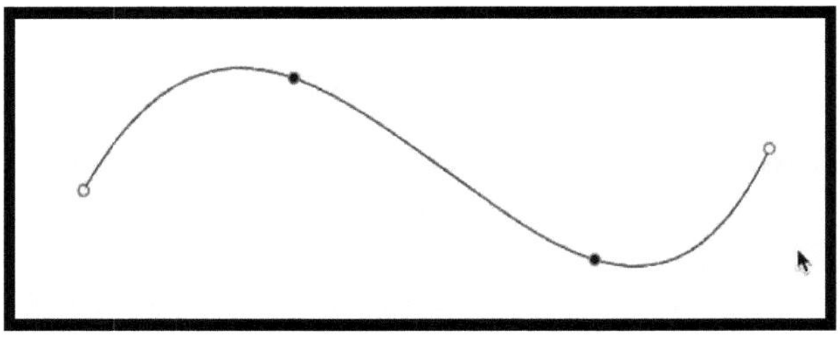

1. On the contextual tab of Sketch, choose **Create > Spline > Fit Point Spline**.
2. Click the canvas to position the initial end point of the spline.
3. Click to locate the next point through which the spline will pass.
4. Continue adding points as necessary.
5. **Finish the spline:**
    a. By clicking the start point, a closed sketch profile is created.
    b. Select the Check Mark symbol.
6. Optionally, repeat steps 2 through 5 to construct a second spline.
7. Press the **Enter** key to finish the command.

The splines are rendered on the canvas.

Control Point Spline

The Control Point Spline command generates a smooth curve controlled by a control frame created by a succession of points. CV Splines are also known as Control Point Splines.

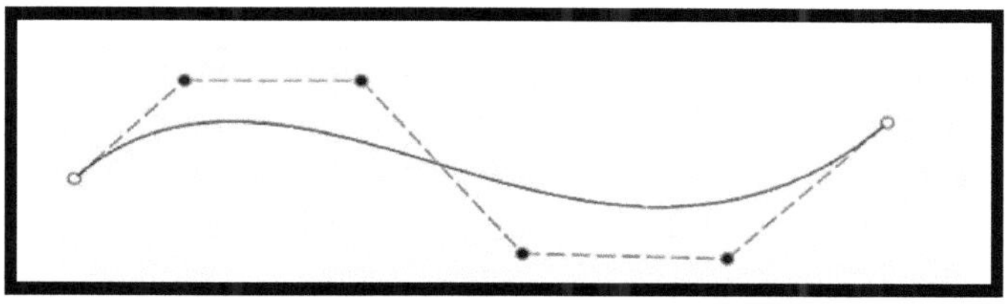

1. On the contextual tab of Sketch, choose **Create > Spline > Control Point Spline**.
2. Click the canvas to position the initial end point of the spline.
3. Click to insert the next point to mold the spline's path.
4. Continue putting points to form the frame of control.
5. Click the **Check** button to finish creating the spline.
6. Optionally, repeat steps 2 through 5 to construct a second spline.
7. Press the **Enter** key to finish the command.

The splines are rendered on the canvas.

- A control point spline often does not pass through the control points, except the initial and final points. Control points, in contrast, to fit points, establish the framework utilized to compute the curve.
- Control points add tension in a particular direction to the spline. Pulling a control point further away increases the stress on the curve in that region. When a control point is moved closer, tension is reduced.
- In the majority of instances, you need more control points than fit points to define a specific form, since each control point has less impact on the entire curve than a fit point.
- Control point splines lack tangent/curvature controls. To improve form control, add more points.

Editing a Spline

1. To view the curvature handles, choose the spline.
2. Adjust the spline's curvature by dragging the end points of a Curvature Handle.
3. **Choose the spline, right-click, and then select one of the choices below:**
    a. **Open/Close Spline Curve** (fit point splines only)
    b. **Insert Spline Fit Point** (fit point splines only)
    c. **Insert Spline Control Point** (control point splines only)
    d. Toggle **Curvature Display**
        i. In the Setup Curvature Display dialog, modify the Curvature Comb Display's Density and Scale.

4. **Pick a Curvature Handle for a fit point spline, then right-click and select one of the following options:**
- Activate Curvature Handle
- Deactivate Curvature Handle

Tips

- To construct a tangent constraint between a spline and other sketch geometry, click the end point of any line, arc, or spline, and then drag the cursor away from it. You may do this by using the mouse. After the spline is finished being created, the tangent constraint will appear on the canvas.
- For both solid and surface modeling processes, pick the **Degree 5** spline type when using the Control Point Spline command in the Sketch Palette dialog's Feature Options section. This applies to both solid modeling and surface modeling. In the Form contextual environment, T-Spline modeling tasks may be completed by selecting the **Degree 3** spline type.
- When you snap to the sketch grid or other geometry in the design, object snap symbols will show near the geometry as you move the mouse pointer. When you snap to a certain place in the drawing, the logical restrictions are applied to the sketch immediately thereafter.
- While using the **Move/Copy** command, you may alter the spline manipulator handles by selecting any point on the spline and then either showing or hiding all of the handles.
- The spline point will stay on the plane when you use the **Move/Copy** command to move it using the manipulator handles. This command is located in the Edit menu.

Spline degree control reference

On a more technical level, the degree of a spline defines the amount of difficulty of the equation that is used to describe the form of the spline. A spline with a higher degree is defined by an equation with a higher degree, and this equation produces a spline that is technically smoother than a spline with a lower degree. Lower-degree splines are often simpler to deal with since higher-degree splines need more points to describe a particular form. As a result, higher-degree splines are more difficult to use. You have the option of selecting between degree 5 and degree 3, which are the spline degrees that are utilized the most often in Fusion 360. While the Control Point Spline tool is active, you have the option to choose this from the Sketch Palette's Spline Degree drop-down menu.

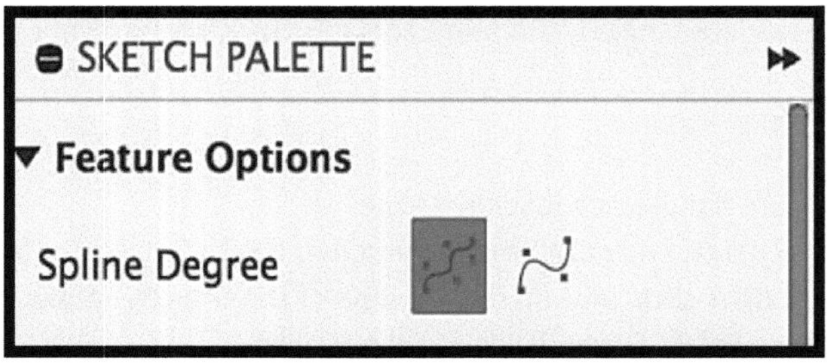

Degree 5: The default setting is degree 5, which provides the optimal outcomes for the vast majority of situations. This offers the optimum balance that can be struck between the smoothness of the geometry and the convenience of usage. Splines of degree 5 are characterized by a high degree of smoothness, which

makes them ideal for establishing principal surfaces on your model and constructing transition surfaces between other types of geometry.

Degree 3: Splines with a degree 3 often call for a lower number of control points, making them potentially simpler to deal with. Technically, they are not as smooth as degree 5 splines since degree 5 splines guarantee G4-continuity internal to the curve, but degree 3 splines only guarantee G2-continuity internal to the curve. When you generate a degree 3 spline with a high number of control points, you could see some abrupt twists or lumps in the curvature comb. These sharp turns and bumps reflect spots on the curve that are not G3-continuous. Note that Degree 3 splines are still guaranteed to be G2-continuous throughout. Surfaces that are formed from G2-continuous curves still have noticeably smooth highlights, which means that they are smooth enough for the majority of use cases.

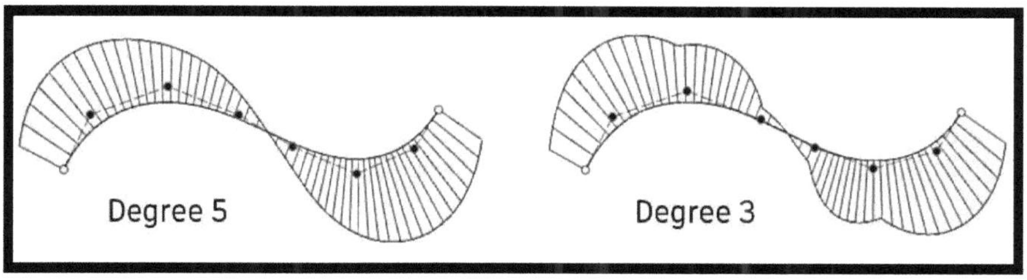

Working with geometry in the Sculpt workspace may benefit from enhanced matching behavior thanks to Degree 3 splines, which is one of the unique behaviors that should be noted about these splines. The reason for this is that the Sculpt tools are based on a technology called T-Splines. This is a technology that is primarily built on degree 3 surfaces. As a result of this, we are going to change the default Spline Degree in the Sculpt workspace to Degree 3. This will allow us to create control point splines. It is also important to remember that the value for the Spline Degree decides the maximum degree that may be constructed for the spline. The degree of a spline can never be more than the number of control points minus one, and it can never be less than that amount. For example, a spline can only be degree 3 or lower if it has four control points. As you pick points to form your control point spline, its degree will steadily rise until it reaches degree 5 or degree 3 (depending on the Spline Degree selection), at which time it will remain at that degree. This will continue until the end of the process. Therefore, regardless of the degree setting, the maximum spline degree that can be achieved is three, even if the setting for the Spline Degree is five. This is because the spline can only be completed after picking four points.

Adding Fit/Control Points in a Spline

Control point splines, also known as CV splines, NURBS curves, and style splines, provide a method for creating more sophisticated curves inside a Sketch. These splines go by a variety of other names as well. Up until this point, this need has been satisfied by the command that is already in place for Splines. When you use this tool, you may pick several points, and Fusion will automatically generate a smooth curve that connects all of those locations. Control point splines provide an additional method that may be used to get the same end goal. You will be asked to choose several points, and the combination of these points will be used to establish a "**control frame**," from which a smooth curve will be generated. We are changing the name of the prior Spline tool to "**Fit Point Spline**" since we will now have two different spline commands. This means that the spline will "fit" the points that you provide. These options may now be accessed in the Sketch tool menu through a flyout titled "**Spline**."

As you begin to combine the usage of these two tools, there are two important distinctions between fit point splines and control point splines that you should bear in mind:

1. A control point spline, as illustrated above, will (typically) not pass through any of the chosen points other than the start and end points. Control points, as opposed to fit points, which specify points that the spline must pass through, simply define the underlying frame that is utilized to compute the curve. Fit points may be defined as follows: You may think of a control point as being something that applies "**tension**" to the spline in a particular direction. If you drag a point farther away, the tension on the curve in that region will grow, and if you push it closer, the tension will decrease.

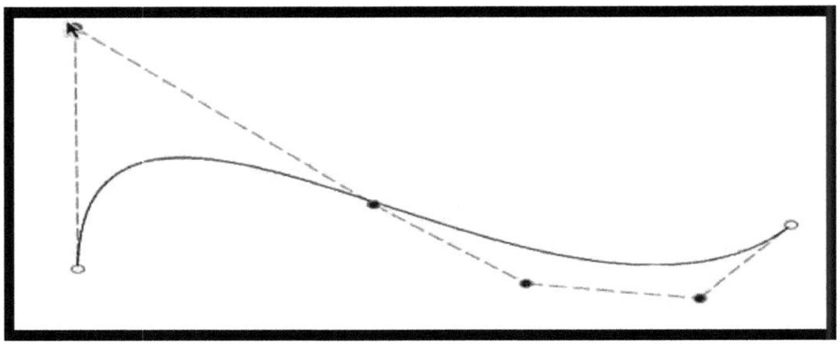

2. To specify a certain form, you will almost always need a greater number of control points than fit points. This is because each control point has less impact on the shape of the curve as a whole than does a fit point. In addition, control point splines do not have tangent or curvature handles; thus, if you want to exercise more sophisticated form control, you will need to increase the number of control points (you can do this by right-clicking the spline and selecting Insert Spline Control Point). Look at the two curves below as an illustration of this concept. A fit point spline with three points will have the sensation of being highly flexible and can be readily manipulated into several different forms. Because it lacks tangent and curvature handles, a control point spline with three points will have a much stiffer feel, and it will restrict the sorts of shape modifications that may be made. In situations like this, the technique that is necessary to provide more flexible form control is to add additional control points as they are required.

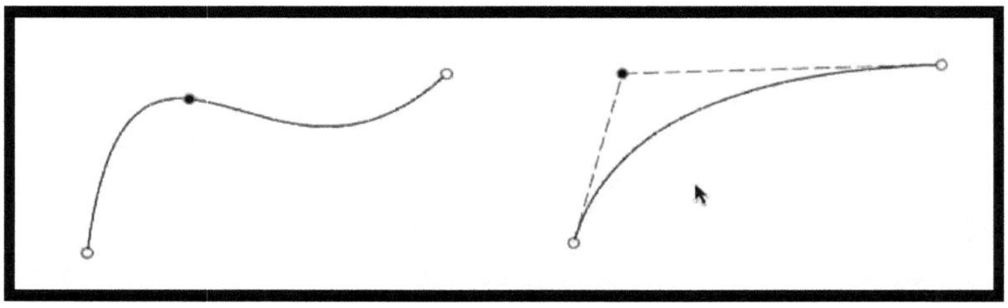

The definition of a spline may be accomplished in a fairly straightforward manner by using fit points. The points that you set will directly limit the curve. On the other hand, behind the scenes, Fusion is the one choosing how the spline form transitions from one fit point to the next. This burden falls mostly on Fusion's shoulders.

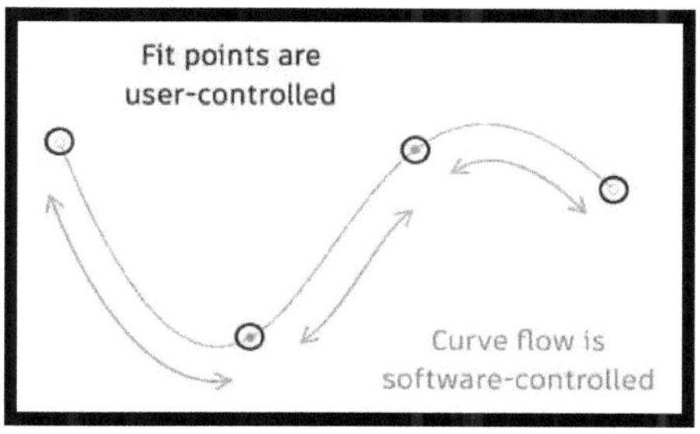

When you're designing products, there are instances when you need to have extremely exact control over the flow of the intermediate form. There are tangent and curvature handles available on fit point splines, which may be used to provide further control if it is required. However, there are times when they don't give precise enough control, and manipulating these handles can have unanticipated effects on other parts of the spline.

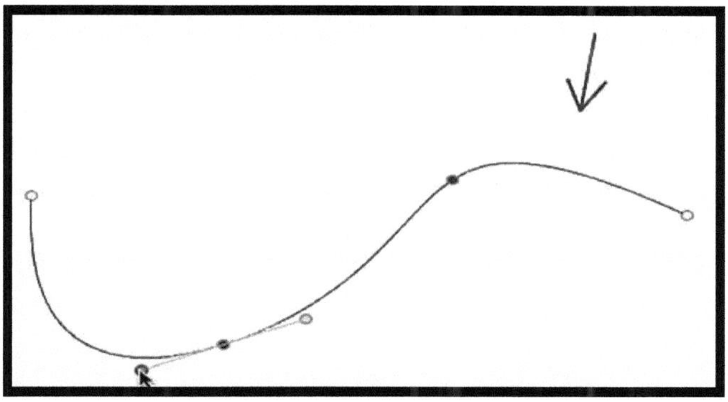

You will have direct access to the underlying control points that determine the whole form of the curve if you choose to work with control point splines. You will have highly fine control over certain aspects of its form as a result of this.

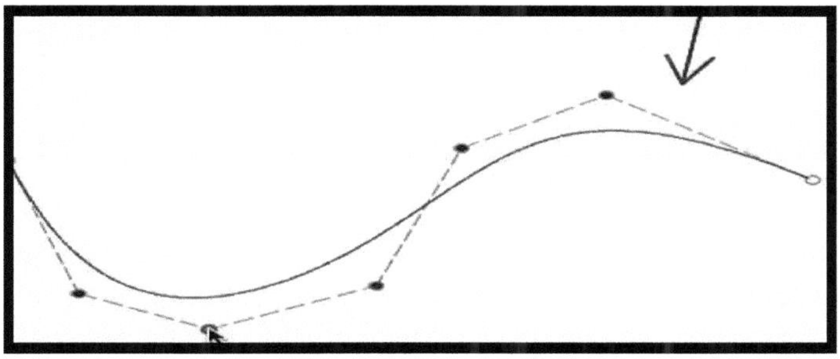

When should I utilize control point splines?

When it comes to defining the major surfaces of your model, the conventional school of thinking maintains that control point splines are superior to fit point splines. They provide you the opportunity to control the math of the surface very clearly, and if you follow the best practices that are outlined below, you can assure that the surfaces that are formed from these splines will be smooth in both an aesthetic and a technical sense.

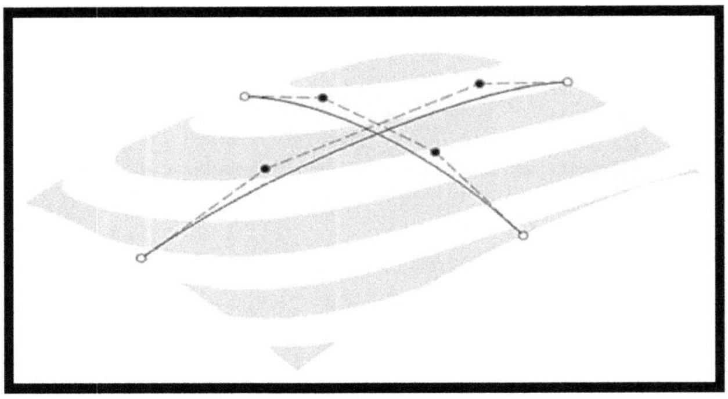

However, because a control point spline will need more points to describe a specific form than a fit point spline would, it may be easier to design complicated shapes with lots of different curvature variations if you use the Fit Point Spline tool. For a small and detailed design task such as this, the high degree of mathematical smoothness provided by control point splines is probably less important, and the shape can be created and edited with much less effort using a fit point spline. An example of this would be a traced logo. Fit point splines allow for the shape to be created and edited with much less effort.

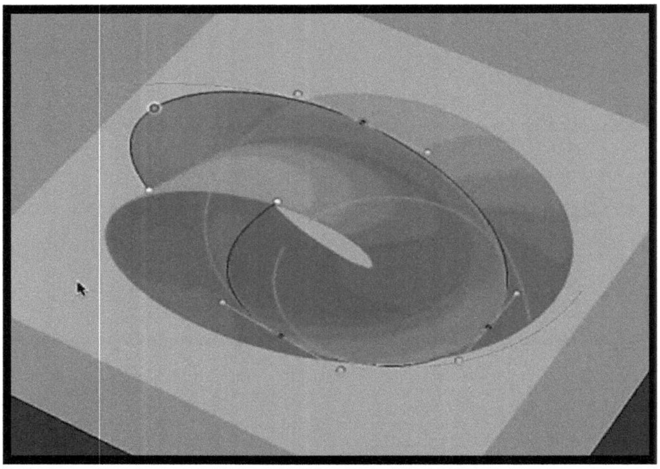

However, the choice of spline tool for many tasks is a matter of personal preference. This is because, although control point splines offer more flexibility for certain scenarios, the two tools fundamentally create the same type of geometry. As a result, you may simply gravitate toward one particular tool that is the most convenient for you!

What are some of the recommended procedures for working with control point splines?

To use the Control Point Spline tool effectively and produce curves of good quality, there are a few fundamental guidelines that must be adhered to.

1. When describing the desired form, use the fewest feasible points possible.

Splines will automatically generate the transition between two spots that are as smooth as is physically feasible. When you create superfluous intermediate points, you are essentially "**overriding**" the inherent smoothness of the curve, which increases the likelihood that it may include unwelcome bumps or wobbles.

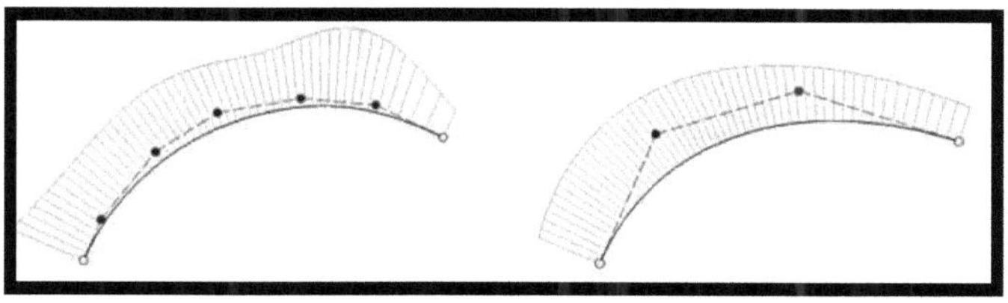

The maxim "**less is more**" applies rather often in this context. A word of caution, though: if you discover that you need to move control points a significant distance away from the curve to obtain the shape you want, you may be attempting to perform too much work with too few control points. In this particular scenario, the amount of form control that may be achieved by adding one or two additional control points may be more appropriate.

2. If at all feasible, try to maintain the points at the same distance apart.

Another element that may create difficulties with the smoothness of a spline is an uneven control point distribution; thus, the spacing between neighboring control points should be kept uniform whenever it is practicable to do so. There are some circumstances in which you will want a denser concentration of control points in certain regions, namely those regions in which you desire a form with a greater degree of curvature. However, bear in mind that in areas where you have transitioned from spread-out control points to bunched-together control points, you need to make sure that those transitions are smooth and natural so that you can maintain a high-quality curve.

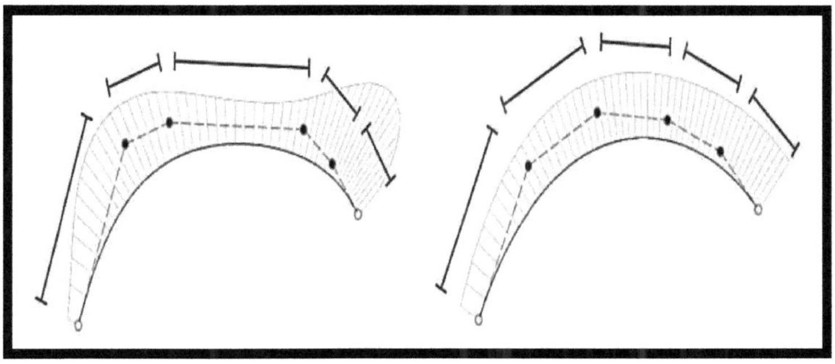

3. Maintain a distance between neighboring locations that are not too great.

Avoid having dramatic changes in distance or direction from one control point to the next. This will result in splines that are difficult to deal with or adapt to in the future. If you discover that you require significant gaps between points to obtain a certain form, it may be preferable to insert a few more control points so that all points sit reasonably near to the curve and one another. This will ensure that the shape is achieved successfully.

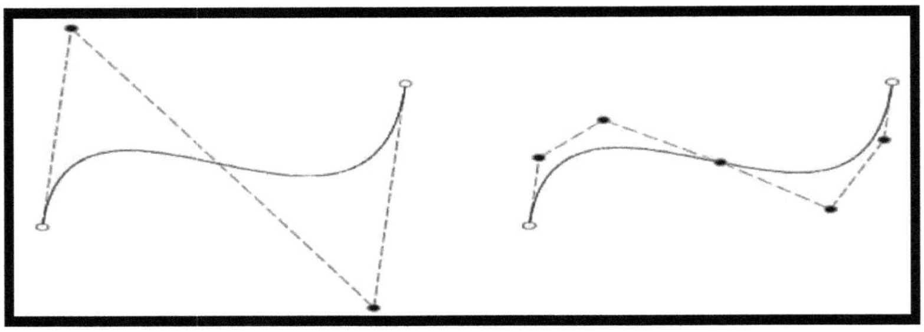

The three guidelines that have been shown above apply to any spline-based geometry, which includes fit point splines and Sculpt geometry. Therefore, you should aim to adhere to these rules as much as possible.

Constraining a control point spline

One of the most distinguishing features of control point splines is the fact that they are always accompanied by a visible control frame. Fusion 360 gives you the ability to apply limitations not only to the control frame but also to the curve itself so that you can get the most out of this feature. The combination of these two approaches may make certain previously unavailable, very effective constraint procedures available. Different kinds of constraints will make more sense to apply to the two distinct kinds of objects because the control frame is made up of straight lines and the curve itself is a form with complicated curvature.

As a general rule:

- The control frame is the optimal location for applying the constraints that are used to regulate the spline's overall dimensions and contours.
- It is recommended that constraints used to explain the spline's connection to other geometry are imposed directly on the curve in question.

The Tangent and Curvature constraints are going to be the ones that get utilized the most when trying to describe a relationship to another piece of geometry. These constraints will establish a smooth link between a control point spline and another curve or edge that is present in the model. When attempting to put tangent or curvature constraints on control point splines, one of the most crucial rules to keep in mind is that you will need sufficient "free" control points for the constraint to be successful. If you want to use a Tangent constraint, you need to ensure that there is at least one free control point near the tangent connection. This is because when you apply the constraint, Fusion will have to move that control point to a new aligned location to ensure that the tangent connection is maintained. For the same reason, you'll need two free control points if you want to apply a Curvature constraint to your model.

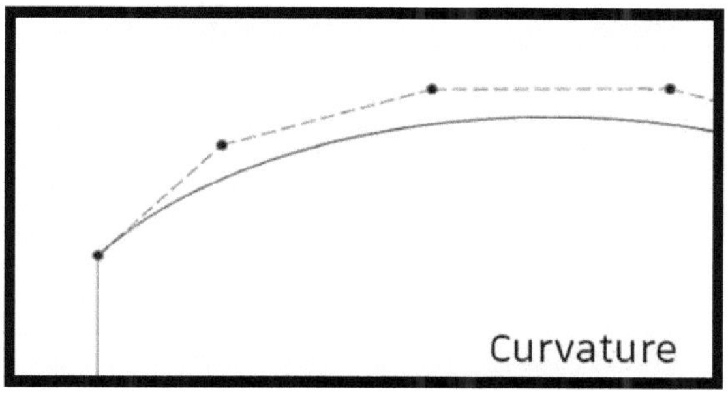

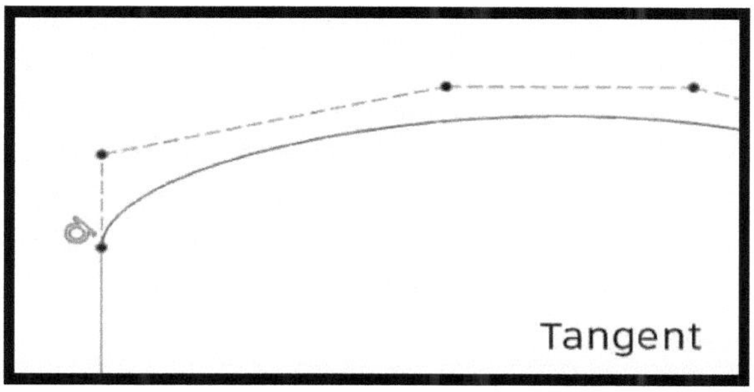

After you have established a tangent or curvature constraint in this manner, the degrees of freedom associated with the shifted control points will be constrained to ensure that the constraint is maintained. Despite this, you should still be able to shift the impacted control points in such a manner that alters the 'weight' of the tangent/curvature connection. This is an effective method for fine-tuning the personality of a curve or surface transition, and it may be used for either.

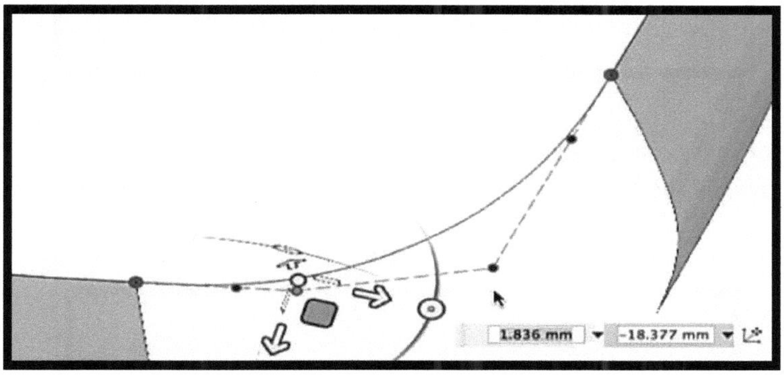

To completely specify the form of a control point spline, you will also need to limit the positions of all of the control points. This is where control frame constraints come into play since they are required. Control frame edges may be constrained in a drawing in the same manner that other straight lines can be constrained there. For instance, you may control the form of the spline in those particular places by applying distance and angle dimensions to the control frame edges. Keep adding them until the control frame is entirely confined, at which time the form of the spline curve will, by definition, likewise be constrained. This process should be repeated until the control frame is fully constrained.

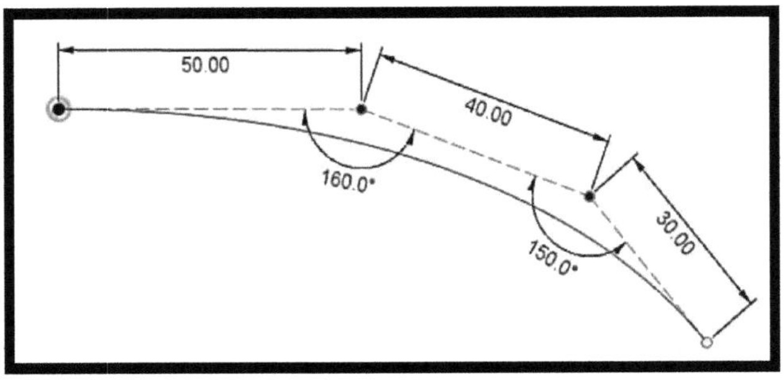

It is important to keep in mind that control point spline shapes can be "**repeated**" by using matching constraints. This means that once a control point spline has been fully constrained, you can get an identical resultant shape by applying the same set of constraints to a second spline (of the same degree). It is also possible to apply restrictions on the control frame to characterize certain aspects of the spline form. By way of illustration, the addition of a horizontal/vertical restriction at one end of the control frame will guarantee that the spline runs properly horizontally/vertically at that end. When constructing a spline that will, at some point in the future, be reflected, this might be of great assistance.

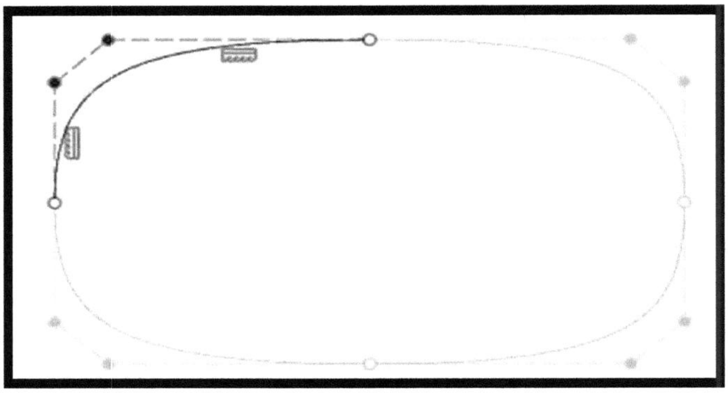

If the manufacture of your product needs a draft angle, you may impose that draft angle on the geometry derived from the spline by specifying an angle between the control frame and a horizontal/vertical datum line.

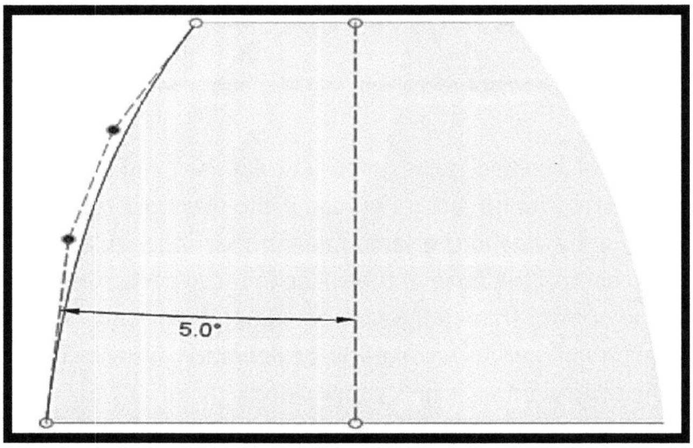

Instead of depending only on Symmetry constraints, you may generate a symmetric control point spline by applying Equal constraints between matching pairs of control frame edges. This can be done in place of the Symmetry constraints. In certain cases, this results in less labor being required while also providing greater freedom than the typical symmetry limits. For instance, you may make a spline with rotational symmetry by applying a mix of Equal and Parallel constraints, which isn't feasible when using **Symmetry constraints** alone. This is because Symmetry constraints only allow for the creation of translational symmetry.

Creating Sketch Points

Using the **Point tool** found in the **Make** drop-down menu of the **SKETCH** contextual tab in Fusion 360, you can generate several sketch points inside the drawing area. These points may then be used to create sketches. The sketch points serve as reference entities inside the context of sketching and may be used to produce additional entities that are part of the drawing. The sketch points may also be used for locating Hole features, establishing reference planes and axes, and a variety of other purposes. Clicking on the **Point** tool after invoking the **CREATE** drop-down menu located in the **SKETCH** contextual tab is required to generate sketch points. The next step is to position the sketch point by clicking the left mouse button on the area of the drawing where you wish to place it. It is now time to build the drawing point. Similarly, by pressing the left mouse button on the drawing area, you may generate many sketch points to utilize in the drawing. After you have finished making the sketch points, right-click anywhere in the drawing area, and when the **Marking Menu** displays, choose the **OK** option. This will allow you to quit the Point tool.

Inserting Text into a Sketch

Inserting Text by Drawing a Rectangular Frame

When you have Fusion 360's Design Workspace open, you have the option to make a new drawing. Navigate to the "Text" option by selecting it from the "**Create**" menu that is located on the "**Sketch**" ribbon. The usual "**Text**" tool is opened when the document is first opened. To make advantage of it, you must first construct a container box within which all of the content will be encapsulated. You may make a boundary box by picking two points that are diagonal to one another. It's important to note that these corner points may snap to already establish sketch entities or model references. In addition to this, you'll notice that the tool window has grown in size and that some text has already begun to appear. To add to or alter the text that appears in the sketch area, use the text box that is located in this window.

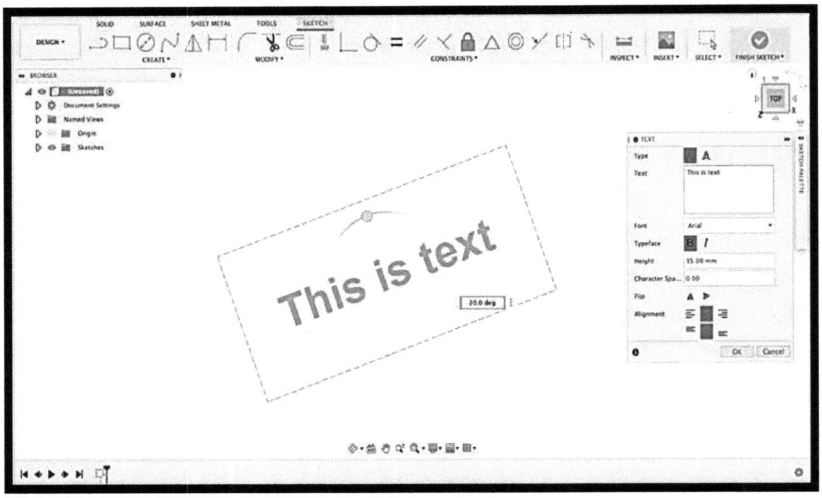

This window also contains stylistic options, which allow the user to pick the font, typeface, alignment, and character spacing, respectively. The height setting determines the actual height of the tallest letters and is reported in millimeters. This option is responsible for controlling the size of the text. The text may be flipped through its container by rotating the box around it. To rotate the text around its central axis, you may do so by clicking and dragging the angular handle. Simply left-clicking on one of the box corners will change the rotation axis so that it points to that particular corner. Make advantage of the flip option to reflect the text by either a horizontal or a vertical line; this function is very helpful for the components that go into stamps and molds. The remaining options function in the same manner as they would in any other text editing program.

Inserting Text along a Path

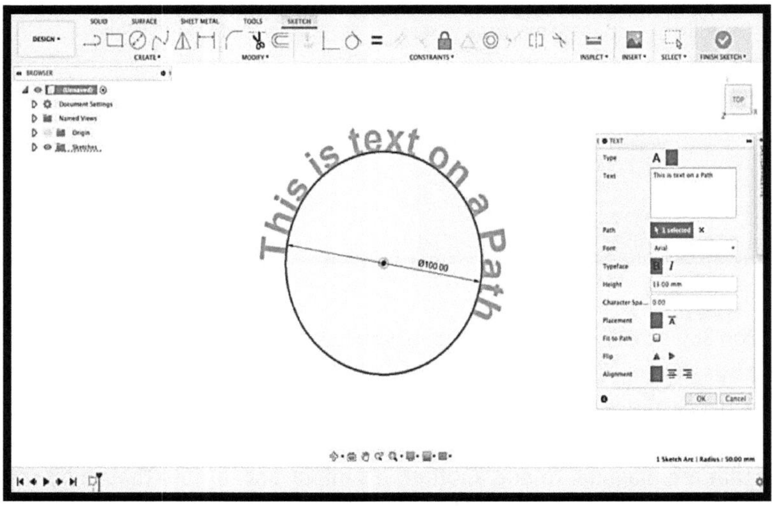

The second tool that comes with the text feature is called "**Text on a Path**," and to use it, you need to have a line, trajectory, or edges already created. You may make use of this tool by choosing the icon located on the right side of the first "**Text**" window, as seen in the previous image. You will not be prompted to create a boundary box; rather, you will be asked to choose a path from the drawing. After the selection has been made, the example text should go along the path rather than in a straight line. The text is wrapped around a circle in the example that is shown above; however, any path may be used with this tool, including curved lines, splines, ellipses, and many more.

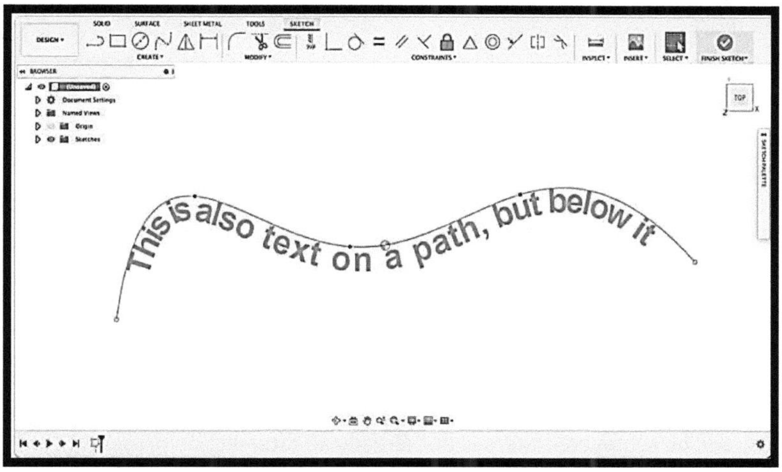

The formatting options for text that is on a path are identical to those for conventional text; the only difference is in the placement, which is slightly altered. The alignment (left, center, and right) is now about the path that was picked rather than the boundary box that was previously used. There are two new options for the text type. The first is called "**placement**," and it allows the text to be put either above or below the path. The second is called "**fit to path**," and it uniformly distributes the text along the path when it is engaged.

Questions

1. What are the two main categories of Features?
2. Which of the features is a sketch-based feature of any real-world component?
3. When drawing an ellipsis, what are the axes you need to define?
4. How do you turn off or on the display of grids in the drawing area?
5. Which tool is used in drawing a rectangle by specifying diagonally opposite corners?
6. When the Rho value of a conic curve is less than 0.5, then the conic curve is what?
7. Can you draw a tangent arc by using the Line tool?

CHAPTER 3

EDITING AND MODIFYING SKETCHES

The procedure of editing and revising a drawing is an essential phase in the process of giving the sketch the form that is intended. In Fusion 360, a drawing may be edited in several different ways, including removing unnecessary sketch entities, expanding sketch entities, mirroring, patterning, scaling, moving, and rotating sketch entities, and more.

Trimming Sketch Entities

1. Select **Modify > Trim** from the contextual menu of the Sketch Tab.
2. While pausing the pointer over the drawing geometry, a preview of the trim will be shown.
3. Trim to the next junction by clicking the **geometry** button.
4. To continue trimming, keep clicking the geometry icon.
5. Press the **Enter** key to finish the command.

Tip: To swiftly trim numerous segments of sketch geometry, click and hold the mouse button, then drag the cursor to touch each section you wish to trim. This will allow you to trim many segments at once. Note that the sketch geometry will be removed if there is not already an intersection present.

Extending Sketch Entities

1. Select **Modify > Extend** from the contextual tab of the Sketch workspace in the Design workspace.
2. To examine a preview of the extension, pausing the cursor over the sketch geometry will allow you to do so.
3. Extend to the next junction by clicking the **geometry** button.
4. To further expand, keep clicking the geometry icon.
5. Press the **Enter** key to finish the command.

Take note that you won't be able to expand the sketch geometry if there are no intersections.

Offsetting Sketch Entities

Note: To edit sketch geometry, you must create a new sketch using the Create Drawing command or right-click an existing sketch and choose **Edit Sketch** from the context menu to enter the Sketch contextual environment. Only then will you be able to alter sketch geometry.

1. Select **Modify > Offset** from the contextual tab of the Sketch Tab.
2. Choose the sketch curve, a chain of related sketch curves, or a sketch profile to offset inside the canvas.
3. Indicate the distance that should be offset.
4. Select a new sketch geometry and repeat steps 2 and 3 if you want to continue offsetting the geometry. This step is optional.

5. Press the **Enter** key to finish the command.

Within the canvas are shown the offset geometry as well as the offset distance dimension. Note that when you pause the cursor over a valid selection, that selection will become highlighted.

Tips

- The outcome of applying an offset will be an ellipse if you choose an ellipse by clicking near either its major or minor axis. The axis is shown when you look at the preview, and the distance of the offset is the same for both the main and the minor axes. Because an ellipse is produced, the distance of the offset fluctuates as it moves around the remainder of the ellipse.
- You will get an oval as the consequence of an offset when you pick an ellipse by clicking away from either its main or minor axis. Both the offset distance and the axis do not appear in the preview, and the axis distance remains constant around the ellipse.
- Deleting the offset glyph will destroy the connection that was previously established between the original sketch geometry and the offset sketch geometry.
- Eliminate the offset dimension to preserve the offset connection while regaining control of the offset distance.
    - To bring back the dimension, right-click the offset glyph, and then pick the **Add Offset Dimension** option from the context menu. If you have removed the offset dimension from the drawing, you may still add a conventional sketch dimension to it.
- It is not possible to produce offset geometry by starting with offset sketch curves.

Creating Construction Entities

By selecting the **Construction tool** inside the **Line type** section of the SKETCH PALETTE dialog box in Fusion 360, users can activate the construction mode, which allows them to create construction entities within the drawing area.

In the **SKETCH PALETTE** dialog box, this tool is disabled by default so you can't use it. As a consequence of this, the only way for you to generate solid sketch entities is to make use of the sketching tools that are accessible through the **CREATE** drop-down menu of the SKETCH contextual tab on the Toolbar. Simply choose the **Construction** tool inside the Line type section of the **SKETCH PALETTE** dialog box to bring up the option to build construction entities. The building mode has been brought into play. Now, the sketch entities you generate in the drawing area by using the sketching tools will operate as construction entities, and you may only use them as references. This restriction applies even if you save them as references. A preexisting solid sketch entity may also be converted into a construction entity or vice versa. To do this, first, pick the entity you want to modify in the drawing area, and then in the SKETCH PALETTE dialog box, under the Line type section, click on the **Construction** tool.

Mirroring Sketch Entities

By selecting the "**Mirror**" option from the "**CREATE**" drop-down menu located in the "**SKETCH**" contextual tab of the Toolbar, you will have the ability to mirror sketch entities around a mirroring line. The figure below illustrates a mirroring line as well as the entities that need to be reflected.

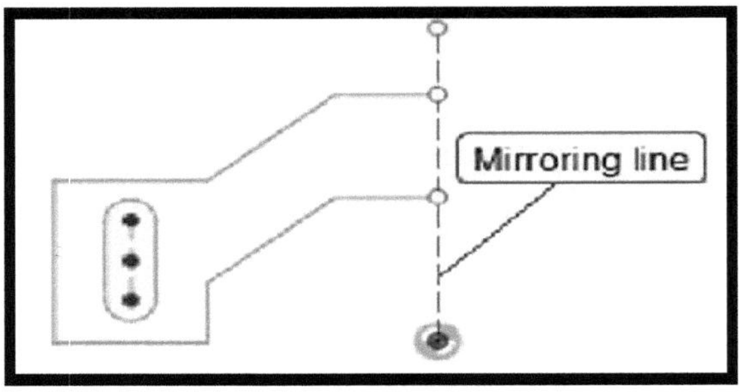

The drawing that was produced as a consequence of reflecting the entities around the mirroring line can be seen in the picture below.

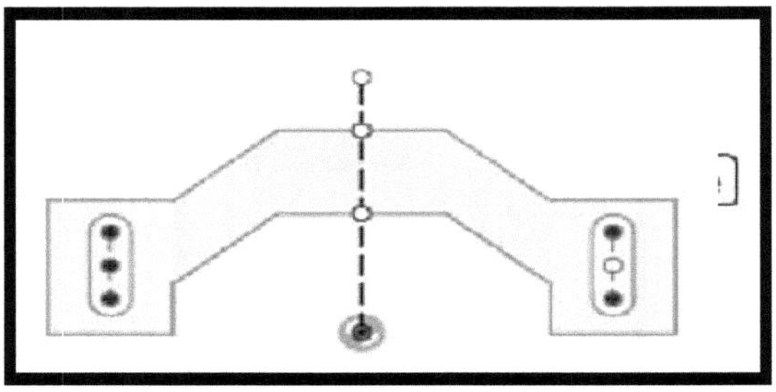

Following is an explanation of the process for mirroring entities by making use of the Mirror tool:

NOTE: When you mirror entities, a symmetric relation is established between the original entities and the mirrored entities about the mirroring line. This ensures that the mirrored entities are an exact reflection of the original entities. As a consequence of this, any changes made to the entities that are being mirrored will immediately reflect in the original entities, and vice versa.

1. Navigate to the **CREATE** panel in the **SKETCH** contextual tab on the Toolbar.
2. Select the **Mirror** tool.
3. Click the **Create** button.
4. You may also choose the Mirror tool by going to the SKETCH contextual tab, opening the CREATE drop-down menu, and then clicking on the tool. A dialogue window labeled **MIRROR** will now display.

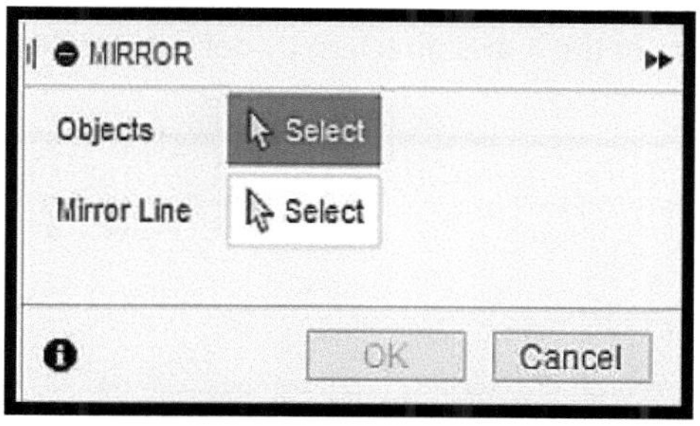

5. Either by clicking the left mouse button one at a time on each entity to be mirrored in the drawing area or by creating a window around the entities to be mirrored, choose each entity to be mirrored individually.
6. In the **MIRROR** dialog box, pick the Mirror Line option by clicking on its corresponding button.
7. Within the drawing area, pick a mirroring line that will serve as the pivot point around which the chosen entities will be reflected. As the mirrored line, you have the option of using either a building entity or a conventional sketch entity. In the sketching area, a preview of the mirrored entities is shown.
8. In the MIRROR dialog box, click the **OK** button to finish the process. The chosen entities will be reflected like that of the mirroring line.

Patterning Sketch Entities

You may construct rectangular and circular patterns of sketch entities in Fusion 360 by utilizing the **Rectangular Pattern** tool and the **Circular Pattern** tool, respectively. Both of these tools allow you to create patterns of sketch entities. The next section will focus on both of the instruments.

Rectangular Pattern Tool

Creating several instances of a sketch object or entities in linear directions may be accomplished with the use of the tool known as a **Rectangular Pattern**. To do this, open the dropdown menu labeled **CREATE** on the **SKETCH** contextual tab of the Toolbar, and then choose the Rectangular Pattern tool from the resulting menu. A dialog window labeled **RECTANGULAR PATTERN** will now display.

Objects

When choosing sketch entities to be patterned, utilize the Objects selection option found in the dialog box. The **Objects** selection option is turned on by default when it may be used. As a consequence of this, you can choose entities one at a time by either repeatedly pressing the left mouse button or creating a window around each one individually.

Direction/s

The first and second linear directions of the pattern may be defined by selecting the appropriate options from the Direction/s selection option. The X-axis and Y-axis will be used to pattern the chosen entities when the default settings are used. Nevertheless, if you activate this selection option, you will have the ability to pick either linear edges or sketch entities to serve as the first and second linear directions of the pattern. The preview of a pattern that runs in the X-axis direction by default can be seen in the picture below.

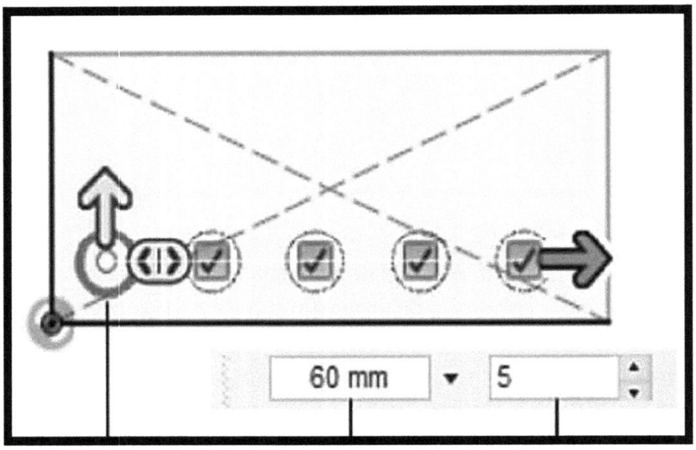

The preview of a pattern that runs along an inclined sketch entity can be seen in the picture below.

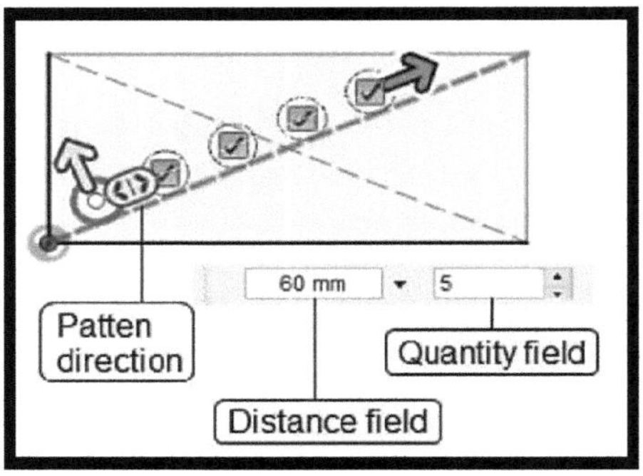

Distance Type

The kind of distance measurement that will be utilized between the pattern instances may be specified by selecting it from the drop-down list titled "**Distance Type**." This drop-down menu has the Extent option selected by default for your convenience. As a consequence of this, the number that you provide in the Distance box will be utilized to determine the amount of space that exists between the first and final pattern occurrences (total pattern distance). When you pick the Spacing option from the drop-down box labeled Distance Type, the value that you enter into the Distance field is the one that is utilized to determine the amount of space that exists between two consecutive pattern occurrences.

Quantity

The number of pattern instances that are to be produced may be specified in the Quantity boxes located in the Direction 1 and Direction 2 portions of the dialog box, respectively. These fields are located on opposite sides of the box. The directions 1 and 2 portions of the dialog box are shown in the picture below.

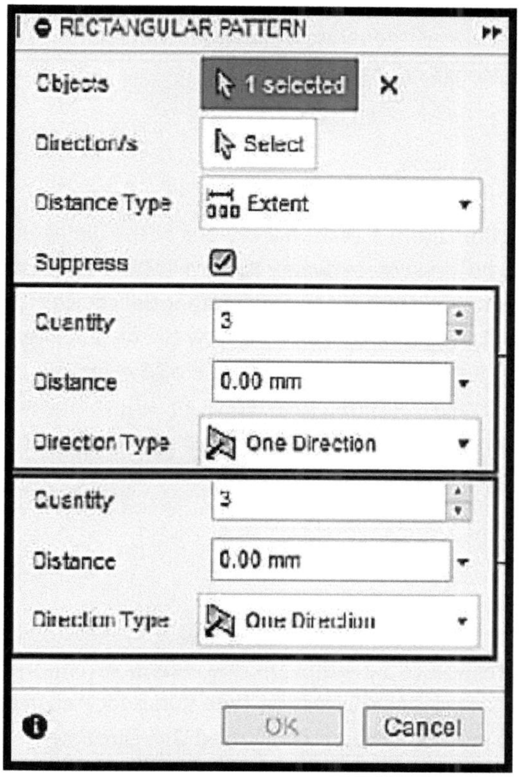

The preview of a rectangle pattern can be seen in the picture below. This design has 5 occurrences in direction 1, and 3 examples in direction 2.

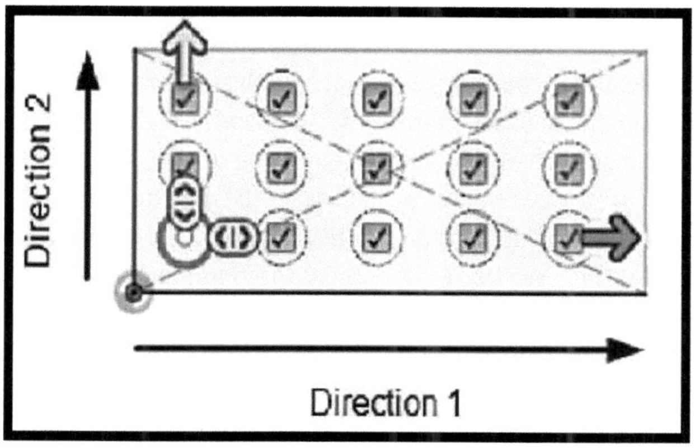

You also have the option of specifying the number of pattern instances that will be drawn in the drawing area by using the Quantity box. Alternatively, you may adjust the number of pattern instances by dragging the spinner arrows that are located next to the parent object in the preview of the pattern. These arrows appear in the vicinity of the pattern.

NOTE: The quantity of pattern instances that you provide in the field labeled "Quantity" is tallied along with the instance that serves as the parent or the original instance. For instance, if the Quantity field is set to 6, then the associated pattern direction will generate 6 instances of the pattern, including the parent instance. This occurs regardless of the pattern's orientation.

Distance

The Distance fields in the **Direction 1 and Direction 2** regions of the dialog box are used to determine the amount of space that should be present between pattern instances in the corresponding directions, Direction 1 and Direction 2. It is important to keep in mind that the choice chosen from the drop-down list labeled "**Distance Type**" in the dialog box will determine how the distance value is stated in these fields. In the Distance field that appears in the drawing area, you are also given the option to specify the distance between individual pattern instances. Alternatively, you can adjust the distance between the pattern instances by dragging the arrow that appears on the final pattern instance in the pattern preview. This arrow allows you to adjust the distance between the pattern instances. In addition, you have the option of entering a negative distance in the Distance box. This will cause the pattern orientation to be reversed.

Direction Type

You can define the pattern direction to be either on one side or symmetric about the parent entity or entities by using the drop-down lists labeled **Direction Type** that is located in the **Direction 1 and Direction 2** areas of the dialog box. To do so, select the option labeled One Direction or Symmetric, as appropriate.

Suppress

In the RECTANGULAR PATTERN dialog box, the **Suppress** check box is selected by default and cannot be deselected. As a direct consequence of this, a checkbox will show up in the middle of each pattern instance that is present in the drawing area. You may exclude some pattern instances from the final pattern by deselecting the check boxes next to those pattern instances in the pattern editor. You may do this by clicking the left mouse button on the instance of the pattern that you want to remove from the pattern. To retrieve the skipped occurrences of the pattern or to include them in the output, choose the check boxes that show next to those instances in the preview of the pattern. Click the **OK** button after you have finished specifying the parameters for patterning the entities inside the **RECTANGULAR PATTERN** dialog box. This results in the formation of a rectangular pattern. NOTE: To modify the parameters of a rectangle pattern that has already been produced, click on a pattern instance that is currently active in the drawing area. In the drawing area, the symbol for the rectangle pattern appears close to the object that is its parent. After that, double-click on the icon that looks like a rectangle pattern. The **EDIT RECTANGULAR PATTERN** dialog box is brought into view. You can make changes to the parameters of the rectangle pattern by utilizing this dialog box.

Circular Pattern Tool

Creating many instances of a sketch object or entities in a circular fashion around a central point is the purpose of the Circular Pattern tool. To do this, choose the Circular Pattern tool from the drop-down menu of the SKETCH contextual tab on the Toolbar. After this, you may begin creating your pattern. A dialog window labeled **CIRCULAR PATTERN** will now display.

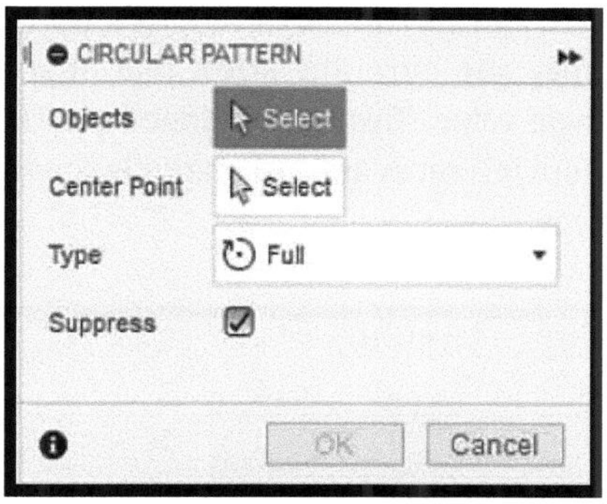

Objects

When using the Objects selection option in the dialog box, sketch entities that are to be patterned may be chosen. The Objects selection option is turned on by default when it may be used. As a consequence of this, you can choose entities one at a time by either repeatedly pressing the left mouse button or creating a window around each one individually.

Center Point

Through the use of the Center Point selection option, a point can be chosen to serve as the focal point of the circular pattern. This allows the instances to be patterned in a way that revolves around the chosen point. To achieve this, you need to activate the Center Point selection option that is located in the dialog box by clicking on it. Next, choose a point inside the drawing area to serve as the focal point of the circular design by clicking on it. In the drawing area, the preview of the circular design is shown with the default values.

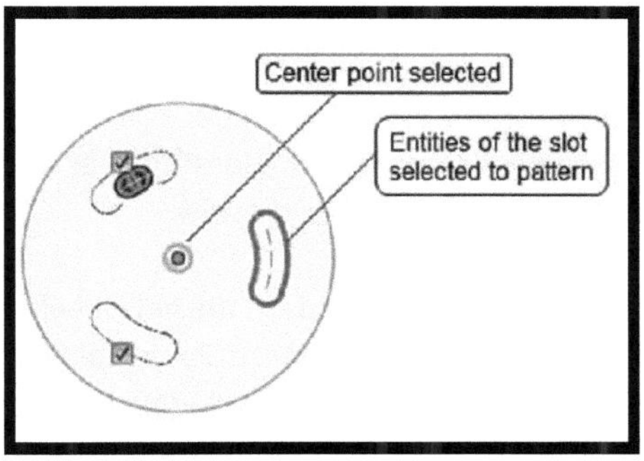

Type

Both the dialog box and the drawing area have the Full option selected by default in the Type drop-down list. This setting applies to both the dialog box and the drawing area. As a consequence of this, the circular pattern is developed in such a way that it encompasses all 360 degrees in the pattern, and the number of pattern instances that are indicated in the field labeled "**Quantity**" is equalized within the context of a total of 360 degrees. The Total Angle field will become visible in the dialog box after the Angle option has been selected from the Type drop-down list. You may define the entire angle value of the pattern in this box, and it will be used appropriately. You may also move the arrow that displays near the most recent pattern occurrence to adjust the overall angle value. This can be done by clicking and dragging the arrow. It is important to take note that the pattern instances are automatically changed so that they remain within the overall angle value that has been given.

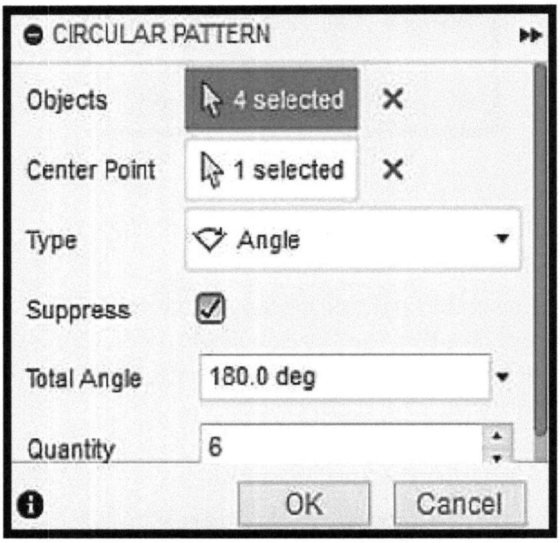

You can generate a circular pattern that is symmetric to the parent entity or entities that you pick when you select the Symmetric option from the Type drop-down list.

Quantity

The number of pattern instances that are to be produced may be specified by using the box labeled "**Quantity**." You have the option of either specifying the number of pattern instances in the dialog box's Quantity field or directly in the drawing area's drawing area. You may also adjust the total number of pattern instances by dragging the spinner arrows that are located near the parent entity or entities in the pattern preview. These arrows appear near the pattern preview.

NOTE: The quantity of pattern instances that you provide in the field labeled "Quantity" is tallied along with the instance that serves as the parent or the original instance. For instance, if the Quantity field is populated with the value 6, then the creation of 6 pattern instances, including the parent instance, will take place.

Suppress

In the CIRCULAR PATTERN dialog box, the Suppress check box is chosen automatically whenever the box is opened. As a direct consequence of this, a checkbox will materialize next to each occurrence of the pattern in the drawing area. You may exclude some pattern instances from the final pattern by deselecting the check boxes next to those pattern instances in the pattern editor. Simply selecting the checkboxes that are shown in the pattern's preview will allow you to either recall or include the occurrences of the pattern that were skipped. Click the **OK** button after you have finished specifying the parameters for patterning the entities in the **CIRCULAR PATTERN** dialog box. This results in the formation of a circular pattern. **NOTE:** To make changes to the parameters of the circular pattern that has already been drawn, choose a pattern instance in the drawing area and click on it. Within the sketching area, a symbol representing a circular pattern emerges. After that, double-click on the icon that looks like a circular pattern. A dialogue window labeled **EDIT CIRCULAR PATTERN** is shown. You can make changes to the parameters of the circular pattern by utilizing this dialog box.

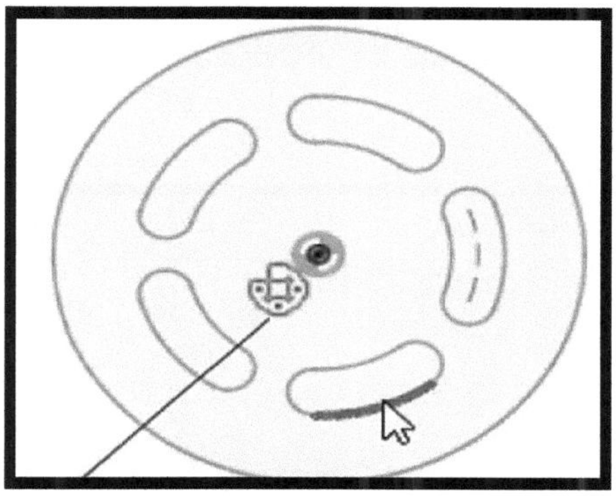

Creating a Sketch Fillet

By drawing a tangent arc with a fixed radius and deleting the corner that results at the junction of two sketch entities (lines or arcs), this is what is referred to as a "sketch fillet." **Using the Fillet tool located in the MODIFY panel of the SKETCH contextual tab will allow you to create sketch fillets.**

1. To use the Fillet tool, go to the MODIFY panel of the SKETCH contextual tab and click on the tool's name. Another option is to choose the Fillet tool from the drop-down menu that appears when the MODIFY button is clicked in the contextual SKETCH tab. It is now possible to use the Fillet tool.
2. Position the cursor on a corner or vertex of the drawing that is generated when two lines, arcs, or a line and an arc meet with one another. In the drawing area, the fillet preview will be highlighted as it is being drawn. You may also choose two lines that cross or run parallel to one another one at a time to construct a fillet between the lines.
3. Depress the left mouse button when the fillet preview window becomes highlighted. Within the drawing, the area is where you will see the Fillet radius field. Additionally, a directional arrow is shown with the fillet preview.

4. In the area labeled "**Fillet radius,**" type in the desired fillet radius. Adjusting the fillet radius may also be accomplished by dragging the arrow that shows in the pre-view. The fillet radius affects the preview of the fillet, and this effect is dependent on the fillet radius.
5. In the same manner, click on each of the other corners of the drawing one at a time to generate fillets with a certain radius.

TIP: If you want to create a fillet of a specific radius between two sketch entities, rather than picking a corner or a vertex, you may choose two sketch entities that intersect or that are parallel to one another.

6. Once the fillets have been created, right-click anywhere in the drawing area, and when the Marking Menu appears, choose the **OK** tool from the list of available options.

Scaling Sketch Entities

By using the Sketch Scale tool, you can manipulate the scale of sketch entities in any direction. To do this, choose the MODIFY option from the drop-down menu located in the SKETCH contextual tab of the Toolbar, and then select the Sketch Scale tool from the list of available options. The **SKETCH SCALE** dialog box is brought into view.

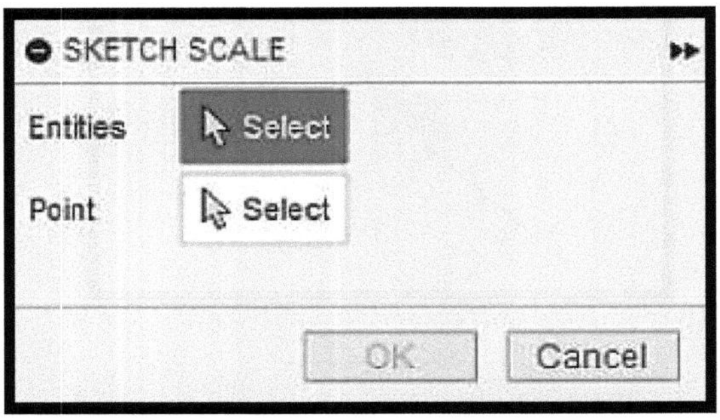

Entities

The ability to pick entities that are to be scaled is referred to as the Entities selection option. The Entities selection option is active in the dialog box when it is first opened by default. As a direct consequence of this, you can choose entities one at a time by either pressing the left mouse button or creating a window around the things that are to be chosen. Either before or after bringing up the SKETCH SCALE dialog box, you may pick entities to work with.

Point

With the Point selection option, you may choose a specific point to serve as the starting position for the scaling of the chosen entities. To do this, first, enable the Point selection option by clicking on it inside the dialog box, and then choose a point within the drawing area by clicking on it. It has been determined that this point will serve as the starting point for the scaling of the entities. Take note that there is an arrow located quite close to the starting place in the sketching area.

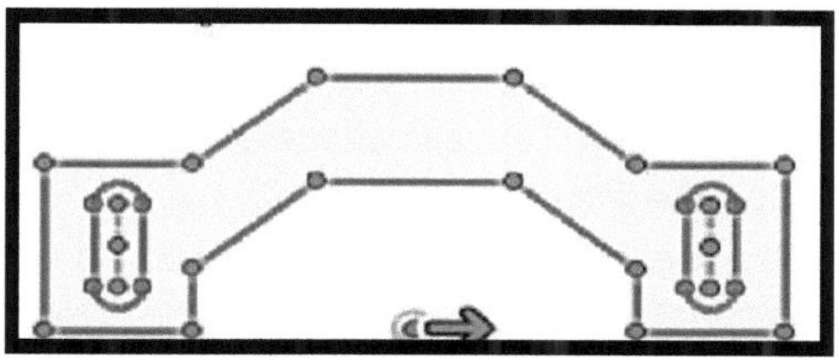

Additionally, the **Scale Factor** field may be found in both the dialog box and inside the drawing area itself. The origin of the picture is chosen to serve as the foundation point for scaling the various things that have been picked. Next, fill up the area labeled "**Scale Factor**" with the scale factor. In the drawing area, you will get a preview of the scaled sketch entities according to the scale factor that you set. Note that to reduce the size of the chosen sketch entities, you must provide a scale factor that is more than 1, and to increase the size of the entities, you must use a scale factor that is higher than 1. To change the scale factor, you may also drag the arrow that appears in the drawing area. This is located on the right side of the screen.

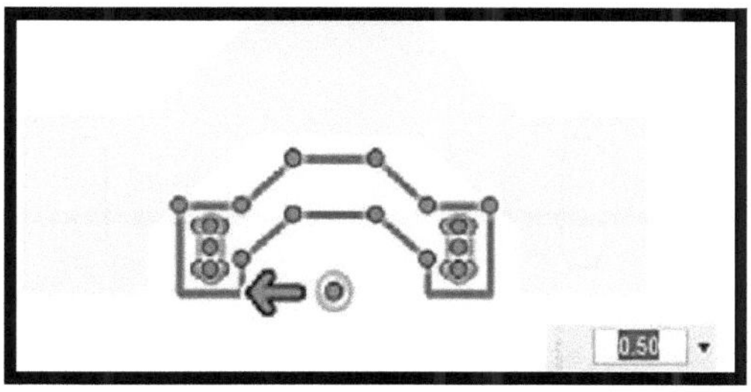

It can be seen that the scale factor for this picture is set at 0.5. As a direct consequence of this action, the preview now displays a reduced version of the chosen entities. After that, you should choose the OK button located inside the dialog box. The scales are set to the specified entities.

Creating a Sketch Chamfer

You are required to either use the Create Sketch command to generate a new sketch or right-click an existing drawing and pick the Edit Sketch option to enter the Sketch contextual environment. Only then will you be able to edit the sketch's geometry.

Equal Distance Chamfer

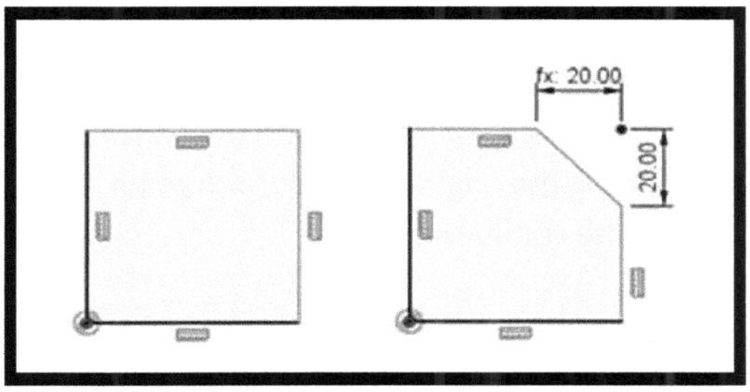

1. Select **Modify > Chamfer > Equal Distance Chamfer** from the contextual tab of the Sketch Tab.
2. Put the cursor in the middle of the first line or one of the vertices.
    a. A preview of the chamfer will appear whenever you stop over a vertex in the editor.
3. Using the mouse, pick either the line or the vertex.
4. If you have already picked a line, move the mouse to the second line and hold it there to obtain a preview of the chamfer.
5. Select the second line by clicking on it.
6. Either move the distance manipulator handle around the canvas or enter a value for the distance.
7. To bring the command to a close, hit the **Enter** key.

The distance measurements as well as the geometry of the chamfer are shown on the canvas. The first distance dimension acts as the catalyst for the development of the second distance dimension. If you modify the first dimension, the second dimension will also be modified automatically, ensuring that the two distances will continue to be proportional to one another. Note that when you pause the cursor over a valid selection, that selection will become highlighted. The first preview of the chamfer shows a distance value that is proportional to the item that is smaller among the ones that have been picked.

Distance and Angle Chamfer

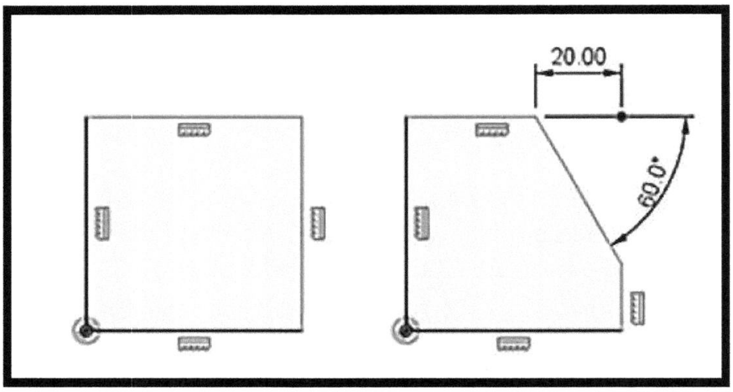

1. Select **Modify > Chamfer > Distance and Angle Chamfer** from the contextual menu of the Sketch Tab.
2. Put the cursor in the middle of the first line or one of the vertices.
    a. A preview of the chamfer will appear whenever you stop over a vertex in the editor.
3. Using the mouse, pick either the line or the vertex.
4. If you have already picked a line, move the mouse to the second line and hold it there to obtain a preview of the chamfer.
5. Select the second line by clicking on it.
6. Either move the distance manipulator handle around the canvas or enter a value for the distance.
7. To change the angle, either drag the angle manipulator handle inside the canvas or enter a value.
8. Press the **Enter** key to finish the command.

The canvas displays the geometry of the chamfer, including the distance dimension and the angle dimension.

Two Distance Chamfer

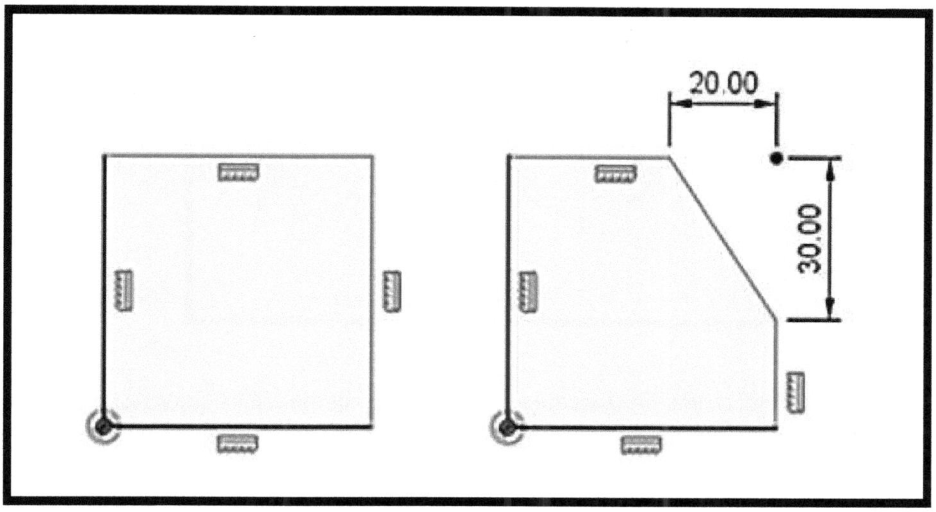

1. Select **Modify > Chamfer > Two Distance Chamfer** from the contextual menu of the Sketch Tab.
2. Put the cursor in the middle of the first line or one of the vertices. A preview of the chamfer will appear whenever you stop over a vertex in the editor.
3. Using the mouse, pick either the line or the vertex.
4. If you have already picked a line, move the mouse to the second line and hold it there to obtain a preview of the chamfer.
5. Select the second line by clicking on it.
6. Move the first distance manipulator handle inside the canvas, or enter the initial distance value, as desired. When you make a change to one of the distance manipulators handles for the first time, both of the distance values are updated.
7. Either move the second distance manipulator handle inside the canvas or enter a new value for the second distance.
8. Press the **Enter** key to finish the command.

The distance measurements as well as the geometry of the chamfer are shown on the canvas. Each distance dimension is independent. If you make a change to the first dimension, the second dimension will keep the previous state that you gave it, and vice versa.

Tips

- While any chamfer command is active, you can swap between different kinds of chamfers by using the **Feature Options** area of the **Sketch Palette** dialog.
- When you snap to the sketch grid or other geometry in the design, object snap symbols will show near the geometry as you move the mouse pointer. When you snap to a certain place in the drawing, the logical restrictions are applied to the sketch immediately thereafter.

Breaking Sketch Entities

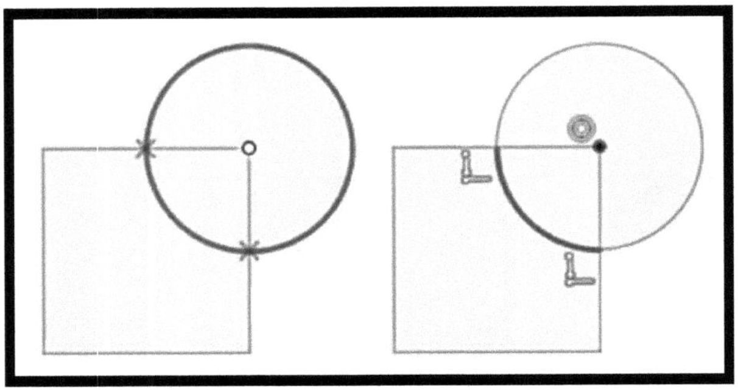

Note: To edit sketch geometry, you must create a new sketch using the Create Drawing command or right-click an existing sketch and choose Edit Sketch from the context menu to enter the Sketch contextual environment. Only then will you be able to alter sketch geometry.

1. Select **Modify > Break** from the contextual tab of Sketch.
2. While the pointer is still above the sketch geometry, a preview of the break will be shown.
3. Use your mouse to destroy the geometry.
4. Keep clicking the broken geometry until it is fixed.
5. Press the **Enter key** to finish the command.

Questions

1. Which tool is used to increase or decrease the scale of sketch entities?
2. Which checkbox in the OFFSET dialog box are you to select while offsetting sketches which will make all the contiguous entities of the selected entity get automatically selected?
3. Which tool is used for offsetting sketch entities at a specified offset distance?
4. The tool used to trim the unwanted sketch entities to their closest intersection is called?
5. Which tool are you to activate in the Sketch Palette dialog box that allows you to create construction entities in the drawing area?
6. Which tool is used for breaking a sketch entity into two or more two?
7. Which tool extends sketch entities up to their nearest intersection?

CHAPTER 4

APPLYING CONSTRAINTS AND DIMENSIONS

Working with Constraints

When creating a drawing, the degrees of freedom may be constrained via the usage of constraints. You can add restrictions to a sketch entity, as well as between sketch entities, as well as between sketch entities and planes, axes, edges, or vertices. When creating sketch entities, some restrictions, such as horizontal, vertical, and coincident, are imposed on their own automatically. When you are drawing a line entity, for instance, if you move the cursor horizontally toward the left or right, a sign of horizontal constraint appears near the cursor.

This indicates that the line entity cannot be drawn in that direction. This shows that for the horizontal constraint to be applied to the line object, you must define the endpoint of the line. When you move the pointer vertically upward or downward, a sign of vertical restriction appears near the cursor. This occurs regardless of the direction you move the mouse. This indicates that a vertical limitation will be applied to the line if you give the terminus of the line.

Horizontal Constraint

The horizontal constraint function allows an object's orientation to be changed to horizontal and then maintains that orientation by forcing the entity to stay horizontal. You may use this limitation on a line, a construction line, or even between two points or vertices.

Vertical Constraint

The vertical constraint tool is used to reorient an entity to a vertical position and then compel it to continue to maintain that orientation. You may use this limitation on a line, a construction line, or even between two points or vertices.

Coincident Constraint

The coincident constraint is used to coincide two points or vertices and then compel them to continue to coincide with one another. This restriction may be applied between any two points, as well as between a point and a line, arc, circle, or ellipse. In addition to that, you have the option of using a coincident constraint between a sketch point and the origin of the drawing.

Collinear Constraint

Collinear constraint is a method for bringing two lines into a collinear relationship with one another and then maintaining that relationship by requiring the lines to stay collinear. You also have the option of collinearly attaching a line object to a linear edge.

Perpendicular Constraint

The purpose of the perpendicular constraint is to first turn two-line entities perpendicular to each other and then to ensure that they continue to be perpendicular to one another. In addition to this, you may draw a line that is perpendicular to a linear edge.

Parallel Constraint

The parallel constraint aligns two-line entities such that they are parallel to one another and then ensures that they continue to be aligned in this manner. You also have the option of creating a line object that is parallel to a linear edge.

Tangent Constraint

A circle and a line are two examples of sketch entities that may be made to be tangent to one another with the use of a tangent constraint. You could also construct two circles, two arcs, or two ellipses that are tangent to each other, or you could build a mix of these three shapes. In addition, you have the option of making a sketch object (such as a line, circle, arc, or ellipse) tangent to an edge that is either linear or circular.

Concentric Constraint

It is possible to make two arcs, two circles, two ellipses, or any combination of these things concentric on each other by using a constraint known as a concentric constraint. In the case of the concentric constraint, the entities that have been chosen all have the same center point.

Equal Constraint

The equal constraint is used to ensure that two things (arcs, circles, or lines) are proportionally equivalent to one another. When the equal constraint is applied, the length of line entities and the radii of arc entities are both brought to the same level.

Midpoint Constraint

A point may be made to correspond with the midpoint of a line object by using a constraint known as the midpoint constraint. A midway restriction may be applied between a sketch point and a line or a sketch point and a linear edge. This can be done in Sketch.

Symmetry Constraint

With the use of the symmetry constraint, it is possible to make two points, two lines, two arcs, two circles, or two ellipses symmetric around an object that is a line.

Curvature Constraint

The curvature constraint is used to preserve a continuous and smooth curvature at the point when two sketch entities are transitioning into one another (two splines or a spline and a line).

Fix Constraint

Fixing a sketch entity's present location as well as its size may be accomplished with the help of the fix constraint. The endpoints of a fixed line or arc entity, on the other hand, are free to travel in any direction without the location of the entity being affected in any way.

Applying Constraints

You can apply restrictions in Fusion 360 by making use of the tools for applying constraints that are located in the CONSTRAINTS panel of the SKETCH contextual tab located in the Toolbar.

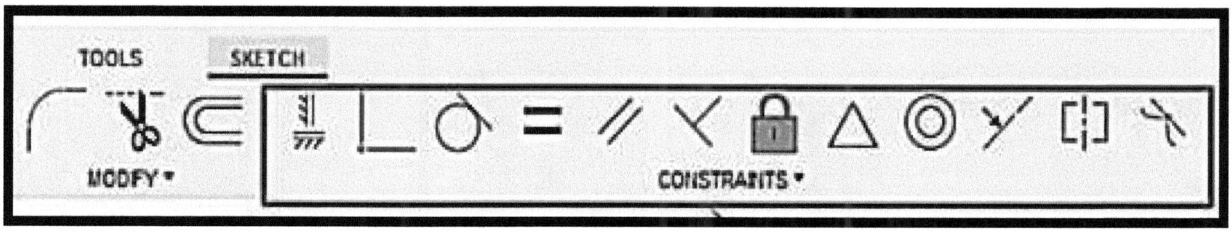

To apply a constraint, first, pick the entities in the drawing area, and then click on the tool that corresponds to the constraint in the CONSTRAINTS panel of the SKETCH contextual tab. Clicking on the concentric tool in the CONSTRAINTS panel, for instance, is all that is required to impose a concentric constraint between an arc and a circle. The next step is to click on the circle, followed by the arc, in the drawing area one at a time. After applying the concentric constraint, the entities that were chosen changed their relationship with one another such that they became concentric and shared the same center point. Additionally, the icon representing the concentric limitation can be seen near the entities in the drawing area.

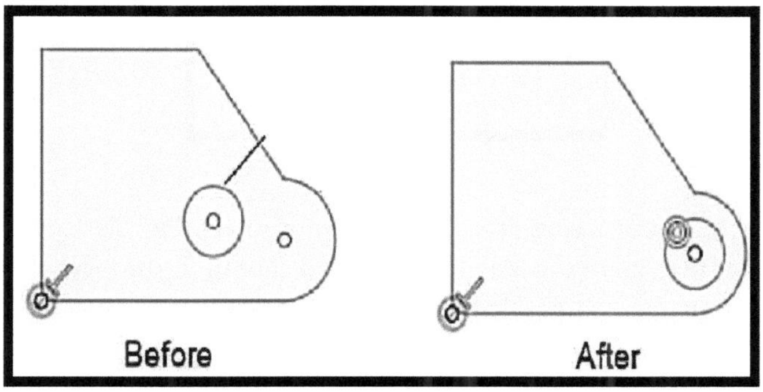

NOTE: You can choose entities to apply a constraint either before or after calling the needed constraint tool in the **CONSTRAINTS** panel. This allows you to apply constraints in any order. **Hint**: The second entity that was picked will often shift to fulfill the constraint condition that was imposed. On the other hand, owing to the previous constraints that have been imposed, there are situations when the first-picked entity shifts to fulfill the constraint requirement.

Click on the **Horizontal/Vertical tool** that is located in the CONSTRAINTS panel of the SKETCH contextual tab. This will allow you to add a horizontal or vertical constraint to an inclined line. After that, in the drawing area, choose the slanted line by clicking on it. If the inclined line is closer to the horizontal or vertical orientation than the chosen line, then the selected line will be constrained horizontally or vertically, depending on which orientation is closest to the inclined line. A limitation on the horizontal plane has been placed on the inclined line seen in this picture. This is because the chosen line is the one that is most aligned with the horizontal orientation. Using the Restrictions panel in the same manner, you can apply additional constraints to the sketch entities as necessary. You may also impose a constraint between the entities that you have chosen by using the **Marking Menu.** To do this, first, pick the sketch entities that should have a constraint put between them, and then right-click anywhere inside the drawing area. The Marking Menu pops up with a list of all of the different restrictions that may be used to define the relationships between the entities that have been chosen.

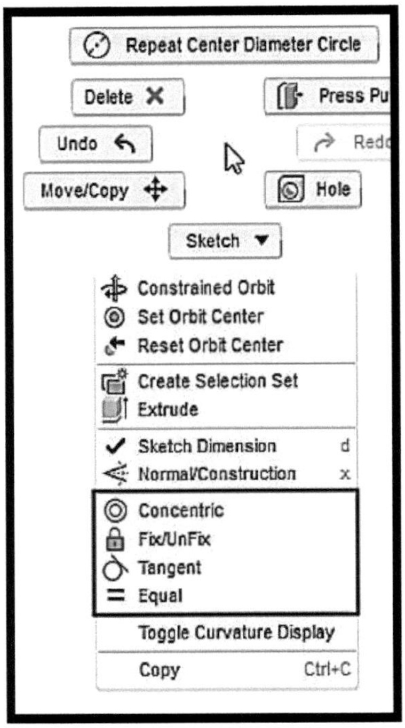

After picking two circles in the drawing area, this picture displays the Marking Menu that was made available to the user. After that, go to the Marking Menu and choose the necessary restriction. The chosen limitation will be imposed on the relationship between the entities.

NOTE: Even after a constraint has been applied, the constraint tool will still be available to use. To disable the constraint tool, you will need to use the **ESC** key on your keyboard. You may also use the **SELECT** tool by clicking on its icon in the toolbar. You also have the option to cancel the tool by right-clicking in the drawing area, which will bring up a **Marking Menu**, and then selecting the **CANCEL** tool from that menu.

Controlling the Display of Constraints

You have control over whether or not the drawing area displays the limitations that have been imposed on the drawing. Selecting or clearing the Show Constraints check box in the Options rollout of the **SKETCH PALETTE** dialog box is how you switch the display of the applicable constraints on or off, respectively. This is done via the SKETCH PALETTE dialog box.

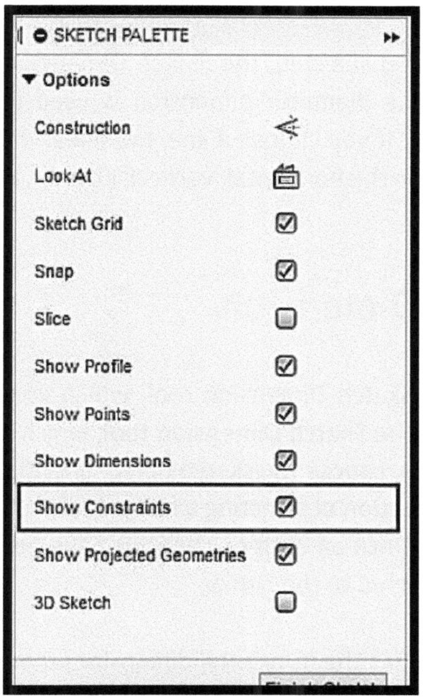

Hint: You may remove a restriction after it has already been applied by selecting the constraint in the drawing area and then clicking the DELETE key.

Applying Dimensions

After you have produced a drawing and applied the necessary geometric restrictions, the next step is to apply the necessary dimensions to the sketch. Since Fusion 360 is a parametric piece of software, the parameters of sketch entities like length and angle are driven or controlled by the dimension values. When you change the value of a dimension, the entity that corresponds to that dimension in the sketch is likewise updated to reflect the change. Using the Sketch Dimension tool included in Fusion 360, you can assign dimensions to objects.

You may use any one of the following approaches to activate the Sketch Dimension tool in your toolbox:

1. In the **CREATE** panel of the **SKETCH** contextual tab, choose the Sketch Dimension tool by clicking on its name.
2. Press the **D** key.

3. After activating the **CREATE** drop-down menu of the **SKETCH** contextual tab, choose the **Sketch Dimension** tool from the available options.
4. Use your right mouse button to click on the drawing area. The Marking Menu will now display.
5. After that, either choose the **Sketch** tool by clicking on it in the **Marking Menu** or by hovering the mouse over it there.
6. The second level of the Marking Menu is where you'll find the tools that are most often used for drawing.
7. After that, go to the **Marking** menu and choose the **Sketch Dimension** tool from there.

Depending on the kind of entity that is selected, the Sketch Dimension tool is used to add dimensions to the selected entity. For instance, the diameter dimension is used if you pick a circle, and the linear dimension is used if you select a line. If you choose a line, the linear dimension is used. By using this tool, you will be able to apply dimensions in the horizontal, vertical, aligned, angular, diameter, radius, and linear diameter categories.

Applying a Horizontal Dimension

Pressing the **D** key will enable the Sketch Dimension tool, which you can then use to add a horizontal dimension. Another option is to use the **Sketch Dimension tool**, which can be found in the **Create** panel of the **SKETCH** contextual tab. After that, choose the sketch object or entities that are necessary. To apply the horizontal dimension, you have the option of selecting a horizontal sketch entity, an inclined sketch entity, two points, or two vertical entities. Once an entity or entities have been selected, the current dimension value for those entities will be connected to the cursor.

Next, to choose the placement point for the horizontal dimension, move the pointer vertically up or down and then click on the left mouse button inside the drawing area. The current dimension value is shown inside a dimension box that appears in the drawing area. In this box, enter the needed value for the dimension, and then hit the Enter key on your keyboard. It is necessary to apply the horizontal dimension. After you have selected an inclined item or two sketch points, you should be aware that the vertical or aligned dimension will get connected to the cursor if you move it in a direction other than vertically up or down.

Applying a Vertical Dimension

Using the Sketch Dimension tool, you can, in a manner analogous to applying a horizontal dimension, apply a vertical dimension to a vertical sketch entity, an inclined sketch entity, between two points, or between two horizontal sketch entities. In addition, you can apply a vertical dimension between two points. It is important to keep in mind that after choosing an entity or entities, you must then shift the mouse horizontally toward the right or left to apply a vertical dimension.

Applying an Aligned Dimension

You can apply an aligned dimension to an aligned sketch entity or between two points by using the Drawing Dimension tool, much as you can apply horizontal and vertical dimensions to a sketch by using the tool.

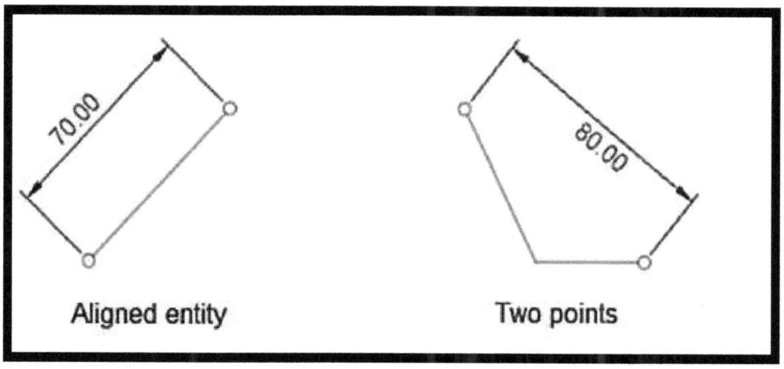

In most cases, the aligned dimension is utilized to determine how long an inclined line is when measured along its aligned direction. It is important to keep in mind that after picking an entity or entities to apply an aligned dimension, you will need to shift the mouse in a direction that is perpendicular to the chosen entity to define the placement point. Alternatively, after choosing an entity or entities, you may right-click anywhere in the drawing area, and when the **Marking Menu** appears, you can pick the **Aligned option** from the list of available options to apply aligned dimensions.

Applying an Angular Dimension

Using the **Sketch Dimension tool**, you can apply an angular dimension between two-line entities that are not parallel to one another or between three points. To do this, first, enable the Smart Dimension tool, and then choose two-line entities in the drawing area that are not parallel to one another. The angular dimension that exists between the things that have been chosen is affixed to the cursor.

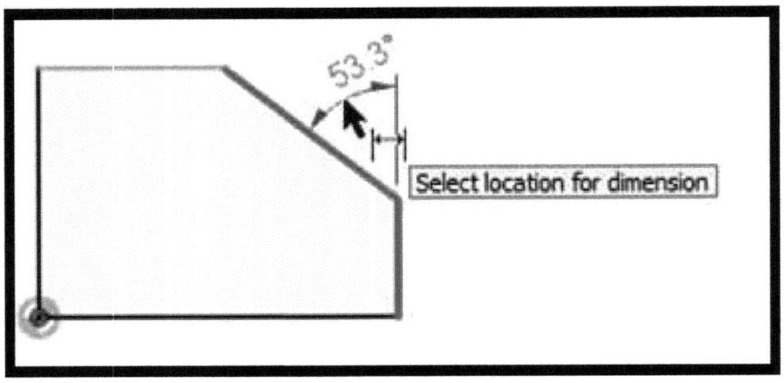

The next step is to drag the mouse to the spot where you want the dimension to be placed, and then click to set the placement point for the dimension. The drawing area now has a dimension box superimposed over it. In this box, enter the appropriate angle value, and then hit the Enter key on your keyboard. Between the entities that have been chosen, an angular dimension will be applied. Note that the placement points in the drawing area determines whether or not an angular dimension is applied between the chosen entities. This is determined by the position of the placement point.

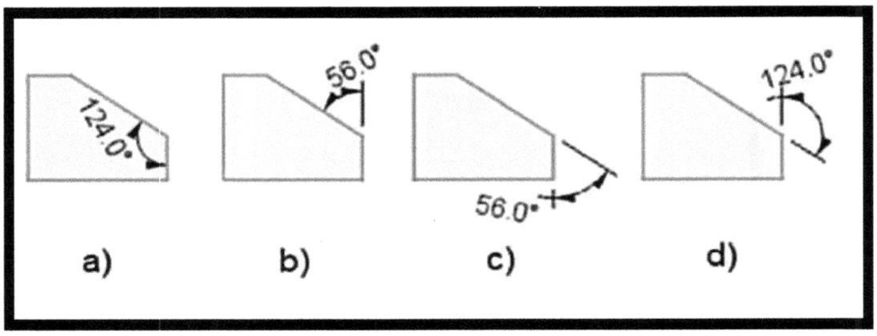

To apply an angle dimension between three points in the drawing area, first, enable the Sketch Dimension tool, and then pick each of the three points individually. This will allow you to apply the angular dimension.

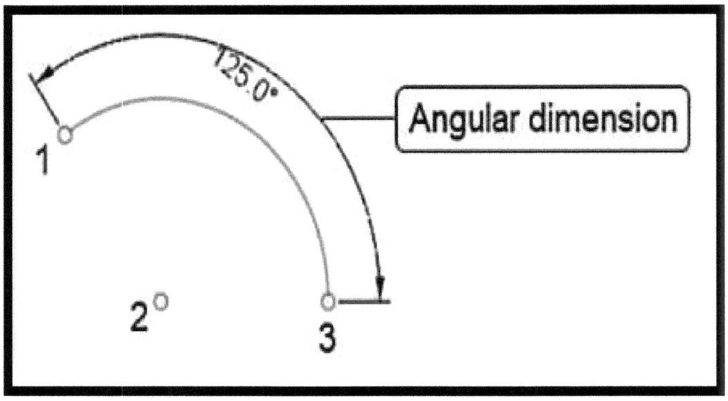

The angular dimension that exists between the points that have been chosen is affixed to the cursor. The next step is to indicate the placement point for the associated angular dimension by moving the mouse to the position where you want to put it and then clicking. A box indicating the dimensions is displayed. In this box, enter the appropriate angle value, and then hit the Enter key on your keyboard. The three spots that were chosen get an angular dimension that is applied between them.

Applying a Diameter Dimension

Using the Sketch Dimension tool, you can give a circle a dimension that represents its diameter. To do this, first, activate the **Sketch Dimension** tool, and then choose a circle from the drop-down menu. The diameter measurement is associated with the cursor. After that, position the cursor where it needs to be, and when it's in the right spot, click it to set a placement point in the drawing area. A box indicating the dimensions is displayed. After you have entered the diameter value in this box, hit the **ENTER** button. A diameter dimension is applied.

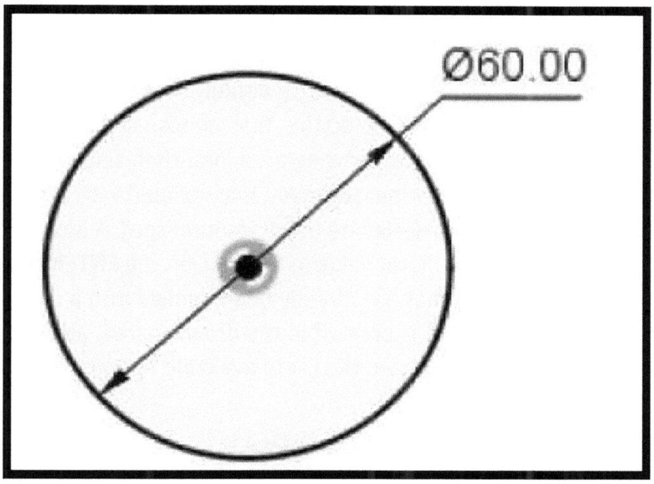

Hint: The diameter measurement will be applied to a circle by default. A circle, on the other hand, may also have a radius dimension applied to it. After choosing a circle to which you want to apply a dimension, right-click anywhere in the drawing area, and when the **Marking Menu** appears, pick the **Radius** option from the list of available options. A connection is made between the cursor and the radius dimension.

Next, you'll need to click anywhere inside the drawing area to designate the placement spot. A box indicating the dimensions is displayed. After you have entered the radius value in this box, hit the **ENTER** button. Additionally, you have the option to transform the currently used diameter dimension into the radius measurement. To do this, right-click on the diameter dimension that is shown in the drawing area, and when the **Marking Menu** opens, choose the **Toggle Radius** option from the list of available options.

Applying a Radius Dimension

Using the **Sketch Dimension tool**, you may give an arc a radius dimension and apply it to the arc. To do this, first, enable the **Sketch Dimension tool**, and then click on the arc that you want to measure. The radius is connected as a dimension to the cursor. To designate a placement, point inside the drawing area, first move the cursor to the spot where it has to be and then click. A box indicating the dimensions is displayed. After you have entered the radius value in this box, hit the **ENTER** button. The radius measurement is being used here.

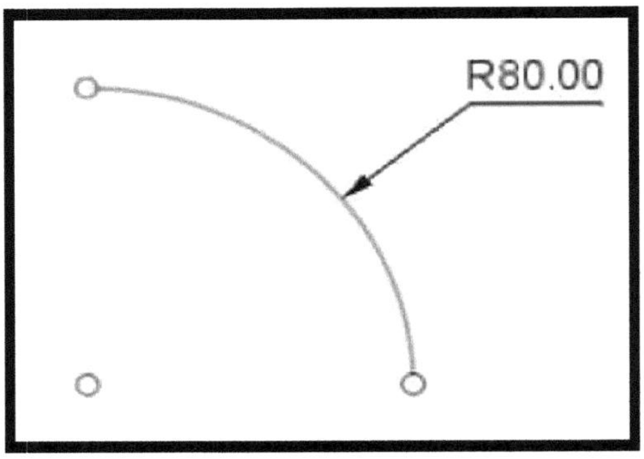

Tip: The radius measurement will be applied to an arc by default. The diameter, on the other hand, is a dimension that may be applied to an arc as well. To do this, first, choose the arc to which the measurement will be applied, then right-click anywhere in the drawing area, and then select the **Diameter** option from the Marking Menu that displays. The diameter measurement is associated with the cursor. Next, you'll need to click anywhere inside the drawing area to designate the placement spot. A box indicating the dimensions is displayed. After you have entered the diameter value in this box, hit the **ENTER** button. You also have the option to transform the radius dimension that has already been applied into a diameter dimension. To do this, right-click on the radius dimension that is present in the drawing area, and when the Marking Menu appears, choose the **Toggle Diameter** option from the list of available options.

Applying a Linear Diameter Dimension

A drawing of a revolving feature may have a linear diameter dimension added to it. To apply a linear diameter dimension, first, enable the Drawing Dimension tool, and then, as the rotating axis of the sketch, pick a linear item (either a line or a centerline).

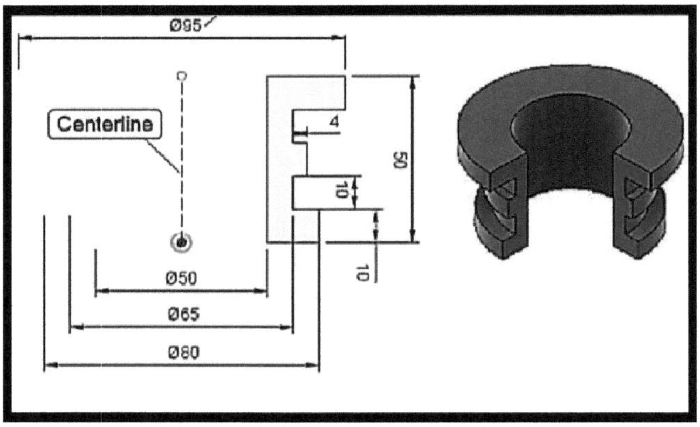

In this particular illustration, the centerline or construction line has been chosen to serve as the rotating axis of the drawing. Next, choose one entity from the linear drawing that makes up the sketch. The linear dimension that exists between the things that are now chosen will be tied to the cursor. Click the right mouse button within the drawing area next. The Marking Menu will now display. To access the **Diameter Dimension** option, use this Marking Menu's drop-down menu. The linear diameter measurement is affixed to the cursor in this step. After moving the mouse to the other side of the object that has been chosen as the axis of rotation, clicking will allow the placement point to be specified. A box indicating the dimensions is displayed. In this box, enter the linear diameter value, and then hit the Enter key on your keyboard. The linear diameter measurement is the one that is used.

Editing and Modifying the Dimensions

It is also possible to adjust dimensions outside of the Sketch Environment. Locate the drawing in the browser tree that you wish to change, right-click it, and pick the **Show Dimension option** from the context menu. The drawing will now display all of the measurements that were included in it. Double-clicking on the dimension you wish to edit after you have already selected it will adjust it.

Working with Different States of a Sketch

Under Defined Sketch

A drawing is considered to be inadequately defined when its degrees of freedom are not completely locked down. This indicates that the entities of the drawing have the capability of altering not just their form but also their size and location when they are moved. The drawing that can be seen below is of a rectangle, and the length of the rectangle is specified as 50 millimeters (mm). Nevertheless, neither the width nor the location of the rectangle about the starting point is specified. This indicates that the width of the rectangle as well as its location may be altered by dragging the entities of the rectangle that correspond to those changes. It is important to take note that the entities of a sketch that is under-specified appear in the drawing area colored blue.

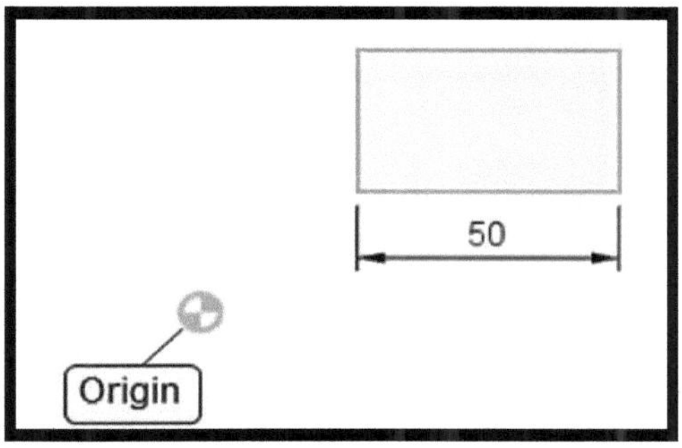

Fully Defined Sketch

A drawing is considered to be completely defined when all of its degrees of freedom have been eliminated. This ensures that the entities of the drawing do not change in any way when they are moved, including their form, size, or location. A rectangular drawing with its length, breadth, and location all determined can be seen in the picture below. Take note that the entities of a drawing that has been completely specified appear in black. Additionally, a little lock symbol is shown on the drawing when it is viewed in the BROWSER under the enlarged Sketches folder.

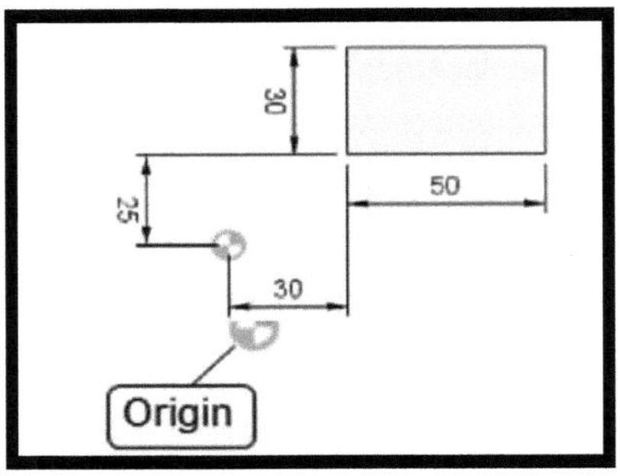

The drawing that was just shown is an example of a completely defined sketch since all of its entities have been dimensioned and the necessary constraints have been applied to the sketch. In this drawing, the horizontal constraints are applied to the horizontal things, while the vertical constraints are applied to the vertical items. During the drawing process, horizontal and vertical restrictions are imposed in an automated manner on the entities. **NOTE**: If you apply a dimension to a sketch that has already been fully defined, the Fusion 360 message window will inform you that adding this dimension will over constrain the sketch and suggest that you apply it as the driven dimension instead. This happens automatically when you apply a dimension. To use the dimension as the driving dimension, choose the button labeled OK from the drop-down menu. The newly applied dimension transforms into a driven dimension but continues to perform its role merely as a reference dimension. As a direct consequence of this, the drawing does not end up being too limited.

Working with SKETCH PALETTE

When a sketch is active, a dialog window labeled SKETCH PALETTE is shown at all times. It offers convenient access to the sketch choices and display settings that are most often utilized.

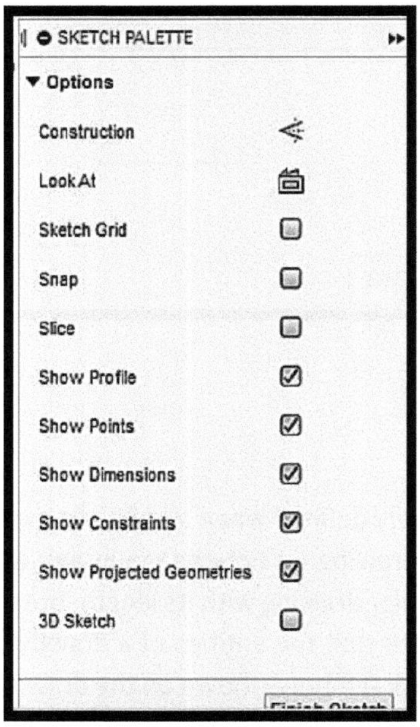

Look At

With the Look At tool, you may alter the orientation of the drawing plane so that it is normal to the direction in which you are seeing it. The orientation of the drawing plane is automatically normalized to the direction that is being seen, which is the default setting. However, if its orientation was altered while you were creating a sketch, you can click on the **Look At** tool in the **Options** rollout of the **SKETCH PALETTE** dialog box to change the orientation of the sketching plane so that it is normal to the viewing direction. This will allow you to view the sketch as it was intended to be viewed.

Slice

Using the drawing plane as the cutting plane, you may slice through an item with the help of the Slice checkbox. If you are creating a sketch on a sketching plane that is passing through an object, then you can select the Slice checkbox to slice the object in such a way that the sketch appears in front of the object. This option is available if you are creating the sketch on a sketching plane that is passing through an object.

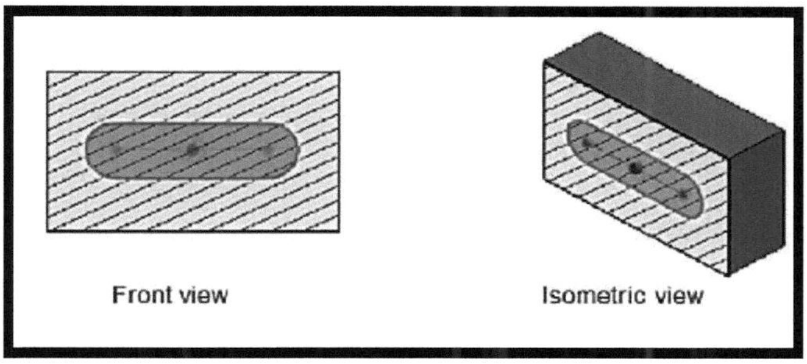

Show Profile

The shaded closed profiles in a drawing can be seen by selecting the **Show Profile check box** and clicking the **Show Profile** button. Within the Options rollout of the SKETCH PALETTE dialog box, this check box is chosen automatically every time it is used. As a direct consequence of this, the shaded display can be seen on all of the closed profiles of the drawing. This makes it much simpler to determine whether or not all of the profiles of the drawing have been completely closed.

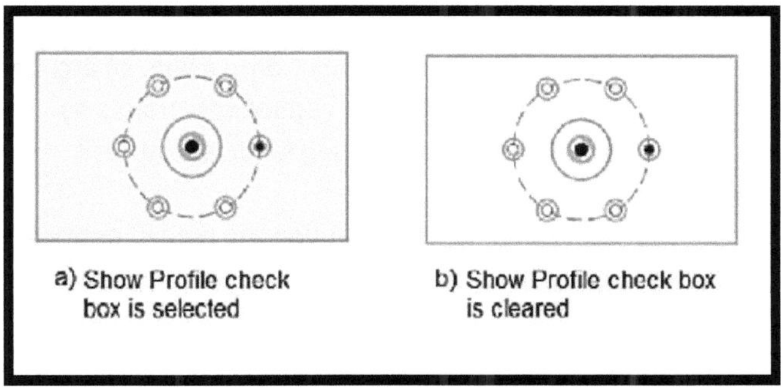

Show Points

To show points on the open ends of the drawing, choose the Show Points check box and click the Show Points button. This facilitates the identification of the sketch's open connections in an easier manner.

Show Dimensions.

The Show Dimensions check box is used to toggle the visibility of the applied dimensions of the sketch in the drawing area. This may be done either by turning them on or turning them off. In the SKETCH PALETTE dialog box, this check box is selected automatically whenever it is used. As a direct consequence of this, all of the dimensions that have been applied can be seen in the drawing area. By removing this checkmark from the box, you will be able to temporarily disable the display of the measurements.

Show Constraints

It is possible to toggle the display of constraint symbols in the drawing area using the Show Constraints check box, which allows for both on and off states.

Show Projected Geometries

The display of projected geometries in the drawing area may be toggled on and off by selecting the Show Projected Geometries check box and selecting either "**On**" or "**Off**."

3D Sketch

After checking the box labeled "**3D Drawing**," you will be able to generate a 3D sketch via the use of various sketching tools, such as Line and Spline.

Questions

1. Which tool is used for changing the orientation of the sketching plane normal to the viewing direction?
2. Which checkbox of the SKETCH PALETTE dialog box is used for cutting the object by using the sketching plane of the sketch?
3. Which constraint is used for coinciding a sketch point onto a line, an arc, or an elliptical entity?
4. How do you control the display or visibility of the applied constraints by
5. Which dimension is applied to a sketch representing revolve features?
6. How do you apply constraints?
7. The tool used for applying dimension, depending upon the type of entity selected is called?

PART 2

CREATING AND EDITING 3D MODELS/COMPONENTS

CHAPTER 5

CREATING BASE FEATURE OF SOLID MODELS

Creating an Extrude Feature

When you add or remove material in a direction that is normal to the drawing plane, you are creating an extrude feature. It is important to note that the geometry of the extrude feature is defined by the drawing. Adding more material is the primary method by which the first or basic extrude features are formed. The next picture demonstrates a variety of basic extrude characteristics that are developed from the corresponding designs. Using the Extrude tool found in the **CREATE** panel of the SOLID tab of the Toolbar in Fusion 360, you can generate an extrude feature in the software.

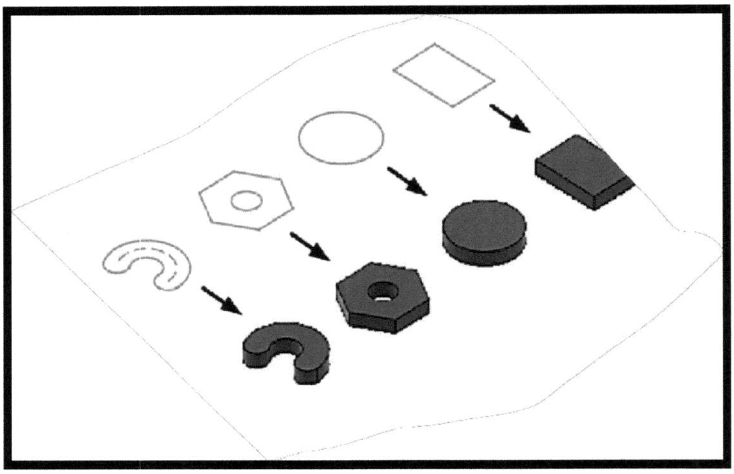

After you have created the drawing by utilizing the tools for sketching, choose the Extrude tool from the **CREATE** panel or the CREATE drop-down menu of the SOLID tab, depending on where you are working in the program. The EXTRUDE dialog box is brought into view. In addition to this, the perspective of the drawing has been altered to be isometric. Alternatively, you may bring up the EXTRUDE dialog box by using the **E** key on your keyboard.

NOTE: After producing the drawing, you may also conclude the production of the sketch by first invoking the **FINISH SKETCH** tool located in the **SKETCH** contextual tab of the Toolbar. After that, you can invoke the Extrude tool to extrude the sketch. When extruding the drawing, the choices in the **EXTRUDE** dialog box are what you use to provide the parameters for the operation.

The following is a discussion of some of the choices available in this dialog box:

Profile

Within the EXTRUDE dialog box, the Profile selection option is one of the options that is turned on by default. As a consequence of this, you will have the option to pick a closed sketch profile whenever you want to add or delete content. When a base feature is being created, the only way to extrude the profile is to first add the material. You may also pick numerous closed profiles to create an extrude feature.

TIP: To deselect a profile that has already been chosen or one that was selected inadvertently, either click once more on the profile that has been selected or press and hold either the **CTRL or SHIFT** key while clicking on the profile that is to be deselected from the selection set.

Start

The start condition for extruding the sketch profile may be specified by selecting one of the alternatives from the drop-down list located in the Start section of the dialog box.

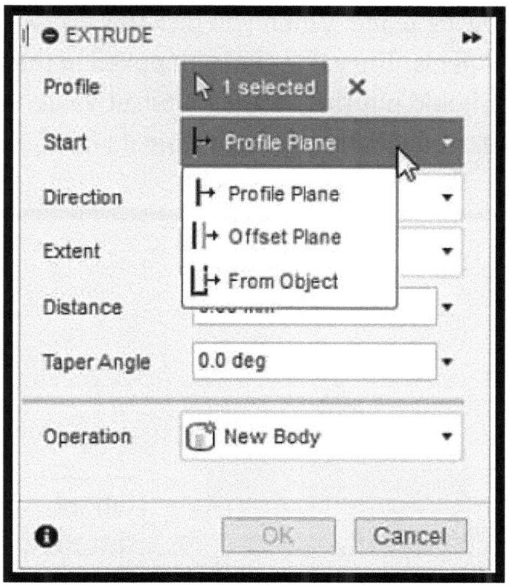

Profile Plane

Within the EXTRUDE dialog box, the Start drop-down list has a selection that is, by default, set to the Profile Plane option. As a consequence of this, the extrusion process begins precisely from the drawing plane of the original sketch. When the Profile Plane option is chosen, the preview of an extrude feature as seen from the front is shown in the picture below.

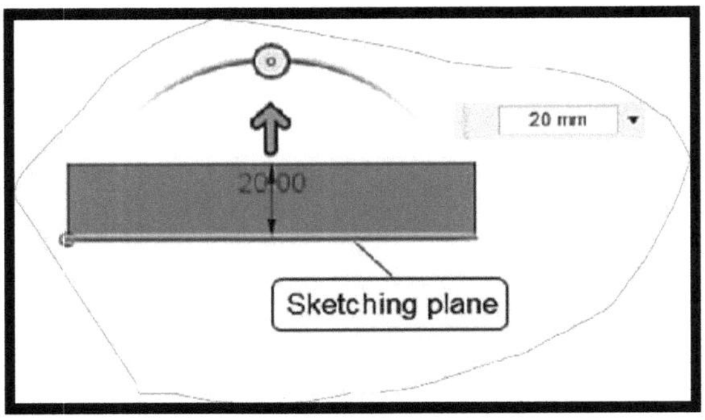

Offset Plane

When selecting the **Offset Plane** option, you will be able to create an extrude feature that is situated at a distance that is offset from the drawing plane. When you pick this option, the EXTRUDE dialog box adds a field labeled Offset to the available fields. The value that is supplied in the Offset field is set to 0 by default (zero). This is the field where you should put the necessary offset value. Following the specification of an offset distance, the preview of an extrude feature as seen from its front can be seen in the picture below.

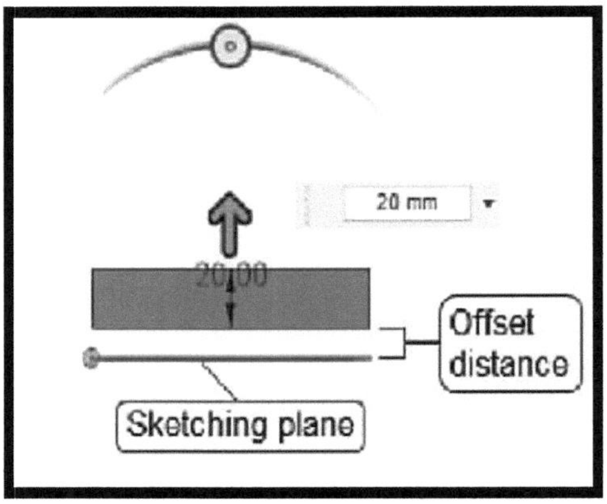

Direction

The direction in which the extrusion will occur may be specified by selecting an option from the EXTRUDE dialog box's drop-down list titled "**Direction.**" Following that, we will go through these available choices.

One Side

The direction of extrusion on each side of the drawing plane may be defined by selecting the **One Side** option from the Direction drop-down list. This can be done for either side of the plane. It is important to keep in mind that the Distance field of the dialog box requires you to provide a number that is in the negative to reverse the direction of the extrusion.

Two Sides

To extrude the sketch profile on both sides of the sketching plane, choose the Two Sides option from the Direction drop-down list. This will cause the profile to be extruded. When you pick this option, a dialog box will display with the rollouts for Side 1 and Side 2 respectively. Both rollouts contain the same options; the only difference is that the options in the Side 1 rollout are used to define the extrusion parameters for one side of the sketching plane, while the options in the Side 2 rollout are used to define the extrusion parameters for the other side of the sketching plane. The options that are available in both rollouts are the same.

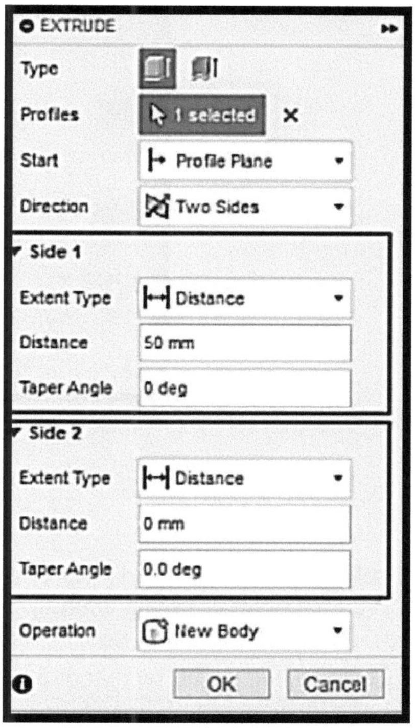

Symmetric

It is possible to extrude the sketch profile symmetrically on both sides of the drawing plane by selecting the Symmetric option from the Direction drop-down list. When this option is selected, the Half Length and Whole Length buttons show in the dialog box below the Direction drop-down list. The button labeled "**Half Length**" is enabled in its default state. As a consequence of this, the value of the distance that is entered in the field labeled Distance of the dialog box is calculated as the extrusion's length divided by two. For instance, if the value of the provided distance is 10 millimeters, the resulting feature will be produced by adding 10 millimeters of material to each side (side 1 and side 2) of the drawing plane. After clicking the Whole Length button, the value of the distance that was entered into the field labeled Distance will be used to calculate the whole length of the extrusion. For instance, if the value of the provided distance is 10 millimeters, the resulting feature will be formed by adding material that is 5 millimeters on each side (side 1 and side 2) of the drawing plane.

Extent

When extruding a sketch profile, the choices included in the drop-down list labeled "Extent" of the dialog box are what are utilized to set the extent or end condition of the extrusion. The subsequent topic of discussion will be the choices available in the Extent drop-down list.

Distance

The distance of the extrusion may be specified in the dialog box by entering a value in the area labeled "**Distance.**" You have the option of entering the distance of the extrusion in either this field or the box labeled Distance that is located in the graphics area. You may also change the distance of the extrusion dynamically by dragging the arrow that displays beside the preview of the extrude feature in the graphics section. This is how you do this. To switch the direction of extrusion from one side of the sketch profile to the other side of the profile, you will need to input a negative distance number into the dialog box's Distance field. This will do this. It is important to take note that the Distance field becomes accessible in the dialog box when the Distance option is chosen from the drop-down list located in the dialog box's Extent section.

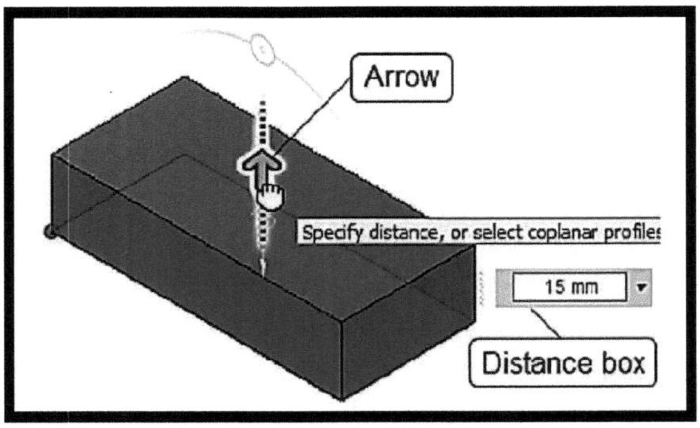

Taper Angle

When using the extrude functionality, you may add tapering by entering a value in the Taper Angle area of the dialog box. By default, 0 (zero) is placed in this field. As a direct consequence of this, there is no tapering present in the extruded feature that is produced. This is the field in which you should put the desired taper angle. To change the taper angle dynamically, you may also drag the manipulator handle that appears in the graphics area alongside the preview of the extrude feature. This allows you to modify the taper angle. Take note that to switch the direction of the taper from the outward to the inward side of the sketch or vice versa, you will need to enter a negative value for the taper angle into the Taper Angle field of the dialog box. This will allow you to switch the direction of the taper in the opposite direction. The sort of operation that will be utilized to create the extrude feature may be selected from the available choices in the drop-down list located in the dialog box labeled "**Operation**."

If you are constructing the initial or foundational feature of a model, then the New Body option that is found in the operation drop-down list will be picked automatically for you. As a consequence of this, the material that is added results in the creation of the consequent base extrude feature, which functions as a new body. After you have created the first feature of the model as a body, you may build the other features of the model by selecting Join, cut, or intersect from the operation drop-down list. This will allow you to generate the remaining features of the model. You may use the Join option to extrude the drawing by adding more material and then merging or combining the newly created feature with the features that are already present in the model. When you choose the **Cut** option, you will be able to extrude the drawing by cutting away material from the model, producing a cut feature. When constructing a feature, the Intersect option is used so that the only material that is kept between the current feature and the feature that is being formed is that which is shared by both features. When putting together a new component for an assembly, choose the New Component option from the drop-down menu. Click on the **OK** button located in the EXTRUDE dialog box after you have finished providing all of the parameters needed to extrude a sketch profile. The extrude functionality is developed further.

Creating a Revolve Feature

A feature that is built in such a way that more material may be added or deleted by rotating the drawing around an axis of revolution is referred to as a revolve feature. Take note that the drawing that is going to be revolved should be placed on either the left or the right side of the axis that the revolution revolves around. The axis of rotation may be a line, a construction line, or a linear edge, depending on your preference. Utilizing the "**Revolve**" tool inside Fusion 360 will allow you to create a feature that revolves. Take note that the fundamental characteristics of the rotation are produced by the addition of material. The picture below shows drawings together with the base revolve characteristics that were produced as a consequence of rotating the sketch along the separate axes of revolution.

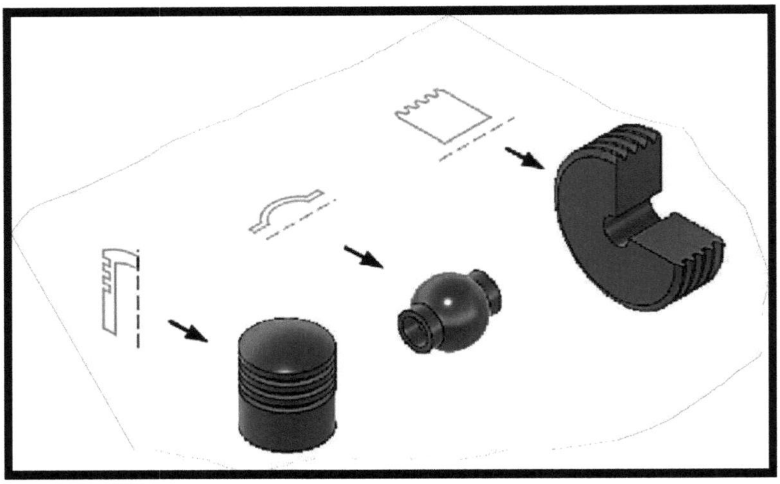

After you have sketched a revolve feature along with the axis of rotation, you should then choose the **SOLID** tab and then click on the **Revolve** tool that is located in the CREATE panel. You may also choose the Revolve tool by going to the SOLID tab, opening the CREATE drop-down menu, and then clicking on the tool. A dialogue window labeled REVOLVE will now appear. In addition to this, the perspective of the drawing has been altered to be isometric.

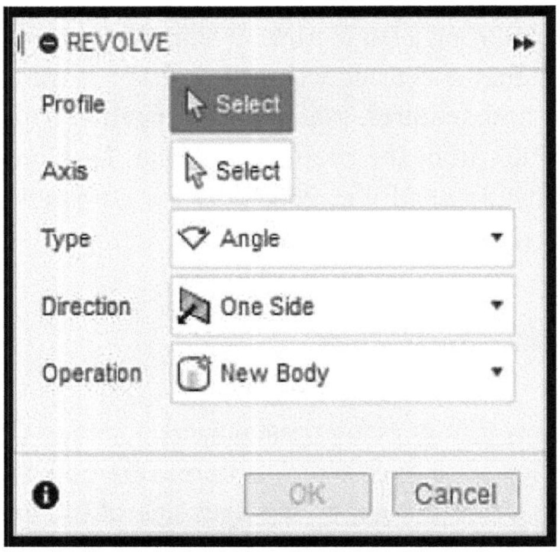

NOTE: After you have created the sketch, you may also conclude the production of the sketch by clicking on the **FINISH** Drawing tool located in the SKETCH contextual tab of the Toolbar. After doing so, you can then activate the Revolve tool to revolve the sketch. The choices included inside the REVOLVE dialog box are what are utilized to determine the parameters of the drawing when it is revolved. The following will go through a few of the choices that may be made inside this dialog box.

Profile: Within the REVOLVE dialog box, the Profile selection option is one of the options that is turned on by default. As a direct consequence of this, you will have the ability to choose a closed sketch profile to circle the axis of rotation. Only by adding more material will you be able to rotate the profile while you are developing a basic feature. In addition, you may build a revolve feature by selecting many closed profiles at the same time.

TIP: To deselect a profile that has already been chosen or one that was selected inadvertently, either click once more on the profile that has been selected or press and hold either the CTRL or SHIFT key while clicking on the profile that is to be deselected from the selection set.

Axis

You may choose an axis of rotation by using the Axis selection option in the drop-down menu. To do this, first, enable the Axis selection option inside the dialog box by clicking on it, and then choose an axis of rotation to work with. As the axis of rotation, you have the option of selecting either a line, a construction line or an edge. The preview of the revolve function will display in the graphics section after a closed profile and an axis of rotation have been selected.

Angle

The end condition of the revolution may be specified by selecting the Angle option from the Type drop-down list and entering a value into the Angle field of the dialog box. This will allow the end condition to be set.

Full

When you choose the Full option, a drawing will be rotated along its axis of rotation through a full 360 degrees.

Angle

The angle of rotation may be specified in the dialog box by typing the value into the area labeled "**Angle**." Either in this section of the dialog box or in the Angle box that displays in the graphics area, you may enter the angle of rotation that you want to use. You may also change the angle of rotation dynamically by dragging the manipulator handle that displays the preview of the revolve feature in the graphics area. This handle is shown with the preview of the revolve function. To change the direction of rotation from one side of the profile to the other side of the profile, you need to enter a number that is a negative angle in the area labeled "Angle" in the dialog box. Take note that the Angle field will not be accessible in the dialog box when the Full option is chosen from the drop-down list located in the dialog box's Type field.

Direction

The direction of the revolution may be defined by selecting one of the choices included inside the REVOLVE dialog box's drop-down list under "**Direction**."

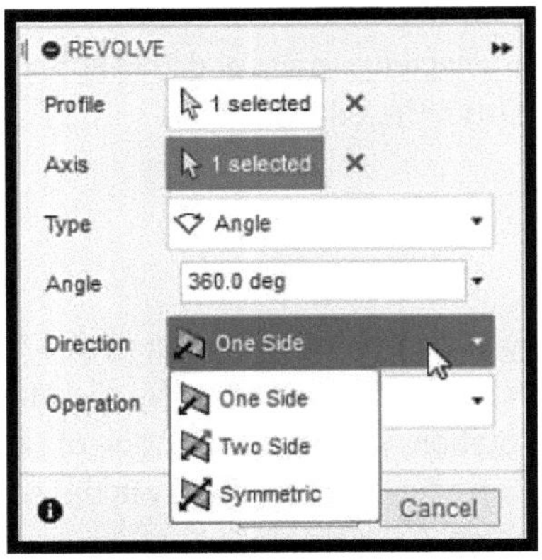

One Side

Defining the direction of rotation on either side of the drawing plane may be accomplished by selecting the One Side option from the menu. Take note that to change the direction that the revolution is going in, you need to enter a number with a negative angle in the area labeled "**Angle**" on the dialog box.

The Two Faces

When you choose the Two Sides option, the sketch profile will rotate so that it is visible on both sides of the drawing plane. When you pick this menu option, the dialog box will display two new fields labeled Angle 1 and Angle 2, respectively. You can define multiple angle values for rotating the drawing on both sides of the sketching plane using the fields that are located here.

Symmetric

By selecting the Symmetric option, the drawing profile may be rotated such that it is the same on both the top and bottom of the sketching plane. For instance, if you select the angle value in the Angle field to be 120 degrees, then the resulting feature will be constructed by rotating the profile by 120 degrees on each side of the drawing plane. This action will be performed when you click the Create button.

Operation

When establishing a revolve feature, the choices included in the drop-down list located in the dialog box titled "**Operation**" are used to describe the sort of operation that should be performed. If you are constructing the initial or foundational feature of a model, then the New Body option that is found in the operation drop-down list will be picked automatically for you. The resulting revolve feature, which is generated by adding material and functions as a new body, is the end product of this process. Using the Join, Cut, or Intersect option of the operation drop-down list, you may build the remaining features of a model (body) after first generating the base feature as a body. This can be done by selecting the option from the operation drop-down list. When putting together a new component for an assembly, choose the New Component option from the drop-down menu. Click the **OK** button in the **REVOLVE** dialog box after you have finished providing all of the settings for the process of rotating a sketch profile. The revolve function is added to the game.

Navigating a 3D Model in Graphics Area

You can move about inside a model in Fusion 360 by using the mouse buttons and the other navigation tools. You may access the navigation tools by clicking on the Navigation Bar located in the center portion of the graphics area. From there, you can also access the Display Settings. You may also browse a model by using something called **View Cube**. This is an alternative method. Having said that, you need to be familiar with the navigation settings before you begin traversing a model. You may control the shortcuts for panning, zooming, and circling a model in Fusion 360 in a manner that is comparable to that of the Fusion, Alias, Inventor, Tinker cad, or SolidWorks CAD software.

Controlling the Navigation Settings

The Preferences dialog box in Fusion 360 gives you the ability to adjust the navigation settings for the program. Simply click on your name located in the top right corner of the Fusion 360 interface to bring up the **Preferences** dialog box. The User Account drop-down option will now be shown. Select the Preferences tool from the menu that drops down from here. The dialog box for configuring preferences is shown.

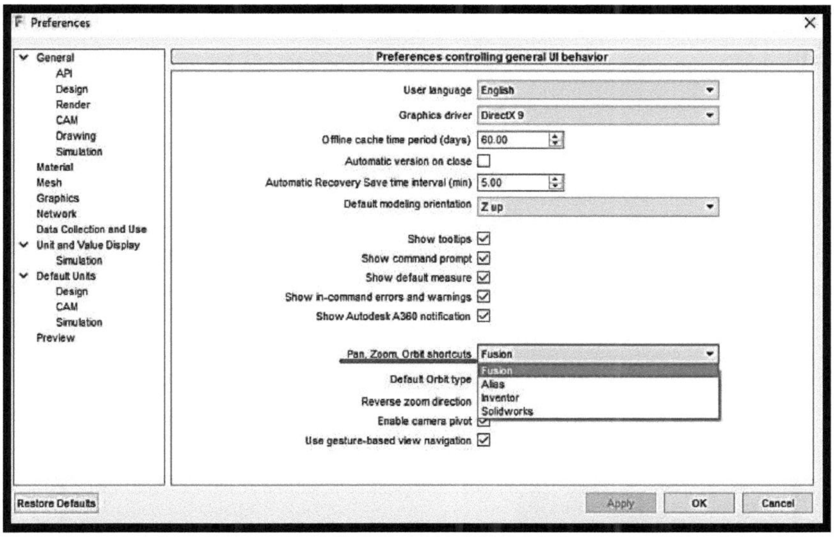

Make sure that the "**General**" option is chosen in the "**Preferences**" dialog box by checking the "**left panel**" of the "**Preferences**" box. The right panel of the dialog box contains the choices that may be used to alter the settings for the navigation. Next, choose the Fusion, Alias, Inventor, or Solid works option from the **Pan,**

zoom, or **Orbit** shortcuts drop-down list that is located inside the dialog box. It is important to keep in mind that the way you traverse the model will change based on whatever choice you choose from the Pan, Zoom, and Orbit shortcuts drop-down list.

For more information on this, please refer to the table that can be found below:

Setup	Pan	Orbit	Zoom
Fusion	MMB	MMB + Shift	Scroll wheel
Alias	Shift+Alt+MMB	Shift+Alt+LMB	Shift+Alt+RMB
Inventor	F2 + LMB	F4 + LMB	F3 + LMB
Solidworks	MMB + CTRL	MMB + Alt	MMB + Shift

Using the Default Orbit type drop-down list that is located inside the dialog box, you have the additional option of setting the default orbit type for the model to either be Constrained Orbit or Free Orbit. When you have finished configuring the navigation settings following the requirements, return to the Preferences dialog box and click the **Apply** button, followed by the OK button. Alternatively, you have the option of modifying the command settings on your computer. It may be possible to specify custom commands for Fusion 360, but this will depend on the operating system you use. (You may discover official solutions from Apple or Windows as well as independent plugins for establishing custom commands that are compatible with your system by searching the internet for anything along the lines of "**set custom commands + [your operating system**].")

Pan

Using the Pan tool in the graphics area enables you to pan or move a model around in the area. To do this, choose the Pan tool from the Navigation Bar and then adjust the Display Settings. The Pan tool is made active at this point. The next step is to push and maintain pressure on the left mouse button while dragging the pointer.

You also have the option of panning the model by moving the pointer while pressing and holding the middle mouse button. This will allow you to do so.

Zoom

By using the Zoom tool, you will have the ability to dynamically zoom into or out of the graphics area. By way of further explanation, using the Zoom tool enables users to dynamically adjust the size of the view of a model. To do this, choose the Zoom tool from the Navigation Bar and then adjust the Display Settings. The Zoom tool has been made available. The next step is to press and maintain your grip on the left mouse button while dragging the pointer upwards or downwards inside the graphics area. When you drag the cursor upward, the view gets smaller; however, when you drag the cursor downward, the view gets bigger. You also have the option to change the direction the zoom is going in. To do this, bring up the Preferences dialog box, and then choose the check box for the "**Reverse zoom direction**" option. It is important to keep in mind that the size of the model does not change regardless of whether you zoom in or out. However, the viewing distance may be adjusted to either enhance or diminish the view of the model depending on the desired effect.

Zoom Window

The Zoom Window tool allows the user to zoom in on a specific section or region of a model by allowing the user to define a window. To do this, open the Zoom flyout in the Navigation Bar and Display Settings by clicking on the arrow that is located next to the tool that is now being used to zoom in. After that, choose the Zoom Window tool by clicking on its icon, and then proceed to create a window by dragging the mouse over the region of the model that needs to be magnified. The space that is contained inside the window expands.

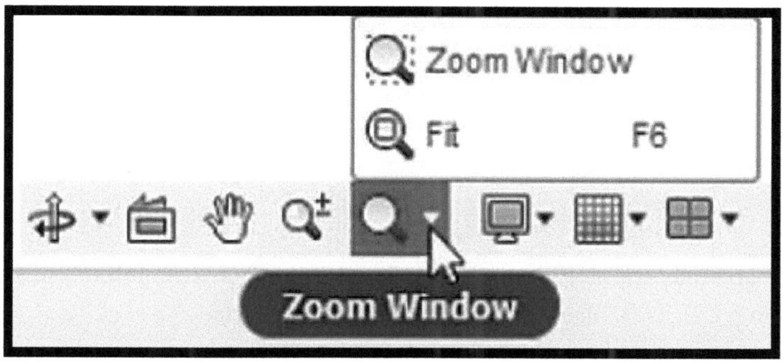

Fit

Utilizing the Fit tool will allow you to entirely accommodate a model inside the graphics area. To do this, first, open the Zoom flyout in the Navigation Bar and Display Settings by clicking on the arrow that is located next to the tool that is now being used to zoom in, and then choose the Fit tool from the available options. The graphics area can accommodate the model without any additional space being required. You may also hit the **F6** key to entirely fit the model into the graphics area that you have selected.

Free Orbit

Utilizing the Free Orbit tool allows for the model to be rotated in any direction inside the graphics area. To achieve this, first, open the Orbit flyout by clicking on the arrow that is located next to the current orbit tool in the Navigation Bar and Display Settings, and then choose the Free Orbit tool from the drop-down menu that appears. In the graphics section, there is a mark in the shape of a cross in the middle of a circular rim that has lines emanating from each of its four quadrants. After depressing and maintaining pressure on the left mouse button in the graphics area, you may freely rotate a model by dragging the pointer around in the region. Alternatively, you may move the pointer by pressing and holding the **SHIFT** key while also pressing and holding the middle mouse button. Move the cursor over the horizontal line that is located in either the right or left quadrant of the circular rim to rotate a model about the vertical axis. The icon representing the cursor transforms into a curved arrow that moves horizontally. The next step is to rotate the model around the vertical axis by dragging the pointer while pressing and holding the left mouse button. You may also rotate the model around the horizontal axis by dragging the cursor after setting it over a vertical line at the top or bottom quadrant of the circular rim. This can be done in the same way as the vertical rotation.

Constrained Orbit

By limiting the user's perspective of the model to the XY plane of the Z axis, the Constrained Orbit tool allows the user to rotate the model in a certain direction. To do this, open the Orbit flyout from the Navigation Bar's Display Settings, and then choose the Constrained Orbit tool from the drop-down menu that appears. The next step is to push and maintain pressure on the left mouse button while dragging the pointer. You may also rotate the model along either the vertical or horizontal axis by utilizing the horizontal or vertical lines of the circular rim that appear in the graphics area, depending on which direction you want to rotate the object.

Look At

With the Look At tool, you may show the chosen face of a 3D object in a way that is normal to the direction in which you are looking at it. To achieve this, go to the Navigation Bar and click on the Look At tool. Then, under the Display Settings menu, click on a face to choose it. The chosen face will now seem typical when seen from this direction. If you are in the Sketching environment, you can use this tool to make the current sketching plane normal to the viewing direction. If you are not in the Sketching environment, this tool is not available to you.

Navigating a 3D Model by Using the View Cube

When the 3D graphics system is turned on, a navigation tool known as View Cube appears. This tool gives you the ability to toggle between the regular perspective and an isometric view of the environment.

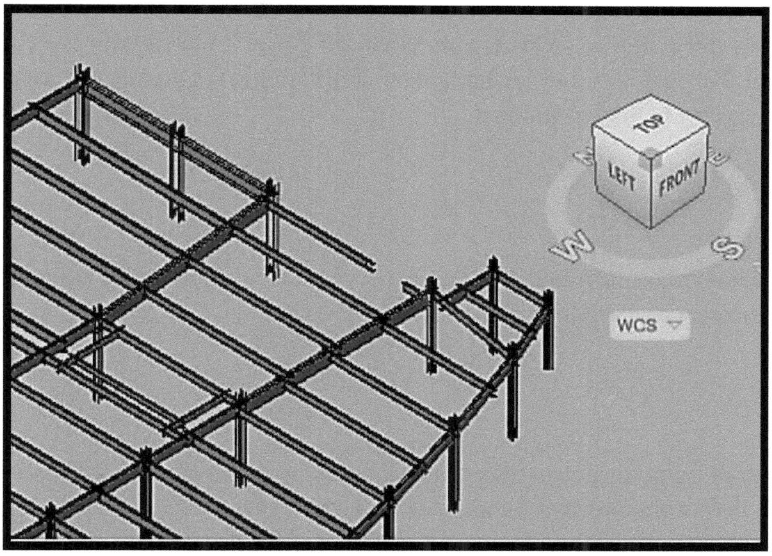

After the View Cube has been brought into view, it will remain in a dormant condition above the model and appear in one of the four corners of the drawing window. The View Cube turns into an active component as soon as the pointer is positioned over it. You have the option of rolling the current view, switching to the Home view of the model, or switching to one of the preset views that are currently available.

In addition, View Cube is presented while using the Object Viewers. In Object Viewers, View Cube will always be visible and active.

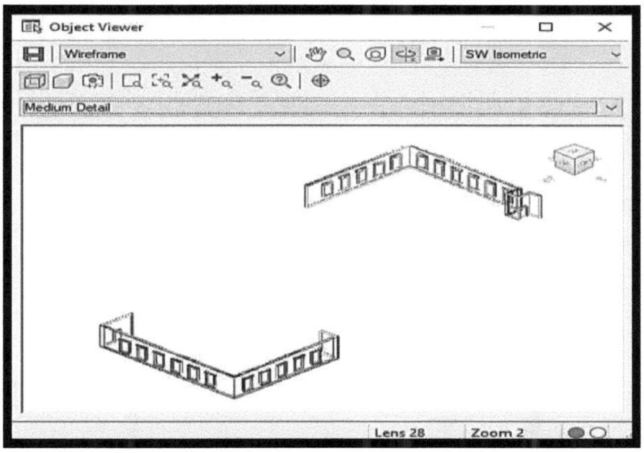

Note:

- By default, the View Cube will be shown on the screen. The 2D Wireframe and 3D Hidden visual styles are two notable exceptions to this rule; in each of those cases, the View Cube is not visible.
- When View Cube is displayed in the drawing area, you have access to a compass and you can define a UCS. This is because View Cube is a 3D model. In an Object Viewer, there is neither a UCS option nor a compass accessible for use.

You can toggle between the conventional view and an isometric perspective by using View Cube. The inactive state is how things are set up by default. When the cursor is moved over the View Cube, it turns into an active tool that may be used for navigation and becomes accessible. By using the View Cube components, it is possible to browse a model.

Home

When you click the Home icon on View Cube, the current view of the model will be changed to the isometric view, which is the home view by default.

Corner

It is possible to get an isometric perspective of the scene by using a corner of the View Cube, as well as freely rotating the view in any direction. Simply click on a corner of the View Cube to switch to an isometric perspective. If you press and hold the left mouse button while dragging a corner of the View Cube, you will be able to freely rotate the view in any direction you want.

Edge

You may rotate the view in any direction you choose by using one edge of the View Cube to do so, or you can obtain a view that is edge-on by using that edge. Simply clicking on one edge of the View Cube will give you an edge-on perspective. To freely rotate the view in any direction, press and hold the left mouse button while dragging an edge. This will cause the view to rotate.

Face

To get an orthogonal view, such as the top, front, or right, you will need to utilize the face of the View Cube. Clicking on the top face of the View Cube, for instance, will provide you with a view of the model from the top. You also can show extra choices, which you may use to manage the view of a model or the settings for View Cube. To do this, click on the arrow that is located at the bottom of View Cube. This will offer choices that allow you to change the settings of View Cube. Alternatively, you may see these settings by right-clicking anywhere on View Cube.

Go Home

By selecting the Go Home option, the currently selected view of the model will be changed to the home view, which is the default view. Orthographic The Orthographic choice is chosen whenever it is shown to the user. As a direct consequence of this, the model is shown in the orthographic view inside the graphics area.

Perspective

You may show a model in a perspective view by selecting the Perspective option from the View menu.

Perspective with Ortho Faces

Putting a model into perspective view while maintaining its orthographic face structure requires the use of the Perspective with Ortho Faces option.

Set current view as Home

You can make the view you are now looking at in a model the **"Home view"** in Fusion 360, with either a fixed distance or fit to view. To do this, place the pointer over the option that says "**Set current view as Home.**" The choices for **Fixed Distance** and **Fit to View** appear in a menu that cascade down the screen. With the Fixed Distance option, you may change the current view of the model to the Home view while maintaining the same view distance that is currently specified for the model. With the **Fit to View** option, you may make the view you are now looking at of the model become the Home view by adjusting the distance to make it fit. This indicates that the perspective of the model will automatically adapt such that it will fit inside the graphics area.

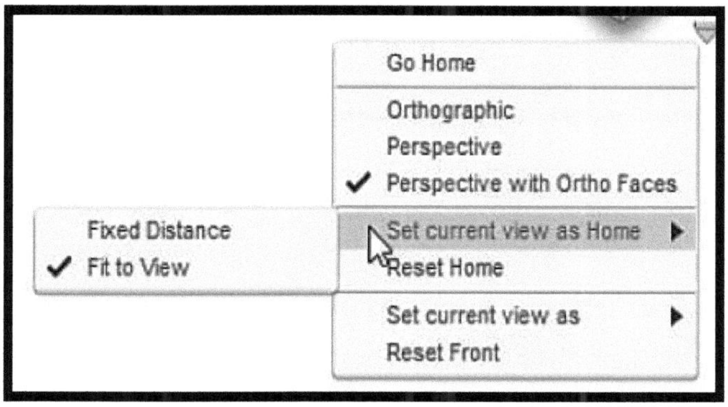

Reset Home

By selecting the "**Reset Home**" option, you can return the model's Home view to the settings that were present when the model was initially loaded.

Set current view as

You have the option of viewing the model from the front or the top at any given time. To accomplish this, place the mouse over the option that says "**Set current view as**," and then click it. There is a drop-down menu that displays selections for the Front and Top. To choose the necessary item, select it from this menu.

Reset Front

By selecting the "**Reset Front**" option, one may return the model's front view to the parameters that were present when the model was first loaded.

Changing the Visual Style of a Model

You can modify the visual or display style of a model to wireframe, wireframe with hidden edges, wireframe with visible edges, shaded, shaded with visible edges, shaded with hidden edges, or shaded with visible edges. You can get to the tools that let you adjust the visual style of the model by going to the **Navigation Bar** and clicking on **Display Settings > Visual Style**. This will bring up the Display Settings menu.

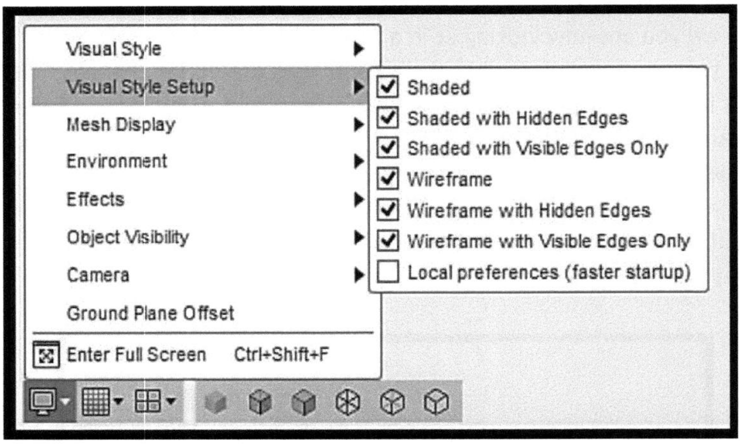

Shaded

The shaded visual style may be applied to a model via the use of the Shaded tool. In this presentation, the model is shown in shaded mode, and the edges are not shown as they would normally be.

Shaded with Hidden Edges

The visual style known as "**shaded with hidden edges**" may be applied to a model via the use of the Shaded with Hidden Edges tool. In this presentation, the model is shown in shaded mode, and the display of both visible and hidden edges is enabled.

Shaded with Visible Edges Only

The model may be shown in a visual style known as "**shaded with visible edges**" by using the tool known as Shaded with Visible Edges Only. In this presentation, the model is shown in its darkened state, with the visibility of its edges being the only aspect that is activated. This instrument has its default settings set to active. As a direct consequence of this, the model will always be shown in the graphics section using the visual style known as "**shaded with visible borders.**"

Wireframe

The model may be shown in a visual style known as "**wireframe**" with the help of the Wireframe tool. In this presentation, the edges of the model, both those that are visible and those that are concealed, are shown as solid lines.

Wireframe with Hidden Edges

The 'wireframe with hidden edges' visual style may be displayed on the model via the use of the tool titled "**Wireframe with Hidden Edges.**" In this presentation style, the edges of the model that are not visible to the user are shown as dashed lines, while the edges of the model that are visible to the user are shown as solid lines.

Wireframe with Visible Edges Only

The Wireframe, Complete with Exposed Edges When showing the model in the "wireframe with visible edges" visual style, the only tool that is utilized is a tool. Only the visible edges of the model are shown in this manner as continuous lines, while the display of the model's hidden edges has been turned off.

Questions

1. The tool used for fitting a model completely inside the graphics area is called?
2. Which field of the EXTRUDE dialog box is used to add tapering in the extrude feature?
3. Which option is used for extruding or revolving a feature symmetrically about the sketching plane?
4. Which tool is used for creating a feature by adding or removing material normal to the sketching plane?
5. The tool used for creating a feature by revolving the sketch around a centerline as the axis of revolution is known as?
6. In which visual style is the model displayed in shaded mode with the display of visible edges turned on?
7. Which tool is used for zooming a particular portion of a model by defining a window?

CHAPTER 6

CREATING CONSTRUCTION GEOMETRICS

Creating a Construction Plane

There are three different building planes accessible to use by default in Fusion 360. These planes are **Front, Top,** and **Right**. You can utilize these building planes to generate the fundamental aspect of a model by extruding or rotating the design. On the other hand, to make a model of the actual world that has various elements, you could need extra construction planes. To put it another way, it's possible that the three building planes that come as default won't be enough to create all of the elements of a real-world model. If you need to develop extra construction planes for your real-world models, Fusion 360 gives you the ability to do so. Utilizing the many tools included in the **CONSTRUCT** drop-down menu of the Toolbar will allow you to generate a wide variety of construction planes of your design.

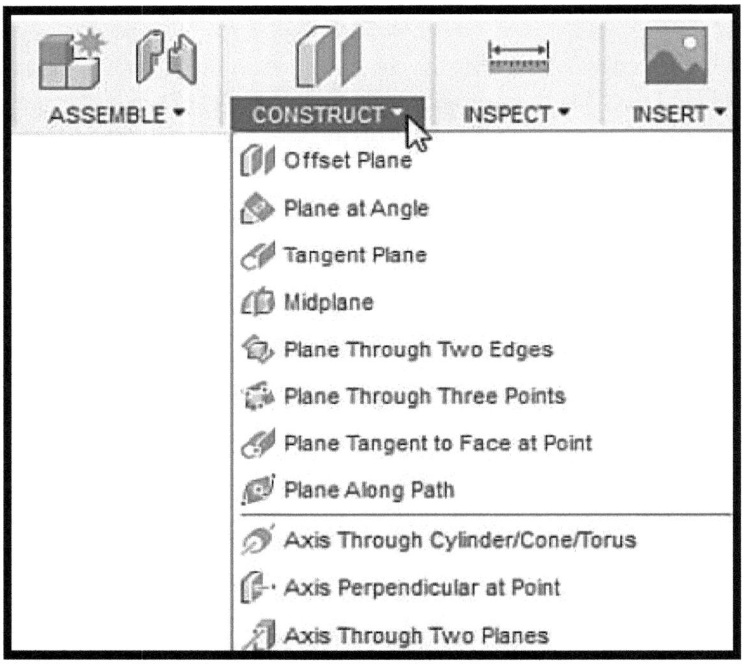

The graphic below depicts a multiple-feature model, which can only be produced by individually producing each of the model's characteristics. This particular model includes six different characteristics. The Top plane is where you'll find its initial feature, which is an extrude feature. The top planar face of the first feature is the location where the extrude feature for the second feature is formed. The top planar face of the second feature was the starting point for the creation of the third feature, which is a cut feature. A construction plane that has been specified by the user and is generated at an offset distance from the top planar face of the model constitutes the fourth feature. The user-defined construction plane is used to generate the fifth feature, which is an extrude feature, and the sixth feature is a circular pattern of the fifth feature.

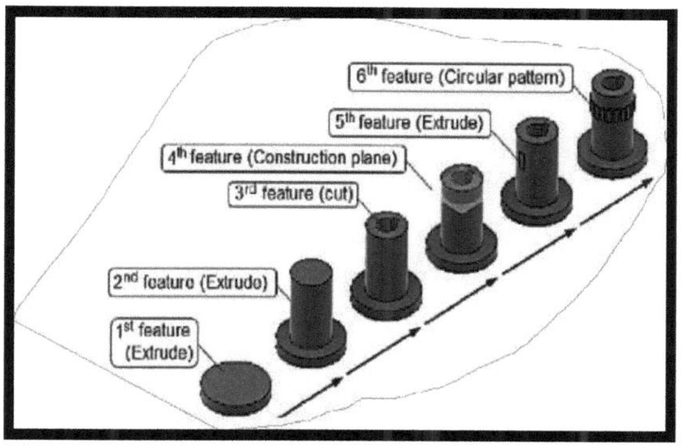

Note that the preceding figure makes it abundantly evident that more building planes would be needed to create the characteristics of a model. You can build construction planes, construction axes, and construction points in addition to generating more construction planes. The CONSTRUCT pull-down option in the Toolbar gives you access to the construction-specific tools that you need to create different kinds of construction planes, axes, and points.

Creating a Plane at an Offset Distance

You can build a construction plane in Fusion 360 in a variety of different ways, including at an angle to an existing plane or planar face, at an offset distance from an existing plane or planar face, tangent to a cylindrical or conical face, crossing between two edges, and so on.

Creating a Plane at an Angle

1. In the toolbar's drop-down menu, choose "**Construct**," and then select "Offset Plane" from the list of available tools. A dialogue window labeled OFFSET PLANE is shown.
2. In the graphics section, choose a planar face or a plane by clicking on it. A preview of the offset plane is shown when the offset distance is set to 0 (zero).
Additionally, the Distance field may be found in both the dialog box and the graphical portion of the screen. This is because the Extent drop-down list of the dialog box has its default setting set to pick the Distance option.
Within this drop-down selection, the Distance option has been chosen as the default setting for the Extent field. As a direct consequence of this, you will have the ability to generate a plane at a chosen offset distance from the selected planar face. When you pick the **To Object** option, you will have the ability to build a plane that extends up to a reference point, a sketch point, or a vertex.
3. In the box labeled "**Distance**," enter the needed value for the offset distance. The preview of the building plane is updated to reflect any changes made to the offset distance that you choose. To dynamically alter the offset distance of the building plane, you can also drag the arrow that appears in the graphics area. This is done in the same manner.
NOTE: If you want to change the direction the construction plane is moving in, you may either input a negative offset distance number or drag the arrow to the other side of the chosen planar face. Either way, the direction of the building plane will be changed.

4. In the dialog box, choose the **OK** button with your mouse. The construction offset distance is used to build a construction plane at the given distance.

Creating a Plane Tangent to a Cylindrical or Conical Face

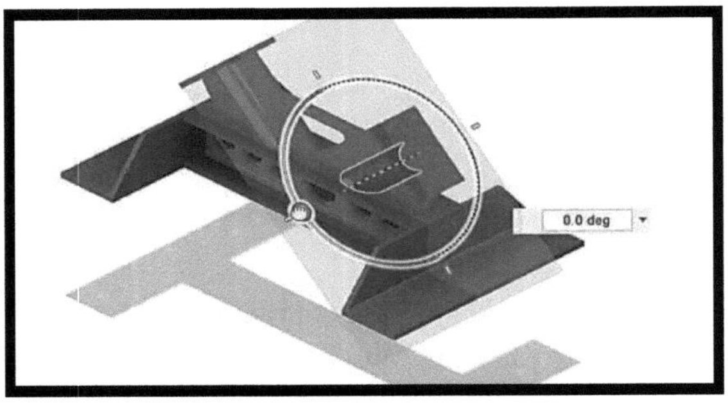

1. On the toolbar, go to the **Construct** menu and pick **Tangent Plane**. The Tangent Plane dialog is what you see at this point.
2. Within the canvas, choose a face that is either cylindrical or conical.
3. If you like, you may choose a Reference Plane here.
4. Within the canvas, drag the Angle manipulator handle to the desired angle, or enter an exact number.
5. Select the "**OK**" button.

The newly constructed plane appears on the canvas, rotated to the degree that you chose in the previous step.

Tips

- When you wish to produce drawings that do not lay on one of the three default planes, you will need to first establish construction planes.
- The input for other commands, such as the cutting tool for the Split Body command, maybe construction planes if you use them properly.

Creating a Plane in the Middle of Two Faces/Planes

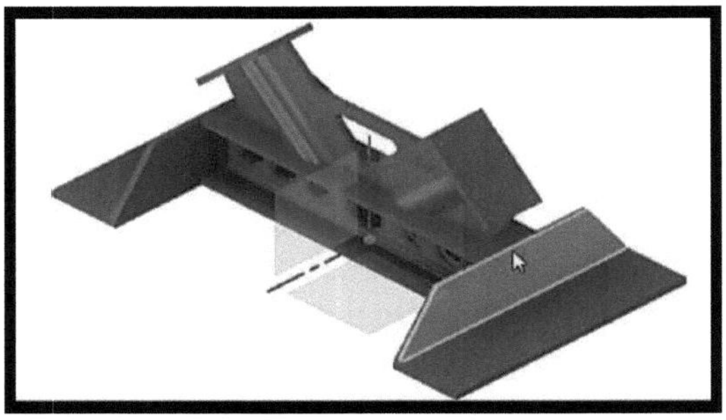

1. Select "**Construct**" > "**Midplane**" from the toolbar. The Midplane dialog appears on the screen.
2. Make a selection of the initial face or plane inside the canvas.
3. Choose the second side, often known as the plane.
4. Select the "**OK**" button.

The new construction plane appears on the canvas, aligned at a distance that is equal to each face or plane that you have chosen.

Tips

- When you wish to produce drawings that do not lay on one of the three default planes, you will need to first establish construction planes.
- The input for other commands, such as the cutting tool for the Split Body command, maybe construction planes if you use them properly.
- To perfectly cut a body in two, you may use a Midplane as a cutting tool.

Creating a Plane Passing Through Two Edges

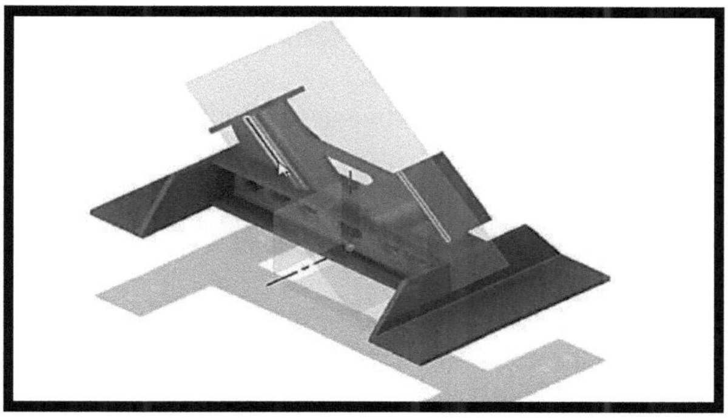

1. Select "**Construct**" > "**Plane Through Two Edges**" from the toolbar. The dialog for the Plane through Two Edges operation appears.
2. Make a selection inside the canvas of the first edge or axis.
3. Make your selection along the second axis or edge.
4. Select the "**OK**" button.

The new construction plane appears on the canvas, and it is positioned so that it will pass between the two edges or axes that you have chosen. Note that you are unable to pick the second edge or axis of a mathematical plane if the plane does not already have both of its edges or axes.

Tips

- When you wish to produce drawings that do not lay on one of the three default planes, you will need to first establish construction planes.
- The input for other commands, such as the cutting tool for the Split Body command, maybe construction planes if you use them properly.

- When you wish to establish a connecting body between two existing bodies, you should use a plane through two edges to do so.

Creating a Plane Passing Through Three Points

1. Select "Construct" > "Plane Through Three Points" from the toolbar. The dialogue box labeled Plane Through Three Points appears.
2. Make a selection of the first point or vertex inside the canvas.
3. Choose the second point, also known as a vertex.
4. Choose the third point, often known as the vertex.
5. Select the "OK" button.

The newly constructed plane appears on the canvas, and it is positioned so that it will pass through the three points or vertices that you have chosen.

Tips

1. When you wish to produce drawings that do not lay on one of the three default planes, you will need to first establish construction planes.
2. The input for other commands, such as the cutting tool for the Split Body command, maybe construction planes if you use them properly.
3. If you wish to make a connecting body between two bodies that already exist, you should use a plane through three points.

Creating a Plane Tangent to a Face and Aligned to a Point

1. Select "**Construct" > "Plane Tangent to Face at Point**" from the toolbar. The dialog titled "**Plane Tangent to Face at Point**" appears on the screen.
2. Within the canvas, pick the cylindrical or conical face depending on your preference.
3. Choose the spot to focus on.
4. Select the "**OK**" button.

You should see the new building plane appear on the canvas, tangent to the face you picked at the spot you specified.

Tips

- When you wish to produce drawings that do not lay on one of the three default planes, you will need to first establish construction planes.
- The input for other commands, such as the cutting tool for the Split Body command, maybe construction planes if you use them properly.
- Make the location selection process simpler by using a Plane Tangent To Face At Point whenever you wish to simplify the process.

Creating a Plane along a Path

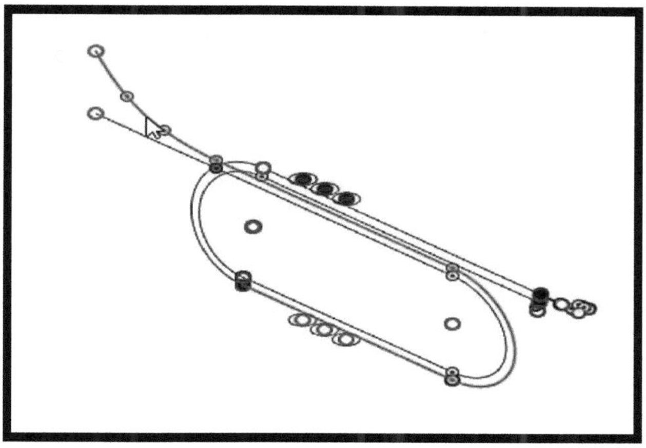

1. Navigate to the Construct menu on the toolbar and pick **Plane Along Path**. The dialog box labeled **Plane Along Path** appears.
2. Within the canvas, choose an edge that you want to utilize as the Path.
3. **Choose a Distance Type from the drop-down menu in the dialog box:**
   a. **Proportional**: Indicate the value of the distance as a percentage of the total length of the path.
   b. **Physical**: Provide a concrete description of the distance.
4. To adjust the distance, either drag the Distance manipulator handle inside the canvas or provide an exact amount.
5. Select the "**OK**" button.

The new building plane is shown on the canvas, normal to the point along the path that you selected.

Tips

- When you wish to produce drawings that do not lay on one of the three default planes, you will need to first establish construction planes.
- The input for other commands, such as the cutting tool for the Split Body command, maybe construction planes if you use them properly.
- If you wish to generate a sketch profile that sweeps along the path, you should use the Plane Along Path tool.
- If you want the position of the construction plane to update automatically whenever you modify the dimensions of the path, you should choose the proportional distance type for the path's distance.
- Make use of the Physical distance type when you want the placement of the construction plane to stay at a set distance along the path regardless of the changes you make to the size and form of the path.
- If you do not want the program to choose tangentially associated geometry automatically, deselect the Tangent Chain checkbox.

Creating a Construction Axis

You may establish a construction axis like constructing a construction plane. To construct elements like revolved and circular patterns, you may utilize a building axis as the axis of rotation. Next, we'll talk about how to make several kinds of building axes.

Creating an Axis Passing Through a Cylinder/Cone/Torus

1. Click **Construct > Axis Through Cylinder/Cone/Torus** in the toolbar. The dialog box for Axis Through Cylinder, Cone, or Torus appears.
2. Pick a cylindrical, conical, or toroidal face on the canvas.
3. Press **OK**.

The center of the cylinder, cone, or torus you choose appears on the canvas as the new construction axis.

Tips

- Only one construction axis may be created at once.
- When referencing an axis or edge that does not already exist or is not one of the three default axes, create construction axes.

Creating an Axis Perpendicular at a Point

1. Click **Construct > Axis Perpendicular to Face at Point** on the toolbar. The dialog box for the axis perpendicular to face at point appears.
2. Pick a face on the canvas.
3. Pick a point or vertex that is not part of the face.
4. Press **OK**.

The new axis, which is parallel to the point you choose outside the face, appears on the canvas.

Tips

- One axis may only be created at a time.
- When referencing an axis or edge that does not exist or is not one of the three standard axes, create custom axes.
- A building plane cannot be used to produce an axis perpendicular to the face at a point.
- If you wish to choose a point that is located directly on the face, use an Axis Perpendicular at Point.

Creating an Axis Passing Through Two Planes

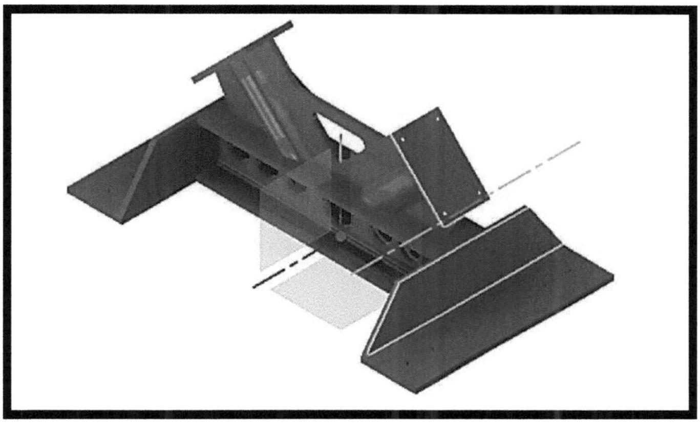

1. Click **Construct > Axis Through Two Planes** in the toolbar. The Axis Through Two Planes dialog will display.
2. Pick the first face or plane on the canvas.
3. Pick the following face or plane.
4. Press **OK**.

Along the expanded intersection of the two faces or planes you choose; the new construction axis appears on the canvas.

Tips

- Only one construction axis may be created at once.
- When referencing an axis or edge that does not already exist or is not one of the three default axes, create construction axes.
- You cannot choose two faces or planes that are parallel to one another.
- When referencing the extended intersection of two planes or faces, use an axis via two planes.

Creating an Axis Passing Through Two Points

1. Click **Construct > Axis Through Two Points** on the toolbar. The dialog box for "Axis through Two Points" appears.
2. Pick the first point or vertex on the canvas.

3. Pick the following vertex or point.
4. Press **OK**.

The canvas shows the new construction axis, which traverses the two points or vertices you choose.

Tips

- Only one construction axis may be created at once.
- When referencing an axis or edge that does not already exist or is not one of the three default axes, create construction axes.

Creating an Axis Passing Through an Edge

1. Click **Construct > Axis Through Edge** in the toolbar. The dialog box for Axis through Edge appears.
2. Pick a linear edge on the canvas.
3. Press **OK**.

The canvas shows the new construction axis along the chosen linear edge.

Tips

- Only one construction axis may be created at once.
- When referencing an axis or edge that does not already exist or is not one of the three default axes, create construction axes.
- You must choose a linear edge for your edge.
- When referencing the linear expansion of an existing edge, use an axis via edge.

Creating an Axis Perpendicular to Face at Point

1. Click **Construct > Axis Perpendicular at Point** on the toolbar. The dialog for Axis Perpendicular at Point appears.
2. Pick a face-related place on the canvas.
3. Press **OK**.

Perpendicular to the point you choose on the face, the new construction axis is visible on the canvas.

Tips

- Only one construction axis may be created at once.
- When referencing an axis or edge that does not already exist or is not one of the three default axes, create construction axes.
- A building plane cannot be used to generate an axis perpendicular to point.
- If you wish to choose a point that is not on the face, use the axis perpendicular to the face at the point.

Creating a Construction Point

A construction point serves as a standard reference point for tasks like measuring distance and drawing planes. The various building point creation processes are then explored.

Creating a Point at Vertex

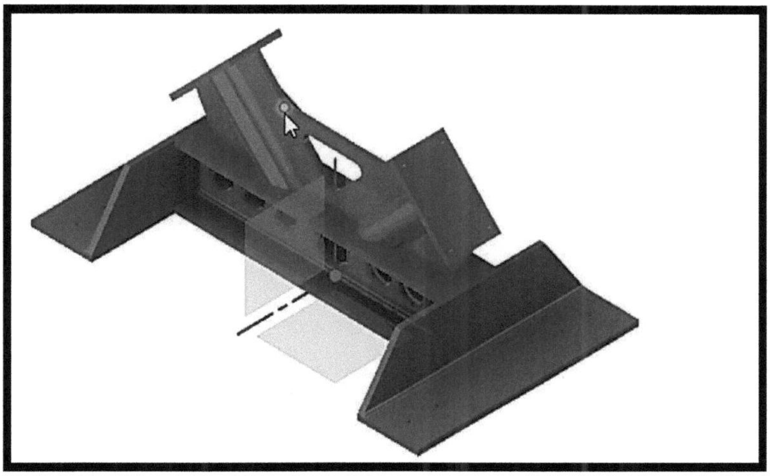

1. Click **Construct > Point at Vertex** in the toolbar. The dialog box for Point at Vertex appears.
2. Pick an existing point or vertex on the canvas.
3. Press **OK**.

At the position of the existing point or vertex you choose, the new construction point appears on the canvas.

Tips

- Only one construction point may be created at a time.
- When referencing a point that doesn't exist, create construction points.

Creating a Point at the Intersection of Two Edges

1. Click **Construct > Point Through Two Edges** in the toolbar. The dialog box for "Point Through Two Edges" appears.
2. Pick the first edge or axis on the canvas.
3. Pick the second axis or edge.
4. Press **OK**.

At the junction or extended intersection of the two edges or axes you choose; the new building point appears on the canvas.

Tips

- Only one construction point may be created at a time.
- You cannot choose two edges or axes that are parallel to one another.
- When referencing a point that doesn't exist, create construction points.
- When you wish to establish a construction point at the intersection or extended intersection of two edges or axes, use a Point Through Two Edges.

Creating a Point at the Intersection of Three Planes

1. Click **Construct > Point Through Three Planes** in the toolbar. The Point Through Three Planes dialog appears.
2. Pick the first plane or face on the canvas.
3. Decide on the second face or plane.
4. Pick the third face or plane.
5. Press **OK**.

At the point where the three planes or faces you choose cross or extend into one another, the new building point appears on the canvas.

Tips

- Only one construction point may be created at a time.
- When referencing a point that doesn't exist, create construction points.
- You cannot choose three planes or faces that are parallel to one another.
- To establish a construction point at the intersection or extended intersection of three planes or faces, use a Point Through Three Planes.

Creating a Point at the Center of Circle/Sphere/Torus

1. Click **Construct > Point at Center of Circle/Sphere/Torus** on the toolbar. The dialog box Point at Center of Circle/Sphere/Torus appears.
2. Pick a spherical, steroidal, or circular face on the canvas.
3. Press **OK**.

The center of the circle, sphere, or torus that you choose is where the new building point appears on the canvas.

Tips

- Only one construction point may be created at a time.
- When referencing a point that doesn't exist, create construction points.

Creating a Point at the Intersection of an Edge and a Plane

1. Click **Construct > Point at Edge and Plane** in the toolbar. The dialog box for Point at Edge and Plane appears.
2. Choose the axis or linear edge on the canvas.
3. Pick a face or plane.
4. Press **OK**.

The expanded intersection of the linear edge or axis with the plane or face you choose is where the new building point appears on the canvas.

Tips

- Only one construction point may be created at a time.
- When referencing a point that doesn't exist, create construction points.

Creating a Point along a Path

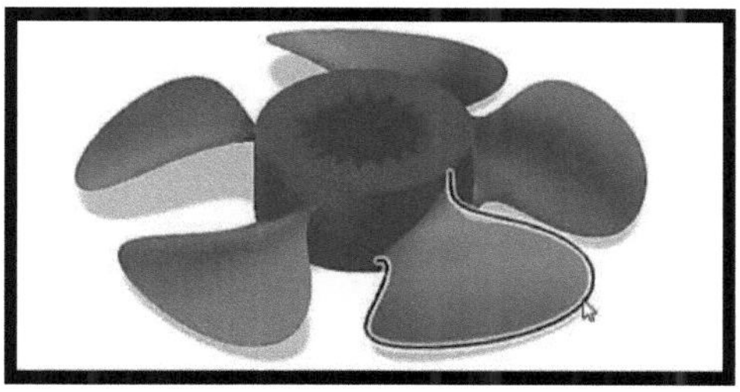

1. Click **Construct > Point Along Path** in the toolbar. The dialog box for Point Along Path appears.
2. Choose a canvas edge to serve as the Path.
3. **Select a distance type in the dialog:**
    a. **Proportional**: Indicate how much of the path the distance measurement represents.
    b. **Physical:** Give a precise measurement of the distance.
4. To define a precise distance, drag the Distance manipulator handle onto the canvas.
5. Press OK. At the location along the path that you selected; the new construction point appears on the canvas.

Tips

- Only one construction point may be created at a time.
- When referencing a point that doesn't exist, create construction points.
- If you want the position of the construction point to vary as the size and form of the path change, use the proportional distance type.

- When the path's size and form vary and you want the construction point's position to stay a set distance from it, use the Physical distance type.

If you don't want geometry that is tangentially related to other objects automatically selected, uncheck Tangent Chain.

Questions

1. You can create a construction plane in the middle of two faces/ planes by using which tool.
2. Which tool is used for creating a construction axis passing through a cylinder, cone, or torus?
3. You can create a construction plane at an offset distance by using which tool?
4. You can create a construction plane at an angle by using which tool?
5. Which is used for creating a construction point at a vertex?
6. Which tool is used for creating a construction point at the center of a circle, a sphere, or a torus?
7. Which tool is used for creating a construction axis passing through two planes or planar faces?

CHAPTER 7

ADVANCED MODELING - I

Using Advanced Options of the Extrude Tool

The EXTRUDE dialog box displays whenever the Extrude tool is used to extrude a drawing in Adobe Illustrator. The following is a discussion of a few of the choices that may be made inside this dialog box:

Start drop-down list

The start condition of the extrusion process may be defined by selecting one of the choices from the drop-down list located in the dialog box labeled Start.

From Object

With the Start drop-down list's From Object option, you may pick a face, a plane, or a vertex to specify the beginning point of the profile from which extrusion begins. This can be done to determine where the extrusion process will begin. After you have selected this option, you will be prompted to choose a face, a plane, or a vertex as the starting condition for the extrusion. You can see a sketch profile that needs to be extruded and a face that has to be chosen as the start condition of the extrusion process in the picture below.

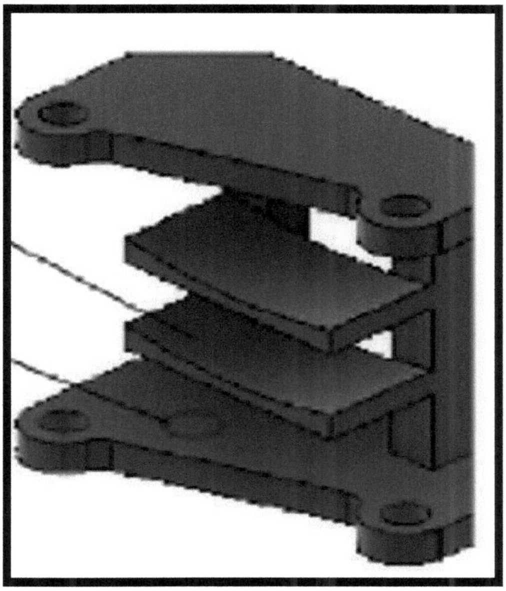

After choosing the face as the start condition, the preview of the extruded feature that would result can be seen in the picture below.

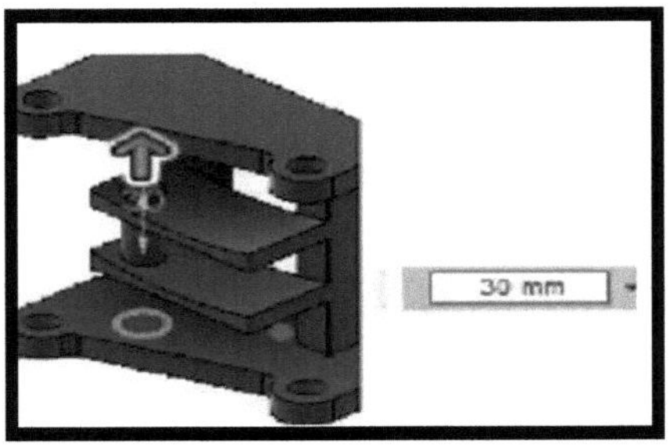

NOTE: The Offset field of the dialog box has a value of 0 (zero) typed in it by default. As a consequence of this, the extrusion begins precisely from the item that was picked (face, plane, or vertex). In this box, you may provide the needed value for the offset parameter.

Extent drop-down list

The extrusion's end condition and manner of termination are both defined by selecting an option from the drop-down list labeled "**Extent.**"

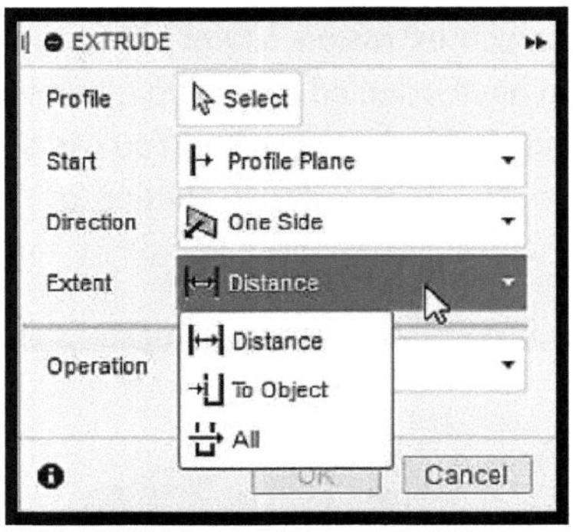

To Object

By choosing a body, a face, a plane, or a vertex, the "**To Object**" option allows the user to define the end condition or termination of the extrusion process. This may be done by selecting a vertex. The picture below illustrates a sketch profile that has to be extruded, as well as a face that needs to be chosen as the end condition/termination of the extrusion process.

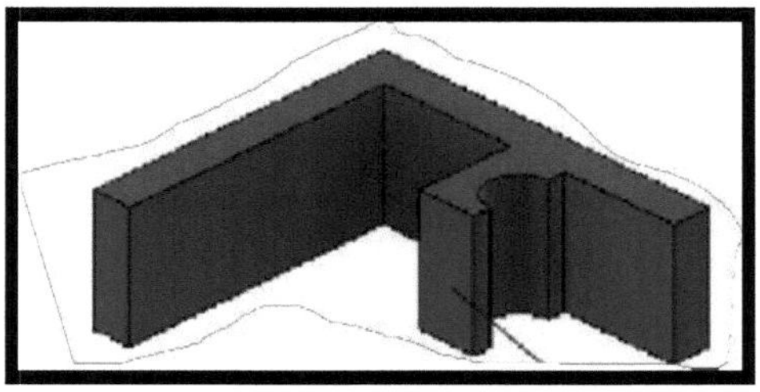

Following the selection of the face as the end condition, the preview of the extruded feature that will result can be seen in the picture below.

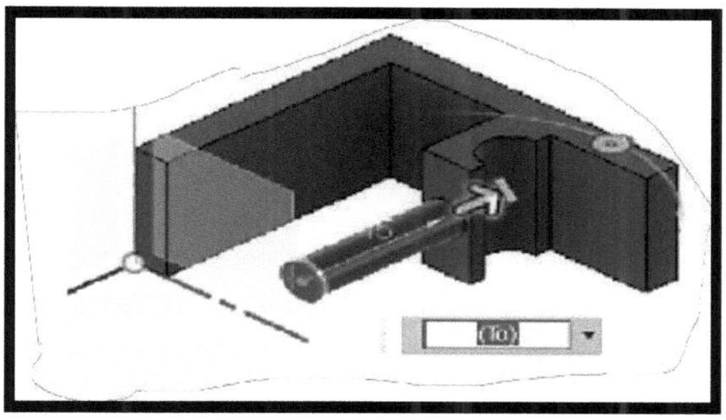

The buttons to Extend Faces and Chain Faces will become available in the dialog box after you have chosen a face to serve as the end condition. The Extend Faces button has its state set to active by default. Therefore, even if the profile that is going to be extruded does not entirely project onto the specified face of the model, the extrusion will end on the selected face of the model regardless of this fact. This occurs as a result of the chosen face of the model being stretched out to the point where it contacts the extrusion.

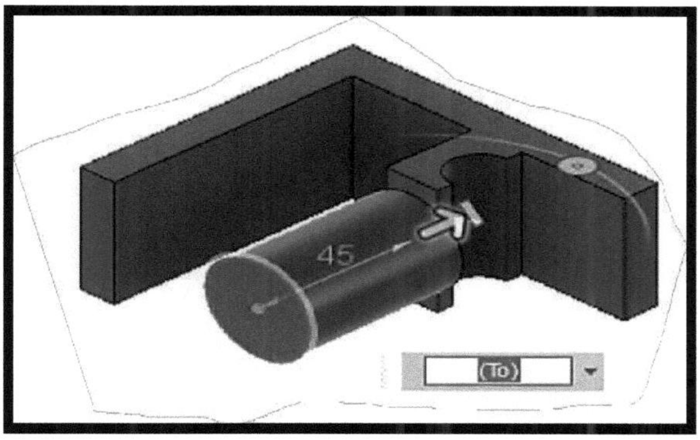

When you select the **Chain Faces** button, if the profile that is going to be extruded does not completely project onto the face that is currently selected, the extrusion will continue over the adjacent faces until it reaches the next intersecting face, at which point it will be completely projected onto that face. It is important to keep in mind that the material of the newly formed feature does not replace the material that is already present in the model.

All

When using the Extent drop-down list, selecting the **All** option allows you to define the extrusion such that it goes across all of the model's faces. You may also flip the direction of the extrusion from one side of the drawing plane to the other by clicking the **Flip button** in the dialog box. This will allow you to reverse the direction in which the extrusion is occurring. As soon as you pick the **All** option in the drop-down menu, the **Flip** button will become active in the dialog box.

Operation drop-down list

The sort of operation that should be utilized to create the extrude feature may be selected from the drop-down list titled "**Operation**."

Join

Extruding the profile by adding the material and merging or connecting the feature with other features of the model may be accomplished by selecting the **Join option** from the **operation** drop-down list. This option is utilized for both of these tasks. When you choose this option, the newly generated feature will combine with any other features that are already present, and the combined features will function as a single body.

Cut

Extruding the profile involves removing material from the model, which is accomplished by selecting the Cut option from the operation drop-down list.

Intersect

When generating a feature, the **Intersect** option of the operation drop-down list is selected. This option is used to build a feature by only retaining the material that is shared by the old feature and the new feature that is being formed.

New Body

When you choose the **New Body** option, the feature that is being produced will not combine with any of the other features that are already present in the model; rather, it will be given its own distinct body. This choice is chosen automatically if a model's base feature is used as the basis for the creation of a new feature.

New Component

Create a new component in the currently active design file by selecting the **New Component** option. This option is used to create a new component. After doing this step, the design file will function as an assembly file, and you will be able to generate all of the assembly's components. With Fusion 360, you can construct both individual components and whole assemblies without ever leaving the same workspace. After you have specified all of the necessary criteria in the EXTRUDE dialog box, you may go on to click the **OK** button. The extrude feature is made.

Using Advanced Options of the Revolve Tool

The **REVOLVE** dialog box appears in the graphics area whenever the Revolve tool is used to revolve a drawing. This box can be seen in the middle of the screen. During the process of developing the fundamental revolve function of a model, a few of the choices available in the **REVOLVE** dialog box were covered in further detail.

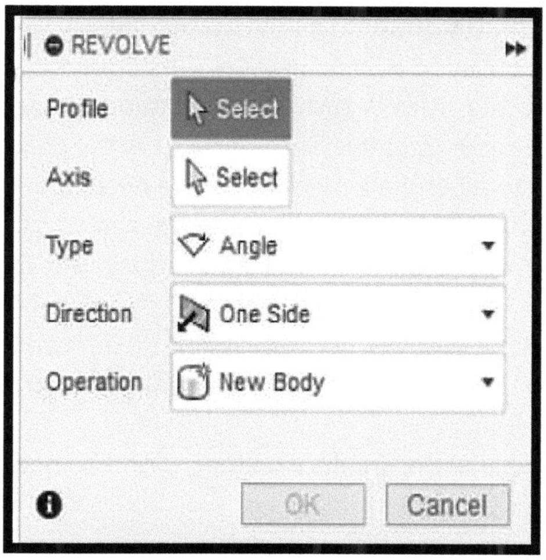

The options such as **Join, cut, and Intersect** in the operation drop-down list of the REVOLVE dialog box are the same as those discussed earlier with the exception that these options are used for creating a revolve feature. The only difference is that the options are located in the REVOLVE dialog box. The choices that are available in the Type drop-down list of the **REVOLVE** dialog box have already been covered, except the "**To**" option. This option is what is used to stop the revolve feature at a face or a plane.

Working with a Sketch having Multiple Profiles

The use of a single sketch in Fusion 360 that contains numerous closed pro-files enables the creation of many features at the same time. The two images that follow the show, first, a drawing that has many closed profiles, and then, second, the multi-feature model that was produced by utilizing the sketch.

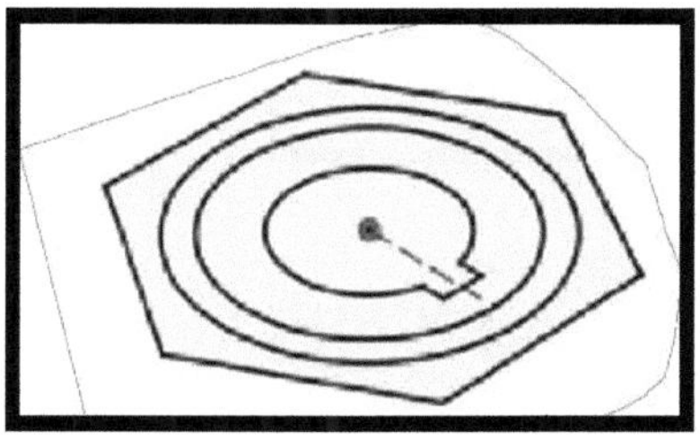

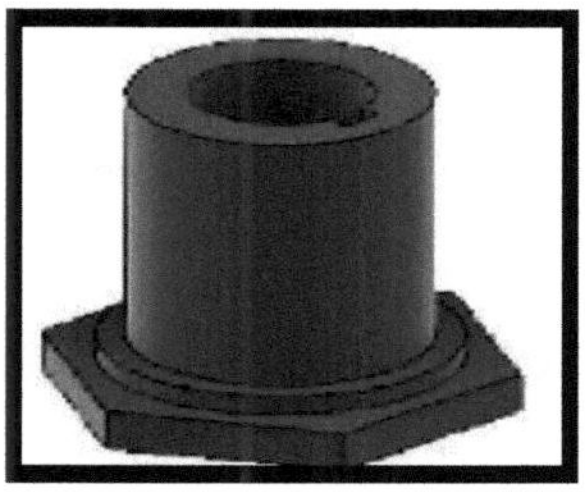

1. By using sketching tools, you can produce a drawing that has many profiles.
2. To see the tools for solid modeling, go to the Toolbar and click on the tab labeled **SOLID**.
3. Either use the E key on your keyboard or click the EXTRUDE tool located in the **CREATE** panel of the SOLID tab. The EXTRUDE dialog box is brought into view.
4. Select the Home symbol located inside the View Cube and click on it to switch the perspective of the drawing to an isometric view.

5. Position the pointer over a closed profile of the drawing that is to be chosen, and when it becomes highlighted in the graphics area, click on it to choose it.
6. Within the dialogue box, you will be able to provide the settings for the creation of the feature.
7. In the dialog box, click the **OK** button. The new component has been developed. In addition to that, its name has been included in the Timeline. Take note that the drawing will no longer be visible in the graphics section. This is because the feature uses up all of the resources from the drawing. As a direct consequence of this, it is absent from the graphics section.
   NOTE: The Timeline shows all of the actions that have been done on a design, such as drawings, features, components, and building planes in the order in which they were created. You may, however, rearrange the sequence of events by dragging and dropping the operations in the Timeline.
8. In the BROWSER, expand the **Sketches** node by clicking on the arrow that is located directly in front of it. The presently active design file displays a list of all of the drawings that have been made in that file.
9. To make the drawing visible in the graphics section, click the Show icon that is located in front of the sketch. This will make it visible.
10. After using the Extrude tool, choose a closed profile from the drawing to use as your starting point.
11. In the dialog box that appears, you will first need to provide the settings for establishing the feature, and then you will need to click the OK button that appears in the dialog box. The extrude functionality is created.
12. Using the same method, you may make the remaining features by drawing closed profiles from a sketch.

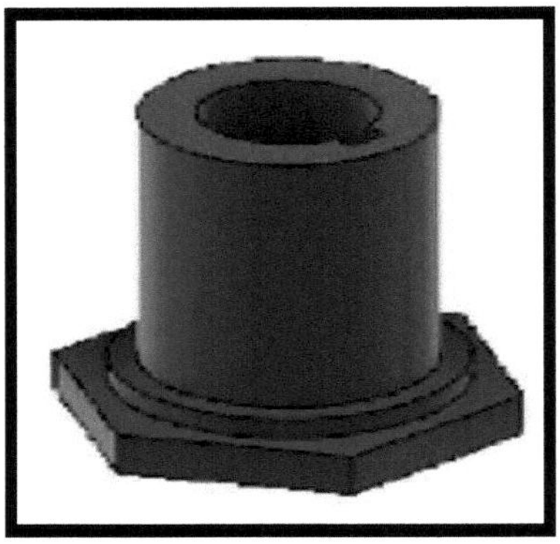

Projecting Edges onto a Sketching Plane

When sketching in Fusion 360, you may use the Project tool to project edges of existing features onto the drawing that is now active. This is possible when using the Sketch tool. The model that is shown in the following picture is one in which the contours of the already present features have been depicted as sketch entities on the active sketching plane.

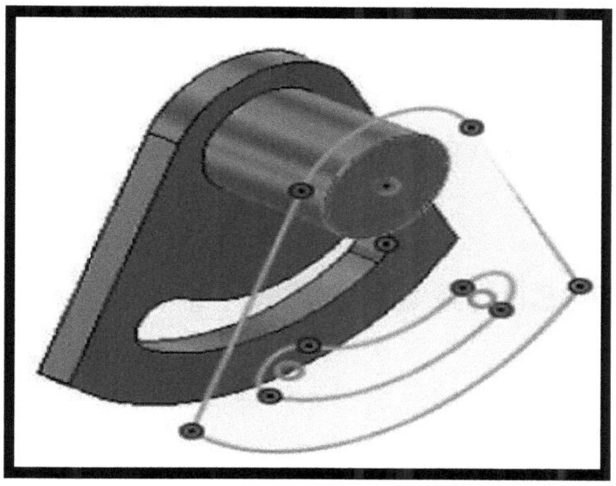

To project the edges of the existing features onto the currently active sketching plane, invoke the CREATE drop-down menu located in the **SKETCH** contextual tab of the Toolbar and then click on **Project / Include > Project**. This will allow you to project the edges of the existing features onto the currently active sketching plane. You might try pressing the **P key** instead. A dialogue window labeled **PROJECT** will now display. The available choices will be discussed below.

Geometry

In the drop-down menu, the geometry selection option is the one that is active by default. As a consequence of this, you will have the ability to pick edges, faces, sketch entities, and bodies as the geometries that will be projected onto the drawing plane that is now active. Take note that once you pick a face, all of that face's edges will automatically be projected into the drawing plane. You can narrow down your choice of geometries by utilizing the buttons located in the dialog box's **Selection Filter** area.

Selection Filter

Within the Selection Filter section of the dialog box, the Specified entities button will always be enabled when it is first opened. You will be able to pick the model's edges, faces, and sketch entities as a consequence of this. To pick bodies, you will first need to activate the button labeled "**Bodies**" located in this section of the dialog box.

Projection Link

When the check box labeled "**Projection Link**" is selected, the projected drawing is connected to the entity that it belongs to. As a consequence of this, if a change is made to the entity that is being projected, that change will immediately reflect on the entity that is being projected. Take note that the projected drawing cannot have its individual properties changed if it is related to the entity that it belongs to. After choosing the necessary geometries to be projected, go to the next step by clicking the OK button in the dialog box. The vertices and edges of the geometries that are currently chosen are projected as sketch entities onto the active drawing plane. You can construct features with the help of these projected sketch entities. **Tip**: When you create a sketch on an existing planar face of a model, the edges of that face will automatically project into the sketching plane if the Auto project edges on the reference check box in the Preferences dialog box are enabled. This may be done by selecting the check box. To choose this check box, first, bring up the Preferences dialog box and then click on the Design option which is located on the left panel of the Preferences dialog box, which is located under the General option. After that, in the right panel of the dialog box, check the box labeled "**Auto project edges on reference**," and then click the **Apply** button to save your changes.

Show or hide projection geometry

You may choose to show projected geometries by checking or unchecking the box in the Sketch Palette.

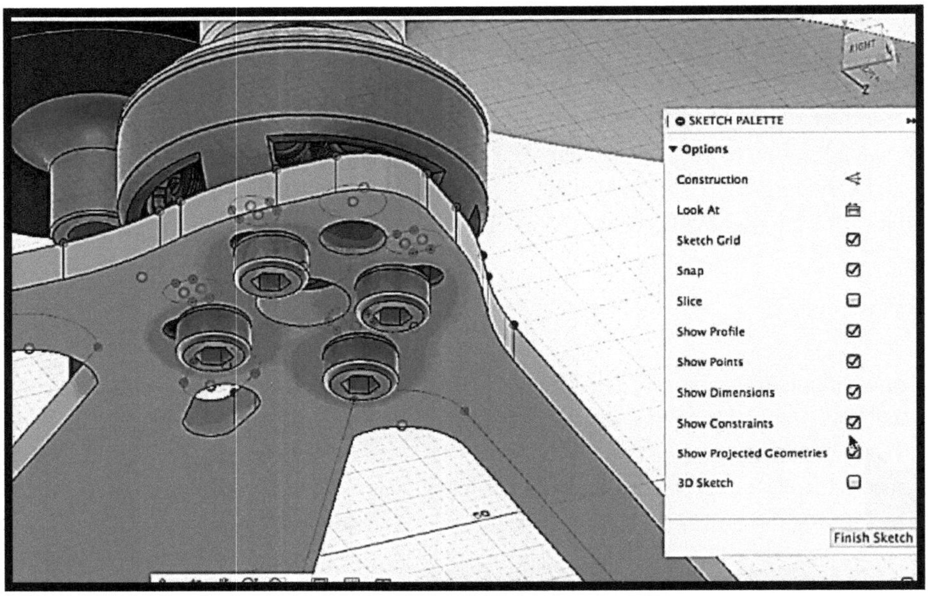

Manage lost predictions

A yellow alert appears on the Sketch feature in the Timeline to signal that the Projection Link has been lost if you modify the items that were projected from the design and the associative link is destroyed.

On the canvas, the altered projection geometry is indicated in orange or yellow.

1. In the Timeline, choose the **Sketch feature** and right-click it.
2. Choose **Manage Lost Projections** from the menu.
   a. The dialogue box labeled Manage Lost Projections appears.
3. Choose a lost projection from the drop-down menu in the dialog box.
4. **Pick one of the Available Operations:**
   a. **Re-link**: To re-establish the associative association, choose a body, face, edge, or point from the object, and then click the "**Re-Link**" button.
   b. **Break Link**: If you want to break the associative link between the actual object and the projection geometry in the drawing, use the "Break Link" command. The drawing will continue to use the non-associative geometry in the same position it is in now.

c. **Delete the geometry**: In the drawing, delete the geometry that represents the projection.

5. Repeat steps 3 and 4 for each projection that was lost.
6. Press the **OK** button.

In the active drawing, the associative linkages are either re-established, disrupted, or removed entirely.

Tips

- If you do not want to keep an associative link between the items you have chosen and the projection geometry, make sure that the "**Projection Link**" checkbox is not checked.
- When you are managing lost projections in complicated designs, you may make it simpler to notice lost projections by checking the box next to Fade Other Geometry.
- In the section labeled **Options**, choose **Remove All or Break Connection All** to simultaneously delete the projection geometry or sever the associative link for all of the lost projections. This may be done by clicking the corresponding button.

Creating 3D Curves

You can design a variety of curves in Fusion 360. These curves serve a variety of purposes, including acting as a path, a guide rail, and so on when you are creating features such as sweep and loft. Next, we will go through the processes that may be used to produce a variety of curved shapes.

Creating a Projected Curve

You may make a projected curve in Fusion 360 by utilizing the **Project To Surface tool** to project a sketch onto an existing face of a model. This will allow you to build a projected curve. When projecting drawing entities, you have the option of selecting between flat faces or curved faces.

The following is an explanation of the procedure for developing a projected curve:

1. To enter the Drawing environment, choose a plane or a planar face to use as the sketching plane. The context-sensitive tab labeled SKETCH has been added to the Toolbar.
2. Select **Project / Include > Project** to Surface from the drop-down menu that appears when you invoke the **CREATE** drop-down menu in the **SKETCH** contextual tab. Within the graphics section is where you will find the **PROJECT TO SURFACE** dialog box.
3. Click on the **Home** symbol located on the View Cube to switch the perspective of the drawing view to an isometric perspective. Within the dialog box, the Faces selection option is the one that is chosen by default. As a consequence of this, you will have the ability to choose a face or faces (either planar or curved) onto which to project the sketch entities.
4. In the graphics section, choose a face of the model, or many faces if necessary.
5. When the Default option in the **Project Type** drop-down list is chosen, the preview of the projected curve is shown in the graphics area. Take note that the curves that are going to be picked should not be included in the sketch that is now being used.

6. It is possible to project the sketch entities to the point on the chosen face that is the closest to them along the face vector by selecting the **Closest Point** option from the Project Type drop-down list.
7. When you select the **Along Vector** option in the Project Type drop-down list, the Project Direction selection option appears in the dialog box. This option allows you to select a vector along which you want to project the entities on the selected face. When you select the Along Vector option, the dialog box appears. In this illustration, the Top plane has been chosen as the direction of the vector.
8. Choose the appropriate alternative from the Project Type drop-down list located within the dialog box. Note that if you choose the Along Vector option in the Project Type drop-down list, you will also need to define the project direction by selecting a face, a plane, or an edge. This can be done by clicking on the appropriate option in the Project Direction drop-down list.
9. Within the dialog box, choose the check box labeled "**Projection Connection**" to create a link between the projected curve and the original design.
10. In the dialog box, choose the **OK** button and click it. On the face of the projection that you have chosen, the projected curve will be generated.

Creating an Intersection Curve

Using the Intersection Curve tool in Fusion 360, it is possible to generate a 3D curve by intersecting two geometries in the workspace. The final 3D curve seen here is produced by intersecting two 2D curves as shown in the picture (splines). You can also make a 3D curve by having a 2D curve collide with a face to make the intersection.

The following is an explanation of the procedure for creating an intersecting curve:

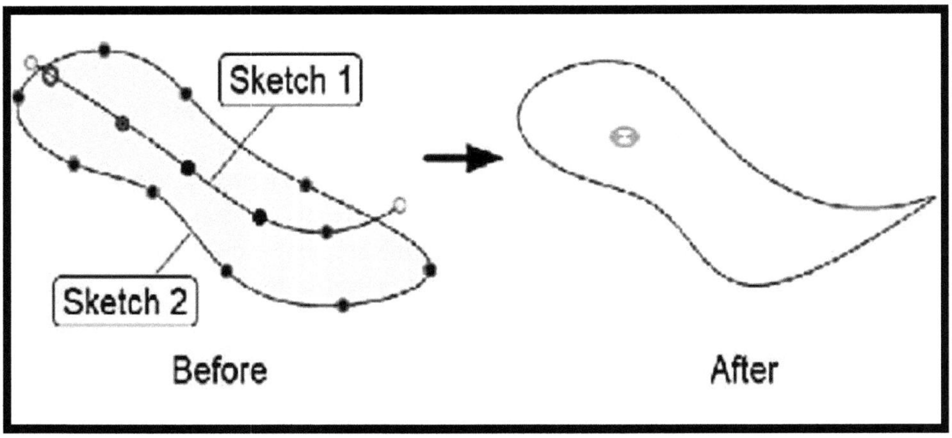

1. To enter the Drawing environment, choose a plane or a planar face to use as the sketching plane. The context-sensitive tab labeled SKETCH has been added to the Toolbar.
2. Select **Project / Include > Intersection Curve** from the drop-down menu that appears after invoking the CREATE drop-down menu that is located in the SKETCH contextual tab of the Toolbar. Within the graphics section is where you will find the INTERSECTION CURVE dialog box.

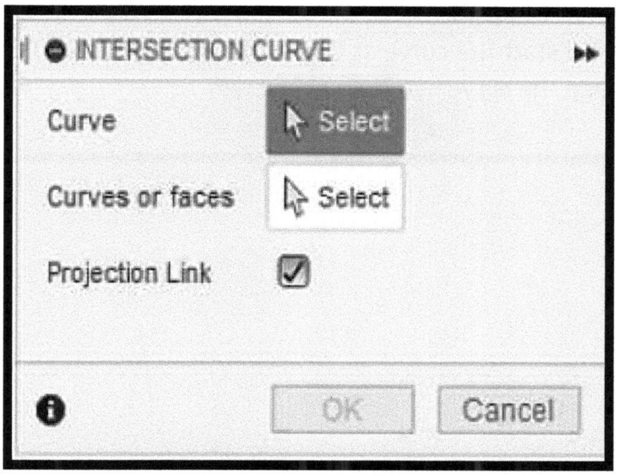

3. Click on the **Home** icon located on View Cube. This will shift the perspective of the drawing view to an isometric perspective.
4. Within the dialog box, the Curve selection option is the one that is chosen automatically. As a consequence of this, you will have the ability to pick either a sketch object or a 2D curve to be projected on the other 2D curve or a face.
5. In the drawing area, choose a curve or sketch item to work with. A selection has been made of the curve, and the Curves or faces selection option in the dialog box has been automatically enabled as a result.
6. In the drawing area, choose another curve or a face to work with. A preview of the curve that intersects appears. Take note that the curves that are going to be picked should not be included in the sketch that is now being used.
7. To connect the projected curve with the parent drawing, you need to make sure that the check box labeled "**Projection Link**" is selected in the dialog box.
8. In the dialog box, choose the **OK** button and click it. It is possible to generate the intersection curve by intersecting the first chosen curve with either the second selected curve or the face.

Projected Compound Curves in Fusion 360

We will begin by defining two orthogonal curves or splines, and then, via a series of stages, we will make use of these splines to build a projected compound curve. The following illustration depicts a basic sweep of the example projected compound curve that we will create in this section.

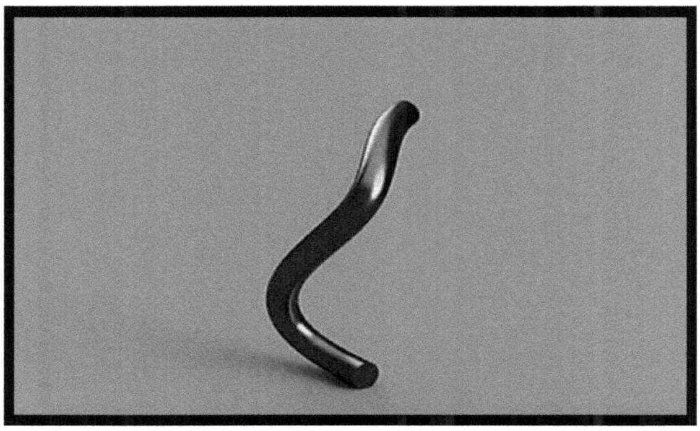

On the Front Plane, we will start by doodling the very first generating curve, also known as a spline. In this particular example, we will start the curve at the origin; however, this is not a requirement for curves in general. It is important that the curve not cross over itself.

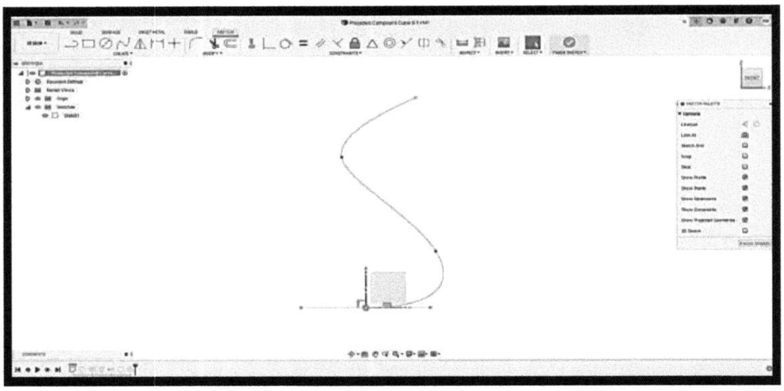

For the sake of this demonstration, we will design our Generating Curves on the Front and Left Planes that are predefined in Fusion 360. In a broad sense, any two planes that are orthogonal to one another may be employed. Next, we will make a rough design of a second Generating Curve, but this time we will do it on the Left Plane. Check to see that it does not self-intersect. Make it a point to check that the **'height'** of this curve is the same as the **Front Plane Curve**. To clarify, what I mean by this is that the domain of both curves needs to be the same along the Z-axis, just as in the illustration below.

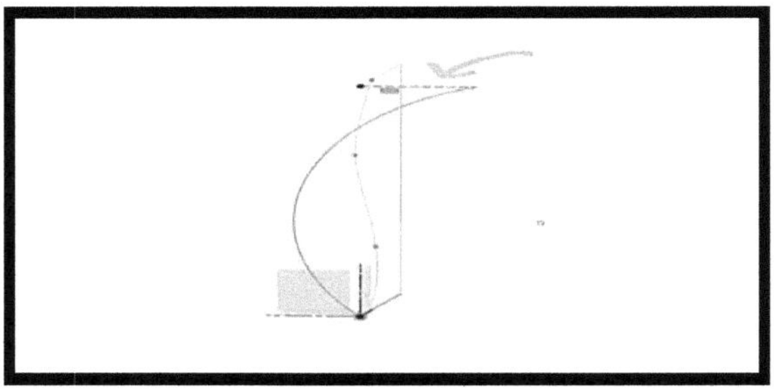

Lastly, at the beginning and the conclusion of this drawing, add a couple of brief vertical lines, as seen in the following example: This assists with the split body step that comes later.

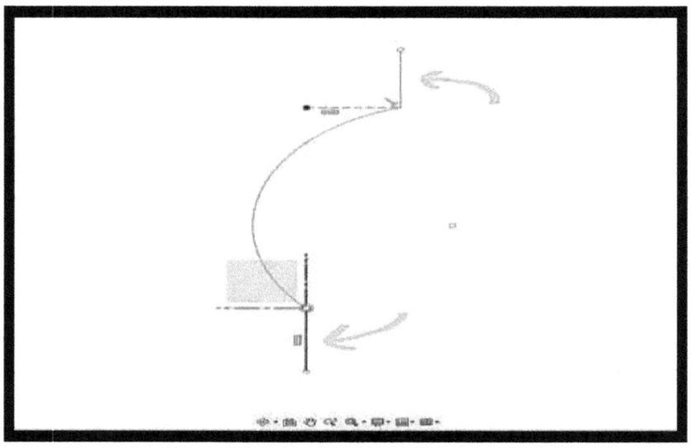

Make any necessary adjustments to the Front Plane Generating Curve that was drawn in the previous stage. To surround the Front Plane Curve on one side of the design, as shown in the example that follows below, you will need to add some more lines.

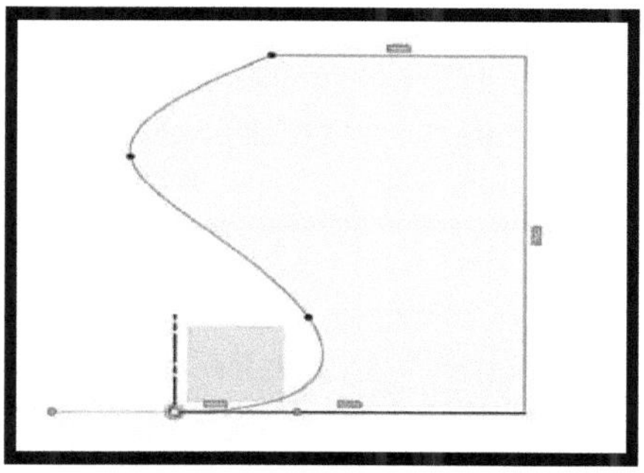

This part of the workflow is arguably the least obvious of the whole process. In the current stage, we are preparing for the extrusion that will be performed in the next step, which will then be adjusted to produce the completed Projected Compound Curve. The drawing of the Front Plane with the modifications should be extruded in both directions. It is sufficient for this purpose that the length of the extruded body spans the left plane sketch in the Y direction; the precise distance is not relevant in any way. Make the extrusion exceedingly lengthy if you are unclear about what to do.

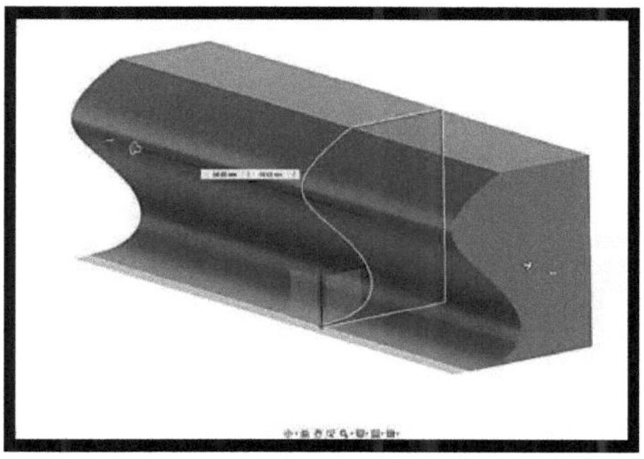

With the use of the **Left Plane Generating Curve** and the **'Split Body' tool**, which can be found in the Modify menu, divide the body that was formed into two halves.

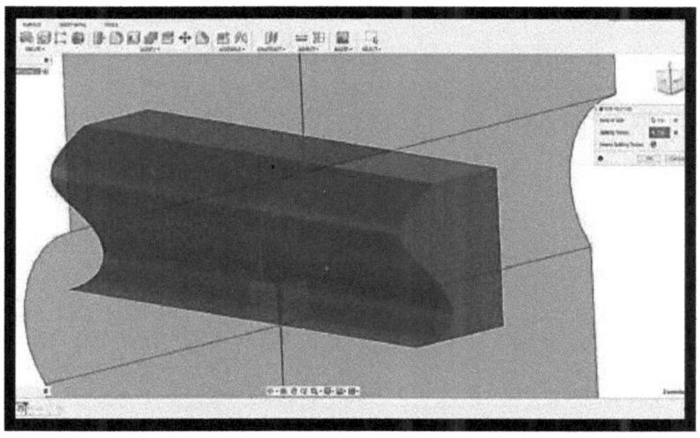

To remove one of the divided bodies, right-click on the body in the left-hand side objects list, then pick "**Remove**" from the context menu. This step is not required, but it is best practice, in my experience. Keeping both bodies might sometimes lead to problems with the sweeps.

For the sake of constructing a **Projected Compound Curve**, even if it may not be immediately clear, we have done what we set out to do. The Compound Curve that we have been attempting to build is located at the leading edge of the split body, which is where the split took place.

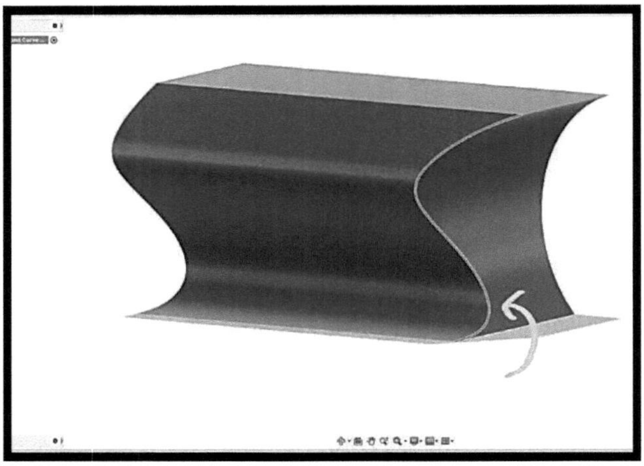

The Compound Curve that was developed is now available for use in sweeps and other applications. We'll utilize the Projected Compound Curve to make a straightforward sweep so that we can bring this example to a close. Start a new drawing on the Left Plane and draw a circle at the point where you want the sketch to begin. It could be easier to draw the circle on the Front Plane, depending on the Compound Curve that you are working with. Alternatively, you might create a new plane that is rotated between the Front and Left Planes. Feel free to experiment with both options.

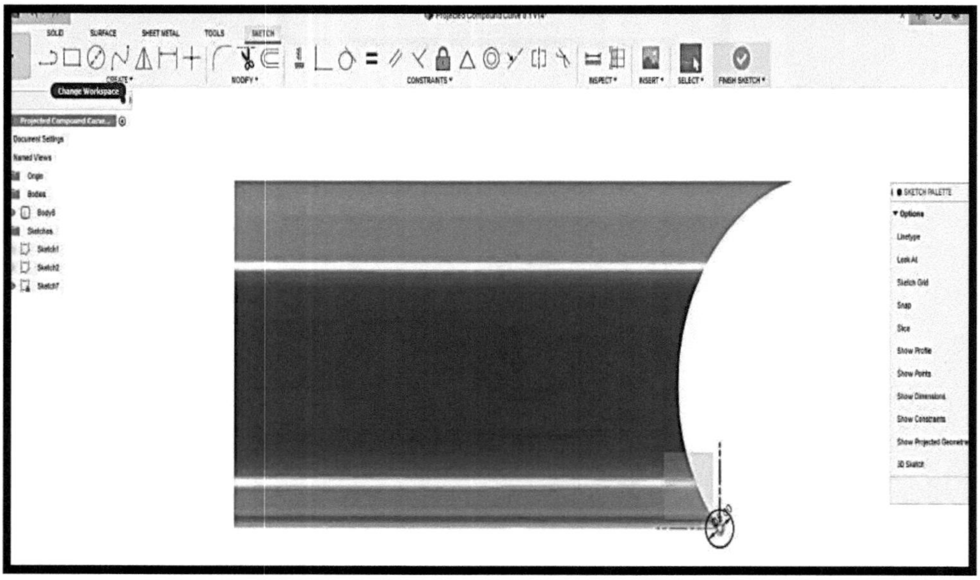

Now, build a sweep by giving it a **'Profile'** that is the circle we just created, and **a 'Path'** that is the projected compound curve. This should result in a smooth sweep of our projected compound curve if everything has gone according to plan.

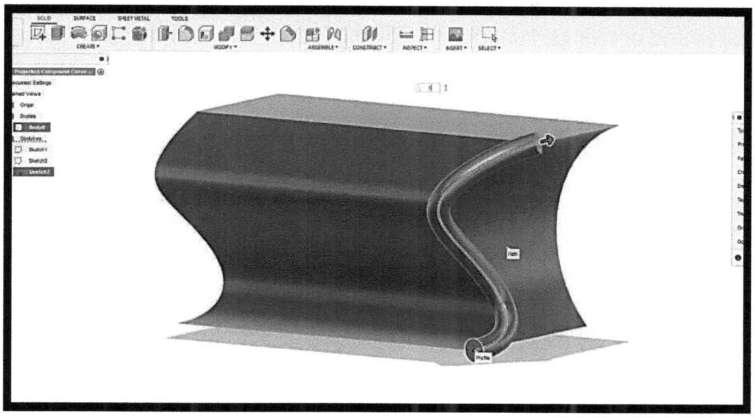

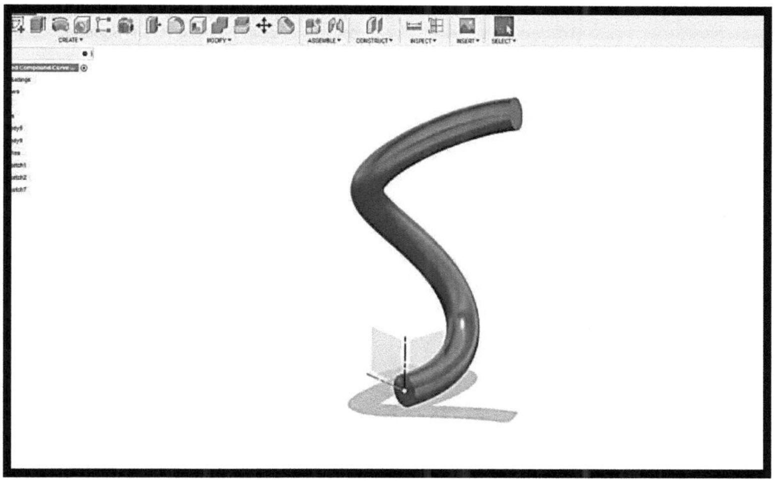

Creating a Curve by Projecting Intersecting Geometries

1. Navigate to the Design workspace and click the Sketch contextual tab. From there, choose **Create > Project/Include > Intersection Curve**.
2. Pick a sketch curve to use for the projection.
3. Choose the items that you want to intersect with.
4. To continue, either click **OK** or press **Enter**.

Objects to intersect on

You have the option of intersecting on workplaces, curves, surfaces, or faces when you use this tool.

Editing a Feature and its Sketch

By utilizing the Timeline, Fusion 360 gives you the ability to alter the characteristics of a model at any moment throughout the design process, regardless of whether the design is being changed or revised. A list of all of the features and drawings, including building geometries that have been developed for a model is shown in the Timeline.

The following is an explanation of the process for modifying a feature as well as a sketch:

1. In the Timeline, choose the feature that needs to be modified. There is a menu for shortcuts that shows.

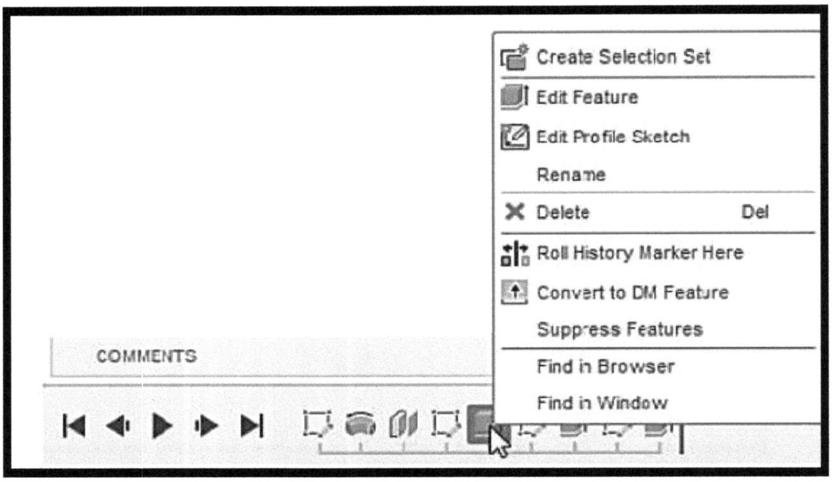

2. To make changes to the feature's configuration settings, use the shortcut menu and choose the "**Edit Feature**" option. In the space reserved for graphics, the appropriate dialogue box for the feature that was chosen is displayed. Take note that to modify the drawing of a feature, you will need to choose the **Edit Profile Sketch** tool from the shortcut menu that will show when you right-click on the feature. When you do this, the drawing of the chosen feature will become active, and you will be able to use the tools for sketching to edit or alter the sketch.
3. Enter new values into the dialog box to change the settings of the features to meet your needs, and then save your changes.
4. Once you have finished customizing the feature's settings, choose the OK button located in the dialog box. It is important to keep in mind that if you need to change the sketch of the feature, you will need to choose the **FINISH SKETCH** tool from the SKETCH contextual tab of the Toolbar to complete the editing process.

An individual drawing may also be edited in Fusion 360, which is a helpful tip. To do this, right-click on the drawing that needs to be altered in the Timeline, and when the shortcut menu displays, choose the Edit Sketch tool from the list of available options.

Editing the Sketching Plane of a Sketch

A sketch's drawing plane may also be edited or redefined after it has been created. To do this, right-click on the drawing whose sketching plane you want to modify and choose "**Edit Sketching Plane.**" There is a menu for shortcuts that shows. Select the **Redefine Sketch Plane** tool from this menu to get started. A dialogue window labeled REDEFINE SKETCH PLANE is shown.

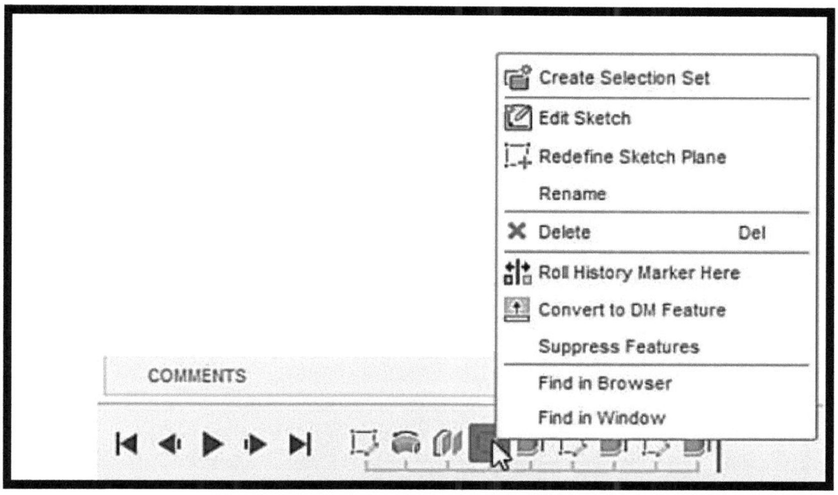

The new sketching plane of the drawing may be changed in the graphics area by selecting a new plane or a planar face as the new sketching plane, and then clicking the **OK** button in the dialog box. The sketching plane of the drawing is either redefined or altered such that it corresponds to the recently chosen planar face or plane. In the graphics section, there is also a shift in both the orientation of the drawing and the feature that is linked with it.

Applying Physical Materials Properties

In Fusion 360, you may create new materials, alter existing ones, and apply them to components and bodies with the use of the Physical Material, Appearance, and Manage Materials commands.

- Physical Material
- Appearance
- Manage Materials

Physical Material

You can add color and engineering qualities to components and bodies with the use of the Physical Material command. The component or body will have the default physical material applied to it whenever you build or import it into the game. Other types of geometry, such as building geometry, drawings, and face geometry, do not contain any actual materials. Within the Preferences window, you have the option of selecting a distinct default physical substance. You may use the drag-and-drop method to apply a physical material by dragging it from the dialog onto a component or body.

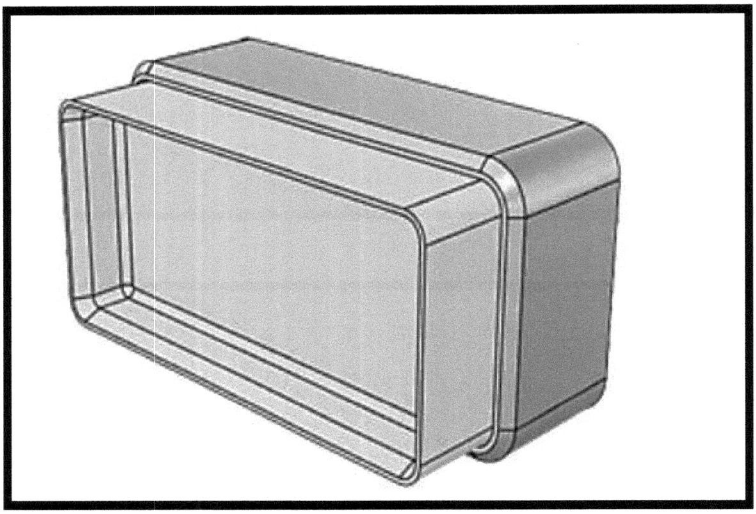

Appearance

You can give components, bodies, and faces color via the use of the Appearance command. The color of a component's body, face, or facet will, by default, be inherited from the underlying physical material. Appearances have precedence over the color that the actual substance has allocated to them and only apply to the occurrence that was chosen. The technical qualities of the material are unaffected by its outward appearance. To apply an appearance, just drag it from the dialog box onto the component, the body, or the face you want to change.

Manage Materials

You can handle the physical materials that are being utilized in your design by using the Manage Materials command. The color as well as the technical qualities of bodies and components are influenced by the materials that make them up. You may move the physical material from the dialog into the body or component of the canvas by dragging it there.

Modify physical materials in a design

1. Navigate to the **Design** menu and choose **Modify > Physical Material** from the toolbar. The dialogue box for the Physical Material appears.
2. In the browser or on the canvas, choose the components, bodies, or faces that you want to change.
3. **Look in one of the following areas for the actual substance you wish to utilize and locate it there:**
    a. **In This Design**: Any tangible components that have already been included in your design.
    b. **Library**: Physical materials that are not yet used in your design but that appear in the Fusion 360 Material Library, the Fusion 360 Additive Material Library, the Fusion 360 Nonlinear Material Library, or your **Favorites library**. These libraries may be accessed using the Fusion 360 app.
4. Select the look by clicking and dragging it inside the browser or canvas, and then dropping it on top of the components, bodies, or faces there. The new look is reflected in the components, bodies, or faces that make up the canvas.
5. Repeat steps 2-4 to provide alternate looks to the various bodies, faces, and components of the character.
6. Click the **Close** button.

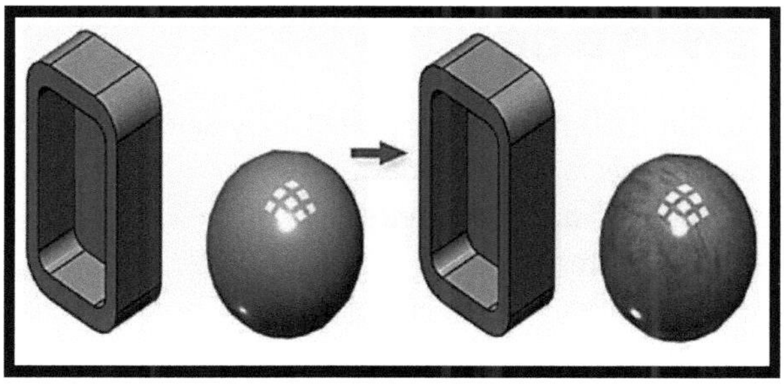

Modify appearances in a design

Applying color to components, bodies, and faces in a Fusion 360 design may be done with the use of the Appearance command.

1. **In the toolbar, choose the following:**
    a. **Design > Modify > Appearance**
    b. **Render > Setup > Appearance**
    c. **Animation > Transform > Appearance**
2. The Appearance dialog is brought up.
3. In the dialogue box, go to the Apply To section and pick the types of objects to **which you would want to apply an appearance:**
    a. Bodies/Components
    b. Faces
    c. All Storyboards
    d. Current Storyboard
4. Choose the components, bodies, or faces that need to be modified in the browser or on the canvas.
5. Navigate to the area of this page that corresponds to the look that you would want to utilize.
    a. **In This Design**: Appearances that are now being used in the design that you have created.
    b. **Library**: Appearances that are not yet used in your design but that appear in the Fusion 360 Appearances library, My Appearances library, or your Favorites library. These libraries may be accessed via the Appearances tab in the Fusion 360 interface.
6. Drag and drop the appearance on top of the components, bodies, or faces in the browser or canvas by clicking and dragging the appearance.
7. The new look is reflected in the components, bodies, or faces that make up the canvas.
8. Repeat steps 2-5 to provide varied looks to the various bodies, faces, and components of the character.
9. Click **Close**.

Tips

- To alter the look of the design's default component in the Browser, modify the default appearance by dragging and dropping an appearance onto the component.
- In the Material area of the Preferences dialog, you can alter the default look that is applied to bodies when new designs are created.

Manage materials in a design

1. On the toolbar, go to the Tools menu and choose Utility before selecting Manage Materials. The Material Browser dialog appears in the window.
2. Under the tab titled "**Physical" or "Appearance**,":
    a. Look for a certain material.
    b. Inside the "**Home**" area, browse one of the libraries and choose a piece of content from within it.

c. You have the option to add a particular piece of content to either your Favorites or a custom library.
d. In a library where reading is not permitted, you may examine the chosen item's identity, appearance, and physical details.
e. You may see and change the Identity, Appearance, and Physical information of a particular piece of content that is stored in either your Favorites or a custom library.
f. You may open a custom library, create one, or delete one.
g. Create or remove a custom material category.
h. Create a brand-new substance.
i. Duplicate an existing material.
j. Either open or shut the popup for the Asset Browser.

3. To put your changes into effect, click the **Apply** button.
4. When you are finished, click the **OK** button to end the Material Browser window.

Physical Material reference

You can assign both visible and physical material to bodies or components via the use of the physical material feature.

Design > **Modify** > **Physical Material**

To the appropriate components or bodies, assign the physical materials and visual materials. Gather resources from several different libraries.

- **Library**: This presents a list of the available resources for the chosen library.
- **Library drop-down**: Make your selection from the available libraries to apply resources by using the menu that drops down. There are a total of three choices open to you: the Favorites list, the Fusion 360 Material Library, and the Legacy Material Library.

Appearance reference

The hue of the bodies, components, and faces is determined by the appearance. Appearances take precedence over the color that is derived from the substance itself.

Design > **Modify** > **Appearance**

Modify the appearance of the materials that are already incorporated into your design. Appearances take precedence over the color that is derived from the substance itself.

The aesthetic qualities have no impact on the engineering properties.

- **Apply To**: Choose this option if you want to alter the look of the whole body or only the face of the component.
- **In This Design:** Provides a list of the materials that are being used in the current design.

Move your cursor over the picture to see the product's name and a brief description of it.

- **Library**: The drop-down menu may be used to pick a library that will be applied to the requested content to customize how it appears.
- **Show downloadable materials**: If you check this option, the items that are accessible for download will be shown. If you wish to get the content that you want, click the **Download Material** button.
- **Cancel all Download**: When the Show Downloadable Materials toggle is turned on, it will be available. Clicking this button will halt any downloads that are currently taking place.

Customize materials in the Generative Design workspace

Within the Material Browser window, you will see the option to create a new material. You are unable to make any additions, deletions, or edits to the content that is included inside the Fusion 360 Material libraries since they are read-only. Only the Favorites library allows you to alter the attributes of the various materials. After you have produced a new item for the content in your Favorites library, you will be able to add it to any user-defined library that you have access to.

Create a new material

1. Select the **Materials** tab on the Define menu, and then select **Manage Physical Materials**. The Material Browser dialog box is brought into view.
2. If you want to add anything new to the Favorites collection, you may do it in one of three distinct methods.

Pick the approach that works the best for your circumstances

- Search the Fusion 360 Material Library or a user-defined library for an existing material that you may use as a model for your new material. You can also utilize a user-defined library. There is a pencil and an arrow icon that displays at the right end of the line whenever the cursor is over a piece of library content. If you click on this icon, the item will be added to the Favorites library, and its characteristics will be shown so that you may alter them.
- In the Material Browser, locate the New Material button in the bottom left corner and then pick the **Create New Material** option. A dialog box labeled Select Material Browser displays.

  Then:

  a. Navigate to the material you want to utilize as a model for your new material, and then double-click on it. The window for the Material Browser is updated with the copied physical characteristics (which may be underneath the currently displayed dialog). The default parameters for both the description and the look are likewise preset.
  b. Exit the Select Material Browser box by clicking the "**X**" located in the top right corner of the window. The Material Browser has been updated to make the newly added material characteristics fully editable and accessible.

- Find an existing piece of content in the Favorites collection that you would want to utilize as a model for your new piece of content, and then click on it once. Even though there isn't any visible sign right now, the material has been chosen.

Then:

c. In the Material Browser window, locate the New Material button in the bottom left corner. From the drop-down menu, pick Duplicate Selected Material. You also have the option to right-click the content you want to copy and pick the Duplicate option.
d. Position your mouse so that it is above the new material item, and then click the Edit button to show the attributes so that you may make changes to them.

3. **Within the editor, the material characteristics are separated into three different tabs for your convenience:**

- **Identity**: Within this tab, choose the sort of material that you are working with (Plastic, Metal, etc.) and add information that is descriptive as well as product-related about the material.
- **Appearance**: Within this page, you may specify characteristics that impact the produced appearance of the material. These include color, roughness, highlight parameter settings, and more.
- **Physical**: Within this tab, you are going to define the mechanical qualities, the fundamental thermal parameters, and the material's strength.

4. To commit the modifications or additions to the property that you have made, click the Apply button.
5. To give the material a name that is entirely its own, right-click the material in the Name column (but not inside the editor itself), and choose Rename from the menu that appears. After entering the chosen name, hit the Enter key.
   Please take note that the material list has been reorganized so that it remains in alphabetical order. As a result, once you rename the material, it could shift position higher or lower in the list.
6. You have the option of deleting a material by right-clicking the item in the Name column, then selecting Delete from the context menu that appears. You can only remove items from the Favorites or user-defined libraries that you have access to.
7. If you want to add a piece of content to another library, you may do so by right-clicking the item in the Name column, selecting the Add fly-out menu, and then selecting the library you want to add it to. It is only possible to copy items into the Favorites or user-defined libraries.

Note: The default material units may be changed by selecting a new option from the drop-down menu labeled "**Material Unit Display**" in the **"Unit and Value Display"** group of the "Preferences" dialog. You can change the default units in some input fields by inserting alternative units after the value (such as psi or MPa). When support is present, the input is automatically translated to the standard unit of measurement for the material. You are unable to alter the default units in other circumstances, such as when dealing with nonlinear or temperature-dependent stress-strain data points. To specify the attributes of the material using the appropriate units for these inputs, you will need to adjust the options of the software.

Create a new material library

The resources in the libraries of Fusion 360 cannot be edited, nor can new ones be added. You will need to use the custom libraries if you wish to add new materials or make changes to existing ones.

You can arrange items that are used often or share collections of materials with other people using a personal library.

1. Select the **Materials** tab on the **Define** menu, and then select **Manage Physical Materials.** The Material Browser dialog box is brought into view.
2. In the Material Browser dialog, locate the **library** button in the bottom left corner and then pick the **Create New Library** option.
3. In the Create Library dialog, locate the File name area and provide a name for the new library you are creating.
4. Locate the folder in which you want to save the new file for the material library.
5. To build the library, click the **Save** button.

The new, bare-bones material library replaces the previous one as the active library. Please be aware that you cannot directly generate new items inside a user-defined library. The Favorites library is the place where all fresh content is generated. Nevertheless, you are free to include the contents of any other library in your user-defined libraries.

Remove a user-defined library from the Material Browser

1. Select the **Materials** tab on the Define menu, and then select **Manage Physical Materials**. The Material Browser dialog box is brought into view.
2. Choose the material library you wish to get rid of from the list of material libraries by using the tree.
3. In the Material Browser window, locate the library button in the bottom left corner, and then pick the Remove Library option.

Note that removing the library does not result in the**.adsklib** file being removed from your computer. Simply removing it from the Material Browser is all that this does. If you decide you no longer need the library file, you may remove it manually. If you did not delete the library, you will need to use the following procedure to open it again.

Copy or reopen an existing user-defined library

Make use of this process to accomplish any of the two objectives that follow:

- To transfer a personalized content collection from one computer to another
- To reopen a library that has been developed earlier but was deleted from the Material Browser.

1. Check to see that a copy of the library is saved on your computer.
2. Navigate to the "**Define**" tab and choose "**Materials**" before selecting "**Manage Physical Materials.**"
3. In the bottom left corner of the Material Browser box, click the library button, and then pick the **Open Existing Library** option.
4. Select the file after navigating to the folder in which it is stored and click on it.

5. Click **Open**.

Manage materials in the Generative Design workspace

The selection of suitable materials is an essential component of successful generative research since it plays a role in determining the ultimate forms that outputs will take. You have the option, within your research, of associating certain materials with particular manufacturing processes; alternatively, you might design many studies based on the same generative model but associate distinctive materials with each of those studies. You have access to a variety of assets inside the Fusion 360 library. You may also alter these materials to build your materials and then utilize those materials for your research if you so want.

Use the **Manage Physical Materials** command if you need to manage or customize materials. The **Materials** panel of the **Generative Design** toolbar is where you'll find the option to access it. Make use of the **Material Browser** window to manage material libraries, alter material parameters, or build a material that is unique to your needs. You can copy things from the Fusion 360 Material Library and paste them into the Favorites folder on your computer. After that, you may establish your personalized material attributes by editing the materials that are stored under the Favorites folder. You also can modify any of the Appearance factors, including Color, Reflectance, Translucency, and many more. Note that the Fusion 360 Materials Library cannot have its properties edited since it is protected by a password (**read-only**).

Select materials in the Generative Design workspace

1. Navigate to the "**Materials**" tab of the "**Define**" tab. Click "**Study Materials.**" The Study Materials dialogue box is brought into view.

Note that the Study Materials dialog may also be accessed through the Browser if you prefer that method. Use the context menu that appears when you right-click a study to access the Study Materials.

2. In the Methods section, expand the list of available production methods, and then choose the desired manufacturing technique from the corresponding drop-down menu.

Note that the list of all production processes that have been specified may be found in your study.

3. Select the material library you want to use from the drop-down list labeled Library. **You have the option to choose from the following libraries:**
    - **Fusion 360 Material Library**. Only materials that are part of the Fusion 360 Material Library will be shown when you open this window.
    - **Fusion 360 Additive Material Library** (default library). Only materials that are part of the Fusion 360 Additive Material Library are shown when you open this window.
    - **Fusion 360 Nonlinear Material Library**. Only materials that are part of the Fusion 360 Nonlinear Material Library are shown when you open this window.
    - **Favorites**. Only the content that has been added to the Favorites library will be shown in this box.

Hint: You may make a resource a favorite of yours by right-clicking the resource in question inside one of the other libraries and selecting "**Add to Favorites**" from the context menu.

4. From the Library area, choose a piece of content, and then drag it over to the **In This Study** section.

- You also have the option to add a material to a method by right-clicking on the material and selecting **Add to Method** or **Add to All Methods** from the context menu.

5. Click the **Close** button.

Hint: The list of items may be modified or reviewed in the browser. Expand the Manufacturing node, then move the cursor over the Materials node for the technique that is now chosen, and then click.

Calculating Mass Properties

After you have assigned all of the necessary material qualities to a model, you may proceed to determine its mass properties such as its volume and mass. To do this, right-click on the name of the design file in the **BROWSER**, and once the shortcut menu opens, choose the Properties tool from the list of options that display.

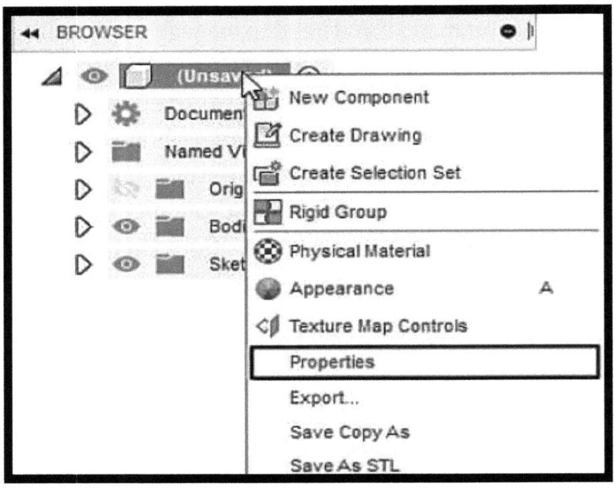

The **PROPERTIES** dialog box appears in the graphics area and displays the properties of the model. These properties include the area of the model, its mass, its volume, the dimensions of the bounding box, the center of mass, the moment of inertia at the center of mass, and the moment of inertia at the origin. You may also use the button labeled "**Copy to Clipboard**" which is located in the **PROPERTIES** dialog box to copy the results to the clipboard and then paste them into the necessary file.

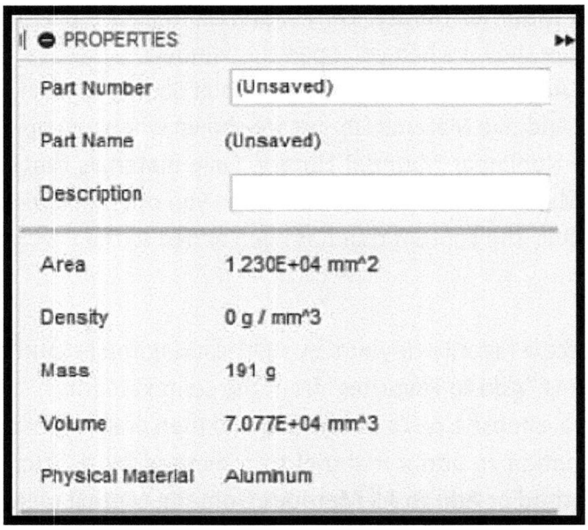

NOTE: If you right-click on the name of the design file, you will be able to bring up the Characteristics dialog box, which will display the mass properties of the whole design. This means that if the currently active design file contains multiple components or bodies, then the **PROPERTIES** dialog box will display the overall properties of the design by combining the properties of all of the components and bodies that are available in the active design file. If the design file does not have multiple components or bodies, then the **PROPERTIES** dialog box will display the properties of the entire design. To see the properties of the individual components or bodies, right-click on the Body or Component in the BROWSER, and then choose the Properties tool from the shortcut menu that appears. This will reveal the properties of each component or body. It is important to take note that the BROWSER has a node titled "Bodies" that lists all of the design file's bodies.

Measuring the Distance between Objects

Using the Measure tool in Fusion 360, you may determine the distance, angle, area, and arc radius of a chosen item or object, as well as a variety of other parameters. To do this, first, open the **INSPECT** drop-down menu located in the TOOLS tab of the Toolbar, and then choose the Measure tool from the menu that appears. You also have the option of pressing the letter "**I**" on your keyboard. The dialog window labeled MEASURE will now display. The next sub-topics up for discussion is the MEASURE dialog box's available choices.

Selection Filter

Within the Selection Filter part of the dialog box, the button labeled Select Face/Edge/Vertex is enabled by default. As a direct consequence of this, you will have the ability to pick a face, an edge, or a vertex of a model as the object for which its measurement data will be shown. When determining the distance between numerous objects (faces, edges, or vertices), you also have the option to choose many items at once. You can pick one or more bodies by clicking the Select Body button, and you can select one or more components to measure the distance values by clicking the Select Component button. Precision to specify the accuracy of the measurement results, which refers to the number of digits that come after the decimal point, utilize the Precision drop-down list that is located in the dialog box.

Secondary Units

Choosing a secondary unit of measurement may be done with the help of the drop-down list labeled Secondary Units.

Restart Selection

The button labeled "**Restart Selection**" may be used to either clear the current selection set or restart the selection process.
Show Snap Points: When the Show Snap Points checkbox is selected, the snap points of an object are shown whenever the mouse is moved over a face, edge, or vertex of the object. In addition, you have the option of selecting a snap point to show the information associated with it in the MEASURE dialog box. It is

important to keep in mind that the Select Face/Edge/Vertex button in the Selection Filter portion of the dialog box must be active for this check box to become visible.

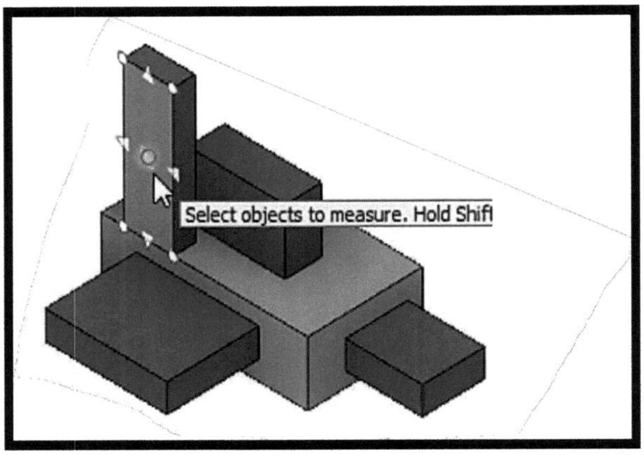

Select the object (face/edge/vertex, body, or component) in the graphics area after you have chosen the proper selection filter and precision in the dialog box. The relevant results of the item that was chosen are shown in the area labeled "**Selection 1**" in the dialog box. The results of the measurements taken on a cylinder face are shown here in this image.

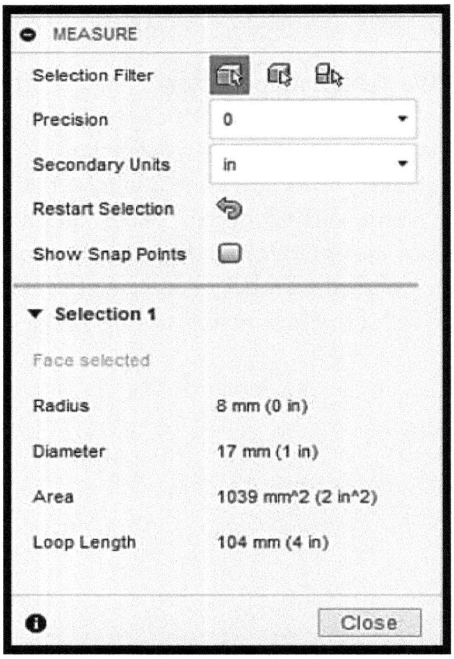

When you choose two items in the graphics area, distance values between those objects will display in the Results rollout of the dialog box as well as in the graphics area itself. This occurs regardless of whether or not you select the objects. In addition to this, the measurement values of each item are shown in the dialog box's Selection 1 and Selection 2 rollouts respectively.

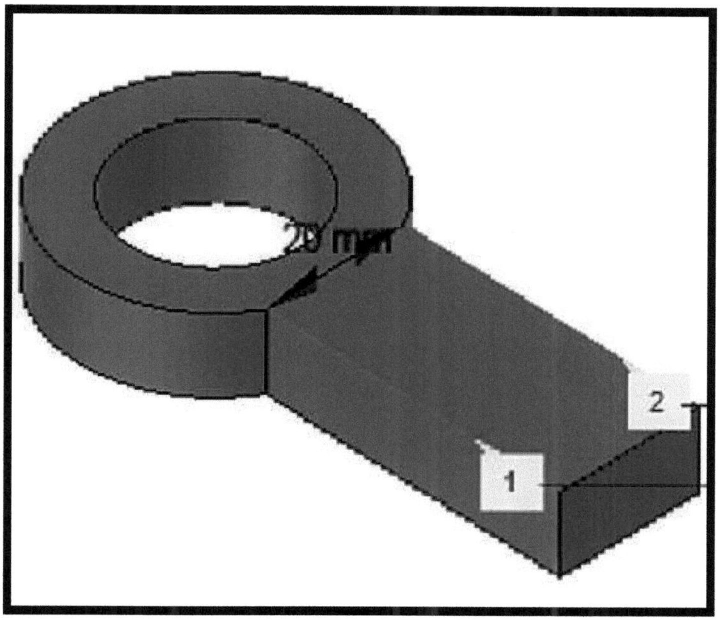

Questions

1. The options in the ________ drop-down list of the EXTRUDE dialog box are used for defining the start condition of extrusion.
2. Which option of the operation drop-down list is used for extruding the profile by removing material from the model?
3. Which option of the operation drop-down list is used for extruding the profile by adding material and merging a feature with the existing features of the model?
4. Which tool is used to project the edges of the existing features onto the currently active sketching plane?
5. Which option of the Start drop-down list in the EXTRUDE dialog box is used for selecting a face, a plane, or a vertex as the start condition of extrusion?
6. Which option of the Extent drop-down list in the EXTRUDE dialog box is used for defining the termination of the extrusion by selecting a face, a plane, a vertex, or a body?
7. The tool used to apply physical material properties such as density, elastic modulus, and tensile strength to a model is known as?

CHAPTER 8

ADVANCED MODELING - II

Creating a Sweep Feature

Adding or deleting material from a profile while sweeping it along a path result in the creation of a sweep feature. The first picture displays a path along with a profile. The subsequent sweep feature that was formed by sweeping the profile along the path is seen in the second picture. Adding more material results in the creation of the sweep feature shown in this picture.

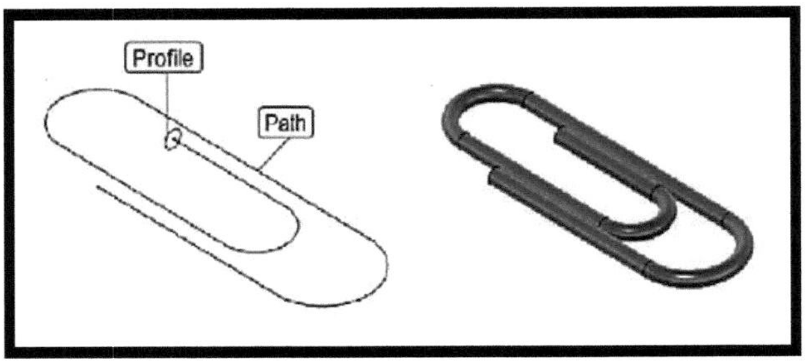

The preceding figures make it abundantly clear that to generate a sweep feature, you first need to generate a profile and a path, with the intention that the profile will then follow the path and generate the sweep feature. You need to determine the cross-section of the feature that will be developed before you can construct a profile for it. To produce a path, it is necessary to determine the path taken by the profile throughout the production of the feature. Using the Sweep tool, which can be found in the **CREATE** drop-down menu of the SOLID tab in the Toolbar, you may generate a sweep feature in Fusion 360.

It is important to keep in mind that to create a sweep feature, you will need to guarantee the following:

1. The drawing must be closed to qualify as a profile. You also have the option of choosing a particular face of a model to serve as the profile.
2. The path may be either an open or a closed sketch, and it can be composed of a collection of sketched entities that are linked from end to end, a curve, or a set of model edges.
3. For more accurate results, the point of origin of the path ought to be such that it intersects the plane of the profile.
4. Neither the profile nor the path nor the resulting sweep feature may cross itself in any way. Following the creation of the path and the profile, choose the Sweep tool from the **CREATE** drop-down menu located in the SOLID tab of the Toolbar. A dialog window labeled **SWEEP** will now display.

Type

Within the SWEEP dialog box, the Kind drop-down list is where the option to pick the type of sweep feature that will be produced can be found. In this particular drop-down list, the option to Use a Single Path is chosen by default. As a consequence of this, you can produce a sweep feature by moving the profile in a sweeping motion down the path.

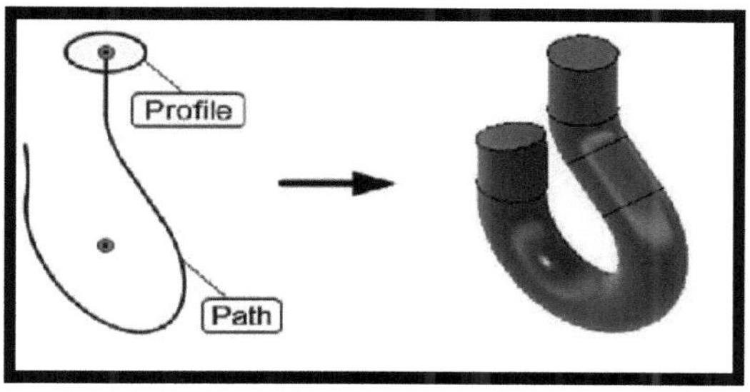

By sweeping the profile along the path while a guide rail controls the feature's size and orientation, the **Path + Guide Rail** option may be used to create a sweep feature. This is accomplished by sweeping the profile down the path.

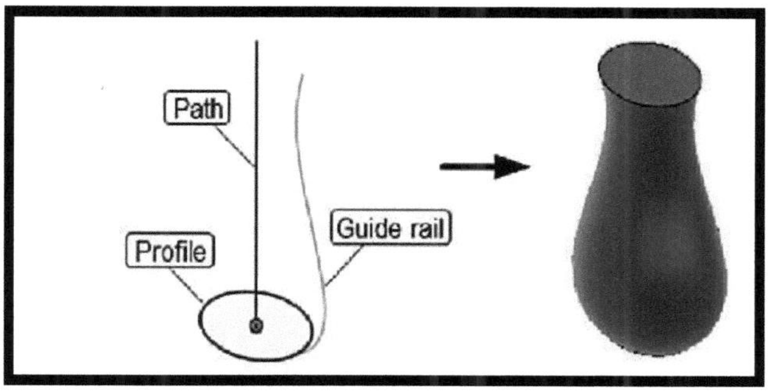

Using the **Path + Guide** Surface option, one may create a sweep feature by sweeping the profile along the path while having the orientation directed by a guide surface. This option is used to create a feature.

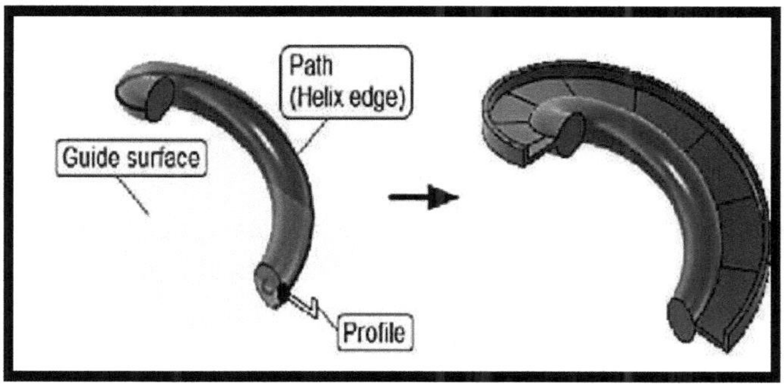

Creating a Sweep Feature with a Single Path

1. Select the **CREATE** option from the drop-down menu located in the SOLID tab of the Toolbar. Next, select the Sweep tool from the available options. The SWEEP dialog box is brought into view.

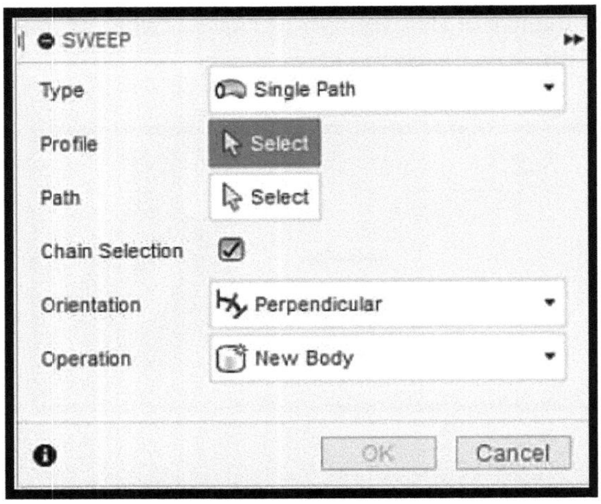

2. Check the box next to the Type drop-down menu in the dialog box and make sure that the Single Path option is chosen there.
   Profile: The Profile selection option in the dialog box is active by default when it is first opened. As a direct consequence of this, you will have the ability to pick the profile of a closed drawing or a face inside the graphics area.
3. Within the graphics section, go to the sweep tool and choose a closed profile to use.

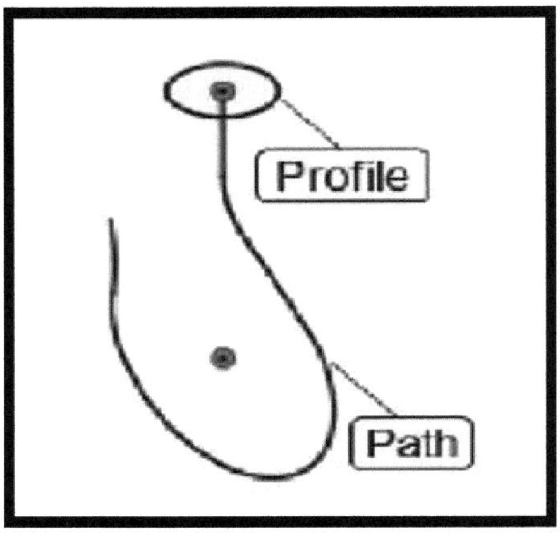

   Chain Selection: The Chain Selection check box in the dialog box is selected by default when it is first opened. As a consequence of this, when one entity of a path made up of many segments (entities) is picked, all of the adjacent entities, regardless of whether they are closed or open loops, of the selected entity, are also automatically selected.
4. In the dialog box, you need to make sure that the check box labeled "**Chain Selection**" is selected.
   Path: This is the name of the option inside the selection menu that is used to choose a path. You have the option of selecting closed or opened sketch entities, edges, or curves that are joined end to end. Take into account that to get better results, the beginning point of the path must intersect with the plane of the profile.
5. Select a path in the graphics area after clicking the **Path selection** option in the dialog box and then make your pick. In the graphics section, there is a sneak peek of the sweep function that emerges.

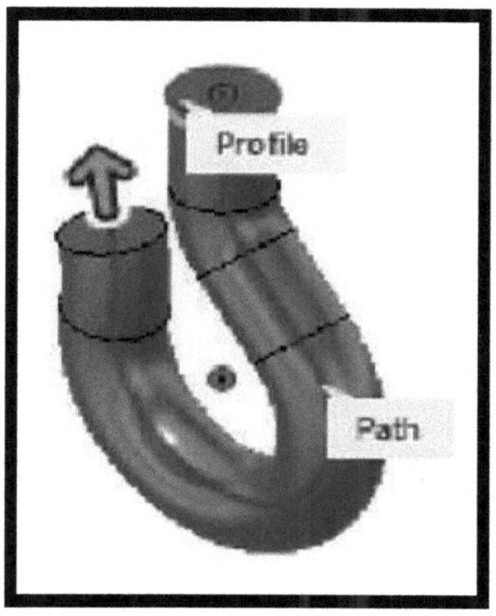

Distance: The number 1 is entered by default in the field designated for "Distance" on the dialog box. Because of this, the pro-file moves throughout the whole path in a continuous motion. By entering the needed percentage number in the Distance area (where it must be larger than 0 and less than 1), you can decide when the sweep function will come to an end. The value of the percentage is determined relative to the entire distance traveled along the course that was chosen. For instance, a percentage value of 1 will cause the profile to be swept along the whole length of the path, but a percentage value of 0.5 will only cause the profile to be swept along half of the length of the path. Additionally, you may dynamically specify the value by dragging the arrow that shows in the preview of the feature.

6. Within the dialog box's Distance field, enter the needed number for the percentage of distance. If you want the profile to be swept throughout the whole length of the path, you need to make sure that the Distance field has the value 1 typed into it. Taper Angle: The Taper Angle field of the dialog box has a default value of 0 degrees in it, which indicates that the taper angle is not defined. As a direct consequence of this, there is no tapering present in the resulting sweep feature. This is the field in which you should put the desired taper angle. The picture below displays a glimpse of the sweep feature with the taper angle set to a value of -2.5 degrees. You will need to input a negative number for the taper angle if you want to change the direction of the taper from the outside to the interior side of the profile or vice versa. It is important to take note that the Taper Angle field becomes accessible in the dialog box when the Perpendicular option in the dialog box's Orientation drop-down list is chosen.

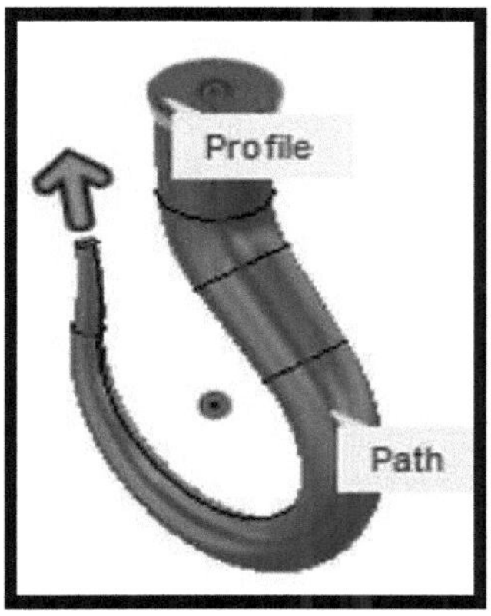

7. In the area labeled "**Taper Angle**," provide the needed value for the taper angle. Make sure that o degrees are placed into this area so that you may design a sweep feature that does not have any tapering.

Twist Angle: The Twist Angle field of the dialog box has an angle of 0 degrees typed into it by default. As a direct consequence of this, the sweep feature that was produced does not include any twisting. To twist the profile along the path, you may twist it by entering the needed twist angle in this box. The first picture displays a preview of a sweep feature that has an angle of twist that is 0 degrees, and the second picture shows a preview of a sweep feature that has an angle of twist that is 90 degrees. Take note that the Twist Angle field becomes accessible in the dialog box when the Perpendicular option in the Orientation drop-down list is chosen in the dialog box.

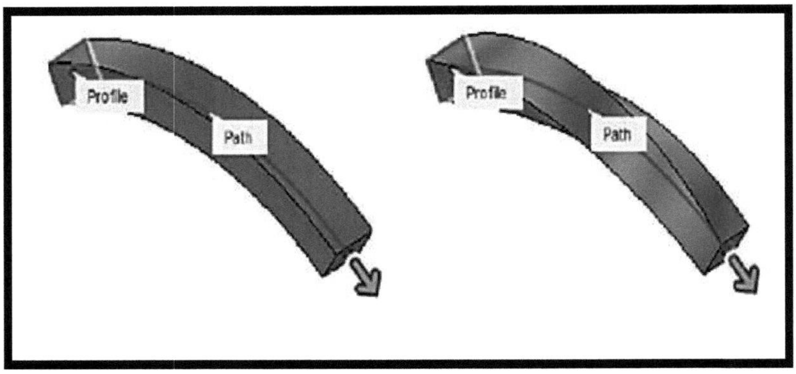

8. Within the dialog box's **Twist Angle field**, enter the necessary twist angle that you want to use. Make sure that you provide 0 degrees into this area if you do not want the ensuing sweep feature to have any twisting. This will allow you to produce no twisting at all.
   Orientation: When you first open the dialog box, the Orientation drop-down list will have the Perpendicular option chosen by default. As a consequence of this, the consequent sweep feature is produced by ensuring that the profile of the feature is maintained in a direction that is perpendicular to the path. If you choose the Parallel option from this drop-down selection, the subsequent sweep feature will be produced with the profile of the sweep feature maintained such that it is parallel to the drawing plane of the profile.
9. In the Orientation drop-down list of the dialog box, choose the option that corresponds to your needs (either Perpendicular or Parallel).
10. In the "**Operation**" drop-down list of the dialog box, choose the option that corresponds to your needs.
11. In the dialog box, choose the **OK** button and click it. The sweep function is triggered when the profile is dragged along the path in a sweeping motion.

Creating a Sweep Feature with Path and Guide Rail

1. Select the **CREATE** option from the drop-down menu located in the SOLID tab of the Toolbar. Next, select the Sweep tool from the available options. A dialog window labeled **SWEEP** will now display.
2. In the Type drop-down list of the dialog box, choose the **Path + Guide Rail** option. The dialog box displays the choices that may be made to create a sweep feature by using the path and guide rail.

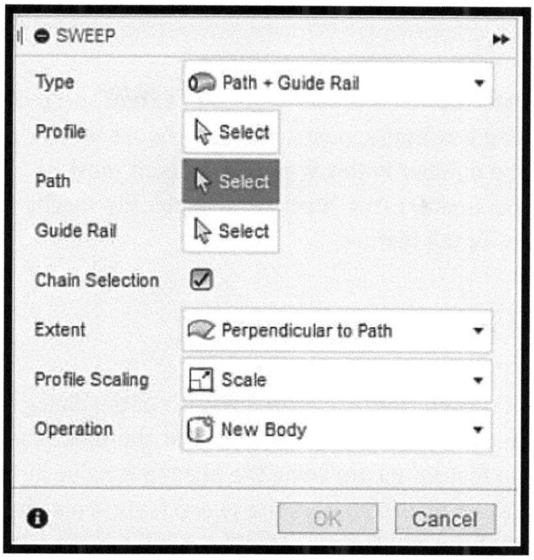

NOTE: After choosing the Path + Guide Rail option in the drop-down menu, the dialog box that appears has some of the same choices as those that were previously mentioned.

3. Within the graphics section, go to the sweep tool and choose a closed profile to use.

4. In the dialog box, pick the path of the sweep feature by clicking on the option labeled **"Path selection**," and then making your selection.

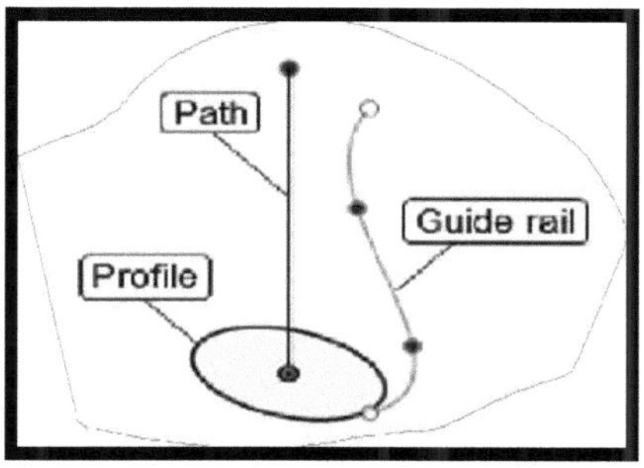

Guide Rail: The Guide Rail selection option is used to choose a guide rail for managing the size and orientation of the sweep feature. This may be done by choosing the appropriate rail from the drop-down menu. For optimal results, make a note that the beginning point of the guide rail must be located at an intersection with the plane of the profile.

5. Select the guide rail for the sweep function by clicking on the Guide Rail selection option in the dialog box, and then selecting the guide rail. A sneak peek of the sweep function is shown here.

Extent: The Extent drop-down list in the dialog box has the Perpendicular to Path option chosen by default. This may be changed by selecting a different option. Consequently, the subsequent sweep feature is produced by maintaining the feature's profile in a perpendicular relationship to the path.

The profile of the resulting sweep feature does not retain a perpendicular connection to the path when the Full Extents option from this drop-down list is selected, and it extends along the whole of the path or the guide rail.

6. In the "**Extent**" drop-down list of the dialog box, choose the option that corresponds to your needs.

Distance

When the "**Perpendicular to Path**" option is chosen from the "**Extent**" drop-down list, the "**Distance**" field becomes accessible in the dialog box that appears. You can choose when the sweep feature will end by entering the needed percentage number in this area. The amount must be larger than 0 and less than 1, and it must fall within those parameters. You may also dynamically specify the % value by dragging the arrow that shows in the preview of the feature.

Path Distance and Guide Rail Distance

When the Full Extents option is chosen from the drop-down list of the dialog box's Extent option, the Path Distance and Guide Rail Distance fields become accessible in the dialog box. These fields are used to designate the end of the sweep feature by providing the needed % value in terms of the path length and guide rail length. This value must be entered before the sweep feature may be terminated.

7. In the corresponding field(s) of the dialog box, enter the needed percentage number to determine the termination of the sweep function, or accept the default values. Alternatively, you may click the "Accept Defaults" button.

Profile Scaling

The size and direction of the sweep feature may be controlled by using the choices found in the drop-down list of the dialog box titled **"Profile Scaling.**" These options are depending on the guide rail that has been chosen. When generating a sweep feature, the Scale option is used to scale the profile (section) of the feature in both the X and Y directions of the guide rail. This allows the feature to be created more precisely.

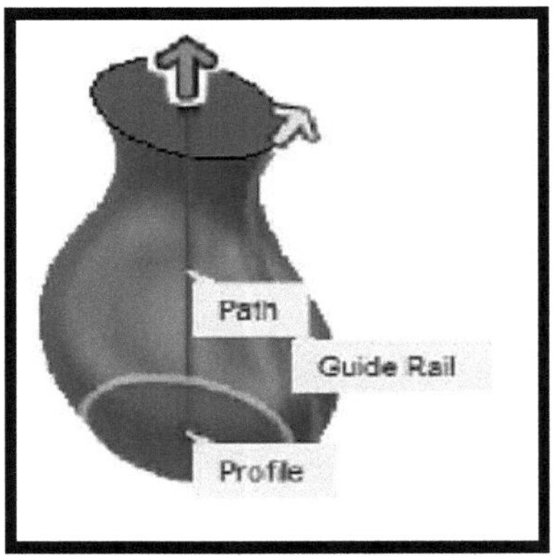

When designing a sweep feature, use the Stretch option to scale or stretch the profile (section) of the feature in the X direction of the guide rail alone. This is the only direction in which the option is applicable. When constructing a sweep feature, the **None** option is selected. This prevents the profile (section) of the feature from being scaled depending on the guide rail and ensures that the feature maintains the same parts down the path.

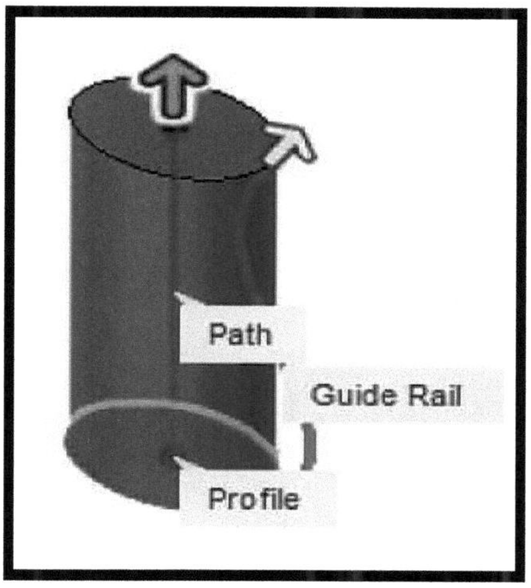

8. In the Profile Scaling drop-down list of the dialog box, choose the option that corresponds to your needs.
9. Choose the appropriate choice from the drop-down menu labeled "Operation" in the dialog box, and then proceed to click the OK button located inside the same dialog box. The sweep function is triggered when the profile is dragged along the path in a sweeping motion. The guide rail is responsible for controlling not just the size of the feature but also its direction.

Creating a Sweep Feature with Path and Guide Surface

1. Select the **CREATE** option from the drop-down menu located in the SOLID tab of the Toolbar. Next, select the Sweep tool from the available options. A dialog window labeled **SWEEP** will now display.
2. Make a selection in the Type drop-down list of the dialog box by choosing the Path + Guide Surface option. The dialog box displays the choices that may be made to generate a sweep feature by using the path and guide surface.

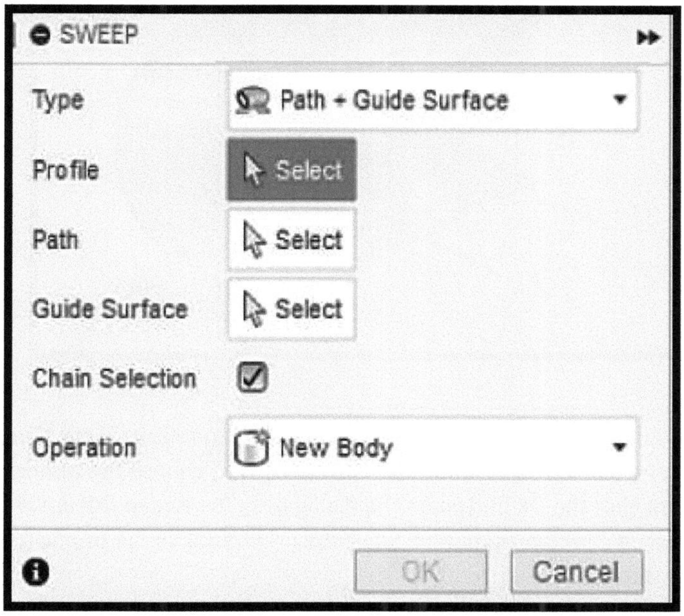

3. Take note that after choosing the Path + Guide Surface option, the majority of the choices that show in the dialog box are the same as those that were covered before in this section. 3. In the graphics section, choose a closed profile for the sweep feature.
4. In the dialog box, pick the path of the sweep feature by clicking on the option labeled "Path selection," and then making your selection.

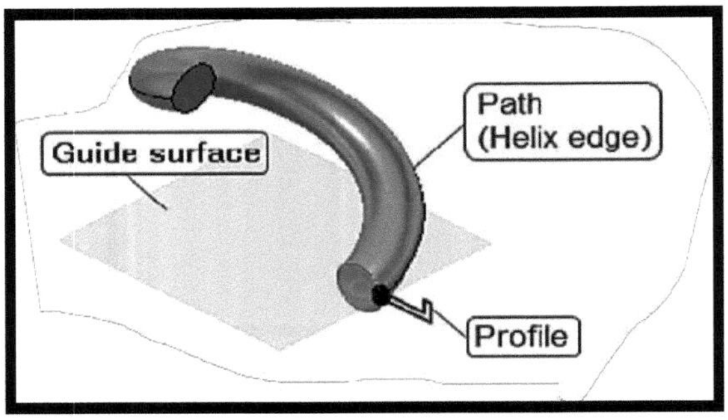

NOTE: The helical edge of a coil feature has been picked as the path for the creation of the sweep feature in the picture above.
Guide Surface: The Guide Surface selection option is used to pick a guide surface (a face or a plane) for directing the orientation of the profile while sweeping along the path. This may be accomplished by using the option to select a guide surface.
5. In the dialog box, pick the **Guide Surface selection** option and then select a face or a plane to use as the guide surface. A preview of the sweep feature is shown in the graphics area, with the orientation of the preview being determined by the guiding surface that was chosen.

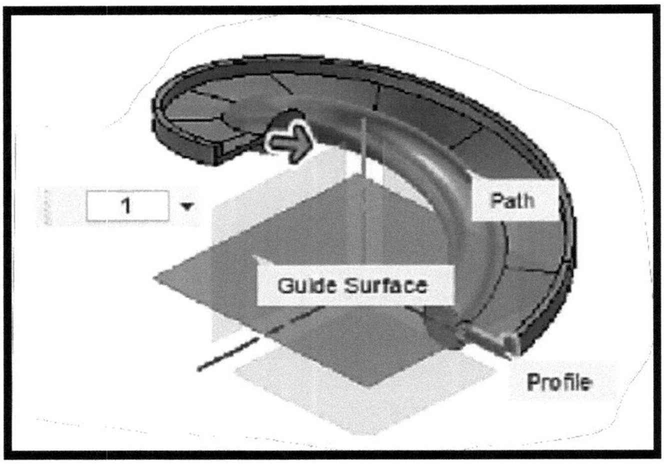

6. Go to the Distance field of the dialog box and enter the needed number for the percentage.
7. In the drop-down menu labeled "**Operation**" on the dialog box, choose the option that corresponds to what you need, and then click the OK button on the dialog box. The sweep feature is produced by moving the profile down the path in a sweeping motion, while the orientation of the profile is kept constant by the guide surface that is chosen.

Creating a Loft Feature

When two or more two profiles (sections) are lofted together in such a way that the cross-sectional form of the loft feature transitions from one profile to another, this results in the creation of a loft feature. The first picture displays two distinct profiles (parts) that were formed on separate planes and have a different distance between each other than what is seen between them. In the second picture, you can see the loft feature that was produced.

The preceding illustrations make it very clear that to generate a loft feature, one must first generate all of the sections that form the geometry of the feature. By selecting the Loft tool from the CREATE drop-down menu located in the SOLID tab of the Toolbar in Fusion 360, you will be able to add a loft feature to your model.

It is important to keep in mind that to create a loft feature, you will need to guarantee the following:

1. Before invoking the **Loft** tool, there must be a minimum of two and a maximum of two profiles in the graphics area that are either comparable or different from one another.
2. All of the profiles have to be deleted. You have the option of selecting closed profiles of drawings as well as faces.
3. Each profile has to be conceived in the form of a unique drawing.
4. The profiles and the lofted feature that results from them cannot self-intersect in any way.

You can create three distinct kinds of loft features in Fusion 360: ones with profiles, ones with profiles and guide rails, and ones with profiles and centerlines. Following this, we will go through the processes that may be used to create a variety of loft features.

Creating a Loft Feature with Profiles

After invoking the CREATE drop-down menu in the SOLID tab and clicking on the Loft tool, you will have successfully created a loft feature with profiles. A dialogue window labeled LOFT will now display.

Profiles

Within the dialog box, the Profiles selection option is the one that is turned on by default. As a direct consequence of this, the loft function gives you the option to pick closed profiles. When constructing a loft feature, you may choose to use two or more two closed profiles that are the same or different from one another. Following the selection of the profiles, a preview of the loft feature will display in the graphics area. This preview will include connection points that will link the profiles. Additionally, the names of the profiles that have been chosen are displayed in the Profiles section of the dialog box in the order in which they were selected.

NOTE: To construct the twist in a loft feature, just drag the connection points that show in the preview of the feature. These points appear in the loft feature. Within the Profiles section of the LOFT dialog box, three columns are labeled respectively as Profiles, Reorder, and End Condition.

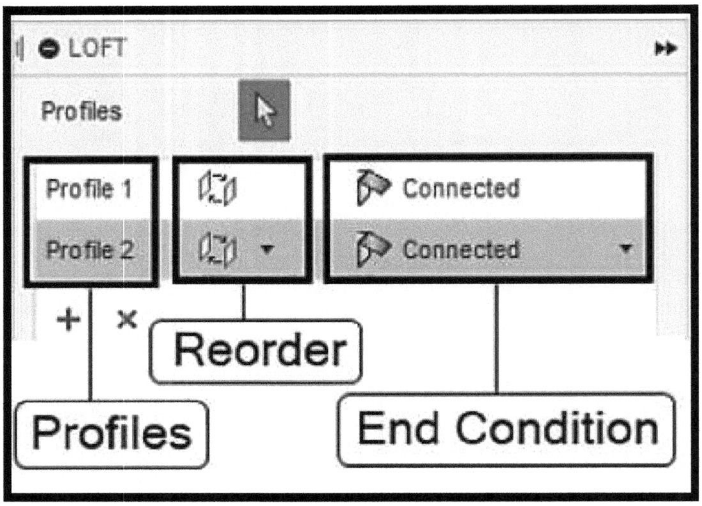

The Profiles column provides a list of profiles that are shown in the order in which they were chosen.

Reorder: Simply click on the "**Reorder**" column that corresponds to the profile that you want to move up or down in the list to do this. A list that can be selected from dropdown. To place your needed pro-file order, choose it from this list's drop-down menu (Profile 1, Profile 2 ... Profile n). The order in which the selected profile is shown is altered to correspond with the order that was chosen from the drop-down list. Final State of Affairs. You can govern the transition of a profile from one profile to another by defining the end condition for a profile in Fusion 360. To do this, click the cell in the End Condition column that is associated with the profile whose end condition is to be specified. The final condition of the chosen profile may be defined by selecting an option from a drop-down list that shows on the screen. It is important to note that the kind of geometry that is picked as the profile will determine the alternatives that are available in this drop-down list. The next section below will go through a few of the available choices.

Connected: The Connected option is used to ensure that the transition from one profile of the loft feature to the next is performed in a completely straight manner.

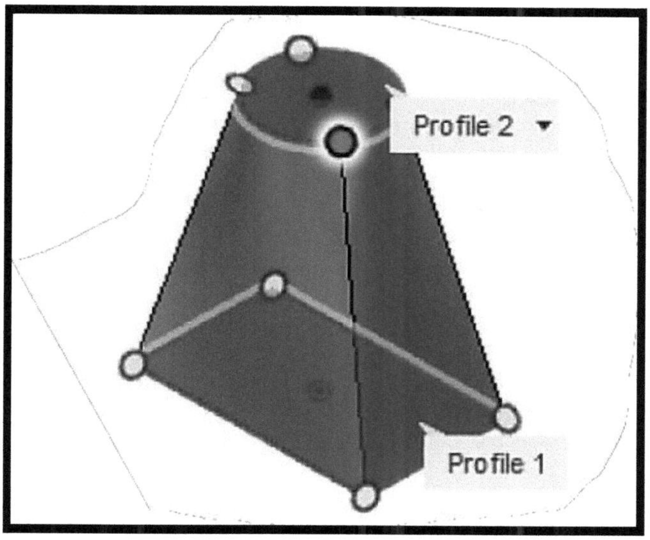

Direction: The Direction option allows the start angle of the transition from the chosen profile to be defined, as well as the degree to which the selected pro-influence files are exerted along the loft path. When you pick this option, the LOFT dialog box's bottom section is reorganized to include new fields labeled Takeoff Weight and Takeoff Angle. The amount of effect that the start angle transition has along the loft path may be defined by entering the desired value in the Takeoff Weight field. The initial angle of the transition is specified by the value entered in the Takeoff Angle box.

Tangent (G1): Use the Tangent (G1) option to define the G1 tangency condition for the loft profile. This option is found under the Tangent submenu. Please take note that this option will appear in the drop-down list only if the loft profile that you have chosen is a face of the model.

The Curvature (G2): This is used to establish the G2 curvature continuity requirement for the loft profile. Please take note that this option will appear in the drop-down list only if the loft profile that you have chosen is a face of the model.

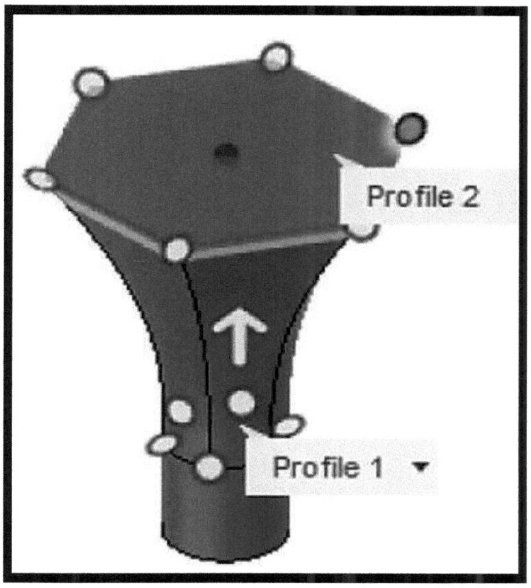

Sharp: You may define a sharp transition to a point profile by selecting the **Sharp** option from the drop-down menu. Take note that you will only have access to this option if the loft profile that you have chosen is a point.
Point Tangent: The Point Tangent option is used to define the tangency at a point and provides a dome shape transition. This option can be found under the Tangency menu. If the loft profile that you have chosen is a point, then you will have access to this option. It is important to take note that the Tangency Weight field displays at the bottom of the dialog box whenever the Point Tangent option is selected. You will be able to describe the tangency transition impact at this moment if you use this field.
Closed: By using the Closed check box while generating a loft feature, one may ensure that the beginning and ending profiles of the loft feature are connected, thus producing a loft feature that is considered to be closed.
Note: A minimum of three parts are necessary to build a closed loft feature. A total angle that is more than 120 degrees should exist between the beginning and ending segments of the line.

Tangent Edges

When the Merge button in the Tangent Edges portion of the dialog box is activated, the tangent edges of the resulting loft feature are combined into a single edge. When the Keep button is activated, the tangent edges of the loft feature that was produced do not blend.

Operation

The choices that appear in the drop-down list of the dialog box titled "**Operation**" are the same ones that were mentioned before and are used to define the sort of operation that will be carried out. Click the OK button in the dialog box once you have selected the profiles for constructing a loft feature and the necessary choice from the operation drop-down list. The loft function is made.

Creating a Loft Feature with Profiles and Guide Rails

The natural path that a Loft will follow through the profiles throughout its length is the one that is the shortest. The usage of guide rails is one method that may be used to modify the way it moves between profiles.

Guidelines for constructing a Loft with the use of guide rails

- Along the length of the loft, draw as many different profiles as the situation calls for.
- Construct guide rails according to the specifications.

Note that the guide rails are required to make contact with each of the profiles for the loft to be successfully formed.

1. Within the Solid / Surface or Mesh menu, locate the construct group and then choose the Loft command.
2. Starting at one end of the loft and working your way to the other, go through and choose each of the profiles.

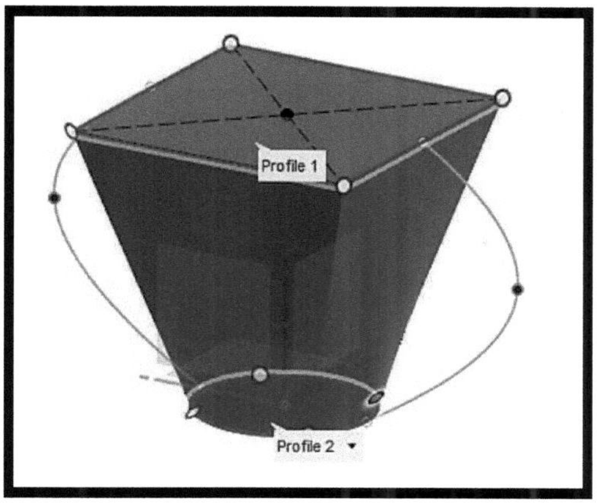

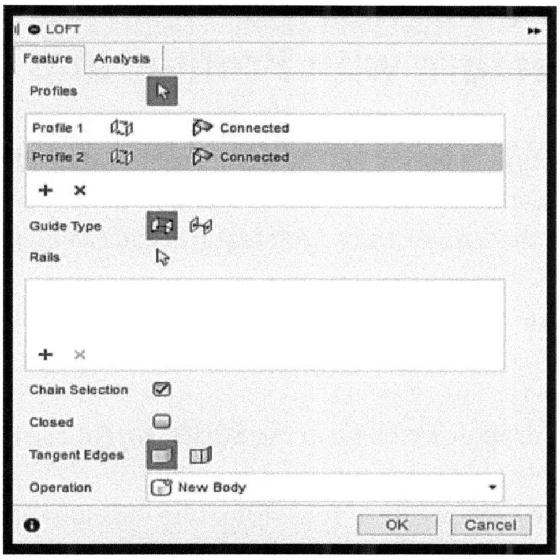

3. Click the **Rails** button, then click the guide rails to choose them.

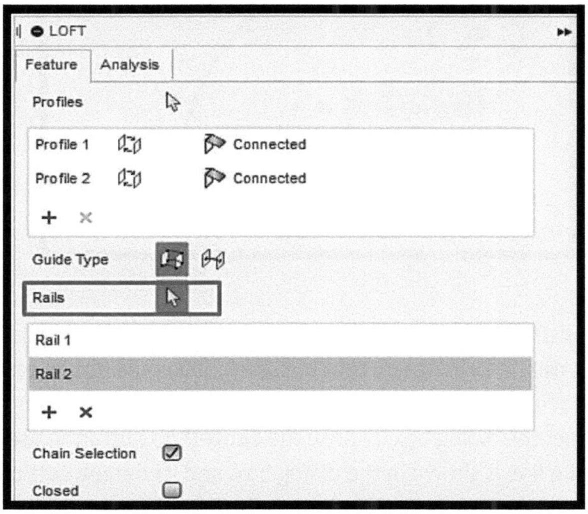

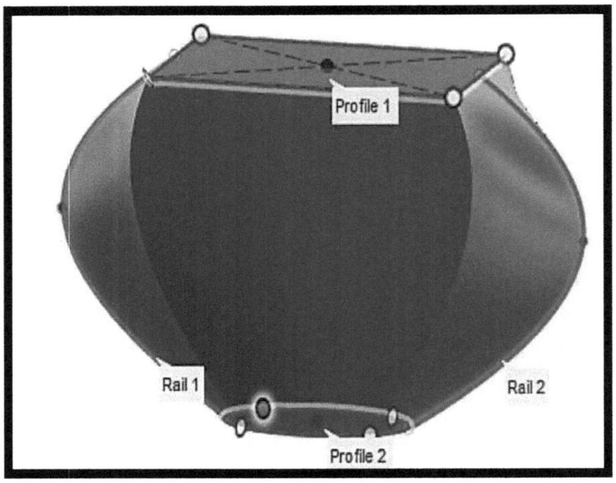

Creating a Loft Feature with Profiles and Centerline

You also can construct a loft feature in Fusion 360 by using profile data and a centerline. The centerline is utilized to ensure that the loft feature has a neutral axis and that there is a consistent transition between the different profiles. Take note that to construct a loft feature, you can only choose one centerline to use.

Follow the procedures that are outlined below to construct a loft feature that has profiles and a centerline:

1. After bringing up the **CREATE** drop-down menu in the **SOLID** tab, choose the Loft tool from the available options. A dialogue window labeled LOFT will now display.
2. In the graphics section, choose each profile of the loft feature individually using the drop-down menu.

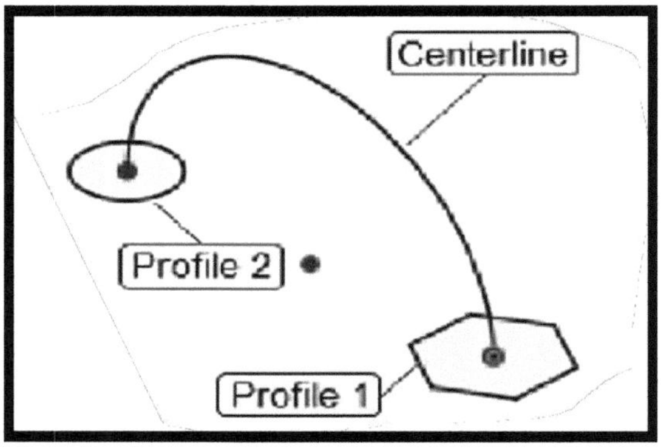

Both of the profiles are constructed on the same plane that makes up this figure. A warning notice will display as a consequence of this, informing you that the operation could not be completed successfully with the default parameters and requesting that you modify the values or alter the geometries that were chosen.
3. In the Guide Type section of the dialog box, choose the **Centerline** button to use as your guide. The arrow for selecting the center of the line is shown in the dialog box, and its default setting makes it active. You are now able to choose a centerline to use in the creation of the loft feature.

4. Choose a centerline inside the graphics area; for reference. Make it a point to check that the plane of each profile has a point of intersection with the centerline. A sneak peek of the loft functionality is shown in the visuals section.
5. In the drop-down menu labeled "**Operation**" of the dialog box, choose the option that corresponds to what you need, and then click the OK button. The loft function is made. You will need to pick the Cut option from the drop-down list of the dialog box's Operation menu to construct a loft feature by removing the material from the model. This will allow you to do so.

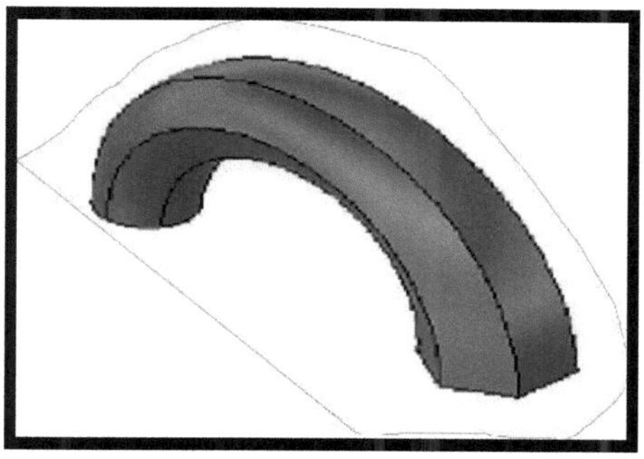

Creating Rib Features

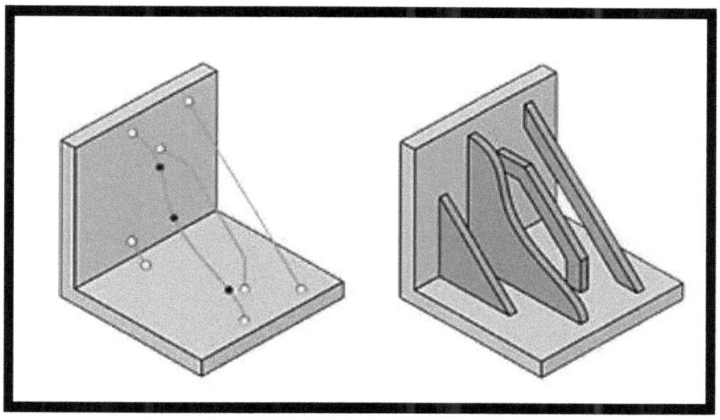

1. On the toolbar, go to the Solid menu and pick **Create > Rib**. The Rib conversation box appears.
2. Make a selection of an open sketch profile inside the canvas to utilize as the Profile.

3. Choose a Thickness Direction from the drop-down menu in the dialog box:

- **Symmetric**: Extrudes one-half of the thickness value to each side of the sketch profile when using the symmetric operation.
- **One Side**: This option will only extrude the entire thickness value onto one side of the sketch profile.

4. Pick one of the following ways to begin:

- **From Top**: This method begins the measurement of thickness from the top.
- **From Bottom**: This method measures thickness beginning at the base of the object.

5. Indicate the value for the Thickness property to extrude the rib in a direction that is perpendicular to the sketch plane:

- To move the distance manipulator handle, drag it inside the canvas.

- Alternatively, a specific value may be provided.

6. Choose an Extent Type, then modify the options that are linked with it:

- **To Next**: Extrudes the rib from the sketch profile to the closest faces on a solid body
- **Distance**: Extrudes the rib from the sketch profile to a depth that you specify.
- **Depth**: Specify the distance to extrude the rib, parallel to the sketch plane, toward the closest faces on a solid body. This distance should be in the direction of the faces.

7. If desired, draft and fillets may be applied to the rib feature:

- Specify a **Draft Angle value**.
- To specify the **Draft Pull Direction**, choose a plane or a face to work with.
- To change the pull direction of the draft, choose the **Flip Pull Direction** option from the menu.
- You will need to provide a value for the **Fillet Radius value** to apply fillets to the base of the rib feature.

8. Select the "**OK**" button.

The rib detail is then projected onto the solid body in the canvas after being extruded in a direction that is parallel to the sketch plane.

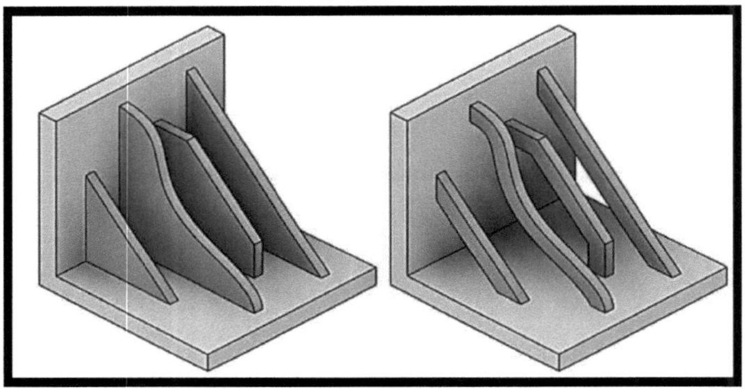

Creating Web Features

You may get creative with the web tool if you need to create some thin walls since it not only offers a fast and super-efficient technique to add cross-bracing to your designs for greater strength but also allows you to do it quickly and easily. Because it is possible that using the web command for the first time will make you feel as if you are participating in a magical experience, we are going to take a deep dive into the functioning of the feature today and show you what's what. If you are developing a thin-walled consumer product, or even if you just want to play around with the additional capability, the Web command is something that you should look into using. Having said that, I've brought up a design in Fusion 360 for a utility knife where I've sculpted the main shape, cut some through-holes for specialized usefulness, then split and shelled the component to make two hollow halves with uniform wall thickness. The next step that we may do is to move a plane away from our split surface by a few millimeters. This will prevent our web from reaching the top of our portion. We are going to make a rough drawing of the outline of our web using this offset plane, and you will soon realize why it is OK for us to do such a sketch.

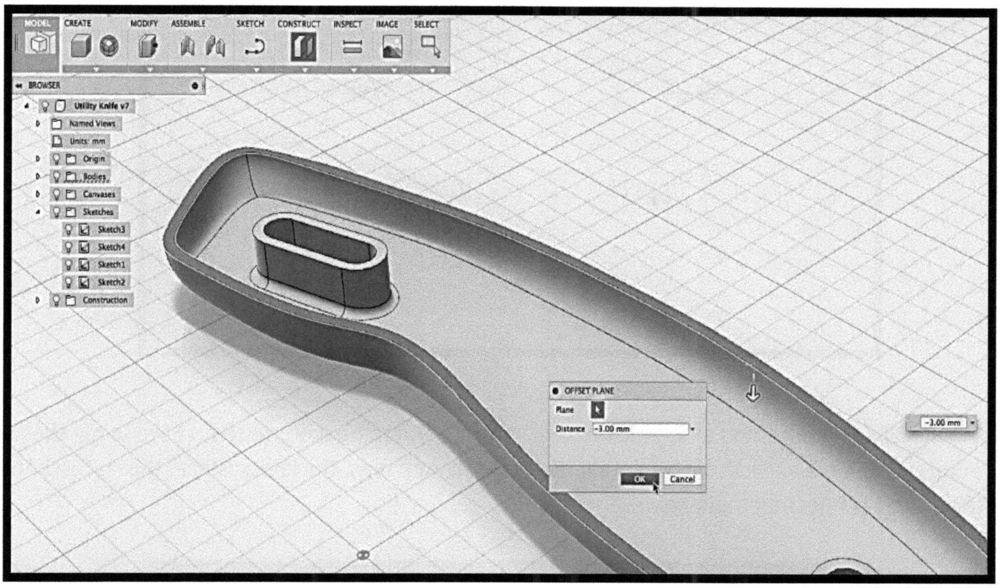

The next step is to make a rough design of the pattern that will be used for our web. The beautiful thing about this is that these lines do not have to stretch to a projection or any other geometry. The web command will make these lines thicker and extend them both outward so that they completely cover the border that the body has formed, as well as downward, all the way to the very bottom of our component.

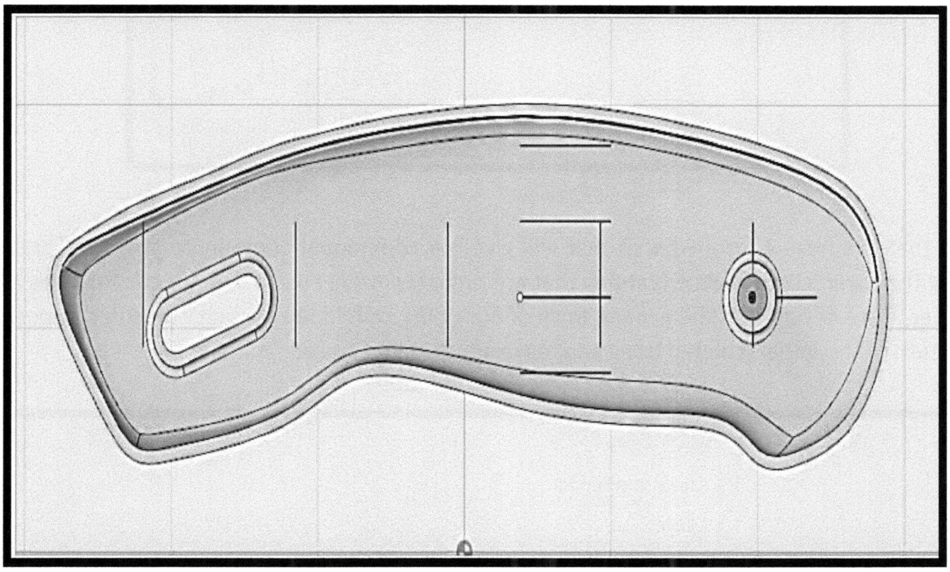

Note: When it comes to the parts of your design that have holes or cavities, be very cautious while sketching such sections. The web command will stretch outward and downward; however, it is possible that it could have complications if a sketch line runs over a hole. You'll see how we shortened the drawing lines to prevent anything like this from occurring. Now that our draft is finished, all that is needed to do is make use of the web command! (Create, then Web)

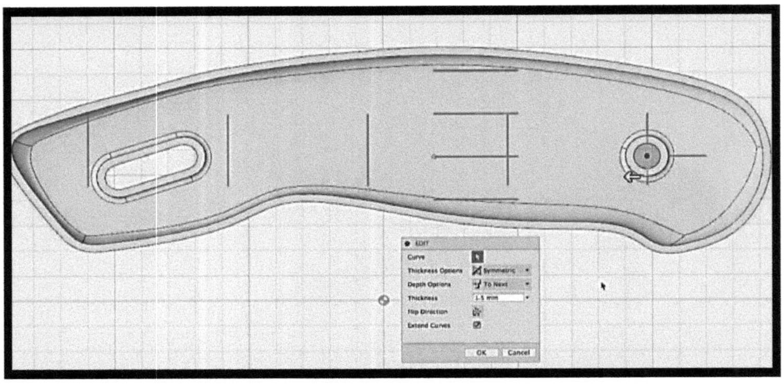

Here, we will provide a thickness of 1.5 millimeters, which is the same amount that I used in my shell script. Bonus points will be awarded for maintaining a consistent wall thickness since this is essential for applications such as injection molding.

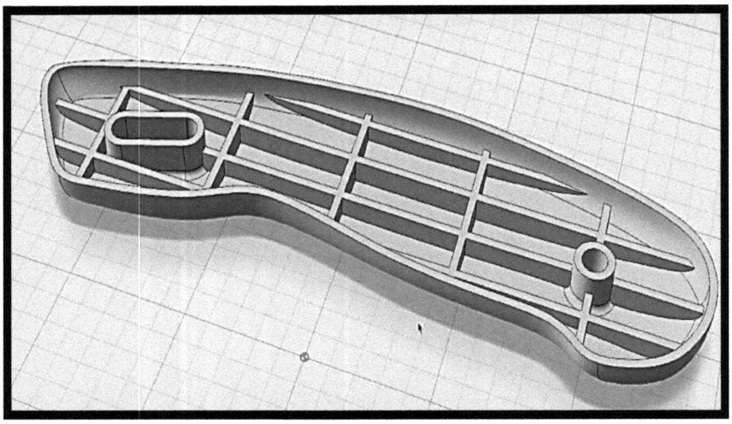

And with that, we have a finished web that will give our component some more structural stability. By employing the parametric timeline features that are available inside Fusion 360, we can take this even one step further. If we decide that the general form of our utility knife doesn't meet our expectations, we can always return to the initial sculpted body and make adjustments there.

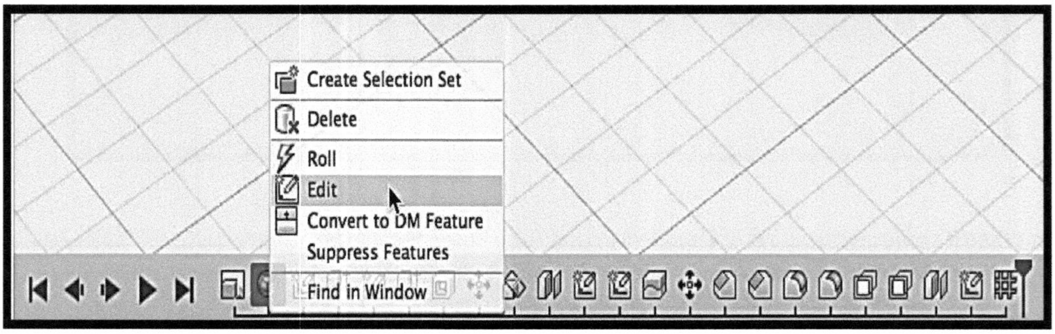

We may alter the web command by right-clicking on the form icon in our parametric timeline, making the modifications that are required, and then click "**Save.**"

Creating Holes

To make holes, go to the CREATE panel of the SOLID tab and click on the **Hole** tool. The HOLE dialog box will now show up. Alternatively, you may bring up the **HOLE** dialog box by using the **H** key on your keyboard or by right-clicking anywhere in the graphics area and then selecting the Hole tool from the Marking Menu that displays. The next section will focus on the choices available in the dialog box.

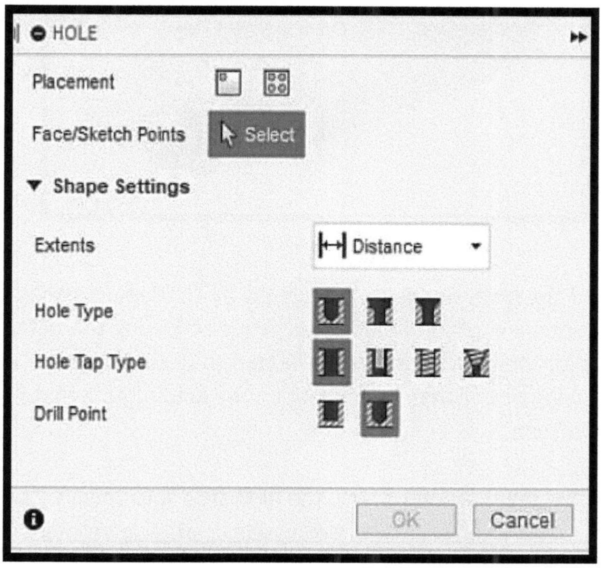

Placement

In the Placement section of the dialog box, there are two buttons: At Point (which creates a single hole) and From Sketch (which creates several holes). The At Point (Single Hole) button is used to create a single hole on an existing face of the model, while the From Sketch (Several Holes) button is used to create multiple holes by utilizing the drawing points of a sketch. Both of these buttons are located on the same toolbar. In the second scenario, the holes in the drawing are produced by a process that propagates to each sketch point in the sketch. After discussing these ways of placement, the following topic is the generation of holes.

Creating a Single Hole on a Face

1. Bring up the HOLE dialog box, and then in the Placement section of the dialog box, click on the At Point (Single Hole) button to produce a single hole on an existing face of the model.

Face: The Face selection option is turned on by default in the dialog box that you're working in. As a consequence of this, you have the option of choosing either a face or a plane as the placement plane while you are making the hole.

2. Position the cursor inside the graphics area such that it is over a face or a plane. The face is brought into focus, and its defining features come into view.

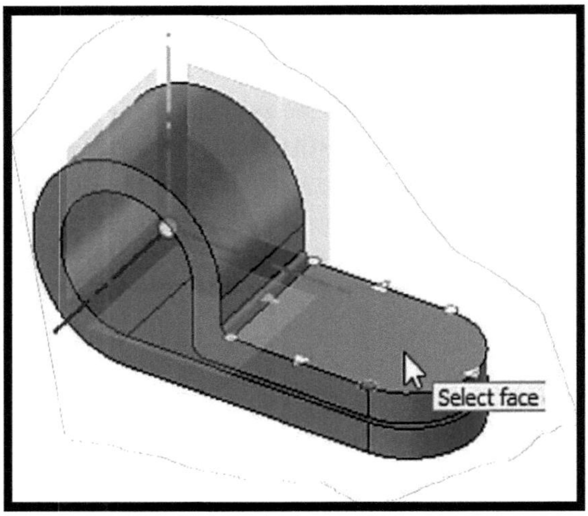

3. To specify the location of the hole, define its placement by clicking on a snap point or the face. In the graphics section, there is a preview of the hole that is generated using the default settings. Additionally, new customization choices for the hole's creation are added to the dialog box. Take note that the choices that are accessible in the dialog box change depending on the kind of hole that is chosen in the section of the dialog box labeled "**Hole Type**."

Following the step of defining the placement face, the next step is to specify its location on the face that was picked.

Reference: The References selection choices provide you the ability to choose which edges to use when positioning the hole.

4. Move the mouse such that it is over one of the model's linear edges. The distance that can be seen from the hole's edge to its center point is shown here. After that, pick the border by clicking on it. Both the dialog box and the graphics area provide a field for the distance that may be changed. Please provide the necessary value for the distance in this field. Similarly, choose an opposite edge from which to put the second direction of the hole. It is important to take note that when you pick a circular edge, the center points of the hole and the chosen circular edge will align to become concentric with one another.

NOTE: You may also set the position of the hole by dragging its center point to the desired location on the placement face that has been chosen. This option is available to you if you have the Advanced Hole Tool. Following the step of determining the placement face and the location of the hole, the next step is to choose the kind of hole that will be made.
Hole Type: The Hole Type portion of the dialog box is where you make your selection for the type of hole (either Simple, Counterbore, or Countersink) that will be made.
5. In the "**Hole Type**" section of the dialog box, click the option labeled "Simple," "Counterbore," or "Countersink."

Hole Tap Type: The Hole Tap Type part of the dialog box is used to pick the hole tap type (Simple, Clearance, Tapped, or Taper Tapped) that is to be generated. This may be done by clicking one of the buttons in this area.

6. In the "**Hole Tap Type**" section of the dialog box, click the button labeled "**Simple," "Clearance," "Tapped,"** or **"Taper Tapped."**

7. In the Drill Point section, choose either the **Flat or Angle** button to construct the hole with either a flat end or an angle end, depending on your preference.

Thread Offset: The Thread Offset section allows you to decide whether to make a full-length thread or a custom-length thread in the hole by choosing the Full or Offset buttons, respectively. This allows you to create either a full-length or a custom-length thread in the hole. Take note that the Tapped button must be chosen in the dialog box's Hole Tap Type area before this section of the box can be accessed.

8. When making the tapped hole, in the box labeled "**Thread Offset**," choose either the Full or Offset button.

9. In the corresponding areas of the dialog box, provide the needed parameters for constructing the hole. It is important to keep in mind that the availability of fields in the dialog box is determined by the buttons that are chosen in the regions of the dialog box titled "**Hole Type," "Hole Tap Type," "Drill Point,"** and **"Thread Offset.**"

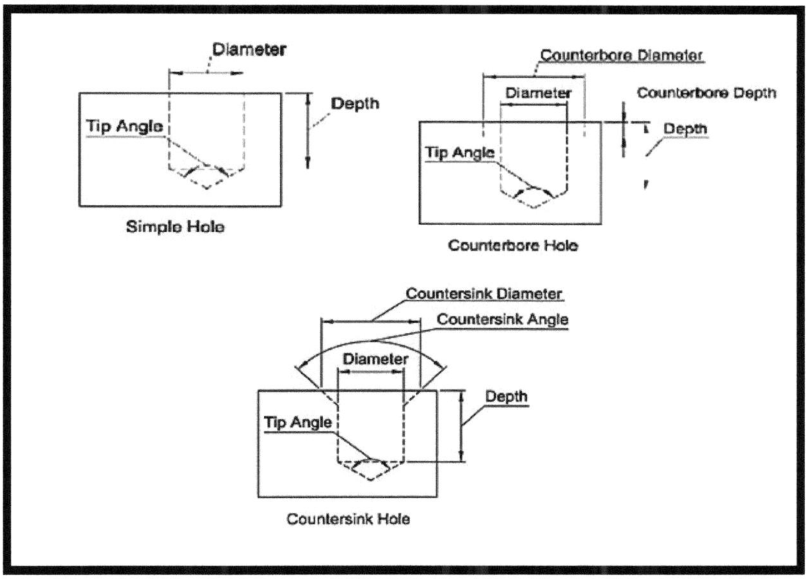

10. In the dialog box for constructing the tapped hole, provide the needed parameters in the **Standard, Fastener Type, Size, Thread Type, Class, Direction, and Fit drop-down boxes**. Take note that these drop-down lists will not display in the Hole Tap Type portion of the dialog box until one of the three buttons labeled Clearance, Tapped, or Taper Tapped has been selected.

11. In the Extents drop-down list of the dialog box, choose the needed option to specify the end condition of the hole, and then click the Define button. The previous topic has been covered by the choices available in this drop-down list. By utilizing the Flip Direction button located inside the dialog box, you will be able to reverse the direction in which the hole is created so that it is created on the other side of the face that is chosen.

12. Select the OK option and click it. The hole is drilled following the specifications that were supplied. On the top planar face of the model is where the counterbore hole is formed in this figure.

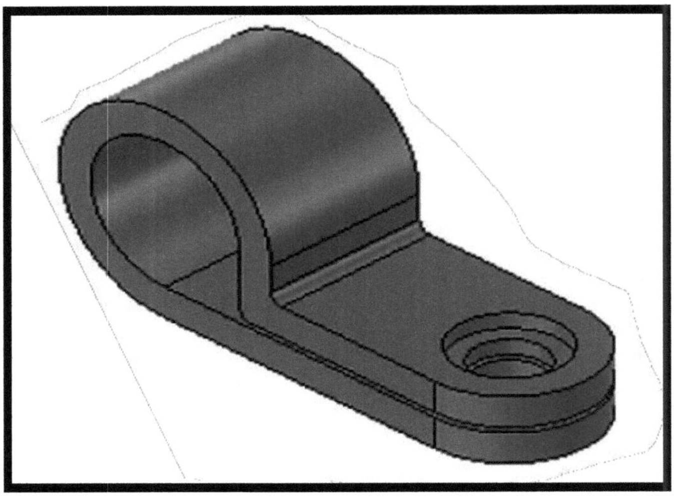

Creating Multiple Holes on Points

If you choose the sketch points or vertices of the model in Fusion 360, you also have the option of creating several holes in the model.

1. Bring up the HOLE dialog box, and then in the Placement section, select the button labeled From Sketch (Several Holes) to start the process of creating multiple holes based on the sketch points.
One additional benefit is that you can select multiple sketch points or vertices of the model to create holes. This can be helpful if you want to create holes in a complex model.
2. In the graphics section, choose the sketch points or the vertices of the model one at a time and move them around. It is important to take note that when you pick the points, a preview of the holes will display in the graphics area with the default settings set in such a way that the center points of the holes will match the points that you have chosen.

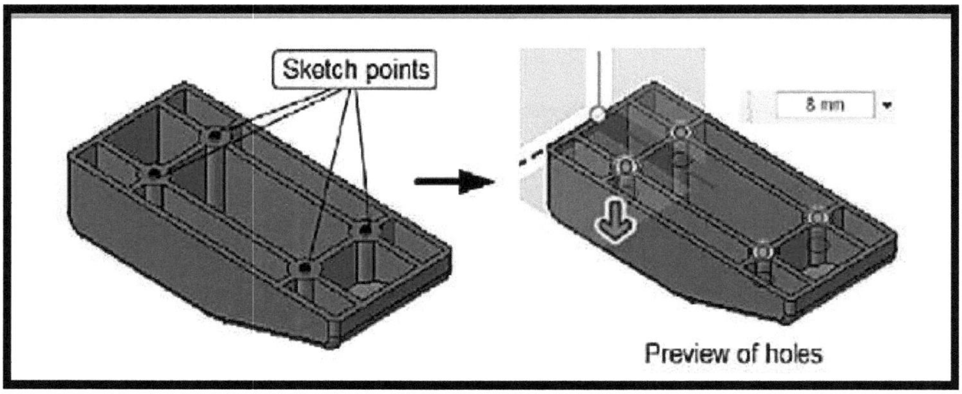

3. In the Hole Type section of the dialog box, choose the kind of hole that you want to create—either a Simple hole, a Counterbore hole, or a Countersink hole.

4. The necessary parameters for the creation of the hole must be specified in the appropriate areas of the dialog box.
5. From the Extents drop-down list, choose the option that corresponds to your needs and then specify the hole's final condition. The previous topic has been covered by the choices available in this drop-down list.
6. Select the **OK** button with your mouse. The spots that you pick will be where the holes are produced. Selecting these four drawing points results in the creation of basic holes, as seen in the picture below.

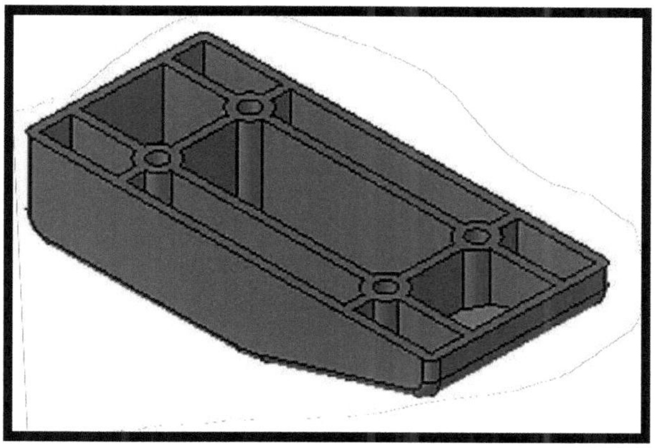

Create a hole at an angle on an angled surface.

Step 1: Sketch a helpline

To begin modeling the hole, begin by drawing a line from the edge of the surface she should start in the direction you want the hole to face and at the desired angle. You can see in the photo below that I am aiming for the first hole as well as the one that is in the center of the par three (dashed line)

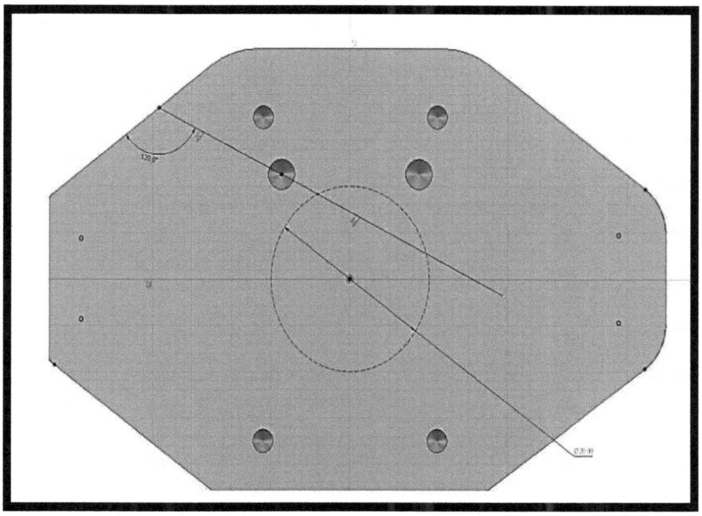

From this vantage point on the part, you could see the hole in the center of the component.

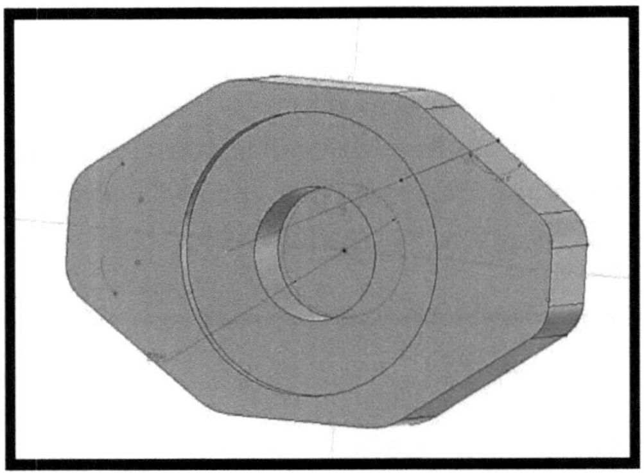

Step 2: Draw the leading line.

Now all you need to do is lightly draw a line where the hole should be located on the surface (marked blue in the pic below). You must make the connection between the line and the terminal of your previous drawing (point is highlighted in the pic below).

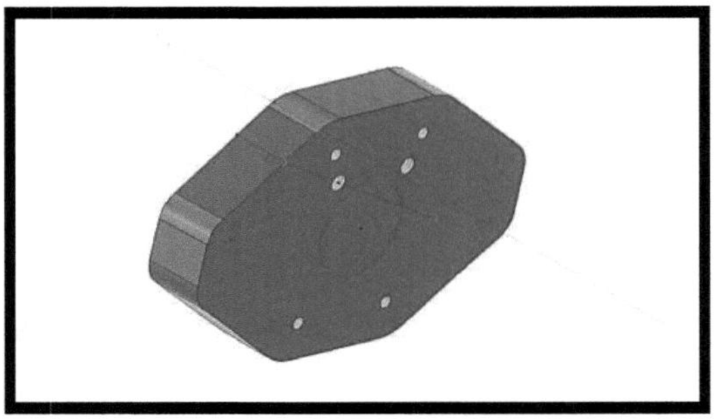

Step 3: Set Plane in angle

In this Step, you will need to utilize a plane, and you will need to place it at an angle to the drawing in "**Step 2.**" To do this, you will need to use the button that is located below.

As you can see in the picture below, under "**Step 1**" you should adjust the angle so that it is 90 degrees to the line of your drawing.

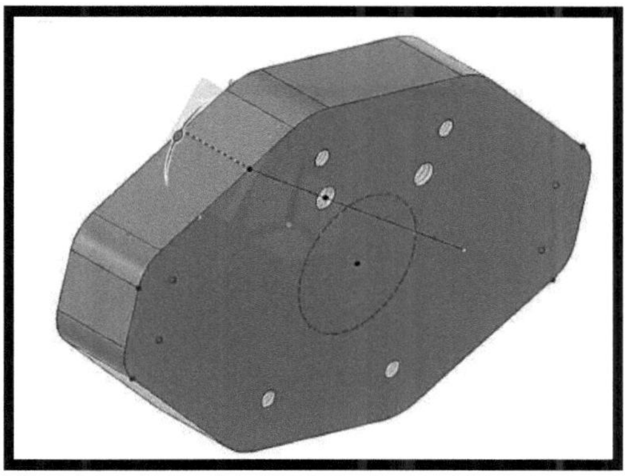

Step 4: Check if the angle is right

To determine whether or not the angle is accurate, just press I on your keyboard to bring up the measurement tool, then measure the angle that exists between your plane and the line that was sketched in "**Step 1.**"

An illustration of this can be seen in the picture below.

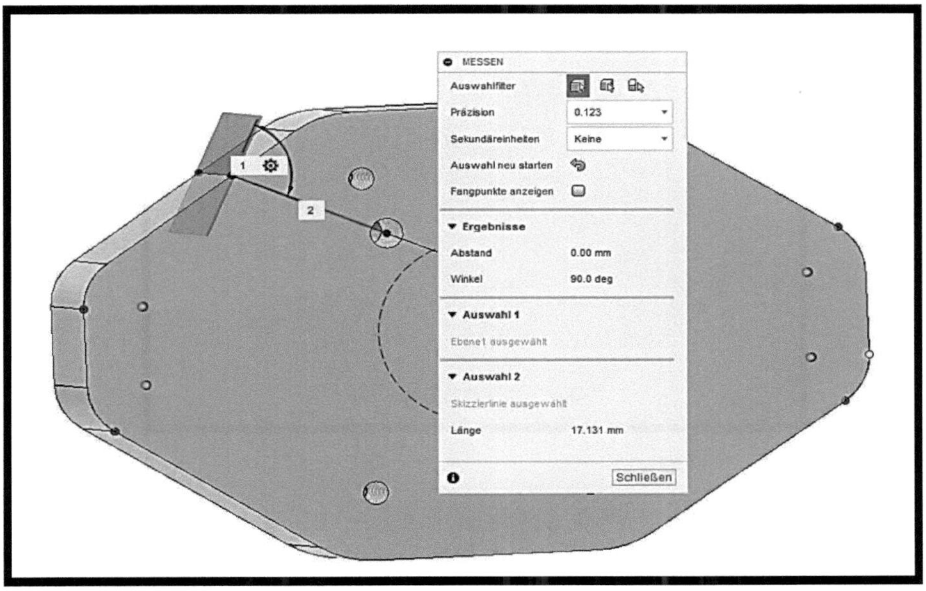

As can be seen, the angle is exactly 90 degrees.

Step 5: Offset planar

For the danze Druchmesser to be expelled from the component while the bore is being created, we need to construct an offset level.

To proceed, you must first click on this icon.

Pull the plane out of the part far enough so that the hole can entirely cut through the component rather than simply partly cutting through it.

An example is down below.

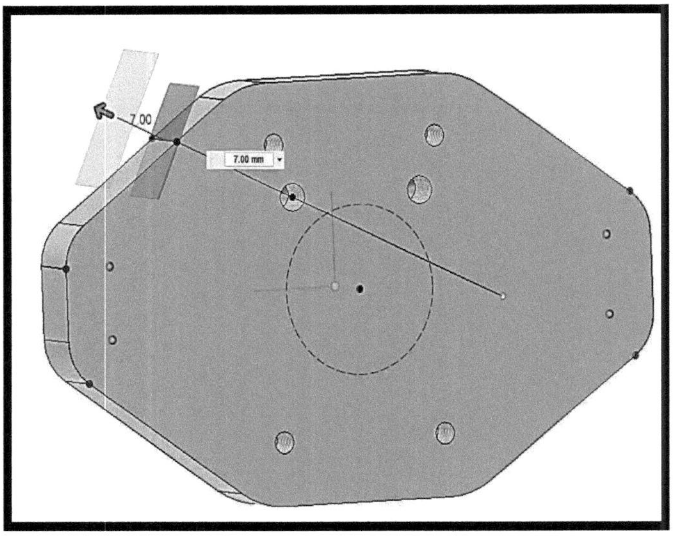

Step 6: Main sketch for the creation of a Hole

Now, build a sketch on top of the newly produced level from "**Step 5**". Despite this, we do not wish to draw a line at this time; rather, we will project the leading line that was established in "**Step 2.**" To project a line, you need to first click on the line you wish to project, and then hit the "p" key on your keyboard. After receiving your confirmation with an ok, the line will be projected. When you make changes to the first drawing, those changes are instantly transmitted to the rest of the sketches. This saves you from having to manually open each sketch and make the necessary edits to it. Additionally, if you alter the component's current thickness.

On this line, you will draw a point and give it the dimensions that you want, just as in the illustration below.

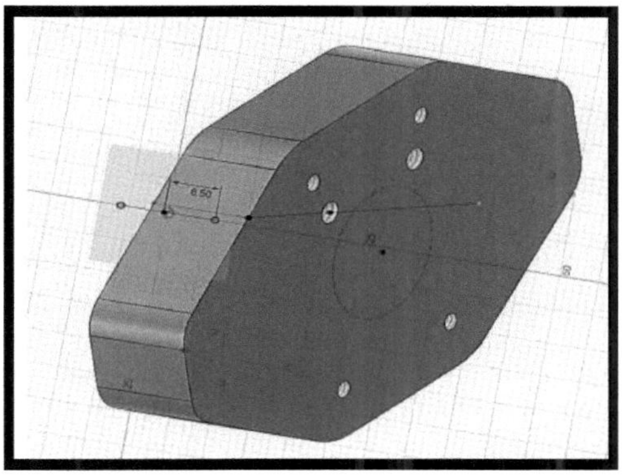

Step 7: Create the Hole

Now that the point has been generated, you may produce the hole by using the button labeled "**drill-hole**" (see the image below for reference). Simply choose the desired diameter and the amount of depth you want to drill.

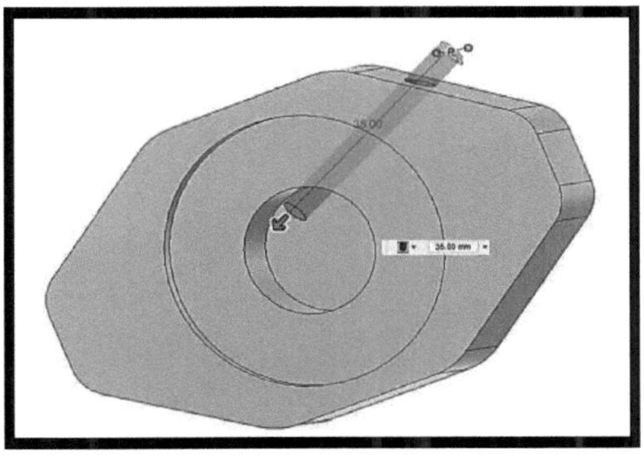

Creating a Thread

1. Navigate to the thread command, which can be found in the toolbar's Create menu option.

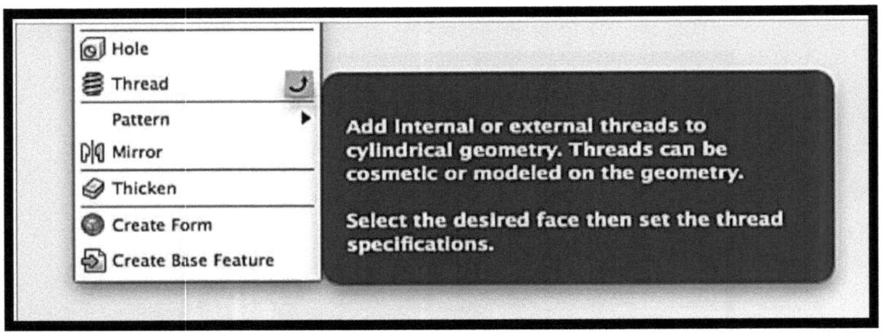

2. Decide which body you want to attach the thread to.

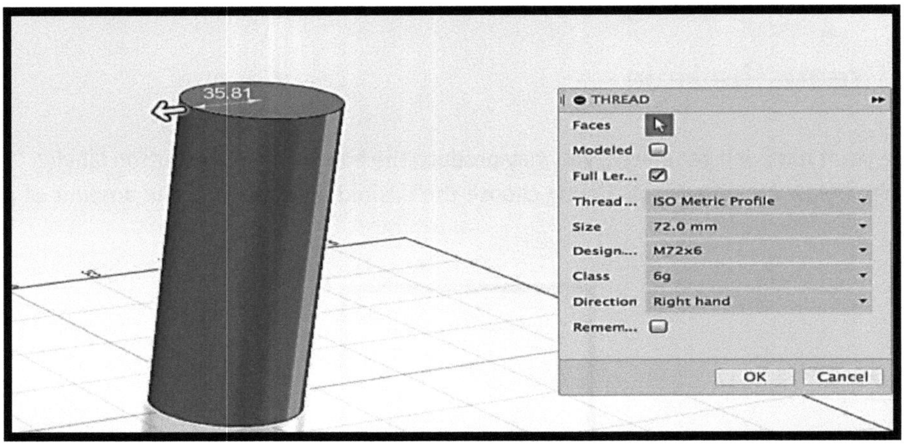

3. Select the "**Modeled**" option to get actual physical threads rather than a graphical depiction of the threads.

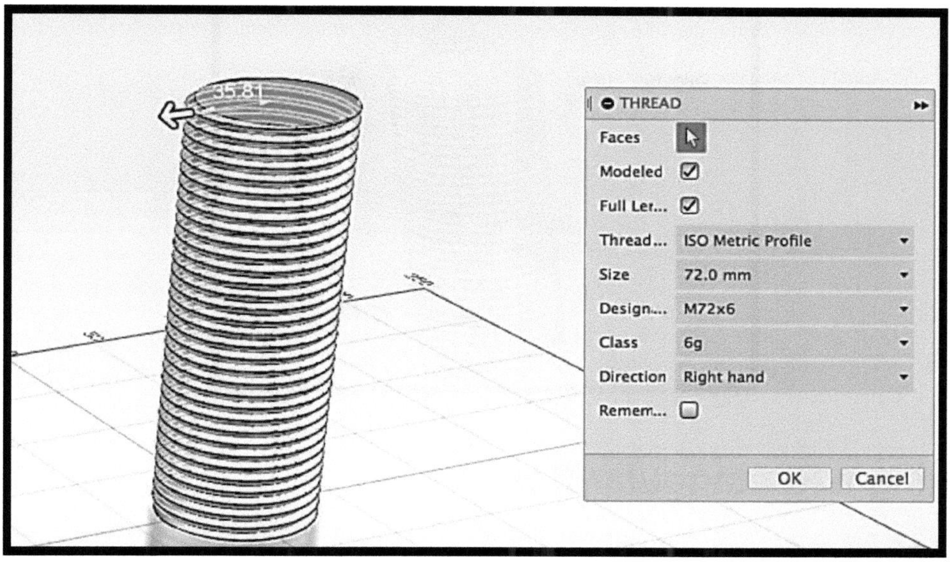

And voila! Before you apply the thread to your component, you could also want to add fillets or chamfers to it depending on the design objective you had in mind.

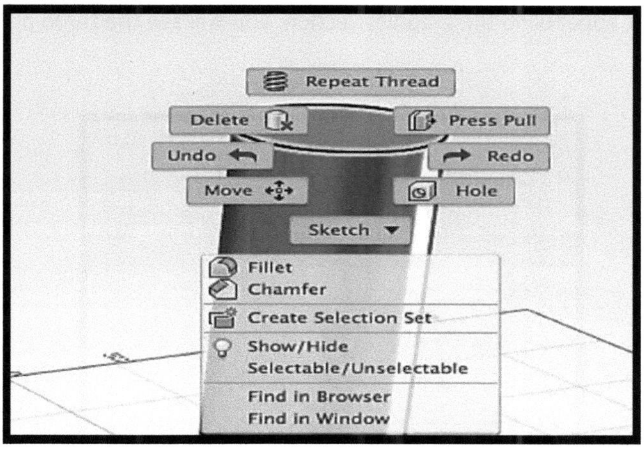

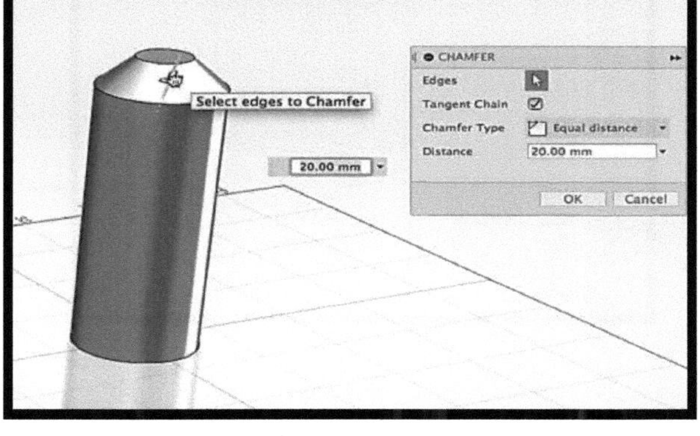

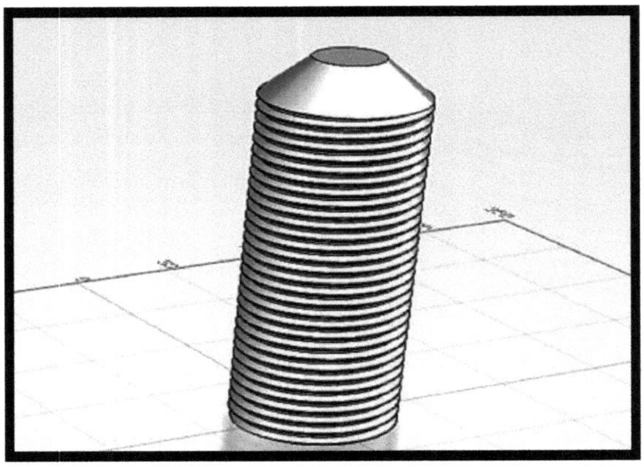

Creating a Rectangular Box

Using the Box tool in Fusion 360, you can make a box that has the dimensions of a rectangle.

The following is an explanation of the procedure for making a rectangular box:

1. Navigate to the CREATE drop-down menu located in the SOLID tab of the Toolbar. Next, choose the **Box tool** from the menu that appears. In the graphics section, you will see the three planes that are preset by default.

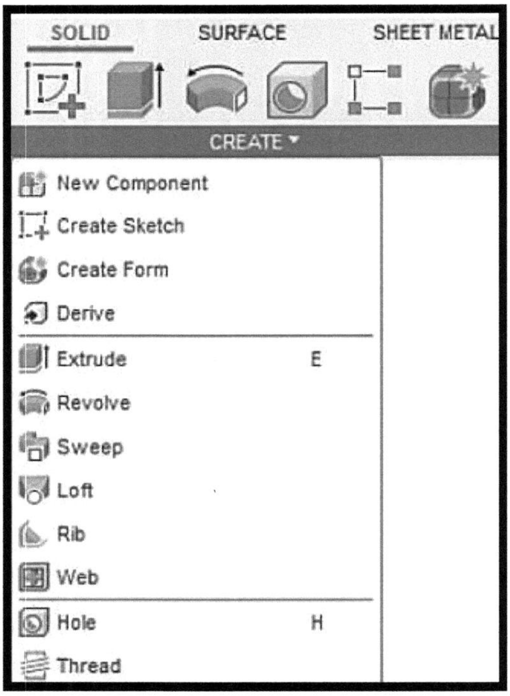

2. If you want to produce a sketch of the rectangular box, choose a plane or a planar face to use as the sketching plane. When you click the **2-Point Rectangle** tool, it will immediately activate, and you will be invited to choose two corners of the rectangle that are diagonally opposite one another.
3. To make a rectangle, start by identifying its two corners that are diagonally opposite one another. In the graphics section, there is a preview of the rectangle box that is shown with the default specifications. In addition, a dialog box labeled **BOX** is shown.

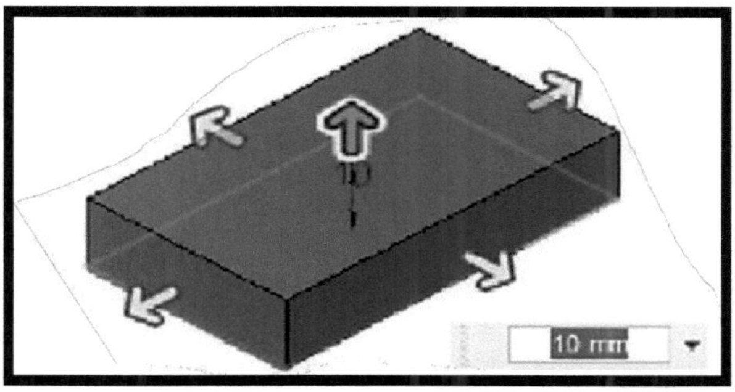

4. In the corresponding areas of the dialog box, enter the dimensions of the box in terms of its length, width, and height. Alternatively, you may adjust the dimensions of the box dynamically in the graphics area by dragging the arrows that show in the preview of the rectangular box. These dimensions include the box's length, width, and height.
5. In the "**Operation**" drop-down list of the dialog box, choose the option that corresponds to your needs. The previous topic has been covered by the choices available in this drop-down list.
6. In the dialog box, choose the OK button and click it. In the space reserved for graphics, a rectangular box containing the parameters that were supplied is produced.

Creating a Cylinder

By using the Cylinder tool, you will be able to produce a cylinder. The following is an explanation of the process of making a cylinder:

1. Navigate to the CREATE drop-down menu located in the SOLID tab of the Toolbar. Next, choose the **Cylinder** tool from the menu that appears. In the graphics section, you will see the three planes that are preset by default.
2. To generate a drawing of the cylinder, choose a plane or a face of the cylinder that is planar to use as the sketching plane. You will then be invited to choose the location that should serve as the circle's center once the **Center Diameter Circle** tool has been automatically enabled.
3. First, click to define the point that will be the circle's center, and then click to specify the diameter. In the graphics section, when the default settings are used, a preview of the cylinder will appear; for example. In addition, the CYLINDER dialogue box is shown.

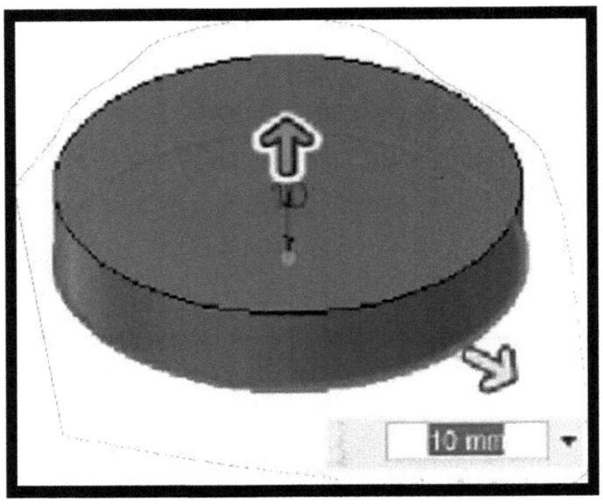

4. Within the corresponding areas of the dialog box, provide the diameter of the cylinder as well as the height of the cylinder. Alternatively, you may adjust the diameter and height of the cylinder dynamically in the graphics area by dragging the arrows that show in the preview of the cylinder.
5. In the "**Operation**" drop-down list of the dialog box, choose the option that corresponds to your needs.
6. In the dialog box, choose the **OK** button and click it. In the graphics section, the cylinder with the parameters that have been supplied is produced.

Creating a Sphere

Utilizing the "Sphere" tool will allow you to make a sphere. The following is an explanation of the process for making spheres:

1. Navigate to the CREATE drop-down menu located in the SOLID tab of the Toolbar. Next, choose the Sphere tool from the menu that appears.
2. To designate the location of the sphere's center point, choose a plane or a planar face to use as the drawing plane. Automatically, the Point tool will be launched, and you will be requested to indicate the point at which the sphere's center is located.
3. Specify the position at which the sphere is centered by clicking. A preview of the sphere will display in the graphics area, and its diameter will be set to the default value. Additionally, the SPHERE dialogue box is shown.

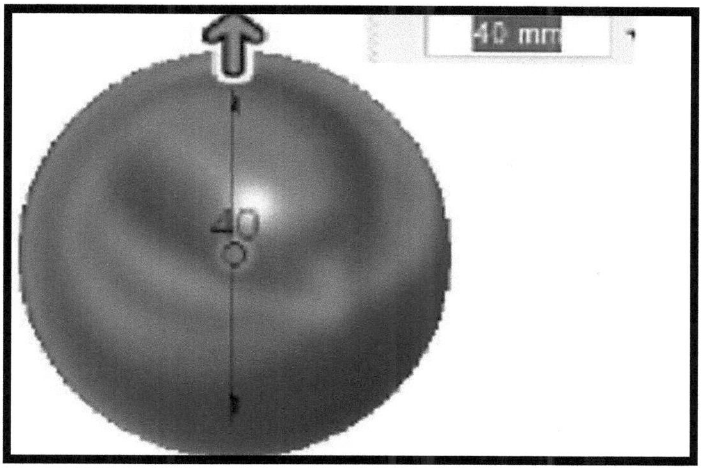

4. Enter the diameter of the sphere into the corresponding area in the dialog box labeled "**Diameter**." You also have the option of dynamically changing the diameter of the sphere by dragging the arrow that shows in the preview of the sphere.
5. In the "**Operation**" drop-down list of the dialog box, choose the option that corresponds to your needs.
6. In the dialog box, choose the **OK** button and click it. The diameter of the sphere that is being produced is taken into account.

Creating a Torus

Utilizing the Torus tool will allow you to design a torus for your needs. The following is an explanation of the process that is used to create a torus:

1. Navigate to the SOLID tab of the Toolbar and choose the CREATE drop-down menu. Then, select the Torus tool from the menu that appears.
2. To generate a drawing of the torus, choose a plane or a face of the torus that is planar to use as the sketching plane. You will be requested to choose the circle's CenterPoint when the Center Diameter Circle tool is automatically enabled after it has been selected by you.
3. First, click to define the point that will be the circle's center, and then click to specify the diameter. In the graphics section, you will see a preview of the torus emerge using the default settings. In addition, the TORUS dialog box is shown. It is important to take note that the circle serves as the axis of rotation for the torus.

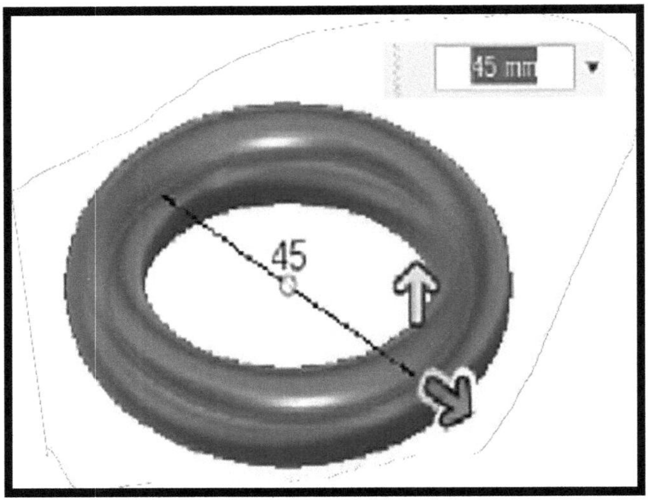

4. In the area labeled "**Inner Diameter**," type in the diameter that should be used for the torus's inner circumference. The axis of rotation of the torus is specified by default as being equal to the inner diameter. You may also adjust the inner diameter of the torus dynamically by dragging the arrow that appears along the axis of rotation of the torus.
5. Enter the diameter of the torus into the area labeled "**Torus Diameter.**" It is important to note that the cross-sectional diameter of the torus is what is measured by the torus diameter. You may also move the arrow that shows in the preview of the torus to dynamically adjust the diameter of the torus in the graphics area. This can be done by clicking and holding the mouse button.
6. Within the dialog box, go to the Location drop-down list and choose the necessary option to determine the position of the torus about the inner diameter that has been selected in the field labeled Inner Diameter. The On Center option is picked whenever there is a choice. The center of the torus section must then be positioned on the inner diameter that was defined to get the desired outcome of a torus. When you pick the **Inside** option, the subsequent torus is created by moving the torus such that it is positioned inside the inner diameter that you have defined. If you choose the Outside option, the subsequent torus will be constructed by moving the torus such that it is positioned outside of the inner diameter that you choose.
7. In the drop-down menu labeled "**Operation**" of the dialog box, choose the option that corresponds to what you need, and then click the OK button. The torus, including the parameters that were supplied, is formed.

Creating a Helical and a Spiral Coil

With the help of the Coil tool in Fusion 360, it is possible to fashion both helical and spiral coils.

1. In the SOLID tab, open the CREATE drop-down menu and then choose the Coil tool from the menu that appears.
2. Determine the drawing plane by picking a plane or a planar face to use. You will then be invited to choose the location that should serve as the circle's center once the Center Diameter Circle tool has been automatically enabled.
3. First, click to define the point that will be the circle's center, and then click to specify the diameter. A sneak peek of a helical coil is shown here.

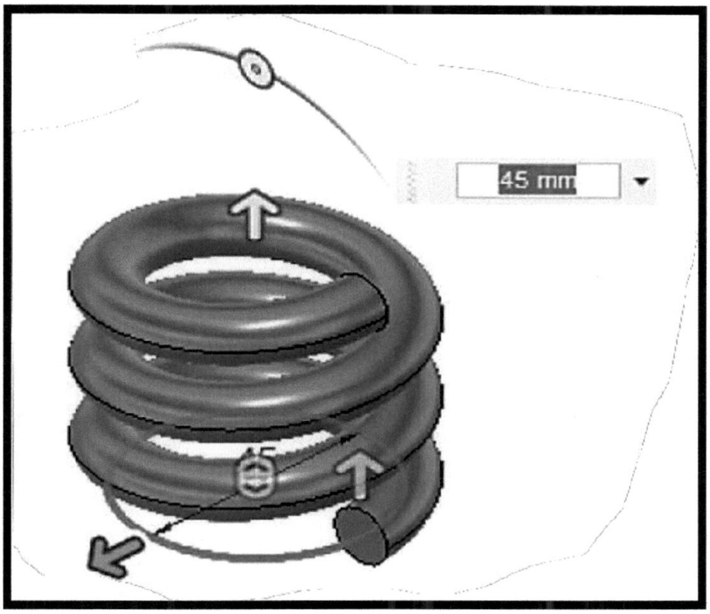

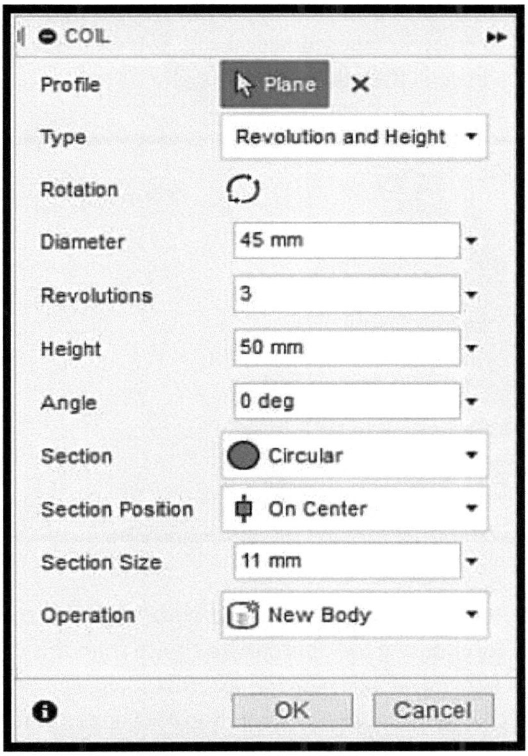

The technique that is to be utilized for producing the coil, as well as the kind of coil that is to be generated (either helical or spiral), may be selected from the drop-down list under "**Type**." The available choices will now be discussed. With the **Revolution and Height** option, you may fashion a helical coil by specifying the total number of revolutions as well as the height of the finished product. When you pick this option, the dialog box provides you with the opportunity to create a helical coil by specifying the number of rotations and the height of the coil.

Through the use of the **Revolution and Pitch** option, one may generate a helical coil by specifying the desired number of revolutions and pitch for the coil. Through the use of the Height and Pitch option, one may generate a helical coil by specifying the overall height and pitch of the coil. You may make a spiral coil by selecting the Spiral option and then setting its pitch and the number of rotations you want it to make.
4. From the drop-down menu labeled "**Type**," choose the appropriate way for fabricating the helical coil by making your selection from either the "**Revolution and Height**," "**Revolution and Pitch**," or "**Height and Pitch**" option, depending on the situation. Take note that the Type drop-down menu must have the Spiral option selected for you to be able to make a spiral coil.
5. In the area labeled "**Diameter**" of the dialog box, enter the initial diameter that you want for the coil. By default, the circle that is drawn will be used to determine the initial diameter of the coil.
6. To generate the coil, provide the specifications in the appropriate areas of the dialog box. Some of these parameters include revolutions and pitch. Take note that the choices that are accessible in the dialog box are determined by the option that is chosen in the drop-down list labeled Type inside the dialog box. You may also dynamically alter the settings in the graphics section by dragging the arrows that show in the preview of the coil. This can be done by clicking and dragging the arrows.

NOTE: You may also make a tapered helical coil by entering the taper angle into the Angle field of the COIL dialog box. This will allow you to create a tapered helical coil. You will need to put a negative angle value into the field to have the direction go in the other way.

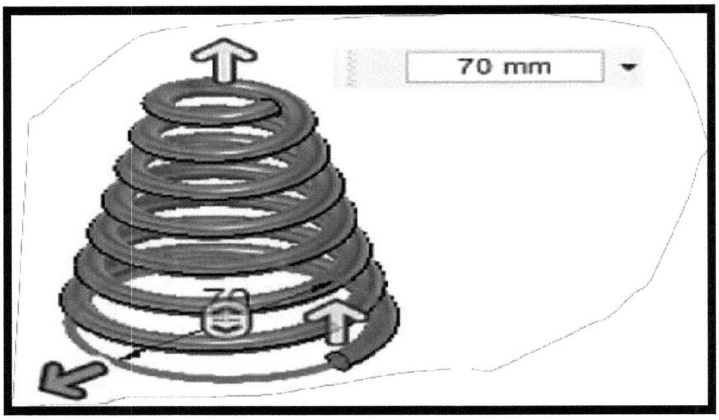

Section: The coil's cross-sectional shape may be specified by using the Section drop-down list, which is located at the top of the page. By choosing the appropriate choice from this drop-down selection, you will be able to make a coil that has either a circular, square, external triangular or interior triangle form. To set the cross-sectional form of the coil, go to the Section drop-down list and choose the option that corresponds to your needs.

Section Position

The location of a cross-section of the coil may be defined by using the drop-down list that is located in the Section Position field. The On Center option is picked whenever there is a choice. Therefore, the final coil is produced by positioning the center of the coil section on the initial diameter of the coil as indicated in the field labeled "**Diameter**." If you choose the Inside option, the resulting coil will be constructed by moving the coil segment such that it is positioned inside the start diameter that you choose. When the Outside option is selected, the resulting coil is produced by moving the coil section beyond the diameter at which the process begins.

8. In the dialog box, go to the Section Position drop-down list and choose the needed option to determine the position of the coil concerning the initial diameter that was selected in the Diameter field. The size of the coil section may be specified in the Section Size box, which is used for entering such information.

9. In the "**Section Size**" area of the dialog box, enter the dimensions of the coil section you want to use. Take note that the size of the coil is determined by the kind of section that is picked from the drop-down list located in the Section option.

10. To change the direction in which the coil is being rotated, use the Rotation button located inside the dialog box.

11. In the drop-down menu labeled "**Operation**" of the dialog box, choose the option that corresponds to what you need, and then click the OK button. It is now possible to generate the coil with those settings.

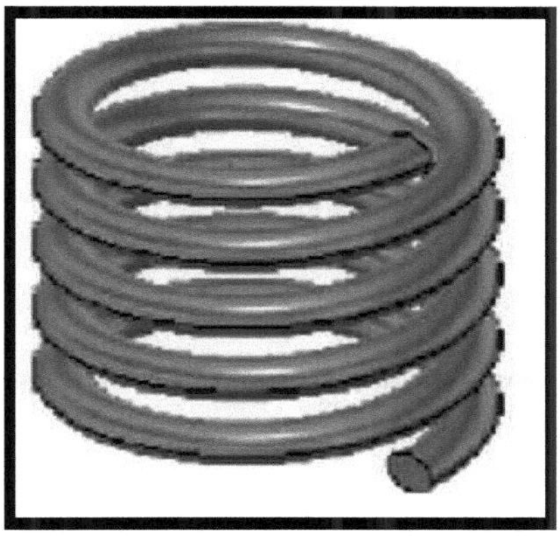

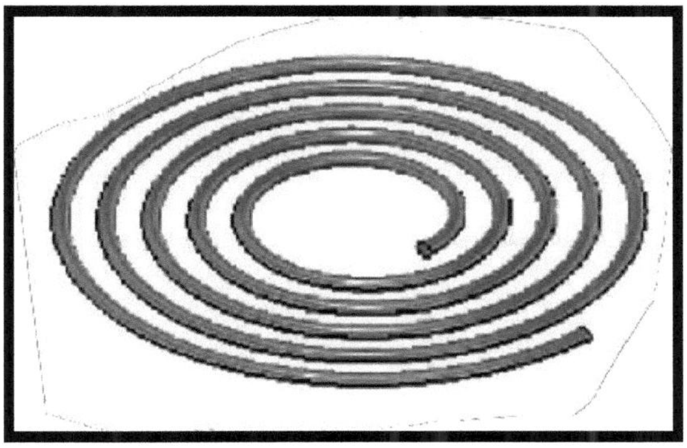

Create a 3D sketch spiral or helix

The sketching capabilities of Fusion 360 do not include the ability to generate a 3D helix or spiral automatically.

The following steps are the most common ones used when making a 3D sketch of a helix or spiral:

1. Make sure that 3D Sketch is active by heading to the Preferences menu, selecting Design, and checking the option that says "Allow 3D drawing of lines and splines."
2. Navigate to the **Create > Coil** menu option and adjust the diameter to your liking.
3. Make sure that the section position is set to "Outside" and that the section shape is set to "**Triangular** (Internal)" This will align the inner border of the triangular spiral to the dimensions that you choose, giving you the look that you want.
4. Complete the information for the spiral by entering the remaining details. Setting the rotation and height of a coil, the revolution, and pitch of a coil, or the height and pitch of a coil may all define a coil. After everything is done, click the OK button to make the coil body.
5. Select **Include 3D Geometry** from the **Project > Include menu** in Sketch.
6. To create a 3D sketch object, select any plane (it doesn't matter which plane is picked for the sketch plane), then select the inner edge of the plane, and then click the **Ok** button. To leave the drawing, use the "**Stop Sketch**" option from the menu. Since it has a projection reference, the spiral sketch object will appear in purple.

The reference may be removed by following these procedures, which will also enable the coil body to be deleted:

1. Make the coil body invisible by turning off the visibility setting.
2. Select "**Edit Drawing**" from the context menu that appears when you right-click on the sketch spiral in the browser or timeline.
3. Select the reference glyph by clicking on it.

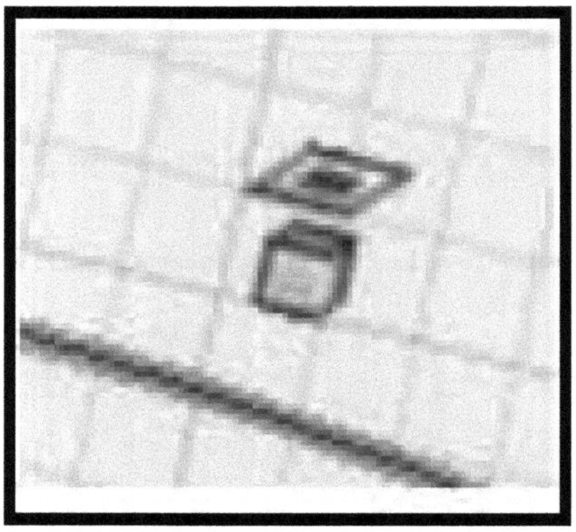

4. Press "**Delete**" on your keyboard. The sketch's spiral should be blue at this point. After that, you may remove the coil body from the system.

Creating a Pipe

Using the Pipe tool in Fusion 360, you can make a pipe that is either completely solid or completely hollow. You may make a pipe by choosing either an open or a closed drawing as the course of the pipe, or you can make use of a curve instead. You also have the option of choosing a single edge or a collection of model edges to act as the pipe's path.

The path that is being followed is a 3D drawing in the picture below.

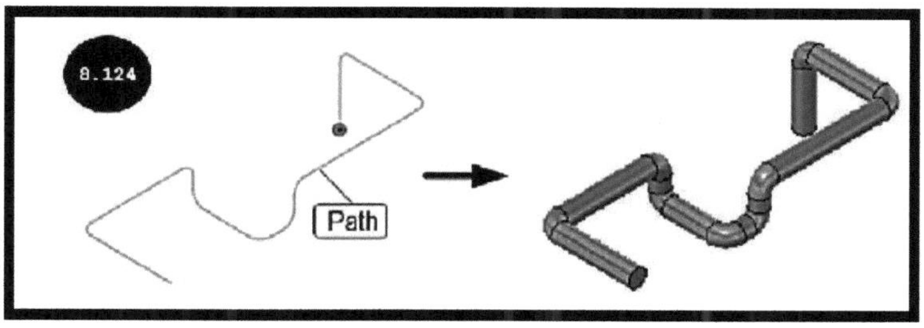

1. Using the sketching tools, create a drawing that is either open or closed or choose to use a curve as the path.
2. In the SOLID tab, open the CREATE drop-down menu and then choose the Pipe tool from the menu that appears. The PIPE dialog box will now show up.

Path: The Path selection option in the dialog box is turned on by default when it is first opened. As the path, you have the option of selecting between an open or closed drawing, as well as a curve. You also have the option of choosing a model edge or collection of model edges to act as the path. Take note that the check box for Chain Selection is already checked. As a direct consequence of this, all of its adjacent entities will be chosen automatically.

3. In the graphics box, choose the path that the pipe will take. The preview of the pipe, complete with fault parameters, is shown in the graphics area in such a way that the specified path is followed by the section of the pipe.

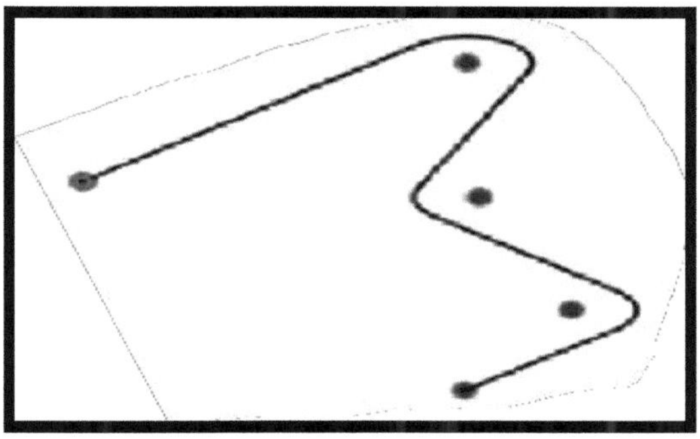

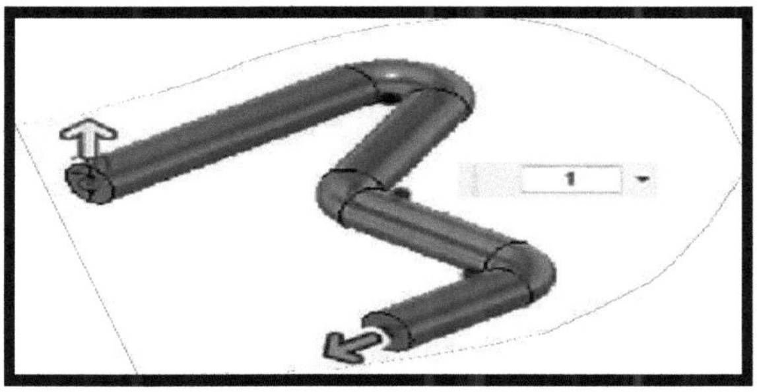

Distance: The number 1 is entered by default in the field designated for "**Distance**" on the dialog box. As a result, a pipe that is the whole length of the path is constructed. You have the option of determining the total length of the pipe as a percentage of the path that was chosen.

4. Within the dialog box's Distance field, enter the needed number for the percentage of distance. Make sure that the number 1 is provided in the Distance box so that you may build a pipe that is the complete length along the path that was chosen.
5. Use the drop-down menu located in the dialog box labeled "**Portion**" to choose the appropriate section for the pipe. One can fashion a pipe with either a circular portion, a square section, or a triangular part.
6. In the "**Section Size**" area of the dialog box, enter the size of the pipe section you want to work with.
7. In the dialog box, make sure that the check option for Hollow is unchecked so that you may create a solid pipe. It is necessary to tick the Hollow box to generate a hollow pipe, and after doing so, you must enter the desired wall thickness for the hollow pipe into the Section Thickness area that appears in the dialog box.
8. In the drop-down menu labeled "**Operation**" of the dialog box, choose the option that corresponds to what you need, and then click the OK button. The pipe is made from scratch. The first picture depicts a solid pipe with a square cross-section, while the second picture depicts a hollow pipe with a circular cross-section.

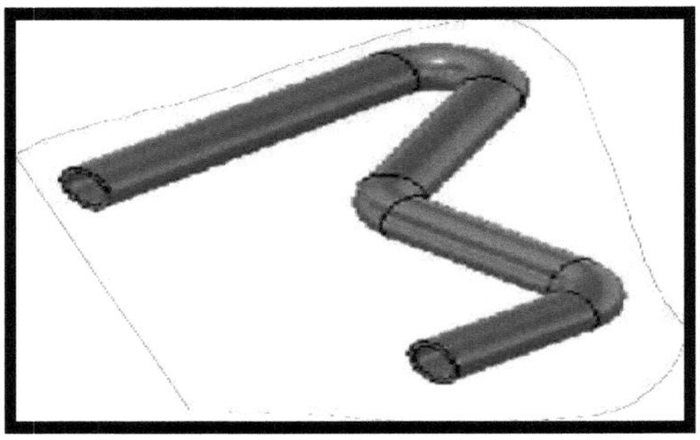

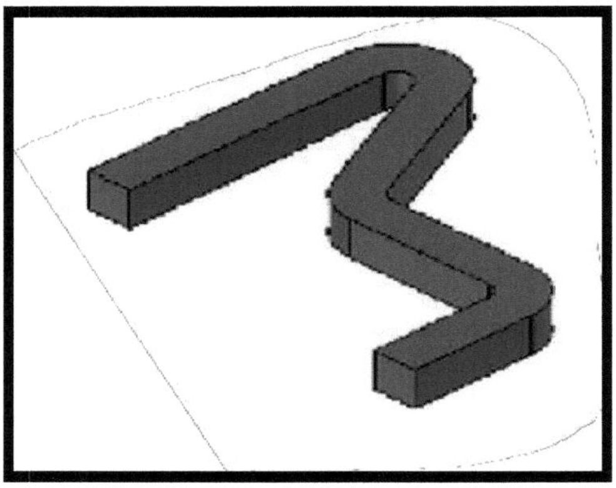

Creating 3D Sketches

Using the many sketching tools available in Fusion 360, such as Line and Spline, it is possible to generate 3D drawings. When constructing architectural elements such as sweeps, lofts, and pipes, 3D designs serve both as a 3D path and as a guide curve.

The following is an explanation of how to use the Line tool to create a 3D sketch:

1. In the toolbar, choose the **Create Sketch tool** and then click it. In the graphics section, you will see the three planes that are preset by default.

2. To begin creating the drawing, choose a plane or a face that is planar to use as the sketching plane. The drawing plane is determined to be the one that was picked. Additionally, the **SKETCH** contextual tab and the SKETCH PALETTE dialog box are shown to the user.
3. To generate a 3D drawing, open the **SKETCH PALETTE** dialog box, and choose the check box labeled "**3D Sketch**."

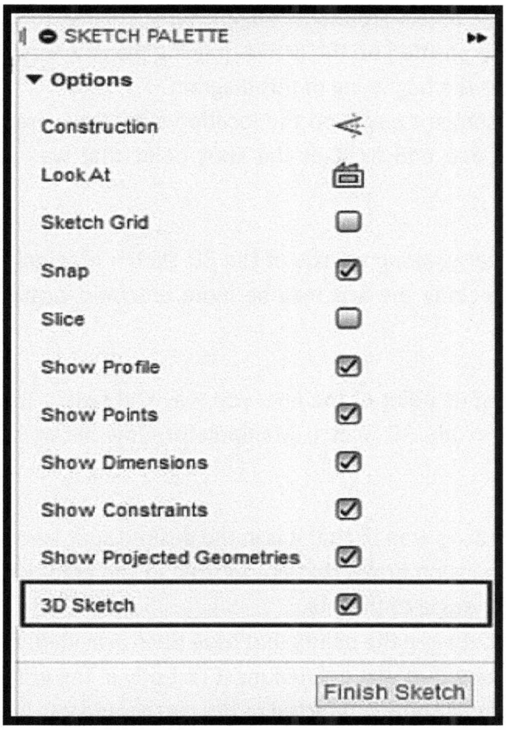

4. Select the **Home** symbol located inside the View Cube and click on it to switch the perspective of the drawing to an isometric view.

5. To create a 3D sketch using the Line tool, go to the **CREATE** panel of the **SKETCH** contextual tab and click on the Line tool. The 3D Sketch Manipulator may be found in the middle of the graphics area at the origin (0,0).

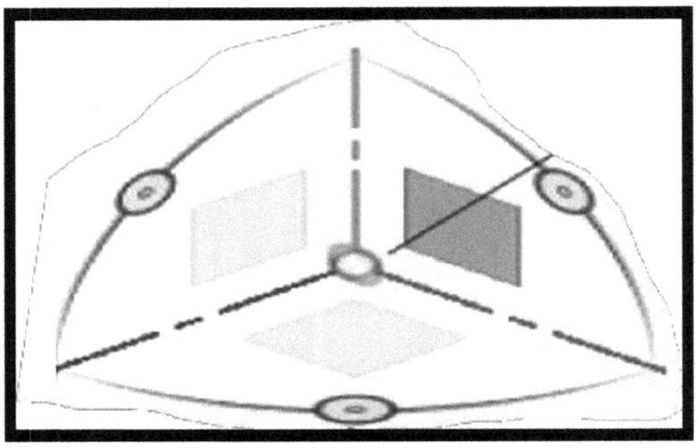

6. Within the 3D Sketch Manipulator, choose the plane you need to use as the current drawing plane by clicking on it.

NOTE: When generating a 3D drawing, you may transition from one sketching plane to another by clicking on the necessary plane (XY, YZ, or XZ) in the 3D Sketch Manipulator. This allows you to sketch in three dimensions. The 3D Sketch Manipulator additionally provides you with a Rotation handle that, when dragged, allows you to rotate the object around its origin.

7. Using the mouse, indicate the position on the active drawing plane where the line should be. The origin serves as the point that denotes the beginning of this diagram.

8. Position the cursor some distance away from the location where you started. There looks to be a line made of a rubber band, with one end fixed at the start point that was provided, and the other end connected to the cursor.

Hint: An extension line will emerge along an axis of the 3D Sketch Manipulator whenever you move the mouse along that axis. A place along the axis may be more precisely located with the assistance of this extension line.

NOTE: Even after defining the start point of the line, you may still switch to a different drawing plane by clicking on the needed plane in the 3D Sketch Manipulator. This allows you to sketch in a variety of orientations.

9. Position the cursor in the drawing area so that it is in the desired spot, and then click to set the terminus of the first line. Within the dimension boxes that are located in the graphics area, you are also given the option to choose the length and angle of the line.

In this example, a line is drawn between the points that have been provided, and the origin of the 3D Sketch Manipulator is moved to the point that was defined most recently in the graphics area. In addition to this, a line that looks like a rubber band is now connected to the cursor, and you will be asked to choose the end point of another line.

10. If necessary, choose the necessary plane to use as the drawing plane in the 3D Sketch Manipulator by clicking on it.

11. On the current drawing plane, move the pointer to the desired spot, and then click to indicate the terminus of the next line.

A line is drawn, and the origin of the 3D Sketch Manipulator is moved to the most recent location that was defined in the graphics area.

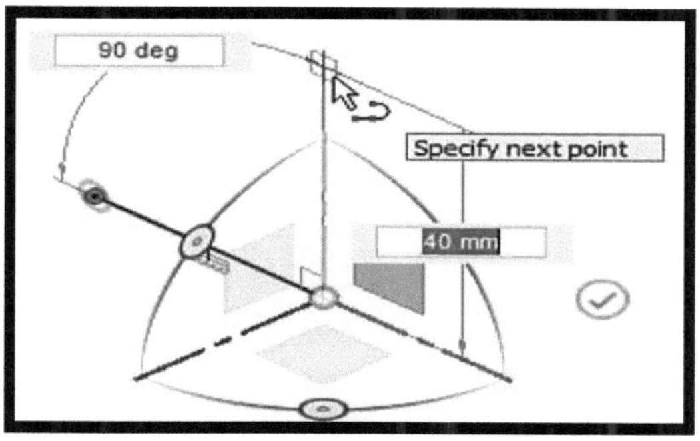

12. In a similar manner, you can build the remaining line entities of the 3D drawing in various planes. NOTE: You may also eliminate the sharp edges of the 3D design by using the Fillet tool to create fillets in the sketch. This will make the corners rounder. Utilizing the Drawing Dimension tool is required to apply dimensions to a 3D design; however, this process is otherwise identical to that of adding dimensions to a 2D sketch.

13. When you have finished generating all of the sketch entities for the 3D drawing, use the ESC key to leave the Line tool. To finish your sketch and quit the Sketching environment, go to the SKETCH contextual tab of the Toolbar and click on the FINISH SKETCH tool. The first picture displays a 3D drawing, while the second picture demonstrates a pipe feature that was generated using the Pipe tool.

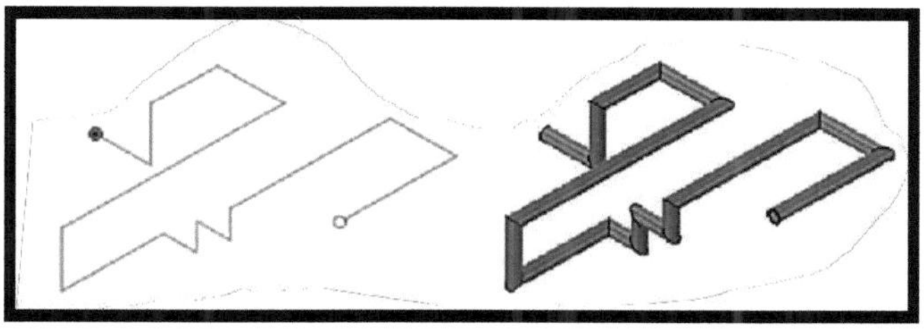

Easily Model Wires and Tubes

To begin, construct a level surface in the shape of a square box. The next step is to fashion a smaller cube with sides that are sufficiently roomy to accommodate the wire or tube's cross-section. We'll simply make a cube that's 10 mm on each side and 10 mm on all sides for our 8 mm tube. A start location and angle may be easily defined with the help of this cube, although its use is not strictly required. In addition to that, it will highlight an essential method that comes up later. In most cases, there is a predetermined location at which to begin and finish your wire or tube project; but, in this particular instance, we do not have anything of the like.

After that, build an offset plane on top of the huge surface with an offset that is equal to the radius of your wire or tube. In our situation, this is equal to 4 millimeters. In addition, make a sketch on one of the sides of the cube at the location where you wish to begin running your wire or tube. As seen in the screenshot below, draw a circle that is tangent to the bottom border of the canvas. Our sweep profile will consist of this information.

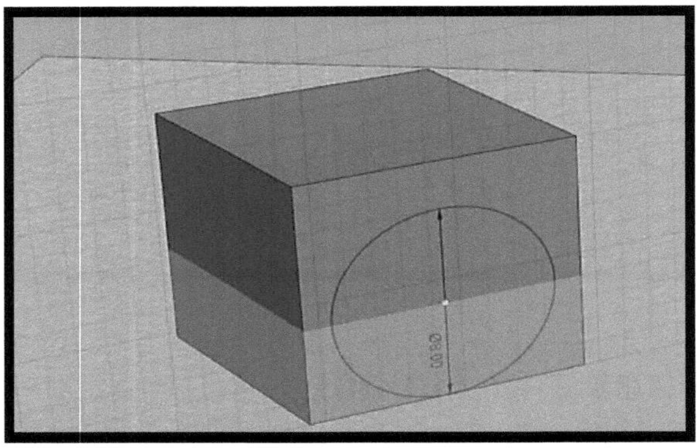

Create a spline on the offset plane that begins at the center-point of the face of your cube that is facing the correct direction next. The form does not matter all that much, but it will reflect the physical features of your wire or tube, which may be as rigid as a garden hose or as flexible as boiling spaghetti. At this point, you shouldn't be concerned about whether or not the spline is perpendicular to the cube edge. You also have the option of drawing a construction line on the same design that is perfectly straight, begins at the point where the spline begins, and continues through the cube. This should be done such that it is perpendicular to the edge or face of the cube.

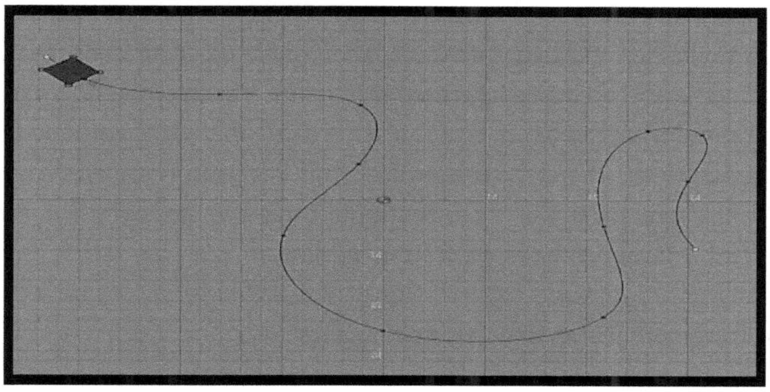

Create a tangent constraint between your spline and your straight construction line. This is a cool little technique that you may try out. By doing it this manner, your wire or tube will begin at an angle that is naturally occurring concerning what it is linked to. It doesn't really make a difference in this particular case, but generally speaking, you want your wire or tube to emerge from a box or other container in a perpendicular direction. You may also experiment with the fit points of the spline, and the start will continue to maintain the same angle in a completely natural way.

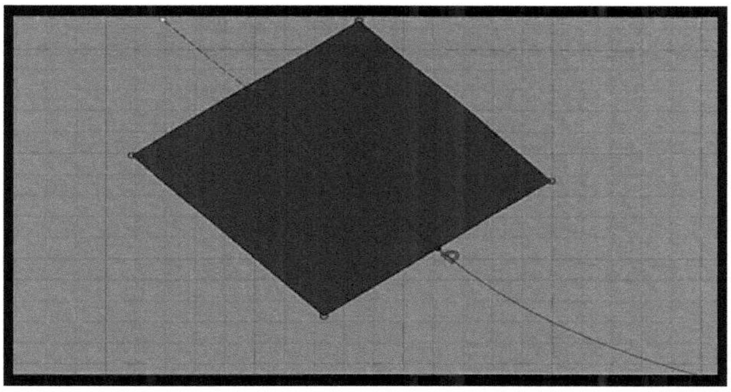

Now we get to the enjoyable part! Employing the sweep tool, choose the circle on the face of the cube as the profile, and decide to use the spline as the patch. Be sure that the orientation is set to perpendicular, and decide whether the operation will include the creation of a new body or a new component.

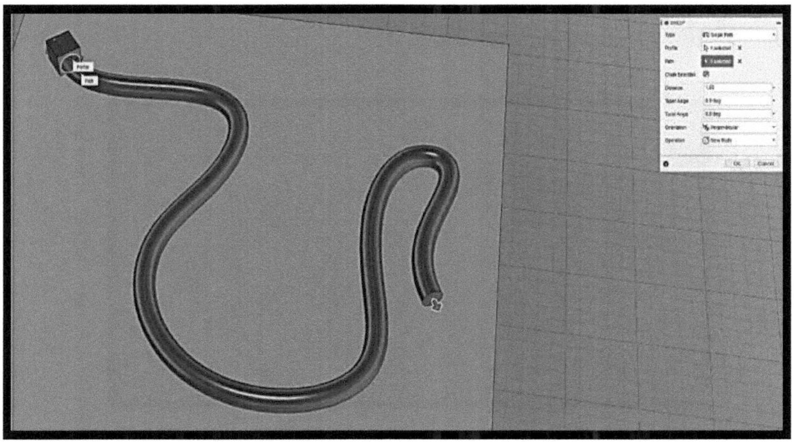

Use the shell tool to make this object seem less like a nicely bent steel rod and more like a tube to fool people into thinking it is the latter. Choose both ends, then enter the wall thickness you want (in our case 1 mm). This will result in our steel rod being hollowed down and transformed into a pipe instead. You could also build two circles on the side of the cube, one for the outside diameter and one for the inner, and then utilize the space in between them as the sweep profile. This is an alternative method. You won't have to utilize the command shell if you do it this way. It should have the look of clear acrylic, and you should execute a rapid render. Don't forget to keep your cube hidden!

The end product might have something like this appearance:

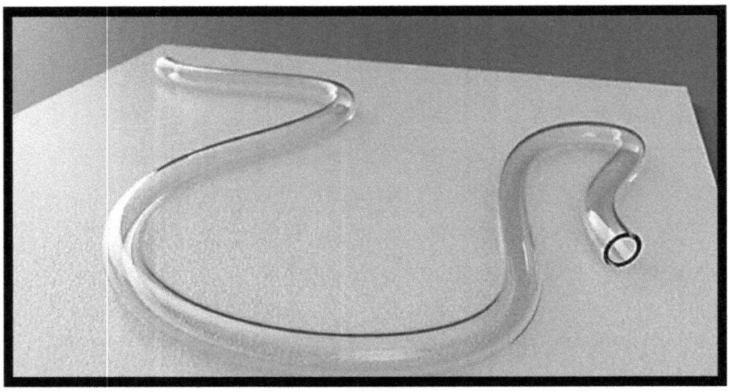

By repositioning, adding, or deleting spline fit points in the schematic, it is possible to effortlessly alter the curvature of the tube. The modifications will be reflected in the completed product. By adjusting the size of the circle that is located on the face of the cube, the outside diameter may be customized. For it to remain stationary on the ground, you will need to go and adjust the offset plane offset.

Uneven Surface

Let's make things a little bit more difficult. Although this approach may be used on any sort of surface, for the sake of this illustration, we will utilize the sculpting environment to create an uneven surface and then proceed from there. The first step is to create a form. This will take you to the workspace for the Sculpt application. Make a plane with as many faces as you want, and then use the **Edit Form** tool to make it "**un-flat**" by dragging the vertices, edges, and/or faces up and/or down. We channeled our inner artists to produce the magnificently undulating surface below.

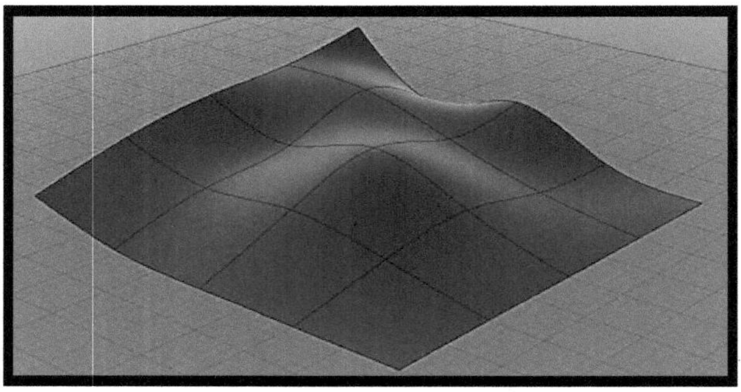

Now, we're going to use the helpful Thicken tool to create two additional surfaces based on this one: one surface that the center of the tube will follow, and another surface that will thicken the original surface and create a solid body. Both of these surfaces will be derived from this one. One of the neat features of the Thicken tool is that it allows a surface to be thickened in either the direction of an axis or in the direction of the surfaces normal. Because the tube will move in a normal plane, we will need to utilize the **No Edge** thicken type, and the **Normal** direction for the plane it moves in. Pick a thickness that's going to be the same as the tube's radius. In our situation, this measures out to **4 millimeters.**

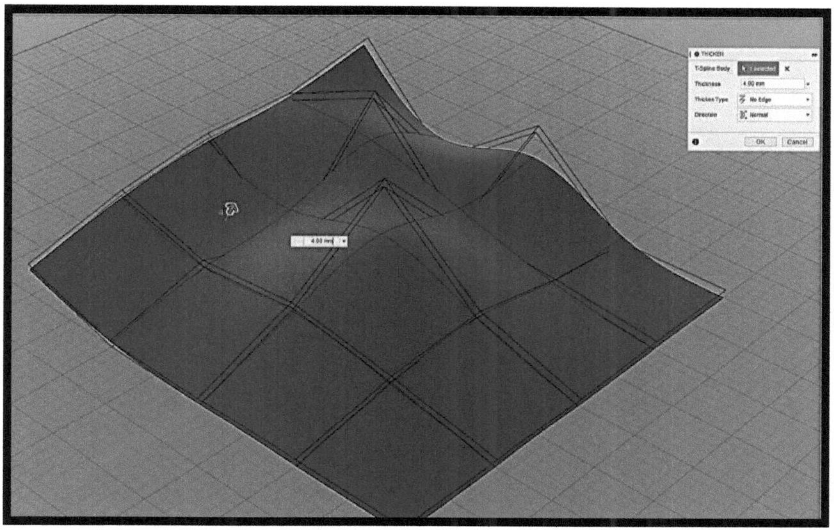

Carry out the process once again, but this time, turn it around; after that, choose either the Sharp or the Soft thickening kind. There is no significance in either the direction parameter or the thickness (we went with **Sharp, Normal and 1 mm**). Make a drawing in the XY plane (assuming the Z-axis is your vertical axis), then use a spline to construct the first form of the tube you want to use. You may check our rough draft down below.

After that, make a new drawing, and then choose the tool labeled "**Project to Surface.**" This is the place where all the magic takes place. With an Along Vector project type, the topmost surface should be used as the face, the spline should be used as the curve, and the vertical axis should be used as the projection direction. The outcome can be seen in the image below, where the spline has been made to follow the selected surface.

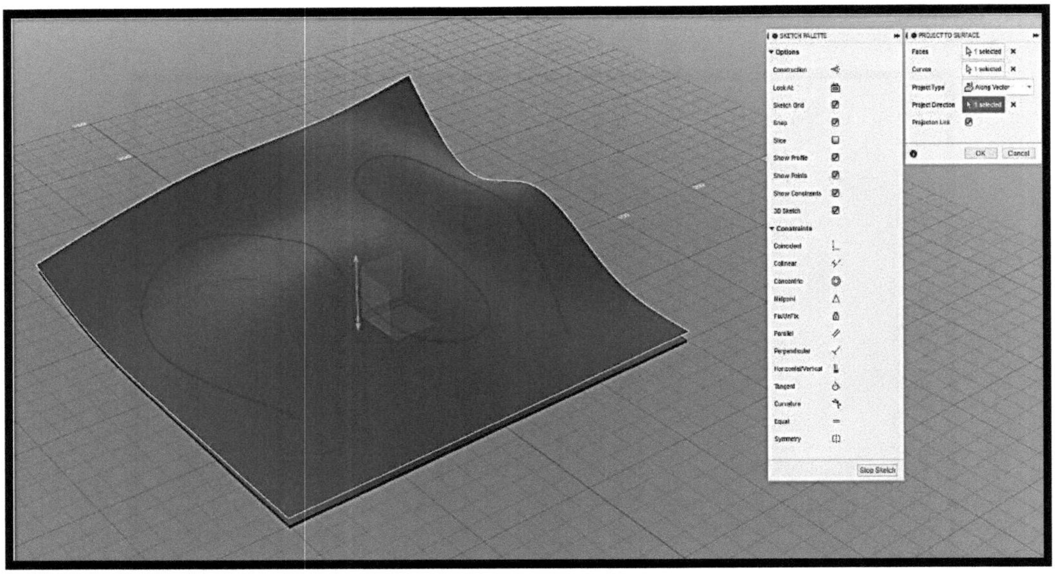

In the first illustration, the sweep profile was defined with the help of a cube. This time around, we are going to engage in a new activity. Construct a plane along the path, select the newly projected curve, and then move the plane until it is positioned at one of the curve's endpoints, as shown below. The curve will consistently be drawn such that it is normal to this plane. Hide the surface that is currently on top; you won't need it anymore.

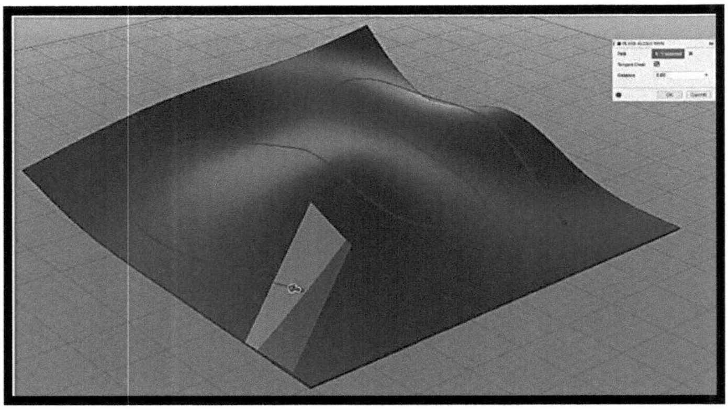

The rest is straightforward. Make use of the sweep tool to fashion the tube after first constructing a tube profile on the freshly built plane that has the appropriate outside radius. There is a possibility that the tube may scratch the base surface, which is one problem that might arise. This makes little sense to us, given that the surface that the projection is meant to hit ought, at any given instant, to be precisely one tube radius away from the surface it is meant to hit. Thankfully, this sum is not all that substantial. You can see in the following image how much of our base surface was chopped away. For the sake of a purely aesthetic experience, this may be ignored. We decided to remove the overlapping section.

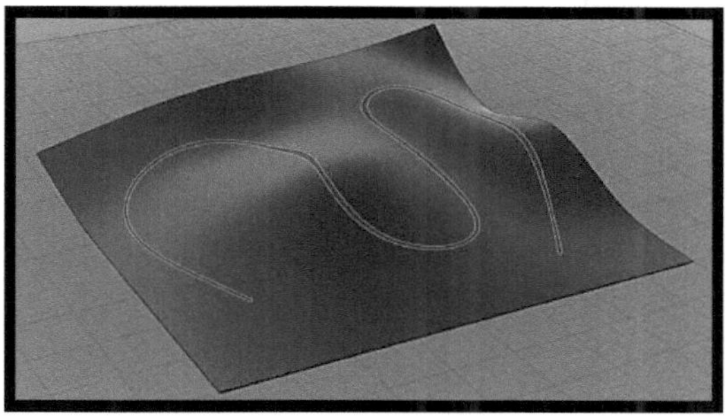

Now, put on some silly textures and render. Here's our outcome.

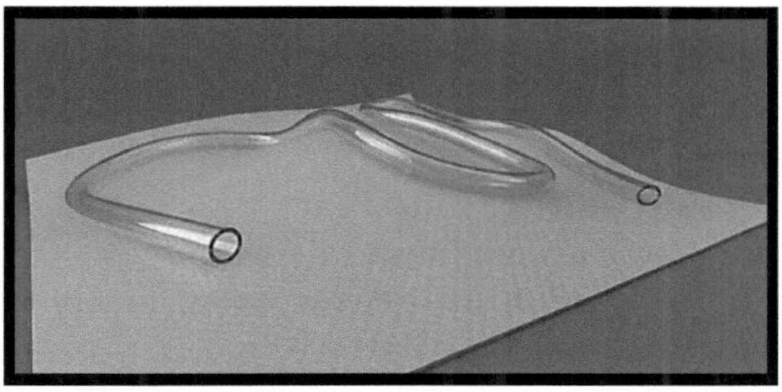

Air Time

Up until this point, all of our wires and tubes have been laid out in a fully flat pattern. This gives the impression that it is incredibly fluffy or heavy. Smaller wires and tubes are often highly rigid in comparison to their weight, and as a result, they will float far higher in the air.

The following is an example of where we have increased the natural rigidity a little bit, but despite this, it still seems to be fairly soft and heavy.

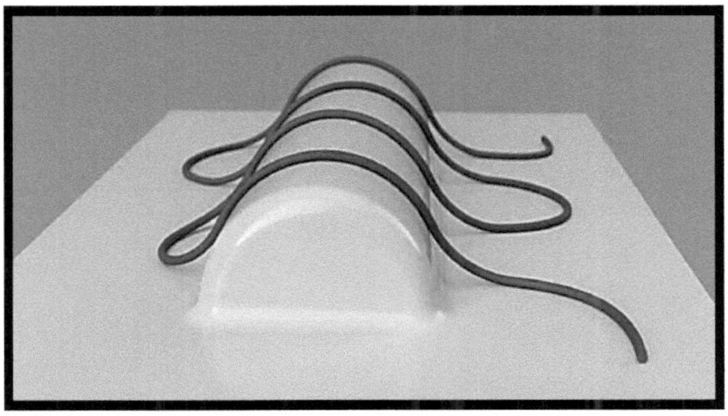

In this case, we followed the identical strategy as we did in the one before it, with the exception that we departed more from the starting surface.

Due to the simple nature of the starting surface, what we performed here was quite uncomplicated:

- First, make a replica of the original body, and then scale it up in the standard direction (larger diameter on the cylinder and a bit thicker flat area).
- Raise the fillet radius on the sides of the cylinder on the bigger body so that it fits more snugly. Because of this, the wire or tube will float somewhat in the air, where it is fairly natural to do so.
- Bring the project up to the surface and sweep.

3D Sketching

If you combine everything you've learned so far with the ability to draw in three dimensions, you'll have a potent set of abilities for constructing wire and tubes. For this to function, you will need to go into the Design options and tick the box labeled "**Allow 3D drawing of lines and splines**." You now can-do things like generate a spline on a drawing and then manually pull the spline fit points away from the sketch plane, which will result in the creation of a three-dimensional spline.

Questions

1. Which tool is used for creating a sweep feature?
2. On selecting the ________ option, the resultant sweep feature is created by keeping the section/profile of the feature perpendicular to the path.
3. What are the two types of threads that you can create?
4. Which button of the HOLE dialog box is used for creating multiple holes by using the sketch points?
5. When you choose the ________ option, you can create a helical coil by defining its pitch and number of revolutions.
6. Which option of the Type drop-down list in the SWEEP dialog box is used for creating a sweep feature by using the profiles and a guide rail?
7. Which field of the SWEEP dialog box is used for specifying the twist angle value for twisting the profile along the path?

CHAPTER 9

PATTERNING AND MIRRORING

Creating a Rectangular Pattern

Using the Rectangular Pattern tool, you may produce a rectangular pattern by producing numerous instances of faces, bodies, features, or components in either one or two linear dimensions. This can be done in either one or two linear directions. To make a pattern consisting of rectangles, use the "Rectangular Pattern" tool, which can be found in the "**CREATE**" panel of the "**SOLID**" tab. A dialog window labeled RECTANGULAR PATTERN will now display. You may also choose **Pattern > Rectangular Pattern** from the drop-down menu that appears when you call the CREATE drop-down menu in the SOLID tab.

Pattern Type

To pick the faces, features, bodies, or components that are going to be patterned, utilize the drop-down list labeled "**Pattern Type**" that is located in the dialog box. When you pick the Faces option, you will be able to select the faces that determine the geometry of a model that is going to be patterned. When you pick the Bodies option, you will be allowed to choose which bodies will be patterned. When you pick the Features option, you will be allowed to choose which features will be patterned. When you pick the Components option, you will be allowed to choose which components will be patterned.

Objects

You can pattern various things, such as faces, bodies, features, and components, by using the Objects selection option. It is important to note that the choice picked in the Pattern Kind drop-down list determines the type of item that may be selected. Within the graphics section, you have the option of selecting bodies, components, faces, or features.

Directions

The Directions selection option is used to indicate the first and second linear pattern directions before the pattern is created. This is done to create the pattern. In the first and second pattern directions, you have the option of choosing either an axis, a linear edge, or a linear sketch object. It is important to take note that after picking the first pattern direction, the second pattern direction will automatically be established as being perpendicular to the first direction that was picked. You have the option of choosing the second pattern direction, depending on what you need. After the pattern directions have been selected, the arrows that depict them will display in the graphics section.

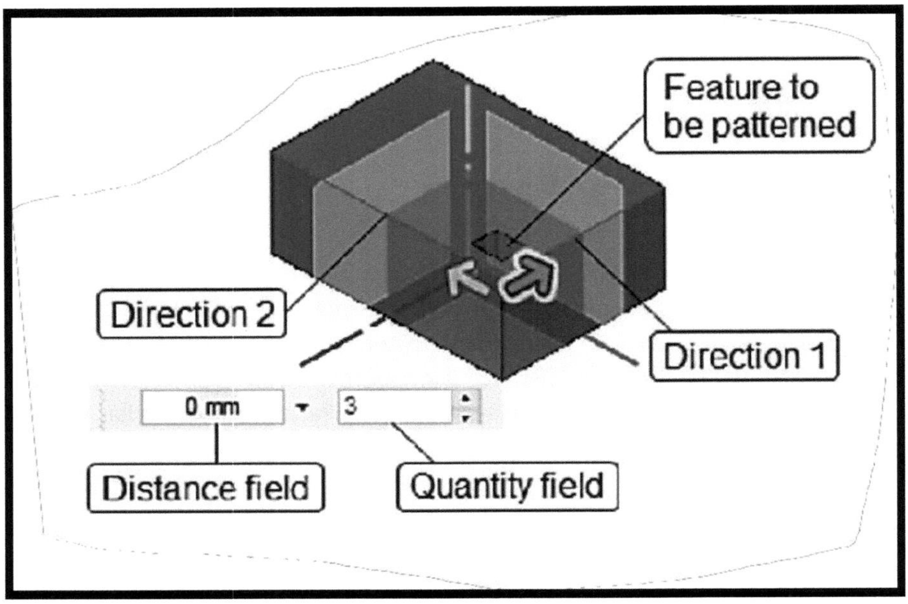

Distance Type

The kind of distance measurement that will be utilized between the pattern instances may be specified by selecting it from the drop-down list titled "**Distance Type**." This drop-down menu has the Extent option selected by default for your convenience. As a consequence of this, the number that is entered into the field labeled Distance inside the dialog box is the one that is used for the spacing between the first and final pattern occurrences (total pattern distance). For instance, if the pattern distance along a pattern direction is defined to be 100 mm, then all of the pattern instances will adapt such that they are contained inside the provided pattern distance while maintaining an equal amount of spacing between each of the pattern instances. When you pick the Spacing option from the drop-down box labeled Distance Type, the value that you enter into the Distance field is the one that is utilized to determine the amount of space that exists between two consecutive pattern occurrences.

Quantity

In the RECTANGULAR PATTERN dialog box, the Quantity boxes in the Direction 1 and Direction 2 sections allow the user to define the number of pattern instances that are to be produced in Direction 1 and Direction 2, respectively. The first picture shows the sections designated as Direction 1 and Direction 2 in the dialog box. A preview of a rectangular design can be seen in the second picture. This pattern has four occurrences in direction 1, and five occurrences in direction 2. You can also adjust the number of pattern instances by dragging the spinner arrows that are located close to the source object in the preview of the pattern. These arrows appear in the vicinity of the source item. In the Quantity box that appears in the graphics area, you are also given the option to define the total number of pattern instances that will be produced.

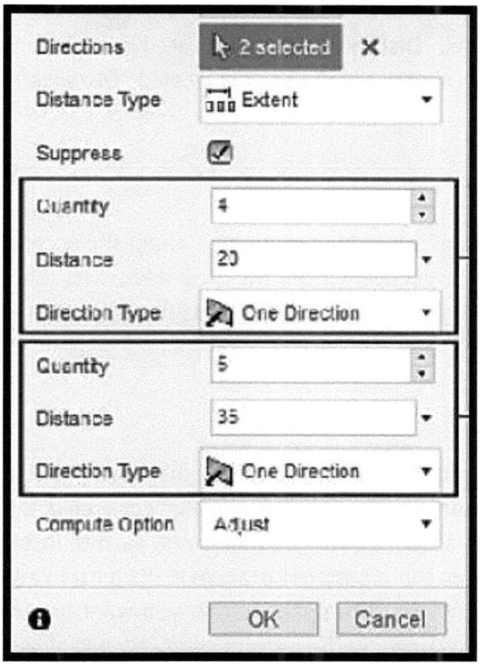

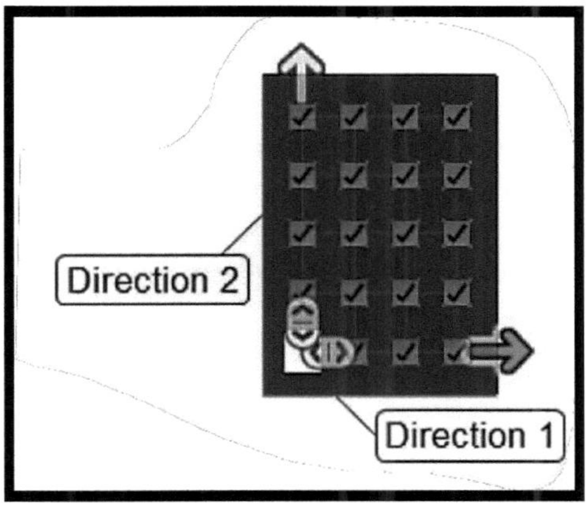

NOTE: The quantity of pattern instances that you provide in the field labeled "**Quantity**" is tallied along with the instance that serves as the parent or the original instance. For instance, if the Quantity field is set to 4, then the associated pattern direction will produce 4 pattern instances in addition to the parent instance. These instances will be constructed in the same order as the parent instance.

Distance

The Distance fields in the **Direction 1 and Direction 2** regions of the dialog box are used to determine the amount of space that should be present between pattern instances in the corresponding directions, Direction 1 and Direction 2. It is important to keep in mind that the choice chosen from the drop-down list labeled "**Distance Type**" in the dialog box will determine how the distance value is stated in these fields. You may also adjust the spacing between the pattern instances by dragging the arrows that show in the preview of the pattern. This can be done to make the space larger or smaller. Another option is to enter the desired distance in the field labeled "**Distance,**" which is located in the graphics area. Additionally, you have the option of entering a negative distance in the section labeled "**Distance**" to invert the pattern direction.

Direction Type

You can define pattern direction on one side or symmetric about the parent object(s) by selecting the One Direction or Symmetric option, respectively, from the drop-down lists that are located in the **Direction 1 and Direction 2** areas of the dialog box. These lists are used to define the pattern direction.

Suppress

In the RECTANGULAR PATTERN dialog box, the Suppress check box is selected by default and cannot be deselected. As a direct consequence of this, a checkbox manifests itself in the exact middle of every pattern instance present in the graphics area. You may exclude some pattern instances from the final pattern by deselecting the check boxes next to those pattern instances in the pattern editor. You may do this by clicking the left mouse button on the instance of the pattern that you want to remove from the pattern. Simply selecting the checkboxes that are shown in the pattern's preview will allow you to either recall or include the occurrences of the pattern that were skipped.

Compute Option

The computational approach for constructing the pattern is defined by selecting one of the choices from the drop-down list labeled "**Compute Option**" which is located inside the dialog box. It is important to take note that the Compute Option drop-down list becomes accessible once the Features option has been chosen in the Pattern Type drop-down list. We will now go through the choices that may be made using the drop-down menu.

Optimized

To create a pattern with a high number of pattern instances while simultaneously optimizing the process of constructing the pattern, choose the Optimized option from the drop-down menu. It is the quickest approach to accomplish that goal.

Identical

When building a pattern, you may utilize the identical option to ensure that the pattern instances do not keep the same geometrical relations as the parent feature when it comes to the pattern's appearance. For instance, the figure below depicts the front view of a model, in which a cut feature is formed by specifying the end condition as being 4 mm offset from the bottom face of the model. This offset is measured in millimeters.

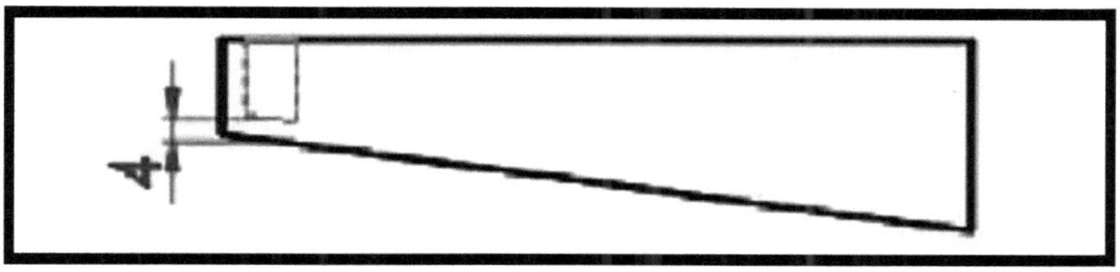

The pattern of the cut feature that was produced as a consequence of choosing the identical option from the drop-down list of Compute Options is shown in the picture below.

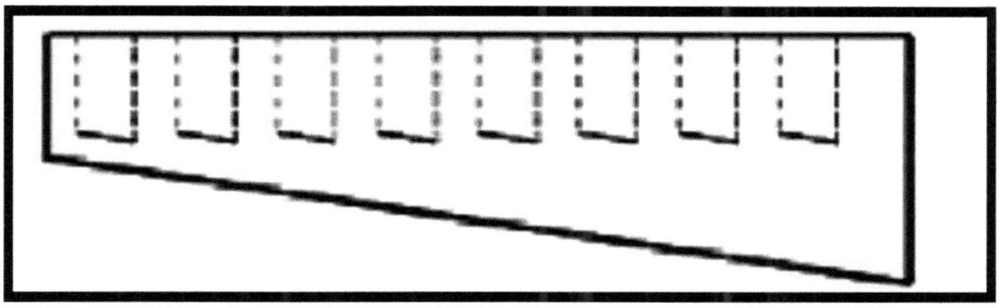

Adjust: Using the Adjust option, you may create a pattern in such a way that all of the pattern instances preserve the same geometrical relations as the parent feature. This is accomplished by ensuring that the parent feature is the active feature. The pattern instances in the picture below keep the geometrical relation of the parent feature, which has a 4 mm offset from the bottom face of the model. This can be seen by looking at the image.

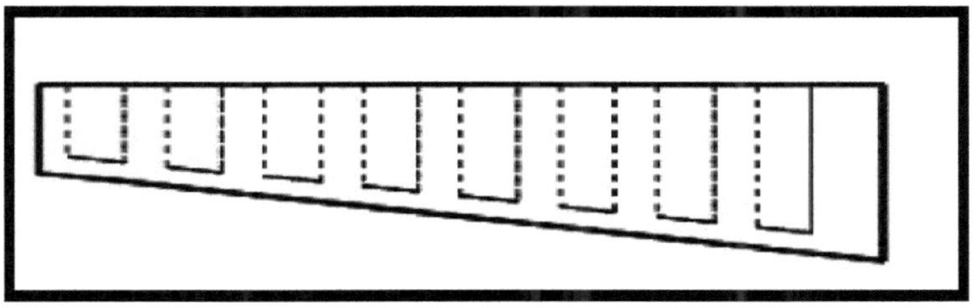

Click the OK button after you have finished specifying the parameters in the RECTANGULAR PATTERN dialog box. This results in the formation of a rectangular pattern.

Creating a Circular Pattern

By utilizing the Circle Pattern tool, you may generate a circular pattern by producing many instances of faces, bodies, features, or components that are arranged in a circular fashion around an axis. To make a circular pattern, go to the SOLID tab, open the **CREATE** drop-down menu, and then choose **Pattern > Circular Pattern** from the menu that appears. We will now go through the choices that are available in this dialog box.

Pattern Type

You may decide which faces, features, bodies, or components are going to be patterned by using the drop-down list labeled "Pattern Type." When you select the Faces option, you will be able to pattern the graphics area with the faces that define the geometry of a model. These faces can be selected by clicking on them in the graphics area. When you pick the Bodies option, you will be allowed to choose which bodies will be patterned. When you pick the Features option, you will be allowed to choose which features will be patterned. When you select the Components option, you will be allowed to select the components that will be patterned. Objects you can pattern various things, such as faces, bodies, features, and components, by using the Objects selection option. It is important to note that the choice picked in the Pattern Kind drop-down list determines the type of item that may be selected. In the graphics section, you may choose to pick either the faces, bodies, or components, while in the Timeline, you can choose to select the features.

Axis

By using the Axis selection option, you may choose an axis that will serve as the center of a circular design that you wish to construct. To do this, open the dialog box and click on the Axis selection option. Next, choose either an axis, a circular face, a circular edge, or a linear drawing to serve as the pattern axis. Note that when you choose a circular face or edge as the pattern axis, the corresponding center axis is automatically identified and utilized as the axis of the circular pattern. This is something that you should keep in mind.

Type

Within the Type drop-down list, the Full option is the one that is chosen by default. As a consequence of this, the circular pattern that was produced is designed in such a way that it encompasses all 360 degrees of the pattern, and the quantity of pattern instances that was entered into the Quantity field of the dialog box is distributed evenly over those 360 degrees. The Total Angle field will become visible in the dialog box after the Angle option has been selected from the Type drop-down list.

You may define the entire angle value of the pattern in this box, and it will be used appropriately. You may also move the arrow that appears near the most recent pattern instance to adjust the overall angle value. This displays near the most recent pattern occurrence. Take note that the pattern instances are automatically changed so that they remain within the overall angle value that you have set. By going to the Type drop-down menu and choosing the Symmetric option, you will be able to build a circular pattern that is symmetric around the parent object that you have chosen.

Quantity

The number of pattern instances that are to be produced may be specified by using the box labeled "Quantity." You can also adjust the number of pattern instances by dragging the spinner arrows that show up in the preview of the pattern. These arrows will appear in the pattern preview.

NOTE: The quantity of pattern instances that you provide in the field labeled "Quantity" is tallied along with the instance that serves as the parent or the original instance. For instance, if the Quantity field is set to 4, then the associated pattern direction will produce 4 pattern instances in addition to the parent instance. These instances will be constructed in the same order as the parent instance.

Suppress

There is a checkmark in the Suppress checkbox by default. As a direct consequence of this, a checkbox manifests itself in the exact middle of every pattern instance present in the graphics area. You may eliminate pattern instances from the final pattern by clearing the check boxes next to those instances in the resulting pattern that you do not wish to use. Simply selecting the checkboxes that are shown in the pattern's preview will allow you to either recall or include the occurrences of the pattern that were skipped.

Compute Option

The same information that was covered earlier can be found in the Compute Option drop-down list's options, which are used for defining the computational method that is used when creating a pattern. Lick the OK button after you have finished specifying the parameters for patterning the items that have been chosen in the CIRCULAR PATTERN dialog box. This results in the formation of a circular pattern.

Creating a Pattern along a Path

Using the Pattern on path tool, you may produce a pattern by producing several instances of faces, bodies, features, or components along a path. This can be done to build a pattern. You have the option of choosing sketch curves or edges as the path, which will cause the pattern instances to be driven along the specified path. To generate a pattern along a path, go to the SOLID tab, activate the CREATE drop-down menu, and then choose **Pattern > Pattern on Path** from the menu that appears. A dialog window labeled **PATTERN ON PATH** will display.

Pattern Type

To pick the faces, features, bodies, or components that are going to be patterned, utilize the drop-down list labeled "**Pattern Type**" that is located in the dialog box. You can pick the faces that determine the geometry of a model when you select the Faces option from the drop-down menu in the graphics section. You will be able to pick bodies in the graphics section if you select the **Bodies** option. When you pick the Features option, you will be allowed to select features in the graphics section. When you choose the Components option, the graphics area will become available for you to pick various components.

Objects

You can pattern various things, such as faces, bodies, features, and components, by using the Objects selection option. Take note that the kind of object selection will change depending on whatever option you choose from the drop-down list labeled "**Pattern Type**" in the dialog box. Within the graphics section, you have the option of selecting bodies, components, faces, or features.

Path

You may choose a curve or an edge to act as the path that drives the pattern instances by using the Path selection option. This option can be found in the Edit menu. To do this, first, choose the path in the graphics area, and then click on the Path selection option in the menu that appears. Take note that when you pick one edge or curve, all the other edges and curves that are adjacent to it will also be chosen automatically.

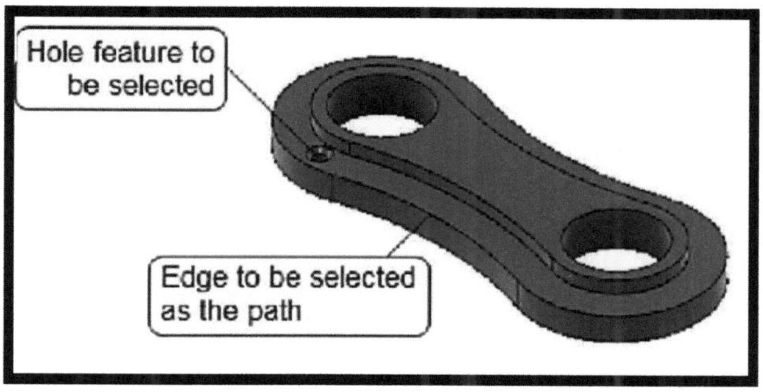

Distance Type

The kind of distance measurement that will be utilized between the pattern instances may be specified by selecting it from the drop-down list titled "**Distance Type**." This drop-down menu has the Extent option selected by default for your convenience. As a consequence of this, the number that is entered into the field labeled Distance inside the dialog box is the one that is used for the spacing between the first and final pattern occurrences (total pattern distance). For instance, if the pattern distance is defined as 100 millimeters, then each instance of the pattern will change such that it fits inside the provided pattern distance while maintaining the same amount of space between each instance. When you pick the Spacing option from the drop-down box labeled Distance Type, the value that you enter into the Distance field is the one that is utilized to determine the amount of space that exists between two consecutive pattern occurrences.

Distance

The Distance field of the dialog box allows you to determine the amount of space that should exist between pattern occurrences along the path that has been chosen. Take note that the distance value that you enter into this field will change depending on the option you choose from the drop-down menu labeled "**Distance Type**" in the dialog box. You may also adjust the spacing between the pattern instances by dragging the arrows that show in the preview of the pattern. This can be done to make the space larger or smaller.

Quantity

The number of pattern instances that are to be produced along the path that has been chosen may be specified by typing a number into the Quantity field of the dialog box. You may also raise or reduce the number of pattern instances by dragging the spinner arrows that show in the preview of the pattern. This can be done in the pattern editor.

Start Point

Within the dialog box, the Start Point field is where you will define the point at which the pattern computation will begin. By default, a 0 (zero) value is placed in this field. As a direct consequence of this, the pattern will begin with the parent object that has been chosen to be patterned. It is important to keep in mind that the value that is supplied in this field is computed as a percentage (ranging from 0 to 1) of the entire length of the path that was chosen. If you put 0.5 in the Start Point box, for instance, the pattern will begin at the midpoint of the path that you have decided to use.

Direction

The choices found in the drop-down lists labeled Direction are what are utilized to define the pattern direction on one side or symmetric around the parent object(s) that have been chosen.

Orientation

When the Identical option is selected from the Orientation drop-down list, the orientation of the pattern instances will remain the same as the orientation of the parent object that has been chosen.

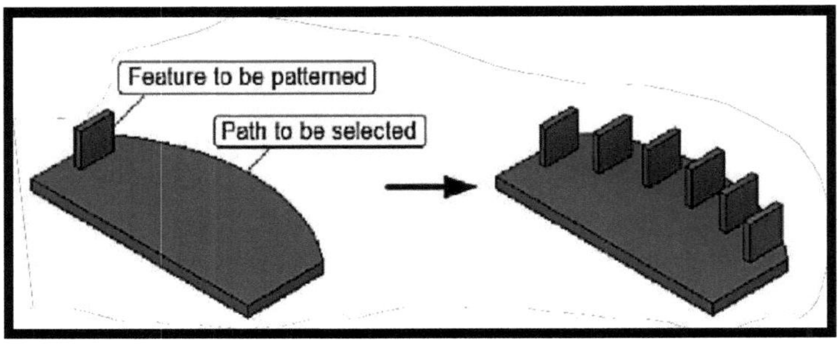

By selecting the path Direction option, you can ensure that the pattern instances continue to keep their orientation concerning the path that has been chosen.

Suppress

In the dialog box, the "**Suppress**" check box is chosen by default when it may be deselected. As a direct consequence of this, a checkbox manifests itself in the exact middle of every pattern instance present in the graphics area. You may exclude some pattern instances from the final pattern by deselecting the check boxes next to those pattern instances in the pattern editor. Simply selecting the checkboxes that are shown in the pattern's preview will allow you to either recall or include the occurrences of the pattern that were skipped.

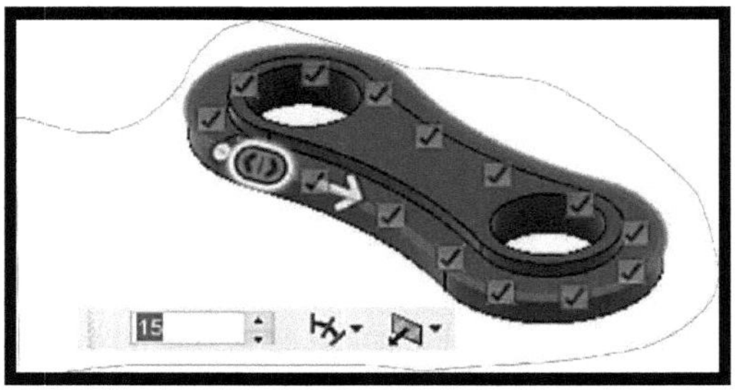

Compute Option

The same information that was covered before can be found in the Compute Option drop-down list's choices, which are used to define the computational approach that will be utilized to create the pattern. After you have finished specifying the specifications for patterning the item that is now chosen, click the **OK** button. Along the path that was picked, the instances of the pattern were constructed. Choosing the Path Direction option from the Orientation drop-down list of the dialog box will result in the creation of the pattern that is seen in this picture.

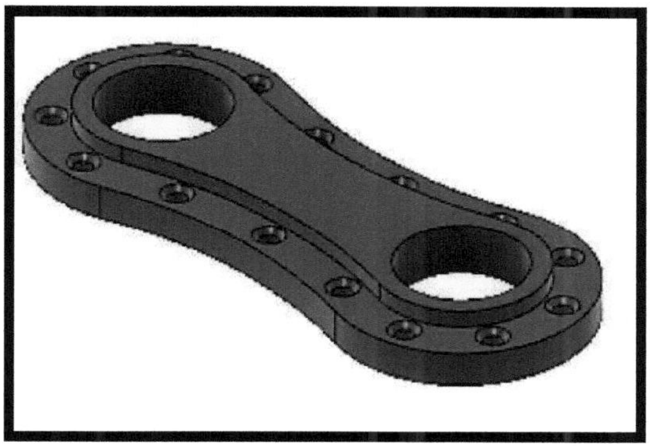

Mirroring Features/Faces/Bodies/Components

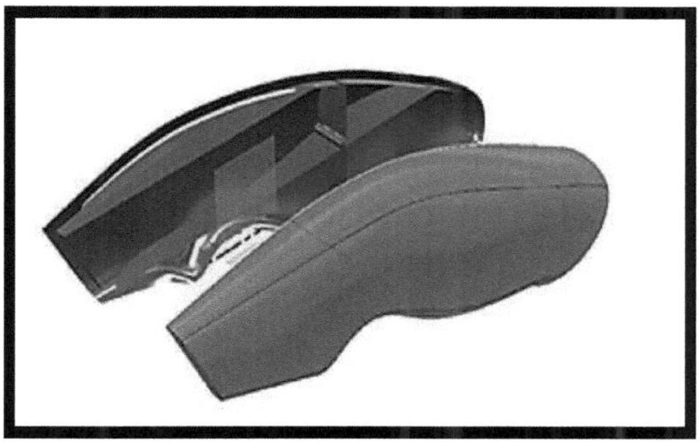

1. Navigate to the Design workspace and pick the Solid or Surface tab. From there, choose the **Create > Mirror** option. The Mirror dialogue box will appear.
2. **Choose the kind of items you want to reflect from the drop-down menu in the dialog box.**
- Faces
- Bodies
- Features
- Components
3. Select the items you want to reflect in either the canvas or the browser.
4. Within the dialog box, pick the plane or planar face you want to mirror the chosen items across, and then click the Mirror Plane button.
5. **If the Type is set to Bodies, choose an operation from the following options:**

- **New Body**: This function creates a new body that is reflected across the mirror plane.
- **Join**: If the mirrored body and the original body intersect, this operation joins the two together.
  - Multiple solid bodies are brought together.
  - The surface bodies are stitched, and the stitch Tolerance may be adjusted by the user.

6. **If the Type drop-down menu is set to Features, choose one of the following to compute options:**

- **Optimized**: Makes exact replicas of features by patterning their faces to create new features. (Fastest)
- **Identical**: This feature replicates the outcomes of the original features to produce exact replicas of those features.
- **Adjust**: This creates possibly unique copies of features by patterning features and calculating the extent or terminations of each occurrence. This allows for potentially unique copies of features to be created. (Slowest)

7. Activate the "**OK**" button.
   Faces, bodies, characteristics, or other components that are reflected appear on the canvas.

Questions

1. The ________ option is used for maintaining the orientation/ position of the pattern instances relative to the path selected.
2. Which tool is used for mirroring faces, bodies, features, or components in a mirroring plane?
3. The tool used for creating multiple instances of features, faces, bodies, or components in one to two linear directions is called?
4. Which option is used for creating a pattern such that all the pattern instances maintain the same geometrical relations as that of the parent/source feature?
5. The tool used in creating a pattern by creating multiple instances of faces, bodies, features, or components along a path is known as?
6. Which tool is used for creating multiple instances of features, faces, bodies, or components in a circular manner around an axis?
7. Which check box in the RECTANGULAR PATTERN dialog box is used for displaying a checkbox at the center of each pattern instance in the graphics area to skip the instances?

CHAPTER 10

EDITING AND MODIFYING 3D MODELS

Working with the Press Pull Tool

Modifying a solid model in a way that is both rapid and dynamic may be accomplished with the assistance of the Press Pull tool. You may dynamically offset a face of a model, fillet an edge of a model, or extrude a sketch profile in the graphics area by using the Press Pull tool. Other options include filleting an edge of a model. To do this, go to the MODIFY panel of the SOLID tab and choose the Press Pull tool from there.

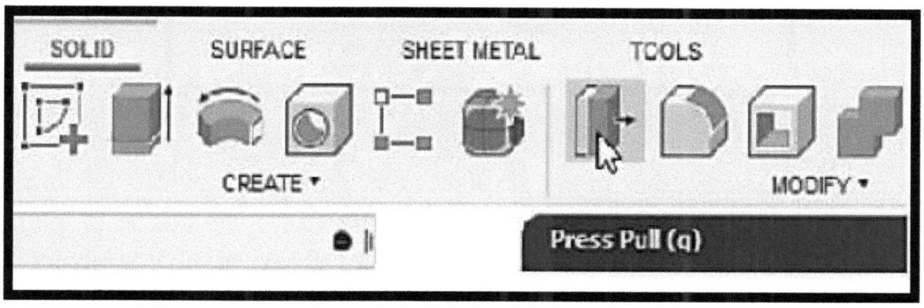

A dialogue window labeled PRESS PULL is shown. Alternatively, you may activate the Press Pull tool by pressing the Q key or right-clicking in the graphics area. After that, go to the Marking Menu and choose the Press Pull tool from the list of available options. Following the activation of the **PRESS PULL** dialog box, you will be able to make a modification selection for the model's geometry. You have the option of selecting the geometry to be adjusted from either a face or an edge of the model. Take note that the editing procedure varies depending on the shape that you choose to work with. For instance, when you choose a face of a model, the **OFFSET FACE** dialog box displays. This box gives you the ability to offset the face of the model that you chose by an amount that you specify. On the other hand, when you choose an edge of a model, the FILLET dialog box appears. This box gives you the option to build a fillet with either a fixed or variable radius on the edge of the model that you chose.

Offsetting a Face by Using the Press Pull Tool

1. Invoke the dialog window labeled **"PRESS PULL."** You will be asked to choose a geometry that will be updated after this prompt.

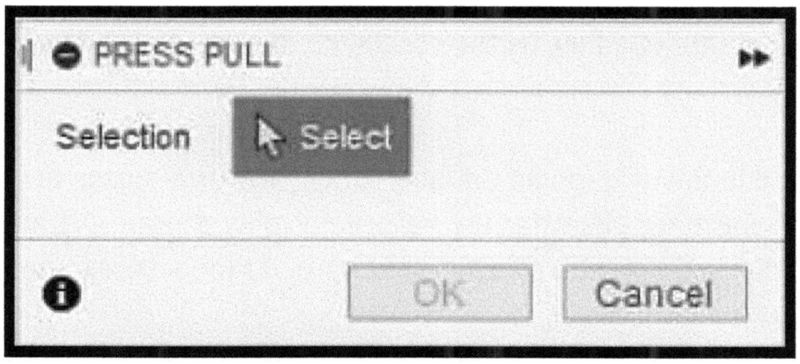

2. Determine which of the model's faces will be altered and choose that face. The OFFSET FACE dialog box is brought into view. Additionally, the face that is now chosen will become highlighted, and an arrow will appear in the graphics area.

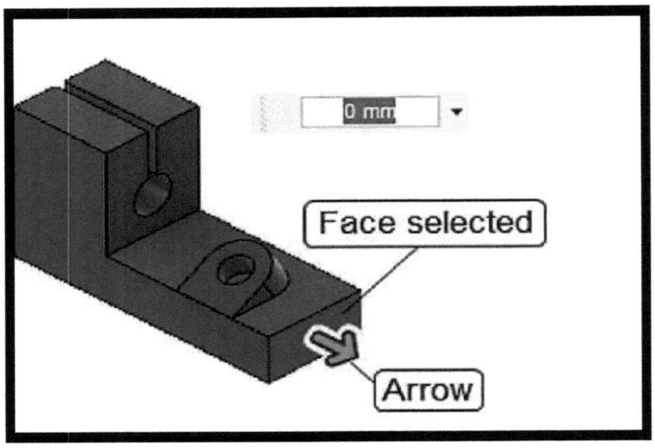

3. To dynamically offset the chosen face in the graphics area, press and hold the left mouse button, and then drag the arrow that appears in the graphics area. You also have the option of inputting the offset distance in the area labeled Distance inside the OFFSET FACE dialog box. In the box labeled "**Distance**" that displays in the graphics area, you also have the option of entering an offset distance. You may change the direction of the offset by dragging the arrow to the other side of the face that is now chosen, or by entering a negative number for the offset distance in the area labeled Distance.

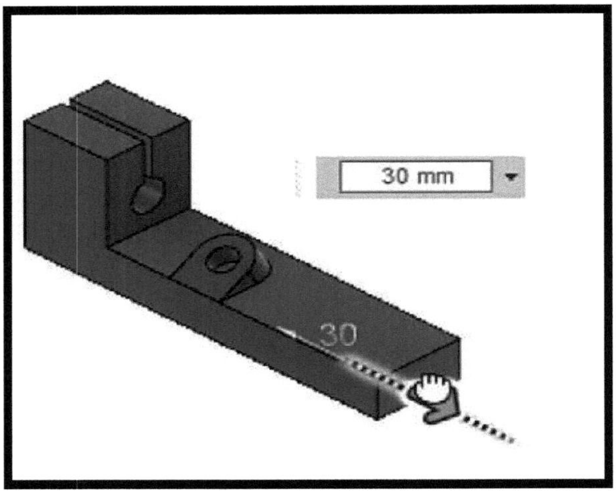

4. Once you have finished offsetting a face by the specified amount, choose the OK button located in the dialog box.

NOTE: The choices included in the drop-down list labeled "**Offset Type**" inside the dialog box are what are utilized to define the mechanism for offsetting the face that is now chosen. Offsetting the face that is now chosen is one of the ways that you may edit an existing feature of a model using the **Modify Existing Feature** option.

When selecting the New Offset option, a new offset feature will be added to the Timeline. This option is used for offsetting a face beginning from zero. When using the Automatic function, the chosen face will have its offset adjusted using the method that provides the best results (either Modify Existing Feature or New Offset).

Filleting an Edge by Using the Press Pull Tool

1. Either use the **Q** key on your keyboard or click on the Press Pull tool located in the MODIFY panel of the SOLID tab. You will be invited to choose a geometry to have its properties updated when the PRESS PULL dialog box displays on the screen.
2. Pick an edge of the model that you want to modify and set it aside. A dialog window labeled **FILLET** will now display. In addition to this, the edge that has been picked will get highlighted, and an arrow will show in the graphics area.

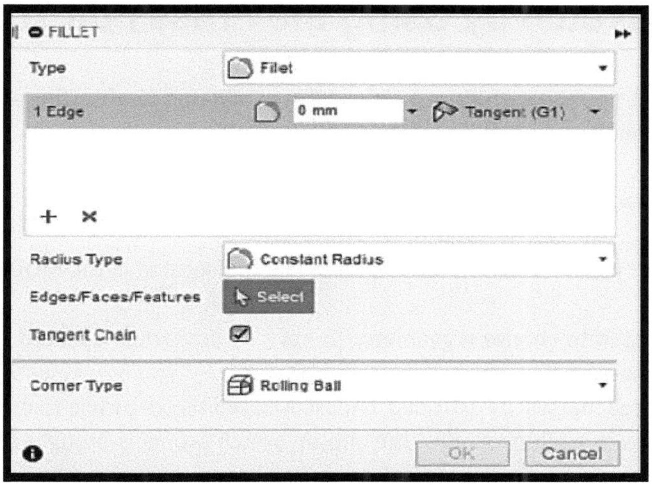

3. While holding down the left mouse button, drag the arrow that appears in the graphics area to dynamically generate a fillet along the edge that was picked. You also have the option of entering the fillet radius in the area labeled Radius inside the FILLET dialog box. Additionally, you have the option of typing the fillet radius into the Radius box that shows up in the graphics area.

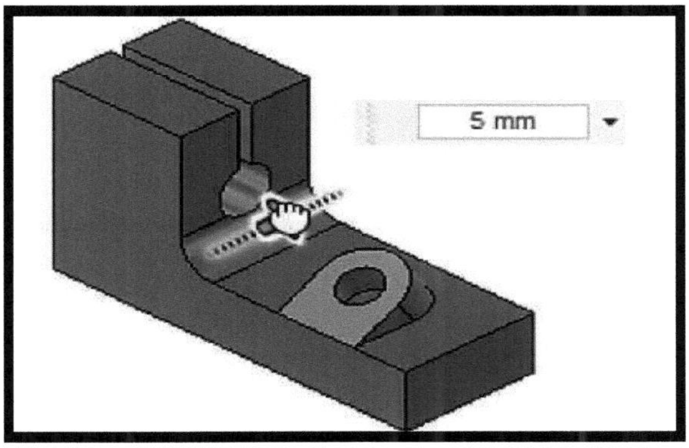

NOTE: The choice chosen in the Radius Kind drop-down list of the FILLET dialog box determines the type of fillet that will be formed on the edge that has been selected. This fillet type will be applied to the edge. The Constant Radius option is chosen whenever it is available. As a direct consequence of this, the edge that was picked will now have a fillet with a constant radius.

You can create a fillet with a variable radius by either entering different radius values for both ends of the selected edge in the Radius fields respectively or by dragging the arrows that appear on both ends of the selected edge after selecting the Variable Radius option. This will allow you to create a fillet with a variable radius. You can make a fillet with a constant radius by selecting the Chord Length option and then manually entering the chord length that you want the fillet to have.

4. After completing the creation of a fillet along the edge that was chosen, pick the OK button located inside the dialog box.

Extruding a Sketch by Using the Press Pull Tool

Using the Press Pull tool, you can extrude a sketch profile in addition to offsetting a face and generating a fillet on an edge. Additionally, you can use this tool to offset a face.

The following is an explanation of the procedure for extruding a sketch profile:

1. Use the **Q key** on your keyboard or click on the Press Pull tool located in the MODIFY panel of the SOLID tab.
    - You will be invited to choose a geometry to have its properties updated when the PRESS PULL dialog box displays on the screen.

2. Within the graphics area that will be extruded, choose a closed sketch profile to use. The EXTRUDE dialog box is brought into view. In addition to this, the chosen sketch profile is brought to the forefront of the screen, and the graphics area is adorned with an arrow and a manipulator handle.

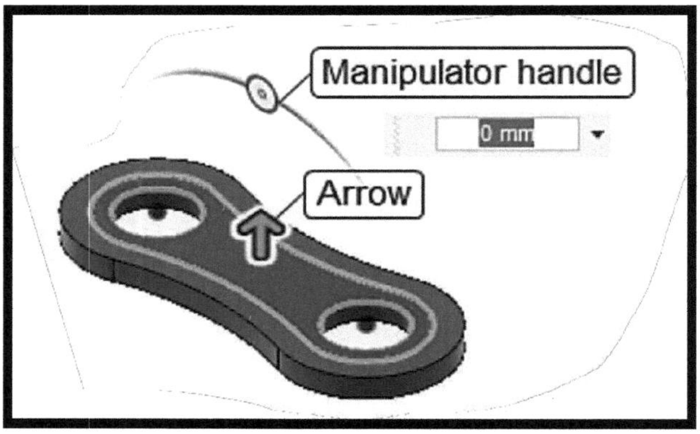

3. To dynamically extrude the sketch profile, press and hold the left mouse button, and then drag the arrow that appears in the graphics area with your left mouse button. You also have the option to enter the extrusion distance into the area labeled Distance inside the dialog box. You can also add tapering to the extrude feature by sliding the manipulator handle or entering the taper angle into the Taper Angle field of the dialog box. Both of these options are available in the Extrude section of the dialog box.

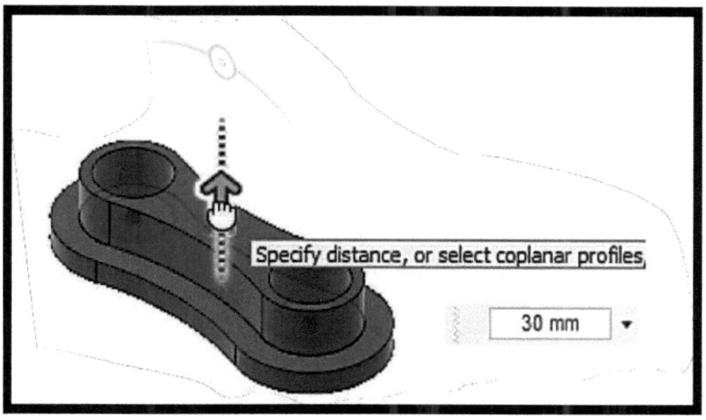

4. In the drop-down menu labeled "**Operation**" of the dialog box, choose the option that corresponds to what you need, and then click the OK button. The extrude feature is developed.

Creating Fillets

A fillet is a curved face with a constant or variable radius that is used to remove sharp edges from a model that might cause harm when the model is being handled. Fillets can have either a constant or variable radius. Using the Fillet tool in Fusion 360, you can create a fillet with either a constant or variable radius, or you can choose the chord length to determine the fillet's length. In addition, the Fillet tool allows you to create rule fillets, which is another useful option.

Creating a Constant Radius Fillet

1. When you choose the Fillet tool from the MODIFY panel of the SOLID tab, a dialog window labeled FILLET will display. You also have the option to bring up the FILLET dialog box by using the F key.
Type: When you first open the dialog box, the Type drop-down list will have the Fillet option selected by default. As a consequence of this, you can produce a fillet with either a fixed radius or a variable radius as well as by providing the chord length. Rule fillets may be crafted by selecting the Rule Fillet option from the Type drop-down list in the Type editor.
2. In the Type drop-down list of the dialog box, you should make sure that the Fillet option is chosen. Fillets with a constant radius, fillets with a variable radius, or fillets with a chord length can be created by selecting the appropriate option (Constant Radius, Variable Radius, or Chord Length) in the Radius Type drop-down list. Alternatively, you can create fillets with a chord length by selecting the appropriate option.
3. In the Radius Type drop-down list of the dialog box, choose the Constant Radius option to build a fillet with a constant radius.

- **Edges/Faces/Features**: Inside the dialog box, the Edges/Faces/Features selection option is the one that is active by default. As a consequence of this, you will have the ability to create fillets by selecting the edges, faces, or other characteristics of the model. In the graphics area, you can choose to select either edges or faces, while in the Timeline, you can choose to select features.
- **Tangent Chain**: The check box denoted by "**Tangent Chain**" is selected in the dialog box's default state. As a consequence of this, when one edge is picked, all of the edges that are tangent to the edge that was selected are also automatically selected.

4. In the dialog box, you need to make sure that the check box labeled "**Tangent Chain**" is selected to add tangentially related edges or faces. Deactivating the Tangent Chain checkbox will allow you to design fillets on specific edges or faces.
5. To make the fillet, choose an edge, a face, or a feature of the model from the available options. When you choose an edge, a face, or a feature, the FILLET dialog box is updated with new possibilities. Additionally, an arrow will display the entity that has been chosen in the graphics section.

- **Hint:** If the Radius field is set to a value other than 0 (zero), then you must use the CTRL key to pick several edges or faces that are to be filleted. In the dialog box, the field labeled "**Radius**" is where the specified value for the fillet's radius should be entered.
- **Continuity**: The choices available in the Continuity drop-down list are what you should select to apply either the G1 tangent continuity or the G2 curvature continuity to the fillet, depending on the type of continuity you want to use.

6. From the Continuity drop-down list, choose the needed choice, either **Tangent (G1)** or **Curvature (G2),** as the kind of continuity to be applied to the fillet to complete the fillet.

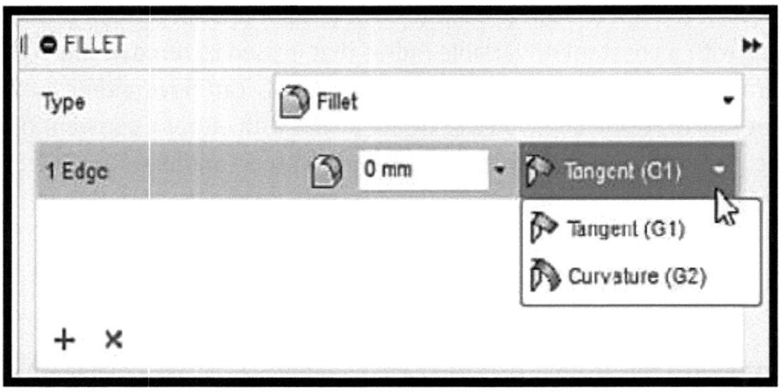

7. To specify the radius value of the fillet dynamically, either enter the value for the fillet's radius in the Radius field of the dialog box or move the arrow that appears in the graphics area. The preview of a fillet with a constant radius is seen here.

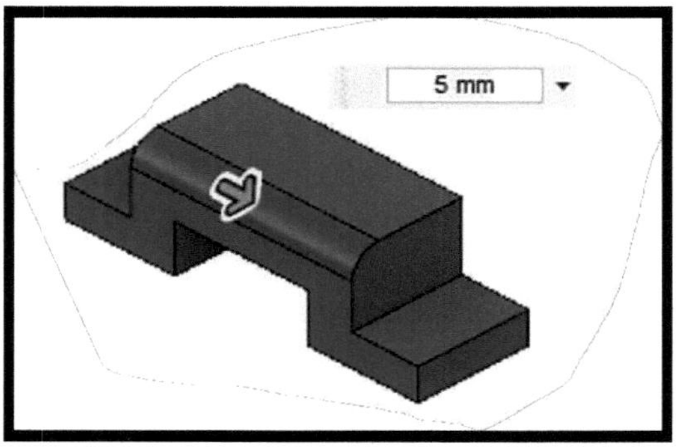

Corner Type: In the dialog box's Corner Type drop-down list, the Rolling Ball option is chosen by default. You may change this if you'd like. As a direct consequence of this, the rolling ball corner is produced at the vertex in the region where three or more than three edges connect. A setback fillet may be created at a corner where three or more than three edges cross one another by selecting the Setback option from the Corner Type drop-down list of the dialog box. It is possible to have a smooth transition from the fillet edges to the common intersecting vertex when you use a setback fillet corner.

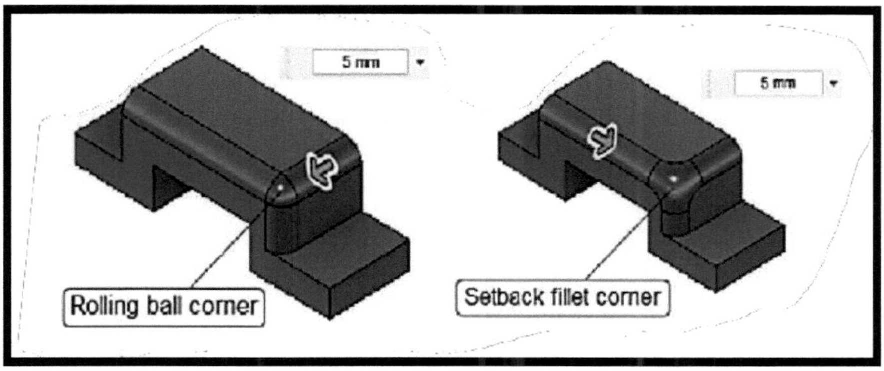

8. In the dialog box, go to the Corner Type field and choose the appropriate choice there.
9. In the dialog box, choose the OK button and click it. The fillet with the constant radius is now created.

Creating a Variable Radius Fillet

You may apply fills and rounds to edges with a configurable radius by making use of the Fillet command. A variable-radius fillet is one whose radius varies as it moves down the length of the fillet. You will set a radius for the starting point as well as the ending point. In addition to this, you may add intermediate spots along the length, and each of these places can have a unique radius. Under the **Solid** tab, open the **Modify** panel, and then choose **Fillet** or enter **F** in the text box that appears. The dialog window for the Fillet operation will appear. Turn on the Tangent Chain. Choose the top of the front edge. Additionally, the tangent edges will be chosen. Make sure that the **Radius Type** is set to **Variable Radius**. The model receives two new manipulator arrows, and the palette receives two new Radius values that match those arrows. These are the beginning and ending radii, respectively. To make changes to the End radius, just drag the back arrow. You should now be able to watch the radius vary as it travels down the length of the chosen edges. The value of the End Radius in the dialog box has been adjusted. Make the **End Radius** equal to **10 millimeters**. Adjust the **Start Radius** to **10 millimeters**.

Hovering your mouse above a chosen edge while adding intermediate points requires you to do so. A crimson dot indicates that a point may be scored for this effort. At either the middle or terminus, there will be a green dot. To both the front and rear edges, add two new points. Now put a point precisely in the middle of the right edge. After each selection, a radius field and an arrow are added to the model and palette, respectively. Because the radius values will be arranged in the palette from beginning to end, it does not matter in what order the picks are made. If you made a mistake and added an intermediate point or if you need to remove a point, choose the arrow on the model, and then click the Delete Point button in the dialog box that appears. Make sure the second arrow is selected near the **Start Radius**. The values in the edit box correspond to the location and the radius. The location is expressed as a percentage of the length of the edge, with 0 indicating the beginning of the edge and 1 indicating its completion. Adjust the second Radius so that it is 5 millimeters and its location so that it is 20 percent, or 0.2. The preview of the fillet has been updated. Now, change the third radius's location to 50% and set it to 20 millimeters. When calculating the fourth radius, use 5 millimeters and an 80% location. Simply selecting the OK button will produce the variable-radius fillet.

Using the Fillet command's Variable Radius option, it is possible to design fillets with a great deal of complexity. The location is determined relative to the length of the combined edges if the edge that was picked has multiple tangent edge segments. Because there are no start and endpoints in a closed loop, such as the end of a cylinder, you are required to add the points at which the radii are determined when you are adding a variable radius fillet to the closed loop. This is because there are no start and endpoints in the closed loop.

Creating a Fillet by Specifying the Chord Length

You can make a fillet by defining its chord length, very similar to how you can create a fillet with a constant radius by supplying the value of the fillet's radius.

1. In the **MODIFY** panel of the **SOLID** tab, choose the Fillet tool by clicking on it or using the F key on your keyboard. The **FILLET** dialog box will now show up.
2. To make the fillet, choose the model's borders, faces, or features from the available options. In the graphics section, you may pick either borders or faces; features, on the other hand, can be chosen in the Timeline.
3. In the drop-down menu labeled "**Radius Type**" in the dialog box, choose the Chord Length option. Additionally, an arrow is shown along the edge that has been picked.

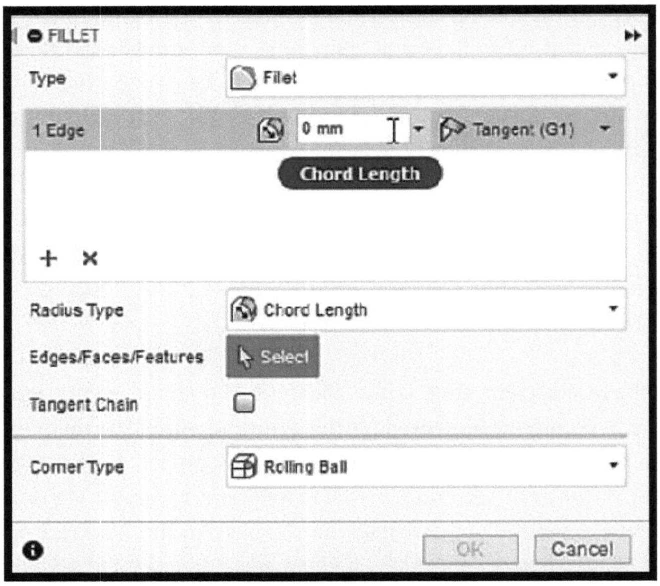

4. To adjust the size of the fillet, go to the dialog box labeled "**Chord Length**" and type the chord's length into the area provided. You also have the option of dragging the arrow that displays in the graphics area to dynamically specify the chord length of the fillet. A glimpse of the fillet is seen here.

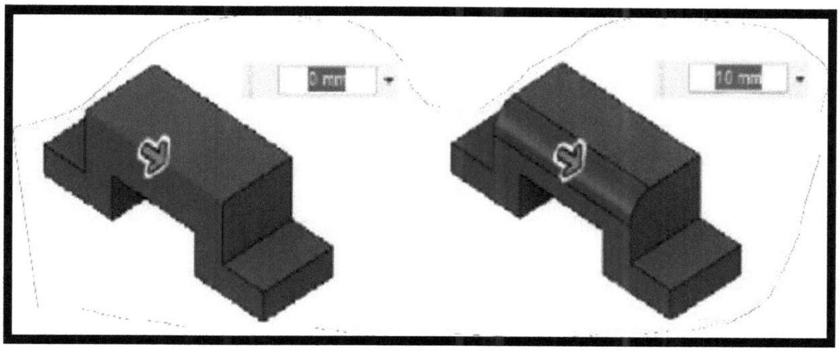

5. Once you have specified all of the necessary criteria for the creation of the fillet, click the OK button located in the dialog box. On the edge of the model that you pick, the fillet will be constructed with the chord length that you specify.

Creating Rule Fillets

Rule fillets are identical to constant radius fillets; the only distinction lies in the fact that with rule fillets, the edges that are used to create fillets are decided by the application of rules. To do this, you will need to choose faces and characteristics.

With the help of the Fillet tool in Fusion 360, you'll be able to fashion rule fillets.

1. In the MODIFY panel of the SOLID tab, choose the **Fillet tool** and click on it. The FILLET dialog box will now show up. You also have the option of using the **F key** to bring up the FILLET dialog box.
2. In the dialog box, locate the Type drop-down menu and choose the Rule Fillet option.

The Faces/Features selection option is used to pick the faces or features that will be utilized to construct a rule for identifying the edges that will be used to generate fillets. Take note that you may pick the characteristics of the model in the Timeline, but you can select the faces of the model in the graphics section.

3. Select the faces or characteristics that will be used as the input to define the rule. In this example, the definition of the rule is determined by selecting a face as the input. It is possible to pick a single face or numerous faces or characteristics.

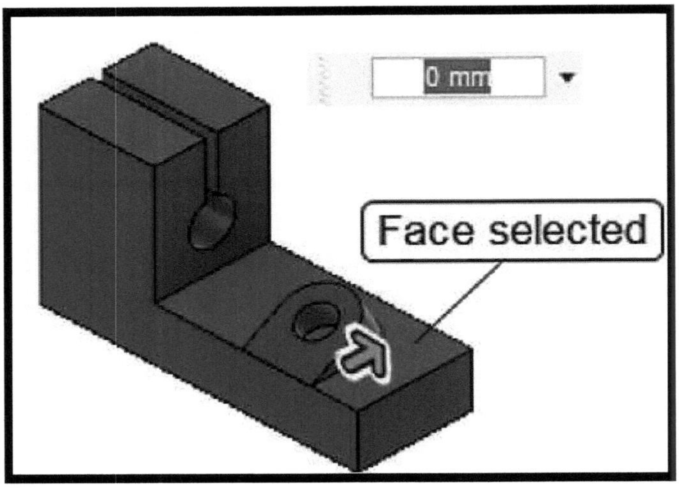

You have the option of entering a radius value into the Radius field of the dialog box or dragging the arrow that appears in the area of the graph. The preview of the fillets displays on the edges that are decided by the default rules that are set in the Rule drop-down list of the dialog box.

The following is an explanation of the choices available in the Rule drop-down list:

Rule: In the dialog box's Rule drop-down list, the All-Edges option is chosen by default. You may change this setting if necessary. As a direct consequence of this, the fillets are produced on all of the face's edges that were chosen. Following the selection of the Between Faces/Features option in this drop-down list, the Faces/Features 1 and Faces/Features 2 selection choices become available in the dialog box.

You may make fillets by selecting two different sets of faces or features and then utilizing these selection choices to determine the edges that connect the two sets. A face is chosen to represent set 1 in this illustration, and a characteristic is chosen to represent set 2.

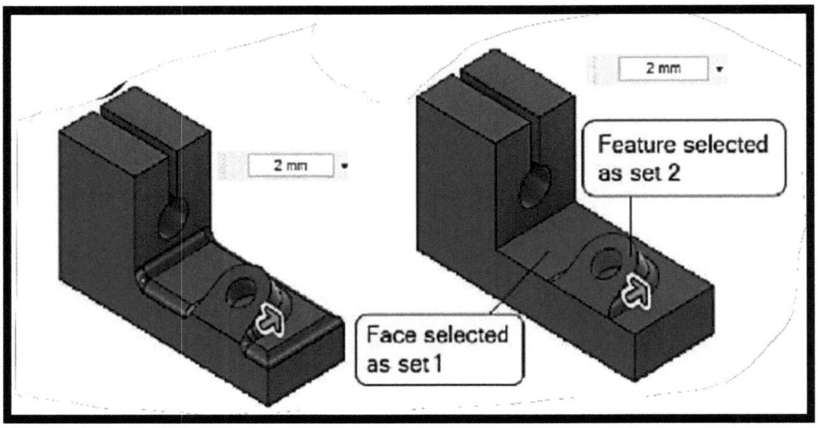

As a direct consequence of this, fillets are only produced at the intersections of the face and the feature that has been chosen. Take note that you may pick the characteristics of the model in the Timeline, but you can select the faces of the model in the graphics section. To identify which edges should be filleted, use the Rule drop-down list in the dialog box to choose the appropriate option (All Edges or Between Faces/Features, depending on the situation). Note that to establish the edges for constructing fillets, you need to pick two sets of faces or features when you choose the Between Faces/Features option in the fillet creation tool.

- **Rounds and Fillets**: The Rounds and Fillets option is chosen by default in the drop-down list of the Rounds and Fillets section of the dialog box. As a direct consequence of this, all fillets and rounds are fabricated on the outlined margins. Only the fillets will be formed on the relevant borders when you pick the **Fillets Only** option from the **Rounds/Fillets** drop-down list. When the option to construct just rounds on the relevant edges is selected, only the rounds will be formed.

You can define the type of fillets (rounds or fillets) that will be created on the determined edges of the selected faces or features by selecting the appropriate option from the Rounds/Fillets drop-down list in the dialog box. The available options are **Rounds and Fillets, Fillets Only, and Rounds Only.**

7. After specifying the appropriate input and choices, choose the button labeled "**OK.**" It is now time to make the fillets.

Creating Chamfers

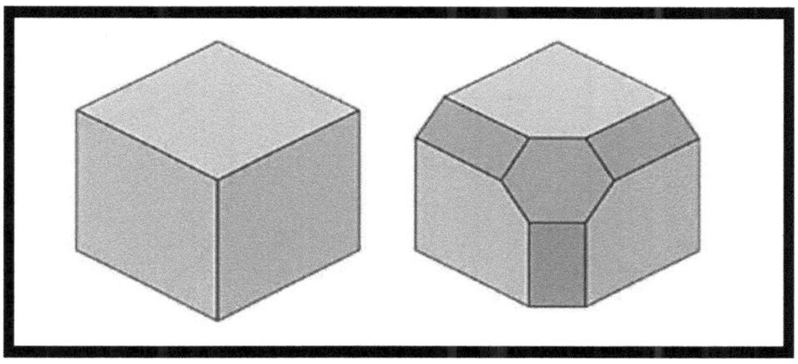

1. Select **Chamfer** from the **Design > Solid > Modify** menu. A Chamfer dialog box appears.
2. Pick the borders, faces, or features you want to chamfer on the canvas. In the selection box, the selection set appears as a row.
3. Choose the **Chamfer Type** in the dialog:
- **Equal Distance**: Bevels edges such that the distances from each side are equal.
- **Two Distance**: Based on a different distance to each side, bevels the edges.
- **Distance and Angle**: Based on a single distance and an angle, bevels are applied to edges.
4. Modify the values for the Distance or Angle for the Chamfer:
- Drag the manipulator handles for distance or angle in the canvas.
- Enter the distance or angle values in the dialog row's selection box.

Tip: To change the selection set after adjusting the Distance or Angle parameters, hold Ctrl (Windows) or Command (macOS).

5. Choose to flip the first and second sides of the Two Distance Chamfer type by clicking the symbol (Optional).
6. Pick a Type of Corner:

- **Chamfer**: A chamfer is made to connect beveled edges at corners.
- **Miter**: Creates a corner point by combining beveled edges.
- **Blend**: Integrates neighboring faces with beveled edges.

7. Optional: To add a selection set to the list, click the Plus button in the selection box. To produce fillets with parameters different from the initial selection set, repeat steps 2 through 6.
8. Press **OK**.

On the solid body of the canvas, the chamfers are visible.

Creating Shell Features

The creation of a model with a shell feature involves making the model hollow on the inside or deleting the model's faces, both of which result in the feature having thin walls. In the first picture, the shell feature is made by hollowing out the model, but in the second picture, the shell feature is made by eliminating the top planar face of the model. Both of these methods provide the same result, which is a shell.

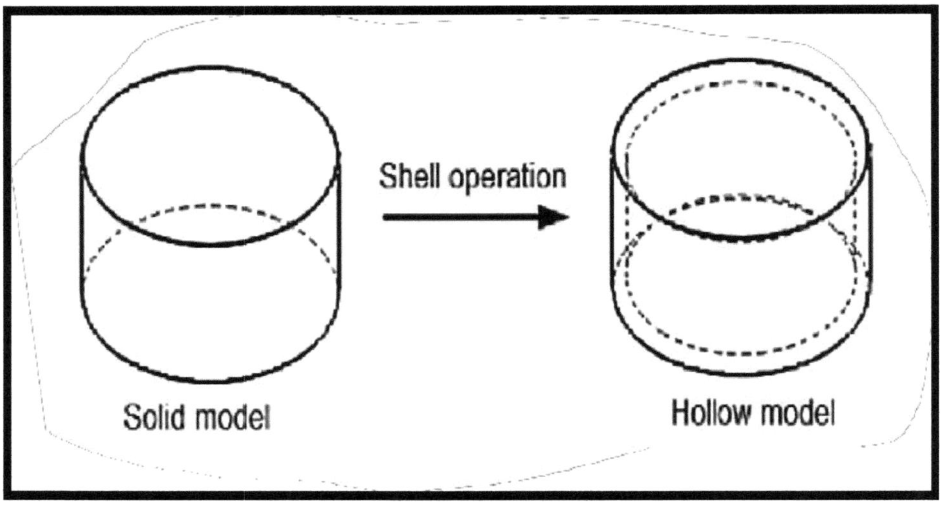

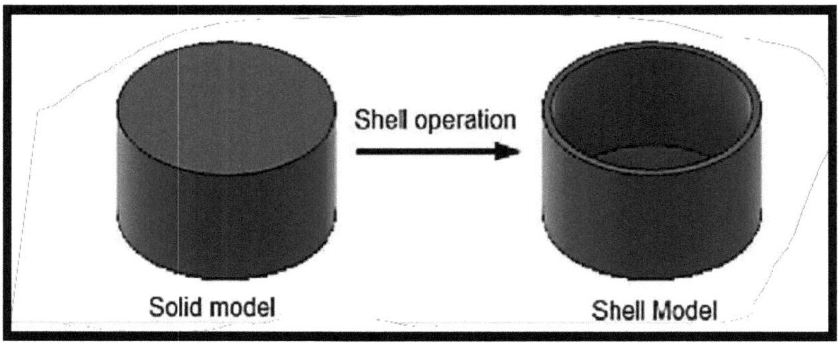

NOTE: The visual style of the model has been modified in the first picture to a "wireframe with hidden edges" visual style so that the hidden edges of the hollow model can be seen. This was done so that the hidden edges of the model could be seen.

Click on the **Shell** tool that is located in the **MODIFY** panel of the SOLID tab. This will allow you to construct a shell feature. A new dialog box labeled SHELL emerges.

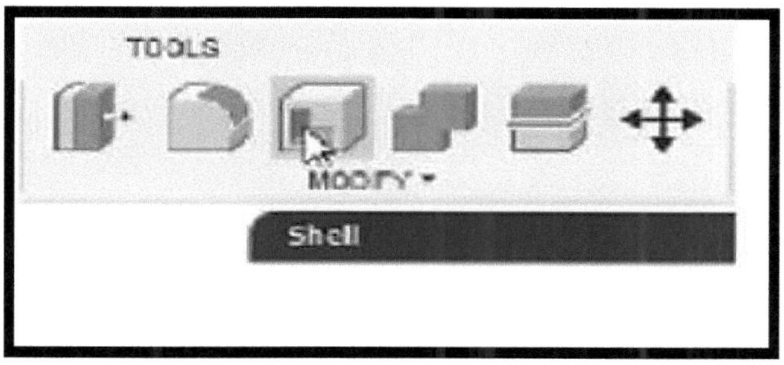

Faces/Body

Within the dialog box, the Faces/Body selection option is the one that is turned on by default. As a consequence of this, you will be able to pick either faces or a body to generate a shell feature with a certain wall thickness. In the area labeled "**Inside Thickness/Outside Thickness"** of the dialog box, you have the option of entering the wall thickness. It should be noted that the closed hollow shell model with the given wall thickness is constructed whenever a body is selected. Either in the graphics area or the Bodies node of the BROWSER, you may pick a body to work with. To choose a body in the graphics area, place the cursor over one edge of the model, and when the whole model becomes highlighted, click the left mouse button. When a face or faces are chosen, a shell feature with a defined wall thickness is generated in such a way that the face or faces that were selected are deleted from the model.

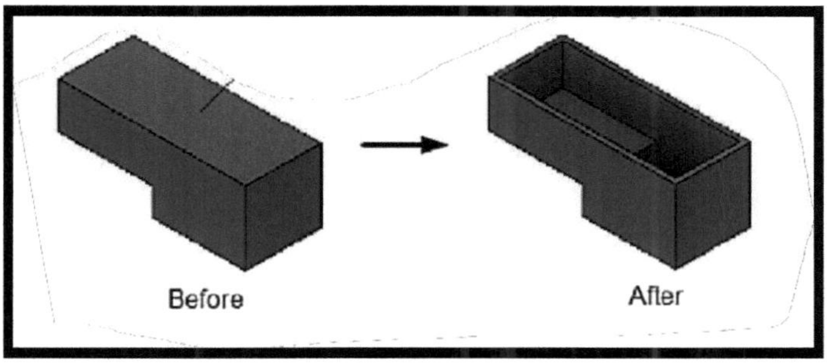

Tangent Chain

The Tangent Chain check box in the dialog box is selected automatically when it is opened. As a consequence of this, while picking a face on the model to be removed, all the faces of the model that are tangentially linked to the face that was picked are automatically selected as well.

Inside Thickness/Outside Thickness

The wall thickness value of the shell feature that is to be introduced inward to the model may be specified by typing in the corresponding number into the Inside Thickness field of the dialog box. Take note that the Inside or Both option in the dialog box's Direction drop-down list must be chosen for this field to become visible in the box. It is possible to define the wall thickness value of the shell feature that will be introduced externally to the model by making use of the Outside Thickness field. Take note that the Outside or Both option in the Direction drop-down list of the dialog box is required for this field to become visible for you to enter data into it.

Direction

Choose the appropriate choice from the Direction drop-down list to define whether the thickness will be added to the inside, outside, or both sides of the model. This may be done by choosing either **"Inside," "Outside," or "Both Sides.**" After you have entered all of the necessary criteria to build the shell feature, you will need to click the **OK** button. The shell component with the desired wall thickness is created.

Adding Drafts

The procedure of adding drafts involves tapering the faces of the model to make it simpler for the model to be removed from its cast during the manufacturing process. By using the Draft tool inside Fusion 360, you'll have the ability to taper the faces of the model. To do this, choose the **MODIFY** option from the drop-down menu located in the SOLID tab, and then select the Draft tool. The DRAFT dialog box is shown to the user. We will now go through the choices that are available in this dialog box.

Plane

Within the dialog box, the Plane selection option is the one that is turned on by default. As a consequence of this, you can choose either a plane or a planar face to use as a neutral plane when defining the pulling direction for adding drafts. In the illustration below, the top planar face of the model has been chosen as the neutral plane, and the draft has been applied to the face of the model that is situated on the side. As soon as you pick the neutral plane, an arrow will appear on the face that you have chosen. This arrow will indicate the direction that will be pulled.

Faces

You may pick one or more faces of the model to be tapered or sketched by using the Faces selection option.

Angle

This field is used to provide the draft angle that will be utilized to taper the face or faces that have been chosen. It is important to keep in mind that the draft angle for the specified faces is computed about the neutral plane that was chosen. You may enter a value with a negative angle in this field to reverse the direction that the draft is moving in. You may also dynamically define the draft angle by dragging the manipulator handle that appears in the graphics area. This is done in the same manner.

Flip Direction

With the press of a button labeled "**Flip Direction**," the direction of the draft may be changed from **"outward" to "inward"** or vice versa.

Direction

In the Direction drop-down list of the dialog box, the One Side option is chosen by default. You may change this if necessary. As a consequence of this, the Angle field of the dialog box will only allow you to enter a single draft angle. When you pick the **Two Side** option from the drop-down list located in the **Direction** section of the dialog box, two Angle fields appear. These fields provide you the ability to set two draft angles, one above the neutral plane and one below it, respectively. The draft angle that is entered in the Angle field will be applied symmetrically above and below the neutral plane that has been chosen when the Symmetric option is selected. Following the selection of a neutral plane and faces to be drafted, as well as the specification of the draft angle, the OK button in the dialog box should be clicked. The chosen faces go through a process of tapering.

Scaling Objects

Using the Scale tool in Fusion 360, you may make components, bodies, or sketch entities larger or smaller. This adjustment can be made in either direction.

The following is an explanation of the procedure for scaling an object, whether it be a component, body, or sketch entity:

1. Select the MODIFY option from the drop-down menu located in the SOLID tab. Then, select the Scale tool from the toolbox. A dialog window labeled **SCALE** will now display.
Entities: The Entities selection option in the dialog box is active by default when it is first opened. As a direct consequence of this, you will have the ability to choose sketch entities, bodies, or components to act as the objects that will be scaled.
2. Choose the components, bodies, or sketch entities that will be resized in the graphics area as the items to be modified.
Point: The Point selection option is used to define a basis point or center point for scaling the chosen items. This may be done by dragging the point around the screen. Note that when you pick a body or a component to be scaled, a point on the chosen object will automatically be selected as the basis point.
This happens regardless of whether you want to scale the body or the component. After selecting the Point selection option and clicking on the point you want to use as the basis point for scaling the chosen object, you will have met the requirements to define a base point.
3. Select a point in the graphics area to use as the basis point by clicking on the Point selection option in the dialog box, and then selecting the point.

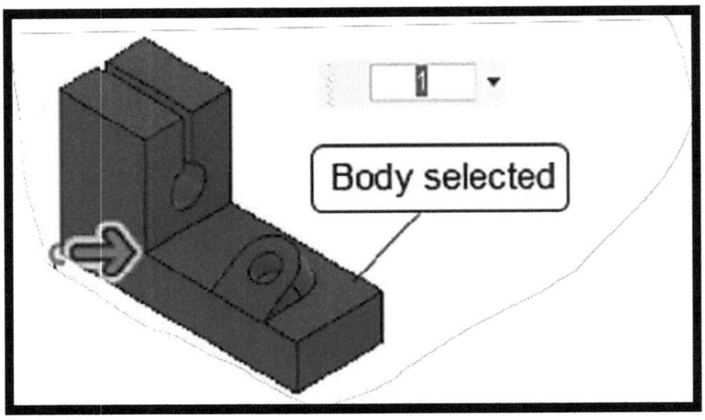

Scale Type: The Scale Type drop-down list of the dialog box allows you to choose whether to scale the chosen objects uniformly or non-uniformly around the base point. You may accomplish this by selecting either uniform or non-uniform from the list. In this particular drop-down list, the option known as "**Uniform**" is chosen by default. As a consequence of this, the chosen objects will be scaled following the scale factor that was entered into the Scale Factor field of the dialog box. This will cause the scaling to be consistent in all directions around the base point. After choosing the non-Uniform option, you will be allowed to enter several scale factors for the chosen objects to be scaled in the X, Y, and Z axes, respectively.

4. In the Scale Type drop-down list of the dialog box, choose the option that corresponds to your needs (either Uniform or Non-Uniform).
5. To scale the items that have been chosen, go to the dialog box's **Scale Factor field** and enter the value for the scale factor there. You may also move the arrow that displays in the graphics area to dynamically choose the scale factor. This option is available to you provided you have the appropriate permissions.
Note that if you choose the non-Uniform option from the Scale Type drop-down list, you will be able to specify different scale factors in the **X Scale, Y Scale, and Z Scale** fields of the dialog box. This will allow you to scale the selected objects in a manner that is non-uniform in the X, Y, and Z directions.
6. In the dialog box, choose the **OK** button and click it. The scale factor that was given is applied to the selected items, and those things are then scaled.

Scale components, bodies, or sketches

1. Choose **Modify > Scale** from the Solid tab of the Design workspace.
2. Pick a fixed anchor point for the scaling and the body or bodies to be scaled.
3. Select a scale type from the drop-down menu:
- **Uniform**: Equally scale the body along all axes.
- **Non-Uniform**: Scale independently along the x, y, and z axes.

4. To adjust the scale distance, use the manipulators or the dialog (-0.5 to halve the size or 2 to double the size, for example).
5. To finalize the task, right-click and choose **OK**.

Scaling a mesh body.

1. To access the Mesh Workspace, right-click on the mesh body in the workspace or the timeline and choose **Edit.** Ensure the **Design History** is enabled.

2. To view the mesh tools, make sure you are on the Mesh Tab in the toolbar if Design History is not enabled.

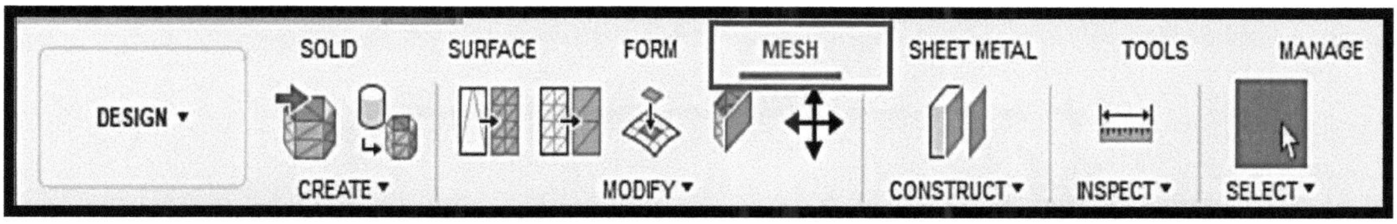

3. Select **Scale** from the Modify menu.

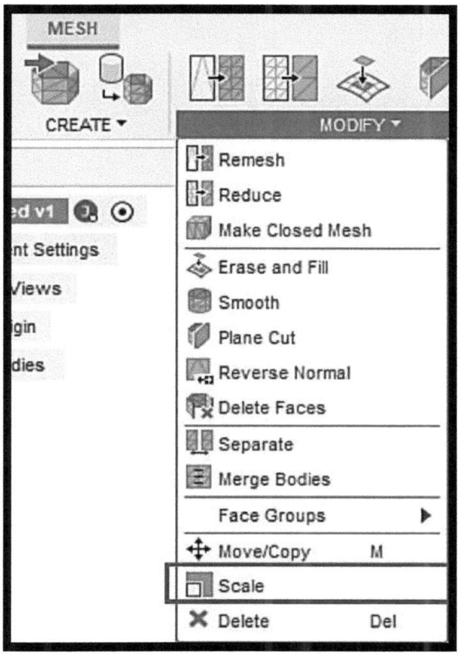

Recall that by choosing a different scale type from the drop-down list, the mesh may also be scaled irregularly.

4. Choose the entity to scale, then type the scale factor.
5. To complete scaling, click **OK**.
6. Click **Finish Mesh** in the toolbar to exit the mesh workspace if design history is enabled.

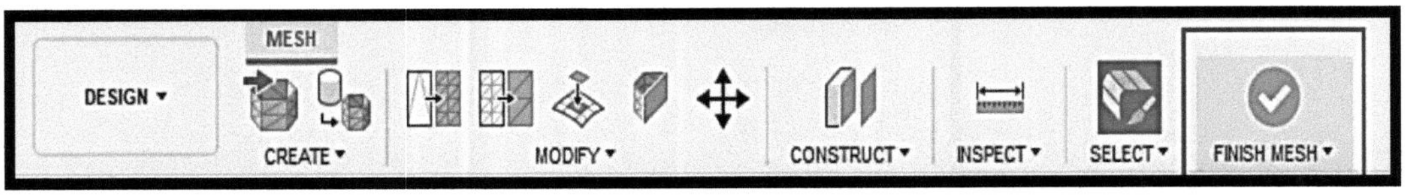

Combining Solid Bodies

Do the following to unite or merge solids or bodies:

1. To begin, choose **Design > Solid > Modify** > **Combine**.
2. Pick the **Target Body** in the Combine dialog.
3. Choose Tool Bodies

4. **Select the Operation:** option in the Combine dialog.
   - **Join**: Consolidates many solid bodies into one.
   - **Cut**: Removes from the Target Body the volume of Tool Bodies.
   - **Intersect**: Maintains overlapping volumes while fusing them into a single solid body.
5. Choosing New Component will allow you to make a new component from the outcome.
6. If desired, choose the option to retain the tool bodies after the solid bodies have been joined.
7. Press **OK**.

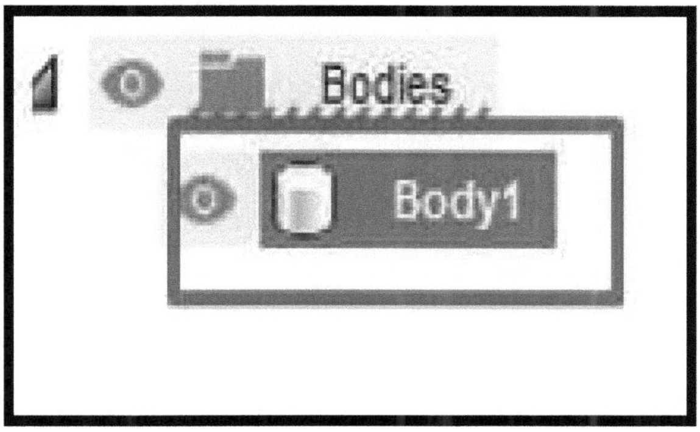

Offsetting Faces of a Model

By using the Offset Face tool inside Fusion 360, users can offset the face of a model that has been chosen by a certain distance.

The following is an explanation of the procedure for offsetting the faces of a model:

1. Select the MODIFY option from the drop-down menu located in the SOLID tab. Next, select the Offset Face tool from the toolbox. The OFFSET FACE dialog box is brought into view.
   - **Faces**: The Faces selection option in the dialog box is active by default when it is first opened. As a direct consequence of this, you will have the ability to pick one or more faces for offset.
2. Choose one or more of the model's faces to have an offset applied to them. The face that is now chosen is brought to the front, and an arrow appears in the graphics area.
3. To dynamically offset the chosen face inside the graphics area, press and hold the left mouse button, and then drag the arrow that appears in the graphics area with the left mouse button. You also have the option of inputting the offset distance in the area labeled Distance inside the **OFFSET FACE** dialog box. You also have the option to specify an offset distance in the box labeled Distance, which is located in the graphics area. You may change the direction of the offset by dragging the arrow to the other side of the face that is now chosen, or by entering a negative number for the offset distance in the area labeled Distance.

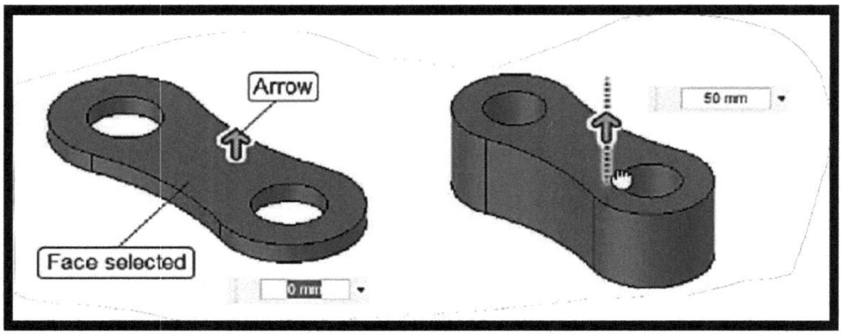

4. Once you have finished offsetting a face by the specified amount, choose the OK button located in the dialog box.

Splitting Faces of a Model

1. Click **Modify > Split Face** on the Solid tab of the Design workspace.
2. Decide which face to divide. To pick numerous faces, hold down the Ctrl (Windows) or Command (macOS) keys.
3. Click the Splitting Tool box in the Split Face dialog and choose one of the following actions:
- Choose a **work plane**
- Choose a **surface or draw on the canvas.**

4. Make sure the Extend Splitting Tool is chosen if you want to pick a drawing or surface.
This setting makes sure your cutting tool intersects your faces entirely.
5. Click **OK.**
6. (Optional) Right-click and choose **Repeat Split Face** to repeat the procedure. Extend Splitting Tool doesn't need to be selected again.

By utilizing Press Pull or the split as a separation line for the manuscript, you may go on editing.

Splitting Bodies

To divide a body, you can use a work plane, surface, drawing, or face. The body must intersect the splitting object, or the expanded body must also intersect the splitting object. Where the split occurs is shown by a red shape. You may choose a surface body and a work plane. You may choose one face or all of them. The red surface, for instance, indicates the points where the faces penetrate the solid.

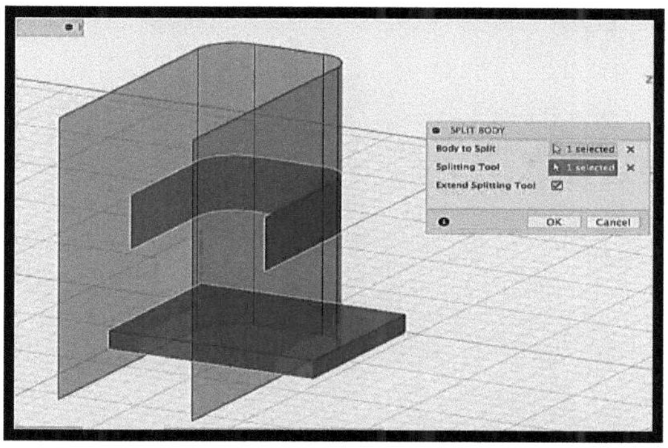

- **A Sketch**. The profile of the drawing may be open or closed. If you extrude the drawing, it must be able to go through the body.
- **A face on a solid body**. For instance, this cylinder would pass through the solid rectangle.

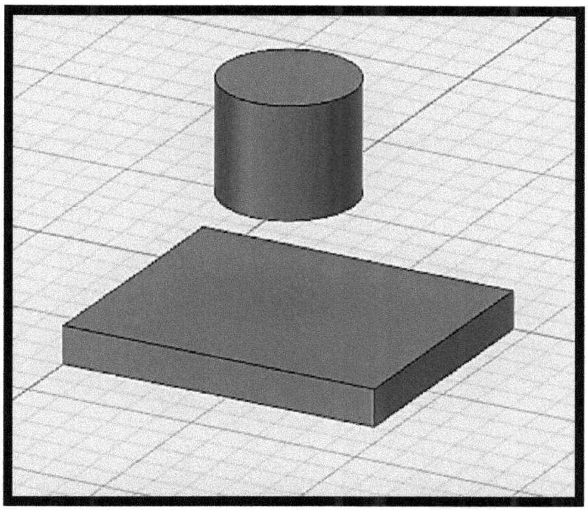

1. Select **Split Body** under **Modify**.
2. Choose the solid you wish to separate under **Body to Split**.
3. Choose the body-splitting item for the **Splitting Tool**.
4. Choose the Extend **Splitting Tool** if the splitting item does not already cross the body.

Remarkably, you can also extrude a sketch profile through a solid with the Extrude command. This leaves a space and clears everything underneath the drawing. For instance, if you extrude this drawing, the portion of the solid underneath it is removed.

Before

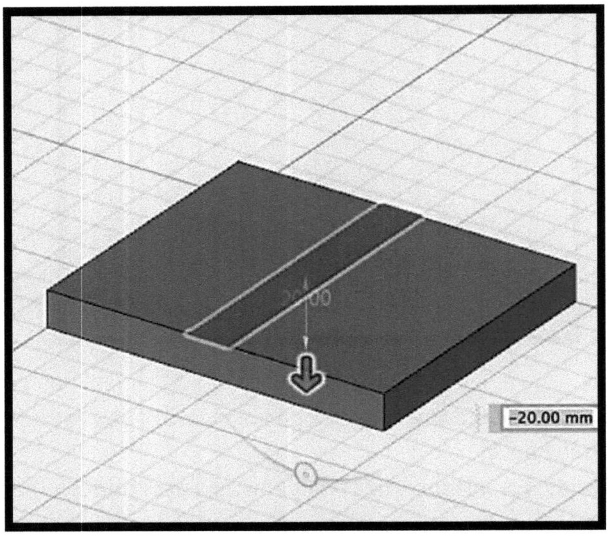

After

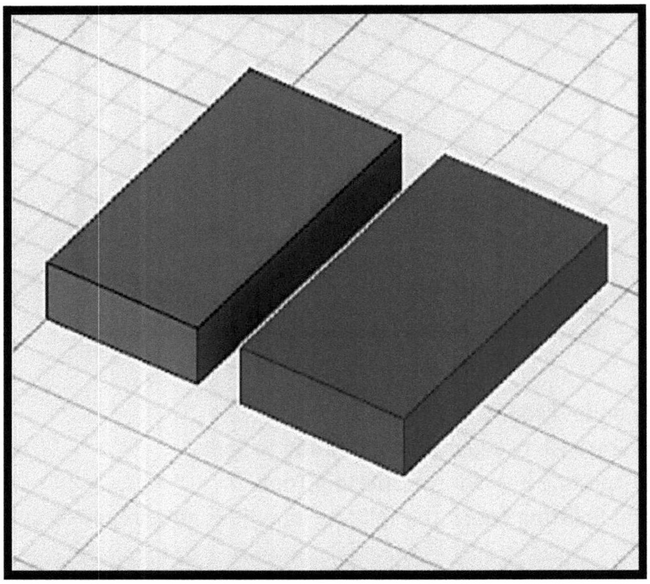

Questions

1. Which tool is used to taper the faces of the model?
2. Which tool is used to increase or decrease the scale of components, bodies, or sketch entities?
3. What can you create with the Fillet tool?
4. The tool used for creating a thin-walled feature by making a model hollow from the inside or removing the faces of the model is known as?
5. The Combine tool is used for combining solid bodies by performing what Boolean operations?

6. Which tool is used for offsetting a face of a model, filleting an edge of a model, and extruding a sketch profile, dynamically in the graphics area?
7. What is the Chamfer tool used for?

PART 3

WORKING WITH ASSEMBLIES

CHAPTER 11

WORKING WITH ASSEMBLIES – I

Assemblies

An Assembly in Fusion 360 is a group of parts that work together to form a single design. An assembly is any design that consists of two or more components.

Depending on the requirements of your design, you may construct assemblies that make use of a range of different methodologies.

- Build assemblies using a combination of internal and external components, or from solely internal components.
- At the start of a project or as the design develops, define the structure and connections in the assembly.
- Approach the whole assembly top-down or bottom-up, or change your strategy for certain components and subassemblies.
- Work alone on a design or with other project participants.
- Work in tandem or asynchronously with other project participants.

Distributed designs

A distributed design includes references to one or more external components in the assembly.

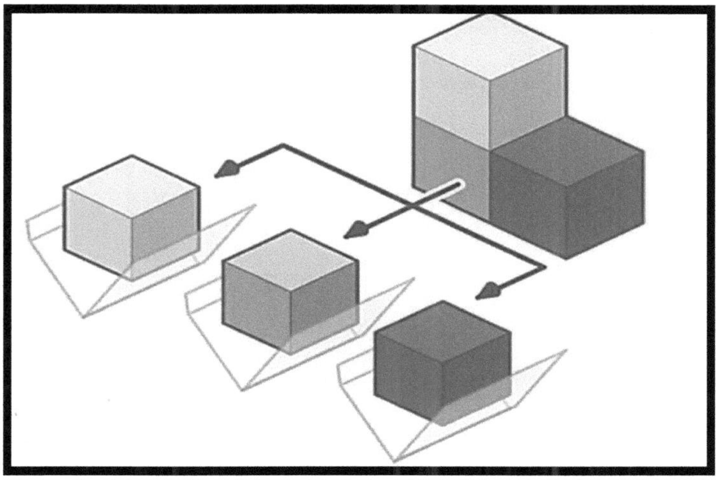

Multiple project participants may change various components in the assembly at once thanks to distributed designs. The whole assembly is updated to reflect the changes made by each project member as they modify components while still in context. Everybody is working with the most recent version of every component in the assembly because you can see who is updating each component, update component versions as team members save them, and keep track of who is altering what.

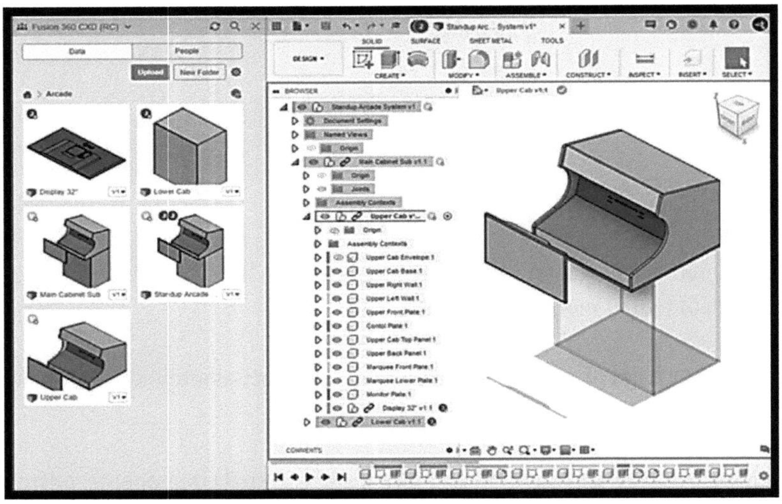

Updates in the assembly

When a project member saves an updated version of the design or an external component in the assembly, the following locations show an Out-Of-Date icon:

- In the Applications window
- Next to a browser's external component
- Next to the browser's default component

The **Subcomponent Out-Of-Date** indicator appears next to the parent external component when a subcomponent nested inside it is out-of-date.

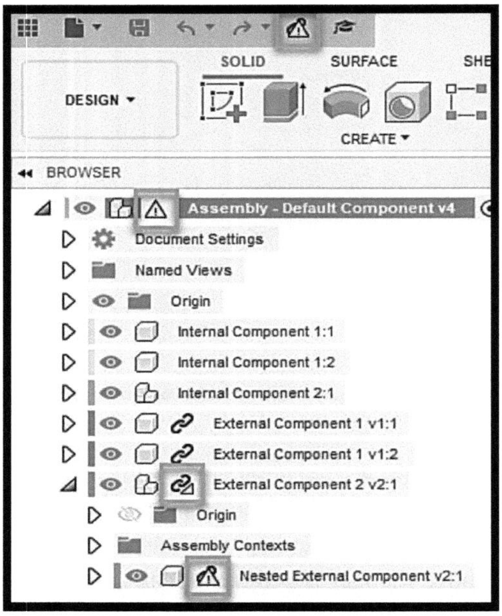

You have the option of updating the current design as well as any outdated external components all at once or one at a time, depending on your preference.

Edit a design directly

1. To open a design, double-click anywhere in the Data Panel to begin.

Your Avatar appears on the thumbnail of the design in the Data Panel, alongside the Avatars of any other project members who currently have the design open in their browser. Additionally, it is shown for other project participants under the current document tab.

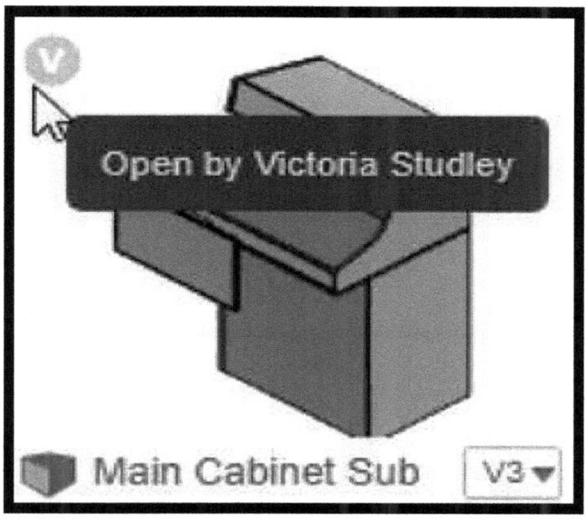

Make a savable change to the design.

The **Reservation Badge** will be shown on your Avatar in the Data Panel, next to the default component in the Browser, and in the current document tab for other project members to see. You will hold onto the design until you decide whether to save or discard your modifications.

1. Continue editing the design.
2. Click the **Save** button located on the Application bar. The Save dialog will now appear.

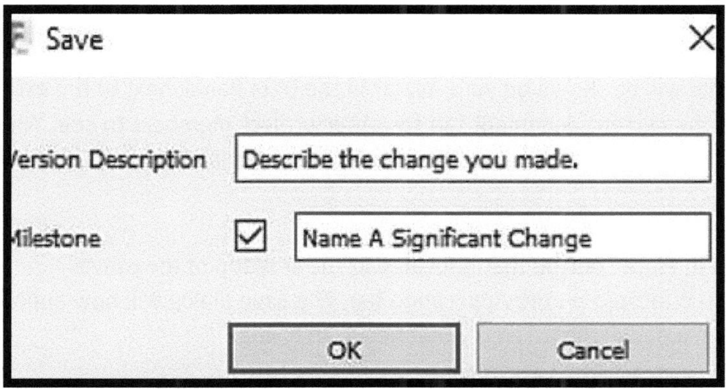

3. Enter a Version Description in the space provided.
4. If the modifications constitute a major iteration of the design, you may choose to check the Milestone box.
5. Press the "**OK**" button.

The design is then posted when a fresh version has been saved of it. After 15 seconds have passed since the completion of the save and upload procedure, the Reservation Badge will be removed from your Avatar. The design is not being held in reserve anymore. Note that the "**Design Reservation**" feature of Fusion 360 is not accessible for individual usage or teams consisting of just one member. Additionally, you will not see any avatars or reservation badges.

Edit an external component in an assembly

1. Double-clicking anywhere inside the Data Panel will open the parent design.
2. While in the Browser, hover your mouse pointer over an external component and then choose the **Edit in Place** option. Your Avatar appears on the thumbnail of the design in the Data Panel, alongside the Avatars of any other project members who currently have the design open in their browser. Additionally, it is shown for other project participants under the current document tab.

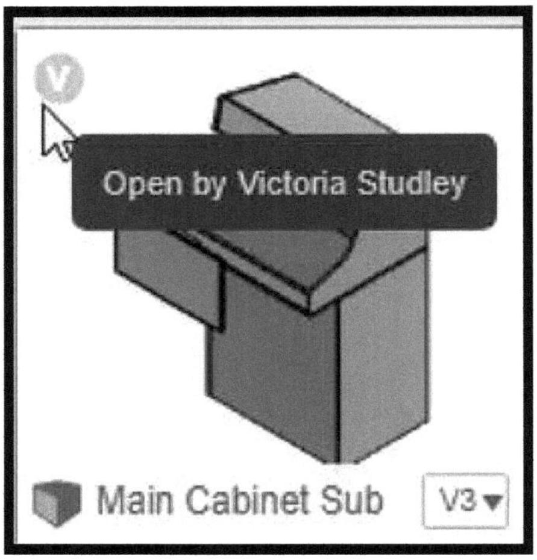

Make a savable change to the design.

The Reservation Badge will be shown on your Avatar in the Data Panel, next to the external component in the Browser, and in the current document tab for other project members to see. You will not trash the external component or its parent designs until you have decided whether or not to save your modifications.

1. Continue editing the design.
2. Click the **"End Edit in Place"** button that is located at the very top of the canvas.
3. Click the **Save** button located on the Application bar. The Save dialog will now appear. It provides a list of all of the designs included in the assembly that needs archiving.

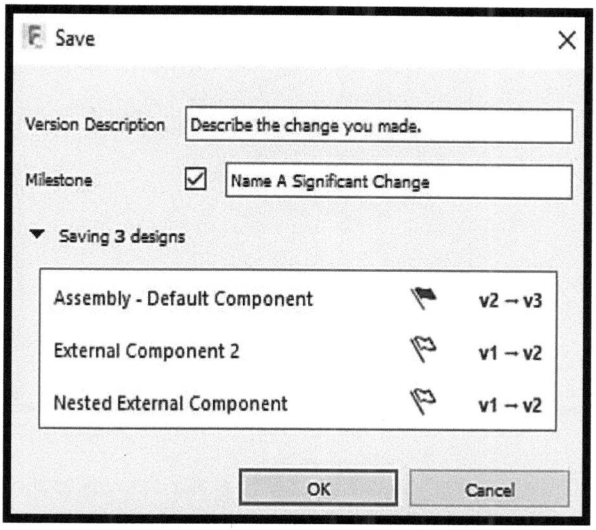

4. Enter a **Version Description** in the space provided.
5. If the modifications constitute a major iteration of the design, you have the option to tick the Milestone box and add a description.
6. Review the list of designs that will be stored once you click the expand button next to **Saving x designs**.
7. If you want to manage which designs receive the milestone version, you may choose them by clicking the Milestone symbol that is located next to each design.
8. Select the "**OK**" button.

The uploaded file includes both the new version of the external component and any updated versions of its parent designs. After 15 seconds have passed since the completion of the save and upload procedure, the Reservation Badge will be removed from your Avatar. There is no longer a reservation for either the external component or its parent designs.

Discard changes

1. In the tab for the current document, click the X button. You will be prompted to Save, Don't Save, or Cancel in a dialog box that appears.
2. Select the **Not Save** option.

The design is closed, and any modifications that you made to the parent design or any external components that were not saved will be lost. Instantaneously, the Reservation Badge will be removed from your Avatar, and any designs that have been reserved will no longer be reserved.

Edit In Place

You may activate and change an external component in the context of an assembly in Fusion 360 by using the Edit in Place feature. This does not need you to leave the parent design.

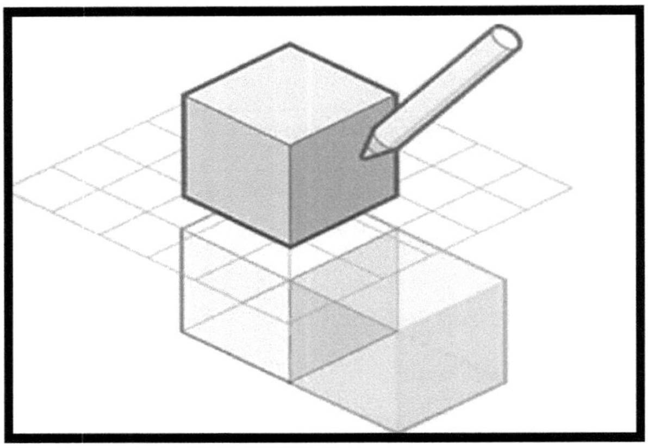

After activating the Edit in Place feature, you will be able to make changes to the component while seeing it in its actual place inside the assembly. Because you can update external components while remaining inside the context of the parent design when using Edit in Place, it is much simpler to employ a top-down design approach.

When you enable Edit in Place for an external component, the following will occur:

- The external component is what is shown on the canvas.
- Other parts of the parent design are rendered inoperable as a result. Although you are unable to make changes to them, they will continue to be shown on the canvas to give you an accurate picture of the overall design.
- You can construct associative linkages between the geometry of the external component and the inactive components, as well as assess relative distances between the two sets of components.

If you make a change to the size or location of a referenced component after you have used the End Edit in Place command, the component that you have just changed will be updated accordingly. Please take into account that the component is only modified in the context of the parent design.

Assembly Contexts

An Assembly Context will be generated in the parent design if it is necessary to refer to the component's parent or sibling geometry to determine the size or form of the component that is currently being edited. The relationship that exists between a parent design and an external component at a certain moment in time is referred to as an assembly context. It stores information relating to the assembly's positions in the assembly. It is the location from which geometry is generated to preserve the connection to the original design.

The following components make up a whole Assembly Context:

An Assembly Context in the browser's Assembly Contexts folder, which is nested beneath the child external component.

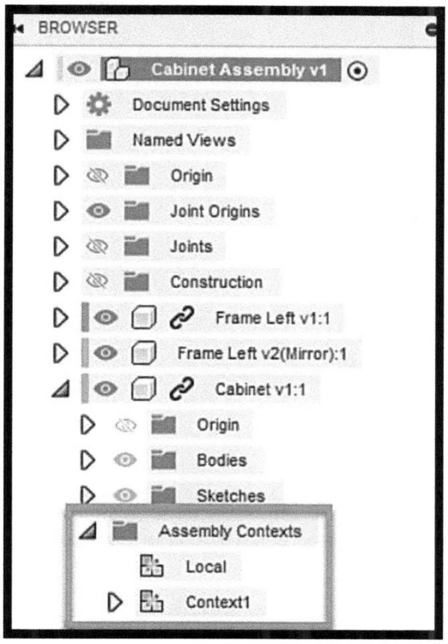

A marking in the parent design's Timeline that identifies the child design. Note that the folder titled "**Assembly Contexts**" stores each Assembly Context individually.

During Edit in Place, an Assembly Context is produced whenever one of the following occurs:

- Connect one of the dimensions with one of the other components
- Connect a limitation or restriction to one of the other components.
- Connect a sketch projection to one of the other components
- Locate a component where you want it to be and record its current position.

Any features that you develop while an Assembly Context is running will be connected to that context. The Timeline of the parent design has had a feature called Assembly Context added to it. When you reference geometry, that geometry is derived into the external component and given the context of an Assembly. When you open the component outside of the assembly, this makes the geometry accessible to the component that is located outside of the assembly.

If any of the following apply to you, it is recommended that you open the external component in a new tab and enable the Assembly Context:

- You have ensured that you have referenced all of the objects that you need to function independently of the assembly's context.
- It is necessary to have access to an enhanced set of modeling tools, in addition to those that are already provided by **Edit in Place**.

Local context

A Local Context can be found inside each folder labeled Assembly Contexts.

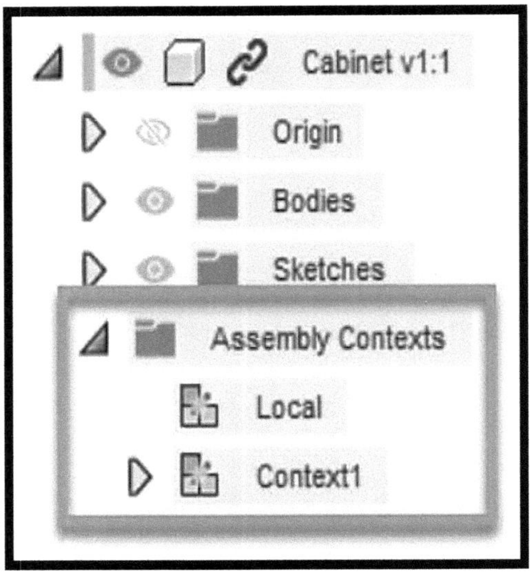

The **Local Context** is a representation of the external component as it would look in the design if it were opened in its separate document tab. It is responsible for the upkeep of its own set of locations for child components.

When you activate the Local Context, the following will occur:

- The geometry in the parent design is unavailable for selection since it has been concealed.
- You will not be able to create any relationships to the geometry in the parent design.
- The locations of the child components inside the external component are determined by those of the parent components within the external component.
- You have access to some instructions that are not accessible in assembly situations. These commands are linked to position, joints, and motion.

Note that you will automatically move to the Local Context if you are working in an assembly context and then activate a command that is only available in the Local context. You will stay in the Local Context even after the command has been completed.

Automatic activation

When you update a feature inside an Assembly Context that is dependent on the geometry of the Assembly Context, the Assembly Context itself will immediately become active.

Reference objects

Creating explicit associative references between an external component and other design aspects in an assembly is the responsibility of the Reference Objects command.

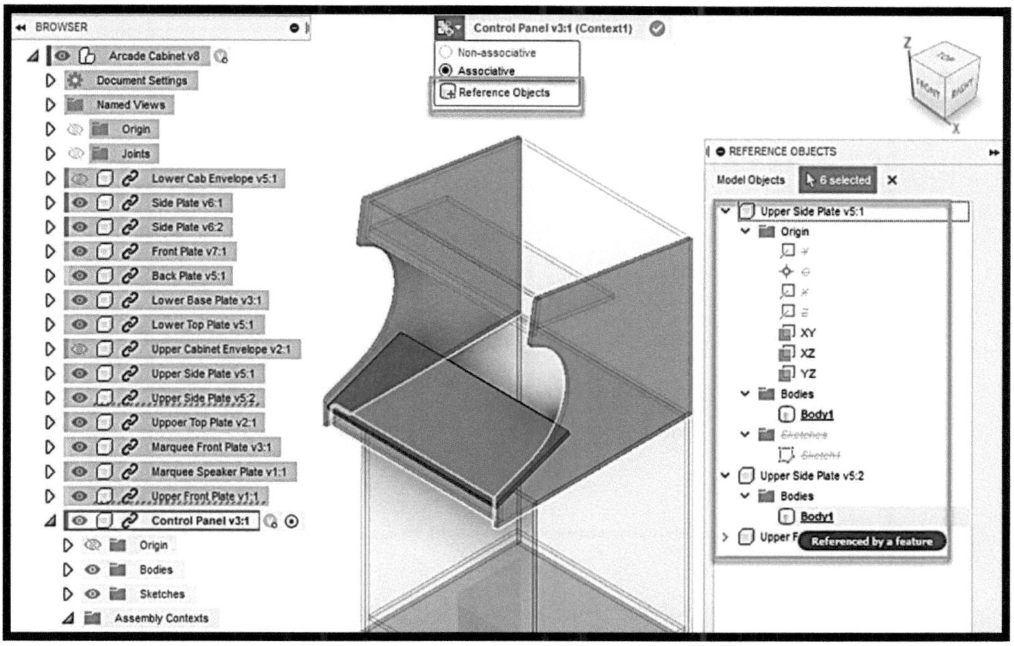

The Reference Objects command may be accessed via the Edit in Place menu, which is located at the very top of the canvas when associative Edit in Place is active. You may pick different aspects of the design either in the Browser or directly on the canvas. The design features that were referred to before may now be derived using an Assembly Context. Before beginning work on the assembly's detailed design, you may reference objects in the assembly in an explicit manner by using the Reference Objects command. If you want your detailed design work to be clearer and simpler to complete, you should only reference the items in the assembly that are essential for understanding the context of a component.

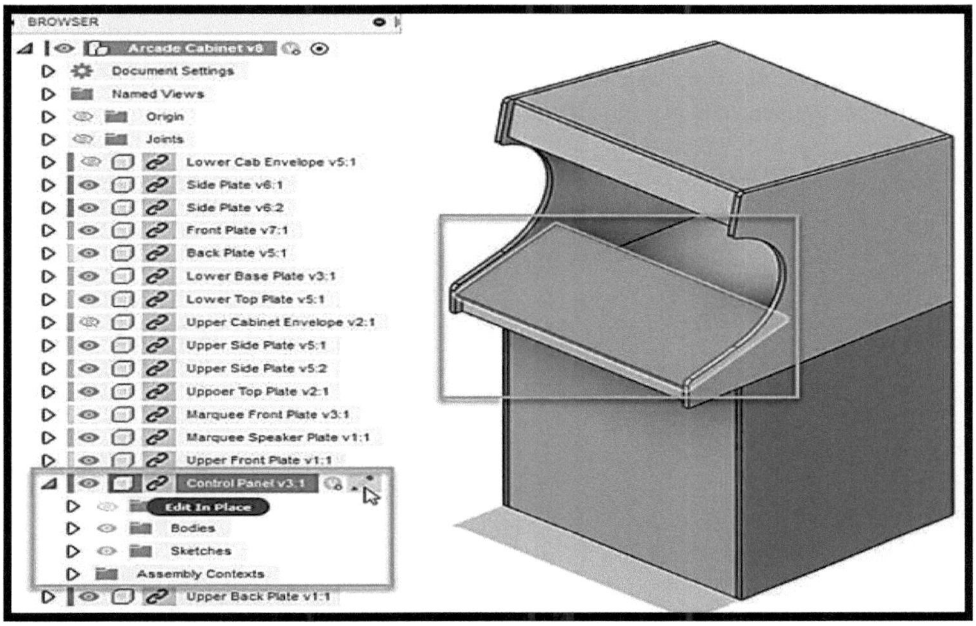

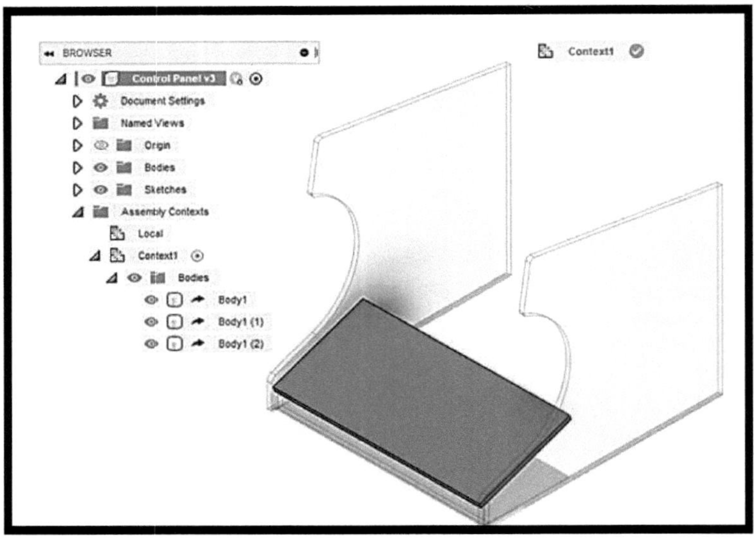

Note that the Reference Objects command cannot be used while doing a non-associative Edit in Place.

Adjust the visibility of objects in an assembly

View or conceal items

1. Find the item you wish to display or hide in the browser.
2. Select the item, then click the visibility symbol.
    - Visibility is on.
    - Visibility is off.

If the item was visible, it is no longer visible in the canvas and the browser. If the item was concealed, it is now discernible in both the canvas and the browser.

Note: The visibility of that particular object is overridden in the assembly when you change its visibility in an external component. In the external design or any other assemblies where the external design is referenced, the visibility is left unchanged.

Override visibility of objects in an external component

1. Expand the assembly's external component in the browser.
2. **Find an item and change its visibility:**
    - Components
    - Bodies
    - Sketches
    - Construction Geometry
    - Documents (Bodies, Sketches, and Construction only)

3. Select the item, then click the visibility icon.

- Visibility is on.
- Visibility is off.

When you mouse over an object's visibility symbol, a tooltip appears and the object's visibility is overridden in the assembly. In the external design or any other assemblies where the external design is referenced, the visibility is left unchanged.

Remove a visibility override from a single object

1. Expand the assembly's external component in the browser.
2. Find the item with the visibility override activated.
3. Select the item, then click the visibility icon.

The visibility override has been eliminated since the object's visibility in the assembly now matches its visibility in the external design.

Remove all visibility overrides from an external component

1. Find the external component in the browser.
2. Right-click on the external component.
3. Press the **Remove Visibility Overrides** button.

The visibility overrides have been eliminated, and all items included inside the external component now match the visibility of the objects in the external design.

Remove all visibility overrides from an entire assembly

1. Right-click the default component in the browser.
2. Press the **Remove Visibility Overrides** button.

All visibility overrides have been deleted, and all objects in the assembly now match the visibility of the objects in the external designs that the assembly referenced.

Tips

- If you change an object's visibility while using Edit in Place, the assembly will override that change. The visibility does not change if you open the external component directly in its document tab.
- Any modifications or overrides made to the visibility of any object types in the Browser are superseded if you choose to hide any of them in the Navigation bar > Object Visibility settings.

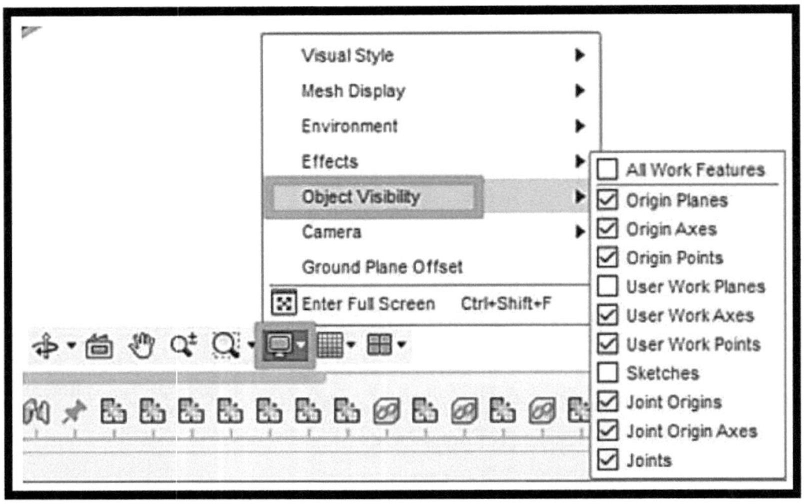

Derived design features

In Fusion 360, you may connect design characteristics from one design into another via the use of the Derive and Insert Derive commands. The modifications made to the derived features in the original design are mirrored in the changes made to the destination design when those features are updated. The process of deriving design features is a time-saving technique to handle elements that are consistent across numerous designs.

The following are examples of design characteristics that may be derived:

- Components
- Bodies
- Sketches
- Construction Geometry
- Sheet metal flat designs
- Favorite parameters
- Feature parameters

Derive command

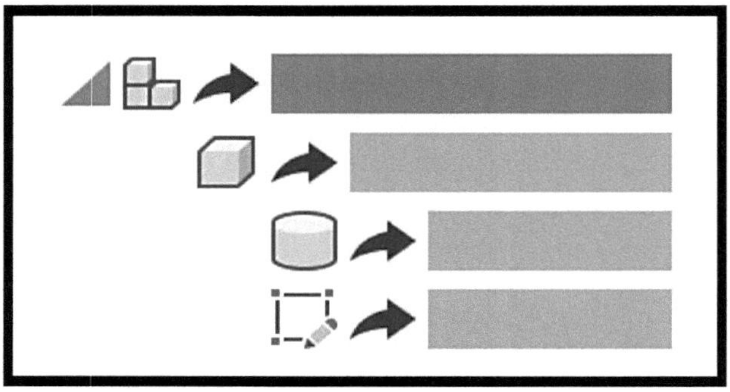

Design > Solid > Create > Derive

When you use the Derive command, design features from the current design will be pushed into a new or existing design and linked to other design elements. The modifications made to the derived features in the original design are mirrored in the changes made to the destination design when those features are updated. You may choose to generate from the current design a single component or a series of components, bodies, drawings, building geometry, flat patterns, or parameters.

Insert Derive command

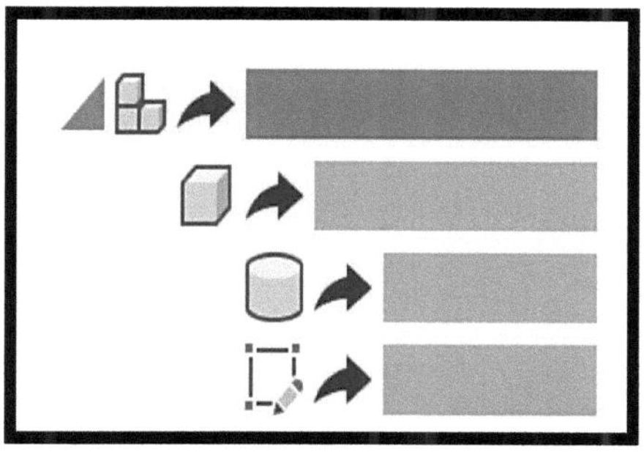

Design > Solid > Insert > Insert Derive

With the Insert Derive command, design features from another design may be pulled into the current design and linked to other design elements. The modifications made to the derived features in the original design are mirrored in the changes made to the destination design when those features are updated. You start by picking a design, and then you choose a collection of components, bodies, drawings, building geometry, flat patterns, or parameters to deduce into the design you choose.

Tip: Activate the component in which you want to place the derived design elements before beginning the **Insert Derive** command. This will ensure that the derived design features are properly placed.

When to use derived design features

Collaborative: Derived design characteristics allow various participants of a project to work on different components simultaneously in top-down assemblies. Meanwhile, the top level of the assembly is kept up to date automatically. When separate components or bodies are combined into an assembly, the overall collaborative design may be completed much more quickly.
Common Parameters: This feature allows you to derive all of the common parameters from only one F3D file. If you need to modify a parameter, you only need to do it in one place, and the change will be reflected in all of the designs that are derived from it.
Reuse: if a component is used in several products, incorporating a part that has already been created might decrease the amount of repetition that occurs in the design process.

Sheet Metal: If you start with a flat design for sheet metal, you can cut numerous flat patterns from a single sheet if you derive the pattern as a flat pattern. The inclusion of many flat designs in a single stock result in cost savings while also lowering the amount of material that is wasted.

Cut the connection between an assembly and a component that is located outside the assembly. Severing the component's association with the initial design should be your first step.

1. Launch the design application that houses the assembly.
2. Navigate to the location of the external component in the Browser.
3. Select the component using the right mouse button.
4. Select the option to **Break Link**.
5. A Break Link window will appear if the external component has any external subcomponents that it depends on.

Choose one of these options:

- **Include subcomponents**: This option, in addition to breaking the connection between the assembly and the specified external component, also breaks the link between any subcomponents and the assembly.
- **Component only**: This option only breaks the connection between the assembly and the component that is now chosen. The associative linkages between the external subcomponents are kept intact.

The associative relationship that previously existed between the assembly and the external component has been severed. The component will only affect the local assembly if any modifications are made to it after it has been changed to an internal component.

Note: Any bodies and features that were part of the external component will be moved into the appropriate folders inside the converted internal component if the external component contains Assembly Contexts.

Working with Bottom-up Assembly Approach

When it comes to putting together individual parts, the method known as **"bottom-up assembly"** is by far the most common. In this method, each component of an assembly is initially given its distinct design file before being compiled together into a single document and stored in a central place. After that, all of the components are loaded into a design file one at a time, and after that, they are put together by applying the necessary joints.

Tip: A useful feature of Fusion 360 is its ability to connect objects in both directions. Due to this, any change or modification made to a component is automatically reflected in the component used in the assembly, as well as in the drawing and other workspaces of Fusion 360, upon updating the respective file. This occurs regardless of whether the change is cosmetic or structural.

Working with Top-down Assembly Approach

When using the Top-down Assembly Approach, a single design file serves as the starting point for the creation of all of an assembly's parts. It is helpful in the process of constructing a concept-based design, which is a design in which new components of an assembly are formed by drawing references from the components that are already in the assembly.

Creating an Assembly by Using Bottom-up Approach

After designing each component of an assembly as a distinct file and storing it in a central place, you will need to create a new design file and insert each component individually into it. Only then will the assembly be complete. To do this, open a new design file in the DESIGN workspace by selecting the **New Design** tool from the File drop-down option on the Application Bar. This will allow you to begin creating your new design.

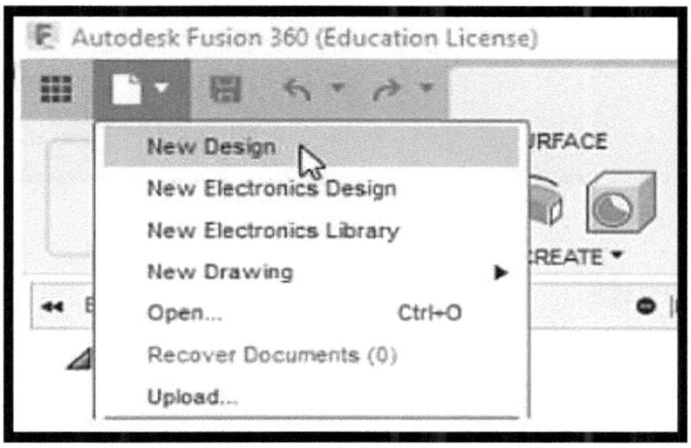

NOTE: When working in the DESIGN workspace of Fusion 360, you may build both a component and an assembly inside a design file at the same time. The production of components and assemblies does not make use of a distinct workstation or environment. When you choose the New Design tool from the File drop-down menu, the new design file is opened with the name "**Untitled," and the BROWSER** is shown to the left of the graphics area. This action triggers the saving of the new design. Take note that the icon for the component displays in front of the name of the design file while you are using the BROWSER. This reveals that the currently active design file corresponds to a component in the overall system. However, in the BROWSER, the component icon will change into the assembly icon as soon as you create a component within the design file or insert a component into the currently active design file as an external file. This occurs regardless of whether you create the component within the design file or insert it from another file.

Internal and External Components

Internal Components

A component that is housed inside the framework of the existing design is referred to as an internal component. When using the "**Top-Down**" assembly method, which requires all of the elements to be designed inside the same file, Internal Components are a need. When you create a new internal component in the Fusion 360 Browser, it will automatically be nested below the component that is now active. To move the component to a different location in the browser, use the Parent selector, which is shown below.

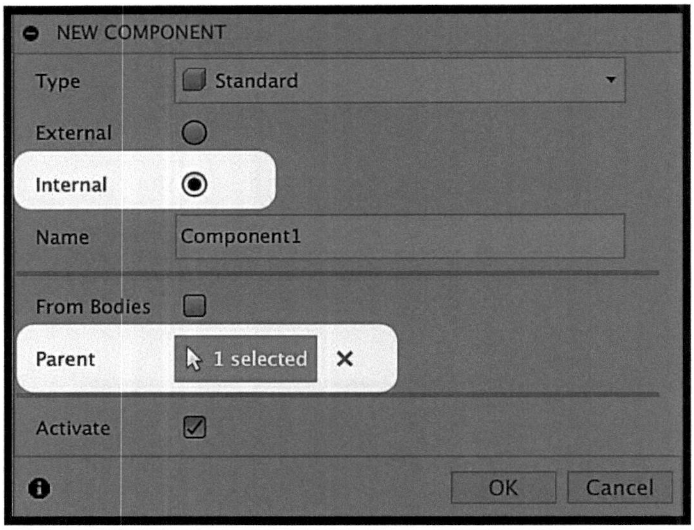

External Components

An External Component, often known as an **Xref**, is a component that is part of a different design but is referenced in the assembly that is currently being worked on (design file). The **"Bottom-Up"** assembly method makes use of external components. With this method, individual design files for each component are kept separate, and the completed product is saved as a single assembly file. When you want to insert a design file (component) inside of another design file, you may use the "**Insert into Current Design**" function instead of utilizing External Components. When working with external components, you will need to provide the Location (of the Data Panel) where the particular file will be kept. To modify the place where the file will be stored, use the "**location selector**" option from the menu. When you add a new external component to a model in the Fusion 360 Browser, it will automatically be nested underneath the component that is currently selected. To move the component to a different location in the browser, use the **Parent selector**, which is shown below.

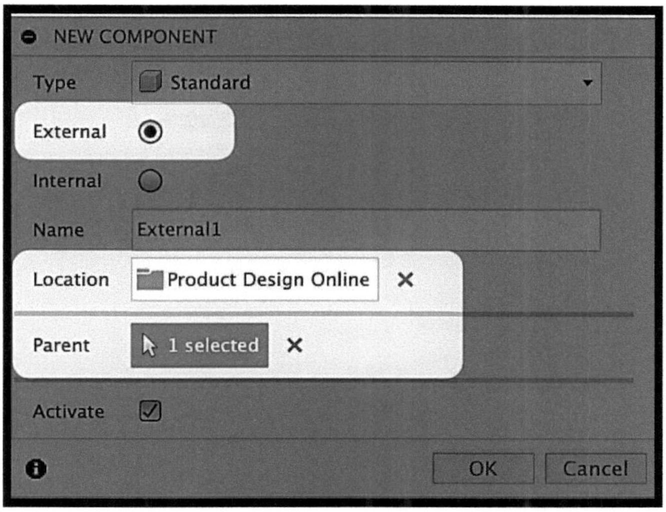

Edit External Components

Within the context of an active design file, you may modify external components by making use of the **Edit in Place** feature (hovering over the component in the browser and selecting the pencil icon). You also have the option of opening the independent design file to alter it outside of the assembly's environment.

Inserting Components in a Design File

1. Ensure that all of the designs have been successfully saved, and upload any designs that have not previously been done so.
2. Launch the "**Assembly**" **file**, which is the design that everything will be integrated into later on.
3. Open the data panel.
4. Use the right mouse button to choose the file's thumbnail that will be placed.
5. Select the **Insert into Current Design** option from the menu.

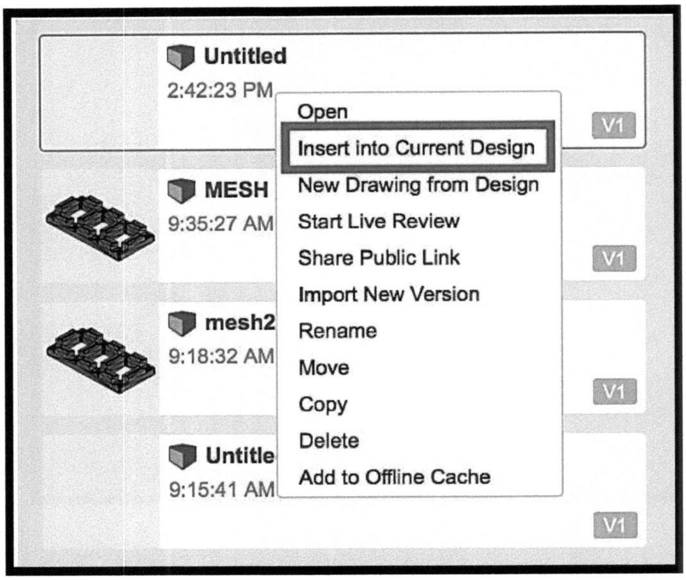

6. At this point, the Assembly file will have all of the bodies, components, and designs from the previous file loaded into it.
7. Place the model in the position you want it to be in.
8. Select the "**OK**" button.

By selecting "**Insert into Current Design**," a component will be added to the assembly file, and that component will have a reference to the original file that had the external design. This indicates that modifications may be made to the design of the initial component, and when the file containing the main body design is changed, the inserted component will convert to its new design along with any improvements that have been made. The chain link indicator that appears next to a file's name in the browser tree indicates that the file is being referenced. When you right-click on the component that has been installed, you will see choices that include "**Get Latest," "Choose Version," and "Break Link**."

- If you use the "**Get Latest**" command, the component will get an update depending on the file it was originally using.
- The "**Choose Version**" command will make it possible to choose between different versions of the component that have been previously stored.
- The "**Break Link**" command will remove the link to the file that was referenced, which is a step that is sometimes required to carry out certain operations.

Note that if you do manage to break the connection, the inserted component will no longer be referred to its original file. This means that any modifications made to the original file will not result in an update to the component in your body design.

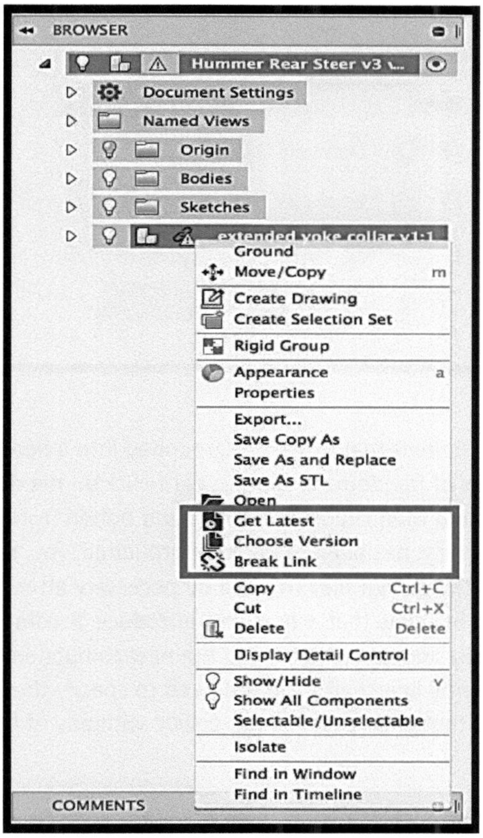

Note that this might result in complications if the timeline of the design that is now being entered contains any outstanding capture position instructions, warnings, or errors. Before utilizing a design as an X-REF, you will need to make sure that the position has been captured and that any timeline warnings and errors have been fixed.

Fixing/Grounding the First Component

When you enter a component into a design file using Fusion 360, that component is a floating one that has no restrictions on any of its degrees of freedom. A floating component does not have any restrictions on its ability to move or rotate inside the graphics area. Fixing or grounding the first component of the assembly is required before you can go on to inserting the second component into the design file. A component that is fixed or grounded does not permit any movement in either the translational or rotational directions. To do this, right-click anywhere inside the BROWSER on the name of the component you want to modify. There is a menu for shortcuts that shows. To access the Ground option in this drop-down menu, click the option. The component that you have chosen transforms into a fixed component, and a push-pin icon is added to the icon that represents it in the BROWSER. Additionally, the sign of a **push pin** can be seen next to the component that is fixed in the Timeline. The push-pin sign denotes that the component has no degrees of freedom and that it cannot move or spin in any direction. Additionally, the symbol implies that the component is immobile.

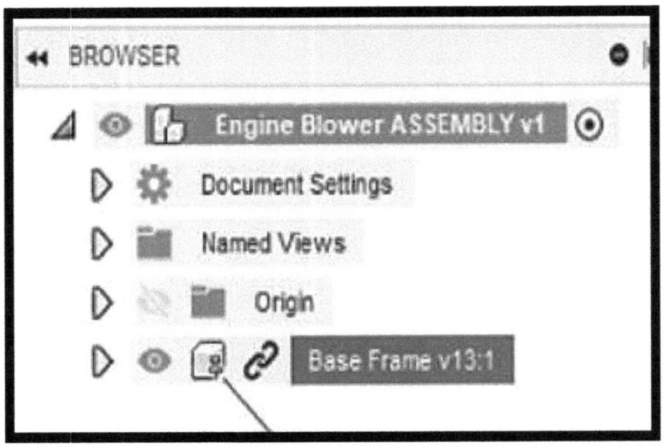

NOTE: You may also turn a component that is fixed or grounded into a floating component, which has no restrictions on any of its degrees of freedom. To do this, right-click on the fixed component that you want to unground in the BROWSER, and then choose the **Unground** option from the menu that displays when you do so. After the first component has been repaired or grounded, you will need to include the second component of the assembly in the design file. This will be necessary after the first component has been fixed. It is important to keep in mind that when you introduce a component, the translational and manipulator handles immediately appear connected to the new component in the graphics area, and the **MOVE/COPY** dialog box is instantly launched. You will need to specify the location of the component by utilizing these handles in a way that ensures it will not collide with any of the other components that are already part of the assembly.

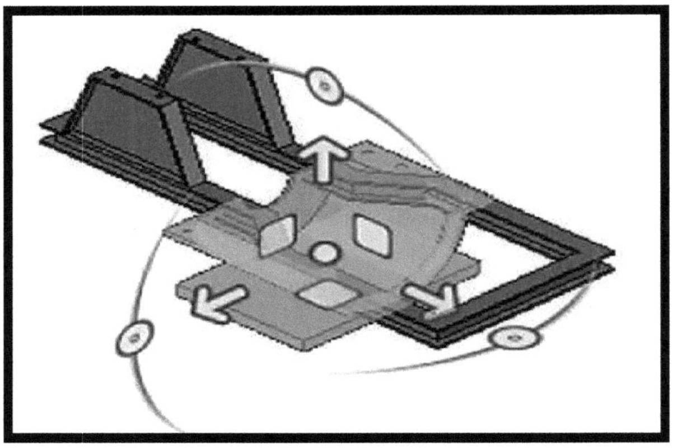

After you have inserted the second component into the assembly, you will need to combine it with the first component by applying the necessary joints between the two components. Joints are used in the process of defining the relationship between the many components that make up the assembly. It is essential, however, that you first have an understanding of the degrees of freedom before moving on to the next step of learning how to apply joints between the components of the assembly.

Working with Degrees of Freedom

Joints and as-built joints are what Fusion 360 uses to establish the interactions between parts, and joint movement is what contributes to the degrees of freedom. When working with other CAD tools, you may restrict one or two degrees of freedom at a time by using a constraint or mate, and then you can continue adding constraints or mates until you have sufficient degrees of freedom. In contrast, the first step in the process of using Fusion 360 is to restrict all degrees of freedom, and then you choose a joint motion type that outlines the available degrees of freedom. Using this strategy, you will be able to gain the necessary degrees of freedom all at once, with only a single command. A component can rotate around one of the X, Y, or Z axes or move translational (back and forth) along one of these axes when it has a joint that permits it to do so. Each joint incorporates the required number of degrees of freedom to achieve the desired range of motion.

Choose one of the following kinds of joints to put between two components when you want to link them together:

- **Rigid**. A stiff joint is a connection between two components that is permanent. There are no degrees of freedom afforded by it.
- **Revolute**. A revolute joint is similar to a hinge in that it only has a single degree of rotational flexibility. This joint may revolve around the X, Y, or typical Z axis, or it can rotate around an edge in the model (a custom axis).
- **Slider**. One and only one degree of translational flexibility is afforded to a slider joint. Components that may glide along one another making use of this material. These alternatives are quite similar to the revolute joint options; the only difference is that the components slide along the axis of rotation rather than rotating around it.
- **Cylindrical**. One degree of freedom is provided by translation, while the other is provided by rotation when using a cylindrical joint. Components that are linked together using a cylindrical joint will always spin along the same axis once the connection has been assembled.
- **Pin Slot**. A pin slot joint provides the same two degrees of freedom as a standard joint, but it additionally permits component rotation around several axes.
- **Planar**. There are three degrees of freedom available at a planar joint. It is possible to translate in two different directions inside a plane, and it is also possible to rotate in one direction that is normal to the plane. It helps attach two components in such a way that allows them to rotate while still sliding over the plane.
- **Ball**. Pitch and yaw are the two degrees of rotational freedom that a ball joint has. Components can spin around the Z-axis when pitch is used. Yaw is a rotational motion that revolves components around the X-axis.

Joint command

Through the use of the Joint command, you can arrange components about one another and then specify the motion that occurs between them.

Make use of this command when the components of an assembly have not yet been positioned concerning one another.

- To specify the location of the joint, you will need to locate the joint origin of each component.
- After that, choose the kind of joint that will be used to define the relative motion.
- Once on the canvas, you may get a preview of the joint motion.

In most cases, the Joint command will shift the component that you selected first to the component that you selected second. To make room for the initial component's movement, Fusion 360 will, if required, loosen any existing connections or change the grounded component status. For animating joints between components is that neither component should be attached to anything if at all possible. When one of the components is locked in place by grounding it, the motion of the joint can be predicted more accurately.

Selection order

The positive direction for joint movement is established based on the sequence in which component selection is performed. **Component 1**, which is the first component you pick, rotates around an axis or travels along an axis in the direction indicated by the arrow that represents the degrees of freedom, relative to **Component 2**.

Component 1 will rotate 30 degrees around the Z axis in the direction that the degrees of freedom arrow points if, for instance, you design a **Revolute** joint and configure it to rotate **30.0** degrees around the Z axis. If you have a door slider lock, you should choose the slider first, and then pick the component that is related to the door second. If you pick the components in the incorrect sequence, the joints could still move appropriately, but you might have to provide negative values for the Joint Alignment parameter to have the motion you want.

Applying Joints

Using the **Joint and As-built Joint** tools in Fusion 360, you may apply several kinds of joints to the components of an assembly to specify the connection that exists between those components. These joints include **stiff, revolute, slider, cylindrical, pin-slot, ball,** and **planar joints.** Simply selecting the **Joint tool** from the **ASSEMBLE** panel and clicking on it will allow you to apply a joint between two components of an assembly using the Joint tool. A dialog window labeled **JOINT** will now display. Alternatively, you may open the JOINT dialog box by selecting the ASSEMBLE option from the drop-down menu found on the SOLID tab, and then either clicking on the Joint tool or using the **J** key. Position and Motion are the two tabs that are available in this dialogue box. You may utilize the settings on the Position tab to define the components that need to be connected and the alignment of those components. The kind of joint that will be applied between the components may be defined by selecting one of the choices found in the Motion tab.

Applying a Rigid Joint

The components are locked or fixed together by the stiff joint, which eliminates all degrees of freedom and does not permit any relative motion between the components. This joint is used for locking or fastening the components together. The term "**rigid joint**" refers, in most cases, to the connection that exists between two components that have been either welded or bolted together such that there is no room for motion between them.

The following is an explanation of the process for applying a stiff joint:

1. To use the Joint tool, either hit the **J** key on your keyboard or click the Joint tool in the drop-down menu of the SOLID tab. A dialog window labeled JOINT will now display. Additionally, the components of the assembly that are fixed are rendered invisible in the graphics area.

NOTE: If the Fusion360 message window appears, informing you that some components have been moved from their previous position, then click the **Capture Position** button to capture the current position of the components. If the message window does not appear, then the current position of the components will not be captured. If you click the **Continue** button in this message box, the components will rearrange themselves according to how they were laid out before you clicked the button. When a tool is used after the location of a component has been changed, this notification box shows every time.

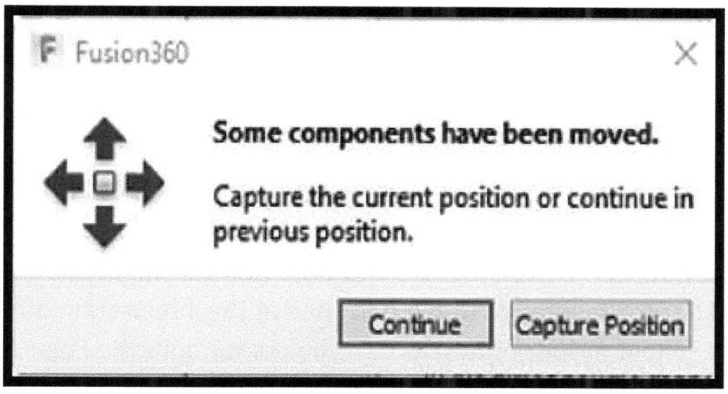

Component 1: To define the joint origin on the first component, go to the Position tab of the dialog box and choose the choices from the Component 1 rollout (moveable component). In the Mode section of this rollout, the button labeled "**Simple**" is the one that is chosen by default. As a consequence of this, you can establish the origin of the joint on a face, an edge, or a point of the first component. When you pick the **Between Two Faces** option, you will be able to establish the joint origin on a plane that is in the middle of the two faces that you have chosen. You may specify the joint origin at the intersection of two edges of the component by choosing the button labeled "**Two Edge Intersection**," and then selecting the button.

NOTE: To specify the joint origin on a plane at the center of two chosen faces of a component, pick the Between Two Faces button in the Mode area of the Component 1 rollout. This will cause the origin of the joint to be placed in the center of the plane. In the Component 1 rollout, the Face 1 and Face 2 selection choices are there for users to choose from. The Face 1 selection option is active by default whenever it is used.

Due to this, you will have the ability to pick the initial face of the component. Following the selection of the first face, the opportunity to choose **Face 2** becomes available for selection. After that, choose the component's second face to work with. Within the Component 1 rollout, the **Snap selection** option is available to be chosen. The next step is to move the pointer over a face, an edge, or a point in between the faces that have already been chosen on the component.

Following the appearance of the snap points, an imaginary plane will emerge in the middle of the two faces that have been chosen. After that, choose a snap point by clicking on it. The location of the joint origin is determined to be in the middle of two different faces chosen for the component in such a way that the selected snap point is projected onto an imaginary plane.

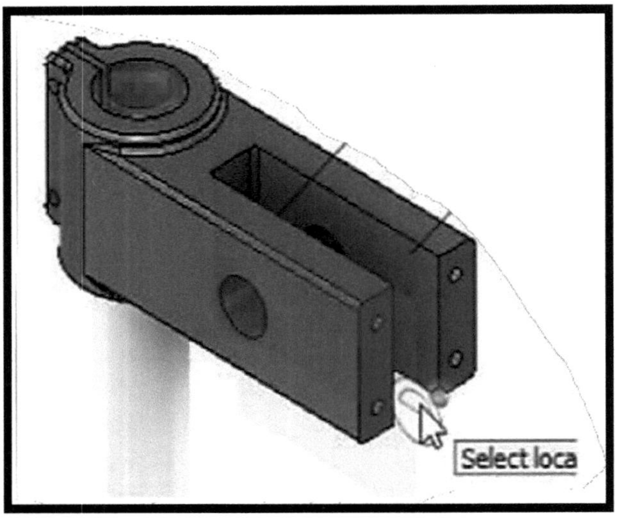

Clicking the **Two Edge Intersection** button in the Mode area of the Component 1 rollout will allow you to specify the joint origin of a component such that it is located at the intersection of two of the component's edges. The Component 1 rollout includes the selection choices for both the Edge 1 and the Edge 2 edges. The Edge 1 selection option is active by default whenever it is used. As a direct consequence of this, you can pick the first edge of a component. Following the selection of the first edge of a component, the option to pick the component's second edge will become active. After that, choose the component's second edge to work with. A snap point will appear at the junction of the two edges that have been chosen, and the pointer will automatically move to that location. After that, you should click on the snap point. The junction of the two edges that were chosen is where the joint origin is determined, and after that, the component in question becomes translucent in the graphics area.

2. When establishing the joint origin on a face, an edge, or a point of the first component, make sure that the Simple button is selected in the Mode section of the Component 1 rollout.

3. Position the cursor such that it is above a face, an edge, or a vertex of the first component (moveable component). The face, edge, or vertex is brought into focus, and its snap points come into view. In addition to this, the origin of the joint seems to be related to the cursor. In this illustration, the pointer has been shifted such that it is now hovering over the face of a component.

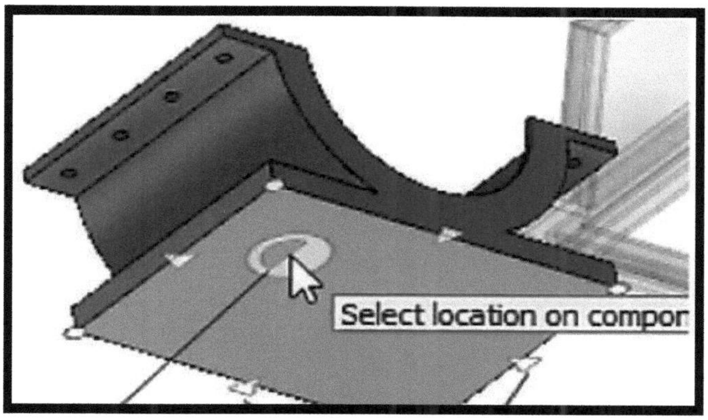

Hint: A snap point with the shape of a triangle suggests a midpoint, a snap point with the shape of a circle indicates a corner, and a snap point with the shape of a square indicates a center. You will now need to specify the location of the joint origin on the face, edge, or vertex of the first component that was highlighted in yellow.

4. By using the left mouse button, you may specify the location of the joint origin on a needed snap point that is accessible on the face, edge, or vertex that has been highlighted on the first component. You will be prompted to define the position of the joint origin on the second component as soon as you have finished defining the position of the joint origin on the first component. This happens because the **Snap selection** option in the Component 2 rollout becomes active as soon as you have finished defining the position of the joint origin on the first component. Additionally, the first component will transform into a translucent state inside the graphics area, and the joint origin sign will appear at the location that you have chosen.

Component 2: The choices available in the Position tab of the Component 2 rollout are identical to those of Component 1, with the exception that the Component 2 rollout options are the ones that are utilized to define the joint origin of the second component.

NOTE: When you are defining the location of the joint origin, you may notice that the snap points of the other face or edge of the component get highlighted when you move the cursor near one of the snap points of the highlighted face or edge of the component. You may get out of this predicament by locking the face or edge of the component that has to have its snap point chosen to define the starting position of the joint. When the snap points of the appropriate face or edge appear, hit the **CTRL** key, and then click the left mouse button on the required snap point. This will accomplish the desired result. After that, let go of the **CTRL** key.

5. When specifying the joint origin on a face, an edge, or a point of the second component, make sure that the Simple button is chosen in the Mode section of the Component 2 rollout. Note that to define the joint origin on a plane either at the center of two selected faces or at the intersection of two selected edges of a component, you will need to select the **Between Two Faces** or **Two Edge Intersection** button that is located in the Mode area of the Component 2 rollout. This will allow you to define the joint origin at either the center of two selected faces or at the intersection of two selected edges.

6. Position the cursor over a vertex, edge, or face of the second component. The snap points are now visible. In addition to this, the origin of the joint seems to be related to the cursor.

7. Click and specify the location of the joint origin so that it is located on a required snap point that is available on the face, edge, or vertex of the second component. The first component travels in the direction of the second component, and as it does so, the joint origins of both components move closer and closer together in the graphics area. Additionally, a preview of the motion that will occur between the components

is shown in the graphics area as an animation. This preview is determined by the default joint type that is chosen in the tab labeled Motion of the dialog box.

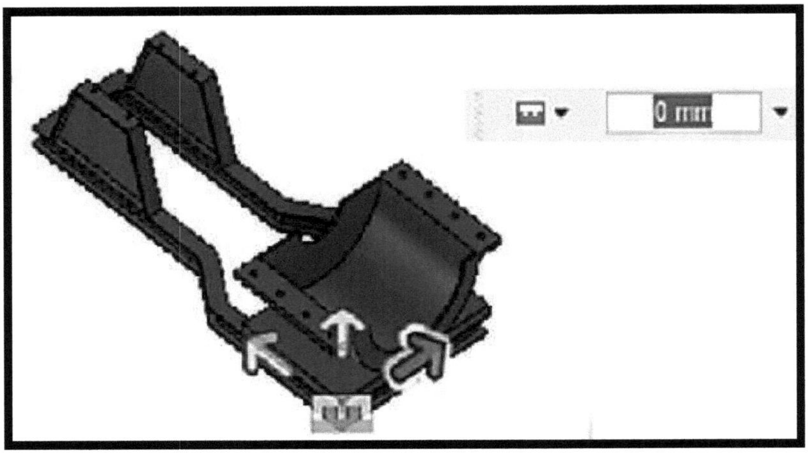

Joint Alignment: When setting the alignment between the components, you may utilize the choices that are found in the Joint Alignment rollout of the Position tab of the dialog box. In the **Offset X, Offset Y,** and **Offset Z** fields of this rollout, the number 0 is shown as the default setting for each field. As a direct consequence of this, the combined origins of the two different components will now coincide with one another. You can put an offset value in any of these fields, depending on what is necessary.

The orientation of the first component about the second component may also be defined by entering the angle value into the Angle field of the dialog box. It is important to take note that the **Joint Alignment** rollout in the Position tab of the dialog box does not include all of these data until after the joint origins have been defined on both of the components. When you click the Flip button on the Joint Alignment rollout, the alignment between the components will be flipped in the opposite direction.

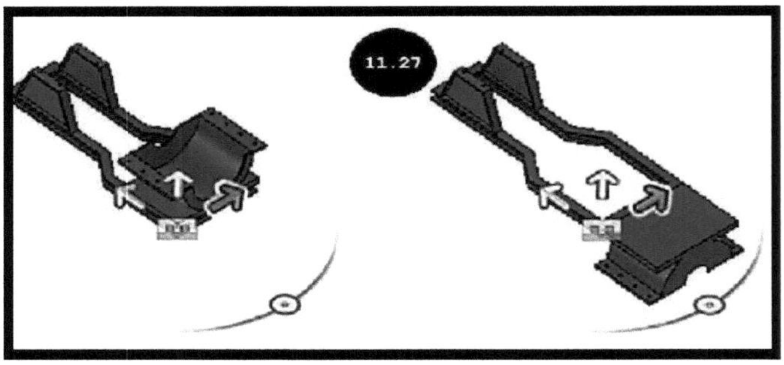

8. If necessary, use the Joint Alignment rollout that is included on the Position tab of the dialog box to specify the alignment that should be used between the components. After you have defined the joint origins of two components by making use of the choices found in the Position tab, the next step is to describe the kind of joint that will be applied between the components by making use of the options found in the Motion tab.
9. In the dialog box, choose the Motion tab and click on it.

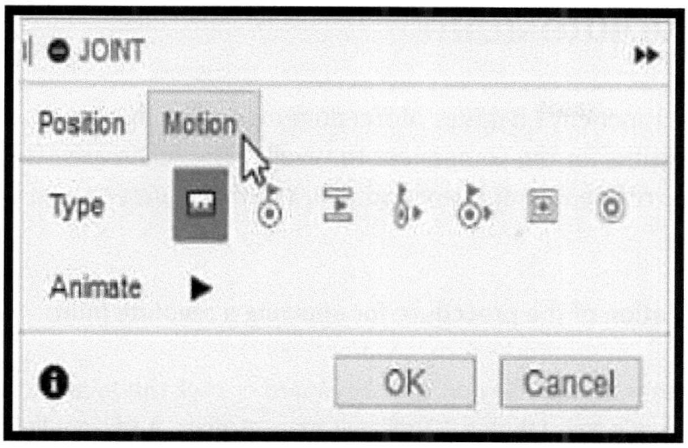

Type: In the dialog box, under the Motion tab, you'll see a section under "**Type.**" This is where you'll define the type of motion or joint that will be utilized between the components. By choosing the appropriate button in this section, you will be able to describe the motion between the components as being either stiff, revolute, slider, cylindrical, pin-slot, planar, or ball motion.

10. To create a hard connection between the components, choose the **Rigid** button located in the Type section of the Motion tab of the dialog box.

Animate: After applying the joint, you may animate the permissible motion between the components by clicking the Play button in the **Animate** section of the Motion tab of the dialog box. This button is located in the **Animate** area. It is useful in determining the free degrees of freedom of the components depending on the joint that has been applied to them.

11. In the dialog box, select the OK button and click it. When the rigid joint is applied between the components, all of the degrees of freedom that the components previously possessed are removed, and the components are then locked into place. Additionally, in the graphics section, there is a representation of a stiff joint.

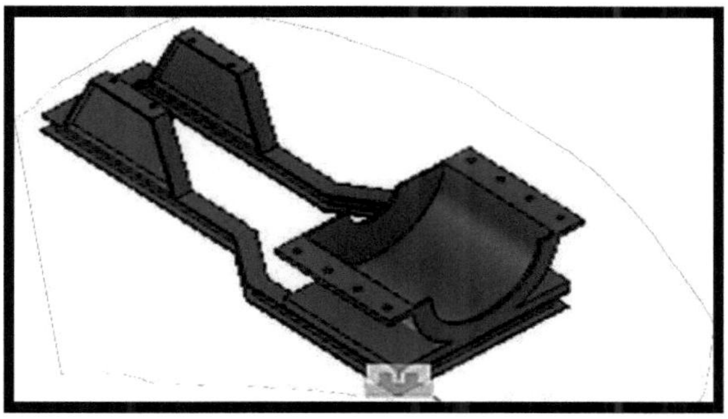

NOTE: The visibility of applied joints is switched on by default and may be viewed here. As a direct consequence of this, the graphics section now has icons representing each of the applied joints. Invoking the Display Settings flyout under the Display Settings menu will allow you to toggle the visibility of applied joints on and off. Next, in the flyout menu, choose the **Object Visibility** option by moving the cursor over it. A menu that collapses into itself emerges. To toggle the display of joints in the graphics area, use this menu to select or clear the Joints checkbox. Doing so will either turn joints on or off. Other joints, such as revolute, slider, cylindrical, pin-slot, planar, and ball joints, which will be addressed in the next section, may also be used similarly.

Applying a Revolute Joint

By eliminating all of the component's degrees of freedom except for the rotating degree of freedom, the revolute joint makes it possible for the component to revolve around an axis. This type of joint is utilized whenever it is necessary to rotate a component about an axis that is determined by the joint origins of the component.

The following is an explanation of the procedure for applying a revolute joint:

1. To use the Joint tool, either hit the **J** key on your keyboard or click the Joint tool in the drop-down menu of the SOLID tab. A dialog window labeled JOINT will now display. Additionally, the components of the assembly that are fixed appear transparent when viewed in the graphics area. In addition, if the message box for Fusion360 displays, click the button labeled "**Capture Position**" to record the components' positions as they are now found. When you click the Continue button in this message box, the components will move to the place they were in before you clicked the button.

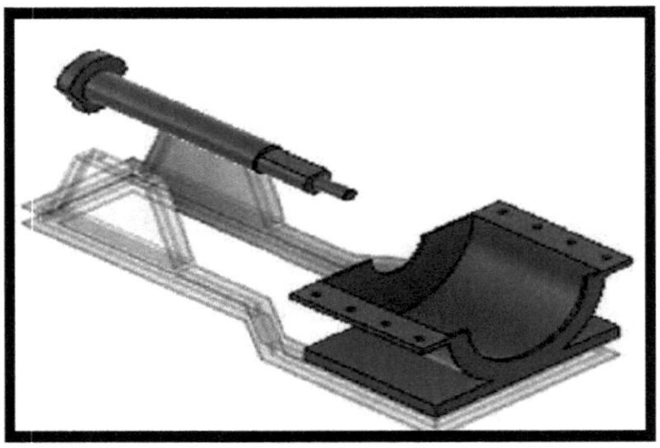

At this point, you must specify the joint origins of both of the components. A revolute joint is one in which the parts revolve around the origin of the joint.

2. In the dialog box for establishing the joint origin on a face, an edge, or a point of the first component, make sure that the Simple button is selected in the Mode section of the Component 1 rollout. Note that to define the joint origin on a plane at the center of two selected faces or at the intersection of two selected edges of a component, you will need to select the Between Two Faces or Two Edge Intersection button in the Mode area of the Component 1 rollout. This will allow you to define the joint origin at the center of two selected faces or the intersection of two selected edges.

3. Place the cursor on a side of the first component or along one of its edges (moveable component). The face or edge is brought into focus, and its snap points and joint origin are brought into view. The pointer has been moved on a circular border of the component in the diagram that may be found further down. As a consequence of this, there is only one snap point that appears in the middle of the edge, and the joint origin is automatically snapped to this point.

4. To determine the location of the joint origin on the first component, select the snap point and click on it. Keep in mind that you need to hit the **CTRL** key to lock a face or an edge so that you can simply pick its snap point. The origin of the joint has been determined, and the component has gained transparency.

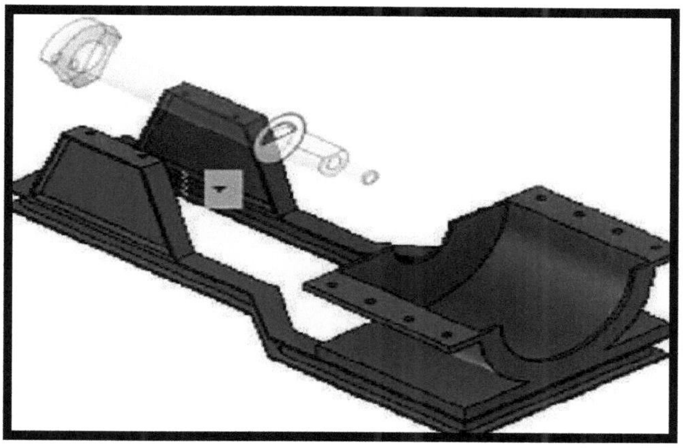

At this point, you must specify the joint origin for the second component.

5. In the dialog box for establishing the joint origin on a face, an edge, or a point of the second component, make sure that the Simple button is selected in the Mode area of the Component 2 rollout. This area is located in the rollout for the Component 2 rollout. Note that to define the joint origin on a plane at the center of two selected faces or at the intersection of two selected edges of a component, you will need to select the Between Two Faces or Two Edge Intersection button that is located in the Mode area of the Component 2 rollout. This will allow you to define the joint origin at the center of two selected faces or the intersection of two selected edges.
6. Move the cursor so that it is over one of the faces or edges of the second component. The face or edge is brought into focus, and its snap points as well as the joint origin are revealed.

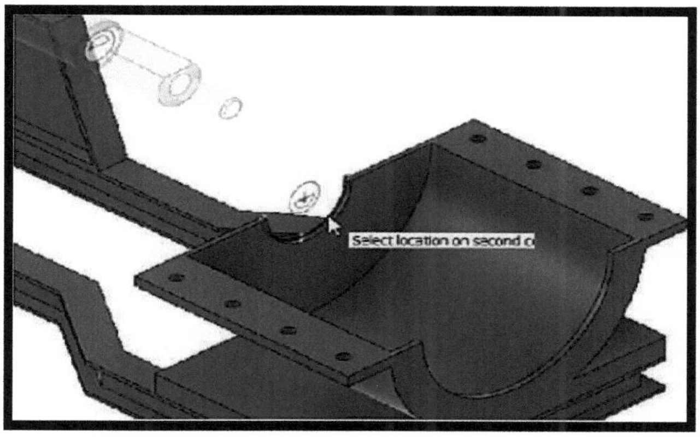

7. To define the position of the joint origin on the second component, click on the snap point that is highlighted in the image. The first component travels in the direction of the second component, and as it does so, the joint origins of both components move closer and closer together in the graphics area. Additionally, a preview of the motion that is taking place between the components is displayed in the graphics area as an animation. This is done following the joint type that is selected by default in the Motion tab of the dialog box.

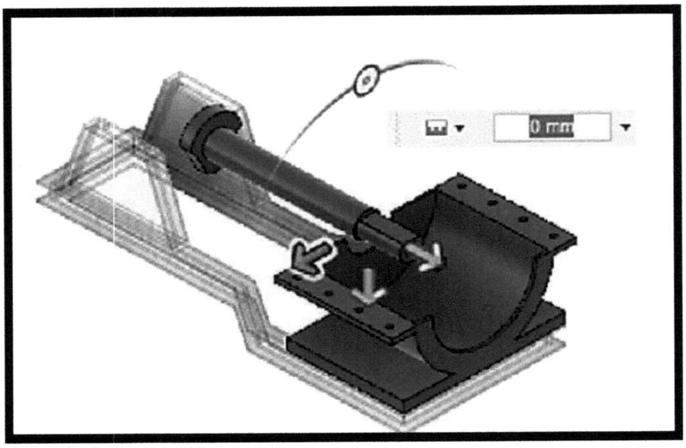

NOTE: If you want to quickly select the component's snap point, you can lock a face or an edge of it by pressing the CTRL key on your keyboard.

8. If necessary, use the Joint Alignment rollout that is included on the Position tab of the dialog box to specify the alignment that should be used between the components. At this point, you need to decide what kind of joint will be put in place.
9. In the dialog box used to pick a kind of joint that will be applied between the components that have been chosen, go to the Motion tab and click on it.

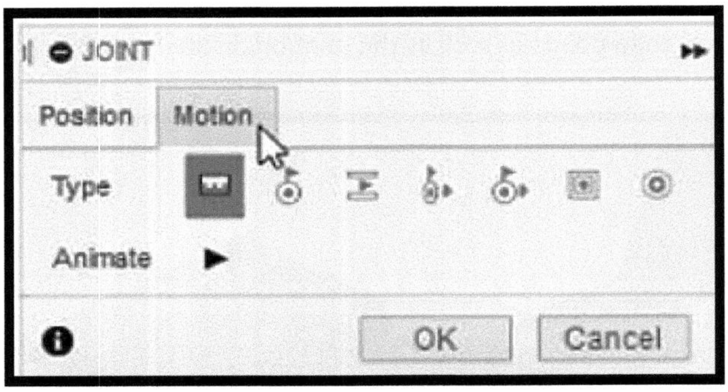

10. To apply the revolute joint and rotate the component around an axis, use the **Revolute** button located in the Type section of the Motion tab.
11. Define the needed axis of rotation for the component by choosing the required option from the drop-down list located in the Motion tab of the dialog box. This will allow you to define the appropriate axis of rotation.

NOTE: You may specify the rotation of the component around the X, Y, or Z axis by choosing the appropriate option in the **Rotate** drop-down list. These axes are shown in order from left to right. Using the **Custom** option will allow you to establish a custom axis in addition to the X, Y, and Z axes that are already available. To accomplish this, select the **Custom** option from the drop-down list located next to the **Rotate** button. Next, choose an edge or a face to define the custom axis for rotating the component about it. The axis that is normal to the selected face is defined when you select a face to work on.

12. In the dialog box, select the **OK** button and click it. The revolute joint is applied between the components in such a way that all of the degrees of freedom of the components, except the rotational degree of freedom, are removed. This allows the component to rotate around the axis that has been specified.

TIP: To check how a component moved after a joint was applied to it, pick the component and then drag it along or about its free degree of freedom. This will show you how the component moved.

Applying a Slider Joint

By eliminating all degrees of freedom other than the degree of freedom associated with translation, the slider joint enables the component to be translated or slid along a single axis. This joint's name comes from its primary function.

The following is an explanation of the procedure for installing a slider joint:

1. Open the dialog box labeled "**JOINT.**"
2. In the dialog box for establishing the joint origin on a face, an edge, or a point of the first component, make sure that the **Simple** button is selected in the **Mode** section of the Component 1 rollout. Note that to define the joint origin on a plane at the center of two selected faces or at the intersection of two selected edges of a component, you will need to select the **Between Two Faces** or **Two Edge Intersection** button in the Mode area of the **Component 1** rollout. This will allow you to define the joint origin at the center of two selected faces or the intersection of two selected edges.
3. Place the cursor on a side of the first component or along one of its edges (moveable component). The face or edge is brought into focus, and its snap points as well as the joint origin are shown.

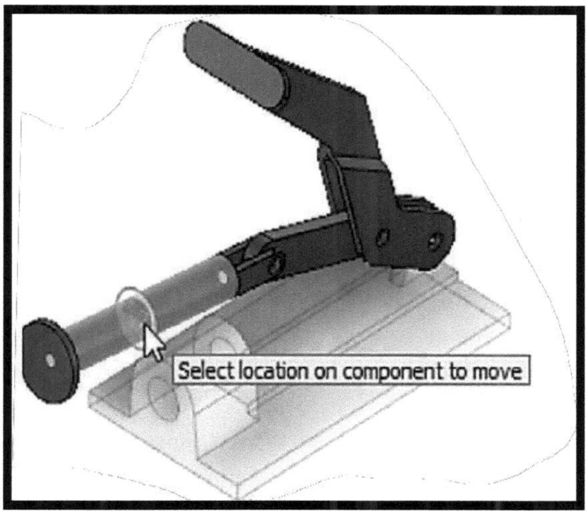

4. To determine the location of the joint origin on the first component, choose a snap point by clicking on it. By hitting the **CTRL** key, you may also lock a face or an edge to make selecting that feature's snap point simpler. At the point at which the snap point is determined, the joint origin is defined, and the component becomes translucent.

- At this point, you must specify the joint origin for the second component.

5. In the dialog box for establishing the joint origin on a face, an edge, or a point of the second component, make sure that the Simple button is selected in the Mode area of the Component 2 rollout. This area is located in the rollout for the **Component 2** rollout.
6. Position the cursor over a vertex, edge, or face of the second component. The snap points are now visible. In this illustration, the cursor has been dragged around the component until it is hovering on one of its round edges.

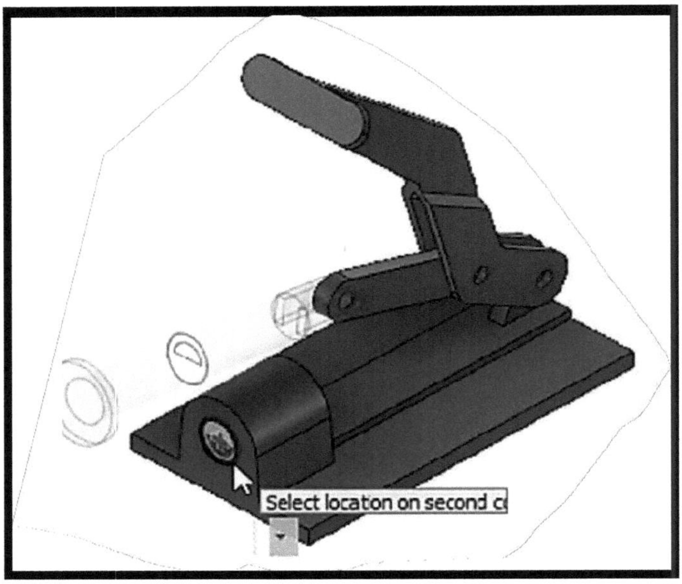

7. To determine the location of the joint origin on the second component, click on the snap point that is highlighted in the image. Within the graphics area, the combined origins of the two different components will eventually overlap with one another. Additionally, a preview of the motion that will occur between the components is shown in the graphics area as an animation. This is done following the default joint type that is chosen in the **Type** section of the dialog box.

- At this point, you need to decide what kind of connection will be made between the components that have been chosen.

8. Sliding the movable component along an axis may be accomplished by selecting the Slider button located in the **Type** section of the dialog box after clicking on the Motion tab.
9. Specify the needed axis to define the movement of the component by choosing the required option from the Slide drop-down list located on the Motion tab of the dialog box. This will allow you to define the movement of the component.
10. In the dialog box, choose the **OK** button and click it. The slider joint is applied between the components in such a way that all of the degrees of freedom of the components, except a single degree of freedom that allows for translation, are eliminated. Additionally, the component can slide along the axis that has been defined.

TIP: To check how a component moved after a joint was applied to it, pick the component and then drag it along or about its free degree of freedom. This will show you how the component moved.

Applying a Cylindrical Joint

The cylindrical joint is utilized for translating as well as rotating the component along the same axis. To accomplish this, the cylindrical joint eliminates all degrees of freedom other than one translational and one rotational degree of freedom. Its primary function is to facilitate the formation of a screw mechanism connecting the various components. **The following is an explanation of the procedure for applying a cylindrical joint:**

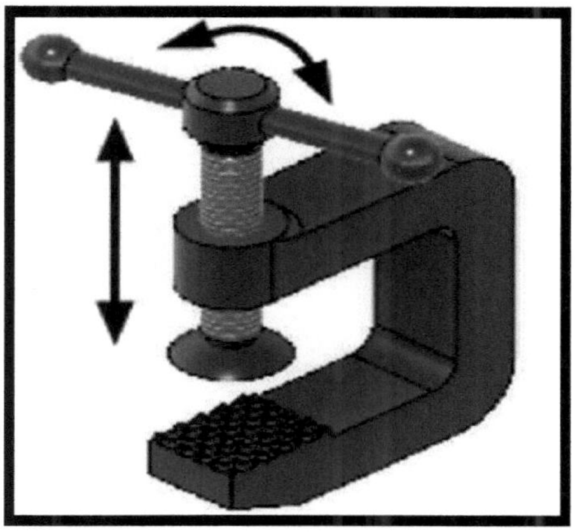

1. Open the dialog box labeled "**JOINT**."
2. In the dialog box for establishing the joint origin on a face, an edge, or a point of the first component, make sure that the Simple button is selected in the Mode section of the Component 1 rollout. Note that to define the joint origin on a plane at the center of two selected faces or at the intersection of two selected edges of a component, you will need to select the **Between Two Faces** or **Two Edge Intersection** button in the Mode area of the Component 1 rollout. This will allow you to define the joint origin at the center of two selected faces or the intersection of two selected edges.
3. Place the cursor on a side of the first component or along one of its edges (moveable component). The face or edge is brought into focus, and its snap points as well as the joint origin are shown.

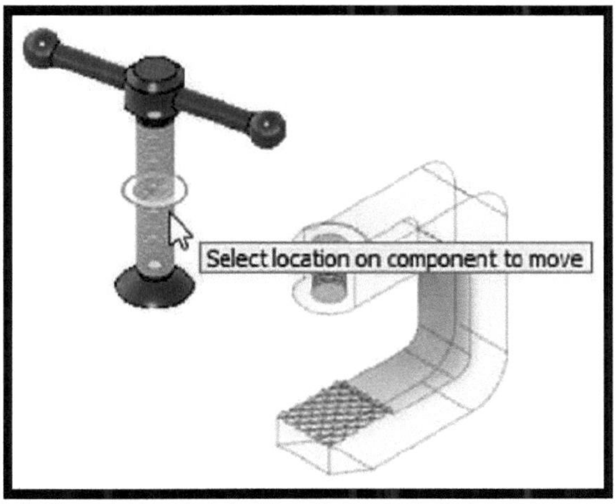

4. To determine the location of the joint origin on the first component, select the snap point and click on it. At the point at which the snap point is determined, the joint origin is defined, and the component becomes translucent. At this point, you must specify the joint origin for the second component.
5. When specifying the joint origin on a face, an edge, or a point of the second component, make sure that the Simple button is chosen in the Mode section of the Component 2 rollout.
6. Position the cursor over a vertex, edge, or face of the second component. The snap points are now visible.

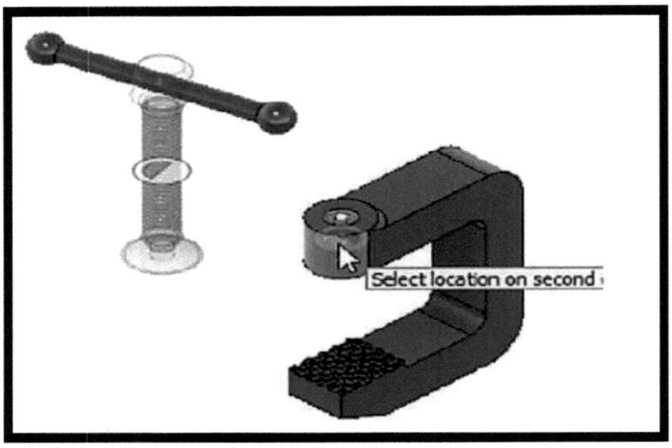

7. To determine the location of the joint origin on the second component, click on the snap point that is highlighted in the image. The first component travels in the direction of the second component, and as it does so, the joint origins of both components move closer and closer together in the graphics area. At this point, you need to decide what kind of connection will be made between the components that have been chosen.
8. Navigate to the Motion tab, then click the **cylindrical** button in the Type box to give the component the ability to rotate in addition to moving along the same axis.
9. Specify the necessary axis to define the rotation and translation of the component by choosing the necessary option from the Axis drop-down list located on the Motion tab of the dialog box. This will allow you to specify the rotation and translation of the component.
10. In the dialog box, choose the **OK** button and click it. For the component to be able to rotate as well as translate along the designated axis, the cylindrical joint must be applied between the components.

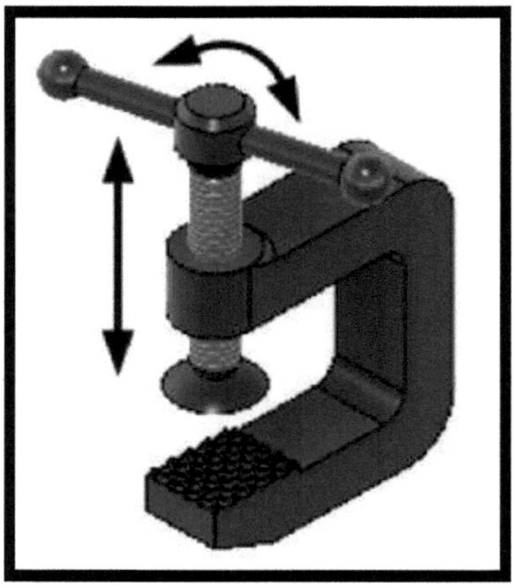

Applying a Pin-slot Joint

The pin-slot joint is used to translate the component along one axis and rotate the component around a separate axis. This is accomplished by eliminating all degrees of freedom from the joint, except one degree of freedom that is translational and one degree of freedom that is rotational. The cylindrical joint and the pin-slot joint both function in the same manner. The pin-slot joint, however, differs from the cylindrical joint in that it allows the user to pick alternative axes for the translation and rotation of the component.

The following is an explanation of the procedure for attaching a pin-slot joint:

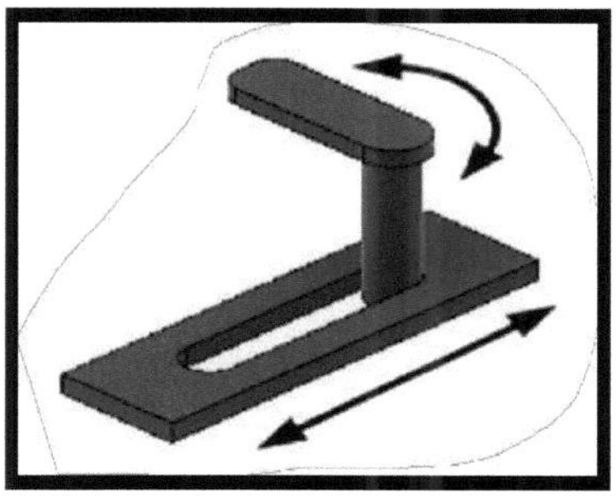

1. Open the dialog box labeled "**JOINT**."
2. In the dialog box for establishing the joint origin on a face, an edge, or a point of the first component, make sure that the Simple button is selected in the Mode section of the Component 1 rollout. Note that to define the joint origin on a plane at the center of two selected faces or at the intersection of two selected edges of a component, you will need to select the **Between Two Faces** or **Two Edge Intersection** button in the Mode area of the Component 1 rollout. This will allow you to define the joint origin at the center of two selected faces or the intersection of two selected edges.
3. Position the cursor so that it is over a face or an edge of the first component (the movable component), and then define the position of the joint origin on the appropriate snap point.
4. Position the cursor so that it is over a face or an edge of the second component, and then define the position of the joint origin on the appropriate snap point.
5. Within the graphics area, the combined origins of the two different components will eventually overlap with one another.

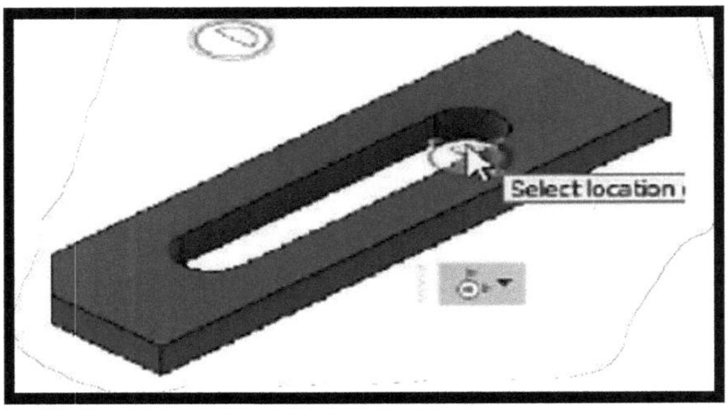

At this point, you need to decide what kind of connection will be made between the components that have been chosen.
5. Navigate to the tab labeled Motion and pick the **Pin-slot** button located in the Type section to give the component the ability to rotate about one axis and translate along another axis.
6. On the Motion tab of the dialog box, locate the drop-down menu labeled "**Rotate**," and choose the axis of rotation that corresponds to your needs.
7. From the drop-down list located in the Motion tab of the dialog box, choose the axis of translation that corresponds to the action that you want to perform.

NOTE: If you choose the **Custom** option, you also can provide a custom axis that will be used for the rotation or translation of the component. To do this, pick the **Custom** option from the drop-down list located in the **Rotate or Slide** section of the interface. Next, select either an edge or a face to establish the custom axis for the component's rotation or translation, as the case may be.

8. In the dialog box, choose the **OK** button. Pin-slot joints are used between the components to allow for rotation and translation along various axes. These joints are applied between the components.

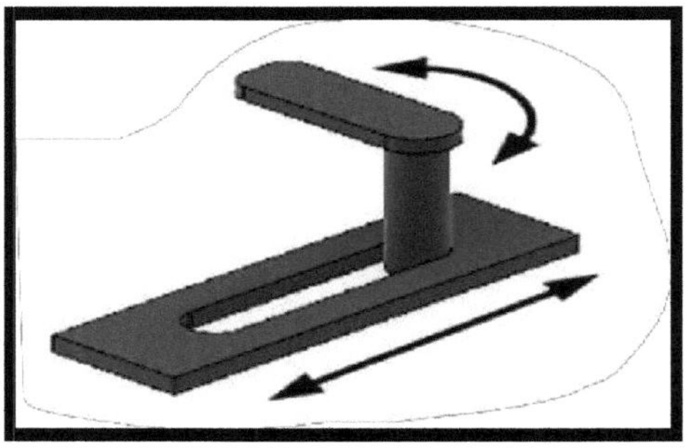

Applying a Planar Joint

In addition to allowing rotation along a single axis, the planar joint also allows for the component to be translated along two other axes. When using this kind of joint, the component may be constrained to a planar face of another component in such a way that its movement in the direction that is normal to the planar face is limited, but the movement is still permitted inside the plane of the face. In addition to this, it enables rotational movement along an axis that is perpendicular to the flat face. An object, for instance, can rotate along an axis that is normal to the planar face of a tabletop in addition to moving along the planar face of the tabletop itself. **The following is an explanation of the procedure for applying a planar joint:**

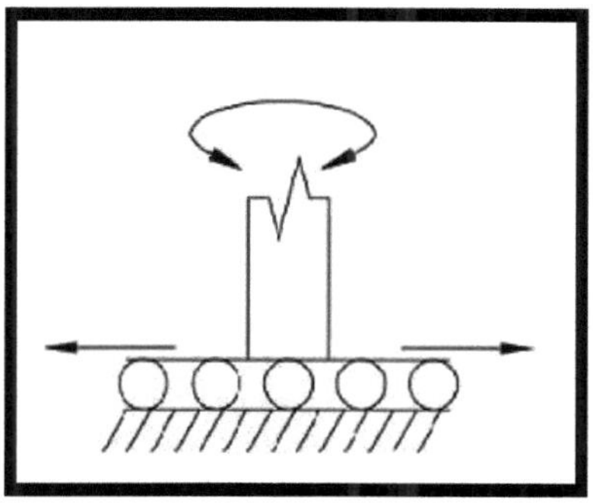

1. Bring up the **JOINT** dialog box, then position the cursor over a face or an edge of the first component (a component that may be moved), and then set the location of the joint origin on a needed snap point. It is important to keep in mind that by using the **CTRL** key, you may quickly lock a face or an edge so that you can pick its snap point.

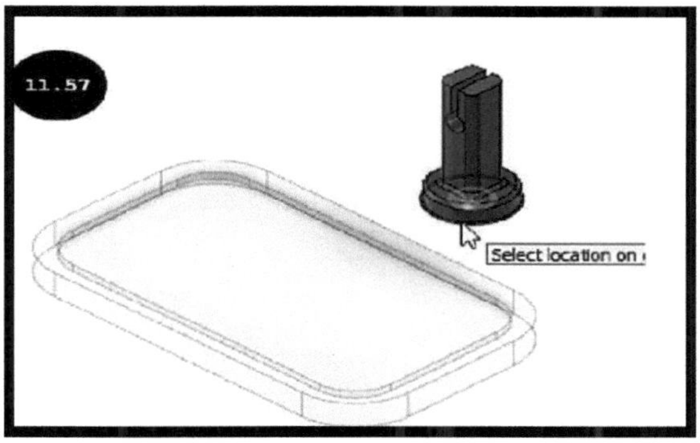

2. Position the cursor so that it is over a face or an edge of the second component, and then define the position of the joint origin on a needed snap point.
3. Within the graphics area, the combined origins of the two different components will eventually overlap with one another.

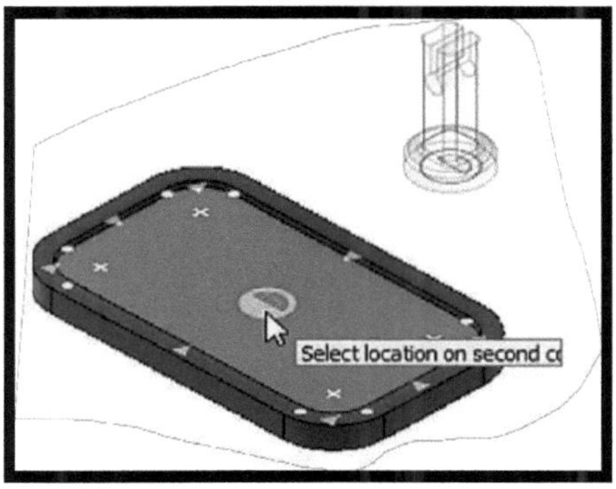

At this point, you need to decide what kind of connection will be made between the components that have been chosen.

4. Navigate to the tab labeled Motion, and then click the **Planar** button located in the Type section. This will enable the component to rotate around a single axis as well as translate along two axes.
6. In the drop-down list labeled **Normal** located on the Motion tab of the dialog box, choose the axis that is necessary to specify the rotation of the component. Using the Custom option found in this drop-down list, you are also able to design a bespoke axis for the chart.
7. Within the Slide drop-down box, choose the axis that you need to use to describe the two different translational motions that the component will make within the face plane. It is determined depending on the choice that is chosen in the drop-down list labeled Normal in the dialog box. This is the default setting. Using the Custom option found in this drop-down list, you are also able to design a bespoke axis for the chart.
8. In the dialog box, choose the OK button and click it. The planar joint is applied between the components in such a way that the component may rotate around the designated axis in addition to being able to translate along two axes (the plane of face).

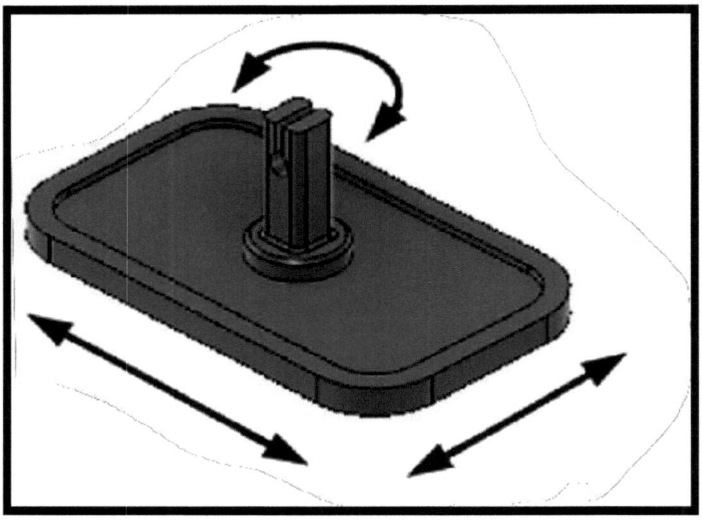

Applying a Ball Joint

The ball joint allows rotation of the component about all three axes of rotation, making it an invaluable component. In this joint, all of the component's translational degrees of freedom are constrained, but the component is allowed to rotate around all three axes concerning a point that is specified as the joint origin.

The following is an explanation of the procedure for installing a ball joint:

1. Open the dialog box labeled "**JOINT**."
2. When you are creating the joint origin on a face, edge, or point, make sure that the Simple button is chosen in the Mode section of the Component 1 rollout.

3. Position the mouse on the spherical face of the first component (the movable component), and then click to define the placement of the joint origin at the center snap point of that component.

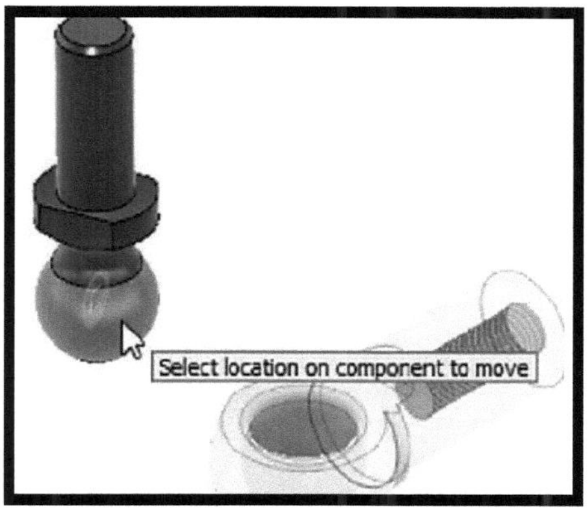

At this point, you must specify the joint origin for the second component.
4. When defining the joint origin on a face, an edge, or a point of the second component, make sure that the Simple button is selected in the Mode area of the Component 2 rollout.
5. Position the mouse on the spherical face of the second component, and when the center snap point appears, click it to designate the location of the joint origin. Within the graphics area, the combined origins of the two different components will eventually overlap with one another.
At this point, you need to decide what kind of connection will be made between the components that have been chosen.
6. Navigate to the tab labeled Motion, and then click the Ball button located in the Type section. This will enable the component to spin around all three axes.

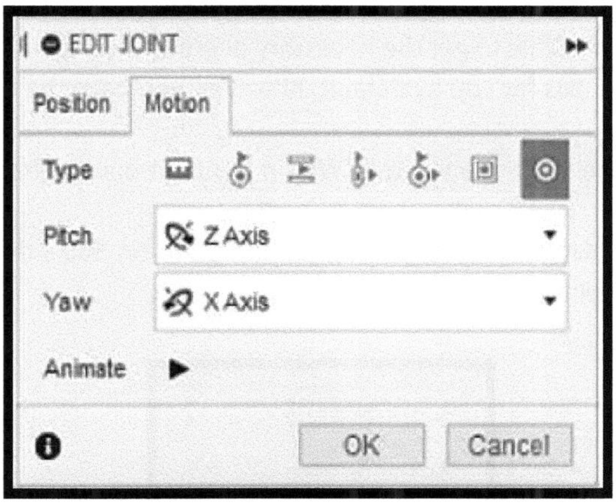

7. Choose the axis from the drop-down list labeled "**Pitch**" on the Motion tab of the dialog box. This will set the axis as the lateral axis of the component. By selecting the Custom option from this drop-down list, you also have the opportunity to create a custom axis as the lateral axis.
8. In the Motion tab of the dialog box, locate the **Yaw** drop-down list and choose the axis to use as the component's longitudinal/perpendicular axis. By selecting the Custom option from this drop-down list, you also can set a user-defined axis as the perpendicular axis.

9. In the dialog box, select the **OK** button and click it. The ball joint is attached between the components in such a way that it allows the component to rotate about three axes while preventing it from moving in any translational direction.

Create a joint between the shaft and the gear housing

In this stage of the process, you will utilize the Joint command to design a **Revolute joint** that will connect the body of a gear housing to its shaft.

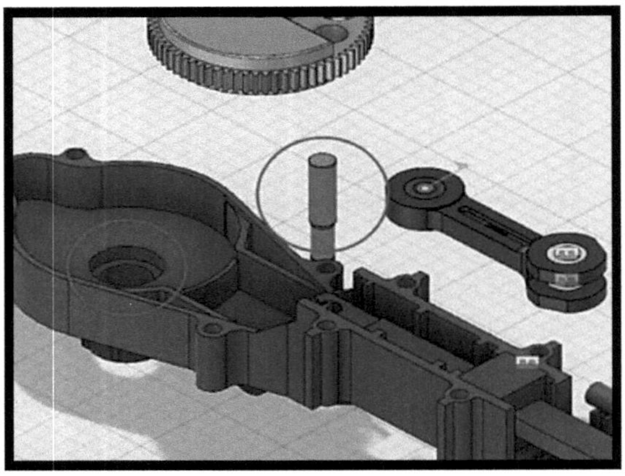

1. If the Data Panel is not already visible, click the **Show Data Panel** button.
2. Navigate to **Projects > Samples > Workshops & Events > Adoption Path > Mechanical Assembly > 5 Assemblies and Joints**. Once there, open the 5 Assembly Joints file in the Data Panel.
3. Select **Assemble > Joint** from the Model workspace.
4. In the Joint dialog, choose the **Revolute** option for the Motion Type drop-down menu.
   - Fusion 360 makes it possible to get the necessary degrees of freedom for the motion type. Fusion 360 will choose the Z axis for you by default; however, you have the option to select another axis if required.
5. Determine which side of the shaft you will use. Within the Joint dialog, the shaft that has been chosen for Component 1 can be seen.
6. There is just one point available to connect to when using Fusion 360's default settings, which in this instance is the edges center point.

7. On the shaft, there is a little symbol that is referred to as the **joint origin**. It serves as the point of reference for the joint that is located on this component.

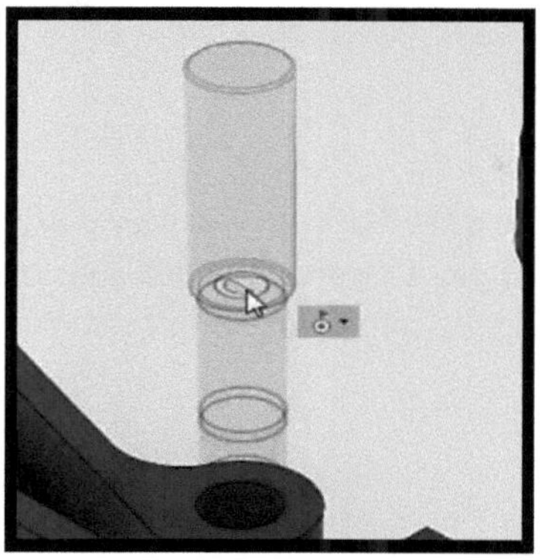

8. Choose a spot on the ring that surrounds the aperture in the gear housing's interior. This option is shown in the Joint dialog for Component 2, which was selected.
9. The shaft is moved to the gear housing, where it is attached to the housing in a revolving connection.

10. Make sure you click **OK**.
11. Rotate the shaft's base in a clockwise direction. The animation is shown on the flag that rotates.

Editing Joints

Editing Options

If you right-click on a joint when you are connected to one of the access points, you will be presented with a variety of choices, most of which are elaborated upon in more depth in this document. If you want to get the most out of your joints, one of the most essential things you can do is make use of the choices that are provided in this menu. This may seem less crucial than the actual process of creating the joint.

Drive Joints

Drive Joints give you the ability to establish exact values for the various degrees of freedom that may be achieved by using the joint. You also can make use of the manipulator to rapidly comprehend the movements.

Edit Joint

You have the opportunity to amend the work that you have previously done with the Joint by selecting the Edit Joint option. This option also provides a means to adjust your component choices by modifying the component's placement or by replacing the component with a sister component.

Edit Joint Limits

You have the opportunity to update and specify the limitations for your Joints when you choose the **Edit Joint Limits** option. In the next sections of this handout, we will go more deeply into this topic.

Lock

Lock makes the values and placement of the Joint permanent as they are now shown. You will still have access to update the Joint and its restrictions, but the Joint's present location will remain unchanged until you unlock it. Lock eliminates the user's ability to drag the Joint in any direction.

Suppress

You now have the power to momentarily stop the Joint from carrying out the activity it was assigned to do by using the Suppress ability. The Joint operates just as if it had been removed, and it does not contribute in any way to the motion that occurs between components. You may put this to use to assist you in resolving any mutual disagreements.

You may also use Suppress when you need to understand the motion of other Joints and you want to temporarily halt the behavior of the Joint you are suppressing while keeping its values intact. This allows you to comprehend the motion of the other Joints.

Animate Joint

When you use Animate Joint, it will simply animate the Joint itself; it will not take into consideration neighboring joints, being grounded, or other external impacts that the Joints may be subject to. When you just need to comprehend the movement of a single Joint, Animate Joint is an excellent tool to use.

Animate Model

Animate Model will animate the model as a whole and will take into consideration grounded as well as any other joints in your model that may have an influence. Make use of this to get an understanding of the connection between several Joints.

Go to Home Position

When you relocate a component that already has a Joint associated with it, you are relocating the component away from its "**home**" location, also known as the position where the Joint was first constructed concerning the connected component. Utilizing the Go to Home Position ability will allow you to return the joint to its previous position. You also have a command that is quite similar to this that is called "**Set as Home Position**," and it enables you to redefine the Home Position.

Select Components

The components that the Joint is related to are selected when you use the Select Components button. This gives you a better understanding of what the joint is doing to your body.

Defining Joint Limits

When a joint is applied to a component in Fusion 360, by default, the component is free to rotate or translate along its free degrees of freedom, without being constrained in any way by the joint. For instance, when the slider joint is used, the component is allowed to freely translate along the axis that was defined without being constrained in any way. To prevent this from happening in Fusion 360, you may define the maximum and minimum limits for a joint to control the movement of a component along or around its free degrees of freedom. This will allow you to keep the component in its desired position. This only permits the component to move or rotate within the boundaries that have been established.

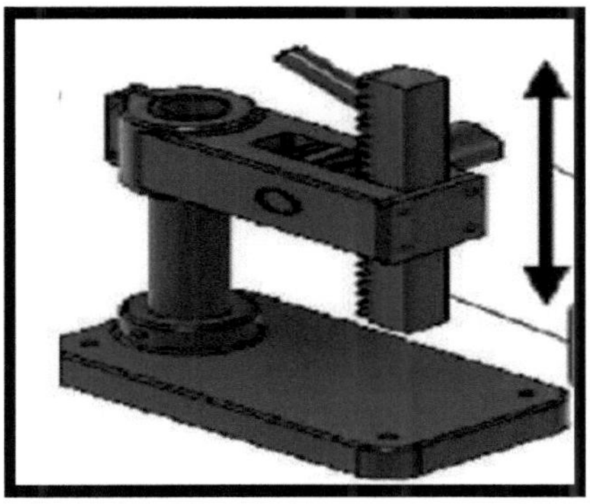

Simply expanding the Joints node in the **BROWSER** will allow you to determine the limitations of a joint. Next, place the cursor over the joint to specify the joint's boundaries in the Joints node that has been extended. The **Edit Joint Limits** icon is shown next to the name of the joint in the joint editor. After that, choose this icon to edit the joint limits. A dialog box labeled **EDIT JOINT LIMITS** is shown. Alternatively, you may open the **EDIT JOINT LIMITS** dialog box by right-clicking on the joint in the enlarged Joints node of the **BROWSER** or in the Timeline. After that, choose the Edit Joint Limits tool from the shortcut menu that appears to make changes to the joint's limits. We will now go through the choices that are available in this dialog box.

Motion

In the **EDIT JOINT LIMITS** dialog box, the Motion drop-down list shows the several types of free movements that are possible for the joint that is now chosen. As an illustration, the slider joint is incapable of any other translational or sliding motions. As a direct consequence of this, the Motion drop-down list only has the **Slide** option, which may be used to define the joint's boundaries for the slider. The cylindrical joint, on the other hand, allows for two different motions: **rotation** and **translation**. As a direct consequence of this, the Rotate and Slide choices have been added to the Motion drop-down list for the cylindrical joint. Furthermore, you can specify the limits for both of the movements that are accessible by choosing them from the Motion drop-down list.

Minimum

The minimal limit for the specified motion of the joint may be defined by selecting the Minimum check box inside the dialog box. This sets the limit to the smallest possible value. When you pick the Minimum check box in the dialog box, a field will appear directly below it. In this area, you can enter the minimum limit for the mobility of the joint that you have chosen. It is important to keep in mind that the limits are measured between the places that have been established as the joint origins of the components.

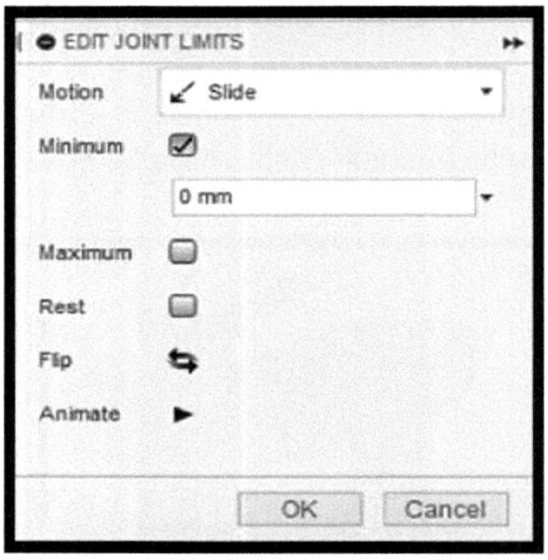

Maximum

The Maximum check box is used to set the upper limit for the motion that the joint is capable of doing in its specified position. When the check box for Maximum is selected in the dialog box, a field appears immediately below it. In this box, you can set the maximum limit for the mobility of the joint that has been chosen. The limits are determined by taking the distance between the points where the joint origins are established on the components.

Rest

The component's rest position may be specified by selecting the box labeled "**Rest**" from the drop-down menu. The position in which the component will be found to be at rest after the motion has been completed is referred to as the component's rest position. When you tick this box in the dialog box, a new field will appear below it. You can define the component's rest position via the use of this field. The component's rest position may be configured anywhere between the minimum and maximum limitations that have been set.

Animate

The motion of the component may be animated by clicking the **Play** button in the **Animate** section of the dialog box. This button is used to animate the motion of the component between the minimum and maximum limitations that have been established for the joint. Click the **OK** button in the dialogue box after you have specified the lowest and maximum limits for the mobility of the joint. The restrictions have been established, and the component can only move inside the boundaries that have been established for it.

Animating a Joint

After adding a joint in Fusion 360, you have the option to animate it so that you may examine its motion. To do this, expand the Joints node in the BROWSER, and then right-click on the joint whose motion is to be animated once the node has been expanded. There is a menu for shortcuts that shows. To use the Animate Joint tool, choose it from this menu of shortcuts. When a joint is chosen, the animation of its motion will begin to play out in the graphics section. Simply using the **ESC** key will put an end to the animation.

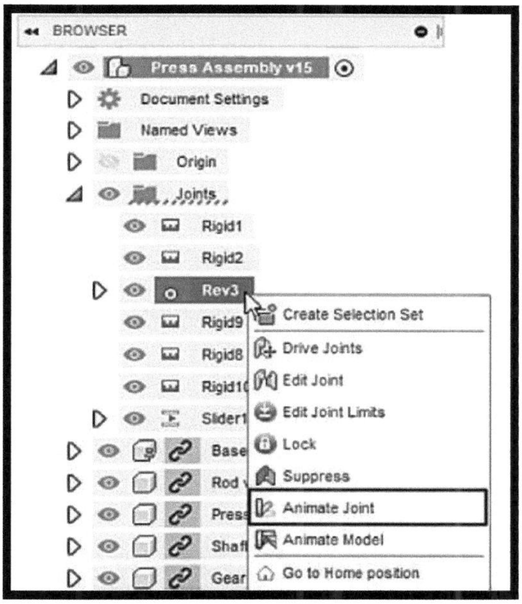

Animating the Model

You may animate a joint in Fusion 360, but you can also animate the model or assembly itself to examine the working conditions of the model or assembly as well as the behavior of its different components about each other. To animate a model, first, choose the joint you want to animate by right-clicking on it inside the enlarged Joints node of the BROWSER, and then selecting the Animate Model tool from the shortcut menu that displays. In the graphics section, the model will begin animating itself depending on the joints that have been added. For instance, in the figure below, animating the revolute joint of the crankshaft causes the crankshaft to begin spinning around its axis. Simultaneously, the piston, which is linked to the crankshaft by the connecting rod, begins moving up and down. Take note that to animate an assembly in precisely the same manner as its functioning in the actual world, you need to apply the appropriate joints between the components of the assembly.

Locking/Unlocking the Motion of a Joint

You can momentarily freeze the motion of a joint in Fusion 360. To do this, right-click on the joint that needs to be locked in the enlarged Joints node of the BROWSER or in the Timeline, and then choose the **Lock** tool from the shortcut menu that appears. This will accomplish the desired result. The movement of the joint that you choose will be frozen in its present position for the time being. When you right-click on a joint that is locked, a shortcut menu will show. From this menu, choose the **Unlock** tool. This will allow you to unlock the motion of the joint. You also have the option of using the **Revert** tool, which can be found in the contextual **POSITION** panel that is located at the very end of the Toolbar.

Driving a Joint

Using the Drive Joints tool in Fusion 360, you may drive a joint within its free degrees of freedom to specify a new location for the component. This can be done to move the component in a new direction. To achieve this, first, open the ASSEMBLE drop-down menu found in the SOLID tab, and then choose the Drive Joints tool from the drop-down menu that appears. A dialogue window labeled **DRIVE JOINTS** is shown. Next, choose a joint by clicking on it in either the Joints node of the Browser or the Timeline. Within the dialog box, you will see the Distance and Rotation fields. Take note that the types of joints you choose will determine which fields in the dialog box are available for your use. For instance, choosing a cylindrical joint cause both the translational and rotational movements of the joint to be driven by the **Distance and Rotation** fields. However, selecting a slider joint cause just the Distance field to be driven by the translational motion of the joint. Next, you will need to input the needed values in these fields to drive the chosen joint, which will allow you to define the new location of the relevant component inside the graphics area.

You may also control the movement of the joint by dragging the arrows that display in the graphics area. When you are finished driving the joint, return to the dialog box and click the **OK** button. You may also move a component along its free degrees of freedom to reposition it in the graphics area. This can be done by clicking and dragging the component.

Defining Relative Motion between Two Joints

Using the Motion Link tool in Fusion 360 allows you to not only describe absolute motion between two joints but also define relative motion between the joints. For instance, you may specify the relative motion between slider joints and revolute joints in such a way that the linear motion of one component translates to the rotational motion of another component and vice versa. You can also describe the relative motion between other types of joints. Click on the **Motion Link** tool after selecting the **ASSEMBLE** drop-down menu located in the SOLID tab. This will allow you to describe the relative motion that occurs between two joints. A dialogue window labeled **MOTION LINK** will now display. After the **MOTION LINK** dialog box has been brought up, pick two joints one at a time from either the Joints node of the Browser or the Timeline. The dialogue box is altered to provide new choices, which may be used to regulate the relative motion between the joints that have been chosen. Take note that the choices that are shown in the dialog box will change depending on the kind of joints that you choose. The slider and revolute joints are highlighted in the figure seen below. As a consequence of this, the Distance and Angle boxes of the dialog box allow you to respectively indicate the distance traveled by one component about the angle of rotation of the other component.

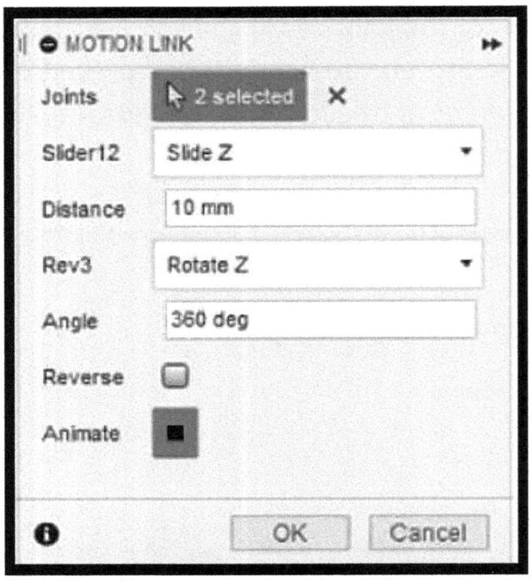

It is important to take note that the relative motion between the joints is animated in the graphics area following the values supplied in the relevant areas of the dialog box. You also have the option to change the direction of motion by clicking the checkbox labeled "**Reverse**" inside the dialog box. You may either play the animation or stop it by clicking the **Play/Stop** button located in the Animate section of the dialog box, depending on which option you choose. Click the **OK** button in the dialogue box after you have finished specifying the relative motion between the joints that have been chosen. You may examine the relative motion that has been specified between the chosen joints by moving the relevant components around in the graphics area. It will show up on the screen.

Grouping Components Together

1. To add a new component, choose "**New Component**" from the **Assembly** menu.

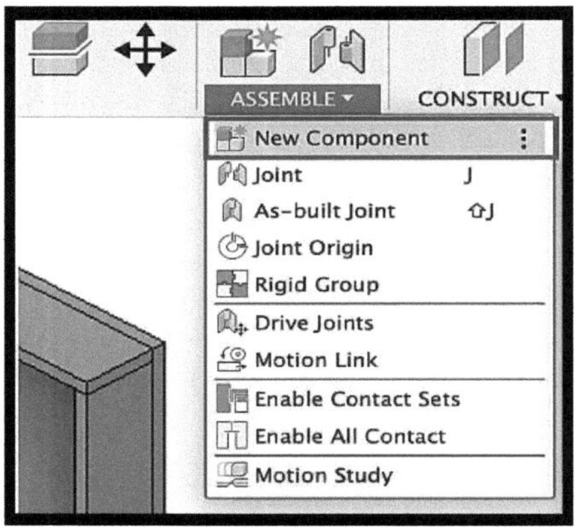

2. To build the new empty component, you need to click **OK** in the dialogue box.
3. Mark all of the components in the browser tree that need to be consolidated or integrated and click the **Edit** button.
4. Move the components that are highlighted until they are on top of the new component that was just made.

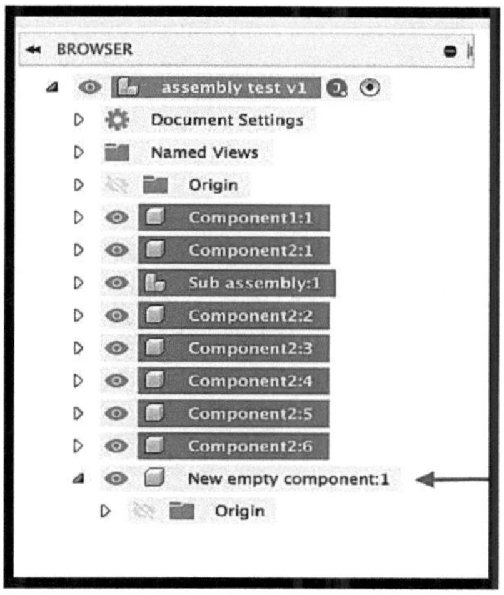

5. Now all of the highlighted components are contained under a single sub-assembly, which may be collapsed to make the browser tree more organized.

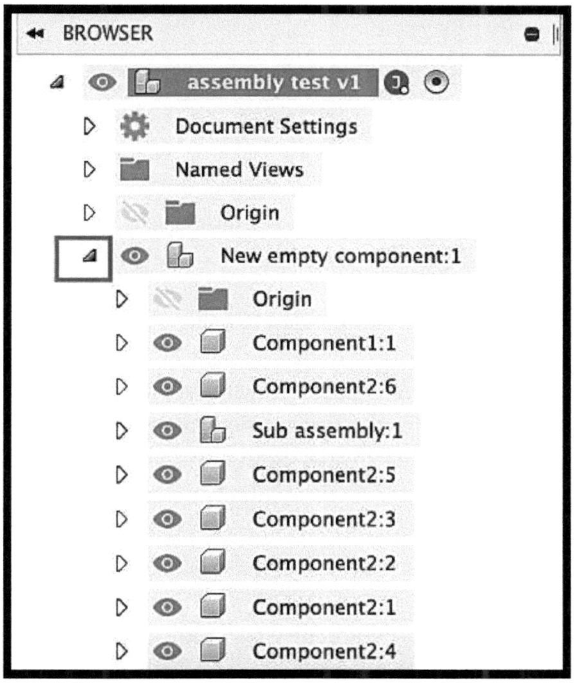

Create a contact set

1. To enable contact sets, go to the toolbar and pick the **Assemble > Enable Contact Sets** option.
2. Choose **Assemble > New Contact Set** from the drop-down menu. The New Contact Set dialog is shown.
3. Choose two or more components to work within either the canvas or the Browser.
4. Select the **OK** button.

The new contact set may be found in the folder labeled Contact Sets inside the Browser. When contact sets are enabled, the chosen components are forced to be near one another.

Edit a contact set

1. Expand the **Contact Sets folder** in the Browser's navigation menu.
2. After selecting Edit with the context menu after right-clicking the contact set. The Edit dialog appears, and the chosen components in the canvas are highlighted in a contrasting color.
3. Simply clicking on components inside the canvas or the Browser will either add them to the contact set or delete them from it.
4. Select the **OK** button.

The contact set will be updated to include or exclude the components that you have added or deleted when you have finished making changes.

Suppress or Un-suppress a contact set

1. Expand the **Contact Sets** folder in the Browser's navigation menu.
2. Click the **Suppress** or **Un-suppress** button that is located next to the contact set.

Until you click the symbol once again, the contact set will be suppressed or unsuppressed, respectively.

Enabling Contact Sets between Components

Components in a design may be given contact sets so that they will only move when they are in physical touch with another component in the design. To restrict movement, contact sets to ensure that components come into direct touch with one another. If interference is found, the components will remain still.

This approach involves more calculation in comparison to using a motion joint.

- **Enable Contact Sets**: This option activates contact analysis between the components in contact sets. The browser is responsible for the management of contact sets.
- **Disable All Contact**: This option deactivates the contact analysis for every component.
- **Enable All Contact**: This option turns on the contact analysis for every component.
- **New Contact Set** - This function creates a contact set between the components that have been chosen. Determine which bodies or components are going to be a part of the contact analysis.

When components are moved, contact sets determine which components are checked for possible contact. Components are constrained by contact sets in such a way that they cannot pass through one another, therefore simulating how they would behave in the actual world. For instance, you may restrict the movement of a component such that it revolves around a joint but does not pass through its bracket. The Enable All Contact command performs an analysis of the contact between all of the design's components, regardless of whether or not those components have specific contact sets. The performance of an assembly is impacted by the total number of its components. When you use the New Contact Set command, the components of the contact set that you define will be constrained.

- The **New Contact Set** command configures the contact analysis for the components that have been chosen. The use of contact sets prevents individual pieces from moving via the space between them.
- The **Drive Joints** command identifies the specific points in the component assembly at which motion takes place and indicates the boundaries of the component's possible range of motion inside the assembly.

Capturing Position of Components

When you want to continue editing and assembling components while keeping the current position of components in the assembly, you may use the **Capture Position** command to save the positions of components that you have recently moved or rotated. Note that positions are discreetly collected as you move components until you execute a command that prompts you to determine whether or not you want to capture the position of components to proceed. Until then, positions will be captured whenever you move components.

Capture position proactively

1. Rotate or move one or more elements on the canvas. In the toolbar, the **Position panel** is shown.
2. Choose **Position > Capture Position** from the toolbar. The assembly's current component positions are recorded.

Capture position when prompted

1. Rotate or move one or more elements on the canvas. In the toolbar, the Position panel is shown.
2. Pick a command like **Joint Origin** that is dependent on the components' present positions. A notice appears alerting you to the movement of specific components and asking you to either capture or restore their original places.

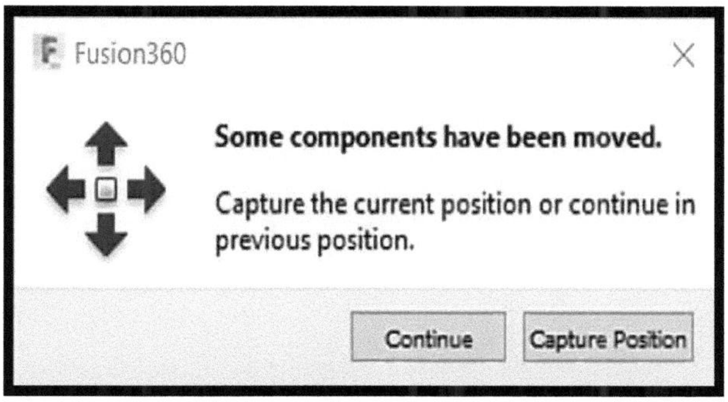

3. To begin, click **Capture Position**.

The assembly's current component positions are recorded. You go on with the order you just issued.

Revert position proactively

1. Rotate or move one or more elements on the canvas. In the toolbar, the Position panel is shown.
2. Choose **Position > Revert** from the toolbar.

The assembly's parts return to the last position they were in when they were captured.

Revert position when prompted

1. Rotate or move one or more elements on the canvas. In the toolbar, the Position panel is shown.
2. Pick a command like **Joint Origin** that is dependent on the components' present positions.

A notice appears alerting you to the movement of specific components and asking you to either capture or restore their original places.

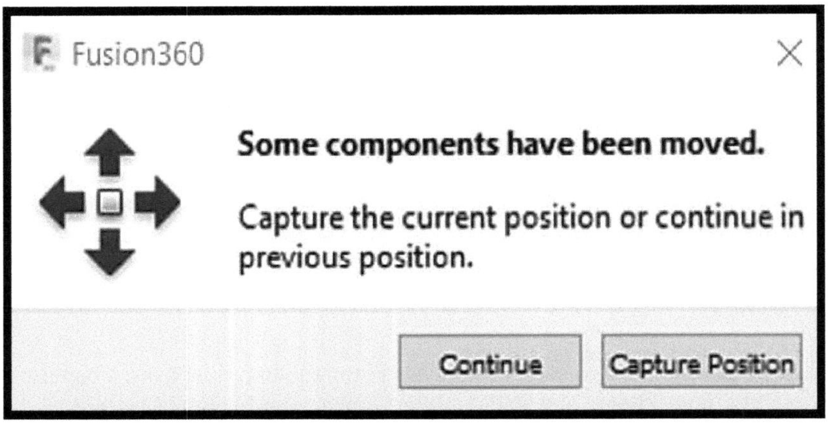

3. Click **Continue**.

The assembly's parts return to the last position they were in when they were captured. You go on with the order you just issued.

Avoiding Coincident Face Rendering Artifacts Using Dielectric Priority

Coincident Faces

When modeling a container with content such as liquid, or anything else that fills a section of the container, you will obtain coincident faces. This is because the fluid or other material fills a portion of the container. This indicates that the space occupied by the faces of the content is the same as the space occupied by the faces of the container's interior. There is no cause for concern about this on its own. You may run into some difficulties, though, if you want this to have a pleasant appearance when it is rendered and the container you are using is translucent. The use of coincident faces is not restricted to containers. You will get a coincident face if you construct a box on top of another box that you have already created.

Rendering Transparent Bodies and Coincident Faces

If you render a glass of water using the default settings, you will see artifacts where the water and the glass meet. This is the case even if the water fills the glass. In the picture that is seen above, you can see something off to the left. It is up to the rendering engine to decide whether the water should be interpreted as entering and reaching inside the glass body, or if it should remain on the outside as it normally would. Because of this, we see this strange and unnatural pattern. The situation may be approached from a few different angles. Making the glass completely opaque may be the simplest solution, but where's the fun in that? Reduce the size of the body of water to take advantage of this second strategy. This is a simple remedy that could work, but the outcome might not get you exactly where you want to go — the water is not filling the glass as it should be doing so. Utilizing dielectric priority is a third option to consider.

Using Dielectric Priority

Some bodies are given preference over others according to something called dielectric priority. This indicates that if there is a collision between two bodies that have different dielectric priorities, the one that has the higher priority will be displayed instead of the other one. The concept of overlap is essential to our discussion, and we will need to elaborate on it more.

Overlapping

In our situation, the volume of the water has to be raised to the point that all of the faces of the water that were coincident with the glass become entirely encased inside the body of the glass. Depending on how complicated the bodies are, this might be a difficult task.

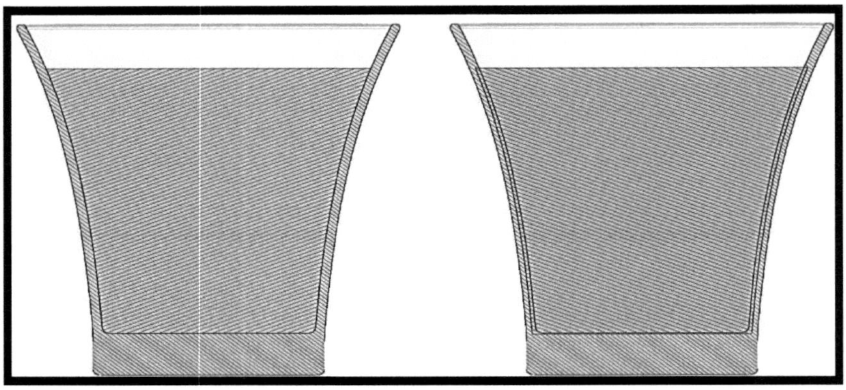

Setting the Priority

As soon as you have overlaps in the places where you need them, you will need to establish an appropriate priority. Enter the render workspace, right-click one of the bodies or components (depending on what you operate with), and pick the **Dielectric Priority Control** option from the context menu.

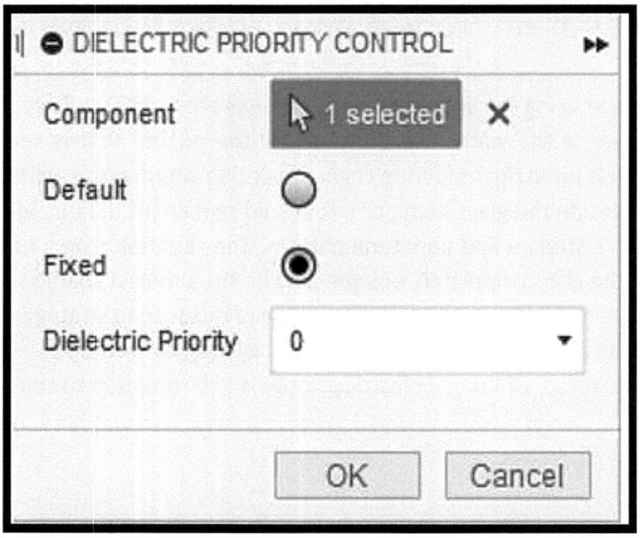

Alter the setting so that it reads Fixed Instead of Default, then choose a priority. Repeat this process for all of the bodies and components that need a certain dielectric priority. It's important to note that the priority will be greater if the number is lower. This indicates that priority 0 is the most important. Since we want to give the glass the greatest priority in this scenario, we will continue to place it in the position of priority 0. Since we wish to depict glass rather than water in the areas where they overlap, we will give the water the highest priority.

Basic Static Stress Simulation in Fusion 360

Static stress, modal frequencies, heat, and thermal stress are all things that may be simulated using the new simulation module that has been added to Autodesk Fusion 360. This module is very straightforward to use. Many people are unaware that these functionalities can be found in the program Fusion 360, which is available for free to students, makers, and small businesses.

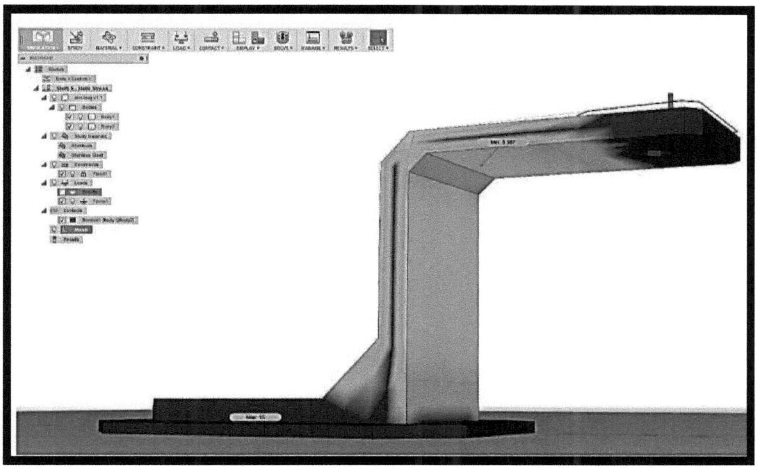

Why do Static Stress Simulation?

When creating mechanical devices, you often want such products to have exactly the right amount of robustness. If you make things overly flimsy, they are more likely to break. If you give the items more stability than they need, they will end up being bigger, heavier, and/or more costly than they should be. Before sending your item to production, you may make it stronger where it needs to be strong while simultaneously making it smaller, lighter, and more affordable by modeling static stress and removing unneeded pieces from it. This can be done by reinforcing weak spots and adding new parts. When you have access to this kind of simulation inside your CAD program, it is quite simple to switch between modifying your model and simulating it. This makes the process much more efficient.

Simulating Static Stress in Fusion 360

The first thing that we need is a model.

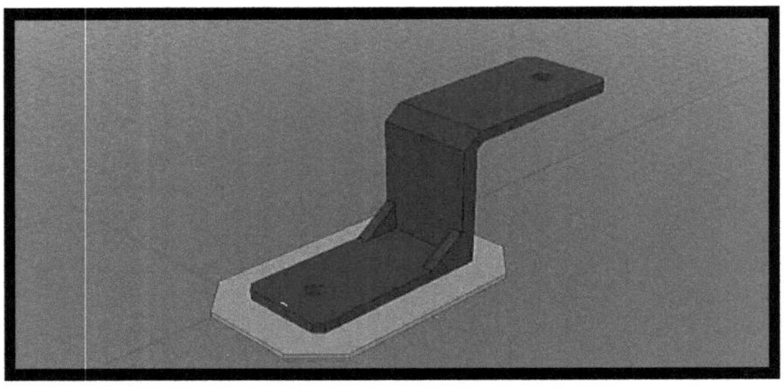

When you have a model, please proceed as follows:

Step 1: Preparations

To access the simulation section, go to the toolbar's upper left corner and choose the corresponding icon. After hitting the **Simulation** button, a new window will appear. In this window, pick the Static Stress option.

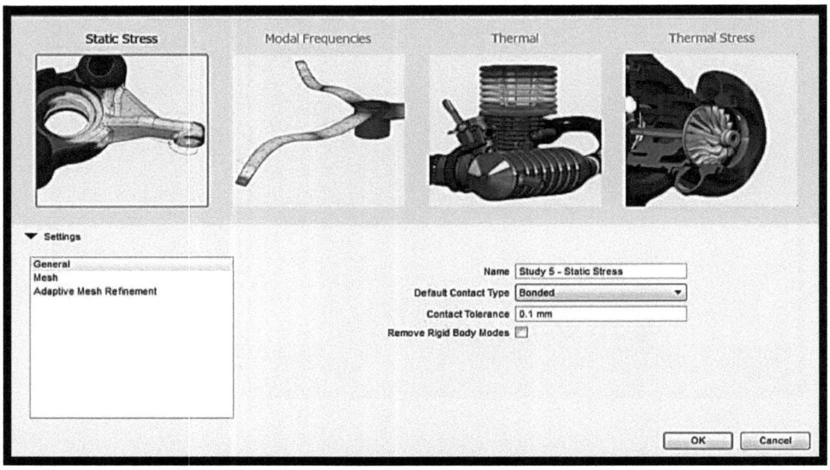

The very first thing that you want to perform is to make a decision about which of the bodies and components in your assembly ought to be a part of the simulation (aka. **study**). You may choose which bodies and components you wish to include by expanding one of the entries in the browser on the left side (the one with the component icon), and then checking or unchecking the boxes next to those bodies and components. You also have the option to pick particular components to conceal here. After that, you should hit the button labeled "**Material**" to pick the material that the various bodies will be simulated as (also known as the study material). There is a LONG list of different kinds of materials available for selection.

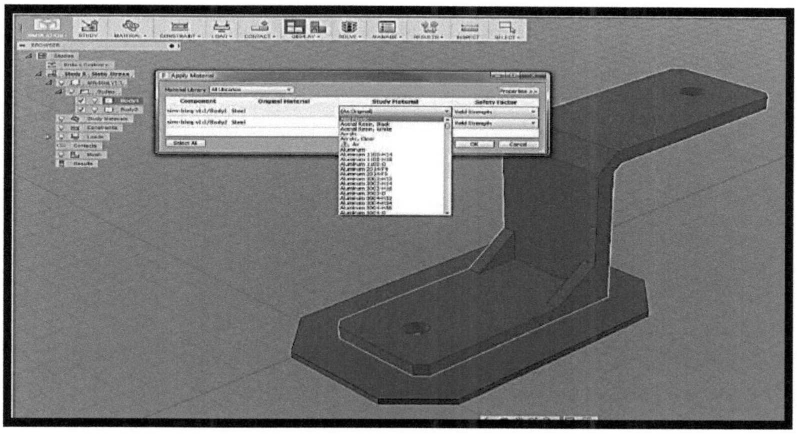

Step 2: Structural Constraints

At a minimum, one restriction is required for your simulation. It would be analogous to attempting to exert force on an item that was only floating in the air or space if there were no constraints.

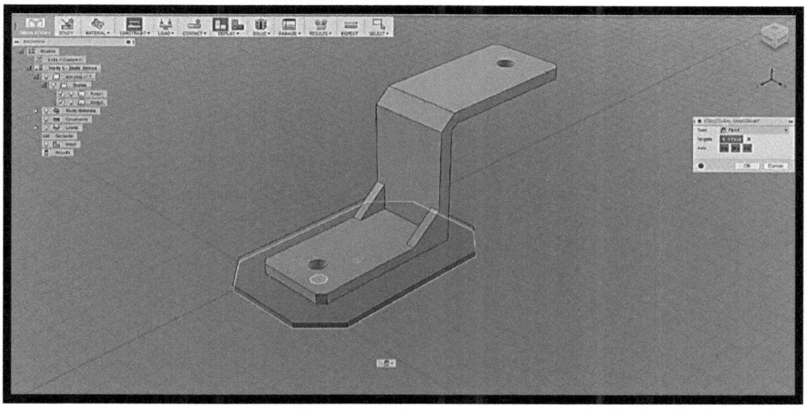

Fixed

The fixed constraint is the most fundamental sort of constraint, and it requires you to choose one or more faces, edges, or vertices that must always remain in their current position. You also have the option of choosing along which axis it should be locked.

Pinned

Constraints that are pinned are imposed on the cylindrical faces. In the same way, as the axes in the type of fixed constraints may be turned on and off, the pinned constraints type has three "**subtypes**" of constraints that can be turned on and off: radial, axial, and tangential.

- As if you had a pin in a hole, activating the radial restriction will stop the cylinder from moving when you try to move it (for example: **insert a bolt**).
- If you enable the axial limitation, the cylinder won't be able to slide along the pin (for example: **fasten a nut**).
- Because of the tangential limitation, the cylinder is incapable of spinning (for example: **tighten the nut**).

Other Constraints

There is also the frictionless constraint, as well as the prescribed displacement, both of which are options, but we are not going to go any deeper into them right now.

Step 3: Load

After the constraint or constraints have been established, it is time to apply the load. Although you may simulate a variety of other kinds of static loads, such as pressure, moment, and so on, in addition to applying gravity, we are just going to focus on the force here. It is possible to apply force to a single face, several edges, or many vertices at the same time. It is necessary to specify the magnitude (in Newtons).

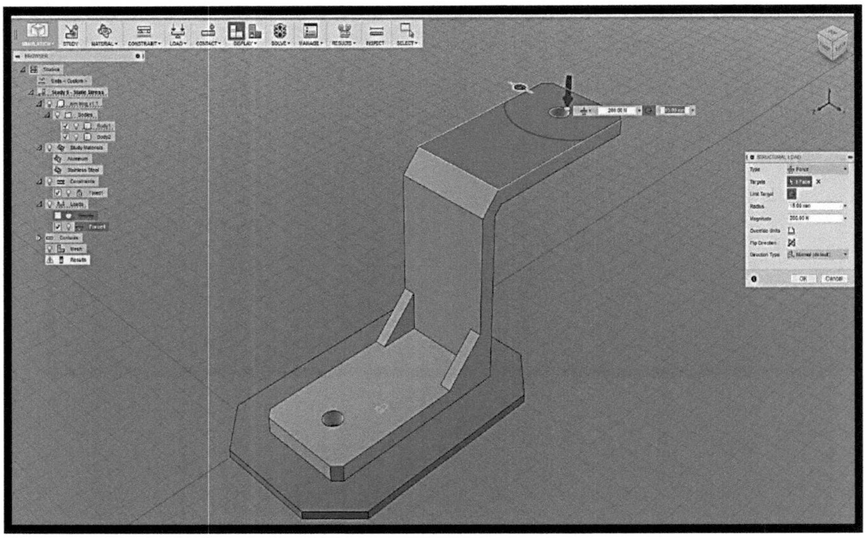

Altering the direction using angles, the XYZ vector, or a reference angle are all viable options (normal on a reference face or axial on a reference edge). By utilizing the Limit Target feature while applying force to a face, you will have the ability to choose precisely where the force will be delivered to the face. After that, you will have the option to choose the radius of the region in which the force will be applied.

Step 4: Contacts

This step is only essential if you are simulating more than one body at a time. The contact function is responsible for defining how different bodies should behave toward one another. These are likewise limitations, but in contrast to the structural limitations that we discussed previously, the contact limitations are not geographical limitations; rather, they are limitations that are exclusively related to the bodies involved. Selecting **Automatic Contacts** from the dropdown menu found under the **Contact heading** is the quickest and simplest method to add contacts. The use of this method will result in interactions being made between bodies that are in sufficient proximity to one another. On the settings page, under Static Stress (which you chose in step 1), you can specify this threshold (default is 0.1 mm). Additionally, you have the option of defining the kind of contact that will be applied to the algorithm (default is bonded). After you have executed Automatic Contacts, you will have the ability to make changes to the contact(s) that have been generated. You may also add new ones or remove some of the existing ones.

There are four different kinds of connections that pretty well explain themselves:

- Bonded
- Separation (no sliding)
- Sliding (no separation)
- Separation + Sliding

You may check to see whether all of the components are adequately restricted for the simulation by clicking the **DOF View** button, which is located just to the left of the Solve button. They should all be brought up to full working order (green).

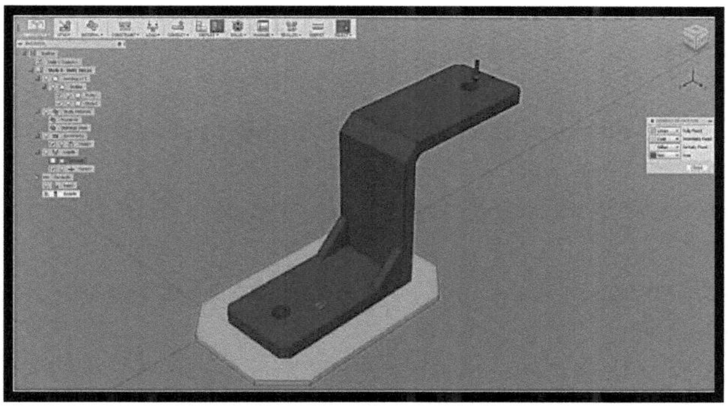

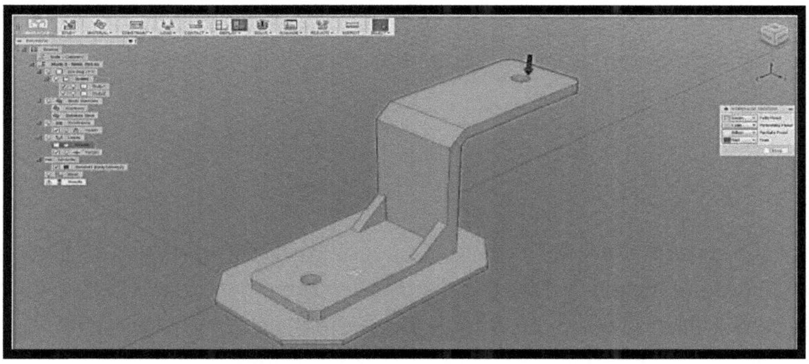

Step 5: Solve

The traffic light symbol in the toolbar that represents Solve should have turned green at this point. If it has, you may go ahead and push it, and the simulation ought to be over in just a few seconds after that. Even if it has a yellow or red light, you should still push it. You will get error messages that are easy to understand and that describe what is wrong with your configuration.

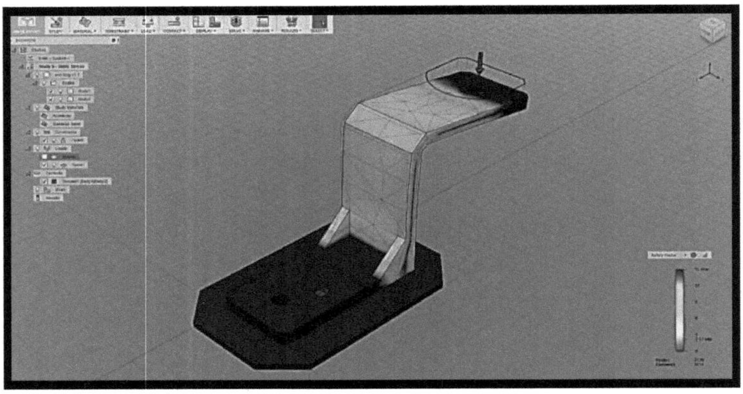

Prepare the simulation model, this stage involves meshing the model. This step comes before the actual simulation. You may adjust the parameters on the options page to get a mesh with a higher (or lower) resolution by playing around with the settings. In the drop-down menu labeled **Display**, you have the option to turn the mesh visibility on and off.

Step 6: Examining the Results

After you have successfully solved the problem, you will be able to view the following 4-5 various results:

- The **Safety Factor** is often referred to as the Factor of Safety (FoS). Please refer to this page for the normal numbers.
- **Stress** is a measurement of how much pressure one particle puts on another particle in its immediate environment.
- **Displacement** refers to the amount that the body has changed in comparison to how it was initially.
- **Strain** is a measurement of the amount of distortion that has occurred in the material as a direct consequence of the stress. Often visually quite similar to the state of tension.
- **Contact Pressure** (if there is any) - The pressure that is exerted between the surfaces that are in contact. In the bottom right corner, above the horizontal bar, you may make your selection of which one to look at.

Deformation

The distortion is not always consistent with reality. Depending on the material, the body may shatter right there where the tension is the highest before it is distorted to the extent that is displayed. You may find the **Deformation Scale** in the dropdown menu that is located beneath the results. You have the option of selecting none, the original deformation, or a scaled version of it here.

Isolating Parts of the Spectrum

You may isolate sections of the assembly by moving the arrows at the top or bottom of the vertical bar at the bottom right of the screen. This will make it easier for you to determine whether areas of the assembly are the most vulnerable or the most robust.

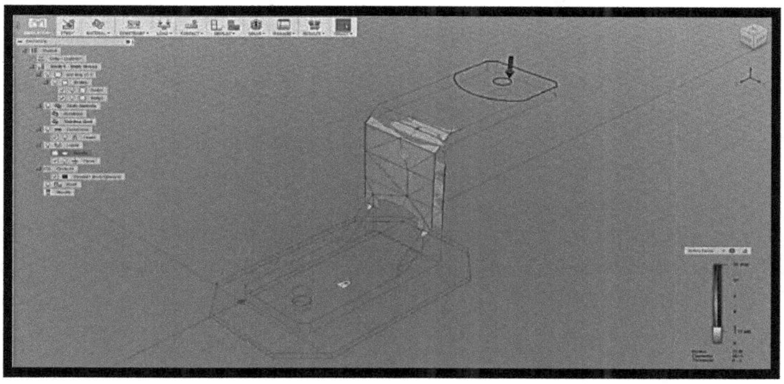

Animation

Animate is yet another option available in the Results drop-down box. This is a fantastic method to see what occurs when you progressively apply more and more force up to your specified load, and it's a good way to observe what happens. To create an animation that is appealing to the eye and runs without hiccups, it is suggested that you raise the total number of steps and choose **Fastest** as the animation speed. In addition, you may manually jerk about using the step slider, and you can even create a video clip to use during your presentation.

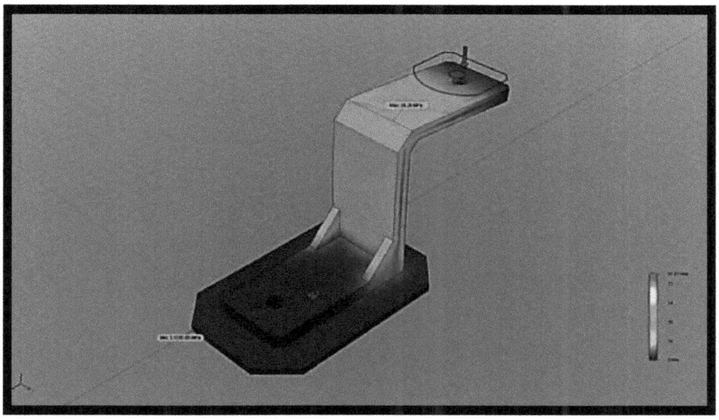

Step 7: Improving Your Design

Consider that we have a minimum requirement of a safety factor of 3. After increasing the thickness of the top inner chamfer and the vertical portion of the bracket by one millimeter each, we obtained the result shown in the figure below.

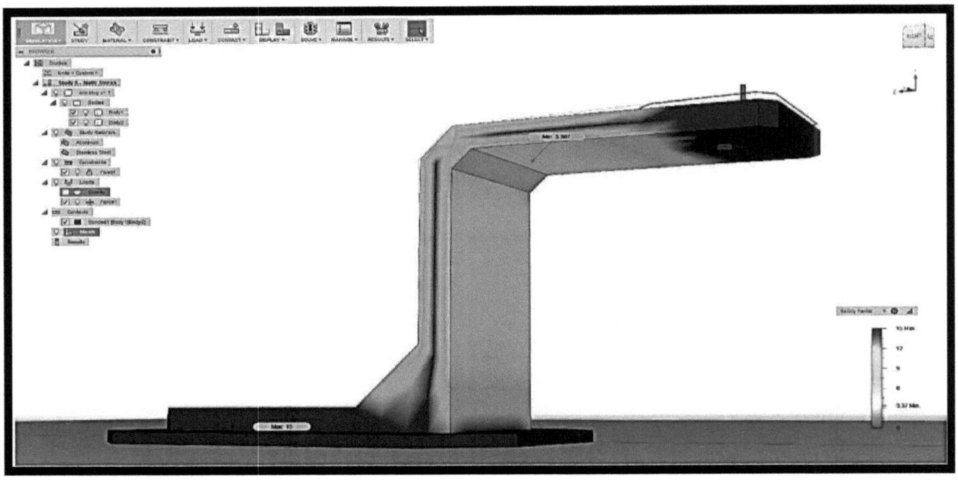

It is essential to simulate for a purpose, and doing so is not always as straightforward as it would first seem to be. You may, of course, mimic for entertainment purposes, which can really be very enjoyable, but doing so is not necessarily particularly beneficial. Becoming an expert at optimizing a design by knowing what to look for and how to modify your model appropriately after reviewing the outcomes of a simulation requires both prior experience and knowledge. **There are three other simulation modules available in Fusion 360.**

- Using **modal frequencies**, you can determine at what frequencies your model will begin to act strangely, as well as how it will behave in certain situations (for instance if you place it in front of a speaker). If your component is delicate, it is in your best interest to steer clear of these frequencies in real life (for instance thin glass).
- Using **heat modeling**, for example, you can create the most effective heat sinks. It is clear how heat travels along and between bodies and can be seen being transferred and lost.
- **Heat simulation** and static stress simulation are both components of the phenomenon known as thermal stress.

Questions

1. Which approaches are used to create assemblies?
2. The joint that allows the component to translate along an axis as well as rotate about a different axis is called?
3. Which tool is used for animating the model or assembly to review its working conditions and the behavior of its components concerning each other?
4. Which joint allows the component to rotate about an axis by removing all degrees of freedom except one rotational degree of freedom?
5. Which joint allows the component to translate along a single axis by removing all degrees of freedom except one translational degree of freedom?
6. Fusion 360 has ________ capabilities. As a result, if you make any change in a component, the same change reflects in the component used in the assembly as well as in the drawing and other respective workspaces of Fusion 360, automatically updating the respective file.
7. Which dialog box appears every time on inserting a component in a design file and allows you to define the position and orientation of the component in the design file?

CHAPTER 12

WORKING WITH ASSEMBLIES - II

Creating an Assembly by Using a Top-down Approach

With a top-down design, all of your components are created using the same design. Relationships between pieces are simple to develop and maintain using top-down design. **There are two different joint instructions in Fusion 360:**

- **As-built Joint** command, which you use when joining components that are already in place.
- **Joint command**, which you use when a component is not at the proper location. The Joint command may be used for top-down designs as well as dispersed designs, which is how it is commonly employed. **You will use the top-down design approach in this case to:**
- Add As-built Joints and create components.

Create components and add As-built Joints

- Drawing a two-dimensional profile for three components.
- Extruding the profile into components using the Press Pull command.
- Grounding a part (larger box).
- Using As-built Joints to secure the smaller box's location and define the motion of the cylindrical component.

Prerequisites

- Check that your units are set to millimeters rather than inches.

Steps

1. Begin drawing a picture on the XZ (Top) plane.

- If required, pick Design from the workspace switcher to access the Design workspace.
- If required, start a fresh design. Click **File > New Design** to start a new design.
- Select **Create > Sketch** from the Solid menu.
- Decide which plane, XZ (Top), to draw on.

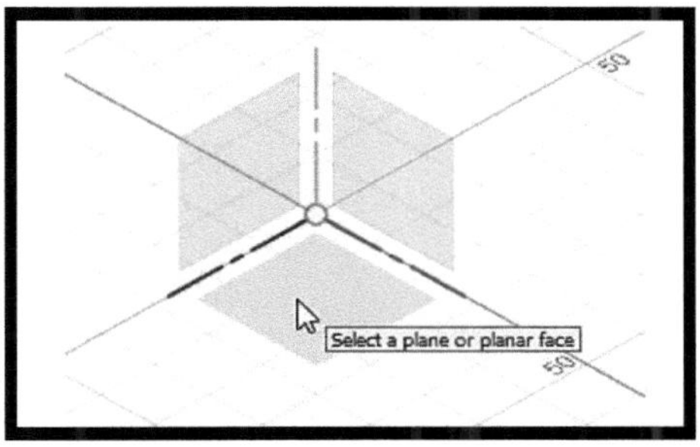

2. After choosing the plane, you are sent to the **Sketch contextual** tab, where you may find frequently used Sketch tools. Additionally, choices pertinent to your current work or the presently chosen sketch entity are shown in the Sketch Palette.
3. Draw a two-dimensional drawing of the three parts. Because we'll change the circle sketch's location later, it is not entirely specified.

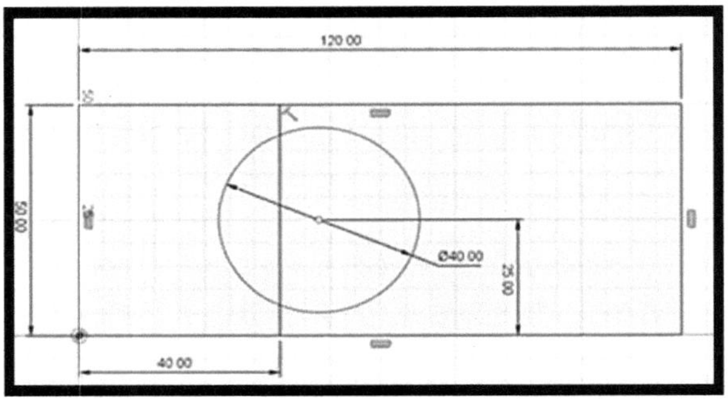

a. Select **2-Point Rectangle** from the **Sketch > Create > Rectangle** menu.
b. Move your cursor over the sketch's origin (or center). The pointer automatically moves to this spot.

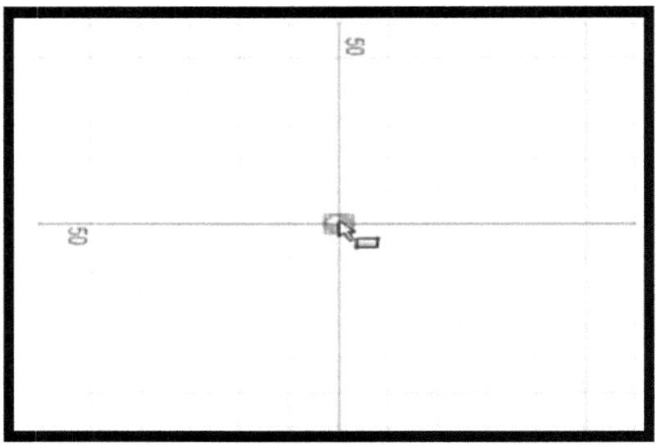

4. Click once to start positioning the rectangle's starting point.

- To draw a rectangle, drag the mouse aside and then click again once it is 50 mm x 120 mm in size to finish.

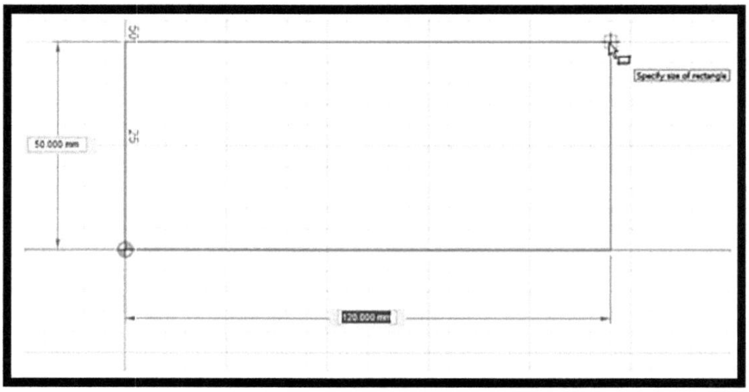

- Select **Line > Create Sketch**.
- Draw a vertical line 40 mm away from the rectangle's left edge.

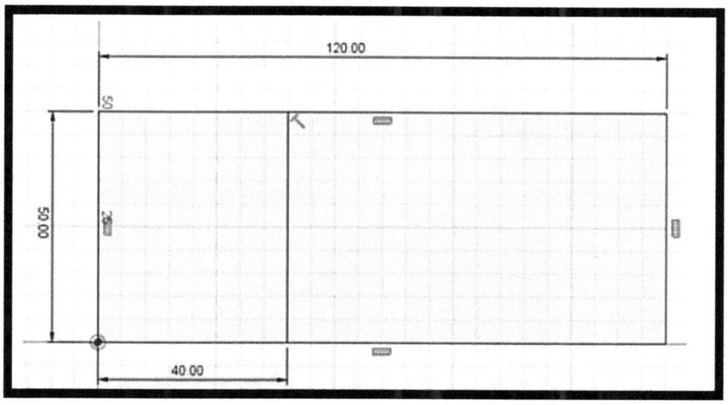

Make sure to draw a circle that is 40 mm in diameter, 25 mm from the bottom border of the rectangle, and close to the vertical line. Since we will modify the circle sketch's location later, it is not entirely specified. Click to **Finish Sketch**.

5. Construct the first element (bigger box) with a 20 mm height. Make sure you add a New Component rather than a Body.

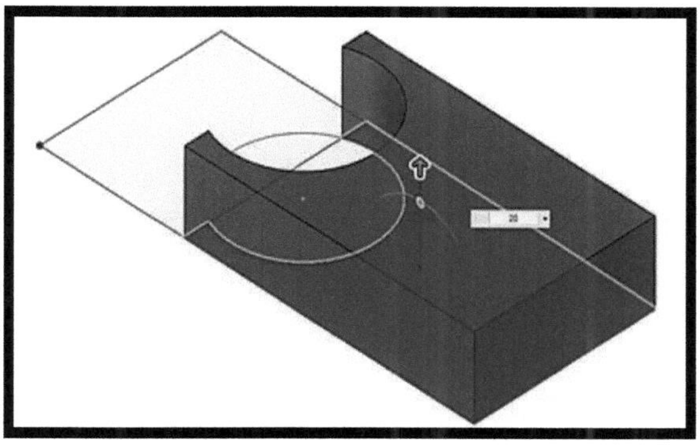

- Click **Solid > Modify> Press Pull**
- Choose the right-hand sketch profile.

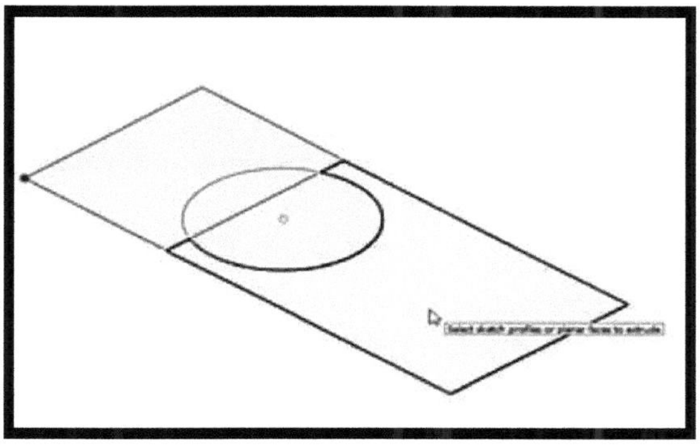

- Choose **New Component** from the Operation list.
- Type 20 mm in the Distance field. Press **OK**.
- To make sure the remaining portion of your drawing is shown, locate the sketch folder in the Browser and click the icon.

6. Design the cylinder component to have a 30 mm outside radius on both sides of the drawing. Make sure you add a **New Component** rather than a Body.

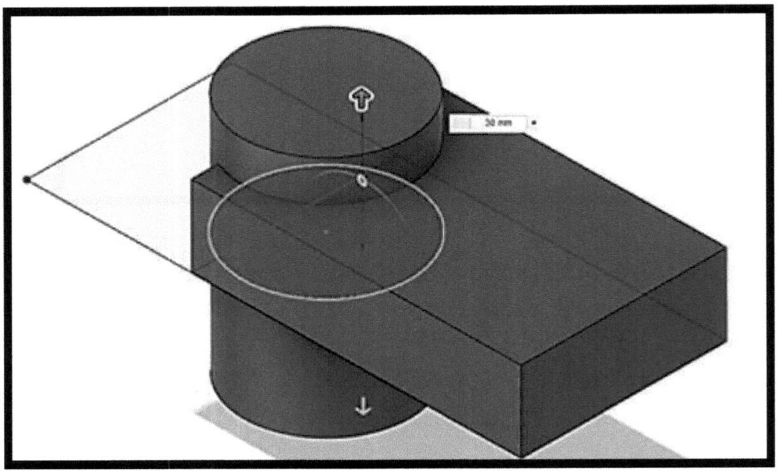

- Click **Solid > Modify >Press Pull**
- Decide which two sketch profiles go together to form the circle.

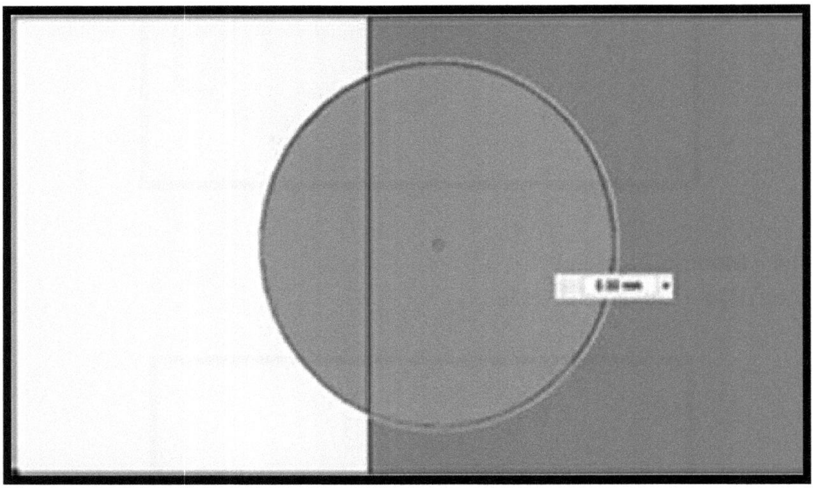

- Choose **Symmetric** under **Direction** from the list.
- Choosing **New Component** from the Operation list in step b.
- Type **30 mm** in the Distance field. Select **OK**.
- Now that there are several components, use **Shift + F** to choose **Inspect > Display Component Colors** to differentiate between them on the canvas.

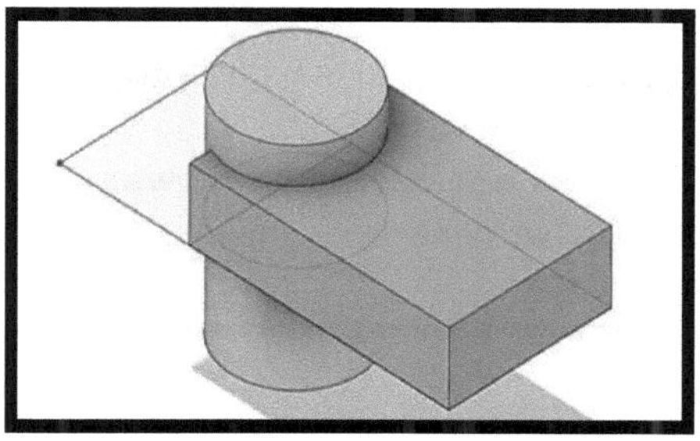

Please take note that the colors are chosen randomly. If your hue differs from what is seen in this guide, do not be concerned. If you so choose. The color coding may be modified.

7. When creating the final component, make sure it is **10 mm** below and **5 mm** above the drawing. Make sure you add a **New Component** rather than a Body.

- Select **Solid > Modify > Press Pull.**
- Select the profile on the left.

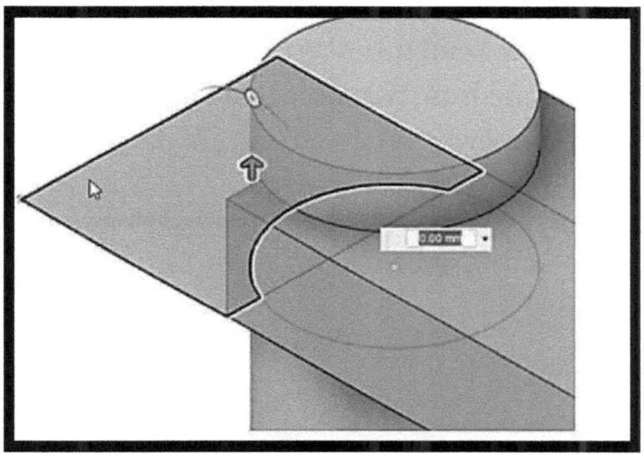

- Choose **Two Sides** from the Direction list.
- Choosing **New Component** from the Operation list in step b.
- For the Distance, enter 5 mm under Side 1.
- Type 10 mm for the Distance under Side 2. Select **OK**.

There are now three parts in the browser, take note.

8. Make the components' outer shells 2 mm thick.

- Select **Solid > Modify > Press Pull**
- Tap each component's top face.

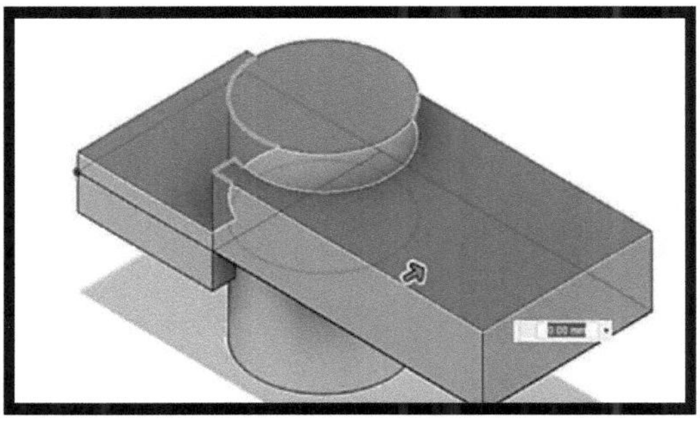

- For Inside Thickness, type 2 mm. Select OK.

9. Make the necessary adjustments to the drawing so that the cylindrical component is only located within the bigger box (it is currently in between both boxes).
    - While the drawing you generated is selected in the Browser, right-click it and choose Edit Sketch from the menu. The drawing in two dimensions emerges.

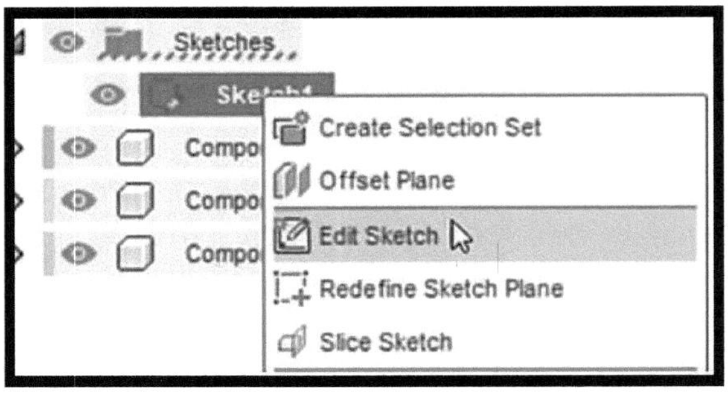

Simply click the point in the middle of the circle, and then click and drag it to the right until it no longer overlaps the two parts. Click the **Finish Sketch** button located in the Sketch Palette. Because all three components of the model were developed from the same drawing, which is an illustration of the advantages of using a top-down design approach, a newer version of the model has appeared.

10. Establish a firm foundation for the bigger box component in outer space. Right-clicking the **Component 1:1 node** in the Browser will bring up the **Ground** menu. Since it is now set in place, you can no longer freely move component 1 about in space.

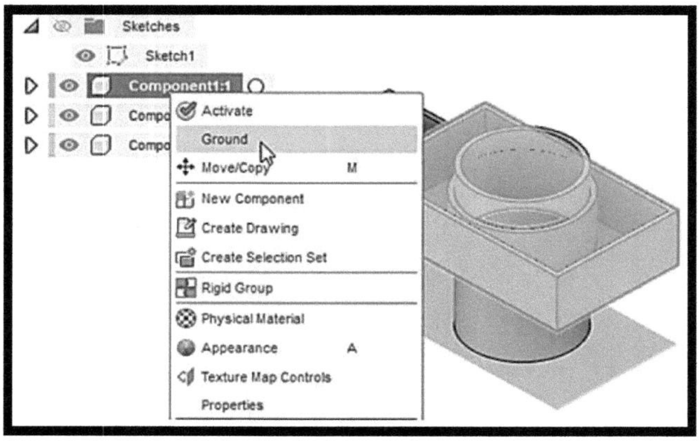

Note: Before you attempt to reattach a component in space, check to see that none of the other components have shifted from their starting positions. If they have been moved, a button labeled "**Revert**" will show in the Position panel of the Ribbon. Clicking this button will allow you to move them back into their original position. If it's essential, click the button labeled **Revert**.

11. To permanently secure the location of the smaller box concerning the bigger box, use a sturdy As-built Joint (which is grounded).

- Navigate to the Solid menu and choose **Assemble > As-built Joint**.
- Choose **Rigid** from the list of types that appears.
- First, choose the component with the bigger box, and then select the component with the smaller box. The canvas displays a preview of the animation for stiff motion. Select the OK button. In the AS-BUILT JOINT dialog, you may preview the joint motion once more by pressing the button that is located next to the word Animate.

12. To permanently set the position of the cylinder, make use of a revolute As-built Joint.

- Navigate to the Solid menu and choose **Assemble > As-built Joint**.
- Select "**Revolute**" from the list of Type options.
- First, choose the cylindrical component, and then select the component that is the bigger box.
- If you need to, click the button that is located next to Position to make sure that it is active.
- Choose the top edge of the cylinder as the Position for the component that is cylindrical. A preview of the rotatory motion animation can be seen on the canvas. Select the **OK** button.

Creating Components within a Design File

- Before beginning the design process, you should first create empty components. This will ensure that the assembly's structure and chronology are well-organized and simple to browse.
- If you have already built the bodies in the default component and you wish to arrange them into an assembly, you should construct new components from the bodies that already exist in the default component.
- During the majority of the operations in the Create panel, a new component should be created.

Creating a New Empty Component

1. Right-click and choose the component that is set as default in the browser.

In addition, the New Component command may be used from the Create panel or the Assemble panel through the toolbar.

The New Component dialog is shown to the user.

2. In the New Component dialog, choose the kind of component you want to add:

- Standard
- Sheet Metal

3. Give the new component a completely original name.

4. Determine where on the design you would want to place the new component, and select that location:

- **Internal**: Produced in-house and included in the overall design.
- **Parent**: The creation of the new component takes place inside the context of the parent component.

  The parent position is assigned mechanically to the component that is now active. To switch the parent:

    - To deselect everything, click **X**.
    - To choose the new parent component, click the component's name in the Browser.
- From **Bodies**: Select this option to convert already-existing bodies into their parts individually.
- If you pick option, you will lose the ability to select the component's parent; however, you will retain the ability to select bodies to convert into components. Please see the following for more instructions.
- **External**: Produced and housed in a distinct design, which is then referred into the assembly that is being designed at the moment.
- **Location**: The new layout that will include the new component has been stored at this location. The folder for the project in which the currently active design is stored is picked automatically. To move to a different location:

To open the folder, click its name.

- Within the Select Folder dialog, go to the new place where you wish to save the design and select it.
- Click the **Select** button.

5. Choose a **Sheet Metal Rule** to use with a component that uses sheet metal.
6. If you do not want to activate the newly created component once you have created it, uncheck the box labeled "**Activate**" (optional).
7. Activate the "**OK**" button.

For Internal Components:

The newly created component will appear in the browser just below the parent component that you choose to work with. If the **Activate** setting was selected, the component will be immediately activated, allowing you to begin working on the new component. This only applies if the **Activate** option was checked.

For External Components:

- The new design will be produced in the project folder that you pick in the Data Panel.
- The new component has been referenced in the existing design, and it will appear in the browser just below the parent component that you have chosen to use.
- If the Activate option was selected, the component will be immediately activated, and an **Edit with Place** session will commence. This will allow you to begin working on the new component within the context of the existing design.

Creating a New Component from Existing Bodies

1. Open up the folder titled "**Bodies.**"
2. Choose the bodies you wish to turn into components and then click "**Convert.**"
3. Select "**Create Components from Bodies**" from the context menu that appears when you right-click.

Note that you can also right-click the Bodies folder and select all of the bodies included inside it to convert them all at once. A new component will appear in the browser's hierarchy underneath the component from which the chosen body originated whenever that body is viewed. The body is relocated from the Bodies folder in the component's first iteration to the Bodies folder in the component's subsequent iteration. Note that even though the body is moving into a new component, any drawings that were used to construct it as well as any adjustments that you make to it will continue to be stored in the component in which they were created. This can make the timeline difficult to understand and interact with, so it is generally best practice to create empty components first, and then create the geometry of that component's entire component entirely within it. This is because doing it the other way around can make the timeline difficult to understand and interact with.

Creating a Component during an Active Tool

1. Select a command from the **Create** panel and begin the command's execution.
2. Within the dialog, go to the operation dropdown menu and choose **New Component**.
3. Modify any other settings that are associated with the command.
4. Select the "**OK**" button.

The newly developed component will appear in the web browser. The bodies that you built while the command was running are shown on the canvas and can also be found in the Bodies folder of the new component.

Important: If you want to produce duplicates of a component, you should not use the **New Component** operation inside command dialogs. Instead, use the **Copy Component** operation. However, both the sketch and the body will continue to use the default component, which will affect the **Save Copy As** command. This option is useful for creating a closed design that needs mobility.

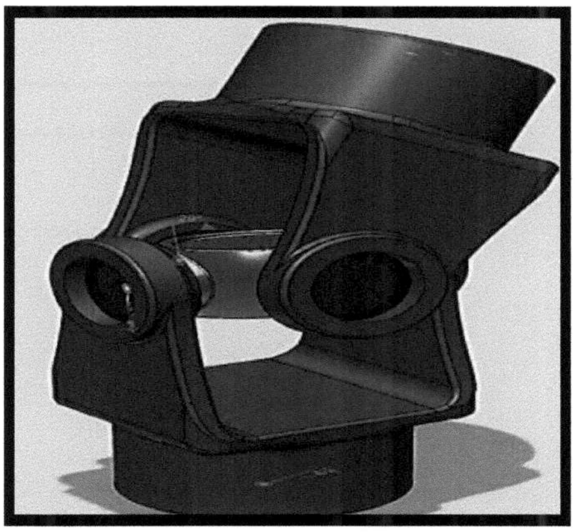

Tips

- Before beginning the process of developing any geometry for a component, you should first construct a new component. This will guarantee that the full parametric history of the component is kept inside the component itself. Because of this, it is guaranteed that any copy of the component will be parametrically complete and will not include references to any other components.
- As you develop each component, give it a name, so that you and anybody else working on the project with you can quickly understand how the assembly is put together.
- Give each body a new name before you attempt to transform them into components. The descriptive name that you have given to the body will be carried over into the naming of the new component, making it much simpler to locate inside the assembly.

- While utilizing the majority of the commands in the **Construct** panel, such as Extrude, Revolve, Box, Cylinder, etc., you can simultaneously create a new component. Change the setting for Operation during the command so that it reads "**New Component**." After you have created the component, you need to make sure that you rename it.
- To activate a component, you will need to click the radio button that is located next to it in the browser. Before adding any geometry to a component, you should always activate it first.

Fixing/Grounding the First Component

When you use the Top-down Assembly technique in Fusion 360 to construct components for a design file, such components are considered floating components since all of their degrees of freedom are unrestricted. As a consequence of this, the components are unrestricted in their ability to move or rotate in any given direction. Because of this, you need to first fix or ground the first component before you can apply joints to components that are joined together. To do this, right-click anywhere inside the BROWSER on the name of the component you want to modify. A shortcut menu will display. To access the Ground option in this drop-down menu, click the option. The component that you have chosen transforms into a fixed component, and a push-pin icon is added to the icon that represents it in the BROWSER. Additionally, the sign of a push pin can be seen in the Timeline. The push-pin sign denotes that the component has no degrees of freedom and that it cannot move or spin in any direction. Additionally, the symbol implies that the component is immobile.

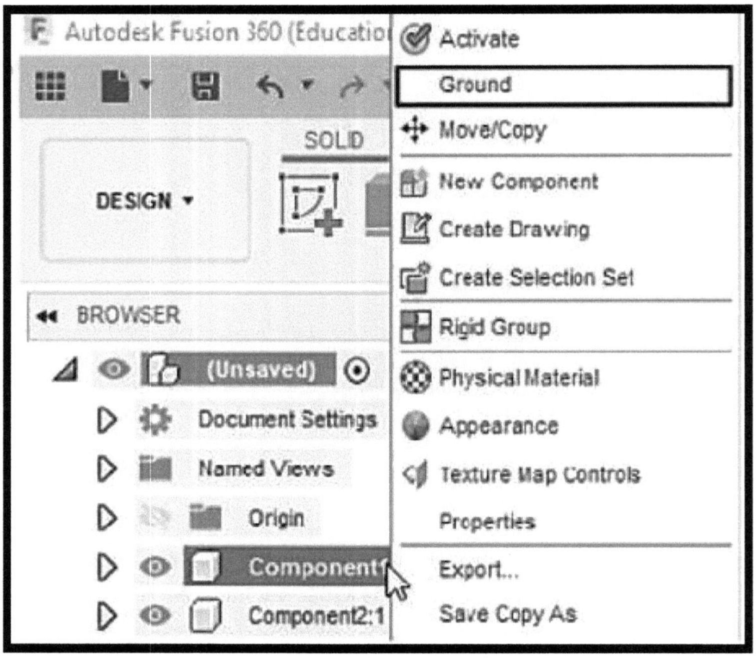

NOTE: It is also possible to convert a fixed or grounded component into a floating component, which has no restrictions on any of its degrees of freedom. To do this, right-click on the fixed component that you want to unground in the BROWSER, and then choose the **Unground** option from the menu that displays when you do so.

Applying As-built Joints

When you use the Joint tool and the As-built Joint tool, you will have the ability to apply many different kinds of joints, including stiff, revolute, slider, cylindrical, pin-slot, ball, and planar joints. The As-built Joint tool is used for adding joints to components in their present location as they are produced so that the relative motion between the components may be defined. When the components of an assembly are built in-context to each other by utilizing the Top-down assembly technique and are already positioned appropriately concerning one another, this is the most common situation in which it is employed.

The following is an explanation of the procedure for applying a joint by making use of the As-built Joint tool:

1. From the **SOLID** tab, choose the **ASSEMBLE** drop-down menu and then select the As-built Joint tool from the list of available options. The dialog box labeled AS-BUILT JOINT will now display. Alternatively, you may bring up the **AS-BUILT JOINT** dialog box by pressing the Shift key together with the **J** key.
2. To apply a joint while keeping the components in their present location, select two components in the graphics area one at a time and do so one by one. An animation depicting the motion that will occur between the components is shown in the graphics area depending on the default joint type that was chosen from the drop-down list labeled Type inside the dialog box.

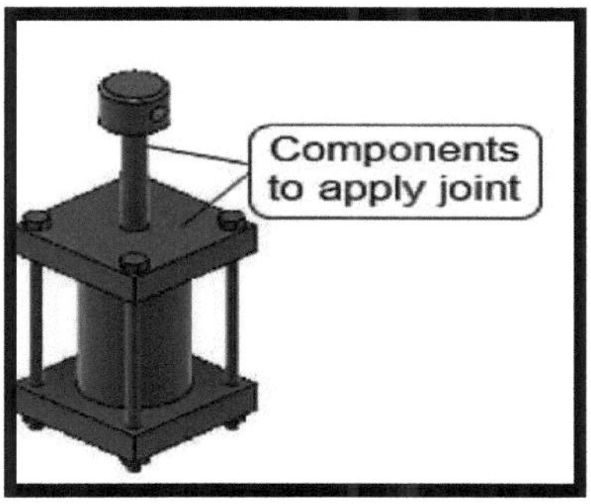

3. Choose the sort of joint you want to use from the drop-down menu labeled Type in the dialog box. Take note that when you pick a joint type other than the **Rigid** joint from the drop-down list in the dialog box's Type drop-down list, the Location selection option appears. This option allows you to define the position of the joint origin and can be found in the dialog box. The joint origin is used to define the point where two components have a relative motion about one other. This location is determined by the motion that occurs between the two components.
4. Indicate the location of the joint origin at which the components may move relatively to one about one another. To do this, move the cursor over a face or an edge of the component you're working with. The face or edge is brought into focus, and its snap points are brought into view. To determine the location of the joint origin, hover your mouse over the highlighted face or edge and then click on the desired snap point.
5. Choose the appropriate choice from the drop-down list or lists that are located just below the Type drop-down list in the dialog box. It is important to take note that the drop-down lists shown below the Type drop-down list are identical and rely on the joint type that is chosen.
6. In the dialog box, choose the **OK** button and click it. The parts are joined together via the joint.

7. You may establish relative motion between the second set of components in the same way by applying joints to the connections between them.

Defining a Joint Origin on a Component

In Fusion 360, the geometry that will be utilized to associate two or more components with joints is defined by a **Joint Origin**. There may be more than one **Joint Origin**.

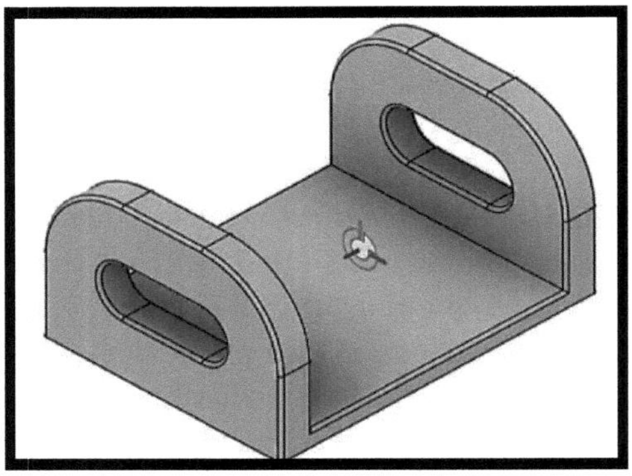

- The **Joint command** is responsible for the creation of joint origins within the framework of a particular joint.
- The **Joint Origin** command is responsible for the creation of independent joint origins, which in turn facilitates the creation of more complicated joint locations.

A graphical representation of the Joint Origin is generated whenever a joint is created. It is a graphical depiction that clarifies the steps involved in the assembly process of a joint. When you make a joint, you must first establish a joint origin on each component by snapping to the geometry of the component or the building. You may conceive of each joint origin as a coordinate system, with the planar face of the Joint Origin symbol representing the XY Plane. **This allows you to see the joint origins more clearly.**

- The positive direction of the X-axis is represented by the red axis in this diagram.
- The axis in the positive direction of the Y-axis is represented by the green axis.

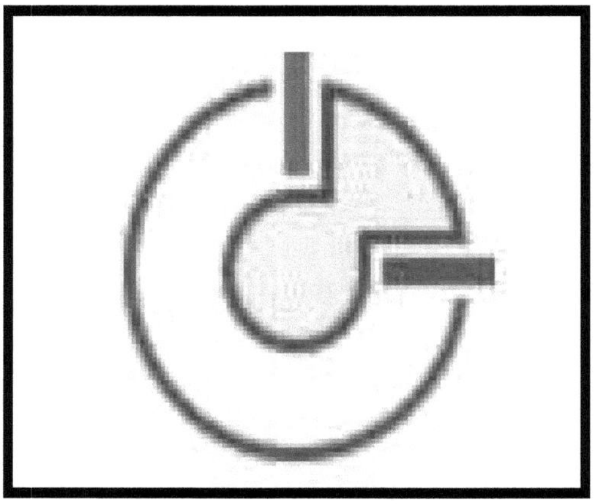

The **Z-Axis** moving in a positive direction is shown by the side of the **Joint Origin** sign that is white.

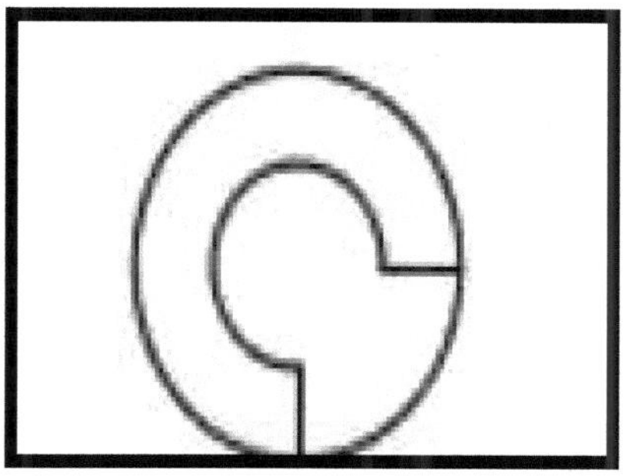

The negative direction of the Z axis is shown by the orange side of the Joint Origin symbol.

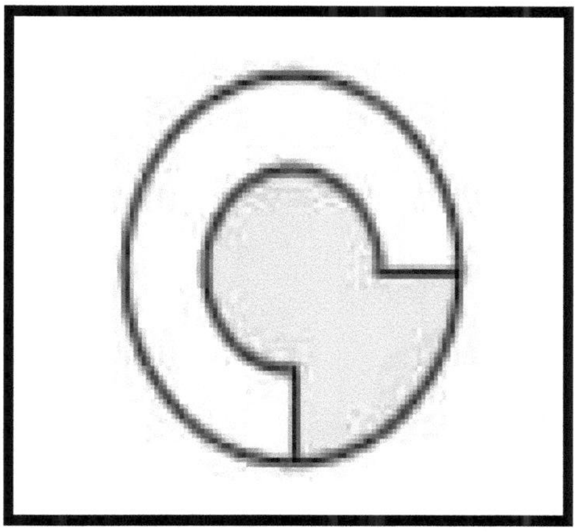

Simple

You may position the joint origin on a face, an edge, or a point of the component by clicking the Simple button in the Mode section of the dialog box. Once the joint origin is in place, you can then manipulate its placement as necessary. To do this, first ensure that the Simple button is selected in the Mode section of the dialog box, and then drag the mouse over a face of a component. This will allow you to create a simple shape for the component. The face is brought into focus, and its defining features come into view. Simply selecting a snap point with your mouse will allow you to determine the beginning location of the joint origin. The graphics area contains the handles for the translational and manipulator functions. In addition, the JOINT ORIGIN dialog box receives updates that include new choices that allow for more precise control over the location of the joint origin. You are now able to specify the location of the joint origin, as necessary, by dragging the translational and manipulator handles that appear in the graphics area. This may be done to meet your needs. You may also give the angle and offset values in the dialog box to define the location of the joint origin. This is done so that it can be defined following the requirements. After you have determined where the joint origin should be placed, choose the **OK** button located in the dialog box. The location of the point of origin of the joint is specified. When you have finished specifying the joint origin on a component, you can use the Joint tool to select the component so that a joint may be applied to it.

Between Two Faces

You may position the joint origin on a plane such that it is in the center of two chosen faces of a component by clicking the **Between Two Faces** button in the **Mode** section of the interface. To do this, click the **Between Two Faces** button that is located in the Mode section of the dialog box. In the drop-down menu of the dialog box, the Face 1 and Face 2 selection choices are shown. The Face 1 selection option is active by default whenever it is used. As a direct consequence of this, you can pick the initial face of a component. When you have finished choosing the first face of a component, the option to pick the component's second face will become active. Next, choose the component's second face using the select-select method. The Snap option is now available for selection inside the dialog box. The next step is to move the pointer over a face, an edge, or a point in between the faces that have already been chosen on the component. Following the appearance of the snap points, an imaginary plane is shown in the center of the faces that have been picked. After that, choose a snap point by clicking on it. Because the joint origin is located in the center of the faces that have been chosen, the selected snap point will be projected onto the imaginary plane that will be found in the middle of the faces. Additionally, the translational and manipulator handles are added to the graphics area, and the JOINT ORIGIN dialog box is changed to provide extra choices for adjusting the location of the joint origin. These additions allow for greater precision while editing the graphics.

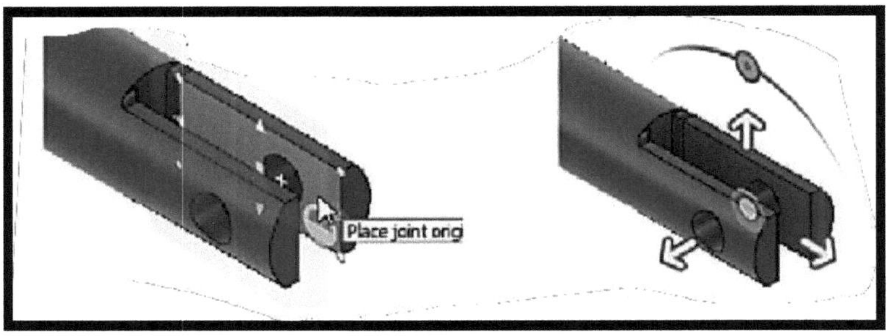

You may either define the location of the joint origin by dragging the translational and manipulator handles that appear in the graphics area or by providing the angle and offset values in the dialog box. Defining the position of the joint origin can be done according to the requirements. After you have determined where the joint origin should be placed, choose the OK button located in the dialog box. The location of the origin of the joint is determined to be in the center of the faces that have been chosen. Using the Joint tool, you can now apply a joint to an object, and by selecting the object, you can specify the location of the joint origin.

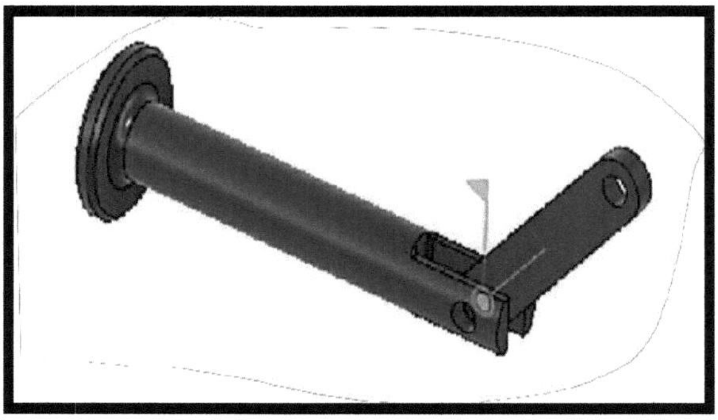

Two Edge Intersection

It is possible to position the joint origin at the intersection of two chosen edges of a component by clicking the button labeled "**Two Edge Intersection**" located in the Mode area. To do this, use the Two Edge Intersection button located in the Mode area of the editor. The dialog box displays the **Edge 1 and Edge 2** selection choices for the user to choose from. The Edge 1 selection option is active by default whenever it is used. As a direct consequence of this, you can pick the first edge of a component. Once the first edge of a component has been selected, the option to pick the component's second edge will become active. After that, choose the component's second edge to work with. A joint origin is established at the junction of the edges that have been picked after the selection of those edges. Additionally, the translational and manipulator handles are added to the graphics area, and the JOINT ORIGIN dialog box is changed to provide extra choices for adjusting the location of the joint origin. These additions allow for greater precision while editing the graphics.

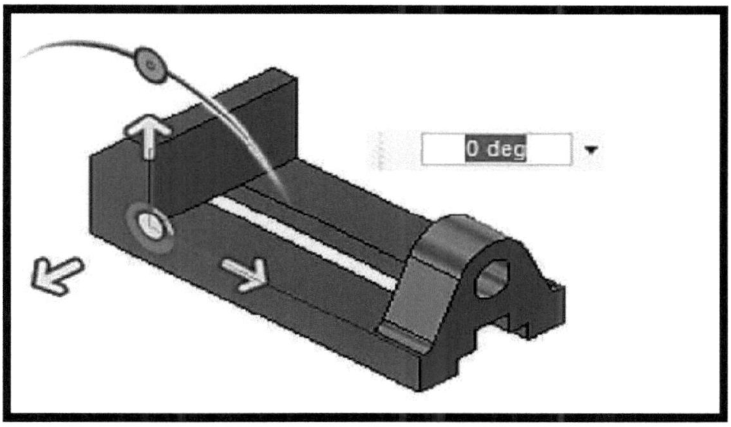

You may either define the location of the joint origin by dragging the translational and manipulator handles that appear in the graphics area or by providing the angle and offset values in the dialog box. Defining the position of the joint origin can be done according to the requirements. After you have determined where the joint origin should be placed, choose the **OK** button located in the dialog box. The point where the chosen edges cross is where the location of the joint origin is determined to be. When you have finished specifying the joint origin on a component, you can use the Joint tool to select the component so that a joint may be applied to it.

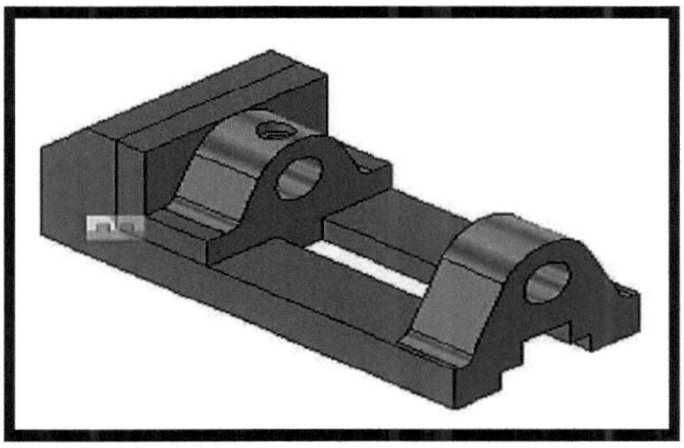

Editing Assembly Components

When you are in the process of developing an assembly, you may find that some of the assembly's components need to be edited. This may be necessary due to changes in the design, modifications, or other factors. You can make changes to individual parts of an assembly at any stage in the design process using Fusion 360.

The following is a discussion of the many techniques for modifying components:

To edit a component of an assembly that was produced inside a single file by utilizing the Top-down Assembly technique, you must first activate the component that is to be altered. After activating the component, you may then edit the component. You will be able to change the component's features and drawings as soon as the component is active. To edit a feature or a sketch, first right-click on the feature or sketch that needs to be modified in the Timeline, and then, from the shortcut menu that displays, choose either the **Modify Feature tool** or **the Edit Sketch tool**, depending on which tool you need to edit. The next step is to make any required adjustments to the feature settings or the drawing that was chosen. By making use of solid modeling tools, it is also possible to add brand-new functionality to the component.

NOTE: If the assembly is made by adding the components as external references, then the component that has to be modified may be opened on a separate file so that its features and drawings can be updated. This is possible if the assembly was created using this method. To do this, right-click on the component that needs to be modified in the BROWSER, and once the context menu opens, choose the Open tool from the list of available options. When you pick a component, a new file will be opened for that component. You now can make changes to its characteristics and drawings. After you have finished altering the component, use the **Save tool** to save it. After that, you should go on to the assembly file. In the assembly file, you will see the **Update** icon on the name of the changed component in both the BROWSER and the Application Bar. This indicates that the file has been updated. To bring all of the components of the assembly up to date at once, use the Update button located in the Application Bar.

Questions

1. The tool used for creating a joint origin anywhere on a component is known as?
2. Which button of the JOINT ORIGIN dialog box is used for placing the joint origin on a face of the component and then manipulating its location, as required?
3. In which approach are all components of an assembly created within a single design file?
4. Which selection option of the NEW COMPONENT dialog box is used for selecting the parent for the component being created?
5. Which tool is used for applying joints between the components in their current position as they are built?
6. Which dialog box is used for creating an empty component or converting the existing bodies into a component?
7. The ________ radio button of the NEW COMPONENT dialog box is used for creating an empty component.

CHAPTER 13

CREATING ANIMATION OF A DESIGN

Invoking the ANIMATION Workspace

You will need to go away from the DESIGN workspace and into the ANIMATION workspace to animate an assembly once you have created it in the DESIGN work plane. To do this in a design file, first, open the Workspace drop-down menu, and then choose ANIMATION from the menu that appears. The ANIMATION workspace's first user interface is shown when it starts up.

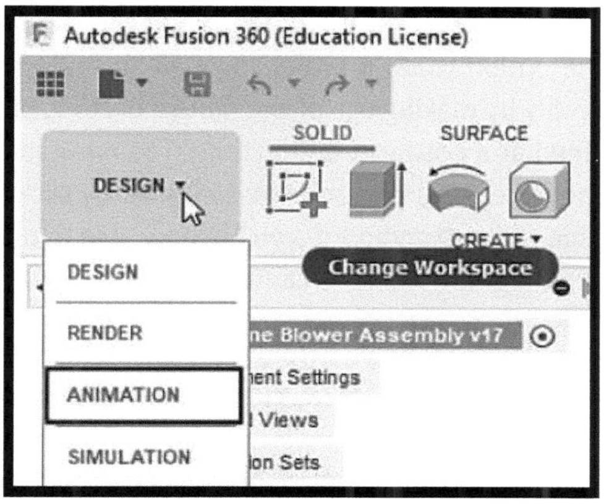

To generate an animation of a design in Fusion 360, you will need to develop a storyboard that documents the views and activities that occur along the Timeline. It is important to keep in mind that any traversing activities, including zooming in and out, orbiting, and zooming in and out, that are done at a particular moment in time on the design or assembly are saved as views on the Time-line. On the other hand, the Timeline will record as actions any transforming operations, such as move and rotate, that are carried out at a certain moment in time on particular components of an assembly.

Capturing Views on the Timeline

To record a view, such as zoom or orbit, you must first establish the location of the Play head on the Timeline at a moment in the future before the action is recorded.

This illustration depicts the Playhead being positioned on the Timeline at the 2-second mark. Note that if the location of the Playhead is specified on the Timeline at Time 0 (the red mark), then the view will not be recorded when navigating any action on the design or assembly. This is because the view is dependent on the position of the Playhead. Simply clicking on the View tool in the toolbar will allow you to record or capture views, and you have the option to do it either manually or automatically. Perform a traversing operation on the design or assembly by making use of the mouse buttons or the navigating tools once the Playhead position has been defined at a positive point in time. The navigation action that was carried out is recorded as a view on the Timeline at a particular instant in time. By clicking on the Play button located in the center of the bottom section of the storyboard, you are now able to play the animation and evaluate the view that was taken. You have the same ability to capture several views of the Timeline at various times during its history.

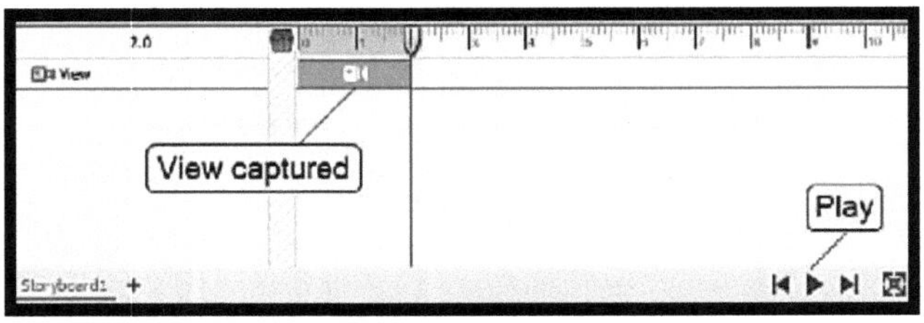

NOTE: After capturing a view, if you then perform any other navigating operation without moving the Playhead position on the Timeline, the previously captured view will be replaced by the newly performed navigating operation. This occurs even if you don't change the Playhead position on the Timeline.

Capturing Actions on the Timeline

You may record activities at a specific moment in time on the Timeline in Fusion 360 by carrying out operations such as moving and rotating individual components of an assembly. You can also capture activities by constructing exploded views of an assembly, turning on or off the visibility of the components, and creating callouts with annotations. These are all examples of things that you can do.

Transforming Components (Move or Rotate)

Components can be manually turned into a variety of different animation sequences as an alternative to, or in addition to, utilizing the Explode command.

1. To define when to move or rotate components, move the playhead to the appropriate position in the storyboard. This will take you to the place where you may make those changes.
2. Initiate the Transform Components command by using any one of the following procedures:

- To transform the components, choose the "**Transform**" menu option. The next step is to choose the components to move or rotate in the graphic window or the browser.
- Within the graphic window or the browser, make your selections for the components you want to move or rotate. After that, pick "**Transform Components**" from the context menu when you right-click.

3. Either use the manipulators to move or rotate the components that have been chosen, or specify the translation and rotation in the Transform Components dialog.

- You may translate the component in the X, Y, or Z direction by specifying the distance in either X, Y, or Z.
- To rotate the component about the X, Y, or Z axis, you must provide the X, Y, and Z angles.
- To move the components along an axis, you need to make use of the directional manipulator.
- To rotate the components, you need to make use of the rotating manipulator.
- To move components around inside the plane, you should use plane manipulators.

4. In the **Transform Components** window, confirm the new location of the component by clicking the OK button, then exit the program. The Actions Panel for the chosen component or components receives an automated addition of a Move or/and Rotate action for each of the components. A quick way to return a component to its default location is to pick the component, then go to the Transform menu and choose the Restore Home option. This activity has been documented as having taken place.

Creating an Exploded View of an Assembly

You can record activities on the Timeline in Fusion 360 by producing an exploded view of an assembly. This allows you to see the parts of the assembly more clearly. An assembly that is shown in exploded view makes it possible to more readily identify the location of each component inside the assembly. Utilizing the **Auto Explode**: One Level, **Auto Explode**: All Levels, or Manual Explode tools inside Fusion 360 will allow you to generate exploded views of your models. After that, we will talk about the various instruments that are used while blowing up an assembly.

Auto Explode

One Level tool is used to automatically explode just the children's components of the first level of the construction. Because of this, if the assembly is made up of sub-assemblies, then the components of those sub-assemblies will not explode when the assembly itself does. To do this, first, expand the Components node in the BROWSER, and then choose the assembly node by clicking on it once it has expanded. The graphics area is updated to show that each component of the assembly has been chosen and highlighted. After that, open the drop-down menu labeled **TRANSFORM** that's located in the Toolbar, and then choose the Auto Explode: **One Level tool**. After selecting an assembly, the process of exploding the first level children's components of that assembly begins, and after it is finished, the preview of the exploded view of the assembly as well as the Auto Explode toolbar appears in the graphics area. Additionally, the activities of the exploded view of the assembly's various components are recorded on the Timeline, and the green and red sliders are shown.

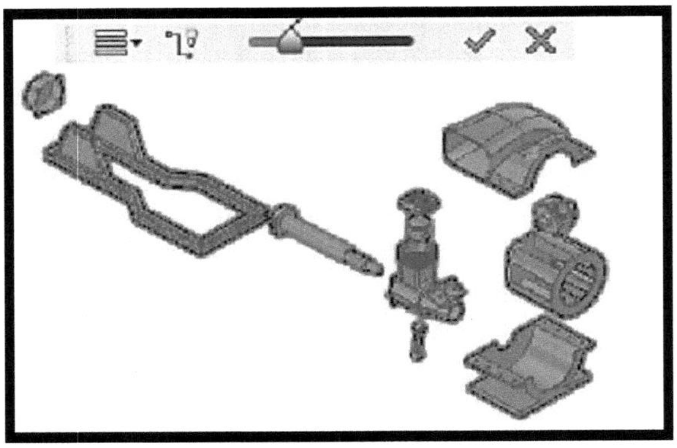

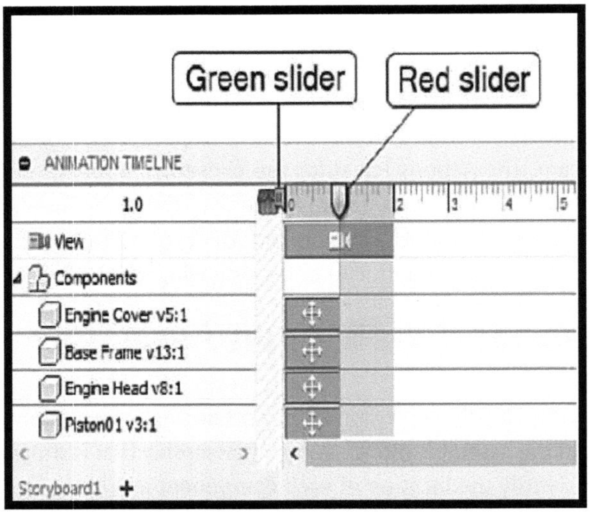

The moment at which the exploded view on the Timeline begins is indicated by the green slider, while the time at which it concludes is shown by the red slider, which appears in the backdrop of the Play head. You can modify the beginning and ending times of the exploded view by dragging the corresponding markers along the Timeline in the appropriate manner. The kind of exploding view, as well as the visibility of the trail lines, and the magnitude of the explosions, may all be controlled using the Auto Explode toolbar that displays in the graphics area. When you click on the **Sort** drop-down menu, the **One-Step Explosion** option will be picked automatically as the type of explosion to use. As a direct consequence of this, each component of the assembly blows up simultaneously. Choose the **Sequential Explosion** option from the Type drop-down list on the Auto Explode toolbar. This will cause each component of the assembly to explode in the order that it was added to the assembly. Take note that the activities of the exploded view are recorded appropriately on the Timeline following the choice that is chosen in the Type drop-down list. Click the **OK** button (shown by a green checkmark) in the Auto Explode toolbar after you have finished specifying the necessary parameters for the exploded view. After the exploded view has been constructed, the activities performed by each component of the assembly that has been exploded are logged into the Timeline. You are now able to animate the exploded view by selecting the Play button located inside the Storyboard.

Auto Explode

All Levels is used to automatically burst each level of the assembly. This indicates that the components of any sub-assemblies that make up the assembly will likewise explode, provided that the assembly itself is made up of other sub-assemblies. The technique for detonating all tiers of the assembly by making use of the Auto Explode feature.

Manual Explode Tool

For manually exploding the components of the assembly, the tool known as "**Manual Explode**" is what you'll need. To do this, open the drop-down menu labeled **TRANSFORM** located in the Toolbar, and then choose the **Manual Explode** tool from the menu that appears. Within the graphics section is where you will find the Auto Explode toolbar. Additionally, a green slider and a red slider can be seen on the timeline. Next, in the graphics section, pick a component to be detonated manually by clicking on it. In the graphics section, the chosen component is accompanied by a triangular diagram that has a variety of axes.

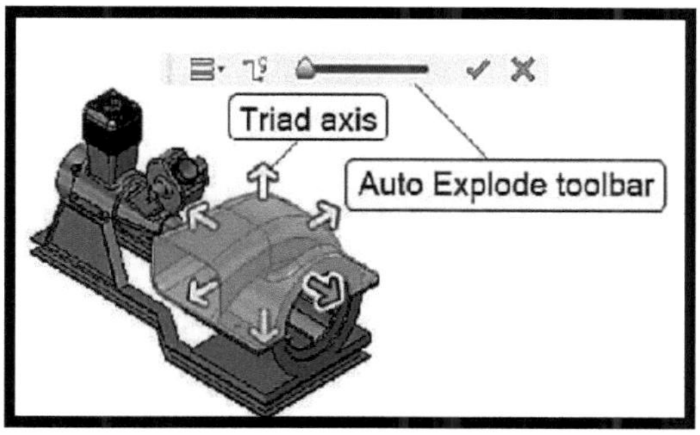

Choose an axis of the triangle to represent the direction in which the explosion will occur for the component that is now chosen in the graphics area. You may pick more components to be exploded in the same manner, and then determine the direction in which each component will explode, one at a time, inside the graphics area. You may also pick many components at once by holding down the **Control** key while making your selections. Following the selection of the components and the establishment of the direction in which the explosion will occur, use the Auto Explode toolbar to make the following adjustments: specify the type of explosion (either **One-Step Explosion** or **Sequential Explosion**), the visibility of the trail lines, and the scale of the explosion. In the graphics section, there will be a preview of the exploded view of the components that you have chosen.

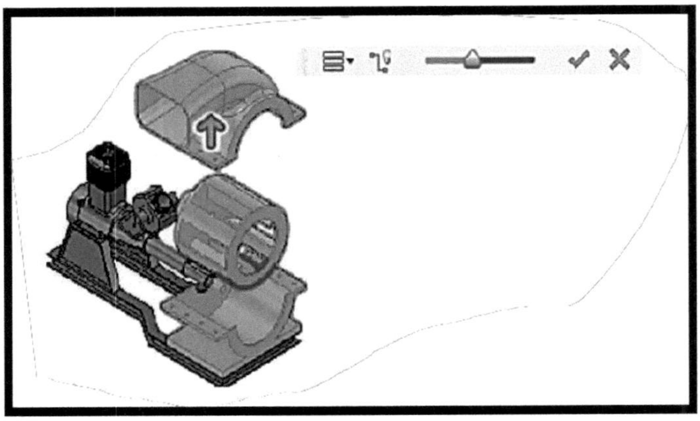

Additionally, the detonated acts have been recorded in the timeline. Now, by sliding the red and green sliders that display in the Timeline, you may set the beginning and end times for the exploded activities that were created. After that, under the Auto Explode toolbar, choose the OK button, which is represented by a green tick mark. The exploded view is generated, and the Timeline is updated to reflect the activities generated by the exploded view. You can burst manually additional components of the construction in a similar fashion. After you have completed the process of constructing the exploded view, you will be able to animate it by selecting the **Play** button located on the storyboard.

Toggling on or off the Visibility of Components

You may record activities on the Timeline in Fusion 360 by toggling the visibility of components at a certain moment in time on the Timeline. This allows you to record actions as they occur. To do this, you must first set the location of the Play head on the Timeline to a positive point in time, which is the point in time at which the component's visibility is to be disabled. After that, choose the component that is located in the graphics area. Once the component has been selected, go to the **TRANSFORM** panel of the Toolbar and click on the **Show/Hide tool** there. In the graphics section, the visibility of the chosen component is hidden away after being disabled. Additionally, a visibility action is recorded and appended underneath the name of the component that was chosen to appear on the Timeline.

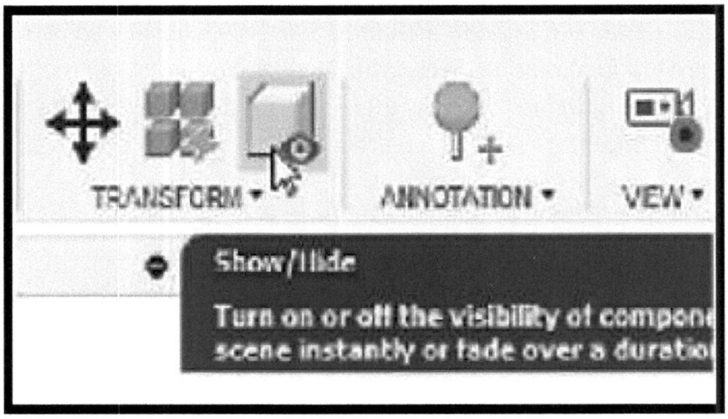

Now, when you play the animation, you will see that the visibility of the chosen component is instantaneously switched off at the desired point in time. This occurs at the moment when the animation is being played. This is since the Instant option for the visible action is predefined in the settings by default. You can set the start and end timings for the visibility action, which will allow you to gradually fade the component out of view. To do this, right-click on the light bulb symbol that represents the visibility action in the Timeline, and when the shortcut menu displays, choose the **Edit Start/End** option from the list of available options. Only the Start field displays the Start/End toolbar when the field is selected. The Duration option may be accessed by first selecting the arrow that is located next to the Instant option in the Toolbar. The Toolbar has a Start field in addition to an End field. You are now able to enter the start and end timings of the activity into the corresponding areas of the Toolbar. Once you are finished, click the OK button to save your changes. When you play the animation now, you will see that the component begins to fade from its start time on the Timeline and then disappears when it reaches its conclusion time.

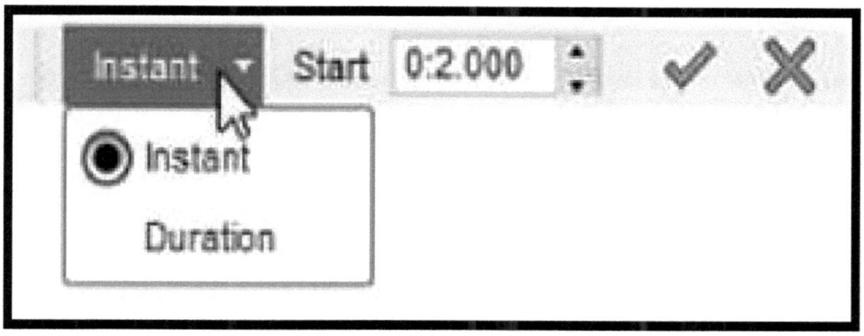

Creating a Callout with Annotation

1. Within the storyboard's timeline, shift the playhead to the moment when the callout is to be shown.
2. Select the **Create Callout** option from the menu.
3. Either click to position the annotation inside the canvas or pick the model geometry to link the annotation to a particular component.

- Note that when you hover over a component of the model geometry, the color of the callout will change from red to green to show that it is associated with the component. Callouts connected to a particular geometry take into account any transformations that are applied to that geometry.

4. Within the Annotation dialog box, type the text that will be shown in the callout.
5. Select the "**OK**" button.
6. If required, move the callout along the timeline by dragging it if you want to adjust the moment at which the callout is displayed in the environment.

Edit the text of an existing callout

- Right-click an annotation in the storyboard timeline's Annotation list, and then pick the **Edit Callout** option from the context menu.
- To alter the wording of the callout, double-click on it, and then open the annotation dialog.

Customizing Views and Actions on the Timeline

After collecting views and activities on the Timeline in Fusion 360, you can change them by changing the start and finish times at which they were captured. To alter the start time of an activity, drag the cursor over its start time (left end) on the Timeline until it transforms into a double arrow. Only then can the start time be edited. Next, move the pointer along the Timeline to reposition the new beginning time for the activity. You also can choose the time at which the activity will terminate, depending on your needs. When you adjust the timings at which an activity begins and ends, you have control over the total amount of time that the action takes up on the Timeline. You also can change the length of an activity. In addition to modifying the times at which an activity begins and ends to alter the amount of time it takes; you can also relocate an action to a new location on the Timeline. Simply move the pointer over the activity on the Timeline to do this. The moving cursor icon replaces the previous one. After that, move the action to where you want it to go along the Timeline by dragging it.

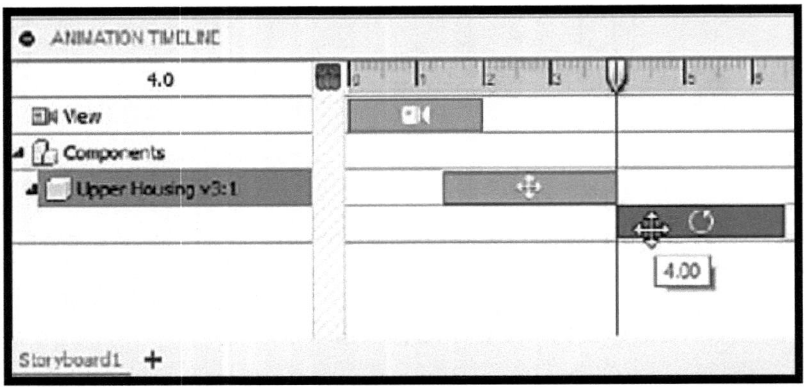

Once all of the necessary actions and views for a storyboard have been created, you will be able to play the animation by clicking the **Play** button that is located in the center of the bottom section of the storyboard.

Deleting Views and Actions of a Storyboard

You can remove views and actions of a storyboard inside Fusion 360. To do this, right-click anywhere on the storyboard's Timeline that has a view or action that you want to remove. There is a menu for shortcuts that shows. To delete anything, choose the option "**Delete**" from this shortcut menu. When you pick a view or action to remove from the storyboard's Timeline, that view or action is removed.

Creating a New Storyboard

When you choose the ANIMATION workspace in Fusion 360, a blank storyboard with the default name (Storyboard1) is immediately produced at the bottom of the screen. This storyboard is given the name Storyboard1. You may build a new storyboard in addition to the storyboard that is produced by default, and then add the necessary views and actions to that new storyboard. To do this, choose the STORYBOARD panel of the Toolbar and then select the New Storyboard tool from inside that panel. A new dialog box labeled NEW STORYBOARD opens. If you choose the **clean** option from the Storyboard Type drop-down list in the dialog box, a new empty storyboard will be produced with no actions, and the transformation of the components will remain the same as it was when they were imported from the DESIGN workspace. When you choose the option to **Start** from the end of the previous storyboard, a new empty storyboard is generated with no actions, and the components retain the same transformation as they had after the previous storyboard.

Choose the appropriate selection from the drop-down menu labeled "**Storyboard Type**" inside the dialog box, and then click the OK button when you are through. The current storyboard is switched to a newly generated, blank storyboard that receives the default naming convention. You are now able to add additional perspectives and actions to the storyboard that was just built. You also have the option of making a new storyboard by clicking on the plus symbol that is located next to the tab for the current storyboard. **IMPORTANT**: When you publish the animation of a storyboard, the name of the storyboard itself will display as the title of the animation on the web. As a consequence of this, it is strongly suggested that the name of the storyboard be changed to reflect this change. To do this, right-click on the storyboard tab located in the bottom-left corner of the screen, and once the shortcut menu appears, choose the **Rename** option from the list of available options.

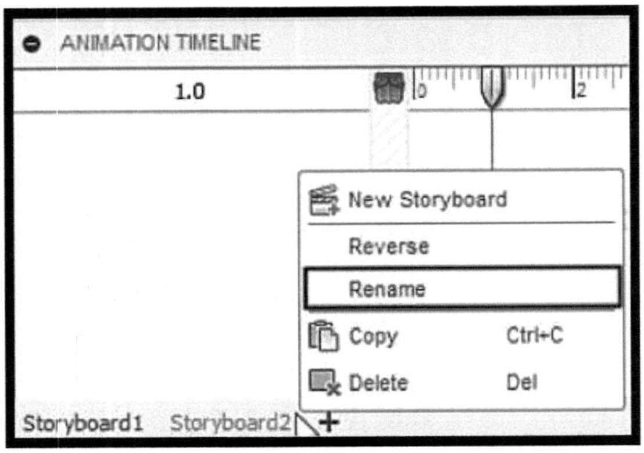

Toggling On or Off Capturing Views

When the Playhead is positioned in Fusion 360 at a positive point of time on the Timeline, the views will be automatically captured or recorded upon conducting the traversing activities. However, if you want to build up a scenario to prepare it for animation, you may need to switch off the feature that captures views. To enable or disable the capture of views, choose the View tool from the Toolbar or press the **CTRL and R** keys simultaneously. Turning either on or off will activate or deactivate the automated recording of navigation activities as views, accordingly. Take note that this button acts as a toggle.

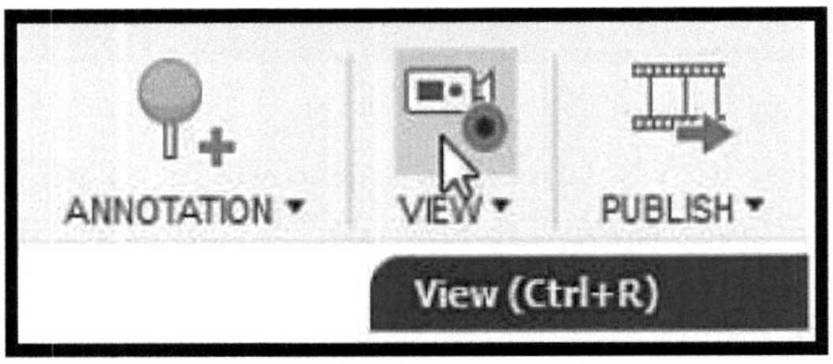

NOTE: If the recording or capturing of views is turned off in Fusion 360, you may still capture actions by using the View tool on the Toolbar. This allows you to capture actions even when recording or capturing views is off.

Playing and Publishing Animation

When you have finished recording all of the views and actions on the Timeline of a storyboard, you will be able to play the animation and publish it in a video file format. To begin viewing the animation, simply click the "**Play**" button located in the middle-lower portion of the storyboard. To save the animation in the form of a video file, either hit the **P** key on your keyboard or select the **Publish Video tool** that is located in the **PUBLISH** panel of the Toolbar. The Video Options dialog box is shown. Choose which storyboards' animations to publish in the Video Scope drop-down list of the dialog box by choosing either the All Storyboards or the Current Storyboard option, depending on whether you want to publish the animation of all storyboards or only the one that is active at the moment. In the section of the dialog box labeled "**Video Resolution**," you may choose the resolution and size of the video file that will be released. The video may be published using the pixel size and resolution of the environment in which it is being viewed by selecting the **Current Document Window Size** option found within this section. After that, you should choose the OK button located inside the dialog box. A dialog window labeled **Save As** will open. Enter the name of the video file that you want to store in this dialog box, and then choose the directory on your computer's local disk where you want the file to be saved. After that, choose "Save" from the drop-down menu. The video file (which ends in.avi) is stored in the place that you chose.

Using the Timeline function

Modifying a feature or editing the profile sketch of a feature is the most powerful thing that the timeline enables you to accomplish, and it's also the thing that you'll probably use it for the most often. If you decide that the fillet that you added to your model is not to your liking, you can easily alter it by right-clicking or double-clicking on the feature. When you've finished extruding your model, you could notice that the shape isn't quite right. If this happens, you can easily correct the issue by editing the **Profile Sketch**. You should edit with extreme care since the farther back you go in history, the more probable it is that you will uncover a feature that relies on earlier characteristics. If you do this, your model might wind up being broken.

Locating a feature using the timeline

In the Browser, just right-click the **Feature or Profile Sketch** in the timeline to find out what model a Feature has altered. This may also be done to locate a Profile Sketch. Under the folder that the sketch or feature is stored in, you will see that a dotted gray line has appeared.

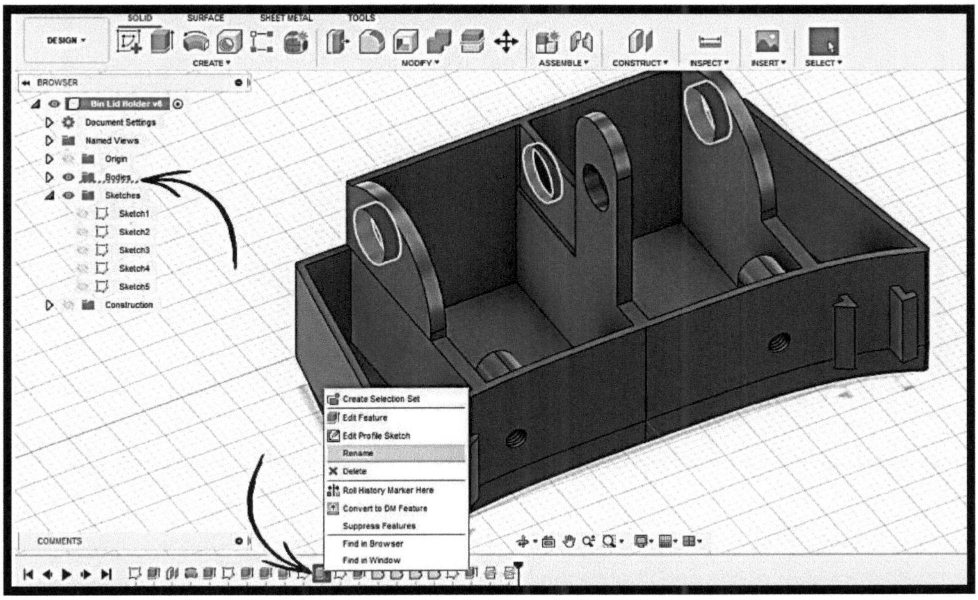

To locate a Profile Sketch from the Browser in the timeline, just right-click the sketch, and then choose the Find in Timeline option from the context menu. After that, the Profile Sketch will have a blue highlighting added to it.

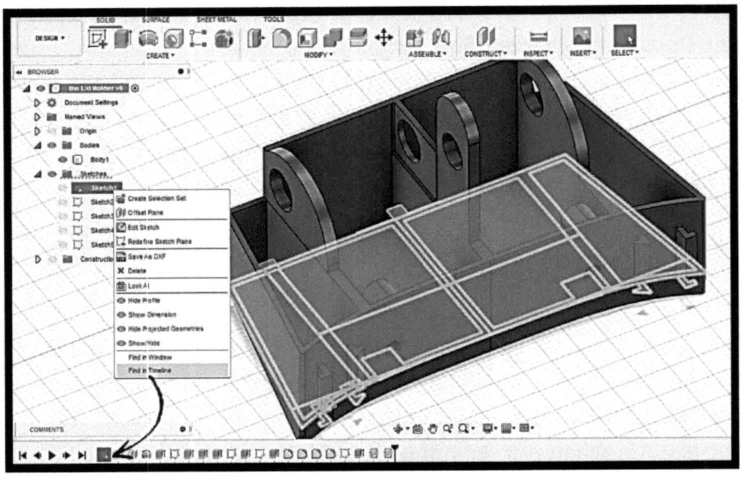

If you've built a complex model with a lot of separate parts and pieces, this tool will be of particular use to you.

Suppress a feature

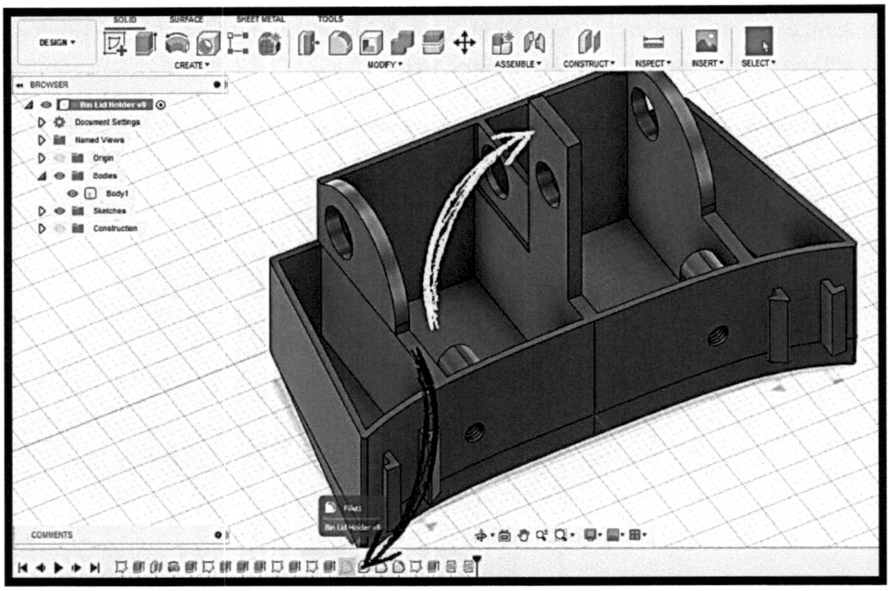

If you want to see what your model would look like if you removed a feature that you have applied, just right-click the feature in question and choose the "**Suppress Features**" option.

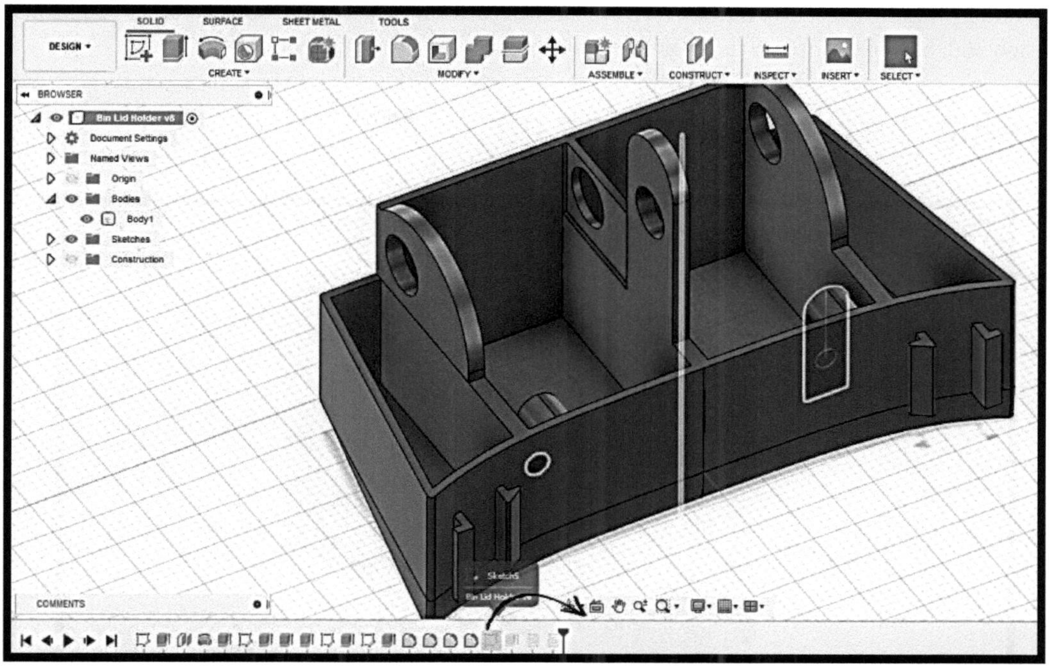

If disabling that feature has an impact on other features further down the timeline, such as extrusion, then disabling that feature will also disable all of the other features that are dependent on it.

Watch your project's history

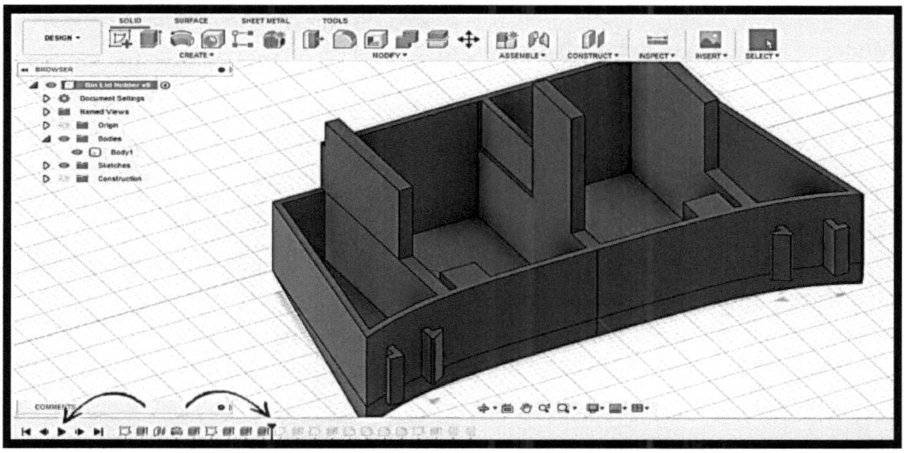

You may utilize the replay buttons located on the far left of the timeline menu to examine the stages that have been completed in a project. The buttons on the very edge of the interface allow you to go directly to the beginning or the very conclusion of the project. You can navigate through the project in one step either ahead or backward by using the two buttons in the middle. You may play the project as if it were an animation by clicking the center button. If you're interested in learning more about how other people model in Fusion 360, having the option to "**re-watch**" the creation of a project might be beneficial.

Turning the timeline on and off

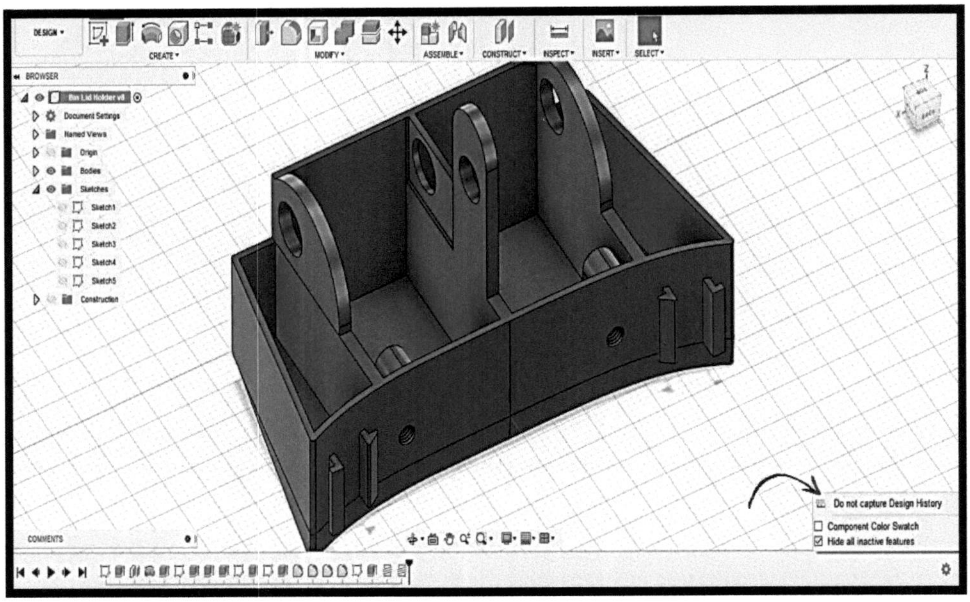

When you import some models, you might discover that your **Design History** is not being recorded. When you switch off Design History, the next option you'll access is called Direct Modeling. This might provide you with strong capabilities to repair a model that was imported. You will exit Design History and re-enter Parametric Modeling when you switch on Design History.

Questions

1. Which tool is used for exploding the first-level children's components of the assembly, automatically?
2. The tool used for exploding all levels of the assembly including the sub-assemblies of the components, automatically is known as?
3. In which workspace can you create the animation of a design?
4. Which button of the TRANSFORM COMPONENTS dialog box is used for toggling the visibility of the trail line on or off in the graphics area?
5. Which tools are used to create an exploded view of an assembly?
6. If the position of the ________ is defined on the Timeline at Time 0 (red mark), then the views and actions will not be captured.
7. Any transforming operation such as move or rotate performed at a point in time on a component of an assembly is captured as what?

PART 5
CREATING DRAWINGS

CHAPTER 14

WORKING WITH DRAWINGS

Invoking the DRAWING Workspace

You will need to go away from the DESIGN workspace and into the DRAWING workspace to create the drawings for a design (either a component or an assembly) once you have created it in the DESIGN work plane. To do this, open a design file, choose the Workspace drop-down menu, and then select **DRAWING** > **From Design** from the menu that appears. A dialogue window labeled **CREATE DRAWING** is shown. You can also invoke the CREATE DRAWING dialog box by selecting **File > New Drawing > From Design** from the Application Menu, or you can right-click on the name of the design (the top browser node) in the BROWSER, which will bring up a shortcut menu, and then select the Create Drawing option from that menu. Both of these methods are alternatives. The next section is the **CREATE DRAWING** dialog box's available choices.

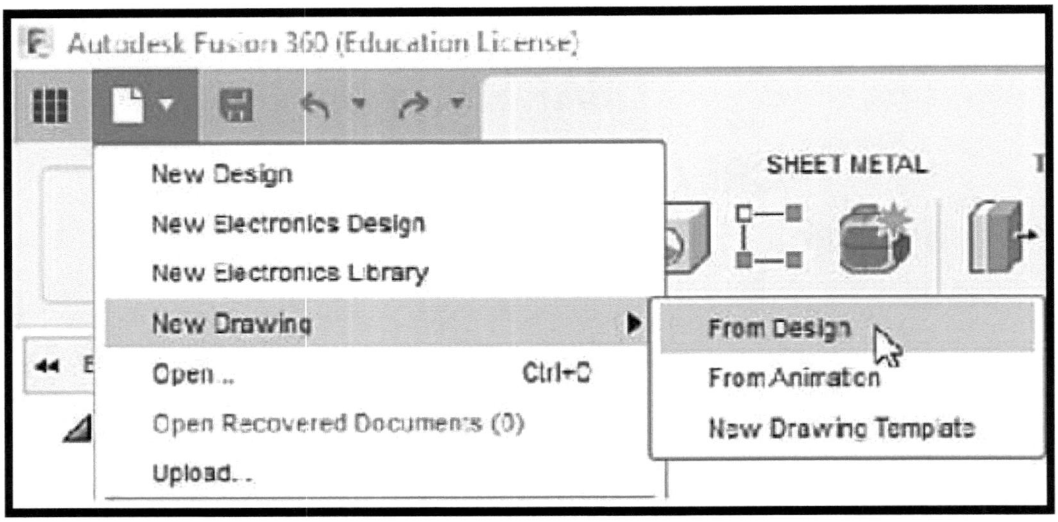

NOTE: You may activate the DRAWING workspace in Fusion 360 from either a design file or an animation file by choosing the appropriate option from the drop-down menu labeled "**From Design**" or "**From Animation.**" While the From Design option is used to create drawing views from the design file (component or assembly), the From Animation option is used to create drawing views from exploded views of the assembly that were created in the ANIMATION workspace. The From Design option is used to create drawing views from the design file (component or assembly).

Reference: You can generate a drawing of the whole assembly by choosing the check box labeled Full Assembly under the Reference rollout of the CREATE DRAWING dialog box. After deselecting the checkbox labeled "**Full Assembly**," the Components selection option will become available in the dialog box.

This option may be used to pick the individual parts of the assembly that will be utilized to create the design. In this illustration, the box labeled "**Full Assembly**" has been unchecked, and the component of the assembly that will be used to generate the drawing has been chosen.

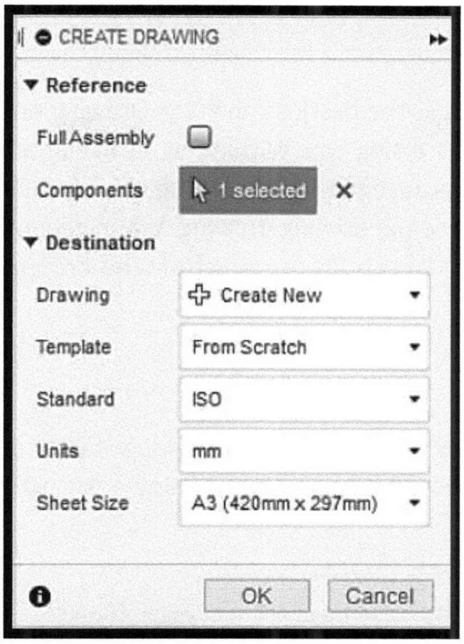

Destination

The choices in the Destination rollout of the dialog box are used to pick a drawing destination (new drawing or add to an existing drawing), template, drawing standard, unit of measurement, and sheet size for the drawing that is now being worked on.

Drawing

In the dialog box's Drawing drop-down list, the option to **Create New** is chosen automatically when the box is opened. Because of this, you will be able to start a brand-new drawing from scratch. A list of previously prepared drawings for the design is also shown under the drop-down menu for the Drawing option. In this drop-down list, you have the option of selecting an existing drawing that was generated for the design. When you do this, you will have the option to either generate drawing views inside an existing sheet of the drawing or add a new sheet of drawing to the current drawing.

Template

The Template drop-down list displays in the dialog box when the Create New option is chosen from the Drawing drop-down list. In this particular drop-down list, the option to **Start From Scratch** is chosen by default. As a direct consequence of this, you will have the ability to start a brand-new drawing inside the default drawing template. You also have the option of choosing an existing template to use while creating the new drawing. To do this, choose the Browse option from the drop-down list that is located next to the Template heading. The dialog box labeled Select Template will now appear. Use the "Browse" button in this dialog box to go to the place where the drawing template was stored, and then pick it when you get there. After that, you should click the Select button located inside the dialog box.

Sheet

When an existing drawing is chosen as the destination in the Drawing drop-down list of the dialog box, the Sheet drop-down list is shown in the dialog box. Within this particular drop-down list, the option to create a new sheet is chosen by default. Because of this, you will be able to build drawing views inside the current drawing as well as add a new sheet to the existing drawing. When generating drawing views, you also have the option of selecting a sheet from an existing drawing from this drop-down list.

Standard

The drop-down list titled "**Standard**" is used to pick a drawing standard before beginning the creation of the drawing. It is important to take note that this drop-down list will become active in the dialog box whenever a new drawing is created.

Units

Utilizing the drop-down menu labeled "**Units**," one may choose the unit of measurement to apply to the design. It is important to take note that this drop-down list will become active in the dialog box whenever a new drawing is created.

Sheet Size

To choose a sheet size before beginning the creation of the design, utilize the drop-down menu labeled "**Sheet Size**." After making your selections in the CREATE DRAWING dialog box that are necessary for the creation of the drawing, you may go on to click the OK button. The DRAWING workspace is activated with the drawing sheet that has been scaled to the required dimensions. Additionally, the DRAWING VIEW dialog box is shown, and the base view of the chosen design (either the component or the assembly) is shown as an attachment to the cursor. In addition, the basic view of the design will need to be placed on the drawing sheet, and you will be asked to identify its location. Click on the drawing sheet to establish the placement point for the base view, and then use the DRAWING VIEW dialog box to set the needed parameters for the base view, such as its orientation, style, and scale. After that, you should click the **OK** button. Within the drawing sheet, a basic view that has certain parameters applied to it is formed.

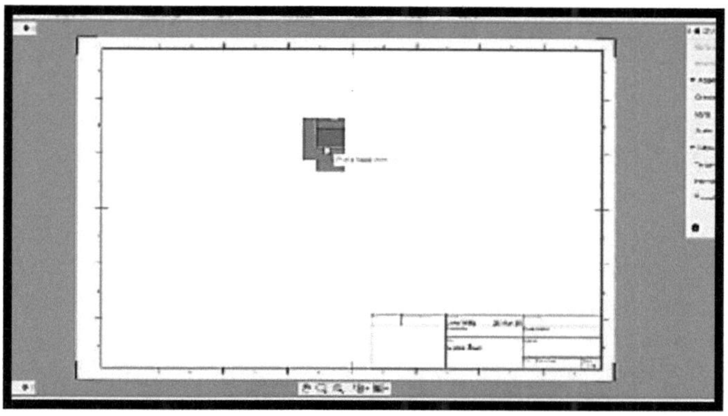

NOTE: When you launch the DRAWING workspace in Fusion 360, the DRAWING VIEW dialog box opens automatically. This is because the Base View tool becomes enabled on the Toolbar automatically when you enter the DRAWING workspace.

Creating the Base View of a Design

An independent perspective of a design is referred to as the base view. In the process of creating the orthogonal and isometric projected views of the design, it is sometimes referred to as the initial view or the parent view. The DRAWING VIEW dialog box, which opens automatically when the DRAWING workspace is used, may be utilized to facilitate the creation of the basic view. A second method for opening the DRAWING VIEW dialog box is to use the **Base View** tool, which is located in the DRAWING VIEWS panel of the Toolbar. The choices that may be made inside the DRAWING VIEW dialog box.

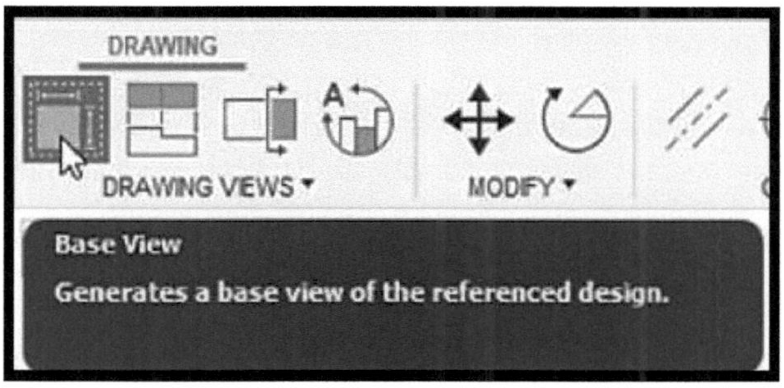

Reference

Within the dialog box's Reference drop-down list, the Create New option is chosen automatically whenever the box is opened. After generating the base view, a new base view reference will be inserted in the BROWSER as a direct consequence of this action. Additionally, a list of existing base view references that have been established on the current drawing sheet is shown in the Reference drop-down list. You have the option of using any one of the pre-existing base view references in this drop-down list as a point of reference for the newly built base view. Note that when the DRAWING VIEW dialog box is launched automatically on launching the DRAWING workspace, the Reference drop-down list will not be enabled.

Representation

You are given the option to define the representation of the base view either as a model or as an exploded view derived from a storyboard by using the drop-down list labeled "**Representation.**" A list of storyboards that were developed for the current design in the ANIMATION workspace can be seen by selecting this option from the drop-down menu. When the DRAWING workspace is opened from a design, the Model choice in this drop-down list is pre-selected by default. Therefore, the model is a representation of the basic view. You may construct an exploded view of the design by selecting a storyboard from this drop-down list and using it as the basis view for the view. Note that the Representation drop-down list is disabled when the DRAWING VIEW dialog box is automatically called on calling the DRAWING workspace from a design. This is something you should keep in mind.

Orientation

The Orientation drop-down list in the dialog box is where you make your selection for the orientation of the basic view of the design that you are going to construct. Possible orientations are Front, Top, and Right.

Style

The field labeled "**Style**" inside the dialog box is where a visual style may be specified for the basic view that is going to be produced. In this section, you may specify the visual style of the model by selecting the button labeled Shaded, Shaded with Hidden Edges, Shaded with Visible Edges, or Shaded with Hidden Edges and Visible Edges.

Scale

In the Scale section of the dialog box, you may enter a scale for the base view that you are working with. The most accurate scale for the base view is automatically determined by Fusion 360 based on the sheet size and the volume of the model. This setting may be changed if necessary.

Tangent Edges

The presentation of the tangent edges of the model in the base view may be controlled using the Tangent Edges field of the dialog box. Tangent edges are smooth transitions (tangent continuity) between faces and rounded edges of a surface (filleted edges). When the Entire Length button of the Tangent Edges section is clicked, the model's base view will show the full length of any tangent edges that are now being shown. Use the Shorter button to show shortened tangent edges in the base view. This button is utilized in the Tangent Editor. The display of tangent edges in the base view may be turned off by selecting the **Off** button from the toolbar.

Interference Edges

The display of the model's interference edges may be toggled on and off using the checkbox labeled "**Interference Edges**," which is located in the base view. Interference edges are edges that develop as a result of the faces of two components intersecting one another and coming into contact with one another. The check box for Interference Edges is not selected in the dialog box's default configuration. As a direct consequence of this, the base view no longer presents the interference edges that were previously shown. When you choose this checkbox, the basic view will immediately begin displaying the interference edges that are present.

Thread Edges

After choosing the check box labeled "**Thread Edges**" in the dialog box, the thread edges will be shown in the drawing views in the form of dashed lines. When you deactivate this checkbox, the thread edges depiction in the drawing views will no longer be shown. When making the necessary adjustments for the creation of the base view, such as the orientation, visual style, and scale factor, click on the drawing sheet to place the base view after you have finished making those adjustments. When this happens, the DRAWING VIEW dialog box's OK button becomes active. To continue, choose the **OK** button located inside the dialog box. The design sheet is where the foundation of the provided settings is created. The orthogonal and isometric projected views of the model may be generated from the base view of the model once it has been first created.

Creating Projected Views

1. Initiate a Projected View.

- Now that we have a basic view of the model assembly, let's move on to creating projected views and editing the characteristics of those views so that we may generate a full drawing layout.
- Choose **Projected View** from the Create Toolbar's drop-down menu.
- To pick the base view as the parent view from which the projected views will be produced and related, click on the base view and then select it from the drop-down menu.

2. Position the Views in the Room

- To preview the projected view, position the cursor to the right of the base view, and then note that the view is being previewed based on this alignment.
- To position a projected view, click to the right of the base view that is already there.
- To position a second projected view, click at the bottom of the currently displayed base view.
- To complete the process, press the Enter key.

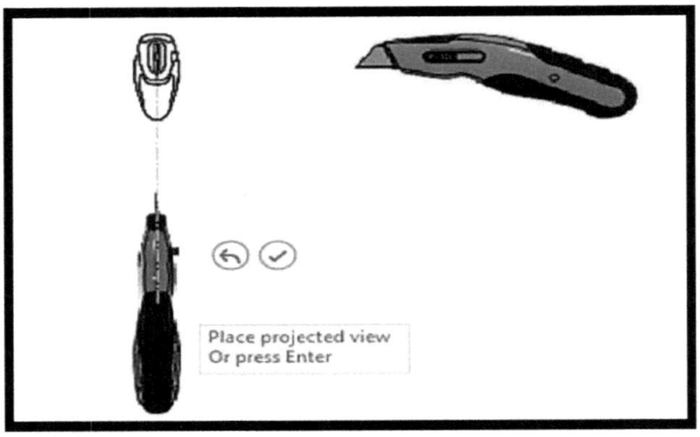

Note: A projected view will take on the attributes of its parent view automatically. When a modification is made to a property of the parent view, that change is reflected as an update to the corresponding property of the projected view. Simply double-clicking a projected view will allow you to make modifications to its settings.

3. Develop a base view using an isometric perspective.

- Select **Base View** from the Create Toolbar's drop-down menu.

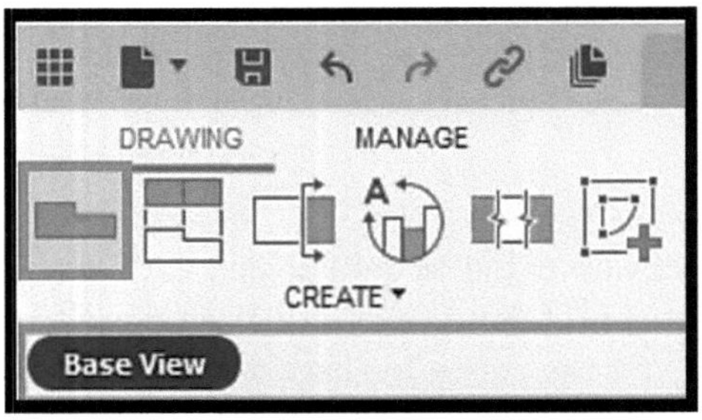

- Click to move the view so that it is located in the bottom right corner of the sheet layout, just above the title block.
- Change the orientation such that it is northeast isometric.
- To commit the view, click the **OK** button.

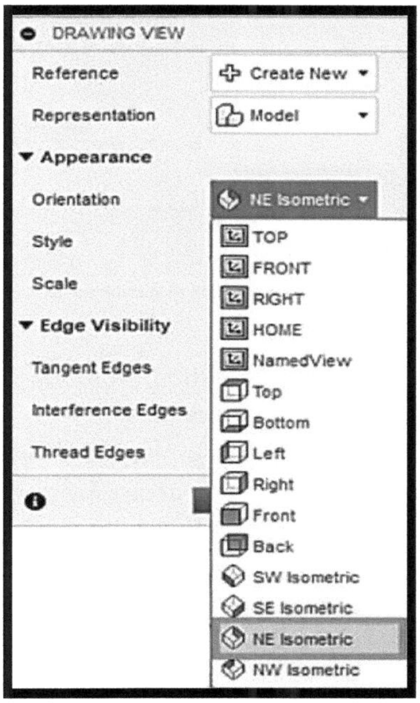

Note: A projected view will take on the attributes of its parent view automatically. When one of the properties of the parent view is modified, the properties of the projected view that correspond to that property are likewise updated. Simply double-clicking a projected view will allow you to make modifications to its settings.

About Projected Views and View Options

The parent-child link between projected views and the underlying views they were derived from is maintained by projected views. They get the attributes of the parent base view that they inherit. After you have created the projected view, you have the option to alter those settings if required.

The projection angle serves as the defining factor for the approach that is used to produce projected views.

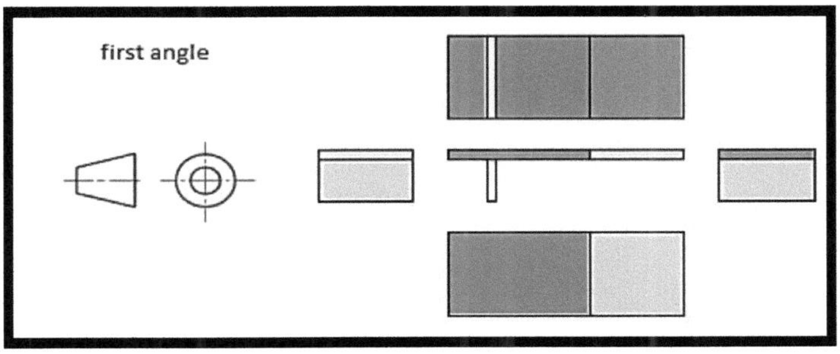

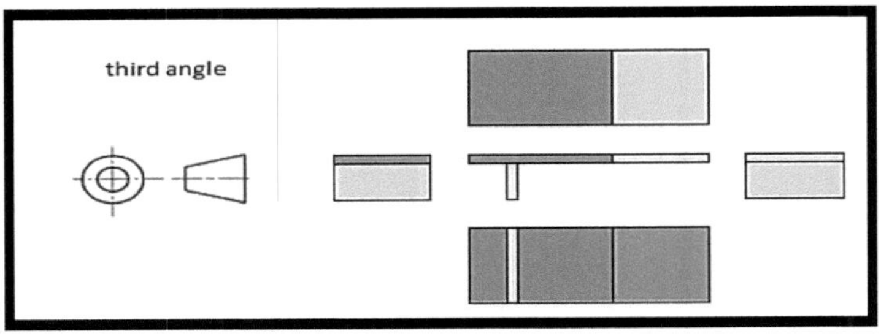

First Angle Projection: When you use first angle projection, projected views that are placed to the right of a base view depict the appearance when viewing it from the left.
Second Angle Projection: When you use second angle projection, projected views that are placed above a base view depict the appearance when viewing. The appearance seen from above is represented by projected views that are positioned below the base view. The ISO drafting standard requires that first-angle projection be used when producing drawings. When the drawing format is set to ISO, the Drawings workspace will utilize first-angle projection as the default projection method whenever possible.
Third Angle Projection: When you use third angle projection, projected views that are positioned to the right of a base view show the look of the scene as it would be seen when seen from the right. The appearance from below is shown via projected views that are positioned below the base view. The ASME drafting standard requires that third-angle projection be used wherever possible in the production of drawings. When the drawing format is set to ASME, the Drawings workspace will utilize third-angle projection as the default projection method whenever possible.

4. Modify the view of the isometric base.

Let's utilize the Drawing View options to further adjust the view layouts now that you have generated a basic view as well as numerous projected views of the model.

- To activate the isometric view, right-click anywhere within the selection border of the view, and then click it again.
- To scale the base view, use the Drawing View dialog's Scale drop-down list to pick 1:1 as the base view's scaling factor.
- To accept the modifications to the drawing view, click the **Close** button.

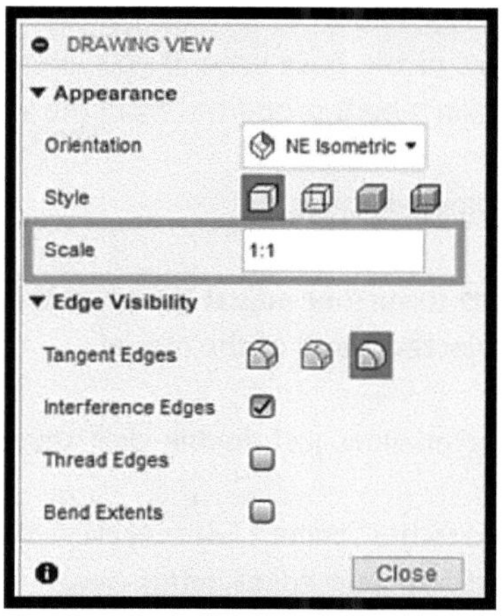

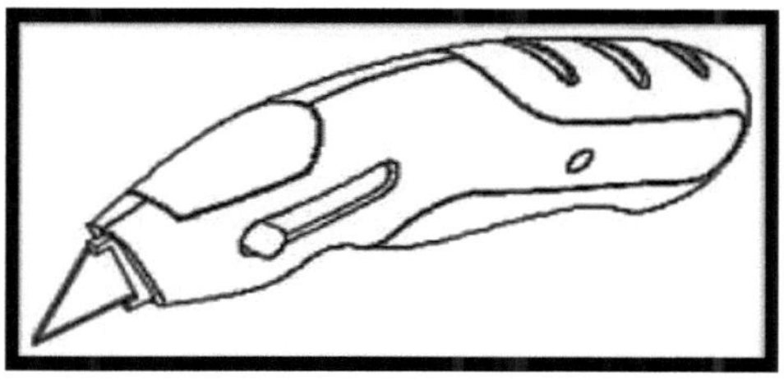

5. Edit the Right Projected View

- To activate the right projected view, just double-click anywhere within the selection boundary of the right projected view.
- To show hidden lines in this view, choose **Visible and Hidden Edges** from the Style choices inside the Drawing View dialog.
- To accept the modifications to the drawing view, click the Close button.

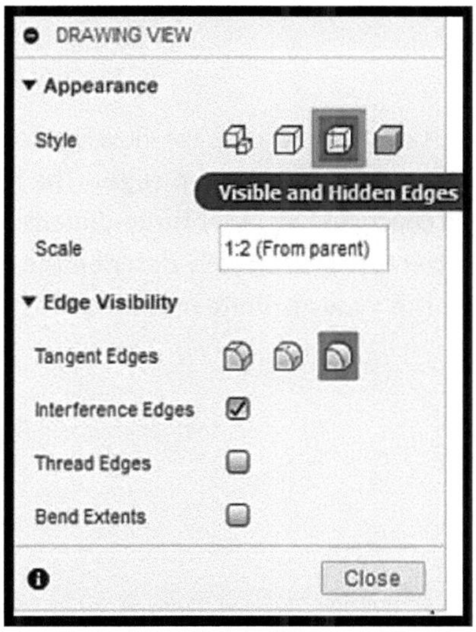

Note: Once the characteristics of the projected view have been altered, it is important to keep in mind that they will no longer inherit the settings of the base view. If you alter the properties such that they read **"From parent,"** then they will once again inherit properties from the view that they are children.

6. Modify the view of the bottom projected image.

Let's utilize the Drawing View options to further adjust the view layouts now that you have generated the basic view as well as multiple projected views of the model.

- To activate the bottom projected view, just double-click anywhere within the selection boundary of the bottom projected view.
- In the Drawing View dialog, go to the Tangent Edges section and choose **Full Length** from the drop-down menu to show full-length tangent edges in this view.
- To accept the modifications to the drawing view, click the **Close** button.

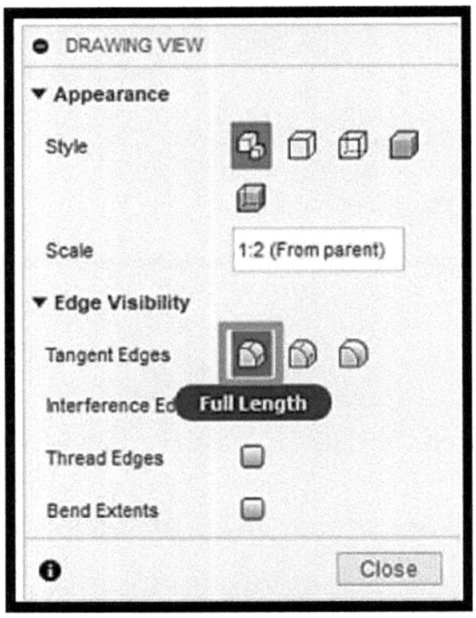

About Drawing View

Hidden Lines To show hidden lines inside the chosen base view, go to the Style settings and pick either Visible and hidden edges or shaded with visible and hidden edges. The Hidden-line format hides or reveals lines, edges, and other things that are concealed by other three-dimensional objects. This representation is used to display hidden data. When attempting to visually describe the inner workings or dimensions of a complicated assembly or component, this view attribute may be quite beneficial.

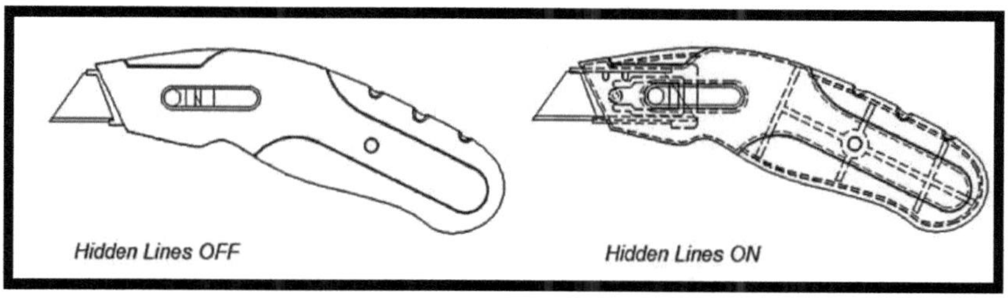

Tangent Edges: To show tangent edges inside the chosen base view, pick **Full length, Shortened**, or **Off** from the drop-down list. The transition from a flat surface to a rounded edge, which is most often observed in the form of filleted edges, is denoted as tangent edges.

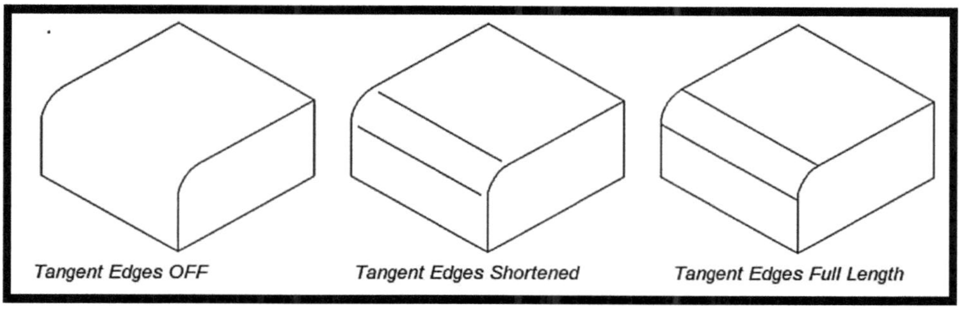

Interference Edges: To show interference edges inside the chosen base view, you may choose to either turn them on or leave them off by selecting or unchecking the corresponding checkbox. When two faces of two different components cross, the result is an interference edge. When the Interference Edges setting is on, an edge will be presented that indicates where the two components collide with one another. When this option is enabled, linked drawing views will show edges, both hidden and visible, that had been previously omitted because of an interference situation. Conditions such as press fit or interference fit, as well as threaded fasteners in tapped holes, are examples of interferences (where the hole is modeled using the minor diameter).

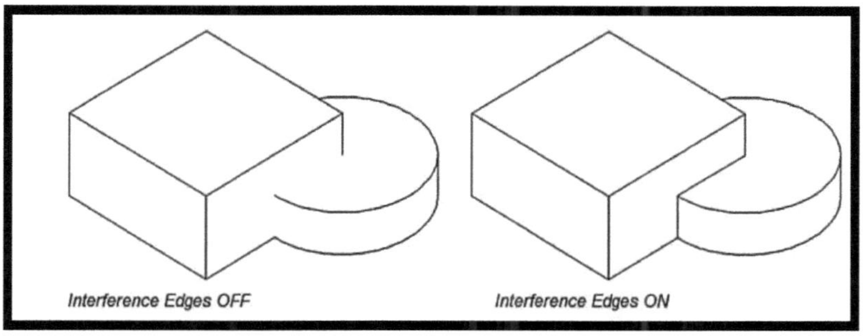

7. Create a Detail View.

A projected image known as a detail view magnifies a particular section of the overall view and displays it at a smaller size.

- Select **Detail View** from the Create toolbar's drop-down menu.
- Make the right-side projected view the parent view in your selection menu.
- Click the spot in the middle of the border for the detail (as shown in the image below).
- Click once more to increase or decrease the size of the detail view border.
- Use the mouse to choose an empty part of the drawing page to position the detail view.
- In the View Properties dialog, make the detail view bigger by selecting 2:1 from the Scale drop-down list.
- To produce the detail view, click the **OK** button.

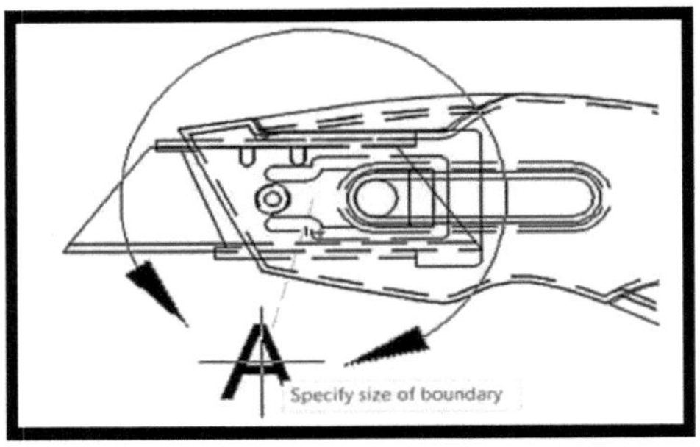

8. Move Objects.

- To choose an item, click on it anywhere on its surface.
- To grab the item, click the gray grip that is located in the middle of it.
- Click on a different place for the thing to be moved to.

Note that the behavior of the **Move** action remains the same regardless of whether it is used to view, text objects, dimensions, or balloons.

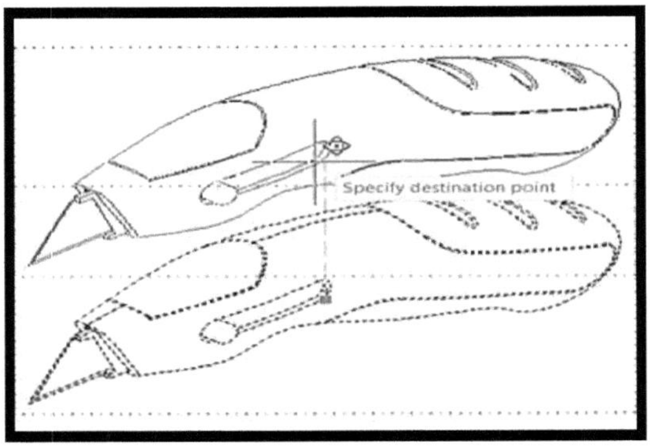

- Rearrange the things on your drawing so that they are evenly spaced apart, and make sure to leave the top right corner of the drawing area blank.

At this point, your drawing needs to resemble something along these lines:

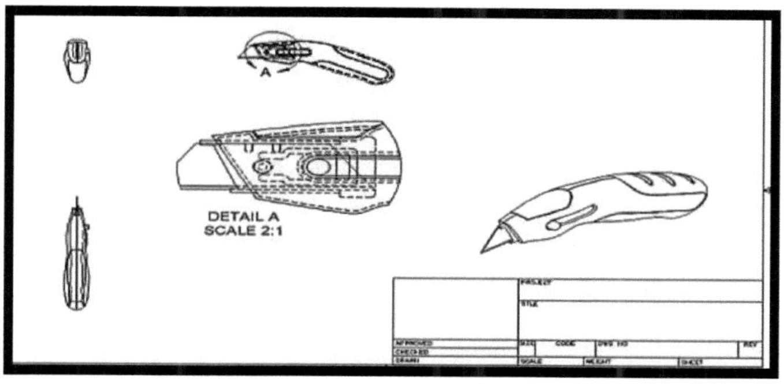

Working with Angle of Projection

There are two different angles of projection that are used in engineering drawings. These are the first angle of projection and the third angle of projection. When using the first angle of projection, it is anticipated that the item will be retained in the first quadrant, and the spectator will approach the object from the direction. Since the object was maintained in the first quadrant, all of its projections of views are located on the appropriate planes. Now that the planes of projection have been unfolded, the front view will appear on the top side, and the top view will appear on the bottom side. Additionally, the left side view is mirrored onto the right side of the front view, and the right-side view is mirrored onto the left side of the front view. Similarly, it is expected that the item will remain in the third quadrant when the third angle of projection is used. In this instance, the projection of the front view appears on the bottom of the drawing, but the projection of the top view appears on the top side. Additionally, the view from the right-hand side is shown on the right, while the view from the left-hand side is presented on the left of the front view.

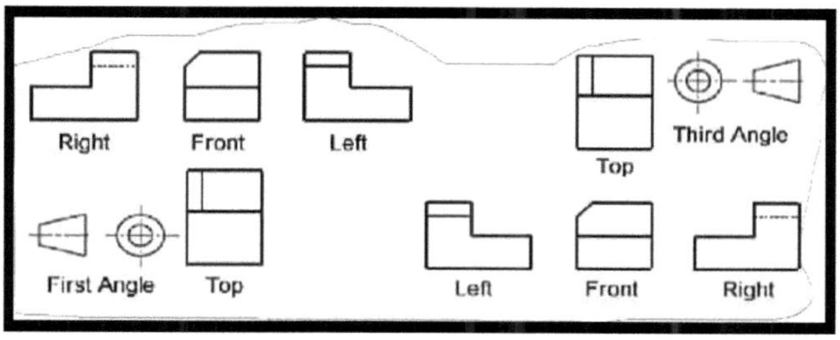

Defining the Angle of Projection

When you make a drawing following the ISO standard, the first angle of projection is used to generate the projected views. On the other hand, when you make a design following the ASME standard, the third angle of projection is utilized. You are, however, able to modify the projection angle that is used by default to suit your needs. To accomplish this, click on your name, which is located in the top right corner of the Fusion 360 interface. The drop-down option for the User Account is shown.

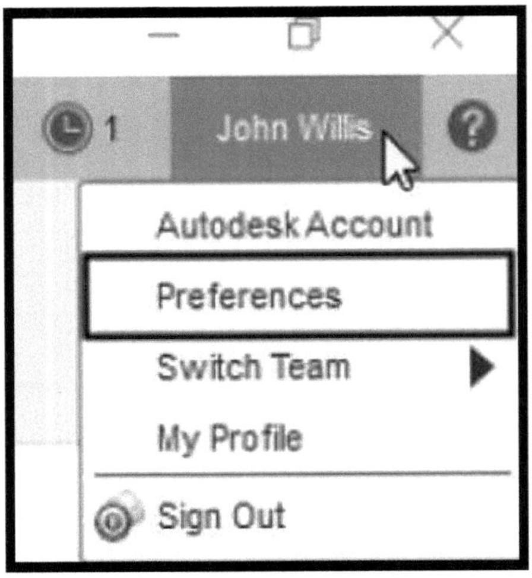

Select the **Preferences** tool from the menu that drops down from here. The dialog box labeled Preferences will now appear. After that, go to the General node on the left side of the dialog box and choose the Drawing option from within it. Next, in the Standard drop-down list, pick the drawing standard (ASME or ISO) to change the default projection angle for that standard. When you have chosen the drawing standard, the dialog box will update to display all of the drawing standard's default attributes and choices. The ASME standard has been used for this particular illustration. After that, choose whether you want to Override or Restore the Format Defaults. To modify the attributes of the chosen drawing standard's default settings, choose the "**Below**" check box in the dialog box. Every single one of the default properties may now be edited. Within the dialog box's drop-down list labeled "**Projection Angle**," you are now able to choose the projection angle that best suits your needs. After that, in the dialog box, click the **Apply** button to confirm that you want to keep the modification, and then click the **OK** button to close the dialog box.

Note that any adjustments made to the projection angle for a standard will only be reflected in new drawings; these alterations will not affect the drawing that is currently being used or any of the drawings that have been used in the past.

Defining Drawing Preferences

You can set the default choices for making drawings in Fusion 360. These default preferences allow you to choose the drawing annotation format, drawing annotation units, drawing sheet size, annotation font, and dimension accuracy. To do this, launch the Preferences dialog box, which was covered in more detail before. After that, go to the General node on the left side of the dialog box and choose the **Drawing** option from within it. The right panel of the dialog box contains the choices that may be used to establish the default preferences for drawing. In the dialog box, the Standard and Annotation Units drop-down boxes both have the "**Inherit from Design**" option selected by default. As a direct consequence of this, every new drawing utilizes the structure and units that have been established for the design. You have the option of picking the necessary standard from the ASME or ISO options in the Standard drop-down list. After that, you can choose to either override or restore the format defaults. Check the "**Below**" box in the dialog box to personalize the preferences that are set by default, if necessary. After you have finished establishing the default preferences for a standard, you may accept the modification by clicking the Apply button in the dialog box, and then you can click the **OK** button to leave the dialog box. Be aware that any changes that you make to the default settings for a standard will only be applied to new drawings; they will not have any effect on the drawing that is now being worked on or any of the drawings that already exist.

Editing Annotation and Sheet Settings

After a new drawing has been created in Fusion 360, the drawing standard and units associated with it cannot be modified. On the other hand, you can change the settings for the annotations and the sheet size for the current drawing. Click on the arrow that is located next to the Annotation Settings tool in the Navigation Bar, and then click on the Display Settings option that is located at the bottom of the drawing area. This will allow you to make changes to the annotation settings for the current drawing. The flyout for configuring annotations will now show.

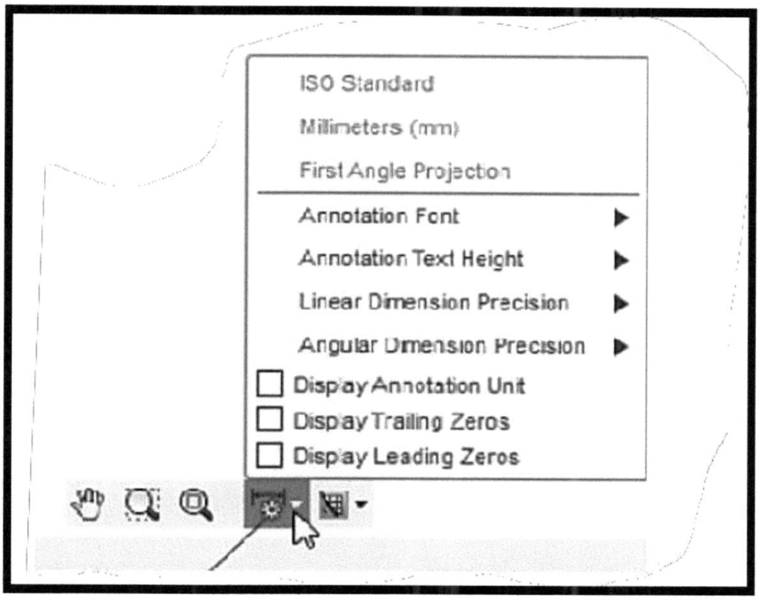

You may modify the annotation font, the annotation text height, the linear dimension accuracy, and the angular dimension precision by utilizing the appropriate cascading menus that are included in the flyout for the **Annotation Settings**. You can also turn on or off the display of trailing and leading zeros in the decimal dimensions of the drawing by using the check boxes labeled **Display Trailing Zeros** and **Display Leading Zeros** in the Annotation Settings flyout, respectively. These check boxes allow you to toggle the display of trailing zeros and leading zeros on and off. The display of trailing zeros in all decimal dimensions is turned off when the check box to Display Trailing Zeros is unchecked. If the dimension is 15.500 units, for instance, deselecting this check box will change it to 15.5 units, whereas deselecting it will change 15.000 units to 15. Similarly, when the check box labeled Display Leading Zeros is deactivated, the display of leading zeros in the decimal dimensions is suppressed.

For instance, if the dimension is 0.800 units, then unchecking this option will change it to.800. Click on the **arrow** that is located next to the **Sheet Settings** tool in the Navigation Bar and Display Settings. This will allow you to make changes to the sheet settings for the current drawing. The flyout for the Sheet Settings can now be seen. In this flyout, you can change the sheet size of the active design by choosing the desired sheet size from the cascading menu located under the Sheet Size heading. You can also toggle the display of the drawing border and title block in the drawing by utilizing the checkboxes of the flyout that are labeled Display Border and Display Title Block. Either one of these features may be turned on or off.

Editing and inserting a New Title Block

Fusion 360 (Fusion) provides users with two primary process options for the creation of individualized Title Blocks. The first option is to make the Title Block in Fusion itself, and the second option is to make the Title Block in AutoCAD and then import it into Fusion. If you do not have access to AutoCAD or are not familiar with how to use it, your best bet is to go with the first choice, which is to create the model from inside Fusion. The second option, "**Create in AutoCAD,**" is intended for those of us who already own AutoCAD and are proficient in its use.

The first step in getting started with any of these options is the same. Proceed with the Following Steps.

It is not required to establish a Project, but it is advised that you do so since it will include your templates and other corporate requirements. It is also advised that before you start, you doodle on a piece of paper what you want the **Title Block** to look like, what information is needed, and what information is optional. This should be done before you start the actual project.

1. Launch a **new drawing template**.

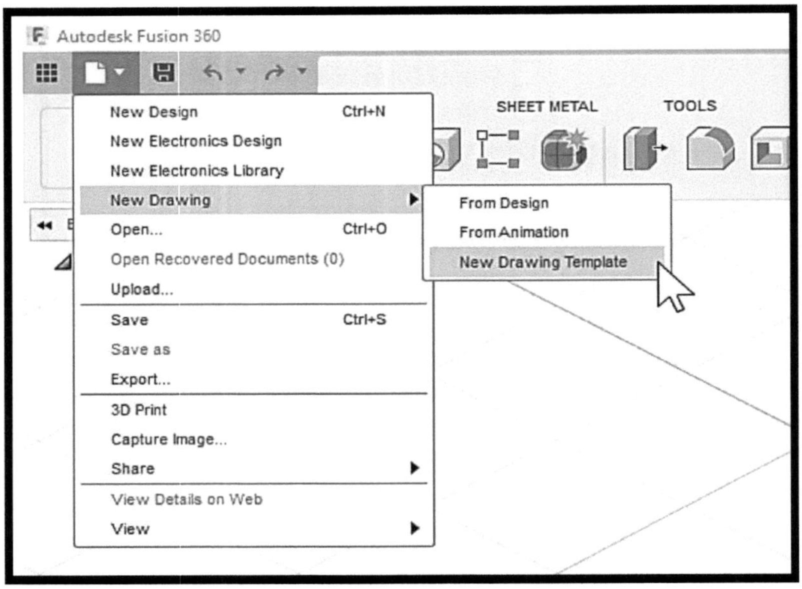

2. Choose "**From Scratch**" as your starting point, then choose the standard, units, and paper size.

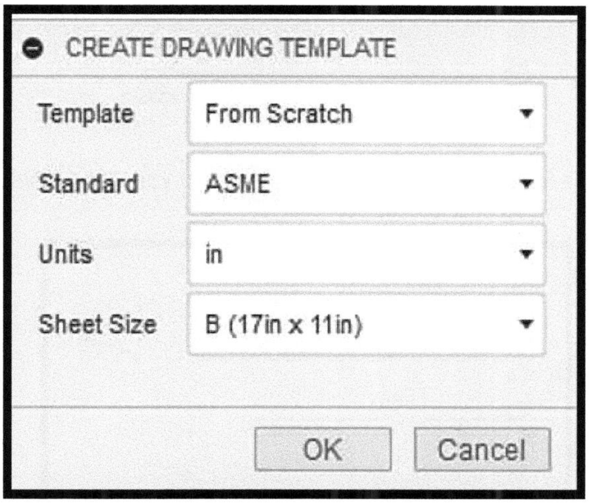

3. Choose "**Add Title Block**" from the menu that appears at the bottom of the screen.

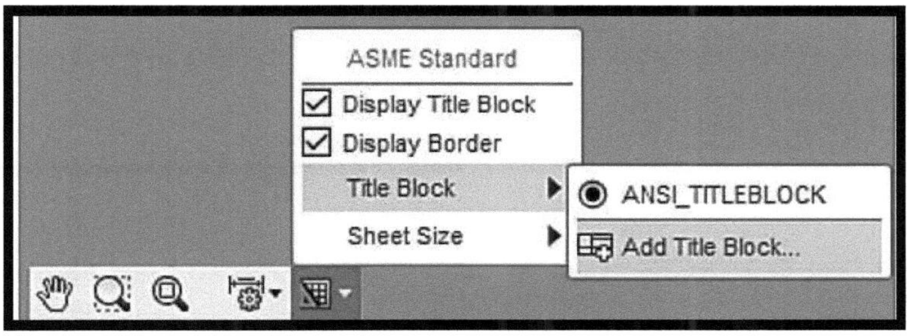

4. You now have a choice between the following three options:

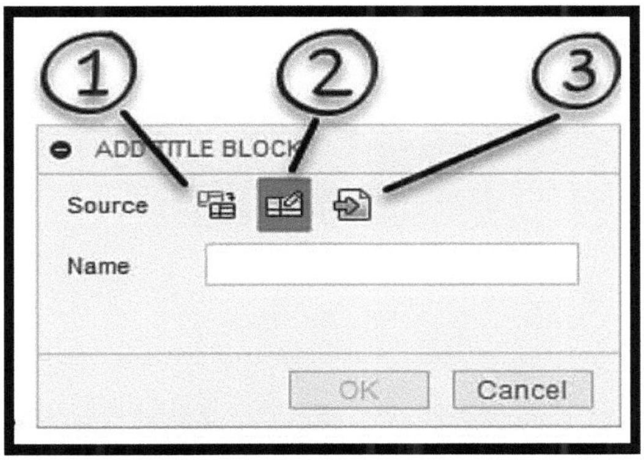

a) From Existing
   - Create Title Block from an existing one
b) From Scratch
   - Create a brand-new Title Block from scratch
c) From DWG File

- Import from an AutoCAD DWG

On Fusion 360

1. Choose Option 2 (from the list above), and provide a name for your Title Block.

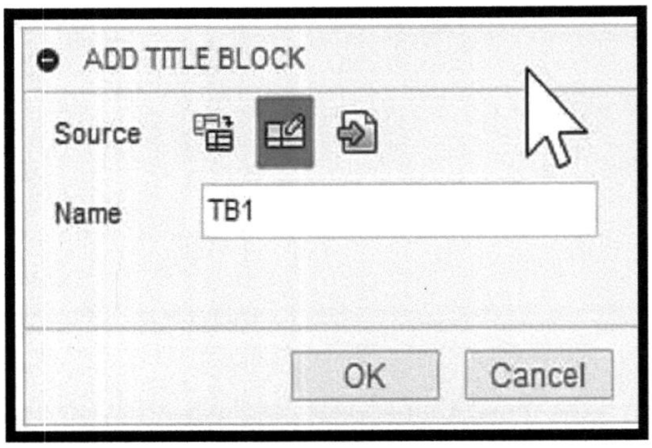

To build the Title Block, Fusion will provide you with fundamental drawing and editing tools, such as the geometry and Modify Panels.

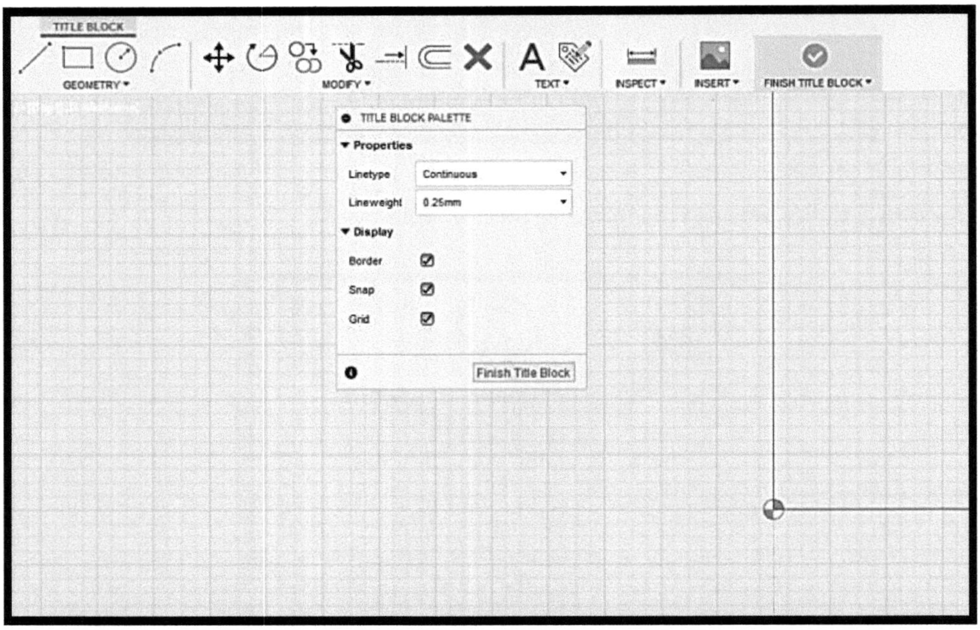

Since the built-in attribute names are already supplied, Attributes (Text Panel) are extremely simple to position (7 built-in attributes). You may also simply set new attributes to add extra data if you desire more information than what is supplied here, which is seven pieces of information.

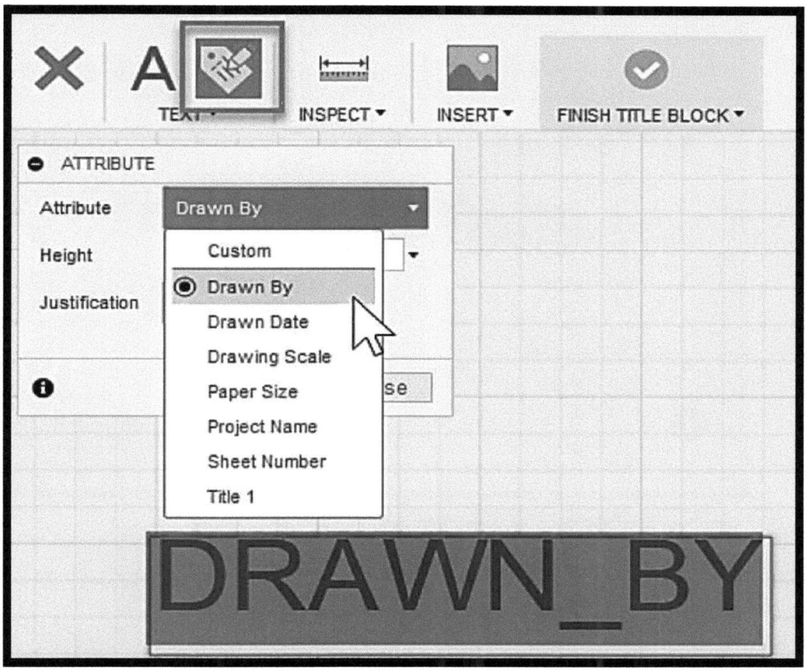

The following is a list of Fusion properties, along with the locations from which they are pulled. Because the majority of the properties are read only once when the drawing is constructed, the attribute value will not update automatically if you modify the model's title, project, or any other property. You will need to manually change the characteristics of the Title Blocks by double-clicking on each property (s).

(Insert frowny expression here) To complete the process of filling up custom attributes, just double-click on the attribute that is located in the Title Block.

- **TITLE 1**
  - This will retrieve the name that you gave the Fusion file when you stored it.
- **SHEET**
  - This will include the sheet number as well as the total number of sheets (1/3, 2/3, 3/3... according to this format).
- **PROJECT**
  - Whenever you save a file, it will do so inside a folder designated for the project. This will get the name of the project folder. Therefore, give careful consideration to how you arrange your data, and if you want all caps, you must enter the name of the project folder using all caps.
- **SIZE**
  - The sheet size of the template will be retrieved as a result of this action.
- **SCALE**
  - This will bring in the scale that was used for the initial view as well as how you entered the scale (1:1, 1/1, 1...) Additionally, if you alter the scale after the first view has been inserted and you want this property to update, you will need to double-click on the Title Block and choose "Reset Attributes." This will cause the attribute to be updated.

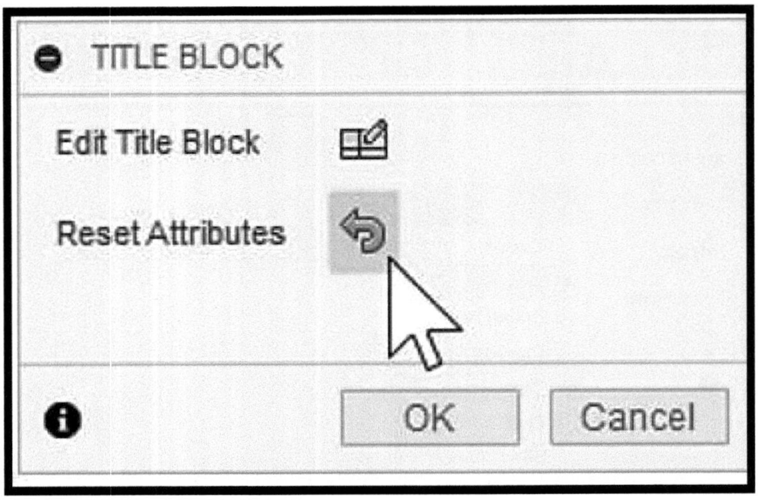

- **DRAWN DATE**
    - The time at which the drawing was produced.
- **DRAWN BY**
    - Brings in the information from your Autodesk profile, which is located in the top right corner of the screen.

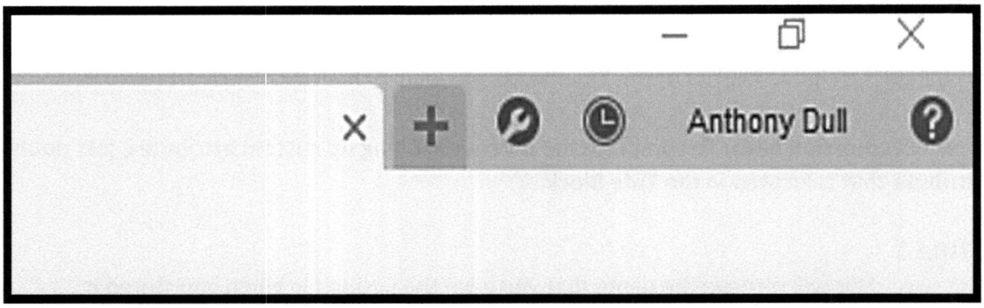

The inability to precisely draw geometry while simultaneously adding dimensions during the process of constructing a Title Block in Fusion is a significant source of frustration. After you have drawn a line, rectangle, circle, or arc, the only way to go back and measure what you have drawn is to use the Inspect command, which is located on the **Inspect Panel**. To make the necessary adjustments to the size, you would have to drag the snap points. I don't see any reason why the same feature that you have in the sketch environment couldn't exist here, making it possible for you to put dimensions as you draw to precisely plan and create the Title Block. If you start by using the rectangle command, for instance, there is no indication of the real dimensions of the rectangle that has been created. You run the risk of drawing the rectangle at a size that is one hundred times larger than it should be. At the very least, the line, circle, and arc commands provide a visual representation of the size of the drawing you are creating. Therefore, if you decide to design your Title Block using this method, you should begin with the line command so that you may have an estimate of how large the picture will be.

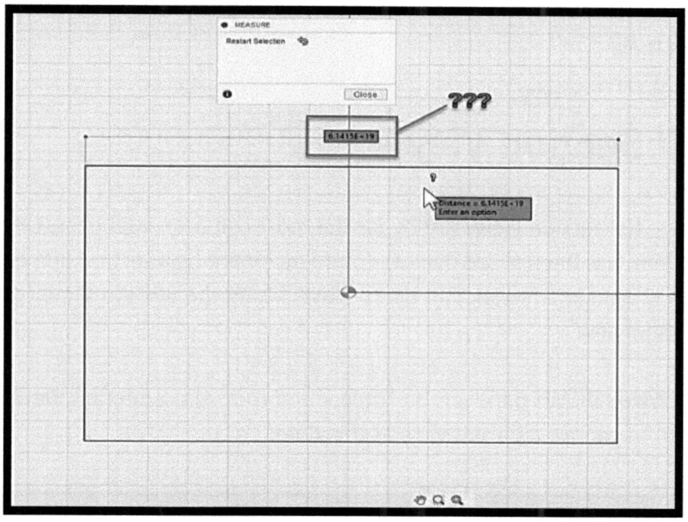

Modifying Title Blocks

To edit an existing Title Block, just pick the Title Block, right-click on it, and choose "**Edit Title Block**" from the context menu that appears. You have successfully navigated back into the area used to create Title Blocks, where you may now make the alterations, you need.

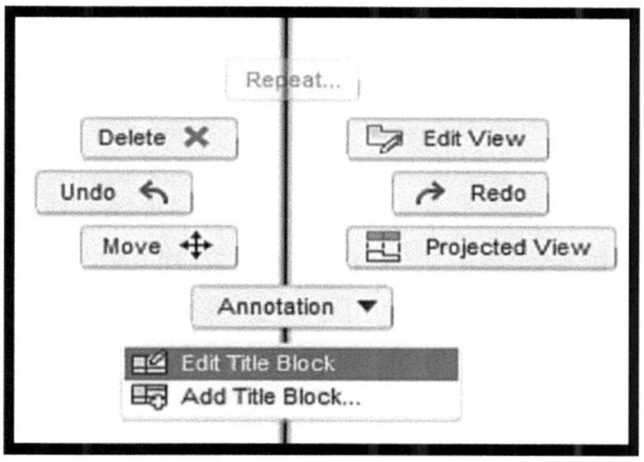

Creating Section Views

To create a section view of an item, first, the object must be sliced through using either an imaginary cutting plane or a section line, and then the object must be seen in a direction that is normal to the section line. The interior characteristics of an item may be more easily understood when shown in a section view. In addition to this, it lessens the number of lines that are used for concealed details, makes it simpler to determine the dimensions of interior elements, reveals cross-sections, and so on.

By using the Section View tool inside Fusion 360, users can generate the following section view kinds.

- Full Section View

- Half Section View
- Offset Section View
- Aligned Section View

Creating Full Section Views

In engineering drawings, full section views are by far the most common kind of section view to be utilized. It is presumed that an item has been sliced over its complete length by a section line or an imagined cutting plane when the object is seen in a full section perspective. Using the Section View tool in Fusion 360, you can generate a full section view.

1. Navigate to the **DRAWING VIEWS** panel of the Toolbar and choose the **Section View tool** from inside that panel. You will be asked to choose a parent view at this time.

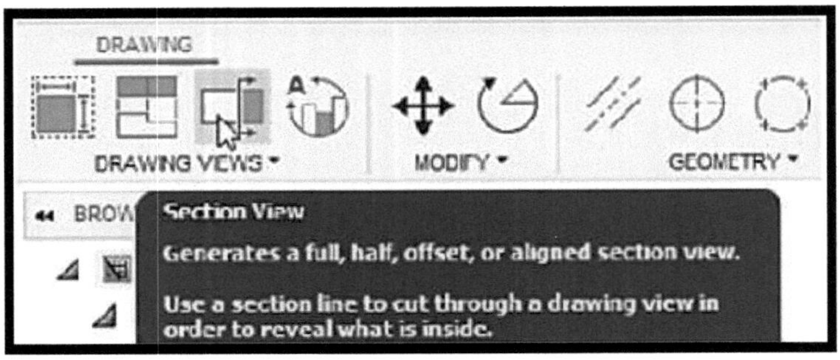

2. Choose an existing drawing view to serve as the parent for the section view that you are building. You will see that the cursor now has an arrow connected to it, and you will be invited to choose the beginning point of the section line. Additionally, a DRAWING VIEW dialog box will be shown.
3. Specify the place at which the section line should begin by clicking there. Note that the object snap tracking line, which appears when you move the cursor away from an object snap point of the parent view, may be used to set the start point. This happens when you move the cursor away from the object's snap point. After the starting point has been specified, the section line will appear in such a way that the arrow pointing to its conclusion will be tied to the pointer. In addition, the termination of the section line will be requested of you to be specified.
4. Specify the endpoint of the section line by clicking the button. Another segment of the section line is now connected to the cursor, and you are requested to either hit **ENTER** to finish creating the section line or define the next point on the section line by clicking the button that appears next to the prompt. You may make a section line in Fusion 360 by setting numerous points one after the other in the order that you want them to appear.
NOTE: To produce a complete section view, you will need to provide the beginning and ending points of the section line in such a way that it travels the whole length of the object. Only then will you be able to generate the view.
5. To finish creating the section line, press the **Enter** key on your keyboard. You will be invited to specify its location in the drawing sheet when the preview of the section view displays tied to the pointer.
NOTE: The section view will automatically maintain a horizontal or vertical alignment to the section line. This alignment may be turned off if desired. Simply using the **SHIFT** key will allow you to disrupt the

alignment of the section view. If you want to restore the horizontal or vertical alignment of the section view, you may do so by pressing the **SHIFT** key once again.
6. Using the mouse, establish the point of placement for the section view in the drawing sheet by clicking. Using the DRAWING VIEW dialog box, you may, after establishing the location for the section view, define the appearance, scale, and visibility of tangent edges in the section view. This is done after defining the placement for the section view.
Objects to Cut: A list of the bodies that will be cut is shown in the **Objects to Cut** rollout of the DRAWING VIEW dialog box. This rollout is part of the **DRAWING VIEW** dialog box. When you create a section view of a component, it will only show the single body that you specified.
When you create the section view of an assembly, on the other hand, it shows a list of all the bodies that are included in the section cut. You may choose to exclude bodies like fasteners from the section cut by clearing the check boxes that appear in front of the bodies in this rollout.
7. In the DRAWING VIEW dialog box, choose the **Default** option, and then click the **OK** button to confirm your selection. The view of the segment is being produced. The first picture below shows a section view of a component, while the second picture shows a section view of an assembly, however, the Jaw Screw component was not included in the section cut for this picture.

Note: The viewing direction may be inferred from the orientation of the arrows on the section line.

Creating Half-Section Views

A half-section view is produced by slicing through an item with an imagined cutting plane or section line that runs through the middle of a drawing view or the middle of a segment of the view. Using the Section View tool in Fusion 360, you can generate a half-section view of your model.

The steps below will show how to generate a half-section view:

1. In the toolbar's DRAWING VIEWS panel, choose the **Section View tool** from the available options. You will be asked to choose a parent view at this time.

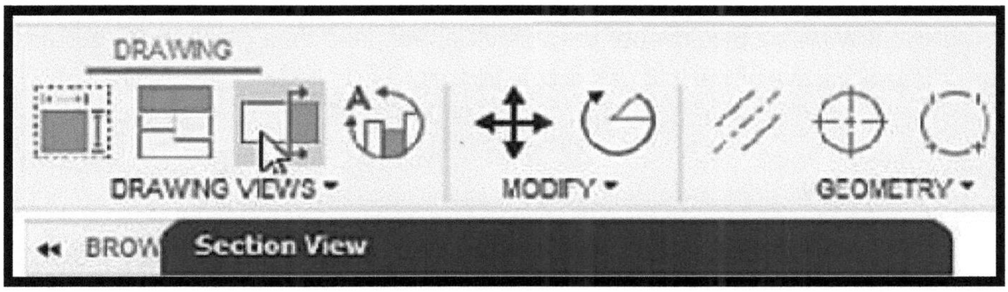

2. Choose an existing drawing view to serve as the parent for the section view that you are building. You will see that the cursor now has an arrow connected to it, and you will be invited to choose the beginning point of the section line. Additionally, a DRAWING VIEW dialog box will be shown.
3. Specify the place at which the section line should begin by clicking. It is important to keep in mind that the object snap tracking line, which appears whenever the pointer is moved away from an object snap point

in the parent view, may be used to designate the starting point. After the starting point has been specified, the section line will appear in such a way that the arrow pointing to its conclusion will be tied to the pointer.
4. In the drawing view, choose the location where you want the first segment of the section line to terminate by clicking on it. You are asked to either identify the next point of the section line or hit **ENTER** to halt the development of the section line once the second segment of the section line appears tied to the cursor.
5. Specify the endpoint of the section line that is located outside the drawing view by clicking the button. The cursor now has what looks to be the third segment of the section line linked to it.
6. To finish creating the section line, press the **ENTER** key. You will get a preview of the half-section view linked to the cursor, and you will be invited to choose a location for it on the drawing page.

NOTE: The section view will automatically keep the horizontal or vertical alignment to the section line as the default setting. Simply using the **SHIFT** key will allow you to disrupt the alignment of the section view. If you want to restore the horizontal or vertical alignment of the section view, you may do so by pressing the **SHIFT** key once again.

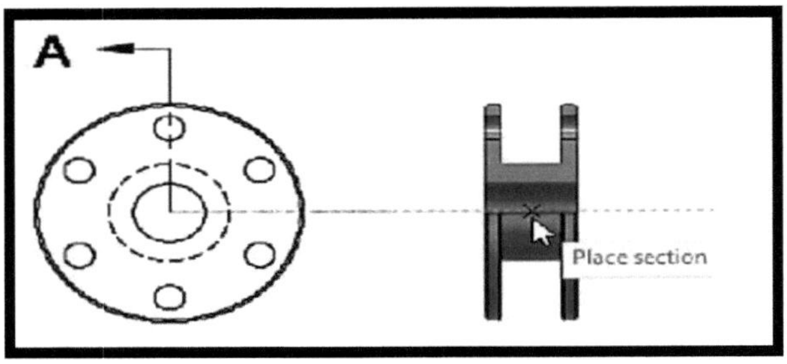

7. Use the mouse to choose the location at which the placement point for the section view in the drawing sheet will be defined. Using the DRAWING VIEW dialog box, you may, after establishing the location for the section view, define the appearance, scale, and visibility of tangent edges in the section view. This is done after defining the placement for the section view.
NOTE: If you are creating the section view of an assembly, you can also define the bodies to be included or excluded from the section cut by using the **Objects To Cut** rollout of the DRAWING VIEW dialog box. This is useful when determining which bodies should be included or excluded from the section cut.
8. In the DRAWING VIEW dialog box, choose the Default option, and then click the **OK** button to confirm your selection. The perspective of the half part is constructed.

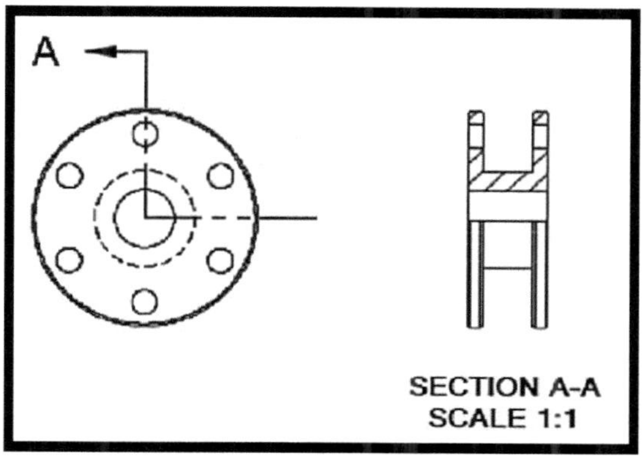

Creating Offset Section Views

You may generate an offset section view by jogging or bending the imaginary cutting plane or section line in such a way that it cuts the piece of the object that cannot be sectioned along a straight line. This creates a view that is offset from the normal section view. By using the Section View tool inside Fusion 360's interface, users can generate an offset section view.

The steps below are steps for creating an offset section view:

1. Navigate to the DRAWING VIEWS panel of the Toolbar and choose the **Section View tool** from inside that panel. You will be asked to choose a parent view at this time.
2. Choose an existing drawing view to serve as the parent for the section view that you are building. You will see that the cursor now has an arrow connected to it, and you will be invited to choose the beginning point of the section line. Additionally, a DRAWING VIEW dialog box will be shown.
3. Specify the place at which the section line should begin by clicking there. You will be asked to provide details on the terminus of the section line.
4. To designate the second point of the section line, click anywhere inside the drawing view.
5. In the drawing view, click where you want the third point of the section line to be specified.
6. Specify the fourth point of the section line outside the drawing view by clicking the associated button.
7. To complete the addition of section lines, you must now press the **ENTER** key. A preview of the offset section view shows as an attachment to the cursor when the jogging section line has been successfully formed.
8. Use the mouse to choose the location at which the placement point for the section view in the drawing sheet will be defined. Note that by hitting the **SHIFT** key, you may toggle between keeping the horizontal or vertical alignment of the section view and breaking it. This can be done in either direction.
9. In the DRAWING VIEW dialog box, accept the default choices, and then click on the **OK** button. It is determined to produce the offset section view.

Creating Aligned Section Views

After cutting an object with the section line, which consists of two lines that are not parallel to one another, and then straightening the cross-section by rotating it around the center point of the section line, one can produce an aligned section view. This is accomplished by cutting the object using the section line. By using the **Section View tool**, you will be able to produce an aligned section view. The process for making an aligned section view is the same as the procedure for making a regular section view; the only difference is that to make an aligned section view, you need to make a section line that has two-line segments that are not parallel to one another.

Creating Detail Views

The purpose of a detail view is to magnify a specific section of an existing drawing view and display it to the viewer. Using the **Detail View tool**, you may create a border to designate the area of an existing drawing view that will be expanded so that you can then expand that view.

The following is an explanation of the process for making a detail view:

1. Locate the **DRAWING VIEWS** panel in the toolbar and choose the Detail View tool from that panel. You will be asked to choose a parent view at this time.

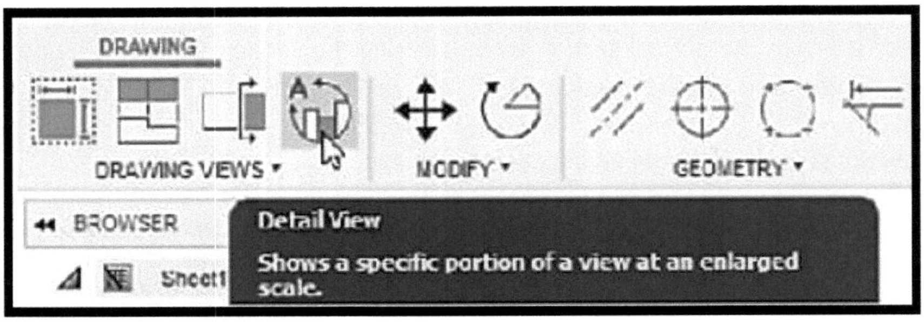

2. Choose an existing drawing view to serve as the parent of the detail view that you will create. You will be asked to identify the point that is directly in the middle of the detail border. Additionally, a DRAWING VIEW dialog box will be shown. Take note that the section of the drawing view that will be magnified may be determined by the detail border.
3. Specify by clicking where the center point of the detail border will be located. By pressing the left button of the mouse, you will be allowed to choose the size of the detail border.
4. Using the mouse, determine the size of the border by clicking. A sneak peek of the expanded image of the section that is included inside the border is appended to the pointer as it moves across the screen.
5. Using the mouse, choose the location at which the placement points for the detail view in the drawing sheet will be defined.
6. In the Scale area of the dialog box, indicate the percentage by which the detail view should be increased. Within the dialog box, you also can define several additional aspects of the detail view.
7. In the dialogue box, choose the **OK** option to proceed. The creation of the detail view has begun.

NOTE: If you adjust the boundaries of a detail view, the view will be dynamically changed once you save your changes. To achieve this, click on the edge of the screen, and the grips will appear. Utilizing these grips will allow you to modify the boundaries. To modify the location of the boundary, for example, click on the center grip of the border, and then click the left mouse button to designate the new location of the boundary on the drawing view. Similarly, to adjust the size of the border by expanding or contracting it, click on a grip that appears along the boundary, and then click again to designate its new location.

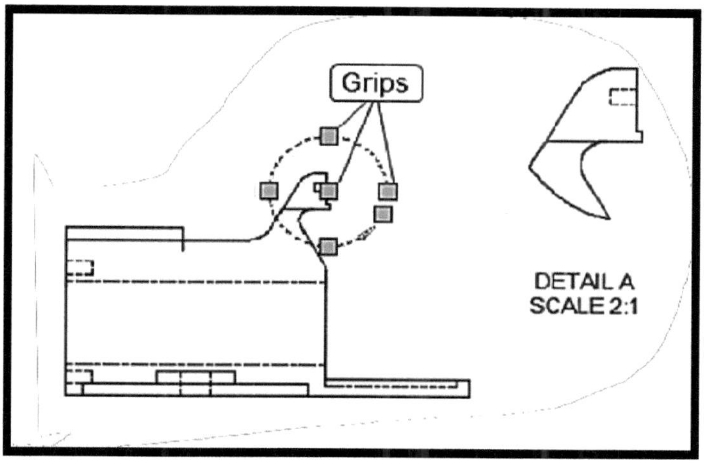

Creating an Exploded Drawing View

Using the Basis View tool in Fusion 360, it is also possible to generate an exploded drawing view of an assembly as the base view for the assembly.

The procedure for producing an exploded view is described below:

1. In the DRAWING VIEWS panel of the Toolbar, choose the **Base View** tool and click on it. The DRAWING VIEW dialog box is brought into view.
2. In the dialog box, choose the Representation option from the drop-down list. The ANIMATION workspace displays a list of all the storyboards that have been generated there.

NOTE: If the animation storyboards for the assembly have not been developed in the ANIMATION workspace, then this drop-down list will just have the Model option.
3. Select a storyboard from the drop-down list labeled "**Representation**" in the dialog box. This storyboard should show an exploded representation of the assembly. Attached to the pointer is a glimpse of the exploded view that was built for the specified storyboard in the ANIMATION workspace.
4. Using the mouse, locate the location at which the exploded view should be placed on the drawing page, and click on it. In the next step, use the DRAWING VIEW dialog box to define the attributes of the exploding view. These properties include orientation, style, and scale.
5. Select the **OK** button with your mouse. A basic view of the assembly in the form of an exploded design is first made in the sheet of drawings.

Creating Break Views

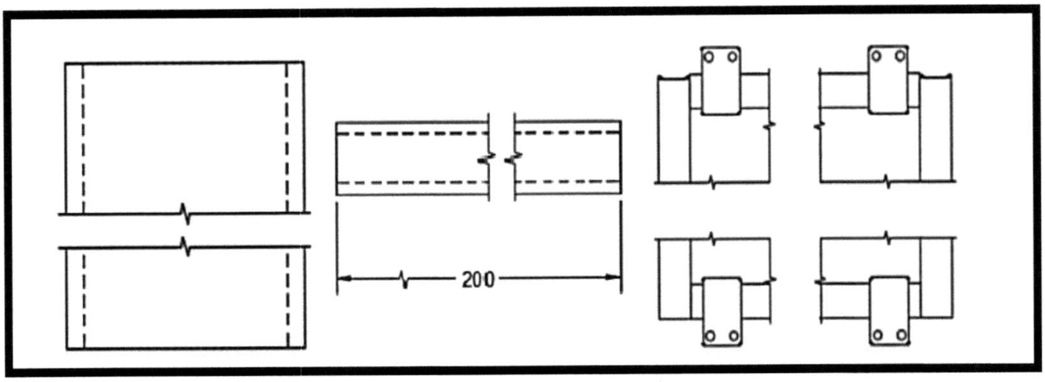

You may show long or tall components as a broken view by using the **Break View** command in the Drawing workspace of Fusion 360. This command allows you to display long or tall parts. You can break base views, projected views, and segment views. An existing drawing view may be shortened using a technique known as "**broken view**," which involves cutting away a piece of the design and highlighting the area of the drawing that has been removed. By making use of broken views, it is possible to present the drawing view at a bigger scale on a drawing sheet that is of a lower size. You may break the view in other situations as well, such as when the component view has extensive portions of geometry that cannot be characterized. For instance, you may be required to annotate both ends of a shaft, even if the piece of the shaft in the middle does not include any characteristics. You are free to include view breaks anywhere you choose throughout the whole of the component's length. Additionally, many breaks may be used inside a single drawing view if desired. Any breaks that are present in the parent view will be immediately inherited by any projected child views. In ASME drawings, dimension lines that pass through a broken view are updated with a break symbol to match the view break lines. This is done when both points of the dimension line are located outside of the region that was removed by the break. You are responsible for defining the direction of the break, which may be either vertical or horizontal, as well as the beginning and ending locations of the break and the width of the space that will be left between the remaining portions of the picture.

Break a view

- Choose **Create > Break View**. The dialog box for Break View appears.
- To break the view, click it.
- Choose the break's orientation in the Break View box.
    - Horizontal
    - Vertical

Note: Based on the length and height of the view, the Orientation is chosen automatically.

- **Decide on a Start Point**. The break will start at the beginning of a line.
- **Decide on an End Point**. The conclusion of the break is indicated with a line.
- You may optionally give a measurement for the space between the two remaining portions.
- You may choose to repeat the process to create more breaks.
- Click **OK**.

The portion between the supplied start and finish points is missing from the shown chosen view. More break symbols are shown on longer break lines.

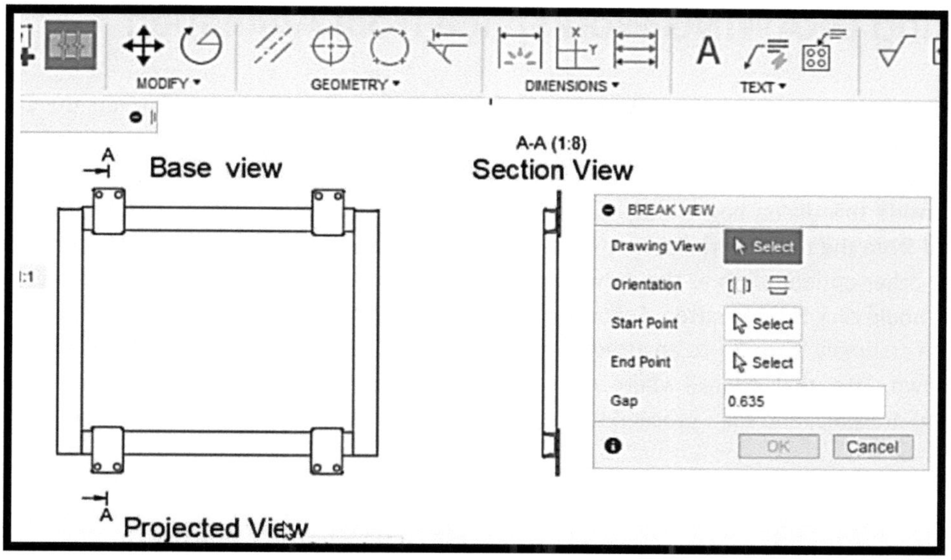

Edit a break in a view

Edit a break in one of the following ways:

Use the Broken View Edit dialog

1. In the broken view, double-click any of the break symbols on the sheet to go to that view. The Broken View Edit dialog is what you see at this point.
2. Make the required adjustments to the break using the Broken View Edit dialog located in the View menu. If you modify either the beginning or the ending point, the whole view will remain uninterrupted, allowing you to choose a new starting or ending point for the break.
Please take note that it is not possible to alter the direction of an existing break. To switch the direction in which a break is placed, you must first erase the break and then create a new break.
3. Click OK.
The chosen view appears beside the newly created break.

Drag the break lines

- Move any of the break lines to a new position on the screen by dragging them. When you let go of the mouse button, a new break will be generated.
- To see more of the scene, you may expand it by dragging one of the break lines past the other break line.

Tip: Click the break line, and then click and drag the break line grips to lengthen the break line. This will make the break line more visible.

Invoking DRAWING Workspace from Animation

In addition to this, you may generate an exploded view of an assembly by calling up the DRAWING workspace and selecting the option to Work from Animation. When you pick the From Animation option, the ANIMATION Workspace is activated, and the CREATE DRAWING dialog box is shown. The choices included inside this dialog box are identical to those that were covered before. Choose the necessary storyboard from the drop-down list located in the dialog box's Storyboard section, and then proceed to define the other options, such as the drawing template, the standard, the units, and the sheet size. After that, you should click the OK button. Following the activation of the DRAWING environment, the exploded view of the assembly is shown as an attachment to the cursor. Additionally, a DRAWING VIEW dialog box will be shown. After that, choose where you want the exploded view to appear on the drawing sheet by clicking and dragging, and then proceed to click the **OK** button on the dialog box. The exploded image is made.

Editing Properties of a Drawing View

After establishing a drawing view in Fusion 360, you can adjust its parameters, including the orientation, style, size, and visibility of tangent edges, among other things. To do this, double-click on a drawing view in the menu. The DRAWING VIEW dialog box is brought into view. You can make changes to the characteristics of the currently chosen drawing view by utilizing this dialog box. It is important to take note that any changes made to the properties of the parent view will result in corresponding changes being made to the characteristics of the projected views. However, if you update the characteristics of a projected view, the properties of the parent view do not reflect any of the changes you make to the properties of the projected view.

Editing Hatch Properties of a Section View

After establishing a section view in Fusion 360, you can make changes to the default hatching settings of that view, including the hatch pattern, scale factor, and hatch angle. To do this, double-click anywhere on the section view's hatch pattern that has to be modified. A dialog window labeled **HATCH** will now display.

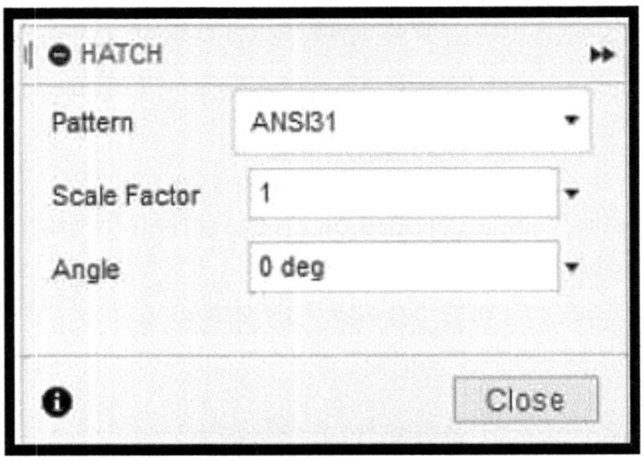

The desired hatch pattern may be selected from the drop-down list labeled Pattern that is located inside the dialog box. The Scale Factor area is where the needed scale factor is entered, and the Angle field is where the angle of the hatch pattern is entered. Both of these fields are utilized to provide the appropriate scale factor. After making changes to the properties of the chosen hatch, you may leave the dialog box by clicking the Close button when you are finished. The characteristics of each hatch may also be edited or modified similarly.

Moving a Drawing View

After putting a drawing view in the drawing sheet in Fusion 360, you have the option to either use the Move tool or the drawing view's grip to move it to a new place inside the drawing sheet. This new position may then be defined.

The process of shifting a drawing view is described in more detail down below:

1. Either hit the **M** key on your keyboard or click the Move tool located in the **MODIFY** panel of the Toolbar. The MOVE dialog box will now show up. In addition, you will be asked to choose which drawing views should be shifted.
2. Choose the drawing view that you want to move. When using the Point-to-Point tool, the dialog box will display a section labeled "**Transform**." You have the option of moving either a single or numerous drawing views at once.

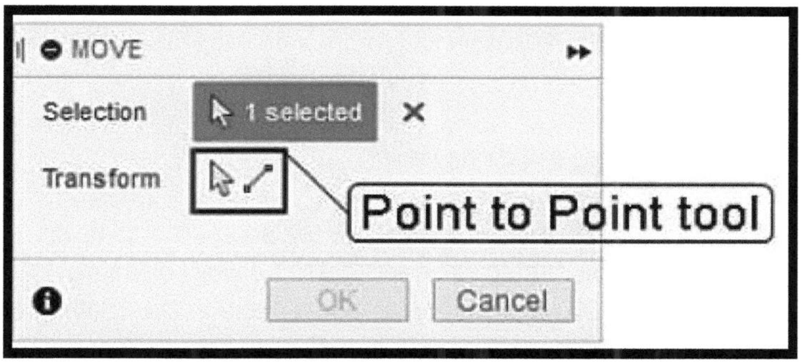

3. Once you have chosen the drawing view or views to work with, click the Point-to-Point tool that is located in the Transform section of the dialog box. You will be asked to select a base point at this time. Take note that the base point functions as a reference point when shifting the drawing view that has been chosen (s).
4. Specify a starting position by clicking the button. You are going to be asked to identify the placement point for the drawing view or views that you have chosen. Additionally, the preview of the chosen view(s) will follow the pointer as it moves about.
5. Specify the second point in the drawing area as the placement point by clicking on it in the drawing area. The drawing view(s) that have been chosen are transferred to the position that has been defined inside the drawing sheet.

NOTE: If you move a drawing view, the related geometries, such as dimensions, centerlines, or section lines, will also move along with the drawing view. These geometries include section lines, centerlines, and dimensions.

You also have the option of moving a drawing view by gripping it and moving it that way. To do this, click the left mouse button and then choose the drawing view that you want to move. The drawing view has been brought into focus, and its grasp has been shown. After that, choose the drawing view's grip by clicking on it. You will be requested to choose the placement point when the preview of the drawing view is tied to the cursor and you move it around. Simply clicking will allow the placement location on the drawing page to be specified. The currently chosen drawing view gets relocated to the place that you specify.

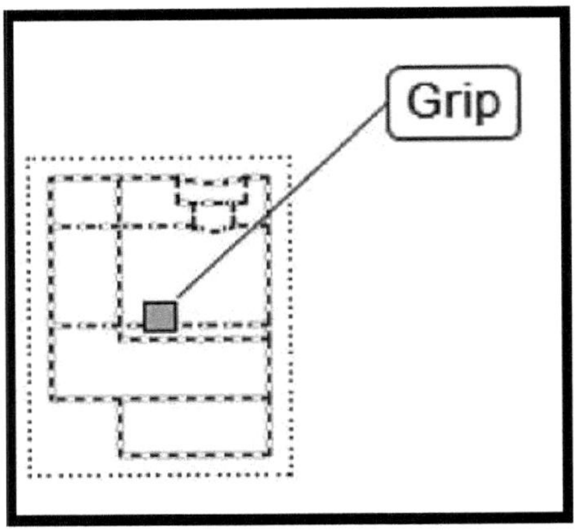

Rotating a Drawing View

By using the **Rotate tool** inside Fusion 360, users can rotate a drawing view in two-dimensional space at whatever angle they want.

Following is the procedure for rotating a drawing view:

1. Navigate to the **MODIFY** panel in the Toolbar and choose the Rotate tool to begin. You will be asked to choose which drawing views should be rotated when the ROTATE dialog box opens. You may also open the ROTATE dialog box by selecting MODIFY from the drop-down menu in the Toolbar, and then select the **Rotate** tool from the drop-down menu that appears.
2. Choose a drawing view to rotate before beginning the process. When you use the Rotate tool, the dialog box includes a section labeled "Transform." You have the option of rotating a single drawing view or numerous drawing views at once.
3. After choosing one or more drawing views, go to the Transform section of the dialog box and click on the **Rotate** tool there. You will be asked to select a base point at this time. Take note that the base point functions as a reference or center point when rotating the drawing view(s) that has been chosen.
4. Specify the position of the base point by clicking. You will then be invited to enter the rotational angle in the Angle field that has appeared in the dialog box. Additionally, a preview of the drawing view(s) that have been chosen is connected to the pointer.
5. In the Angle area of the dialog box, enter a rotational angle value and then click the ***OK*** button to confirm your entry. Clicking anywhere in the drawing area will also work as an alternative method for determining the rotational angle. The drawing view(s) that have been chosen are rotated inside the drawing sheet according to the rotational angle that has been set.

Deleting a Drawing View

To remove an existing drawing view, first, open the MODIFY drop-down menu located in the Toolbar, and then choose the Delete tool from the toolbar's toolbox. A box labeled DELETE appears in the dialogue. After that, choose the drawing view that will be discarded. You have the option of selecting a single drawing view or many drawing views. Click the **OK** button after you have chosen the drawing view you want to use. The drawing view that was chosen to be deleted is removed from the drawing sheet and is no longer included in the drawing. Note that you may pick drawing views to be erased either before or after running the Delete tool. This flexibility allows you to work more efficiently. Another option is to pick the drawing views that are to be removed and then hit the **DELETE** key to remove the views that have been chosen.

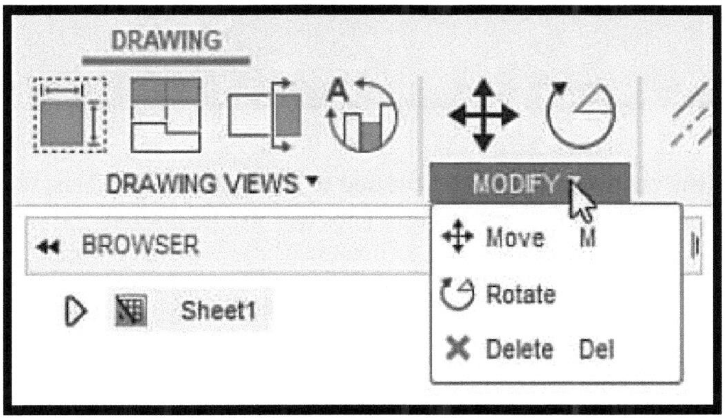

NOTE: If you remove a drawing view, the geometries connected with it, such as dimensions, centerlines, or section lines, will also be destroyed. This is because removing a drawing view deletes all related geometries. Furthermore, if you delete a parent view, all of the dependent views, such as section views and detail views, will also be removed from the tree. Despite this, the projected views will still be accessible on the drawing sheet even after the parent view has been deleted.

Adding Geometries in Drawing Views

Following the creation of the drawing views of an item, the next step in determining geometric connections is to include geometries such as centerlines, center markings, and center mark patterns. For instance, the center marks in the drawing views are used for identifying the center of the rounded or circular edges, and the centerlines are used for identifying the center between two lines or edges representing hole features in the drawing views. Additionally, the center marks in the drawing views are used to identify the center of the rounded or circular edges.

Adding Centerlines

This tool will put a center line between any two lines, regardless of whether or not those lines are parallel to one another. Clicking on the two lines while using the Centerline tool, which can be found in the Centerlines panel of the Annotate tab, will create a centerline.The chosen lines will have the center line inserted into the gap between them automatically. If the lines are intersecting, then the center line will pass through the angle bisector of the lines, as illustrated in the graphic below. If the lines are not crossing, then the angle bisector will not be involved.

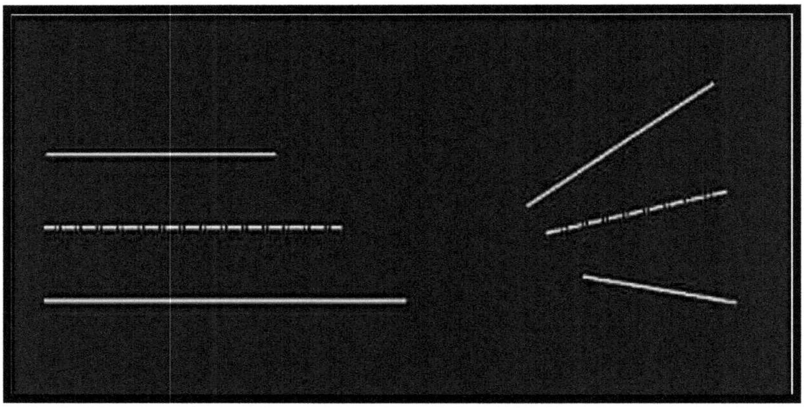

If this is the case, then the center line will also continue to be linked to their lines; however, if the location or orientation of the lines is altered, then the center lines will also be altered.

Changing properties of center lines

Using system variables, it is possible to alter the characteristics of these center lines and the center mark. These characteristics include the linetype, the linetype scale, and the linewidth. You might also try using the CHPROP command as an alternative. For illustration purposes, I will alter the linetype scale as well as the linewidth for the existing center line. On the command line, start by typing CHPROP and pressing enter. After that, choose the center line and hit enter once more. You will see that the command line now displays a variety of choices that are associated with the middle line.

Choose **Lweight** from the menu that appears below the command line, then type 1 and hit enter. Repeatedly selecting **ltScale** from the command line and then modifying its value to 1.5 will increase the **linetype** spacing which is 1.5 times more than the previous value. Simply accepting the settings and exiting the command requires you to press enter twice. You will see that the new attributes will be applied to the center line; however, to see it in the drawing area, you may first need to enable the lineweight option that is located in the status bar.

Adding Center Marks

You can pick this tool from the Centerlines panel of the Annotate tab to add a center mark to a circle or arc. After the cursor transforms into a Pickbox, all that needs to be done to finish the command is to click on the circle or arc and then hit **enter**. You will see that a default center mark has been added, and an example of this can be seen in the picture that follows.

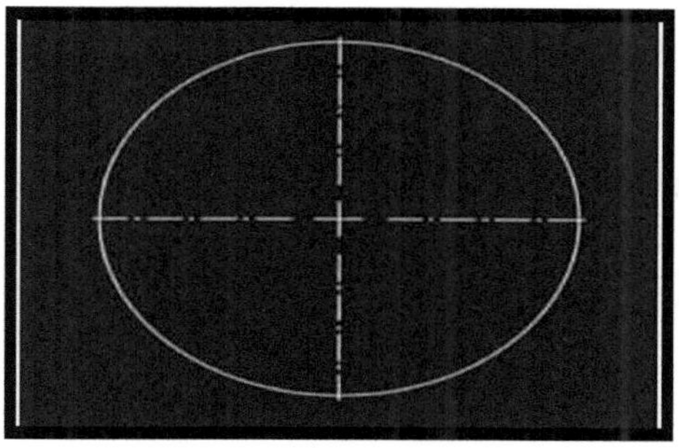

The center mark will, by default, extend throughout the whole of the circle's diameter; this behavior will be preserved, even if the circle's radius is altered. When the radius of this circle is altered using the grips or the properties palette, the size of the center mark will automatically adapt to match the newly determined parameters of the circle. Using the properties palette, you can make changes to the characteristics of this center mark. You may bring up the fast properties menu by doing a double click on the center mark. At the very bottom of the quick property's palette, you will discover an option that allows you to hide the extension line. To conceal the extension line from the center mark, you must first disable the display extension option by selecting "**No.**"

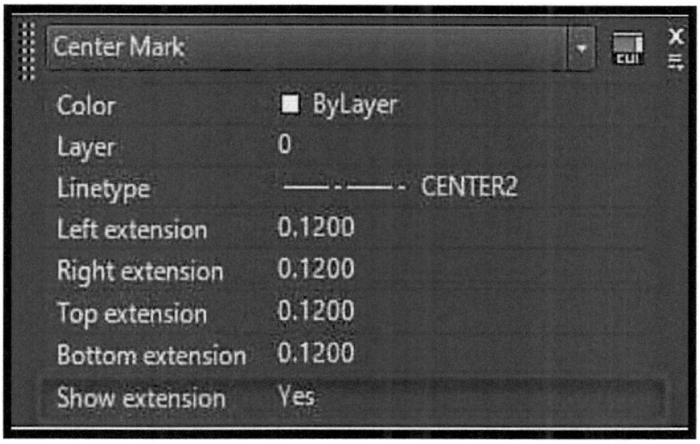

The centerline that is used by default goes beyond the diameter of the circle. You have the option of manually adjusting the grasp of the center mark or modifying the size of this extended length utilizing the fast properties panel.

Adding Center Mark Pattern

1. Choose **Geometry > Center Mark Pattern**.

Note: By default, the Auto-complete option is selected. When you click only one hole or rounded edge, the Center Mark Pattern is immediately generated. If you are unhappy with the outcomes of the automated creation, uncheck the option to build the Center Mark Pattern manually.

2. Pick a rounded edge or a hole.
3. Pick out more edges.
4. Choose the desired choices from the dialog.
5. Click **OK**.

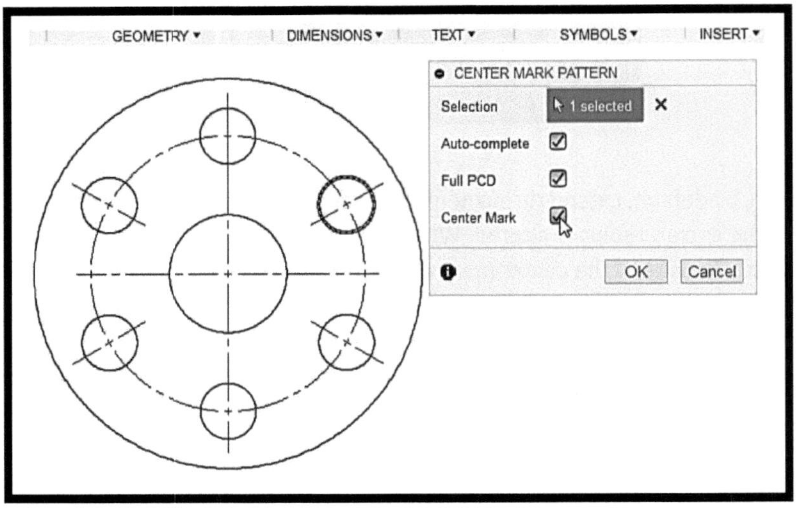

The center mark pattern for a slot must be created with a Reference Edge chosen.

1. Choose **Geometry > Center Mark Pattern**.
2. Remove the check mark next to Auto-complete.
3. Choose rounded edges.
4. In the window, click Select next to the Reference Edge.
5. Choose the reference edge.
6. Click **OK**.

After it is finished, the center mark design will still be connected with the edges that were chosen. As a direct consequence of this, the center mark pattern is automatically updated whenever there are modifications made to the model. For instance, if a hole is removed from the model, the center mark pattern will be updated properly during the drawing update by removing the center mark from the edge that corresponds to the hole that was removed. Note that the center mark pattern will not be updated even if a hole is added to the model; this is because the command does not provide feature detection. You will need to make some adjustments to the preexisting center mark design and include the edge. Double-clicking the pattern will bring up the editing options, from which you may choose the new hole to modify the center mark pattern.

The annotation associativity feature is supported by the center mark pattern, just as it is for current centerlines and center markings. As a result, you can link the center mark pattern to the dimensions, leaders, and symbols. When modifications are made to the model and/or the center mark pattern, any annotations that are linked with that pattern are likewise brought up to date automatically. If the center mark pattern is removed, any annotations that were previously connected with the center mark pattern will likewise be removed. Likewise, if all of the edges that were used to construct the center mark pattern on the drawing are removed from the model, then the center mark pattern will be removed from the drawing when the drawing is updated.

The following are some examples of typical circular and one-way rectangular center mark designs.

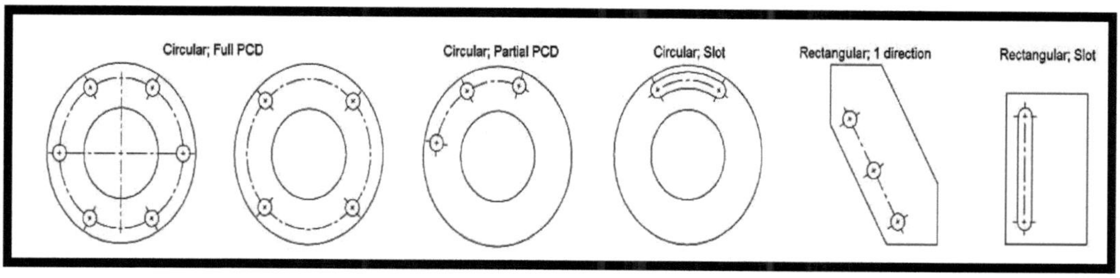

Adding Edge Extension between Two Intersecting Edges

By using the Edge Extension tool inside Fusion 360, users can apply edge extension between two crossing edges that are not parallel to one another. This device is used to show the extension as well as the junction of two edges that are not parallel to one another. In addition to that, it serves as a reference for determining appropriate dimensions. The following is the procedure for adding edge extension:

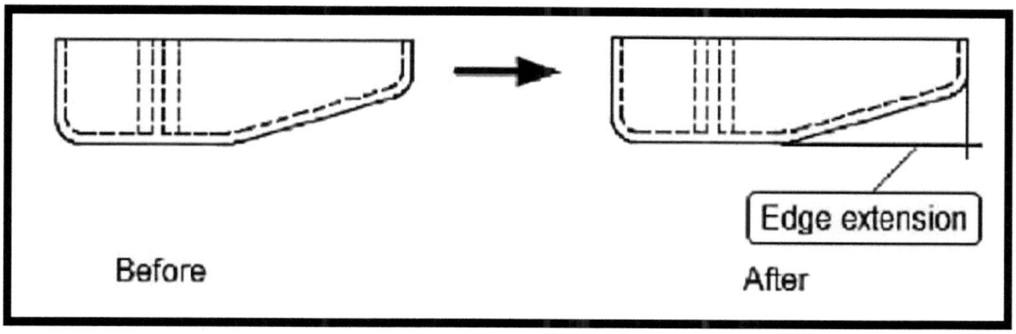

1. To use the tool, go to the **GEOMETRY** panel of the Toolbar and click on the **Edge Extension tool**. You will be asked to choose the first edge to proceed.

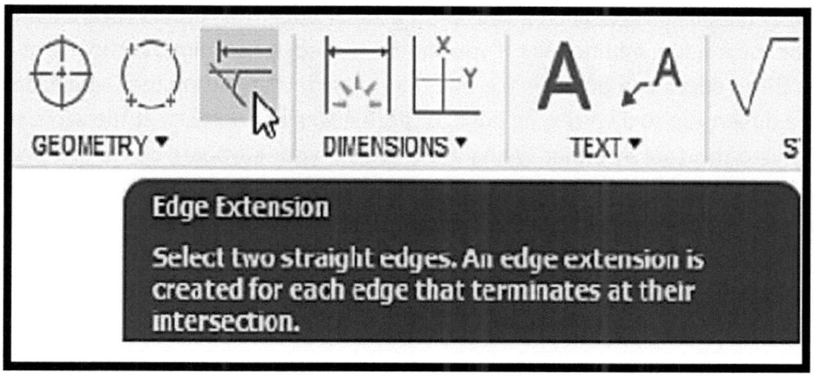

2. Using the mouse, choose the very first edge in the drawing view. You have been given the option to choose the second edge.
3. Using the mouse, choose the second edge of the drawing view that is not parallel by clicking on it. An extension of the edge is added in between the edges that were chosen. After that, you need to quit the **Edge Extension tool** by using the **ESC** key.

Applying Dimensions

It is necessary to apply dimensions to the different design views of a component or assembly that has been created once you have completed this step. The DIMENSIONS drop-down menu of the Toolbar in Fusion 360 gives users access to a variety of tools that may be used to apply different kinds of dimensions to their models.

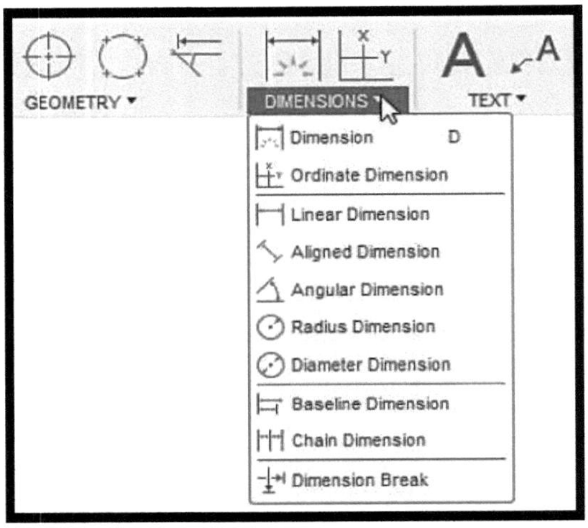

Applying Linear, Aligned, Angular, Radius, and Diameter Dimensions

When utilizing the Dimension tool in Fusion 360, you can apply many kinds of dimensions, including linear, aligned, angular, and radius dimensions. Depending on the kind of entity that is chosen, this tool is used to add dimension to the specified entity. For instance, the diameter dimension is applied if you pick a circular edge, and the linear dimension is applied if you select a linear edge. This occurs regardless of whether you select a circular or linear edge. Additionally, if you choose two edges or points/vertices, the dimension that applies between those edges and points is the one that is used. When using the Dimension tool, you may choose to apply a dimension to a vertex, an edge, or both edges and vertices at the same time. Take note that you may activate this tool by either typing the **D** key on your keyboard or clicking on the Dimension tool that is located in the Toolbar's **DIMENSIONS** panel. You also have the option to right-click anywhere in the drawing area, then pick **Dimensions > Dimension** from the Marking Menu that appears. This will have the same result. To apply a dimension, after activating the Dimension tool, choose either one edge, two edges, or two vertices from the available options. The dimension is bound to the cursor in a manner that varies according to the entity or entities that are chosen. Click to go to determine the placement point for the dimension in the design sheet. Note that after applying a dimension, the Dimension tool will stay enabled, and you will be able to apply the remaining dimensions in the drawing views one at a time.

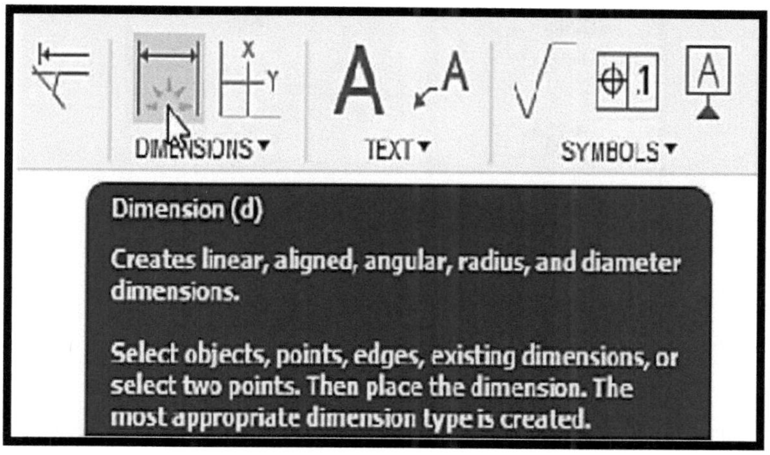

You can apply various types of dimensions by using the Dimension tool, but you can also apply individual dimensions by using the respective dimension tool that is available in the DIMENSION drop-down menu of the Toolbar. This allows you to apply individual dimensions in addition to applying various types of dimensions. For instance, you may apply linear dimensions by activating the **Linear Dimension tool**, and you can apply radius dimensions by activating the Radius Dimension tool. Both of these tools are located in the Dimensions folder.

Applying Ordinate Dimensions

1. Go to the **Dimensions** menu on the toolbar and pick **Ordinate Dimension**.
2. Using the mouse, position the origin point (0, 0) on a drawing view on the sheet by clicking.
3. Position the origin point leader by moving the mouse pointer to the desired location.
4. Position the leader of the origin point by clicking.
5. Decide on a point to use for the measurement.
6. Using the mouse cursor, place the ordinate dimension leader at the desired location.
7. To position the ordinate dimension leader, click the appropriate button.

Repeat steps 5 through 7 if you want to set more ordinate dimensions.

The dimensions will show up on the sheet, and they will have a connection to the geometry that they are measuring in the drawing view.

Align ordinate dimension leaders

1. After selecting a location to measure, move the mouse pointer over an existing ordinate dimension. An Object Snap displays.
2. While holding down the left mouse button, dragged the cursor in the desired direction to align the measurements. The dimension leader aligns itself with the dashed object tracking line that appears on the screen.

3. Position the ordinate dimension leader by clicking the corresponding button.

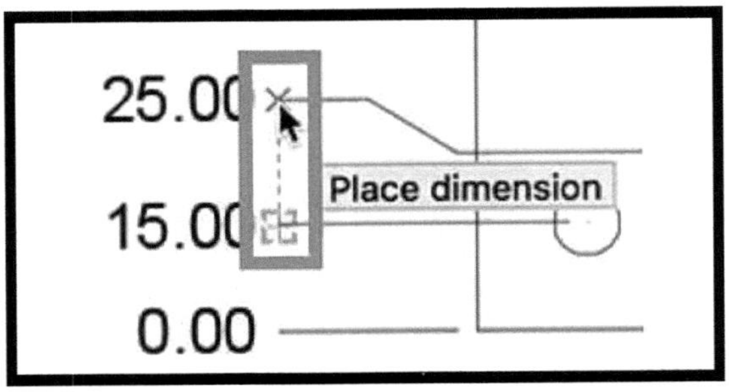

Applying Baseline Dimensions

Before you can utilize a linear or aligned dimension as a baseline, you will first need to establish one.

1. On the toolbar, go to the **Dimensions** menu and pick **Baseline Dimension**.
2. Choose the extension line of an existing linear or aligned dimension on the sheet to serve as the baseline for the measurement.
3. Choose a point to use as the starting point for the following dimension.
4. If you want to establish extra dimensions that are measured from the baseline, you may choose additional points to measure from.
5. Press **Enter**.

All of the dimensions that are shown on the page were measured concerning the baseline. The dimensions have some kind of connection to the geometry in the drawing view that they are measuring.

Applying Chain Dimensions

Before you can utilize a linear or aligned dimension as a baseline, you will first need to establish one.

1. On the toolbar, go to the **Dimensions** menu and pick **Baseline Dimension**.
2. Choose the extension line of an existing linear or aligned dimension on the sheet to serve as the beginning point for the next dimension.
3. Pick a second point to use as the starting point for the following dimension in the chain.
4. If you want to construct extra dimensions in the chain, you may choose additional points at this stage.
5. Press **Enter**.

On the sheet, the measurements are written down, with each one being measured from the conclusion of the one that came before it in the chain. The dimensions have some kind of connection to the geometry in the drawing view that they are measuring.

Editing a Dimension

After applying a dimension in Fusion 360, you can modify it to change its dimension value, include symbols, establish tolerances, and do many other things. To do this, double-click the dimension view that has to be modified. A dialogue window labeled **DIMENSION** will now display. Additionally, the value of the dimension is shown in an edit box as "**value**>."

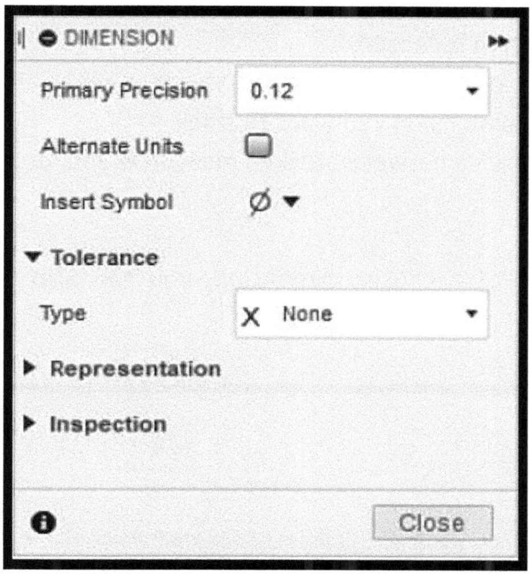

Entering a new dimension value into the edit form that displays allows you to replace the current value of the dimension. You can choose the precision for the specified dimension by utilizing the drop-down list labeled **Primary Precision** which is located inside the DIMENSION dialog box. To show a different unit for the dimension, make sure the check box for "**Alternate Units**" is selected. Alternate Accuracy is a drop-down list that displays in the dialog box when you click the check box for the Alternate Units option. Using this list, you can choose the level of precision that applies to the alternate unit. To enter a symbol, you must first position the cursor so that it is over the needed side of the dimension value in the edit field that corresponds to the location where you wish to put the symbol. After that, under the dialog box's **Insert Symbol** field, choose the down arrow and click on it. The flyout of the Symbol appears. Choose the appropriate symbol from the drop-down menu seen in this flyout. The dimension value in the edit field is changed so that the selected symbol appears on the side that was provided.

Using the drop-down menu that's located in the dialog box's Type section will allow you to pick the needed kind of tolerance for the dimension that has been chosen. The **None** option is used by default whenever it is presented. As a direct consequence of this, tolerance is not provided for the dimension that was chosen. In addition, you can use the Representation and Inspection rollouts of the dialog box to define representation and inspection options for the specified dimension. These options may be found in the drop-down menus. After you have finished making changes to the dimension, you can exit the dialog box by selecting the **Close** button.

Arranging Dimensions

Stack dimensions

- **Set the distance between angular or linear dimensions.**

1. Click **Dimensions > Arrange Dimensions** on the toolbar. The dialog for setting dimensions appears. By default, the Stack option is chosen.
2. Choose the base dimension that will be stacked above or below all other measurements.
3. Choose each additional dimension you want to stack.
4. Accept the standard distance between stacked measurements or provide a custom value instead.
5. Press OK.

Note: From the marking menu of a chosen dimension, you can also activate the Stack Dimensions command.

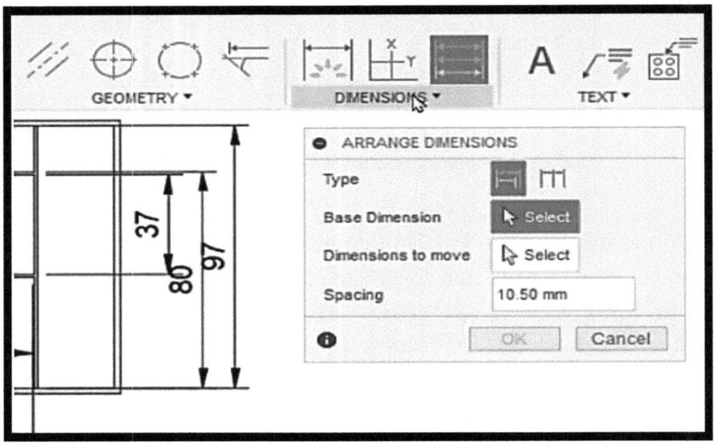

Align dimensions

Align angular or linear dimensions inside an image or between views.

1. Click **Dimensions > Arrange Dimensions** on the toolbar. The dialog for setting dimensions appears. By default, the **Stack** option is chosen.
2. Choose the **Type's Align** option.
3. Decide which dimension will serve as the basis for all others.
4. Choose each additional dimension you want to align.
5. Press **OK**.

Breaking Dimension Lines

You may prevent overlapping or confusion in Fusion 360 by using the Dimension Break tool to break any dimension or leader lines that are intersecting with other dimensions or leader lines. This can be done for any dimension or leader lines that are intersecting. The first picture demonstrates the dimension lines crossing with one another, while the second image shows the dimensions after a dimension line has been broken.

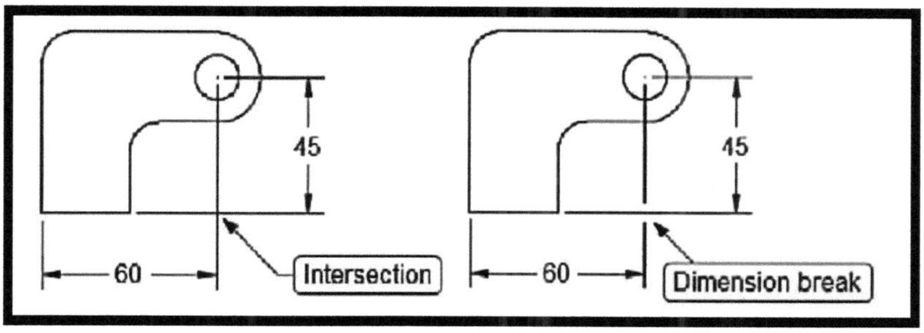

1. In the toolbar, activate the DIMENSION drop-down menu and then choose the Dimension Break tool from the menu that appears. A dialogue window labeled DIMENSION BREAK will now display.

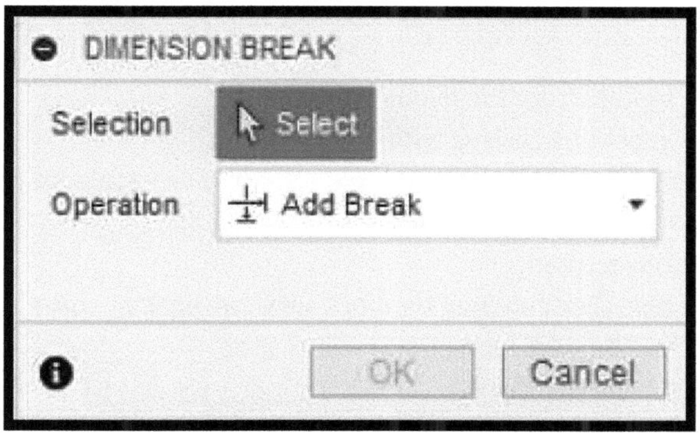

2. Choose, one at a time, the dimensions or leader lines that are overlapping or crossing with one another.
3. In the Operation drop-down list of the dialog box, make sure that the **Add Break** option is chosen.

NOTE: The Remove Break option is used to remove an existing break from the dimension lines that have been chosen, whilst the Add Break option is used to add a break between the dimension lines that have been selected or the leader lines that have been selected.

4. In the dialog box, choose the **OK** button with your mouse. To prevent overlapping, the initial dimension line that was picked was broken.

In a manner analogous to breaking dimensions or leader lines, you can remove the existing break that has been applied between the dimensions or leader lines by selecting the Remove Break option from the drop-down list of the DIMENSION BREAK dialog box. This option is located in the same place as the option to break dimensions or leader lines.

Adding Text/Note

Create text

1. Click **Text > Text** on the toolbar.
2. Click to position the text box's opposing corners. The text box appears on the sheet, along with the Text dialog.

3. Modify the text settings in the Text dialog as follows:

- **Typeface**: Pick a font to use for the text.
- **Height**: Specify the text's height.
- **Bold**: Increase the focus.
- **Italic**: Add italic emphasis.
- **Underline**: Emphasize using underlining.
- **Bulleted**: Make a list with bullets.
- **Numbered**: Make a list with numbers.
- **Lettered**: Make a list that is lettered.
- **Justification**: Decide a justification for which paragraph to use.
    - Left
    - Center
    - Right
    - Justify
    - Distribute
- **Symbols:** Choose a symbol from the flyout symbols.

4. Type the text you wish to appear by clicking within the text box.
5. As an optional step, you may choose a portion of text after you've entered it and change the settings in the dialog box to just affect that area of text.
6. **Optional**: Modify the text box to read:
    - To enlarge the text box, click and drag the horizontal, vertical, or corner grips.
    - To insert indents, click the ruler along the text box's top.
7. Either click Close or click outside the text box.

- On the currently selected sheet, the prepared text appears.

Note: To stop the Text command, use **Esc**.

Change text

1. Click the text item twice.

The text box appears on the sheet, along with the Text dialog.

2. Change the words in the text field:

- To set the cursor's location, click and begin typing.
- To change the settings for highlighted text, click and drag the text to highlight it.
- To enlarge the text box, click and drag the horizontal, vertical, or corner grips.
- To insert indents, click the ruler along the text box's top.

3. Either click **Close** or click outside the text box.

On the currently selected sheet, the updated text appears.

Note: To stop the Text command and undo your modifications, press Esc.

Create bulleted, numbered, or lettered lists

In multiline text, you have the option of creating lists that are either lettered, numbered, or bulleted. The order of the list will automatically update itself whenever you make changes to it by adding, removing, or rearranging items on the list. When formatting a list, you have the option of using either bullets, numbers, or letters to denote items. When followed by letters or numbers, a period comes next. The usage of a double bullet, letter, or number is required for nested lists. The tab stops on the ruler serve as the basis for the items' tab placement. The formatting of a list is applied automatically to any text that has the appearance of a list.

A list may be deemed to exist when the following conditions are met in the text:

- The line starts with one or more characters, numerals, or symbols, depending on the case.
- A letter or number is always followed by a period, space, or comma.
- To add a space after the punctuation, hit the Tab key or the Spacebar on your keyboard.
- After the space, you will either hit **Enter or Shift + Enter**.

Create Stacked Characters

The fraction and tolerance format that is applied to characters included inside multiline text objects and multi-leaders is referred to as stacked text. Characters that represent fractions and tolerances may be formatted in a way that makes them correspond to some different standards.

When you want to specify how a selection of text should be stacked, you utilize special characters.

- The **forward slash**, or **/**, arranges the text such that it is stacked vertically and is separated by a horizontal line.
- The **pound symbol #** stacks text in a diagonal manner, with each line of text being separated by a diagonal line.
- The **Caret symbol ^** generates a tolerance stack that is vertically layered and is not delineated by a line in any way.

When you insert numeric characters before and after a forward slash, pound sign, or caret, the numbers will automatically stack in that position according to the default settings. Additionally, when stacking tolerances, the plus sign (+), the negative sign (-), and the decimal point (.) stack automatically.

Adding Text/Note with Leader

1. Select **Note** from the menu located on the toolbar.
The Note dialog is brought up, and the Type drop-down menu is currently set to **Automatic**.
2. On the sheet, locate the feature whose border you want to annotate and click on it:

- **The Leader Note**: This functionality enables the creation of a multiline text object with a leader that connects the note to a feature or component.
- **Hole and Thread Note**: This function associates a hole or thread note with a hole or thread feature that has been created. Also generates a thread remark for an internal thread that was added to an extruded cut or an extruded circular profile (external thread).
- **Bend Note**: This feature enables the creation of a bend note that is linked with a sheet metal flat pattern bend. The Type setting adapts itself to the nature of the thing you most recently clicked on.

3. While using the Leader Note type, you must first click to put the leader line, then you must:

- Type in the text that will be shown.
- You may format the text by using the Text dialog.
- To finish filling out the leader note, either click anywhere on the page or the Close button.

4. When working with the **Hole and Thread** Note type, click to position the leader line. The text is going to be filled in for you automatically.

- To add more notes, you may insert them by clicking the extra hole or thread features.

5. To set extra notes, for the Bend Note type, click additional bend centerlines.
6. Activate the **OK** button.

Notes such as bend notes, leader notes, hole notes, and thread notes are shown on the sheet that is now active.

Adding the Surface Texture Symbol

- Go to the Symbols menu and choose **Surface Texture**.
- Pick an edge of an item to work with.
- Determine the precise position of the first point of departure.

Note: To generate a leader that emerges in a direct line from the specified edge, you must first provide a starting point that falls inside the bounds of the edge. Alternately, to construct a surface extension, choose a starting point that is outside the boundaries of the edge.

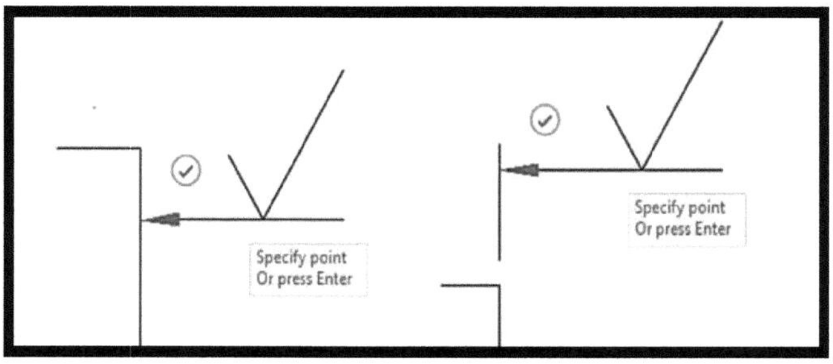

- Click the mouse once more to go on to the next step.
- **Carry out any one of the following actions:**

- To put the surface texture, you may either click the check mark or hit Enter on your keyboard.
- First, click to make a bend line in the leader, and then either click the check mark or press Enter to position the surface texture.

- Select the symbol type from the Surface Texture dialog, and then add annotations.
- Click **OK**. Note that the drawing standard (ASME or ISO) and the symbol type determine which choices are accessible in the Surface Texture dialog.

Create a Surface Identification Leader

Please take note that the surface identification feature is only available for the ISO standard.

- Go to the **Symbols menu** and choose **Surface Texture**.
- Pick an edge of an item to work with.
- Activate the **Marking Menu** by using the right mouse button, and then pick **Surface**.

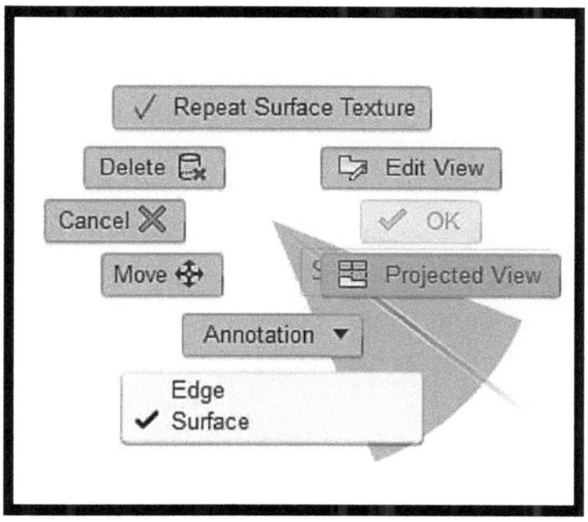

- Determine the geographic position of the first starting point.
- Choose the spot where the next point will be placed, and then position the surface texture leader.
- **Choose one of the following actions to take:**
  - To put the surface texture, you may either click the check mark or hit **Enter** on your keyboard.
  - Click again to add leader segment.

Edit a Surface Texture

1. Select an existing surface texture and double-click it. The surface texture dialog is shown to the user.
2. Make changes to the identification.
3. Press the **Close** button.

Move a Surface Texture

1. Select an existing surface texture using the left mouse button.
2. To move it, make use of the gray grips.

Creating the Bill of Material (BOM)/Part List

After you have finished producing all of the necessary design views for an assembly, the next step is to produce the Bill of Materials and Part list. All of the necessary information is included in the Bill of Material (BOM)/Part list. This includes the number of components used in an assembly, the part number, the amount of each part, the material, and so on. Because it includes all of the information, the Bill of Material (BOM) is used as the main source of communication between the manufacturer and the vendors, and the suppliers. **The following is an explanation of the procedure for developing a Bill of Material (BOM) and Part list for an assembly:**

1. Navigate to the **TABLES** panel of the Toolbar and choose the **Table tool** to get started. The preview of a table will display linked to the cursor as you move it around. Additionally, a box labeled **TABLE** appears in the dialogue.
NOTE: If the active drawing sheet has more than one base view reference created when you invoke the Table tool, you will be prompted to select a drawing view before you can create the part list or add the balloons.
This occurs only if there are multiple base views referenced in the active drawing sheet. Clicking on the icon that corresponds to the drawing view inside the drawing sheet will bring up that view. You have the option of selecting the name of the base view reference in the Reference drop-down list of the **TABLE** dialog box, which will allow you to create a part list as well as add balloons to a drawing view of the reference you have chosen. You may build an empty table on the drawing sheet by opening the TABLE dialog box and choosing the Empty Table option from the Reference drop-down list. This will bring up the option to create an empty table.
2. Specify the location of the bill of materials and part list by clicking on the design sheet. After the BOM/Part list has been positioned in the drawing sheet at the location that has been designated, balloons will be added to each component of the assembly in the drawing view that has been chosen. Note that the part numbering goes from top to bottom if the Part list is put on the upper half of the design sheet, but it goes from bottom to top if the Part list is placed on the lower half of the page. This is something to keep in mind.

PARTS LIST				
ITEM	QTY	PART NUMBER	DESCRIPTION	MATERIAL
1	1	BASE		STEEL
2	1	VICE JAW		STEEL
3	1	JAW SCREW		STEEL
4	1	SCREW BAR		STEEL

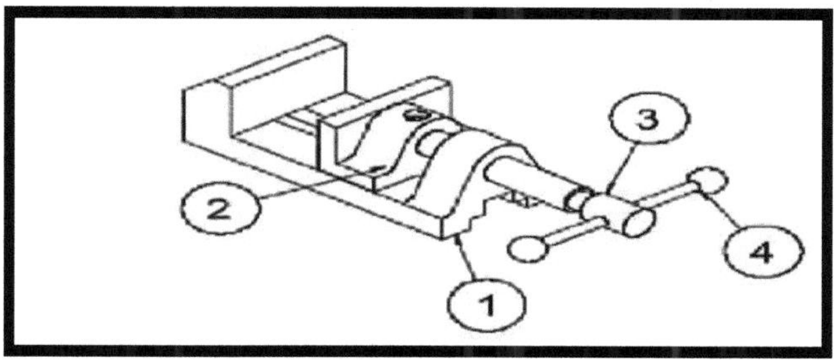

TIP: Before you define the location of the **Parts list**, you may flip its position to either side of the cursor by using the SHIFT key. This can be done before you provide the position of the Parts list.

NOTE: You can personalize the BOM and Parts list in Fusion 360 by either adding or deleting item columns, depending on what the BOM requires. To do this, double-click the Parts list that is included on the design page. A dialog window labeled **PARTS LIST** will display.

You may choose the checkboxes of the columns that are to be added to the Parts list in this dialog box, and you can clear the checkboxes of the columns that are to be deleted from the Parts list or are not to be included in the Parts list. Next, make sure the dialog box is closed.

NOTE: The balloons will be inserted into each component of the assembly after the components list has been entered. However, to correctly organize the balloons on the drawing sheet, you may need to make some adjustments to the default balloon positions. To do this, first, pick the balloon, and then using the grips on each side of it, move it to a new position inside the drawing sheet.

Adding Balloons Manually

A leader line is used to secure a balloon to a component, and the balloon itself shows the part number that corresponds to that component according to the Bill of Materials (BOM) or parts list. In the drawings, balloons are often placed on the separate components of an assembly to make it simpler to identify them concerning the part number that has been allotted to them in the Bill of Materials (BOM)/Parts list. When you use the Table tool in Fusion 360 to add the BOM or Parts list, the balloons are automatically attached to each component of the assembly. This happens when you upload the BOM or Parts list. Besides, you may also add balloons to the components of an assembly, manually by using the Balloon tool.

The procedure for adding balloons manually is given below:

1. To use the Balloon tool, either click on its icon in the **TABLES** panel of the Toolbar or use the B key on your keyboard. You will be invited to pick an edge of the component in a drawing view to create a balloon when the BALLOON dialog box displays.
2. To add a balloon with a standard leader type, check the BALLOON dialog box's Type drop-down list and make sure that the Standard option is chosen. If you choose the Patent option from this drop-down list, you will also have the option to add a balloon with a curved leader.
3. In a drawing view, choose an edge of a component by clicking on it. After selecting an edge, the leader arrow will be connected to that edge, and you will be given the option to designate where the balloon will go.
4. Select the location of the balloon on the drawing page by clicking the corresponding button. The balloon is appended to the edge of the component that has been chosen, along with a display of the component's part number.

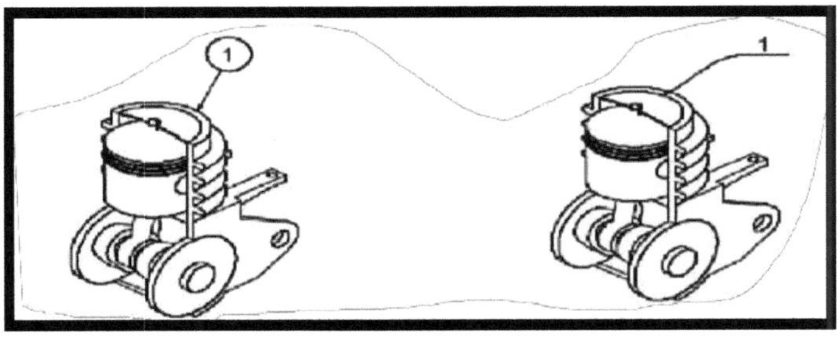

5. You may use the same procedure to manually add balloons to the other components one after the other.

NOTE: If you want to suppress or Un-suppress the components of an assembly in the drawing view in Fusion 360, clear or select the checkboxes of the components in the BROWSER. This will allow you to suppress or Un-suppress them, respectively. When you suppress a component of the assembly in the BROWSER by deselecting its check box, the component will be deleted from the drawing views, and the Part list will be updated to reflect this change.

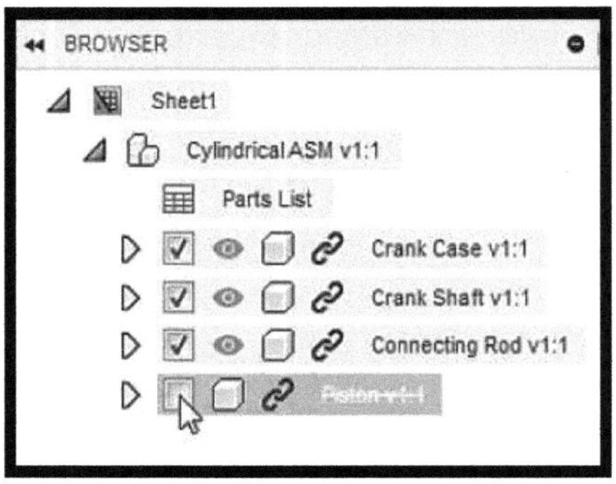

Renumbering Balloons

After adding balloons to each component of the assembly in a drawing view inside Fusion 360, you will be able to renumber them by making use of the tool known as the Renumber. To do this, open the **TABLES** drop-down menu located in the Toolbar, and then choose the Renumber tool from the menu that appears. The **RENUMBER** dialog box is brought into view. The **Starting Number** area of the dialog box is where you should enter the starting number for a balloon. After that, choose a balloon to work within the drawing view. The numbering of the chosen balloon is changed following the instructions given. Additionally, the numbering of the other balloons has been changed, and the Part list has been modified to reflect these changes. Simply renumbering the other balloons by clicking on each one in turn will get them back to the initial number you chose. Next, to close the dialog box, choose the **OK** button.

Adding Drawing Sheets

Simply adding a new sheet is as easy as pressing the "+" button located on the Sheet Bar.

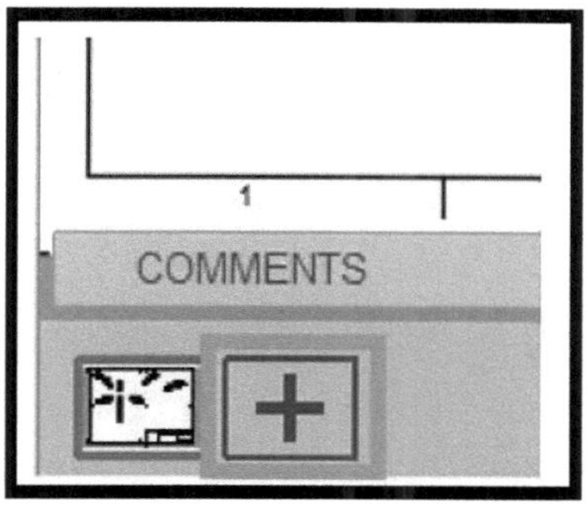

This plus button will automatically add a new sheet, without the need to open a dialog box. The new sheet is put inside the Sheet Bar as the very last sheet, and it is highlighted in blue to show that it is now the active sheet. The new sheet replaces the old sheet that was there. The **Add Sheet command** may also be accessed through the menu that appears when you right-click on the thumbnail shown for each sheet inside the Sheet Bar.

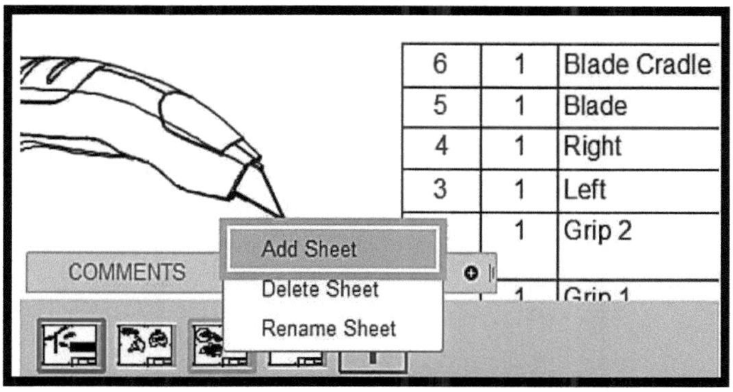

When you click on the **Add Sheet button**, the Add Sheet dialog box will also open. This dialog box includes some properties, such as **From** and **Sheet**, which allow you to select the source of the new sheet's configuration. It also includes information properties, such as Standard, Units, and Sheet Size, which provide you with information about the configuration of the selected source. Clicking on the **Add Sheet** button will also open the **Add Sheet** dialog box. If you don't modify any of the properties, the newly added sheet will automatically inherit the properties of the current sheet. This only applies if you don't change any of the properties. This technique is very useful in situations in which you need to create a new sheet in a certain area, such as between **Sheet3 and Sheet4**, for example. Adding a new sheet directly after a **Sheet3** may be accomplished by right-clicking on its thumbnail and selecting the **Add Sheet** option from the context menu. You may also add a new sheet between two specified sheets by hovering your mouse between those pages when you need to add a new sheet between those two sheets. There is an insertion mark there.

The newly added sheet will, by default, inherit the attributes, such as sheet size, border and border visibility, title block properties, and title block visibility, of the current sheet. These properties include sheet size, border, and title block properties. After the sheet has been uploaded, the Sheet Settings tab allows for the sheet's settings such as its size and title block to be updated. Additionally, it is possible to include a sheet that is based on a sheet that is included inside a drawing template. In this particular instance, the configuration of the drawing template must have the same Standard and Unit settings as the design that is now being worked on. A notification alerting you to the mismatch will appear on the screen if the settings of the chosen drawing template do not match exactly. The new sheet inherits the sheet size, border and border visibility, title block (default ISO and ASME, or custom), and title block visibility, as well as all free-standing annotations from the selected sheet if the configurations of the current drawing and the drawing template that was selected are the same. None of the annotation settings from the drawing template are applied to the new sheet, and the annotation settings from the current drawing are kept even though a different drawing template was selected. This is because the configuration of annotation settings such as font, text height, precision, and other such things could be different between the selected drawing template and the current drawing.

Sheet Bar

The Sheet Bar is a vertical navigational tool that can be found at the bottom of the Drawing workspace. It lists all of the sheets that are included inside the current drawing. The Sheet Bar gives you the ability to alter the order of the sheets, add a new sheet, rename an existing sheet, remove an existing sheet, and convert sheets to PDF format.

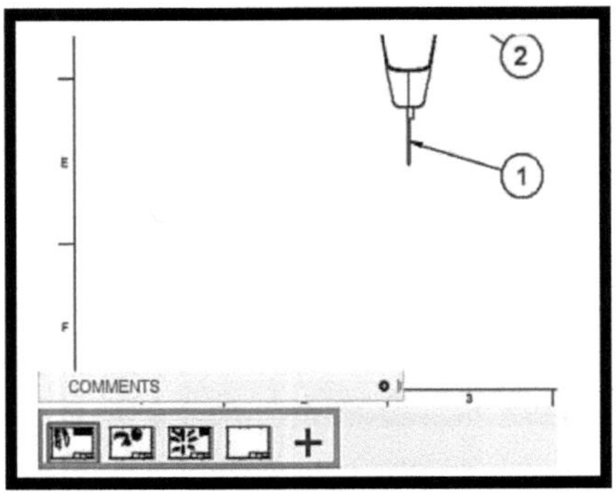

When you move your mouse over a sheet's thumbnail, a larger preview of the sheet will appear, and clicking on the thumbnail will activate the sheet. Blue is used to highlight the sheet that is now active. The contents of the current sheet are shown in both the workspace and the browser.

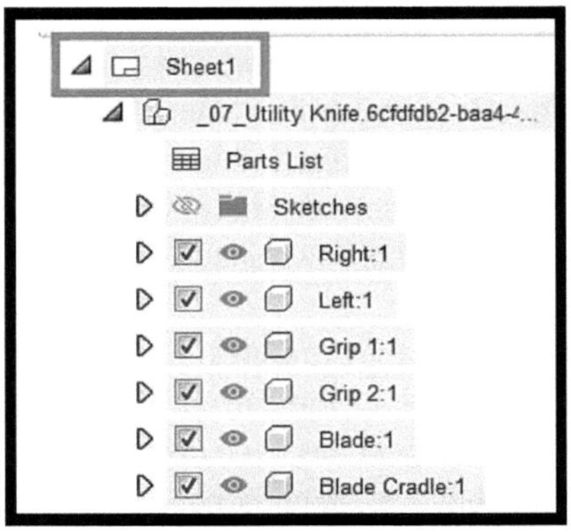

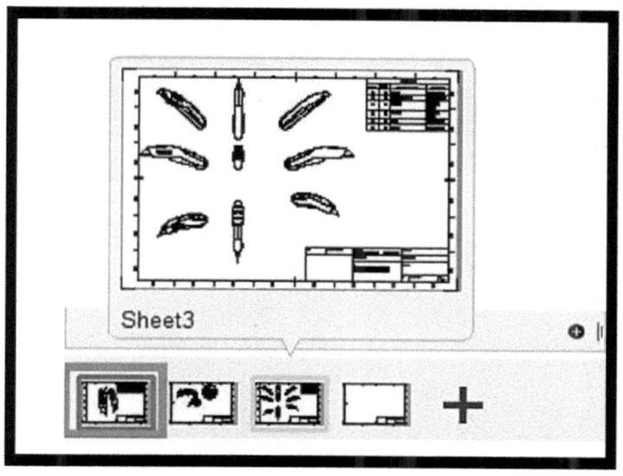

In the title block, you will see both the number of sheets you are now viewing as well as the overall number of sheets included inside a design.

Creating a New Drawing Template

In the Drawing workspace of Fusion 360, you can build drawing templates. These templates allow you to apply uniform standards to new drawings that you and your team generate, which ultimately saves you time and effort in the long run. A drawing template is a file that saves previously preset title blocks, borders, document settings, sheet settings, placeholder views, table placeholders, text, and picture placeholders. If you use a drawing template, you won't have to go through the process of configuring your drawing preferences from the ground up every time you make a new drawing. **Fusion 360 analyzes the referenced design whenever you generate a new drawing by using a drawing template. The following actions are then carried out automatically:**

- Uses the parameters that you have customized for the document
- Produces sheets that have your sheet settings, title block, border, text, and photos in them
- Creates drawing views for the design assembly, placing them in the appropriate locations for base and placeholder views
- Produces components list for the design assembly at the location where the table placeholder was positioned.

You may also design a new drawing template and use it to make drawings; this can be done following the requirements of the project or the standard of your firm. To do this, click the File drop-down menu located in the Application Bar, and then choose the **New Drawing > New Drawing Template tool** from the list of available options.

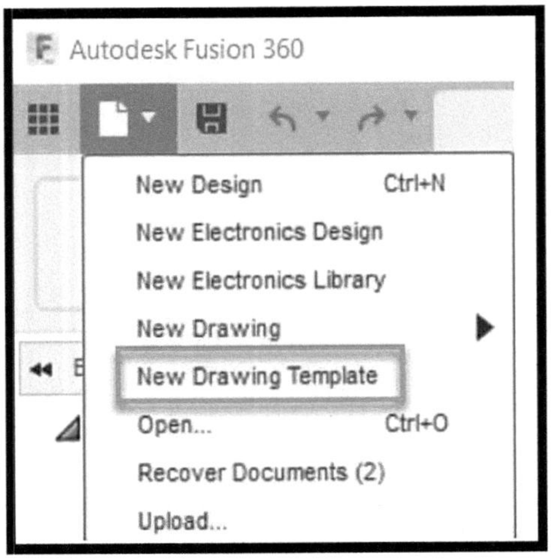

A dialogue window labeled **CREATE DRAWING TEMPLATE** is shown. After making your selections in this dialog box, which may include the standard, the units, and the sheet size, you may then proceed to click the OK button. A brand-new drawing template that may be customized using the selected choices emerges. Now, modify the sample drawing by adding the necessary number of sheets, text, tables, and so on. Additionally, make any necessary adjustments to the title block. After customizing the drawing template to your specifications, go to the **Application Bar** and choose the **Save** tool. The **Save** dialog box will now show up. You will need to provide the name of the drawing template and the place where you want to store it in this dialog box. After that, choose "**Save**" from the drop-down menu in the dialog window. The individualized drawing template is going to be stored in the place that you specified. You are now able to start a new drawing file using this individualized drawing template that you may use to create drawings.

Exporting a Drawing

Exporting a Drawing as a PDF File

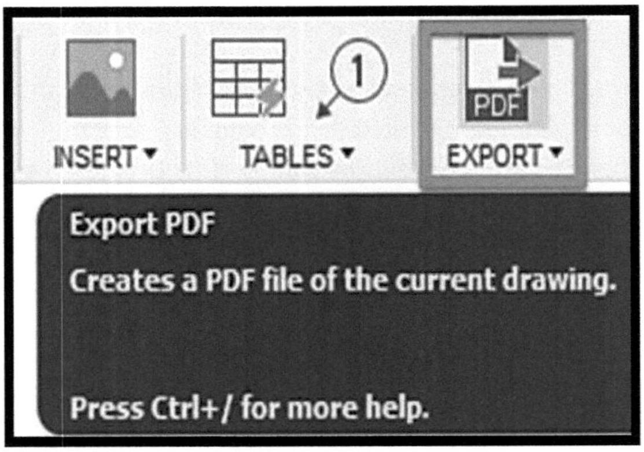

It is possible to export not just the current sheet but also all sheets, chosen sheets, a range of sheets, or just the current sheet by itself. Keep pressing the Shift or Ctrl key to pick many sheets at once or to choose a range of sheets that you want to select, such as 1–3, 5–7. When the export is complete, the PDF will be opened automatically if you have the **Open PDF** check box checked. It does not matter how many sheets are included inside a design or how many sheets you want to export; you will only be able to produce a **single PDF** file regardless. You may also use the right-click menu on the **active** sheet to export the active sheet just as a PDF file if you need to do so. This is an option while using the current sheet.

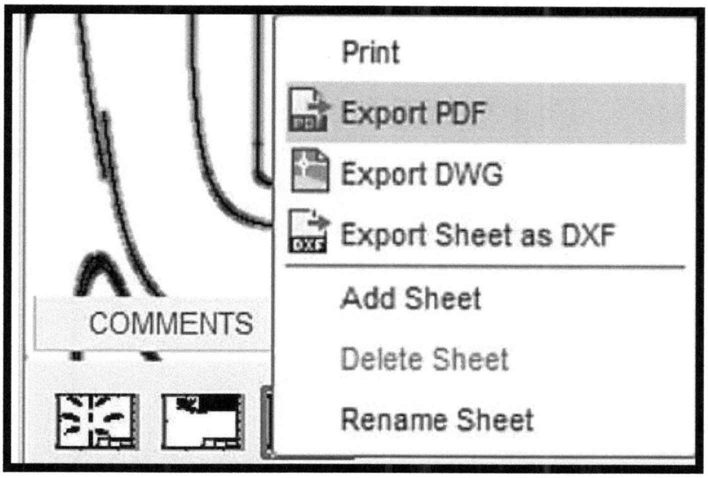

This generates a PDF file that contains just the active sheet.

Note that an error notice will be presented if you attempt to export a drawing that contains material that is no longer up to date. Clicking the **Get Latest** button that displays on the toolbar is all that is required of you to bring the drawing up to date. It is the sole method for keeping the drawing up to date. When you attempt to export a drawing that has annotations that are not related to each other, an error message will be shown, and a Warning Badge will appear in the thumbnail for the sheet. All pages that have one or more annotations that are not related to one another will show the warning badge.

Because the caution icon has no purpose other than to provide information, clicking on it has no effect. However, if you click on the Annotation Monitor badge in the sheet, you will be given the choice to either re-associate the annotation or remove the annotation that has been disconnected.

Exporting a Drawing as a DWG File

It is not able to specify the export while using DWG as the destination format. The outcome will make use of the base view scale, and all of the data will be presented only in the paper space. There will be a transformation of the data into chunks.

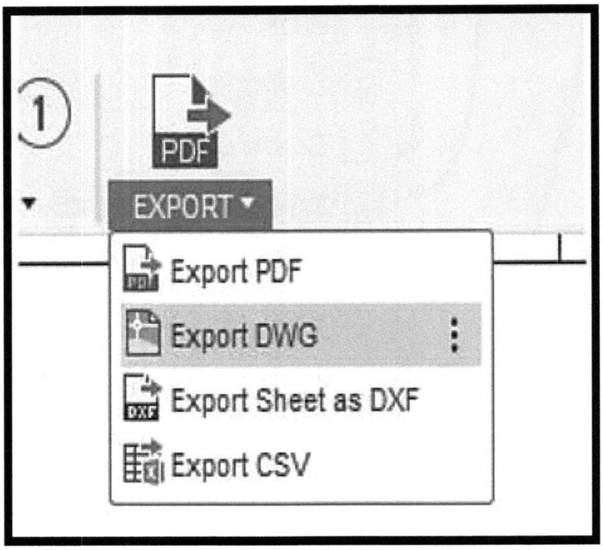

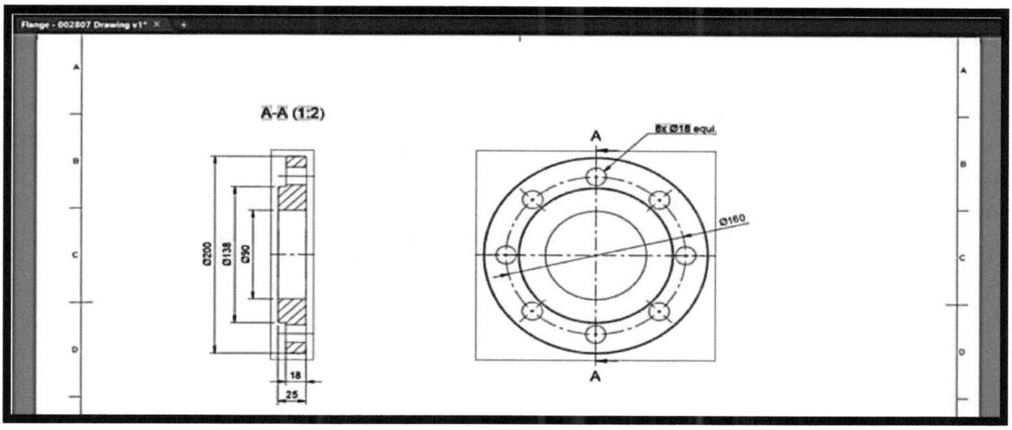

If it turns out that further changes need to be made to the drawing, the EXPORTLAYOUT command may be used to export the relevant data to a model space drawing for use in the editing process. Following the selection of a filename and destination folder, the export will begin to be processed. A popup will appear to enable accessing the new drawing once it is ready. The end output will maintain the same proportions as the layout view it was based on.

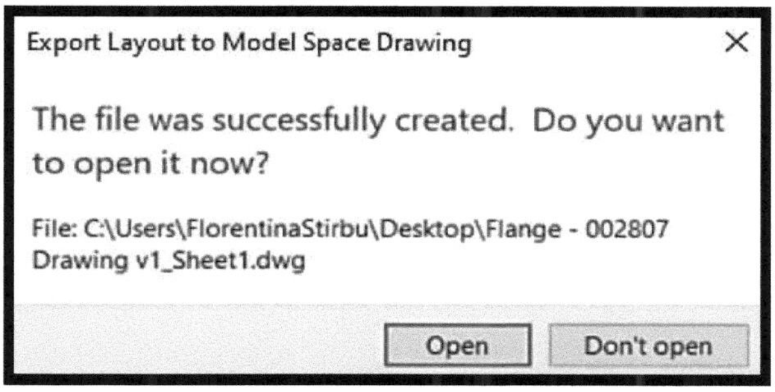

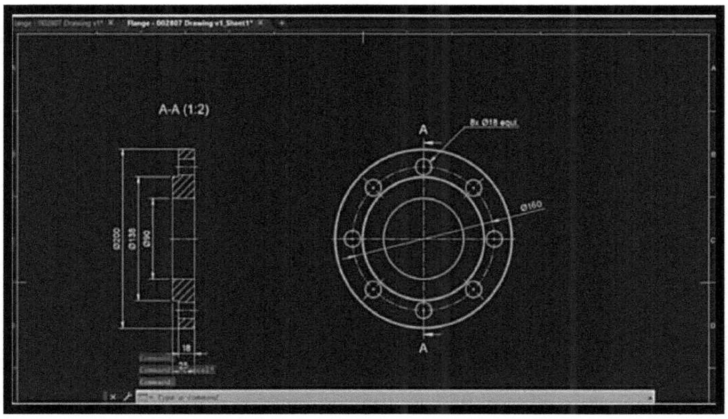

After that, the drawing may be altered, and if required, the EXPLODE command can be used to separate the blocks that make up the artwork into their constituent components.

Exporting a Drawing as a DXF File

Select "**Save as DXF**" from the context menu that appears when you right-click on the newly produced drawing. You are now able to import the dxf file into the program of your choice to submit the component to be **laser cut or CNC'd**.

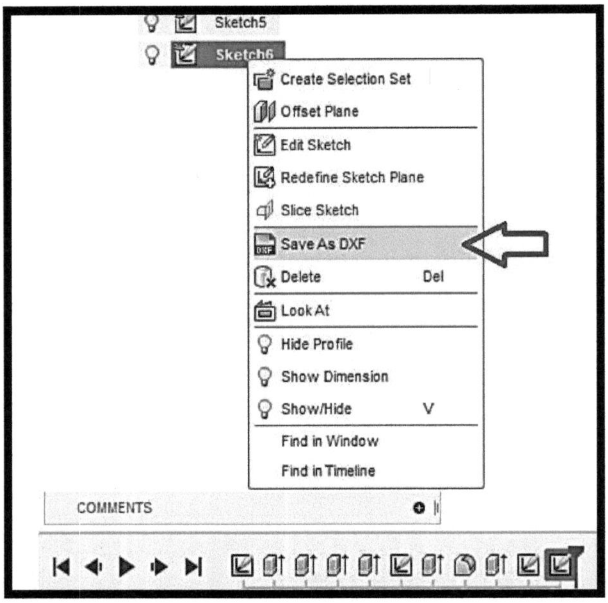

Exporting a Drawing Part List as a CSV File

1. To export a **CSV** file, first, click the **Export** button.
2. In the area labeled "File name," provide the name of the CSV file that you want to work with. Next, you will need to go to the needed place to save the file.
3. Select the "**Save**" option from the drop-down menu. The CSV file with the Parts list has been stored in the place that you requested.

Questions

1. Projected views are ________ and ________ views of an object, which are created by viewing the object from its different projection sides.
2. Which view is created by cutting an object by using an imaginary cutting plane or a section line and then viewing the object from the direction normal to the section line?
3. In which workspace of Fusion 360 can you generate 2D drawings of a component or an assembly?
4. On selecting the ________ check box in the DRAWING VIEW dialog box, the thread edges are represented as dash lines in the drawing views.
5. Which angles of projections do engineering drawings follow?
6. Fusion 360 allows you to invoke the DRAWING workspace from a design or an animation file by selecting which option?

7. On clearing the ________ check box in the CREATE DRAWING dialog box, you can select individual components of the assembly for creating the drawing.

CHAPTER 15

CREATING AND EDITING PARAMETRIC MODELS

This chapter focuses solely on parametric modeling in Fusion 360 as a top-tier computer-aided design (CAD) program. Parametric modeling is the foundation of effective and adaptable design, which enables engineers and designers to easily generate, edit, and manage intricate 3D models. With an emphasis on understanding parameters and dimensions, creating parametric connections, utilizing parameters to drive design changes, and effectively maintaining parametric models, this chapter will guide you through the basis of parametric modeling in Fusion 360. We'll start by explaining what parameters and dimensions are in simple terms. Parameters are like the driving force behind design variables that help you adjust and personalize your 3D models. We will learn how to set up parameters and link dimensions to them, giving you the ability to easily modify and improve your ideas. Parametric modeling in Fusion 360 is all about making different parts of your design work together. You will explore the complexities of creating equations to determine these connections, giving you control over your model's mathematics. We will also learn how to use geometric and numerical restrictions to give you complete control over the shape and functionality of your 3D designs. One advantage of parametric modeling is the simplicity in facilitating design modifications. You will learn how to modify the values of parameters that will make your designs update automatically. This ability promotes experimentation and iteration while also streamlining the design process. We will also explore the concept of "**What-If**" scenarios, which will help you experiment with a lot of design options by modifying parameters and learning from the results. As your parametric models get more complex, it becomes important to keep things organized. In this chapter, we'll show you how to arrange parameters and components inside your Fusion 360 models in a way that's clear and easy to manage. We'll introduce you to parameter tables, a helpful tool that makes it easier to handle and change parameters in an organized and efficient way.

Understanding Parameters and Dimensions

Fusion 360's fundamental component is **parametric modeling**. Fundamentally, parametric modeling is based on two ideas: **dimensions and parameters**. You can look at parameters as the blueprint for your design to understand functions in Fusion 360. The factors that influence your design are called **parameters.** They serve as building blocks that form the framework of your entire design. In Fusion 360, parameters consist of a wide range of things from dimensions (such as length, width, and height), material properties, colors, or any other design details you want to change. By acting as design variables, parameters let you easily modify your model. A perfect example is seen where adjusting one parameter can transform the entire design instead of manually altering each feature. This flexibility becomes important in iterative design processes where you make frequent modifications. Thanks to parameters, these adjustments can be made quickly and accurately. While parameters are powerful on their own, their true potential shines when combined with dimensions. Dimensions determine the sizes and positions of various components in your design. When you connect dimensions and parameters, you establish a dynamic connection. This means that whenever you adjust a parameter, any connected dimensions automatically update, leading to changes in your model's shape and size.

The idea behind Fusion 360's parametric modeling is this relationship. It helps you maintain your design's original nature throughout the modeling process, ensuring that your design meets specific standards and requirements. Parameters are the key to creating customizable designs. For example, when designing a chair, you can specify the parameters for the seat height, backrest angle, and armrest width. Users can then customize the chair by adjusting these parameters to suit their needs. Parameters are essential for optimizing a design to meet specific requirements. Engineers, for instance, can use parameters to adjust dimensions for optimal strength or minimal weight in structural components while maintaining the design's integrity. Parameters also enhance the readability of your design documentation. When dimensions are linked to parameters, it's easier to explain your intentions to stakeholders or colleagues. In Fusion 360, parameters serve as the basis for design automation. You can create parametric models that generate different versions of a design automatically. This is useful for products with customizable features, like consumer goods or modular furniture.

Dimensions: Precision at Your Fingertips

In Fusion 360, dimensions help you describe the sizes, positions, and connections of different parts of your 3D model. You can set dimensions without using parameters, but linking them to parameters gives you more flexibility and control over your design. Your design's measurable qualities are its dimensions. They provide definitions for angles, lengths, and other geometric features that are essential to accurately rendering a 3D model. Fusion 360 offers different types of dimensions, such as radial dimensions for circles and arcs, angular dimensions for angles, and linear dimensions for lengths, etc. When you link dimensions to parameters, it creates a connection between the shape of your design and its driving variables. So, when you change the value of a parameter, all the connected dimensions automatically change too. This means your design stays in line with the specific parameters you've set.

In Fusion 360, dimensions are dynamic components that enable you to obtain control and precision in your designs rather than merely being static measures. Here is how:

1. **Design Accuracy:**
    - Dimensions give you a means of expressing and defining design purposes. They are tools for accuracy, whether you're defining a production critical tolerance or assuring component alignment.
2. **Consistency Across Iterations:**
    - Iterative design processes inevitably involve adjustments. You can change the features of your design and still keep geometric relationships by assigning dimensions to parameters. To keep your design's integrity intact, you must be consistent.
3. **Efficiency in Design Changes:**
    - Trying to change a design without dimensions and parameters can be a stressful and error-prone process. With dimensions, you can make changes to your model easily with confidence that the geometry will be in sync.
4. **Adaptability to Requirements:**
    - You could run against changing limitations or requirements in a lot of design scenarios. When it comes to responding to stakeholder comments or tolerating changes in material thickness, dimensions give you the flexibility to quickly modify your design.

In Fusion 360, parameters and dimensions both have duties and functions to go through, but their performance is seen when they come together.

Let's examine how these two ideas work together to make 3D models that are adaptable and flexible:

1. **Maintaining Design Intent:**
   - You create a clear connection between the geometry of your design and its guiding variables when you associate dimensions with parameters. This makes sure that regardless of the changes made to the parameter, your model stays in its intended shape.
2. **Streamlined Design Modifications:**
   - Imagine you are trying to create a product design that needs exact fitment between several components. Critical dimensions can be easily adjusted when necessary by utilizing parameters, and all components will adapt accordingly. This lowers the possibility of mistakes and streamlines the design change procedure.
3. **Facilitating What-If Scenarios:**
   - For investigating "**What-If" scenarios**, parameters and dimensions are very important. You can easily tweak various design choices by changing its parameters. When developing a mechanical part, you can choose to analyze different parameter values to see how the item performs under different circumstances.
4. **Iterative Design:**
   - As part of the iterative design process, designers must consistently make improvements in response to input. A methodical approach to reacting to criticism and making modifications while maintaining the original design objective is offered by parameters and dimensions.

Defining parameters to drive design variables

Fusion 360's design parameters are very important. This is because they let you modify and control different parts of your design. You can decide to increase the adaptability, flexibility, and ease of modification of your designs by using parameters. There are also various ways to define parameters that efficiently drive design variables in Fusion 360.

These include:

1. User Parameters:

- **Definition**: Custom variables you make to change different design elements are called user parameters.
- **Usage**: To define user parameters, go to the "**Modify**" dropdown menu, choose "**Change Parameters**," and then click "**Create User Parameter**." In this screen, you can give the parameter a name, establish its starting value, and, if necessary, provide units.
- **Advantages**: Changing design dimensions is simple with user parameters which removes the need to manually update each feature. They also improve the clarity of the design.

2. Equations:

- **Definition**: You can relate parameters and use mathematical expressions to control design variables using equations in Fusion 360.
- **Usage**: To define equations, select "**Change Parameters**" from the "**Modify**" dropdown menu, then click "**Create Equation**." From there, you can link various parameters to mathematical expressions.
- **Advantages**: Equations allow you to quickly adjust to changes and preserve design integrity by automating design revisions based on pre-established rules.

3. **Design Tables**:

- **Definition**: Design tables are important in organizing complex designs with several parameters, and are tabular representations of parameters and their values.
- **Usage**: This opens a spreadsheet where you can enter parameter values for several design iterations. To construct a design table, go to the "**Modify**" dropdown menu, select "**Change Parameters**," and then click "**Create Design Table**."
- **Advantages**: Design tables simplify the handling of multiple parameters, facilitating methodical investigation of design alternatives and modifications.

4. **Parametric Modeling:**

- **Definition**: In Fusion 360, parametric modeling enables you to establish connections between various components and features depending on parameters.
- **Usage**: Parametric modeling can be used to control dimensions and behaviors by defining parameters within sketches, features, and assemblies.
- **Advantages**: By guaranteeing that modifications made to one aspect of the design flow through the entire model, parametric modeling preserves consistency in the design and lowers the possibility of errors.

5. **External Parameters**:

- **Definition**: Imported parameters from external files or sources are referred to as external parameters.
- **Usage**: By connecting your Fusion 360 design to external databases or spreadsheets, you can import external parameters. Updates to the external source will cause Fusion 360's parameters to change.
- **Advantages**: This approach works especially well for parameters (such as material attributes or cost variables) that are often updated from outside data sources.

6. **Design Automation**:

- **Definition**: Design automation is the process of programmatically controlling design parameters through the use of application programming interfaces (APIs) or scripting.
- **Usage**: You can write custom scripts to automate parameter-driven design changes with Fusion 360 thanks to its API.
- **Benefits**: You can build bespoke tools that drive design variables based on calculations or specified criteria by using design automation, which is a valuable technique for repetitive and difficult design jobs.

Access Parameters Dialog

From the Design workspace, select **Modify > Change Parameters** to open the Parameters dialog.

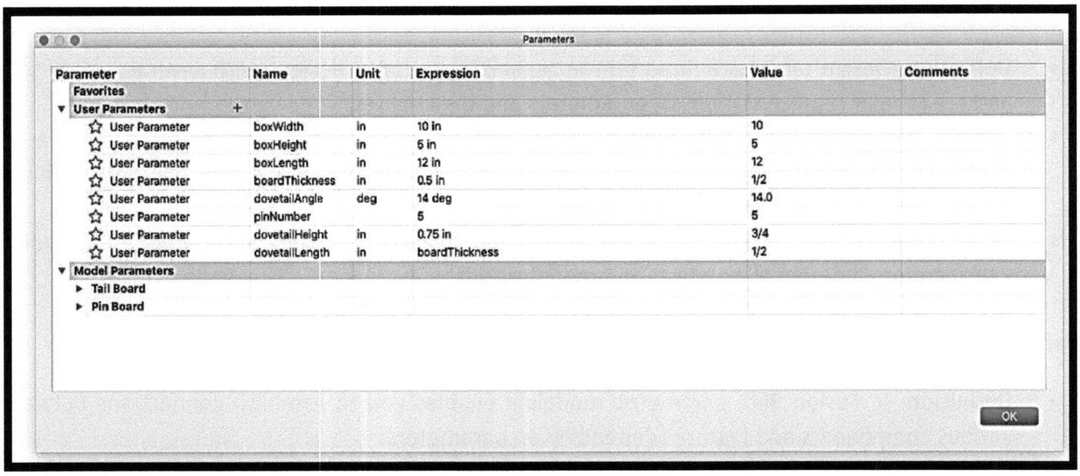

Create New Parameters in Fusion 360

You can set up user parameters in Fusion 360 before you start working on your design file, or after you start working on it.

1. Get the Parameters dialog box open. Select **Design Workspace > Adjust > Adjust Parameters**.
2. Choose the **plus (+)** symbol that is situated next to the "**User Parameters**" heading.
3. Specify the **Expression Value, Parameter Name, Unit, and (optional) Comment**.
4. Upon clicking **OK**, the parameter value can be utilized using **Sketch Dimensions** and **Model** features.

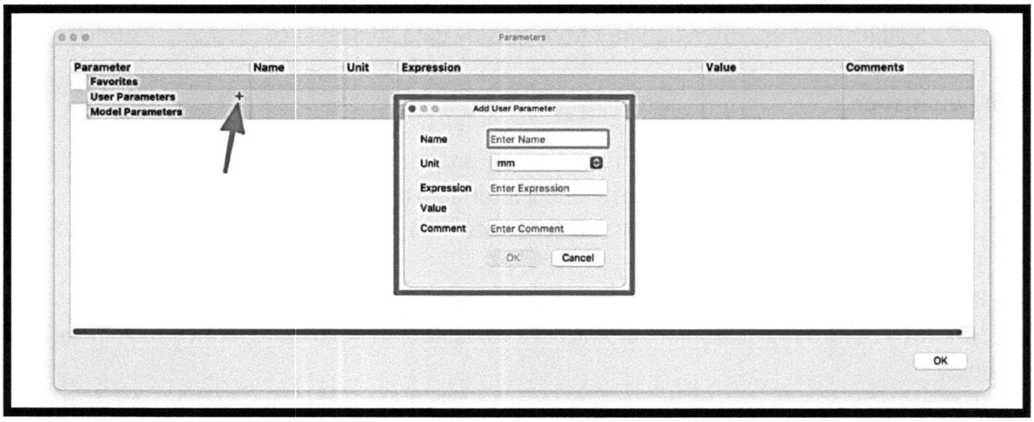

Create User Parameters "On the Fly" in Fusion 360

Create parameters "on the fly" as you are directly entering data into the input areas. Without even having to visit the Change Parameters dialog, you can create parameters with this. To make parameters easily accessible in the Parameters dialog, Fusion 360 automatically adds "on the fly" parameters to your favorites. Because they are obtained from the model itself, parameters that are developed on the fly are referred to as "**Model Parameters**" rather than "**User Parameters.**" Essentially, you can call the parameter name in both sketch dimensions and modeling features, so you can utilize model parameters and user parameters in the same way.

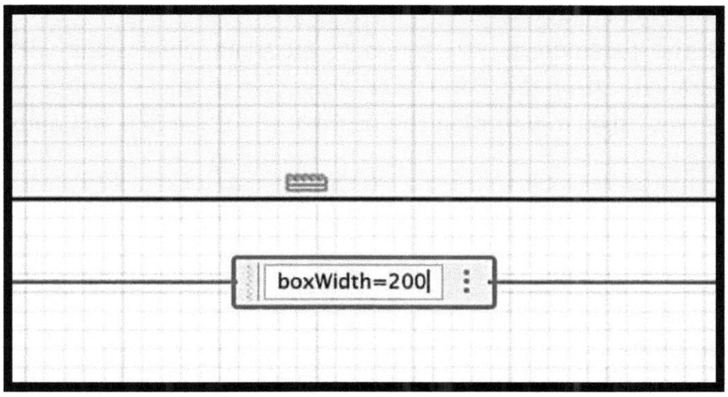

1. Define the parameter name within a dimension input (**Sketch or Model feature**).
2. Use the equal symbol **(=)** and the desired value after the parameter name.

Note: The parameter name and equal symbol are separated by no spaces. Additionally, you will find out that as soon as you save the "**on-the-fly**" parameters, the parameter name is not displayed. But the parameter (and all the places you use the parameter) will keep updating if you change the initial dimension.

Associating dimensions with parameters

In Fusion 360, linking dimensions to parameters is an essential part of making flexible and easily adjustable 3D models using parametric modeling. This approach consists of you giving specific numerical values or parameters, to the dimensions in your design.

By changing these parameters, you can alter the model's size.

1. Open a New or Existing Design:
- Launch Fusion 360 and open a new design or load an existing one.

2. Construct a Sketch:
- The first step in linking dimensions to parameters is often to draw a sketch. Choose the surface or face that you wish to sketch.

3. **Sketch Your Geometry**:
- To build the desired geometry, use the sketch tools. This can involve arcs, circles, lines, and other shapes.

4. **Apply Dimensions:**
- Use dimensions to specify the shape and size of your geometry. Pick the geometry you wish to dimension, then click the dimension tool (often **'D'** on the keyboard). As needed, align the text and dimension lines.

5. **Name Parameters**:
- This is the important part. You must give these parameters names to link dimensions to them. Launch the **'Modify'** menu, then choose **'Change Parameters**.' This will cause the Parameters dialog box to appear.

6. **Establish New Parameters**:
    - By selecting the '+' button in the Parameters dialog box, you can add new parameters. Give a distinct and informative name to every parameter. For instance, you can define parameters like "**Width" and "Height**" if you're working on a rectangular sketch.
7. **Connect Measurements to Constraints:**
    - After creating the parameters, you can now associate dimensions with them. Choose the appropriate parameter from the **'Parameter'** dropdown in the Properties window after selecting a dimension in your sketch. Based on the parameter, Fusion 360 will automatically update the dimension value.
8. **Modifying the Parameters**
    - Return to the Parameters dialog box and modify a parameter's value to test the effectiveness of the parameter-driven design. You'll see that the integrity of the design is preserved as all related dimensions and geometry are updated appropriately.
9. **Formula Creation (Optional):**
    - You can create formulas between parameters with Fusion 360. Using mathematical relationships between various dimensions with this sophisticated tool will give you even more control over your design.

Creating Parametric Relationships

By using Fusion 360's parametric relationships feature, you can effectively specify how various parts of your 3D model communicate with one another. You can make your design process more effective and adaptable by ensuring that modifications to one element automatically impact others by establishing these relationships.

This is a comprehensive tutorial on using Fusion 360 to establish parametric relationships:

- Open Fusion 360 and start creating a new design or opening an existing one.
- Construct the geometric components that you wish to parametrically associate. These could be designs, attributes, or parts.
- The variables that will guide your design are called parameters. To add the necessary parameters, select "**Change Parameters**" from the "**Modify**" menu. Give them descriptive names (such as "**Length,**" "**Width,**" "**Radius,**" and so on) according to what they stand for.
- **Utilizing mathematical expressions, you can establish relationships between parameters. Here are a few typical methods for doing this:**
    - **Equations**: You can make sure that the length parameter is always twice the value of the width parameter by using equations like "**Length = 2 * Width**" in the "**Change Parameters**" window.
    - **Dimensions**: This can be linked to parameters in sketches. You can set the width and height dimensions of a rectangle, for instance, to match your "**Width**" and "**Height**" parameters.
    - **Feature Dependencies**: You can combine a feature's size or dimension with a parameter for features such as extrusions and fillets. After choosing the feature, pick its characteristics and then the parameter under dimensions.
    - **Assembly Constraints:** Constraints such as "**coincident,**" "**collinear,**" or "**parallel**" can be used in assembly designs to create relationships between components. For instance,

using parameters, you can ensure that two faces are always aligned or that components stay apart from each other.

- As soon as these relationships have been established, try them out by comparing the parameter values. With the result, you will find out that the related dimensions, features, or components update automatically.
- In the Parameters dialog, you can organize relevant parameters into folders to maintain an arranged design. This is helpful for complex designs with plenty of parameters.
- You can construct user parameters in Fusion 360. These parameters are not related to geometry directly but can be used as variables in your equations. They are useful when designing user-friendly interfaces or complex relationships.

Building equations to establish relationships

In Fusion 360, you can make use of equations to show how different sizes and values in your designs relate to each other. This is an effective way to make parametric models, which will make your designs more flexible. When you change one size or value, the related ones update automatically. Equations can include functions, constants, and variables, and are built using mathematical expressions. **These equations describe how different sizes or values in a design are connected to start creating equations, do the following:**

- Open your design or start from scratch by using the Fusion 360 application.
- Choose a dimension or parameter from your design that you wish to relate to other values to generate an equation. You can do this by double-clicking on the dimension.
- Give a name to the dimension. It is now easier to refer to in equations as a result. A line's length, for instance, can have a dimension named "**L.**"
- Using the context menu, select "**Edit Equation**" after using a right-click on the dimension you named to open the Equation Dialog. If you have done so, the Equation dialog box will open.

Constructing Equations

You can start creating your equations as you're in the Equation dialog. Complex relationships can be created using Fusion 360 by making use of mathematical operators, functions, and variables. **Key points are as follows:**

- **Operators:** Fusion 360 uses basic arithmetic operators like **"+,"** **"-"**, **"*"**, **"/"**, and **"^"** for addition, subtraction, multiplication, division, and exponentiation, respectively.
- **Functions:** You can use built-in functions like "**sin,**" "**cos,**" "**sqrt,**" and "**abs**" to perform mathematical operations within equations.
- **Variables:** Variables are used to act as dimensions or parameters. You can use the parameter names you assigned earlier in your equations. For example, if you named a dimension "**L,**" you can use it as a variable in your equation.
- **Constants:** You can also use numerical constants in your equations. For instance, you can use **"3.14"** to represent the constant pi (**π**).
- **Logical Operators:** Fusion 360 uses logical operators like **"="**, **"<"**, **">"**, **"<="**, **">="** to create conditions and comparisons within equations.
- **Units:** You have to make use of consistent units in your equations. Fusion 360 supports a variety of units, and you can convert between them if needed.

Example Equations:

Here are some examples of equations you can build in Fusion 360:

1. **Simple Equation:** Let's say you want a rectangle's width (W) to always be half of its length (L). You can set the equation for W as **W = L / 2**.
2. **Using Functions:** To create a parametric circle diameter (D) based on its area (A), you can use the equation: **D = 2 * sqrt(A / pi)**.
3. **Conditional Equations:** You can create conditional equations to control dimensions. For example, if you want a hole's diameter (D) to be 5 mm if a toggle parameter "use_large_hole" is set to true, you can write: **D = if(use_large_hole, 5, 3)**.
4. **Linked Dimensions:** To link the radius (R) and diameter (D) of a circle, you can use the equation: **D = 2 * R**. If you change either D or R, the other will automatically update.
5. **Complex Relationships:** You can create complex equations involving multiple dimensions, constants, and functions to model intricate designs, such as mechanical linkages, gears, or parametric architectural elements.

Benefits of Using Equations in Fusion 360

- **Parametric Modeling:** Equations make your designs parametric, allowing you to easily make changes and iterate on your designs.
- **Efficiency:** Equations reduce the risk of errors by automating calculations and ensuring consistency.
- **Flexibility:** You can quickly explore various design options by adjusting a few parameters.
- **Real-time Updates:** When you modify a parameter linked to an equation, all related dimensions and features update in real time.

Utilizing geometric and numeric constraints

- **Geometric Constraints:** The relationships between sketch entities, such as lines, arcs, circles, and points, are defined by geometric constraints. These limitations make sure that the drawing preserves particular dimensions, angles, and forms. Concentric, parallel, perpendicular, and coincident constraints are examples of common geometric constraints.
- **Numerical Constraints**: In a sketch, you can use numerical constraints to choose accurate sizes, angles, and distances. These constraints give you the power to control exactly where and how your drawings appear. They work for things like lengths, angles, and curved shapes.

Making Geometric Limits

- Open Fusion 360 and start drawing a sketch. The "**Create Sketch**" option can be accessed by selecting a plane or face in your 3D workspace.
- Using Fusion 360's sketch tools, create the required sketch entities, such as lines, circles, and arcs.
- A panel will be displayed on the right side of the screen once you choose the sketch entities you wish to constrain.
- Next, pick "**Constrain**" from the "**Sketch**" menu.

- Choose the kind of geometric constraint you wish to use from the constraints panel. For example, you can choose "**Coincident**" to align two points, "**Parallel**" to align lines, or "**Tangent**" to make circles tangent to one another.
- Click on the **sketch entities** you wish to confine after selecting **Entities**. The chosen constraint will be automatically applied by Fusion 360.
- Constraints can be edited or removed by clicking on them directly on the sketch entities or by choosing them in the constraints panel.

Applying Numeric Constraints

- From the sketch toolbox, use the "**Dimension**" tool to impose numerical constraints.
- Click on the sketch entities you wish to enlarge by selecting Entities. Fusion 360 will show a value box and a dimension line.
- Type the value you wish to assign to the dimension in the value box. Accordingly, Fusion 360 will modify the drawing entities.
- Double-click a dimension to alter its value. Fusion 360 will change the drawing in an additional dimension.

Best Practices for Using Constraints

- Although they are important to keep the integrity of your design, too many limits can make your designs less flexible.
- Before imposing numerical limitations, whenever feasible, establish relationships between sketch items using geometric constraints. More flexibility is frequently offered by geometric limitations.
- Recognize the tolerance levels in your design. Numerical constraints should not be used excessively as this can result in conflicts between constraints, which makes modification difficult.
- After imposing restrictions, make sure the design comes out just as you had intended by adjusting the sketch's dimensions and angles.
- To help others (or your future self) understand the intention of the design, you should consider documenting your limitations for complicated designs.

In conclusion, using Fusion 360's geometric and numerical restrictions is key for producing parametric, accurate sketches and models. These limitations offer the basis for creating adaptable and simple-to-modify designs while preserving accuracy and originality. You can make your Fusion 360 design workflow more efficient by making use of different limitations and keeping to the best practices.

The constraints sketches

In Fusion 360, these sketch limitations are important tools used to ensure design correctness, manage relationships, and make sure your models and sketches perform as you planned. You can efficiently develop exact and parametric designs by applying these limitations.

These include:

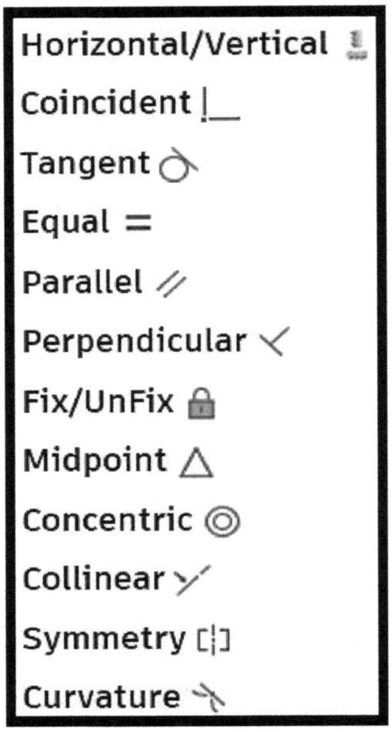

1. **Horizontal/Vertical Constraint: Function:** These force a selected sketch line or edge to be perfectly horizontal or vertical, respectively. They are useful for aligning objects accurately.
2. **Coincident Constraint: Function:** This makes two sketch points or endpoints coincide at the same location, ensuring they share the same position.
3. **Tangent Constraint:** It enforces a tangential relationship between a sketch line or arc and another curve, ensuring a smooth transition between them.
4. **Equal Constraint (Equal Icon):** It makes the lengths of two selected sketch entities equal, ensuring symmetry or equal spacing.
5. **Parallel Constraint (Parallel Icon):** This ensures that two selected lines remain parallel to each other, regardless of their orientation.
6. **Perpendicular Constraint:** It enforces a 90-degree angle between two selected sketch lines or edges, making them perpendicular.
7. **Fix/Unfix Constraint:** Fixing a sketch entity prevents it from moving or changing size. Unfixing allows it to be modified again.
8. **Midpoint Constraint (Midpoint Icon):** It constrains a point to be at the exact midpoint of a selected sketch line, dividing it evenly.
9. **Concentric Constraint:** It forces two circles or arcs to share the same center point, ensuring concentricity.
10. **Collinear Constraint:** This makes two sketch lines or edges lie on the same straight path, ensuring they are collinear.
11. **Symmetry Constraint:** It creates a symmetrical relationship between sketch entities to a selected line, allowing you to mirror geometry.
12. **Curvature Constraint:** This controls the curvature of a spline or arc allowing you to specify the curvature radius accurately.

Driving Design Changes with Parameters

You can use parameters to your advantage as it is important in making dynamic design modifications in Fusion 360. The first steps in the art of pushing design modifications are equations and relationship creation. **You can control the size, dimensions, and behavior of your design by using these mathematical functions.**

- **Change Parameters Command**: The "**Change Parameters**" command is one of the tools available to you. This command gives you the ability to change design parameters on the fly, redefining the rules of your creation. Fusion 360's dynamic feature makes sure that your changes flow through your design as you work, automatically altering it to suit your preferences.
- **Parameter Organization**: Fusion 360 improves your user experience by automatically adding newly improved parameters to your favorites. This feature ensures that your parameters are always visible in the Parameters dialog, which encourages productivity and user-friendliness.

A Practical Example

Let us look at a practical example. Imagine a member of a forum who is committed to streamlining their production process. They hope to construct a model of a fifth-axis trunnion and use joints and sketches to easily get X and Z work offset coordinates at different angles of the B-axis.

It is what they accomplished:

- **Joining Components**: The user skillfully establishes the Z position to the center of rotation by joining a part of their fifth axis.
- **Parameter Magic**: This is where the parameters' true power is displayed. They were able to auto-generate new offsets by transforming a parameter to modify the angular position of their component.

Difficulties and Solutions

There was a little issue in the user's programming. This was clear enough as adjustments to the parameter showed up correctly in the sketch, but the joint was different. **This was the remedy:**

- **Rigid Attachment**: Instead of depending on a revolute joint, the user was recommended to choose a stiff attachment to the sketch geometry to make sure that the parameter-driven modifications were made consistently throughout their design. This calculated move made sure that every single design piece worked together.

Modifying parameter values to update the design

In Fusion 360, you can modify parameter values to update your design. Here's how you can do it:

1. Access the Parameters Dialog

Navigate to the "**Design**" option to get started. From there, choose "**Solid**," then "**Modify**," and lastly "**Change Parameters**." This will bring up the Parameters box, which will serve as your command center for making changes to the parameters that will shape your design.

2. Create a New User Parameter

If you're in the Parameters dialog, you can create new parameters that meet your design requirements. This is done simply by clicking the '+' symbol labeled "**User Parameter**." This action opens a dialogue box.

3. Define the Parameter

You can specify your parameter's primary characteristics in the parameter creation dialogue:

- **Name**: You can give your parameter a unique name. It should be easy to understand and manipulate, showing its role and purpose within your design.
- **Expression**: This is where your parameter's core is located. It is the mathematical logic that controls the behavior of your parameter. You can adjust it to precisely define the parameter value based on your design requirements.
- **Notes**: You can add notes or annotations to your parameter that would describe its intent and other necessary details. It serves as a record for you and the other team members you're working with.

4. Select a Unit Type.

The secret to successful parametric modeling is accuracy. To make sure your parameter works with the right units, choose the preferred unit type from the drop-down menu. Fusion 360 allows us to make accurate calculations in different units—millimeters, inches, degrees, etc.

5. Verify and Close

Click "**OK**" after you've carefully defined your parameter. In this final step, you can introduce your new parameter into your design, where it will play a crucial role in creating dynamic shifts.

Design Optimization

In addition to exploration, changing parameter values is essential for design optimization:

- **Performance**: In engineering applications, parameters can be changed to maximize a design's performance. For example, you can enhance a structural component's strength-to-weight ratio.
- **Cost Reduction**: By modifying material thickness, cutting waste, or simplifying production processes, parameters can be used to identify cost-effective alternatives.
- **Compliance**: To guarantee adherence to rules, guidelines, or particular specifications, design parameters can be changed.

Parametric Modeling vs. Direct Modeling

With parametric modeling, you can achieve the design purpose in 3D CAD by adjusting features and constraints. You can also create mathematical relationships (modeling features) between sketches and the final model. Over time, these get on top of one another and interconnect. You can see it as changing one feature's settings will affect others.

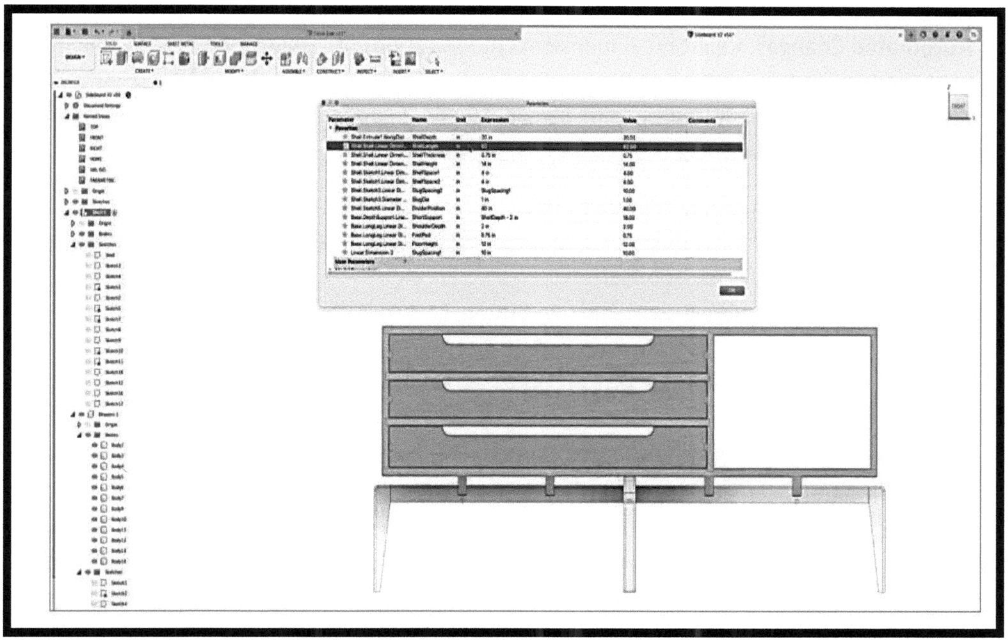

In comparison, direct modeling has to do with rapidly establishing geometry without wasting time fine-tuning features, constraints, and the original design intent. With direct modeling, designers can add or remove parts of solid models without altering sketches or relationships. Additionally, within Direct Modeling, you can import and modify models created using parametric design tools.

How to select an appropriate modeling feature

It's not surprising that each modeling method has its pros and cons. What matters is considering them within the framework of the project you are using them for. For example, parametric modeling enables the designer to change related features and parameters at one time. Although this might limit artistic flexibility, it ensures the design stays intact and permits production to proceed. On the other hand, direct modeling works well for fast prototyping.

Advantages of Parametric Modeling in Fusion 360

In industrial design projects where precise dimensions are required to prevent production problems, parametric modeling is highly effective. When the concept design is already finalized, which is usually throughout production, parametric modeling is most useful.

These are the main advantages.

- **Design intent** –Parameters ensure that your model remains true to your initial concept. Features are adjusted automatically through algorithms when you make changes to other parts of the model.
- **Creation log**: In the design process, the application keeps record of feature modifications that you can access.
- **Structure**: Features that enable exact alterations and spatial changes are controlled by geometric dimensions.
- **Automated Changes**: Real-time dimensional modifications are reflected on the visible model.

Apart from the essential tools found in most parametric CAD applications, Fusion 360's flexible toolkit provides much more. Other features offered by Fusion 360 are:

- Changes to the downstream feature timeline in real-time
- Natural press/pull commands that recognize design elements and, based on the chosen geometry, generate fillets, cuts/joins, or offsets
- Creation of geometry-dependent end conditions

Managing Parametric Models

Before working on your Fusion 360 project, take some time to plan it carefully. You will need to understand the project requirements, jot down your ideas, and create a clear design concept. This will help you determine the relationships and parameters you'll need to set while creating your model. When working with parametric models, being organized is very important. Fusion 360 offers tools for naming and organizing bodies, sketches, and parts. These features will keep your design well-organized and easy to navigate. It will be easier to locate and modify particular model elements if your components have proper names. In parametric modeling, parameters are essential. Instead of setting numbers directly, like dimensions, use parameters to describe these values. This way, it's easy to change dimensions throughout your entire design, which helps refine your ideas. Fusion 360 provides tools like constraints and relationships that help define the interaction between different parts of your design work. This ensures that when you modify one part, it won't mess up the overall design. Depending on what you're designing, these constraints can do things like making parts line up, keeping them parallel, or ensuring they're at right angles. You can create custom parameters which are also known as user parameters and are used to control various aspects of your design. These parameters offer flexibility and make it easy to make design changes quickly. For example, you can easily adjust the thickness of a material used throughout your model by changing a user parameter.

When working on complex parametric models, you need to have good documentation. Use Fusion 360's annotation tools to add dimensions, notes, and labels to your design. This helps other people understand your design goals, especially if they are potential partners or colleagues. Fusion 360 keeps a full record of your designs, showing every step you took to reach your current point. This helps you to easily make changes and history is important when you need to make changes. Parametric modeling allows you to create different design variations quickly. You can experiment with other configurations within a single model file by just changing the parameter values or using design states. This makes it very efficient as it compares options and also saves time. If you're working on a project with a team, Fusion 360 offers collaboration features. These tools support real-time collaboration, version control, and cloud storage, making it easier to work together on even complex designs. Before making final adjustments make sure that you experiment and validate your design thoroughly. Fusion 360 provides modeling and analysis capabilities that can help you identify potential issues like stress concentrations or interference. Addressing these issues early can save a lot of time and resources. If you want to avoid data loss, make regular backups of your Fusion 360 project files. Although version history and cloud storage are helpful, having an extra offline backup adds extra security to your parametric models.

Organizing Bodies & Components

To become experienced in using Fusion 360, you will need to understand the relationship between bodies and components. However, the concept of components is quite confusing except if you are already familiar with manufacturing 3D CAD products or have been using Fusion 360 for some time. Many Fusion 360 users were taught that **Rule #1** to begin a project is to **"start your files with empty components,"** but what does this mean? Let's explore how and why we use components and bodies in Fusion 360 and finally settle the "bodies vs. components" debate.

Components vs. Bodies

This puzzle is quite interesting. To put it simply, you can't say that components are like bodies because bodies make up components. Let's take a step back and understand how the data structure in Fusion 360 works from the top down. When you start a file in Fusion 360, the tab stays pretty empty. If you don't use any components, files like sketches, bodies, buildings, and so on will start to fill up automatically. It's important to remember that all these elements are arranged accordingly. The top assembly is the umbrella that covers everything else. It's the final phase of your file and a type of component in itself.

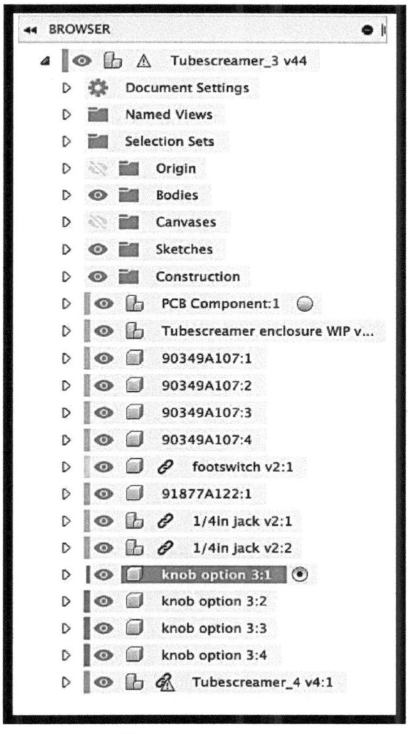

This is all about how you organize your data and structure. What does it mean? How does this fit into **bodies vs. components**? We can start to comprehend their relationship now that we know the top part is a component and the bodies are inside of it. You can't compare bodies to components because bodies are part of components. To make it clearer, think of it this way: When your top assembly has more than one separate body that isn't part of a component or a sub-assembly, those bodies can't connect like components usually can. This is because joints don't work on bodies. After all, you are trying to connect one component with itself.

Bodies vs. Rule #1

Is there any difference between bodies and components? Yes, but it was important to make sure immediately that what people are asking might be if **Rule #1** is even a rule, or if they should create empty components and move on from there. That being said, there isn't a clear answer to this question, which is probably a good thing. If there was, everyone would probably do the same things which would be less exciting. The real answer is: to do whatever makes the most sense for your workflow. In my product creation process, I usually start by exploring ideas. As I work on an idea, it naturally becomes more organized. I prefer to begin with everything as separate bodies. This way I can figure out the interface, where things will go, and how I will use everything. And then I start a new file from scratch, making sure that my components and sub-assemblies are laid out in the browser first. Of course, you can also plan your components and parts if you have a clear picture of what you're working on in your mind.

Why does Rule #1 exist then?

It doesn't matter the strategy you go for as long as you sort out your data into components and sub-assemblies as early in the planning process. When you do that, you'll get the following:

Condensed timelines

Have you ever noticed that when you turn on a component, you have a shorter schedule that displays only the essential things related to that component? This feature is helpful when dealing with large assemblies or complicated models that have so many steps in their schedules. It simplifies things, making them easier to modify.

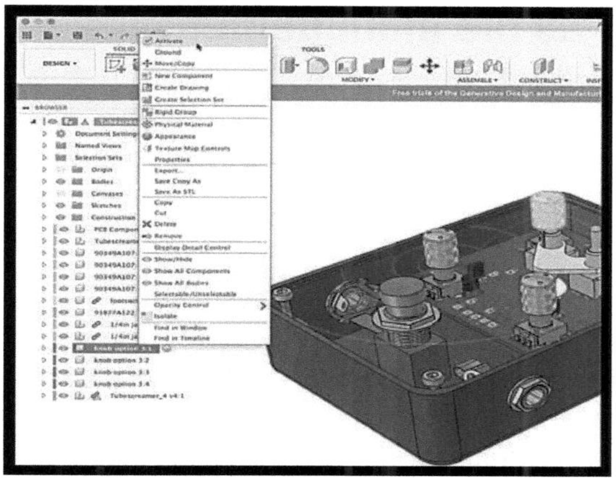

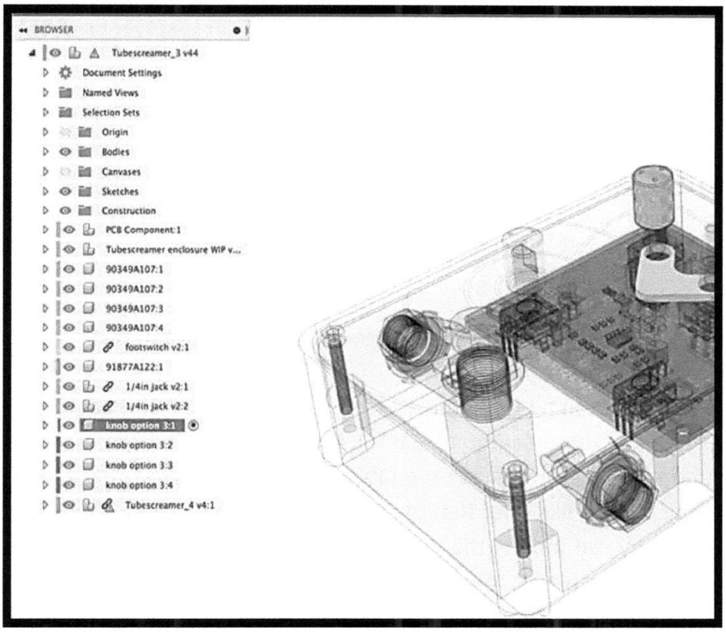

Associated root parts

If you want to create a new component and then fill it, pattern it, or copy it, all the components will change in the same way. This can be hard when you have multiple bodies within one component. To avoid this issue, it's best not to have multiple bodies in one component. This is because certain processes, like joints, only function at the component level. If you have several bodies in one component and try to use a joint, it affects the entire component and applies the restriction to everything.

Sub-assemblies as file management

However, sub-assemblies aren't built for managing files, they are great at organizing your information. They are useful in terms of arranging the different parts of your physical setup which can also assist in combining your timelines.

Portability

This might seem like a big challenge when dealing with lots of files, but there's a smart way to go about it; using components. On the other hand, does make your info movable. Components make the process of moving your data around very easy. You can remove parts of a whole dataset for drawing or exporting and even save copies to try out different styles and split data out for analysis.

Using parameter tables for efficient management

Using parameter tables to create equations that link various parameters is a powerful feature of Fusion 360. This software provides a wide range of mathematical functions and expressions, so you can make connections between different parameters. You can easily modify the input numbers and have your designs updated.

Here's how:

- **Make a Table**: From the "**Modify**" menu, choose "**Change Parameters**" and then "**Add Table.**" A new setting table will be made.
- **Add Parameters**: You can go for parameters on your design list and add them to the table. It will be possible to modify these parameters in the table.
- **Create Equations**: Next, you can use the table to create equations. These equations can be easy, like **A = B + C**, or harder, like ones that use trigonometry or conditional functions.
- **Change Values**: You can modify the values in the table, and Fusion 360 will automatically make changes to your plan based on the equations you made.

When you're designing something, like a product with different size options, parameter tables are very useful. With just little changes in these tables, you can quickly create different versions of your design. This speeds up the planning process and ensures all the versions look the same. You can save these parameters as a **CSV (Comma-Separated Values) file**, which is best for keeping track of your design parameters or sharing them with your team. If you decide to change a value in the table, Fusion 360 will automatically update your design based on the equations you've set. You can also manually refresh the design to see the changes instantly. To keep you right on track, it's important to make sure that your parameter equations are correct. However, Fusion 360 is still packed with tools that can help you scan for errors and fix problems.

These are some benefits of using parameter tables in Fusion 360:

- **Flexibility**: It is quite easy to switch styles and check out other versions.
- **Time-saving**: It saves time automatically while making changes to your model.
- **Consistency**: It ensures that linked parameters remain the same.
- **Documentation**: It is used to write down your design goals by putting them in equations.

- **Work together**: You can also share your parameter tables with your team members to create consistent design practices.

CHAPTER 16

ADVANCED MODELING TECHNIQUES

This chapter gives readers the skills and information they need to feel confident taking on difficult 3D design projects. This chapter gives you a solid basis for advanced modeling in Fusion 360, whether you want to make smooth changes, build organic shapes, or add lots of small details. You will know how to solve a lot of different design problems and make their creative ideas come to life in the world of 3D modeling and design by the end of this chapter.

Lofting between Non-Parallel Profiles

Fusion 360's lofting between non-parallel profiles lets you make complicated 3D shapes by mixing between two or more profiles that are not parallel to each other. This advanced modeling method works best for making smooth changes or links between different geometric shapes or for making things with organic, flowing shapes. **In Fusion 360, here's a quick look at how to loft between curves that aren't parallel:**

1. **Choose a Profile**: To start, pick two or more sketch profiles that show the shape's cross-sections. At different points or on different planes, these shapes can be made.
2. **Guide Curves**: You can change the lofting process with guide curves as well as profiles. Guide curves help Fusion 360 figure out the best way to blend the shapes that were chosen. They make it possible to precisely control the shape of the raised surface.
3. **Adjusting the Parameters**: Fusion 360 has some parameters that you can use to control the lofting process. There are options in these parameters that let you choose how the lofting process moves between profiles and how it interpolates between guide curves. These parameters can be changed to get the shape and continuity you want.
4. **View and Change**: As you change the parameters in Fusion 360, you can see a live sample of the lofted surface. This lets you see how changes affect the end shape and make changes as needed.
5. **Complex Shapes**: Lofting between shapes that are not parallel is very useful when working with complex geometric changes. It's useful for industrial design, product design, and more because it lets you make designs that flow smoothly from one shape to the next. **Now, let us carry out an example.**

Making Simple LOFT

First, let's look at the simplest part of this command. There are three different shapes on these three different but parallel lines.

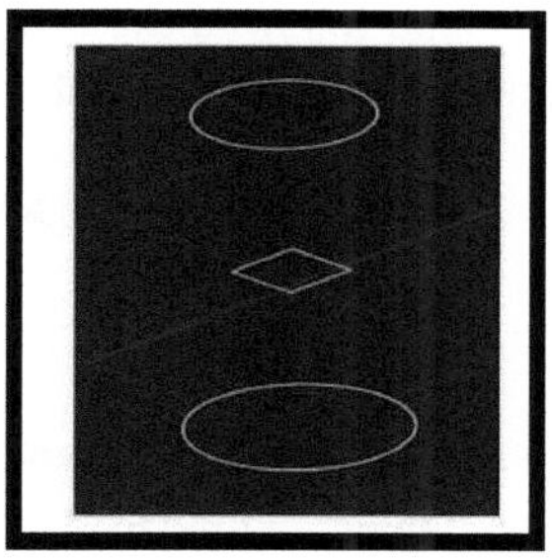

To make it 3D, choose the **LOFT** command and then pick out the items in the way they will be lofted. Changing the lofting order makes the end geometry, and you can make different 3D shapes from the same set of geometries by changing the lofting order. To begin, I will choose the bottom circle, then the middle square, and finally the top circle. I will then press enter twice. As you can see in the picture below, this will make geometry.

To go back to the last 2D drawing, press CTRL+Z a few times and then choose the LOFT command again. I will change the lofting order this time. First, click on the circle at the bottom of the geometry. Then click on the circle at the top. Finally, click on the square in the middle of all three geometry. After you're done, the shape will look like the picture below.

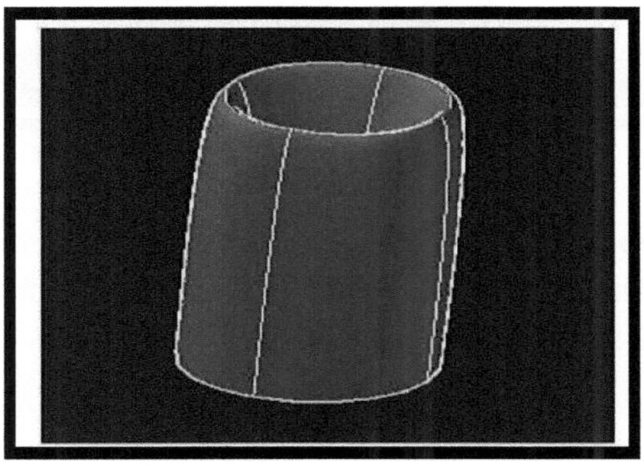

You saw that in both cases, the LOFT command followed the order in which you clicked on the items to make the 3D shape. This means that you need to make sure that the geometry is made in the right lofting order.

Adding Path

The shapes of the 3D loft are determined by the forms you choose in a lofting order. You can add Guides and Path to better control the 3D geometry, though. In this case, there are many circles on different planes, and as you can see in the picture below, a spline goes through all of them.

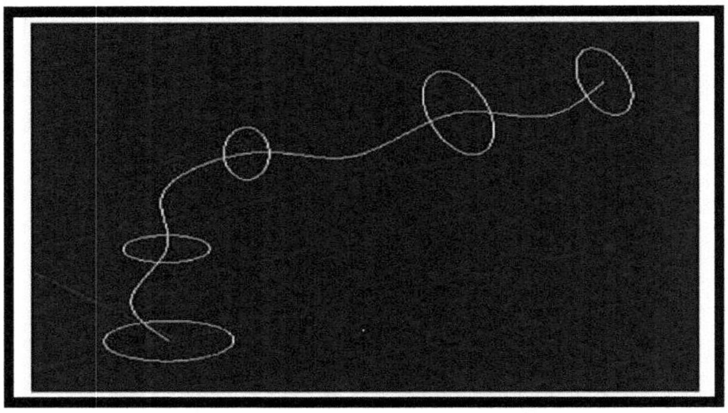

Once more, choose the loft tool and pick out the circles starting with the circle on the horizontal plane. Pick them out in a straight line. After choosing all of the circles, press "**Enter**." Then you will see a sample of the loft like the one below.

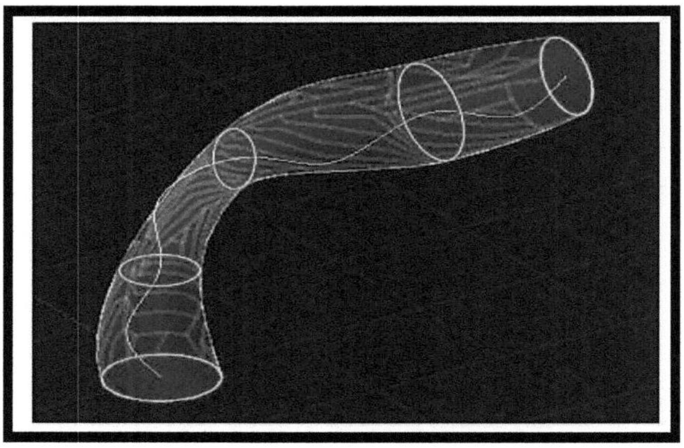

The command line options let you choose a path, and then you choose the curve that goes through the middle of the rings. It will be clear that the 3D model has changed to match the shape of the road you choose. In the end, the lofted 3D shape will look like this.

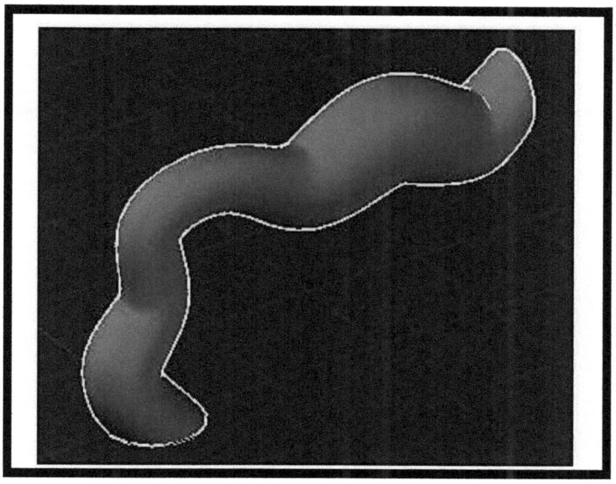

Working with multiple profiles and guide curves

1. **Profile Selection:**

Choose at least two 2D sketch images that show the shape of the item you want to make across its length and width. You can draw these shapes on different planes or in different places in the pattern.

2. **Guide Curve Definition:**

You can set up one or more guide shapes along with the profiles. Through these guide curves, the lofted shape will be able to find its way. You can either make guide shapes in Fusion 360 or bring them in from somewhere else.

3. **Loft Command Execution:**

Press the "**Loft**" button in Fusion 360. Depending on your location, you can find it in the "**Create**" or "**Solid**" menu. Fusion 360 will use the order in which you choose the profiles and guide curves to make the lofted shape, so make sure you do it right.

4. **Editing Parameters:**

You can change the lofting parameters in Fusion 360 to control the shape of the lofted object. There are options in these parameters that let you choose how the lofting process moves between profiles and how it interpolates between guide curves. These parameters can be changed to get the shape and continuity you want.

5. **Preview and Modification:**

Fusion 360 shows you a sample of the lofted surface in real-time as you change the lofting parameters. This lets you see how changes affect the end shape and make changes as needed. To fine-tune the lofted shape, you can try out different parameter choices.

6. **Curvature and Continuity:**

The guide shapes are very important for controlling how curved and continuous the lofted surface is. You can make sure that the change between patterns is smooth and looks good by changing the position and shape of the guide curves.

7. **Editing and Fine-Tuning:**

The profiles, guide curves, and lofted shapes can be edited and fine-tuned with Fusion 360's tools. Because of this, you can make changes to your plan until you get the result you want.

Boundary Patch Modeling

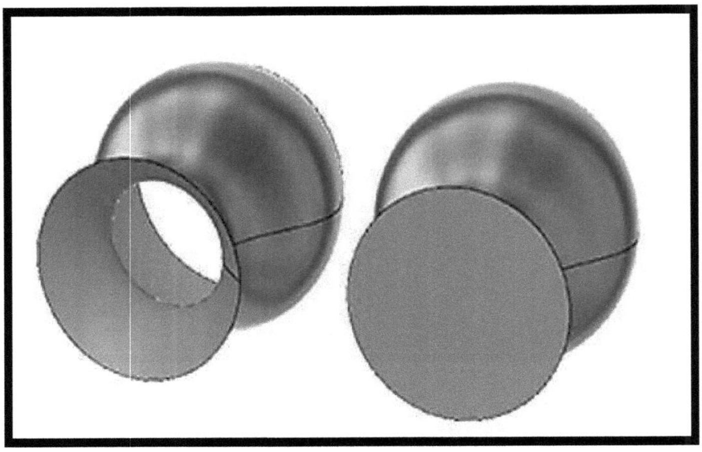

Boundary patch modeling in Fusion 360 is a technique used to create complex and organic 3D surfaces by defining boundaries or profiles that guide the shape of the surface. This is very helpful for producing visually beautiful and smooth surfaces for applications requiring freeform forms, such as automobile or product design. Fusion 360 provides a range of boundary patch modeling tools and procedures.

This is a basic rundown of how boundary patch modeling works in Fusion 360:

1. **Create a New Component**: In your Fusion 360 design, begin by creating a new component. This will assist you in organizing and managing the boundary patch modeling tasks.
2. **Turn on the Surface Workspace**: There are distinct workspaces in Fusion 360 for different kinds of work. Turn on the "**Surface**" workspace to work with surfaces. The workspace drop-down option is located at the top of the screen, and you can pick it to do this.
3. **Make Sketch Profiles**: The first step in boundary patch modeling is usually to make 2D drawings that show the boundaries or profiles of the desired surface. Draw these profiles as necessary on various faces or planes. To design your profiles, you can use a variety of sketch tools, including arcs, circles, splines, and lines.
4. **Define limits**: Make sure your drawing profiles adhere to your design specifications by adding any relevant limits and dimensions. Dimensions, coinciding points, tangent connections, and other things can be constraints.
5. **Make the Surface Patch**: After your sketch profiles are complete, make the boundary patches in the Surface workspace by using the "**Patch**" tool. Usually, you'll use the Patch tool to create the surface that lies between two or more profiles that define the surface's boundaries.
6. **Adjust Surface Continuity**: The options for controlling the continuity between several surface patches are provided by Fusion 360. Depending on what you require for your design, you can define G2 continuity, tangency, or curvature. This guarantees a seamless transition between patches on your surface.
7. **Refine and Modify**: To get the right shape, you may need to make some adjustments to the first surface patches you created. Employ editing tools such as "**Edit Form,**" "**Offset Face,**" "**Extend,**" **or "Trim**" to make any required modifications.

8. **Stitch Surfaces**: You could need more than one surface patch in intricate patterns. To create a single, continuous surface, merge these patches using the "**Stitch**" or "**Surface Fill**" tool.
9. **Analyze & Inspect**: To determine which regions may need further refining, use analysis tools such as "**Curvature Comb**" or "**Zebra Stripes**" to assess the quality of your surfaces.
10. **Convert to Solid (Optional):** You can use the "**Thicken**" **or** "**Solidify**" commands to turn the surface model into a solid if your design calls for a solid 3D model.

Once you are happy with your boundary patch model, you can proceed to the next step of the design process, which is to finalize and export your design in the format you have chosen for printing or rendering. In Fusion 360, boundary patch modeling calls for proficiency with the necessary tools and methods. To get the ideal outcomes for your unique design project, try out several profiles and surface continuity options.

Controlling curvature and continuity

In 3D modeling, curvature and continuity control are essential, particularly when dealing with surfaces, to produce designs that are visually pleasant and smooth. With Fusion 360, you can use a variety of methods and tools to manipulate the curvature and continuity between distinct surface patches.

It can be done as follows:

1. Understand Continuity: The smoothness of surface transitions is referred to as continuity in 3D modeling. Various degrees of continuity exist:

- **Positional continuity (C0):** A smooth transition is not always present when surfaces meet.
- **Tangential continuity (C1):** A seamless transition from one surface to another at the tangent (slope) point.
- **Curvature continuity (C2 or G2):** This is the seamless and aesthetically pleasant joining of surfaces that meet and have a smooth curvature transition.

2. **Use the Correct Tools**: When working with surfaces, Fusion 360 offers the following tools and options to manage continuity:

- **Patch Tool**: Using the Patch dialog, you can select continuity options like "**Tangent**" **or** "**Curvature**" when generating a surface patch between sketch profiles.
- **Blend Tool**: To achieve seamless transitions, you can select continuity options when blending or filleting surfaces.
- **Stitch Tool**: To merge many surface patches while preserving continuity between them, use the Stitch tool.

3. **Tangent Continuity (C1):** At the common boundary, make sure that the tangent lines or vectors of neighboring surfaces match to establish tangent continuity (C1). This can be accomplished by using the "**Tangent**" option in the Patch, Blend, or Stitch tools.

4. Curvature Continuity (C2 or G2): Seamless matching of the curvatures of neighboring surfaces is necessary to achieve curvature continuity (C2 or G2). To adjust this, use the "**Curvature**" option found in Fusion 360's Patch, Blend, or Stitch tools. Fusion 360 will modify the surface geometry to provide seamless curvature transitions when the Curvature option is selected.

5. Continuity analytic: Fusion 360 provides visual analytic tools for examining surface continuity, such as:

- **Zebra Stripes**: To see the continuity, apply Zebra Stripes to the surfaces. Good continuity is shown by stripes that run smoothly.
- **Curvature Comb**: To examine the curvature across the surface, use the Curvature Comb tool. The comb lines should ideally be continuous and smooth.

6. Iterate and Refine: It could take many iterations to achieve perfect curvature continuity. To get the required smoothness, play about with the control points, profiles, and continuity settings of the surfaces.
7. Evaluate using Physical Models: To determine how well your design flows and maintains its continuity in the actual world, it can be useful to make physical prototypes or models.
8. Learn from Tutorials and Practice: Curvature and continuity control are two sophisticated surface modeling methods that you can learn via tutorials and practice. You will eventually become an expert in these abilities by practicing, studying real-world examples, and learning through tutorials.

Recall that obtaining more advanced surface modeling approaches can be necessary to achieve greater degrees of continuity, such as G2 curvature continuity, which can be difficult to achieve. Creating beautiful, high-quality 3D models requires continuity control, particularly in fields where aesthetics are important, like product or vehicle design.

Using Sculpting Tools for Organic Shapes

Fusion 360's sculpting capabilities are among its most intriguing and imaginative features; they allow users to create organic objects with a degree of depth and skill that was previously only possible for professional sculptors. Unlike geometric forms, organic shapes have no exact mathematical description. They imitate the uneven and erratic patterns seen in flora, fauna, and even the human body. Traditional parametric modeling of such forms can be difficult and time-consuming, including several restrictions and intricate mathematical equations. Fusion 360's sculpting capabilities provide a creative and user-friendly way to address these problems. They let designers work with digital clay, allowing them to mold and shape their works in the same way that a sculptor would work with real clay or stone. Artists and engineers can give their creations a degree of realism and aesthetic appeal that is hard to accomplish with conventional modeling approaches by using sculpting tools to give them life.

Getting Started with Sculpting Tools

Fusion 360's sculpting tools can be thrilling and satisfying to use. To begin, adhere to these basic steps:

1. **Activate the Sculpt Workspace:**

Launch Fusion 360, then use the workspace switcher to choose the "**Sculpt**" workspace. With a distinct collection of tools and options particularly suited for the job, this workspace is made for sculpting.

2. **Create a Sculpt Body:**

To begin, make a fresh sculpt body. You can keep your sculpted geometry apart from your parametric models using this special container. It allows you to try new things without compromising your current ideas.

3. **Choose a Sculpting Tool:**

Fusion 360 provides a range of sculpting tools, each intended for a particular purpose. The main tools used for sculpting are:

- **Bristles**: These function similarly to digital paint brushes, letting you push and tug on your model's surface.
- **Sculpting planes**: These provide a regulated surface for sculpting, which facilitates the achievement of exact results.
- **T-Splines:** A powerful tool for creating smooth, freeform surfaces.

- **Sculpting symmetry**: This allows you to work symmetrically, such that any modifications you make to one side of the object will also appear on the other.

4. **Sculpting Techniques:**

To produce organic forms, you'll need to experiment with different sculpting methods, such as:

- **Push and Pull**: Apply pressure to the model's surface using brushes, adding or removing material as necessary.
- **Smooth and Refine**: To get the right amount of detail, smooth off any rough spots and refine the surface.
- **Sculpt Symmetrically**: To keep your design balanced, use symmetry where appropriate.
- **Use Reference photographs**: When sculpting, particularly when replicating real-world things or organic shapes, import reference photographs or drawings to help direct your work.

Sculpting freeform designs with T-splines

"Torsion splines," or T-Splines for short, are an amazing technique that enables users to create complex, organic structures with unmatched beauty and accuracy. **T-Splines have revolutionized the way experts tackle design difficulties across a range of industries:**

1. **Automotive Design**: T-Splines are now a standard technique for creating svelte, curved exteriors and precisely tailored interiors in the automotive sector, where aerodynamics and aesthetics are highly valued. Vehicles with complex surfaces that flow smoothly from one area to another can be created by designers with ease, producing aesthetically arresting cars.
2. **Product Design**: T-Splines are valued by product designers for its capacity to convert conceptual drawings into prototypes that can be manufactured. When designing complex industrial equipment or ergonomic consumer goods, T-Splines provide the flexibility required to strike a balance between form and function.
3. **Architecture**: Architects use T-splines in their work. They may create distinctive and flowing building forms using the program, exploring new avenues for contemporary design. Previously difficult, curved surfaces are now rather simple to achieve.
4. **Animation and Gaming**: T-splines are very useful in the fields of gaming and animation. With the accuracy needed for smooth animation and convincing depiction, they enable artists to create lifelike people, animals, and settings.
5. **Jewelry Design**: T-Splines provide a simplified process for creating stunning, elaborate items in a field where organic and detailed forms are the norm. The boundaries of conventional jewelry design can be pushed by designers who can play with shape and material.

Key Features of T-Splines

T-spline design is partial to T-splines due to some important features:

1. **Control Points**: T-Splines provide control points that can be directly manipulated by designers to shape surfaces. The tactile quality of classical sculpting is reproduced by this easy method, which makes it available to designers and artists.
2. **Local Refinement**: T-Splines are capable of providing local refinement. Without changing the overall design, designers can add more detail to certain parts of a model. This adaptability is quite useful for complex designs.

3. **Smooth Transitions**: T-Splines make it simple to create smooth transitions between various model components. Surfaces can be blended smoothly by designers, preventing sharp variations in curvature.
4. **Compatibility**: T-Splines work with well-known 3D modeling programs including Maya, Rhino, and Autodesk Fusion 360. Professionals may effortlessly incorporate T-Splines into their current processes because of this compatibility.
5. **Analysis Tools**: T-Splines provide customers with analysis tools to evaluate and improve the curvature and continuity of surfaces, allowing them to keep control over the design's quality. This guarantees that the finished work satisfies technical and aesthetic standards.

Challenges and Future Developments

Although T-Splines have made 3D modeling more feasible, they are not without difficulties. The learning curve involved in becoming proficient in T-Spline modeling is one of the main obstacles. Gaining the necessary skills to use control points to get the intended effects can take time for designers. The need for strong computing resources presents another difficulty. High-detail T-Spline models can be computationally demanding, necessitating strong gear for optimal performance. In the future, T-Spline technology development will continue to progress. We can anticipate more T-Spline integration across a wider range of businesses as processing power and software algorithms advance. More innovation and creativity in the fields of manufacturing and design might result from the convergence of T-Splines with other cutting-edge technologies like 3D printing and generative design.

Refining and detailing organic shapes

Mastering Fusion 360's organic shape refinement and intricacy is crucial for any project requiring complex, seamless 3D models, such as product design, character modeling, or creative works.

Fusion 360 offers some methods and resources to assist you in doing this.

1. Make the Base Shape

- Use one of Fusion 360's modeling tools, such as T-Splines, sculpting, or parametric modeling, to begin by generating the main organic shape.

2. Increase and Modify Control Points:

- Use control points to alter the shape when using T-splines or other freeform modeling techniques. By choosing the control points and modifying their locations, you can improve the overall shape of your design.

3. Use Sculpting Tools

- Sculpting tools are included in Fusion 360's Sculpt workspace. Select the suitable sculpting tool, such as the "**Pull,**" "**Push,**" "**Smooth,**" or "**Grab**" tools, after activating this workspace.
- Sculpting gives you the ability to smooth out flaws and add delicate details. Change the brush's falloff, strength, and size to manipulate the sculpting effect.

4. Referencing Pictures:

- Bring any reference photos or drawings you may have of your organic shape into Fusion 360. To guarantee correctness in your modeling, you can use these pictures as a reference.

5. Subdivide the Mesh:

If you're sculpting with a mesh model, you can use the "**Subdivide**" or "**DynaMesh**" tools to improve the mesh's resolution. Finer detail is made possible by this.

6. Put Surface Detail:

- Utilize tools such as "**Stamp" and "Crease**" to include surface features. If you want to add sharp edges or transitions, you can use creasing to produce the same patterns or features straight onto the surface.

7. Mirror and Symmetry:

- Use the symmetry function to keep your organic shape symmetrical. Fusion 360 will instantly replicate any changes you make from one side to the other.

8. Dynamic Evaluation:

- Turn on dynamic analysis tools, such as "**Curvature Combs**" and "**Zebra Stripes,**" which let you see and assess how smoothly and curved your organic shape is. Based on the findings of the analysis, make modifications.

9. Blend and Transition:

It is important to observe how your organic shape transitions from one section to the next. To prevent sudden changes in curvature, use the "**Blend**" tool to make smooth transitions across surfaces.

10. Surface Modeling (Optional):

- You can use the "**Mesh to BRep**" tool to generate a parametric surface model from your organic shape if you need to turn your mesh model into a solid.

11. Color and Texture (Optional):

- Apply these to your model in the render workspace if they are needed for your project. You can paint and texture your organic shape in Fusion 360 to get a realistic depiction.

Creating Custom Patterns and Embossing

Adding complex textures, ornamental embellishments, and branding to your 3D models is possible using Fusion 360's custom patterns and embossing feature. Whether you are working on an artistic project, industrial components, or product design, these strategies are crucial for improving the beauty and usefulness of your ideas.

Using custom patterns and embossing, you may give your 3D models distinctive textures that are aesthetically attractive. These patterns can improve the overall appearance and feel of your designs, increasing user or consumer appeal. You can add trademarks, logos, or branding aspects to your items by using custom patterns and embossing. To promote and differentiate products, it is crucial to strengthen brand identification and familiarity. Functional goals like enhancing grip, decreasing slipperiness, or maximizing airflow can be achieved by patterns and embossed elements in handles, grips, and ventilation systems. Custom patterns and embossing allow you to add realistic elements that mirror real-world textures and surfaces, improving the overall authenticity of your models in industries such as architecture, character modeling, and product design.

1. Onto the curved surface, create a drawing or text that you want to emboss or deboss.
2. Locate and choose the "**Create**" option.
3. Choose "**Emboss.**"
4. **The Emboss dialog box displays:**
    - Select the desired drawing or text to be used as the drawing Profile.
    - On your model, choose the curved surface to be the Face.
    - Select "**Emboss" or "Deboss**" under "**Effect**" depending on the result you're going for.

- Modify any other parameters or changes as needed.

5. Click "**OK**" to apply the settings after you've adjusted them to your preference.

Apply appearances to components, bodies, and faces in a design

In a Fusion 360 design, use the Appearance command to apply color and texture overrides to faces, bodies, and components.

1. On the toolbar, click:
    - **Design > Modify > Appearance**
    - **Render > Setup > Appearance**
    - **Animation > Transform > Appearance**

The **Appearance** dialog displays.

2. **Choose which kind of items you wish to apply an appearance to in the dialog's Apply To section:**
    - Bodies/Components
    - Faces
    - All Storyboards
    - Current Storyboard
3. **Look in one of the following areas for the look you want to use:**
    - **In This Design**: Elements that are currently used inside your design.
    - **Library**: This refers to appearances that are available in the Fusion 360 Appearances, My Appearances, or Favorites libraries but are not currently used in your design.
4. Drag and drop the appearance onto faces, bodies, or other components in the canvas or browser.

The components, bodies, or faces on the canvas exhibit the new look.

5. To apply distinct looks to various components, bodies, and faces, repeat steps 2 through 5.
6. Select **Close**.

Tips

- To set an alternate look for objects in new designs by default, open the **Preferences dialog** and go to the Material section.
- To modify the default look given to new items in the design, drag and drop an appearance onto the browser's default component.
- To apply a new look to all of the components, bodies, and faces at once, pick them beforehand in the browser.

- Drag and drag an appearance to apply an override to a particular part of the body, face, or component.
- Drag and drop an appearance onto a parent component. You can then choose whether to delete the overrides so that the objects inherit the appearance from their parent component, or to maintain the overrides applied to the components, bodies, and faces inside it.

CHAPTER 17
SHEET METAL DESIGN

An overview of the importance of sheet metal workspaces in computer-aided design (CAD), particularly in Autodesk Fusion 360, is given in this chapter. Workstations specifically designed for creating sheet metal components are known as sheet metal workstations. They guarantee that designs adhere to production requirements and expedite the process of creating 3D forms from flat metal sheets. It includes a variety of characteristics and tools specific to sheet metal design, including the production of bends and flanges. It also describes how documentation tools, regulations, and sheet metal parameters improve the accuracy and efficiency of sheet metal design.

Introduction to Sheet Metal Workspaces

To create intricate three-dimensional structures from flat metal sheets, sheet metal fabrication is an essential component of current industrial processes. Autodesk Fusion 360 has a specialized workspace called the **"Sheet Metal"** workspace to expedite and simplify the design and manufacture of sheet metal components. Sheet metal is a versatile material used to make a vast array of items, from consumer electronics to industrial gear, and from automobile components to domestic appliances. Because of its strength, malleability, and affordability, it is quite popular. Due to its thin nature, which can readily distort if not handled appropriately, dealing with sheet metal presents special problems. The process of fabricating sheet metal includes various important processes, such as design, cutting, bending, and assembly. Precise modeling and careful consideration of elements including material thickness, bend radius, and production limitations are necessary for designing sheet metal components. This is where Fusion 360's Sheet Metal workspace is useful.

Exploring the Sheet Metal Workspace

The process of designing with sheet metal is made easier and more effective thanks to the Sheet Metal workspace in Fusion 360. This workspace is a specialized environment. It gives engineers and designers access to a wide variety of specialized tools and capabilities, which makes it possible for them to swiftly build correct sheet metal components.

Let's take a closer look at some of the most important features of this workspace:

1. **Sheet Metal Rules:** You can establish particular rules for sheet metal design, including material thickness, bend radius, and relief cuts, among other parameters. These criteria make it much simpler to modify designs so that they work with a wider variety of materials and processes, as well as ensuring that designs are compliant with production requirements.
2. **Sheet Metal Parameters**: Users can create sheet metal parameters, which are variables that affect different parts of the design. Some examples of these variables are the size of the flat pattern, bend angles, and flange lengths. Using a parametric approach like this makes it simple to make design changes and facilitates rapid iteration.
3. **Creation of Flanges and Bends**: Fusion 360 provides users with user-friendly tools that allow them to easily create flanges and bends in sheet metal components. Users can provide

parameters for flanges, such as height, angle, and edge offset, and Fusion 360 will automatically build the geometry matching those specifications.

4. **Sheet Metal Features:** The program has a variety of features that are specifically designed for sheet metal, such as corner reliefs, miter flanges, and edge flanges. These capabilities make it easier to create intricate designs for sheet metal and guarantee that components can be fabricated precisely.
5. **Unfold and Refold**: With the Sheet Metal workspace, you have the option to unfold and refold sheet metal designs, which is one of the most powerful capabilities available. Because of this, designers can envision the flat pattern of a three-dimensional object, which is a vital step in the process of producing correct cutting patterns for manufacture.
6. **Sheet Metal Documentation:** Fusion 360 makes it easy to create comprehensive drawings and documentation for sheet metal components. This comprises the generation of flat patterns, dimensioning, and the addition of annotations to effectively express design intent.
7. **Integration with 3D Modeling:** Unlike the Sheet Metal workspace, which focuses on sheet metal-specific tools, the normal 3D modeling workspace can be seamlessly integrated with Fusion 360. Because of this, users can mix sheet metal components with other parts and assemblies, resulting in complicated designs that include both sheet metal components and solid components.
8. **Simulation and Validation**: As part of its feature set, Fusion 360 features simulation tools that customers can use to assist them in analyzing and validating their sheet metal designs. This guarantees that components will work as planned regardless of the loads or environments they are subjected to.
9. **Integration of production and CAM**: The CAM capabilities of Fusion 360 allow for the direct translation of sheet metal designs into production processes. This makes the integration of manufacturing and CAM possible. The transfer from design to production is streamlined as a result of this integration, which reduces the number of mistakes and saves time.

Understanding sheet metal-specific tools

To do a good job working with sheet metal in Fusion 360, you will need to be familiar with the various sheet metal tools and features and know how to utilize them.

The following is an overview of some of the most important tools and processes in Fusion 360 that are unique to sheet metal:

- **Sheet Metal Environment**: Fusion 360 has a specific "**Sheet Metal**" workspace that offers specialized tools for creating and modeling sheet metal components. This workspace is referred to as the "Sheet Metal Environment." To switch to this workspace, use the workspace switcher in the top left corner of the screen and pick "**Sheet Metal**."
- **Base Flange**: The "**Base Flange**" tool gives you the ability to design the first flat sheet metal component by allowing you to define the length, breadth, and thickness of the part. A new component can be created, or an existing one can be used.
- **Flange**: Bends or flanges in the sheet metal portion can be formed using the "**Flange**" tool, which gets its name from its primary function. You can design flanges at any angle, and you can also define parameters relating to the flange, such as its length, angle, and radius.

- **Bend**: Use the "**Bend**" tool to add bends to your sheet metal item to complete the process. You can choose a straight edge, and then choose the angle and direction of the bend. The resultant bend will be automatically calculated by Fusion 360, and the model will be updated to reflect the calculation.
- **Corner Seam**: The "**Corner Seam**" tool allows you to link two or more sheet metal components at their corners and is used to create a corner seam. You can pick the components that need to be linked, and Fusion 360 will automatically build the seams and corner reliefs that are required.
- **Junctions**: Fusion 360 offers a variety of options for junctions, allowing users to regulate how sheet metal components cross and join with one another. You can describe how the components interact at their edges by selecting one of the available options, such as "**Butt Joint," "Overlap Joint," or "Underlap Joint."**
- **Unfold and Fold**: The **"Unfold" and "Fold"** tools enable you to move between the flat pattern and the folded shape of your sheet metal item. This is done by unfolding and folding the pattern, respectively. This helps verify the design, make adjustments, and get the component ready for manufacture.
- **Sheet Metal Rules**: Fusion 360 gives you the ability to set particular sheet metal rules for your design. Among these regulations are parameters such as the bend radius, the K-factor, and the material thickness. It is very necessary to construct precise sheet metal rules to get accurate flat patterns.
- **Bend Tables**: If you want to set bespoke bend allowance values depending on your material and the manufacturing procedures you utilize, you can use bend tables to do so. This guarantees that the sheet metal pieces you use are bent precisely to specification.
- **Flat Pattern**: Utilize the "Flat Pattern" tool to inspect and export the flat pattern of the sheet metal item you are working on. This offers a two-dimensional picture of the unfolded sheet metal component, which is necessary for the industrial processes of cutting and shaping.
- **Sheet Metal Manufacturing**: Fusion 360's CAM capabilities allow you to produce toolpaths for laser cutting, punching, and other manufacturing techniques that are particular to sheet metal fabrication. These toolpaths can be used in the fabrication process.
- **Documentation**: Fusion 360 provides the tools necessary to create precise drawings and documentation of your sheet metal designs. This documentation might include dimensioning, comments, and a bill of materials.

You must get acquainted with the tools and processes that are unique to working with sheet metal in Fusion 360 if you want to deal with sheet metal efficiently. In addition, if you want to have a better grasp of sheet metal design in Fusion 360, you should think about looking into the tutorials and training materials that are supplied by Autodesk. Here, we are going to examine its Create and Modify tools. We will not go into the specifics of sheet metal design such as **bends, relief notches, or K-factors**; rather, the goal is to demonstrate how they operate.

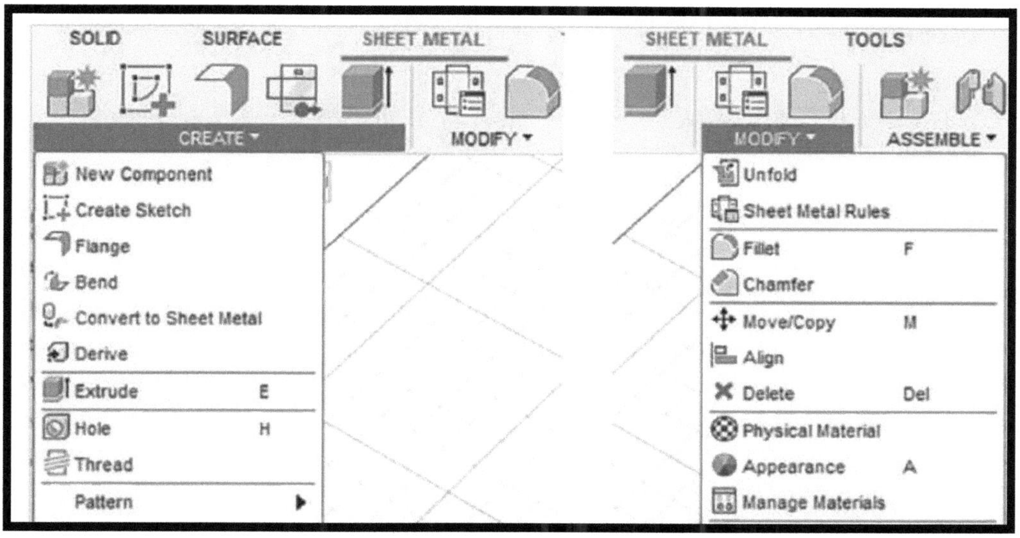

Important Information

- The sketch environment in the Sheet Metal workspace operates in the same manner as the sketch environments in all of the other workspaces.
- The design of sheet metal can only be done parametrically. No option allows for direct modeling.
- A sheet metal body cannot be transferred to another component or copied and pasted into it.
- You can turn a conventional component into a sheet metal component by bringing it into the workspace designated for working with sheet metal. On the other hand, it cannot be reverted to a standard component in any way.

Folded and Unfolded Modes

Folded mode is the appearance that a model has by default. You can either unfold it, which means you can lay it down horizontally, to check that the model will unfold, or you can do so to offer yourself a larger flat space on which to draw. While in unfold mode, you can make further adjustments and add cuts across bends, but you cannot add new flanges to the model. This state is only temporary. On an item that has been unfolded, simple bends and corner reliefs will be seen; however, complicated bends and corner reliefs could not be visible depending on their size, thickness, and bend radii. To refold, click the button labeled "**Refold Faces**" which is located in the upper-right corner of the screen.

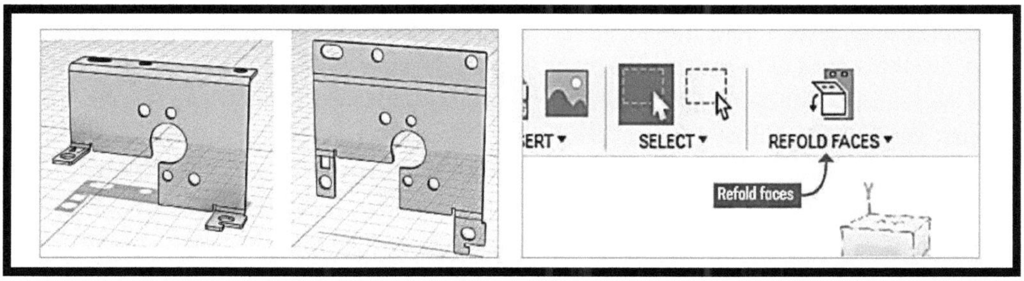

Flat Pattern

A flat pattern is a layout that is produced after the design has been completed and is prepared for cutting. It's something that can be produced using the folded model. At curves and corners, any relief forms and miters, also known as corner joints, will be visible. The bend lines are presented so that the user can see where on the portion the bending should take place. You only need to make one flat pattern for each body and component if you use Fusion's Manufacture workspace. From there, you can generate toolpaths using the flat patterns you made. Flat patterns that can be used by laser, water, and plasma jet cutters, as well as press brakes and punch presses, can be generated using fusion. It is best not to modify in this mode since any changes you make will be visible in the unfolded pattern but not in the folded model. Simply choose the "**Create**" menu option and then select "**Create Flat Pattern**" from the menu that appears. You will be prompted to choose a stationary face on the object whose flat pattern you want to create before proceeding. After a flat pattern has been developed, a listing for it will appear in the Browser. Select and click on the listing to re-enter the Flat Pattern. You can leave the Flat Pattern by clicking on the green icon labeled "**Finish Flat Pattern**" in the upper-right corner of the screen.

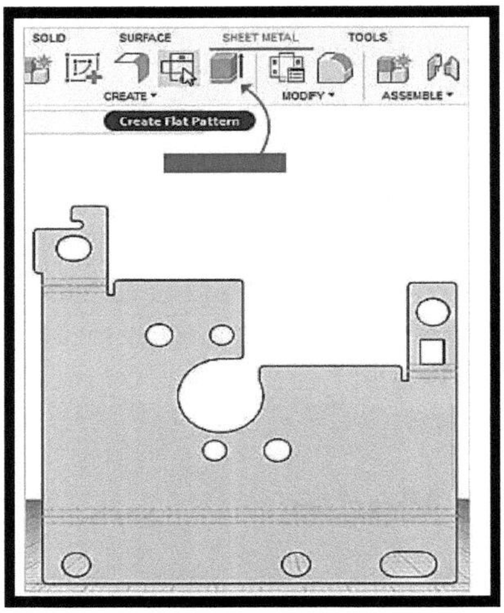

Sheet Metal Rules

Sheet metal rules are settings for different sheet metal properties such as the thickness of the metal, the minimum radius you can bend the sheet without destroying it (called the bend radius), and reliefs. Other sheet metal rules include the bend radius, which is the lowest radius at which you can bend the sheet without damaging it. When a rule is added to a component, it cannot be removed after it has been implemented. To see Fusion's default rules, go to the Modify menu and choose Sheet Metal Rules. To see all of them, use the arrows to slide down the menu. When you move the mouse pointer over each one, an **Edit pencil icon** and a **Create New Rule** icon will appear. You can update rules; however, it is recommended that you first click on the button labeled "**New Rule**," then make any necessary modifications to the information that is populated by default, and then save the result as a new rule. You might consider creating and saving a design that is made up of square flanges and has various rules related to each flange. The next step is to integrate it into a new Sheet Metal design and call it a "**template**." This makes it possible for you to simply add new rules to the design's library, and it also makes it possible for you to share these rules with other people. A component made of sheet metal begins its life as a piece of metal that is flat and has a constant thickness. Since the component is created using a single sheet of material, the thickness will remain consistent at all times. Details such as bend radii and relief sizes are often consistent across the whole of the item for the sake of production. Simply enter the values that you want Fusion to use for those aspects, and it will use them as you desire. During the manufacturing process, the item may fracture or deform as a result of the stretching that occurs when sheet metal is bent. Therefore, you should plan for the particular manufacturing process that will include cutting and bending. Fabricators may need to change the flat plan to make room for the tools, machinery, and materials that are available. The typical bend radii of the most popular sheet metals, composites, and polymers can be found in the generic tables that are provided in many technical handbooks and by sheet metal distributors.

The Flange and Bend Tools

A flange is a lip that is placed on the edge of an item to add strength or attach it to another element. Five different sheet metal flange commands, including base, edge, contour, miter, and sweeping, are rolled into Fusion 360's single Flange tool. This tool will automatically apply the one that is best suitable for the edge that you have picked. A shift in orientation on a steel component is known as a bend. Let's have a look at those tools. When constructing any component in the Sheet Metal workspace, it is recommended that one begin by selecting "**New Component**" from the drop-down menu. If there are numerous components in one design, give each component a name that is easily distinguishable, and adjust the Rules accordingly. At this point, we are going to go ahead and use the defaults. A piece of metal that is flat and has a curve in it is called a flange. The flange tool allows you to generate flat pieces of metal from scratch if you have not imported a model to work with. To draw a rectangle, you need to choose the green plus sign. Leave the sketch mode, then choose **Create > Flange** from the menu.

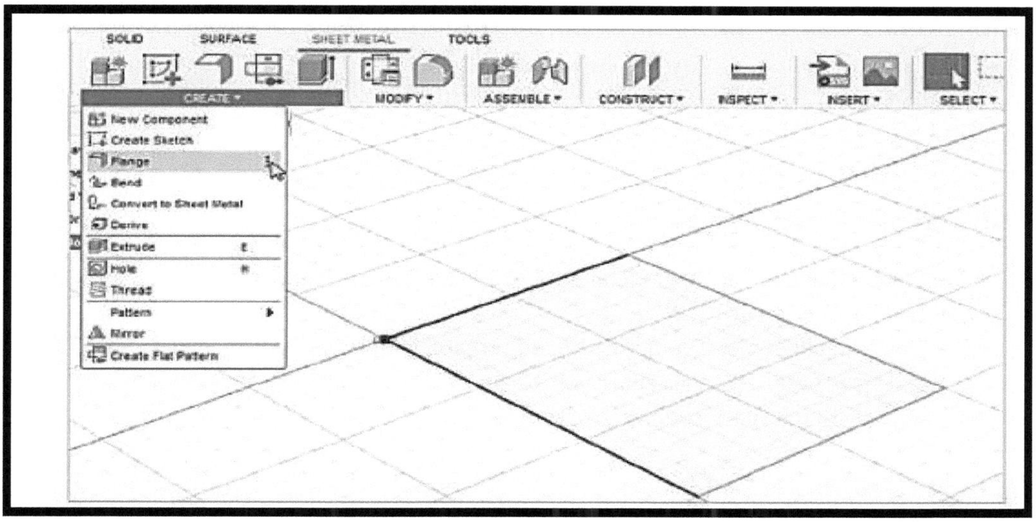

After that, pick the face of the rectangle. Take a look at the new dialog box that has appeared. You can add to the selection by using the plus symbol, and you can remove it from the selection by using the minus sign. When you click **OK**, the drawing will transform into a piece of sheet metal that is flat.

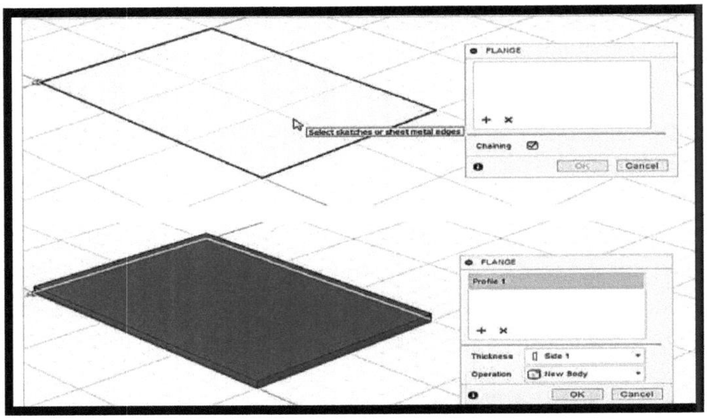

Now we need to give it a little bit of a curve. After selecting an edge with your mouse, return to the Flange tool and click on it once again. Take note of the options that are available in the dialog box. Use the Full Edge setting as the default if you want the bend to be continuous from one end to the other. Choose the Symmetric option to create a symmetrical flange. Using the **transformer button**, you can additionally angle the flange and set the precise location of the bend position. The bend position can be inside, outside, adjacent, or tangent to the edge. There is a Flip option in the dialog box that you can use if the flange does not travel in the direction that you want it to go.

BEND

After entering the Sketch mode, sketching a line on a face to act as the bend line, and then exiting the Sketch mode, you should get the desired result. To use the Bend tool, click it. First, click on the stationary side, and then click on the line that bends. If you wish to, choose an angle for the rotation, and then click the **OK** button.

Creating Sheet Metal Bends

1. Create or Select the Sheet Metal Base:

- A foundation made of flat sheet metal is required to get started. Either a new one can be created, or an existing one can be used.
- To outline your sheet metal item, click on the "**Create**" dropdown menu and pick "**Base**" if you are making a new base. This will allow you to create a new base. Define the size and shape in accordance with the specifications of your design.

2. Activate the "Bend" Tool in the Toolbox:

- Now that the foundation is constructed out of sheet metal, it is time to add bends. You can activate the "**Bend**" tool in the toolbar or by using the keyboard shortcut "B."

3. Choose the Bending Edge:

- When you use Fusion 360, you will get a popup asking you to choose the edge along which you want the bend to be created. Simply click on the base edge of the sheet metal where you wish the bend to take place using the mouse.

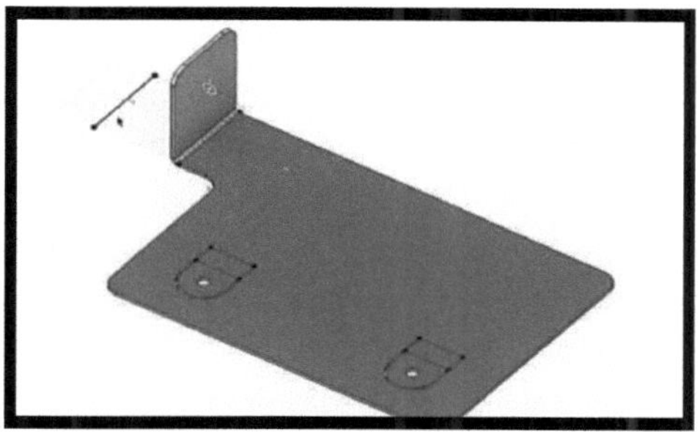

4. Define Bend Parameters:

- Once you have chosen the edge that will be bent, Fusion 360 will provide you with a dialogue box in which you can specify the parameters of the bend.

The following are some important parameters to take into account:

- **Angle**: The angle at which the bend will take place must be specified. You have the option of directly entering the angle, or you can use the protractor tool to measure it from an already-established edge.
- **Inside Radius**: This step involves determining the radius that will be used for the inner curve of the bend. This determines how smoothly the bend will take place.
- **Bend Position**: This field allows you to indicate where the bend will occur along the specified edge. Either a distance from the beginning or the conclusion of the edge can be specified, or a reference point can be used instead.

5. Preview the Bend:

- While you are adjusting the bend parameters, Fusion 360 will offer a real-time preview of how the bend will influence the sheet metal foundation. This gives you the ability to adjust the parameters to get the desired outcome.

6. **Confirm and Create the Bend:**

- When you have adjusted the bend parameters to your liking and verified that they produce the desired result in the preview, click the "**OK" or "Create**" button to confirm the bend.

Repeat for Additional Bends:

- You can carry out the operation many times if your design calls for multiple bends. Repeatedly activating the "**Bend**" tool, selecting the next edge to bend, and defining the parameters are required.

CHAPTER 18
ASSEMBLY CONSTRAINTS AND MOTION

The purpose of this chapter is to further develop our knowledge of assembly constraints and to explore the complex relationships that exist within assemblies. It discusses the use of joint limits, contact sets, and motion links in the process of constructing complex assembly connections. Motion Studies, which enable the construction of dynamic animations inside assemblies and simulate realistic motion for mechanics, are also discussed in this chapter. The simulation of mechanisms and animations is also covered in this chapter. A strong emphasis is placed on the significance of examining assembly motion for the presence of possible interferences and determining the performance and behavior of mechanisms. In addition to this, it provides information on how to create exploded views as well as assembly instructions. This comprises documenting the procedures and directions for assembly to facilitate clear communication and provide production assistance, as well as displaying assembly sequences via exploded views, which aid in understanding the arrangement of components.

Advanced Assembly Joints and Constraints

In Fusion 360, the use of Assemblies enables users to mix and arrange many components to construct complex designs and simulate how those designs would perform. To get the most out of assembly workflows, let's look into the essential tools and processes that are involved.

The following are six fundamental tools that any user of Fusion 360 should be familiar with to comprehend the notion of assemblies:

1. **Component browser**: The component browser is a sophisticated tool that enables you to manage and arrange components inside an assembly. It also displays the relationships between these components. It offers a hierarchical representation of the structure of the assembly, which makes it simple to explore, modify, and manage the various components.
2. **Assembly context**: To construct different variants or configurations of an assembly inside a single design, you can make use of assembly context, which was introduced in the previous section. It gives you flexibility and control over design iterations by allowing you to handle distinct states of your assembly, such as exploded views, subassemblies, or alternate component placements.
3. **View representations:** These are what allow you to construct and manage many views of your assembly. View representations can be found in view representations. You can specify individual component visibility, location, and display settings for each view, which makes it simpler to convey and record various parts of your design.
4. **Exploded views**: The exploded views tool gives you the ability to create exploded views, which you can then use to graphically convey the assembly process or the disassembly sequence. It is possible to exercise fine-grained control over the location, orientation, and spacing of components, thus demonstrating how they can be assembled or disassembled.
5. **Section analysis**: Fusion 360 provides you with tools to do section analysis, which enables you to cut through your assembly and investigate its constituent parts. You can construct cross-

sectional views to acquire insights into the component interactions, clearances, and interference, which will make design validation and verification much easier.

6. **Design timeline**: With the help of the design timeline, you'll be able to view and manage the order in which events occur inside an assembly. You can use it to monitor modifications, assembly animations, and assembly dependencies. This gives you a clear perspective of how the assembly has evolved.

Creating and Managing Components

- **Insert component**: The Insert Component tool gives you the ability to construct new components directly inside an assembly as well as bring in external models. Using this tool, you will be able to make complicated designs by mixing a variety of components that already exist or that you have just made.
- **Component properties**: With the help of component properties, you can specify and adjust the attributes of individual components, such as their mass, appearance, and material. This feature makes it easier to provide an accurate picture and conduct an examination of the components once they have been built.

Techniques

- Make use of assembly patterns to produce many instances of components that recur in a certain pattern or sequence. The assembly process can be greatly sped up as a result, and design alterations can be made more easily.
- Investigate the possibility of making use of derived components to generate variants of components already present inside the assembly without having to alter the initial element.

Factors that should be considered

- When maintaining the components of an assembly, be aware of any potential design modifications or updates that might have an impact on the assembly. Using the functionality called "timeline and rollback," Fusion 360 allows users to monitor and control the changes made to their projects.
- Whenever you make any alterations to the assembly structure or the interactions between the components, you should always be sure to evaluate and confirm the effect such changes have before moving further.

Animating and simulating assemblies in Fusion 360

Visualizing and understanding the functioning and behavior of your ideas is made much easier by the tremendous capabilities offered by the animation and simulation of assemblies in Fusion 360. You can build dynamic animations, evaluate clearance and interference, check structural integrity, and maximize performance with the use of tools like joint motion, exploded views, motion studies, physical simulation, and stress analysis. You will be able to acquire useful insights on the movement of the assembly, replicate real-world circumstances, and make educated design choices for increased functionality and dependability as a result of these capabilities.

The following is a list of five tools that any user of Fusion 360 should be familiar with to animate and simulate assemblies:

1. **Joint motion**: Fusion 360 gives you the ability to specify and control the motion of joints inside an assembly. You can animate the movement of components by specifying joint parameters like rotation angles, limits, or ranges. Other examples of joint parameters include limits and ranges. You will be able to verify the kinematic behavior of your assembly and see how it performs with the help of this tool.
2. **Exploded views**: These are available to users of Fusion 360, which allows users to generate exploded views of assemblies. You can deconstruct components and display each of their distinct pieces in a way that is well-organized and comprehensible if you use this tool. Exploded views aid in the communication of assembly sequences and provide a clearer comprehension of how individual components connect.
3. **Motion studies:** Fusion 360 has tools that enable you to simulate and evaluate the dynamic behavior of assemblies. This allows you to create motion studies. You can construct motion routes, simulate forces and loads, and analyze the performance of moving components using this software. Motion studies provide you the ability to evaluate the operation of your assembly, as well as the clearance and any interferences that exist inside it.
4. **Physical simulation**: Fusion 360 contains tools that can be used to do physical simulations on assemblies. These simulations can be used to validate design decisions. You can simulate the behavior of the assembly under a variety of stress circumstances, apply actual material characteristics, and create connections and constraints, and more. The structural integrity and performance of your design can be validated with the assistance of this tool.
5. **Stress analysis**: Fusion 360 provides you with tools for doing stress analysis, which enables you to assess the structural integrity of assembled parts. You can analyze the stress distribution, deformation, and safety aspects of your design by adding loads and restrictions to it. Utilizing this tool helps in the process of identifying probable areas of failure and improving the design's overall robustness and dependability.

You can animate and simulate assemblies in Fusion 360 by making use of these tools, which will allow you to obtain useful insights into the operation and behavior of the assemblies.

Techniques

Joint selection and type: When applying constraints and joints, it is essential to pick the proper joint type depending on the behavior that is intended. This decision must be made when choosing a joint type. Fusion 360 provides a wide range of joint types, including cylindrical, revolute, and slider, amongst others. By gaining an understanding of the functions performed by the various types of joints as well as their features, you will be able to choose the kind of joint that is most suited for the assembly. In addition, make sure that the joint selection is proper by meticulously determining the connection locations that are wanted between the various components.

Constraint limitations: It's important to be aware of constraint limitations and their impact on the assembly. Constraints in Fusion 360 can be coincident, concentric, or parallel, for example, and they are designed to ensure that components maintain the proper connections with one another. On the other hand, implementing an excessive number of constraints or requirements that clash with one another can lead to outcomes that were not intended. It is important to be aware of the constraints of the constraint and to avoid over-constraining the assembly since this can limit the motion that is wanted or cause the assembly to become unstable.

You can successfully employ constraints and joints to build components in Fusion 360 so long as you pick the proper joint type with care and have a good grasp of the limits of the constraints. These methods assist in ensuring that the assembly will move and behave as planned while preventing problems caused by excessive constraint, which might reduce the assembly's overall usefulness.

About joints in Fusion 360

Joints and as-built joints are what Fusion 360 uses to establish the relationships between components. Joint movement is what gives components their degrees of freedom. When working with other CAD tools, you can restrict one or two degrees of freedom at a time by using a constraint or mate, and then you can continue adding constraints or mates until you have sufficient degrees of freedom. In contrast, the first step in the process of using Fusion 360 is to restrict all degrees of freedom, and then you choose a joint motion type that outlines the degrees of freedom that are available. Using this strategy, you will be able to gain the necessary degrees of freedom all at once, with only a single command. A component can rotate around one of the X, Y, or Z axes or move translationally (back and forth) along one of these axes when it has a joint that permits it to do so. Each joint incorporates the required number of degrees of freedom to achieve the desired range of motion.

When you insert a joint between two components, you choose one of the following types:

- **Rigid**. A rigid joint is a connection between two components that is permanent. There are no degrees of freedom afforded by it.
- **Revolute**. A revolute joint is similar to a hinge in that it only has a single degree of rotational flexibility. This joint can revolve around the X, Y, or Z axis that is typical, or it can rotate around an edge in the model to create a custom axis.
- **Slider**. One and only one degree of translational flexibility is afforded to a slider joint. Components that can glide past one another are made of it. These options are quite similar to the revolute joint options; the only difference is that the components slide along the axis of rotation rather than rotating around it.
- **Cylindrical**. One degree of freedom is provided by translation, while the other is provided by rotation when using a cylindrical joint. Components that are linked together using a cylindrical joint will always spin along the same axis once the connection has been assembled.
- **Pin Slot**. A pin slot joint likewise permits two degrees of freedom, but the components involved can rotate around separate axes.
- **Planar**. There are three degrees of freedom available at a planar joint. It is possible to translate in two different directions inside a plane, and it is also possible to rotate in one direction that is normal to the plane. It helps attach two components in such a way that they can rotate while sliding over the plane.
- **Ball**. Pitch and yaw are the two degrees of rotational freedom that a ball joint has. The Z axis can be rotated by components thanks to pitch. Yaw is a rotational motion that revolves components around the X-axis.

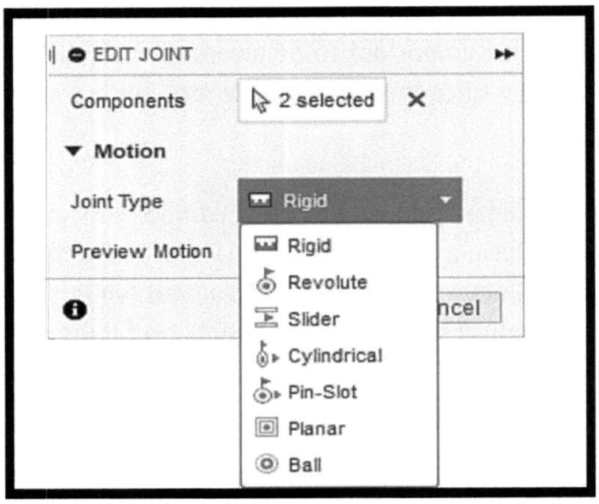

Applying Motion Studies

1. **Create the Motion Study**:
- To get started, you need to first develop the motion study for your design. During this step, you will establish joints, constraints, and keyframes to specify how the components of your assembly move over time. Check to see that the motion study you've created appropriately depicts the motion you want your design to have.
2. **Save the Design**:
- Before you go on to the rendering process, make sure that you have saved your design so that you have the most recent version of your assembly recorded. Because the rendering process will utilize the current state of the design, including any modifications that were made while the motion study setup was in progress, this phase is very important.
3. **Create or Re-render Still Images**:
- It is necessary to have a sequence of still photographs that each represents a frame of the animation to produce a motion study. You can render these photos if you haven't done so before by establishing a rendering job on your computer.

  Proceed in the following manner:

  a. Proceed to the workspace titled "**Render**"
  b. Adjust the options for the rendering so that it looks the way you want it to, including the quality, resolution, and camera views.
  c. To begin the process of rendering, click on the "Render" button. The parameters you choose in Fusion 360 will determine the still photographs it produces.
  d. After the rendering process is finished, you will find a collection of still photographs in the gallery that was created for you.
4. **Open the Rendering Preview**:
- Navigate to the rendering preview where the still photos that you wish to utilize for your motion study are stored. The Render Gallery is the location where you can discover this.
5. **Choose the Image That You Want to Re-render**:
- Navigate to the **Render Gallery** and look for the picture or frame that you want to re-render so that you can include it in your motion study. Make sure that it is a significant part of the story that your animation is telling.
6. **Re-render the Image**:

- Following the selection of the picture, there ought to be a "**Re-Render**" option available to you. Click on this path to select it. Fusion 360 will begin the process of producing this particular frame, taking into consideration any updates or modifications that have been done since the previous time the frame was rendered. To access the capability to produce Motion Studies, click the Play button.

Creating Assemblies Animation

Step 1: Switch to the Animation Workspace

After opening your Fusion 360 assembly in Fusion 360, we will need to go to the animation workspace to begin the process of generating an animation for the assembly. Throughout the process of creating your components, you most likely make use of a variety of different workspaces inside Fusion 360. For example, I split my time mostly between the Model and Render workspaces here in the program. Additionally, the Drawing workspace is quite beneficial to have. Here, we will be working in a workspace known as the Animation workspace, which you may not have used previously. So, in the top-left corner of the window, choose the **Change Workspace** dropdown menu and then select the **Animation workspace** from the list of available options.

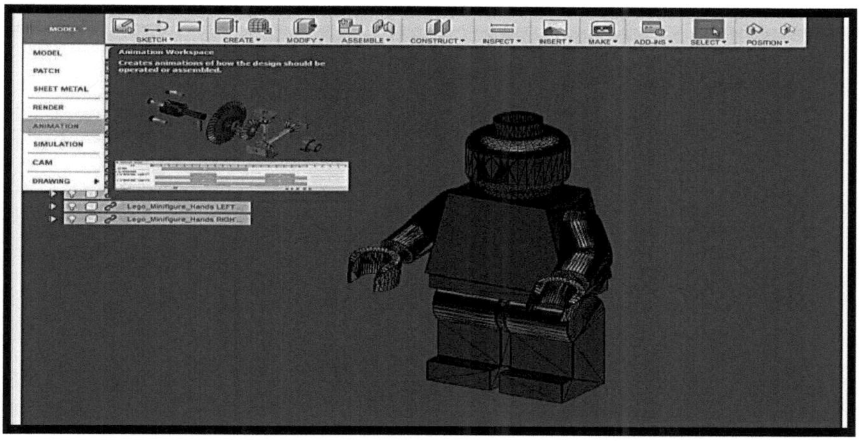

Step 2: Set Initial Positions

Explore the Animation Workspace.

When you first start using the Animation workspace, it can be a little bit perplexing. ***So, before we go any further, let's go over some of the fundamentals of using this workspace, shall we?*** The Timeline is a feature that is only available in the Animation workspace and can be found at the bottom of the screen. This is maybe the most essential function that you will discover. The animation that you see is the result of a series of changes that were made to the Fusion 360 assembly over time and are shown in the Timeline. On the Timeline, there is a row for each component in the assembly, and that row details the modifications that were done to that component. A component's appearance can be modified in some ways, including showing or hiding it, moving it, or rotating it. The majority of the work that needs to be done to complete our assembly animation will be carried out in the Timeline.

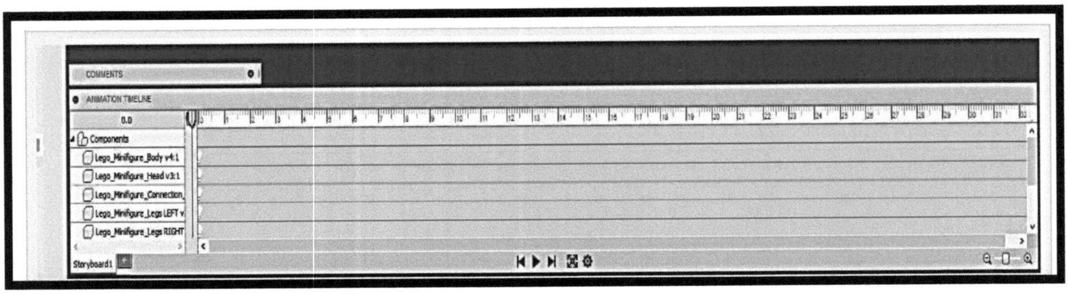

The ribbon menu at the top of the screen is the second component of the Animation workspace that you will want to get acquainted with. Each of the many workspaces, including the Animation workspace, has its own unique set of controls that are accessible on the ribbon. In contrast to many of the other workspaces, the ribbon in the Animation workspace has a far lower number of controls than the other workspaces. The **Transform** menu will be used the most here. Using this menu, you can generate an animation by modifying the location and orientation of the pieces that make up the assembly. You can also get access to a good many of the controls in this menu by right-clicking on individual components inside the assembly. At the very conclusion of this demonstration, we will save the assembly animation by selecting "**Publish**" from the menu bar.

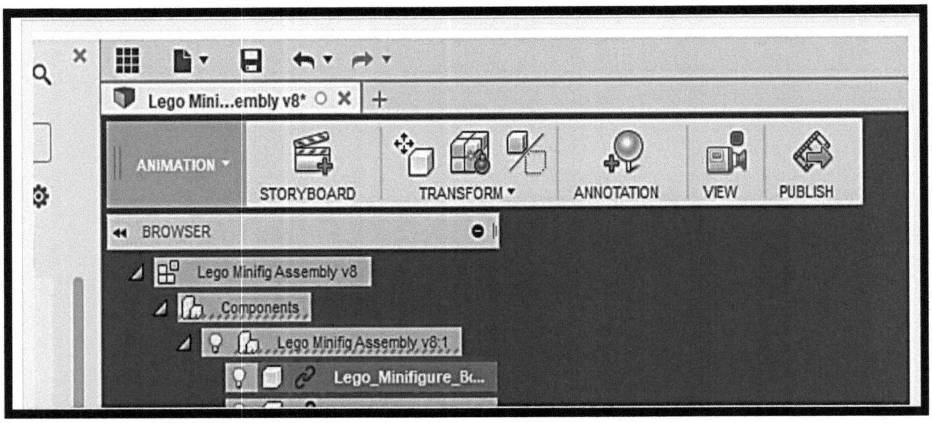

Set Initial Component Positions

After becoming comfortable with the Animation workspace, the first step in the process of designing the assembly animation will be to determine the beginning location of the components. As we build the assembly, you can manipulate the Timeline by moving the scrub head forward and backward in time. There is a red curtain icon located on the very far left side of the timeline. When you select the curtain symbol, it allows you to move the scrub head to the very left side of the Timeline. Now that the scrub head is at the beginning of the Timeline, we can adjust the visibility of the components or move them about freely, and the animation will start with the components in the places that we choose at this time. Use the "**Manual Explode**" command, which can be found in the "**Transform**" menu of the ribbon, to relocate the components.

You can relocate a component in your assembly away from the rest of the assembly by using the **Manual Explode** function. This function enables you to pick a component in your assembly. You will need to set aside some time to use the **Manual Explode** tool to reposition all of the components so that they are in their appropriate starting places for the assembly. You will get a better sense of appropriate beginning locations in the assembly animations that you create in Fusion 360 as you put in more effort.

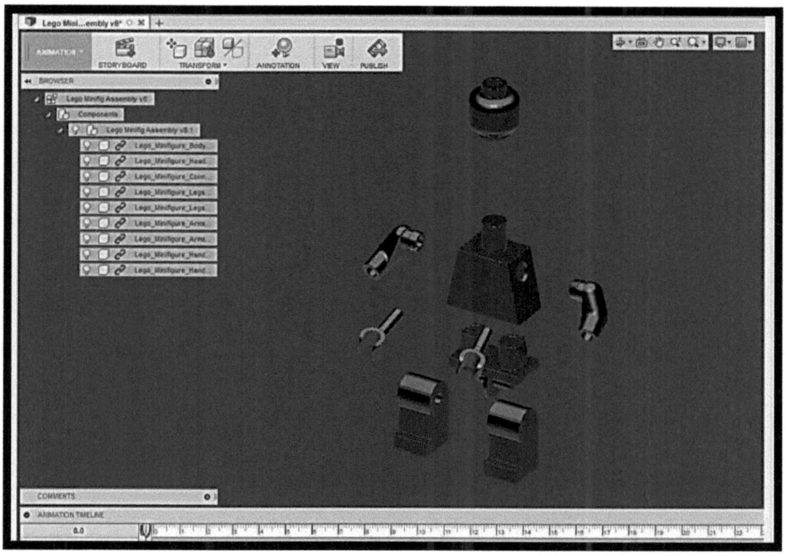

You can also decide to conceal some of the components at the beginning of the assembly animation. This will allow you to reveal those components at the appropriate moment when it is appropriate for them to be combined with the other elements of the assembly. You can choose to reveal or conceal a portion by using the **reveal/conceal** command, which is located in the **Transform** menu.

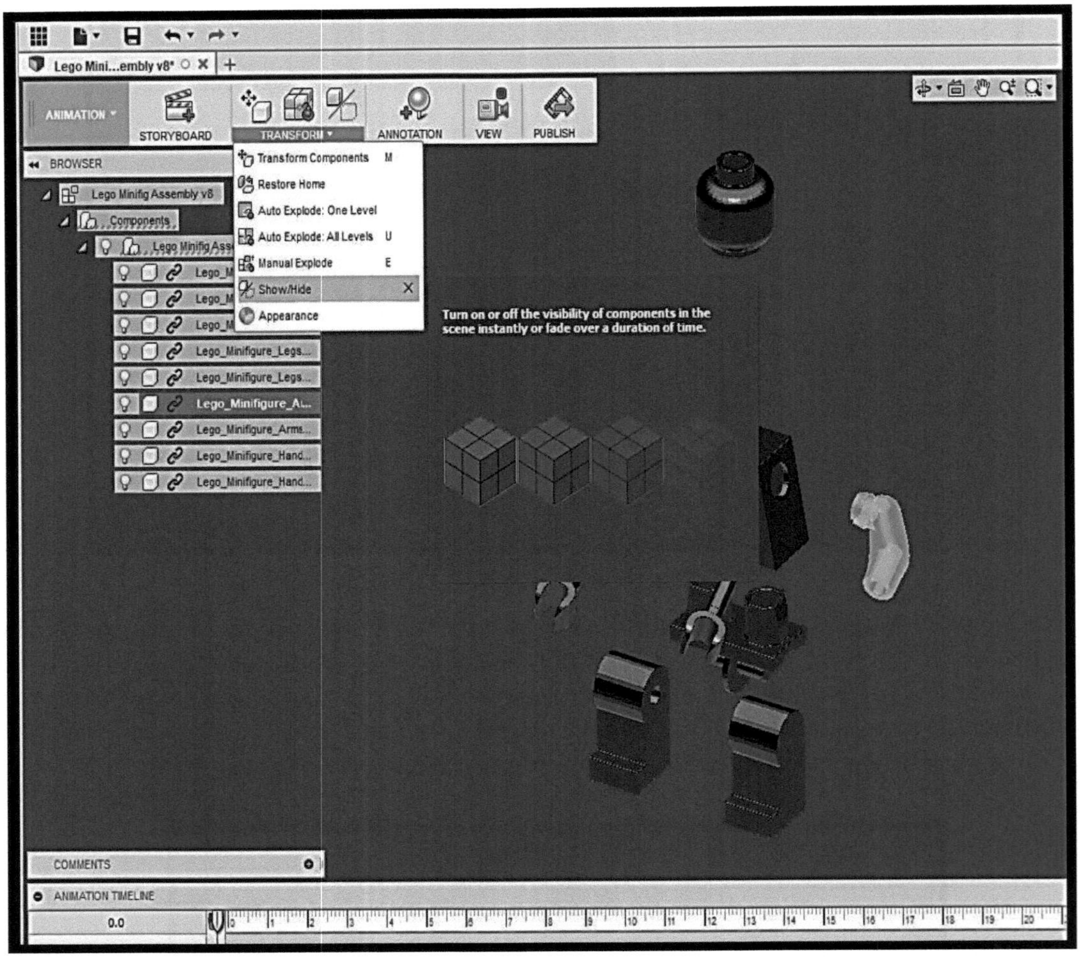

Step 3: Create First Animation Frame

Now that we've determined the starting locations and visibility for each of the components that make up our Fusion 360 assembly, we can go to work on constructing the actual animation itself. To begin, forward the scrub head in the Timeline by one or two seconds so that it is about halfway through the animation. Any adjustments you make to the assembly will be recorded and incorporated into the Timeline as soon as the scrub head has moved to a new location on the Timeline. The animation will have seamless transitions between frames thanks to Fusion 360's intelligent handling of the process. I started building the animation for the example **Lego Minifig model** by moving the hip part of the assembly onto the body with the scrub head positioned at 1.5 seconds. The **Restore Home command** can be used by right-clicking on a component in the assembly or by selecting it from the Transform menu on the ribbon. This command is quite helpful when it comes to reassembling the components.

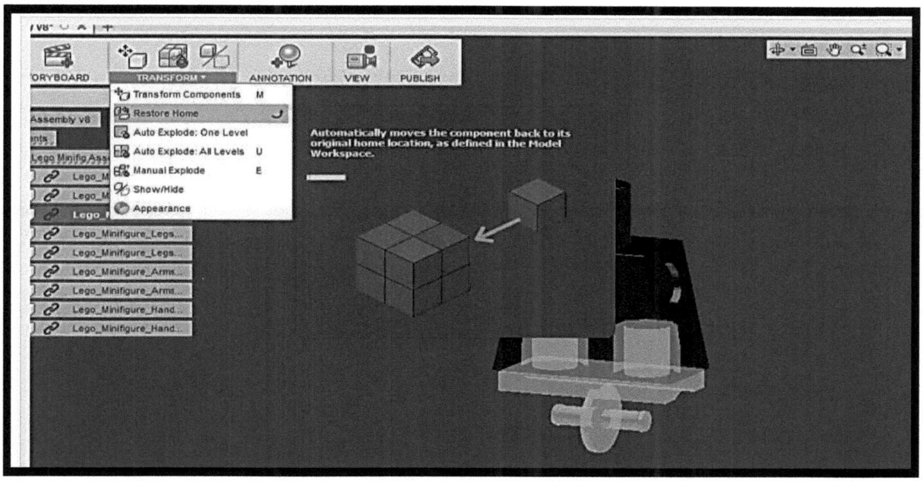

The Timeline will reflect any modifications that you make to it. This involves repositioning components or altering their visibility, as well as adjustments you make to the way you see things. Fusion 360 will automatically animate the change in the camera angle in the Timeline whenever you make a change to it. My animation begins with the hip being moved into position such that it is linked to the body, and the camera also moves very little at this point.

Step 4: Create Remaining Animation Frames

After the first frame of the animation has been completed, the subsequent frames can be constructed using the method that was used to produce the initial frame. Simply reposition the components in the assembly and set the scrub head in the Timeline such that it is a few seconds past the frame that was most recently shown. When you make changes to the assembly, including movements of the camera, Fusion 360 will automatically generate a seamless transition for you, just like it did when it rendered the initial frame. Because developing assembly animations in Fusion 360 is more of an art than a science, you should experiment with a variety of transformations, camera motions, and timings until you reach a point where you are satisfied with the animation that has been produced.

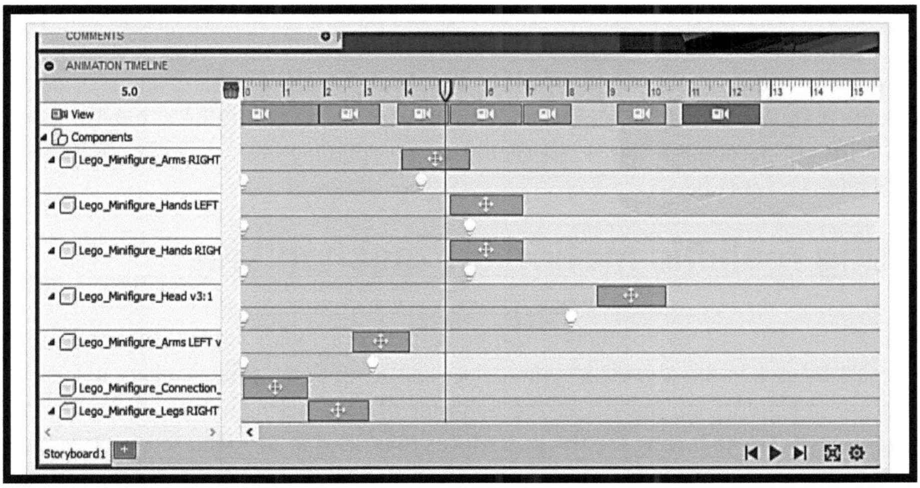

Step 5: Publish Your Animation

After you have completed developing your animation using the Timeline, the next step is to publish the animation. Putting out the animation won't be a problem at all. To publish your animations, use the **Publish button** from the ribbon menu.

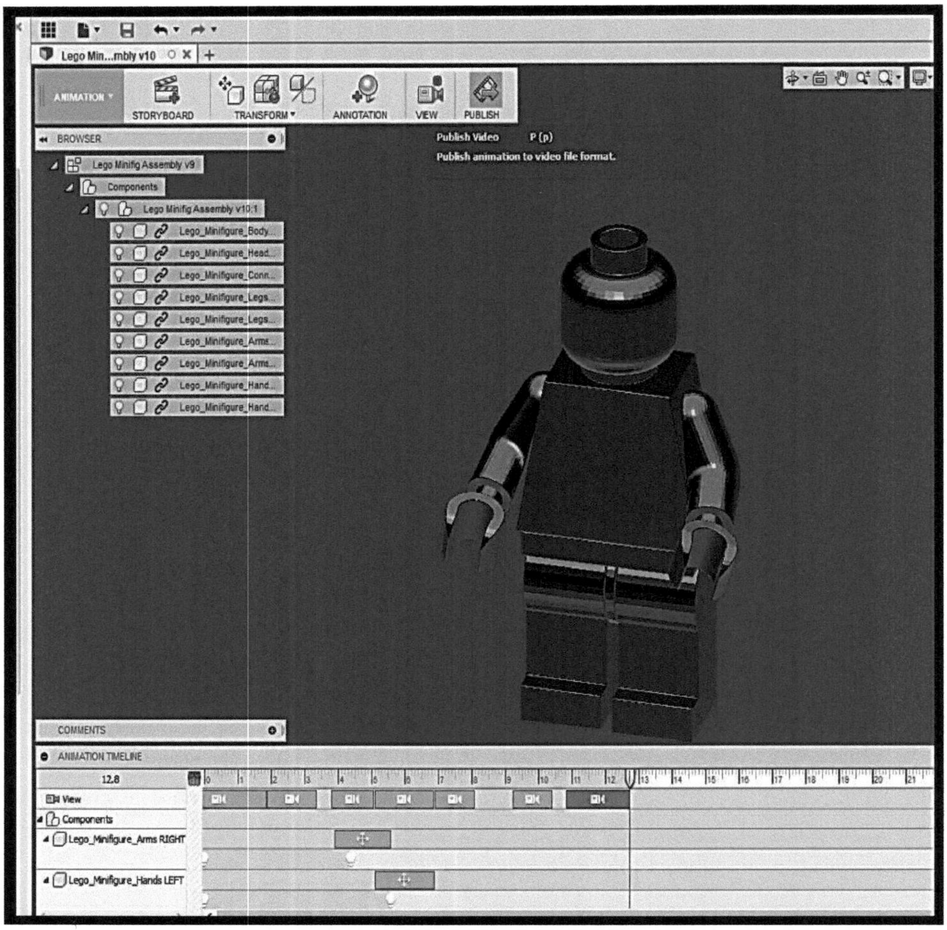

Simply choose the location on your computer where you want the movie to be saved by using the Save As dialog box. After that, you can either immediately share your movie with others, publish it to YouTube, convert it to a GIF (to accomplish this, I use Giphy), or do anything else you want with the wonderful assembly animation you created.

Simulating realistic motion for mechanisms

Creating accurate models of how mechanical components interact with one another and move inside a design is a necessary step in the process of simulating realistic motion for mechanisms in Fusion 360. This is very necessary to conduct an analysis of the behavior of your mechanisms and verify that they are operating as designed. **The following are the procedures that need to be taken to create realistic motion in Fusion 360:**

1. **Create or Open Your Assembly**:
   - Start by either creating a new assembly or opening an existing one in Fusion 360. Your assembly should include all the mechanical components that you want to simulate.
2. **Define Joints and Constraints:**
   - If you want to be able to mimic realistic motion, you will need to specify how the components are related to one another and how they are limited. Different forms of joints, such as revolute, slider, and cylindrical, are available in Fusion 360. These sorts of joints replicate real-world linkages. Insert and configure these joints such that they behave in a manner that is analogous to that of your mechanical system.
3. **Add Motion Inputs**:
   - You need to identify the external forces or motion inputs that will be responsible for driving the motion of your machine. Motors and actuators, as well as human inputs like keyframes, can be considered to be examples of these inputs. To build and manage these inputs, you can use the "**Motion**" workspace.
4. **Adjust the Motion Settings**:
   - To configure the simulation parameters such as time step size, length, and convergence criterion, you must first access the "**Motion Study" or "Simulation**" settings. These options affect the simulation's accuracy as well as its speed.
5. **Set Initial Conditions**:
   - If your mechanism begins in a certain starting state (for example, certain positions or orientations), you can configure these conditions to recreate real-world events more exactly.
6. **Run the Simulation**:
   - Start the simulation so you can track how your mechanism behaves and how it progresses over time. Fusion 360 will do the computation for the motion depending on the circumstances, inputs, and restrictions that you describe. You can get a visual representation of the motion by using the animation timeline.
7. **Analyze Results**:
   - You can analyze the behavior of your mechanism in many different ways while the simulation is taking place or after it has been completed. Examine the system for any collisions, interferences, stress, and other performance indicators to identify problems and locate places where improvements can be made.
8. **Iterate and make adjustments**:
   - If you find any issues when running the simulation or if the behavior of your mechanism doesn't match your expectations, make any required revisions to your design, restrictions, or inputs, and then restart the simulation. If you still find issues, you can also try running the simulation again. The iterative process is very necessary to get practical outcomes.
9. **Generate Reports and Graphs**:
   - There are tools included in Fusion 360 that allow users to make reports and graphs that summarize the outcomes of simulations. These reports can be helpful for recordkeeping as well as communication with coworkers or other stakeholders.
10. **Optimize and Validate**:
    - You should continue to improve both your design and your simulations until you have a behavior model that is both satisfying and accurate in representing your mechanism's operation. To verify the performance of the system, compare the simulation results with the requirements and specifications of the design.

11. **Save and Document**:
    - For future reference, be sure to save your simulation setup, results, and any significant discoveries you make. Create a design document that details the simulation process, including the assumptions used and the outcomes obtained.

Analyzing assembly motion for interference

Fusion 360 assembly motion analysis for interference entails examining an assembly for collisions or interference between individual components. Ensuring that your design functions as intended and that there are no physical collisions between pieces during movement or interaction is essential.

1. To begin an analysis, start Fusion 360 and go to the assembly you want to examine. Inserting your components into a new assembly workspace is the first step in creating an assembly, if you haven't before.
2. Fusion 360 has a tool named "**Interference**" that lets you assess if any of the components in your assembly are interfering with one another.
    - Select the "**Assemble**" tab from the upper toolbar.
    - Click the dropdown menu and choose the "**Interference**" tool.
3. You must choose the components you want to check for interference by selecting them in the "**Interference**" dialog box. You can choose to evaluate all of the components in the assembly or you can pick specific components.
4. To accommodate for tolerances, Fusion 360 lets you set a clearance value. The minimum distance between components that should not be regarded as interference is represented by this number. Enter the clearance value that corresponds to your design specifications.
5. Click "**Compute Interference**" after components have been chosen and the clearance has been defined. Fusion 360 will conduct the analysis and identify any regions in which the chosen components interact with one another.
6. Fusion 360 will show you where parts of the assembly are having interference problems by displaying the interference results in the graphics section. The color-coded visual aid can be used to pinpoint the locations of the issues.
    - **Red**: Indicates interference.
    - **Green**: Indicates no interference.
    - **Yellow**: Indicates that the clearance is close to the defined value.
7. **Modifications to the design may be necessary, depending on the kind of interference. Here are a few typical techniques for removing interference:**
    - Adjust component positions or orientations.
    - Modify component sizes or features.
    - Add clearances or tolerances to your design.
8. To be sure that the problems have been fixed after making adjustments to address interference, you can rerun the interference analysis.
9. Recording the interference analysis findings and any design modifications is a recommended practice.
10. To preserve the adjustments made to address interference, save your assembly and any related files.

Evaluating mechanism performance and behavior

1. To evaluate a mechanism, use Fusion 360 and open the assembly containing the mechanism. The components should be assembled in a new assembly workspace if you haven't already established the assembly.
2. Press the "**Animate**" tool icon located in the toolbar. A play button or the "**Assemble**" tab is where you can find it.

- Decide which mechanisms' components you wish to assess. Fusion 360 will animate their motion according to the limitations placed upon them.

3. **Examine Motion:**
    - Launch the animation to see the mechanism in action.
    - Observe how components work together, if they clash or obstruct one another, and whether the motion is consistent with your design goals.
    - To examine certain movements or interesting points in the animation, use the timeline controls to stop, rewind, or slow it down.
4. **Assessing Interference**
    - Check for collisions or interference between components while the animation is running using the "**Interference**" tool.
    - Locate any trouble spots, and if interference is found, fix the problems by making changes to the design.
5. **Verify Motion Restrictions**:
    - Check that the components' motion limitations (mates, joints, etc.) are appropriately established and provide the intended range of motion.
    - To get the desired behavior, fine-tune or alter the restrictions as needed.
6. **Analyze the Forces and Loads:**

- You can do stress, deformation, or motion studies using Fusion 360's "Simulation" workspace if your system has moving elements that are exposed to loads or forces.
- To test how your mechanism performs under real-world situations, apply forces, torques, or other loads.

7. **Evaluate Performance Metrics**:
    - Depending on the aim of your mechanism, take into account certain performance indicators. You might monitor cycle time, displacement, torque, or speed, for instance.
    - Compute these metrics using Fusion 360's simulation and analysis capabilities, then compare the results to your design specifications.

Iterate on the design of the mechanism's behavior that falls short of your expectations or performance requirements. Make the required modifications, such as altering the shape of the mechanism, adding more restrictions, or changing the sizes of the parts, and then reassess its performance. Through these stages, you can assess a mechanism's behavior and performance inside an assembly in Fusion 360 in a comprehensive way, enabling you to make well-informed design choices and guarantee the mechanism performs as intended.

Creating Exploded Views and Assembly Instructions

Creating an Exploded View

1. **Open Assembly:**
    - Launch Fusion 360 and open the assembly you want to create an exploded view for.
2. **Switch to the Animation Environment:**
    - In the top toolbar, click on the "Animate" tab to switch to the Animation environment.
3. **Explode the Assembly:**
    - **Within the Animation environment, you have several options to explode the assembly:**
        - **Manual Explosion:** Select components and use the "Move" command to reposition them as desired to create the exploded effect.
        - **Auto Explode - One Level:** Under the "Transform" menu, choose "Auto Explode: One Level" to automatically separate components by a single level.
        - **Auto Explode - All Levels:** Similar to the above, but separates all components by their full hierarchy levels.
4. **Apply Trail Lines and Split Transforms (Optional):**
    - If needed, you can apply trail lines to components as they move or choose to split transforms using options in the Move dialog to enhance the exploded view's visual clarity.

It is also possible to animate the exploded view and export it as a video file:

1. Follow the steps above to create the exploded view.
2. Click on "**Publish**" in the Tool Ribbon
3. Select the desired Storyboard and Video Resolution.
4. Click **OK**.
5. On the next window; Name the video file and select where to save it locally and/or in the cloud. Be sure to check the boxes.

To create a video of the exploded view moving in reverse to assemble instead of explode:

1. Follow the steps above to create the exploded view.
2. Right-click on the Storyboard name in the bottom left of the Animation workspace.
3. Select "**Reverse**" on the pop-up.

CHAPTER 19

COLLABORATIVE WORKFLOWS AND DATA MANAGEMENT

This chapter provides an essential examination of how Fusion 360 promotes cooperation, improves project collaboration, and guarantees effective data management for engineers and designers. The chapter opens with a thorough explanation of how to use Fusion 360's features to promote cooperation. It explores the subtleties of configuring and overseeing access control, permissions, and user roles in the program. This is essential to guarantee safe cooperation while maintaining an organized workflow. A critical component of design history, version control, and design management is explored in detail. This chapter explains how Fusion 360 enables users to keep a close eye on design modifications, keep an extensive revision history, and easily go back to earlier design iterations as needed. Maintaining design integrity, traceability, and accountability requires these qualities. This chapter also explores how easily Fusion 360 can be integrated with a wide range of different software products. It talks about how design data can be easily imported and exported, which makes it easier to integrate disparate CAD systems. Furthermore, Fusion 360's versatility in integrating with other design and analytic tools is emphasized, highlighting its function as a key hub in all-encompassing design processes.

Working with Teams in Fusion 360

Fusion Team can be seen as a one-stop shop for all of your requirements related to project collaboration. When we refer to cooperation, we encompass procedures such as:

- Creating and managing projects
- Sharing project data
- Reviewing and discussing designs
- Tracking project updates
- Commenting and marking up projects

This can all occur with a different departmental team member, another designer, or even a manufacturer or other outside expert. All things considered, the Fusion Team serves as the gathering place for all the individuals and procedures involved in your project.

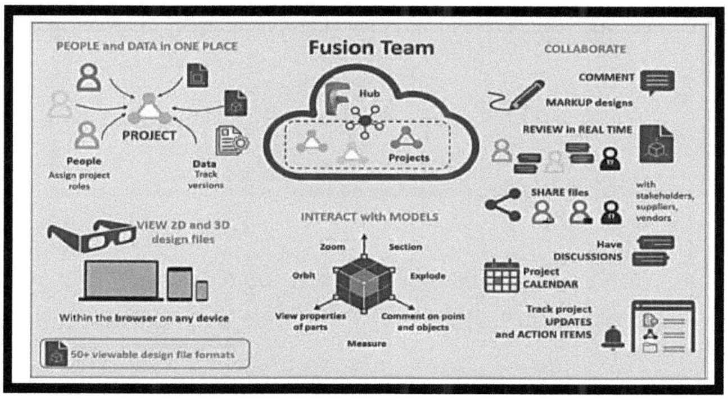

Is Fusion Team, a cloud-based platform for collaboration, something you have never used before? What you can do with it is as follows:

- **Connect teams and suppliers**. Anyone within or outside of your organization can safely access and share your Fusion project. This facilitates stakeholders' ability to easily examine your design as required.
- **Have real-time conversations**. Fusion Team comes with a ton of markup, commenting, and real-time chat tools that facilitate collaboration. Discuss your design back and forth without ever exchanging an email.
- **Centralize project activity**. The Fusion team consolidates all of the communications and version history for your project into a single, central area. This facilitates tracking the development of your design.

Fusion Team offers collaborators the best possible access to your project from almost anywhere. Without Fusion 360 installed, anybody can examine your design on any computer, tablet, or smartphone as long as they have a web browser! We'll begin our journey in Fusion 360. Assume you are the principal designer and you must distribute your project to your manufacturer and a few other team members. Expand the version history for your project after opening your Data Panel in Fusion 360 to access Fusion Team. To launch your project in Fusion Team, click the **Open Details on Web** link.

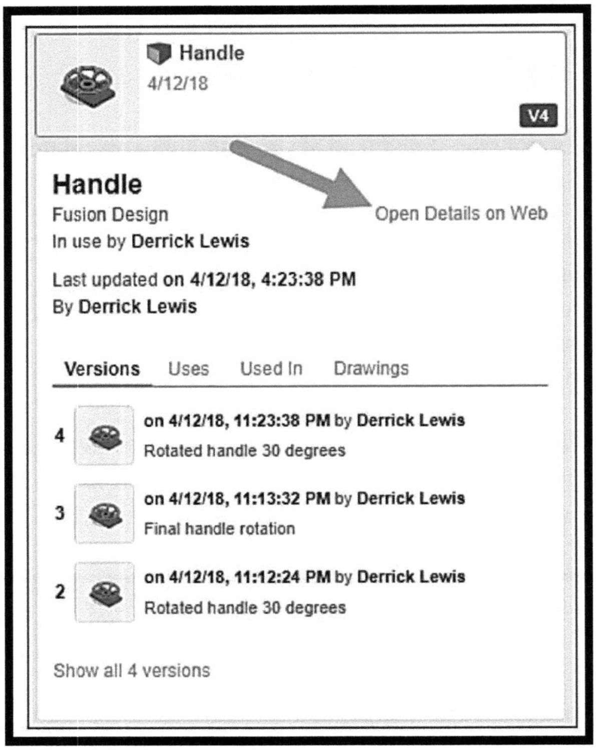

Now, the same design that you saw in Fusion 360 ought to be shown on your web browser. This is the perspective in which you will collaborate. Before sharing your project with others, let's go over a few essentials.

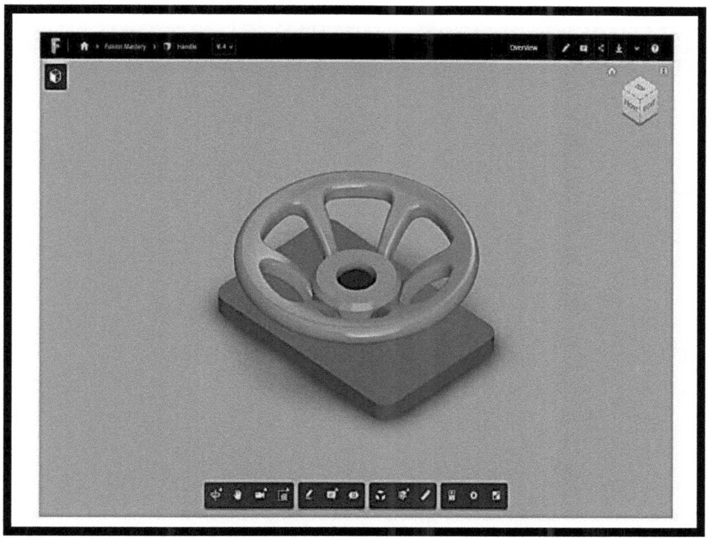

Viewing a design

In Fusion Team, there are several methods to see your design. This view cube located in the upper right corner will allow you to examine your design from several angles. In the toolbar at the bottom, you can also change your viewpoint by using the Pan, Zoom, and Orbit options.

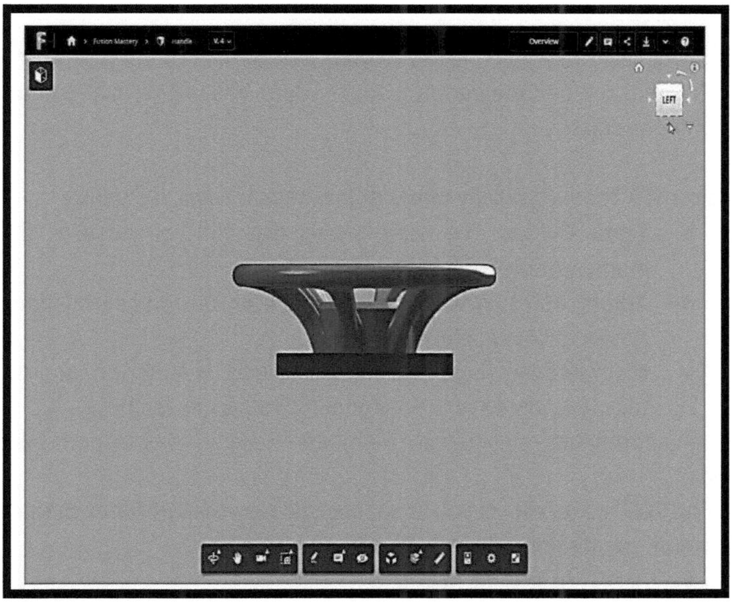

Finally, your Design panel will open if you pick the cube in the upper left corner. You can see your design from some preset angles using this panel. Additionally, you can see your model's various component bodies using this window.

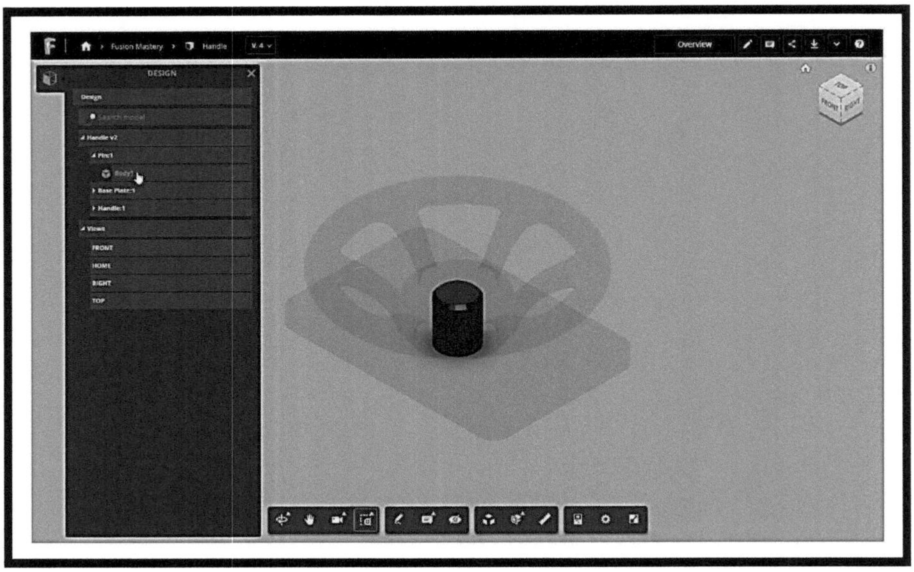

To reset your view if it becomes erratic, just click on the Home symbol located in the upper right corner.

Managing user roles, permissions, and access

1. **Inviting Users to Your Team:**
    - You need to be the team owner or have administrative privileges to manage user roles and permissions.
    - To invite team members, log in to your Autodesk account, go to the Fusion 360 Teams dashboard, and find the option to invite users. You will typically need their Autodesk IDs or email addresses.
2. **User Roles:**
    - **Fusion 360 Teams typically offers different user roles, including:**
        - **Team Owner:** The team owner has full control over the team, including managing roles, permissions, and billing.
        - **Admin:** Administrators can manage user roles and permissions but may not have access to billing information.
        - **Member:** Members can access projects, collaborate, and use Fusion 360, but they typically have limited administrative capabilities.
    - Assign appropriate roles to team members based on their responsibilities.
3. **Permissions:**
    - **Fusion 360 Teams allows you to set specific permissions for each team member or role. Common permissions might include:**
        - Access to specific projects
        - Edit and view permissions for designs
        - Commenting and markup privileges
        - Exporting and sharing capabilities
    - You can typically customize these permissions based on the needs of each team member or role.

4. **Access Control:**
    - Control who can access your Fusion 360 projects by specifying the team members or roles that have permission to view, edit, or collaborate on specific projects.
    - You can also revoke access if needed.
5. **Project Management:**
    - Organize your design projects within Fusion 360 Teams. Each project can have its own set of permissions and access controls.
    - You can typically create, archive, or delete projects as needed.
6. **Collaboration and Version Control:**
    - Fusion 360 provides collaboration features, including version control and commenting, to ensure that team members can work together efficiently and track changes.
7. **Monitoring and Auditing:**
    - Depending on the features offered, Fusion 360 Teams may provide auditing capabilities to track changes and user activities for security and compliance purposes.
8. **Billing and Subscription Management:**
    - If you're the team owner, you can typically manage billing and subscription details for your team.

Version Control

Put simply, version control lets you keep track of all the file changes made to your project. It can be compared to capturing a picture. A version control system keeps track of what was modified, by whom, and when, for each file modification. You'll have access to a full history of versions as your project develops, which you can evaluate or restore as needed. It seems like a straightforward method, so what's the big deal? Think back to the times before version control. On their computers, designers in a team would usually have separate versions of the same file. If you make a change, how is it communicated to others? Do you yell at people in the office? Forward an email? Perhaps you might create a spreadsheet to help you stay organized? Handling this can be rather messy. Version control serves as a safety net by taking a picture of your work at certain intervals and making earlier iterations or versions retrievable.

Version control provides solutions to important problems at its core:

1. **What has changed?**
2. **Who made the changes?**
3. **When were the changes made?**
4. **Why were the changes made?**

Version control offers a systematic framework that reduces mistakes, fosters cooperation, and guarantees responsibility throughout the design and development process by addressing these concerns.

Types of Version Control Systems

There are two primary categories of version control systems:

1. **Centralized Version Control Systems (CVCS):** All file and directory versions are kept in one repository using CVCS. Colleagues can take files out of the central repository, edit them, and

then commit their modifications back in. Subversion and CVS (Concurrent Versions System) are two instances of CVCS.

2. **Distributed Version Control Systems (DVCS):** DVCS transfers the whole repository, together with its complete version history, to every user's local computer. Faster operations and offline access are two benefits of this decentralization. Git is the most well-known DVCS and is used by many businesses.

Why Use Version Control?

Your design project is, let's face it, your top priority. You already have too much on your plate; attempting to pull together a manual version control system is simply another task. Because of this, Fusion 360 now has a version control component.

It works automatically straight out of the box. Why then utilize it?

- **Working together is simple**: You and your team can collaborate on the same project at any time without worrying about modifications getting in the way of each other's work. You don't have to worry about who has what version of a file. Everything is monitored properly and is kept in one single spot for easy access.
- **Version tracking is easy**: As you work on your project, you probably already have a practice of saving it, but how do you know how frequently to do so? What will the names of each version be? Above all, how do you find out what was altered in each version? The Fusion 360 version control system automatically handles all of these queries.
- **Visible**: Fusion 360's version management system creates a new version of your project file whenever a design modification is made. A description that can quickly inform you of the changes made, by whom, and why is also included with each version. When you need some accountability in your workflow and have numerous individuals working on the same design, this is a huge assistance.
- **Restoring versions is quick**: Perhaps after a team discussion, you concluded that your most recent design change isn't quite working. How will you go back to a previous version? I hope you haven't already undone the modifications you made before! Fusion 360 has version control, so you can easily go back to a prior version whenever you'd like.
- **Restoring data is worry-free**: Fusion's cloud storage allows for secure and central storage of all versions that are made. Has your computer suddenly become unreliable and does it need to be replaced? Your design project is not permanently gone. Any device that supports Fusion 360 will have your whole project history available when you open it.

How to Use Version Control in Fusion 360

Fusion 360's version control system is really easy to use, even though it offers a ton of customizable features. We'll be going over our example file to help you understand how the procedure works. Before anything else, we must upload our example file to Fusion 360 so that it can begin tracking changes. To do this, choose the **Upload** button in a project.

The version control mechanism starts operating as soon as the file is successfully uploaded to Fusion 360. You can see the first version of the sample file, designated as V1, by opening your Data Panel.

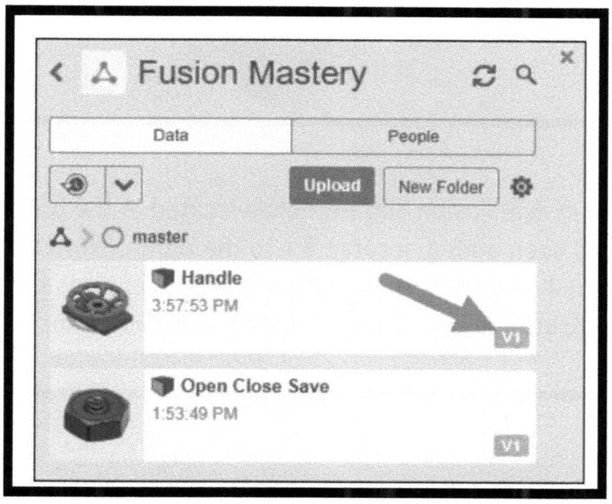

Let's open this file in our canvas, make some changes, and see the operation of the version control system. A handle that can be turned around a base plate is included in this example file. Left-click to rotate the handle left or right. When you release the left click, the new placement is fixed.

A model must be captured when its location is altered. Choose the **Capture Position** button located at the top of your interface once you have moved the handle. From the same option, you can also move the handle back to its initial position if necessary.

Now would be a good time to look at Fusion 360's timeline located at the bottom of the canvas. You'll see that a new Position action has been added, located far to the right of the timeline. Don't worry if you're examining the timetable for the first time. Although there are a lot of icons there, what's there is a history of all the modifications made to your design. View the most recent addition:

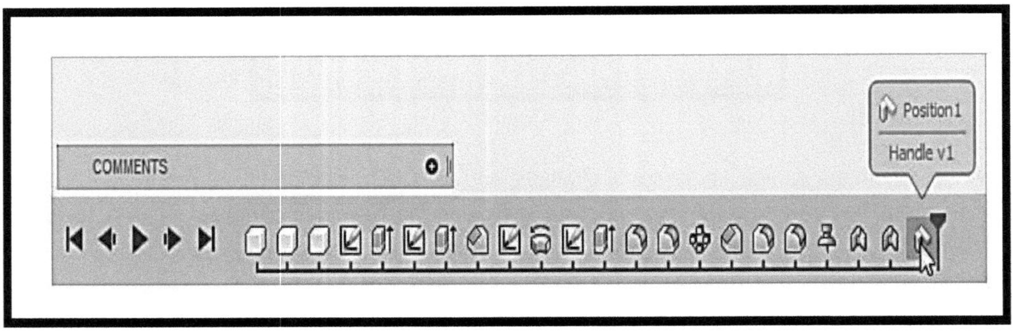

Adding a version change description

We can save our design now that the new location has been effectively recorded. Your interface will open with the **Add Version Description** dialog box when you choose **Save** at the top. Everyone with access to your project will be able to see the description you provide here. Provide as many details as necessary to explain the changes you made.

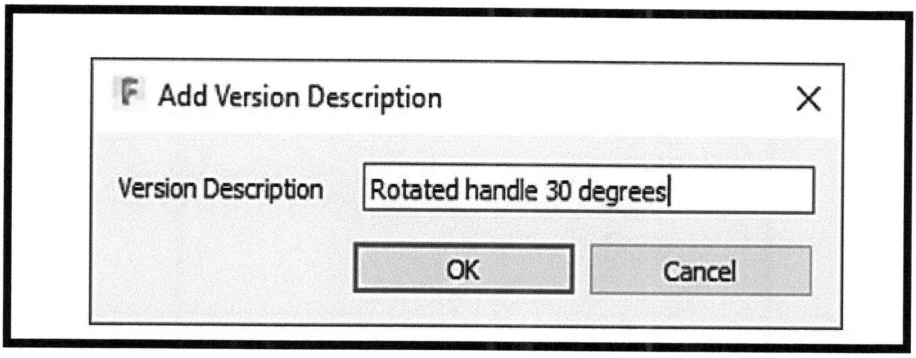

Once you've added a description, click **OK** and give Fusion's version control system a moment to save your snapshot. Once the Data Panel is open, we can see V2 for the handle file listed:

To get a third version, we will do one last rotation to our handle and save it once more. Working with the version control system has been mostly hands-off up to this point. When you save a file after making modifications, an automated new version is produced. What happens, however, if you choose to access an older version, examine the changes made, or go back to a previous version? Everything takes place inside the Data Panel.

Viewing the version history

A full version history will appear when you choose the Handle file's V2 (or V3) icon while your Data Panel is active. As you can see, all three of the variations are mentioned, each with a unique time and description.

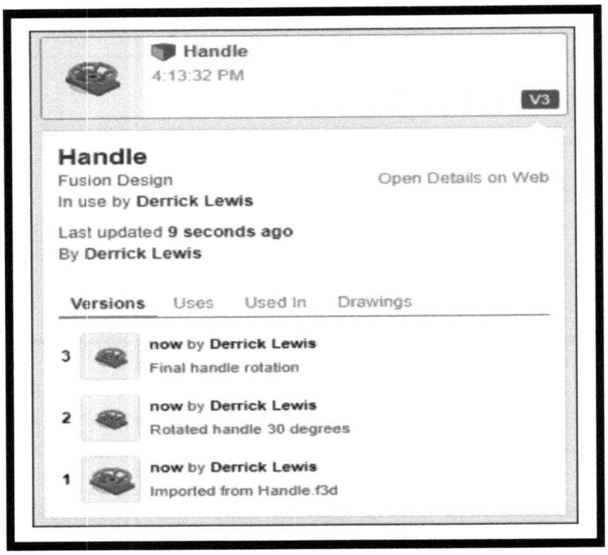

Additionally, there are tabs to show if this file includes any drawings, is used in other designs, or uses any reference designs. Please feel free to explore these tabs on your own; however, they are not covered in this walkthrough.

Returning to the Versions page, you have two choices when you hover over a version that is not currently in use:

- **Promote**. A previous version can be promoted, and that version will become the current one.
- **Open**. An earlier version can be accessed; it will open in a new tab.

Promoting old versions

Let's take a test spin and see what happens. We want to advance the present version above the second one. Note the chronology in our most recent version:

Here's how it appears after the promotion of V2 to the most recent version:

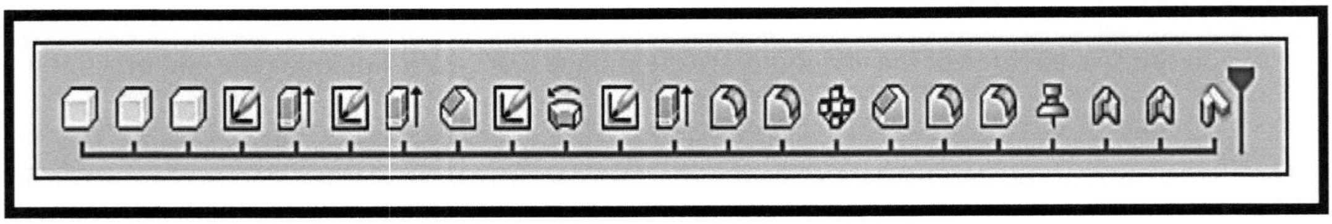

As you can see, the timeline was altered to eliminate the second rotation capture when we promoted an earlier version.

We can also see from our version history that boosting an earlier version results in the creation of a new version:

Opening multiple versions

Just want to open multiple versions of the same file and compare them side by side? The Open action is your best bet. This will open each file version in a separate tab, like so:

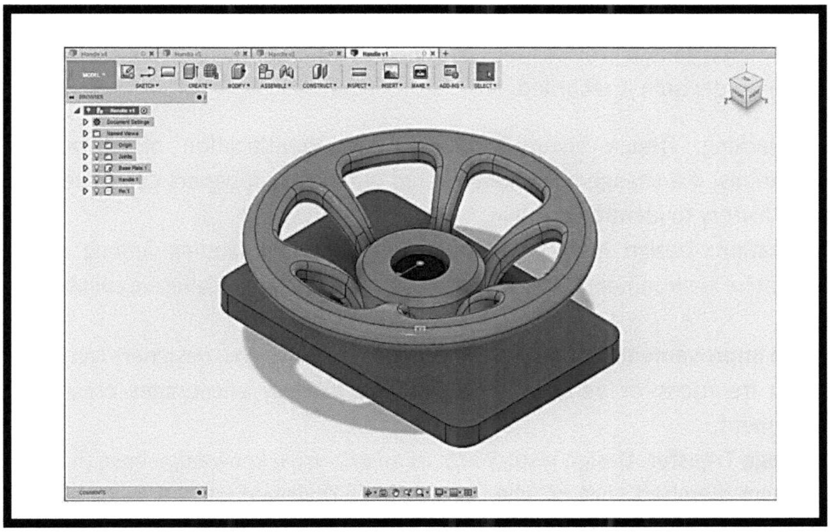

Remember that any earlier version you open is read-only. This implies that you must save a previous version as a whole new design if you need to make any changes to it. Assume for the moment that we want to keep V2 as a new design for use in projects other than this one. We can do this by starting V2 and choosing **File > Save As**. You now have a new, version-controlled handle to deal with if you give that file a name.

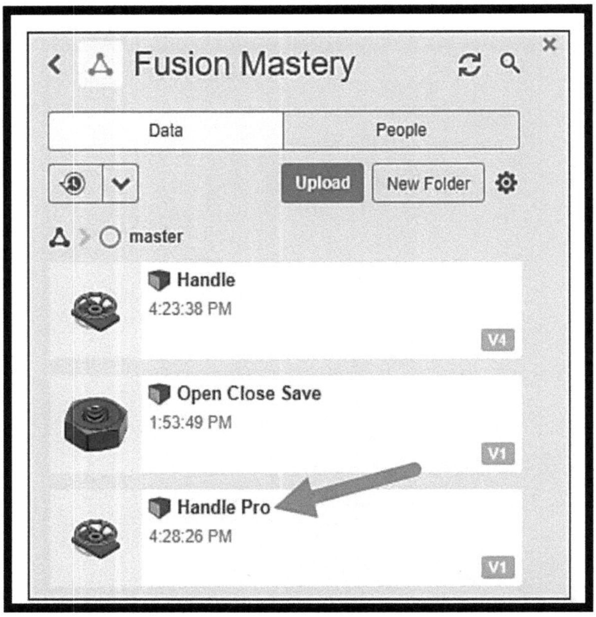

Design History

Design history broadens the definition of version control to include the whole creative process in addition to code, papers, and digital assets. Design history is a dynamic record of all the actions made throughout a design process. It is often seen in programs like Autodesk Fusion 360, SolidWorks, or Adobe Creative Cloud. It provides a thorough overview of a design's development by recording adjustments, alterations, and iterations sequentially. In disciplines like computer-aided design (CAD), industrial design, and 3D modeling, design history is very important. It provides several benefits by guaranteeing that each modification, change in parameter, or design decision is recorded.

1. **Error tracking**: Design history promotes fast identification of mistakes or unwanted modifications. If a change has unanticipated outcomes, designers can trace the problem back through history to identify its origin.
2. **Collaboration**: Design history facilitates mutual understanding among team members in collaborative environments. Better communication and more cohesive collaboration result from this.
3. **Iterative Improvement**: To perfect and enhance their designs, designers can go back and review previous iterations or versions. This iterative process encourages creativity and ongoing improvement.
4. **Knowledge Transfer**: Design history acts as an extensive knowledge base that can be consulted when team members shift or when projects are reviewed later. It helps new team members quickly understand how the project is progressing.

Turning on design history;

1. Navigate to the browser tree.
2. Right-click on the name of any component.
3. Click "**Capture Design History**".

Manipulating a design

In Fusion Team, you have several options for controlling how your design is shown. They can be quite helpful in your correspondence with your manufacturer. Initially, there is the option to "**explode model,"** which will break your design into its component pieces. If your manufacturer wants to see how the various parts will be put together, this is a perfect solution.

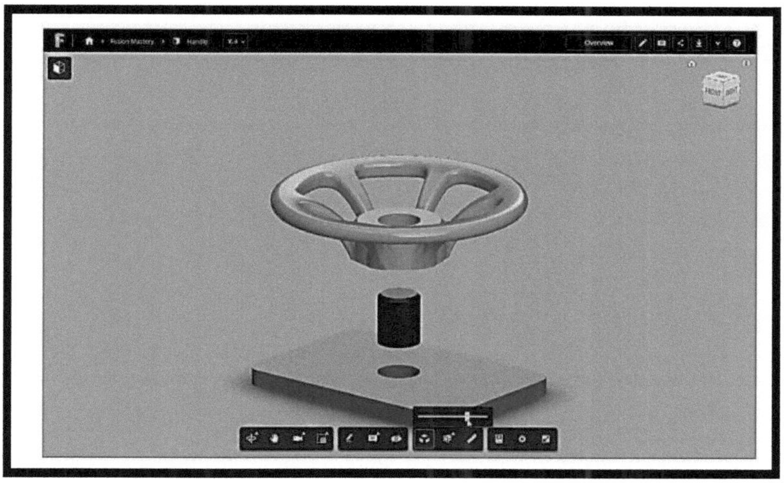

Additionally, sectional planes in the X, Y, and Z axes can be added to your design. Choose one of these choices to display your model's crossview quickly.

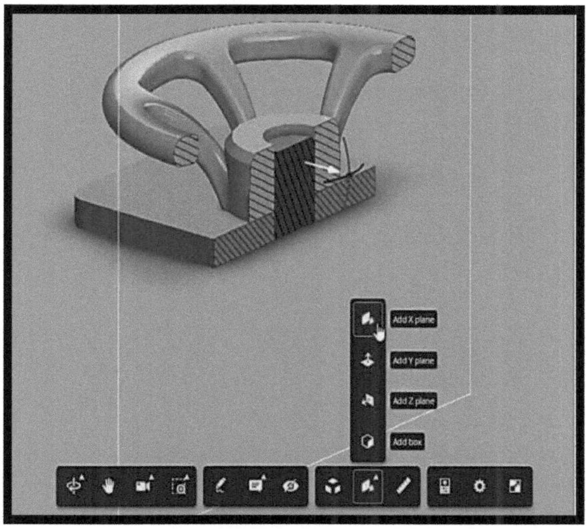

Sharing your design

Now that you understand the fundamentals, let's include some others in your project. There are two approaches to taking on this task:

- **Sharing information among your project's team**. For internal team members that must actively participate in your project, this is perfect. A member of your project can contribute markups and comments that other members can see.
- **Sharing with others not involved in your project**. For those who only need to see your project, such as vendors or customers, this is perfect. Though they can contribute their markup, these individuals won't be able to see any comments made by internal team members.

Every project in Fusion Team has its own set of participants. In Fusion Team, click the Home icon located in the upper left corner before adding a new member to a project. This will direct you to a list of all the Fusion Team projects that you have accessible.

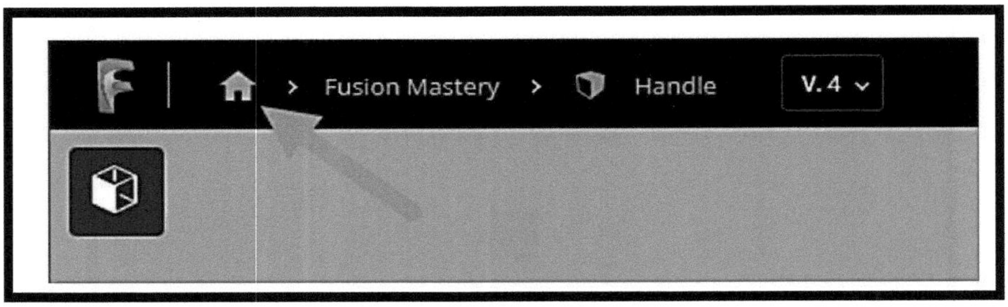

Once you've chosen a project to invite someone to, a Details panel will appear on the right. You can invite them to your project by using the Invite button. Remember that everyone you invite will have access to every file in your project! Once someone accepts your invitation to join your project, they can see a view like yours by opening your design in their browser. The beauty of cooperation can now occur.

All other team members will be able to see any comments or markup added by that individual, as seen here:

Click the **Share** button at the top of the Fusion Team interface, then pick **Share** to distribute outside of your project. This will launch the Share window, from which you can send an email, embed code, or direct link to your design. Pay attention to the privacy settings! You can choose here whether you want users to be able to download your project file to their computer or whether they will need a password to access it.

If you send the share link to an outside vendor, Fusion Team will provide the following view to them:

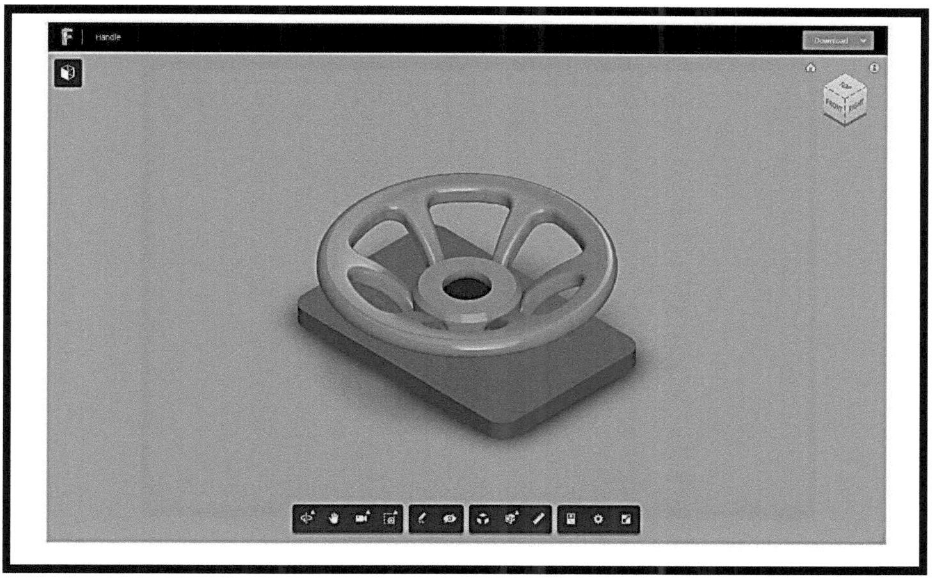

As you can see, certain functionalities are missing. In particular, every sharing and editing option is located in the upper right corner. You can add markup choices in this view, but the other internal contributors on your project won't be able to see them and they can only be saved as a PNG file.

Connecting Fusion 360 and Fusion Team

Assume that after exchanging comments with a teammate and sharing your project, you need to make adjustments in Fusion 360. ***How will this work***? Returning to Fusion 360, click the **plus** symbol that appears next to the Comments panel in the interface's lower left corner. All of the comments that our team members made in Fusion Team are visible in Fusion 360, as you can see in the picture below! There is an immediate workflow between Fusion Team and Fusion 360.

Your model will be positioned in the identical orientation that the commenter placed it in if you choose the link icon next to the comments. The markup comments can then be seen in detail by selecting the picture thumbnail. Do you want to leave a comment or add one of your own? Fusion 360 does not need you to depart. Similar to Fusion Team, you have many choices for leaving a remark on a point, an item, or a picture of your design.

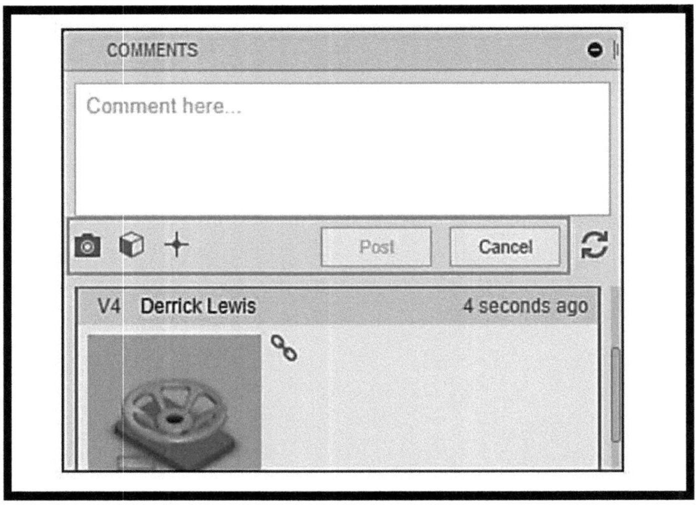

Anybody may watch your remark that you publish in Fusion 360 since it will instantly appear in Fusion Team.

Some Finishing Touches

You've learned the basics of Fusion Team so far, congrats! To finish up, let's cover some extra features that will make your life easier:

Reviewing comment history

To access the **Comments** panel in Fusion Team, click the **Comments** icon located in the upper right corner. An exhaustive history of all team member communications is provided in this area. Choosing a certain remark will make it stand out in your design.

Switching from Fusion Team to Fusion 360

Do you need to return to Fusion 360 from Fusion Team quickly? In Fusion Team, choose the **Edit** design icon located in the upper right corner and select between **Edit in Browser** and **Edit on Desktop**. Selecting any option will launch the project in your design workspace.

Integrating Fusion 360 with Other Software

For your design and engineering processes to function more efficiently and effectively, as well as to increase production, you must integrate Autodesk Fusion 360 with other software programs. A variety of tools and alternatives are offered by Fusion 360 for integration with other programs and services.

Essentially, Fusion 360 can be integrated with other applications in the following ways:

1. **Integration with the Autodesk Ecosystem:**
   - Fusion 360 is a component of the Autodesk ecosystem, which also contains programs like Inventor, Revit, and AutoCAD. By importing and exporting files with ease, you can work together on projects using these programs.
   - In addition, Autodesk supplies developers with the Autodesk Forge platform, which gives tools and APIs for creating unique apps and interfaces that function with Fusion 360 and other Autodesk products.
2. **Cloud Storage and File Sharing Services**: You can establish connections with Autodesk Drive, Dropbox, Google Drive, and Microsoft OneDrive, among other cloud storage services, using

Fusion 360. With the help of this connection, you can save your design files in the cloud, which allows you to access them from anywhere and facilitates team collaboration.

3. **Simulation and Analysis Software**: Fusion 360 is compatible with programs for simulation and analysis such as Autodesk Simulation CFD, SimScale, and ANSYS. This enables you to run sophisticated simulations on your designs, including thermal, fluid dynamics, and stress analyses.
4. **CAM (Computer-Aided Manufacturing) Software:** Fusion 360 has built-in CAM features, but it can also be integrated with other CAM programs, like Mastercam or HSMWorks, to generate toolpaths and do more sophisticated machining.
5. **3D Printing and Manufacturing Services**: Fusion 360 can be connected to Autodesk Print Studio and Autodesk Fusion 360 Additive Build, which facilitates the preparation and submission of 3D models for manufacturing or printing.
6. **Data management and PLM (Product Lifecycle Management):** Fusion 360 interfaces with Autodesk Vault and Autodesk Fusion Lifecycle, which are PLM systems, for managing design data and monitoring changes. Throughout the product life cycle, these technologies provide data management, collaboration, and version control.
7. **Rendering and Visualization Software**: Fusion 360 has rendering capabilities built in, but for more complex rendering and animation needs, you can combine it with external rendering and visualization programs like KeyShot or V-Ray.
8. **CAD and BIM (Building Information Modeling) Software**: Fusion 360 can be connected with CAD and BIM programs, such as AutoCAD or Revit, if you work in the architectural or construction fields. This will improve the interoperability of design data and models in interdisciplinary projects.
9. **Project Management and Collaboration Tools**: Fusion 360 can be integrated with Asana, Trello, Slack, and other project management and collaboration platforms. This makes it possible to coordinate projects, monitor tasks, and communicate more effectively.
10. **Custom Scripting and Automation**: Fusion 360 has an Application Programming Interface (API) that enables you to automate processes and write custom scripts. Scripting languages such as Python can be used to expand Fusion 360's features and connect it to other programs or services.
11. **Plugins and Add-Ins**: Fusion 360 has a marketplace where you can purchase a range of third-party-developed plugins and add-ins. These add-ons can improve Fusion 360's functionality and provide specialized features for certain sectors or jobs.
12. **Internet of Things (IoT) Integration**: Fusion 360 can be integrated with IoT platforms and services to build and simulate IoT systems and devices if you're working on IoT projects.

It's essential to take compatibility, data interchange formats (such **STEP, IGES, or STL for 3D** models), and the particular requirements of your projects into account when integrating Fusion 360 with other applications. Efficient and error-free product development can be achieved via well-thought-out integrations between design, engineering, manufacturing, and other departments.

Importing and exporting design data

Upload a design as a new version of an existing design

1. Find the design that you want to import a new version of in the Data Panel.
2. Right-click on the design, then select **Import New Version**.

- It shows the Upload dialog box.

3. Select a file to import as a new version.
4. Select "**Upload.**"
    - The **job status** dialog box appears.
5. Select "**Close.**"

After being converted to the F3D file format, the chosen file is stored as an updated version of the design that you provided. The Data Panel shows the revised design. You can access the updated version using the Data Panel, Notification Center, or Job Status dialog after it has been imported.

Export designs

1. Open the design you want to export.
2. In the **Application** bar, click **File** > **Export**.

The Export dialog displays.

3. Give the exported design a name in the Export dialog box.
4. Decide which file type to export.

5. Choose the file's saving location.
6. Select "**Export.**"

The design is exported to the file type you selected and saved in the specified location.

Integrating Fusion 360 with other design and analysis tools

Working with Autodesk Fusion 360 in conjunction with other design and analytical tools can significantly improve productivity and efficiency. There are several methods offered by Fusion 360 to interact and work together with other programs and services.

The following are some typical integration points and techniques:

1. The Autodesk Ecosystem: Fusion 360 is a component of the Autodesk ecosystem, which also contains Revit, AutoCAD, and Inventor. Often, these technologies can be smoothly incorporated. For instance, AutoCAD DWG files can be imported straight into Fusion 360 for 3D modeling.

2. Simulation and Analysis capabilities: Fusion 360 comes with integrated simulation and analysis capabilities from Autodesk. You can import your designs into Autodesk Simulation Mechanical or Autodesk CFD for more sophisticated analysis.

- Third-Party Simulation Software: STEP, IGES, and STL are just a few of the file types that Fusion 360 can import and export. These formats can be used to import your designs into simulation programs from other parties, such as ANSYS, SolidWorks Simulation, or COMSOL.

3. CAM and CNC Tools: Fusion 360 offers CNC machining and toolpath generation with integrated CAM capabilities. Additionally, Fusion 360 can be directly connected to CNC machines for toolpath transfer.

- You can export your drawings as G-code files and import them into the CAM program of your choice if you use more sophisticated CAM software.

4. Product Lifecycle Management (PLM) Systems: Fusion 360 provides integration options to sync your design data with PLM systems, such as Siemens Teamcenter or PTC Windchill, for improved version control and collaboration.

5. Additive Manufacturing and 3D Printing: Fusion 360 can export designs in some file formats for 3D printing, including STL and OBJ. After that, you can utilize slicing software for 3D printing, such as Ultimaker Cura or PrusaSlicer. Fusion 360 also has a direct link to Autodesk Netfabb, a company that specializes in producing 3D models for additive manufacturing.

6. Cloud Services: Fusion 360 is a cloud-based platform that works well for cloud data management and collaboration. To save and share your designs with team members, you can utilize Autodesk's cloud services. Furthermore, Fusion 360 can produce high-quality renderings of your ideas by integrating with cloud-based rendering providers.

7. Custom Scripting and API: Fusion 360 has an API (Application Programming Interface) that enables you to create personalized scripts and plugins to expand its capabilities and link with other outside resources and applications. Here's a great method to customize Fusion 360 to meet your unique requirements.

8. Data Management solutions: To better organize and govern your Fusion 360 design data, think about using data management solutions like Autodesk Vault or other PLM systems.

You may need to employ third-party connectors or plugins, refer to documentation, work with IT experts who can help with the technical parts of integration, or all three to put these connections into practice. Your organization's tools and unique design and analysis needs will determine which integration is best for you.

CHAPTER 20

INTRODUCTION TO CAM AND CNC MACHINING

This chapter delves into the fundamentals of Computer-Aided Manufacturing (CAM), explaining the workflows and processes involved. It emphasizes the importance of linking design models to manufacturing processes, highlighting the integration between design and production. The crucial job of configuring toolpaths for CNC (Computer Numerical Control) machining is also covered in detail. It addresses things like setting up cutting tools, establishing machining procedures and strategies, and working out feeds and speeds for cutting. To achieve accuracy and effectiveness in machining operations, these factors are essential. A key component of CAM and CNC machining is simulation. This chapter describes how to use simulation to see how tools move and remove material. To guarantee safe and effective machining processes, it also discusses how crucial it is to identify collisions and optimize toolpaths. CNC machines speak a language known as G-code. The method of creating machine-readable G-code instructions using defined toolpaths is covered in this chapter. It also describes how to program CNC machines to do manufacturing tasks by sending the resulting G-code to them.

Basics of Computer-Aided Manufacturing (CAM)

A universe full of real objects, such as locations, goods, or components, is made feasible via computer-aided manufacturing (CAM). CAM is the solution if you need something manufactured rather than merely planned. ***What is CAM?*** Computer Aided Manufacturing (CAM) is the use of software and computer-controlled machinery to automate a manufacturing process.

Based on that definition, you need three components for a CAM system to function:

- Toolpath-generating software that instructs a machine on how to manufacture a product.
- Industrial machinery that can convert raw materials into completed goods.
- Toolpaths are translated into a language that computers can comprehend via post-processing.

These three elements are fused with a great deal of human effort and expertise. No design is too difficult for a competent machinist company to tackle these days.

Understanding CAM workflows and processes

1. Design Model Importation:
- The importing of a 3D design model made using computer-aided design (CAD) software often kicks off the CAM procedure.
- The creation of toolpaths and manufacturing process instructions is based on this design model.

2. Material Selection:
- One crucial first step in CAM processes is material selection.
- To ensure that the manufacturing process is customized for the material being used, CAM software allows users to select the material's qualities, dimensions, and stock size.

3. Create Toolpaths:

- Toolpaths are the exact pathways that machine heads or cutting tools will take when being manufactured.
- The geometry of the design and the chosen machining operations (such as milling, turning, and drilling) are used by CAM software to create toolpaths.
- When creating a toolpath, variables like feeds, cutting speeds, and tool shape are taken into account.

4. Machining Techniques and Procedures:

- A variety of machining operations and methods are available with CAM systems.
- Users specify the roughing, finishing, and detailing procedures that will be used to remove the material.
- Using specialist tools or figuring out the best cut order are two possible strategies.

5. Configuring Feeds and Speeds:

- To ensure the quality of machined components and manage material removal rates, cutting speeds and feeds must be properly configured.
- For each toolpath operation, CAM software allows users to set the feed rate, cutting depth, and spindle speed.

6. Simulation and Visualization:

- Simulation features that allow users to see the whole machining process are often included in CAM software.
- In addition to seeing how the tool operates, users can also view how material is eliminated and how the completed item will appear.
- The identification of problems like tool collisions, excessive material removal, or other machining defects depends heavily on simulation.

7. Optimization:

- To increase productivity and shorten manufacturing times, CAM workflows may include optimization stages.
- Optimizing a process can include reducing tool changes, smoothing the toolpath, or identifying more productive machining paths.

8. **Post-Processing and G-code Generation**:

- G-code instructions are generated by CAM software when toolpaths are finished.
- CNC (Computer Numerical Control) machines employ G-code, a machine-readable language, to carry out machining operations.
- Creating setup sheets and manuals for the machine operator may also be a part of post-processing.

9. Verification and Quality Control:

- Making sure everything is right is crucial before submitting the G-code to the CNC machine.
- To make sure the produced components will satisfy the necessary criteria, quality control procedures are often included in CAM processes.

10. CNC Machine Operation:

- The G-code is transferred to the CNC machine for manufacturing once it has been created and validated. By executing the toolpaths, the CNC machine removes material from the workpiece and produces the finished product.

11. Data Logging and Reporting:

- Data on quality control and machining operations can be recorded throughout the CAM workflow. - This information can be used for compliance, traceability, and process optimization.

CAD to CAM Process

There can be no CAD without CAM. The design of a product or component is the main emphasis of CAD. Both its appearance and operation. The emphasis of CAM is on making it. Even if you use your CAD tool to create the most gorgeous item, you're better off kicking rocks if you can't manufacture it quickly and effectively using a CAM system. Every engineering procedure starts with the realm of computer-aided design (CAD). Whether it's a car crankshaft, the internal workings of a kitchen faucet, or the concealed electronics on a circuit board, engineers will create a 2D or 3D drawing of it. Any design in CAD is referred to as a model, and it includes a collection of physical characteristics that a CAM system will use. A CAD design can be put into CAM after it is finished. Traditionally, to do this, a CAD file must be exported and then imported into CAM software. CAD and CAM are in the same universe when using a technology like Fusion 360, therefore import/export is not necessary. Your CAD model is loaded into CAM, and the program begins to get it ready for milling. The regulated process of shaping raw material into a predetermined shape by operations like drilling, boring, or cutting is called machining.

Computer Aided manufacturing software works through some steps to get a model ready for machining, such as:

- Verifying if any geometry flaws in the model will affect the manufacturing process.
- Creating the model's toolpath, which is a collection of instructions the machine will use to manufacture the model.
- Adjusting the machine's necessary settings, such as voltage, cut/pierce height, and cutting speed.
- Nesting configuration, in which the CAM system will determine a part's optimal orientation to enhance machining productivity.

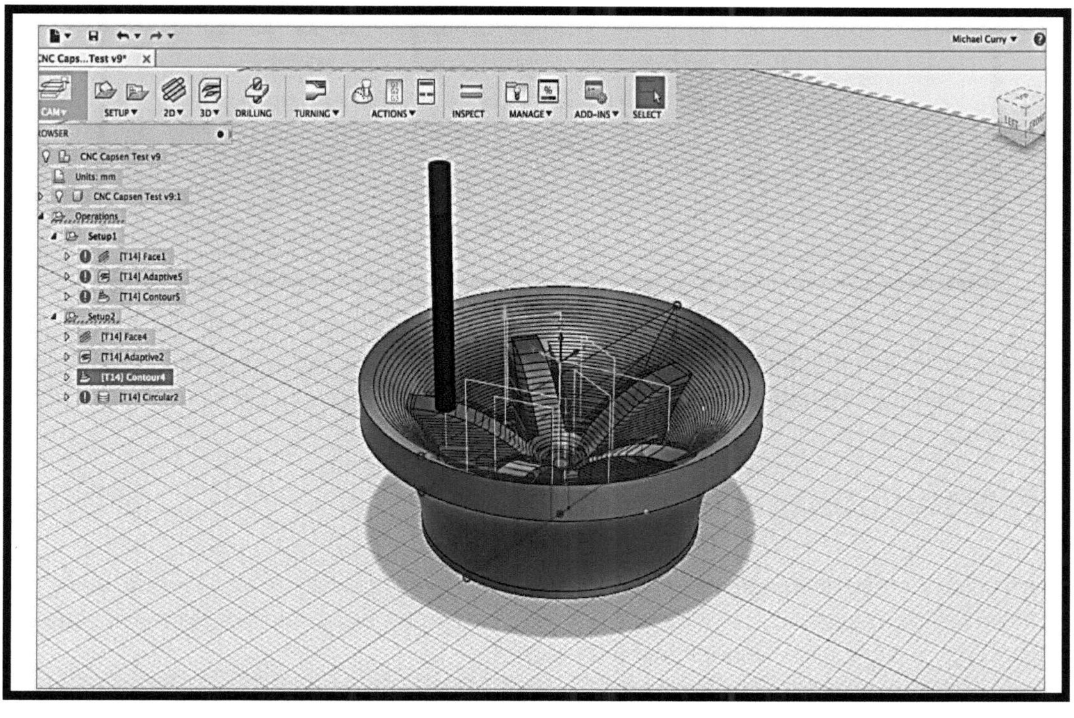

All data is supplied to a machine to physically construct the item once the model is ready for machining. But we can't simply spit out a lot of English instructions to a computer. We must converse in the language of the computer. We translate all of our machining data into a language known as G-code to do this. This is the instruction set that governs the functions of a machine, such as feed rate, coolant flow, and speed.

Reading G-code is simple if you know how it is formatted. For instance, consider this:

G01 X1 Y1 F20 T01 S500

This breaks down from left to right as:

- G01 denotes a linear shift using X1 and Y1 as the coordinates.
- The feed rate, or the distance the machine moves in a single spindle rotation, is adjusted by F20.
- S500 adjusts the spindle speed, while T01 instructs the machine to utilize Tool 1.

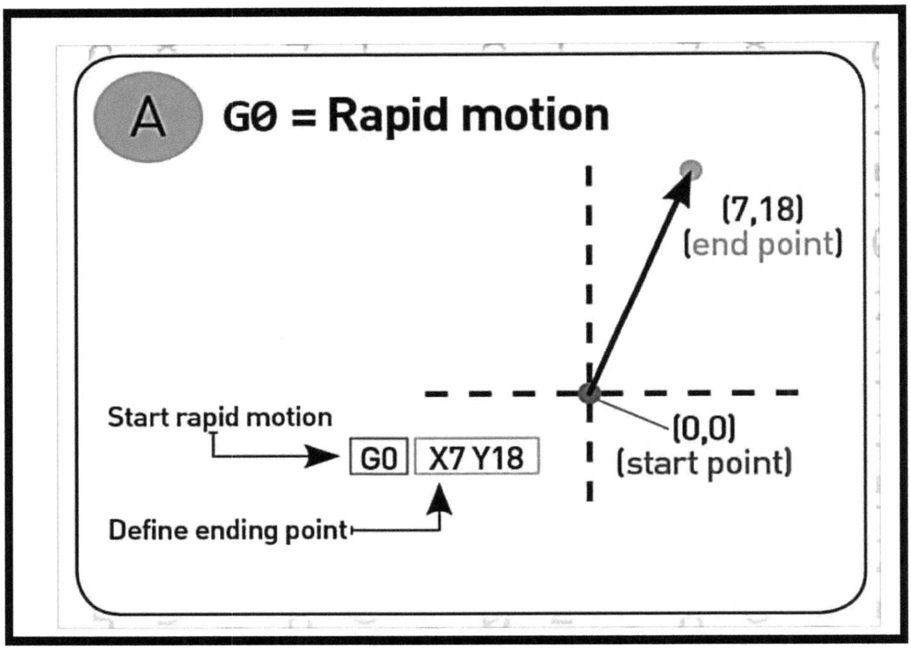

Our work is over when the operator loads the G-code into the machine and presses the start button. It's now time to hand over the task of running G-code to the machine to convert a block of raw materials into a final product.

CNC Machines at a Glance

We have been referring to the components of a CAM system as mere machines up until now, but it is not doing them justice. Every time I see a Haas milling machine cut through a chunk of metal like butter, my face lights up. I couldn't do my work without this equipment

To create designed components, a variety of Computer Numerical Control (CNC) equipment will be used in all contemporary production facilities. CNC machining is the process of programming a CNC machine to carry out certain tasks. Before the invention of CNC machines, industrial facilities were run manually by seasoned machinists. Of course, automation came shortly after, as with everything related to computers. These days, loading a program, adding raw materials, and unloading a final product are the only human actions necessary to operate a CNC machine.

There are respectable assortment of CNC equipment in the Autodesk Pier 9 facility, which includes:

CNC Routers

These devices use high-speed rotating components to cut pieces and sculpt a range of forms. Using a CNC router for woodworking, for instance, can simplify the process of cutting plywood into cabinet components. Additionally, it can handle intricate ornate engraving on a door panel with ease. The 3-axis cutting capability of CNC routers allows them to move along the X, Y, and Z axes.

Water, Plasma & Laser Cutters

These devices provide a controlled cut or engraved finish using high-pressure water, precision lasers, or a plasma torch. While manual engraving methods can take months to do by hand, modern machines can finish the same task in a matter of hours or days. Metals and other electrically conductive materials can be easily sliced through with the use of plasma cutters.

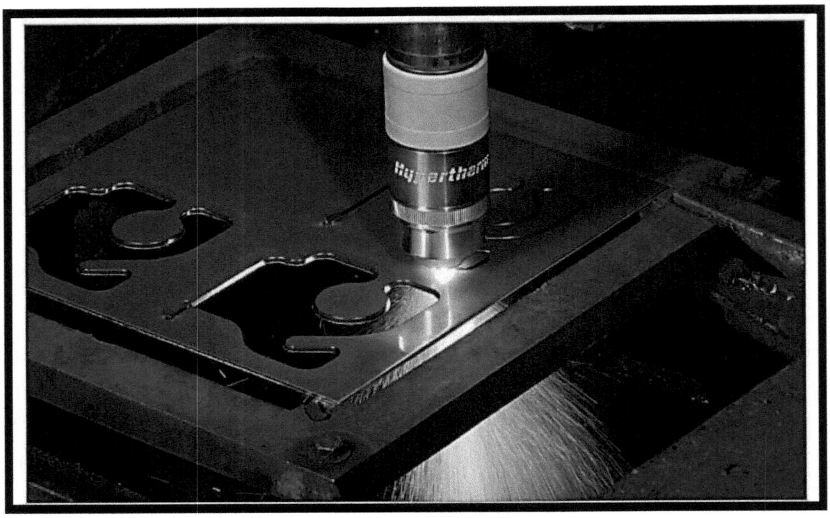

Milling Machines

Metal, wood, composites, and other materials are among the materials that these machines can chip away at. Because they come with a wide range of tools that can fulfill particular material and form requirements, milling machines are very versatile. The main objective of a milling machine is to effectively remove mass from a raw block of material.

Lathes

In addition, these devices grind away raw materials similarly to a milling machine. Their method is distinct. A lathe spins the material while a stationary tool makes cuts in a milling machine that contains both a spinning tool and stationary material.

Electrical Discharge Machines (EDM)

These machines use an electrical discharge to cut the required form out of the raw material. When an electrode and a raw material come together, an electrical spark is produced that may reach temperatures of 8,000 to 12,000 degrees Celsius. This allows an EDM to melt almost anything in a precise and controlled manner.

Linking design models to manufacturing processes

Assume you are in charge of a product development project and that you have just finished utilizing advanced Computer-Aided Design (CAD) software to complete the digital design phase. You have created complex 3D models, thorough product specifications, and well-thought-out assembly plans.

Linking your design to the production procedures that will make it a reality is a crucial step that must be completed before you can turn this digital beauty into a tangible reality.

- **Design Validation**: The digital design is rigorously validated at the start. It is examined closely by engineers and designers to make sure it is both aesthetically pleasing and sound operationally. They use cutting-edge methods for analysis and simulation to confirm structural soundness and functionality.
- **Design for Manufacturing (DFM):** A design must be able to be manufactured in addition to being aesthetically pleasing. To do this, the design must be optimized for the selected production techniques. Efficiency is taken into consideration while choosing materials, machining ease, and assembly needs.

- **Seamless Integration with CAM Software**: This is the point at which software for computer-aided manufacturing (CAM) comes into play. It allows for a smooth transition from digital design to the factory floor by integrating smoothly with the design process. The CAM program receives the 3D CAD model.
- **Toolpath Generation**: Based on the CAD model and the precise machining operations needed, CAM software creates complex toolpaths, which is where its magic starts. The exact actions of cutting tools or machine heads are indicated by these toolpaths, which specify how raw materials are to be shaped into the required components.
- **Material and Machining Parameters**: CAM software allows for fine-tuning of the material and machining parameters. Dimensions and material characteristics are given. Cutting speeds, feeds, and tool selection are among the parameters that are fine-tuned for the best possible machining results.
- **Simulation and Verification**: CAM software offers a useful preview before the removal of every single material chip. The machining process is seen by engineers and machinists in virtual reality. They examine each action closely, looking for any problems such as tool collisions and confirming that the toolpaths are accurate.
- **The Creation of G-code**: G-code is created by CAM software when toolpaths are optimized. CNC (Computer Numerical Control) machines speak this language. Through the course of production, the CNC machine is guided by a precise set of instructions.
- **CNC Machine Setup:** The CNC machine is ready to go after being equipped with the G-code. Precisely loaded raw materials are tightly fastened, and the necessary cutting tools are set up. Production is about to begin on stage.
- **The Dance of Production:** The CNC machine springs to life, following the dance of the G-code. It meticulously carves, mills, or shapes the material, transforming it into the envisioned product with unparalleled precision.
- **Quality Control and Inspection**: Throughout the process, quality control acts as a vigilant watchdog. Measurements are taken, visual inspections are performed, and functional testing is conducted. Ensuring the finished product complies with strict quality requirements is the aim.
- **Post-Processing and Documentation**: Depending on the product's complexity, post-machining procedures like assembling, welding, or finishing may come next. For traceability and reference, comprehensive documentation is kept, including records of the design model, CAM toolpaths, G-code, and quality control reports.
- **Constant Improvement**: The manufacturing process's lessons are applied when the product becomes its ultimate form. They contribute to a cycle of ongoing improvement that aims to maintain flawless product quality, cut costs, and increase efficiency.

From concept through production, this process is a complex, but well-balanced symphony of the digital and physical worlds, driven by state-of-the-art technology and painstaking workmanship. It is evidence of the harmonious coexistence of ingenuity and accuracy that drives the contemporary industrial scene.

Setting Up Toolpaths for CNC Machining

A key idea in computer-aided manufacturing (CAM) and computer numerical control (CNC) machining is toolpaths. They provide the exact paths that other machining or cutting tools used to produce a part or component. CAM software creates toolpaths based on a 3D CAD model of the component and the precise machining operations needed. **Key elements of toolpaths are as follows:**

1. **Definition of Geometry**: Generally, the geometry of the part or component is used to determine the toolpath. This covers all elements that need machining, such as outlines, curves, pockets, and holes. This geometry is used by the CAM program to determine the toolpath.

2. **Machining processes**: A variety of machining processes can be performed using different toolpaths, including:
   - **Roughing**: Material removal at high speeds and feeds to quickly remove excess material.
   - **Finishing**: Precision passes to achieve the desired surface quality and dimensional accuracy.
   - **Drilling**: Toolpaths for drilling holes of various sizes and depths.
   - **Contouring**: Cutting along the perimeter or contours of the part.
   - **Pocketing**: Toolpaths for machining inside closed regions or pockets.
   - **Thread Milling**: Creating threads using helical toolpaths.
   - **Engraving**: Toolpaths for adding text or graphics to a part's surface.

3. **Tool Selection**: When creating toolpaths, the selection of a cutting tool (such as an end mill, ball mill, drill bit, etc.) and its characteristics (such as diameter, flute length), are crucial. Certain machining jobs need the use of different tools.

4. **Toolpath Parameters**: CAM software allows users to set toolpath parameters, such as:
   - **Feed Rate**: The tool's speed through the material, usually expressed in millimeters or inches per **Feed Rate**: The speed at which the tool moves through the material (typically in inches per minute or millimeters per minute).
   - **Spindle Speed (RPM)**: The rotational speed of the tool.
   - **Stepover**: The distance the tool moves laterally between passes (usually a percentage of the tool diameter for finishing operations).
   - **Cutting Depth**: The distance the tool moves vertically in each pass.
   - **Clearance Height**: The height above the workpiece at which the tool moves during non-cutting movements.

5. **Optimization**: The goal of CAM software is to maximize productivity by optimizing toolpaths to reduce material waste, machining time, and tool wear. This might include techniques like adaptive toolpaths, which modify tool engagement according to the part's shape.

6. **Simulation**: The CAM software often has a simulation capability that is used before transmitting toolpaths to the CNC machine. This allows users to see the machining process in action and look for possible problems like tool collisions or toolpath mistakes.

7. **Post-Processing**: The CAM software transforms the data into a format that the CNC machine can comprehend after toolpaths are produced and simulated. Usually, this format is G-code, which includes instructions for spindle speed, tool motions, and other things.

8. **Tool Changes**: During machining processes, toolpaths may include directives that define when and how to change tools.

9. Multi-Axis Toolpaths: These toolpaths allow for more complicated and detailed machining in advanced CNC machining by controlling the movement of the cutting tool in several directions.
10. Customization: To meet particular production needs, tooling configurations, or material concerns, CAM software often allows for toolpath modification.

Because they have a direct influence on the accuracy, speed, and quality of the machining process, toolpaths are an essential part of CNC machining. When toolpaths are set up correctly, the CNC machine can produce components that satisfy design criteria, minimize tool wear, and maximize production times. Toolpaths are often discussed in terms of 2D, 3D, and full 5-axis simultaneous use. So what exactly do these phrases mean? Here, we'll go over it in detail and show you how you can create these toolpaths in Fusion 360.

What are 2D Toolpaths?

Computer-aided design (CAD) and computer-aided manufacturing (CAM) software produce 2D toolpaths, which are instructions or pathways used in machining processes, especially CNC (Computer Numerical Control) machining. These toolpaths direct the motion of a cutting tool—a router or milling cutter, for example—in two dimensions so that the workpiece can be precisely shaped or contoured.

Key elements of 2D toolpaths include the following:

1. **2D Geometry**: When a machining process solely requires two-dimensional geometry, such as engraving on a workpiece, flat profiles, pockets, or holes, 2D toolpaths are usually used. They are often used for operations including drilling holes, surface engraving, and cutting off components from sheet materials.
2. **X and Y Axes**: The X and Y axes of the machining system are the only places where the tool may travel in 2D toolpaths. The tool must travel along the X and Y axes, horizontally and vertically, in accordance with the toolpath instructions, to follow the intended geometry.
3. **Types of 2D Toolpaths**:
   - **Contour Toolpaths**: These toolpaths are designed to cut a 2D form along its inner or outer edges. Profile cutting is a popular use for contour toolpaths.
   - **Pocketing Toolpaths**: These toolpaths are designed to extract material from within a predetermined pocket or boundary. They are often used to remove material to create voids or slits.
   - **Drilling Toolpaths**: A toolpath, which is usually a vertical Z-axis movement of the tool, indicates the sites to be drilled during a drilling operation.
4. **Optimizing Toolpaths**: CAM software creates two-dimensional toolpaths by using the design and material requirements. For precise and productive machining, these toolpaths can be adjusted for variables including feed rates, cutting speeds, and tool selection.
5. **Simulation and Verification**: To make sure the toolpath follows the intended design and won't cause collisions or mistakes during machining, it is usual to simulate and validate it using CAM software before starting real machining.
6. **Multi-Pass Machining**: To get the appropriate depth or polish, the cutting tool may need to pass through a material many times, particularly when working with thicker materials. For these repeated passes, toolpaths can be created by the CAM program.

In general, 2D toolpaths are essential to CNC machining to precisely create two-dimensional features and forms on a workpiece. They also have a major part in the automation and precision of contemporary production processes.

What are 2.5D Toolpaths?

Beyond simple 2D toolpaths, 2.5D toolpaths provide more possibilities for CNC (Computer Numerical Control) machining. Even though machining is essentially a two-dimensional process, they are used to produce pieces or characteristics on a workpiece that seem to be three-dimensional.

The following are the main characteristics of 2.5D toolpaths:

- **Three-Dimensional Appearance**: 2.5D toolpaths allow for tool movement in the Z-axis, while 2D toolpaths are restricted to moving the cutting tool in the X and Y axes (flat plane). This makes it possible to create features that seem to be three-dimensional.
- **Depth Control**: 2.5D toolpaths are often used for jobs like texturing, embossing, and engraving workpieces. By sliding the tool up and down along the Z-axis while adhering to the design's shape or profile, they can adjust the depth of cut.
- **Variable Depths**: In contrast to pure 2D toolpaths, 2.5D toolpaths can change the tool's depth as it moves along the design's contour. This feature helps produce complex patterns or cut surfaces with different heights.
- **Milling and Profiling**: 2.5D toolpaths are often used in profiling operations, where the tool follows the outline of a 2D form while altering the depth to generate a contoured edge, or in milling operations to remove material to a predetermined depth.
- **CNC Drilling and Tapping**: 2.5D toolpaths are often used in drilling and tapping operations, in addition to milling and profiling. They enable different depths or threads to be created by the tool by allowing it to move in the X, Y, and Z axes.
- **Relief Carving:** A typical use for 2.5D toolpaths is relief carving, which involves carving a design into a workpiece to produce a raised or lowered relief pattern that gives the impression of depth and dimension.

- **Toolpath Optimization**: CAM (Computer-Aided Manufacturing) software is used to develop and optimize 2.5D toolpaths, just as it does for 2D toolpaths. It considers several aspects, including feed rates, cutting speeds, and tool selection.
- **Simulation and Verification**: To be sure the tool will follow the appropriate route and produce the necessary 3D effects without mistakes or collisions, 2.5D toolpaths must be simulated and verified using CAM software before being machined.

In conclusion, even though the machining process is generally restricted to two dimensions, 2.5D toolpaths allow CNC machines to produce the appearance of three-dimensional forms and features on a workpiece. These toolpaths are frequently used to add detailed and aesthetically pleasing features to components and products in a variety of industries, including engraving, metalworking, and carpentry.

What Are 3D Toolpaths?

The instructions or pathways produced by CAD and CAM software for CNC (Computer Numerical Control) machining processes entailing the fabrication of three-dimensional components and features are known as 3D toolpaths. 3D toolpaths allow the machining of intricate three-dimensional geometries, in contrast to 2D and 2.5D toolpaths, which are mostly focused on two-dimensional forms or giving depth to 2D profiles.

Key components of 3D toolpaths are as follows:

- **Three-Dimensional Geometry**: When machining procedures call for the production of complex, three-dimensional features or pieces, 3D toolpaths are used. This can include 3D models, freeform forms, and intricately sculpted surfaces.
- **Movement in X, Y, and Z Axes:** Three-dimensional toolpaths (three dimensions) allow the cutting tool to travel in all three of the main axes (horizontal, X), horizontal, and vertical, Y), as opposed to two- and three-dimensional (2D) toolpaths. This allows the tool to follow different depths inside a workpiece in addition to curved and contoured surfaces.
- **Complicated Surfaces**: 3D toolpaths are often used to machine complicated surfaces, including those seen in elaborate artistic sculptures, automobile parts, aircraft components, and medical implants. They can manage surfaces with different undercuts, curves, and slopes.
- **High Precision**: A signature feature of 3D toolpaths is their ability to achieve both high accuracy and exquisite detail. To create precise and smooth surfaces, these routes allow for fine-tuning the tool's movement.
- **Scallop Height and Stepover**: The CAM software in 3D machining determines toolpaths depending on variables such as stepover and scallop height. While stepover specifies the tool's lateral movement between passes to reduce tool marks and flaws, scallop height relates to the intended surface finish.
- **6.5-Axis Machining**: To access intricate angles and surfaces, 5-axis CNC machines, which can tilt and rotate the tool, are often utilized in combination with 3D toolpaths. Its capacity to machine complex three-dimensional components is essential.
- **Toolpath techniques**: A variety of 3D toolpath techniques, including contouring, radial finishing, and parallel finishing, are available with CAM software. Every tactic is customized for the part's unique shape and intended finish.
- **Simulation and Verification:** The intricacy of 3D machining necessitates the simulation and verification of toolpaths before real machining to guarantee that the tool will follow the intended path error-free.

All things considered, 3D toolpaths are critical to manufacturing complicated three-dimensional components. They make it possible to create very precise and detailed pieces, from aesthetic sculptures with minute details to aerodynamic aeronautical components. Creating accurate three-dimensional toolpaths is an essential component of contemporary CNC machining and production.

What Are 5-Axis Toolpaths?

Computer-aided design (CAD) and computer-aided manufacturing (CAM) software create 5-axis toolpaths, which are instructions or routes for CNC (Computer Numerical Control) machining processes that require a cutting tool moving concurrently in five axes. These toolpaths allow for the very accurate machining of delicate and sophisticated three-dimensional objects.

The following are the main features of 5-axis toolpaths:

1. **Five Axes of Movement**: The cutting tool in 5-axis machining can move concurrently along five distinct axes:
    - X-axis (horizontal)
    - Y-axis (horizontal)
    - Z-axis (vertical)
    - A-axis (rotational around the X-axis)
    - B-axis (rotational around the Y-axis)
2. **Complete 3D Machining**: For completely 3D machining processes, where the tool can access and cut material from different angles and orientations, 5-axis toolpaths are used. This feature is especially crucial for machining intricate, curved, and multi-sided surfaces.
3. **Reduced Setup Time:** With 5-axis machining, many sides of a product can often be machined in a single setup, eliminating the need to realign the workpiece and cutting down on setup time and error-proneness.
4. **Complex Geometries**: Parts with complex geometries, such as turbine blades, medical implants, impellers, and aerospace components, are perfectly machined using these toolpaths. The tool can navigate difficult-to-reach places, undercuts, and intricate bends.
5. **High accuracy**: Five-axis machines are suited for applications where smooth surfaces and tight tolerances are crucial because they can achieve very high levels of accuracy and surface polish.
6. **Optimal Tool Angles:** CAM software creates toolpaths that optimize tool angles to reduce tool interference, guarantee effective material removal, and preserve a uniform surface quality.

7. **Simultaneous Movements**: Compared to 3- or 4-axis machines, 5-axis machining allows for smoother and more efficient cutting since the tool can move simultaneously along numerous axes.
8. **Trimming and Contouring**: These toolpaths are used for these processes, which are typical in the manufacture of aircraft, automobiles, and medical equipment.
9. **Toolpath methods**: CAM software provides a range of 5-axis toolpath methods, such as hybrid techniques that include both continuous and indexed motions, indexing (in which the tool repositions itself between passes), and continuous toolpaths.
10. **Simulation and Verification**: To guarantee safe and precise machining, it is essential to simulate and validate toolpaths due to the intricacy of 5-axis machining and the possibility of tool and workpiece collisions.

In conclusion, 5-axis toolpaths are an effective tool in CNC machining that makes it possible to produce intricately geometrized, very exact products. Their advantages include shorter setup times, better surface finishes, and the capacity to handle complex and diverse machining jobs. They are indispensable in sectors that need sophisticated machining skills.

What Are 3+2 Toolpaths?

3+2 toolpaths, also known as positional 3+2 machining or 3+2-axis machining, are a compromise between conventional 3-axis machining and complete 5-axis machining. Other names for this kind of machining include positional 3+2 machining and 3+2-axis machining. In 3+2 machining, the cutting tool travels in three major axes (X, Y, and Z) for rough placement, and then two extra rotational axes (A and B) are utilized to orient the workpiece to attain varied tool angles. X, Y, and Z are called the primary axes.

This strategy has some benefits, including the following:

1. **Access to More Complicated Features**: 3+2 machining allows you access to more complicated features and undercuts than typical 3-axis machining can achieve. The cutting tool can approach the item from a variety of directions if the workpiece is rotated or tilted using the two extra axes.
2. **Reduced Setup Time** Even though it is not as adaptable as complete 5-axis machining, 3+2 machining nonetheless decreases the amount of time needed for the first setup in comparison to 3-axis machining. Machining can typically be done on many sides of the workpiece in a single setup, which reduces the amount of time spent adjusting the piece.
3. **Improved Surface Finish:** Being able to machine from a variety of angles can help enhance surface finish and decrease tool marks, especially on complicated components with curved surfaces.
4. **Tool Life Extending Capabilities**: 3+2 machining can improve tool engagement angles, which reduces tool wear and allows for longer tool life, particularly in difficult machining processes.
5. **Reduced Risk of Collisions:** 3+2 machining can boost machining safety by orienting the workpiece to minimize tool and holder collisions. This decreases the possibility that the machine or the workpiece would be damaged.
6. **Versatility:** 3+2 machining is suited for a broad variety of applications, such as aircraft components, automotive parts, molds, and dies. Although it is not as flexible as complete 5-axis machining, it is still useful for a wide variety of applications.

The toolpaths for 3+2 machining are created with the rotary axes locked at precise angles for each machining operation. This is a key difference between 3+2 machining and simultaneous 5-axis machining, which is an essential point to keep in mind. Because of this, the toolpaths are positional as opposed to continuous. To provide a variety of angles, the machine moves the workpiece to a new location between each machining cycle. 3+2 toolpaths provide a realistic compromise between the capabilities of 3-axis and complete 5-axis machining. This allows for greater access to complicated features, decreased setup time, and higher surface smoothness in some applications that include machining.

Taking This Knowledge to Fusion 360

Now that we have an understanding of the various kinds of toolpaths, let's take a peek inside Fusion 360 to determine how the toolpaths can be programmed. The toolpath techniques for milling in Fusion 360 can be divided into 2D, 3D, and multi-axis categories. We can see the application of a 2D profile route here, which takes place solely in the x and y dimensions. If I edit this, I'll be able to add several depths, and then I can turn it into a 2.5D toolpath.

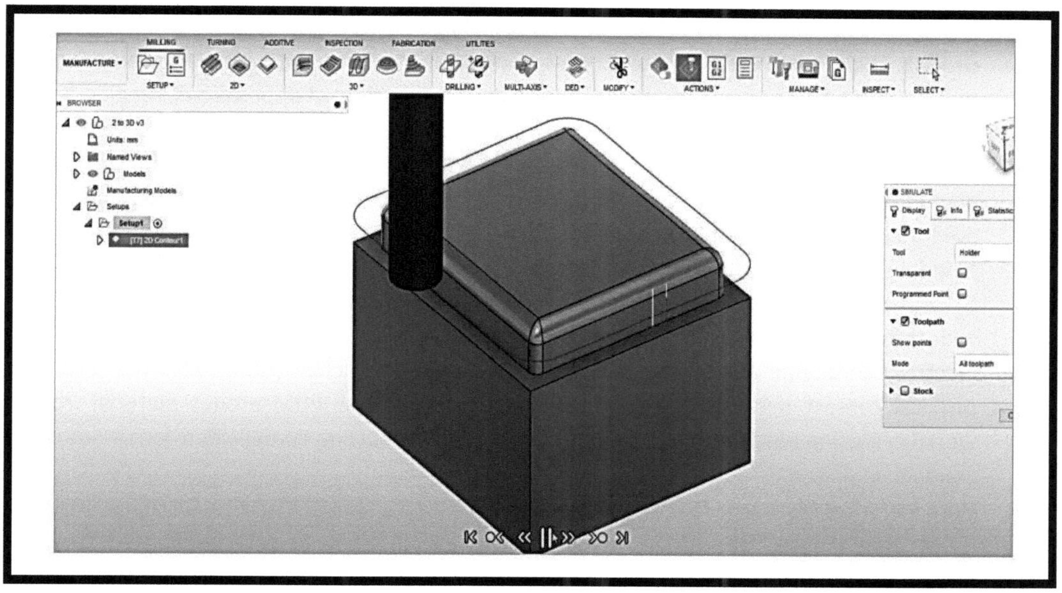

I have included a ramp toolpath on the list of 3D techniques that I use. This toolpath moves the toolpath along the x, y, and z axes simultaneously while it is running. Moving on to the multi-axis choices, I have something called a rotary toolpath, which is a 4-axis toolpath that makes use of one rotating axis. In addition to that, I have a swarf, which is a synchronous route along all five axes. You'll recall that we also went through 3+2 toolpaths, which refer to the situation in which rotational axes are used but exclusively for positioning purposes. I can convert any of the toolpaths from their 2-axis or 3-axis form into a 3+2 toolpath by using tool orientation. To activate this option, I must first go to the geometry tab and then specify the directions of my new axes using the card. After that, the remainder of the code for the toolpath is the same.

Defining machining operations and strategies

Machining operations and strategies refer to the processes and methods used in the manufacturing sector to shape, cut, and finish raw materials (such as metal, plastic, wood, or composites) into the parts or products that are required. Examples of these raw materials include metal, plastic, wood, and composites. Machine tools, also known as CNC (Computer Numerical Control) equipment, are used to do these tasks in today's industrial facilities. The following is a rundown of some of the most typical machining procedures and approaches:

Machining Operations

1. **Turning:** Turning is a machining operation used to make cylindrical components by rotating a workpiece on a spindle while a cutting tool removes material from the part's outer surface. Turning is one of the more common machining processes. This method is often used for the production of shafts, pins, and a variety of other round components.
2. **Milling:** This is a flexible machining operation that removes material from a workpiece using a revolving cutter to form flat surfaces, slots, pockets, curves, and complicated 3D structures. Milling is one of the oldest machining processes. Milling can be done in some different ways, including face milling, end milling, and profile milling.
3. **Drilling:** This is the creation of holes in a workpiece by means of a drill bit that rotates in a rotary motion. It is a basic operation that is utilized in a wide variety of applications, ranging from the creation of simple holes to the production of threaded holes.
4. **Boring**: Boring is a process that is quite similar to drilling; however, it is used to increase the diameter of an existing hole or enhance its concentricity. To attain accurate tolerances in cylindrical components, it is often used.
5. **Grinding:** Grinding is a precision machining operation that employs the use of abrasive wheels to remove material and create surfaces that are exceedingly smooth and precise. It has widespread use in the finishing of materials like hardened steel.
6. **Electrical Discharge Machining (EDM)**: This is a kind of machining that does not involve any physical contact between the machine and the workpiece. EDM erodes material from the workpiece using electrical discharges. It works well for cutting complicated forms out of hard conductive materials.
7. **Wire Electrical Discharge Machining (Wire EDM)**: This is a kind of Electrical Discharge Machining (EDM) that employs the use of a thin wire as an electrode to cut complicated structures, including interior features, with great accuracy.
8. **Laser Cutting:** Laser cutting utilizes a high-powered laser beam to melt, burn, or vaporize material, creating precise cuts or intricate patterns. It's often used in sheet metal fabrication.

Machining Strategies

1. **Rough Machining:** This requires the removal of a substantial volume of material in a very short length of time. In this method, the machining time is reduced by using cutting tools with a coarser cutting surface and a greater feed rate.
2. **Finish Machining**: This is the last phase in the machining process, and its purpose is to obtain the required component dimensions and surface polish. To attain great accuracy and a smooth surface, the use of fine-cutting tools and moderate feed rates is required.
3. **Contouring:** The process of contouring requires carefully following a predetermined route or contour to produce intricate forms or profiles. Milling is one of the most prevalent applications for it, and it can be used for either rough or final machining.

4. **Pocketing** The process of generating pockets, cavities, or recesses in a workpiece is referred to as pocketing. During pocketing, material is removed from the inside of a workpiece.
5. **Drilling and Tapping**: Drilling activities generate holes while tapping procedures add threads to these holes, which allows screws or bolts to be placed into the holes.
6. **3D Machining:** 3D machining strategies are used to create intricate three-dimensional shapes, contours, and surfaces on a workpiece. This often necessitates the use of 3-axis, 3+2-axis, or 5-axis machining strategies.
7. **High-Speed Machining** (HSM): This is an approach that takes advantage of high spindle speeds and quick feed rates to enable rapid material removal while preserving accuracy. HSM is an abbreviation for high-speed machining.
8. **Toolpath Optimization**: The process of modifying cutting tool pathways to decrease the amount of time spent machining, limit the amount of tool wear that occurs, and increase the surface polish.
9. **Adaptive Machining**: Adaptive machining optimizes both the cutting conditions and the tool life by adjusting the route of the cutting tool depending on data that is collected in real time.

The choice of machining operation and strategy is determined by some criteria, including the material being machined, the geometry of the component that is wanted, the tolerances, the requirements for the surface polish, and the available tool. Machining that is both effective and accurate is necessary in contemporary production to produce high-quality goods and components.

Configuring cutting tools, speeds, and feeds

Configuring cutting tools, speeds, and feeds is a critical aspect of CNC (Computer Numerical Control) machining to ensure efficient and precise material removal. Proper tool selection and cutting parameters are essential for achieving desired results, including accurate dimensions, surface finish, and tool longevity.

Here's a step-by-step guide on how to configure cutting tools, speeds, and feeds:

1. **Selecting the Right Cutting Tool:**
    - Choose the appropriate cutting tool based on the material you are machining (e.g., high-speed steel, carbide, ceramic).
    - Consider the tool's geometry (e.g., end mill, drill bit, turning insert) and coating (e.g., TiN, TiAlN) for the specific machining operation.
    - Ensure the tool's size, shape, and cutting-edge geometry are suitable for the job and workpiece material.
    - Select the proper tool holder and tool-holding system to securely grip the cutting tool.
2. **Determining Cutting Speed (SFM or MPM):**
    - Calculate the cutting speed in **Surface Feet per Minute (SFM)** or **Meters per Minute (MPM)** based on the type of material being machined. You can use reference tables or cutting speed formulas.
    - Cutting speed depends on the material's hardness and the type of cutting tool. Harder materials generally require lower cutting speeds.
3. **Selecting Feed Rate (IPM or mm/min):**
    - Determine the appropriate feed rate in **Inches per Minute (IPM)** or **Millimeters per Minute (mm/min).** This rate governs the tool's linear speed along the workpiece.

- Consider factors such as tool material, workpiece material, and tool engagement (depth of cut) when selecting the feed rate.
- Consult machining reference materials and manufacturers' recommendations for starting values.

4. **Calculating RPM (Revolutions per Minute):**
    - Calculate the spindle speed or RPM needed for the cutting tool using the formula: **RPM = (Cutting Speed × 12) / (π × Tool Diameter).**
    - Ensure the spindle speed is within the machine's capability and is compatible with the tool and workpiece.
5. **Setting Depth of Cut (DOC):**
    - Determine the appropriate depth of cut, which is the distance the tool penetrates the workpiece. It depends on the material, tool, and machining operation.
    - Consider the tool's strength and the machine's rigidity when selecting the depth of cut.
6. **Establishing Cutting Tool Coolant/Lubrication:**
    - Implement an appropriate coolant or lubrication system to dissipate heat and remove chips from the cutting zone.
    - Different materials may require different coolant types (e.g., oil-based, water-based).
7. **Toolpath Optimization:**
    - Use CAM (Computer-Aided Manufacturing) software to generate toolpaths that optimize cutting conditions, minimize tool wear, and achieve the desired surface finish.
    - Consider factors like toolpath strategy, tool engagement, and chip evacuation.
8. **Testing and Fine-Tuning:**
    - Perform test cuts on scrap or test pieces to validate your chosen cutting tool, speeds, and feeds.
    - Monitor the results for dimensional accuracy, surface finish, and tool wear.
    - Adjust the parameters as needed to optimize the machining process.

9. **Safety and Monitoring:**
    - Always follow safety guidelines and wear appropriate personal protective equipment (PPE) when operating CNC machines.
    - Continuously monitor the machining process to ensure that the cutting tool is performing as expected and make adjustments if necessary.
10. **Documentation:**
    - Keep records of the cutting tool specifications, speeds, feeds, and other relevant parameters for future reference and quality control.

When configuring cutting tools, speeds, and feeds, it is necessary to strike a balance between maximizing the amount of material removed while also protecting the cutting tool. Experimentation and expertise are two key factors that play a big part in determining which machining operations need the most optimum parameter settings. In addition, studying the advice provided by tool makers as well as machining handbooks can give very helpful direction.

Simulating Toolpaths and Material Removal

The process of CNC machining includes an essential step that involves simulating toolpaths and the removal of material. It helps you verify that your machining processes are precise and safe and allows you to envision how your CNC machine will interact with the workpiece.

The following is an explanation of how toolpaths and material removal can be simulated:

1. CAD Model Preparation:
You need to have a 3D CAD model of your component before you can simulate the toolpaths that will be used or the removal of the material. This model establishes the geometry that you want to manufacture in the future.
2. CAM Setup:
Set up the following components of your machining project in a CAM (Computer-Aided Manufacturing) program such as Fusion 360:

- **Define the stock material**: Specify the material and dimensions of the raw material or workpiece you'll be machining.
- **Select the machine and tooling**: Choose the CNC machine you'll be using and the cutting tools for your operations.
- Set the machining parameters: Specify feeds, speeds, and other cutting parameters based on your material and tooling.

3. Generate Toolpaths:
Using the CAM software, create toolpaths for your machining operations. This involves selecting the toolpath strategy (e.g., contouring, pocketing, drilling) and configuring the toolpath settings. The CAM software will generate a sequence of tool movements that the CNC machine will follow to remove material from the workpiece.

4. Simulation Setup:

Before simulating, set up your simulation environment:

- In Fusion 360, navigate to the CAM workspace.
- Select the Setup you want to simulate.
- Ensure the stock model and toolpath are correctly selected.

5. Simulate Toolpaths:

Once your setup is complete, you can begin the simulation:

- Click on the "**Simulate**" option in Fusion 360's CAM workspace.
- Choose the "**Machine**" option to simulate the toolpaths.
- The software will provide a visual representation of how the tool moves and interacts with the workpiece.

6. Review and Analyze:

During the simulation, you can:

- Play, pause, or stop the simulation at any point to review the tool's movements.
- Adjust the simulation speed to see the process in real-time or slow motion.
- Enable or disable toolpath display, tool holder, and other visualization options for a clearer view.

7. Material Removal Visualization:

Fusion 360 and similar CAM software often provide tools to visualize material removal. This feature displays the areas where material will be removed during machining, helping you ensure that your toolpaths effectively achieve the desired geometry.

8. Verify and Fine-Tune:

While simulating, be vigilant for any issues or anomalies, such as collisions between the tool, workpiece, or fixtures. If you encounter problems, return to the CAM workspace to make necessary adjustments to toolpaths, tool settings, or machining parameters. Simulating toolpaths and material removal is a crucial step in the CNC machining process, as it allows you to identify and resolve potential issues before they occur on the CNC machine. This enhances machining accuracy, minimizes material waste, and reduces the risk of damage to your equipment.

Detecting collisions and optimizing toolpaths

In the process of CNC machining, where precision and productivity are of the utmost importance, vital duties include the detection of collisions and the optimization of toolpaths. These procedures are essential to ensuring that your CNC machine operates in a manner that is both safe and efficient, allowing you to get the machining results you want.

Collision Detection

Collision detection is the first line of defense against possible catastrophes in the realm of computer-aided manufacturing (CAM), also known as computer numerical control. The most up-to-date computer-aided manufacturing (CAM) software, like Fusion 360, has highly developed collision detection algorithms that serve as sentinels protecting the machining process. These fictitious watchdogs monitor every action that your CNC machine does to guarantee that it performs the delicate dance of cutting, carving, and shaping without causing any potentially catastrophic collisions. The machine simulation is the most important part of the collision detection process. Fusion 360 allows you to painstakingly build your toolpaths, and while you do so, it provides a visual picture of each action that the CNC machine will carry out. As the simulation progresses, it analyzes each aspect, paying close attention to everything from the agile dance of the tool to the stance of the machine. It examines the distance between the tool holder and the workpiece, the fixture, and even the machine itself. If a collision is hiding in the digital shadows, the simulation carried out by Fusion 360 does not simply end with its detection. It provides a chance to look into the abyss by allowing you to halt or terminate the simulation at any time, enabling you to analyze the possible problem. You can scrutinize each movement frame by frame thanks to the speed controls, which ensure that nothing escapes your observation.

In the unfortunate case that you are involved in a collision, Fusion 360 bestows upon you the ability to masterfully use your digital tools. You can go back to the CAM workspace and make some subtle adjustments to the toolpaths so that you can avoid the impending risk. Alter the entrance and exit locations of the tool, make necessary adjustments to the depths of cut, and perfect the stepovers. Alter the order in which the procedures are performed, or choose a new tool entirely. You can also adjust the lead-in and lead-out motions with the dexterity of an artist to guarantee that the tool travels harmonically. Never to be neglected, the clearance requirement of Fusion 360 must also be met. It performs checks and double-checks to guarantee that your toolpaths keep a safe distance from the workpiece, clamps, and fixtures, as well as the machine itself. Because of this painstaking attention to detail, a collision that may have potentially been fatal is reduced to little more than an afterthought.

Optimizing Toolpaths

The process of optimizing toolpaths is an art form that exists outside the area of collision detection. When it comes to machining, every second matters and every action has a specific function. You will be able to build toolpaths with surgical precision with the help of Fusion 360, which will save waste and increase productivity. To get started, choose the appropriate toolpath strategy for each of the operations. There are a plethora of different tactics available for your pick, including contouring, pocketing, adaptive clearing, and numerous more. Each one is a new stroke that you're going to put on the canvas that is your machining masterpiece. The concept of optimization encompasses even the minutest aspects of the machining process. Think about the path that the tool will take through the workpiece and ask yourself whether or not it can take the path that is least obstructed. You can fine-tune entrance and exit strategies with the help of Fusion 360, which minimizes moves that aren't essential and maximizes efficiency. In addition, improving toolpaths requires selecting the tool that is most suited for the activity at hand. The toolbox that comes with Fusion 360 is loaded with possibilities, ensuring that you will always have the appropriate tool for the job at hand. This not only increases the effectiveness of your work but also makes your tools last longer. In the world of CNC machining, the two most important factors for achieving success are collision detection and toolpath optimization. Your CNC machine will move with precision, efficiency, and safety when you use Fusion 360 because of its digital capabilities, which equip you to traverse this delicate dance.

Exporting G-code for CNC Machines

It is the climax of a journey that has been methodically thought out to export G-code for CNC machines. This is the point at which digital designs are translated into physical things. It is the instant at which the virtual world effortlessly converges with the actual world, and it all starts inside the constraints of a CAM (Computer-Aided Manufacturing) software program such as Fusion 360. You have one more stop to make on your journey through CNC machining, and before you do so, you need to make sure that your CAM setup is as close to ideal as it can be. The stock material must be precisely determined, the CNC machine must be picked with precision, the tools must be chosen to fulfill your vision, and the machining settings must be properly calibrated. This is the canvas that your artwork will be painted on, so be creative! After you have finished configuring your CAM software, it is time to check your toolpaths. Every motion, plunge, and sweep of the tool must be carried out in accordance with your vision. Check the toolpaths carefully to see if there are any inconsistencies, irregularities, or flaws. This is a preview of the performance that will shortly take place in the real world, and it's done in digital form. When everything is in place and the performers are prepared, it is time to bring the show to a climactic conclusion. You choose the CAM configuration that encompasses the whole of your machining process, checking to make sure that it has all of the necessary information before making your choice.

Post-processing, sometimes known as the moment of alchemy, has finally arrived. This is the point at which your digital design in Fusion 360 is translated into the motions of the CNC machine. With only a few mouse clicks, you can bring up a dialog box that, in essence, serves as the doorway to the beating heart of your CNC machine. Here, you will configure the post-processor, which is a specialized translation engine that translates the abstract notions generated by your CAM setup into G-code, the language that is understood by CNC machines. This step is where the digital and the physical worlds collide, and it requires extreme accuracy. You must define several specifics, such as tool change instructions, coolant settings, and coordinate systems, to make sure that your G-code is suitable for your particular CNC machine. The process of configuring the post-processor is like writing a symphony as you go. The conclusion of your decisions will decide the harmony of the machining operation you are doing, and each setting is like a note in the symphony. It's a point in time when experience collides with originality and comprehension converges with imagination. After all of the post-processing steps have been finished, you will be presented with the final masterpiece, which is the G-code file. This file contains all of the details that characterize your CNC machining process, including your toolpaths, as well as your design. It is the score that the conductor will use, and your CNC machine is prepared to interpret it. This G-code file serves as a connection between the world of your imagination and the real world. It is the formula for the transformation of the material as well as the blueprint for the motions of your CNC machine. When you give it over to your CNC machine, you are giving it the authority to transfer your digital dreams into the real world and make them a reality.

Generating machine-readable G-code instructions

The process of computer numerical control (CNC) machining requires, as one of its primary steps, the generation of G-code instructions that are readable by machines. G-code is a language that CNC machines understand; it is made up of a sequence of alphanumeric codes that inform the machine how to move, position, and operate the tool to build a physical product based on a digital design.

This language is called "G-code." Instructions in G-code that are readable by machines can be generated as follows:

1. **Prepare Your CAM Setup:**
- Before you can generate G-code, you will need to set up your machining project in a CAM (Computer-Aided Manufacturing) program like Fusion 360. This must be done before you can generate G-code.
- Specify the stock material, decide which CNC machine to use, decide which cutting tools to use, and define the machining parameters.
2. **Generate Toolpaths:**
- To carry out your machining operations, you need to first define toolpaths using the CAM program. Specifying the toolpath approach (such as contouring, pocketing, or drilling, for example) and modifying variables such as cutting depths, stepovers, and tool engagement are required to complete this step.
3. **Simulation and Verification:**
- It is recommended that you do a simulation of your toolpaths inside the CAM program before moving on to the next step of generating G-code. This makes it easier for you to visually verify that the toolpaths are correct and that there are no collisions or motions that are unexpected.

4. **Post-Processing:**
- **The following phase, which comes after confirming your toolpaths, is the post-processing stage. At this point, your CAM configuration will be converted into G-code, which is readable by machines:**
    - In Fusion 360, go to the "**Actions**" panel and select "**Post Process.**"
    - Choose the appropriate post-processor for your CNC machine. This post-processor translates your CAM data into G-code specific to your machine.
    - Configure the post-processor settings, including tool change commands, coolant activation, coordinate systems, and file format options.

5. **Generate G-code:**
- Carry out the post-processing procedure after ensuring that the post-processor parameters are properly established. The G-code file will be generated for you depending on your CAM configuration and the post-processor that you choose when you do this activity.
- The G-code file will be saved to the directory that you choose as a text file with either the **".nc" or ".gcode"** extension, depending on which you want.

6. **Review and Save:**
- Perform a thorough inspection of the G-code file that was created to confirm that it appropriately reflects the machining goals you had.
- Make sure that the G-code file is stored in a place that can be accessed by your CNC machine. You may also think about naming it after your project so that it is easier to go back to later.

7. **Load and Execute G-code:**
- After the G-code file has been produced, transfer it to your CNC machine. This is often accomplished with the use of a USB drive or other suitable techniques.
- Open up the control software for your CNC machine and load the G-code file into it.
- Start the CNC machine and run the G-code program, which will command the machine to follow the toolpaths and machining processes that have been defined.

The most important step in bridging the gap between your digital design and the real world is to generate instructions in a machine-readable format called G-code. It guarantees that your CNC machine will faithfully copy the geometry you desire and will bring your creative ideas to life with precision and repeatability.

Sending G-code to CNC machines for production

The last phase in the CNC machining process is the sending of G-code to the CNC machines that will be used for production. The language that CNC machines comprehend is called G-code, and it consists of a sequence of instructions that explain to the machine how to move, position, and operate the tool so that a real thing can be created based on a digital design.

Here's how you can send G-code to CNC machines for production:

1. **Generate G-code:** As described in the previous responses, you must first generate the G-code instructions using CAM software. Ensure that your CAM setup is correctly configured, and you've generated the G-code file specific to your machining project.
2. **Transfer the G-code File:**
    - Save the generated G-code file with the appropriate file extension (e.g., ".nc" or ".gcode").

- Transfer the G-code file to a storage medium that can be used with your CNC machine. Common options include USB drives, SD cards, or network connections. Ensure that the storage medium is compatible with your CNC machine's control system.

3. **Prepare the CNC Machine:**
    - Make sure the CNC machine is in good working condition and properly calibrated.
    - Securely mount the workpiece and ensure it is clamped or fixtured according to your CAM setup.
    - Load and secure the correct cutting tool in the machine's tool holder.
4. **Access the CNC Control Software:**
    - Power up the CNC machine and access its control software. The exact steps for accessing the control software may vary depending on the machine's make and model.
5. **Load the G-code File:**
    - Use the CNC control software to load the G-code file from the storage medium you transferred it to. Follow the machine's user manual for specific instructions on how to load G-code files.
6. **Set Work and Tool Offsets:**
    - Verify and set any work and tool offsets as specified in your CAM setup. These offsets ensure that the machine positions the tool accurately relative to the workpiece.
7. **Execute the G-code Program:**
    - Start the CNC machine's control software and initiate the G-code program. The machine will begin executing the commands in the G-code file, guiding the tool through the specified toolpaths and machining operations.
8. **Monitor the Operation:**
    - During production, closely monitor the CNC machine to ensure it is operating as expected. Keep an eye on tool wear, coolant levels, and any potential issues.
9. **Quality Control:**
    - After the machining process is complete, inspect the finished part to ensure it meets your quality standards. Make any necessary adjustments to your CAM setup or tooling if needed.
10. **Repeat as Necessary:**
    - If you have multiple parts to produce, you can repeat the process by reloading the G-code file and changing the workpiece if required.
11. **Shutdown and Maintenance:**
    - After production is complete, safely shut down the CNC machine, perform any necessary maintenance tasks, and store the G-code files and setup information for future use.

The pinnacle of your machining project is the process of sending G-code to CNC machines for manufacturing. This is the stage at which the digital design is converted into a real thing with precision and accuracy. To guarantee a good end, it is necessary to pay close attention to the details during the whole process, pay careful attention to how things are set up, and monitor everything carefully.

Manufacturing in Fusion 360

The manufacturing phase of the product development process is an extremely important step. To meet your production requirements, Fusion 360 provides a complete variety of tools and processes to choose from. Let's investigate some of the most important features of manufacturing in Fusion 360.

Introduction to manufacturing workflows in Fusion 360

The integration of production capabilities into the same software environment that Fusion 360 delivers enables a smooth transition from the design phase to the manufacturing phase. Fusion 360 provides a variety of tools and workflows that may help you simplify the manufacturing processes you use, whether you work with subtractive processes like CNC machining or additive manufacturing techniques like 3D printing. For example, you can import CAD files directly into Fusion 360.

In addition to the smooth transition from design to manufacture, Fusion 360 provides various proof points that show its strengths in manufacturing processes. These proof points include the following:

- **Integrated CAM functionality**: The integrated computer-aided manufacturing (CAM) feature of Fusion 360 enables you to build toolpaths from inside the program itself. This removes the need for separate CAM software and provides a process that is more effective from the design phase through the machining phase.
- **Toolpath optimization**: The CAM tools that come with Fusion 360 feature a variety of sophisticated techniques for optimizing toolpaths. These solutions increase overall production efficiency by optimizing cutting pathways, reducing machining time, minimizing tool wear, and optimizing tool wear.
- **Simulation and verification**: Before you send your ideas out to be manufactured, Fusion 360 gives you the ability to simulate and validate the machining process so that you can be confident in the results. To identify any possible problems or collisions, you can see the toolpaths, simulate the material removal process, and do so. This feature helps to guarantee that the machining is done without errors and decreases the danger of making expensive mistakes.
- **Support for multiple manufacturing methods**: Fusion 360 offers support for some different manufacturing processes. Among them are CNC machining, 3D printing, manufacturing of sheet metal, and other similar processes. Within the confines of a single software platform, you have the flexibility to choose the method of production that is most suited to meeting the needs that are unique to your business.
- **Cloud collaboration**: The cloud-based infrastructure that Fusion 360 utilizes makes it possible for seamless cooperation with manufacturing partners. It is simple to exchange design files, you can interact in real-time and can monitor the progression of the project. During the phase of the manufacturing process when decisions are being made, this simplified method of collaboration helps to develop effective communication and efficient decision-making.

Fusion 360 users are given the ability to accomplish high-quality production that is cost-effective by exploiting these features, which also enable users to simplify their manufacturing operations.

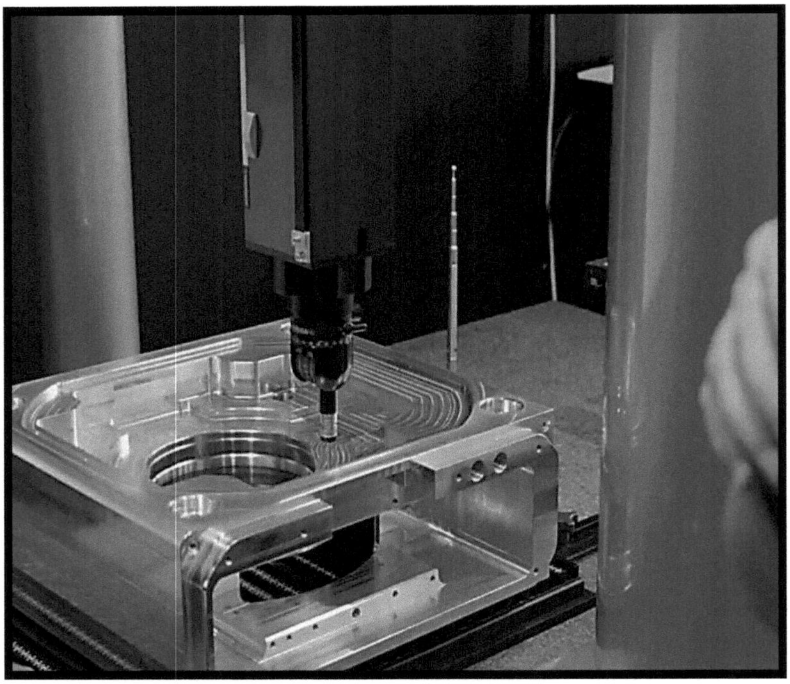

Fusion 360 manufacturing capabilities

The following are five elements that showcase the potential of Fusion 360 in regards to manufacturing workflows:

1. **Adaptive clearing**: The CAM elements of Fusion 360 include sophisticated algorithmic implementations of adaptive clearing. This toolpath method maximizes the amount of material that can be removed by dynamically altering the level of interaction between the cutting tool and the material being cut. The machining time can be cut down, the tool life can be extended, and higher-quality finishes can be produced all thanks to adaptive clearing.
2. Fusion 360's support for **multi-axis machining** enables you to design intricate toolpaths for CNC machines with four and five axes, respectively. With multi-axis capabilities, you can manufacture complicated geometries and obtain more flexibility in your production operations. You can also make undercuts with greater ease.
3. Fusion 360 has **post-processing tools** that can create machine-specific code for CNC machines. These capabilities are part of the software's **machine simulation** feature. This assures compatibility and seamless integration with the CNC machine you have specifically chosen. In addition to this, the machine simulation capabilities are included in Fusion 360. Because of this, you can view and check the machining process, which enables you to identify and avoid any possible problems or collisions.
4. **Design for Manufacturability (DFM) analysis:** The Design for Manufacturability (DFM) analysis tools that are included in Fusion 360 may assist you in optimizing your designs for production. These tools help identify places in the design where adjustments can be made to enhance the product's ability to be manufactured, such as limiting the number of difficult setups, reducing the number of tool changes, and enhancing accessibility for machining processes.

5. Fusion 360 interacts with a **variety of manufacturing services** and partners, which enables a faster process for ordering components straight from inside the program. By providing access to a reliable network of manufacturing services, this integration makes the process of shifting gears from design to production much more straightforward and straightforward.

Fusion 360 helps to expedite the production process and guarantees that your ideas are successfully realized by harnessing the resources that are available to them.

Creating 3D prints and exporting files for additive manufacturing

Fusion 360 offers tools used in additive manufacturing techniques, such as 3D printing, to prepare models and create optimal files. You can create support structures, alter print parameters, and export files in a variety of formats that work with different 3D printers. Fusion 360's additive manufacturing features enable you to generate end-use components as well as workable prototypes.

Here are five proof points that highlight Fusion 360's capabilities in additive manufacturing workflows:

Fusion 360 additive manufacturing functionality

1. **Parametric design for flexibility**: Fusion 360's parametric design features allow you to simply generate models that can be adjusted and updated for additive printing, giving you flexibility in your design process. Your design can be optimized for certain 3D printing techniques, materials, or desired properties by changing its size, parameters, and features.
2. **Mesh editing and repair**: Fusion 360 offers strong tools for these tasks. This is very helpful when using models or 3D scans that you got from other sources. Meshes can be altered, cleaned up, and repaired to get them ready for 3D printing. You can deal with a variety of geometries thanks to this.
3. **Slicing and print preparation**: Fusion 360 has slicing capabilities that let you get ready for printing 3D objects. Print parameters include layer height, infill density, support structures, and more that you can customize. Before sending the file to the printer, it is simple to customize and see the printing process thanks to Fusion 360's user-friendly interface.
4. **Fusion Team integration**: Fusion 360 and Fusion Team, a cloud-based platform for collaboration, work together effortlessly. Colleagues, customers, or manufacturing partners can securely access your ideas and evaluate the 3D models and production files, offering input. The production process is streamlined and communication is improved in this cooperative setting.
5. **Additive manufacturing simulation**: Fusion 360's simulation features include additive manufacturing procedures. To anticipate and improve elements such as component deformation, residual stresses, and warping, you can model the 3D printing process. This enhances the general quality and dependability of the printed components and helps guarantee the successful printing of complicated geometries.

Fusion 360 provides a comprehensive solution for harnessing the capabilities of additive manufacturing technologies.

Sheet metal fabrication and manufacturing considerations

For modeling sheet metal pieces, Fusion 360 provides a specialized sheet metal environment. You can design bends, flanges, tabs, and other sheet metal elements in this environment. Fusion 360 offers production data and flat layouts as well as tools for precisely displaying sheet metal designs. Successful production of sheet metal components can be ensured by being aware of manufacturing restrictions and having a thorough understanding of sheet metal fabrication procedures throughout the design phase.

Fusion 360 sheet metal functionality

Dive into these five points that highlight Fusion 360's capabilities in sheet metal workflows:

1. **Overview of sheet metal tools**: Fusion 360 provides an extensive collection of tools designed especially for sheet metal design. These tools can be used to make a variety of flanges, such as base, edge, and miter flanges. With ease, you can also include characteristics such as reliefs, bends, and corners to precisely depict the required sheet metal geometry.
2. **Creation of flat patterns**: With Fusion 360, you can create flat patterns from your sheet metal drawings. The unfolded geometry of your sheet metal components can be seen and exported using this capability, which is crucial for the fabrication and production processes. You can verify that the dimensions and features are accurately represented before manufacturing by looking at the flat pattern.
3. **Manufacturing information**: Sheet metal designs include manufacturing information with the use of Fusion 360's tools. To guarantee correct production, you can provide bend radii, bend allowances, and other manufacturing-specific information. This data can be used internally to expedite the fabrication process or directly shared with manufacturing partners.
4. **Design validation**: You can verify the structural soundness and producibility of your components by using Fusion 360's simulation capabilities for sheet metal designs. The bending processes can be simulated to detect any problems like excessive deformation or material failure. This raises the efficiency and dependability of your sheet metal manufacturing by optimizing your designs.

You can easily produce high-quality components and optimize the sheet metal manufacturing process by using Fusion 360's sheet metal tools.

Collaborating with manufacturing partners

Fusion 360's extensive network of top companies in the sector improves its production operations. Fusion 360 helps smooth operational throughput by forming alliances with suppliers, machine tool makers, and work-holding organizations. Through these partnerships, you have access to a large selection of specialty tools, fixtures, and machinery made especially for accurate and productive manufacturing.

You can gain from more productive workflows, refined manufacturing capabilities, and better manufacturing capabilities by using this ecosystem. Fusion 360's dedication to partnering with top industry players guarantees that you will have access to the tools and assistance required to realize your ideas with optimal quality and efficiency.

Fusion 360 manufacturing partnerships

Check out these five proof points that highlight Fusion 360's capabilities in manufacturing partnerships:

1. **Access to specialized tools**: Users have access to a wide variety of specialized tools thanks to Fusion 360's agreements with suppliers, machine tool manufacturers, and work-holding businesses. Through the use of these tools, users may get the best possible outcomes in industrial processes by increasing efficiency and precision.
2. **Improved workflows**: Fusion 360 optimizes manufacturing processes via integration with leading companies in the sector. By facilitating smooth data interchange, tool compatibility, and process integration, the partnership lowers human labor and boosts operational effectiveness.
3. **Enhanced productivity**: Users may enhance their production processes by using the ecosystem of leading industries. Fusion 360 users can cut time-to-market and improve overall project efficiency by achieving greater levels of productivity with access to cutting-edge tools and solutions.
4. **Quality and consistency**: Fusion 360 customers can depend on top-notch tools and equipment thanks to partnerships with leading industry players. Renowned manufacturers produce these tools and subject them to rigorous testing, ensuring consistent performance and trustworthy outcomes.
5. **Integration of materials and suppliers**: Fusion 360's network of top companies in the sector goes beyond tools and equipment to include material suppliers. Collaboration with suppliers is made easy by this connection, which also guarantees access to a large variety of materials and expedites the procurement procedure for manufacturing projects.

Fusion 360's community of industry experts provides tools and experience that customers can use to improve their manufacturing skills, optimize workflows, and accomplish more efficiency and quality in their projects.

CHAPTER 21
FINITE ELEMENT ANALYSIS (FEA)

The chapter starts with a description of FEA and how it can be used in engineering and design. It draws attention to how important FEA is to stress modeling and analysis. It talks about how to define loads, materials, and boundary conditions for Finite Element Analysis (FEA) simulations. These elements are necessary for a precise analysis. The practical features of configuring FEA studies in Fusion 360 are also covered in this chapter. To replicate real-world situations entails building simulation models, meshing them for analysis, and adding loads and restrictions. It explores how to evaluate FEA data. The analysis of stress, displacement, and safety considerations derived from simulations is explained. It also highlights the need to determine crucial areas in which design modifications are necessary in light of the outcomes. The chapter's last section covers the iterative design process that is motivated by simulation discoveries. It describes how to improve designs using FEA data, which will eventually improve performance and guarantee that designs adhere to efficiency and safety standards.

Understanding Stress Analysis and Simulation

In Fusion 360, the terms "**stress analysis" and "simulation**" relate to the process of examining how a mechanical assembly or component will respond to different loading scenarios using computer-aided design (CAD) software. By using this research, engineers and designers can make sure that their creations are safe, strong, and able to endure the stresses they will face in practical applications. Envision yourself as a designer or engineer who is about to produce a ground-breaking item, such as a sophisticated assembly of pieces or a complicated mechanical component. You recognize that your invention will encounter a variety of loads, stresses, and pressures in the actual world. It is crucial to ensure its structural integrity, which is where Fusion 360's simulation and stress analysis tools come in handy. Making a digital blueprint of your project is the first step in your quest. Fusion 360's CAD modeling tools enable you to easily shape complex geometry. You can see what you want to happen on your computer screen and arrange the scene with a few clicks and swipes. For an engineer, every material has a personality of its own. Assigning material properties like Poisson's Ratio and Young's modulus gives your virtual creation life. How the material will bend, stretch, or compress under stress is determined by these properties. Anchors are necessary for your design, just as in real life. You can specify boundary constraints using Fusion 360 to make sure your virtual prototype acts as if it's securely fastened to the actual world. You choose which points are free to move, where it's fixed, and how it's supported. Your digital masterpiece is now separated into a tangle of little components.

Imagine it as a huge web around your design. This model is essential; the precision of your simulation depends on how intricate it is. More information can be captured with a finer mesh, but it also requires more processing power. Time to apply the laws of physics. To simulate the conditions your virtual model will face in the actual world, you apply forces, pressures, and torques to it. Limitations help to keep your design in check and prevent it from straying into the virtual void. A virtual mathematician plays a role behind the scenes. Similar to a conscientious investigator, the solver is set up with certain settings. It is in charge of figuring out how loads and limits will cause your design to deform and respond. Once everything is set up, you start the big experiment: executing the simulation. As Fusion 360's virtual laboratory comes to life, finite element analysis (FEA) is performed by the program like a skilled alchemist. It computes the complex dance between deformation and stress in your model. The findings are revealed as the curtain rises. Fusion 360 creates a clear image of the reaction to your design. You see graphs that show the inner workings of your design, arrows that show displacement, and colors that illustrate stress distribution. It's a time of exploration. As the artist of this virtual world, you examine the outcomes. You verify that your design satisfies performance and safety requirements. Conversely, you iterate. You make adjustments, restart the simulation, and polish your work of art. You are the one who planned this trip, and you record your discoveries. With Fusion 360, you can create thorough reports that track the effectiveness of your design. These reports provide a guide for future revisions and interactions with stakeholders and colleagues. An experiential exam is the best in the actual world. If required, you conduct physical trials to confirm your virtual results and make sure the digital mirror you have constructed accurately reflects reality. You can do the impossible using Fusion 360's stress analysis and simulation features. Within the limits of your computer screen, you develop, test, and enhance. You bring concepts to life, making sure that your creations are not just creative but also resilient against the forces that confront them in the actual world.

Here's an overview of stress analysis and simulation in Fusion 360:

1. **CAD modeling**: To start, a 3D CAD model of the component or assembly you want to examine must be made. For this reason, Fusion 360 has strong modeling tools that let you design intricate shapes.
2. **Material Properties**: Give the elements in your CAD model **material properties.** It is necessary to include material properties like Poisson's Ratio and Young's Modulus to correctly simulate how the material will flex under stress.
3. **Boundary Conditions**: Define boundary conditions, which are sometimes referred to as limitations. These requirements define how the component is supported or fixed throughout the analysis. Supports, applied forces, and fixed points are typical boundary conditions.
4. **Meshing**: Fusion 360 divides the geometry into smaller components using a process known as meshing. How precisely the program can model stress distribution depends on the mesh. Although fine meshing demands more processing power, it yields more accurate results.
5. **Loads and Constraints**: Give your model loads. Different types of loads, such as pressures, torques, and forces, can be identified. For your design to behave as it would in the actual world, you also establish limitations.
6. **Solver Setup**: Set up the solver by adjusting its parameters, including the simulation time and convergence criterion. Based on the input circumstances, the solver determines the stress and deformation in your model.
7. **Running the Simulation**: The simulation can be launched when the analysis has been configured. Finite element analysis (FEA) methods will be used by Fusion 360 to determine the part's response to applied loads.
8. **Viewing the Results**: You can examine the results after the simulation is finished. Fusion 360 offers stress, displacement, and other pertinent parameter visualizations. Additionally, reports that document your results can be generated.
9. **Interpretation and Optimization**: Examine the outcomes to make sure your design satisfies performance and safety standards. If problems are found, you can optimize the design by making modifications to the design and running the simulation again and again.
10. **Documentation**: Write reports and documentation outlining the analysis's conclusions. These reports help inform stakeholders about the performance of your design and ensure that it complies with industry standards.

11. **Validation**: If required, confirm your simulation findings with physical testing. By doing this step, you can make sure that your virtual analysis correctly depicts behavior in the actual world.

Both inexperienced and seasoned engineers and designers may easily do stress analysis and simulation using Fusion 360's user-friendly interface. By identifying any design problems and making improvements to your ideas before production or prototyping, you can save time and dollars by using these simulation tools.

Introduction to finite element analysis (FEA)

In science and engineering, **finite element analysis (FEA)** is a potent numerical method for resolving intricate issues pertaining to the behavior of materials, physical systems, and structures. Through the use of computing, a complex system can be broken down into smaller, more manageable parts known as "**finite elements**" to estimate and evaluate its behavior under different scenarios. Finite Element Analysis (FEA) has emerged as a crucial tool across several domains, such as mechanical, civil, aerospace, biomedical, physics, and materials research.

An overview of the core ideas of finite element analysis is provided below:

1. **Mathematical Approximation**: Essentially, FEA is the process of breaking down a continuous system (such as a solid item or a fluid) into a limited number of smaller, linked pieces to approximate its behavior. These are often basic geometric forms such as polyhedra, tetrahedra, or other 3D polyhedra, or 2D triangles or quadrilaterals.
2. **Discretization**: A mesh is created by connecting the discretized nodes of the continuous problem to a limited number of other nodes. FEA is based on the mesh, and the mesh's ability to accurately reflect the underlying geometry determines how accurate the analysis is.
3. **Governing Equations**: Under different circumstances **(such as mechanical loads, temperature changes, or fluid movement),** the behavior of every element in the mesh is determined by physical equations that explain how stress, strain, and other properties vary inside the element. These formulas change based on the particular issue being resolved.
4. **Boundary requirements**: FEA has to have established boundary conditions to be applied to real-world issues. These criteria define how the system or structure is loaded or restricted at its borders. You might, for instance, apply pressures and temperatures to certain nodes or repair others.
5. **Solution Process**: FEA employs numerical methods to solve the governing equations after the mesh, boundary conditions, and equations are determined. The "**finite element** method," which solves a set of linear or nonlinear equations repeatedly, is the most often used technique. **ANSYS, Abaqus, and COMSOL** are FEA software systems that manage the intricate mathematics needed for this stage.
6. **Visualization of the Result**: FEA solves the equations and offers insightful information on the behavior of the system. To understand how the system reacts to various situations, scientists and engineers can visualize the outcomes, such as stress distribution, deformation, temperature, and fluid flow patterns.
7. **Verification and Optimization**: **Finite Element Analysis (FEA)** is used in some processes, such as verifying designs, forecasting failure sites, streamlining structures, and assessing performance in diverse contexts. To increase the effectiveness, security, and dependability of their systems, engineers can make well-informed judgments.

8. **Applications**: **Finite Element Analysis (FEA)** is widely used in engineering disciplines, such as electromagnetics (e.g., antenna design and electromagnetic interference), fluid dynamics (e.g., aerodynamics and fluid flow in pipelines), thermal analysis (e.g., heat transfer in electronics), and structural analysis (e.g., bridges, buildings, and mechanical components).

In conclusion, engineers and scientists may simulate and understand the behavior of complicated systems by disassembling them into smaller, more manageable components using a computer process called finite element analysis. It has completely changed the way we conceptualize and build physical systems, resulting in creative, safe, and effective solutions across many different sectors.

Defining materials, loads, and boundary conditions

To set up and run Finite Element Analysis (FEA) simulations, which are often used in engineering and scientific applications, materials, loads, and boundary conditions must be defined. To effectively represent and analyze the behavior of structures, components, or systems, certain concepts are necessary. **Let's take a closer look at each of these features:**

1. Materials:

Using an FEA simulation, you can specify the physical properties of the structures or components by using their materials. **The following are important material properties:**

- **Young's Modulus (E):** This term describes the stiffness or the degree to which a material resists deformation, under a load. Stiffer materials are indicated by higher values.
- **Poisson's Ratio (v):** This parameter describes the deformation-response behavior of a material. It connects the lateral and axial strains. Values typically fall between 0 and 0.5.
- **Density (ρ):** This quantity is crucial for mass and gravity simulations as it influences how a material reacts to gravitational forces.
- **Thermal Conductivity (k)** and **Specific Heat (C)**: The properties of Thermal Conductivity (k) and Specific Heat (C) are essential for thermal simulations because they define a material's ability to transmit heat and store thermal energy.
- **Yield Strength, Ultimate Strength, and Failure Criteria**: You may need to provide parameters about material strength and failure in simulations involving mechanical loads. These parameters include yield and ultimate strengths as well as failure criteria (such as Von Mises stress).
- **Isotropic or Anisotropic Properties**: When examined in various orientations, many materials display distinct properties. Behavior can be classified as anisotropic (having distinct properties in various directions) or isotropic (having the same properties in all directions).
- **Temperature-Dependent Properties**: It is important to include temperature-dependent properties in thermal simulations as materials can have them.

2. Loads:

The FEA model is subject to external forces, pressures, or limitations, which are represented by loads. Typical loads consist of:

- **Force**: An external force exerted on a particular area or node inside the model. It can be used at different angles and intensities.

- **Pressure**: Pressure can be delivered as a point load at a particular spot or as a dispersed force over a surface.
- **Moment**: To represent rotational effects, a moment or torque is supplied to the model.
- **Gravity**: To account for weight and deformation caused by gravity, structural assessments must simulate the influence of gravity.
- **Thermal Loads**: Essential to thermal simulations, they consist of applied heat sources and temperature gradients in the model.
- **Velocity or Acceleration**: To simulate fluid flow, you can set intake velocities or accelerations in fluid dynamics models.

3. Boundary Conditions:

The FEA model's boundary conditions define how it is supported or limited at certain points. They make sure the model doesn't move or deform randomly and acts realistically.

Typical border circumstances consist of:

- **Fixed Support**: Nodes or surfaces that are fully restrained and cannot move or deform.
- **Roller Support**: Limiting movement in a single direction (allowing movement in a plane or along a line, for example).
- **Pinned Support**: Complete restriction of motion, except rotation.
- **Symmetry or Anti-Symmetry**: These circumstances make use of geometric symmetries to minimize the problem's dimensions.
- **Remote Displacements**: a common technique in structural assessments, this technique simulates the impact of a remote support or constraint.
- **Periodic Boundary Conditions**: For repeated patterns or periodic structures.
- **Constraints on Temperature**: Determining the temperature at certain locations or surfaces (crucial for thermal simulations).

Get relevant results from FEA simulations with precise definitions of materials, loads, and boundary conditions. By simulating and analyzing the behavior of structures, parts, or systems under many situations, these definitions enable engineers and scientists to optimize their designs and make well-informed design choices.

Setting Up FEA Studies in Fusion 360:

1. Open Your Design:

- Visualize taking a seat at your computer and starting Fusion 360. You open the design or CAD model that you have been working on nonstop with a feeling of purpose. This design ought to be an accurate representation of the thing or structure you are going to examine. Every little thing counts.

2. Get the Simulation Environment Started:

- By navigating to Fusion 360's "**Simulation**" workspace, you can quickly access the simulation world with a few clicks. This is the area where you will test your design and discover its latent features.

3. Create a New Study:

- This is where you start your trip by starting a new study. It's similar to starting a new chapter in your simulation journey, where you set the parameters for the activity.

4. Define the Material:

- Envision imparting material properties to your model by reaching out to it. You carefully choose parts and materials from Fusion 360's collection, indicating density, Poisson's Ratio, Young's modulus, and other crucial parameters. You are aware that your simulation's fundamental properties are these.

5. Create the Mesh:

- At this point, you start the mesh creation process. Your design has been discretized into a variety of interrelated pieces rather than remaining as a single, continuous entity. The size and complexity of the mesh are chosen by you, just as an artist chooses the ideal brushstroke. The precision of your simulation will be impacted by your choices.

6. Set Up Boundary Conditions:

- Now is the time to provide the parameters for your simulation. You impose restrictions, acting as the defenders of your model's motion. They establish the model's interaction with the virtual world as well as which components are free and which ones stay attached. In the virtual world, realism is guaranteed by your limits.

7. Apply Loads:

- You exert loads, forces from outside that will influence what you've created. It might be a torque, force, pressure, or even a heat load. As a result of these forces acting upon it, your model starts to obey the rules of the virtual world.

8. Configure Simulation Settings:

- It's you who adjusts the simulation parameters behind the scenes. You can pick the kind of analysis (static, thermal, modal, or another), establish convergence conditions, and choose between linear and nonlinear solvers. The parameters that control the behavior of your simulation are these settings.

9. Run the Simulation:

- The crucial moment occurs when you press the "**Run**" button. The computer engine of Fusion 360 roars to life, and the virtual laboratory comes to life. It deciphers the intricate FEA calculations and reveals the secrets buried in your design.

10. Review and Interpret Results:

- You enter the "**Results**" workspace after the simulation comes to an end. The behavior of your model is revealed here. Vibrant graphics show temperature distributions, deformations, stress patterns, and other important information. It's a canvas of data that you examine closely and critically.

11. Iteration and Optimization:

- If the outcomes prompt inquiries or identify opportunities for improvement, you begin a cycle of refinement and optimization. Equipped with your acquired information, you revisit your CAD model, making deliberate modifications before repeating the experiment. It's a repetitive dance that leads to mastery.

12. Generate Reports:

- Reports are created at the end of your tour. These files are proof of your work; they are an all-inclusive account of the setup, outcomes, and lessons learned throughout the simulation. For cooperation and communication, they serve as tools.

13. Save and Share:

- You save your simulation research in Fusion 360, feeling proud of yourself. If required, you distribute it to coworkers or other relevant parties, encouraging cooperation and understanding among everyone.

Every move in Fusion 360's FEA studies realm is a well-planned dance of science and engineering. It's an exploration voyage where the virtual and the real come together, enabling you to confidently and precisely hone and polish your concepts.

Interpreting Simulation Results

One important element in the Finite Element Analysis (FEA) process is interpreting the findings of the simulation. After completing your simulation in a program like Fusion 360, you are shown a variety of statistics and visuals that offer you an understanding of how your design performs in different scenarios. **Let's delve into the art of interpreting these results:**

1. Stress Distribution:
- Show the distribution of stress across your model. Diverse stress levels are represented by colors. Potential failure spots can be indicated by high-stress locations, which are often highlighted in warm or red hues. Keep a watchful eye out for locations with high loads, fillets, and sharp corners where stress concentrations may occur.

2. Deformation and Displacement:
- Pay attention to how your model flexes when weights are applied. Plots of deformation show how much the structure bends or moves. This is essential for determining if the design satisfies safety requirements and whether the deformation is within allowable limits.

3. Safety Factors and Margins:
- Examine margins of safety or safety considerations. These numbers show you how near failure your design is. Your design can withstand the imposed loads if your safety factor is over 1.0; numbers below 1.0 might point to a possible failure.

4. Strain Distribution:
- Analyze the strain distribution to comprehend the deformation of materials. High strains might be a sign of weariness or injury to certain parts of the body. Make sure stresses don't exceed allowable limits to avoid material failure.

5. Modal Analysis (if applicable):
- Examine mode forms and natural frequencies in modal analysis. Determine which mode shapes and resonance frequencies might cause instability or vibrations in your design. If required, modify the design to prevent these problems.

6. Thermal Analysis (if applicable):
- Examine temperature gradients and dispersion while doing thermal analysis. Locate hotspots or areas when temperature thresholds are surpassed. If necessary, modify the thermal boundary conditions or enhance the thermal management.

7. Factor of Safety (FOS):
- Compute and verify the safety factor, if your program does not provide it automatically. Greater design resilience is indicated by a higher factor of safety. To make sure it's safe, compare it to your design specifications.

8. Stress Concentration and Critical Points:
- Determine the crucial spots and stress concentration factors (SCFs) in your model. Significantly more stress than the component's average stress is present in these regions. To lessen stress concentrations, take into account design changes.

9. Deflection and Displacement Limits:

- Examine the displacements and deformations in real terms against the tolerances and design limitations. Make sure the deflections stay within permissible limits in terms of both appearance and operation.

10. Convergence and Solution Quality: - Verify if the outcomes of your simulation are converging. Verify if a stable state has been achieved by the solution. Your model or simulation setup may be having problems if there is poor convergence or non-convergence.

11. Sensitivity analysis (if applicable): - Analyze the effects of changing factors (such as material properties, loads, or dimensions) on the functionality of your design. This can assist in determining important design elements.

12. Validation and Correlation (if applicable): - If at all feasible, do physical testing to verify the outcomes of your simulation. Examine both actual and simulated data to make sure your model is accurate.

13. Documentation and Reporting: - Keep a record of your results, analysis, and suggested modifications to the design. Write summaries of the analysis's findings and conclusions in reports. These reports are necessary for decision-making and stakeholder communication.

Finding significant technical insights from the data and visualizations is just one aspect of interpreting simulation results. It calls for an acute attention to detail, a thorough comprehension of the relevant physics, and the capacity to convert information into useful design advancements. By optimizing for efficiency and cost-effectiveness, efficient interpretation guarantees that your design satisfies performance and safety requirements.

Analyzing stress, displacement, and safety factors

Analyzing Stress

Consider that you are analyzing a FEA simulation's output. A brightly colored stress distribution plot that shows the tensions in your intricate engineering design greets you. Every hue in this visual spectrum has a meaning; warmer red and orange tones indicate high-stress zones, whereas chilly blue and green tones denote low-stress zones. Finding stress concentrations, or those hotspots that stick out like beacons, is your first duty. These are the areas, which are often found close to jagged edges, abrupt transitions, or places prone to strong forces, where the model experiences the brunt of the imposed stresses. Examining these high-stress areas closely, you take into account the materials involved. Do the stress levels stay within the yield strength of the material, or do they approach the ultimate strength? Because it indicates if the material is close to failing under the simulated circumstances, this study is essential. The safety margin, often known as the **factor of safety (FOS),** is then computed.

The outcome of dividing the material's yield strength by the maximum stress yields this numerical guarantee. An elevated factor of safety (FOS) signifies a more robust design, implying that the framework can reliably and comfortably support the loads. Depending on how the FOS value compares to your design objectives, it's either a moment of comfort or a call to action. Your investigation is not over yet. You examine several load instances, each of which is a distinct situation with distinct stress patterns. This gives you a comprehensive understanding of how your design performs in different scenarios. You are aware that a design has to be strong in a variety of real-world situations in addition to meeting safety regulations. You've entered the realm of design alteration if your astute eye spots areas of tension. You consider ways to lessen these areas of high stress. Perhaps you'll add reinforcements, distribute the weights differently, or avoid those steep turns. It's a dance between form and function, the inventiveness of engineering.

Analyzing Displacement

Now turn your attention to the plots of deformation. These striking illustrations show how your work changes as the simulated stresses press down on it. Your design comes to life as it reacts to the applied pressures, bending, stretching, and twisting. Your first concern is magnitude. The amount that your structure moves or deforms is examined. Is the deformation within the limits of the use that you have in mind? Is there enough deformation present for your bridge, structure, or mechanical component to jeopardize its intended use, or does it retain its shape and functionality? You have an analytical mind. You superimpose design assumptions and tolerances on top of the displacement data. Changes are required if the deformations are greater than predefined thresholds. Maybe a mechanical part is playing around too much, or a beam is deflecting more than you'd want. Stiffness, a measurement of your design's resistance to deformation, is another thing you take into account. High stiffness is essential for structural stability and functioning since it guarantees that your structure will keep its shape under stress. You investigate mode shapes if your investigation involves modal analysis. These are the rhythmic patterns that correspond to the frequencies at which your design vibrates or deforms. They make your structure's dynamic qualities clear. You listen for frequencies that can cause instability or vibrations in this symphony of motions.

Analyzing Safety Factors

Safety elements serve as your moorings throughout your evaluation. The factor of safety (FOS), a numerical watchdog that prevents failure, is calculated. It's a comforting presence that makes sure your design holds up well under duress. You follow your engineering instincts. You evaluate the FOS, examining its proximity to **1.0.** It's reassuring to know that your design can withstand applied loads with a margin of safety when the value is higher than **1.0.** A score below 1.0, however, raises red flags since it might indicate that your design is stretching the boundaries and necessitates close observation. Every load case has its narrative, and you look at the **FOS** under various conditions. Lower FOS values in certain load circumstances may serve as an early warning system for particular problems that need your attention and can benefit from design improvements. As a protector of safety, you set out on a mitigation mission if the FOS is not met. You think about making adjustments to the design that will increase the margin of safety. You can use reinforcements, changes in geometry, and material selections as tools in your toolbox. Stress, displacement, and safety factor analysis is essentially a laborious process. Numerical data and visualizations become windows into the behavior of your invention in the art of engineering. It's an endeavor driven by experience, knowledge, and the unwavering pursuit of technical greatness in the search for safety, dependability, and optimization.

Identifying critical areas for design improvement

Finding the most important places to improve your design is like dressing up as a design investigator and going through every aspect of your work with a fine-tuned eye for improvement. Layer by layer, the process is revealed, driven by insights gleaned through experiments, simulations, and in-person observations.

1. The Analytical Canvas:

- Imagine an analytical canvas that displays the outcomes of your simulations as a plethora of numerical and color patterns. Your starting points will be stress distribution charts, temperature profiles, and deformation maps; each tells a different tale.

2. The Heat of Stress:

- The stress distribution plot is the first thing you see, where the colors change to represent stress gradients. This is where the flaming oranges and reds appear, indicating areas that are under stress. These are the crucial spots when your design's fundamental framework is put to the test. Concentrations of high stress become focal areas and possible indicators of impending collapse.

3. The Dance of Deformation:
- Turning your attention, you see the displacement and distortion dance. Your design comes to life as simulated stresses cause it to flex and stretch. Your keen sight assesses the extent of this motion. Is it within reasonable limits? Does it put safety or functioning at risk?

4. Safety by the Numbers:
- Counts appear as guardians of safety. Safety factors (FOS) are like sentinels, waiting to shield your design from impending disaster. A greater FOS is your reassuring comrade, telling you that your work can withstand the severe storm that is administered. Nonetheless, a score less than 1.0 causes caution since it may indicate weaknesses.

5. The Temperature Tapestry:
- Temperature distributions offer a picture of heat and cold in the field of thermal analysis. Hotspots, or places where the temperature rises beyond bearable levels, form. You see them as possible danger spots, where overheating might result in malfunctions or material deterioration.

6. Vibrations in Mode Shapes:
- If modal vibrations are a part of your analysis, you explore the modes' frequencies and forms. It's a symphony of motion, with every mode form displaying a different vibration pattern. You turn your attention to resonant frequencies to locate possible causes of structural instability.

7. The Material Odyssey:
- You navigate a maze of material consumption on your quest. You look for a balance between the weight and the strength of the material, pointing out spots where the material is either too much or not enough. Not only may material distribution be optimized for strength, but it also offers cost savings.

8. Pruning Redundancies:
- In the process, you find redundant information and too complicated elements. These are the excesses that make your design heavier and more intricate. Pruning them turns into an art, simplifying your work for grace and efficiency.

9. The Real-World Feedback Loop:
- Prototypes and real-world testing whisper insights into your ears. They provide an observable reality check, highlighting differences between performance as predicted by simulation and actual. These seasoned voices are priceless.

10. A Confluence of elements:
- You encounter a confluence of insights as you examine and sort through various elements. Cost considerations, standard compliance, customer input, and manufacturing viability issues are all woven into the improvement fabric.

With this abundance of knowledge at your disposal, you are ready to master the art of prioritizing. Which areas need to be addressed right away? Which adjustments can have the most influence on efficacy, safety, and efficiency? Finding important areas for design advancement requires multifaceted investigation. It's an adventure across the engineering world's data-rich landscapes, led by the pursuit of excellence and optimization as a compass. It is a perfect example of the engineering spirit, combining creativity and experience to produce ideas that not only fulfill requirements but beyond them.

Optimizing Designs with Simulation Data

Using simulation data to optimize designs is like having a virtual laboratory where every pixel on your computer screen might be an innovative opportunity. It's a dynamic process that reshapes the limits of what engineering and design can achieve, a symphony of digital exploration. Envision entering this digital playground, an environment where the tangible limitations of prototypes vanish. Here, mathematical models and lines of code take the place of steel and concrete to represent your thoughts and notions. It's an environment free from the constraints of the material world, where creativity flourishes. A key component of this domain is the vast amount of simulation data. It seems like you've dipped a net into the ocean of technical expertise and hauled up an abundance of fish. This data includes fluid dynamics, temperature gradients, stress distributions, and more. Every data point is a pearl of knowledge, a hint to the riddles around the behavior of your design. Finding your shortcomings is the first step in your path. Patterns become apparent when you examine the simulation data. The colors red and orange indicate areas of susceptibility in stress plots. Deformation maps illustrate the movement of the structure, while thermal profiles identify hotspots that should be taken seriously. It's a trail of abnormalities and possible dangers for a detective. The process of optimization is an iterative dance. The design changes are a waltz, with each step dictated by revelations from the simulation data. You make both little and major adjustments before submitting your design to the online competition. Your invention develops with every round, becoming more powerful and sophisticated.

You're the conductor of a magnificent symphony in this digital world, deftly adjusting settings. You play with geometries, change dimensions, and modify material properties. Motivated by the quest to find the ideal arrangement, it's an exploration of the wide world of design options. Your compass becomes efficient. You look for methods to make your design work better while using fewer resources. Is it possible to use less material without sacrificing strength? Is it possible to adjust fluid flow to use less energy? The compass that directs you toward these efficiency gains is simulation data. Losing weight turns into a beautiful art. You weigh every gram and ounce because you are aware that even the slightest adjustment can have a significant effect. Choosing where and how to remove extra weight is based on simulation data, to achieve beauty and economy. The design turns into a canvas with every iteration, and the simulation data becomes the brushstroke. You are getting closer to the perfect design as you iterate and optimize; this is a creation that optimizes efficiency, reduces waste, and precisely meets your goals. The real-world benefit of this trip is what makes it even more amazing. You can experiment, test, and improve designs using simulation data before they are even taken off the computer screen. It protects against expensive errors and spurs creativity. In essence, using simulation data to optimize designs is a journey of change and discovery. It's the synthesis of science and art, where the real world is shaped by digital discoveries. It's evidence of the combined strength of human creativity and technology, enabling us to push the limits of engineering and design.

Iterating designs based on simulation insights

Design iteration based on simulation insights is a dynamic, iterative process that goes through many cycles of analysis, correction, and validation to improve and refine your structure or product. This method makes use of the plethora of data gleaned from simulations to provide designs that are more reliable and in line with your intended objectives.

Here's a closer look at this procedure:

1. **Simulation as a Design Compass:**
   - Imagine simulation insights as a guiding compass in your design journey. They provide direction, illuminating the path toward optimization and innovation.
2. **The Insight Harvest:**
   - Start by harvesting insights from your simulation data. Dive into stress distributions, deformation patterns, thermal maps, and any other relevant data. These are your clues, your keys to understanding how your design behaves in a virtual world.
3. **Identifying Weaknesses:**
   - The first step in the iteration process is to identify weaknesses or areas that require improvement. High-stress concentrations, excessive deformations, or thermal hotspots are red flags that signal potential issues.
4. **Design Adjustment:**
   - Armed with these insights, embark on the journey of design adjustment. This could involve modifying dimensions, materials, geometries, or load conditions. Each adjustment is a deliberate step toward a better design.
5. **Virtual Testing Ground:**
   - Simulation serves as your virtual testing ground. It's where you introduce these design changes and observe how they affect your product's or structure's performance. The virtual environment allows for rapid testing without the cost and time associated with physical prototypes.
6. **Data-Driven Decisions:**
   - Your decisions are driven by data. You carefully analyze how each adjustment influences stress levels, deformation, temperature distribution, or other relevant parameters. This data becomes your feedback loop, informing your next move.
7. **Iterative Loops:**
   - The iteration process involves multiple loops. After each adjustment, you evaluate the results, fine-tune your design further, and repeat the analysis. It's a cycle of continuous improvement, where each iteration brings you closer to an optimized solution.
8. **Performance Assessment:**
   - Throughout the process, you assess performance rigorously. Does the design meet or exceed performance targets? Does it align with safety and reliability criteria? Are there efficiency gains or cost savings?
9. **Balancing Trade-Offs:**
   - Optimization often involves trade-offs. You might need to balance factors like weight reduction, structural integrity, energy efficiency, and manufacturing feasibility. Simulation insights help you strike the right balance.

10. Real-World Validation: - As your design evolves through these iterations, you're preparing it for real-world validation. The insights gained from simulations guide the development of physical prototypes or production-ready designs.

11. Prototyping and Testing (if applicable): - If physical prototypes are part of your process, you create and test them, comparing their performance with simulation predictions. Any discrepancies or differences inform further refinements.

12. Documentation and Reporting: - Each iteration is documented meticulously. This documentation includes design changes, simulation results, and performance improvements. These reports serve as valuable records for future reference.

13. Stakeholder Collaboration: - Collaboration with stakeholders, including engineers, designers, and decision-makers, is crucial. Simulation insights are shared and discussed, leading to informed decisions and a collective vision for the design's evolution.
14. The Quest for Excellence: - The overarching goal is excellence. With each iteration, you're not just refining a design; you're pursuing the pinnacle of performance, safety, and efficiency.
Iterating designs based on insights from simulations is essentially an ongoing process of improvement. It is evidence of the effectiveness of data-driven decision-making, in which each iteration brings you one step closer to an exceptionally good design. To investigate, hone, and develop until you've arrived at the best answer is the essence of engineering.

Using simulation-driven design to enhance performance

A revolutionary method for improving performance is to use simulation-driven design, which makes use of computer simulations to maximize systems, processes, or products. This process enables engineers and designers to perform better across a range of industries, from manufacturing and architecture to aerospace and automotive engineering, by making data-driven choices and iterating quickly.

This is a thorough explanation of the procedure:

1. **A clear definition of the design challenge is necessary:**
   - This journey is first led by a precise and in-depth comprehension of the design issue. The objectives are clearly stated, regardless of whether the goal is to create an airplane that flies more efficiently or to improve a manufacturing process's thermal performance. Performance measures serve as your compass, guiding you in the right direction. Examples include lift-to-drag ratios, stress limits, and temperature profiles.
2. **The Craft of Simulation Modeling:**
   - Within the digital environment, the concept materializes as a painstakingly constructed simulation model. This model, which captures every subtlety and detail, is a digital twin of the real system. Meticulously specified are the geometry, material properties, and physics regulating the behavior of the system.
3. **Selecting the Ideal Simulation Tool:**
   - You choose the best simulation software for a task, just as a craftsman picks the best tools for the job. Different tools are needed for different design challenges: multi-physics simulations that weave complex webs of interactions, computational fluid dynamics (CFD) for fluid behavior, or finite element analysis (FEA) for structural integrity.
4. **Parameterization: The Puppet Strings of Design:**
   - When you use parameterization, your design takes on the complexity of a marionette. The simulation model identifies and regulates design factors. This is where creativity finds its canvas: the production parameters, material compositions, and wing form factors become your palette.
5. **The Dance of Optimization:**
   - An algorithmic and computational dance of sorts, optimization is started. The stage when design factors are tweaked and refined is the simulation model. You are looking for the sweet spot, the set of factors that, when compared to your predetermined measurements, produces better performance.
6. **The Vigilance of Performance Metrics:**
   - Performance metrics are your watchful partners in this dance. They act as sentinels, comparing each iteration of the design against the intended performance standards. Metrics might include

reductions in processing time, improvements in load-bearing capability, or increases in fuel economy.

7. **Iterative refinement:**
   - Optimization is a process that involves several iterations. You examine the simulation results, draw conclusions, and improve the design with every cycle. To meet and surpass performance goals, your design must constantly learn from its mistakes and evolve.
8. **The Performance Visualization:**
   - Visualization serves as a window into improved performance. Visual representations of simulation findings include temperature gradients, fluid streamlines, and stress contours. In addition to demonstrating your accomplishments, these visualizations open your mind to fresh concepts and directions for development.
9. **Validation and Real-World Testing:**
   - Your design is prepared for validation as it develops in the virtual world. Real-world testing is done after actual tests or prototypes are created. This is the point at which simulation-driven improvements are proven reliable and the virtual and physical worlds merge.
10. **Knowledge capture and documentation:**
    - Precision is used to record every stage of this process. Documents and reports are maintained, acting as a knowledge base for future tasks and designs. The knowledge acquired via simulation-driven design is preserved through the codification of lessons learned.
11. **Exceeding Perfection in Iterations:**
    - In the end, the journey is about adopting the idea of continuous improvement rather than merely improving performance. Even once performance targets are reached, the process of iteration never stops in search of the pinnacle of perfection.

To put it simply, performance enhancement via simulation-driven design is a creative fusion of science, imagination, and an unwavering quest for excellence. It is a process whereby the physical and digital realms come together to create inventions that stretch the bounds of what is possible. It is evidence of the ability of data, technology, and human creativity to revolutionize designs and performance benchmarks.

CHAPTER 22

RENDERING AND VISUALIZATION

In this chapter, the emphasis is on improving Fusion 360's visual representation of your creations. You will learn how to allocate materials to bodies and components in your design in this chapter. You'll learn how to modify the properties of materials to attain realism and give your models a more tactile, realistic appearance. You will see how crucial scene lighting and surroundings are to producing aesthetically attractive renderings. Learn how to adjust the lighting in your sceneries to create the right ambiance and mood. Learn also how to set up cameras such that they render in perspectives that accentuate the greatest features of your design. You will explore the realm of producing top-notch graphics and animations here. Learn about the benefits of cloud rendering, which can provide very high-quality results. Discover how to render individual photos and animation clips so you can dynamically present your designs. The skill of crafting visually arresting presentations is also emphasized in this chapter. You'll pick some tips and tricks for successfully showcasing your design ideas and aesthetics to clients and stakeholders. In conclusion, this chapter gives you the abilities and information required to improve the way your concepts are visualized in Fusion 360. You can create stunning drawings and animations that improve your design presentations and persuasively convey your ideas by using materials, arranging lighting, and utilizing cameras.

Applying Materials and Textures

You will first need to enter the rendering workspace. To go to the render workspace, click the **Model** icon located on the far left of the toolbar. You may notice a little difference in the surroundings when you do this. This occurs as a result of the surroundings you use for modeling not being the same as those made expressly for rendering.

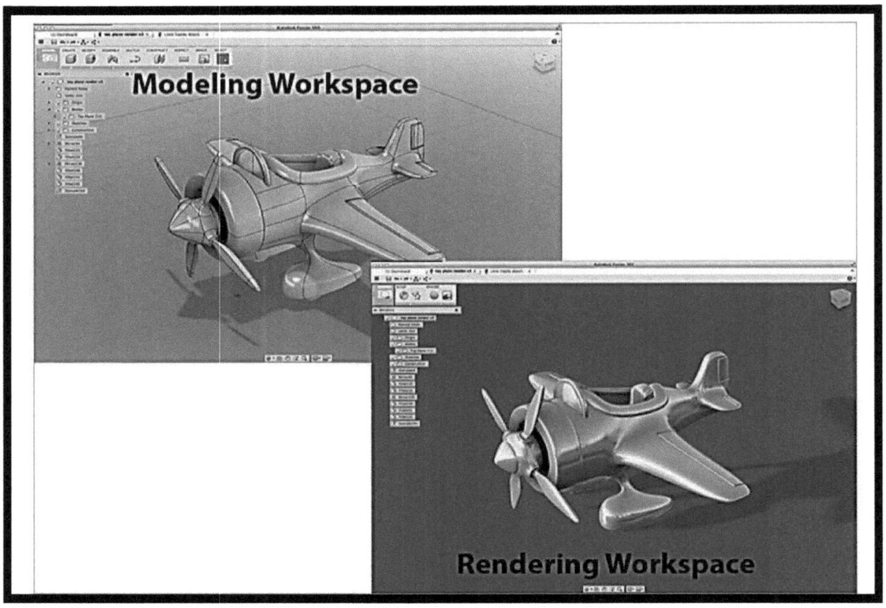

- New tools will appear in the toolbar once you are in the rendering workspace.

SETUP is the name of one collection of tools for configuring your model's look. And **RENDER**, a different collection of tools for rendering and producing images.

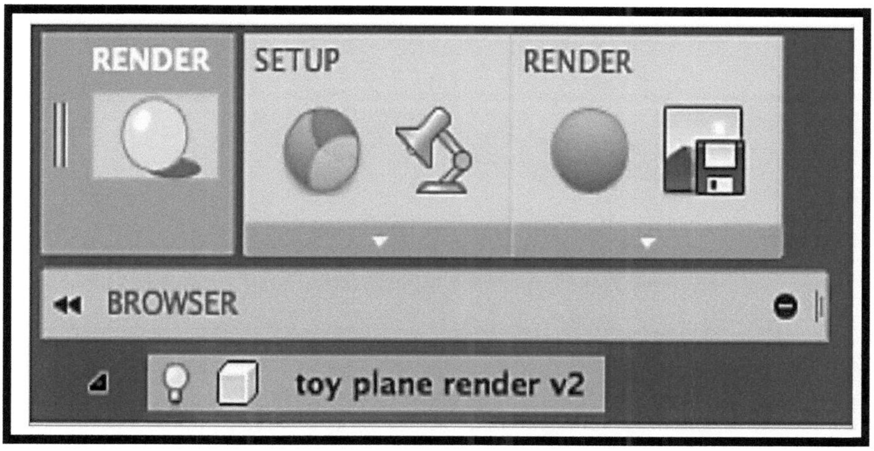

Side Note about Materials in Fusion 360

Were you aware that Fusion360 offers two different kinds of materials? Materials can be either Physical materials or appearance materials. Physical materials are utilized in mass calculations and determine the composition of the thing. It is the appearance materials that determine how the thing will appear when displayed.

The Appearance Dialog Box

Double-click the Appearance icon on the toolbar to open the appearance dialog box. There are many sections in the Appearance dialog box:

- **Apply To:** This feature lets you alternate between applying materials to specific faces or bodies/components.
- **In This Design** - This displays the materials that have been allocated to the various components of your design. **Note:** In the ***In This Design section***, the same material will only appear once if it is allocated to several components on your model.
- **Library** – You can flip between the Legacy Appearance Library and the new Fusion 360 Appearance Library of materials in this area. In addition, it includes sample swatches of the materials as well as folders and subfolders with materials arranged according to common categories.

Assigning Materials

A component, a single body, a collection of bodies, or a set of faces on a body can all have materials allocated to them.

Assigning Materials to Bodies

Single Body

The selected material will be applied to the body when you click and hold it and drop it there.

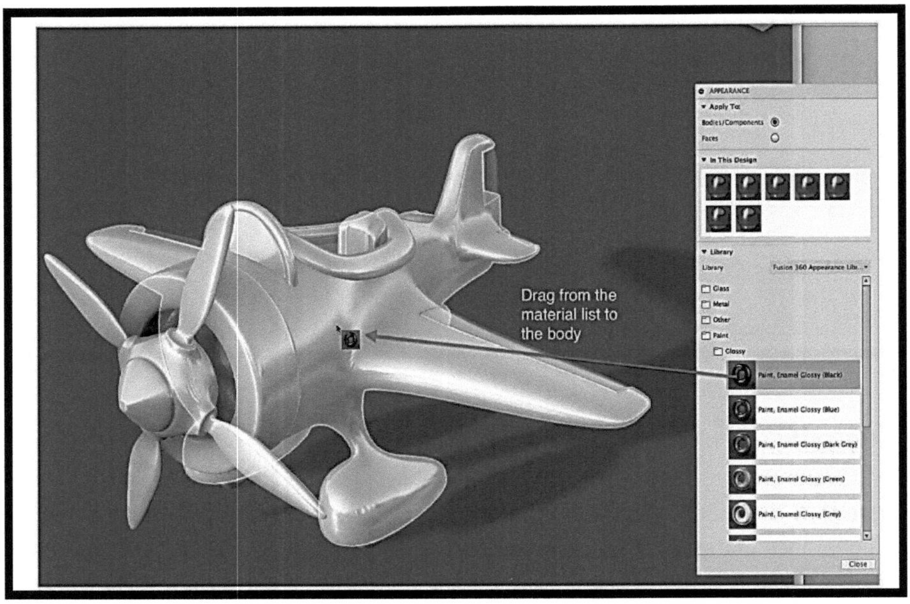

Multiple Bodies

When you drag a material onto one of the pre-selected bodies in the browser, it will be applied to that body.

Replace Applied Material

In the *In This Design* section of the Appearance dialog box, drag a material from the materials library and drop it on top of an existing material. The new material will now be applied to all the objects where the previous material was applied.

Bodies in a Group Folder

If you drag a material to the top of the Bodies folder in the browser, it will be applied to all the bodies inside that folder.

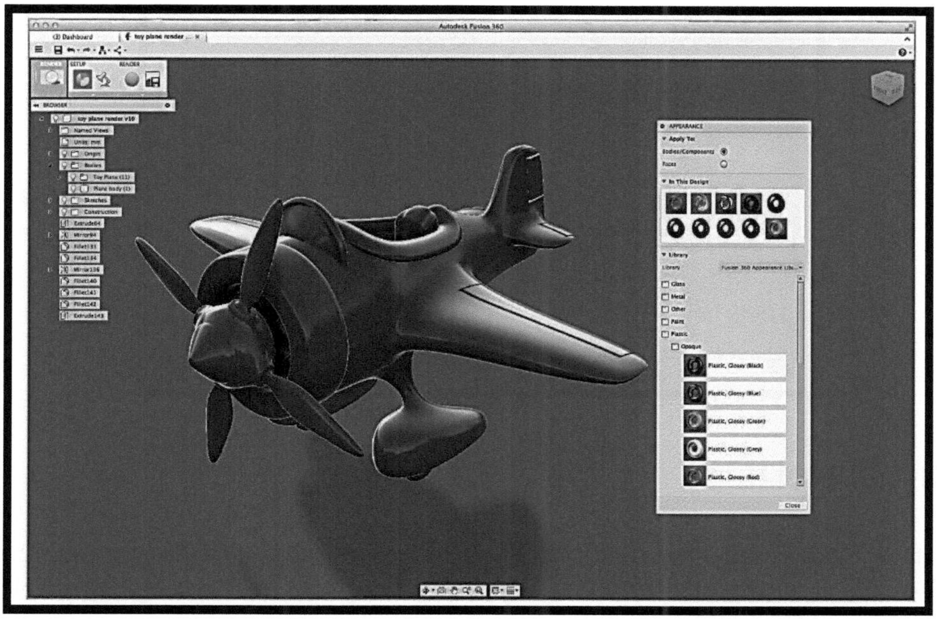

Note: The following question will appear if you apply a material to a set of bodies when one or more of those bodies have already received a material application:

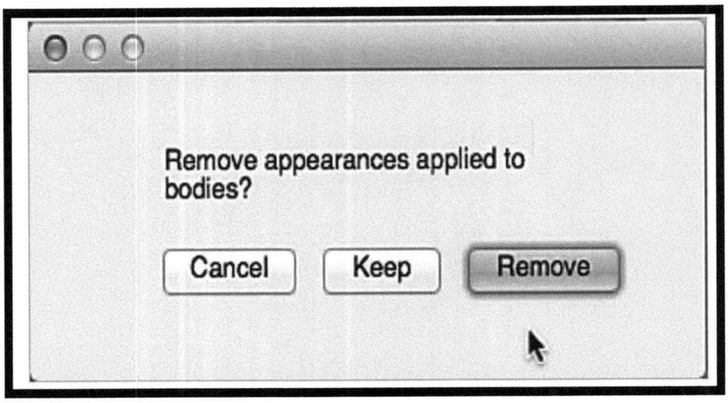

Remove: The new material you applied will completely replace any previously applied materials.
Keep: The new material will only be applied to the bodies you specified that haven't previously had it applied.

Assigning Materials to Faces

Additionally, materials can be allocated to specific model faces.

1. Choose **Faces** in the **Apply To** area located at the top of the Appearance dialog box.
2. Individual faces on the body will illuminate as you hover over them when you drag a material from the material library onto the body. When the mouse button is released, the newly added material will be applied to the highlighted face.

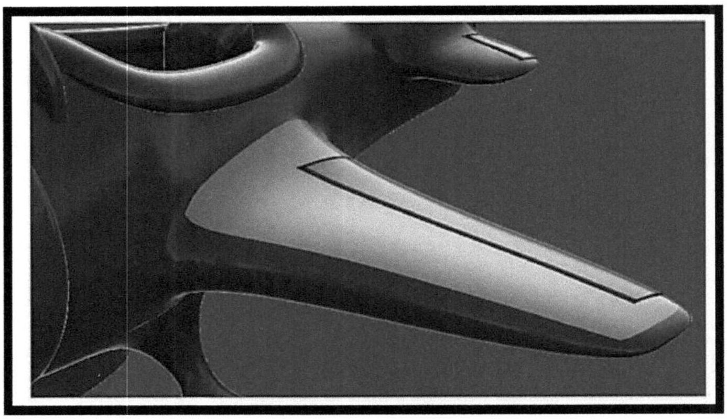

Editing Materials

You can alter a material's appearance after it has been applied to a body or face in your design by editing it. Double-clicking on a material swatch in the Appearance dialog boxes ***In This Design*** section allows you to change it. There will be a little editing window that opens beside the Appearance dialog box.

With this editor window open, you can:

- Rename the material.
- Adjust the color by inputting an RGB value or moving the color sliders.
- Adjust the texture map's scale inside the content (if applicable).
- Rotate the texture map in that area of the substance, if necessary.
- Select **Advanced Options**.

Advanced Option.

Upon selecting the advanced options button, a new dialog box with more settings to alter the material's appearance will appear. Depending on what you are altering, the advanced editor's choices will change. The possibilities for textured plastic are shown in the example below.

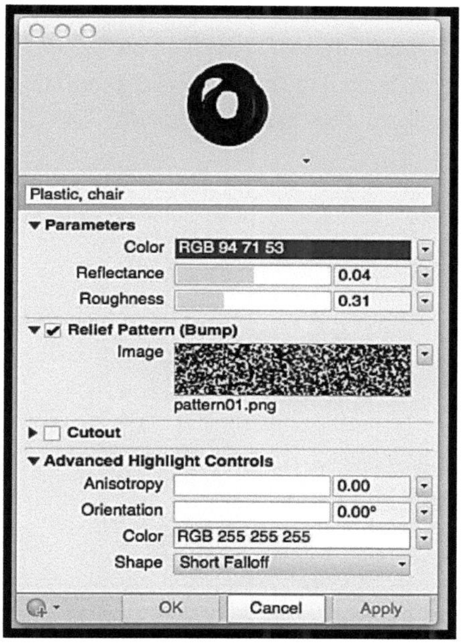

- **Reflectance:** The surface's ability to reflect light.
- **Roughness:** Regulates the surface's level of roughness, which impacts how glossy it seems.
- **Relief Pattern (Bump):** This displays the applied bump map.
- **Advanced Highlight Controls**
  - **Color:** modifies the highlight's hue. For a genuine effect, you will usually leave this white.
  - **Shape:** switch between highlights that are sharper (Short Falloff) and smoother (Long Falloff).

After you've completed modifying, choose OK or select Cancel to return to the original settings.

Duplicate a Material

Sometimes generating new materials from scratch takes longer than copying an existing material and changing one parameter. To make a copy of a material, just right-click on the swatch in the Application dialog box *In This Design* section and choose Duplicate. A version of the content displays that can be assigned and changed.

Deleting Materials

There will be times when you have been testing or assigning several materials, and you can find that you have several swatches in the "In This Design" area that are not on any faces or bodies. Right-click on any swatch and choose Delete All Unused to tidy things up. Material swatches that are not applied will be removed.

Check Your Work: Quick Render Mode

You should start the render in Quick mode after you have completed applying and adjusting your materials to see how they will appear while the Rapid Ray Tracer (RRT) is generating the picture. Choose **Enable Ray Tracing** under **RENDER** from the toolbar. The dialog box for **RAY TRACING** will open. Select **Quick** under the **Quality setting**.

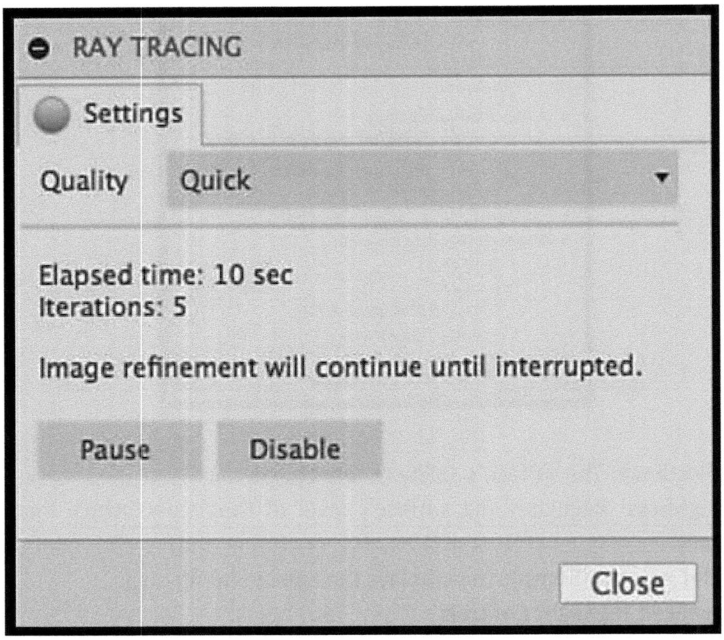

Setting up Lighting and Cameras

Configuring scene lighting and environment

Achieving realistic and aesthetically pleasing renderings in 3D design tools such as Fusion 360 requires careful configuration of scene lighting and surroundings. Setting up the lighting and surroundings correctly can have a big influence on your 3D sceneries' overall quality, mood, and ambiance.

1. **Scene Lighting:**
   - The foundation of a realistic 3D rendering is lighting. It has a direct effect on how people see your things, drawing attention to details like texture, form, and mood. Fusion 360 offers several tools for efficient lighting control.
   - By selecting the "Setup" option, you can see the lighting settings in the "Render" workspace. When setting up stage lighting, **keep the following important factors in mind:**
     - **Directional Lighting:** Fusion 360 provides a sun-like directed light source. To create the illusion of sunshine striking your items realistically, adjust its hue, angle, and intensity. To produce natural shadows, pay attention to the direction of the light.
     - **Point lighting**: This can be included in your picture to replicate artificial or specific lighting. To accomplish desired effects, like emphasizing certain parts or adding warmth to your picture, adjust their location, intensity, and hue.
     - **Ambient Lighting:** This kind of lighting makes sure that every item in your scene can be seen, even in low light. To change your rendering's overall brightness and contrast, adjust the ambient light.
2. **Environment Lighting:**
   - The atmosphere and lighting of your scene are greatly influenced by the environment you choose in Fusion 360. It's similar to selecting a background for a picture.
   - On the "Render" workspace, click on "**Setup**," and select the "**Environment**" tab, to access the environment settings. You can import your own HDR (High Dynamic Range) environment maps for unique lighting conditions in addition to the collection of standard environments that Fusion 360 gives.

The following factors should be taken into account while using ambient lighting:

- **HDR Environments:** Realistic lighting situations are captured in high-quality HDR pictures, giving your scenarios realistic and captivating lighting. Try out several HDR settings to see which one best suits your design.
- **Intensity and Rotation:** You can modify the lighting in the surrounding area to regulate how it affects your model. You can change the direction of light sources and hence the shadows and reflections on your objects by rotating the environment map.

3. **Sun and Sky Lighting:**
   - Fusion 360 has a sun and sky system for architecture renderings and outdoor settings. It's very useful for simulating daylight environments realistically.
   - In the "**Environment**" menu, activate the sun and sky system. This method operates according to the time of day and place that you choose.

Vital factors to consider for sun and sky lighting:

- **Geographic Location:** Align the scene's location with the real-world environment you want to replicate. The direction and angle of the sun are impacted by this.
- **Time and Date:** You can create different lighting conditions, like dawn, noon, or dusk, by adjusting the time and date settings to manipulate the sun's position in the sky.

- **Shadow Control:** To add depth and authenticity to your picture, you can adjust the shadow settings to manage the strength and softness of the shadows.

4. **Test Renders and Iteration:**
   - Finding the ideal lighting arrangement sometimes involves trial and error. To assess the effects of various lighting combinations, surroundings, and settings on your design, create test renderings.
   - Don't be afraid to experiment and fine-tune your lighting and environment selections until your 3D scene has the required appearance and feel.
5. **Advanced Techniques:**
   - As you acquire expertise, you can experiment with more sophisticated lighting approaches, such as adding **IES (Illuminating Engineering Society)** profiles for very realistic artificial lighting simulations or utilizing **HDRI (High Dynamic Range Imaging)** for exact control over lighting and reflections.

Set the lighting, background, and camera in your render

1. Choose **Scene Settings** under **Setup**.
2. Environment Library tab
   - **Current Style:** Shows the style implemented in the environment.
   - **Library:** Choose a lighting design from the collection. Before applying, certain styles need to be downloaded.
   - **Attach Custom Environment**: Open the custom style selection dialog box. File formats supported include **EXR, HDR, PIC, RGBE, and XYZE**.
3. Utilize the Environment options to adjust the illumination. Using the Style drop-down menu, choose the environment style. This sets the lights' default rotation and exposure. Adjust using the sliders.
   - **Brightness:** Adjusts how bright the lights are based on the style.
   - **Position:** Manages the lights' rotation and position.
   - **Background**: Solid Color to choose a color, or **Background Select Environment** to utilize the picture of the surrounding area.
4. **Configure the Ground effects.**
   - **Ground Plane**: A ground plane is shown on the canvas via the Ground Plane. If the option is on, the aircraft permits reflections and shadows on the ground.
   - **Flatten Ground**: Allows the environment picture to be mapped as a texture, creating a "**textured**" ground plane.
   - **Reflections:** The ground plane reflects objects inside the canvas.
   - **Roughness**: When Reflections is turned on, roughness is available. Regulates how crisp the reflection is.
5. **Set the Camera settings.**
   - **Camera:** Select perspective or orthographic view.
   - **Focal Length:** Adjust the focal length using the slider or by providing a numerical number.
   - **Exposure:** Set the exposure of the camera.
   - **Depth of Field:** If necessary, enable **Depth of Field**. Only in the case of enabled ray tracing is the depth of field shown.
     a. Decide which item will serve as the Center of Focus.
     b. You can use the slider or input a number to adjust the blur.

- **Aspect Ratio:** This specifies the workspace aspect ratio for the render.

6. After you have the settings adjusted the way you want them, choose **Close**.

Rendering High-Quality Images and Animations

1. **Preparing Your 3D Model:**

The first step in creating high-quality renderings is making sure your 3D model is ready. It includes:

- **Materials:** Give each component of your model realistic materials. Fusion 360 has a vast collection of materials, or you can design your own to meet your unique needs.
- **Lighting:** Be mindful of how the lighting is configured. To create the right atmosphere, play around with the lights in your scene, adjusting their location, intensity, and color.
- **Camera:** Adjust the focal length, location, and angle of the camera. Try out several camera settings to see which one gives your render the greatest viewpoint.

2. **Select the Appropriate Render Environment:**

Fusion 360 has many render environments, each customized to meet distinct requirements:

- **Ray Tracing:** Using ray tracing results in renderings that are crisp and lifelike. It produces realistic materials, reflections, and gentle shadows by simulating the course of light rays.
- **Real-Time:** It is appropriate for rapid prototypes and iterative design. Your model will be visualized more quickly but with fewer details if you choose real-time rendering.

3. **Adjusting Render Settings:**

Achieving excellent results requires fine-tuning the render parameters. Among these settings are:

- **Render Quality:** Renders with higher quality settings will take longer to finish but will be more realistic and detailed. Take into account the needs of your project while balancing speed and quality.
- **Resolution:** Select a suitable resolution for the finished product. For elaborate presentations or huge printouts, higher resolutions are required.
- **Advanced Settings:** To further improve realism, experiment with advanced settings like ambient occlusion, caustics, and global lighting.

4. **Rendering Images:**

Launch the rendering process when your scenario is ready. Fusion 360 will forward your project to the cloud, where robust servers will handle its processing. Downloads of the rendered pictures will subsequently be possible.

5. **Creating Animations:**

Use Fusion 360 to create animations by doing the following steps:

- **Define Keyframes:** Use keyframes that are positioned at various times to animate your model. To produce fluid animations, Fusion 360 will interpolate between these keyframes.
- **Camera Animation:** To help the viewer navigate your scene, animate the camera's location and perspective. This is very helpful for showing off products.
- **Render Animation:** Use the same render parameters as static photos to create your animation. To make sharing and embedding videos easier, think about using an MP4 or MOV file type.

6. **After Processing:**

After rendering, post-processing programs like Adobe Photoshop or Premiere Pro can help you improve your pictures and animations even further. By adjusting brightness, contrast, and color balance, you can provide a more polished look to your renderings.

7. **Iterate and Experiment:** Rendering is a science and an art. It is okay to make adjustments and try various materials, lighting configurations, and settings. Your outcomes will become better the more you practice.
8. **Cloud Rendering Tips:**
   - **Queue Management:** You can control rendering queues using Fusion 360. You can submit several render tasks and keep an eye on their developments at the same time.
   - **Cost Consideration:** Pay close attention to cloud rendering expenses, particularly for intricate or time-consuming tasks. Cost estimates are provided by Fusion 360 before rendering.

Utilizing cloud rendering for high-quality output

You will see a new icon under **Render > Cloud Rendering** in the Rendering workspace. A new "carousel" window for the Rendering Gallery has also been introduced at the bottom of the rendering workspace.

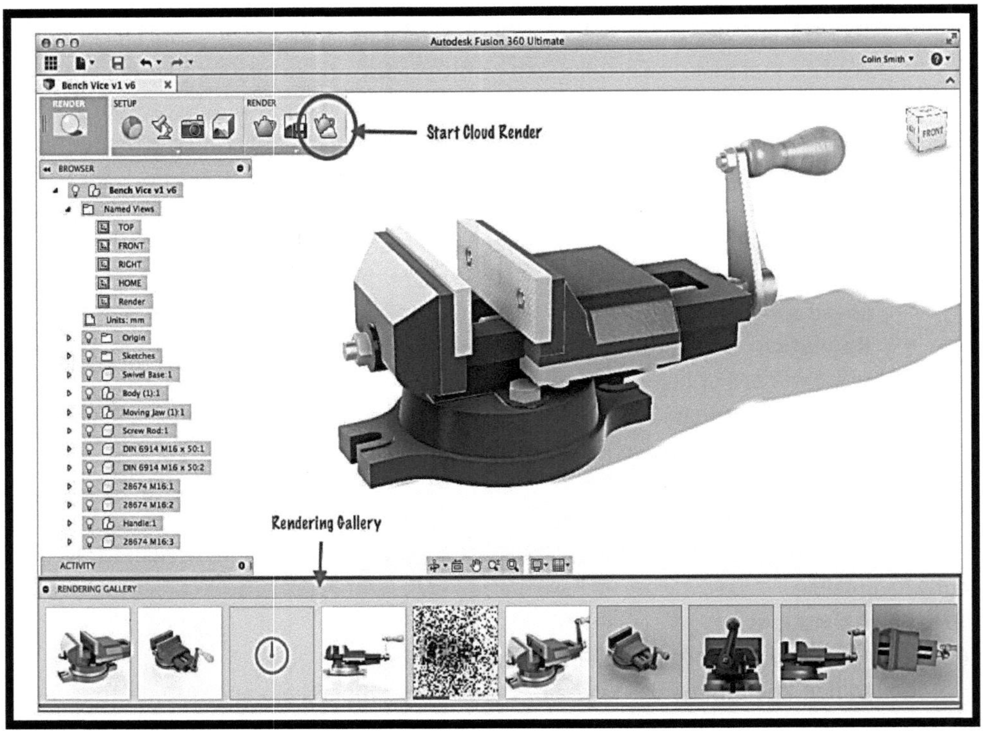

How it all works

After adjusting the materials, environment, and camera settings on your model to your liking, click the **Cloud Render** button to begin a cloud render.

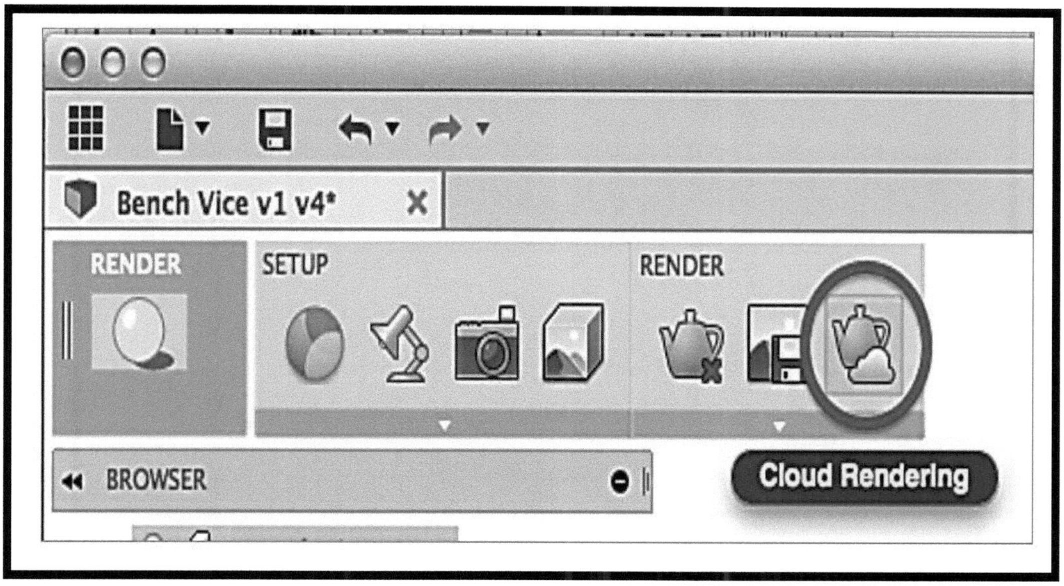

The model and camera location are automatically saved by the cloud render, which also displays a dialog box similar to the one below:

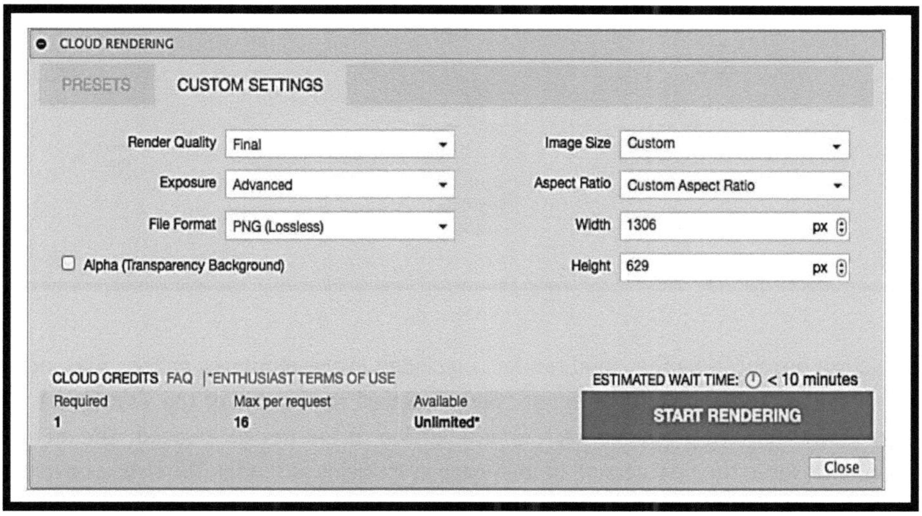

NOTE: You can be asked to save the file before beginning the cloud render if this is your first time using it or if you haven't previously saved a version. The default picture size for a cloud render is determined by the size of your screen by design. You can modify the settings to your preference or go with the defaults as they are. To choose from a list of preset picture settings that are divided into categories based on the kind of output you are making the image for—web, mobile, print, or video—you can also click the **PRESETS** tab at the top of the window.

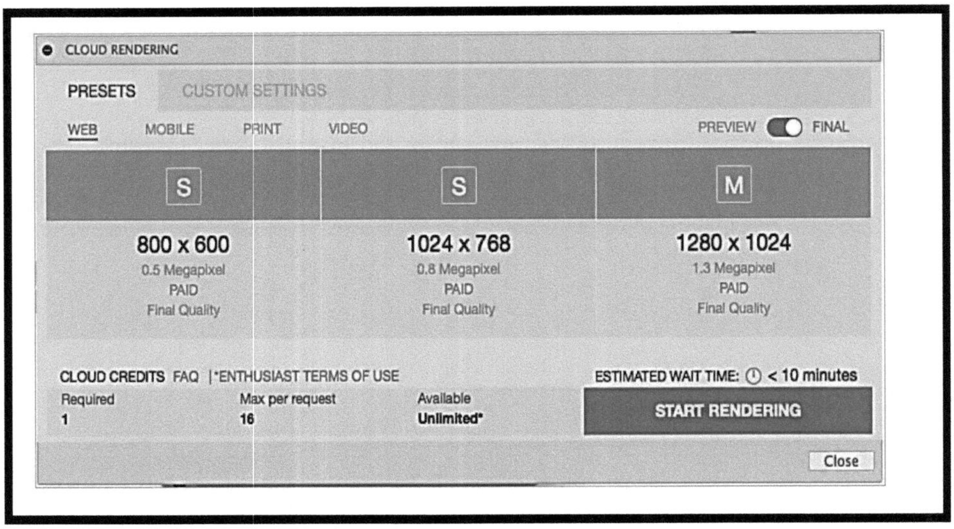

Click the **START RENDERING** button at the bottom of the window to send the data to the cloud renderer after you have the picture parameters configured as you want. A new picture icon in the **RENDERING GALLERY** will appear after the cloud render has begun, indicating that the render is queued in the cloud.

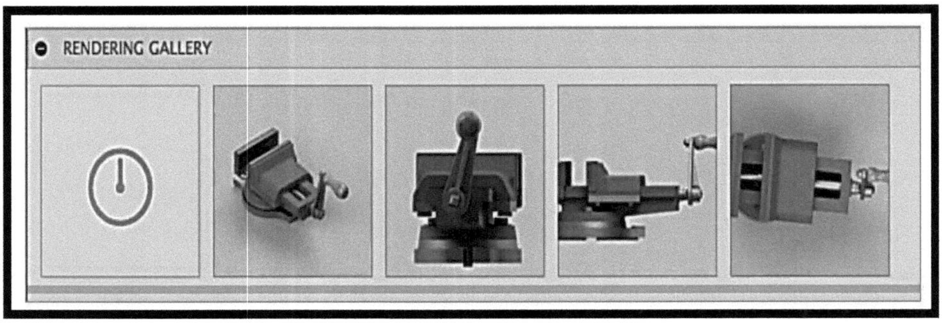

Note: Every picture produced by the cloud render is included in the rendering gallery. This included both the designer's initial pictures and the automatically generated renderings of the **Top, Front, Right, and Home Named Views** that are produced each time a version of the design is saved. The picture tile will gradually become closer to the final version of the image as it begins to render. When you hover the symbol over a final picture, it will provide the image's item data, including size, format, quality, time, and size.

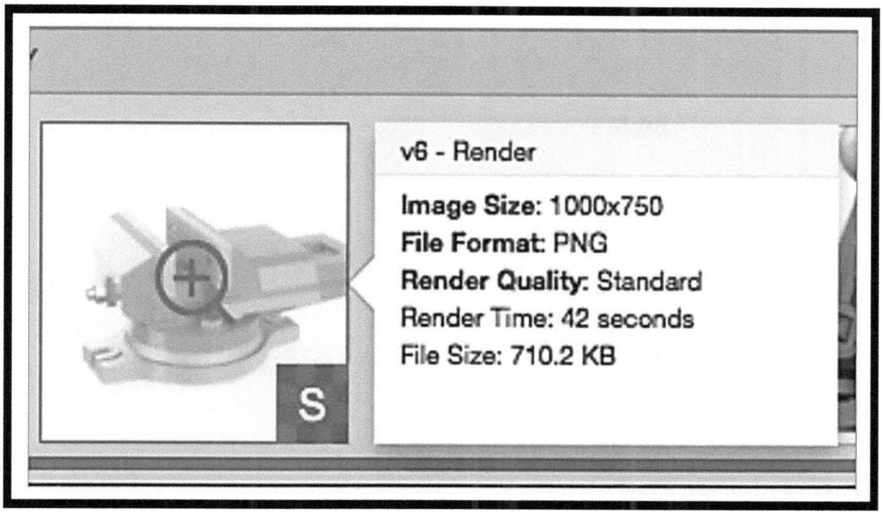

Note: You can cancel the cloud render by clicking on the picture tile in the Rendering Gallery, which will bring up the Cloud Rendering window. The picture will open in a **Cloud Rendering window** when you double-click on the image tile in the Rendering Gallery. You can download the picture to your desktop, remove it, share it through the Fusion 360 Gallery, or use it as an A360 activity all from this window. Starting a turntable rendering of the file in the cloud is another option available to you.

Five Tips for Creating Exceptional Renderings

It's possible that engineers and designers already understand how important quick prototyping is to bringing goods to market. Teams can develop several versions of a project quickly and more effectively by using 3D renderings to help projects come to life. Making precise visualizations isn't always easy, however. Obstacles arising from creative issues can impede production, as can constraints in the process. Groups need to think about how renderings can improve their physical designs. Both novices and seasoned pros can enhance their workflows.

To produce even better representations, adhere to these five suggestions:

1. **Incorporate Intelligent Lighting and Shadows**

Adding a little photorealism to a rendering by taking reflecting surfaces, shadows, and light principles into account is one of the easiest methods to make it seem better. By adjusting the lighting, professional photographers and film studios can provide fascination and reality to every scene. This gives a product additional depth, realism, and eye-catching appearance while rendering it. The goal of a depiction is to approximate the actual equivalent as much as possible, making it difficult to distinguish between idea and reality. Among the most important factors to take into account while producing a realistic render are shadows and reflections. Similar rules apply to shadows and illumination. Using X-Y-Z matrices, we can do shadow mapping and various types of shading. In a 3D (realistic) setting, we can examine how light sources from different angles interact with our creations. There's a ton of flexibility available for these options.

2. **Choose Accurate Colors**

Aiming for maximum realism while creating your renderings is undoubtedly a wise decision. Your drawings should correspond with what your consumers have in their hands or see on the shelf, and vice versa. The significance of lighting and shadows has already been discussed. Accurate perception of your finished product's look in various lighting scenarios depends on tone matching. The key is consistency. Our representations can, of course, be used for more than simply tangible goods; consider the field of video game creation. The player's immersion is fostered and maintained through the in-game environment. When simulating natural elements like sunsets, grassy meadows, cliffs, or breaking waves, color can be used to spectacular effect. From personal experience, we know exactly how these natural aspects should seem, and players will have similar expectations. If your goal is to visually replicate the actual environment, your audience will respond more strongly to colors that they are acquainted with.

3. **Consider Your File Sizes and Formats**

Graphically complex files called renderings can take up a lot of disk or internet drive space. Nevertheless, formats are smaller in size than equivalent video files. The size of a complete, uncompressed video render can reach tens of terabytes. Selecting the appropriate file format for the sort of material you use is tricky. Exporting your work in an uncompressed (lossless) format (think TIFF, RAW, and to some degree PNG) can be the best option if disk space is not a concern. These facilitate the next changes while maintaining the original quality. When there is a space constraint, however, you will have to make a compromise. Achieving the proper balance makes JPG a good choice for static renderings. Using the H.264 codec when exporting movies is a wonderful technique to reduce file sizes without sacrificing quality.

4. **Keep Ergonomics and Spacing in Mind**

Buildings and public areas are examples of designs that can be portrayed in addition to products. It takes a lot of attention to design spatial visualizations, particularly for builders. Above all things, public gathering spaces need to be operational. They must be aesthetically pleasing, user-friendly, and navigable. We can approach concepts from every perspective thanks to detailed renderings. A virtual tour can provide an idea of how accommodating the finished area is before the design is completed.

5. **Embrace Cloud-Based Rendering Software**

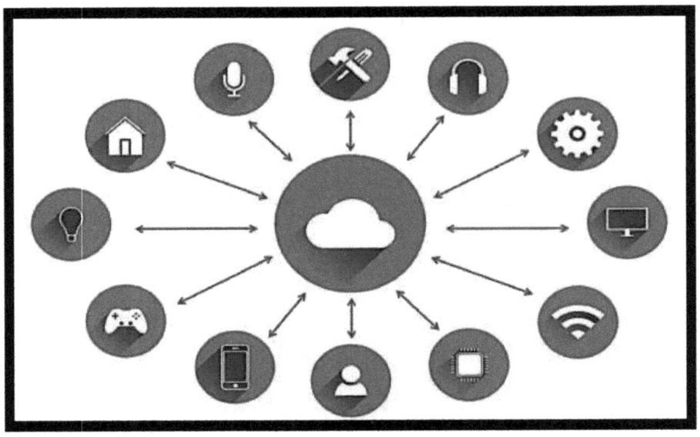

You don't have to be one of the many businesses that haven't embraced the digital revolution yet. Since more workers than ever before are collaborating virtually, localized solutions might be counterproductive to the effectiveness of the team. It is impossible to link distant engineers with even the greatest offline rendering tools. Since frequent iterations, flexibility, and brainstorming are the foundations of good design, allowing your peers to make global changes from a distance will keep everyone informed. However, cloud rendering is not limited to teamwork. It can strain your system's computing resources to render 3D images. System resources are required for textures, colors, shadows, and lighting effects. While we can finish these renderings locally, such procedures take time. Fortunately, more intelligent cloud technologies let us plan cloud renderings. By transferring those responsibilities to someone else, you can free up time to work on your next major project as soon as feasible. Rendering is a simple operation when cloud-based software such as Autodesk's Fusion 360 is integrated. Using the combined CAD, CAM, and CAE applications, you can develop and invent for yourself with the necessary tools. Look to Fusion 360 to enhance your product development process, whether you're creating representations of places or products.

Presenting Designs with Visual Impact

Creating visually appealing presentations

Creating visually appealing presentations in Fusion 360 involves combining effective design principles with the software's capabilities to showcase your 3D designs and ideas in an engaging and professional manner. **Here's a step-by-step guide to help you create visually appealing presentations in Fusion 360:**

1. **Plan Your Presentation:**
    - Define your presentation's purpose and target audience.
    - Outline the key points you want to convey and the order in which you'll present them.
2. **Prepare Your 3D Models:**
    - Ensure your 3D models are complete and well-organized in Fusion 360.
    - Apply materials and appearances to make your models realistic.
    - Use Fusion 360's rendering tools for high-quality images if needed.
3. **Create Views:**
    - Set up different camera views to capture the important angles and details of your 3D models.
    - Use the "Create View" function to save these views for easy access during the presentation.

4. **Storyboarding:**
    - Create a rough storyboard or outline for your presentation. Determine which views and information will be included in each section.
5. **Presentation Environment:**
    - Choose a suitable environment for your presentation. You can use Fusion 360's built-in environments or import custom backgrounds.
6. **Lighting:**
    - Adjust the lighting to highlight your models. Fusion 360 allows you to control the direction, intensity, and color of lights.
7. **Annotations and Text:**
    - Add annotations, labels, and text to explain key features or concepts.
    - Make sure the text is legible and not too cluttered.
8. **Camera Animation:**
    - Use Fusion 360's animation tools to create camera movements between different views. This can make your presentation more dynamic.
9. **Timing and Transitions:**
    - Time your camera movements and transitions between views carefully. Avoid abrupt changes that might confuse the audience.
10. **Render Images and Videos:**
    - Render high-quality images and videos of your presentation to show off your designs. Fusion 360 provides rendering options with various settings for quality and file format.
11. **Assemble Slides or Video Clips:**
    - Depending on your presentation format, create slides or video clips using the rendered images and videos. You can use external presentation software like PowerPoint or video editing software if needed.
12. **Narration and Voiceover:**
    - Consider adding a narration or voiceover to explain the content as you present it. You can record audio separately and synchronize it with your slides or video.
13. **Practice:**
    - Practice your presentation multiple times to ensure smooth transitions and timing.
14. **Feedback and Revisions:**
    - Seek feedback from colleagues or peers and make necessary revisions to improve the presentation.
15. **Present with Confidence:**
    - When presenting, speak clearly and confidently, and engage with your audience. Use your prepared visuals as aids to your explanation.
16. **Save and Share:**
    - Save your presentation in the appropriate format, whether it's a video file, slide deck, or Fusion 360 project, and share it with your intended audience.

CHAPTER 23

ADDITIVE MANUFACTURING (3D PRINTING)

The subject of this chapter is additive manufacturing or 3D printing. This chapter explores several topics about 3D printing, such as material selection, model preparation, design considerations, and typical problem troubleshooting. It talks about how important it is to consider layer-based additive manufacturing while designing. To enable effective 3D printing, it addresses ideas such as managing overhangs, the need for support structures, and setting tolerances. It also highlights how important it is to optimize 3D models so that they can be successfully printed. It assists users in producing printable STL files—a common 3D printing format—by guaranteeing that the geometry is appropriate and error-free. Here, you will examine the vast array of materials that are suitable for 3D printing and learn how to choose the best one according to design specifications. Additionally, you will be aware of the many 3D printing technologies, each with unique advantages and disadvantages. The chapter ends with insightful advice on how to deal with typical problems and flaws that can arise during 3D printing. It offers instructions on how to change print settings to improve print quality and fix problems that could occur during printing.

Design Considerations for 3D Printing

With the help of additive manufacturing, which is a potent technology, you can realize your ideas rather rapidly. When developing your components, you need to take into account the production limitations of the technology, just as with any other manufacturing technique. It's not a guarantee that you can produce something just because you can design it. Seeking advice from printer makers is always the best option since these limitations will vary depending on the kind of additive technology you are utilizing and the particular machine you are using.

Overhangs

Which faces of the model will need support is one of the key factors to take into account while creating an additive construct. In the majority of additive technologies, if the material is produced on top of the preceding layer, no support will be required. This implies that if you're constructing straight up, you won't often require support. Additionally, most of the time, building out to an overhang angle eliminates the requirement for support. The material will need to be supported if the overhang angle needed to construct your item is very large—typically more than 45 degrees.

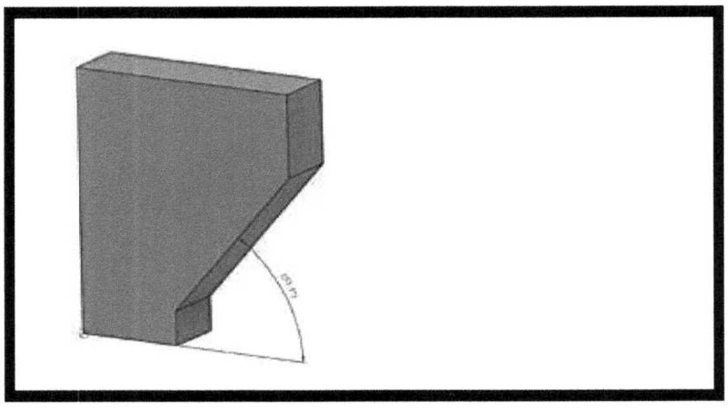

Verify that you are not exceeding the critical overhang angle to minimize the number of support structures you employ, either to cut down on construction time or material consumption or to minimize the amount of post-processing work required to remove these supports.

You can make sure that you don't go over the overhang angle while creating with Fusion 360 by:

- Use the Draft tool to avoid draft angles that are bigger than the overhang angle; or
- Defining any drawings that will result in an angled face to be less than the essential overhang angle.

If required, you can also modify the model using the Draft tool to make the faces' angles smaller. It is also compatible with all imported models.

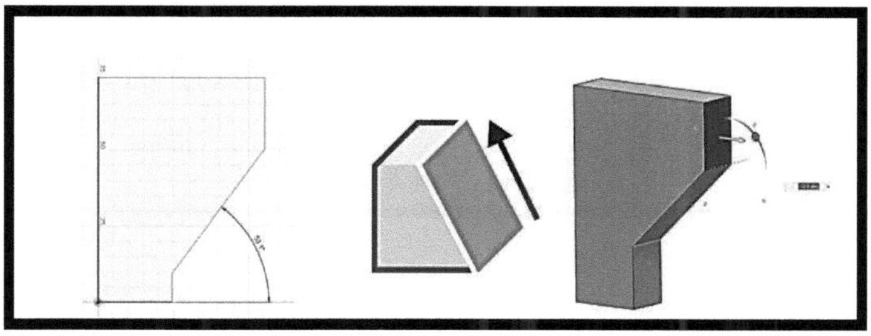

Characteristics

Certain characteristics will print more clearly than others. Avoid using sharp edges or corners since they are more likely to distort. When feasible, fillets should be utilized in place of this. With Fusion 360, you can quickly and effectively replace any sharp edges with rounded fillets by utilizing the Fillet tool.

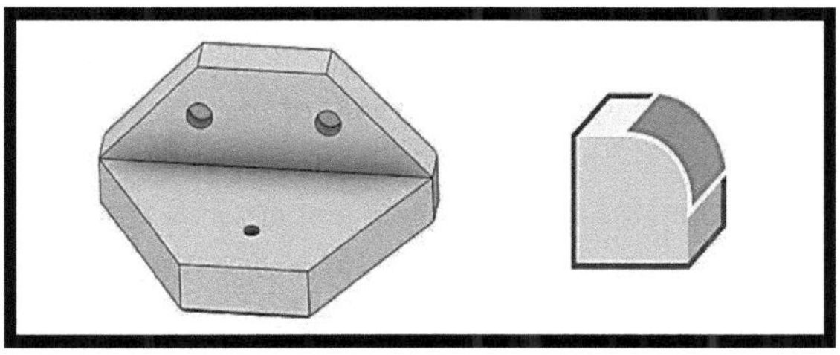

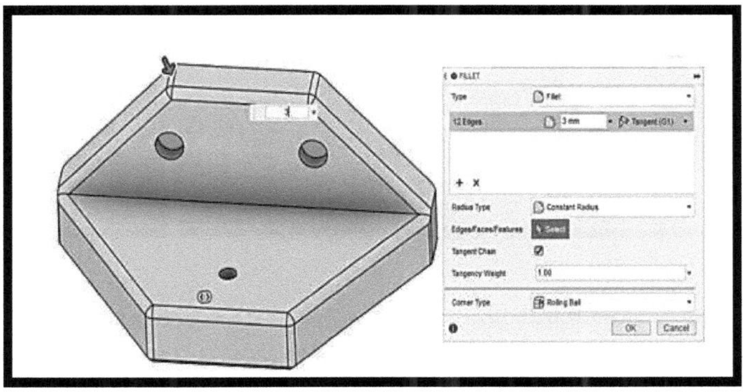

This guideline is not applicable if the fillet curves onto the construction plate, in which case a chamfer should be utilized. This is because a fillet is more likely to pull off of the construction plate and distort. As an alternative, you can quickly include them into your model using Fusion 360's Chamfer tool. If required, you can choose to remove the fillets by choosing the Fillet item from the Timeline or the model's faces.

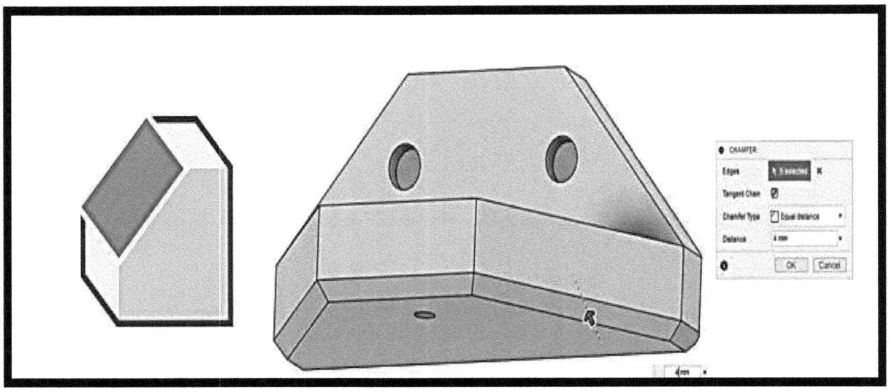

Minimum detail size

Even if very fine detail on a model might be a lovely touch, additive manufacturing might not always be able to provide it. The smallest level of detail that can be achieved depends on the kind of additive technology and might be as small as the printer's nozzle size, the layer height, or even the width of the laser beam. It is crucial to ascertain the smallest detail size compatible with the printing device you want to use. Knowing this value will help you while creating or modifying a model for additive manufacturing.

Prototyping

The ability to quickly produce prototypes of a design is one of the main benefits and a more popular use case for additive manufacturing. This enables you to quickly conceptualize and make necessary changes before committing to mass production or a more involved and possibly more costly form of manufacturing. If design changes are necessary, however, you don't want to have to start the procedure again from scratch. You can rapidly alter a CAD model using Fusion 360's Timeline feature. Any feature or sketch that was made throughout the design process can be edited using the Timeline, and your changes will be reflected across the model, altering the surrounding geometry as needed.

Additionally, you can utilize User Parameters to have greater control over this. These let you specify dimensions and other parameters by giving them a name and a value. These parameters can then be used as a guide for establishing further dimensions. When building a basic rectangular box, for instance, we can designate the width as a user parameter and provide a particular value to it. The length can therefore be defined as an additional user parameter, which we can define as width times two. Likewise, we can specify width multiplied by 1.5 for the third user parameter we can add, which will be the height.

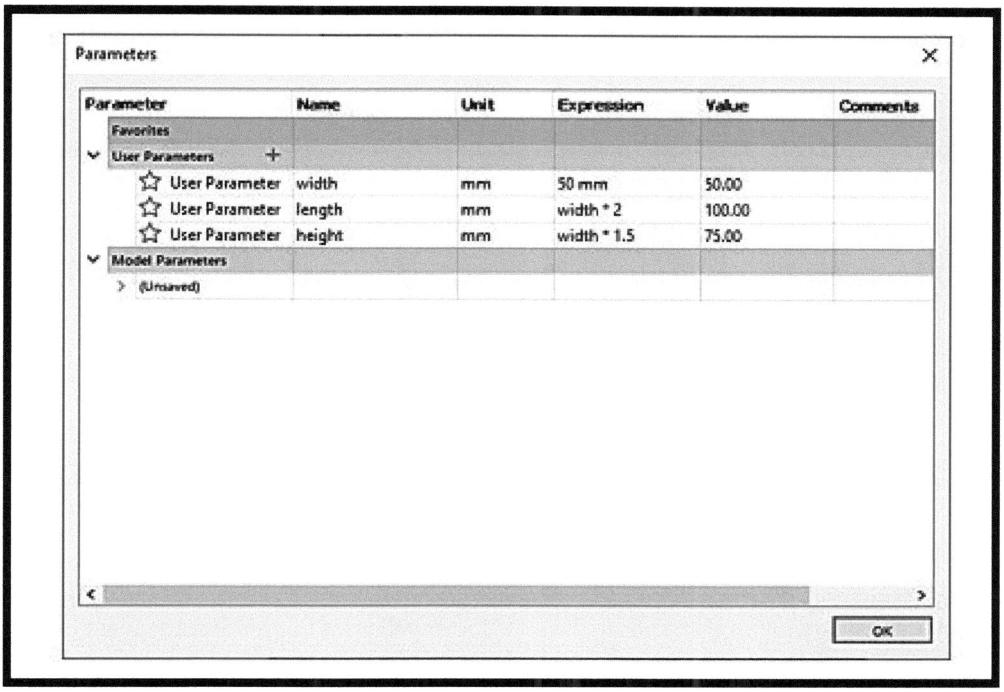

This implies that we won't have to go back and change each dimension and value if we change the width value since the length and height will update immediately. When creating your model, using these User Parameters can be quite effective, particularly if you're using additive manufacturing for iterative prototyping. The Change Parameters dialog box allows you to add and modify User Parameters, or they can be set at the time of sketch creation.

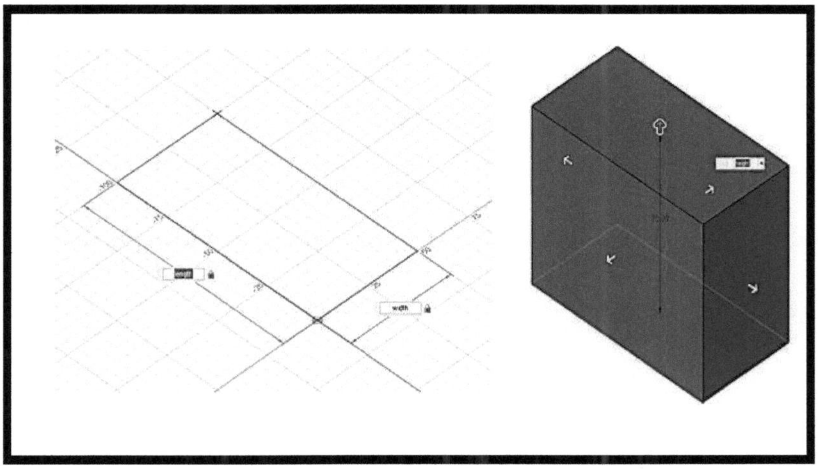

Whole-model edits

Due to the material's loss of heat, all additive manufacturing techniques include some degree of warping and shrinking. As a result, certain models may seem to be created undersize. You may need to make adjustments for this shrinkage if the final part's fit is crucial. Scaling your model up to account for the anticipated shrinkage is one approach to do this while utilizing Fusion 360. The Scale tool can be used for this.

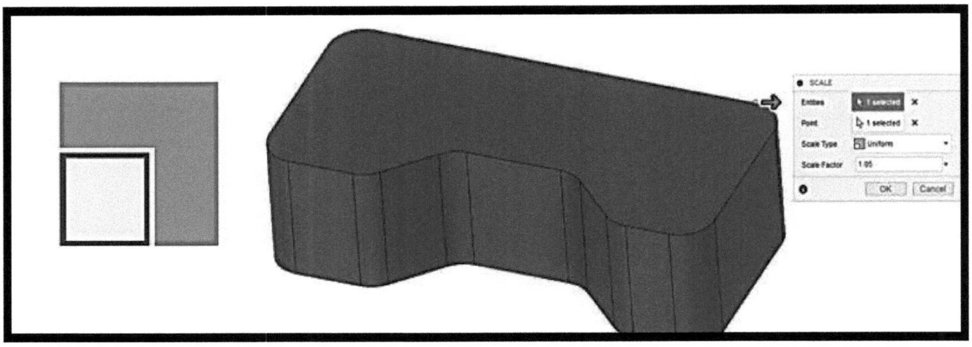

The easiest way to determine the scale factor for your model is to print a test component, measure a few features, and record the difference between the nominal CAD model size and the actual printed size. Using the same print settings, you can then choose the scale factor you want to use for subsequent prints. How big your design is about the size of your construction plate is another thing to think about. Depending on the equipment you are using, you may not be able to print your huge model all at once. It would be wiser to divide the model into smaller components and print each one independently. If this becomes necessary, the Split Body tool can help dissect a body into its component pieces.

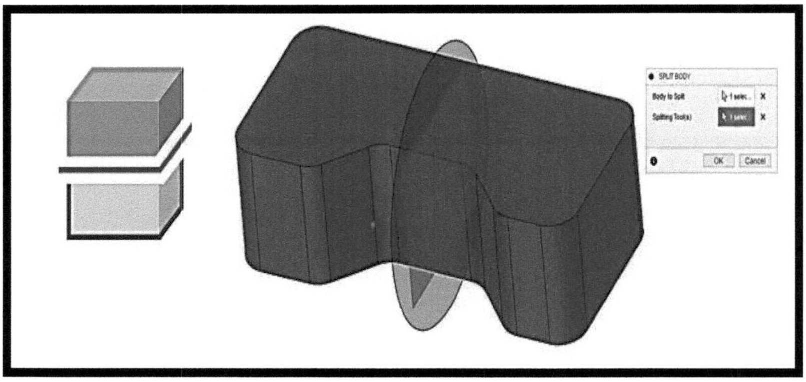

Post-print assembly

It may be necessary to make some adjustments to the model if it is going to be printed as a component of an assembly. To guarantee that the item will be printed to tolerance and fit the other assembly components as needed, the initial update might include using the scaling approach. It's also possible that the parts will be fastened together by bolts or another kind of thread. For this, it would be tempting to attempt printing the thread as part of the model, but utilizing metal heat-set inserts to put these in afterward can sometimes provide superior results. These inserts can be inserted into the printed model by heating them, melting the surrounding material, and then chilling the model once more to secure the inserts. Compared to printing the threads or tapping the printed material, which is an additional alternative, they will be stronger and more resilient. To effectively accommodate and arrange these inserts, include cutouts in your design. These can be simply inserted in Fusion 360 by making a Sketch item and drawing a circle that is marginally smaller in diameter than the insert that will be utilized. To ensure that the circle is positioned appropriately, it could be helpful to measure the circle's center from other drawing elements.

The circular profile can then be used to carve material out of the model using the Extrude tool.

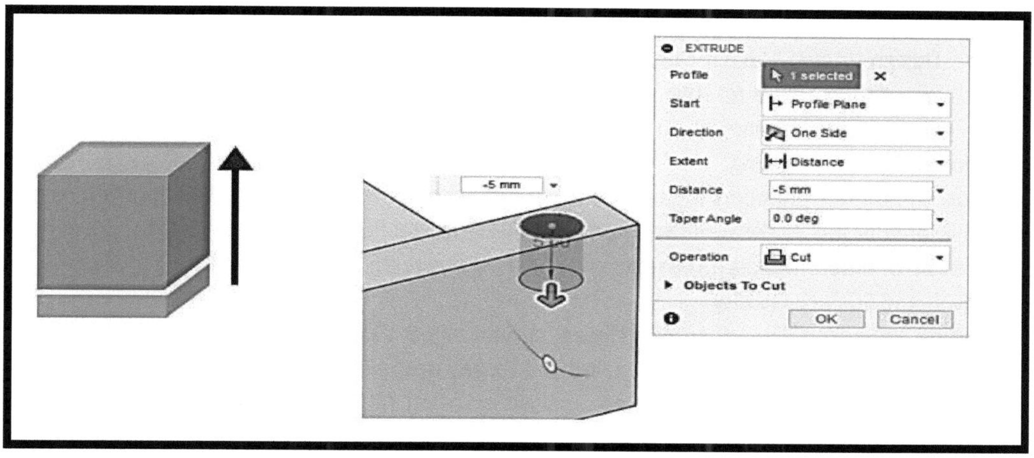

Gluing parts of a unit together is another option. Depending on the material used, this can be a quick and effective way to join them. Dowel pins are a good way to make sure that the parts line up correctly when you're doing this. To do this again, you will need to make holes in your model for the dowel pins. A simple way to do this is to use Sketch and Extrude together. Whether you use dowel pins, a bolt, or a screw with a hole, you will need to make sure that the places of these things line up with the parts that need to be put together. The Joint tool in Fusion 360 will let you place the parts with one another in an assembly, which is the best way to accomplish this.

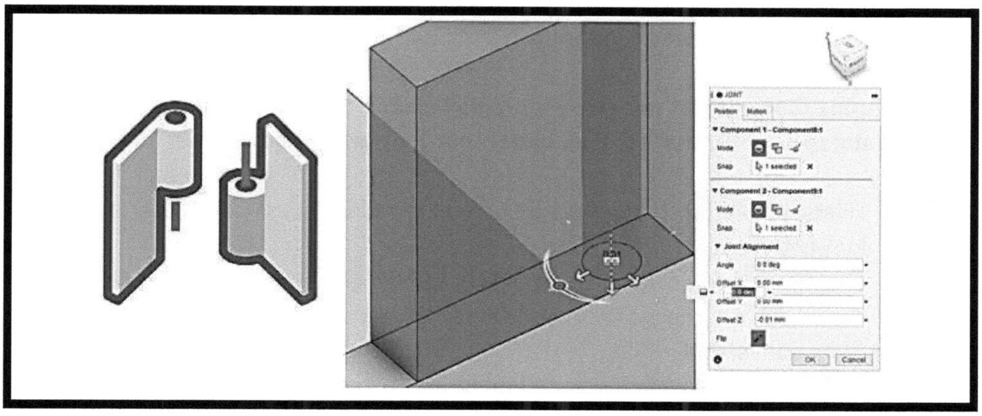

Once they are in place, you can sketch and extrude to make any necessary cuts on multiple parts at once, making sure they will line up correctly and the printed parts will fit together properly.

Preparing Models for 3D Printing

1. **Model Design and Accuracy**

Before you get into the details of 3D printing in Fusion 360, you need to make sure that the design of your model is correct and full. Some important things to think about are:

- **Parametric Design:** This is called parametric design, and Fusion 360 is famous for being able to do it. Use these to their fullest by making a well-defined model with variables, limits, and connections. It is easier to make changes to parametric designs later on if needed.
- **Design Intent:** Make it clear what your 3D-printed item is for and what it needs to do. Think about things like size, style, and purpose. Knowing what the designer wanted to achieve helps you make smart choices during the drawing process.

2. **Model Units and Scaling**

You can work in different numbers in Fusion 360, like millimeters and inches, so it's important to choose the right one for your job. Make sure that the scale of your model fits the size you want it to be in real life. 3D prints can be of different sizes if the units are not set up correctly.

3. **Mesh and Surface Quality**

For 3D printing, your model needs to be a closed, curved object that doesn't leak. The mesh and surface quality of your model should be checked to find and fix any problems:

- **Mesh Analysis:** To do a mesh analysis in Fusion 360, use the "Inspect" tool. This will make any trouble spots in your model stand out, like lines that don't form a manifold or surfaces that cross themselves.
- **Patch or Repair:** Use the "Patch" or "Stitch" tools to fix any mesh problems. These tools fill in gaps or holes in the shape.

4. **Wall Thickness and Tolerance**

To figure out the right wall thickness and limits, you need to know what your 3D printer can do and what material you're using.

- **Minimum Wall Thickness:** The minimum wall thickness needs for each 3D printer are different. Find out what your printer can do and set the wall thickness of your model to match.
- **Clearances and Tolerances:** Think about how your design needs to fit and be put together. If you need to, add limits or gaps to make sure that the parts fit together properly. You can be very specific about these numbers in Fusion 360.

5. **Fillets and Chamfers**

Fusion 360 has strong tools that let you give your model fillets (rounded edges) and chamfers (beveled edges). These features not only make it look better, but they also make it easier to print on and last longer:

- **Fillets:** Round off sharp edges with fillets to reduce stress points and make your model look better overall.
- **Chamfers:** If you need curved surfaces to fit together, chamfers can make the process easier. You can change the chamfer's curves and sizes to fit your design.

6. **Mesh to BRep Conversion**

Models should be in BRep (Boundary Representation) format instead of mesh format for 3D printers. You can turn your mesh model into a solid BRep model in Fusion 360:

- **Mesh to BRep:** The "Mesh to BRep" tool turns your mesh model into a solid BRep model that you can change. For correct 3D printing and slicing, this step is very important.

7. **Checking for Intersecting Geometry**

Geometry that crosses or overlaps can make printing go wrong. Carefully look over your model to find and fix any areas or parts that overlap.

- **Interference Analysis:** Fusion 360 has a tool called interference analysis that can help you find and fix parts of your model that overlap.

8. **Support Structures**

Think about whether your design needs support systems, especially if it has overhangs or a complicated shape:

- **Automatic Support Generation:** Fusion 360 has tools for automatic support generation that can help you add support where they are needed. Change the support settings to get the best print quality and use of the material.
- **Manual Support Placement:** If you want more control, you can use Fusion 360's support-building tools to add support structures by hand. This is especially helpful for models with a lot of details.

9. **Print Bed Orientation**

How your model is placed on the print bed can have a big effect on the quality of the print and the number of supports you need:

- **Optimal Orientation:** Try out different orientations to see which ones require the fewest supports while still keeping the surface quality and structural stability you want.

10. **Exporting and Slicing**

Once your model is complete, you need to save it in a file that your 3D printer can read. Fusion 360 works with many file types, including STL and OBJ, which are often used for 3D printing. Once you're done exporting, bring the model into the slicing software of your choice, like Ultimaker Cura or PrusaSlicer, to make the G-code that the 3D printer will use to print.

11. **Print Options and Setting**

Understanding what your 3D printer can do and how the material you've chosen works is important for setting up the print settings:

- **Layer Height:** Change the layer height to get the best print quality and speed. When you lower the layer height, you get smaller features, but it takes longer to print.
- **Infill Density:** You can change the internal structure of your print by setting the infill density. Higher densities make things stronger, while densities that are lower use less material.

12. **Test Prints and Iteration**

Before you commit to a large-scale print, you might want to do some test prints to make sure your model can be printed and works properly. Iteration is a common part of 3D printing because it lets you make changes to your design based on how it works in the real world.

13. **Post-Processing**

You might need to do post-processing after the 3D build is done to get the finish or features you want:

- **Sanding and Smoothing:** You can get rid of obvious layer lines and improve the finish of the surface of your print by sanding and smoothing it.
- **Assembly and Integration:** If your design has more than one part, you need to plan for how they will be put together and how they will work together. For easy setup, think about adding things like holes, threads, or adjustment pins.

14. **Quality Control and Testing**

Look over your 3D-printed item very carefully to see if it has any flaws. Make sure it works the way you want it to and meets your design purpose. Do any testing that needs to be done to make sure it works in the way it was meant to.

Optimizing models for successful printing

1. **Start with a Solid Foundation**

Before you get too involved with Fusion 360, make sure your idea is good in the most basic ways:

- **Closed Geometry:** Make sure that your model is a closed curved object that doesn't have any holes or gaps. Print mistakes can happen when you use open shapes.
- **Check for Overlaps:** Check your model for areas or parts that meet. Overlaps can make printing more difficult than it needs to be.

2. **Using the Right Units and Scaling**

In Fusion 360, make sure you set the right units and scale to match the sizes you want them to be in real life. When written, units that are not set up correctly can lead to wrong numbers.

3. **Design Intent and Functionality**

Make it clear what your 3D-printed item is for and how it works. Knowing what you want the design to do helps you make modeling decisions and makes sure the finished print meets your needs.

4. **Wall Thickness and Tolerance**

Figure out the right wall thickness for your model by taking into account what your 3D printer can do and the material you've chosen for printing:

- **Minimum Wall Thickness:** Look at the printer's specs to find out what the thinnest walls it can safely handle are. Set the wall thickness of your model to match.
- **Tolerances and Clearances:** If you need to, add limits and gaps to make sure the parts fit together properly. You can correctly enter these numbers in Fusion 360.

5. **Fillets and Chamfers**

Fusion 360 has tools for adding fillets (rounded edges) and chamfers (beveled edges) to make the design look better and make it easier to print:

- **Fillets:** To make your model look better and reduce stress, use fillets to round off any sharp edges.
- **Chamfers:** Chamfers with slanted connecting sides can make installation easier. You can change the chamfer's curves and sizes to fit your design.

6. **Optimal Print Orientation**

Try printing in different ways to see which ones require the least amount of support structures while still getting good results:

- **Overhangs:** Hold your model in a way that reduces overhangs. Features with curves greater than 45 degrees might need support structures.
- **Critical Surfaces:** For the best print quality, make sure that important areas are lined up.

7. **Support Structures**

Think about whether your plan needs any support structures:

- **Automatic Support Generation:** Fusion 360 has tools for making automatic support generation. Change the settings to get the best support spot for your model.
- **Manual Support Placement:** For more control over where support structures go in complex models, add them by hand where they are needed.

8. **Hollowing and Infill Density**

Depending on what you want to use the model for, you might want to hollow it out to save material. Change the depth of the filling to control the structure inside:

- **Hollowing:** You can make things hollow in Fusion 360 by removing shape from the inside while keeping the outside solid.

- **Infill Density:** Choose the infill density based on what your model needs. Densities that are lower save material and cut down on print time while higher densities make things stronger.

9. **Mesh to BRep Conversion**

Models should be in BRep (Boundary Representation) format instead of mesh format for 3D printers. Use Fusion 360's translation tools to turn your mesh model into a solid BRep model.

10. **Intersecting Geometry**

Check your model for geometry that overlaps or intersects with other shapes, and fix any problems you find to avoid printing mistakes.

- **Interference Analysis:** To find and fix parts of your model that overlap, use Fusion 360's interference analysis tools.

11. **Export and Slicing**

You should save your model in a file that your 3D printer can read, like STL or OBJ. To make a G-code for printing, import the model into the slicing software of your choice (for example, Ultimaker Cura or PrusaSlicer).

12. **Print Settings and Parameters**

Set up the print settings based on what your 3D printer can do and how the material you want to use works:

- **Layer Height:** Change the layer height to get the best print quality and speed. It takes longer to print smaller features because the layer heights are smaller.
- **Infill Percentage:** Set the filler percentage to manage the structure inside. More strength comes from higher numbers.
- **Print Speed:** Change the print speed to get the finish and strength you want on the surface. Most of the time, slower speeds mean better quality.
- **Temperature Settings:** Make sure the print temperature is right for the type of material you are using. Read the instructions that came with your material.

Creating printable STL files

When you create printable STL files in Fusion 360, you are essentially sculpting a digital masterpiece; you are painstakingly building a 3D item that can be brought from the realm of your imagination into the actual world via the process of 3D printing. Let's get started on this adventure step by step, keeping a close watch on the details to make sure that the STL file we create is error-free and ready to print. As soon as you step into the world of Fusion 360, you are greeted with a blank canvas, a stage that is waiting to be decorated with your 3D creations. When you click on "New Design," it's like you're an architect imagining a building for the first time. This is the beginning of your creation. Now that your canvas is prepared, it is time to begin sketching the outline of the 3D item you want to create. This is analogous to the first few strokes of an artist's pencil on paper, and it helps shape the basis of your idea. Click the "**Create Sketch**" button to choose the plane (XY, XZ, or YZ) in which your idea will be developed by.

Now, in the manner of a skilled draftsman, build the 2D profile of your item by making use of the sketching tools at your disposal, which include lines, circles, rectangles, and arcs. Accuracy is of the utmost importance in this situation; make sure that your drawing is confined and that it creates a closed shape, exactly as an artist would delineate the borders of their subject. You can go from the 2D world into the 3D world by clicking on the "**Create**" button and then choosing the "**Extrude**" option. At this point, you are analogous to a sculptor who is giving a block of marble new life. You can extrude your design into the third dimension by selecting your drawing and either clicking a button or inputting a specified depth into the text box. Your work is beginning to take shape, and the anticipation of seeing it develop is causing you to feel a rush of enthusiasm. It is now time to improve your product, just as an artist would do by adding complex details or a sculptor would do by smoothing off the rough edges once the fundamental shape has been formed. Fusion 360 gives you access to a wide variety of design tools, such as fillets, chamfers, and more, to help you refine your creation. During this phase, your vision will start to take concrete form, and you will see the intersection of creativity and precision.

You need to make sure that your digital artwork is ready to be printed in three dimensions before it can become a reality in the real world. This will be the last time you verify the product's quality; think of it as an art curator looking for flaws in a masterpiece. Make use of the "**Inspect" and "Modify**" tools included in Fusion 360 to do a thorough analysis of your design to identify any potential flaws, such as non-manifold geometry or open edges that can cause problems during the printing process. You polish your digital product to the same level of excellence that a conservator would achieve by carefully mending a damaged artwork. When you finally export your work in STL format, you will have reached the pinnacle of your adventure. At this point, the digital masterpiece you have been working on is going to be converted into a format that can be understood by your 3D printer. Simply go to the "**File**" menu, choose "**Export**," then select the "**STL**" file type and make any other adjustments you need. Your work is now ready to be introduced into the material world.

Choosing Printing Materials and Technologies

When it comes to making decisions on the types of printing materials and processes available to you inside the domain of Fusion 360, you are traversing a digital terrain from which your creations will emerge into the real world. Your decisions in this step are just as important to the final product as it is for an artist to choose the appropriate digital tools for their work; similarly, they will determine whether or not your 3D-printed item has the intended shape and function.

Within the framework of Fusion 360, let's conduct a comprehensive investigation of this decision-making process:

Printing Materials: The Digital Palette

1. **Fusion 360 Material Library:** Fusion 360 provides its users with a comprehensive material library that consists of a wide array of alternatives including plastics, metals, and composites. You can model how your design will function in the actual world because of the distinctive properties that each material has.
2. **Custom Material Creation:** Fusion 360 gives you the ability to create unique materials that are adapted to the needs of a particular project. This function is analogous to how an artist chooses their colors while painting. You can modify the properties of the material, such as its density, tensile strength, and thermal conductivity, to match materials that exist in the actual world, or you can experiment with made-up, fictitious substances.
3. **Material Simulation:** The simulation features of Fusion 360 enable you to assess how your design will function under a variety of different circumstances. This is comparable to getting a sample of how an artwork will look in a variety of lighting situations or settings. It provides you with the information you need to make educated judgments about the kind of materials you should use depending on elements like stress, heat, or fluid movement.

Printing Technologies: The Digital Tools

1. **Additive Manufacturing Workspace:** The Additive Manufacturing workspace in Fusion 360 serves as your digital workshop, providing you with a variety of tools for 3D printing. This includes the ability to construct support structures for your model, modify print parameters, and prepare your model for 3D printing.
2. **Generative Design:** The generative design capability included in Fusion 360 functions much as an AI assistant would for creative professionals. It does this by investigating several different design choices depending on the parameters you supply and then providing you with optimum forms and structures. After that, you can choose the layout that caters to your material and production requirements the most effectively.
3. **Exporting STL Files:** Once your design is complete, you can export it to an STL file format, which is globally compatible with 3D printing technology. This process can be completed fluidly. This process is analogous to preparing your artwork for printing, in which you make certain that it is in the appropriate format and is ready to be brought to life.

Exploring different 3D printing materials

Exploring the vast landscape of materials available for 3D printing within the framework of Fusion 360 is analogous to setting out on a digital adventure through an infinite number of artistic possibilities. Fusion 360 is a complete platform for design and engineering that not only gives you the capacity to create elaborate 3D models but also allows you to simulate and analyze the behavior of different materials.

This ensures that your designs not only look amazing but also function in the most effective way possible. Let's get started on an in-depth investigation of some of the most well-known 3D printing materials that are available in Fusion 360:

1. **PLA (Polylactic Acid):** PLA, also known as the adaptable workhorse of 3D printing materials, is easily accessible in the material catalog of Fusion 360. It is analogous to a basic hue on an artist's palette and is suitable for designers of all levels, from novices to seasoned professionals. You'll be able to imagine how your ideas will come to life in this common material by simulating PLA's cheap cost, convenience of usage, and eco-friendliness when you utilize Fusion 360. This feature will let you see how easily your concepts can be implemented.
2. **ABS (Acrylonitrile Butadiene Styrene):** ABS, which stands for acrylonitrile butadiene styrene, is another notable substance that can be found inside Fusion 360's material collection. ABS is well-known for its durability and adaptability. You can mimic ABS's resilience to higher temperatures using Fusion 360, as well as the material's appropriateness for the creation of functioning prototypes. To get the best possible results from your printing, you can also try experimenting with the various parameters.
3. **PETG (Polyethylene Terephthalate Glycol):** Fusion 360 allows you to explore PETG, a material that strikes a balance between the ease of PLA and the durability of ABS. You can simulate PETG's resistance to moisture and UV rays, making it an excellent choice for outdoor applications.
4. **Nylon**: Nylon is a material that is often used in industrial settings. It is well-known for both its strength and its flexibility. You can mimic the toughness of nylon inside Fusion 360, which enables you to create components such as gears and bearings that need these properties.

5. **TPU, or thermoplastic polyurethane**: This is a flexible filament that simulates the properties of rubber. Fusion 360 gives the tools necessary to do experiments with TPU. You can conceptualize how **thermoplastic polyurethane (TPU)** can be used in the production of items that need flexibility, such as shoe bottoms and phone cases.
6. **Custom Material Creation**: Going beyond the established materials, Fusion 360 gives you the ability to create bespoke materials that are suited to the specific needs of your projects. This function is analogous to being able to mix your paints to get the precise color and texture that you like. You can design virtual materials that exactly fit your concept by modifying material properties like density, tensile strength, and thermal conductivity in the material editor.
7. **Material Simulation**: The possibilities of Fusion 360's material simulation are comparable to having a laboratory available to you whenever you need it. You can evaluate the resilience of your virtual objects by subjecting them to a variety of situations, including stress, heat, and fluid movement. This enables you to make educated judgments regarding the material selections you need to make depending on the needs of your project.
8. **Metal Filaments:** Fusion 360 does not restrict your creative journey to the use of plastics alone; it also allows you to work with metal filaments. You can also investigate the universe of filaments that include metal in them. You can construct and imagine products with a metallic look when you use these materials since they comprise metal particles such as copper, bronze, or stainless steel. You can imitate the appearance and feel of these materials using Fusion 360, and even play around with different post-processing processes to get genuine metal finishes. Fusion 360 encourages you to experiment with metal-infused filaments in all of your creations, whether you're making sculptures out of metal or manufacturing practical metal parts.
9. **Resin Printing**: The possibilities of Fusion 360 go beyond those of standard printing methods based on filament. It also includes methods for 3D printing based on resin, such as Stereolithography (SLA) and Digital Light Processing (DLP). You can create and view complex items with a high resolution using Fusion 360. These designs can capture the fine details and smooth surfaces that resin printing is known for. You can also mimic the curing process and the support structures that are involved in printing with resin, which ensures that your designs are optimized for the more modern technology.
10. **Wood and Composite Filaments**: The addition of wood-infused filaments is one of the ways that Fusion 360 satisfies the needs of the artist's palette. These materials blend the natural beauty of wood with the adaptability of three-dimensional printing. To create items with a rustic, earthy appeal, you can experiment with the simulation of wood filament's texture and look. In addition, Fusion 360 enables the use of composite filaments, which combine a variety of materials to extend the creative possibilities available to users. Fusion 360 gives you the ability to imbue your digital creations with the richness and coziness of composite materials and the natural beauty of wood, regardless of whether you're working on the design of a piece of furniture, a decorative item, or an artistic installation.
11. **Biodegradable and Eco-Friendly Materials**: Fusion 360 enables you to explore biodegradable filaments such as PLA or PVA. These materials are options that are better for the environment, much like using organic foods and ingredients in the kitchen. The environmental effect of your ideas can be simulated using Fusion 360, allowing you to contribute to the development of environmentally responsible solutions. Fusion 360 is here to back up your efforts to create a more environmentally friendly future, whether you're making components with a low carbon footprint or disposable things with a low impact on the environment.
12. **High-Performance Materials:** The adaptability of Fusion 360 extends to high-performance materials like carbon fiber filaments and other similar materials. These materials, which have

carbon fibers woven into their structure, provide outstanding strength and stiffness while maintaining their low weight. You will have the ability to see the mechanical properties of such materials using Fusion 360, which will make it possible for you to design components for applications in the aerospace, automotive, or athletic industries that need the ideal combination of strength and weight.

The Art of Selection and Simulation in Fusion 360

The process of selecting and simulating different materials for use in 3D printing in Fusion 360 is not only a technical one; rather, it is an art form. It is about fusing your creative vision with the specific properties and qualities of the many kinds of materials. You can explore, simulate, and fine-tune your material selections in Fusion 360's dynamic and iterative environment until they exactly correspond with the design objectives you set for them. Your choice of 3D printing material inside Fusion 360 will ultimately impact the end of the thing you print, similar to how a great artist chooses colors to portray emotions or a master chef mixes components to produce a culinary masterpiece. However, unlike these examples, the outcome of your printed object is entirely up to you. It's a voyage of discovery, experimentation, and endless possibilities, where each substance acts as a brushstroke on the canvas of creation. This is a journey of discovery, experimentation, and boundless possibilities. You can explore, experiment, and bring your concepts to life with the highest level of precision, creativity, and sustainability with the help of Fusion 360, which functions as your digital workshop.

Matching materials to design requirements

When it comes to 3D modeling and product design, choosing the appropriate materials is equal parts science and art. It's a crucial choice that can have a huge impact on a product's performance, looks, and price tag all at the same time. Autodesk's cutting-edge computer-aided design (CAD) software, known as Fusion 360, gives designers and engineers the ability to seamlessly incorporate the process of matching materials to design requirements into their workflow. Fusion 360 was created by Autodesk. Every design starts with a vision, a concept that strives to present itself in the actual world. Those two things come together to form a design. This concept can be executed in a myriad of ways, from a sleek and aerodynamic component for an automobile to a jewelry item that is delicate and complicated in its design. Nevertheless, for a design to be effective, it has to strike the appropriate balance between aesthetics and practicality. Consider, for example, the process of designing the frame of a bicycle. In this particular instance, the shape may need a look that is lightweight and streamlined to improve both aesthetics and agility. However, the function requires a certain level of toughness and longevity to endure the pressures that come with regular usage. At this point, the painstaking process of material selection comes into play, helping to bridge the gap between the intangible idea and the finished product.

As a computer-aided design (CAD) platform, Fusion 360 is lauded for its adaptability. Not only does it give a strong canvas for visually representing design ideas, but it also provides a broad array of tools for studying and modeling the behavior of materials under a variety of different scenarios. Since it combines design and engineering in a single environment, it is an obvious option when it comes to matching the specifications of the design to the appropriate materials.

The process in Fusion 360 can be divided into several stages:

- **Defining Design Requirements**: It is vital to define precise design criteria before entering into the process of selecting appropriate materials. Mechanical properties (such as tensile strength and flexibility), temperature parameters, aesthetic concerns, and financial limitations are some examples of these kinds of factors.
- **Material Library**: The material library in Fusion 360 is rather broad and includes a wide variety of materials, including metals, polymers, composites, and more. Each material is accompanied by a plethora of data, such as its density, thermal conductivity, and tensile strength, which enables designers to make selections based on accurate information.
- **Simulation and Analysis**: One of the most notable characteristics of Fusion 360 is its capacity to model how the behavior of materials will change in response to a variety of environmental factors. To determine whether or not a certain material is suitable for use in their projects, designers can use a tool called finite element analysis (FEA) to simulate the effects of different stresses, temperatures, and other environmental conditions. In the context of the bicycle frame, this would include modeling the stresses and strains that the frame will be subjected to while in use.
- **Iterative Design**: Equipped with data from simulations, designers can repeat their designs to optimize not just for appearance but also for functionality. To achieve the proper balance between the frame's strength and weight, it can be necessary to make adjustments to the material, thickness, or geometry of the frame.
- **Cost and Sustainability**: The material selection process in Fusion 360 takes into account more than just how well the material performs. In addition to this, it takes considerations of cost and sustainability into account. The cost of materials can be compared by designers, and the environmental effect of their decisions can be evaluated, allowing for the creation of designs that adhere to environmentally friendly standards.
- **Visual Representation**: When it comes to presenting a visual representation of the many material options, Fusion 360 shines. Designers can simulate how the final product will look by rendering their models with realistic textures and finishes.

To continue with the design of the bicycle frame, Fusion 360 provides the designer with the ability to investigate a variety of different possibilities. They may start with a frame made of carbon fiber because of the material's remarkable strength-to-weight ratio. They determine via simulation that certain stress spots need reinforcing. Fusion 360's library of composite materials comes into play at this point, giving the designer the ability to fine-tune the composition of the material to ensure that it satisfies the requirements. The iterative process continues, with the designer analyzing not just the success of their decisions in terms of performance but also how cost-effective those choices are. The cost estimate tools in Fusion 360 give insights into how the entire project budget is affected by changes in the materials being used. In addition, designers who are concerned about the environment can calculate the carbon footprint connected with their decisions and look for environmentally beneficial options wherever they can. The rendering features of Fusion 360 enable the designer to have an increasingly accurate mental image of the finished bicycle frame as the design progresses. They have the option of experimenting with a variety of paint finishes, demonstrating how the chosen materials can be arranged to achieve the desired look.

The process of selecting materials in Fusion 360 is not a sequential one; rather, it is a journey that is both dynamic and iterative. The decisions that designers make are continually refined depending on the results of real-world simulations and studies. This positive feedback loop guarantees that the final product not only satisfies but often frequently surpasses the criteria of the original design. In addition to this, Fusion 360 encourages cooperation among members of design teams. Designers, engineers, and other specialists in materials can easily collaborate and share their thoughts to make the best possible material selections. The design process is improved in both quality and efficiency via the use of this collaborative method.

Achieving Better Additive Manufacturing Outcomes in Generative Design

Using the New Additive 2.0 Algorithm

To begin, go to the User Preferences menu on your computer and make sure the Experimental Generative Solvers and Features preview is turned on.

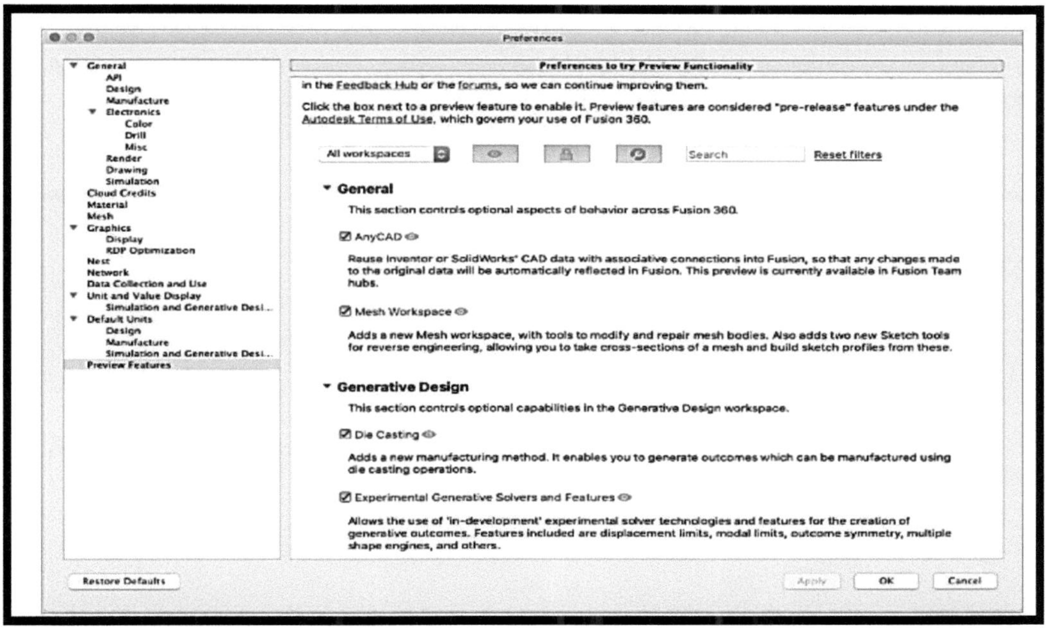

Because you have the preview turned on, you will need to go into the Study Settings and activate the Alternative Outcomes option. After that, you can just organize your study space as you would normally. Turn on the **additive manufacturing** constraint in the **Manufacturing Constraints** window, choose the print orientations you want, and our solvers will handle the rest of the process for you.

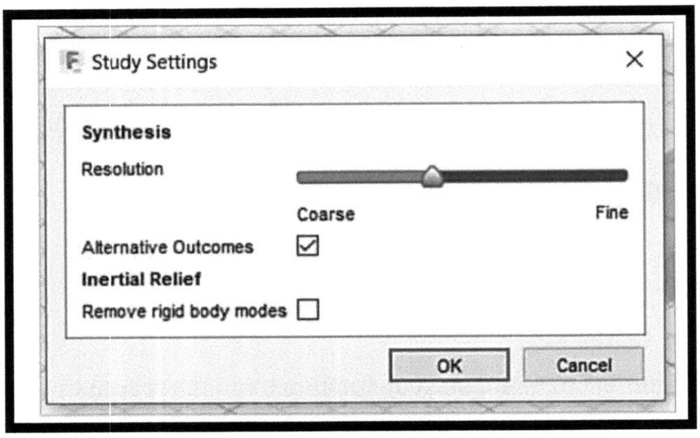

When you are in the Explore mode, Additive 2.0 will produce the second result of each additive set (where a set is defined as the combination of a specified material and a direction) for each additive set. ***Tip: if you want to see this in the most straightforward manner possible, go to the properties view, narrow your focus to the additive manufacturing process, and then choose set the Sort By dropdown to Material.***

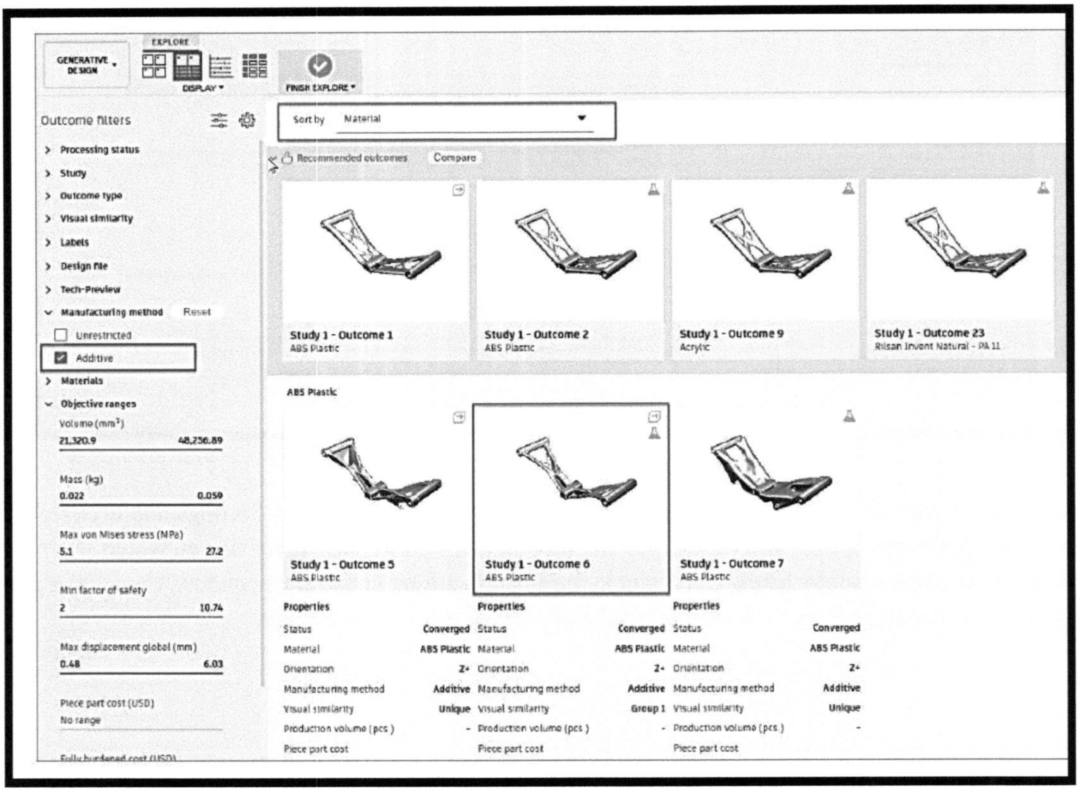

How is Additive 2.0 Better?

In many different contexts, the quality of the shapes generated by our original technique to produce additive results was significantly lacking. As we worked toward satisfying overhang criteria and being self-supporting, it was not uncommon to have results that displayed strong stair-stepping as well as other artifacts. Our solvers now perform a far better job of achieving minimum thickness requirements, balancing design mass, and reducing the amount of support material with the help of our new methodology. For this new strategy to be completely self-sufficient, the form quality will not be compromised.

Let's look at a few instances to see how these changes are going to affect the results that we produce.

The straightforward generative structure presented below is our first example (loads and restrictions are masked for clarity). We intend to produce this component using the orientation shown in **Figure 1 (below),** with the exception that the construction plate will take the place of the red obstruction.

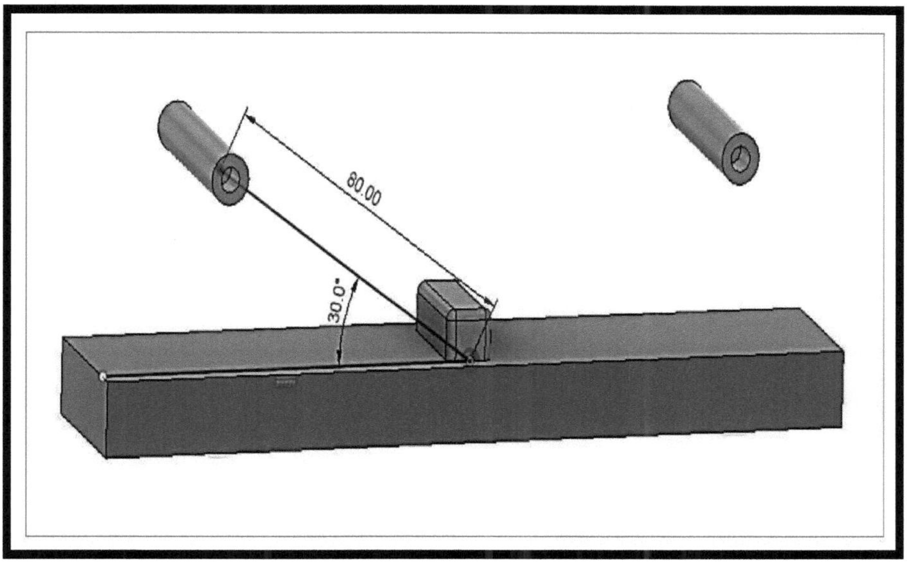

This configuration results in an unrestricted output, which, as can be shown in **Figure 2 (below),** is challenging to manufacture for some different reasons. To begin, a significant portion of the space underneath the component shape calls for the addition of support structures (the portions marked in red in the second half of the picture). In addition, the thin features that are close to the center of the component are brittle, and they may shatter when the support is removed. Although this design can be made via additive manufacturing, it is not in any way optimized.

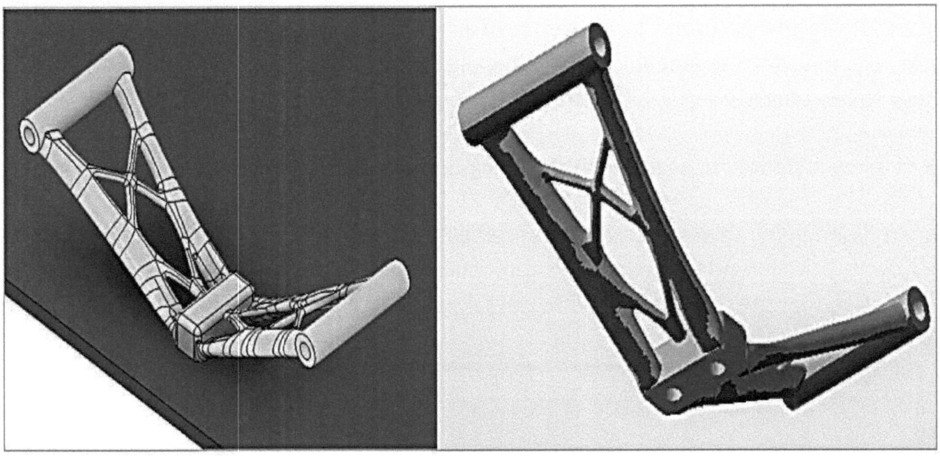

As we begin to compare Additive 2.0 with our previously established additive restrictions (Additive 1.0), the distinctions between the two become readily apparent, as can be seen in **Figure 3**, which can be seen below. In both instances, we specified the additive constraint to require a minimum thickness of three millimeters and an overhang angle of forty-five degrees.

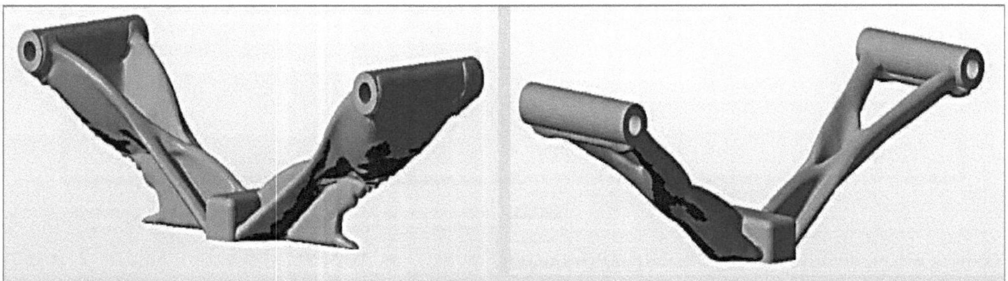

Additive 1.0 result, overhang violations highlighted

Additive 2.0 result, overhang violations highlighted

In either scenario, the quantity of the necessary support material is cut down, but it is not entirely removed. However, the result of using Additive 1.0, which builds material up from the build plate to support the whole structure, is fifty percent heavier than the result of using unconstrained. It suffers from the stair-stepping aberrations that plagued the first additive manufacturing technology, which was a popular source of frustration for users. The quantity of support material that must be used is also greatly reduced by Additive 2.0; however, this is accomplished via more subtle modifications to the geometry, and the overall mass of the model is only increased by 11% as a result. The minimal feature size of 3 millimeters can be met by both additive designs, however, the Additive 2.0 design maintains a structure that is considerably closer to the unconstrained design by combining the lattice beams that are too thin into a thicker organic structure. The new Additive 2.0 outcomes, in addition, get rid of a significant portion of the previous outcome's undesirable surface quality. In principle, the additional limits introduced by Additive 2.0 will lessen the supported area and do away with thin beams while only slightly increasing the total mass of the component. But do these designs make it easier to produce the product? Let's go through the steps of getting the print ready and see what happens.

Validating the Print Process

FFF Example

Figure 4 (which can be seen below) presents a comparison of the results obtained with Additive 1.0 and Additive 2.0 in addition to the initial unconstrained result. Every one of these outputs was obtained by running the standard FFF process inside the additive workspace in Fusion 360. Before the models were printed on a desktop FFF machine, they were prepared for printing by being sliced and post-processed in Fusion 360. After printing, each component was post-processed utilizing the same print settings, machine, and PLA filament throughout the whole process. The findings shown in **Figure 3** unequivocally demonstrate the progression made from Additive 1.0 to Additive 2.0, which resulted in a considerable 41.3% decrease in component mass. The advantage of using Additive 2.0 rather than using unlimited restrictions is also brought to light, as it results in a decrease of support material requirements by 47.8 percent.

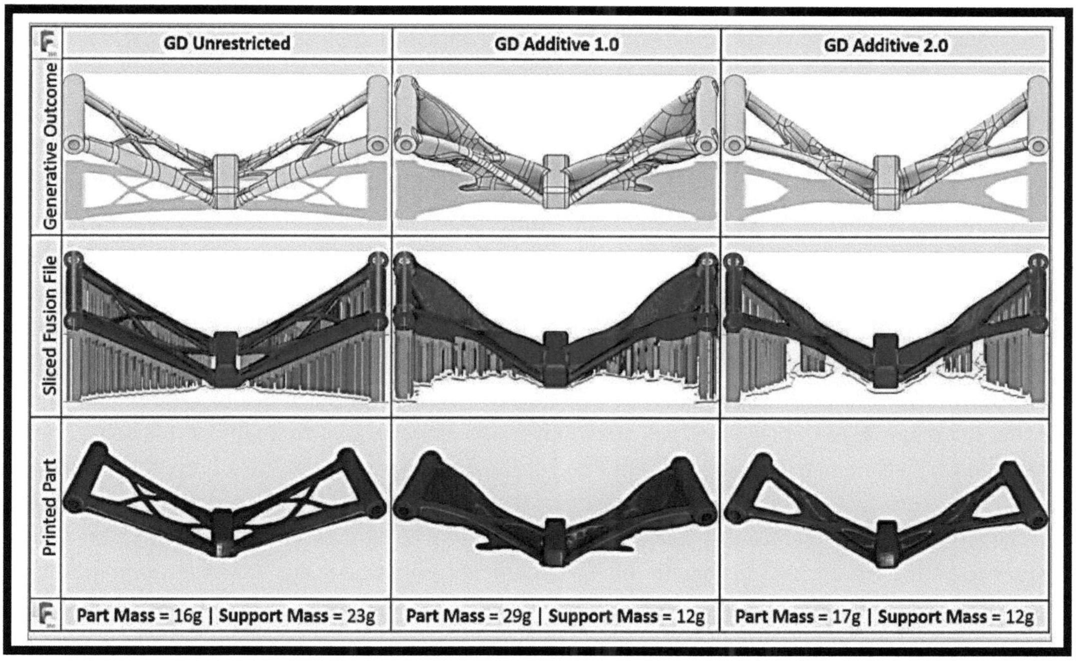

SLA Example

The outputs of the SLA printing process using Additive 1.0 and Additive 2.0 are compared in **Figure 5 (below),** together with the initial unconstrained result that was prepared for printing using the SLA technique. Each of these findings was obtained by running Netfabb through a generic version of the SLA methodology. In a manner comparable to the findings shown before, **Figure 5** elucidates the progression from Additive 1.0 to Additive 2.0. This technique was also necessary for the component mass as well as the support material.

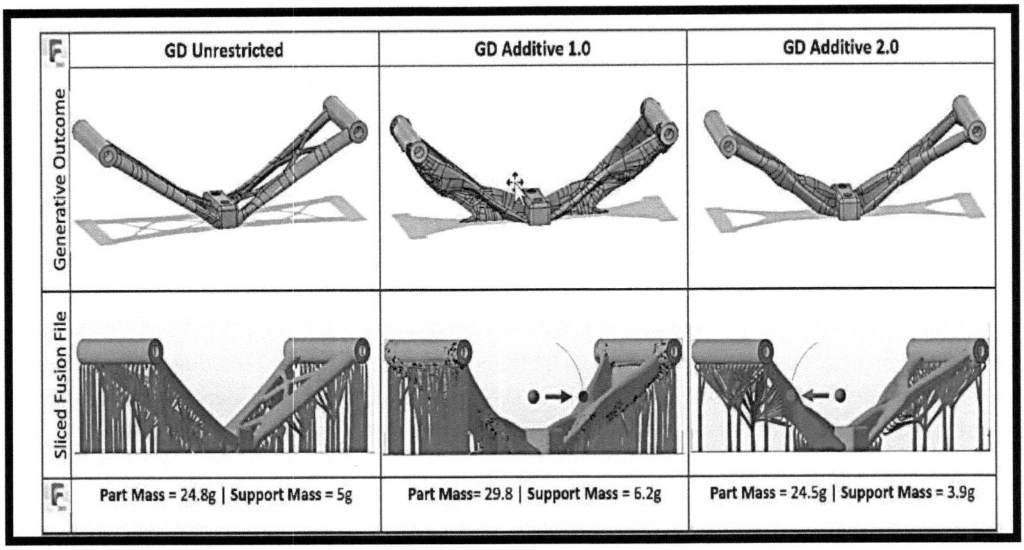

SLM Example

Let's look at another example, this time one that is more relevant to real life. In the generative design training materials, the example issue known as the **motorbike Triple Clamp** guides the user through the process of developing a structural component that attaches the fork tubes to the steering stem of a motorbike. For this illustration, we plan to use selective laser melting (SLM) to do additive manufacturing of the components out of aluminum. Before beginning the generative research, we chose the construction approach that will be used with the component. Because the build height is such a significant factor in overall costs, we decided to avoid going in the **+X** direction. Because of our previous experiences, we are aware that the majority of the big holes will need to be filled with material while the part is being printed, and then the part will need to be post-machined to get the desired tolerance. The **+Y** orientation will have a quick shift in cross-sectional area at the top face of the component after the holes have been filled in, which causes rapid cooling of a big surface and can create construction complications. As a direct consequence of this, we decided to go with the +Z construction direction rather than the +Y orientation.

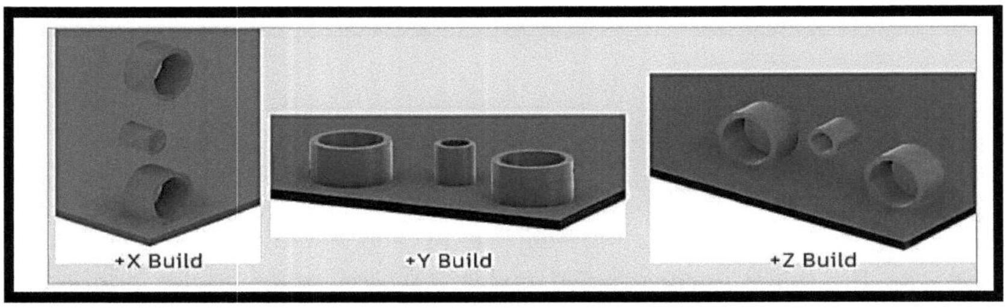

We decided on a minimum feature size of 0.25 inches (6.35 millimeters) to guarantee that any beams formed would be of sufficient size to withstand the forces that result from the lack of support. To maintain consistency with the settings of the SLM process, the overhang angle was adjusted to 45 degrees. The output of Additive 2.0 is shown in the picture below.

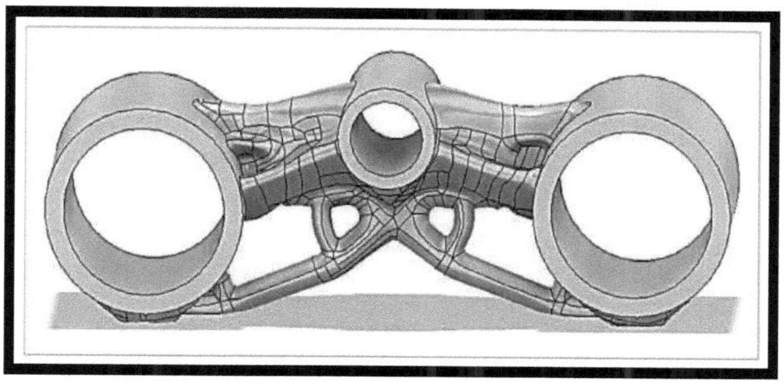

At this stage in the design process, we would normally test design performance and maybe make some design adjustments to the organic shape. For the time being, we will bypass those procedures and go immediately to the manufacturing workstation to get it ready for printing. To manufacture the design, we will be using a **Renishaw AM250**, which needs the Additive Build Fusion extension to be installed. To begin, we will need to fill the huge holes with material so that we can subsequently mill them to the appropriate tolerances. To accomplish this goal, we will go to the Manufacture workspace and create a Manufacturing Model. Using this model, we will **Press/Pull** the holes to reduce their diameter.

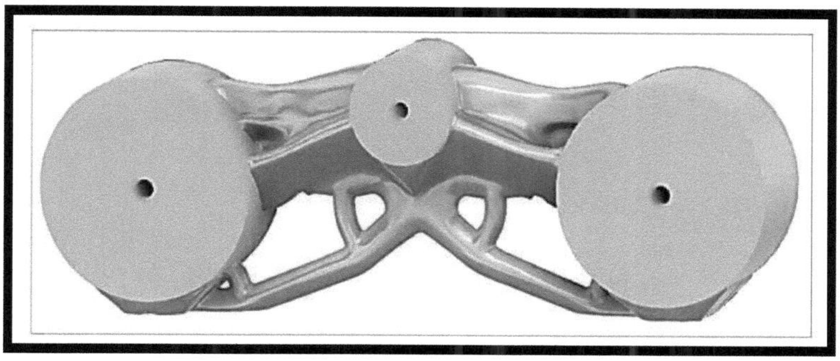

We will now construct a fresh setup, during which we will pick the Renishaw machine as well as our revised geometry. Following a brief interaction with the Move command, our component has been moved to the appropriate location on the build platform.

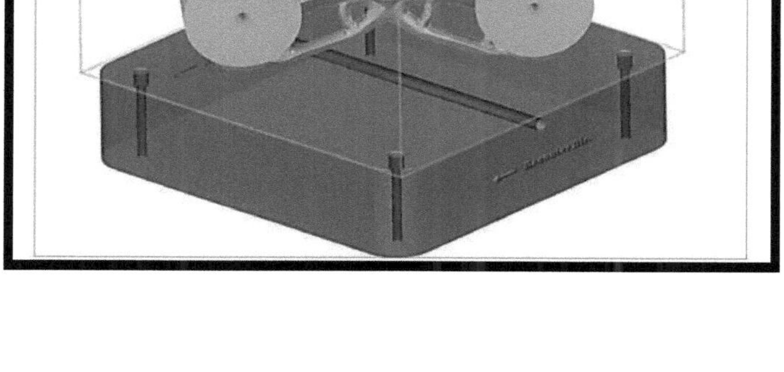

At this point, to produce support material, we will utilize the **Volume Support** command.

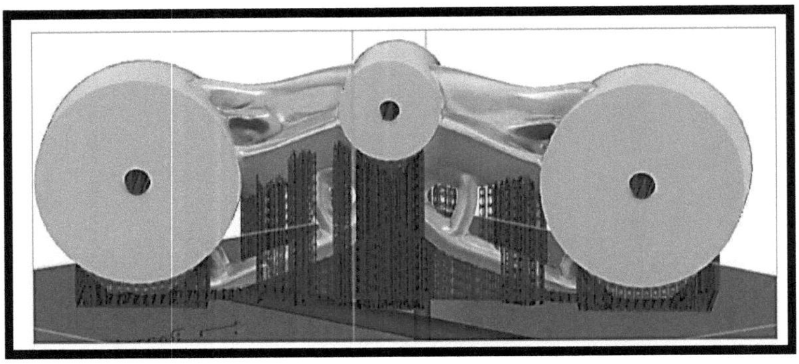

At this stage, we are prepared to run the print simulation, after which we will build the g-code and send it to the machine. The Additive 2.0 design is compared in **Figure 7 (below)** with the unconstrained and current options for additive manufacturing, and we see a pattern that is comparable to the one we saw in the earlier illustration. The effects of adding additive 1.0 make the component heavier, need the same amount of support as the unconstrained item, and have problems with the surface quality. The shape quality is improved by Additive 2.0, which also decreases the amount of support material that is necessary and puts the component mass back to approximately the same level as it was with the unconstrained output.

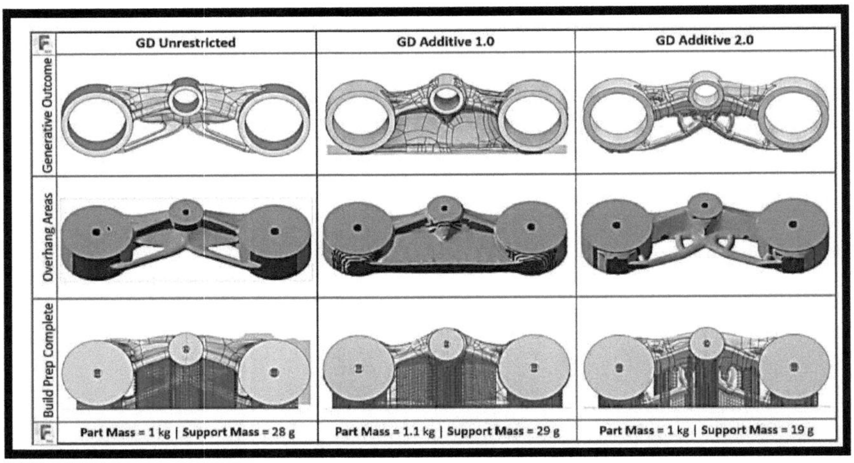

How to Use Generative Design Tools for Additive and Subtractive Manufacturing

Generative design is a technique that aids in the exploration of novel approaches to the resolution of engineering and product design challenges. It enables us to investigate what is outside the usual limitations of design, which is particularly helpful in situations where minimizing weight, maximizing stiffness, and material use are among the most critical objectives. Many people continue to believe that generative design is a method for developing concepts that can only be realized via the process of additive manufacturing. While that may have been true originally, it is no longer the case. Generative design can maximize solutions that are suited for a wide variety of production processes. To be more specific, generative design can provide designs that are ready for production for 2D cutting, 2.5-axis, 3-axis, and even 5-axis CNC machining, as well as die-casting. Take into consideration the findings of this research on generative design. All of them are viable design possibilities, with each one being customized to a different production process. In generative design, each was created using just a single configuration of the system.

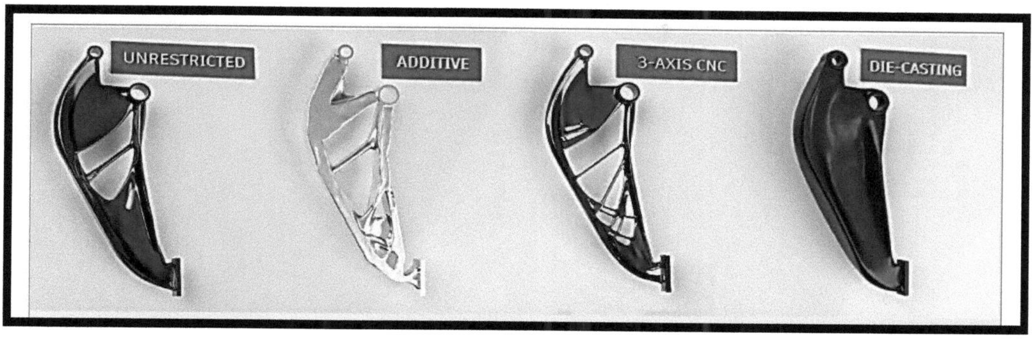

The depth of these capabilities is intriguing for the simple reason that additive and subtractive processes are often considered to be incompatible with one another. As we will see in this section, combining additive and subtractive approaches with generative design can often result in quite positive outcomes. The process of additive manufacturing is sometimes hindered by the fact that unsupported overhangs are not just undesirable but also perhaps impossible to create in the first place. It is now feasible, for instance, to use material filaments that are densely loaded with metal powder and are transported inside a polymer binder by 3D printers that use the Fused Filament Fabrication (FFF) printing method. Parts can be 3D printed on desktop machines using these materials, and then they can be placed through catalytic de-binding and sintering procedures to create a final metal component that is very near to being 100% dense.

However, the material that I planned to use, BASF Forward AM Ultrafuse 316L, does not have a suitable material for detachable support, which means that overhangs cannot be created with it. (During the debinding and sintering processes, overhanging portions can also lead to problems with the part's stability.) To find a solution to this issue, I turned to the 2.5-axis CNC machining limitation that is available in Fusion 360. The minimum tool diameter can be specified while defining the production goals for 2.5-axis CNC machining in the setup for the generative design research. In a normal situation, you would give the exact dimensions of your tool; however, the program does not restrict you to using just real-life tools. If you need to devise a solution for FFF 3D printing, you can choose 0.4 millimeters as the diameter of the material extrusion from the nozzle. This will allow you to develop a solution.

The following is research that I conducted for the design of a gripper arm:

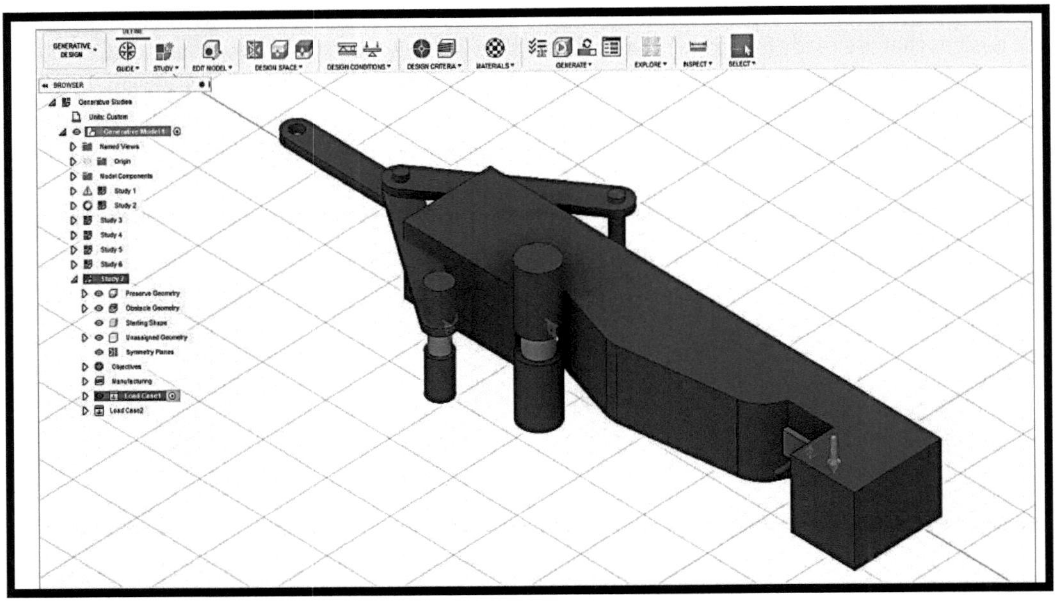

I knew I would use additive manufacturing, so while I was setting up the research, I made sure to incorporate the 2.5-axis limitation. To create a workable environment for 3D printing, I decided to set the tool diameter at a very modest 2 mm (even though a nozzle of 0.6 mm would be used), and I decided to put the wall thickness at 2.5 mm. The orientation of the tool was adjusted to Z to exclude the possibility of creating any overhangs. This is one of the potential solutions that was conceived, and it seemed worthwhile to investigate it further. Before beginning the 3D printing process, I exported the result and made just a few small adjustments.

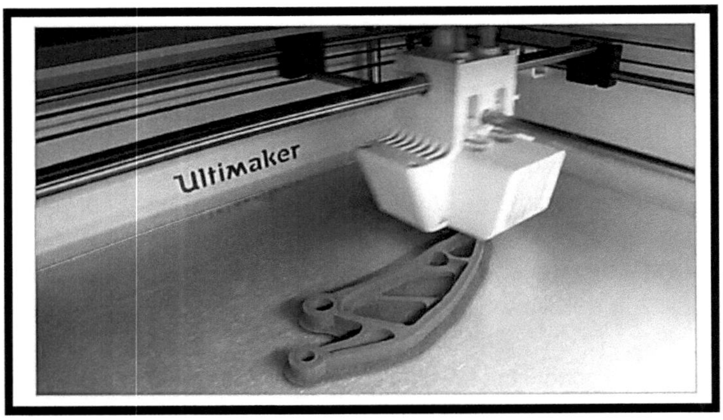

Assigning Plastic Rules to Your Designs with the Fusion 360 Product Design Extension

The Fusion 360 Product Design Extension is a collection of sophisticated 3D design and modeling tools that make it possible to create complicated product designs in an automated manner. Let's go over the steps of assigning and using plastic rules in your designs with the extension so we can get started.

Plastic Rules in Fusion 360 Overview

You can designate a particular plastic rule to the components in your design by using the designate **Plastic Rule** command. A number of the properties of the features included inside that component are automatically controlled by the plastic rule. These include the material, thickness, and radius of the physical object, utilizing the parameters and physical properties that are automatically created. You can rapidly apply the properties of any component in your design that you want to be made of plastic with this tool. You can also change these settings at any moment since they are parametric. After that, have those modifications propagated to any components that have the corresponding material rule applied to them. To guarantee that future parametric features, such as **Shell and Thicken**, inherit settings and parameters from the plastic rule, it is best practice to assign the plastic rule before employing later parametric features such as Shell and Thicken.

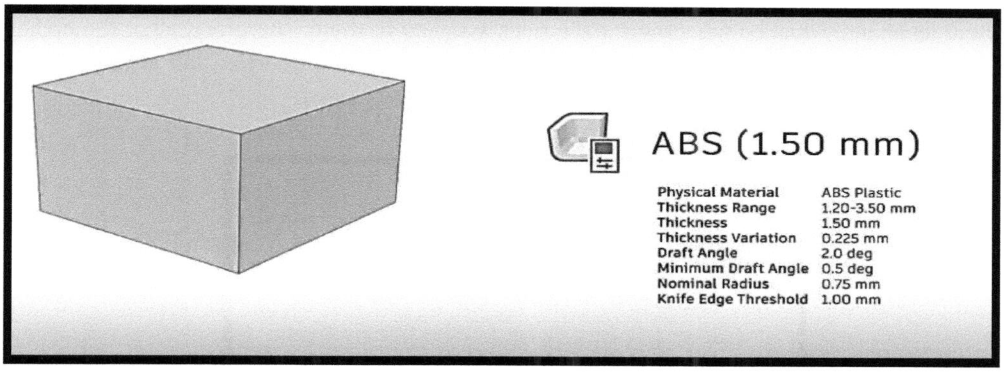

How to assign plastic rules in Fusion 360

To get started, you will need to go into the **Design workspace** and access the command. Then switch to the **Plastic** tab and locate it on the toolbar. You can pick a component in either the browser or the canvas when the **Assign Plastic Rule dialog** shows. This allows you to see the available plastic rules after the dialog has been presented. After that, you can open each rule to see the particular parameters for that rule. **These fall into three categories:**

Physical Material

- Applied to the component

- Affects physical/mass properties based on plastic material

Physical Values

- Thickness, Draft Angle, and Nominal Radius, which are referenced as parameters and used by modeling commands such as Extrude, Rib, Web, Boss, Snap Fit, Emboss, Thicken, Shell, Draft

Design Advice Values

- Thickness range, thickness variation, minimum draft angle, knife edge threshold
- Used by design advice to identify manufacturability concerns based on best practices for plastic injection molding, and provide recommendations to address them. After that, choose a **Plastic Rule**, and after that, click the OK button. After that, the plastic rule is given to the component, at which point it is shown in the browser. You can see the name of the rule as well as the settings for it here.

Physical material and appearance

When you open the **Physical Material** dialog, you'll see that the material also applies at a physical level, complete with the right look and physical properties. These properties are updated in accordance with any changes made to the plastic rule for a component in the future. Plastic rules can only be assigned at the component level; individual bodies cannot have rules assigned to them. Therefore, all of the bodies that reside inside a component will inherit the specific physical material properties and appearance of that component, as specified by the plastic rule.

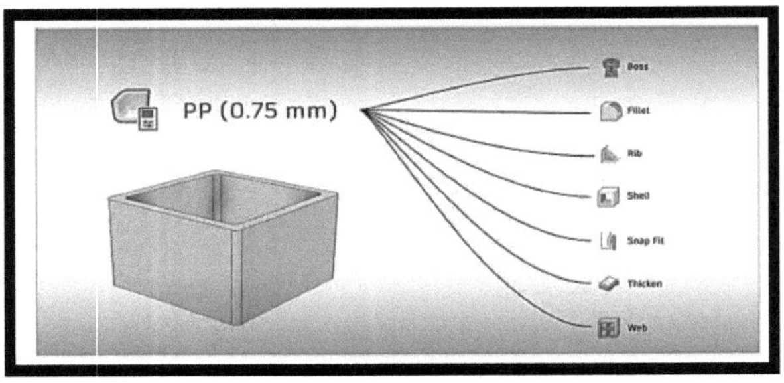

Plastic rule parameters in Fusion 360

When you are allocating materials, you will see that some settings in the settings window are automatically supplied. You will see that the parameter values in the Model section correspond to the materials that have been allocated to the model. These parametric values will now be automatically assigned whenever you carry out operations such as **Shell, Thicken, Draft,** or **Fillet**. If you want to alter any of the material's values, you will only need to alter a single value for these modifications to be propagated across all of the instances that share the same parameter reference.

Troubleshooting Common 3D Printing Issues

1. Poor Layer Adhesion

Issue: Your 3D prints have gaps or weak bonds between layers, causing structural instability.

Troubleshooting:

- **Verify the print temperature**: Set the nozzle temperature to the maximum that is advised for the filament type you are using.
- **Check the print speed**; layer adhesion may be improved by slower print speeds.
- **Make sure the bed is heated**: To avoid warping and encourage adhesion, certain materials need a hot bed.

2. Warping and Bed Adhesion Problems

Issue: Your prints are lifting or warping away from the print bed, causing print failures.

Troubleshooting:

- **Appropriate bed leveling**: Verify that the nozzle-to-bed distance is accurate and that your print bed is level.
- **Use a heated bed:** Heating a bed helps lessen warping, particularly when using ABS or other similar materials.
- **Apply adhesion aids:** Take into account utilizing tools such as adhesive sheets for beds, painter's tape, or glue sticks.

3. Filament Jamming

Issue: The filament gets stuck in the extruder, leading to print interruptions.

Troubleshooting:

- **Verify the quality of the filament**: Filament that is dusty or of low quality can jam.
- **Preserve the extruder**: Maintain a smooth filament path and clean the nozzle on a regular basis.
- **Modify the extruder's temperature**: Jams can occasionally be avoided by a little higher temperature.

4. Under-Extrusion

Issue: Your 3D printer isn't extruding enough filament, resulting in weak prints with gaps.

Troubleshooting:

- **Clear nozzle clogs:** Unclog blocked nozzles to allow filament to flow freely.
- **Set the extruder's calibration**: Modify the extrusion multiplier inside your slicer's configuration.
- **Examine any loose belts**: The movement of the print head may be impacted by loose belts, leading to under-extrusion.

5. Over-Extrusion

Issue: Too much filament is extruded, leading to messy prints with blobs and stringing.

Troubleshooting:

- **Adjust temperature settings:** In order to minimize extrusion, lower the nozzle temperature.
- **Calibrate the extruder:** Fine-tune the extrusion multiplier in your slicer.
- **Inspect for excessively tightened belts**: excessively tightened belts may cause inaccurate movement.

6. Print Bed Leveling Issues

Issue: Your print bed isn't level, causing poor first layers and print failures.

Troubleshooting:

- **Consistent bed leveling**: Before every print, level the bed again.
- **Examine the build surface**: Make sure the surface on the bed is clean and appropriate for your filament.

- **Use auto-leveling features**: Turn on and calibrate your printer's auto-leveling feature if it exists.

7. Error Messages and Print Pauses

Issue: Your 3D printer displays error messages or pauses during printing.

Troubleshooting:

- **Examine connections**: Make sure all wires and connectors are tight.
- **Update firmware**: If required, update the firmware as outdated versions can lead to issues.
- **Keep an eye on the power supply**: To avoid print outages, make sure the power source is steady.

8. Bridging and Overhang Problems

Issue: Prints with bridges or overhangs have sagging or drooping sections.

Troubleshooting:

- **Enable supports**: Utilize the support structures that your slicing software has produced.
- **Modify fan settings**: Cool bridges and overhangs more effectively.
- **Optimize print orientation**: Rotate the model wherever it is practical to reduce overhangs.

CHAPTER 24

USING FUSION 360 FOR ELECTRONICS DESIGN

The usage of Fusion 360 for electronics design is the main subject of this chapter. The first section introduces electronics design workspaces, emphasizing the usage of schematic and PCB (Printed Circuit Board) design tools as well as the investigation of electrical design capabilities. It gives readers an overview of the Fusion 360 workspaces devoted to electronics design. The capabilities of these workspaces are examined, with a focus on their importance while designing electronic systems. Along with exploring these features, the chapter offers insights into how Fusion 360 can be utilized in electrical design. The actual use of Fusion 360's schematic and PCB design tools is shown to readers. This entails learning how to use the software's functionality to design PCB layouts and produce electrical schematics. This chapter describes the schematic development technique for creating electrical circuits and making connections. In addition, it discusses PCB components and trace layout, which is essential to the creation of working electrical devices. You will learn how crucial it is for the mechanical and electrical design teams to work together in this section. It goes through how Fusion 360, which enables the smooth integration of electrical components into mechanical designs, can support this kind of cooperation. The design of enclosures to hold electronic assemblies is also touched upon, demonstrating the comprehensive approach to product development.

Overview of Electronics Design Workspaces

Fusion 360 Electronics workspace enhances Fusion 360's electronic design skills. The printed circuit board (PCB) workspace and the schematic workspace are now integrated into one platform and operate simultaneously. The Computer-Assisted Manufacturing (CAM) Processor can be used to export finished designs into the appropriate manufacturing file. Included in the workspaces are extensive Design Rule Checks (DRC) to ensure compliance with manufacturing requirements and schematic simulation based on SPICE.

Differences from EAGLE

Fusion 360 Electronics is modeled after the Autodesk EAGLE product in terms of both capabilities and behavior. However, users of EAGLE who migrate to Fusion 360 Electronics will see many significant distinctions:

- It will be necessary for users to manually associate the Schematic and Board files to maintain real-time forward and backward annotating capabilities when opening current EAGLE designs.
- The UI of several of the EAGLE tools that used icons has been replaced.

Standard controls run down the bottom of the schematic design user interface, which is seen in the image above with two menus opened.

The relevant controls show up when you go to board layout, as seen below:

Electronics Area

The two workspaces in the electronics area are utilized to construct electronic designs and libraries. Together, the workspaces provide a meaningful design experience since they are connected and synchronized.

Electronics Design Workspace

There are three contextual workspaces in this workspace. They are **2D PCB, 3D PCB**, and **Schematic. Four papers** in the Electronics design represent these workspaces.

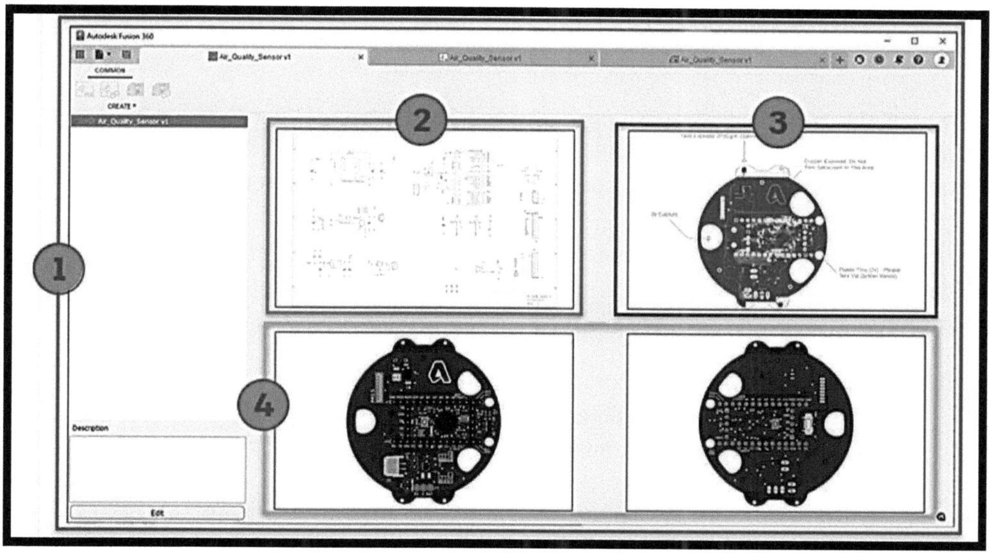

The ability to import the libraries for usage inside Fusion 360 is offered if EAGLE library files are found.

1. The main (umbrella) document that oversees the synchronization of the three other papers is the **design document**. The design and schematic documentation are the first step in each new design.
2. The **schematic document** is where you add symbols to represent the different board components and their connections to demonstrate the logic and functioning of the design. Up to 999 pages can be used in schematic papers if necessary to record the design reasoning. The Electronics Design Workspace automatically maintains consistency between the schematic and 2D PCB papers.
3. You arrange the components with one another in a **2D PCB document**. With a simple mouse click, you can construct the corresponding circuit board at any moment. The schematic components are all arranged next to the empty board in a 2D PCB document that has been opened. Thin yellow lines, commonly referred to as air wires, on components, indicate point-to-point, unrouted connections between them. After defining or importing a board form, you can find components on the board using the 2D PCB tools.
4. A 3D model created from 2D PCB data is referred to as a **3D PCB document**. The schematic is used to create the 2D and 3D PCB documents, which also include parts from the libraries you mentioned. This collection, known as a 3D package, includes the component 3D models in addition to the logical symbol and component footprint. When creating the 3D document, a placeholder shape (rectangle) is used instead of a component if it lacks an accompanying 3D model. In the 2D PCB workspace, 3D models can be mapped to components.

Electronics Library Workspace

Library collections for electronics are part of Fusion 360. It is possible that a library does not have every element in a particular design. Thus, Ultra Librarian is also available, including thousands of electrical components together with their footprints, schematics, and three-dimensional models.

Libraries aid in the upkeep and organization of design-related artifacts. Fusion 360 libraries consist of a minimum of three, and sometimes four, elements:

- **Component**: A completely specified component is made up of one or more footprints, a single symbol, and, if desired, a 3D package. Libraries are where they are kept.
- **Component variant**: When a component exists in two or more configurations, they are called variations.
- **Symbol**: The logic of each component is represented by a single symbol.
- **Footprint**: A minimum of one footprint is present in every component. If there are variations, there is a footprint for every variation. Pin assignments for variations can vary.

- **3D Package** – a 3D model of the component.
  - Each variant can have a different 3D model.
  - The 3D model and footprint must match.
  - For a component to be included in the library it doesn't require a 3D model. In such cases, when pushing the design to 3D PCB, a placeholder shape is used.

Working with schematic and PCB design tools

Schematic design

A schematic, which outlines the logic and functioning of the design, should be the first step in any electrical design. With a single mouse click, the corresponding circuit board can be generated at any moment. Following the switch to Electronics, the packages are positioned adjacent to an empty board and linked by air wires, which are thin yellow lines that show point-to-point connections.

You can continue creating using the Layout Editor as normal from this point on. The Electronics Workspace (**Forward & Back Annotation**) automatically maintains consistency in the schematic and layout. Schematic designs can include up to 999 pages in total. The sheet preview is shown on the left side of the Schematic Editor window. Drawing basic electrical wiring diagrams, such as connection schemes and contact layouts, may also be done using the Schematic Editor.

Work with a new schematic

Build a schematic diagram and include the necessary parts. Later on, you can utilize the schematic to build a circuit board.

Create a schematic

1. Select **File > New Electronics Design** in Fusion 360.
2. On the Electronics toolbar, choose New Schematic. You are presented with a blank canvas on which to draw your schematic.
3. Save the file.

Make sure the grid is set to 0.1 inch

When creating a schematic, always utilize the default grid value of 0.1 inch. If not, there's a chance that your schematic's connections won't work properly on a circuit board. Don't alter this number.

1. Click **Grid Settings** on the Schematic toolbar.

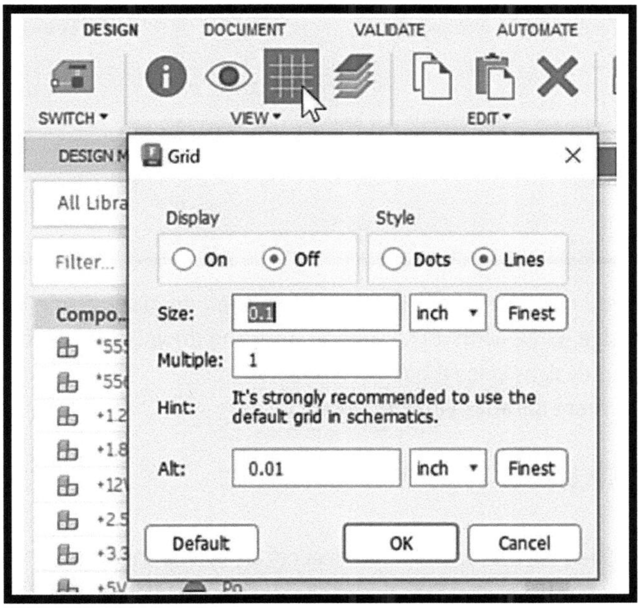

2. Verify that the Size in the Grid dialog is set to 0.1 inch.

Add component libraries with the Library Manager

For your schematic, add any component libraries that you will need using the Library Manager.

1. Click **Place component** on the Schematic toolbar. The Place panel opens up to show the components that are accessible on your PC.
2. To the right of the libraries menu, choose **Open Library Manager**. Three columns appear when the Library Manager opens.

- **Filters**: To focus your search for the library you wish to utilize, use filter criteria.
    - **Status**: Select what is either not in use or used in the current design.
    - **Source**: Restrict the sources of info that you look up.
    - **Updates**: Limit libraries with available updates.
    - **Used in**: Limit the display to components already in use in the current design.
- **Outcomes**: Shows the libraries that meet the specified filters.
- **Details**: Offers details about the chosen library, including its name, folder, and managed or local status. When available, further information is shown.

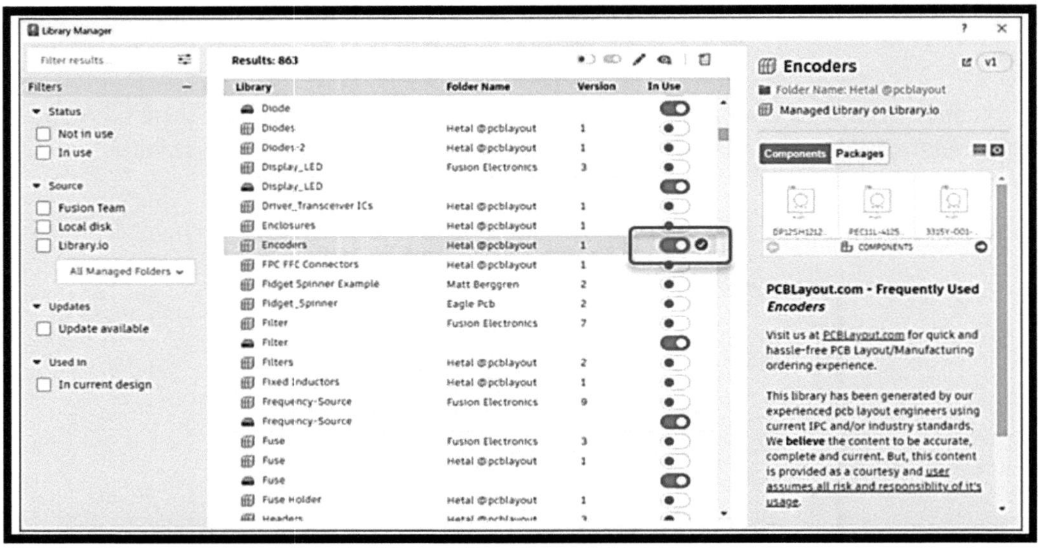

3. If you believe you might use any libraries, turn their **In Use** setting on. The library shows a confirmation badge (circle with a checkmark) after the download is finished. You can now utilize the library in your designs since it has been enabled.
4. Repeat with any more libraries you want to include.

SPICE simulation in the schematic

Circuit designs can be verified via simulation. Electrical circuit simulation using **SPICE (Simulation Program with Integrated Circuit Emphasis)** is possible. Activities can involve checking that all diodes are getting the current they need based on preset values or confirming that an analog amplifier's frequency response and gain match calculations made by hand. Electronics includes a copy of **ngspice**, an open-source mixed-level/mixed-signal circuit simulator, based on Berkeley spice3f5. Full digital and mixed-signal simulation modes, as well as **Operating Point, Transient (time), AC (frequency),** and **DC Analysis types,** are supported by ngspice. Any legitimate SPICE circuit can be simulated, indicating that every element in your schematic has been mapped to a SPICE model, whether it be model-based or primitive. A small library of simulation-ready components named ngspice-simulation is included with electronics. These components have been pre-mapped to the appropriate **SPICE** types and, where necessary, models have been supplied. Thus, with these elements, you can simply design schematics that are suitable for simulation. Along with creating your simulation-ready library pieces, you can also set them up inside an already-existing schematic, regardless of the library from whence they originated. Digital circuits using elementary gates of digital logic, such as **AND, OR, and NOT**, can be simulated using digital simulation. Numerous digital primitives are pre-installed, and some of them are mapped to library components in the ngspice-digital shared library by Fusion 360 Electronics.

Simulate circuit performance with SPICE

1. Using parts from the **ngspice-digital and ngspice-simulation** libraries, create a schematic. If needed, you can load them from the list of options. These libraries already have their components mapped to SPICE models, which is necessary for precise simulations.

2. Assign suitable values for resistance, capacitance, etc. to the components in your schematic. Place a Phase or Voltage probe where it makes sense, for instance:
    a. Click Voltage Probe
    b. Click **location in circuit** to install the probe.
    c. Lengthen the VOUT arrow.

Sample schematic

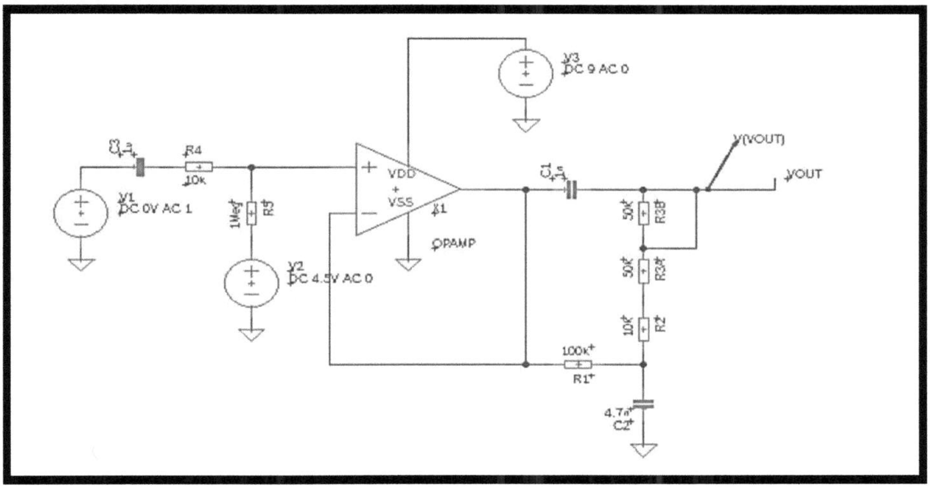

3. Select the complete circuit design by drawing a rectangle around it, then click **SIMULATE** > **Add Model**. When asked whether you wish to convert any Ground (GND) components to **SPICE** ground, click **Yes**.

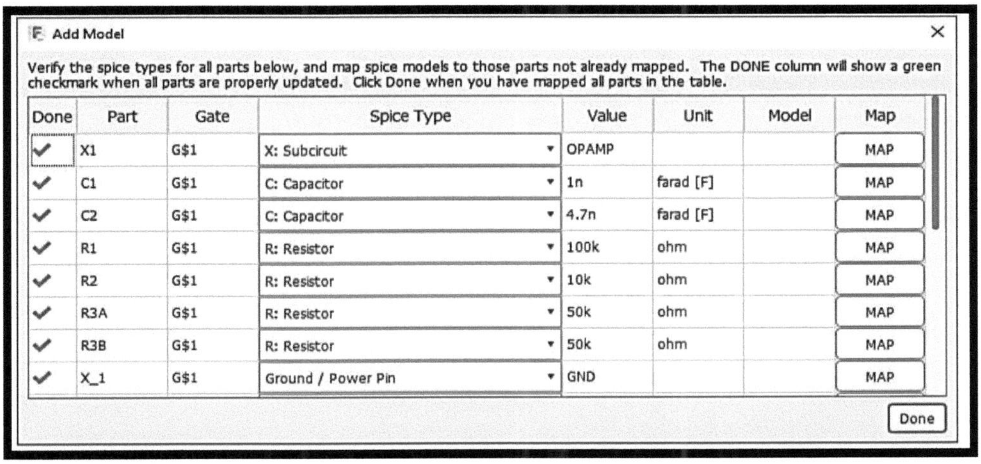

Add Model

Verify the spice types for all parts below, and map spice models to those parts not already mapped. The DONE column will show a green checkmark when all parts are properly updated. Click Done when you have mapped all parts in the table.

Done	Part	Gate	Spice Type	Value	Unit	Model	Map
✔	X1	G$1	X: Subcircuit	OPAMP			MAP
✔	C1	G$1	C: Capacitor	1n	farad [F]		MAP
✔	C2	G$1	C: Capacitor	4.7n	farad [F]		MAP
✔	R1	G$1	R: Resistor	100k	ohm		MAP
✔	R2	G$1	R: Resistor	10k	ohm		MAP
✔	R3A	G$1	R: Resistor	50k	ohm		MAP
✔	R3B	G$1	R: Resistor	50k	ohm		MAP
✔	X_1	G$1	Ground / Power Pin	GND			MAP

Done

Every component of the circuit is shown in the Add Model table, along with a green checkmark in the Done column. You can check and adjust any component values in this table. You can initiate the process of mapping a component to **SPICE** by selecting the **Map** button if you have utilized any components that weren't mapped to a **SPICE** model. An alarm indicator would appear.

4. Select **Simulate** from the ribbon.
5. Choose the appropriate Type value (Operating Point, DC Sweep, AC Sweep, or Transient) in the **SIMULATION** dialog box. Other parameters should usually be left at their default settings.
6. Choose **Simulate** from the dialog box. Several output graphs are shown to you after the simulation is complete. The voltage graph is the most helpful in this AC sweep example.

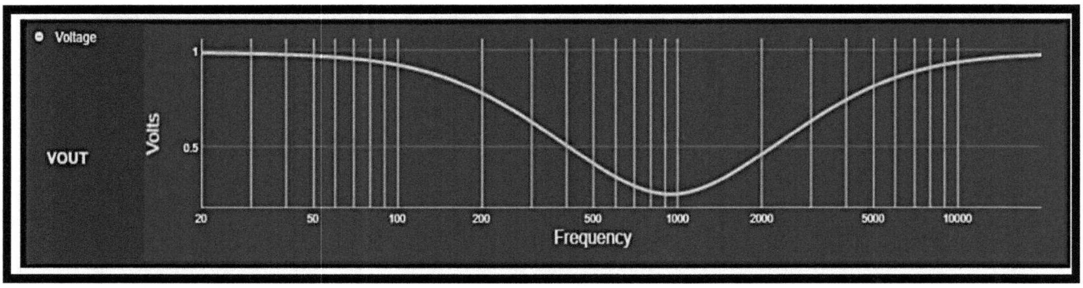

Creating PCB Design

Fusion 360 comes with a PCB design suite, which is an extremely sophisticated tool that can be used by any firm that works with electronics. The user-friendly PCB design suite lets users create 2D schematic drawings, automatically create a 2D PCB design, and optionally transform that 2D model to a 3D model at the touch of a button. Any modifications made to the schematic drawing are instantly sent to the 2D and 3D board designs since the files are continuously connected.

SCHEMATIC DESIGN

Making a 2D schematic drawing is the first stage in producing a full PCB design. Fusion 360 simplifies this process by integrating a large library of frequently used electrical components, which saves the user time. If a component is missing from the libraries, users can add their parts to their libraries. A preview of the schematic representation, the 2D PCB representation, and the 3D model are provided for every component.

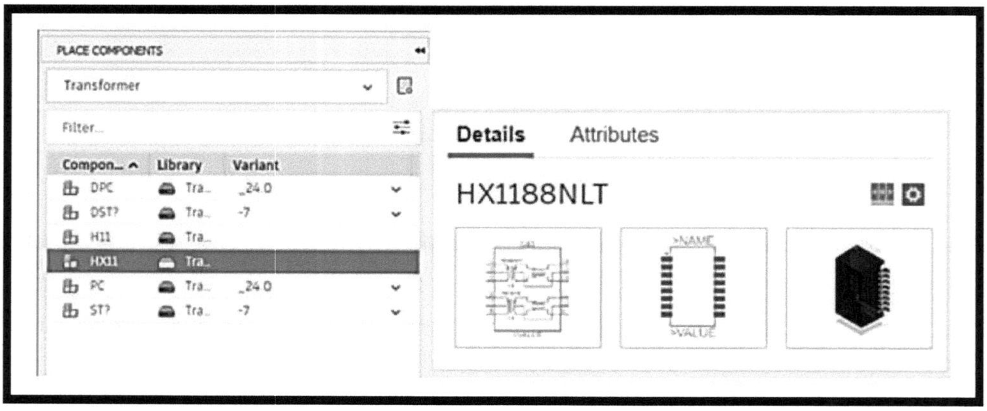

The designs can have bespoke title blocks attached to them for seamless revision history and document management. The NET command can be used to connect all components. When the components are converted to a 2D PCB, air wires will be created, allowing the wiring to be further improved.

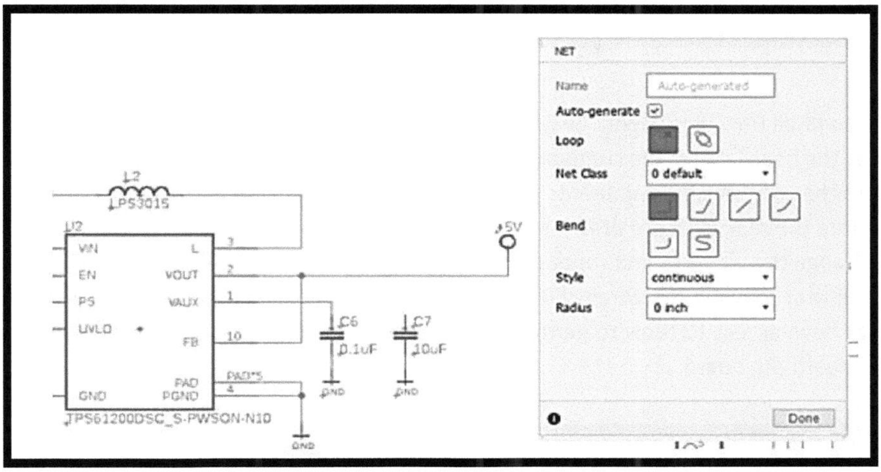

The user can utilize the ERC validation tools at this level of design to look for design-related problems and warnings. This can reduce the need for design modifications by averting problems from arising during subsequent simulation and testing phases.

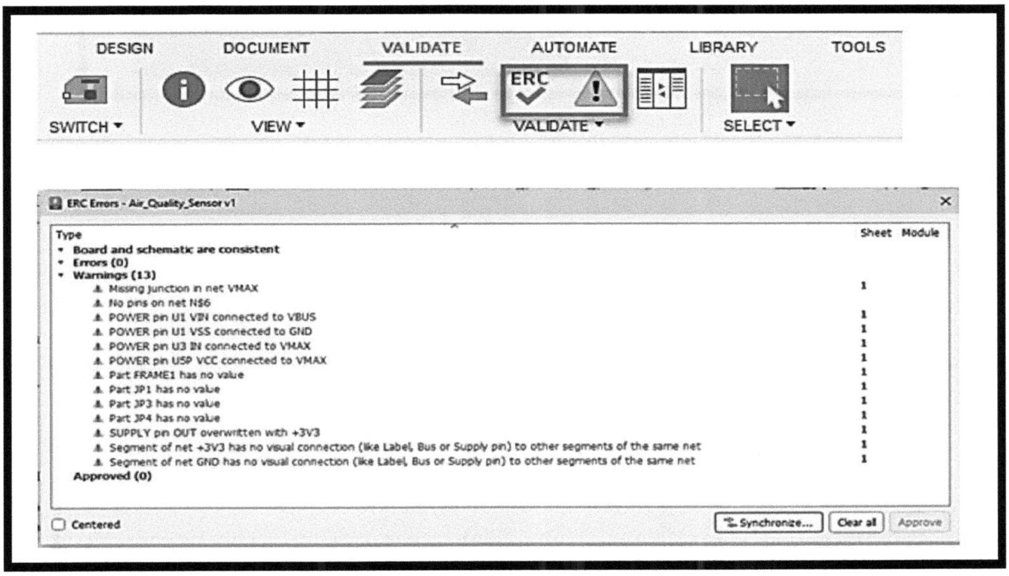

2D PCB DESIGN

Following the construction and error-checking of the schematic drawing, the design can be transferred to the 2D PCB file. Alternatively, you can import a schematic file from another application, such as Eagle, by using the command to reference a schematic document while creating a new electrical design.

As you design to fit all the components neatly and make boards that operate under pre-established limits, you can change the board's size. The components are attached using "**air wires**," which are temporary wires that indicate to the user which components are connected when the schematic is transformed into the 2D PCB space. Before the real wires are drawn in, these air wires serve as a stand-in. After everything is set up, the user can change the air wires and route all of the cabling to fit neatly on the board. By dealing with the 2D PCB file, the user may lay the wires without worrying about collisions because of the complete layer visibility. Users have access to tools to generate an automated copper pour for a signaling layer and can route wires beneath the board.

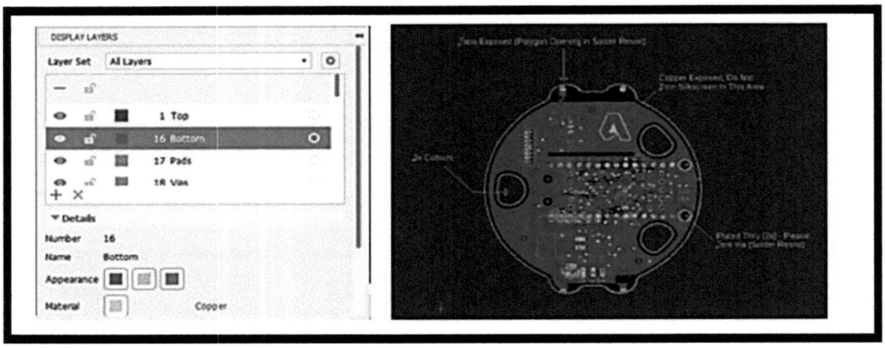

Testing

In addition, users can conduct checks on the design and establish specified clearances, distances, and wiring rules using the **DRC (design rule checker)**, which will once again highlight any mistakes or warnings.

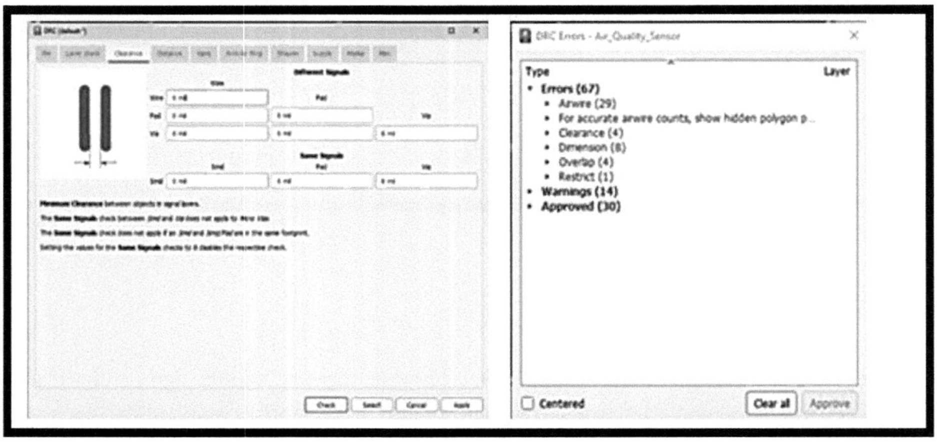

3D PCB DESIGN

Users can choose to export their 2D design into a 3D PCB file when it is finished. This can help the other members of the design team since they can include a full-scale model of the PCB in their assembly rather than just a reduced version. The user just has to choose "**push to 3D PCB**" to generate the 3D board; after that, the file is prepared for export. This is a very fast method since the board can be sent out in a variety of forms, including an Inventor.ipt file, a STEP file, or a Solidworks file, without requiring much modeling.

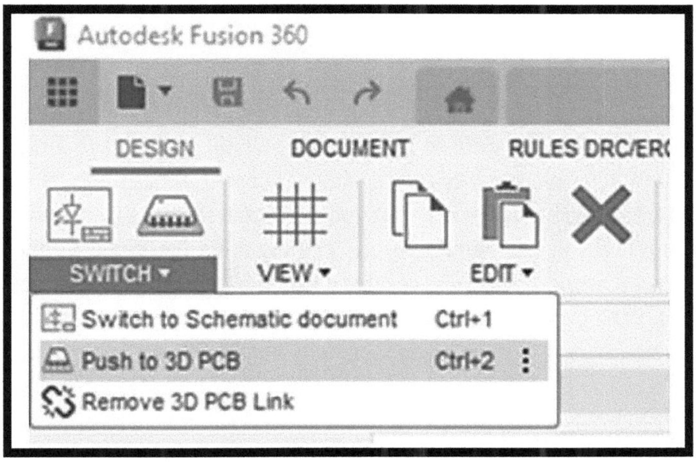

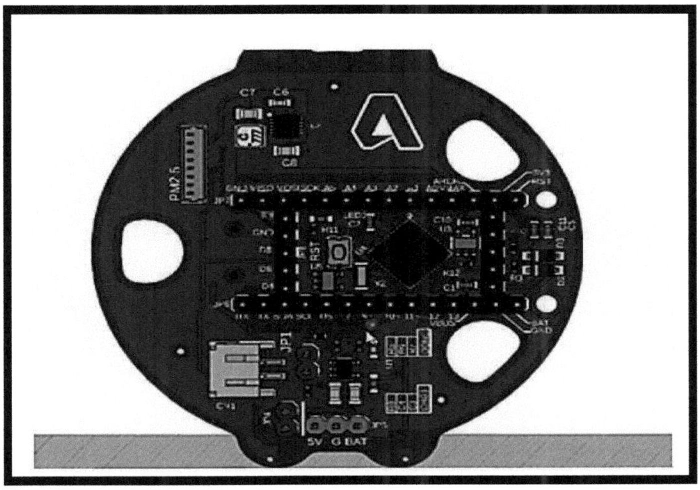

Laying out PCB components and traces

PCB design is a science as well as an art. Concerning trace lengths, layer stackups, schematics, and other related areas, a great lot of technical knowledge and measurements must be taken into account. However, the intriguing part of PCB design comes when you approach the creative aspect of component arrangement. The fact is that there is no one "**right**" method to arrange components, and it is this creativity and fulfillment that ultimately drives the PCB designing process. Everything depends on what you want to design. It does not mean, however, that you can act any way you like. To optimize your component placement flow, keep in mind that your digital design must still be able to be manufactured in physical form. Here are some helpful hints to help you with this.

What's So Important about Component Placement?

One popular statement is that *"**90% of PCB design is placement and 10% is routing**"*. This is true to the letter. It will be much simpler for you to route everything if you take the time to correctly locate your components, and it will also provide the finest electrical performance for your board. What would happen, however, if you simply put your components down carelessly?

- **Lost Hours**. When you discover that some of your components are packed too closely together and don't even have enough room to be routed, you'll probably make a nightmare for yourself. The poorest component placements can result in a board that has to be completely redone.
- **Cracked boards**. Assume for a moment that you are successful in setting up certain parts and traces and sending your files to your manufacturer. The next thing you know, your components may not have been soldered properly, and you receive a board back that doesn't function.
- **Ugly Aesthetics.** Seeing a board that wasn't given the appropriate love and care during component placement can be quite unnerving. Let's face it, as engineers, we adore symmetry and precision. It's only indolent.

Make sense? Here's the real kicker – there's no universally "**right**" way to do it. Give a schematic to 100 different engineers, and you'll likely get 100 different layouts back. This is why the PCB layout process is viewed as an artistic process. Dislike all the nebulous concepts of "**right**" and "**wrong**"? To check whether you're on track with your component placement, use this tip. Once you've assembled all of your components, run Autodesk EAGLE's autorouter. If you don't get a completion grade of at least 85%, it's likely that you still have some component placement work to perform. Now that we've got the **Why** out of the way let's move on to some practical tips you can use in your first design project!

Tip #1 – Understand Your Mechanical Constraints

You should know precisely where your mounting holes and edge connections go as well as what form of mechanical enclosure will work best for your board before you even set a component down.

Why? Comprehending these factors will impact your board's dimensions and form. Many engineers have designed boards that are too large for their enclosures, only to find themselves having to spend hours redesigning the whole thing. In your design guidelines, you can do yourself a favor by entering the clearance requirements for your mounting holes before starting the component placement process. This will free you from thinking about your technical limitations so you can concentrate on the creative things.

Tip #2 – Understand Your Assembly Constraints

Once again, you should be aware of a few details from your manufacturer before setting a component down, such as:

- How will your board be put together and tested?
- Do you think your board will need any additional permissions for v-scoring?
- Will you be hand soldering, wave soldering, or selective soldering your components together?

Why? What kind of room you have to deal with during component placement will ultimately depend on how your board is produced. To avoid any damage during assembly and processing, for instance, you should keep pieces away from the edge of your board if it will be installed along a conveyor belt. You can safely utilize the whole surface of your board when inserting components if your manufacturer fabricates and assembles it using a pallet array technique. Make sure that all of your parts and traces are at least 20 miles away from the edge of your PCB, but, if assembly constraints force you to avoid putting components on the board's edge.

Tip #3 – Give your Integrated Circuits (ICs) Room to Breathe

Whenever possible, aim to space out each integrated circuit (IC) on your board by at least 0.3500" to 0.5000". Even more room should be left for bigger ICs.

Why? The biggest error that novice circuit designers consistently make is aligning their integrated circuits too closely together. Integrated circuits come with a ton of pins for different connections. What results from doing this? When it comes time to routing every pin on your IC, you'll probably run out of room and have to rearrange a lot of stuff, which will take hours or even days of effort.

Tip #4 – Keep Similar Components in the Same Direction

When assembling identical components, take care to align them all in rows or columns that are uniformly spaced out in the same direction.

Why? Your manufacturer will find it easier to install, check, and test all of the items you put in if you do this. When dealing with **Surface Mount components, or SMDs**, which use a wave soldering method, this becomes very important. The bottom of your board will travel across a wave of hot solder during this wave soldering process and any exposed metal parts that the wave hits will be covered with solder. Hence, a solder bond will develop when the wave solder travels over two exposed metal surfaces, such as a lead in a hole, enabling an electrical connection to flow between your board and component. A board with several shorts or open circuits will result from improper soldering of these connections.

Tip #5 – Group Your Parts to Minimize Connection Paths

Reduce the number of connecting pathways that cross and intersect when you arrange your components.

Why? Each component in Autodesk EAGLE has a very tiny line connecting it to another part when you convert a schematic into a PCB layout. In other PCB design tools, these lines are referred to as ratsnests and are also known as airwires. All of the connections between the components that you made with your schematic design are represented by these. Reduce the number of junctions and crisscrosses in your connection pathways, and your routing task will become simpler and easier. To easily recalculate your airwires as you move pieces about, Autodesk EAGLE provides a useful Ratsnest tool on the left side of the interface.

Tip #6 – Place All of Your Edge Components First

Connectors, switches, jacks, USB ports, and other parts that can't be relocated because of a mechanical enclosure should be placed first.

Why? When working with a mechanical designer, the positioning of these parts is usually predetermined and beyond your control. Additionally, by arranging these edge components first, you'll provide yourself with a solid foundation for figuring out how your board layout should develop to include all of your input and output connections. You can begin working on your internal components creatively and enjoyably after you've locked these edge components into place.

Tip #7 – Avoid Overlapping Any Parts

When dealing with a tiny board size, never, ever save on quality by overlaying the pad or the component outline. Make sure there is a minimum of 40 millimeters between each component.

Why? One copper pad for each footprint you put on your PCB will be connected to an electric source. A stream of electricity may flow between components and cause some unintentional short circuits if two parts overlap and the pads come into small contact. Additionally, it will be much simpler for you to route all of your copper traces if you leave room between sections during the installation procedure. Remember to account for the vias holes as well! If they don't have enough room, those green rings—which are a bunch of exposed copper—would love to short-circuit your board.

Tip #8 – Keep Your Parts on One Layer

It is usually best to arrange all of your pieces on the top layer of a straightforward two-layer board.

Why? It takes a lot of time and money to manufacture a physical PCB, especially if you want to put components on the top and bottom layers of the board. The reason for this is that a rapid-fire pick-and-place machine will be used to install your SMD components on your PCB during the assembly process. Putting all of your components on the top layer of your board will simplify this procedure and just need one pass through the pick-and-place machine. However, if you begin attaching pieces to your bottom layer, the pick-and-place machine will need to go through it again, adding to the needless expenses associated with production.

Tip #9 – Keep IC Pins and Polarized Components in the Same Direction

You can take advantage of this by making sure that pin 1 on each of your integrated circuits (ICs) is always oriented in the same direction. Each IC includes an identification that indicates where pin 1 is located. The same goes for polarized components, make sure that the positive leads are all placed in the same direction.

Why? When soldering and inspecting your board, you may be sure that no errors are made by aligning all of your integrated circuits (ICs) in the same direction. It would be disastrous to have to construct a board with every IC facing the incorrect way!

Tip #10 – Design Your PCB Layout like Your Schematic

Place components in logical groups on your PCB layout just like you did with your schematic design.

Why? Throughout the process, you'll save a ton of time and simplify the comparison of your design between the schematic and the PCB layout. This will help reduce the length of the traces since your schematic has already logically grouped the pieces you're putting together.

If you have a large microcontroller, for instance, you should install it first, followed by all of the surrounding resistors and capacitors. This will simplify the routing of your integrated circuit and any linked components using the shortest trace lengths feasible.

Contained Creativity

Excellent component placement is the cornerstone of the greatest PCB layouts, therefore don't hurry this procedure. You're doing something well if you discover that you spend 90% of your time putting pieces together! Keep up the good work! This is a satisfying creative process that is one of the hardest parts of the PCB design process to master, but it is well worth the effort. Ultimately, by making the effort to arrange your components correctly, you will get a board from manufacturing that functions as intended straight out of the box. And that's the best part for any engineer.

PCB Layer Stack Fundamentals: Using Multiple Copper Layers

Copper layers are carved away to form tracks, also known as routes, on printed circuit boards. To create circuits, these rails connect the PCB's parts. We'll look at the things to be aware of in this section while employing several copper layers in your PCB layer stack.

PCB Construction

Single Layer PCBs

For low-cost PCBs with a limited number of components, the most basic PCB has only one copper layer.

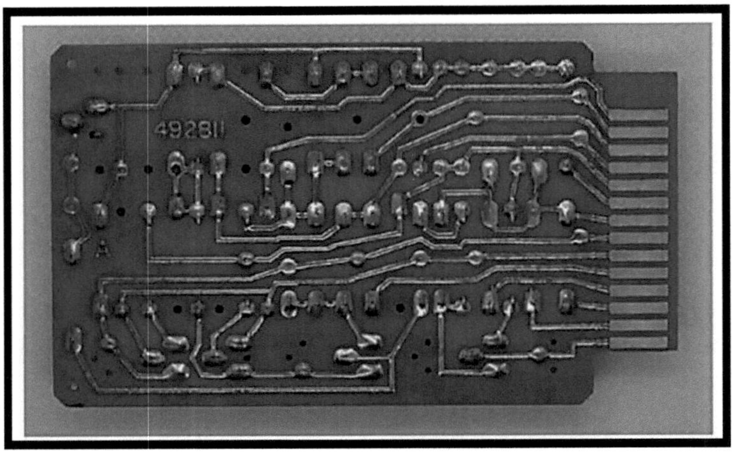

Double-Sided PCBs

When it comes to moderately sophisticated PCBs with a modest component count, double-sided boards are common. Because the PCBs are pre-manufactured with copper foil attached on both sides, they are cheap. Most modern PCBs need additional layers to route component connections as needed.

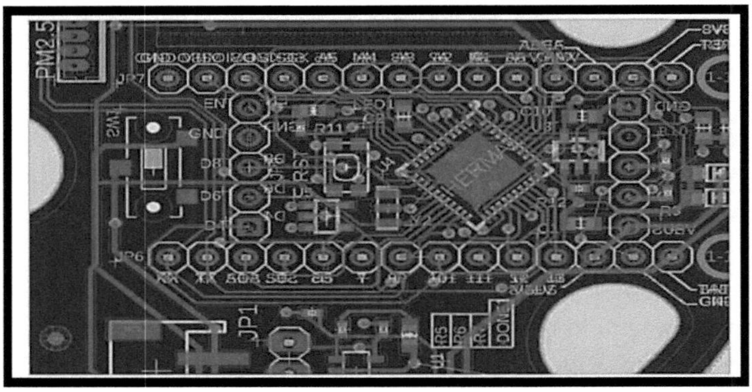

Multi-layer PCBs

Copper solid planes encased on a PCB are known as power planes. Two layers are insufficient at some point, and more layers are required. Power planes are sometimes provided by additional layers. In comparison to traditional decoupling capacitors, this offers superior power supply decoupling, functioning as a large power supply decoupling capacitor that is suitable for frequencies considerably higher. They also serve another vital purpose, which is to limit the electric field to a tiny region to reduce **EMI (Electromagnetic interference)** and crosstalk. The arrangement and distance between the layers on your PCB constitute the layer stack. Attaching two copper foil layers to the top and bottom of a double-sided PCB is the easiest and least costly method of creating a four-layer PCB. Glass fiber cloth that has been pre-impregnated with uncured epoxy serves as a barrier between the upper and lower layers. This so-called pre-preg is malleable and soft, and it will mold itself around traces that have already been carved out of the center of the double-sided PCB, also referred to as the core.

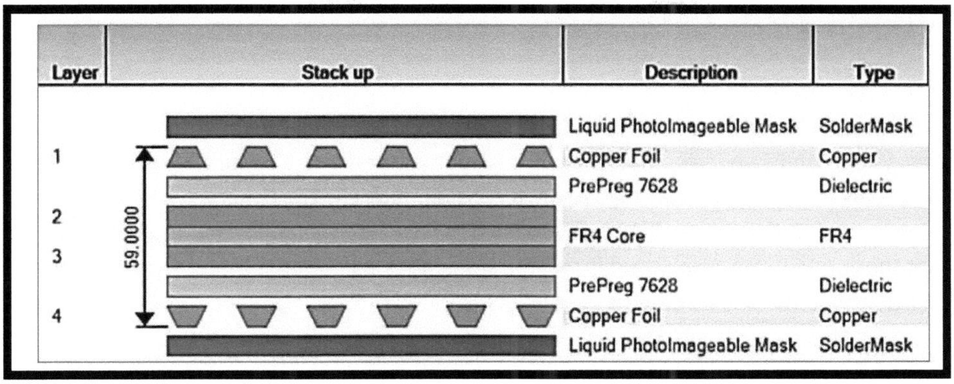

It's The Electric Field That Drives Current

We explain that voltage "**pushes**" electron current across conductors when first introducing electric circuits. It isn't like that. The force is applied by the electric field. The electric field must be taken into account in your stack-up to prevent it from expanding to locations where it can disrupt power lines and signaling. For a PCB designer to confine the field and stop cross-talk or common mode currents from introducing noise into signals or power rails, the stack-up's layer order is essential.

Fusion 360 PCB Layer Stack Manager

You can create and view your layer stack using the layer stack manager that comes with Autodesk Fusion 360.

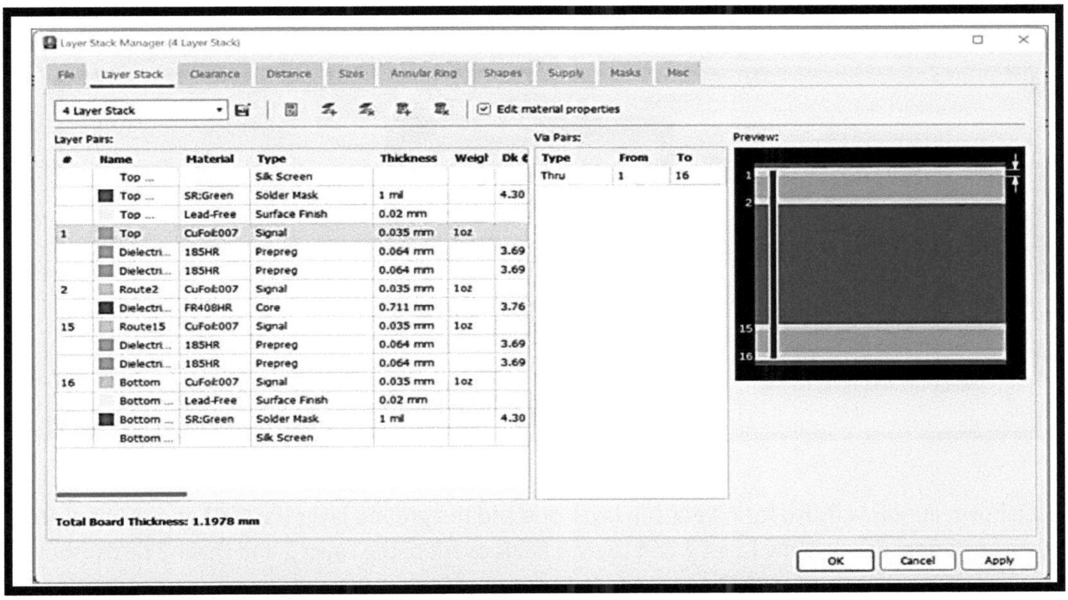

Although layers in Fusion 360 are numbered from 1 to 16, we often refer to layer stacks by their PCB order when we talk about them. Layers 15 and 16 in this four-layer example correspond to layers 3 and 4.

Organizing your PCB layer stack

Your layers must be arranged in a way that confines the electric fields and reduces their interaction with one another. With a ground plane on layer three, a signal/power plane on layer four, and a signal/power plane on levels one and two, take a look at this subpar four-layer stack-up. Although it contains three routing layers, why is this a bad stack-up? We must consider how electric fields will manifest themselves on the board to respond to that query. Suppose you have two traces: one on layer 1 and the other on layer 2. Assume that these traces are being used for digital transmissions. Assume that layer 2 has a logic 0 or 0V and layer 1 has a logic 1 or 5V. An electric field will be created between the two traces as a result.

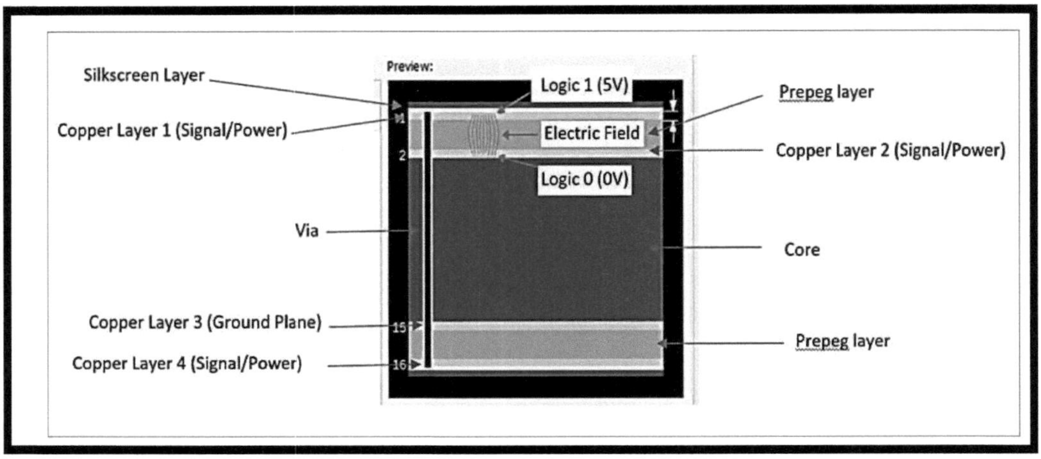

The issue is that signals from layer one will cause the ground plane's layers one through three to generate an electric field.

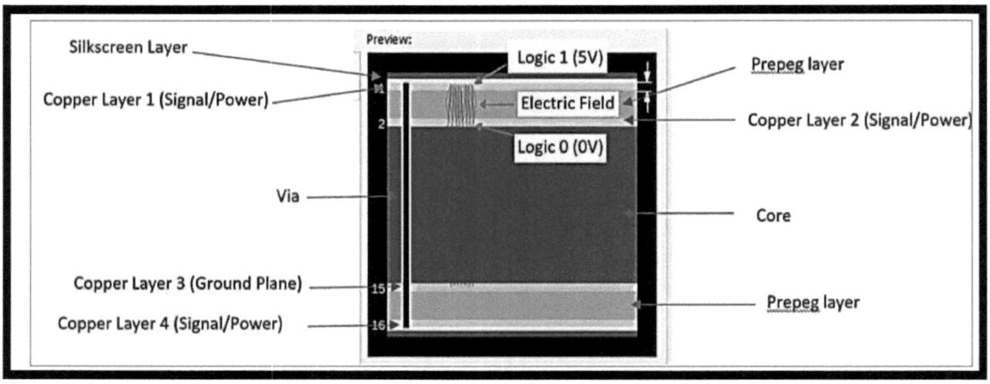

A field (shown in red) will also form between layer one and the ground layer (layer 3) as a result of the 5V signal on layer one. Because the Layer 1 and Layer 3 fields overlap, the Layer 1 and Layer 2 fields (shown in blue) will couple onto the ground. The ground plane becomes loud as a result.

Signal integrity (SI) and **power integrity (PI)** problems are caused by fields interacting with one another. Notably, the signals from the layer 4 couple to the layer 3 ground plane are segregated and do not interfere with one another.

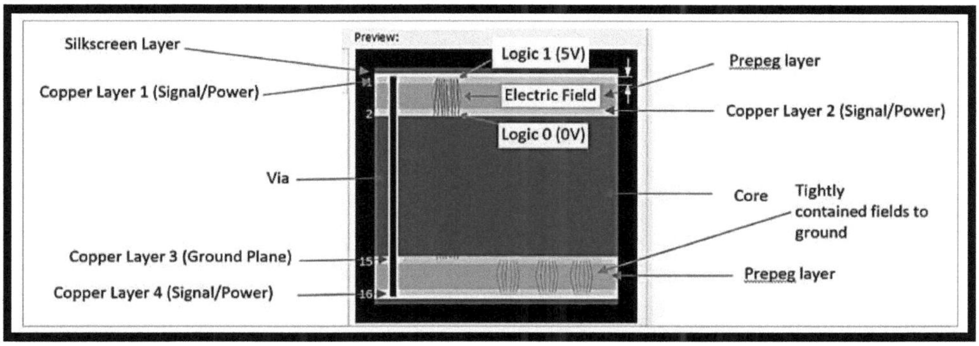

That provides a clue as to how the stack-up can be set up to reduce these interactions.

A Better PCB Layer Stack Up

The ground layer one ground plane and the signal layer two electric fields will be closely connected in this stack-up configuration.

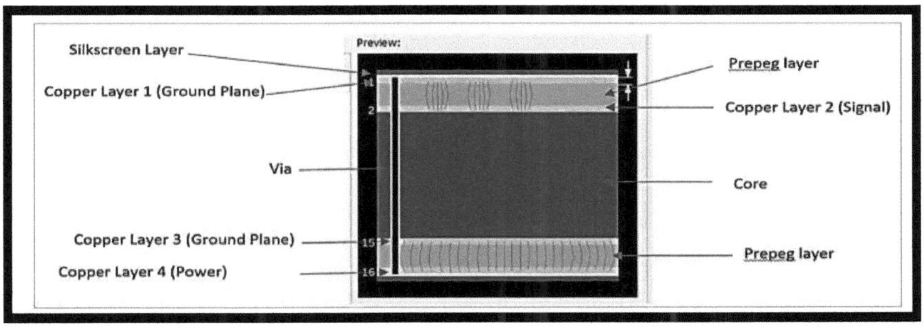

Naturally, the main drawback of this improved stack-up is that it only has one layer for routing signals. Our PCB would ideally merely have extra layers added to it. Here is an excellent six-layer stack-up, for instance. But because there are just two routing layers, it's once again not particularly cost-effective.

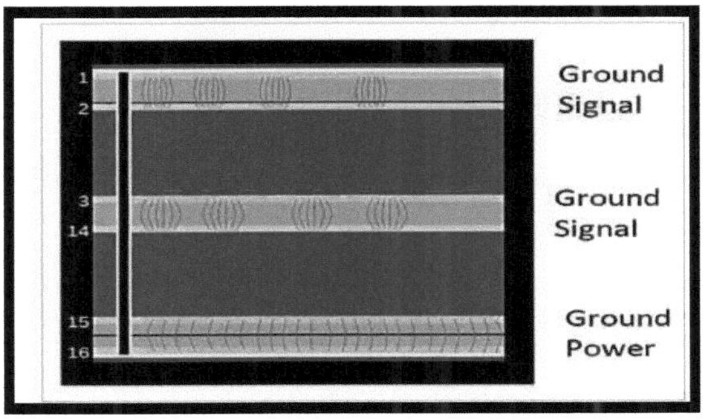

So What Can We Do?

The signal layer must be added, and power pours must be combined with it. This six-layer stack achieves the same goal. The ground planes underneath the fields enclose them firmly. In addition to increasing ground and supply capacitance, large power plane pours also improve PI (Power Integrity). To keep fields confined, a 4-layer stack with ground in the center of layers 2 and 3 and power and signal on levels 1 and 4 also works well. Better still, as shown in b), sig/pwr and sig/pwr as it permits strip-lining between the two grounds on layers 2 and 4.

Example A

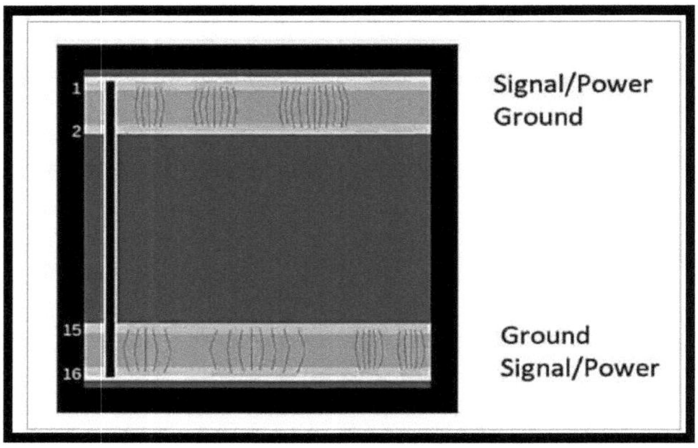

Example B

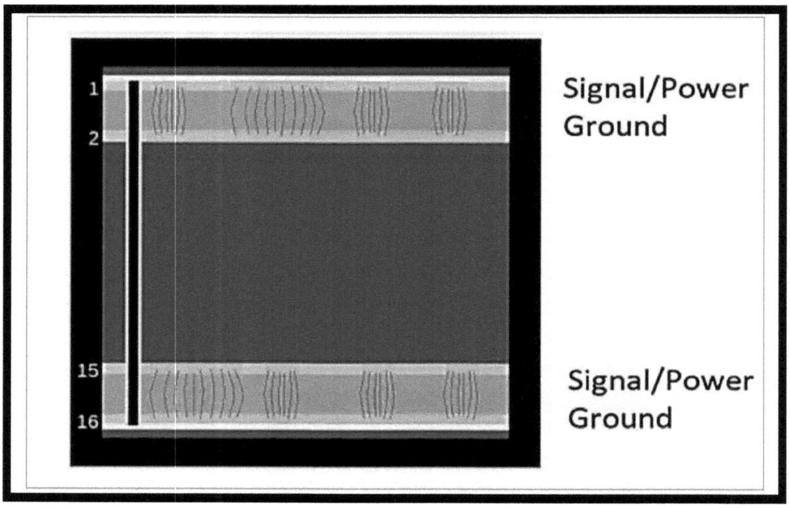

Keep in mind that by ensuring that the signal and power fields do not overlap, all of these topologies reduce the interactions between them. Let's take a closer look at a poorly designed stack of fields that overlap.

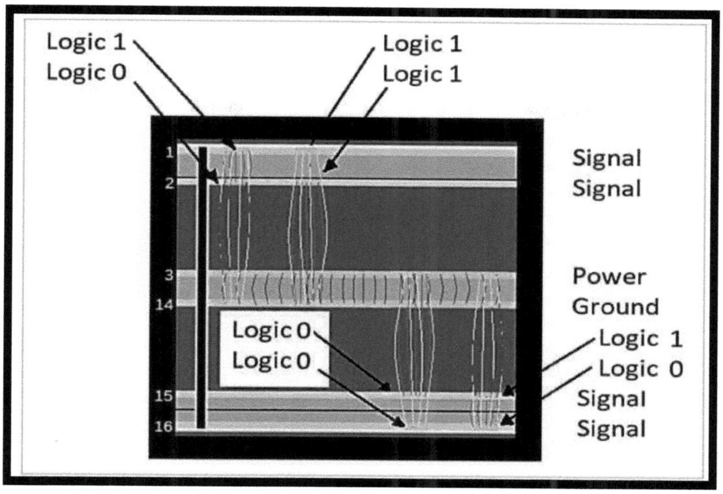

Optimizing the stack-up is the first step in creating a PCB with as few SI and PI problems as possible. Between the layers of copper are electric fields from power and signals, which induce current flow. Ensuring that electric fields are confined and do not overlap is very important. Overlapping fields due to poor stack-ups causes SI, PI, and EMI issues. Effective stack-ups reduce SI, PI, and EMI problems and closely control electric fields. Make sure your stack-up is correct.

How to Design PCBs for Harsh Environments

Any contemporary electrical gadget worth looking into will reveal that the PCB is a crucial component of the system. The materials used to make **printed circuit boards** are typically water-resistant FR-4 fiberglass, which can tolerate high temperatures and act as insulation between copper layers to reduce interference and maintain excellent signal integrity. FR-4 fiberglass is an ideal material for general-purpose PCBs because of these characteristics. They are extensively used in the majority of consumer electronics products. These qualities do have certain restrictions, however. For instance, you could want a circuit that can survive in certain severe conditions based on the planned use cases for your PCB. You'll need to take into account a few additional elements to make the circuit completely functioning under these harsh circumstances.

Harsh Environments Examples

- Extreme temperatures, both hot and cold
- Temperature or humidity fluctuations
- Rain/moist environments
- Dirt, dust, or other contaminators
- Power surges, either natural (i.e., lightning) or human-made
- Electrostatic or electromagnetic interferences

To guarantee that the finished product can last longer in such circumstances, designing a PCB that will survive severe conditions needs specialized knowledge and abilities. Let's examine the difficulties we may encounter with each circumstance and how to get through them.

Temperature

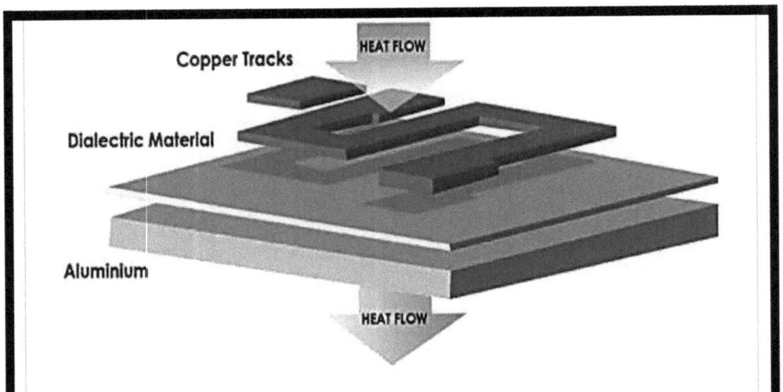

General componsition of a Aluminium Single Sided PCB

Any electrical gadget that operates, produces some heat, as you are well aware. This heat production is caused by several factors. The quantity of heat generated is insufficient to destroy a conventional circuit. Covering the unused portion of a circuit with a copper surface layer is a common method of dissipating heat from the circuit. Although the FR-4 material is not a very good heat conductor, the copper pour aids in the circuit's cooling. This method is limited in its effectiveness, however. We often use metal-clad PCBs, in which the PCB base is an electrically insulated aluminum sheet, if the heat generated is excessive. Aluminum prolongs the life of PCB components by absorbing heat much quicker than FR-4 material and preventing overheating. LED light panels are often made using aluminum printed circuit boards.

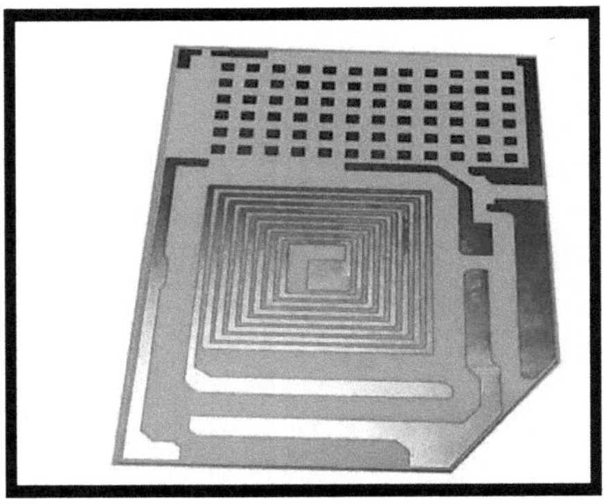

And if that's not enough, there's always the ceramic PCB to think about. The foundation of the PCB is made of ceramic and highly thermally conductive materials including beryllium oxide, alumina, and aluminum nitride (which are often coated with immersion gold). Heat can be swiftly transferred from hot spots to the whole surface via this coating. In terms of heat dissipation, ceramic provides a major advantage over more conventional materials such as FR-4 and metal-clad PCB. Since the components are directly on the boards and there is no isolation layer between them, heat can go through the board much more quickly. Furthermore, the ceramic material may be harmed by high working temperatures (up to 350°C). It's very low thermal expansion coefficient (CTE) opens up more possibilities for PCB design compatibility. Generally speaking, it is more efficient to address a problem at its root. This isn't always feasible, however.

In the case of PCBs that must function at very cold temperatures, there are many solutions available:

- The product's operating temperature rating should be tightened. If you advise users that the product must be used below +85°C, it may not need to be built for temperatures as high as **+125°C.**
- Use outside heating and cooling systems and decide whether the circuit board's temperature has to be controlled by heating, cooling, or both.
- Include components on the circuit board that can survive a broad temperature range in the design.

Moisture, Humidity, and Dust

Water, dirt, and dust are examples of natural factors that the PCB has to be protected against if it is outdoors or exposed to the environment. If you don't take any measures, you will damage the circuit or equipment.

Use conformal coatings to spray or "paint" the PCB components after assembly to keep the circuits dry and dust-free to avoid this.

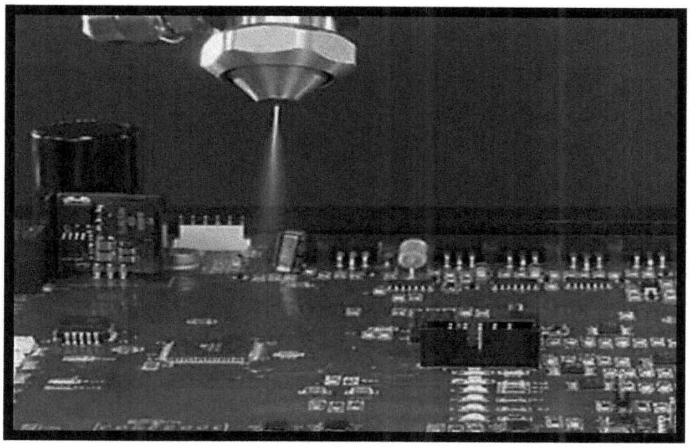

One way to keep electronic components working in less-than-ideal settings is to apply conformal coating. Each of the four main categories of conformal coatings has benefits and drawbacks.

- Acrylic Resin
- Epoxy Resin
- Silicone Resin
- Parylene

The application and its functional needs are taken into consideration while selecting the coating.

High Power Application

PCB circuits are constructed from thin copper traces, as you are well aware. Since the current flowing through a conductive material is directly proportional to the width and thickness of the trace's cross-section area, these copper traces are certified for low-power applications. The layer thickness for general-purpose PCBs is 1 oz. Therefore, to expand the cross-sectional area of the trace and enable it to carry larger currents, we can widen the trace or create many layers on the trace. If that's not a possibility, we'll need to utilize thicker PCB traces to ensure that the board can readily manage larger currents by using more copper.

Signal Interferences

The PCB will only be shielded from the elements and weather by the covering we have already covered. But sometimes, transients caused by electromagnetic interference and other factors can damage individual parts or the circuit board as a whole. Furthermore, several surge kinds can happen, thus it's critical to know how to effectively safeguard your PCBs throughout the design stage. Among surges, **electrostatic discharge (ESD)** is the most prevalent kind. A surge that damages or destroys semiconductor components can be caused by an accumulation of charge on nearby objects or persons. Particularly vulnerable components on the PCB, such as the CPU and other ICs, are harmed by ESD. Memory chips can be corrupted or erased by it. It can also cause erroneous data to appear on its properties or eventually harm the sensors. Maintaining the pad's distance from the PCB ground can help minimize ESD by preventing any shock at the input from instantly reaching every other component on the board. To safeguard the board and its delicate components, use an ESD suppressor at each external connection rather than connecting to ground.

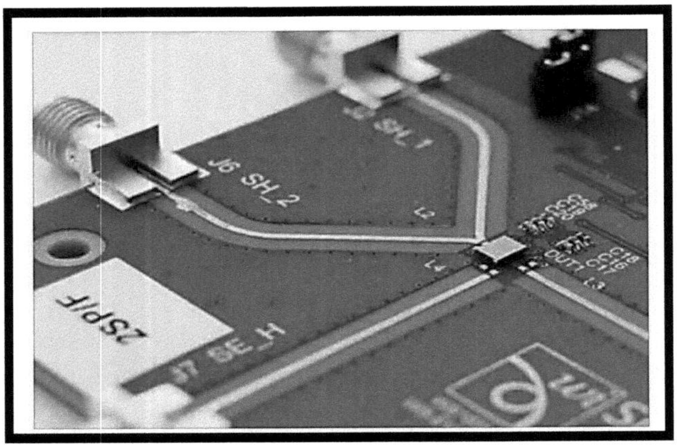

An electrical fast transient (EFT) occurs with the activation of an inductive load. Fans and water pumps, for example, are examples of inductive loads. An inductor is a large coil made of metal wires that is wound around a non-conductive core. When necessary, these inductors discharge the energy they have stored in their coil, which can potentially be harmful. In most cases, the released energy can be sent back into the circuit that controls it. The energy can seriously harm the circuit since its voltage potential is greater than the operational voltage. To prevent voltage spikes, we can add a Schottky diode, sometimes called a flyback diode, across inductive coils to stop energy from returning to the circuit. Optocouplers can also be used to provide galvanic isolation between the low and high sides.

Electromagnetic Interference

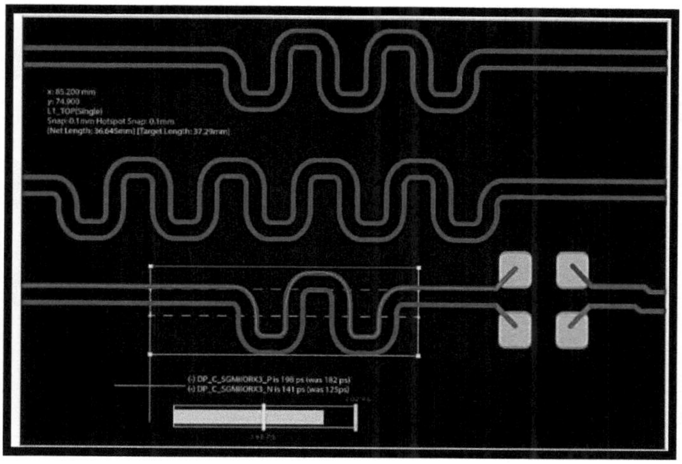

Electromagnetic disturbances also referred to as EMIs, occur when energy is transferred from one electronic equipment to another via radiation or conduction and tampers with the signal quality, leading to malfunctions. The testing specifications and interference between adjacent equipment are the main areas of EMI. It can happen at any frequency, although it's more common on high-speed, analog, and radio frequency circuits.

Consider the following design guidelines to reduce EMI in a PCB:

- The signal traces form a fully radiating antenna that is susceptible to outside noise when they intersect, bend, or form a huge loop inside the circuit.
- By adding ground planes or extending the distance between lines, parallel crosstalk caused by having the output and input traces over a long distance can be reduced.
- It is not advisable to bend the traces at a 90° angle. The corner should have a 45° gradient or be shaped like an arc.
- To minimize the interference signal coupling route, I usually advise keeping the signal lines as short as feasible. It is usually best to route sensitive and clock signal lines first. The high-speed signal lines follow, and then the unimportant signal lines.
- Using **differential pair routing** as a design approach, a balanced transmission system can be produced. Signal traces that are differential—that is, equal and opposite—are routed together to achieve this. The difference between the two lines that comprise the differential pair is interpreted as the signal at the receiving end.
- Lastly, while designing PCBs, a ground plane with a low inductance value is essential to reducing the multiplication of interference issues. A PCB's ground area can be increased to decrease the system's ground inductance, which in turn minimizes EM emission and crosstalk.

Lightning and other forces can also harm the integrity of electronics in addition to these three forms of pulses. Creating PCB designs that protect against these surges aids in preserving the efficiency and integrity of the circuit.

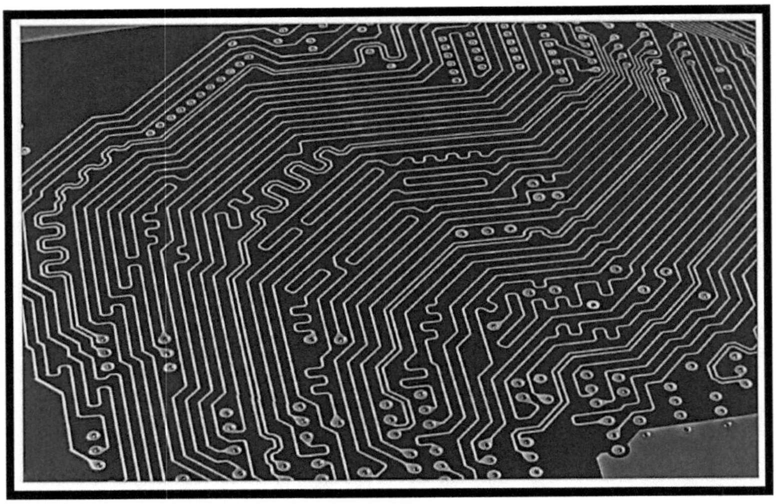

It is not an easy challenge to design PCBs that can resist all these severe conditions. To overcome these obstacles, you'll need to have some advanced knowledge and expertise. Problems become even more critical to a product's survival in severe unfavorable environments, such as the heat and dust of a desert or the frigid vacuum of space. Thus, from a design perspective, solutions become increasingly complex. Designing interconnects with the circuit diagram, including all active circuits that will operate correctly within the constraints of any permitted changes in component characteristics, is a difficulty when creating PCBs for hostile environments.

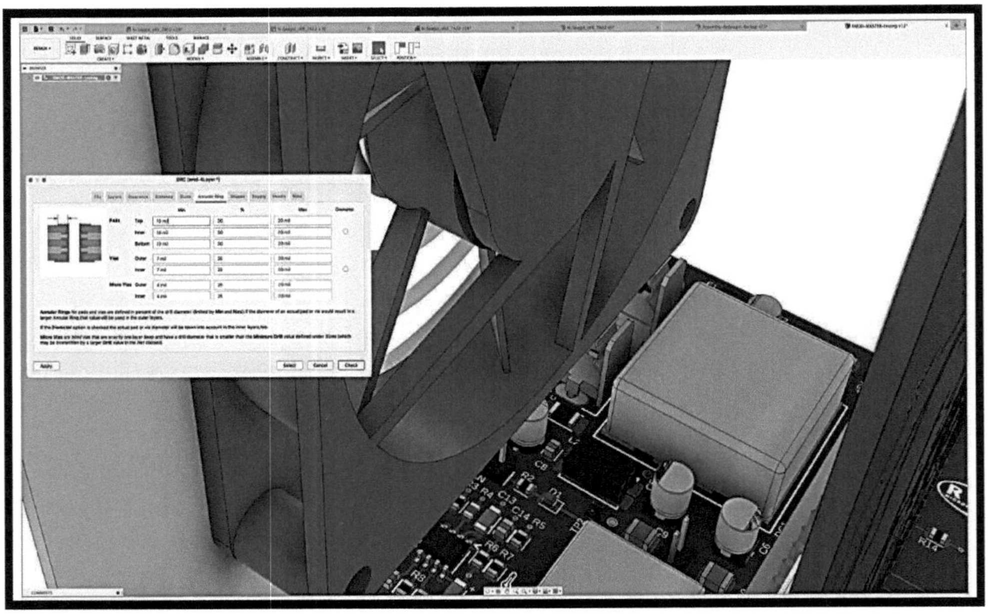

Designing Your Next Printed Circuit Board (PCB) Like a Pro

The process of developing a printed circuit board is quite labor-intensive. All the components of this jigsaw are not handled equally, however. Are you guilty of not showing the respect your PCB layout merits? You probably spend a lot of effort selecting the finest components or creating the ideal schematic. But what use is all of that information and theory if it cannot be implemented into a practical solution? Be sure you use the advice below to design your next PCB like an expert and avoid making your manufacturer and yourself both miserable with a board that's a pain to create.

Drop Those Components like It's Hot

Your components must locate their homes before you install one of those scorching copper lines. A designer must grasp problem-solving via this method, putting on the hats of both a scientist and an artist. These pointers can help to ease this delicate balancing act:

Keep your parts in the same direction

Make sure that every component of the same kind is oriented in the same direction. This will facilitate a flawless soldering procedure when your board passes through the soldering oven. You should not be shocked if your PCB has a lot of unsoldered connections if you arrange your components carelessly. The end effect is that your board is inoperable.

Place like parts together

Make careful to align any **Surface Mount (SMT)** components on the same side of your board if you want to use them. Components that are **Through-Hole (TH)** must all be positioned at the top of your board. Why do you like certain placements?

- This will enable you to use a pick-and-place machine to position your surface mount components all at once without needing to take an additional step.
- Cutting down on the amount of time you need to spend manually assembling your through-hole components, will also help you save money.
- Having components with comparable purposes on the same layer facilitates simpler manufacturing and review processes for your board.

Look one step ahead

Always consider how lengthy your traces will need to be to link your pins together while positioning your components. You can store related routing tasks in one section of your board and greatly simplify and speed up your routing process by aligning essential portions adjacent to each other.

It's Getting Hot in Here

Whatever electrical gadget has to worry about heat dissipation. Particularly when all of your busy traces and components are producing a lot of heat. As PCBs are packed progressively more tightly and enclosures are smaller, use these suggestions to reduce the heat:

Add more copper.

Do yourself a favor and add additional copper around your surface mount pads if you want to have any heat dissipation on your board. This will provide more surface area for heat dissipation. See your component datasheets for all the information you need to utilize the surface area of your pad as a heatsink.

Channel heat with vias

Vias can be used to transfer heat from one side of your PCB to the other, in case you weren't aware. This can be useful if you need to transfer some heat to the other side of your board to reduce the operating temperature of your components.

Keep those hot parts separate

Numerous components, including diodes, MOSFETs, inductors, resistors, and bridge rectifiers, generate a lot of heat. These parts should be kept apart from other heat-sensitive items like electrolytic capacitors and thermocouples. Those capacitors will begin to lose their capacity to hold a charge if they get too hot.

Just Integrate It

Integrated Circuits (ICs) provide a great deal of sophisticated capability in a tiny, portable design. However, they also provide a unique set of difficulties; some require routing hundreds of pins.

To help with your IC placement and routing, consider the following advice:

Give them some space

For ease of routing, ICs with a lot of pins—or any IC, really—need to have enough room between them on your board. Too many inexperienced designers will pack their ICs too closely together, which will leave little to no space for routing all of the necessary pins. Try to leave between each of your ICs a general buffer of **0.350" to 0.500"**, and even more room for bigger components.

Keep them in line

Try arranging your ICs in an up/down or left/right orientation to keep them neat and orderly. This will enable you to align the first pin of every IC in the same direction, which will greatly simplify your work when it comes to routing and design review.

Power with common rails

Our recommendation is to use common rails for each supply to appropriately power your ICs. To ensure that power reaches your energy-hungry integrated circuits (ICs), utilize broad, solid traces. Additionally, avoid daisy-chaining power connections between components to avoid any voltage drop problems.

Route like a Boss

Your best bet for connecting every component on your PCB layout is to use signal traces. In addition, routing your signal traces provides a wonderful chance for some structured artistic license, assuming you're an engineer like the rest of us. Keep the following advice in mind when routing your PCB layout:

Take the sharpness out of angles

In none of your signal traces, use any acute 90° angles. Because of this, maintaining the consistency of your traces' width becomes very difficult, particularly as they go thinner. Alternatively, use 45° bends to maintain a smooth flow.

Figure out those trace widths

Make sure you utilize a trace width calculator (credit to Advanced Circuits) before you put down any traces. Using this calculator will make it simple for you to figure out the necessary thickness and width for each trace depending on your unique design specifications. Use traces with bigger widths if you find that your board has more room than you anticipated since your manufacturer won't charge you more for them.

Remember where your heat goes

Remember that all of the traces on your exterior layers may cool far more effectively than the traces on your inside layers if you're designing a multilayer printed circuit board (PCB). Place those internal traces on top and bottom if at all feasible, since they have a much longer distance to travel through layers of copper and other materials before their heat can be dispersed.

Power It Up, Power it down

Even after placing all of your signal lines, you still need to worry about placing your power and ground traces so that everything is switched on. These power rails, which you can simply install with these pointers, will transmit the current required to power all of that PCB wizardry.

Current capacity is important: To meet the larger load, traces carrying a lot of current will need to be wider than conventional signal traces.

The following numbers can help you determine how broad to construct your traces for separate currents:

Trace Width and Currents Reference

• 0.010 inches	0.3 Amps
• 0.015 inches	0.4 Amps
• 0.020 inches	0.7 Amps
• 0.025 inches	1.0 Amps
• 0.050 inches	2.0 Amps
• 0.100 inches	4.0 Amps
• 0.150 inches	6.0 Amps

Keep that noise away

Make sure that any noisy ground traces are routed as far away from signals that need silence as practicable. A ground plane placed immediately underneath noisy signal traces can also be used to reduce the impedance in high-speed circuits.

Houston, We Have Liftoff

After your printed circuit board (PCB) layout is complete, you can proceed to the next, and most crucial, phase: the design review! At this point, make sure you verify once again that each signal trace's route is correctly linked. This can be accomplished by going through your schematic wire-by-wire and comparing the paths of the traces on your PCB layout with those on your schematic.

Integrating Electronics Components with Mechanical Design

To create creative products that smoothly mix digital and physical features, current engineering requires the integration of electrical components with mechanical design. Fusion 360 is a multifunctional computer-aided design (CAD) program created by Autodesk that is essential to this integration.

The Value of Combining Mechanical and Electrical Design Integration

For several reasons, mechanical design and electronics must be integrated:

1. **Functionality**: It enables engineers to design products with features like touchscreens, sensors, motors, and communication capabilities, which go beyond simple mechanical operations.

2. **Form Factor**: Good integration makes sure that the electrical parts blend in perfectly with the product's design, improving both ergonomics and looks.
3. **Performance**: Reliability and performance are maintained when electronic components are integrated properly, which guarantees that they function as best they can within the given environmental constraints.
4. **Cost-effectiveness**: By including electronics early in the design phase, possible problems can be found and expensive redesigns or changes can be avoided later in the development cycle.

Key Considerations for Integration

Planning and paying close attention to details are essential for a successful integration of electronics and mechanical design.

Here are a few important things to remember:

1. **Component Selection**: Pick small, lightweight, and application-appropriate electronic components. Take into account variables like heat dissipation, power consumption, and ambient conditions.
2. **Thermal management**: The heat produced by electronics can have an impact on the mechanical parts as well as the device's functionality. It is important to integrate cooling systems and heat sinks into the design to provide adequate thermal management.
3. **Cable Management**: Arrange for the routing and management of cables to guarantee that wires and connections are placed neatly and effectively. This makes maintenance easier and lowers the chance of interference.
4. Consider how the electronic components will be installed and accessible to perform maintenance or repairs. Access points and detachable panels are examples of design elements that can significantly impact the situation.
5. **EMI/RFI Shielding**: To stop electronic components from interfering with one another or external devices, take into account electromagnetic interference (EMI) and radio-frequency interference (RFI) shielding, depending on the application.

Utilizing Fusion 360 for Integration:

When it comes to combining electronics and mechanical design, Fusion 360 provides a wide range of capabilities and tools.

- **3D Modeling**: Fusion 360 offers a strong foundation for producing intricate 3D models of electrical and mechanical parts. This makes it possible for engineers to see how parts work together and spot any conflicts or design flaws.
- **Analysis and Simulation**: Fusion 360 has simulation tools that can be used to evaluate vibration analysis, thermal performance, and structural integrity. For integrated systems to be reliable, this is essential.
- **Electronics Design Integration**: Fusion 360's electronic design automation (EDA) tools facilitate the integration of electronic components. Printed circuit boards, or PCBs, can be designed by users and inserted straight into their mechanical assembly.

Collaboration: Cross-functional teams may collaborate easily using Fusion 360's cloud-based collaboration tools, which guarantee that mechanical and electrical design elements are in sync all the way through.

- **Manufacturability**: To expedite the production process, Fusion 360 has options for creating manufacturing documents, such as bills of materials (BOMs) and assembly drawings.
- **Version Control**: Fusion 360 provides engineers with history tracking and version control, enabling them to keep an eye on modifications and go back to earlier design iterations as necessary.

Electromechanical Integration Using Fusion 360

Conventional concepts of electromechanics are often restricted to certain component classes, such as motors, solenoids, relays, and the like, where a mechanical structure is driven by electrical forces. But electromechanics goes well beyond these discrete parts, bridging the gap between mechanical engineering, printed circuit board (PCB) design, and industrial design. In actuality, the union of electrical components and printed circuit boards with physical enclosures and mechanical pieces is what makes almost every electronic product successful. Figure 1 illustrates how a PCB is attached to a plastic enclosure using two push-button switches, four screws, and an interface jack that lines up with holes in the enclosure.

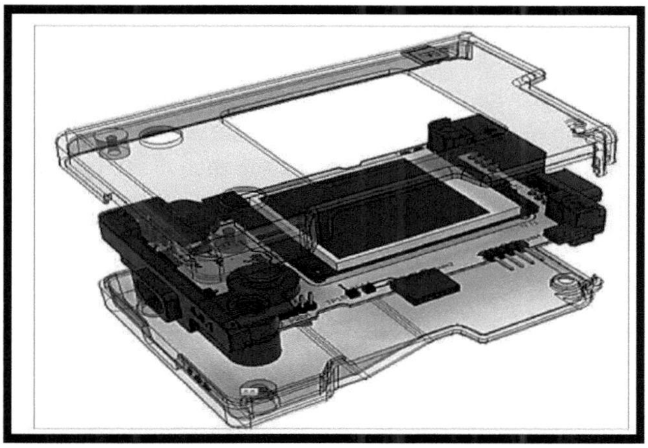

To produce such a device requires engineering efforts across multiple disciplines by designers who must collaborate to ensure their respective components interface properly. In addition to fundamental concerns for physical construction, an industrial designer must provide specifications for the device's overall shape and function. At that point, a mechanical engineer might optimize the construction for weight, strength, and manufacturing feasibility. Last but not least, an electrical engineer has to design and layout the circuit board while staying within the given physical parameters, placing each component in the most advantageous places. All of this technical work has resulted in a common electromechanical integration type that depends on highly specialized design platforms.

An Illustrative Example

Figure 2 illustrates the design of a unique medical device casing created in Autodesk Fusion 360. The gadget has two front ports, a single USB connection on the side, one square connector, four round push buttons, and a tiny LCD screen. The design was industrial and utilitarian, with filets and basic outlines. There are several interior ribs, bosses, and supports for attaching the PCB and other electrical parts.

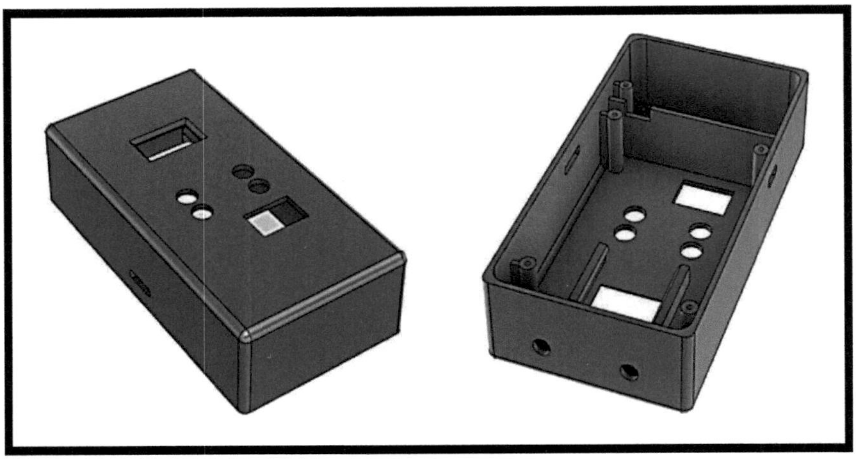

Stage 1 - Definition of Printed Circuit Board Shape

The mechanical engineer must provide the electrical engineer with a PCB board form for the electrical design process to start. This can be done in Fusion 360 in a few different methods, but the most popular one is to create an offset plane with the mounting bosses and then draw the board form on that plane. In Fusion 360's electronics persona, a command that will transform this single sketch straight into a PCB is available for further design. This procedure and the resultant 2D PCB that is prepared for handoff are shown in Figure 3.

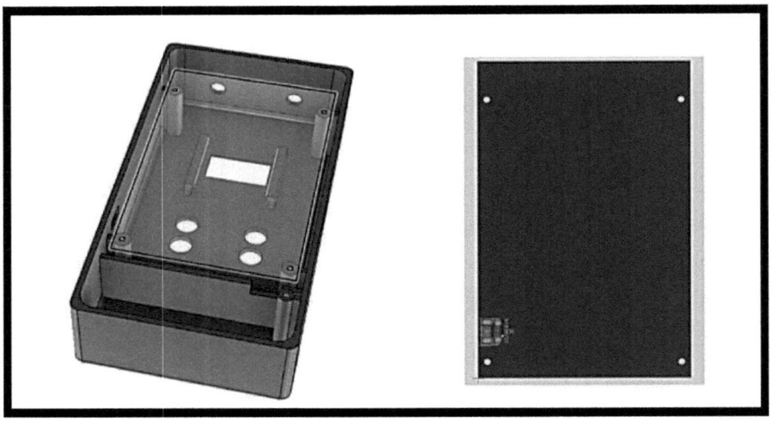

Stage 2 - Component Selection and Placement

The electrical engineer is now given the 2D PCB and utilizes the schematic to choose the proper component packages and form factors. These components are all connected to 3D body models, which can be positioned appropriately on the 2D PCB. These locations could include some electrically powered ones. A voltage regulator, for instance, may be positioned close to the battery connections, although various arrangements might be determined by the enclosure's holes and other characteristics. This data is transmitted to the 3D PCB for further examination by the mechanical team once the components have been chosen and placed on both sides of the PCB. It will be necessary to make adjustments since, as Figure 4 illustrates, the chosen USB location is not in line with the enclosure opening.

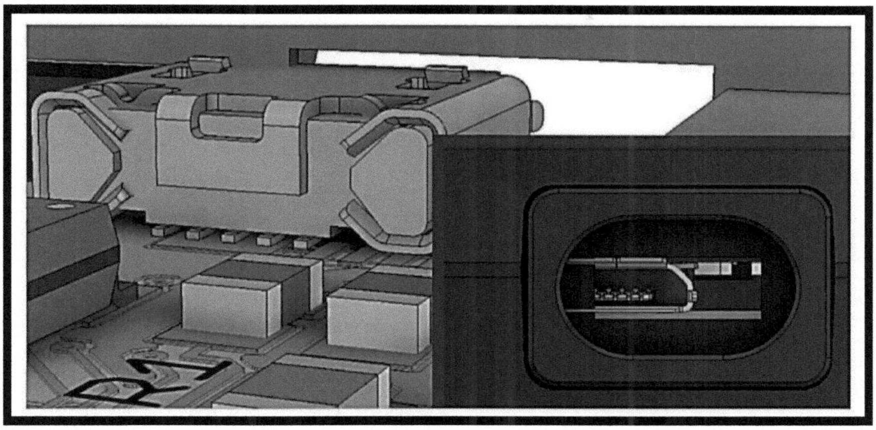

Stage 3 - Refinement of Component Placement

The mechanical team can offer refinement instructions to the electrical designers to remedy any such placement difficulties that may arise. Regarding the USB example that was shown before, the component has to be relocated to the other side of the board and adjusted in the Y direction by one hundred mils. Before the beginning of any work on the electrical routing, all of these placement difficulties must be resolved. In the absence of this precaution, a substantial amount of time and effort may be spent tearing up traces and rerouting for relatively simple component swaps. As can be seen in Figure 5, when the PCB placements have been modified, the USB connection will align exactly with the aperture of the container.

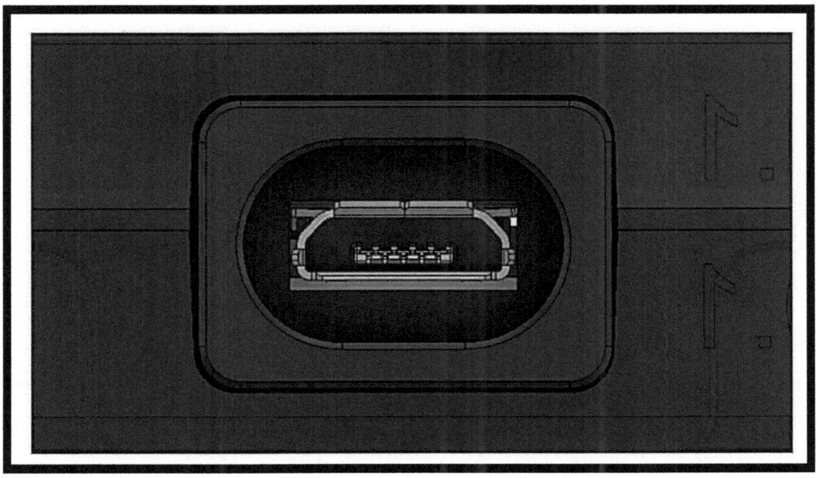

Stage 4 - Routing of PCB Traces

The electrical engineer can now lock all of the important component placements and route the PCB signals at this stage. For improved routing, passive components and other components with a lower level of importance are often allowed more freedom of movement on the printed circuit board. Because of this, a final interference check has to be done on the PCB before it can be sent out to be manufactured. The whole routed PCB has to be brought back into the 3D domain and checked for any mechanical difficulties that may arise, such as concerns with regulatory clearances and the ability to be manufactured. For example, the USB connector above may require that the PCB be inserted at an angle before securing with screws. This must be verified in Fusion 360 by analyzing the interaction of the printed circuit board (PCB) with the various components of the enclosure as it is being assembled.

Using 3D Electronic Component Models to Synch PCB and Enclosure Designs

When creating a product that combines a printed circuit board (PCB) with a mechanical enclosure, the interactions between all of the electrical elements, the circuit board, and the enclosure itself need to be thoroughly evaluated. Additionally, the design of the product has to take into account the constraints of the enclosure. This might be difficult to do because, in the world of electronics, the design process is often carried out in the 2D domain. In this domain, schematics and copper traces are developed in parallel with the primary intention of ensuring that electrical continuity is maintained. Fusion 360 takes this concept and extends it into the three-dimensional space by giving tools for modeling electrical components and parallelizing the design of the enclosure's mechanical components in such a manner that they are constantly in sync with the PCB.

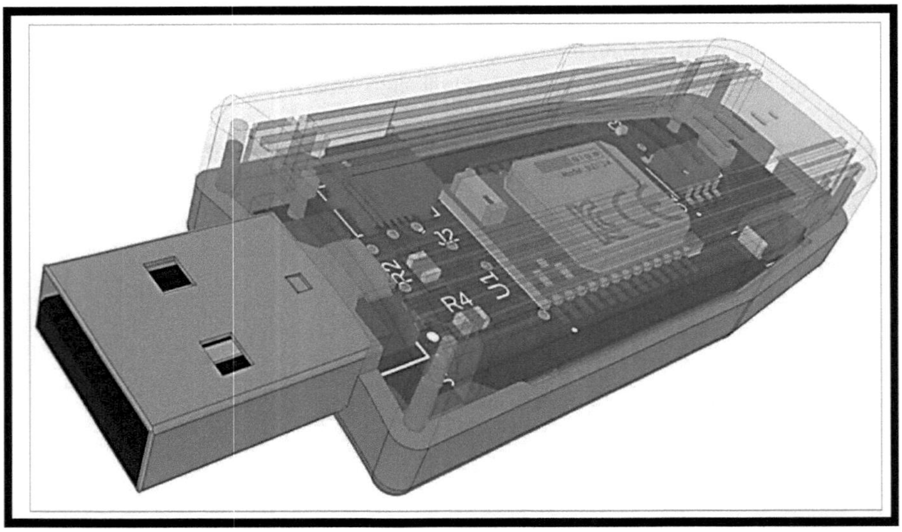

The image above illustrates an example of a USB Bluetooth attachment that is created across three domains at the same time: mechanical, electrical, and electromechanical. The enclosure connects to the printed circuit board (PCB) by the use of alignment pins made of plastic, and the USB connector extends forth from the clamshell enclosure. Multiple components, such as an intricate Bluetooth module and some passives that provide support, are represented in three dimensions and linked electronically via the traces in the printed circuit board (PCB). The printed circuit board (PCB) and the schematic can be shown in the conventional 2D electrical domain inside Fusion 360 by only switching environments.

The component outlines, the two layers of copper, the silkscreen, and the shape of the printed circuit board (PCB) can all be easily seen and changed, as illustrated in the image below. Any modifications made to the schematic are reflected in the PCB layout very quickly, and any modifications made to the PCB layout are promptly propagated to the 3D electromechanical view.

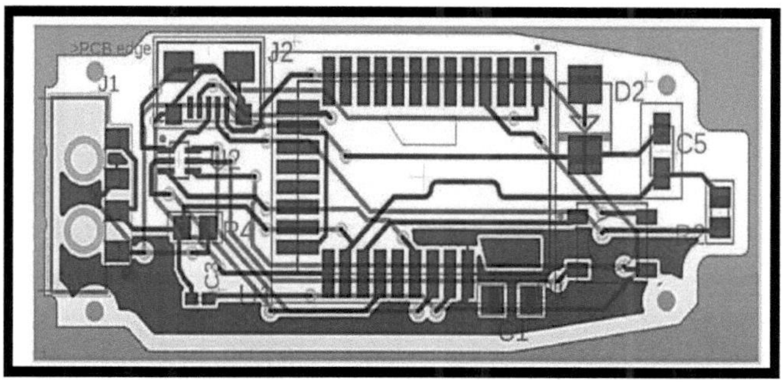

Each of the electrical components must have an exact 3D model connected to it to get the most out of this sort of capability. Importing STEP models provided by the manufacturer or developing models from scratch inside Fusion 360 are the two methods available to accomplish this goal.

Importing 3D STEP Models

STEP files, which stand for **Standard for the Exchange of Product Data**, are a popular format for the representation of 3D CAD models. These files are made available for download and import into electrical computer-aided design (ECAD) tools by a wide variety of electronic component makers. A schematic representation (also known as a symbol) and a PCB representation (also known as a footprint) are the very minimum requirements for an ECAD design, as seen in the image below. Although it is possible to assign numerous footprints to a single symbol to account for variances of a particular component, Fusion 360 needs both to ensure consistency between the PCB and the schematic.

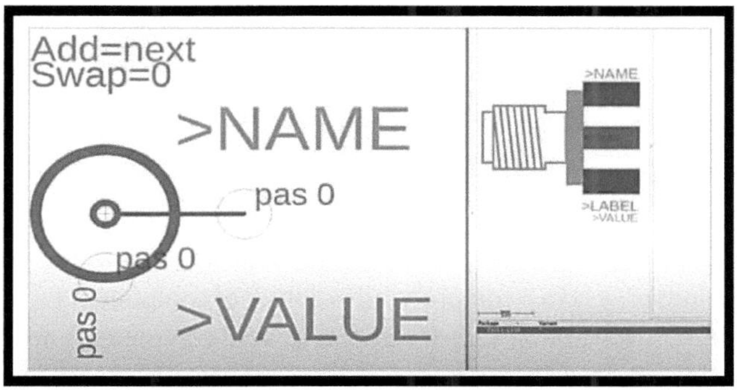

Downloading and importing the STEP file is required to complete the 3D electromechanical integration. This can be accomplished from inside the component library of the software platform, and doing so involves just a few simple steps. After the model has been imported, it has to be aligned to the footprint in the way that is seen in the image below. To put it simply, each of the PCB pads has to be physically connected to a feature somewhere on the 3D model. After this alignment has been finished, the top-level electromechanical design will immediately reflect the presence of the 3D component body.

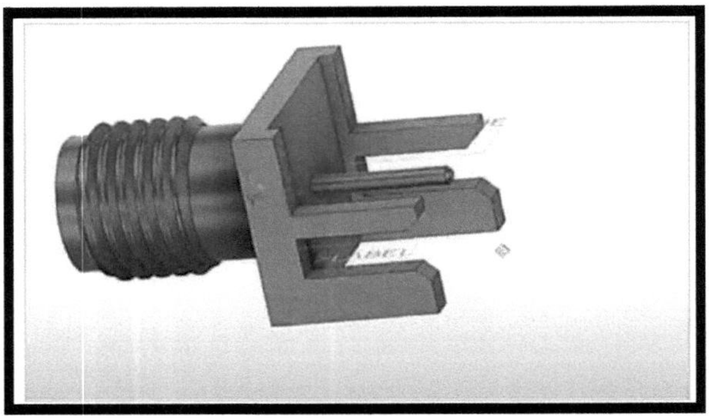

There is a good chance that a specific STEP file for an electrical item will not be accessible. This might be because the manufacturer does not supply the file or because the part is bespoke. In this instance, the 3D body generator that is included in Fusion 360 is beneficial and is based on IPC package requirements. As an example, the footprint of a typical 8-pin SOIC device is shown in the image below. It is possible to call the model generator to build an exact 3D model of this component. The settings of the model generator can then be changed so that they appropriately match the actual device.

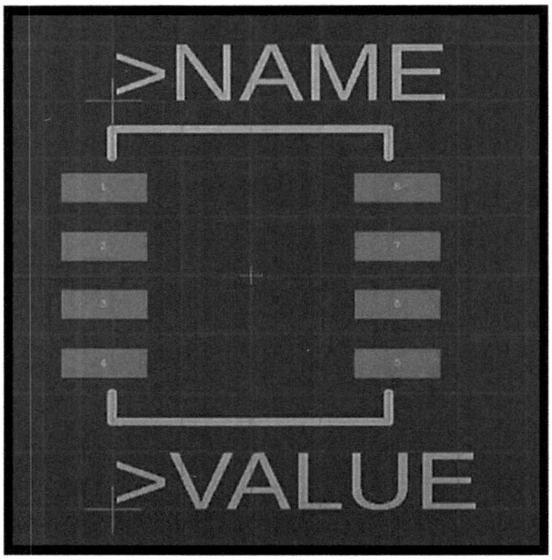

The model generator provides access to a comprehensive library of component families for users to choose from. The image below demonstrates that some examples of axial components are through-hole resistors, surface-mount passives, complicated BGA ICs, and surface-mount chip arrays. Other examples include surface mount chip arrays.

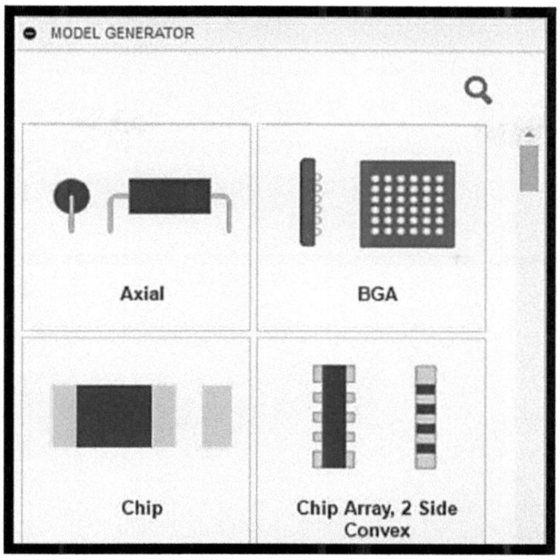

Following the selection of the SOIC family from the model generator, Fusion 360 displays a dialog box with a variety of characteristics. These parameters range from fundamental aspects such as pin count to more complicated IPC tolerances such as placement and manufacturing. The image below presents the SOIC parameters, any of which can be adjusted without much difficulty to accommodate the 8-pin device that is the focus of this discussion.

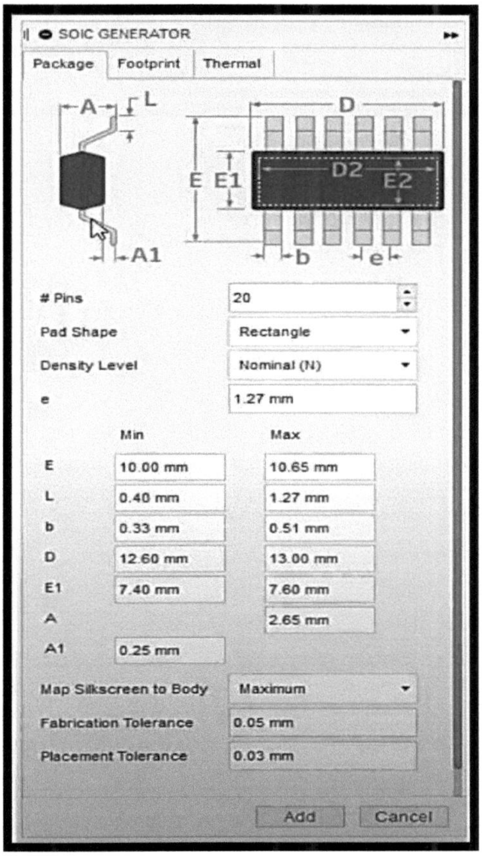

After the relevant parameters have been input to match the actual device, Fusion 360 will generate a functioning 3D representation as well as a 2D footprint model based on established approaches for the packaging of electronics. The footprint and the 3D model are both associated with the components that can be found in the library. The 8-pin SOIC chip, which can be used to verify electromechanical interference and form factor, seems to be a precise match to the 3D physical device, as illustrated in the image below.

CHAPTER 25

WORKING WITH LARGE ASSEMBLIES AND PERFORMANCE OPTIMIZATION

This chapter focuses on "**Working with Large Assemblies and Performance Optimization.**" This chapter gives significant insights into properly managing complicated assemblies inside Fusion 360. It provides methods, procedures, and guidelines for the most efficient administration of huge gatherings. You will get the knowledge necessary to simplify the structure of the assembly and effectively manage its separate components to enhance the overall workflow and performance. This chapter goes into some of the more practical methods for handling big assemblies, with a particular emphasis on arranging components, cutting down on clutter, and keeping a workstation orderly.

You will get an understanding of the significance of simplifying the assembly structure by optimizing the placement of the components, and you will use this understanding moving forward. This entails structuring the components hierarchically and logically to provide easier browsing and modification. This chapter also discusses methods for increasing overall productivity, decreasing the size of files, and improving assembly performance to achieve these goals. It addresses ways that can be used to guarantee that the program operates without any hiccups despite the presence of complicated assemblies. You will get an understanding of how to increase performance by using representations of assemblies that are both lightweight and simple. These representations make it possible to load and manipulate big assemblies more quickly without compromising the integrity of any crucial features.

Strategies for Handling Complex Assemblies

When it comes to 3D modeling and design, dealing with complicated assemblies in Fusion 360 can be a difficult but necessary component of the process. It doesn't matter whether you're creating sophisticated mechanical systems, complex architectural structures, or elaborate consumer products: having a firm grasp on the techniques for managing complex assemblies is very necessary for achieving efficiency and precision in your work. In this in-depth tutorial, we will go through a variety of different approaches and procedures that will assist you in navigating the complexities of complicated assemblies in Fusion 360.

1. **Component Organization**:

Managing complicated assemblies successfully requires a solid foundation of proper organization. To begin, you should organize the components into logical groups. To keep similar pieces together, Fusion 360 provides tools for establishing folders and sub-assemblies. To facilitate easy identification of components, give them meaningful names and labeling.

2. **Top-Down and Bottom-Up Approaches**:

The top-down and bottom-up methods of assembly design are both available to you to work with in Fusion 360. When using a top-down strategy, the primary assembly is developed first, followed by the development of the sub-components. On the other hand, the bottom-up technique begins with the design of individual components and then moves on to the assembly of those components. Pick the strategy that best accommodates the complexity of your project and the way you think about design.

3. **Simplified Representations**:

When dealing with very complicated assemblies, you can find it helpful to create simpler representations of the parts. You can conceal or simplify components in Fusion 360 that are not required for the work at hand by using the Level of Detail (LOD) tool. The performance is enhanced, and the navigation is made easier to handle as a result.

4. **Component Colors and Appearances**:

Components can be visually differentiated from one another by being given separate colors or looks. When making modifications, this can help you locate components in huge assemblies more quickly and lessen the likelihood of making mistakes.

5. **Use of Joints and Constraints**:

Fusion 360 provides users with access to a diverse collection of joint and constraint types, including cylindrical, revolute, and slider joints. If the connections between the components are not properly defined, there is a risk that they will not move or interact as planned. Be cautious to test and mimic these moves before continuing to prevent any collisions or interferences.

6. **Component Patterns**:

Make use of the pattern tools that are available in Fusion 360 for any components of your assembly that are repeated. Components can be replicated effectively using linear, circular, or mirror patterns, which helps reduce the amount of human positioning and adjustment that is required.

7. **Interference Detection**:

Conduct interference detection tests regularly to locate component conflicts and find a solution to them. The interference detection tool in Fusion 360 assists you in locating and fixing these problems, which ultimately leads to a fully working assembly.

8. **Design for Manufacturability (DFM)**:

When designing complicated assemblies, you should keep in mind the production procedures involved. The analysis of manufacturability can be performed using the tools that are provided by Fusion 360. These tools include interference checking, material selection, and weight estimate. Performing DFM optimization can result in cost reductions and improved production flow.

9. **Collaboration and Version Control**:

Complex projects almost always need some kind of teamwork to be successful. Real-time communication, version control, and file sharing among members of a team are made easier with the cloud-based Fusion

Team platform, which is connected to the Fusion 360 application. It makes it easier to guarantee that everyone is working on the most recent design modifications.

10. **Simulation and Analysis**:

Consider using the simulation and analysis tools that are available in Fusion 360 depending on the intricacy of your project. Within your assembly, they can assist you in evaluating elements like stress, heat distribution, and fluid flow, guaranteeing that your assembly will satisfy the standards for its performance.

11. **Documentation and Exploded Views**:

Generate comprehensive documentation and exploded views inside Fusion 360 to facilitate clear communication and assembly instructions. As a result, people are better able to grasp how the components fit together, which in turn makes the production process easier.

12. **Regular Backups and File Management**:

In the end, you should put in place a reliable system for managing files and a backup plan. You won't have to worry about losing data or the integrity of your projects because of the version-saving and data-management tools that Fusion 360 provides.

Managing large assemblies effectively

The ability to effectively manage big assemblies in Fusion 360 is an essential skill for anybody engaged in the 3D modeling and design process. Working with large assemblies can be difficult owing to the intricacy of the parts they include and the possibility of problems with their performance.

1. **Component Organization:**

When it comes to the management of huge assemblies, one of the most basic aspects is effectively arranging your components. Imagine that your group is organized as a hierarchy with many levels. To begin, divide the design you are working on into a series of logical sub-assemblies or groups. Not only does this make it simpler to deal with, but it also improves the general structure of the project you're working on.

2. **Simplify When Possible:**

It is easy for large assemblies to rapidly use a lot of resources, which can result in latency and poor performance. You can generate simpler versions of components in Fusion 360 by using a feature called "**Simplified Representations**," which gives you the ability to remove unneeded features for improved speed throughout the design and review processes.

3. **Use Component Suppression:**

Another useful method for controlling the presentation and behavior of components in an assembly is called suppression. To reduce the amount of computational stress placed on your system, you can suppress components that are not presently required.

4. **Level of Detail (LOD):**

You can produce several degrees of detail for your assemblies while using Fusion 360. You can create several LODs depending on criteria such as distance from the camera. This enables you to show simpler copies of your assembly when zoomed out and detailed ones when zoomed in, which dramatically increases performance. You can read more about how you can establish different LODs here.

5. **Component Patterns:**

Utilize component patterns or arrays if your assembly consists of several components that are the same or quite similar to one another. This function cuts down on the amount of separate parts that make up your assembly, which can make management and performance more straightforward.

6. **Collaboration and Data Management:**

It is very necessary for groups working on big assemblies to have effective data management. The cloud-based collaboration tools that are provided by Fusion 360 make it possible for numerous members of a team to work concurrently on the same project. This guarantees that everyone is working with the most up-to-date data and that collaboration can go without a hitch.

7. **Use Named Views:**

You can store individual camera locations, angles, and settings using the "Named Views" functionality that is included in Fusion 360. This is excellent for swiftly navigating across big assemblies, particularly if you need to return to certain sections regularly.

8. **Hardware Considerations:**

Putting together large assemblies can be taxing on the hardware of your computer. Make sure that your computer is capable of meeting or exceeding the criteria set out by Fusion 360 for the system specifications. When dealing with huge assemblies, investing in a high-performance workstation that has enough RAM and a fast graphics card can substantially enhance your experience with the task at hand.

9. **Regularly Save and Backup:**

It is essential that your work be saved often and that backups be kept for every complicated project you undertake. Even though Fusion 360 features an automatic saving mechanism, it is still a good idea to save your work manually and keep track of different versions in case any data is accidentally deleted.

10. **Rendering and Visualization:**

When working with big assemblies, the use of rendering and visualization tools that operate in real-time can be advantageous. Fusion 360 gives you choices for realistic rendering, which you can use to get a better sense of how your design will look after it's finished.

Streamlining assembly structure and components

1. **Establish a Clear Design Hierarchy:**
   - To begin, you need to establish a distinct hierarchy for your assembly. To achieve this, the design has to be disassembled into its many sub-assemblies, pieces, and components.
   - Make certain that the hierarchy accurately depicts the structure of your product in the actual world. This will ensure that it is easy for everyone who is working on the project to comprehend.
2. **Use Standardized Naming Conventions:**
   - Components and sub-assemblies should all adhere to a naming standard that is both consistent and understandable.
   - You should include information such as part numbers, descriptions, and revision numbers in the names of the components so that it is simple to identify individual parts and conduct a search for them.
3. **Component Reusability:**
   - To encourage reuse, components should be designed such that they can be utilized in several different assemblies.
   - To generate instances of components that are based on a master component, you can use the "Derived" capability that is included in Fusion 360. This guarantees that all of the assemblies are consistent and makes it easier to make modifications.
4. **Keep Components Modular:**
   - Make sure that each component is designed to be modular, which means that it only carries out one function or serves one particular purpose. The process of diagnosing and replacing or upgrading components is facilitated as a result of this simplification.
5. **Component Simplification:**
   - Reduce the amount of complexity that each component has. Take away any features, fillets, chamfers, or internal elements that aren't essential and don't add anything to the functioning or appearance of the product.
   - To generate simpler versions of components that will perform better in big assemblies, you should use the "Simplify" tool that is included in Fusion 360.
6. **Standard Fasteners and Hardware:**
   - To prevent unnecessary duplication of effort, use only standardized fasteners and hardware components. The libraries that come with Fusion 360 provide a diverse selection of standard components.
   - Establish a centralized repository for the hardware that is regularly utilized to guarantee consistency.
7. **Component Suppression and Level of Detail:**
   - Making use of component suppression to deactivate unused components in the assembly when doing so will not compromise the integrity of the system.
   - To switch between simple and detailed views of components depending on your requirements, you need to implement Level of Detail (LOD) representations for the components.
8. **Group and Mate Components Logically:**
   - Get your assembly organized by putting similar parts together in the same group. This not only makes it easy to pick and modify pieces, but it also makes navigating simpler.

- When defining component connections, you should use logical mates. The "As-Built" joint in Fusion 360 is useful for correctly locating components without restricting the mobility of those components.

9. **Document and Annotate:**
   - To record component interactions, tolerances, and assembly instructions, you should create assembly drawings with comprehensive views and comments.
   - Using the drawing tools in Fusion 360, you can develop manufacturing documentation that is both accurate and thorough.
10. **Collaboration and Version Control:**
    - When working in a group, make sure everyone has access to the most recent design data by using the cloud-based collaboration tools that are provided by Fusion 360.
    - Put in place version control so that changes can be monitored and a history of design iterations can be kept.
11. **Regular Audits and Maintenance:**
    - At regular intervals, do an audit of your assembly's structure and the components to search for more possibilities to streamline.
    - Remove any components that are no longer needed or no longer supported, and make sure your hierarchy stays orderly.
12. **Performance Optimization:**

- When dealing with big assemblies, be sure to monitor the operation of the system. Adjust the settings for the visuals, simplify the components as required, and take into consideration upgrading the hardware if necessary.

Techniques for Reducing File Size and Enhancing Performance

Optimizing assembly performance

For users working on complicated design projects in Autodesk Fusion 360, one of the most important tasks is to optimize the performance of the assembly. Even though Fusion 360 is a strong and adaptable computer-aided design (CAD) program, performance can become an issue as assemblies get more complicated. It is vital to use a variety of tactics and approaches to properly maximize assembly performance to guarantee that the workflow will be smooth and effective.

1. **Component Simplification**: Simplifying Individual Components within Your Assembly Your first step should be to simplify each of the components that make up your assembly. There is a function in Fusion 360 called "**Simplify**" that gives you the ability to generate representations of components that are simpler. Make use of this function to simplify some components, particularly those that are not required for the stage of design that you are now working on. This simplification will result in a considerable reduction in the amount of necessary computing work.
2. **Level of Detail (LOD) Representations**: Make the most of the LOD representations that are available in Fusion 360. LOD enables the creation of numerous variants of an assembly, each of which may have a different degree of detail. Use representations with a lower level of detail (LOD) while you are working on certain aspects of your design to lessen the amount of computational work that has to be done. Save the higher LODs for final evaluations and presentations.

3. **Suppress or Isolate Components**: Components That Are Not Directly relevant to the present Design job Should Be Suppressed or Isolated For the Time Being Suppress or isolate components that are not directly relevant to the present design job. Your assembly will be more responsive as a result, and this eliminates the need for any extra computations. Make use of the context menu that appears when you right-click inside the browser to easily hide or isolate components as required.
4. **Use Assemblies and Subassemblies**: Organize the components of your design into subassemblies that make sense. This contributes to the more effective management of complicated tasks. By combining similar components into a single set, known as a subassembly, a main assembly's workload can be lightened, and the design hierarchy can be made more straightforward.
5. **Component Optimization**: Simplify the geometry of the individual components and reduce the number of polygons they include to optimize their performance. Utilize the "Mesh to BRep" function to transform components of your mesh into BRep bodies, which are more computationally efficient. In addition, get rid of any fillets and chamfers that aren't essential and aren't contributing to the functioning of your design.
6. **Graphics and Display Settings**: You can improve performance by adjusting the graphics and display settings. When working on big assemblies, decreasing the amount of detail shown in the graphics, turning off shadows, and switching to the "Shaded with Edges" mode from the "Shaded" option can dramatically increase the responsiveness of the program.
7. **Hardware Considerations**: Check to see that the hardware on your computer either meets or exceeds the specifications set out by Fusion 360 for the system. Having a fast CPU, enough random access memory (RAM), and a graphics card that is solely devoted to rendering can make a significant difference in speed, particularly when working with big assemblies.
8. **Save Incrementally**: Do not forget to save your work regularly and make good use of the version history. This enables you to return to earlier design phases if necessary while preventing the present assembly from being bogged down by a large version history.
9. **Use Simplified Reps in Drawings**: When Creating Drawings of Your Assembly, Use Simple Reps Instead of the entire Assembly Model to create drawings of your assembly, use simple representations rather than the entire assembly model. When working on drawings, the program will experience less strain as a result of this change.
10. **Network and Cloud Settings**: You will need to adjust the settings for both your network and your cloud storage. Be sure that your instance of Fusion 360 is not continuously synchronizing data, since this can have a negative influence on performance while you are actively designing.

Using lightweight and simplified representations

Utilizing representations that are lightweight and simple is a crucial strategy for improving assembly speed in Autodesk Fusion 360. The use of these representations enables designers to achieve a compromise between the essential level of detail that must be maintained and the reduced computational needs that must be met, which ultimately results in a design process that is more streamlined and effective.

In this section, we will go into the intricacies of how to successfully employ lightweight and simple representations:

1. **Lightweight Representations:**
   - **Purposeful Component Selection**: Identify components inside your design that can be assembled as lightweight. These are often components that do not demand a high degree of

detail for the design process that is currently underway. If you right-click on a component in the browser Fusion 360 and pick "Set as Lightweight," the software will automatically simplify the geometry and lower the computational cost for that section.

- **Selective Detailing:** You can pick which details to keep and which features to reduce when constructing lightweight representations. The amount of detail for features like holes, fillets, and chamfers can be adjusted using the choices that are provided by Fusion 360. This degree of control guarantees that essential components of the design will be protected while simultaneously enhancing performance.
- **Regular Updates:** As your design progresses, it is important to regularly examine and update any lightweight representations. When particular components attain a higher level of significance, you will be able to convert them back to full detail as required.

2. **Simplified Representations:**
   - **Creating simpler Versions:** Fusion 360 allows you to build simpler versions of your whole assembly using its "Creating Simplified Versions" feature. This can reduce the amount of work that has to be done on the computer by eliminating some components or replacing them with simpler ones. To generate a representation that is easier to understand, go to the "Assemble" tab, click the "Simplify" button, and then follow the on-screen instructions.
   - **Hierarchical Approach**: When developing complicated Products If you are developing complicated products, you should consider using a hierarchical approach to simplifying representations. To do this, numerous degrees of simplification need to be created. For instance, you can have a version that is very simplified for the first exploration of the idea, a version that is simplified to a medium degree for the design refining, and a version that is highly detailed for the final presentation.
   - **Interference Checks**: Even though components are being simplified, it is very necessary to do regular checks for interferences between the parts in simplified representations. Fusion 360 has tools for interference detection that can operate with reduced representations, guaranteeing that your design will continue to perform as intended even after it has been modified.
   - **Alternative Materials**: In Simplified Representations Not only can you reduce the geometry, but you can also apply alternative materials to individual components. This can help differentiate between materials used in the prototype and those used in the production, which is beneficial for both cost analysis and weight estimate.
3. **Performance Benefits:**
   - **Enhanced Responsiveness**: Making use of lightweight and streamlined representations is one of the best ways to greatly increase the responsiveness of the Fusion 360 assembly you're working on. This becomes most apparent while traveling, turning, or making modifications to the design.
   - **Faster Load Times**: Loading assemblies that use simplified representations happen more quickly, which makes it simpler to access and work on your design without having to wait for extended periods.
   - **Collaboration Efficiency**: Since sharing simplified representations cuts down on file sizes and makes it simpler to express design intent, there is an increase in the efficiency with which team members or other stakeholders can work together.
   - **Improved Presentation:** When it's time to show or share your design with others, you can switch to higher-detail representations for a polished, professional appearance without sacrificing real-time performance while you're working on the design. This feature allows you to display your design in a more polished and professional manner.

In conclusion, one of the most important best practices for improving the speed of an assembly in Autodesk Fusion 360 is to make strategic use of representations that are lightweight and simple. It provides designers with the ability to keep control over the amount of detail while also ensuring that the program operates smoothly, which ultimately results in design processes that are more effective and productive.

Simplifying and Representing Large Assemblies

When it comes to effectively managing complicated projects with Autodesk Fusion 360, one of the most important aspects is the ability to simplify and depict huge assemblies. When dealing with significant assemblies, it is very necessary to use tactics that will expedite the design process, improve performance, and make it easier for people to work together. **Let's look at several ways to simplify and represent huge assemblies, as well as some of the considerations that go into doing so:**

1. **Hierarchical Structure:**

Create a framework for your assembly that is hierarchical and consists of subassemblies and components by organizing it. Because of this structure, the administration of huge projects is made much easier, the clarity of the design is enhanced, and it is much simpler to concentrate on individual components of the assembly.

2. **Simplified Components:**

Locate components within your assembly that can be simplified without affecting the overall reliability of the design. Take into consideration the following strategies:

- **Level of Detail (LOD) Representations:** To transition between high-detail and low-detail versions of components, you need to create LOD representations. Having this capability enables you to work with streamlined versions throughout the design phase, and then transition to working with comprehensive information for the final analysis or presentations.
- **Suppressing or Isolating Components**: Temporarily suppress or isolate components that are not directly related to the design job that you are working on at the moment. This reduces the amount of computing work that has to be done and makes the assembly more responsive.
- **Using Simplify Workspace**: Fusion 360 has a workspace called "**Simplify**," in which users can methodically reduce components by merging bodies, deleting features, or lowering the geometric complexity of their designs. This is especially helpful for sections that are both complex and substantial.

3. **Lightweight Mode:**

Turn on the "**Lightweight**" mode for any subassemblies or components that do not need to be updated often. This mode lightens the burden on the computer by showing the components in a more straightforward fashion, which also makes the interactions more fluid.

4. **Simplified Representations:**

Develop representations of the complete assembly that are simpler. This includes making simultaneous reductions in the degree of detail for numerous components at the same time. Fusion 360 provides users with the tools necessary to quickly generate these representations.

5. **Section Analysis:**

Make use of the "**Section Analysis**" tool to single out certain aspects of the assembly for further in-depth investigation. Working on a more manageable chunk of content at one time can help improve both productivity and concentration.

6. **Visual Styles:**

Adjust the options for the visual style to get the best possible performance. When you need to work on complicated components, or when real-time rendering is not required, switch to a visual style that uses wireframes or concealed lines.

7. **Configuration Management:**

Utilize the "Configure" tool to effectively handle a large number of various configurations or variants of your assembly if it is very big. This gives you the ability to swap between setups without having to load all of the components at the same time.

8. **Hardware Considerations:**

When working with big assemblies, it is extremely important to check that the system requirements of Fusion 360 are met or exceeded by the hardware of your computer. Performance can be substantially improved with a powerful graphics card, a sufficient amount of RAM, and a faster CPU.

9. **Collaboration and Sharing:**

When working on a project with other members of your team or sharing your design with others outside of your organization, you can consider providing a reduced version of the assembly to cut down on the file size and speed up the data interchange. The cloud collaboration capabilities of Fusion 360 ensure a smooth flow throughout this procedure.

10. **Regular Optimization:**

Review the assembly regularly and make adjustments as needed so that it can accommodate any changes to the design. Eliminate any features, components, or specifics that aren't essential for the present phase of the project and have become irrelevant as a result.

Representing complex assemblies efficiently

A critical ability for designers and engineers who want to improve the efficiency of their workflow, guarantee that their models are correct, and make it easier for others to work together is the ability to effectively depict complicated assemblies in Fusion 360.

1. **Component Organization:** If you want to properly handle complicated assemblies, the first step is to organize your components methodically. You can organize your pieces into subassemblies using Fusion 360's hierarchical structure, which the program provides. Taking this method not only makes your design more comprehensible but also makes navigating it simpler. You will be able to develop a straightforward assembly that other people can comprehend if you structure your model in this manner.
2. **Component Naming:** Naming conventions play a crucial part in the efficiency of the assembly process. Make sure to give each component a name that is understandable and specific. Steer clear of terminology that is too vague or general, and make sure there is coherence across the whole assembly. By following this procedure, certainly, everyone working on the project can easily recognize and comprehend the function of each component.
3. **Component Suppression:** Suppressing components is a feature that is available in Fusion 360, and it allows you to temporarily hide components. Because it lowers the amount of computational overhead, this function is quite helpful when working on complicated assemblies. The performance of the software used during assembly processes will be improved as a result of suppressed components not being included in simulations or drawings.
4. **Simplified Representations:** When dealing with complex assemblies of a big scale, you should think about employing simplified representations. These lightweight versions of your assembly only include the necessary components; this makes it much simpler to work with the model

without compromising its level of accuracy. When working together with other members of the team on less powerful gear, this is a really helpful feature.

5. **Component Patterns:** Leverage component patterns to speed up the assembly process. Patterns can be created with Fusion 360 in several different ways, including linear, circular, and mirror patterns. You can repeat components without the need for manual duplication if you use them properly, which will save you time and reduce the danger of mistakes.
6. **Design for Manufacturability (DFM):** During the design process, you should always have manufacturability in the back of your mind. This is known as "design for manufacturability," or DFM. This strategy can reduce the complexity of your assembly by removing any extra components or features that aren't essential. The procedure can be made more straightforward by designing components that are straightforward to produce and put together.
7. **Design Variants:** Because Fusion 360 supports parametric modeling, you can develop design versions for an assembly even if it is the same model. By setting criteria and tying them to other components or features, you can explore multiple design alternatives without cluttering the workspace with superfluous pieces by doing so.
8. **Subtractive Assembly Modeling:** When modeling assemblies with intricate geometries, subtractive assembly modeling is an option to explore. This entails producing pieces as the consequence of subtracting one body from another, which can lower the total number of components and make the assembly process more efficient. It is particularly helpful for pieces that are complicated and interlock with one another.
9. **Component Relationships:** Make intelligent use of assembly limitations and connections between components. To specify how components interact with one another, Fusion 360 provides several different sorts of constraints, such as mate, flush, and tangent. To prevent misalignments or collisions, you must make sure that these connections appropriately reflect the assembly in the actual world.
10. **Documenting Assembly Instructions:** To make cooperation and assembly by others easier, develop assembly instructions inside Fusion 360 that are simple and to the point. Make use of the tools that are already integrated into the software to create assembly drawings, exploded views, and step-by-step animations. This documentation contributes to the process of ensuring that your assembly is appropriately understood and created.

CHAPTER 26

CASE STUDIES AND REAL-WORLD APPLICATIONS

This chapter demonstrates the adaptability of Fusion 360 across a variety of different fields and gives you some useful insights into how Fusion 360 can be used in real-world design situations. It investigates how Fusion 360 can be used in the process of product design for consumer goods. It emphasizes how the software can be used to handle the particular issues and needs connected with the design of consumer items. These challenges and requirements include concerns for aesthetics, functionality, and the user experience. You will get a grasp of how Fusion 360 can be utilized to address certain design difficulties that are often seen in the consumer products market. This can involve factors like ergonomics, the selection of materials, and the viability of the production process. This course explores the convergence of engineering and industrial design ideas via the use of the software Fusion 360. It highlights how important it is to design products that are not only useful but also aesthetically pleasing and easy to use for the final consumer. This chapter demonstrates how to put Fusion 360 to work in the real world by building products that achieve a balance between beauty and utility using the software. This section highlights the tools and features included in the program that contribute to the accomplishment of these objectives. You will be led through the process of developing a functioning prototype with Fusion 360 by way of a step-by-step case study that is presented to you. This hands-on example demonstrates how design concepts and best practices can be used successfully while using the software during the prototype phase by including them in the example itself. Another case study is presented in this chapter, and it focuses on using Design for Manufacturing and Assembly (DFMA) approaches inside Fusion 360. It demonstrates how the software can be used to simplify production and assembly procedures, which will eventually result in manufacturing that is both cost-effective and efficient.

Designing Consumer Products with Fusion 360

Applying Fusion 360 to Consumer Goods Design

The design of consumer goods is a multi-faceted discipline that involves the construction of products that are meant for usage by the general population. These products can consist of everything from electronics and home appliances to furnishings, cookware, and even clothing and accessories. The design of aesthetically pleasing, useful, and user-friendly consumer items must also take into account their capacity to be mass-produced. Fusion 360 is the perfect tool for thoroughly addressing these design considerations.

Key Features of Fusion 360 for Consumer Goods Design

1. **Parametric Modeling:**

Because it supports parametric modeling, Fusion 360 enables designers to construct 3D models with parameters that can be modified in a variety of ways. This capability is especially helpful for the design of consumer products since it makes it possible to do fast iterations of the design to fine-tune the product's size and features.

2. **Realistic Rendering:**

To attract customers, consumer items need to have an attractive appearance. The rendering tools that are included in Fusion 360 provide designers with the ability to generate lifelike renderings of their products. This facilitates the successful presentation of design ideas to stakeholders as well as prospective clients.

3. **Collaboration and Cloud-Based Storage:**

Collaboration is very necessary in the design of consumer products since the process often includes interdisciplinary teams working together on a single project. The cloud-based platform that Fusion 360 uses enables real-time collaboration, which ensures that all members of the team have access to the most recent design modifications and can continue to work on them.

4. **Simulation and Analysis:**

It is of the utmost importance to check that consumer items are structurally sound and adhere to all applicable safety regulations. Fusion 360 provides tools for simulation and analysis that can assist product designers in evaluating internal aspects of a product, such as issues relating to stress, thermal performance, and fluid flow.

5. **CAM (Computer-Aided Manufacturing) Integration:**

When the design is complete, Fusion 360 can go on to the next step, which is the production phase, without any hitches. Its CAM features help in the generation of toolpaths for CNC machines and 3D printers, which ensures the exact fabrication of prototypes and final products.

6. **Design Optimization:**

The generative design elements included in Fusion 360 make use of AI algorithms to provide suggestions for designs that are ideal depending on the parameters you specify. This can lead to designs for consumer items that are inventive and efficient, hence lowering the amount of material waste and the costs of manufacturing.

7. **Customization and Personalization:**

Customization is a factor in the design of many consumer items. It is possible to create parametric models in Fusion 360, which can then be readily modified to fit the specific tastes of individual customers, hence increasing the desirability of the product.

Workflow in Fusion 360 for Consumer Goods Design

1. **Conceptualization:** The first step in the conceptualization process for designers is to draw their ideas inside Fusion 360. The sketching tools in the program make it possible to create designs in two dimensions that can then be expanded into three dimensions.

2. **Prototyping:** When it comes to prototyping after a basic design has been developed, designers can utilize the parametric modeling feature of Fusion 360 to produce 3D models. These models can undergo iterative refining, during which elements like ergonomics and aesthetics can be taken into consideration.
3. **Simulation and Analysis:** To test the functionality and security of the consumer items they create, designers use computer simulations. For instance, stress testing can be used to locate vulnerable areas in the construction of a product.
4. **Rendering and Visualization:** When presenting the design idea to stakeholders or for use in marketing, high-quality renders are created as part of the rendering process. The rendering tools in Fusion 360 make it simple to generate pictures and animations that have a lifelike appearance.
5. **CAM Integration:** After the design has been validated, Fusion 360 offers assistance in the generation of toolpaths for production machinery. The transition from design to manufacturing is streamlined as a result of this.
6. **Collaboration:** The cloud-based infrastructure that Fusion 360 utilizes makes it possible to collaborate at any stage of the design process. Feedback can be provided by designers, engineers, and other stakeholders in real-time, and any required adjustments can be made.
7. **Customization:** Fusion 360's parametric modeling and scripting features allow the production of design variants that can suit individual tastes and are useful for products that provide customization possibilities.

Addressing design challenges and requirements

Using the 3D modeling and CAD software Fusion 360 from Autodesk, which is very adaptable, successfully meeting design difficulties and requirements calls for a mix of innovative problem-solving and the efficient use of the product's capabilities. Fusion 360 offers a powerful platform for developing, visualizing, and modeling the performance of goods while adhering to predetermined design standards. Let's investigate the many ways in which Fusion 360 can be used to address design issues and meet needs that are specific to this program.

Identifying Design Challenges

1. **Complex Geometries:** It may be difficult to design goods with complicated or complex designs, particularly when using typical CAD tools that struggle to handle such geometries well. This can make the task more difficult.
2. **Material Selection:** Selecting the appropriate materials to satisfy design parameters, such as those about cost, weight, and strength, is of the utmost importance. Maintaining a healthy equilibrium between all of these aspects may be difficult.
3. **Prototyping Costs:** Developing physical prototypes may be a time- and money-consuming and costly process. It is vital to reduce the number of prototypes while maintaining a high level of design correctness.
4. **Simulation and Analysis:** Robust simulation and analysis skills are required to guarantee that the product will operate as expected in addition to meeting all applicable safety and performance criteria.
5. **Collaboration:** Without the Right Tools, Collaborating Effectively Among Design Teams, Engineers, and Stakeholders Who Are Often Located in Different Locations Can Be a Challenging Task.

Addressing Design Challenges with Fusion 360

1. **Complex Geometries:**
   - Parametric Modeling: Fusion 360 excels in parametric modeling, making it easy for designers to develop and alter complicated shapes. This feature enables designers to rapidly prototype their ideas.
   - Generative Design: Use Fusion 360's generative design feature to automatically produce creative and effective design solutions based on particular criteria. This feature is available inside Fusion 360.
2. **Material Selection:**
   - **Material Libraries:** Fusion 360 comes with a vast collection of material libraries, which makes it much simpler to choose the materials that are most suited for your design.
   - **Simulation:** The simulation capabilities in Fusion 360 can be used to determine how the use of various materials will impact the product's performance as well as its longevity.
3. **Prototyping Costs:**
   - **Virtual Prototyping:** Fusion 360's capabilities include the ability to create virtual prototypes, which eliminates the need for physical prototypes. When it comes to the design process, this helps save both time and money.
   - **3D Printing Integration:** If you need to create physical prototypes, Fusion 360 interfaces with 3D printing technologies, which enables you to do it in a way that is both quick and inexpensive.
4. **Simulation and Analysis:**
   - **Integrated Simulation:** Fusion 360 has capabilities for integrated simulation, which enable designers to examine and optimize their designs about elements like stress, thermal performance, and fluid dynamics. These capabilities are provided by Fusion 360.
   - **Finite Element Analysis (FEA):** The advanced FEA tools that are included in Fusion 360 assist in confirming that the product complies with all of the applicable safety and performance criteria.
5. **Collaboration:**
   - **Cloud-Based Collaboration:** Regardless of Location Fusion 360 works in the cloud, making it possible for design teams to collaborate in real time regardless of where they are physically located.
   - **Version Control:** Fusion 360 has facilities for version control, which ensures that all users are working on the most recent iteration of the design.

Meeting Design Requirements

1. **Aesthetics:** The rendering and visualization features in Fusion 360 enable designers to generate photorealistic 3D renderings and animations, which help guarantee that the final product has a pleasing appearance.
2. **Customization:** Make use of the parametric modeling and scripting features offered by Fusion 360 to develop designs that can be quickly modified to accommodate the specific tastes of individual customers.
3. **Regulatory Compliance:** Fusion 360 includes capabilities that aid in annotating and explaining how a design complies with regulatory standards. It also helps users to record modifications to designs and document those changes.

4. **Sustainability:** Use Fusion 360 to analyze the potential effects of your design choices on the environment, including how they will affect the selection of materials and the execution of manufacturing processes.
5. **Cost Efficiency:** The cost analysis capabilities in Fusion 360 can assist designers in optimizing their designs to achieve more cost-effectiveness without sacrificing quality.

The Fusion 360 Product Design Extension

The Fusion 360 Product Design Extension is geared toward streamlining and simplifying the design process for consumer goods, as well as automating it. You now have access to design tools that automate and simplify the process of creating features that are aware of the production process. You will also acquire the ability to gather design knowledge to make certain that the plastic components you create can be manufactured.

What kind of features can users expect to see in the Fusion 360 Product Design Extension?

Materials with Intelligence

When making a plastic component, making the right choice of material is essential. The Fusion 360 Product Design Extension requires that you identify material at an early stage in the design process because of this reason. This is the point at which the magic begins. When you create a component out of sheet metal, for instance, choosing the material of the part will let you build up rules that will automate certain characteristics. The wall thickness, draft angles, fillet radius, and other dimensions are among them.

As a result, one of the advantages of switching from one kind of plastic material to another is that your plastic features will be automatically updated following the requirements for the new material. If you have any possible problems with face drafts, wall thickness, knife edges, or undercuts, these material rules can provide design suggestions to help you solve them. In addition to this, they come pre-populated, but you also have the option to personalize them as you see fit.

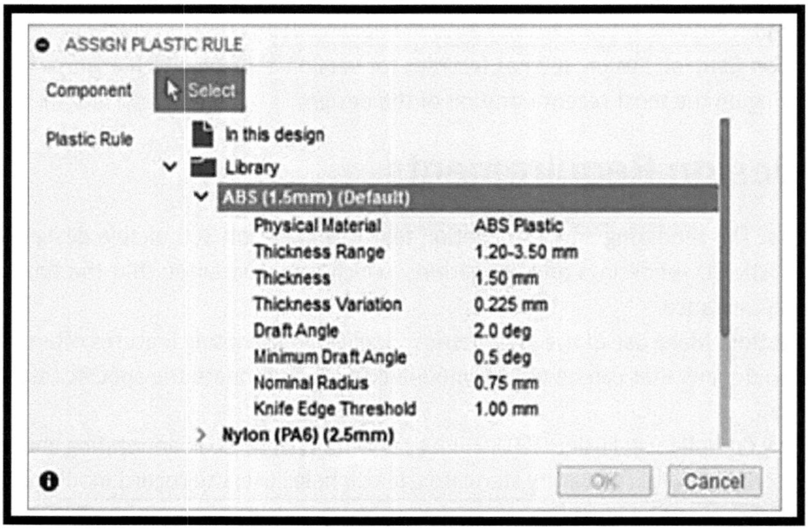

Embedded Plastic Parts

The Fusion 360 **Product Design Extension** provides additional features that were developed specifically to automate the production of bosses, snap features, and rib/web features. Additionally, these plastic features automatically form secondary objects such as drafts and fillets, in addition to associated top and bottom features. You'll be able to finish your designs more quickly and cut down on the number of steps in your timeline if you combine these capabilities. In addition, each of these traits can be traced back to the material in some way. Take, for instance, the case where you change the material of your component from ABS to Nylon. You'll notice that each feature ties to the rules update with the appropriate wall thickness, draft angle, and inner fillet radius when you look at it. Using normal modeling processes to construct a basic boss (top and bottom, including a fastener) takes more time and offers fewer features than using the **Boss command** in the Product Design Extension. The same goes for all the material-aware features.

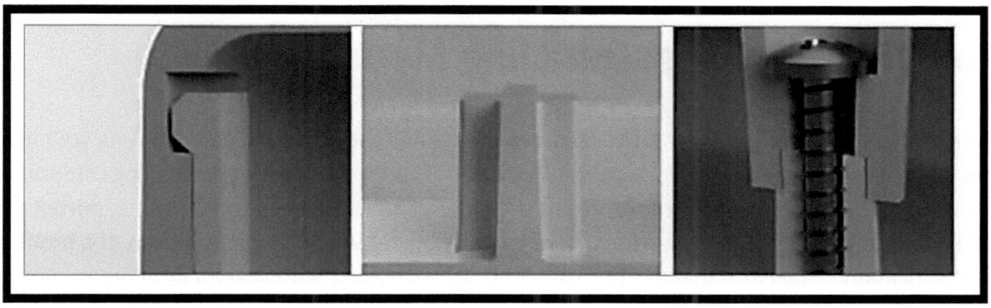

Geometric Pattern

We have included a Geometric Pattern that is exclusive to this market so that the design of your consumer goods may be taken to the next level. Because of this, it is possible to pattern a solid form on a surface that is either flat or curved using a variety of distribution types. The Geometric Pattern function may help you automate the process of adding a pattern to your design for ventilation, lighting, grip/texture, or flair, depending on what you're trying to accomplish.

From Sketch to Final Product: Autodesk Fusion 360 Design & Engineering Highlights You Don't Want to Miss

Volumetric Latticing

One feature of the expansion that deserves special mention is its capacity for volumetric latticing. Using this function, you will be able to design complicated structures that are still very lightweight while retaining their strength and integrity. This is an excellent method for conceptualizing consumer goods, aeronautical components, or cutting-edge medical innovations. This not only makes it possible to cut down significantly on design time and material costs, but it also paves the way for more environmentally responsible production processes. In Fusion 360, the term "**volumetric latticing**" refers to the process of producing intricate, three-dimensional lattice structures inside of a solid model to maximize the amount of material used, as well as its mechanical qualities and weight. Because of the volumetric latticing capability, engineers and designers can replace the bulk material inside a component with a lattice structure while still keeping the component's outside geometry intact. There are many different ways in which lattices can be personalized. To satisfy criteria such as tensile strength and compressive strength as well as weight, these characteristics—which include cell type, size, and density—must be met. The use of volumetric latticing enables designers to produce components that are not only more lightweight but also just as strong or, in some situations, even stronger than the completely solid versions of these components. This is notably useful in the aerospace, automotive, and medical sectors, all of which place a premium on minimizing weight while maximizing material economy. To put this into action, Fusion 360 offers a simple user interface that can be used to specify the area that will be latticed. After the lattice has been constructed, the component can be examined by utilizing the simulation tools in Fusion 360 to check that it satisfies the necessary mechanical requirements. After the design has been finalized, it may be sent out for additive manufacturing, which is a technique that works particularly well for the production of delicate lattice structures.

Fusion 360 Drawings: Detailing Made Easy

The drawing workspace in Fusion 360 is the resource you should use if you are documenting your ideas for production purposes. The Drawings workspace in Fusion 360 is a specialized area for making comprehensive 2D engineering drawings from 3D models. These drawings can be exported as PDFs or exported directly from the software. This workspace is an important connection between the digital design of a product and its actual fabrication or construction in the real world. The Drawings Workspace's intuitive user interface makes it possible for engineers and designers to produce drawings that are compliant with industry standards. These drawings may include measurements, comments, notes, and any other relevant information that may be required. You can quickly and simply project views from a 3D model onto a 2D plane inside the Drawings workspace.

This workspace provides a variety of typical view choices, including top, front, side, and isometric views. The addition of measurements, tolerances, and any other essential criteria for production is based on these predictions, which serve as the foundation. There is also the possibility of adding auxiliary views, section views, and detail views to draw attention to certain design aspects or difficulties. The dynamic relationship that exists between the two-dimensional sketch and the three-dimensional model is one of the most useful characteristics. Any time a modification is made to the 3D model, the drawing receives the update immediately. Consequently, this will ensure consistency and will reduce the possibility of mistakes occurring. This is very important in fields where even relatively little errors may result in considerable issues or expenses. The Drawings workspace allows for the final drawings to be exported into many formats, including PDF and DWG, which makes it simple to share the designs with customers, coworkers, or manufacturers. In general, the drawings workspace offers a comprehensive collection of tools that may be used to transform complex 3D designs into accurate 2D documentation.

Automated Modeling: A Future in Design

The concept of automation is not restricted to drawings in Fusion 360. In addition to that, it encompasses modeling. You can enter design criteria into Fusion 360, and then sit back and watch as the program creates several solutions that are optimal for your needs thanks to generative design techniques. The iteration cycles that are often necessary in the design process are drastically cut down as a result, which enables you to move the timelines of your projects up.

Automated Modeling takes a more balanced approach than standard modeling commands such as Loft and Sweep, which are only able to link a start point and an endpoint. Generative Design, on the other hand, calls for extensive preparation inputs such as loads and restrictions. This tool is included in the Design Workspace and gives you the ability to enter basic criteria such as "**Faces to Connect**" and "**Bodies to Avoid**." With these inputs, it uses generative algorithms to quickly develop various design possibilities.

This tool serves multiple purposes:

1. It does this by instantaneously displaying a variety of design choices that are compliant with key space restrictions, which speeds up the brainstorming process and makes the first design phase go more quickly.
2. The obtained results can be used as jumping-off points for subsequent, more thorough development; alternatively, they can be used in their current state or further refined with the individual needs.
3. Because it creates some different options for the design, the tool stimulates creative thinking outside of the box and enables you to tackle well-known challenges.

Automated Modeling in Fusion 360 is a feature that helps users save time while also fostering their creative potential. It makes the process of generative design easier to understand and provides a route that is both speedier and more direct to feasible design solutions. You are empowered to solve design difficulties with enhanced efficiency and creativity by giving yourself the ability to explore multiple ideas with a small amount of setup.

Performance Improvements: Optimizing Your Experience

Continuous speed enhancements in Fusion 360 increase not just where and how you can accomplish what you can already do, but also what you can do. For example, the software is designed to operate natively on Apple Silicon, which results in up to 30 percent higher computation rates and approximately 50 percent less demand placed on the battery.

Enhanced User Interface

There has been a major improvement made to the user experience thanks to UI enhancements such as the native macOS trackpad engine for gesture processing and high DPI scaling support on Windows. Your design process will be more fluid if you use typefaces that are crisp, icons, and canvas navigation that is seamless.

Assembly Performance

If you deal with assemblies regularly, you will be glad to learn that Fusion 360 has made substantial advancements in this area. Now, activities such as **'insert into current design'** are up to 84% quicker, making your workflow more efficient.

The Power of Cloud-Native Capabilities

Cloud-native architecture is one of the key components that contribute to Fusion 360's formidable capabilities. The cloud features of the program make it eternally scalable and accessible, regardless of whether you are a single user, a startup that is just getting off the ground, or an established business. Collaboration in real-time, rendering on the cloud, and online file management are just some of the features that make Fusion 360 a global design solution.

Seamless Design for an Interconnected World: Fusion 360 is the Future of Engineering and Manufacturing

Fusion 360 stands out as the cloud-native, all-in-one design environment that expands with your demands and skill level in a world that is becoming more interconnected and fast-paced. Fusion 360 offers a level of value that cannot be matched, regardless of the sector in which you operate or the size of your company, since its performance is always being improved. It's not merely a tool for designing things. It is your collaborator in turning concepts into reality, improving processes, and attaining levels of productivity that were previously thought to be unachievable.

Using Fusion 360 in Industrial Design

Industrial design and engineering go hand in hand in the realm of product creation, and their union is analogous to the coming together of art and science in other contexts. Industrial designers are the artists who imagine goods that are visually beautiful and user-friendly, and engineers are the scientists who make sure that these creations are structurally sound, functional, and safe to use. Industrial designers are the artists, and engineers are the scientists. This integration is becoming more fluid and productive than it ever has been before owing to innovative software such as Fusion 360, which is making it possible to bridge the gap that exists between these two worlds, which may be a difficult task. Fusion 360 is a one-of-a-kind environment for industrial designers and engineers to work together, develop, and bring their shared ideas to life.

Designing aesthetically pleasing and functional products

Aesthetics

When it comes to product design, aesthetics refers to the visual components that can capture our attention and elicit feelings in us. Aesthetics are what people notice first about a product, whether it's the slick lines of a sports car or the understated beauty of a smartphone. **Fusion 360 offers designers a flexible working environment that enables them to create visually pleasing things:**

1. **Parameters Modeling**: The parametric modeling functionality of Fusion 360 enables designers to precisely generate and modify three-dimensional forms. Consider it to be the digital equivalent of sculpting clay, where each change influences the way the finished result looks.

2. **Sculpting Tools**: The program provides a variety of sculpting tools, which can be used to create organic and freeform shapes. Imagine you could sculpt virtual clay into whatever form or shape you choose.
3. **Material & Texture Libraries**: Fusion 360 features a vast library of materials and textures, which enables designers to experiment with a variety of surface finishes, ranging from matte to glossy, and simulate how these decisions influence the aesthetic attractiveness of the final product.

Functionality

Functionality is what keeps us interested and happy with anything once we've been drawn in by its beauty. The aesthetic value of a product is not sufficient; in addition, it must effectively fulfill the function for which it was designed.

Fusion 360 provides the tools that designers need to guarantee that form follows function in their creations:

1. **Simulation and Analysis**: The program is equipped with robust simulation capabilities that analyze the performance of a product under a variety of different circumstances. Stress, fluid movement, heat distribution, and other phenomena can all be analyzed by engineers and designers. It is quite similar to a virtual laboratory in which you can test the functioning of your idea.
2. **Design for Manufacturability** (**DFM**) feature helps users optimize their designs so that they are more easily manufactured. This entails making certain that the product can be manufactured at a low cost while preserving its functioning as much as possible.
3. **Interdisciplinary Collaboration**: Working with different specialists, such as mechanical engineers and industrial designers, is a breeze with Fusion 360 because of its intuitive interface. Teams can work concurrently on the same project, which helps to ensure that aesthetics and functionality are taken into consideration at every stage of the design process.

The Fusion 360 Workflow

1. **Conceptualization:** Within Fusion 360, designers can immediately draw their ideas. It's like having a digital notebook where all of your ideas can be turned into 3D models in a flash.
2. **Iteration and refinement**: Design is an iterative process. Fusion 360 makes it simple for designers to implement adjustments and make improvements. These tweaks can be changed smoothly, so if a curve has to be made more graceful or if a button needs to be made easier to push, they can both be done.
3. **Photorealistic Visualization:** Because of Fusion 360's powerful rendering capabilities, designers can build representations of their products that are very lifelike. This is analogous to snapping a picture of the product before it has even been produced by the manufacturer. It lends a hand in presenting design ideas to stakeholders and prospective clients in a more compelling way.
4. **Simulation and Analysis**: This is the point in the process when the art and science of functioning collide. The simulation capabilities in Fusion 360 allow engineers to conduct tests that predict how a product will behave in various real-life settings. It's similar to giving a virtual car a spin around the block or putting a structure through its paces before it's even built.

5. **Collaborative nature**: The collaborative aspect of Fusion 360 makes it possible for all stakeholders, including designers, engineers, and project managers, to work together efficiently. Everyone can offer their knowledge to improve the aesthetics as well as the functioning.
6. **Prototyping and Manufacturing:** Fusion 360 facilitates the transition from digital design to physical product. It generates the necessary files for manufacturing equipment such as 3D printers or CNC machines. Imagine your design blueprint being transformed into a tangible product.
7. **Personalization:** In a society that places a premium on customization, Fusion 360 makes it easy for product designers to make goods that can be customized to the user's specifications. The program guarantees that individual preferences can be accommodated, whether it be in terms of the size, color, or features of a product that is being purchased.

Case Study: Creating a Functional Prototype

Everything You Need to Consider for Prototyping

When you have decided to create a new product, the next step is to consider the benefits and drawbacks of introducing it to the market. Only when you have determined that your new product would be beneficial to your company do you start the process of developing the product. After creating a 3D model of a design, the next stage in the process of developing a product is to create a prototype. The development of a prototype is an essential step in determining both the appearance of the finished product and the modifications that must be made to improve the functionality of the product.

What is Prototyping?

Before a product developer moves forward with fabricating a final design, they make a sample of it called a prototype. Depending on the sort of product being developed, a prototype might be anything from a PCB mockup to a replica of a much bigger product that has been manufactured using 3D printing technology. To put it another way, prototyping is the process of making a first sample of the final product or a rough model of it. It gives the product creators the ability to try out the product's functionality as well as preview how the final product will appear.

The development of a successful product must first begin with the creation of a prototype. It helps save expenses and prevents product developers and designers from squandering their time and effort in fruitless efforts to enhance their products, which saves both of them time and money. Developers can construct an early design of their product with the assistance of prototyping, which they can then use to test the functioning of their final design. Product creators, for instance, may use a 3D printer to produce a prototype of their product and test how well it functions. If they did so, it would assist in identifying flaws, which would then allow them to focus on addressing those issues.

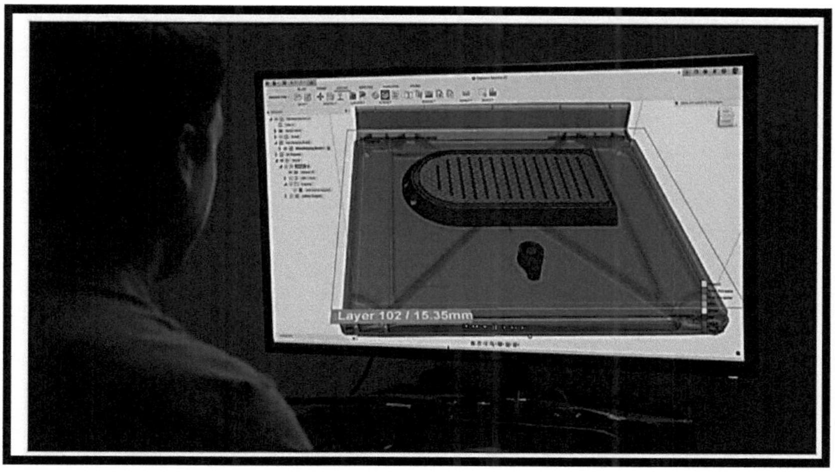

In addition, prototyping makes it possible for designers to construct many prototype models, each of which might have a unique set of capabilities. They can construct some prototypes, put them through various tests, and choose the one that best meets their criteria. They can save the money that they would have needed to spend to make the final product and incorporate the adjustments using this method instead. Product designers can take their ideas and make them a reality by using a prototype. This not only saves them from having to spend thousands of dollars to develop their final product, but it also helps them bring their ideas to life. They may be able to better communicate their vision to others and save time that they would otherwise spend discussing their final product if they have a 3D model of their finished product. This assists product developers when reaching out to investors for financing or showing early concepts to customers and larger internal teams, both of which are important steps in the product development process. They may get buy-in or clearance to continue ahead by using the 3D model of their eventual product to illustrate what their product would look like and how it would function. You, as a product developer, may also utilize a prototype to get information from potential customers in this way. You will be able to get useful feedback early on, which you can then use to focus on improving the design and functioning of the product. It is also possible that it may assist you in determining more appropriate pricing for your goods in the market.

What are the best steps for prototyping?

The time required to create a prototype might range anywhere from a few days to many months. It is dependent on the design, level of detail, technique of prototyping, and the size of the team. For the process to go well, your team has to be composed of knowledgeable individuals who are already accustomed to the creation of prototypes. The process of prototyping is never linear and necessitates the participation of individuals who are versatile in their skill sets. In an ideal world, they would be familiar with areas such as 3D modeling, 3D printing, simulation, and other related areas. You need to choose a budget for the product prototype process first and foremost. When designing a prototype of your final product, you can avoid going over budget by following these steps. Having a budget in mind ensures that you will make responsible use of the resources at your disposal. Everyone on your team has to have a solid understanding of the prototype process in its entirety. They need to be aware of the goals of your product's prototype process. The next step is to design a strategy for your team that will guarantee everything runs smoothly and efficiently during the whole process. The characteristics of your product must be tailored to the preferences of your target audience. When you are developing the prototype for your product, you absolutely must keep the end user in mind at all times. You will be able to design the ideal prototype that fulfills the requirements of your clients if you keep the end-users in mind while you work.

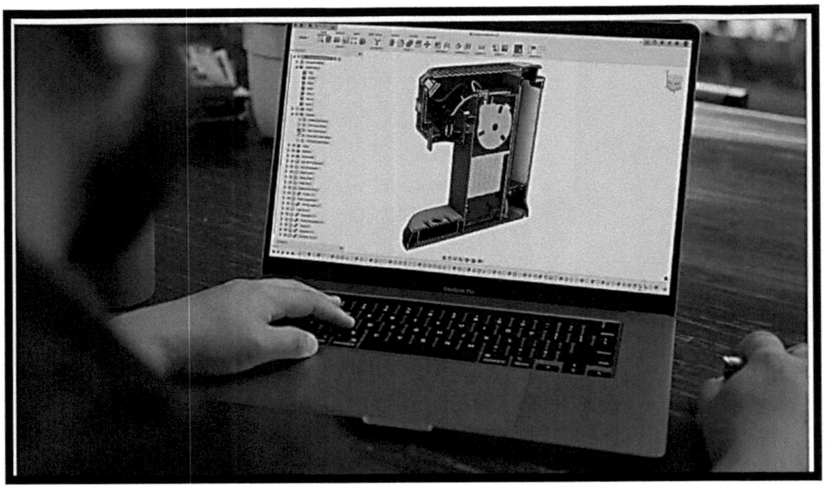

To ensure that the process of product prototype goes as smoothly as possible, your team should be aware of the resources and tools to employ. They need to work quickly and effectively to save time, which they can then use in testing and improving the product. The greatest prototypes are created by designers and engineers who test their prototypes repeatedly and change them until they get the outcomes they are looking for. While you are validating your prototype, you should talk to a variety of individuals, such as contractors, prospective consumers, investors, and other specialists who may be able to contribute to the development of your product. You will be able to develop a flawless final product by incorporating their suggestions into your prototype so that you can make the necessary adjustments. Another useful piece of advice is to keep detailed records of each stage of the prototyping process. You are required to maintain a record of your prototype throughout each step. Take notes on everything, including the designs, the improvements, the comments, the performance metrics, and so on. When you work on producing another prototype for a new product in the future, doing so may save you time and help you work more efficiently. Having a record on hand can also relieve tension if you need to go back to an earlier version of the process.

Incorporating design principles and best practices

Creating 3D models and products that are effective, practical, and visually beautiful requires the utilization of design principles and best practices, both of which must be included in Autodesk Fusion 360. Because Fusion 360 is such a powerful piece of software for computer-aided design (CAD) and computer-aided engineering (CAE), sticking to design principles can help you improve your ability to optimize your designs for a variety of applications. **In this section, we are going to investigate how to properly use these best practices and principles:**

1. **Functionality and Purpose:**
    - To begin, you need first to clearly define the objective of your design as well as the functionality it will provide. Gain an understanding of the issue that you are attempting to

resolve as well as the requirements of your end users. The first step in ensuring that your design serves its intended function is to ensure that it corresponds with that aim.

2. **Sketching and Constraints:**
    - Make exact 2D outlines of your idea by using the sketching tools that are available in Fusion 360. Utilize geometric and dimensional limitations to keep your design accurate and make certain that it responds to changes in the way you anticipate it would.
3. **Parametric Design:**
    - Incorporate the ideas of parametric design into your work by developing equations and parameters. This enables you to make design modifications quickly and easily, as well as experiment with a variety of variants without having to start from zero.
4. **Modularity:**
    - When designing anything complicated, you should think about dividing it up into modular parts. This encourages reusability, makes design revisions easier, and makes it easier for members of the team to collaborate.
5. **Material Selection:**
    - Fusion 360 provides access to a variety of content libraries. Choose materials that are suitable for your design, making sure to take into account acceptable levels of weight, strength, and any other relevant material attributes.
6. **Assembly Design:**
    - When working on assemblies, make use of the assembly environment that is available in Fusion 360. Check that there aren't any improper clearances, interferences, or functioning issues between the components, and use motion studies to verify the movement and interactions.
7. **Sustainability and Environmental Impact:**
    - Maintain an awareness of sustainability by maximizing the use of materials, eliminating waste, and cutting down on the amount of energy you use. The simulation features of Fusion 360 might be of assistance in determining how your plans will affect the surrounding environment.
8. **Aesthetics and Ergonomics:**
    - Pay attention to the user experience and how appealing the design is to the eye. Make convincing visual representations of your idea with the help of Fusion 360's built-in rendering capabilities. Take into account ergonomic elements to improve the comfort of users and the functionality of a product.
9. **Simulation and Analysis:**
    - To test your design's performance, structural integrity, and thermal behavior, make use of the simulation and analysis tools offered by Fusion 360. Take care of any problems that were uncovered throughout these tests.
10. **Documentation and Collaboration:**
    - Produce in-depth documentation, which should include drawings, BOMs (Bill of Materials), and assembly instructions. Fusion 360 has capabilities that can be used to generate these types of documents. Share your design files with the other members of your team and keep track of the changes you make.
11. **Prototyping and Testing:**
    - Before finishing your design, you should construct prototypes or 3D-printed models so that you can test their functionality and see whether they work in the real world. Files that can be used for 3D printing and CNC machining can be exported from Fusion 360.
12. **Version Control:**

- To maintain track of design iterations and modifications, you need to use version control techniques. This guarantees that you will always be able to refer to prior versions or revert to them if necessary.

13. **User Feedback:**
    - It is important to get feedback from prospective users or other stakeholders and to integrate their input into your design. The cloud-based collaboration tools provided by Fusion 360 can make this process more efficient.

You will be able to build high-quality, well-engineered designs in Fusion 360 by using these design concepts and best practices, which will help you satisfy both practical and aesthetic standards with your creations. You will be able to get the most out of this flexible CAD/CAE software if you keep your knowledge of Fusion 360's features and capabilities up to date regularly.

What is Rapid Prototyping?

In the past, designers would build iteration after iteration, print them out, and test them via data transfers between various tools. The repetitive nature of conventional physical prototyping can be alleviated by the use of rapid prototyping. Using computer-aided design (CAD) tools like Autodesk Fusion 360, rapid prototyping is the process of rapidly fabricating a physical component, model, or assembly to test its functionality. The usual steps involved in the fast prototyping process include taking a 3D model and rapidly transforming it into a physical prototype, generally via the use of 3D printing.

How does Autodesk Fusion 360 help with rapid prototyping?

The Autodesk Fusion 360 program combines the capabilities of computer-aided design (CAD) with computer-aided manufacturing (CAM). The all-encompassing nature of its 3D modeling environment, in conjunction with plug-ins for generative design and additive manufacturing, makes it possible for designers to rapidly produce several versions of the same design. Before sending a 3D model to a 3D printer, Fusion 360 may also perform tests to determine the tolerances, durability, and other design aspects of the model.

Designers don't need to export any of their creations out of Fusion 360 for the production process to proceed. Instead, they can swiftly transition from CAD to CAM, which enables them to simply manufacture or 3D print a prototype. Rapid prototyping with the assistance of Fusion 360 allows you to generate numerous iterations daily, as opposed to just being able to build a single iteration that takes place for multiple days. Iterations can be revised and modified by designers throughout the day, and then they can be printed out after midnight.

Fusion 360: professional prototyping and fabrication tools at your fingertips

In the process of developing a product, every step, from prototype to manufacture, can be connected with the help of Fusion 360. Your team will be able to swiftly and effectively bring product ideas to life thanks to the extensive tools that it provides for **CAD, CAM, CAE,** and **PCB**. The following is a list of the ten ways that Fusion 360 assists product designers and engineers throughout the development process:

1. 3D model parts and assemblies

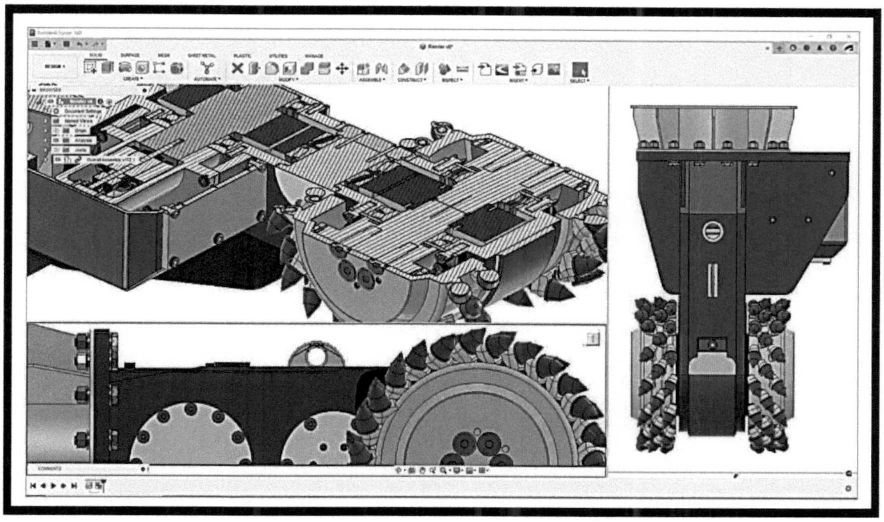

Fusion 360's 3D modeling tools provide teams with the ability to build whatever they can imagine. Sketching, surfacing, parametric modeling, freeform modeling, and many more types of modeling are only some of the professional-level capabilities that are offered by Fusion 360 for the creation of 3D models. Because of its user-friendly design, which includes readily available menus and toolbars, it is simple for teams to adopt.

2. Seamlessly collaborate with Assembly Concurrency

The foundation for successful product development is laid at the outset of a project via good cooperation. The days of using antiquated, piecemeal procedures and exchanging files manually, which took a lot of time, are over. Through the use of Assembly Concurrency, you and your coworkers, contractors, or customers can work together in an assembly in a fluid manner. Additionally, internet access enables simple work site access for anyone who wants instantaneous entry into 3D models. Would you want to swiftly share a model to explain the concept that you have? You can immediately share models with other people at any stage of the development process thanks to the public link sharing feature.

3. Enhance designs through automated modeling and generative design

Automated modeling and the Generative Design Extension make it possible for you to produce feasible concepts based on limitations in a short amount of time. Explore new atypical design ideas using automated modeling, or take things one step further with generative design to integrate factors like production techniques, design limits, or prices.

4. Generate detailed manufacturing drawings

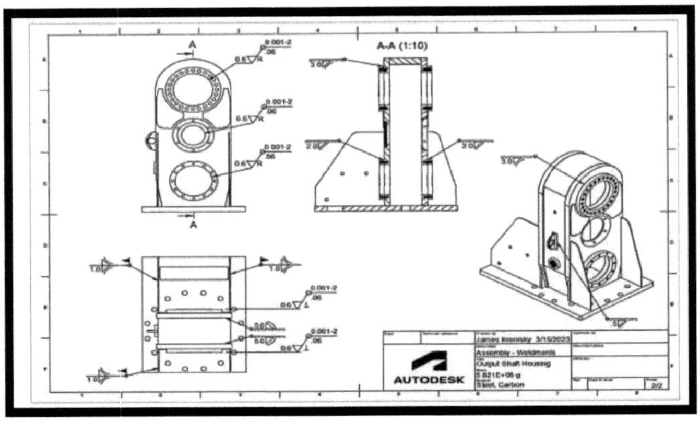

It is very necessary to provide manufacturers with documentation that is simple to understand, accurate, and precise. The Drawings Workspace in Fusion 360 guarantees that your design goals are conveyed clearly, hence limiting the likelihood of any possible misunderstandings or differences in interpretation. If you want to successfully convey crucial manufacturing information, you should publish the fabrication blueprints for your product. These plans should include detailed pictures of the model and the assembly process.

5. Incorporate electrical components with ECAD/MCAD

PCBs and schematics need to be updated to keep up with the increasingly competitive marketplace of today's consumer products. Why not utilize the same tool that you use for 3D modeling while designing them instead? Fusion 360 is one of the only products that offers integrated ECAD and MCAD. In addition, without first conducting simulations before manufacture, ninety percent of boards end up failing. If you are interested in unlocking further ECAD capabilities, the Fusion 360 Signal Integrity Extension provides you with a visual representation of all the information you want before the fabrication of a PCB prototype.

7. Simulate Finite Element Analysis (FEA) and Design for Manufacturability (DFM)

Checking to see that your concepts have a solid foundation before investing money in their manufacture is never going to do any harm. The ability to do static simulation, sometimes known as stress testing, is an integral part of Fusion 360. Additionally, the Simulation Extension may be used if you are interested in gaining access to even further developed simulation capabilities.

8. Create parts for sheet metal fabrication

The Nesting & Fabrication Extension enhances the sheet metal capabilities of Fusion 360 by allowing you to construct optimal and associative multi-sheet layouts for cutting on CNC machines.

9. Generate toolpaths for additive (3D printing) and subtractive (CAM) processes

Components can be made using additive manufacturing technologies, such as fused filament fabrication (FFF) and metal additive, or CNC machining using subtractive computer-aided manufacturing (CAM) toolpaths after a design is suitable for physical testing and evaluation. Because of this dual approach, designs are guaranteed to be optimized for both additive and subtractive manufacturing, which, in the end, results in speedier prototyping, higher-quality final products, and decreased time-to-market.

Case Study: Designing for Manufacturing and Assembly (DFMA)

Implementing DFMA methodologies in Fusion 360

Design for Manufacturability and Assembly (DFMA) is a critical set of methodologies aimed at optimizing product design for efficient manufacturing and assembly processes. By incorporating DFMA principles into your designs, you can reduce production costs, improve product quality, and accelerate time-to-market. Autodesk Fusion 360, a powerful CAD/CAE/CAM software, provides a robust platform for implementing DFMA methodologies effectively.

Understanding DFMA Principles

Before delving into the practical aspects of implementing DFMA in Fusion 360, it's crucial to have a clear understanding of the core principles behind DFMA:

1. **Simplicity:** Simplify your design wherever possible. Reduce the number of parts and assembly steps, as this directly impacts manufacturing and assembly costs.
2. **Design for Ease of Manufacturing:** Choose manufacturing processes that are readily available, cost-effective, and compatible with your design. Minimize the need for specialized tooling or complex machining.
3. **Design for Ease of Assembly:** Optimize your design to facilitate straightforward assembly without the need for highly skilled labor or complex procedures. Use features like self-locating and self-fastening components.
4. **Standardization:** Utilize standardized components and materials to streamline procurement and reduce inventory costs. Avoid unnecessary complexity in specifications.
5. **Modularity:** Design modular components that can be easily replaced or upgraded, reducing downtime and maintenance costs.
6. **Minimize Fasteners:** Where possible, minimize the use of fasteners, as they can be time-consuming to install and may require additional tools.

Now, let's see how you can apply these principles within Fusion 360.

Step-by-Step Implementation in Fusion 360

Step 1: Define Your Design Goals

Before you start designing your product in Fusion 360, it's essential to define your design goals and constraints. Consider factors like cost, production volume, assembly time, and performance requirements. These goals will guide your design decisions throughout the process.

Step 2: Sketch and Create the Initial Design

Begin by creating a sketch of your product's basic shape and dimensions. Use Fusion 360's sketching tools to create 2D profiles. Then, extrude these profiles to create 3D solids that represent the initial design.

Step 3: Design for Manufacturing (DFM)

DFM focuses on designing parts that are easy and cost-effective to manufacture. In Fusion 360, consider the following DFM principles:

a. **Material Selection**: Choose materials that are readily available and suitable for your application.
b. **Standard Components**: Use standard fasteners, bearings, and other components to reduce manufacturing costs.
c. **Minimize Complexity**: Simplify part geometry to reduce machining or fabrication complexity.
d. **Tolerance Analysis**: Ensure that your design has appropriate tolerances for manufacturing processes, such as machining or 3D printing.

Step 4: Design for Assembly (DFA)

DFA focuses on designing parts that are easy to assemble. In Fusion 360, consider the following DFA principles:

a. **Modular Design**: Divide your product into modules or sub-assemblies that can be assembled independently.
b. **Minimize Fasteners**: Reduce the number of screws, bolts, and other fasteners by using snap-fit, press-fit, or adhesive joints where possible.
c. **Self-Locating Features**: Design parts with features that guide their alignment during assembly.
d. **Accessibility**: Ensure that assembly workers can easily access and manipulate parts during assembly.

Step 5: Perform Finite Element Analysis (FEA)

Use Fusion 360's simulation tools to perform FEA on critical components. This will help you identify potential weaknesses or areas of stress concentration that may affect both manufacturing and assembly.

Streamlining production and assembly processes

It is essential to streamline the manufacturing and assembly processes in Autodesk Fusion 360 if one wants to raise one's level of productivity, lower one's costs, and raise one's level of product quality. Fusion 360 provides a wide variety of tools and capabilities that can assist you in accomplishing the aforementioned goals:

1. Model Optimization:

- **Parametric Modeling:** Start by creating a parametric model of your design. Because Fusion 360 enables you to set parameters and equations, it simplifies the process of making necessary adjustments to a model's dimensions and characteristics. Because of this flexibility, your design will be able to accommodate any changes that may occur during the production process.
- **Simplify Geometry**: Remove any unwanted complications from your 3D model by following this step. Utilize the direct modeling capabilities found in Fusion 360 to reduce curves, eliminate unnecessary features, and optimize shapes for production and assembly.

2. Design for Manufacturability (DFM):

- **Material Selection**: You should select materials that are easily available and appropriate for the production techniques you will be using. The material libraries offered by Fusion 360 come with a diverse selection of options, one of which is mechanical characteristics.
- **Design Validation**: Utilize Fusion 360's simulation capabilities to perform stress analysis, thermal analysis, and dynamic simulations. Fusion 360 also includes a thermal analysis tool. This ensures that your design can endure the manufacturing conditions and assembly stresses that are encountered in the real world.

3. Design for Assembly (DFA):

- **Component Reduction:** One of your goals should be to reduce the amount of components in your design. You can explore a variety of assembly configurations within the environment provided by Fusion 360's assembly feature, which also helps you locate chances to combine pieces.
- **Standardization**: Whenever possible, use standardized components to ease procurement and cut down on part variation. The content libraries in Fusion 360 provide access to a comprehensive assortment of standard parts.
- **Assembly Sequencing**: Utilizing Fusion 360's assembly environment, plan and visualize the order in which components will be assembled. Determine the best order in which to assemble the components to reduce the amount of handling and tool changes.

4. Collaborative Workflows:

- **Cloud Collaboration**: To streamline your work with your team members, suppliers, and other stakeholders, make use of the cloud-based collaboration options that are available in Fusion 360. Files for design can be shared, modifications can be monitored, and input can be gathered in real-time.

- **Design Review**: Run design reviews inside of Fusion 360, where all members of the team can discuss and make recommendations directly on the design. The feedback loop is streamlined as a result of this, and everyone is on the same page as a result of this.

5. Documentation and Visualization:

- **Bill of Materials (BOM):** Using the documentation tools provided by Fusion 360, you can generate an exhaustive BOM. Make sure that an accurate listing of all of the components, including the numbers and the specs, has been created.
- **Exploded Views:** Construct exploded views and assembly animations to assist assembly teams in comprehending the appropriate sequence and positioning of components. The animation features in Fusion 360 make this process quite easy to complete.

6. Prototyping and Testing:

- **3D Printing Integration**: For rapid prototyping and testing, you can export files that are instantly printable in 3D from within Fusion 360. Before committing to manufacturing in large quantities, you will be able to confirm the design's functionality and fit thanks to this.
- **Physical Testing**: To guarantee that prototypes meet the design criteria and assembly requirements, it is necessary to put them through physical testing. The results of your simulations in Fusion 360 can act as a guide to help you identify potential problems that need to be addressed during testing.

7. Continuous Improvement:

- **Feedback Loop**: Make sure to keep an open line of communication with the teams responsible for manufacturing and assembly so that you can resolve any problems that may crop up during production. Maintaining open lines of communication is beneficial for making modifications in the here and now.
- **Cost Analysis**: Constantly evaluate the costs of manufacturing and assembly, searching for opportunities to cut costs and enhance efficiency. The tools for cost estimation that are included in Fusion 360 can be of assistance with this procedure.

CHAPTER 27
CUSTOMIZING FUSION 360

This chapter digs into the fascinating realm of customization, which provides users with the chance to shape this flexible software into a tool that is exactly aligned with their particular design requirements and workflows. This chapter reveals a world of possibilities in which users can extend the capabilities of Fusion 360, automate actions that are performed repeatedly, and design personalized workflows to increase their productivity. The chapter commences with an exploration of Fusion 360's API, an Application Programming Interface that serves as a gateway to harnessing the software's underlying power. Users are introduced to the concept of add-ins, which are custom programs that extend Fusion 360's functionality beyond its standard features. This section illuminates how programming can be employed to create tailored tools and features that cater to unique design requirements. Designing individualized workflows that maximize efficiency is a crucial component of customization. This chapter also teaches readers how to create their custom commands, which enables them to automate mundane chores and improve the efficiency of their design processes. Designers and engineers can navigate Fusion 360 with pinpoint accuracy by first customizing their workflows and then integrating those workflows into the ecosystem of the software. Scripting emerges as an effective tool when it comes to the field of customization. Users are given an introduction to the world of scripting in this chapter. In this world, lines of code can automate chores, increase productivity, and orchestrate complicated operations. This chapter gives insights into the production of scripts as well as their applications for those who are interested in making their design work more efficient. Scripts are a wonderful asset for individuals who are looking to make their design work more efficient.

Introduction to Fusion 360 API and Add-Ins

Imagine you're immersed in the world of 3D design, working on intricate models and product prototypes. Autodesk's Fusion 360 is your trusty companion, offering a digital canvas for your creativity. But what if you could mold Fusion 360 into a tool that dances to your unique tune? That's where **Fusion 360's Application Programming Interface (API)** comes into play. The Application Programming Interface (API) for Fusion 360 is not merely a feature; rather, it is the magic wand that transforms Fusion 360 into a customized powerhouse. You can think of it as a backstage ticket to the inner workings of Fusion 360, where you can construct bespoke tools, orchestrate activities, and change designs with only a few lines of code.

Within the Fusion 360 API realm, you have an array of creative outlets:

- **Script Add-Ins:** These are similar to small, sophisticated scripts that can automate actions that are performed repeatedly. Imagine being able to effortlessly generate complex reports, crunch figures, or make design adjustments with the precise accuracy of a surgeon. These agile scripts make it feasible to accomplish everything.
- **Command Add-Ins**: This allows you to expand upon your creative potential. Imagine being able to design bespoke commands that are completely integrated into the Fusion 360 user interface. These commands eventually become indistinguishable from the tools that are pre-installed with Fusion 360, and you can manipulate them with the same ease.

- **Panel Add-Ins:** There are also add-ins for the panel available for the virtuoso. These tools allow you to create immersive panels without leaving the UI of Fusion 360. Imagine having your very own design dashboard, replete with tools, configurations, and features that are well-suited to your specific requirements.

The Power of Fusion 360 API in Action

The Fusion 360 API should be thought of as your automation partner. Imagine that you are a designer working on a project that requires a large number of processes that are identical to one another, such as the generation of part drawings. You can automate this tiresome task by using a script that connects to an API, which will both guarantee its accuracy and save you a ton of time. Alternatively, you could be an engineer who is tasked with consistently applying intricate design standards. You can construct a specialized command with the help of a command add-in that monitors compliance with these guidelines across all of your projects and ensures that they are followed without fail. The Fusion 360 Application Programming Interface (API) makes it feel like you're opening a treasure chest when you first start using it. Installing Fusion 360, using a coding editor such as Visual Studio coding, and having a little bit of creative spirit are all requirements. The comprehensive documentation and tutorials provided by Autodesk serve as your treasure map, directing you through the complexities of the API as well as its potential. As you begin your adventure with the Fusion 360 API, you should give some thought to the prospect of sharing the creations you make. You can promote your add-ins to a community of designers and engineers located all over the world by using the marketplace that Autodesk provides. Your creativity has the potential to revolutionize how others in the Fusion 360 ecosystem do their work. When it comes to the realm of three-dimensional design, the Application Programming Interface (API) of Fusion 360 is not merely technical; rather, it is your artistic canvas, your automation ally, and your gateway to personalization. Fusion 360 exceeds its default capabilities and transforms into a mirror of your vision and requirements in the realm of digital design when you have it.

Extending Fusion 360's functionality through programming

You can transform Fusion 360 into a design and engineering tool that is highly effective thanks to a game-changing strategy that involves extending the capabilities of Fusion 360 through the use of programming. Let's go even deeper into this interesting domain and investigate how programming can release the full power of Fusion 360. The Application Programming Interface (API) of Fusion 360 is the essential component in expanding the capabilities of the software. This application programming interface (API) acts as a conduit between you, the user, and the complex mechanisms that lie at the heart of Fusion 360. It enables you to access a vast treasury of functions and data that can be manipulated through the use of programming. Imagine the numerous hours that you have to spend doing mundane, uninteresting work. You can eliminate the need for performing these tedious tasks entirely by using programming. For instance, you can write scripts that generate standardized reports, do batch file conversions, or methodically update design parameters across numerous projects. All of these tasks can be automated. This automation not only helps save time but also decreases the likelihood of mistakes being made by humans.

Fusion 360 is a versatile tool, but there is a possibility that it may not always correspond exactly with the requirements of your particular project or business. This is where the programming comes into its own. You can create bespoke design tools that fit in well with the UI of Fusion 360. These tools can enforce design standards, make complex computations easier, or give modeling functions that are unique to themselves. For instance, if you work in the automobile business, you can develop a bespoke tool that determines the optimum aerodynamics of a car by basing its calculations on a set of specified factors. You can design a technology that generates parametric building structures if architecture is your field of study. Workflows in the modern day frequently make use of a wide variety of software tools and computerized technologies. The API that comes with Fusion 360 gives you the ability to bridge these gaps. Fusion 360 can be integrated with third-party systems, databases, and even Internet of Things (IoT) devices. Imagine that your 3D printer is connected to Fusion 360 and can receive real-time design updates. This would ensure that your physical prototypes are constantly current with the most recent design revisions. The process of designing better products is a difficult one. On the other hand, if you know how to program, you can construct algorithms that can automatically fine-tune your designs. For instance, you can design a script that iteratively modifies the settings to decrease the amount of material used while still achieving the standards for structural integrity. Obtaining such a high level of optimization with human labor is quite unlikely.

The management of one's data is an essential component of design initiatives. Through the use of Fusion 360's programming capabilities, users can construct scripts that can organize and categorize design files, making it simple to find and refer to important information. In addition, you can generate extensive reports on design statistics, the progress of the project, or any other metrics that are necessary for making informed decisions. The importance of consistency in design and working together cannot be overstated. You can ensure that every member of your team adheres to the same best practices by using the API that is provided by Fusion 360 to construct add-ins that enforce design standards. You can also create tools that facilitate collaboration, making it easier to share and discuss designs within your business or with external partners. This is something you can do.

User-Interface Customization with Fusion 360's API

When it comes to personalizing the user interface of Fusion 360, there are two distinct principles to keep in mind: adding buttons that provide the user the ability to perform instructions and designing individualized dialogs for your actions. This section explains the process of adding buttons to the user interface of Fusion 360. When you add a new button to the user interface of Fusion 360, you need to give great consideration to where that button will be placed. There is a finite amount of space, and if every add-in writer placed their command in a location where it was always visible, there would not be enough room for all of the commands. Think about the functionality that your command delivers and where the user would reasonably seek other options that are comparable to what your command offers. For instance, if a command alters an existing model, it ought to probably be added to the MODIFY panel in the Design workspace. This is because the **MODIFY** panel is located in the Design workspace. If you want to have more control over how the design is seen, you should probably add it to the Navigation toolbar that is located at the bottom of the window. You should only think about creating additional tabs or panels if your command is doing some action that cannot be accomplished by using existing Fusion capability. When dissecting Fusion 360's user interface, it can be broken down into two main areas; structure and contents.

Structure

As will be shown below, the presentation of the commands in the user interface is given structure by some elements. The workspace is displayed in blue, the toolbars are displayed in red, the toolbar tabs are displayed in yellow, and the toolbar panels are displayed in green. The controls of the toolbars that are used to represent the buttons in toolbars and panels are referred to in the next section as the "**Contents**" section.

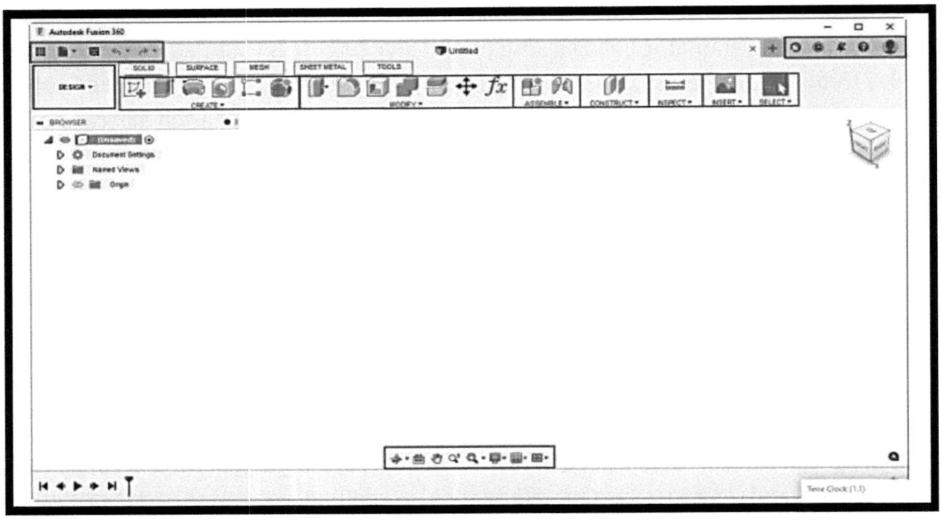

Toolbars

A toolbar is a collection of controls organized in a container. A control can take the form of a command button or a drop-down menu that contains further controls. These control types and their descriptions can be found below. Some toolbars can be used, but just the first three will be shown to you by default. Because the content of these three is independent of the context in which it is being used, it does not change no matter what is going on in Fusion 360. You can access a particular toolbar by using its unique ID, which is contained throughout each toolbar and all of the other user interface elements. The toolbar located in the top-left corner of the screen is typically referred to as the QAT, which stands for the Quick Access Toolbar. "**QAT**" is its identifier. It grants access to all of the commands that are associated with files. The user account and commands relating to help can be accessed using the toolbar that is located in the upper-right corner of the screen. Its ID is "**QATRight.**" The toolbar that can be found in the middle of the bottom of the window is called the navigation toolbar. It contains all of the instructions that are associated with the view, and its ID is "NavToolbar." Through the UserInterface object's toolbars property, which in turn returns an instance of the Toolbars class, you have access to each toolbar. If you already know the ID of the toolbar you want, you can utilize the itemById field on this object to retrieve it. The following snippet of Python code obtains the Toolbar object, which stands in for the QAT.

```
app = adsk.core.Application.get()
ui = app.userInterface

qatToolbar = ui.toolbars.itemById('QAT')
```

Workspaces

Workspaces are the primary proprietors of the UI structure at the top level. As illustrated in the image below, the user selects the active workspace by using the huge drop-down menu located in the top left corner of the Fusion 360 window. When switching between workspaces, the complete user interface shifts to display only the elements that are suitable for the workflow that is required by the workspace. Here, we will concentrate on the toolbar tabs and the contents of those tabs; however, modifying the workspace can also alter the contents of the browser as well as the graphics for the model.

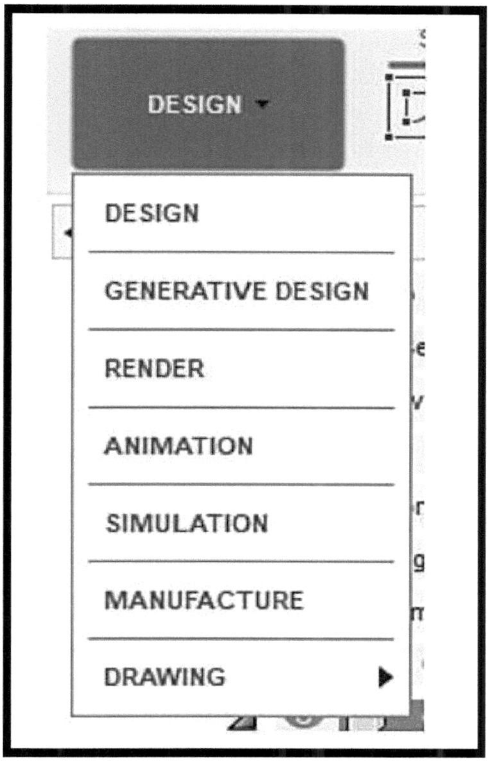

Toolbar Tabs

Every workspace has its collection of tabs for the toolbar. The commands that are required by the workspace can be arranged in logical categories thanks to the toolbar tabs that are available. In the Design workspace, for instance, you will find tabs labeled **SOLID, SURFACE, MESH, SHEET METAL, and TOOLS.** Each of these tabs represents a different kind of data and workflow. For instance, you can have access to the instructions utilized in the process of constructing and changing a solid model by selecting the tab labeled **SOLID**. Nevertheless, when the **MESH** tab is selected, only those instructions that are helpful when interacting with a mesh are displayed.

Toolbar Panels

One or more toolbar panels can be found inside of a toolbar tab. Within each toolbar tab, commands are categorized into categories using the toolbar panels. Every panel on the toolbar has two components: the panel itself, and a drop-down menu. For illustration purposes, the **ASSEMBLE** panel in the image below has a red outline, while the drop-down menu associated with it has a yellow outline.

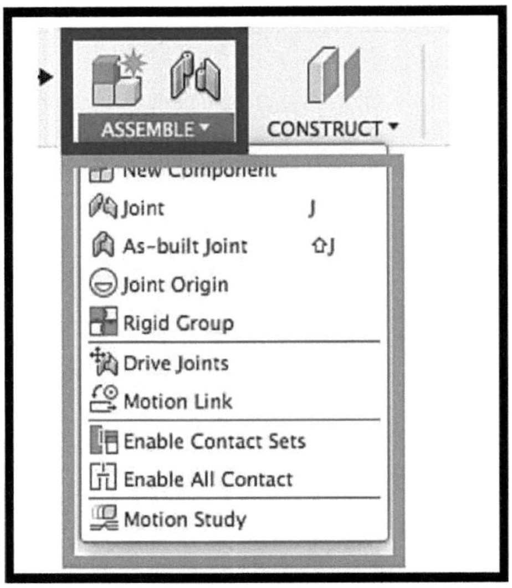

The panel displays only a fraction of the options available in the drop-down menu, making it possible to quickly retrieve frequently employed commands. By pressing the ⋮ **More** button and then checking or unchecking the **"Pin to Toolbar"** option, the user can control which instructions from the drop-down menu are displayed in the panel.

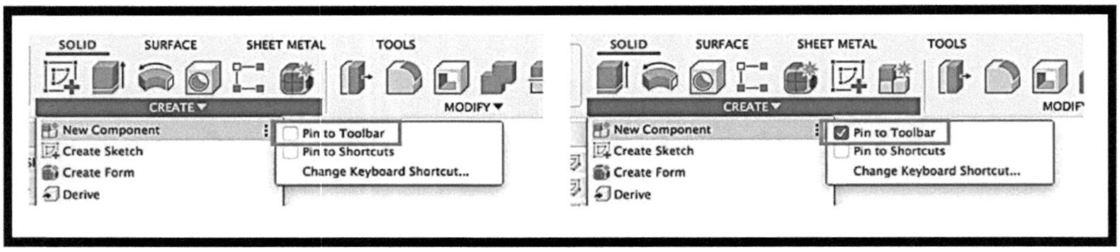

Through the **Application Programming Interface (API)**, toolbar panels can be accessed in one of two locations: either from the tab of the toolbar that contains the panel or from a WorkSpace. Panels are certain to be one-of-a-kind within a workspace; hence, you can access a particular panel if you are aware of both the workspace and the panel ID. The panel can also be accessed by selecting it from a tab on the toolbar, which is yet another method. If you loop through the toolbar panels in a workspace, you will discover that many of them have a value for the **isVisible** property that is set to **False**. This indicates that the panel is not currently visible in the workspace. Fusion 360 toggles the visibility of toolbar panels as the user switches between tabs, allowing the user to only view the panels that are relevant to the tab that is now active.

Contents

After examining the components that are responsible for the formation of the structure, we will now investigate the controls that are used to determine the contents of the toolbars and panels.

Controls

Toolbars and toolbar panels both serve for toolbar controls. There are several distinct kinds of controls, including command, drop-down, split-button, and separator controls. When you click any of the command controls that are displayed in the sketch toolbar panel and the drop-down menu that is linked with it, a command will be initiated. When you click on the **Rectangle, Circle, Arc, or Polygon** objects, a drop-down menu will appear for you to select from. This classifies these elements as drop-down controls. A separator control is a control that is used to visually separate and structure the items of a menu. In this case, the divider line between the "**Create Sketch**" and "**Line**" commands is a separator control.

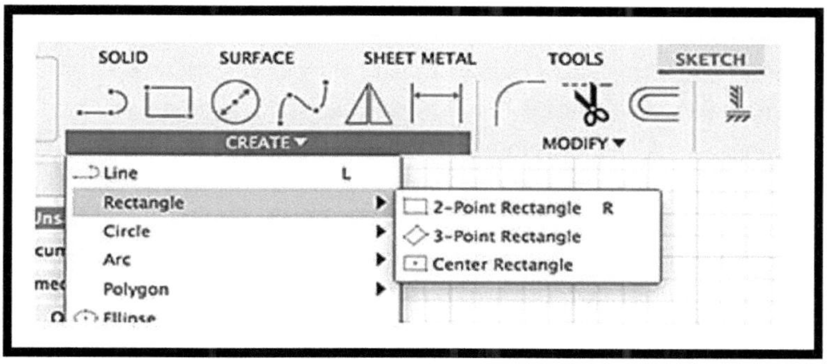

The control that is displayed below is a split-button control. A split-button control consists of a button that also contains a little arrow pointing to the right. When the button is clicked, the command that is printed on the button is carried out. Clicking the arrow opens a drop-down menu, from which the user can select one of several additional commands. The top-level command can optionally take the form of the last command selected from the drop-down menu. As stated earlier, controls are the part of the user interface that are visible to the user. On the other hand, a control only acts as a placeholder within a toolbar, and all of the intelligence (text, icons, tooltips, and so on) that we see comes from the command definitions that are linked with the control. Because of this, each control must refer to a command definition to display itself properly.

Command Definitions

Command definitions include all of the information that specifies how a control appears and works, including its appearance and behavior. A control will refer to a command definition, and the control will use the information included in the command definition to show itself. A command definition is not directly visible to the user. It is possible to have the same command in more than one place in the user interface if the command definition is kept separate from the control. For instance, you can add your command to the **MANUFACTURE** workspace in addition to the DESIGN workplace. Even if you add your command to a single toolbar panel, the user will still have two controls available to them if they want to pin the command to the toolbar. In this particular instance, there are two distinct controls (one in the panel, and another in the drop-down of that panel), but both controls reference the same command definition, and choosing either control will result in the same behavior. If you modify a property of the command definition, that change will immediately be mirrored in each control that refers to that command definition. If, for instance, the **isEnabled** property of the command definition is changed so that it reads "False," then every control that refers to that command definition will lose its ability to function. In addition, the commandCreated event of the command definition will be triggered if the user clicks on any of the controls that are associated with the command definition. This means that you can carry out the action that the command is intended to carry out.

The creation of a command definition is the first step in the process of developing a new control. The concept of a command and what an end-user understands to be a command are often synonymous with one another. This one-to-one correspondence holds in most cases. There are three distinct sorts of command definitions: buttons, checkboxes, and lists. You choose the type of command definition you want to use based on how you want the command to be presented to the user in the user interface. For instance, the definition of a button command will result in the creation of a button, whereas the definition of a checkbox command will result in the creation of a single check box. An example of a drop-down control with four checkbox commands is provided below. These controls are referred to as **Layout Grid, Layout Grid Lock, Snap to Grid**, and **Incremental Move** respectively. In addition to that, it has two button commands—"**Grid Settings' ' and "Set Increments' '**—that you can use.

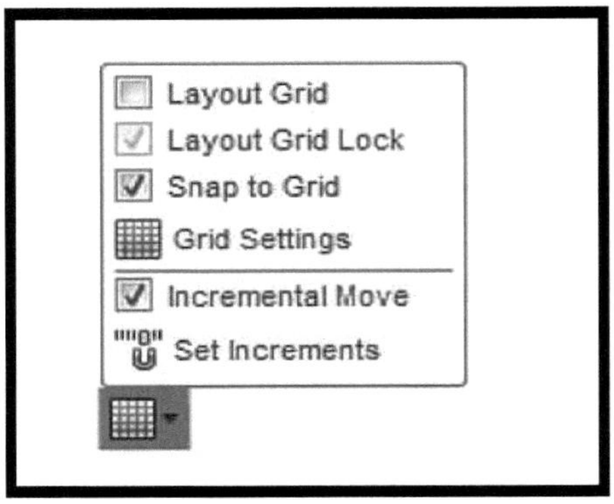

A command that is defined as a list command is presented in the form of a drop-down menu and has an accompanying list of checkboxes, radio buttons, or text items. An example of a checkbox list can be found below. When the user clicks the "**Effects**" button, the drop-down menu is presented, and they can check and uncheck items as they go down the list. The list can remember any modifications that have been made and will present itself in its current condition the next time it is presented.

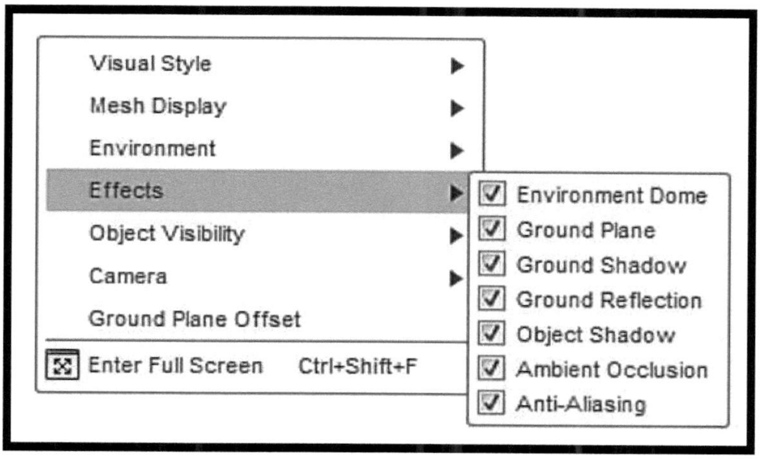

An example of a radio button list can be found below. The drop-down menu appears once the user clicks the "**Visual Style**" button. Once making a selection from the available options, the user can then close the menu by pressing the "**X**" button. The user can only choose one option at a time, just as you would anticipate with radio controls. Because the list remembers which item has been selected, it will always display the item that is currently selected when it is displayed again.

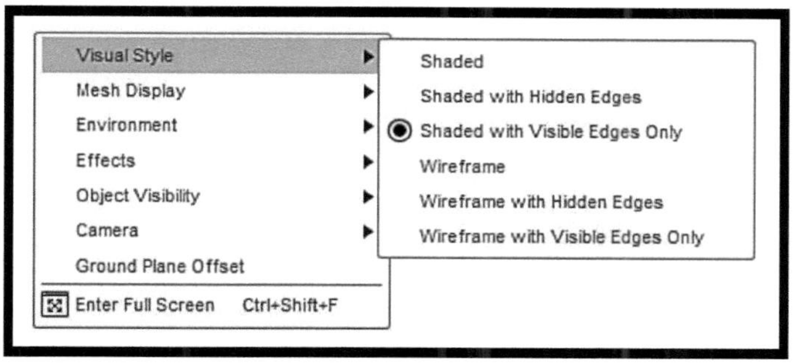

Here is an illustration of a typical item list, which in this case takes the form of a list of text items. When you click on "**Programming Resources**", it brings up a drop-down menu from which you can select a single item before the menu is cleared away again. Because there is no such thing as a "**selected**" item or state in a standard item list, nothing is ever chosen for display by default when the list is brought up for the first time.

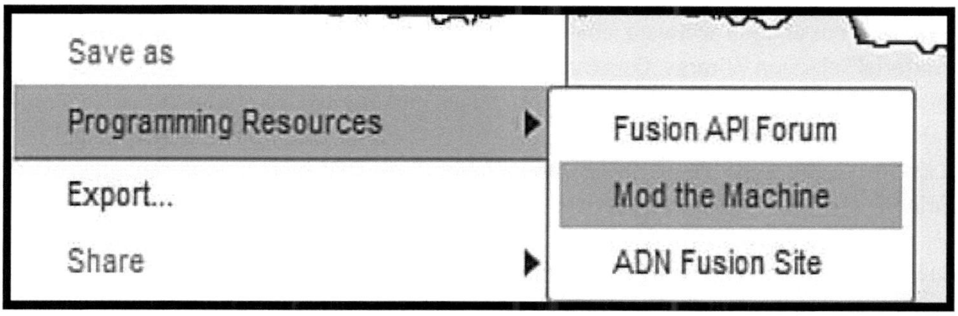

Creating custom tools and features with APIs

Using Fusion 360's Application Programming Interfaces (APIs) to build bespoke tools and features is analogous to wielding a digital blacksmith's forge; doing so enables you to mold this flexible design and engineering software to meet your requirements. Let's explore how you can leverage the power of application programming interfaces (APIs) to create bespoke solutions that improve the efficiency of your workflow and take your engineering and design projects to the next level.

1. The Fusion 360 API: Your Workshop of Creativity

The **Application Programming Interface (API)** for Fusion 360 serves as the nerve center of your journey toward greater customization. It is the equivalent of having access to a vast toolkit that is packed with a variety of functions, data, and opportunities. You can create one-of-a-kind tools and features by using the API as your hammer and anvil, and then seamlessly integrating them into the environment of Fusion 360.

2. Designing Custom Tools: Precision Tools for Your Craft

Imagine you had access to a technology that could automate the processes that are unique to your industry or project. You can make these tools by using the Fusion 360 Application Programming Interface.

Take, for instance:

- **Automated Parametric Design**: Create scripts that generate parametric designs and give you the ability to easily adjust dimensions and other parameters. Iterative design approaches can benefit greatly from having access to this information.
- **Specialized Calculators**: Develop calculators that answer difficult engineering equations directly within Fusion 360. Some examples of these equations are stress analysis and heat transfer calculations.
- **Geometry Generators**: Construct tools that can build complex three-dimensional geometries, such as gears or lattice structures, in accordance with the specifications of your project.

3. Integrating Custom Features: Elevating Fusion 360's Capabilities

Because Fusion 360 is extensible using application programming interfaces (APIs), you can include bespoke features that behave as though they were always a part of the program. **Some instances are as follows:**

- **Simulation and Analysis Plugins**: Create plugins that connect Fusion 360 with specialized simulation or analysis software, enabling you to perform simulations directly within Fusion 360.
- **Material Selection Wizards**: Construct wizards that guide you through the process of selecting the most appropriate materials for your ideas, taking into account criteria such as cost, strength, and influence on the environment.
- **Custom Visualization Tools:** Design visualization tools that offer unique rendering styles or 3D printing previews, enhancing your ability to present and communicate your designs.

4. Workflow Enhancements: Boosting Efficiency

APIs empower you to optimize your workflow. Consider these enhancements:

- **Batch Processing Scripts:** Automate batch tasks like file conversions, rendering, or exporting data, ensuring consistency and saving valuable time.
- **Data Management Add-Ins:** Create tools that organize and manage your Fusion 360 data, making it easier to find and reuse designs.
- **Custom Reporting Tools:** Generate detailed reports on design changes, project progress, or performance metrics, providing valuable insights for decision-making.

5. Collaboration and Standardization: Bringing Teams Together

Your organization's internal collaboration and standardization can also be encouraged with the use of specialized tools and features:

- **Design Review Workflows:** Create bespoke processes for design reviews, enabling members of your team to submit input directly within Fusion 360.
- **Design Standards Enforcement:** Create add-ins that impose design rules and guidelines to guarantee that there will be no inconsistencies across projects.
- **Custom Collaboration Portals:** Construct portals within Fusion 360 to share project-specific information and facilitate contact with coworkers, customers, or suppliers.

Creating custom tools and features with APIs in Fusion 360 involves a series of steps and requires some programming knowledge. Here's a high-level overview of the process:

1. Set Up Your Development Environment:

- You'll need a code editor for writing scripts and add-ins. Autodesk provides a built-in code editor in Fusion 360, or you can use an external code editor like Visual Studio Code.
- Ensure you have a Fusion 360 account and the software installed on your computer.

2. Choose the Type of Custom Tool or Feature:

- Determine what specific tool or feature you want to create. Is it a script add-in, a command add-in, or a panel add-in?
- Understand the functionality and purpose of your custom tool. Consider the problem you're trying to solve or the workflow you want to enhance.

4. Write the Code:

- Start writing the code for your custom tool using Fusion 360's API. This will involve using JavaScript (Fusion JavaScript) to interact with Fusion 360's objects and functions.
- Depending on your chosen type of add-in, you'll write code to define the behavior of your tool. For example, if it's a script add-in, you'll create a script that automates a specific task.

5. Test Your Custom Tool:

- Regularly test your code within Fusion 360 to ensure it functions as intended. You can run your scripts or add-ins directly from the "**Scripts and Add-Ins**" workspace in Fusion 360.

6. Debug and Refine:

- Debugging is an essential part of the development process. Use the debugging tools in your code editor to identify and fix any issues in your code.
- Continuously refine your custom tool based on feedback and testing. Pay attention to usability and user experience.

7. Documentation and User Interface (UI):

- If your custom tool has a user interface (UI), design it to be user-friendly and intuitive.
- Provide documentation or instructions for users on how to install and use your tool effectively.

8. Package and Share:

- Package your custom tool or feature as an add-in that can be easily installed by others. Fusion 360 allows you to package add-ins as .ZIP files.
- Consider sharing your add-in with the Fusion 360 community through Autodesk's App Store or other relevant platforms.

9. Maintain and Update:

- Continue to maintain and update your custom tool as needed, especially when Fusion 360 undergoes updates or changes to its API.
- Listen to user feedback and make improvements accordingly.

10. Seek Help and Collaboration:

- Don't hesitate to seek help or collaborate with other developers in the Fusion 360 community. Forums and online communities can be valuable resources for troubleshooting and learning.

Searching the API Documentation

The Fusion assistance system has support for searching that is integrated right in. As can be seen in the image to the right, the page has a search bar close to the top. When using this aid, filters are supported to restrict the results; nonetheless, users still frequently wind up with a vast list of results, which can make it challenging to refine the list and select the most relevant area. When searching, it is recommended that you use Google because it typically returns superior results. Google has indexed every single part of the assistance system.

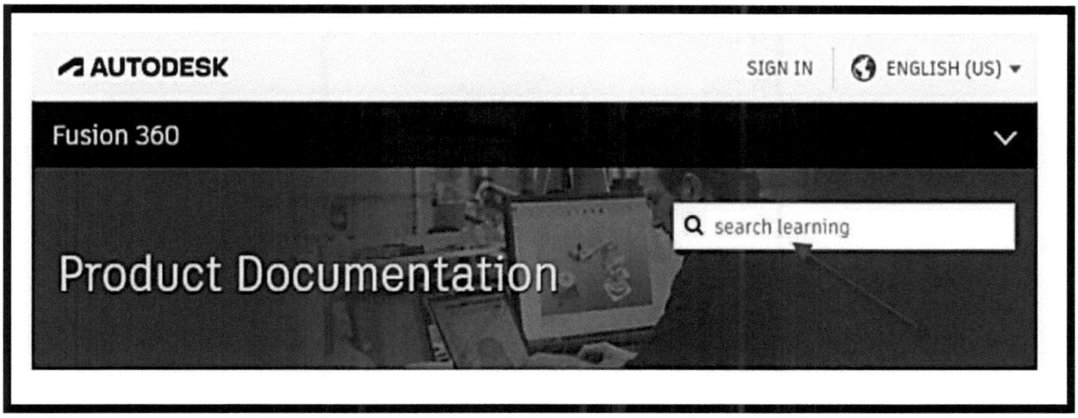

What's New in the Fusion 360 API

Enhancements

1. **Python Version Update**

The version of Python that is built into Fusion has been updated to version 3.11 in this release, which brings it from version 3.9. This modification affects add-ins that are shipped as compiled Python modules (files ending in.pyc). Add-ins that were created with Python 3.9 will not load properly with Python 3.11 because compiled modules are only compatible with the minor release version of Python that was used to produce them. This only affects add-ins that only deliver.pyc files or rely on libraries that only provide the.pyc files because Python automatically recompiles the.py source files to create new.pyc files. If the add-in folder already contains the.py source files, then there is no issue because Python automatically recompiles them.

2. **Named Views support**

The functionality of Fusion's Named Views is now fully supported by the API in its entirety. Take note of the "**Named Views**" folder, which is located towards the top of the browser tree, if you are not familiar with named views. Four named views are normal, and you can also create new views with names of your choosing. When a named view is established, the camera orientation is saved within the named view, which allows you to quickly return to the previous view you were using.

3. **Rip Features**

The application programming interface (API) now provides users with the capability to build and change the newly introduced sheet metal Rip Features.

4. **New Sketch Constraints**

Some new sketch constraints have been added to Fusion, and the API now also supports the creation of those constraints. Look for the new addCoincidentToSurface, addLineParallelToPlanarSurface, andaddLineOnPlanarSurfaceaddPerpendicularToSurface methods on the GeometricConstraints object. Two of the new constraints are dimension constraints and the new addDistanceBetweenPointAndSurfaceDimension,addDistanceBetweenLineAndPlanarSurfaceDimension methods have been added to the SketchDimensions object.

New objects that represent each type of constraint have also been added to the API.

5. **Rendering**

Adding support for rendering "in canvas" brings this version closer to its goal of fully exposing the Rendering functionality contained within the API. There was already support for local rendering, which is carried out on the local machine but in a separate process that runs in the background. When rendering is done in the Fusion window, this is referred to as "In Canvas" rendering. Depending on your requirements, you can now select the best option.

6. **CAM Hole and Pocket Feature Recognition**

In the version that took place in July 2023, a preview feature was included that gave users the capacity to spot holes and pockets. It is no longer in the preview stage and the complete version is now supported. Because of this new edition, the **Feature Recognition** user guide has been updated to include a new item that explains the functionality of the program as well as its capabilities. In addition to that, there is a fresh example that displays the capability of it.

7. **Canvases**

The ability to create and update canvases is moving out of preview, and a new Canvases subject has been developed in the user guide. It describes the specifics of how to use the API, along with providing some examples.

8. **Project Axis in Revolve Feature**

When you are creating a revolve feature, the option to "Project Axis" is now supported by the API.

Basic API Concepts

Some basic concepts are used throughout the Fusion 360 API and understanding these concepts will make the API much easier to understand and use.

Objects

The Fusion 360 Application Programming Interface (API) is an object-oriented API that is accessed through a collection of objects. As a user of Fusion 360, you should find that many of these objects have a one-to-one correlation with features or functions that you are already familiar with. For instance, the **ExtrudeFeature** object is what the Fusion 360 API uses to describe an extrusion in a model that was created with Fusion 360. You can perform the same actions that you can perform through the user interface by utilizing the capabilities offered by the **ExtrudeFeature** object. You can, for instance, make a new extrusion, retrieve and set its name in the timeline, suppress it, remove it, and even access and change the sketch that is linked with it. In addition to the API objects that represent elements in the Fusion 360 UI that you are already familiar with, there are additional objects that are specific to working with the API that provide functionality that cannot be accessed any other way. These objects are referred to as "**API only**" objects. Using the Application Programming Interface (API), it is possible, for instance, to query a model and obtain all of its geometry. The ability to generate new commands and add them to the user interface of Fusion 360 is another example of a capability that is only available through the API.

Object Model

How particular objects are accessed is one of the fundamental distinctions that can be made between using the Fusion 360 user interface and the API. Dedicated commands are used to construct new things, such as "**Extrude**" to generate an extrusion or "**Box**" to build a new box. These commands are used to create new objects. Access to objects is handled by something that is known as "**Object Model**" when using the API. The section of the object model that is displayed below is the one that is used whenever extrusions are being created. At the highest level, the Application object stands in for the entirety of Fusion 360. The Application object grants access to attributes that apply to the entire application in addition to providing access to its immediate descendants (Documents being the most important of these). Modeling and CAM data are two examples of the types of information that can be stored in documents. All of the data that was modeled for use in the document is represented by the Design object. There is one component at the very top level of the Design object, and it is referred to as the root component. The root component serves as the entry point for accessing all of the sketches, features, construction geometry, components, and other elements that are present within the Design. The object model contains a hierarchical structure that is structured in a parent-child fashion for all of the items. It ought to be fairly obvious, in most circumstances, what the path is that one must take to reach a specific object. Consider, for instance, what would be responsible for the ownership of a sketch line if you wanted to gain access to a particular drawing line. A sketch is the entity that owns all of the different kinds of sketch entities, while a component is the entity that owns a sketch. The browser will frequently represent the same structure in multiple instances.

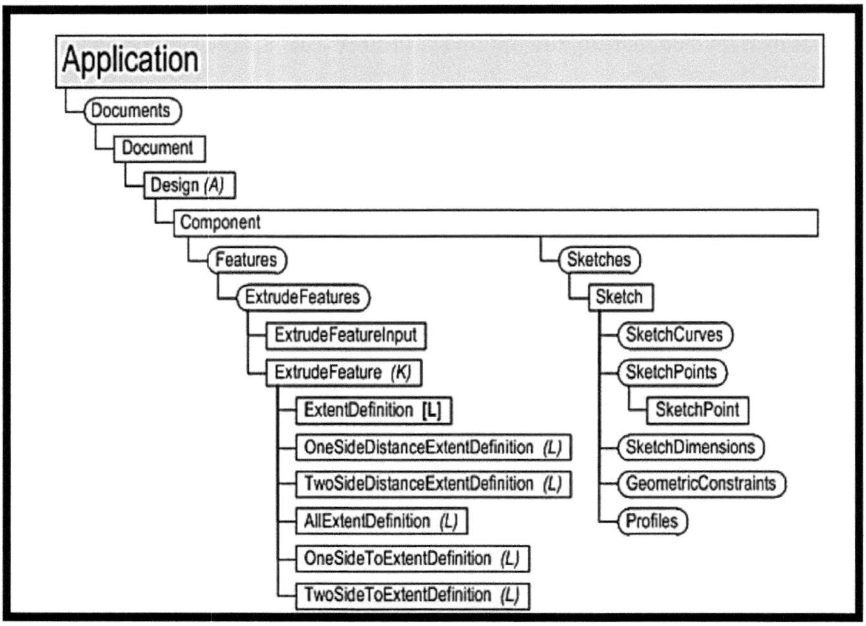

Creating Custom Commands and Workflows

The process of developing custom commands and workflows in Fusion 360 is similar to developing a finely tuned tool that is in tune with the specific requirements of your design and engineering projects. This method requires careful planning, a deft hand with coding, and some measure of creative thinking.

The following is an in-depth guide that will teach you how to get started on your voyage of customization:

1. Articulate Your Vision:

- Before delving into the realm of code, you must articulate your vision. Define the problem you want to solve or the workflow you aim to optimize. This clarity is your North Star throughout the customization journey.

2. The Fusion 360 API: Your Craftsmanship Toolkit:

- Fusion 360's Application Programming Interface (API) is your virtual workshop, filled with tools and materials for creating custom commands and workflows. Dive into the API documentation, gaining insight into the intricate workings of Fusion 360's core.

3. Choosing the Right Path:

- **Determine the nature of your customization**: Is it a custom command, a panel add-in, or a script add-in?
- **Custom Commands:** These are finely crafted tools in your digital toolbox, enabling you to add specific actions that seamlessly blend with Fusion 360's native commands.
- **Panel Add-Ins:** Picture a customized control center within Fusion 360, where you can orchestrate a symphony of commands and tools, elegantly organized in a panel of your design.
- **Script Add-Ins:** For quick automation and streamlined tasks, script add-ins are your swift brushes, allowing you to automate repetitive tasks with finesse.

4. Artistry in Code:

- Embrace JavaScript, the artist's palette of Fusion 360 customization. Your code will sculpt your vision into reality, breathing life into your commands and workflows.
- Define the behavior of your custom command or workflow. For a custom command, this could involve complex parametric modeling or intricate simulations. A panel add-in might require a sophisticated UI design, while a script add-in handles repetitive tasks with graceful precision.

5. Refinement through Testing:

- Like a sculptor fine-tuning their masterpiece, continually test your creation within Fusion 360. Ensure it functions harmoniously with your design and engineering processes.
- Debug any imperfections, refining your code to ensure seamless execution.

6. Documentation and User Experience:

- A custom command or workflow should be as intuitive as a masterful piece of art. If it includes a user interface (UI), design it with user-friendliness in mind.
- Provide clear documentation or instructions, ensuring that users can seamlessly incorporate your customizations into their workflows.

7. Packaging and Sharing Your Craftsmanship:

- Package your custom command or workflow for easy distribution. Fusion 360 allows you to bundle your creation as an add-in, simplifying installation for others.
- Consider sharing your customizations with the wider Fusion 360 community, contributing to a collaborative ecosystem of innovative tools.

8. Ongoing Artistic Maintenance:

- Just as art requires preservation, your customizations need upkeep. Regularly maintain and update your commands and workflows, especially when Fusion 360 evolves or the API changes.

- Stay attuned to user feedback and adapt your creations accordingly, ensuring they remain finely tuned to meet evolving needs.

Creating a Script or Add-In

Creating, Editing, and Running Your First Script

There is not much of a distinction between a script and an add-in from a technical standpoint. Because the procedures for generating, revising, and debugging them are, for the most part, equivalent, the description that follows applies to both of these processes. Before delving into the specifics, let's take a look at the fundamental actions required to write, edit, and execute a Python script or add-in. Creating a C++ script or add-in follows a procedure that is fairly similar to that.

1. Run the **Scripts and Add-Ins** command from the **UTILITIES** tab in the toolbar, as shown below.

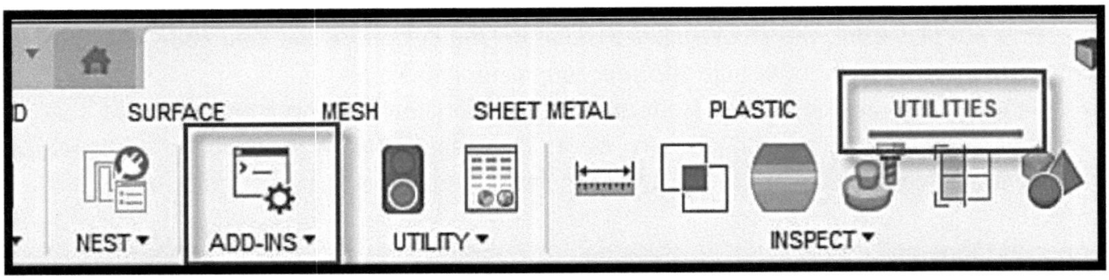

2. To create a new script or add-in, select the "**Create**" button in the Scripts and Add-Ins dialog.
3. After selecting "**Script**" and "**Python**" as the programming language in the "**Create New Script or Add-In**" box, enter a name for the script name, and then optionally enter some information in the "**Description" and "Author**" columns before pressing the "**Create**" button. This will return you to the "**Scripts and Add-Ins**" dialog that you were previously in.

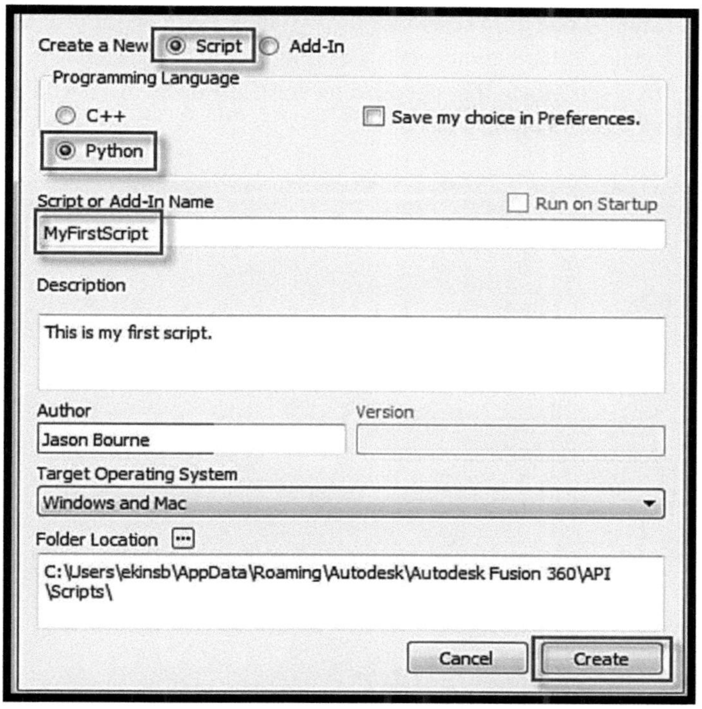

4. You now have a script, and it will be visible on the "**Scripts**" tab's list of programs when you select that tab. To make changes to it, you must first select it and then click the "Edit" button.

Fusion's development environment for Python projects is called **Visual Studio Code (VS Code),** and it is used by Fusion. When you try to edit or debug in Fusion 360, if Visual Studio Code is not already installed on your computer, the following installation prompt will appear. This step is only necessary the very first time you make any changes to a script or add-in. Repeat the **Edit step** to open the script in VS Code once the installation of VS Code has been completed.

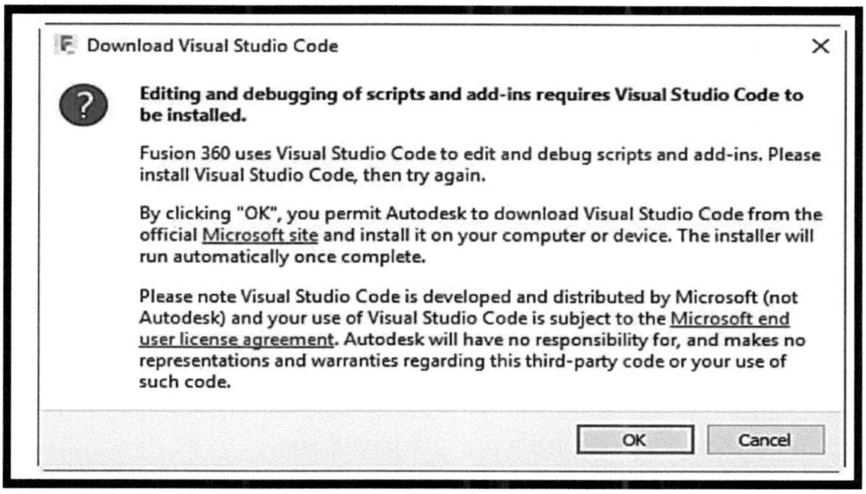

When you launch Visual Studio Code from Fusion for the first time, a box will appear informing you that an extension is now being installed. The Python plugin for Visual Studio Code is being installed by Fusion 360 right now. In addition, this is something that needs to be done just once. In the end, once everything has been installed, VS Code will open, as shown below.

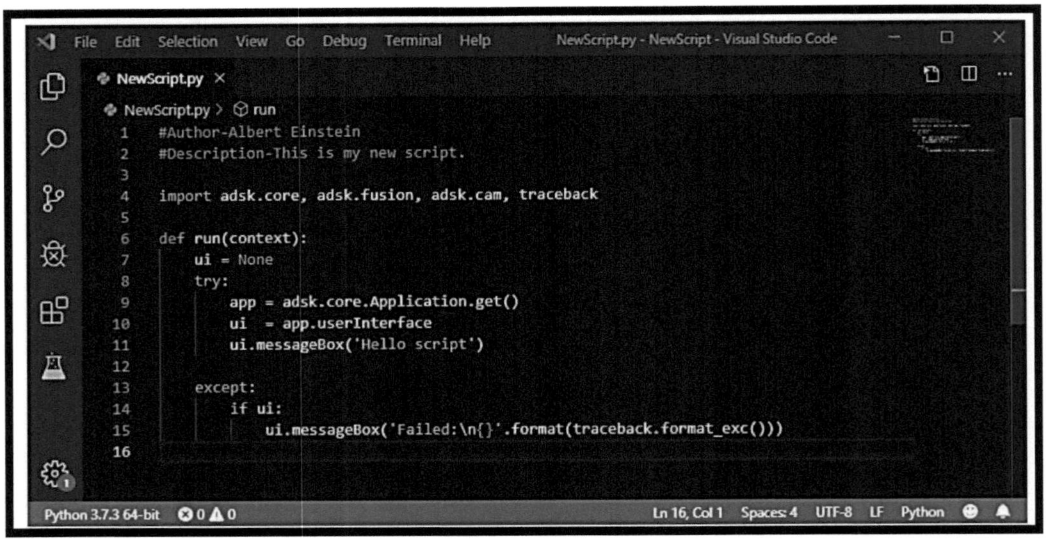

5. Your program can now be edited through the use of VS Code. Save the modifications you make after modifying the text for the messageBox to any message you desire, such as the one that is shown below. This will complete the easy example.

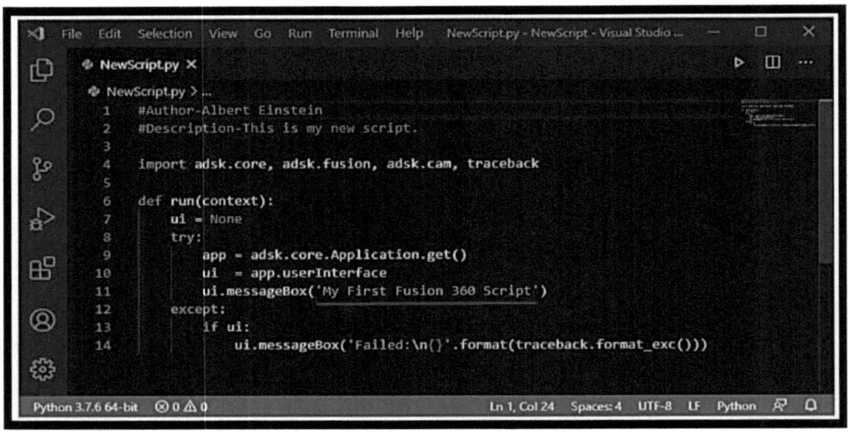

6. You should be proud because you've just finished writing your first script. To execute your script, you will need to first invoke the Scripts and Add-Ins command, choose your script from the list of available scripts, and then click the "**Run**" button.

- The script will execute and carry out the instructions that it was given to carry out. In this particular instance, it will show the message box that is displayed below.

7. The ability to debug your software is the aspect of a development environment that is considered to be the most crucial. **Python and C++** have significantly distinct approaches to the debugging

process. In the language-specific subjects, you'll find information about debugging your **Python and C++** applications, which you can then put to use.

Script and Add-In Details

Now that you are familiar with the fundamental steps involved in writing and debugging a script, I will provide you with some additional information regarding the specifics of scripts and add-ins. Users and programmers alike will find that the **Scripts and Add-Ins** dialog is their primary point of entry when it comes to scripts and add-ins. It consists of two tabs, one of which lists the accessible scripts, and the other of which lists the available add-ins. You can choose a script or an add-in from these lists, and then either run it or update it. It is unnecessary to utilize the "**Debug**" option because it performs the same function as the "**Edit**" option in the drop-down menu located directly under the "**Run**" button.

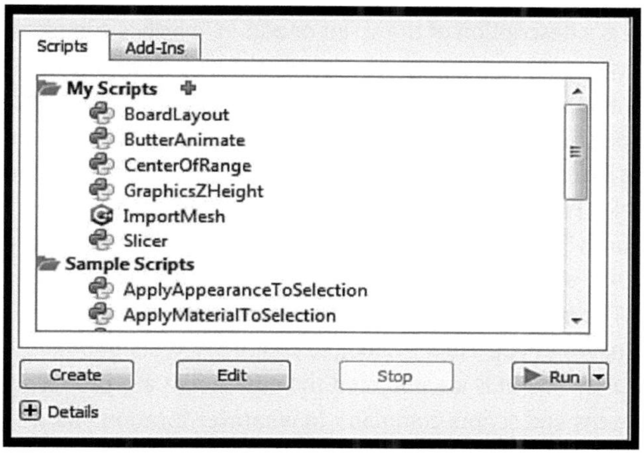

The "**Create New Script or Add-In**" box is presented whenever a new script or add-in is created. This is the place where you enter information regarding the script or add-in you are generating.

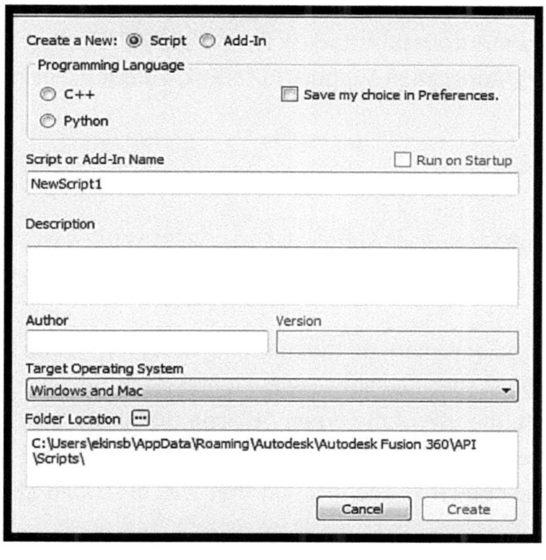

The various settings in the dialog are described below.

- **Programming Language**: Select **Python or C++** as the programming language for the script or add-in that you want to write. If you tick the box labeled "**Save my choice in Preferences**," the current settings will be saved, and the next time you generate a new script or add-in, they will be applied immediately.
- **Run on Startup** – This is an add-in-specific setting that defines whether or not the add-in should be run automatically whenever Fusion 360 is started. The vast majority of add-ins will want to make use of this capability so that the commands they describe can be made accessible to the user as soon as Fusion 360 is launched.
- **Name of Script or Add-In** – This is the name of the script or add-in that you have created. This name will be used to create a new folder in the location indicated by the "Folder Location" field, and it will also be used for the name of the script or add-in code files that are generated by the process.
- **Description**: This is a description of the script or add-in, which is completely optional.
- **Author:** This is a name that can be used to specify the person who wrote the script or add-in.
- **Version** – This is an optional setting that is add-in-specific and is the version of the add-in. This is a string and can be any form of a version label, for example, “1.0.0”, “2016”, “R1”, “V2”, etc.
- **Target Operating System** – This specifies the operating systems in which the script or add-in should be made available. For instance, if your script or add-in requires Windows-only libraries, you should change this to "**Windows**" so that Fusion 360 will not attempt to display or load it on a Mac. This will prevent any errors that may occur.
- **Folder Location**: This is the location where the script or add-in will be produced when you click the "**Location**" button. When you use the dialog to create a new script or add-in, a new folder with the name of the script or add-in is created, and the add-in files are produced within that folder. You can point the add-ins and scripts command to whatever location you wish by editing the default path in the "**General" -> "API section**" of the Preferences command. The default locations for add-ins and scripts are listed below for your reference.

Add-Ins

- **Windows** – %appdata%\Autodesk\Autodesk Fusion 360\API\AddIns
- **Mac** – $HOME/Library/Application Support/Autodesk/Autodesk Fusion 360/API/AddIns

Scripts

- Windows – %appdata%\Autodesk\Autodesk Fusion 360\API\Scripts
- Mac – $HOME/Library/Application Support/Autodesk/Autodesk Fusion 360/API/Scripts

Scripts and add-ins can be stored anywhere on the machine; however, Fusion 360 will only search for add-ins in the locations that have been specified above when it first starts up. Any script or add-in that is stored in another location will require the use of the green "+" icon that is situated near the top of the "**Scripts and Add-Ins"** dialog box to be manually located. When you are transferring or installing an add-in onto another computer, you should copy it to the location that was described above so that Fusion 360 will discover it automatically.

Script and Add-In Files

When a new script or add-in is made, a new folder is made with the name that was supplied, and the code files (a.py file for Python and a.cpp file and other relevant files for **C++**) are created at the same time. In addition to the files containing the script's or add-in's code, a file with the extension.manifest is also generated. This file stores additional information regarding the program. If you build a Python add-in and name it MyAddIn, for instance, a folder named "**MyAddIn**" containing the files listed below will be created in the "**.../Autodesk/Autodesk Fusion 360/API/AddIns" directory**. To ensure that the add-in is self-contained, additional files associated with the script or add-in, such as icons, should be added to this folder. Once these files are in place, the add-in can be "**installed**" by merely copying this folder to the appropriate location.

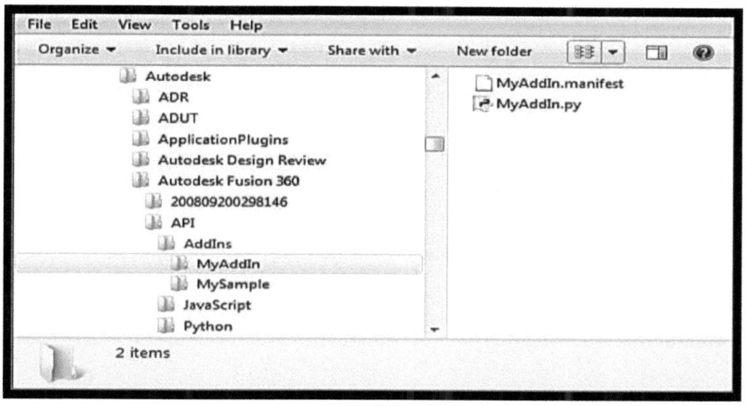

The Manifest File

The information that you gave in the "**Create New Script or Add-In**" window when you initially created the script or add-in is stored in the.manifest file that is associated with the script or add-in. It also contains extra information that Fusion 360 uses to determine when it should be shown and loaded. This information is contained in the file. The add-in and the manifest file share the same name, but the manifest file's name is followed by the extension.manifest. The file in question is a **JSON-formatted** text file. An example of a common manifest file for an add-in is provided below.

```
{
    "autodeskProduct":  "Fusion360",
    "type": "addin",
    "id":   "62a9e55a-dbe4-408d-ad8b-cb802473725e",
    "author":   "Brian Ekins",
    "description":  {
        "": "This is a test add-in."
    },
    "version":  "V1",
    "runOnStartup": true,
    "supportedOS":  "windows|mac"
}
```

A description of each of the items included in the manifest can be found below.

- **Autodeskproduct**: The value **"Fusion360"** will remain assigned to this attribute at all times.
- **Type**: This property can have the value "**addin" or "script**" to indicate whether the software in question is an add-in or a script.
- **Id**: This attribute is a GUID that identifies this add-in in a way that is not shared with any other add-in. If you ever create a new add-in or script by copying an existing add-in or script, you should replace this ID with a new GUID so that the ID of each one is unique. This is necessary to ensure that the add-ins and scripts you produce are compatible with each other. Fusion 360 does not take advantage of this at the moment, but there is a good chance that it will shortly.
- **Author**: This property is a string that contains the author's name; it is referred to as the "author" property. The "**Scripts and Add-Ins**" window presents this information to the user.
- **Description** - This is a JSON object with properties that define the add-in's description. It can be found in the "**description**" property. It is supplied as an object in the JSON format, with one or more properties, so that descriptions can be specified in a variety of languages. The example that is shown below contains one property that does not have a name. This is the default description, and it will be used for any language that does not have a specified description. Using language codes that are industry standard, the other attributes determine the text that will be used for the various other languages that are supported by Fusion 360.

```
"Description":{
                "":"Default description",
                "1028": "說明在中國",
                "1031": "Beschreibung auf Deutsch",
                "1033": "Description in English",
                "1034": "Descripción en Español",
                "1036": "Description en Français",
                "1040": "Descrizione in Italiano",
                "1041": "日本語での説明",
                "1042": "한국어 설명"
}
```

- **Version**: This property defines the version of the add-in and can be any string, for example, "**1.0.0", "2016", "R1", "V2**", etc.
- **runOnStartup**: This is a property that can be set to either true or false to indicate whether or not this add-in should be automatically started by Fusion 360 whenever Fusion 360 is started.
- **supportedOS**: This attribute can take the values "**windows,**" "**mac," or "windows|mac.**" This identifies the computer operating systems on which the add-in will load. This is utilized, for instance, in the situation where an add-in needs OS-specific libraries, which means that the add-in will not function properly on any other operating system. For instance, if I were to build an add-in that required the usage of a Windows-specific library, I could set the supportedOS property of the add-in to "**windows,**" which would prevent Fusion 360 from displaying the add-in in the "**Scripts and Add-Ins**" menu on a Mac and from attempting to launch it automatically when the program started up. This should be set to "windows|mac" to indicate that the add-in can be loaded for both Mac and Windows computers. Since the vast majority of Python scripts and add-ins should be

compatible with both operating systems, this setting is unnecessary. Because C++ scripts and add-ins need to be generated separately for each platform, it is more probable that the developer will choose this option when they do not have access to both a Windows and a Mac system to compile the code.

- **sourcewindows and sourcemac**: For both Windows and Mac, a C++ script or add-in possesses two additional characteristics that identify the filename of the project file. These properties are the same. When you select the "**Edit**" option in the "**Scripts and Add-Ins**" dialog box, Fusion 360 will open the related project file utilizing the program that is typically used for opening files of that particular type. For instance, a.vcxproj file is supplied for the sourcewindows property in the example that can be found further down on this page. As a result, Visual Studio will be launched since Windows has designated it as the application that should be used to open.vcxproj files. You can select any code editor you prefer by editing this file and saving the changes.

```
"sourcewindows":    "NewCPPTest.vcxproj",
"sourcemac":    "NewCPPTest.xcodeproj"
```

It is important to take note that the name of the script or add-in is not provided anywhere in the manifest file, except for the **sourcewindows and sourcemac** properties. The name is determined by the name that is given to the directory that contains all of the files. If you want to alter the name of a script or add-in, you must first modify the names of the directory and the files to reflect the new name.

Script Code

This is the code that gets generated whenever a new Python script is produced, and it can be found below. Please take note of the "**run**" function. When the script is executed in Fusion 360, the run function will be called automatically by the program. In addition, Fusion sends information to the script via the "**context**" option, which indicates whether the script is being loaded during a session or whether it is being run when Fusion 360 first starts up. This can be ignored for a script since this code is only ever executed during a session of Fusion 360 and never at the program's beginning. Your script begins execution when you call the run function, and when that function returns successfully, Fusion recognizes that the script is done and unloads it.

```
Import adsk.core, adsk.fusion, traceback

def run(context):
    ui = None
    try:
        app = adsk.core.Application.get()
        ui  = app.userInterface
        ui.messageBox('Hello script')

    except:
        if ui:
            ui.messageBox('Failed:\n{}'.format(traceback.format_exc()))
```

Scripts vs. Add-Ins

There is virtually little difference, from a technological standpoint, between a script and an add-in, as was mentioned earlier. The fundamental distinction lies in the manner in which they have carried out and the length of their existence. The user can run a script by selecting the **"Scripts and Add-Ins"** command, and the script will terminate its execution as soon as the "**run**" function has finished its processing. After a script has completed running, the process is over. When Fusion 360 first starts up, an add-in will normally be loaded automatically by the software. During the initialization process, an add-in will often generate one or more user-specific instructions and add them to the user interface. The add-in remains active for the duration of the user's session in Fusion 360 so that it can respond immediately whenever any of its commands are carried out by the user. The add-in will continue to run until either Fusion 360 is terminated or the user stops it directly through the "**Scripts and Add-Ins**" box. When it stops, it cleans away any user interface customizations that it produces in its stop function. This occurs when the program exits.

There is no difference between a script and an add-in in terms of how they use the Fusion 360 API. It is the same API, and none of the API calls are restricted to being used only by add-ins or scripts. On the other hand, there are a few parts of the API that are more beneficial to an add-in than they are to a script. The first component of the application programming interface (API) is the part that focuses on dealing with the user interface of Fusion 360 and adding buttons or other controls to access your custom instructions. If you build a custom command that draws geometry in a sketch, for instance, you will want to add a new button to the Sketch panel so that it is simple for the user to locate. This will ensure that the command is used correctly. Because an add-in can be loaded at startup, it can add its unique commands to the user interface whenever Fusion 360 starts up. This ensures that the instructions are always available to the user and gives the impression that they are a normal Fusion 360 command.

The Commands interface is a second part of the API that can be beneficial for add-ins. The usage of commands is not restricted to add-ins, and there may be occasions when it is necessary to make use of the command capabilities within a script; however, it is more common to utilize commands within an add-in, where they also make more sense.

Conclusion

This guide to Autodesk Fusion 360 has gone into great detail about one of the most powerful and flexible pieces of design and engineering tools on the market right now. A lot of advanced tools and methods have been looked at that can help people elevate their design and engineering projects to a higher level. By using simulations and analysis, parametric models, and generative design, Fusion 360 lets professionals come up with new ideas, make designs better, and test how well they work—all in a single, unified space. Using cloud-based tools for teamwork and data management together has made it easier than ever to work together with teams from around the world. This has increased output and sped up the product development process. The information and skills you learn from this guide will come in handy in the world of design and engineering right now, where things change quickly. Whether you're an experienced worker who wants to stay on top of your game or a beginner who wants to get the most out of Fusion 360, the advanced techniques and tips in this book will help you stay on top of your game and be successful. As you move forward with Fusion 360, keep in mind that the quest for greatness in engineering and design is a continuing process. Don't be afraid to try new things, and keep pushing the limits of what's possible. Fusion 360 is more than just a tool; it's a creative partner that can help you make your unique ideas come to life.

Thanks for coming along with us on this trip through advanced Fusion 360. We hope everything goes well with your design and engineering projects, and we can't wait to see the amazing things you make.

Fusion 2D 360 Practice Exercises

Exercise one

Sketch the model shown in the image below. The dimensions and the model shown in the figure are for your reference only. All dimensions are in mm.

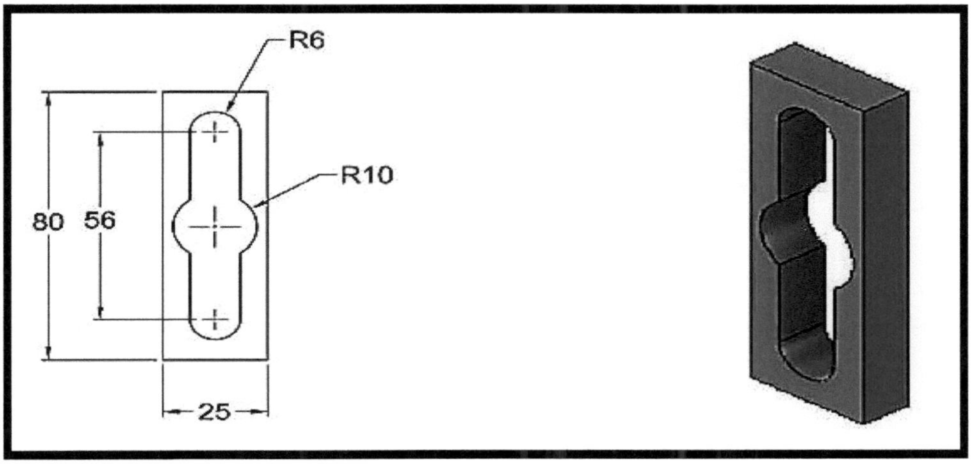

Exercise Two

Draw the sketch shown in the image below and make it fully defined by applying all dimensions and constraints. The model shown in this figure is for your reference only.

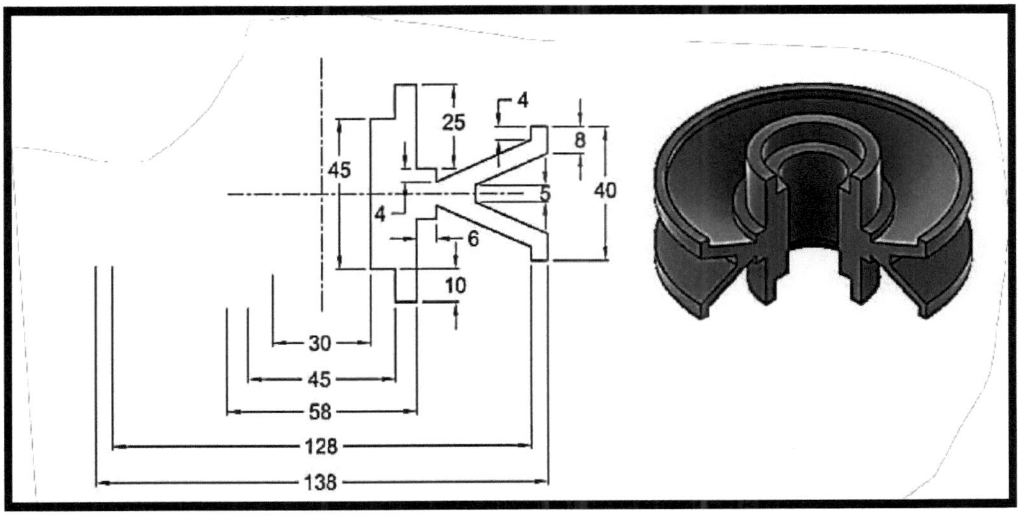

Exercise Three

Draw the sketch shown below and make it fully defined by applying the dimensions and constraints. The model shown in this figure is for your reference only.

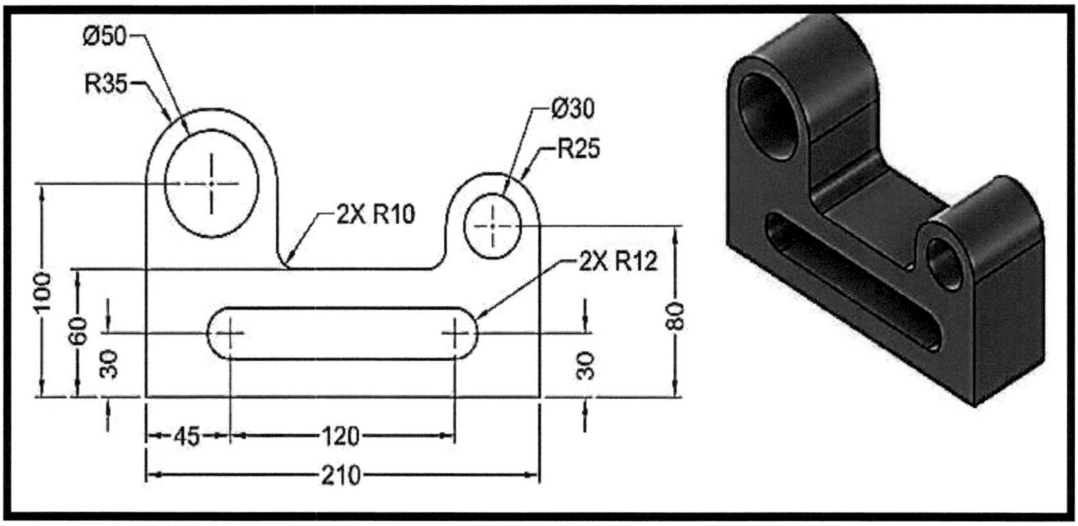

Exercise Four

Draw the sketch shown below and make it fully defined by applying all dimensions and constraints. The model shown in this figure is for your reference only.

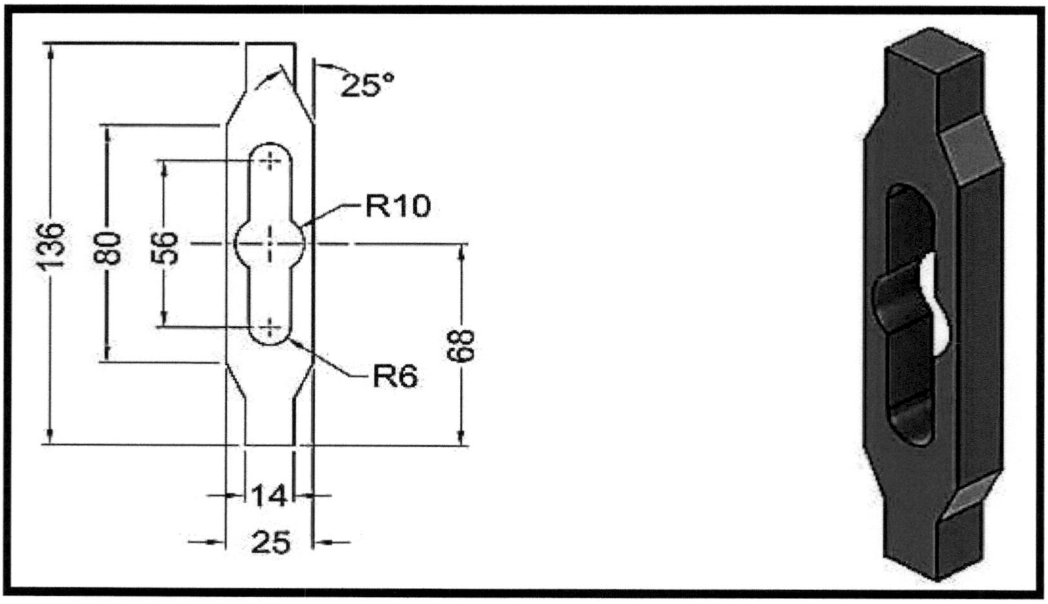

Exercise Five

Sketch the model shown below. You need to apply dimensions to make it fully defined. The model shown in the figure is for your reference only.

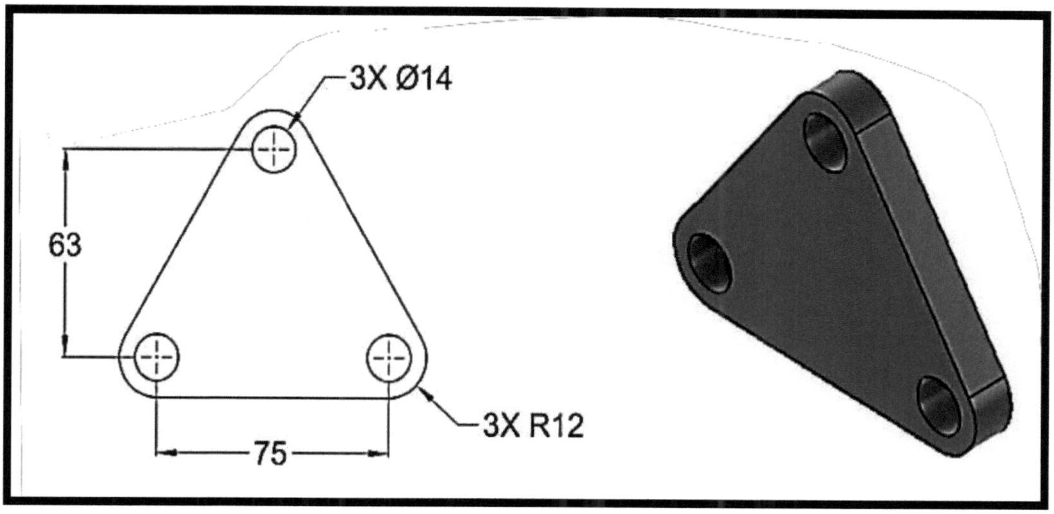

Exercise Six

Create the revolve model, as shown in the image below. All dimensions are in mm.

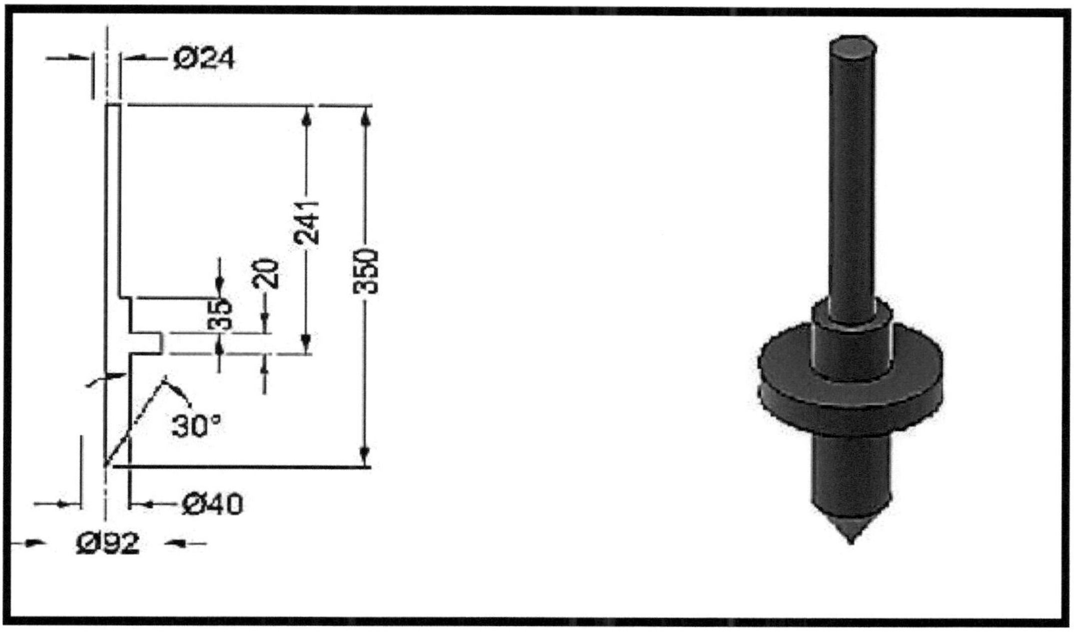

Exercise Seven

Create the extruded model, as shown in the image below. The depth of extrusion is 2 mm. All dimensions are in mm.

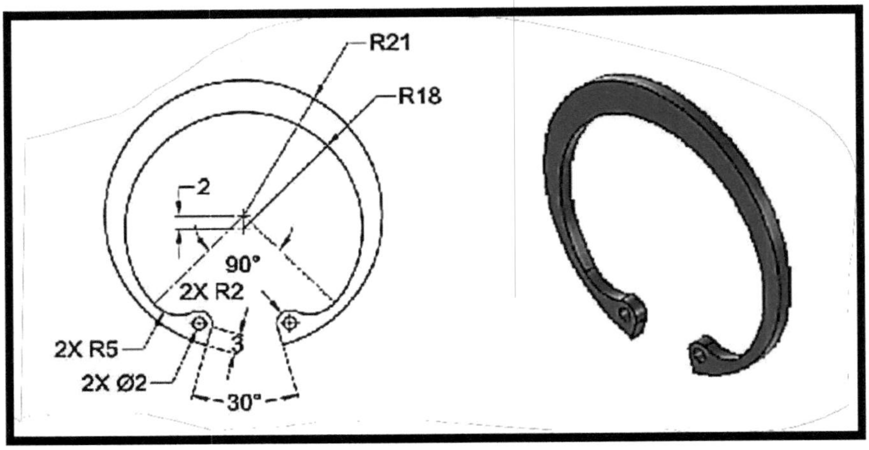

Fusion 3D 360 Practice Exercises

You can put your Fusion skills to the test by working through the 3D Fusion Exercises and practice drawings that are provided below.

Exercise One

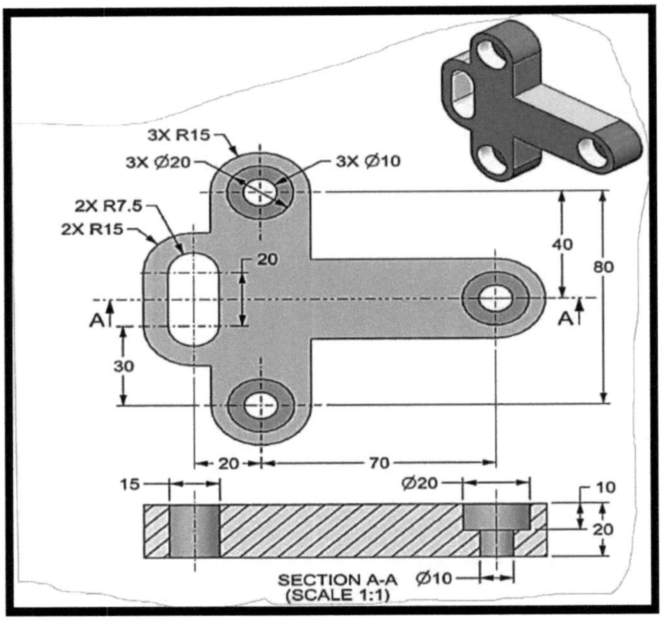

Exercise Two

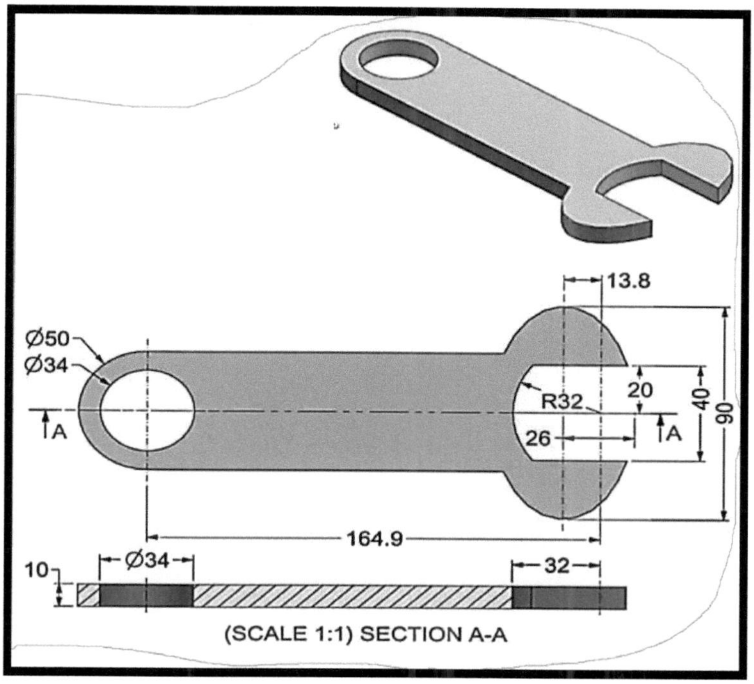

Exercise Three

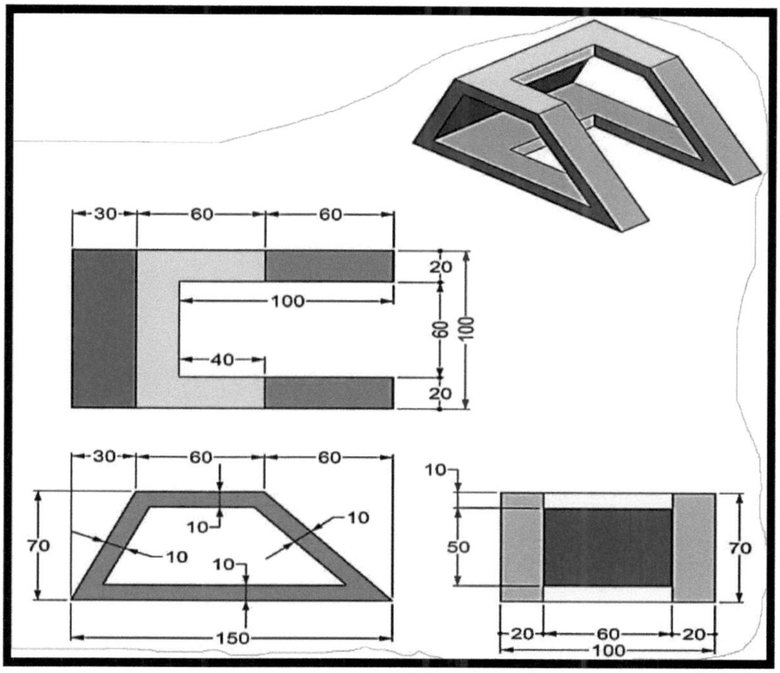

Exercise Four

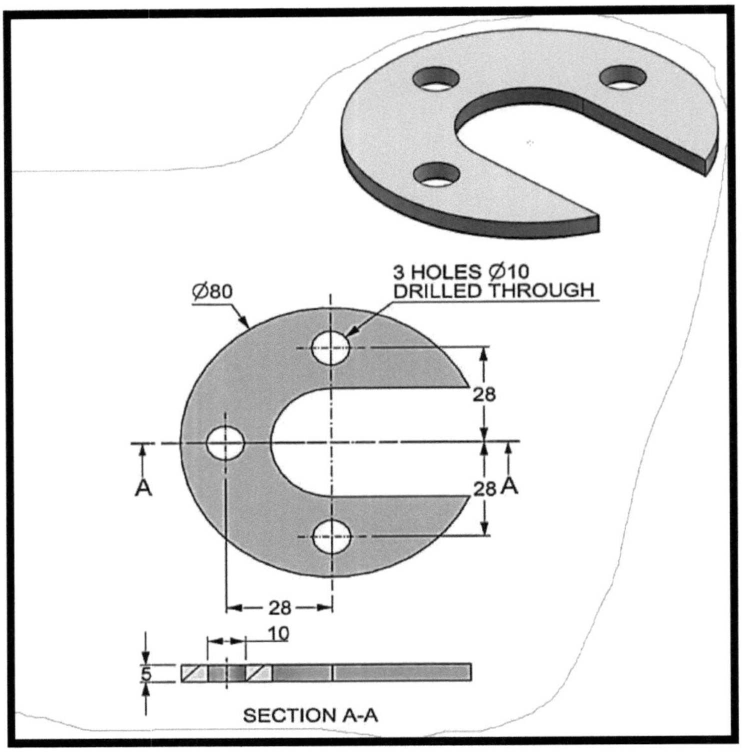

Exercise Five

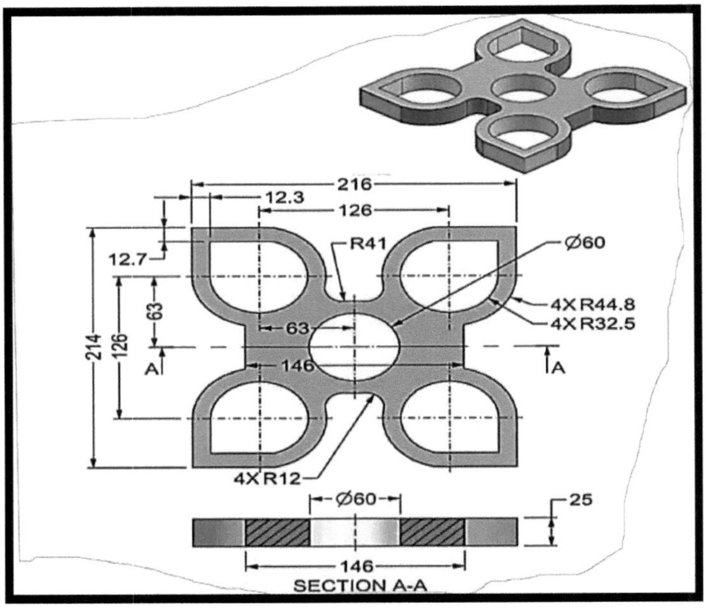

Exercise Six

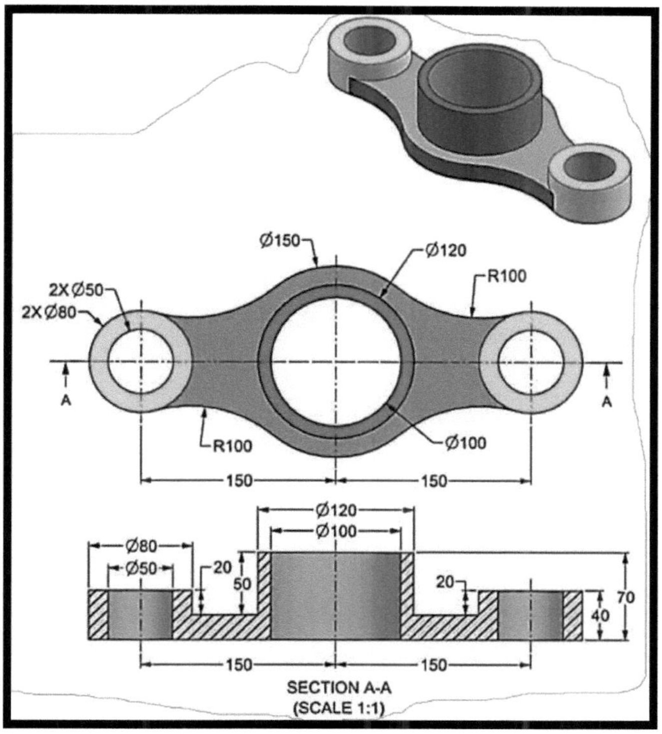

Exercise Seven

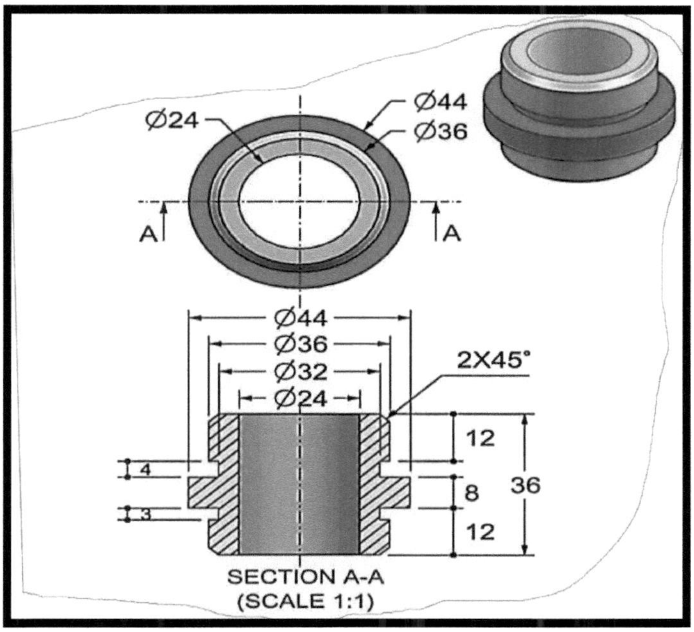

Exercise Eight

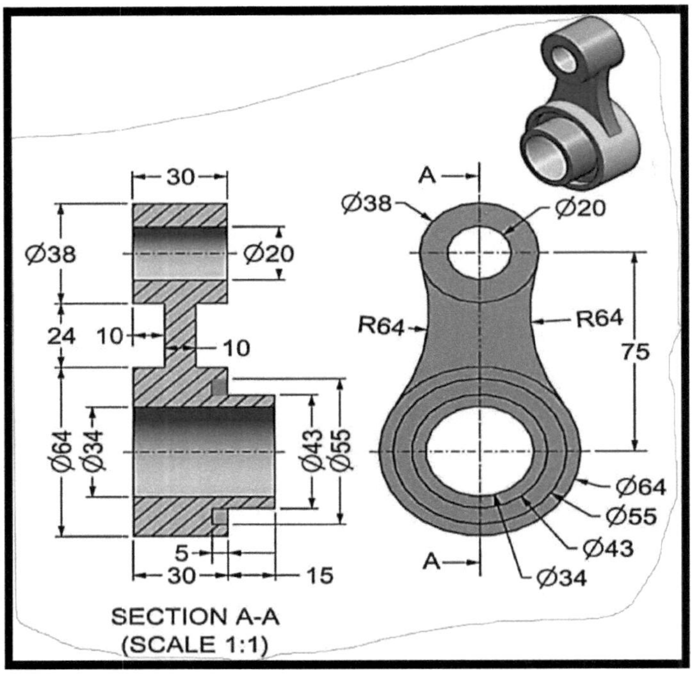

Exercise Nine

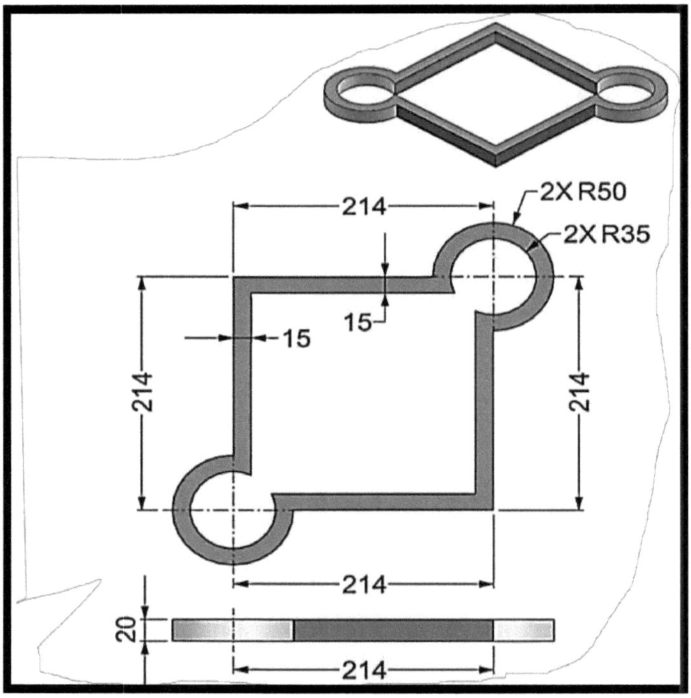

Exercise Ten

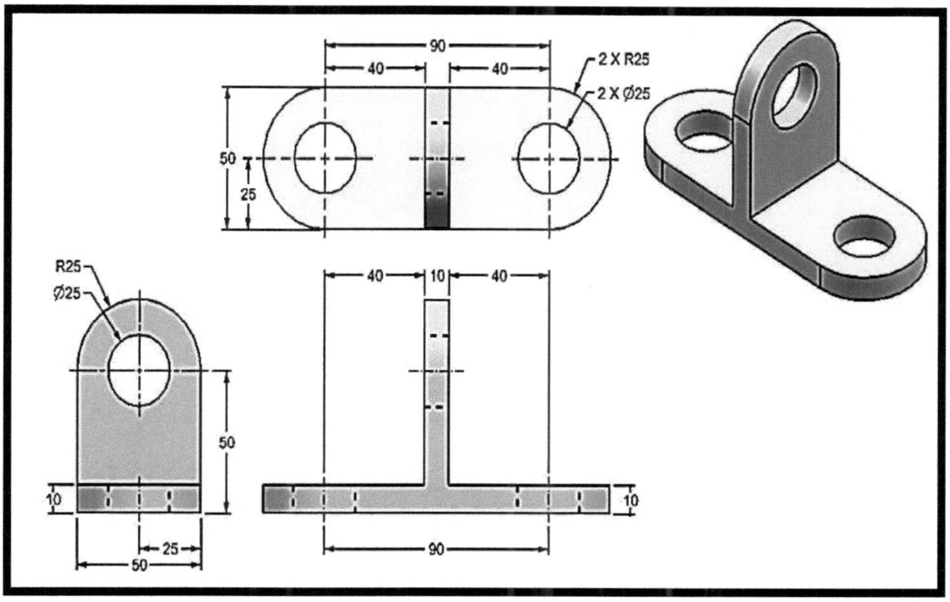

Exercise Eleven

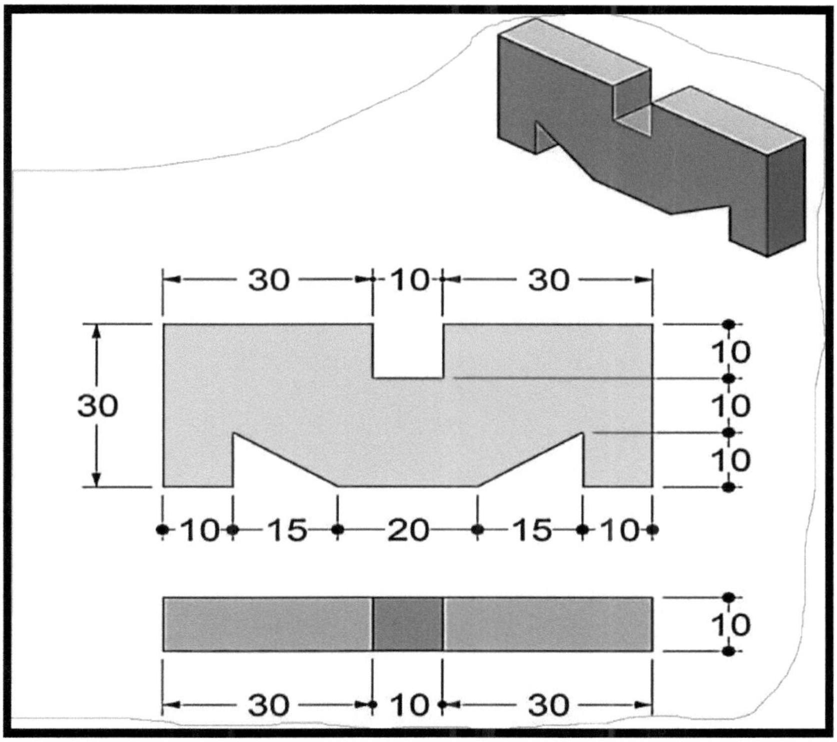

Exercise Twelve

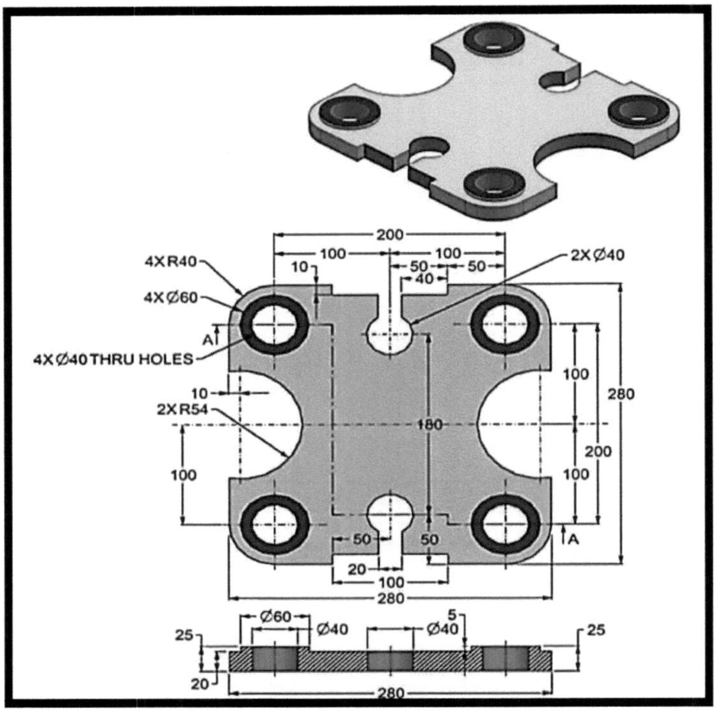

Exercise Thirteen

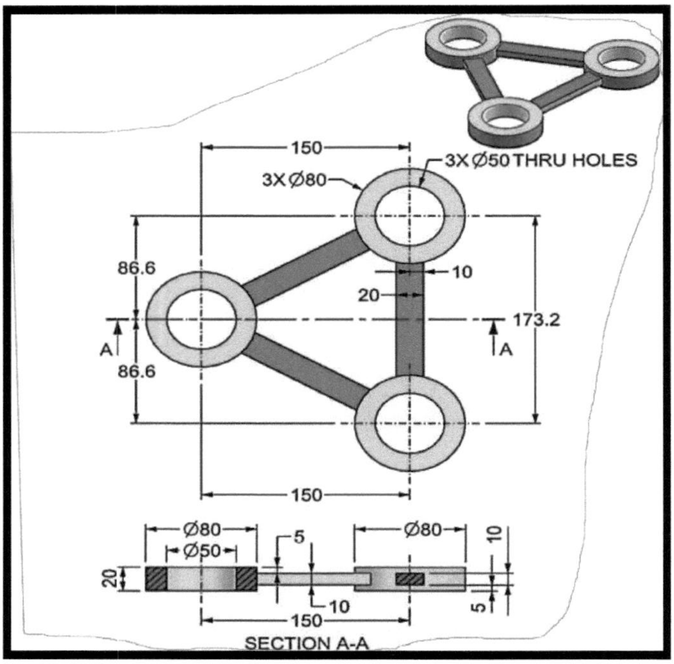

Exercise Fourteen

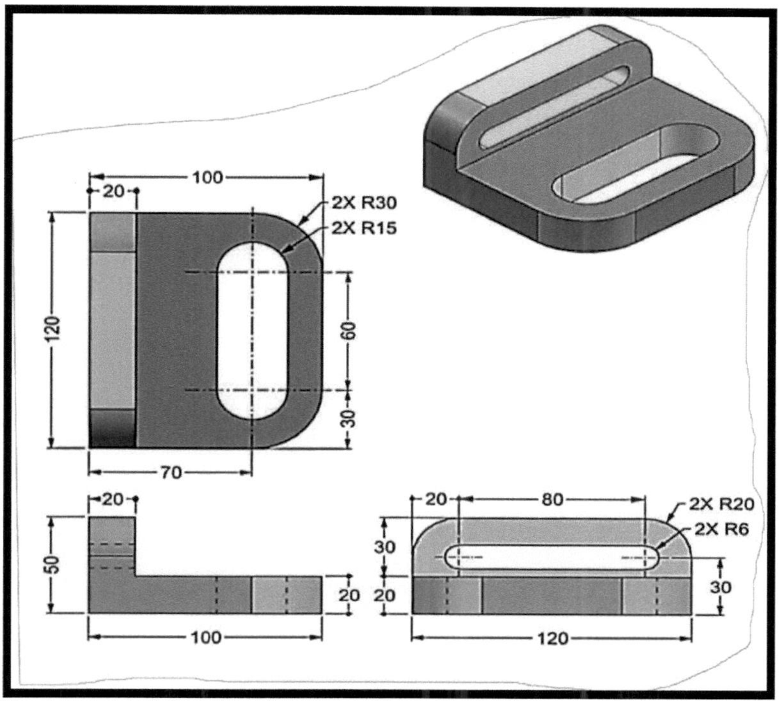

Exercise Fifteen

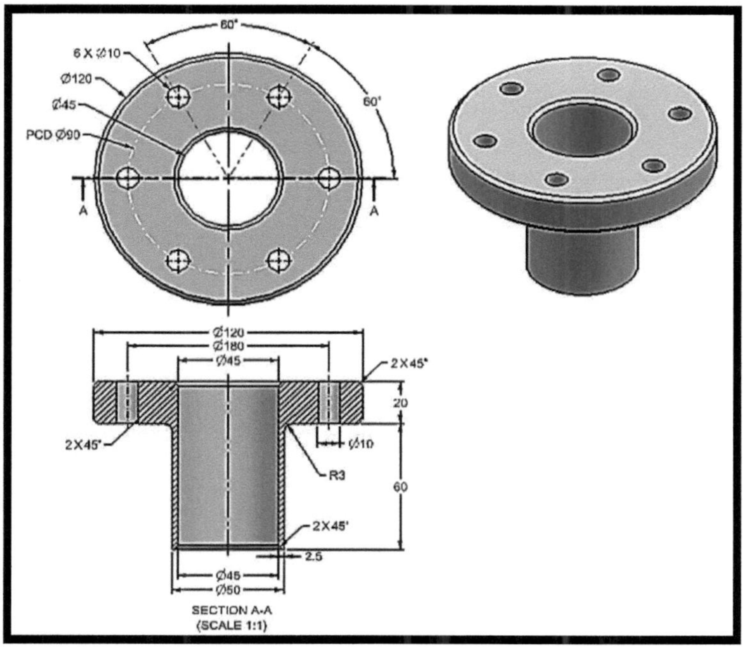

FUSION 360 ADVANCED PRACTICE EXERCISES

These exercises offer a variety of 3D Models & Drawings suitable for everyone, whether you're a beginner, intermediate, or advanced user. Each picture comes with clear measurements for each part of the model. We highly recommend practicing with these exercises to improve your skills and create some amazing things. Take your time, put in the effort, and you'll be crafting impressive items that reflect your growing expertise in no time.

Exercise 1

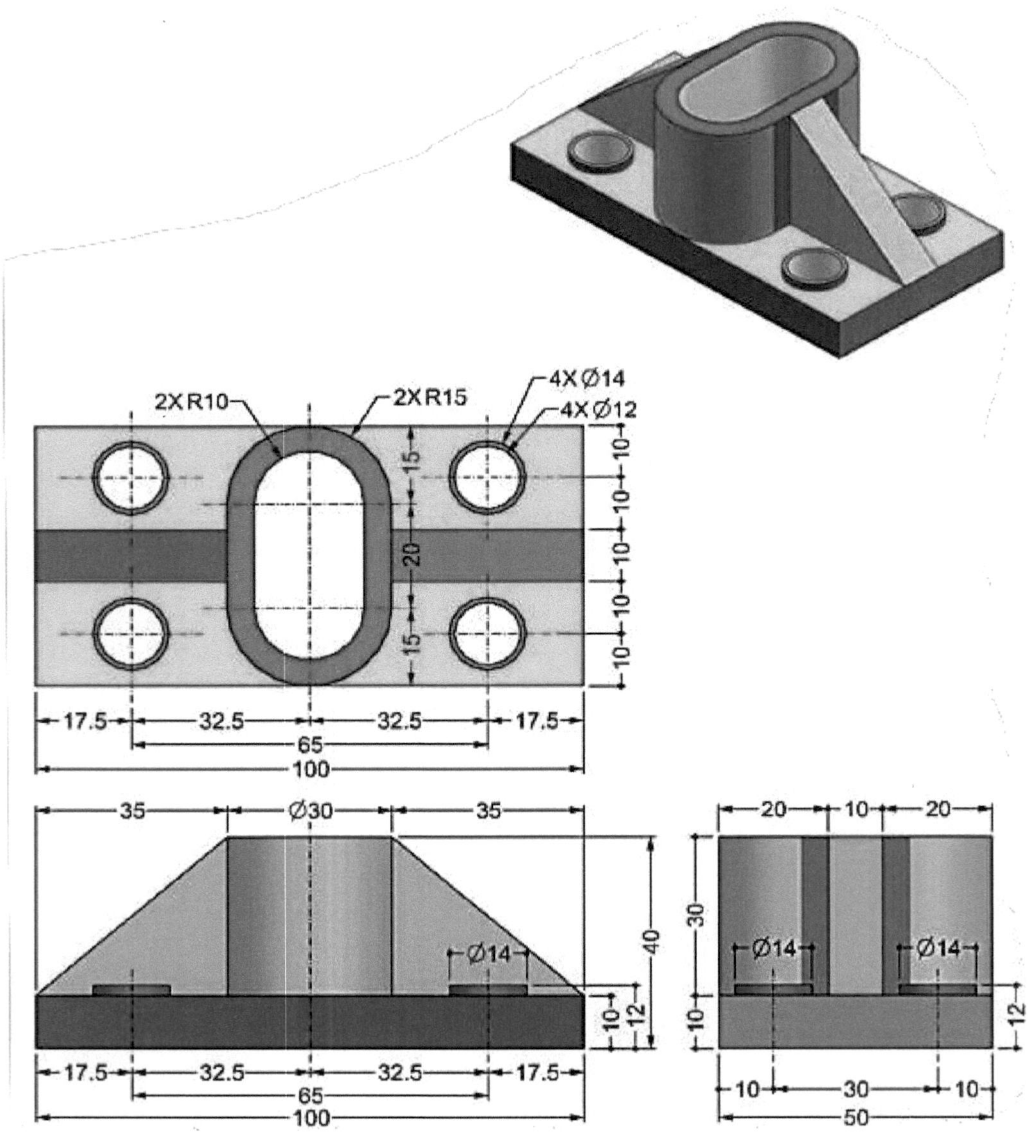

Exercise 2

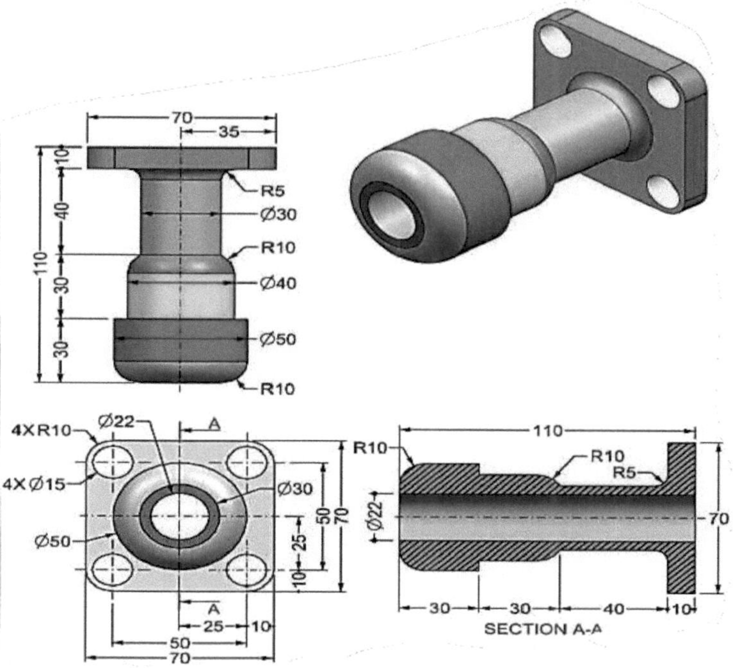

Exercise 3

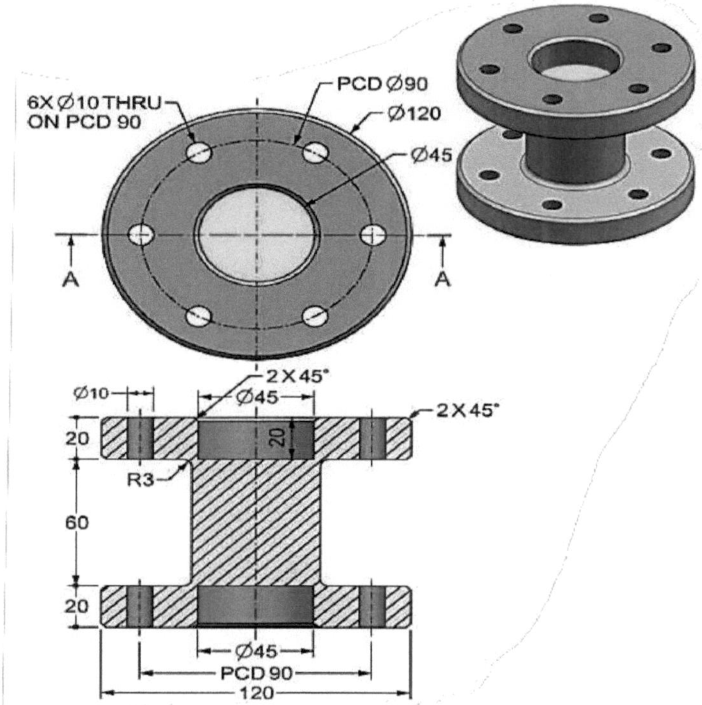

Exercise 4

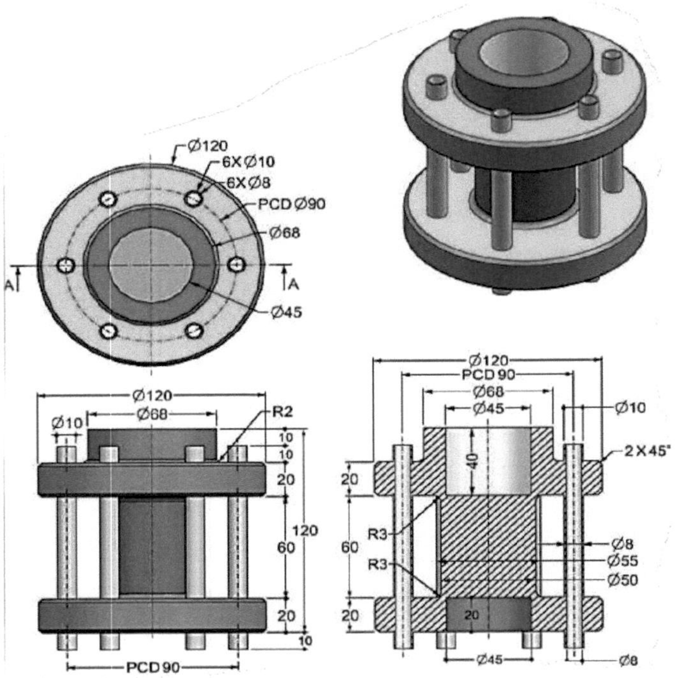

Exercise 5

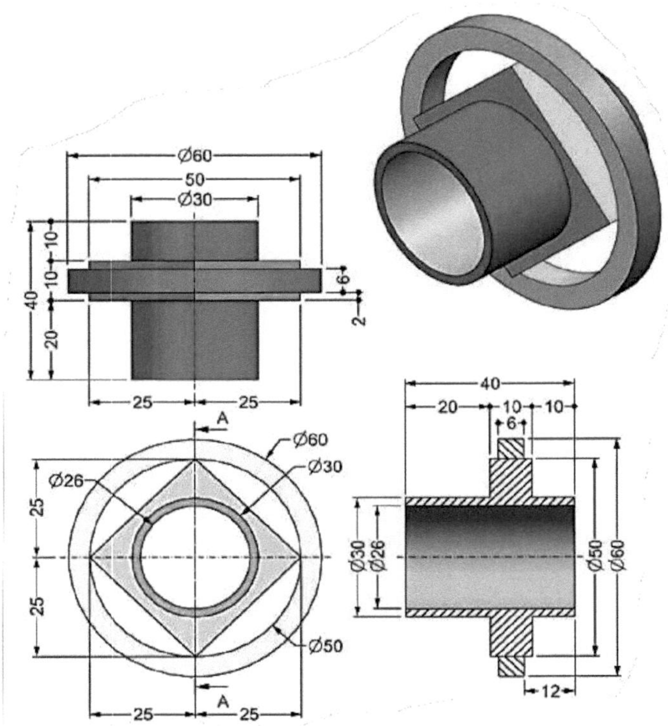

Exercise 6

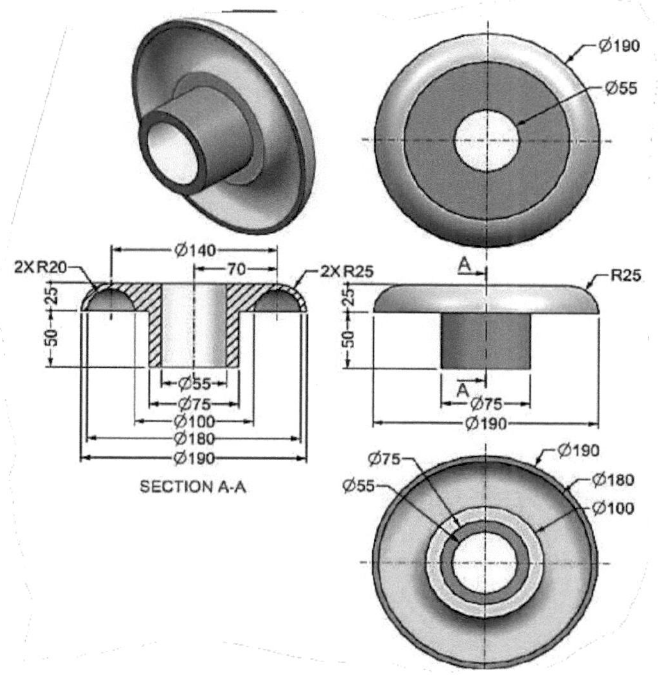

Exercise 7

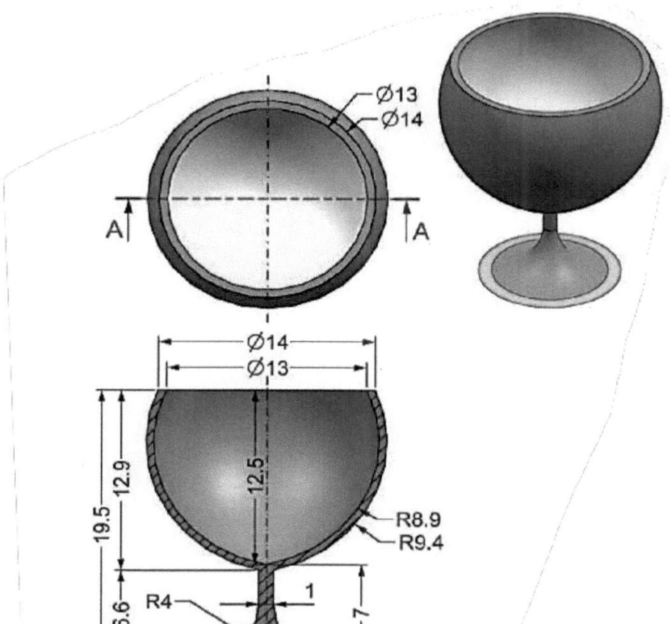

Exercise 8

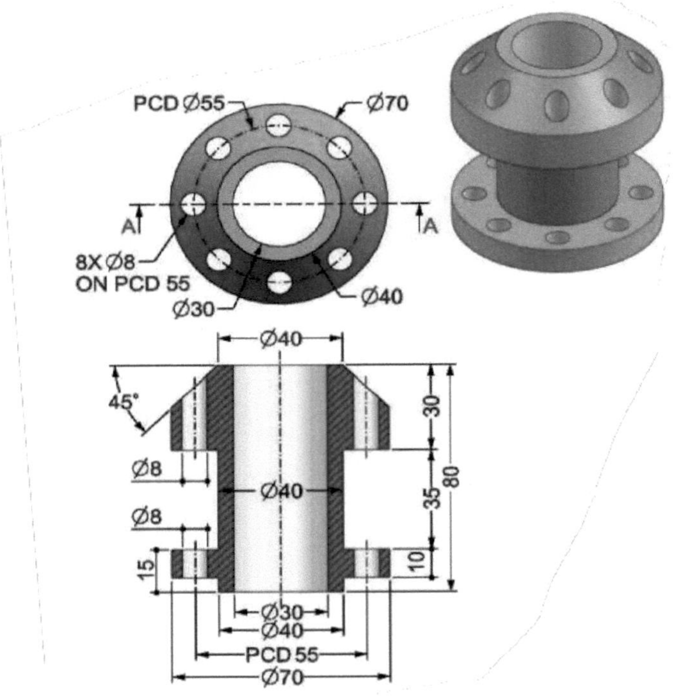

Exercise 9

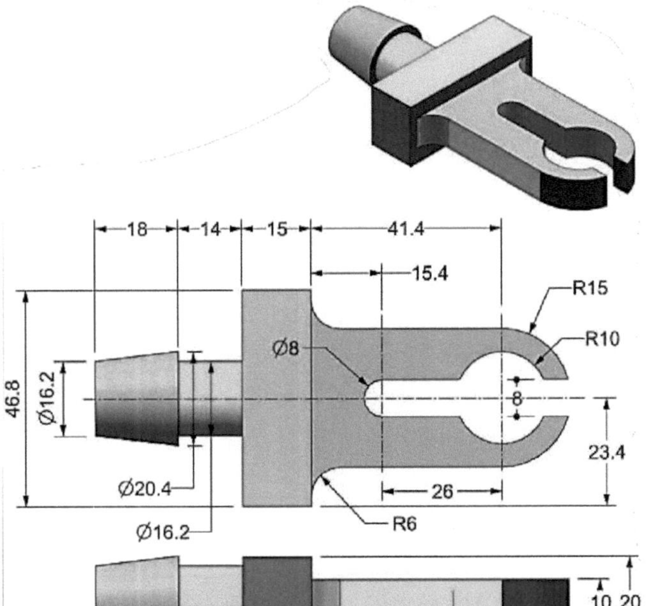

Exercise 10

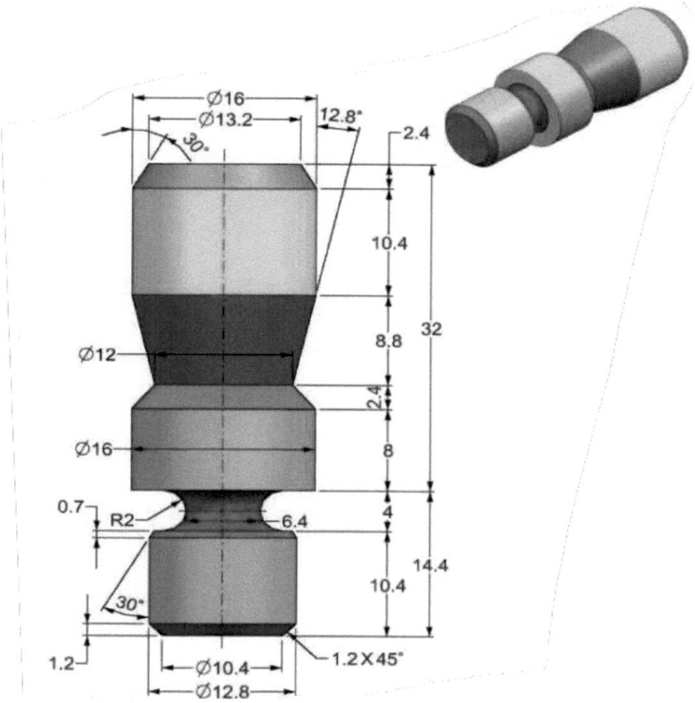

Exercise 11

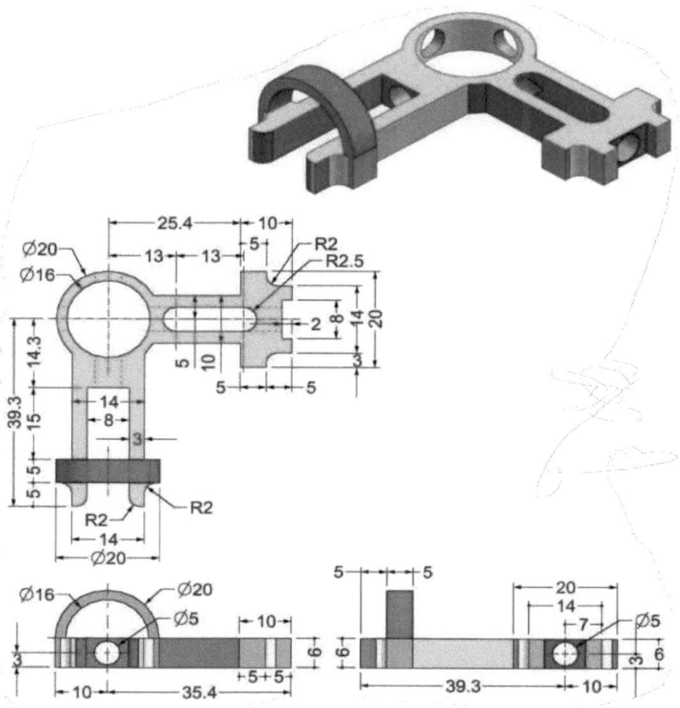

Exercise 12

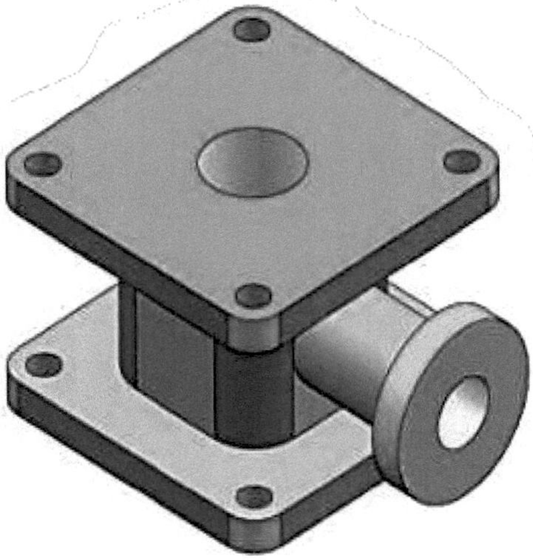

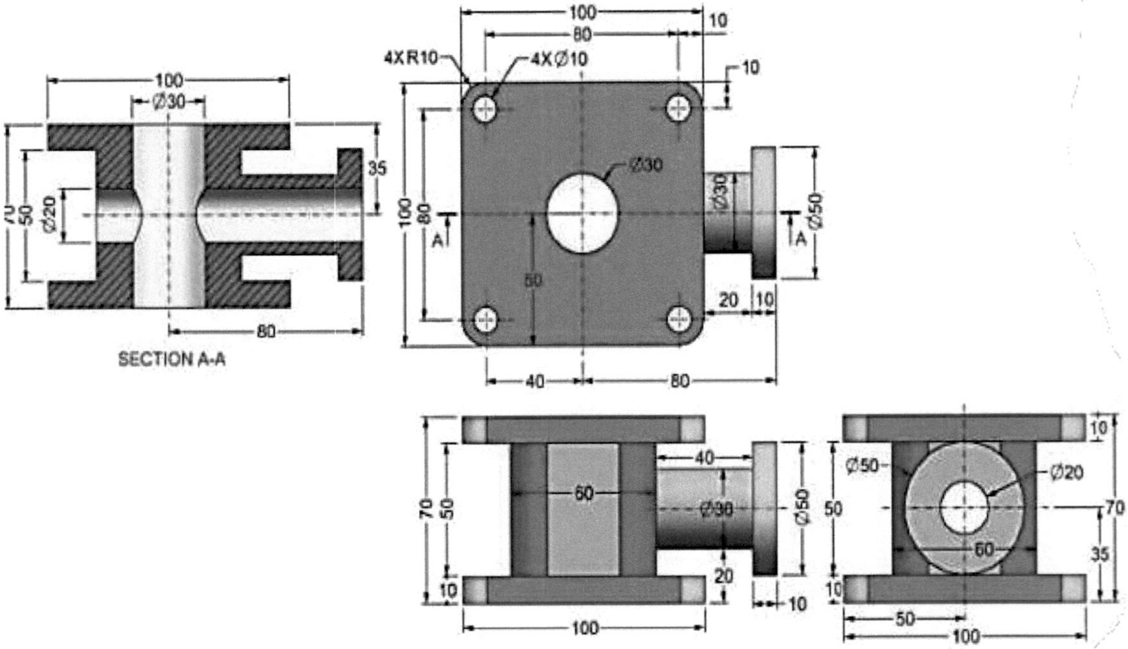

Exercise 13

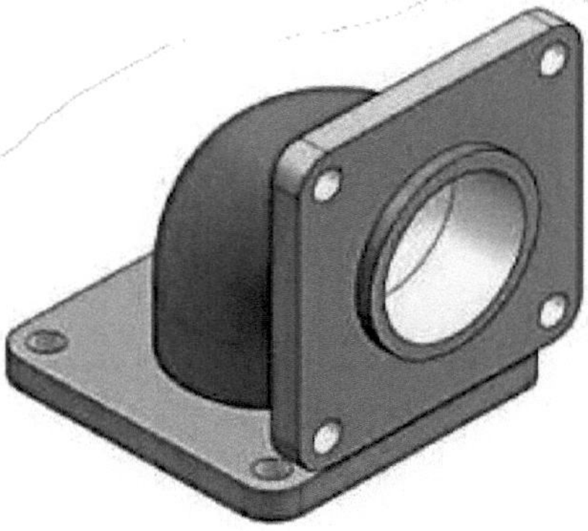

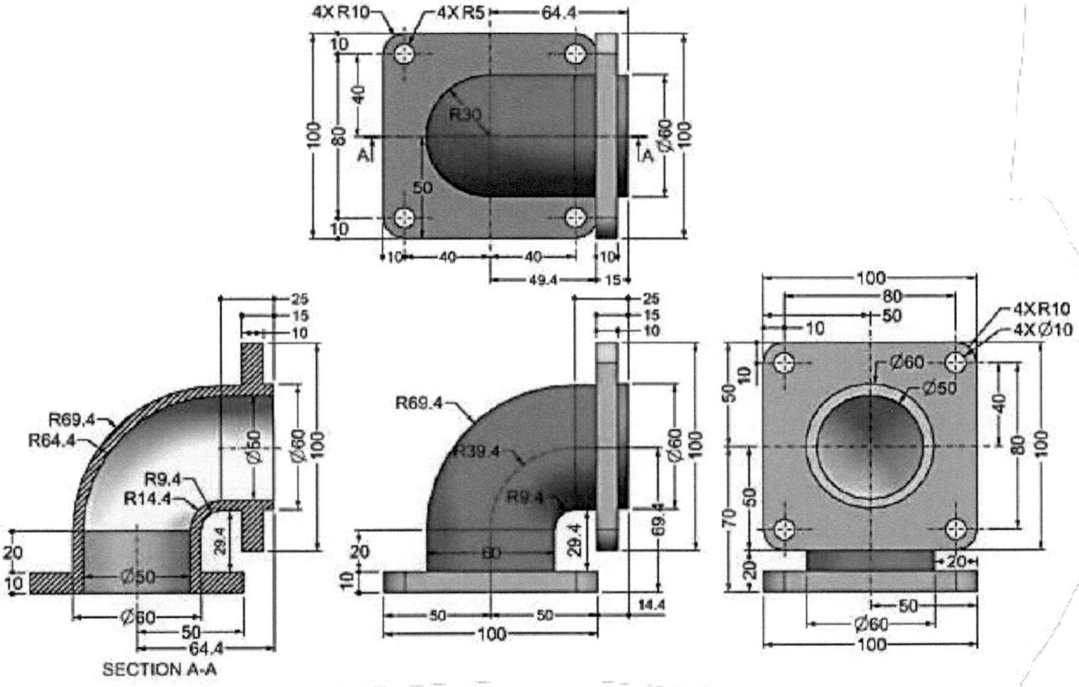
4X R10
4X R5
64.4
10
40
100
80
A
A
R30
50
Ø60
10
40
40
10
49.4
15
25
15
10
R69.4
R64.4
R9.4
R14.4
Ø50
Ø60
100
29.4
20
10
Ø50
Ø60
50
64.4
SECTION A-A
R69.4
R39.4
R9.4
60
29.4
69.4
14.4
50
50
100
4X R10
4X Ø10
100
80
50
Ø60
Ø50
70
20
Ø60

Exercise 14

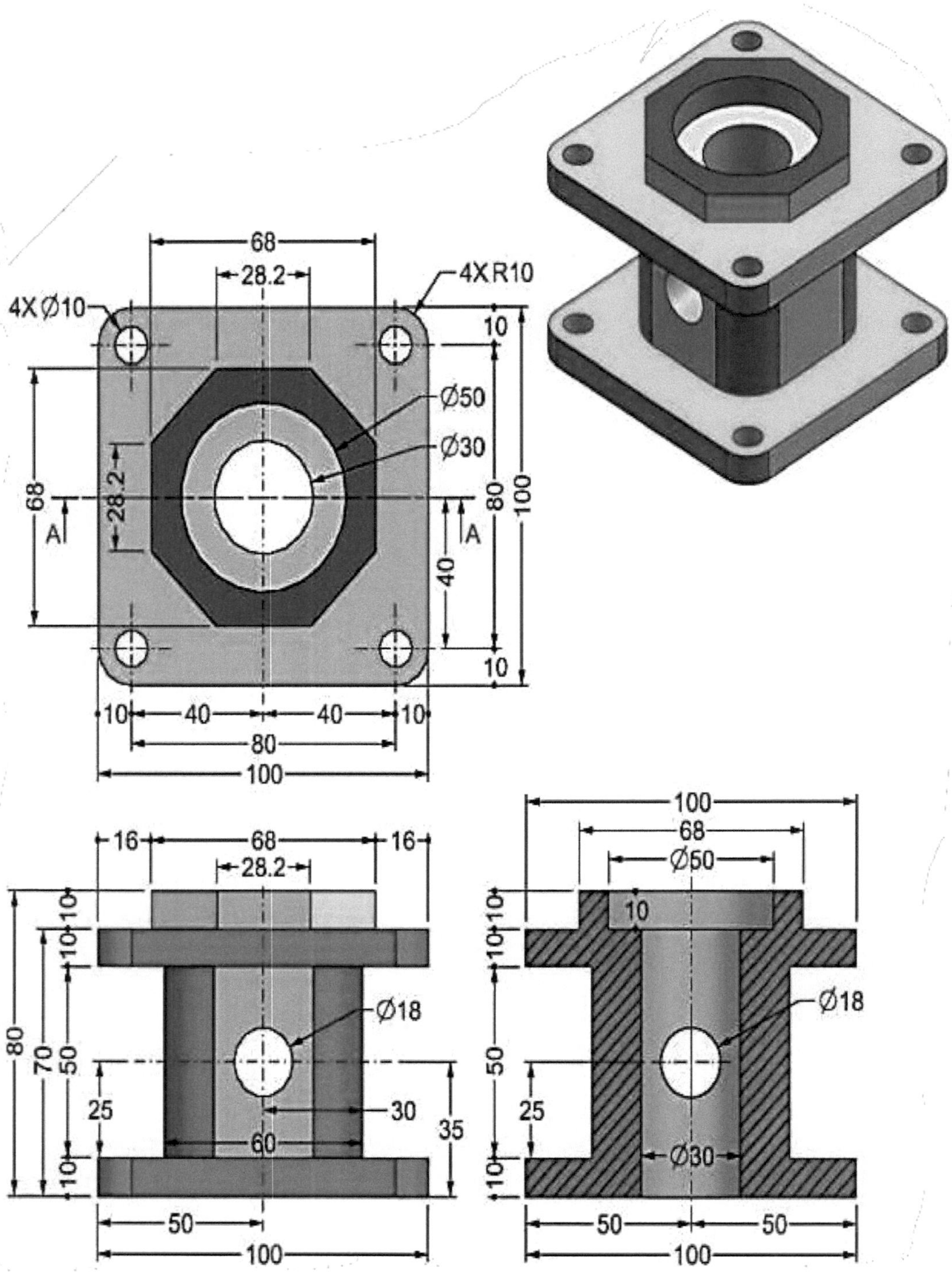
4X Ø10
4X R10
68
28.2
Ø50
Ø30
A
A
10
80
100
40
10
10
40
40
10
80
100
16
68
16
28.2
Ø18
80
70
50
25
30
35
60
10
10
10
50
100
100
68
Ø50
10
Ø18
25
Ø30
50
50
100

Exercise 15

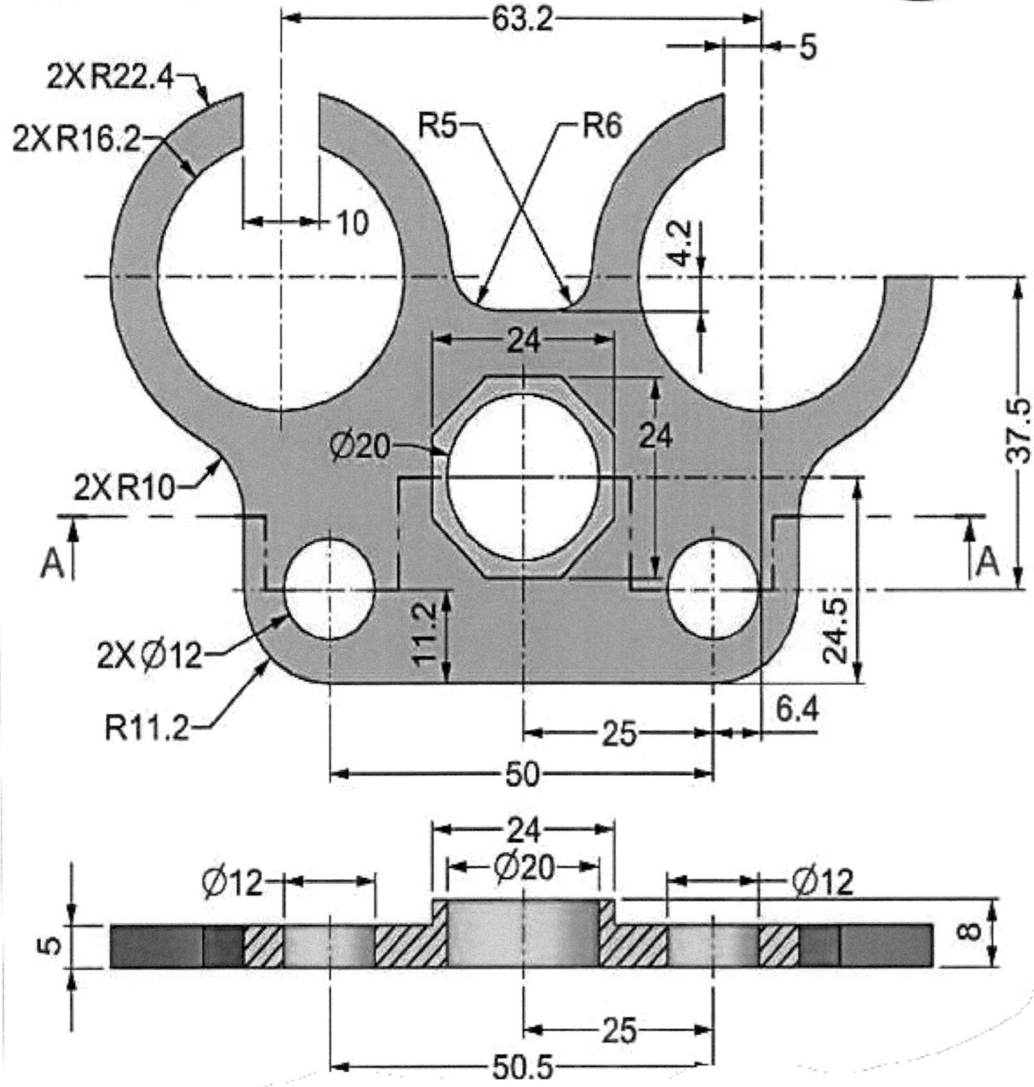
63.2
5
2X R22.4
2X R16.2
10
R5
R6
4.2
24
24
Ø20
2X R10
A
A
37.5
2X Ø12
11.2
24.5
R11.2
6.4
25
50
24
Ø20
Ø12
Ø12
5
8
25
50.5

Exercise 16

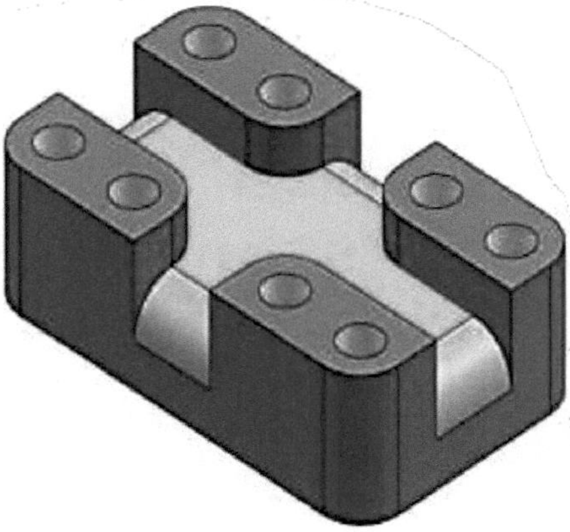

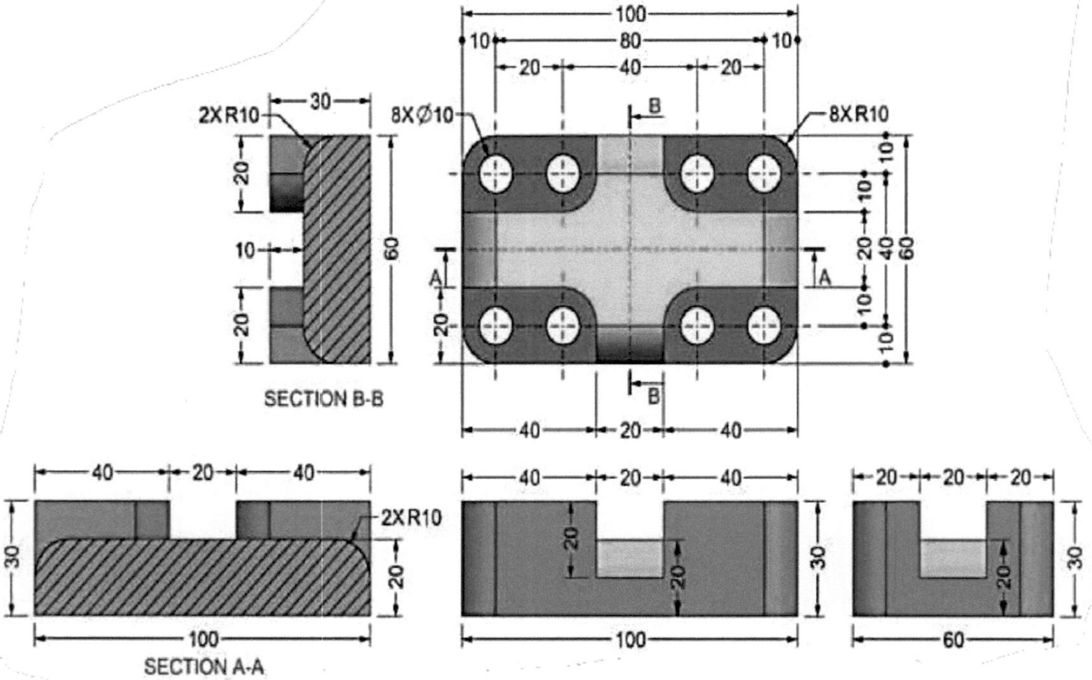
100
10
80
10
20
40
20
2XR10
30
8XØ10
B
8XR10
10
10
20
40
60
10
10
A
A
60
SECTION B-B
B
40
20
40
2XR10
30
20
100
SECTION A-A
40
20
40
30
100
20
20
20
30
60

Exercise 17

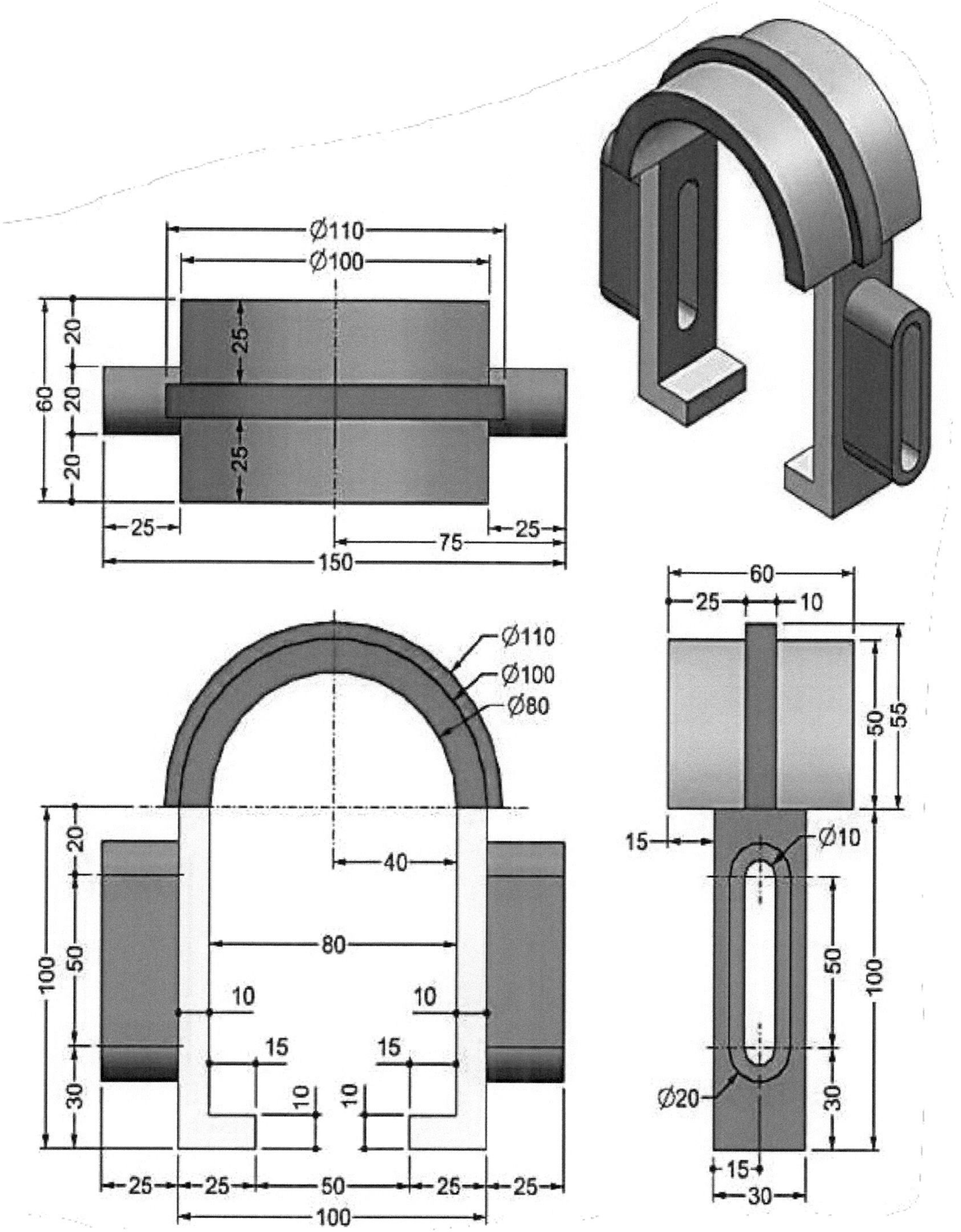

Ø110
Ø100
60
20
20
20
25
25
25
25
75
150
Ø110
Ø100
Ø80
40
80
100
20
50
30
10
10
15
15
10
10
25
25
50
25
25
100
60
25
10
50
55
15
Ø10
50
100
30
Ø20
15
30

Exercise 18

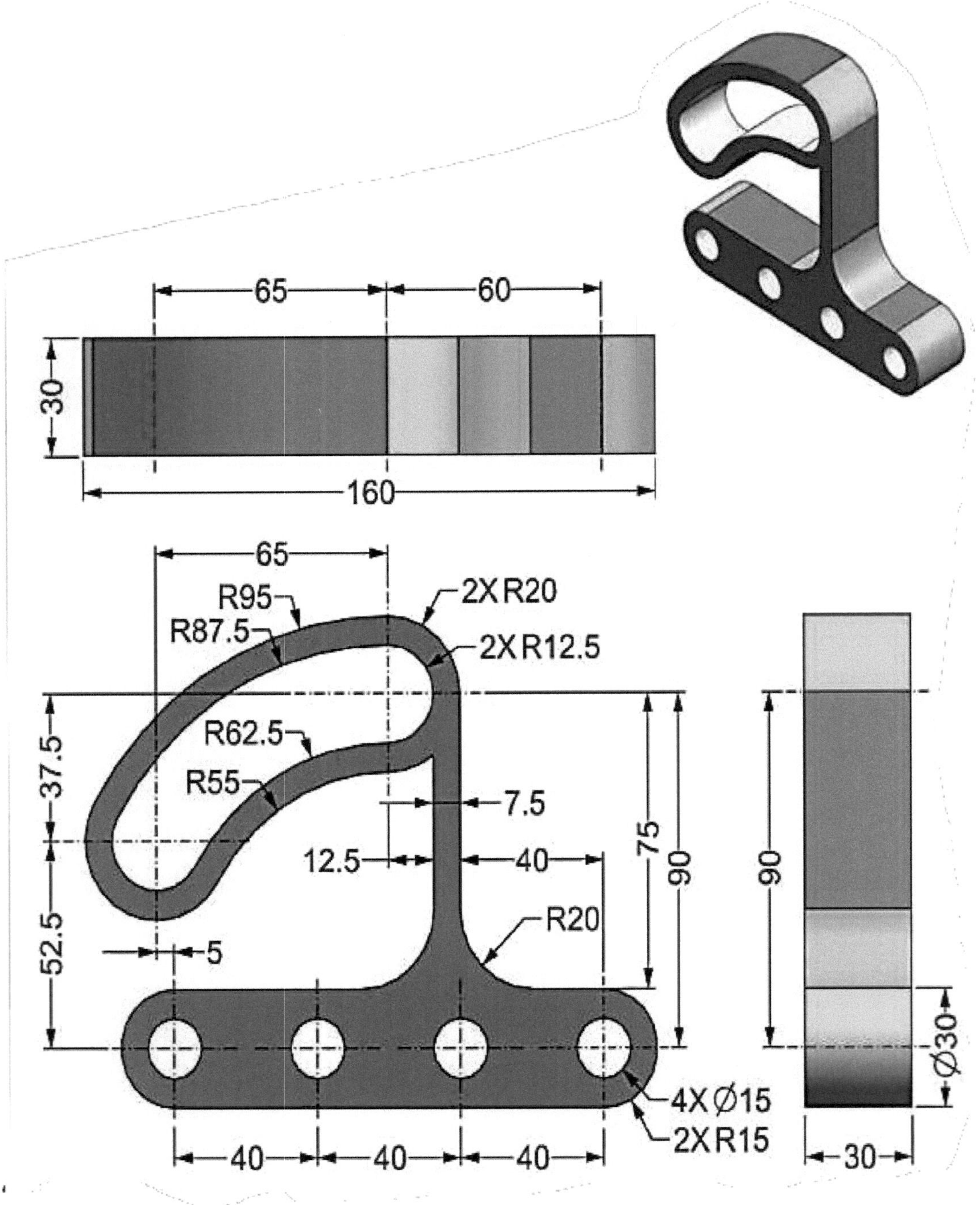

65
60
30
160
65
R95
R87.5
2X R20
2X R12.5
R62.5
R55
7.5
37.5
12.5
40
75
90
R20
52.5
5
4X Ø15
2X R15
40
40
40
90
Ø30
30

Exercise 19

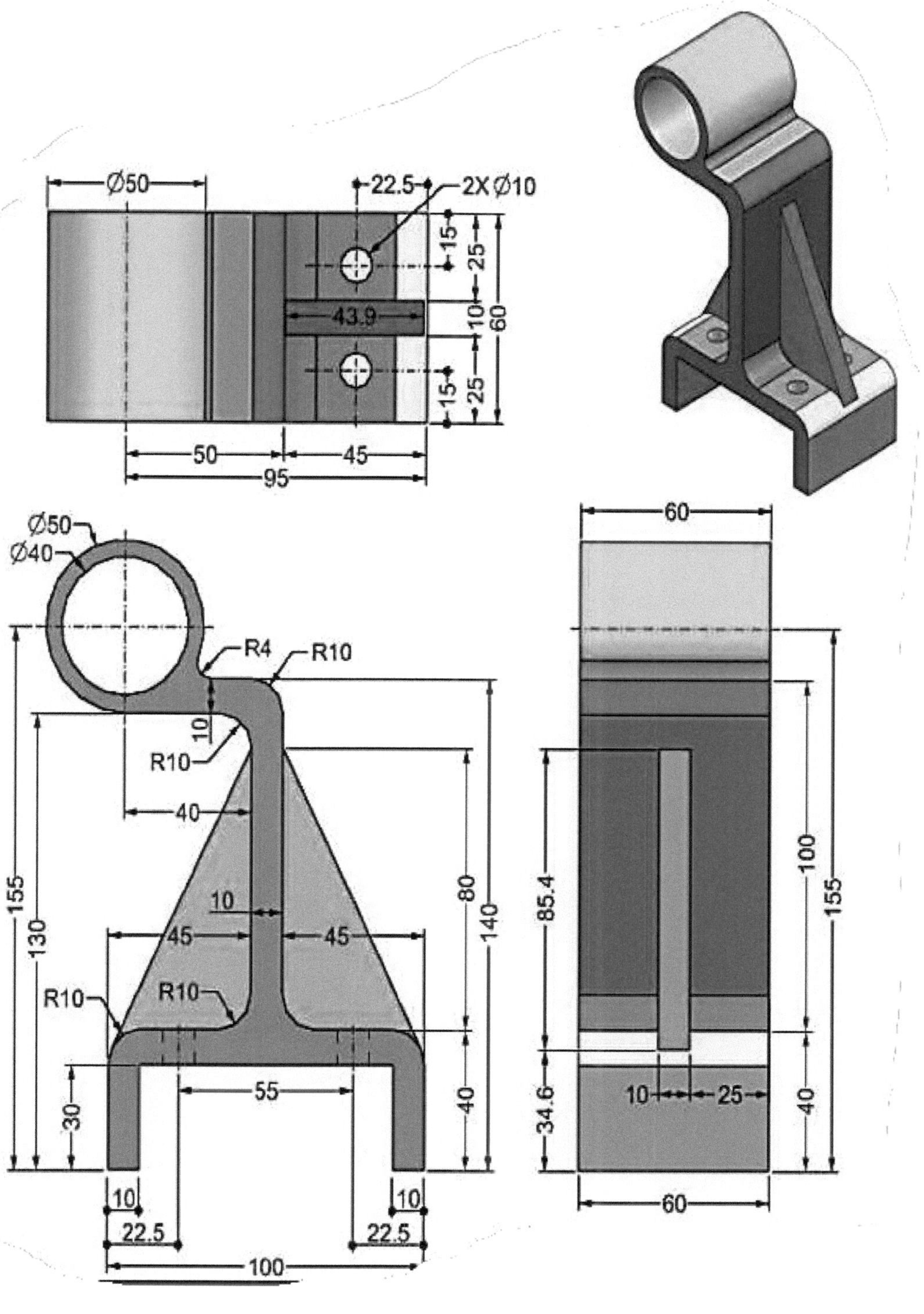
Ø50
22.5
2X Ø10
15
25
43.9
10
60
25
15
50
45
95
Ø50
Ø40
R4
R10
10
R10
40
10
45
45
R10
R10
155
130
80
140
55
30
40
10
10
22.5
22.5
100
60
85.4
100
155
34.6
10
25
40
60

Exercise 20

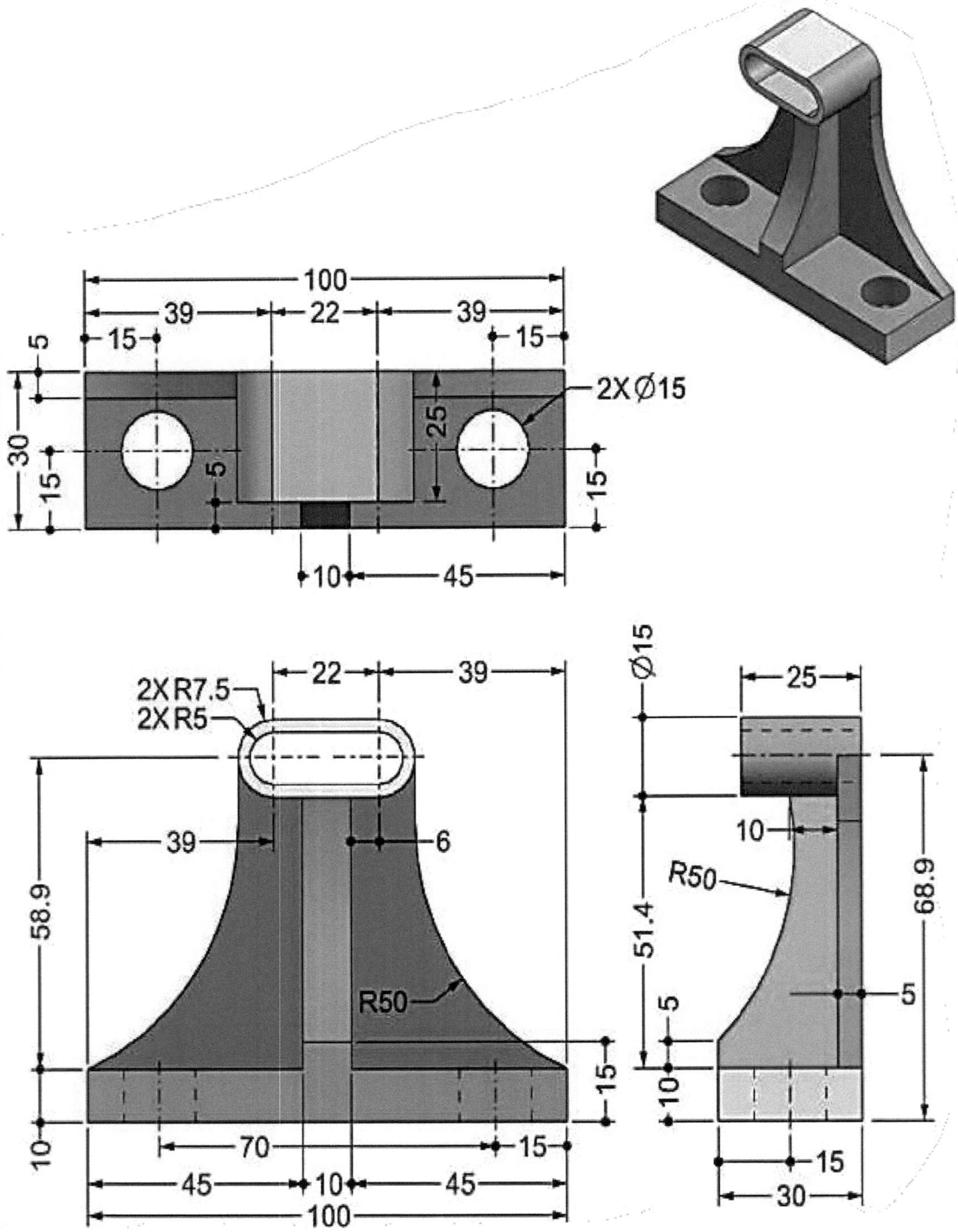
100
39
22
39
15
15
5
2XØ15
25
30
15
5
15
10
45
2XR7.5
2XR5
22
39
39
6
58.9
R50
15
10
70
15
45
10
45
100
Ø15
25
10
R50
51.4
68.9
5
5
10
15
30

Frequently Asked Questions

What are the primary elements that make up a design project using Fusion 360?

The 3D model, the 2D drawings, and the CAM file are the most important aspects of a design project that was created using Fusion 360. The 2D drawings are utilized to produce the CAM file, which is then used to build the toolpaths for the machining of the component. The 3D model serves as the foundation for the design.

How does SolidWorks or AutoCAD compare to the capabilities of Fusion 360?

Fusion 360 is a 3D CAD/CAM application that is hosted in the cloud that allows engineers, designers, and machinists to work together more effectively. Both SolidWorks and AutoCAD are conventional computer-aided design (CAD) programs that run on desktop computers. Fusion 360 is a more recent and forward-thinking product, with a primary emphasis on cloud-based collaboration and design.

Can you explain what Joints are in the context of Fusion 360?

In Fusion 360, assemblies, which are essentially 3D models made up of several pieces, are created by joining multiple sections together via joints. These pieces are joined together by joints, which may either be hard or flexible, depending on the situation. While flexible joints let the components move about one another, rigid joints maintain the parts' current location about one and restrict them from moving.

In the context of Fusion 360, what do you understand about the CAM system?

The technique of employing computer software to control and automate the manufacturing process is referred to as computer-aided manufacturing (CAM), which stands for computer-aided manufacturing. CAM, when applied to the context of Fusion 360, may be used to build toolpaths that can then be utilized to drive a CNC machine to make components and finished goods.

Can you list any examples of how Autodesk Inventor and Fusion 360 may be used?

Autodesk Inventor is a 3D computer-aided design (CAD) program that is used for product and mechanical design. On the other hand, Fusion 360 is a 3D computer-aided design (CAD), computer-aided manufacturing (CAM), and computer-aided engineering (CAE) program that is used for product, mechanical, and industrial design.

What is the most effective method for creating a drawing with the Fusion 360 software?

Using the sketch tools in Fusion 360 to draw your geometry is the most effective method for creating a sketch Fusion 360. Draw freeform curves with the pencil tool, create straight lines with the line tool, and draw arcs with the arc tool. These three tools are found in the Draw menu. After you have created your geometry, you may use the constraints tool to apply restrictions to your design. Once you have done this, your sketch is complete. Because of this, you will be able to maintain the right position and size of your geometry.

In Fusion 360, what is the most efficient technique to add parameters to an already existing sketch?

Utilizing the "**Add Parameters**" function in Fusion 360 is the most effective method for adding parameters to an already existing drawing in the program. The "**Modify**" menu is where you'll find the "**Command**" option. After using this command, you will be able to pick the entities to which you would want to apply the parameters that you have specified.

What is the most efficient approach to switching the view orientation in Fusion 360?

Utilizing ViewCube is the most effective method for modifying the view orientation inside Fusion 360. You can make rapid adjustments to the view of the model by using ViewCube, which is found in the top right-hand corner of the Fusion 360 window.

In Fusion 360, what is the most effective method for scaling a model?

Utilizing the Scale command is the most effective method for adjusting the size of a model in Fusion 360. The menu labeled "**Modify**" is where you'll find this command. After choosing the Scale command, you will be able to pick the faces, edges, or vertices that you want to scale once you get to that point in the process. After that, you will be able to input the scale factor that you like.

What is the most effective method for rotating a model?

Utilizing the rotate tool inside Fusion 360 is the most effective method for rotating a model. You can find this tool under the edit tab, and it gives you the ability to choose a point to rotate around as well as the angle at which you want the object to rotate around that point.

What is the most effective method for mirroring a model?

Using the command titled "**Mirror**" in Fusion 360 is the most effective method for mirroring a model. The menu labeled "**Modify**" is where you'll find this command. Following the selection of the Mirror command, you will be prompted to choose the plane or axis on which you want to center the mirrored model. When you have chosen the mirroring plane or axis, the model will be reflected around that point once you have finished making your selection.

What is the most efficient approach to moving a model around?

Using the move command in Fusion 360 is the most effective method for moving a model in this program. Using this command, you may choose a model and then relocate it to a different spot in the scene. Altering a model's orientation and size may also be accomplished with the use of the rotate and scale commands, respectively.

What is the most effective method for joining two models together?

Using the Assemble command in Fusion 360 is the most effective method for joining two models together in the program. This command will enable you to pick the two models that you want to snap together, and it will then automatically align the models and make a joint between them. You will have the ability to do this by selecting the models from the drop-down menu.

Can you list any real-world examples of projects that were constructed utilizing Fusion 360?

There are a lot of projects from the real world that were made with Fusion 360, and you may look at samples of them. The Mars 2020 rover is one illustration of what may be accomplished using Fusion 360's design capabilities. Another example of this would be the Airbus A350, which, like many other modern aircraft, was created using Fusion 360.

In the context of Fusion 360, can you describe your understanding of the concept of freeform modeling?

The capacity to construct three-dimensional models using freeform modeling means that the models do not have to conform to conventional geometric shapes or forms. When creating models, this enables a wider degree of creative and aesthetic expression than was previously possible. It is also possible to utilize it to construct models that are more realistic and better depict things that exist in the actual world.

Can you explain the steps of extruding a surface in Fusion 360?

To begin the process of extruding a surface in Fusion 360, you will first need to pick the surface from which you want to extrude. After you have chosen the surface, go to the toolbar and pick the "**Extrude**" tool. You will then need to click on the "**Extrude**" tool. This will bring up a menu where you may set the parameters for the extrusion, such as the height of the extrusion, and it will bring up the menu immediately. To extrude the surface, you will need to click the "**OK**" button once you have completed the previous step of specifying the parameters.

Can you explain the steps for sweeping a profile along a route in Fusion 360?

To sweep a profile along a route in Fusion 360, you will first need to sketch the profile you want to sweep. After that, you may proceed to sweep the profile down the path. After that, you will need to make a rough sketch of the route you want to follow when sweeping the profile. After you have finished creating both drawings, you will need to make use of the Sweep command so that the profile may be swept down the route.

Can you explain how to rotate a profile in Fusion 360 around a certain axis?

You will need to utilize the Revolve tool in Fusion 360 if you want to revolve a profile around an axis in the program. Within the Model workspace's Modify panel is where you'll find this particular tool. To begin, you will have to decide which of the many profiles you wish to circle. Next, you will need to choose the axis that the profile will circle before you can go on to the next step. In the end, you will be tasked with providing details on the angle of revolution.

Why Are My Components Grayed Out?

We expect that you are already aware of the idea of components, regardless of how long you have been using Fusion 360—whether it's been a day or a year. To recap, you may think of components as reusable elements or as anything that would exist in the actual world. Components can also be thought of as building blocks. To begin working on a particular component while using design files, you will first need to activate that component. After that, the opacity of each of the other components will be reduced by itself automatically. This is something that happens automatically and is designed to make it simpler for you to concentrate on the component that you now have active. After all, you are expected to be focusing on the component that is currently active. If you activate the component at the top level, you will see that all of the components included inside your assembly file will give the appearance of being active, also known as having an opacity of 100%. Since other CAD programs do not provide this function, it seems that quite a few users are taken aback by this. However, this was developed due to the top-down structure of Fusion 360, which allows you to construct all of your pieces (as components) from inside your assembly file. This led to the implementation of this feature.

Turning Component Visibility on And Off

You may modify your preferences by selecting "**Preferences**" from the dropdown menu that appears when you click on your username in the top right corner of the screen. This will bring up the dialogue box for configuring your preferences. From this point on, you will need to pick the "**Design**" tab which is located on the left side of the screen. The "**Active Component Visibility**" option, which is located at the very top of the list, will need to be checked or unchecked for you to be able to activate or deactivate this function. You will need to click the "apply" button regardless of whether you choose to tick or uncheck this option. For the modifications that you made to take effect in Fusion 360, you will need to restart the program.

How Do I Preview New Features?

Choose your **Username** from the menu that appears in the top right corner, and choose "**Preference**" from the list that appears below it. After that, you will need to pick the "**Preview**" tab that is located on the left-hand side of the screen. You will have the ability to activate and deactivate certain features that are currently undergoing testing through the Preview tab. A good number of you, for instance, have seen or experimented with the UI preview, which is the more recent user interface that Autodesk intends to adopt (at some point). It is essential to keep in mind that the aforementioned preview functions have not yet been completely pushed out. Many times, for valid reasons, they are not shared in their entirety. As a result, you must use extreme care while using them. There are often flaws in the preview features, which might cause Fusion 360 to crash or lead you to lose access to other functions. If you wish to modify any of the preview settings, as usual, you will need to "apply" the settings and restart your Fusion 360 application for the changes to take effect and be visible.

How Do I Make Changes to My Preferences Regarding Navigation?

To access your account, go to the top right corner and click on your **Username**. After that, choose **Preferences** from the menu that drops down. After that, you'll see a few different parameters that you may adjust to better configure your navigation process to better suit your particular requirements. You may "**reverse the zoom orientation**" by going to the "**general**" page and finding the option there. You will need to toggle this option to make the scroll wheel on your mouse zoom in the other way.

The "**Default Orbit type**" may be found just above that option. You may utilize the orbit tool by pressing and holding the shift key on your keyboard while moving your mouse around. This will allow you to use the tool. You also have the option of using the orbit tool, which is located at the very bottom of your screen. When you choose it at the bottom, you'll see that you have the option of selecting either a constraint orbit, which rotates the model about a certain point or a free orbit, which gives you complete control over how the model is moved around the screen. If you discover that you use one of these orbit tools more often than the other, then you may adjust this preference to the orbit setting that best suits your needs. The next time you use the orbit function with your keyboard and mouse, this will be the setting that is selected by default. Next, you will see that above the orbit setting, you have the ability to modify your navigation settings following a few different CAD software. When you apply any one of these other options, you'll discover that the navigation will behave in a manner that is analogous to the settings that come preconfigured with the program you've chosen. However, it is essential to keep in mind that each of these CAD packages has its own unique set of features and capabilities, which means that not everything will operate the same as it does in the other. This is a helpful way to bridge the gap, particularly for those of you who are still utilizing a different program.

Why Is My Z-axis In the "Up" Direction?

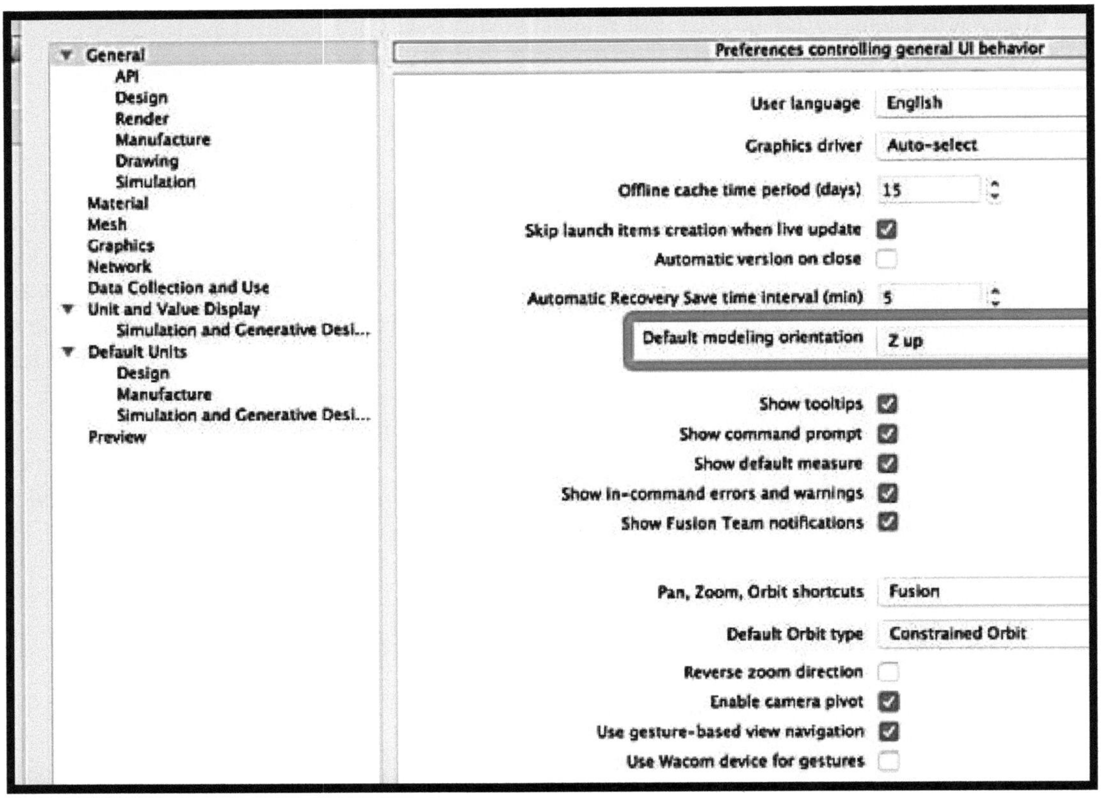

If you look at the viewcube in the upper right-hand corner of your screen, you'll notice that it's most likely configured so that the Z-axis serves as the vertical axis. This is because the Z-axis is currently set as the default in Fusion 360. When you make a change to this parameter, it will only affect design files that are created in the future. This is a very crucial point to keep in mind when working with the Z vs Y orientation. Unfortunately, if you change this setting, it will not have any effect on the files that you already have open at this time. There is, however, a simple workaround that you can utilize to simulate the reorientation of your model.

By clicking the caret symbol that appears next to the viewcube, you will be able to reset both the top view and the front view of your model. After that, choose the "set current view as" flyout folder, which will allow you to pick the "front" or "top" face of the object. If you set the front and top faces of your model, you will be able to reorient it without having to rotate it using the move command if you do so by setting those faces. It might be challenging to achieve perfection while using the move command. To recap the Y-axis orientation against the Z-axis orientation, does not have much of an impact on the actual model you are working on in Fusion 360. The only actual difference between the two is the orientation of your model, which is usually only relevant after you have exported your model for another purpose, such as for the slicing software that comes with a 3D printer. This is the rationale for the change that the engineers at Fusion 360 made to make the Z-up orientation the default setting. They discovered that the majority of their customers were using CNC milling machines or 3D printers, both of which normally operate with the Z-axis up since this position most accurately depicts the third dimension.

INDEX

B

C

D

E

F

G

H

I

J

K

L

M

N

O

P

Q

R

S

T

U

V

W

X

Y

Z

This book has been produced in line with the EU GPSR guidelines about the safety of products.

The General Product Safety Regulation is the European Union's updated framework for ensuring that all consumer products, including books, are safe for consumers.

This book has been printed by Libri Plureos GmbH. The printer has issued safety certificates for the materials - like ink, paper and glue - being used.

The product identifier is: 9789403877075

The author is responsible for the content of the book and had it produced by Bookmundo.

Should there be any questions in regard to the safety of the product, please contact us.

Bookmundo
Delftsestraat 33
3013AE Rotterdam
The Netherlands
info@bookmundo.com